A HISTORY OF THE
ROMAN PEOPLE

69 - 81
83 - 107
108 - 145
146 - 245

THIRD EDITION

A HISTORY OF THE ROMAN PEOPLE

ALLEN M. WARD

UNIVERSITY OF CONNECTICUT

FRITZ M. HEICHELHEIM

CEDRIC A. YEO

PRENTICE HALL, UPPER SADDLE RIVER, NEW JERSEY 07458

Library of Congress Cataloging-in-Publication Data

Ward, Allen Mason.
   A history of the Roman people / Allen M. Ward, Fritz M.
Heichelheim, Cedric A. Yeo. — 3rd ed.
     p.   cm.
   Rev. ed. of: A history of the Roman people / Fritz M. Heichelheim,
Cedric A. Yeo, Allen M. Ward. 2nd ed. 1984.
   Includes bibliographical references and indexes.
   ISBN 0-13-896598-6
   1. Rome—History. I. Heichelheim, Fritz M. (Fritz Moritz)
II. Yeo, Cedric A. III. Heichelheim, Fritz M. (Fritz
Moritz). History of the Roman people. IV. Title.
DG209.W33 1998
937—DC21   98-11923
                                             CIP

Acquisitions Editor: Todd Armstrong
Editorial Assistant: Holly Jo Brown
Editorial Director/EIC: Charlyce Jones Owen
Director of Marketing: Gina Sluss
Marketing Manager: Sheryl Adams
Production Editor: Louise Rothman
Manufacturing Buyer: Lynn Pearlman
Manufacturing Manager: Nick Sklitsis
Cover Design: Jayne Conte, Bruce Kenselaar

This book was set in 9.5/11 Times Ten by the Composing Room of Michigan, Inc. and was printed
and bound by RR Donnelley & Sons Company. The cover was printed by
Phoenix Color Corp.

Printed in the United States of America

10 9 8 7 6 5

ISBN 0-13-896598-6

Prentice-Hall International (UK) Limited, *London*
Prentice-Hall of Australia Pty. Limited, *Sydney*
Prentice-Hall Canada, Inc., *Toronto*
Prentice-Hall Hispanoamericana, S.A., *Mexico*
Prentice-Hall of India Private Limited, *New Delhi*
Prentice-Hall of Japan, Inc., *Tokyo*
Pearson Education Asia Pte. Ltd., *Singapore*
Editora Prentice-Hall do Brasil, Ltda., *Rio de Janeiro*

Contents

v

V   The Rise of the Roman Republic, 509 to 287 B.C.   50

VI   The Roman Conquest of Italy and Its Impact, 509 to 264 B.C.   69

PART TWO
THE HIGH POINT OF THE ROMAN REPUBLIC

VII   The First Punic War and the Beginning of Overseas Imperialism, 264 to 241 B.C.   83

VIII   Between the Wars, 241 to 218 B.C.   91

IX   The Second Punic War, 218 to 201 B.C.   99

X   War and Imperialism in the Hellenistic East, 200 to 133 B.C.   108

XI   Roman Imperialism in the West, 200 to 133 B.C.   118

XII   The Transformation of Roman Life, 264 to 133 B.C.   124

XIII The Great Cultural Synthesis, 264 to 133 B.C. 136

PART THREE
THE WORLD OF THE LATE REPUBLIC

XIV The Gracchi and the Struggle over Land Reform, 133 to 121 B.C. 146

XV The Breakdown of the System, 121 to 88 B.C. 156

XVI Marius and Sulla: Civil War and Reaction, 88 to 78 B.C. 167

XVII Personal Ambitions and Public Crises, 78 to 60 B.C. 175

XVIII   The Rise of Caesar, 60 to 52 B.C.   190

XIX   Caesar Wins and Is Lost, Mid-50s to 44 B.C.   198

XX   The Last Days of the Republic, 44 to 30 B.C.   209

PART FOUR
THE EARLY ROMAN EMPIRE

XXVI   The First Two Julio-Claudian Emperors: Tiberius and Gaius (Caligula), A.D. 14 to 41   295

XXVII   Claudius, Nero, and the End of the Julio-Claudians, A.D. 41 to 68   307

XXVIII   The Crisis of the Principate and Recovery under the Flavians, A.D. 69 to 96   318

XXIX The "Good" Emperors of the Second Century, A.D. 96 to 180   329

XXX Imperial Culture and Society in the First Two Centuries A.D.   345

PART FIVE
CRISIS, CONTINUITY, AND CHANGE IN THE THIRD AND FOURTH CENTURIES

XXXI Crisis and Temporary Recovery A.D. 180 to 235   373

XXXII   The Third-Century Anarchy, A.D. 235 to 285   384

XXXIII   Changes in Roman Life and Culture during the Third Century   396

XXXIV   Diocletian: Creating the Fourth-Century Empire, A.D. 285 to 305   415

XXXV   Constantine the Great and Christianity, A.D. 306 to 337   427

Maps

Preface

There are now whole fields of Classics and Ancient History that scarcely, if at all, existed when the second edition of *A History of the Roman People* was published in 1984. The intervening years have produced a flood of fascinating research on old and new topics, which has necessitated a thoroughly revised third edition. Extensive new archaeological evidence combined with a greater appreciation of the Romans' own antiquarian research has completely reshaped our understanding of the origins and early development of Rome. Advances in historical demography and vast quantities of recently excavated or restudied artifacts have produced a far more sophisticated understanding of urbanization and the role of cities in the ancient Roman economy. The luxuriant growth of Late Antiquity as a major field of study has produced a fertile synthesis between Classical and Medieval studies that puts the history of the late Roman Empire in a new light socially, economically, politically, and culturally.

Gender studies, literary criticism, and art history have brought to bear new theories, paradigms, and perspectives on the study of ancient Roman society and culture in all periods. Similarly, the application of new methods in analyzing vast amounts of data from inscriptions and coins and paying closer attention to previously underutilized texts such as law codes, popular romances, and the enormous volume of Jewish and Christian texts have also opened up new vistas in social and cultural history. Accordingly, women, slaves, common citizens, provincial subjects, and other marginalized groups occupy a much larger place in scholarship beside the highly educated and articulate aristocrats who used to be the primary focus of historians' attention.

In the belief that a comprehensive history of Rome is still useful for assignment in undergraduate courses, I have tried to incorporate this greatly expanded body of work into the new edition without an increase in size. To do so, I have cut down on the density of the traditional political and military narrative without sacrificing the comprehensive coverage of important trends and events or the depth of interpretation and explanation. The great strength of history as a discipline is its insistence that the general must be supported by the specific and that the specific is meaningful only in the context of the general. Therefore, I have tried always to strike a balance between the two even at the expense of brevity. I have also maintained and even reinforced the previous editions' chronological organization and frequent citation of dates. My experience is that students are not familiar enough with the basic sequence of events to avoid being confused by a purely topical or thematic presentation and that they need frequent chronological signposts. I have elected to retain the B.C./A.D. system that some scholars have abandoned under the influence of those who fear that its historical links with Christianity may be offensive to people of other faiths and non-Western backgrounds. To me, however, the assumption that everybody in the world shares the Western dating system is still ethnocentric, and the B.C.E./C.E. system ends up serving no purpose other than confusing students with unnecessary complexity.

Fritz M. Heichelheim, who originally conceived this book, died only six years after it first appeared. The fact that it has survived for over 35 years in two editions speaks for the enduring value of this work. His colleague, Cedric A. Yeo, who helped him shape the text for an English-speaking audience, died soon after the publication of the second edition. While Professor Yeo published basic research in Roman economic history that is still cited in new scholarship fifty years later, he never lost sight of the fact that educating undergraduates is the most important service that scholars render to society. To that end, he sought to make the facts and ideas come alive with clear and lively writing accessible to undergraduates or even good students in the higher secondary grades. I have tried to keep that standard in mind throughout and still do justice to the complexities and subtleties that it is the historian's duty to convey.

Other helpful features are the frequent inclusion of the modern versions and ancient alternatives of Roman place names and fuller maps better coordinated with the text. I have also included many more cross-references in the text to make students aware of the numerous interconnections that give texture and depth of meaning to events. At the same time, a more comprehensive index should make it easier to use for reference.

As always, it is a pleasure to acknowledge those who have aided and encouraged me. The University of Connecticut and its History Department have generously provided the space, time, and staff without which my task would have been far more difficult. Mrs. Diedra Gosline did most of the word processing, while Mrs. Roberta Lusa, Mrs. Lisa Ferriere, and my graduate assistant, Mr. Drane Wilkinson III, helped in many different ways. I should also like to thank the reviewers of this edition, Kevin K. Carroll, Arizona State University, and Sarolta A. Takacs, Harvard University, for their helpful suggestions.

Many hands at Prentice Hall have shepherded the manuscript around numerous obstacles on the road to publication. The *sine qua non* in the whole process has been the production editor, Louise Rothman. Her skill, tact, and attention to detail have saved me much anxiety and embarrassment.

I owe a special debt of gratitude to Dr. Alston Hurd Chase, late master of Latin and Greek at Phillips Academy in Andover, who bequeathed to me an invaluable library of reference works and ancient texts that have spared me innumerable trips across campus.

Finally, I must express my deepest appreciation for the abiding love and friendship of my former colleague Prof. Albert E. Van Dusen and his wife, Wilda, who proofread the manuscript, provided strong encouragement and support, and gave me a home away from home during my labors.

Allen M. Ward
Storrs, Connecticut

I

The Foundations
of Early Rome and Italy

When most people think of Rome, they think of the Roman Empire, Rome of the emperors, which starts with the Emperor Augustus in 27 B.C. and lasts for centuries thereafter. The death of Maurice in A.D. 602, which marks the shift to more characteristically Byzantine history, provides a convenient date for the end of this book, although one could continue until the Islamic conquests and beyond. Before the seemingly endless Empire, however, there was the period of the Roman Republic. Then public business, *res publica,* was controlled by the adult male citizens in public assemblies, upper-class officials (magistrates) elected by the assemblies, and the senate, a body of experienced advisors made up of all current and former holders of certain offices (magistracies). The traditional date for the founding of the Republic is 509 B.C., which may not be far from wrong. Before the Republic stretches the period of the Monarchy, when Rome was governed under a simple form of kingship.

Under Augustus, April 21, 753 B.C., was accepted as the date of Rome's founding by Romulus, supposed to be Rome's first king. Modern archaeologists used to accept the idea that 750 B.C. was approximately correct, but newer archaeological work in Rome and the surrounding territory of central Italy has made that date untenable as either the date of first settlement or the beginning of a formally orga-

nized city. Now it appears that the site of Rome has been continuously inhabited since the late Bronze Age, between 1200 B.C. and 1000 B.C. It is here that one must begin the story of Rome, for to understand how the Roman Empire and its culture were created, it is necessary first to understand the geographic, demographic, and ethnic conditions that shaped the development of Rome from a primitive village in prehistoric Italy to the urban republic whose confederacy embraced all the peoples of Italy. That accomplishment gave the Romans the resources and outlook that helped them to conquer the greater part of Western Europe, much of the Ancient Near East, and most of North Africa and unite them into the single political and cultural entity of the Roman People.

Geography Unlike Greece, which was closer to the ancient centers of civilization in the Near East and Egypt, Italy did not reach a high level of civilization in the early Bronze Age. It simply took longer for the influence of civilization to spread west to Italy. Nevertheless, despite this initial geographic disadvantage, Italy was geographically favored to dominate the Mediterranean Sea and the older centers of civilization around its eastern basin once it had achieved an internal level of development on par with them.

1

Ancient Italy

First, separated from the rest of Europe by the Alps on the north, Italy is naturally oriented toward the sea. The west coast has access to the Tyrrhenian Sea; the southeast coast overlooks the Ionian Sea; and the east coast from the "heel" of the peninsula's "boot" northward fronts the Adriatic. Italy juts out like a giant pier from the continental mass of Europe southwestward 750 miles into the middle of the Mediterranean proper. Therefore, it and its geological extension, the island of Sicily, separated from it by only the narrow Straits of Messana (Messena, Messina) and from North Africa by only ninety miles of water, naturally dominate the sea lanes that link the eastern and western Mediterranean basins and the lands around them. Accordingly, before the rise of greater powers to the north and west, strategically and economically the power that controlled Italy was in an ideal position for dominating the whole Mediterranean world.

Second, Italy enjoyed internal geographic advantages that made it possible for a single city to unite it and become strong enough to use its great strategic and economic advantages overseas. Although the Apennine Mountains cut through Italy in a great arc swinging out from the northwest southeastward along the Adriatic coast and then back to the southwest coast along the Tyrrhenian Sea, they are not a serious barrier to internal unity. On the average, they are 4,000 to 6,000 feet high and are pierced by numerous easy passes. Moreover, the plains of Italy and Sicily were among the largest and best agricultural areas in the Mediterranean world.

Bounded by the Alps on the north and northwest and by the Apennines on the south, the northern part of Italy is a vast alluvial plain watered by the Po and Adige rivers. On the west coast, between the Apennines and the Tyrrhenian Sea, are the wide lowland plains of Etruria, Latium, and Campania, fertilized by a layer of volcanic ash and weathered lava ejected by the many volcanoes that had been active in earlier geologic times. These plains are watered by the Arno, the Tiber, the Liris, and the Volturnus, which were easily navigated by small ships in ancient times and provided convenient communication between the coast and the interior. These fertile plains supported dense populations that made Italy, in Vergil's words, the "mother of men," the main source of ancient military might.

Wood and Mineral Resources The physical geography of Italy also made available other valuable resources. Although ancient Italy was not rich by modern standards, it was for its time. Until they were overcut in the late first millennium B.C., extensive forests provided abundant wood for fuel and timber for ships and buildings. The most abundant mineral resources were stone building materials: hard stones like marble, granite, basalt, and flint; and softer, more easily worked types like sandstone and various kinds of tufa (cappellaccio, Peperino, Grotta Oscura, and travertine), as well as volcanic pozzolana for making cement. Etruria not only possessed these resources but also was the area richest in metals important for the ancient economy. It produced lead, zinc, copper, silver, and tin and controlled most of ancient Italy's iron ore on the island of Elba (Ilva).

The Site of Rome Geographically, Rome was ideally situated to take full advantage of Italy's resources and strategic position. As the Roman historian Livy (Book 5.45.5) duly noted, Rome benefited from its location on the Tiber River and "a site uniquely adapted to the growth of a city." It was centrally located on the naturally favored west coast of Italy fifteen miles up the Tiber on the northern edge of Latium. Here the Tiber River has a big bend and is slowed somewhat by Tiber Island midstream. In ancient times, the curved shore provided an ideal landing spot, and Tiber Island provided the first convenient ford and bridgehead nearest the river's mouth. Also at this point, seven hills ranging from 200 feet to 700 feet above sea level rise above the river's east bank and make the site easily defensible. The hills nearest the Tiber are the Capitoline, the Palatine, and the Aventine, separated from one another by intervening valleys. Farther to the east and enclosing them in a kind of arc stand

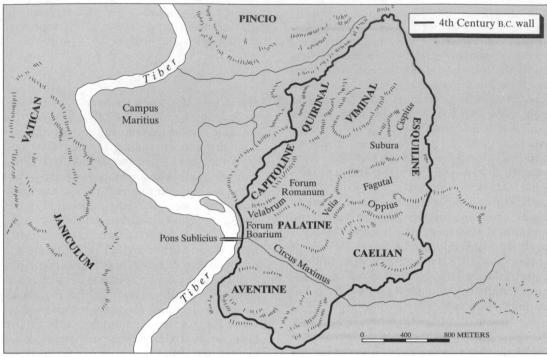

Site of Ancient Rome

the other four: the Quirinal, the Viminal, the Esquiline, and the Caelian. On those seven hills stood the later city of Rome. Two other hills across the river, the Janiculum and the Vatican, were ultimately incorporated, too.

Although the importance attributed to the Tiber alone can be exaggerated, it was significant. In early times, the Tiber and its valley were important routes for bringing salt from the coast into central Italy. Eventually, Rome became Italy's largest river port as Greek, Phoenician, and Etruscan merchants took advantage of its ideal location for trade with central Italy. Sandbars at the Tiber's mouth prevented the passage of large warships so that Rome was safe from naval attack. The river itself helped to block attacks by land from the north.

While the Tiber River and its valley provided communications north into central Italy, having the bridgehead nearest to the mouth of the Tiber also gave the Romans easy access to the coastal route between Etruria and the plains of Latium and Campania. Thus Rome's

geographic position in Italy made her the focal point of the communication routes running up, down, and across the peninsula; communications that enriched her through trade and permitted her armies, with minimum expenditure of effort, to strike in almost any direction at will. The seven hills made possible the observation of enemy movements, and the proximity of the hills to one another facilitated the fusion of several village communities into a single state, ultimately the largest in area and population not only in Italy but also, perhaps, in the whole premodern world. Strategically located for both defense and offense, Rome, as a river port, bridge town, road center, and magnet of trade and population, was thus favored by nature to be the capital of a unified Italy and, given Italy's central location and large population, the seat of a Mediterranean empire.

The Peoples of Pre-Roman Italy Demographic factors are another source of economic, social, political, military, and cultural strength. The population of Italy by the beginning of the Roman Republic (ca. 500 B.C.) was the product of a diverse ethnic and cultural heritage that stretched back thousands of years. The Romans recognized part of this diversity in their own early legends, which, for example, told how Romulus attracted settlers to Rome by establishing a place of asylum for outcasts and exiles from all over Italy; how those men stole their wives from neighboring Sabines; how an Etruscan immigrant named Tarquin rose to become the fifth king of Rome; or how the powerful Sabine Attus Clausus (Appius Claudius) and his whole clan of four thousand relatives and dependents added their strength to Rome's in return for citizenship. This recognition of their own heterogeneous origins, as opposed to the highly exclusive attitude of the ancient Greek city-states, allowed the Romans to assimilate other people and unite Italy into a strong federation based on an unusual degree of equality and fairness for ancient times.

From Paleolithic Times to the End of the Bronze Age, 700,000 to 1000 B.C. Human habitation in Italy goes back to at least 700,000 B.C. during the Lower Paleolithic period (2,500,000 to 200,000 B.C.). At that time, it was limited to the Apennine Mountains, where limestone caves provided shelter, and supplies of flint and chert were available for toolmaking. At the end of the Middle Paleolithic period (200,000 to 40,000 B.C.), finds of *Mousterian* tool types in caves at Sacropastore and Monte Circeo in Latium indicate the presence of Neanderthal groups. During the Upper Paleolithic period (40,000 to 10,000 B.C.), there are numerous finds associated with human beings of the present type. Caves in Liguria, for example, have preserved stone tools and wall paintings closely resembling similar finds in the Paleolithic caves of Spain and France.

Paleolithic hunters and gatherers adapted to changing environmental conditions during the Mesolithic period (10,000 to 5000 B.C.), and there is continued evidence of connections with people in France and Spain. Rapid changes began to take place after 5000 B.C. during the Ne-

olithic period (5000 to 2500 B.C.). Painted pottery appears in southern Italy that has links eastward to Dalmatia and the Peloponnese and westward to Capri and the Lipari Islands. In northern Italy, people who produced small clay female figurines and dark, polished square-mouthed pottery decorated with incised geometric decorations had links with people on the northeastern Adriatic coast and possibly eastern central Europe. People in northwestern Italy, however, had stronger connections with people of western Switzerland and eastern France.

It is clear that there were flourishing internal and external trade networks during the middle and late Neolithic periods. What is not clear, however, is to what extent developments in Italy were the result of cultural contacts with others and to what extent, if any, they were caused by immigration. Beginning around 2500 B.C., the use of copper and then bronze is connected with central Europe in northern Italy and with the Aegean in the South. Material culture and the technology of metalworking advanced more rapidly in the North, where the trade in amber from northern Europe crossed the Alps into the Po valley on its way to the Aegean world via the Adriatic.

At the beginning of the Bronze Age, around 1700 B.C., substantial villages of rectangular huts framed in timber began to appear in the Po valley. They flourished for a long time and built up rich deposits of organic matter that mark their sites with layers of rich black earth, *terramara*. Their inhabitants, known as the Terramaricoli, hunted bear, boar, and deer; cultivated flax, beans, and two varieties of wheat; raised cattle, sheep, and pigs; produced various types of pottery decorated with grooves, dimples, and bosses; and were skilled casters of bronze tools and weapons. The related Peschiera culture represented by lakeside villages in the Alps shared many of these characteristics.

At the beginning of the late Bronze Age (1300 to 1100 B.C.), there may have been some migration of newcomers across the Alps and into the Po valley, where they mixed with the Terramaricoli. Certainly, major cultural changes took place. New types of pottery appeared, and horses were added to the inventory of domestic animals. Representations of chariots and four-wheeled wagons carved in Alpine rocks may also indicate the arrival of such vehicles at the same time, but as yet there is no direct evidence of their presence. If these changes were produced by newcomers, they may represent the first wave of Indo-European-speaking peoples to arrive in Italy. The term *Indo-European* is a purely linguistic one used to identify the family of related languages that include Sanskrit in India, Persian, Armenian, the Slavic tongues, Greek, the Celtic dialects, the Germanic languages, English, Latin, and all the Latin-derived Romance languages.

The spread of what is called the Apennine culture at the same time also seems to reflect an influx of Indo-European speakers who probably came from the Balkans and entered Italy on the east and southeast coasts by way of the Ionian Sea. Their pottery styles and decoration are similar to ones found in Greece and the Balkans. They gradually spread throughout the Apennine range and established a fairly uniform culture. They lived in simple huts or even mountain caves and buried their dead in rock-cut tombs or simple earthen graves. One of their major sources of livelihood was transhumant pastoralism. That is, they moved their flocks between winter pasture on the coastal lowlands and summer pasture in the mountains (as high as 6,000 feet up). They and the Terramara people had access to late Bronze-Age trade goods such as pottery and metalware that were brought from Greece by Mycenaean traders along the Italian coast. In fact, the stimulus of Mycenaean trade created a common style of bronze artifacts from central Europe, across Italy, and around the Aegean.

Around 1100 B.C., another influx of Indo-European-speaking migrants occurred. They were part of the widespread disturbances and movements of peoples that characterized the late Bronze Age all over central Europe and the eastern half of the Mediterranean. These immigrants came from central Europe. They were representatives of the Urnfield culture that flourished there and evolved into the later

culture that came to be associated with the Celts by 500 B.C. The name *Urnfield* is taken from their distinctive practice of cremating their dead and placing the ashes in urns that were buried close together in cemeteries. The urns were all variations of a general design called biconical because they were tapered toward the top and bottom. The upper part was usually covered with a top shaped like a bowl or helmet.

The spread of a material culture is not always accompanied by the migration of particular people, but often it is. For example, no one would deny that the spread of Greek material culture in southern Italy between 800 and 600 B.C. was accompanied by the immigration of Greeks or that the spread of European material culture in North and South America between A.D. 1500 and 1900 was accompanied by the immigration of Europeans. In view of certain linguistic similarities between the Celtic languages, which evolved north of the Alps in association with the later stages of the Urnfield culture, and the Italic dialect group, which evolved south of the Alps in the areas where Urnfield material culture appears, it is hard to deny that some significant influx of people from north of the Alps occurred. People do not adopt language through mere cultural contact nearly so readily as they adopt material culture.

Urnfield settlements spread rapidly from the Po valley to the southern limits of Italy. Sometimes they may have taken over or been assimilated into some of the existing Terramara and Apennine villages. Often they established new settlements on high ground; sometimes they added fortified walls for increased protection. Their funerary urns show local variation in shape and decoration. Collections of bronze status goods have been found in graves and individual hoards. They include various types of large bronze "safety pins" called *fibulae* (sing. *fibula*), knives, embossed cups, and pieces made from sheets of bronze. While their settlements were numerous, they in no way replaced or overwhelmed previous populations. Instead, they and the older inhabitants interacted to produce several distinctive local cultures and populations in the Iron Age.

Early Iron-Age Italy, 1000 to 750 b.c. The Villanovan culture marks the transition from the Bronze to the Iron Age during the tenth century B.C. in Italy. The term *Villanovan* comes from Villanova, a small hamlet five miles east of Bologna, where many of the artifacts typically associated with Villanovan culture were first discovered. The earliest examples of Villanovan culture have been found farther south in southern Etruria and northern Latium, including the site of Rome. It is not possible, however, to give any particular ethnic meaning to the term *Villanovan*. The people who produced the Villanovan culture probably evolved from interaction between those associated with the earlier Urnfield culture and various other people with whom they traded and intermingled.

Villanovan culture carried on many of the traditions associated with the Urnfield culture. People lived in curved-sided huts made of wattle and daub on a frame of poles, cremated their dead, and buried their ashes in tall biconical urns placed in round holes or rectangular stone-lined tombs. Various metal tools, weapons, and small ornaments, such as brooches, bracelets, and razors, were placed inside or around the tombs. In the South, the ashes of the dead were sometimes placed in clay hut-urns, which were miniature versions of the curved-sided huts used by the living.

Evidence of the kinds of cultural interactions that took place can be seen at or near the southern Villanovan sites where some people did not cremate their dead but buried them in long rectangular pits or trenches, *fossae* (sing. *fossa*), lined with stone. This tradition is probably derived from the Apennine culture that appeared earlier in this region. To distinguish "*Fossa* People," however, from "Villanovans" as different ethnic groups on the basis of their different burial practices is methodologically dubious.

The Peoples of Italy, ca. 750 to 400 B.C.

The people of various prehistoric cultures known in Italy only from archaeology evolved into a number of distinctive groups identified in

A typical biconical cinerary urn for cremation burials in the Villanovan period. (Courtesy Fratelli Alinari, Florence, Art Resource, New York)

the written sources of Roman history and further classified by archaeological research. Numerous factors contributed to their evolution: first, specific local conditions; then, commercial contacts with outsiders like the Phoenicians, Greeks, and emerging Celtic peoples north of the Alps; and eventually, the immigration of newer settlers in large numbers such as the Greeks in the South and the Celts in the North. The Romans themselves had come into existence through this same process. They contin-

Peoples of Early Italy

ued it as they interacted with the other peoples of Italy, who helped to shape the later course of Roman history. The names of these people will occur often in the next few chapters, and it will be helpful to give a brief overview of them now.

Ligurians (Ligures) The Ligurians were composed of several different subgroups who inhabited the northwest corner of Italy between the Alps, the Ticinus River, and the western flank of the Apennines down to the Arno River. They were probably descended in large part from the early Neolithic inhabitants of the area, and their linguistic affiliations are unclear. In their predominantly mountain terrain, most of the Ligurians never reached a high level of development and were often the convenient targets for Roman commanders looking for easy triumphs in the second century B.C. On the coast, however, several fine harbors like Genua (Genoa), Savo (Savona), and Albingaunum (Albegna) offered their inhabitants the chance to become skilled sailors and merchants, and establish prosperous communities.

Etruscans To the west and south of the Ligurians were located those people collectively known as Etruscans. Like their Greek contemporaries, they shared a common language and general culture but were politically fragmented and had many local differences. They spoke a non-Indo-European language. The words of surviving texts can be read because they are written in an alphabet borrowed from the Greeks, but they cannot be fully understood because the language has no identifiable connection with any better-known language. The Etruscans were concentrated in Etruria, between the Arno and the Tiber rivers, but extended north across the Apennines into the Po valley from the Rubicon River to Lake Maggiore and southward into Campania. They developed a rich, powerful urban culture and will be treated more fully in the next chapter.

Gauls (Celts) By the late fifth century B.C. the central part of the Po valley between the Ligurians and the Veneti had been heavily settled by Gauls (*Galli*). They overwhelmed the earlier

Etruscan inhabitants and eventually caused the area to be known as Cisalpine Gaul, "Gaul this side of the Alps." They were a branch of the Celts, another Indo-European-speaking people. The Celtic family of languages and the Italic dialects seem to share a common origin among the Indo-European-speaking people of the Urnfield culture of the late Bronze Age. The Celts had spread out from central Europe, first by moving west into France, the British Isles, Spain, and then south and east into Italy, the Balkans, and finally Asia Minor, where they settled as the Galatians.

Latins On the west coast of central Italy south of the Tiber lies the fertile, well-watered plain of Latium, home of the Latins. They were another Indo-European-speaking group that had evolved out of the general spread of such speakers throughout most of Italy in the late Bronze and early Iron ages. Their Italic dialect and that of the neighboring Faliscans made up one of the two major Italic dialect groups that predominated in the central Apennine region. The foothills of the Apennines in eastern Latium and the rolling central plain were ideal for herding and the cultivation of grain. Latium was well forested until late in the first millennium B.C. and provided an abundant supply of wood for building and fuel. Accordingly, the Latins grew in numbers and developed many prosperous towns—Alba Longa (destroyed ca. 600 B.C.), Antium, Ardea, Aricia, Cora, Lanuvium, Lavinium, Praeneste, Rome, Tibur, and Tusculum. Rome would eventually unite them all, and through Rome their Italic dialect would become one of the most important languages in the world.

Umbro-Sabellians Throughout the central Apennines, from the Rubicon in the North, where the mountains come close to the Adriatic at Ariminum (Rimini), and down through Campania and Lucania, dwelt a group of tribes speaking related Italic dialects previously called Osco-Umbrian and now often referred to as Sabellic. Among these tribes were the Umbrians, Vestini, Frentani, Sabines, Aequi, Marsi, Volsci, Campani, Lucani, and Samnites.

Though their family of Italic dialects was Indo-European, these dialects retained a large element of the non-Indo-European language spoken by earlier inhabitants of the region. The tribes represented by these dialects were primarily pastoralists and peasant farmers, whose constant need for more land to support their growing populations brought them into frequent and bitter conflict with the wealthier, more urbanized people of the neighboring plains, especially Latium and Campania, who also often sought to expand their own territories. The external history of Rome during the early Republic (509 to 264 B.C.) revolves primarily around wars with these neighboring tribes, particularly the Aequi, Marsi, Volsci, and Samnites.

Oscans and Iapygians The Oscans originally dwelt in Lucania around Campania. They were largely descendants of an earlier non-Indo-European-speaking people. Sabellic speakers, particularly the Samnites, gradually moved into their territory and superimposed their Sabellic dialect. Even before that, however, the Oscans already may have been influenced by earlier Indo-European-speaking migrants. Across the Apennines, along the lower Adriatic and around the Gulf of Tarentum, were several tribes known collectively as Iapygians. They had evolved in close cultural and commercial contact with Mycenaean and post-Mycenaean Greece, and there may well have been some admixture of migrants from the Balkans but certainty is impossible. One of these tribes was the Massapii, who have given their name to Massapian, the language of the Iapygians. It, too, was Indo-European but was not part of the two Italic dialect groups.

Piceni (Picentes) Various subgroups generally identified as Piceni or Picentes inhabited the mid-Adriatic coast north and south of Ancona between the Aesis and Pescara (Aternus) rivers. Their culture is not so uniform as once thought, but there are enough similarities to continue to treat them together. They had a long tradition of stockraising supplemented with hunting and fishing. From the ninth century onward, they maintained active trade networks across the Adriatic, north and south along the Italian coast, and even west into Etruscan territory. The abundance of weapons found in early graves is compatible with their later reputation among the Romans as tough and warlike people. Linguistic evidence for the northern area is not clear, but the people in the southern region seem to have spoken a tongue firmly linked to the Sabellic dialects. A number of leading men from Picenum became important at Rome in the second and first centuries B.C., the most important of whom was Pompey the Great.

Greeks All around the coast of southern Italy from the Bay of Naples to Tarentum, Greeks had established important colonies since the end of the ninth century. Several were prosperous trading centers and exercised significant cultural and economic influence upon the other peoples in Italy. They will be discussed further in the next chapter.

All these various peoples of diverse ethnic and geographic origins and having distinctive cultural heritages made up the population of Italy between 500 and 400 B.C. At this time, therefore, Italy was fragmented and disunified. Later, however, as the descendants of these various peoples were absorbed into the Roman state through peaceful alliance or, most often, violent conquest, they merged into the Roman People (*Populus Romanus*).

II

Etruscans and Greeks
in Pre-Roman Italy

Complex urban communities in Italy evolved first in the area corresponding to Etruscan settlements from the central Po valley down through Etruria, Latium, and Campania between 800 and 600 B.C. A similar phenomenon occurred in the Greek lands of the Aegean after starting a little earlier in places like Cyprus and Phoenicia. In fact, the origin of complex urban communities in Italy must be seen as part of a general pattern connected with increasing population and commerce in the eastern Mediterranean.

By 800 B.C., Phoenician traders looking for metals like silver, copper, lead, tin, and iron were active along the west coast of Italy. They found significant sources in Etruria and on the island of Elba (Ilva). Greek traders soon joined the Phoenicians. Both brought the native peoples of Italy into contact with the advanced cultures and economies of the eastern Mediterranean. That contact stimulated the growth of correspondingly complex societies in Italy. On no one was that impact stronger than on those who came to be known in English as Etruscans. The ancient Greeks called them Tyrsenoi or Tyrrhenoi, and the Romans called them Tusci or Etrusci, but they seem to have called themselves Rasenna.

The Land of the Etruscans   Early Etruscan centers have been found at such places as Ca-

pua in Campania, Praeneste (Palestrina) in Latium, Veii and Volaterrae (Volterra) in Etruria, and Marzabotto and Felsina (Bononia, Bologna) in the Po valley. By 400 B.C., however, the expansion of other peoples had limited the Etruscans to a triangular area between the coast of the sea that bears their name (the Tyrrhenian Sea) and the Arno and Tiber rivers. Called Etruria in ancient times and Tuscany today, it, too, still echoes their name.

Geographically it falls roughly into northern and southern halves. In the North there are fertile river valleys, plains, and rolling sandstone or limestone hills with metal-bearing strata. The southern part is wilder and rougher, shaped by the actions of volcanoes, wind, and water. The soft, volcanic stone called tufa has been carved into deep valleys or gullies surmounted by peaks or small mesas on which many of the earliest Etruscan cities are found.

At a time when village life predominated in the largest part of Italy, the centers of Etruria had already become towns, and some of the towns were becoming cities. These cities were often built on or near Villanovan sites, sometimes on the coast or near it on a river—Caere (Cerveteri), Tarquinia (Tarquinii), Vulci, and Populonia (Populonium)—and sometimes inland—Volsinii (Orvieto), Clusium (Chiusi), Perusia (Perugia), Arretium (Arezzo), and Volaterrae. Ancient sources say that at their height the Etruscan people were leagued in a federation of twelve cities. To list the twelve is not easy because the various sources do not agree on the names and more than one league existed. In addition to the towns mentioned above (which found a place in written history by fighting against the Romans), archaeology is constantly finding others.

Sources for Etruscan History

Most modern knowledge of the Etruscans is derived from the ruins of their cities and, more particularly, their tombs. Tombs of various sizes, shapes, and types—the well and trench tombs of Villanovan times, the *tumuli* (great mushroom-shaped, grass-covered mounds with bases of hewn stone), the circular stone vaults built into hillsides, and the corridor tombs cut out of rock—whether containing pottery, metalware, furniture, jewelry, or wall paintings, all help to reveal the cultural life of the Etruscan people.

Nearly ten thousand Etruscan inscriptions (some dating back to the seventh century B.C., others as late as the age of Augustus) have been found. Many can be translated with a fair degree of confidence, although the Etruscan language is not fully understood. They have not yet shed much light on early Etruscan political history because only about a dozen contain more than thirty words, and most are only lists of proper names, religious formulae, dedications, or epitaphs. Nevertheless, useful social, religious, and cultural inferences can be made from their stylistic and statistical patterns.

Unfortunately, surviving historical accounts of the Etruscans were all written by their Greek and Roman enemies. Greek stories of Etruscan origins appear in Herodotus from the fifth century B.C. and in Dionysius of Halicarnassus and Strabo, both from the late first century B.C. They and Diodorus Siculus, another late first-century-B.C. Greek historian, also describe Etruscan conflicts with the Greeks and Carthaginians for domination of the sea in the West. To these and other Greek writers, the Etruscans are infamous as pirates and immoral lovers of luxury. Livy and later Latin historians describe a period of supposed Etruscan domination of Rome in the sixth century B.C. and concentrate mainly on Rome's wars with

Etruscan cities. Cicero and other Roman writers also comment on Etruscan religion and its influences.

Etruscan Origins

The question of where the Etruscans originated has been generating speculation and controversy for at least twenty-five hundred years. According to Herodotus (Book 1.94), the earliest Etruscans were Lydians who had migrated from Asia Minor to find a new homeland when their own was suffering from famine. About 450 years later, Dionysius of Halicarnassus (Herodotus' birthplace), took the opposite view in his *Roman Antiquities* (Book 1.25–30) and claimed that the Etruscans were native to Italy.

Some modern historians have argued that the Etruscans migrated from central Europe before 1000 B.C. and settled in the Po valley and later in Etruria. This view has been largely rejected. Archaeological evidence now indicates that Etruscan towns and cities evolved from villages that were part of the Villanovan culture during the late Bronze and early Iron ages. This change began after the Phoenicians and Greeks started trading and settling along Italy's western shore. Most early Etruscan towns appear on or near earlier Villanovan sites without a radical break in the archaeological record to indicate an invasion of new people. For example, as at Tarquinia (Tarquinii), one of the earliest Etruscan cities, different styles of burial and the kinds of objects found in graves appear as a progressive development: first, early Villanovan cremation and burial in simple urns; then either cremation and burial or inhumation (burial of the whole body) in trench graves (with more luxurious grave goods in each case); and finally, the general practice of inhumation in elaborately decorated and furnished rock-cut chamber tombs, which are an outstanding feature of high Etruscan civilization.

The early "Orientalizing" period of Etruscan civilization in the late eighth and early seventh centuries B.C. shows many Near Eastern and Aegean influences in art, jewelry, dress, and weaponry. These influences were not limited to the Etruscans but were part of a more general cultural development among the peoples of central Italy. They are rightly seen as the result of trade and contact, not the wholesale influx of outsiders. As will be seen, Greeks did begin to settle in the Bay of Naples in Campania with the establishment of the earliest Greek colonies in Italy at Pithecusae (Aenaria, Ischia) and Cumae around 750 B.C. That they did not, however, either settle farther north or even move into the interior of Campania may indicate that the indigenous population was already too numerous and strong. These colonies were primarily the vehicles of trade and contact. For example, the Etruscan alphabet quite clearly seems to have been borrowed from the Greek alphabet used at Cumae. There is no evidence of Etruscan literacy before contact with the Greeks, and the Greek colonies along the Bay of Naples remained resolutely Greek while sites elsewhere in Campania became Etruscan.

Etruscan Economy Etruscan civilization could not have existed without the natural wealth of its territory. The fertility of the soil and the mineral resources of the region were major economic assets (p. 3). The Etruscans exploited them on a large scale through agriculture, mining, manufacturing, lumbering, and commerce.

The alluvial river valleys produced grain for domestic use and export and flax for linen cloth and sails. Less fertile soils provided pasture for cattle, sheep, and horses, whereas the hillsides supported vineyards and olive trees. As the population expanded, an ingenious system of drainage tunnels (*cuniculi*) and dams won new land by draining swamps or protected the old by checking erosion.

The Etruscans energetically exploited the rich iron mines on the coastal island of Elba (Ilva) and the copper and tin deposits on the mainland. At Populonia (Populonium) the iron ore from Elba was smelted into pig iron. The mining and refining of copper was carried on around Volaterrae (Volterra) and Vetulonia (Vetulonium). Many Etruscan cities exported finished iron and bronze wares, such as helmets, weapons, chariots, urns, candelabra, mirrors, and statues, in return for other raw materials and luxury goods. They also made linen and woolen clothing, leather goods, fine gold

jewelry, and pottery. Virgin forests of beech, oak, fir, and pine fueled the fires of Etruscan smelters; supplied wood for fine temples, houses, and furniture; and provided timbers for the ships of war and commerce.

Trade kept Etruscan Italy in close contact with the advanced urban cultures of the Mediterranean world. It led ultimately to the introduction of a money economy in Italy and a standard coinage. The earliest coins found in Etruria were minted by Greek cities in Asia Minor. After 480 B.C., Etruscan cities began to issue their own silver, bronze, and gold coins.

Etruscan foreign trade was mainly in luxury goods and high-priced wares. It enriched the trading and industrial classes and stimulated among the upper class a taste for elegance and splendor. That explains the Etruscans' reputation for excessive luxury among contemporary Greeks.

Etruscan Cities and Sociopolitical Organization By the end of the seventh century B.C., the Etruscans had developed several strong states, each centered on a rich and powerful city. For economic reasons, they built cities in fertile valleys or near navigable streams; for military reasons, they built on hilltops whose cliffs made them easily defensible. At first they fortified their cities by wooden palisades or earthen ramparts and then with walls of masonry, often banked with earth.

Inside the walls, the Etruscans seem to have laid out some of their cities on a regular grid plan, as the Greeks had begun to do. In some cases they appear to have centered the plan on two main streets intersecting at right angles like the *cardo* and *decumanus* of the later Roman military camp. The first monumental buildings to go up were temples for the gods and palaces for the king. Then, as the population increased, side streets were paved, drains dug, and places built for public entertainment. These cities, as in Greece, were the political, military, religious, economic, and cultural centers of the various Etruscan states, which formed leagues, usually of twelve members, primarily for the joint celebration of religious festivals. The jealousy of the member cities and their insistence on rights of sovereignty prevented the formation of a federal union, which might have acted to repel the aggression that later threatened to destroy them one by one. When events at last forced the cities to unite, it was too late.

During the early period of state formation, the executive power of the Etruscan city-states was in the hands of kings elected and assisted by councils of aristocratic chiefs, who were their colleagues. The king was the symbol of the state, commander-in-chief of the army, high priest of the state religion, and judge of his people. He wore purple robes and possibly a golden crown, and he rode in a chariot inlaid with ivory. As he passed through the streets, heralds preceded him and lictors accompanied him with the fasces (bundles of rods) and double-bitted axes, symbols of judicial, military, and religious authority. Yet he was neither a hereditary monarch nor an absolute ruler. Sometime during the sixth or fifth century B.C., the nobles stripped him of his political, military, and judicial powers, and set up republics governed by aristocratic senates and headed, as in Rome, by magistrates elected annually. The real power in the state was at all times in the hands of a small circle of landowning families who, having acquired or seized large tracts of the best land, became the landed aristocracy and enjoyed all the privileges of a warrior aristocracy and priestly class. In some cities they were later forced to share the government with a small group of wealthy outsiders who had won wealth and social standing through mining, craftsmanship, or commerce. The middle and lower classes consisted of small landowners, shopkeepers, petty traders, artisans, foreign immigrants, and the serfs or slaves of the wealthy.

Women and the Etruscan Family   Women and the family played prominent roles in Etruscan life. Etruscans came to have two or three names corresponding to the Roman *praenomen, nomen (gentilicium),* and *cognomen* (p. 40). The first indicated the individual, the second the family at large, and the third a particular

branch. Those who could afford them built large family tombs capable of holding many individuals. Epitaphs frequently recorded both the father and mother of the deceased, and tomb paintings and sarcophagi (coffins) often portrayed husbands and wives reclining or seated together in mutual respect and affection.

The Etruscan wife often appeared in public with her husband. She went to religious festivals with him, and, unlike her Greek counterpart, she reclined beside him at public banquets. The common practice of decorating women's hand mirrors with words indicates a high degree of literacy among those who could afford these expensive items. Many Etruscan women also took a keen interest in sports, either as active participants or as spectators. Their presence at public games, where male athletes sometimes contended in the nude, made them appear worse than immodest to the Greeks, who usually forbade their women to witness such exhibitions.

Etruscan Culture and Religion   Etruscan as a spoken language persisted as late as the second century A.D., and enough written materials survived till the first century to enable the Emperor Claudius I (A.D. 41–54) to write twenty books on Etruscan history. Nevertheless, all Etruscan literature is now lost. There were probably many works on religion and the science of divination and, perhaps, annals of families and cities. There were also some rustic songs and liturgical chants. If the Etruscans composed poetry, dramas, or sophisticated works of philosophy, history, or rhetoric, no trace of them has been preserved or recovered.

If there was an intellectual vacuum in their society, the Etruscans redeemed themselves partially by their passion for music. They had a predilection for the flute, whose shrill strains accompanied all the activities of life—banquets, hunting expeditions, athletic events, sacrifices, funerals, and even the flogging of slaves. As flutists, trumpeters, and lyre players, they were renowned in Rome and throughout Greece. Dancing was also a major element of their culture. They danced at banquets, religious festivals, and funerals. In tomb paintings, they seem to dance with ecstasy and abandon and with an almost orgiastic physical exuberance.

Sports Tomb paintings show that outdoor sports assumed an important place in Etruscan life. Because of their association with religion and rites for the dead, sports were serious affairs, and to neglect them was considered a sacrilege. There were also sociological reasons for the popularity of games. The growth of cities, the expansion of industry and commerce, and the rise of a wealthy leisured class gave the time, opportunity, and money for indulgence in sports of all kinds. Hunting and fishing, which for prehistoric people had been a labor of necessity, became a form of recreation for the Etruscan rich. Next to hunting, riding and chariot racing were favorite sports. Organized athletic competitions, such as were common in Greece, were especially popular. They gave the upper-class youth a chance to display their skill and prowess; they served also as a source of entertainment for the masses. Most illuminating in this regard is the great frieze in the *Tomb of*

the Chariots at Tarquinia, which shows a vast stadium and a large number of spectators of both sexes applauding and cheering the charioteers, the runners, the boxers, the wrestlers, and acrobats. Several paintings reveal the popularity of the equivalent of the Roman gladiatorial contest. This deadly sport, thought to have been a relic of the primitive custom of human sacrifice, formed part of the funeral games and originally was intended to supply blood to sustain the spirit of the deceased.

Religion Most modern writers assert that the religion of the early Etruscans was pervaded with fear and gloom and dominated by a superstitious and authoritarian priesthood. This view seems inconsistent with the wall paintings found in tombs, which reveal the early Etruscans as a joyous, life-accepting people. They believed that the ruling powers of the universe manifested themselves in every living thing: in human beings, in trees, in every flash of lightning, in lakes and streams, in the mountains and the sea. To penetrate their mystery, to make these powers speak, to wrest from them their secrets, called for elaborate ritual. Once discovered, the

Etruscan Sarcophagus from Cerveteri. Late sixth century B.C. (c. 525 B.C.), Terracotta. Museo Nazionale di Villa Giulia Museum, Rome, Italy. (Alinari/Scala, Art Resource, New York)

will of the deity had to be obeyed and executed with meticulous care. As time went on, Etruscan religion became more and more formal, theological, and legalistic in the struggle to guarantee the goodwill of powerful deities.

The Etruscan gods paralleled those of the Greeks and Romans. First among them was Tinia, who, like Zeus and Jupiter, spoke in thunder and hurled his lightning bolts across the sky. He executed the decrees of destiny. With him were associated two goddesses of Italic origin, Uni (Hera, Juno) and Menrva or Menerva (Athena, Minerva). Together they formed a celestial triad whose temple (*kilth*) stood in every Etruscan city and on the Capitoline Hill at Rome. With nine other deities they formed the council of the Twelve Gods, six male and six female. The Etruscans believed that an infernal triad ruled over the lower world: Mantus (Hades, Pluto), Mania (Persephone, Proserpina), and Tekum (Demeter, Ceres), the goddess of the harvest.

Minor Etruscan deities included Vertumnus, the god of vines and gardens, and several other gods peculiar to certain cities and sacred places. In addition, there were the inferior deities or demons, of whom the most horrid was Charun, whose Greek namesake was Charon, the conductor of the dead to the underworld. He was represented in Etruscan art with a big nose, pointed ears, bluish skin, and snakes crawling over his head and shoulders.

The most striking aspect of Etruscan religion was the so-called *Disciplina Etrusca*. It was an elaborate set of rules that aided the priests in their study and interpretation of natural phenomena in order to forecast the future, know the will of the gods above, and turn away the wrath of the malignant spirits beyond the grave. There were several kinds of divination, but the most important was hepatoscopy, the inspection of the livers from sheep and other animals slaughtered for sacrifice by special priests (*haruspices*). Thunder, lightning, and numerous other omens were also studied as tokens of the divine will. The flight of birds, which the Romans studied with scrupulous care before battles, elections, or other affairs of state, was for the Etruscans of secondary importance.

Etruscan Art and Architecture   The art of the Etruscans was their most remarkable and enduring achievement. Religion gave it occasion and impulse. As in Greece, Etruscan temples and precincts were lavishly decorated with ornamental reliefs and paintings. Believing, as did the Egyptians, in the survival of life after death, wealthy Etruscans provided elaborate tombs for the dead, some of gigantic size, such as the tumulus of Regolini-Galassi (about 158 feet in diameter) at Caere (Cerveteri), and they spared no expense in their construction and decoration. In his grave, the Etruscan noble or merchant prince had his chariot and hunting gear, his jewels and favorite Greek vases, his best wines, and beautiful pictures that magically brought to life pleasant hours at home, in the country, and at the seaside. When she died, his wife, decked out in her costly robes and finery, was buried with him so that they could enjoy the afterlife together.

In these tombs are preserved many masterpieces of both Greek and Etruscan art—black-figured vases imported from Athens, sarcophagi (coffins) with sculptured lids, statues, silver goblets, gold and silver jewelry, engraved gems, and wall paintings. The desire to perpetuate the personality of the dead gave rise to the tradition of portrait sculpture similar to that of the Romans.

Origin, Development, and General Features
Three major traditions shaped Etruscan art: the simple geometric designs of the Villanovan culture; the "Oriental" represented by Assyrian, Hittite, Persian, and Egyptian motifs from the East; and the contemporary styles of the Greeks. Throughout the sixth century B.C., Greece exerted a powerful influence upon the art of Etruria and the entire Mediterranean world. Attic black- and later red-figured vases were imported in tremendous quantities and were much admired and imitated by the Etruscans. Numerous Greek artists and craftsmen appeared in the harbors and cities of southern Etruria to ply their trades for wealthy Etruscan patrons.

During the fifth century, the political, social, and economic crises brought on by wars with Rome and an outlook that was not in sympathy with the restrained classicism of the Greek Golden Age saw the Etruscans prefer the older, more archaic Greek styles. Later, however, the more exuberant and emotional Greek art in the period after Alexander the Great found much favor with the Etruscans, whose situation had improved after peace with Rome.

Architecture Etruscan architecture was also part of a larger Italic pattern in central Italy. Houses had the characteristic *atrium,* an unroofed central court around which the living rooms were arranged. Etruscan temples had the low, squat, top-heavy look of Italic temples in general. Often set on a hill, the Etruscan temple was also raised up on a stone base mounted in front by a broad flight of walled-in steps. The walls of the temple itself were built of brick, and the roof and columns of wood. Columns were used only for a deep porch in front. The solid walls of the cella (main chamber) were directly behind it. The cella itself, almost square in shape, was subdivided into three smaller chambers, one for each of a triad of gods. Each chamber had its own door at the front of the temple. Topping the whole structure was a long, low-pitched wooden roof.

The brick and woodwork were sheathed in molded terra-cotta (baked-clay) panels decorated with Greek motifs like leaf moldings and acanthus scrolls. The pediment and gable were adorned with terra-cotta friezes and statuary of gods and mythical scenes. The overall effect was somewhat jarring because the highly ornamented pediment and gable clashed with the plain columns below.

The Arch Etruscan architects were famous for their use of arches and vaults. Early Etruscan builders formed arches and vaults by corbeling (projecting out each course of stones in a stepped pattern until everything met at the top to form a solid whole). In the third century B.C., however, the Etruscans borrowed the familiar round arch made from bricks or voussoirs, stones cut into truncated wedges to fit the desired curve. They then applied it to the construction of city gates, sewers, bridges, and tombs.

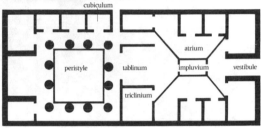

Roman atrium house with a peristyle and hortus *(garden) off the back, drawing and plan of, from* Roman Art, *second edition, Nancy and Andrew Ramage, Prentice Hall, 1996*

Sculpture Etruscan sculpture is truly outstanding, and though influenced at first by Near Eastern and later by Greek sculpture, it developed into a genuinely national art—vital and true to nature. Clay, not marble, was the medium used by the early Etruscan sculptors in some of their best work. Their skill in handling this soft, flexible material is evident in numerous sofa-shaped sarcophagi with complicated reliefs sculptured on the sides and figures of married couples on the covers. Solemn or gay, attractive or ugly, the faces of the men and women reclining on these elaborate terra-cotta sofas belong to real people. The realism exhibited in this portrait sculpture and carried at times to the extreme of caricatured violence is as alien to archaic Greek taste as is the naked physical strength and vigor of motion displayed

Artist's reconstruction of temple at Veii. (Marina Mueller)

in the celebrated *Apollo* of Veii. Except for the smile, typical of Greek archaic statues, the naturalism of the *Apollo* is apparent from the vigor of the god's stride and the tenseness of his powerful leg muscles as he advances boldly upon his enemy.

The special forte of later Etruscan sculptors was bronze. In this medium were created several masterpieces, such as the celebrated *Capitoline Wolf* (sixth century B.C.) and the equally famous *Chimaera* of Arretium (Arezzo) (fifth century B.C.). They show the blend of Greek and Near Eastern influences with a realistic spirit that characterizes the best Etruscan art. You can almost feel the wolf's alert gaze, and the realism of the *Chimaera* is such that one can almost hear the roar of pain torn from the brute when he was hit by the deadly darts of Bellerophon. Another famous Etruscan statue is that of an orator from the second century B.C. With stern features and commanding personality, he has all the dignity of an Appius Claudius or Cato the Elder.

Painting Painting, although perhaps not the greatest of the Etruscan arts, is the best preserved. It is preserved in tombs, especially those at Tarquinia and Caere, which surpass even the tombs of ancient Egypt as repositories of ancient painting. Although the Greeks probably excelled in painting as they did in sculpture and architecture, their paintings (except those preserved on pottery) have been lost, dispersed, or destroyed with the buildings that housed them. The Etruscan works are therefore of particular historical importance because they furnish the sole link between the lost Greek and later Roman paintings.

The drawings are bold and incisive; the colors are bright and achieve fine effects through juxtaposition and contrast. The themes, usually taken from life, are developed with direct and uncompromising realism and are often brutally frank. In the Tomb of the Augurs at Tarquinia (sixth century B.C.), one scene shows two wrestlers locked together in struggle. Another scene in the same series depicts a sport as brutal as the gladiatorial contests of the later Roman arena: a burly, thickset man, his head covered by a sack, is trying to knock down a savage dog whose leash is held by an opponent. If the man wins, he has his adversary at his mercy; if he loses, he will be left to the dog.

The festive side of life is a favorite theme in tomb paintings. In the *Tomb of the Lionesses* men and women are depicted reclining at a banquet. Everybody is in high spirits. In one scene a massive bowl is wreathed with ivy, and musicians are playing. To the right of the bowl, a dancing girl is performing a lively and voluptuous dance. A male dancer, shown in darker color, matches the rhythmic movements of the girl. Scenes of this kind are very commonly depicted in tomb paintings and, taken together, provide an interesting commentary on Etruscan social and religious life.

The Fate of the Etruscans   By 600 B.C., the Etruscans had become the most powerful people in Italy. In the Po valley, they battled the Ligurians in the West and expanded eastward to take advantage of trade coming into the North through the Adriatic Sea. In fact, the Adriatic takes its name from Atria (Adria), a city originally founded by Greeks at the mouth of the Po and taken over by Etruscans in the fifth century. Many rich and powerful cities had risen in Etruria, with one league of twelve in the North and another in the South, while Capua eventually headed a league of twelve cities in Campania.

Etruscan expansion and conquests in new areas stemmed not so much from the concerted drive of any expanding state as from the uncoordinated efforts of individual war chiefs and their retainers. On land, Etruscan warriors had begun to adopt the Greek hoplite style of warfare, in which soldiers wore metal helmets, breastplates, and greaves (shin guards) and fought in ranks instead of as individual "heroes." Etruscan seafarers had also adopted the latest advances in naval architecture. In 540, a combined Etruscan and Carthaginian fleet won a naval battle over the Phocaean Greeks near Corsica and forced them to withdraw to Massilia (Marseille), a powerful

Apollo of Veii. Etruscan. c.500 B.C. Painted terracotta. Height ca. 5ft 10ins (1–8m). (Museo Nazionale di Villa Giulia, Rome. Scala, Art Resource, NY.)

The Capitoline Wolf, *sixth-century Etruscan bronze. (National Gallery of Art, Washington, D.C.)*

The Chimaera, *fifth-century Etruscan bronze. (Art Resource, New York)*

Phocaean colony on the southeast coast of what is now France. In 525/24, however, the Greek colony of Cumae on the Bay of Naples repulsed an Etruscan attack, and in 504 Cumae and some Latin allies defeated an army of the Etruscan adventurer Lars Porsenna at Aricia, sixteen miles southeast of Rome. In 474, Cumae joined forces with the Greek tyrant Hieron I of Syracuse and won a great naval victory over an Etruscan fleet. From that point, the Etruscans' fate as independent peoples was sealed. The Gauls were moving into the Po valley, the Samnites began to take over Campania, and the Romans soon started expanding into Etruria.

A wall painting (ca. 475 B.C.) in the "Tomb of the Lionesses" at Tarquinia showing a ritual dance. (Fratelli Alinari, Art Resource, NY)

A wall painting (ca. 500 B.C.) in the "Tomb of the Augurs," showing wrestlers and a masked figure trying to beat down a dog. (Archivi Alinari, Art Resource, NY)

The Greeks in Italy Beginning in the eighth century B.C., traders familiar with Italy and Sicily pointed the way for permanent settlers from Greek cities wishing to gain strategic commercial outposts and find relief from a growing shortage of agricultural land and associated problems. Although it may have maintained sentimental, religious, and commercial ties with its mother city, each new colony became a completely independent political entity (*polis*), just like the individual city-states in the Greek homeland. Therefore, the same divisiveness and lack of unity that characterized the Greek homeland characterized the colonies.

Greek Colonies in Italy It is significant that the chief sponsor of the first major Greek settlement in Italy at this time (ca. 750 B.C.) was Chalcis on the island of Euboea, just off the east coast of central Greece. Chalcis, whose name means copper in Greek, was a center of metalworking and fought a famous war with its neighbor Eretria in the eighth century for the rich Lelantine plain, which lay between them. The need for copper and land brought settlers from Chalcis to Italy, which was relatively well endowed with both.

Along with the Chalcidians came some people from Eretria and two other neighboring towns, Cumae and Graia. They settled first about 750 B.C. on the island of Pithecusae (Aenaria, Ischia) just off the northern tip of the Bay of Naples. As they expanded, they moved across to the mainland and established Cumae, named for Cumae in Euboea. Later, a little farther east on the bay, they founded a separate port town, and when they outgrew those two places, they established another city, Naples (Neapolis, "New City"), to handle the overflow.

All of these towns left their marks on the Romans. It was probably from Cumae, either directly or through Etruscan intermediaries, that the Romans derived the Latin alphabet, in which these words are written. Through Cumae, many Greek gods became familiar to neighboring Italic tribes—Heracles (Hercules), Apollo, Castor, and Polyduces (Pollux), for example. The oracle of the Sibyl at Cumae won great renown, and a collection of her supposed sayings, the *Sibylline Books,* was consulted for guidance at numerous crises in Roman history.

Although the Greeks called themselves Hellenes, the Romans called them Greeks because of the Graians (Graioi, Graei), whom they first met in settlements around the Bay of

Naples. The port for Cumae became Puteoli (Pozzuoli), the most important trading port in Italy throughout most of Roman history. Naples became the most populous city in the rich district of Campania and opposed Roman expansion there for many years. After the Romans took control of it, however, wealthy Romans built sumptuous seaside villas all around its bay, and many, like Vergil, learned Greek literature and philosophy from Naples' poets and philosophers.

Numerous other Greek settlers soon followed the founders of Cumae. Attracted by fertile soil, Achaean Greeks settled on the western shore of the Gulf of Tarentum at Sybaris around 720 and Croton around 700. They established so many cities in southern Italy and Sicily that the Romans called the whole area *Magna Graecia*, Great Greece. Sybaris became so famous for its wealth and luxurious pleasures that such things are still referred to as sybaritic, and people who indulge in them are called sybarites. Sybaris was eventually destroyed by its rival Croton, which is renowned as the seat of Pythagoras and his community of philosophers. The Romans even believed (quite wrongly) that one of their early kings, Numa Pompilius, was a disciple of Pythagoras.

To the north of Croton and Sybaris, the Spartans founded Taras (Tarentum, Taranto) also about 700 B.C. It became a great manufacturing center and gave its name to the whole gulf by which sailors seeking its wares reached it. Two hundred and fifty years after the settlement of Tarentum, Athenians founded Thurii near the site once occupied by Sybaris. Eventually, jealousy and suspicion between Tarentum and Thurii involved Rome in their affairs and led Tarentum to call in King Pyrrhus of Epirus against the Romans. That fateful move led to the final Roman takeover of all the Greek cities in southern Italy.

Sicily   Across from Italy on the fertile island of Sicily, the Greeks founded even more cities than in Italy proper. There they were the rivals of the Phoenicians, who settled Panormus (Palermo), Solus, and Motya in the West, while the Greeks eventually occupied most of the rest of the island at the expense of the older, native inhabitants. The oldest of the Greek cities here, as in Italy proper, was founded under the leadership of Chalcis. Founded about 730, it was named Naxos for some fellow settlers from the island of Naxos and was located at the base of Mt. Aetna, where it guarded the Straits of Messana (Messina) between Sicily and Italy. Within the next few years, the Chalcidians also founded Catanae, Leontini, and Zancle (later called Messana) on Sicily and Rhegium (Reggio di Calabria) across the straits on the toe of Italy.

Dorian Greek cities predominated on the southeastern and southern coasts of Sicily at places like Selinus, Gela, Acragas (Agrigentum, Gigenti), and Syracuse. Of them, Syracuse, founded by Corinthian settlers around 730, was the most important. Growing even larger than Athens, it rivaled her in wealth, power, and culture. While the Syracusan tyrant Hieron I led the Greeks of the West to victory over the Etruscans in the naval battle of Cumae in 474, Dionysius I briefly gained ascendancy in southern Italy and Sicily at the beginning of the fourth century. In 264, the rivalry between Carthage and Syracuse over the city of Messana contributed to Roman intervention and the First Punic War, which ended with the Romans in control of Sicily.

Decline of the Greek Cities in Italy and Sicily

As was the case with the Etruscans, the Greek city-states founded in Italy and Sicily, though achieving a high level of prosperity, culture, and political sophistication, ultimately failed to stop the Roman conquest of Italy in the fourth and third centuries B.C. The individual Italian and Sicilian Greek cities were unable to find a middle ground between uncooperative independence and predatory imperialism. Rather, they perpetuated the fierce independence and predatory rivalries of Greek city-states everywere. Therefore, their alliances were weak and their empires unstable. The Romans ended their independence one by one while borrowing heavily from their artists, writers, and philosophers.

III

Early Rome to 500 B.C.

The stories of Rome's founding and the so-called Monarchy or Regal period, which ended ca. 500 B.C., present many problems for the modern historian. The traditional accounts found in ancient literary sources were not formed until hundreds of years after the events narrated therein. For example, it was an antiquarian named Marcus Terentius Varro in the late first century B.C. who calculated the canonical date of April 21, 753 B.C., for Rome's founding. Moreover, the ancient literary sources do not always square either with each other or with the vast amount of physical evidence excavated by archaeologists since the late nineteenth century, much of it from tombs and graves. Since the 1960s, the sheer volume of bones, buildings, monuments, sculpture, pottery, furniture, jewelry, tools, weapons, other metalwork and items of daily life, and the organic remains of food and sacrifices has been overwhelming. Therefore, trying to construct a coherent and credible picture out of the disparate literary and archaeological evidence is a major challenge.

The Ancient Literary Tradition and Its Sources The oldest extant literary accounts of any significance all come from the second half of the first century B.C. The first is the second book of Cicero's dialogue *De Re Publica* (ca. 50 B.C.). Much longer is Book One of Livy's 142-book history of Rome, *Ab Urbe Condita*

(ca. 25 B.C.), and longer still are the first four books of the *Roman Antiquities* by the Greek author Dionysius of Halicarnassus (ca. 7 B.C.). Books Seven to Nine of the world history of Diodorus Siculus, a Greek from Sicily, are fragmentary but still important (ca. 30 B.C.). All four authors approached the writing of history as a branch of rhetoric, however, and their views of Rome's past were shaped by their own political concerns and experiences during the civil wars that destroyed the Roman Republic.

Similar things can be said about Plutarch and Cassius Dio. Plutarch, a Greek biographer and essayist who wrote in the late first or early second century A.D., supplements the earlier historians, particularly in his "biographies" of the supposed early Roman kings Romulus and Numa Pompilius. Cassius Dio, a Bithynian Greek who was a high Roman official in the late second and early third centuries A.D., covers early Rome in the first three books of his *Roman History*, but they are preserved only in fragments. Later Imperial writers like Florus, Aurelius Victor, Eutropius, Festus, Orosius, and Julius Obsequens in the fourth and fifth centuries basically summarize Livy for early Rome and only repeat what had become the dominant historical narrative.

The Augustan poets, Vergil, Horace, Ovid, and Propertius, are another important part of the literary tradition. They and their later commentators often refer to people, events, and practices from Rome's remote past. Other bits and pieces can be found in later poets as well.

Sources of the Literary Tradition As it now exists, the literary tradition rests on the mostly lost works of antiquarian researchers, earlier historians, and the writers of patriotic epics and drama. In the late third and early second centuries B.C., a number of historians (many of them called annalists because they narrated events on a year-by-year basis) and patriotic epic poets tried to present coherent versions of early Roman history (see pp. 138–142). These accounts are all lost, but they established the outline on which all later narratives ultimately depend. In the second and third centuries, antiquarian researchers interested in preserving and explaining interesting or obscure facts about early Roman institutions, religion, life, and art compiled detailed and learned studies that became raw material for other writers.

The data on which the poets, annalists, and antiquarians had to draw were not so scanty or worthless as many have assumed. Various traditional practices and oral sources preserved much authentic information, however imperfectly understood or distorted in details during transmission. Important families maintained wax images (*imagines*) and carved portraits of great ancestors and kept alive the memories of their deeds to be sung or recited during banquets, at funerals, and on military campaigns. Stories of major civic events were retold from generation to generation on significant public occasions. Hereditary priests passed on the lore of cult and ritual, and archaic hymns continued to be sung long after the words were commonly understood. Archaic political institutions and practices were never abandoned but simply overlaid with new ones as changed conditions required. No people ever respected the customs of their ancestors more or were more tenacious in holding on to them in however attenuated form than the Romans.

There were also other customs, oral traditions, monuments, and records among Rome's Latin, Etruscan, and Greek neighbors that Romans could utilize in reconstructing Rome's early days. Although it is now lost, there once existed a large body of Etruscan records and writings that could have been consulted. The same must have been true of the Latin and Greek cities that Rome eventually conquered. Indeed, the earliest written accounts of Roman history were found in Greco-Sicilian historians like Timaeus (ca. 356 to 260 B.C.) and Philinus (ca. 250 B.C.). They were the models for early Roman accounts and preserved information from the traditions of the cities of *Magna Graecia,* which had had contacts with early Rome.

Some documents, archives, and monuments from early Rome were also available to antiquarians, annalists, and poets. For example, the Regia or "King's House" sat on one of the most hallowed sites in the Roman Forum. Beneath it, archaeologists have found a series of successive buildings going back to around 770 B.C.

Literacy had long been known in Latium and Rome. The earliest-known inscription in a Greek alphabet has not been found in Greece or the western Greek colonies, but in Latium. It appears on a small vase from a grave dated to ca. 770 B.C. In Rome, the earliest-known piece of writing is the Greek name *Ktektos* inscribed on a small Corinthian pot from a grave dated between ca. 730 and ca. 625 B.C. The earliest public inscription yet found at Rome is the *Lapis Niger* or Black Stone inscription, named for the black stone under which it was found in the Roman Forum (see p. 30). It is dated to some time in the sixth century.

By 625, Rome had reached a significant level of urbanization, and some kinds of documentary records were needed. It is not likely that there were any kinds of systematically connected records from that era, but some records may have been kept on papyrus, cloth, or wood, and major items like laws, religious dedications, treaties, and commemorative inscriptions on public buildings were set up on durable stone or bronze. In the late first century B.C., schoolchildren were still memorizing the text of Rome's first law code, the Twelve Tables, which was compiled in the mid-fifth century and preserved some of the customs and laws of earlier centuries (pp. 59–60).

Many have assumed that little of the documentation that existed before ca. 500 could have survived the sack of Rome by marauding Gauls ca. 390 B.C. Recent research, however, indicates that the devastation has been exaggerated. Records on durable materials like stone and bronze probably were largely unaffected. More perishable records were housed in buildings such as the temple of Saturn, the Capitol, and the Regia, where the *pontifex maximus* (Chief Pontiff) performed important duties and kept his archives during the Republic (p. 56). Those buildings remained intact, and the records kept therein may well have survived. Also, since the Romans sent the Vestal Virgins and their sacred paraphernalia across the Tiber to Caere before the sack, they probably took similar precautions to protect other important personnel and materials such as records.

Reconstructing Early Roman History

For the period before 500, however, the surviving oral materials and written documentation were not enough for constructing the rather detailed picture presented by the existing literary tradition. The problem is that although much oral, monumental, and documentary material was available to later poets, historians, and antiquarians, particularly for the period after 625, its original context and meaning was not always clear by their day, and it existed in no systematic chronological or narrative form. They had the task of making sense out of it. Where there were gaps, they filled them as suited their own needs and circumstances. Thus they produced the basic outline that was further enhanced, embellished, and modified by the writers of the late first century B.C. and the early Empire. The story created contains valuable information that helps scholars make sense of raw archaeological data. Those data, in turn, help scholars to correct and fill out the story.

According to the basic outline of Rome's beginning in the ancient literary tradition, it all started with the Trojan hero Aeneas, who escaped the fall of Troy and after many years of wandering landed in Latium. There he met the Greek hero Evander, who already had settled at the future site of Rome on the Palatine Hill. He also met Latinus, king of the Latins, won the hand of Latinus' daughter Lavinia after a war with her native suitor, and founded a city named Lavinium in his new wife's honor. Aeneas' son, Ascanius (Iulus), subsequently founded Alba Longa. Numitor, the twelfth Alban king after Ascanius, had a daughter, Rhea Silvia (Ilia). Numitor's brother, Amulius, overthrew him and forced Rhea Silvia to join the Vestal Virgins. She became pregnant by the god Mars and bore two sons, Romulus and Remus. When Amulius ordered them to be killed, they were set adrift on the Tiber and washed up on shore near the site of Rome. There a she-wolf found them and suckled them. They were discovered by a shepherd, Faustulus, who raised them. Subsequently, they each founded a settlement near the site of their miraculous rescue, but Romulus soon killed Remus in an argument. Romulus populated his city with men who were exiles and fugitives from all over Italy. Lacking wives, Romulus and his men carried off the women of a nearby Sabine village. The resultant war ended in a reconciliation of the two groups and an amalgamation under the joint rule of Romulus and Titus Tatius.

This account reflects the combination of various Greek, Etruscan, Latin, and Roman traditions. Greek settlers in Italy and Sicily were naturally anxious to link their area with the glorious epic traditions of their native land. The wanderings of Odysseus in the *Odyssey* provided a handy link. Sometime (ca. 600?) after the founding of Greek colonies on the bay of Naples, the anonymous Greek author of the appendix to the main text of Hesiod's *Theogony,* called Latinus a son of Circe and Odysseus and made him king of the Tyrrhennians. The Greeks often did not distinguish between the Etruscans and the Latins, and archaeologically their early material remains are scarcely distinguishable. Latinus is obviously a manufactured eponym (person for whom something is named or supposedly named) for Latium and the Latins. In the sixth century, the Sicilian Greek poet Stesichorus may have added the story of Aeneas' journey to Italy. The story definitely appeared in the work of the late fifth-century Greek historians Hellanicus of Lesbos and Damastes of Sigeum. Aeneas quickly became associated with the Etruscans, who were the great foes of the Greeks in Italy, as the Trojans had been of the earlier Greeks in the Homeric epics.

The Etruscans eagerly adopted Aeneas as their own. Through him, they could have a past as ancient and glorious as their Greek rivals. Sixth-century votive statues of Aeneas carrying his father, Anchises, have been found at Veii, and the same scene appears on seventeen vases found in Etruscan tombs of the late sixth and early fifth centuries. Perhaps the kings of Etruscan origin who ruled Rome during the sixth century popularized the links with the Greek epic tradition.

The Etruscans may have added the story of the she-wolf to the legend of Rome's founding. The great bronze she-wolf that still adorns the Capitol is usually considered an Etruscan work of about 500 B.C. (p. 20). The baby twins were not added until the Renaissance, but there is an Etruscan relief sculpture of about 600 B.C. that shows a wolf suckling a baby boy.

The story that Romulus and Remus came from Alba Longa and founded Rome is part of the earliest Latin tradition. In the early period, Alba Longa was Rome's chief rival for leadership of the other Latin towns, and the story would have been useful propaganda to bolster Alba's claim to leadership. Archaeological evidence does show close connections between early Rome and Alba but cannot be used to prove any Alban origin for Rome.

The characters Romulus and Remus look like two slightly different versions of the typical eponymous (giving one's name to) hero whose name is actually derived from that of the city which he is supposed to have founded. The later Romans would have been familiar with such stories from the Greek settlers in southern Italy. In fact, one Greek legend claims that Rome was founded by Rhomus, another son of Odysseus and Circe.

One of the last elements to become part of the standard legend was the list of Alban kings. As Greek scholars and historians became more skilled, they became concerned with es-

tablishing precise chronologies. In the early part of the third century B.C., the Sicilian Greek historian Timaeus, the first comprehensive writer on the western Greeks and events relevant to them, equated the foundation date of Rome with that of Carthage, supposedly 814 B.C. About fifty years later, another Greek, Eratosthenes, established the standard date in antiquity for the fall of Troy, 1184 B.C. Clearly, Aeneas could not have wandered 370 years before getting to Italy, and a large gap existed between his son's founding of Alba Longa and Romulus' founding of Rome. The Alban king list was handy for bridging this gap, and its tradition was flexible enough to be adapted to fit changes in the accepted date for Rome's foundation as the ancient equivalents of 748 B.C. and finally 753 B.C. gained favor.

Early Rome and Latium   It is clear that the traditional narrative of Rome's founding is completely unhistorical in its details. Nevertheless, this eclectic mixture of Greek, Etruscan, Latin, and Roman material does reflect a larger historical reality. Archaeological evidence shows that the evolution of Rome as a city-state cannot be separated from the larger pattern of urbanization taking place from the Po valley to the Bay of Naples during the eighth and seventh centuries B.C.

Although excavations indicate that the site of Rome has been continuously inhabited since between 1200 and 1000 B.C., it seems that important changes leading ultimately to urbanization began around the middle of the eighth century B.C. Some ancient Roman religious institutions, rites, and monuments that still existed in later centuries may have had their origin in the mid-eighth century B.C. and may account for calculations like Varro's that place the permanent settlement and foundation of Rome around that time. Indeed, the archaeological evidence is compatible with the idea that small Iron Age villages found on some of the hills associated with Rome began to expand and coalesce into a larger entity in that era.

Prior to then, their Indo-European-speaking inhabitants, who were similar to people who inhabited the rest of Latium, pursued simple lives as farmers and herders, lives that are reflected in their graves and later Roman legends, religious customs, and language. For example, Rome's legendary eponymous founder and his twin brother, Remus, allegedly were raised in a sheepherder's cottage; the festival of the *Parilia* on April 21, the day on which Romulus supposedly founded Rome, celebrated a cleanup day for stalls and stables; in honor of *Tellus,* or Mother Earth, the primitive goddess of the fruitfulness of animals as well as of crops, the early Romans twice annually celebrated the festival of the *Fordicidia,* at which they sacrificed a pregnant cow in the spring and a pregnant sow in early winter.

Because of this pastoral tradition, the Romans, like the Jews of the Old Testament, sacrificed animals to their gods: to Juno a goat, to Mars a bull, to Jupiter a white bullock. Traces of the same background are evident in the name given to one of their city gates, the "Mooing Gate" (*Porta Mugonia*), as well as in the words *egregius* (meaning "out of the flock" and, therefore, "excellent") and *pecunia* (meaning "wealth in flocks" but later "money in general").

Even so, pasturage could not have been pursued on a very large scale until the Romans had access to wider grazing lands and gained command of the trails to summer pastures in the Apennines. Perhaps standing behind the story of the Sabine women and amalgamation with Latium's Sabine neighbors are later battles for those trails and treaties giving the Romans access to summer pastures in the mountains, the Sabines winter pastures in the lower Tiber valley, and both the right of intermarriage.

Meanwhile, the Iron Age villagers had other sources of livelihood. They fished; raised pigs and chickens; and planted gardens of turnips, peas, beans, lettuce, and cabbage. On small plots of land adjacent to their houses, they cultivated *spelt,* a hard kind of emmer wheat, which, like durum, was more suitable for making porridge than bread. They probably also gathered wild grapes and figs, which they either ate as fruit or brewed into wine.

They wore coarse, homespun clothing and used crude, handmade pottery fired without kilns. They seem to have imported little except some simple jewelry and bronze or iron tools. Their houses were round or eliptical huts with thatched roofs and wattle-and-daub walls supported by a framework of posts and poles. Smoke from the fireplace escaped through a hole in the roof, and a single large doorway served for additional lighting and ventilation. Foundations of just such houses have been found on the Palatine Hill, in the Roman Forum, and at other sites in Latium.

Evidence from Graves The earliest graves at Rome have been found in the Roman Forum. The oldest are dated between 1000 and 900 B.C. They are simple cremation burials consisting of a large jar (*dolium*) containing miniature versions of the pottery and tools used in daily life. The pottery sometimes contained food and drink, and the urn for the ashes was often a miniature version of the typical huts in which people lived. Many similar burials have been found elsewhere in Latium and reflect the Proto-Villanovan culture of the late Bronze Age shared by other people in Italy. From about 900 to about 830 B.C. cremation burials continued in the Forum, but along with them appear simple inhumation burials typical of the Latial culture that emerged in the early Iron Age throughout Latium. Around 830 B.C., a new cemetery with only inhumation burials was opened up on the Esquiline. The inhumation burials in both the Forum and Esquiline cemeteries between ca. 900 and 770 B.C. contained only two or three ordinary vases, a bronze *fibula,* and no weapons in the case of a man. A female burial usually contained a *fibula* and jewelry like rings and glass or amber beads along with spindle whorls and loom weights for spinning and weaving.

Clearly no radical changes took place during this period, but evidence of population growth appears at the site of Rome and other places in Latium between 830 and 770 B.C. At Rome, dwellings spread from the Palatine to the Capitoline and Forum. The increased population and the habitation of the Forum probably necessitated the opening of the new burial ground on the Esquiline. By about 770 B.C., the

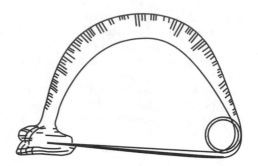

*Thickened-bow bronze fibula
from Latium*

growth of Rome and many communities in Latium had caught up with that of communities in Etruria. Now they were both poised to develop in tandem under the stimulus of increasing trade.

Long before Rome was settled, people from the hill country of the central Apennines had been beating a path along both sides of the Tiber to and from the salt beds near the river's mouth. (Salt was a valuable commodity in Europe even as late as the French Revolution. It was the special treasure of the lower Tiber.) While it was relatively simple to get down the river by raft, the strong current made it next to impossible to go back upstream, so that trails along the banks were used instead. The trail along the west bank was less broken and irregular and led to the best and most easily worked beds. When this trail came under the control of Etruscan Veii, independent salt miners and merchants had to use the Old Salt Road (*Via Salaria*), which ran along the east bank. When Veians later crossed the river and seized the fortress of Fidenae in the mid-seventh century, the salt men lost the use of this road. To save their lives or escape tolls, they had to bypass Fidenae by a wide detour inland via Nomentum on the Allia. Returning to the Tiber at Antemnae, they followed the Old Salt Road to Rome. The vicinity of Rome provided the only safe and convenient place to cross the Tiber, both because it was beyond Veii's range of control and because Tiber Island made it easy to ford. The earliest bridge built at Rome was the Sublician Bridge (*Pons Sublicius*). Made of wood in the late seventh century to replace a ferry be-

low Tiber Island, it attracted even more traffic and helped the early city to grow.

Beginning with the founding of the Greek colony at Pithecusae (Aenaria, Ischia) in the first half of the eighth century, the trickle of trade and outside influence that had been flowing through the slowly growing Iron-Age farming villages of Latium turned into a floodtide. This tide produced a sea change clearly marked in the archaeological record and lifted many Latin, Etruscan, and Campanian centers to the level of complex urban communities between ca. 750 and ca. 625 B.C.

By 770 B.C., graves in Latium and Etruria begin to show the influence of Greek imports on local cultures. As previously noted, the earliest example of writing in a Greek alphabet has been found on a pot from about 770 B.C. in a grave near the Latin town of Gabii. From a tomb in Veii comes Greek-style geometric pottery dated about 750 B.C. Greek influence on local pottery is evident from tombs on the Esquiline Hill dated between 770 and 730 B.C. Excavations in the Forum Boarium near the Tiber River at Rome have turned up eighth-century Greek pottery from Euboea, Corinth, the Cycladic Islands, and the colony of Pithecusae. Between 730 and 625, Greek imports appear in the Esquiline graves. One item is the Corinthian vase bearing the Greek name *Ktektos* (p. 24). It may indicate the burial of a resident Greek. Phoenician wine amphorae begin to show up in seventh-century Latin graves, and the foundation of a cult of the Greek god Hercules, associated with trade, in the Forum Boarium has been linked to resident Greek traders, or possibly even to Phoenician traders, because the Phoenician god Melqart was equated with Hercules.

The Seventh Century The level of material culture in Rome and Latium had changed enormously in the seventh century. Princely orientalizing tombs rivaling those of the Etruscans have been excavated south of Rome at Castel di Decima and Acqua Acetosa, Laurentina, and to the east at Praeneste. Graves at the first two sites contained men and women richly dressed with gold, silver, and bronze ornaments. Swords, lances, shields, and even chariots accompanied many of the men. At least one of the women at each site also had a chariot, the one at Acqua Acetosa, Laurentina, resembling a type found in Assyria. Some of the women had all the equipment for presiding over a sumptuous banquet—imported Greek pottery and Punic wine amphorae included. The tombs from Praeneste contained elaborate gold jewelry from Etruscan workshops, silver bowls with pseudo-Egyptian reliefs, bronze tripods from the Near East, bronze cauldrons decorated with oriental motifs like griffen heads, and many items carved from elephant ivory that could have originated only in Syria or Africa even if the carving was done by local craftsmen.

Parallels exist at Rome. One of the mid-seventh-century trench graves on the Esquiline contained a unit of armor and a chariot. A seventh-century grave in the Forum contained glass-paste beads, a bracelet of ivory, and a disc of amber from northern Europe. Others show that imports of expensive Etruscan metalware and pottery increased greatly after about 625 B.C.

During the seventh century B.C., Rome acquired substantial private and public buildings similar to those appearing at the sites in central Italy and decorated in similar style. Architectural remains excavated in the Forum show that by the end of the seventh century B.C. substantial houses were being built with stone walls made of square blocks of tufa and roofs of heavy terra-cotta tiles supported on wooden beams. They also had archaic terra-cotta decorations like those found on Etruscan buildings

from the same period. At about the same time, the Forum received its first pavement, a formal drain (the *Cloaca Maxima*) was put in, and a new street was laid over fill between the Palatine and the Velia, a low hill between it and the Esquiline. By 625 B.C., therefore, what had once been a loose collection of Iron-Age hilltop villages by the Tiber had truly become the city of Rome.

The growth of separate villages into a significant town during the eighth and seventh centuries B.C. can be traced in some of the archaic Roman religious practices that survived into historical times. The religious festival of the Septimontium (Seven Hills or Enclosed Hills) seems to have originated in the establishment of a common religious festival by the communities on the Palatine, Esquiline, and Caelian Hills, which actually embrace seven separate heights: the Esquiline and its three projections, the Oppius, the Cispius, and the Fagutal; the Palatine; the Velia; and the Caelian. Religious association seems to have led to political union under the Palatine community prior to the later incorporation of the Quirinal.

Two ancient priesthoods, the Salii and the Luperci (p. 57), were each divided into two groups representing the Palatine and the Quirinal. This practice indicates that the priesthoods originally were common to two independent communities. According to Livy (Book 2.13), the combination of the Palatine and Quirinal communities resulted in what is known as Rome of the Four Regions: the Palatine, Esquiline, Caelian, and Quirinal Hills. These four regions also fall generally within the ancient sacred boundary of the city of Rome.

The Early Roman State The combined archaeological and literary evidence indicates that not only the city but also the state that can be called Rome came into existence around 625 B.C. There had been, no doubt, recognized religious and community leaders before then, but the evidence regarding the traditional kings of Rome accords well with the idea that a self-conscious political identity and formally organized monarchic state crystalized at about the same time the Forum was paved and began to receive monumental shrines and temples. These projects required a greater coordination of labor and resources than an informal community could have commanded.

A state implies some kind of formal political institutions and practices that are collectively identified as its constitution. In all of her history, Rome never had a written constitution but, as in Great Britain today, only a constantly growing and changing body of custom, precedent, and legislation that determined what the "constitution" was at any historical moment. The archaic constitution of the Regal period was not complex. The basic outline was still preserved in the Republic that followed. Much may be deduced or inferred from information preserved in the Roman literary tradition and from what is known about similar monarchies in archaic Greece.

The Kings According to tradition, from its founding to 509 B.C., Rome was ruled by seven kings (Titus Tatius, Romulus' brief Sabine colleague, being excluded). The first four were alternately Latin and Sabine: Romulus, Numa Pompilius, Tullus Hostilius, and Ancus Marcius. The last three were Tarquinius Priscus (Tarquin the Elder), Servius Tullius, and Tarquinius Superbus (Tarquin the Proud). The two Tarquins were always recognized as Etruscan, but the question of Servius' Latin or Etruscan origin is in doubt. The names notwithstanding, it is a reasonable assumption that early Rome came to be ruled by kings, and so, too, did other archaic Latin city-states, such as Aricia, Tusculum, and Lanuvium.

That kings ruled at Rome in the sixth century is supported by two pieces of archaeological evidence. The first, dated to the last quarter of the century, is part of a bucchero cup clearly inscribed with the word *rex,* meaning "king." Moreover, it was excavated at the site of the Regia, whose name means "King's House." The second piece of evidence is the *Lapis Niger* (Black Stone) inscription on a block of Grotta Oscura tufa under the black pavement of the Forum. It is dated to the late sixth century and has RECEI, a form of the word *rex* in its inscribed text. In later times, it was believed to mark the grave of one of the early kings.

The existence in Republican times of certain terms and titles related to kings also indicates the existence of kings in an earlier stage of political development. In the Republic when death, resignation, or the failure to hold elections on time removed the regularly elected leaders, the senate declared an *interregnum,* which literally meant "a period between kingships," and appointed an *interrex,* "interim king," to hold elections. One of the priests of the Republican period was even called the *rex sacrorum,* "king of sacrifices." His wife was called *regina,* "queen," and his job was to carry on religious functions that must originally have belonged to the kings.

There are, however, many historical difficulties in accepting the detailed accounts of the kings found in the literary sources. First of all, Romulus seems obviously a made-up eponym. Second, even with Romulus, there are not enough kings to cover the period from 753 to 509 B.C. without improbably long reigns averaging thirty-five years. It is more probable that the earliest records went back to only ca. 625 B.C. Depending on the inclusion or exclusion of Titus Tatius, six or seven kings between ca. 625 and 509 B.C. would yield much more probable average reigns of seventeen to twenty years. On the other hand, there is no reason to reject the story that an Etruscan immigrant named Tarquin successfully established himself in Rome and eventually became king. The archaeological record shows that Greeks, Etruscans, and Phoenicians frequented the important trading center that was archaic Rome, and there is every reason to believe that a number settled there.

An apparently independent Etruscan tradition antedating the earliest Roman historical speculations corroborates the existence of the Tarquins. A fourth-century wall painting in the François Tomb near Vulci bears, among others, the name of Gneve Tarchu Rumach (Gnaeus Tarquinius of Rome). Macstrna (Mastarna), also named in this painting, cannot with any certainty be identified with King Servius Tullius, to whom some ascribe the Etruscan name

Mastarna, although the name Caelius Vibenna (Caile Vipinas), the legendary friend of Servius Tullius, also appears here. Other Etruscan inscriptions prove that the Tarchna (Tarquins) were Etruscan nobles.

What probably should be rejected, however, is the idea of a long-term Etruscan takeover of Rome. It is clear from the material remains that seventh-century B.C. Rome must have looked little different from contemporary Etruscan cities. That would have been even more clear to later Romans, who were still able to see many old buildings and monuments from that era as late as the first century B.C., when the Romans had long developed a more distinctive style of their own. It would have been perfectly logical to assume that Rome's earlier Etruscan appearance was the result of some Etruscan takeover associated with the Etruscan dynasty of the Tarquins. In light of current archaeological evidence, however, it is much more probable that seventh-century- B.C. Rome looked like an Etruscan city because both Rome and the Etruscan cities were part of a larger, central Italian cultural complex.

That is not to say that there were not attempts or even temporarily successful ones by individual Etruscan and non-Etruscan warlords to seize control of Rome in the sixth and early fifth centuries B.C. The literary tradition and a recently discovered Latin inscription of ca. 500 B.C. confirm the existence of powerful aristocratic chiefs who controlled private bands of armed dependents called "clients" (*clientes*) or "companions" (*sodales*). Such individuals seem to be represented in the stories of the Etruscans Lars Porsenna of Clusium and Aulus Vibenna of Vulci, who are said to have seized strategic hills and ruled at Rome for a time. Attus Clausus the Sabine chief (p. 53) and the renegade Romans Gnaeus Marcius Coriolanus and Appius Herdonius, who reportedly tried to seize the city for themselves in the early fifth century, probably were all cast from the same mold.

Indeed, it is not unlikely that the last of the Tarquins, Tarquin the Proud, murdered his predecessor and ruled Rome as a tyrant, as tradition records. That he initiated the building of the great temple of Capitoline Jupiter accords well with the archaeological evidence. It is not unlikely that Rome, just as other contemporary cities in Italy, was subject to the same forces that produced similar tyrants in the contemporary archaic Greek world. Therefore, the "Etruscan" appearance of Rome should not be attributed to a period of Etruscan domination but participation in a shared social, economic, political, and cultural world.

The Nature of Early Roman Kingship The living symbol of the unity, power, and authority of the early Roman state was the king. Though he held his office for life, he acquired it neither wholly by inheritance nor by popular election. It is clear that a king could influence the choice of his successor by bestowing favors on him or entrusting him with important duties, but the ultimate choice was not his. On the death of each king, the right of *auspicium,* determining the will of the gods by taking auspices, which gave divine sanction to royal authority, reverted automatically to the *patres* ("fathers") of the community. Often identified as being synonymous with senators, perhaps the *patres* at this time are best understood as only senators from certain *gentes* (clans), namely, the patrician *gentes,* whose members enjoyed the exclusive right of holding the priesthoods of various archaic cults (see p. 55).

The *patres* chose one of their members to serve for five days as *interrex*. He, in turn, appointed another *interrex* if necessary, and so it went until a new ruler pleasing to both gods and men was found. Interestingly, none of the known kings came from *gentes* that can be identified as patrician. Apparently, the *patres* always preferred candidates outside their own ranks to prevent divisive competition among themselves, or powerful leaders of war bands may have constrained them to do so.

The last *interrex* presented the accepted nomination to a popular assembly known as the *comitia curiata* (Curiate Assembly) for confirmation. Made up of all adult arms-bearing men (the *populus*), the Curiate Assembly witnessed the last taking of the *auspices,* expressed their approval of the new king by acclamation, and bestowed on him the power of command (*imperium*) as it pledged him loyalty and obedience. This formal investiture of the king gave him official sovereignty and the power to punish or even kill wrongdoers, a power symbolized by the fasces carried by the lictors who attended him (p. 14).

As chief of state and supreme commander of the army, the king had the power to make peace and war, direct foreign affairs, and conclude treaties with other states; to enforce military discipline, draft citizens into the army, and levy taxes in time of war; and to distribute booty among his soldiers or land among citizens in repayment of wartime loans. As director of internal affairs and administrator of justice, the king probably possessed both lawmaking and law-enforcement powers and issued edicts deemed necessary for the security and government of the state. Nevertheless, he had little to do with the formulation of private or civil law, because in early Rome that seems to have been created neither by royal decree nor by statute, but evolved out of use and custom and the social conscience of the community. The king promulgated the so-called "royal laws" in his capacity of high priest, for at that time law, not divorced from religion and custom, was regulated by priests.

As supreme head of the state religion, the king was personally inviolable and sacrosanct. His duties were to represent the people in their relations to the gods of the state, to perform certain public sacrifices, to take the *auspices* and so learn the will of the gods, to appoint the priests and supervise their activities, to draw up the calendar, and to proclaim the feasts acceptable to each of the gods. The gods had to be consulted before every important act of state—the election of rulers, the calling of the people to assembly, and the departure of armies for battle.

During the late sixth century B.C., kings such as the reputed immigrant Tarquin the Elder; Servius Tullius, who was said to be the son of a captured slave; and Tarquin the Proud, who was branded a hated tyrant in Roman tradition, may well have been comparable to the popular tyrants appearing in contemporary Greece.

Stories of them enjoying the favor of certain goddesses like Fortuna and Minerva and their utilization of purple robes and triumphal chariots may reflect their attempts to legitimize their power with the mythology and trappings of Near Eastern divinely sanctioned kingship, a model with which they could well have been familiar from contact with traders from the eastern Mediterranean. At the same time, they probably reduced the role of the traditional king (*rex*), whose political and military power they had usurped, to the performance of his cultic duties as the priest known in the Republic as the *rex sacrorum*, king of sacrifices (p. 52).

The Senate   In the Republic, the senate came to be the most powerful institution of the state. Under the kings, however, it was just what its name implies, an advisory body of elders (*senes*) to the king. It was his private council, appointed by him from among his friends and the important members of the city's leading families. The senate could not legislate and could give advice only when summoned by the king. He did not always accept its advice, but it was not politically wise for a king habitually to ignore or reject it, particularly on major issues. If he did, he would sooner or later incur the enmity of too many powerful men and might, as did the last Tarquin, even lose his throne.

The Curiate and Centuriate Assemblies (Comitia Curiata and Comitia Centuriata) The Curiate Assembly was based upon the groups to which the adult arms-bearing men (*populus*) originally belonged for the purpose of military service. All citizens were divided up into three tribes (*tribus,* literally "by threes")—Ramnes, Tities, and Luceres. Each tribe probably represented a district of the earliest city and was subdivided into ten smaller districts called *curiae,* from which is derived *curiata,* for a total of thirty. In assembly, all the men from each *curia* mustered together just as they would if called up for active military duty.

The role of the *comitia curiata* in government during the Monarchy was varied but not strenuous. The law of custom seldom required modification or change, and the men who constituted the *populus* were summoned into assembly by the king not to speak but to listen. Though they are said to have possessed even then ultimate sovereign power (*maiestas*), that power was latent, theoretical, still in a state of development. Nevertheless, the king was wise not to ignore it, if only to win the armed citizens' cooperation and consent to major changes in law and policy. They not only took part in the inauguration of a new king, but they also heard proclamations concerning peace, war, and other important affairs of state. The *comitia curiata* even attended the king in the performance of his religious duties, confirmed the appointment of public priests, witnessed, if not authorized, wills and adoptions, and dealt with other matters connected with private law.

This primitive assembly became politically obsolete during the early Republic, if not before the end of the Monarchy. It was superseded by another assembly of the people in arms, known as the *comitia centuriata* (Centuriate Assembly) (p. 55). This new assembly owed its existence to a reorganization of the Roman *populus* to integrate new immigrants and newly incorporated territory into the civic and military life of a rapidly growing city, probably in the latter part of the sixth century B.C.

The Early Roman Army The creation of a formal state organization that accompanied the full urbanization of Rome in the last quarter of the seventh century B.C. paralleled and was integral with the spread of new arms, armor, and military tactics in central Italy at the same time. A similar pattern had occurred at the beginning of the seventh century B.C. in Greece. The old heroic style of combat involving a few elite warriors backed up by a rather disorganized mass of retainers as seen in Homer gave way to tactics based on the hoplite phalanx.

The hoplite phalanx was a formation in which heavily armed infantry troops advanced to the attack in tight ranks several deep. Each soldier now carried a long spear for thrusting and a sword for close combat. He was protected by a *hoplon* (*clipeus* in Latin), a round shield smaller than earlier "body shields" and fastened to the left arm through a loop in the mid-

dle and a hand grip near the edge. A helmet, breastplate or corselet, and greaves (shin guards) all made of metal completed the panoply. Each man's right side was protected by the shield on his neighbor's left. So long as each man kept in formation, the hoplite phalanx was almost indestructible. Introduced by the Greeks into Italy in the seventh century B.C., the hoplite panoply spread rapidly among the native peoples, as the evidence from late seventh-century graves show.

The first formal Roman field army was a legion (*legio*) drawn from the three tribes, with each tribe's ten *curiae* providing a quota of ten to forty cavalry and one hundred heavy infantry for the hoplite phalanx. The one thousand heavy infantry of each tribe were commanded by a tribune ("tribal officer") of the soldiers, *tribunus militum,* and the cavalry unit of each tribe by a tribune of the cavalry, *tribunus celerum* (*equitum*). At the top, the supreme command belonged to the king or his appointee the *magister populi,* master of the army. Next to the king or *magister populi* in rank was the commander of the whole cavalry, the *magister equitum,* master of the cavalry. Outside of the phalanx were twelve-hundred light-armed troops, who could not afford the full hoplite panoply.

By the latter part of the sixth century B.C., the tribally organized *curiae* became obsolete for military purposes. The growing size and importance of the heavily armed hoplite phalanx, the *classis* as it came to be called, resulted in a reorganized and expanded field army associated with the reforms ascribed to King Servius Tullius in the literary tradition (p. 52). All of the changes credited to Servius Tullius could not have happened at once and probably were not fully developed until well into the Republic. Still, it is entirely possible that a king named Servius Tullius or someone like him in the latter part of the sixth century B.C. sought to increase Rome's military might and his own power by incorporating more men into the ranks of the *populus.*

It seems likely that "Servius" added a fourth tribe, perhaps in conjunction with incorporating the Quirinal into the Roman state, and increased the *classis* to 4,000 infantry made up of 40 units now called centuries (*centuriae*), "hundreds," instead of *curiae*. Later, the *classis* expanded to 6,000 infantry in 60 centuries. The officer in charge of each group naturally became known as a *centurion*.

That is probably all that the original "Servian" reform entailed. As the state grew in population and territory, new "rural" tribes were added to the original 4 urban tribes until a limit of 31 rural tribes was reached. Each tribe contributed an equal number of men to groups from which the field army, the legion (*legio*), was drawn. These groups also came to be called centuries because originally most to men taken from each group formed one of the centuries of the hoplite *classis*. The number of centuries eventually grew to 193 and were made up of people ranked by the value of their property. As this centuriate organization grew, it replaced the *comitia curiata* as the primary citizen assembly of the Roman Republic (p. 55).

During the Regal period, therefore, a group of small agricultural villages had evolved into a true city and state by the last quarter of the seventh century B.C. Location on advantageous trade routes had greatly stimulated this development and created a thriving urban center, although agriculture remained the primary way of life for the vast majority of the population. Rome, as it could now truly be called, had acquired a relatively sophisticated political and military organization on par with the major archaic city states of Greece and the rest of central Italy and had become a significant force in Latium and southern Etruria. Although there is no reason to declare the tradition that there were kings of Etruscan origin like the Tarquins at Rome to be totally unfounded, there is no reason to see Rome under the control of some external Etruscan power near the end of the Regal period. Rather, Rome had developed at the same time in the same cultural context as the cities of Etruria, and they would overthrow their increasingly "tyrannical" kings at about the same time. In the process, however, Rome would create the most powerful republic ever seen in the ancient world.

IV

Early Roman Society, Religion, and Values

The Principle of Hierarchy To understand Roman history, it is necessary to understand the nature of Roman personal and social relations and the religious and ethical frameworks within which they functioned. The operative principle in all aspects of Roman life was hierarchy. Inequality was an accepted condition of life in the Romans' view. There were higher authorities everywhere to whom those lower down in the hierarchy owed obedience and from whom they expected benefits in return for the greater privileges enjoyed.

Nowhere was this situation more clear or more crucial than in the Roman family. It was the basis of the early state, which was simply a community organized to protect the interests of its constituent families. Each family was controlled by a patriarch called the *paterfamilias*. What concerned the families as a group, particularly the most powerful among them, was the state, the *res publica* (literally the "common wealth" or "common thing"). Its close connection with the fathers of the leading families is confirmed by the Latin word for country, *patria,* which comes from the adjective *patrius,* "belonging to the father." Roman religion and law are basically extensions of the religious and ethical practices of the families and fathers who made up and controlled the community.

The Family The predominance of the family over the state never completely disappeared in Roman history, as can be seen in the dynastic ambitions of Roman emperors right up to the end. The family was a living thing, as the state was not. Citizens could be motivated to benefit the state not so much for the state's sake as for the honor and prestige that could be gained for themselves and their families. The approval of one's ancestors, whose presence was always felt in the *mos maiorum*—the traditions handed down from generation to generation—and in the death masks and busts that adorned the upper-class Roman home, and the chance to perpetuate oneself in the memory of future generations, were powerful incentives to civic action. On the other hand, where the interests of the family seemed to be at variance with those of the state, there was always a great temptation to sacrifice the state's interests if the two could not be reconciled. Therefore, the state could easily become the battleground of competing interests among the powerful families that controlled it.

The English word *family* is used to translate the Latin word *familia,* from which it is derived, but the Roman concept is not so wide-ranging as the English concept in some respects and is more extensive in others. The Romans distinguished among several different types of kinship connections that English often loosely lumps under the term *family.* Kin by marriage were affines (*adfines*). Relations with one's *adfines* could be very useful and important, but ties of blood or adoption, as one might expect, were more important. The least important of the blood or adoptive relatives were those in the female line, the *maternum genus*. On the other hand, there were two very important types of blood or adoptive relatives. The first, emphasized most in early Roman law, constituted one's agnates (*agnati*), blood or adoptive relations through the male line: father's siblings, father's other children, father's brothers' children, sons' children, grandsons' children, and so on down the male line. The second type of blood relatives embraced one's cognates (*cognati*), who were by blood or adoption the immediate family or "house" (*domus*), a person's parents, siblings, children, and siblings' children.

The *familia* proper was closely associated with one's cognates but included much more. It was, rather, a hierarchical association of housemates: cognates, clients (freeborn dependents), freed slaves (*liberti*), and slaves. Moreover, it included the spirits of deceased agnatic ancestors, the "greater ones" (*maiores*). They stood at the top of a generational hierarchy that included the living generations and those yet unborn. The living were expected to serve the spirits of the dead, *Di Manes,* in the afterlife through maintaining the sacrifices and rituals of the family cult and to follow the "custom of the ancestors" (*mos maiorum)* with the utmost respect. Three festivals were eventually devoted to propitiating the *Di Manes* with sacrifices and feasting, the *Lemuria* in May and the *Parentalia* and *Feralia* in February. The living also would seek to earn the respect of the unborn generations by enhancing the wealth and status of the family of which they would be the heirs. Finally, the *familia* consisted of property as well as persons. Legally the *familia* included the house property: dwellings, outbuildings, land, animals, crops, and other forms of wealth.

The Roman family was not only a hierarchical community of people and property but also a system of defense, law, and government—a miniature state. In the earliest Roman law it was recognized as a closed, self-sufficient, self-contained association, an economic unit operating under self-given rules within the

Junius Brutus, a Roman noble, with busts of his ancestors; lifesize marble, first century A.D. *(Art Resource, New York)*

larger framework of the economic system then prevailing and completely free from interference by the state. It was also a religious organization, a community of worship centered around the cult of the hearth and the cult of the dead.

***The* Paterfamilias *and* Patria Potestas** Within the living family the principle of hierarchy could be seen most vividly in its patriarchal head, the *paterfamilias.* He was not necessarily a begetter of children. The word meant simply "master of the household." He might have no children of his own; he might even be a bachelor. The only qualification was that he be subject to no authority save that of the state, that he be legally independent and self-sufficient in dealing with other families and the state. In a legal sense, he was the family, and without him there was no family or household.

The father's power (*patria potestas*) within the family was almost absolute, unlimited by the state or any other organization outside of the *familia* unless he was demonstrably insane or mentally incompetent. He was the legal owner of all family property. Only he could loan, mortgage, or sell it or engage in contracts involving the family. He was also the source of law within the family, and his orders were recognized by the state as having the force of law. His authority was based on ancestral custom, of which he was legally the sole judge and interpreter. He was the judge of the household, and his rulings normally could not be set aside by any external authority, even though he might kill, mutilate, expel, or give into bondage his sons or housemates, and though he might break or dispose of the household property.

Nevertheless, the father's absolute power, the *patria potestas,* was not supposed to be despotic or tyrannical. He had a duty to consult other members of the family, especially the adult males and his wife, the *materfamilias,* who constituted the family council. His function was to promote the welfare of the entire family, not destroy it by abuse. Respect for and obedience to tradition implanted by religious precept usually rendered his exercise of authority not a brutal display of force, but a recognized distribution of the only justice that could be secured until the "moral imperative" of custom was replaced later by the "legal imperative" established by the state.

Women within the Family and Marriage
Within the family hierarchy, women and children were always subject to the power of some adult male. In a world where labor was scarce, and only a father's legitimate offspring could inherit the property on which a family's welfare depended, men viewed the strict control of access to women's labor and power of reproduction as an absolute necessity. Attitudes and practices that were codified in the Law of the Twelve Tables (p. 59) about sixty years after the traditional end of the Regal period doubtlessly reflect earlier attitudes and practices regarding women. There, it is specified that a woman was always to be in the position of a daughter or ward to some adult male: her father, her husband, or a guardian (*tutor*). Her *tutor* could be a close male relative among her father's or husband's agnates, or someone named in her father's or husband's wills. A woman under guardianship could not buy or sell property or make contracts without the permission of her *tutor.* The only exceptions were the Vestal Virgins, the six virgins dedicated around the age of ten to at least thirty years of service to the cult of Vesta, goddess of the communal hearth and its procreative power. During the Republic, they were free of both the *patria potestas* and the requirement of a *tutor.* Still in the performance of her duties and upholding her vow of chastity, a Vestal Virgin was supervised by the *pontifex maximus,* Rome's male chief priest.

A husband acquired control over a wife through transference to his *manus* (hand). A husband could acquire *manus* over his wife in three ways. The first involved a religious marriage ceremony known as *confarreatio,* which involved the sacrifice to Jupiter of a special cake made from a variety of wheat called *far.* *Confarreatio* involved difficult, cumbersome rituals and was largely replaced over time by a simpler form of marriage with *manus* called *coemptio,* which involved the nominal sale of the bride by her *paterfamilias* or guardian to her husband. In the third form of marriage, which was like a common-law marriage, *manus* was established through *usus* (use). If a man and woman consented to live together as man and wife without interruption for a full year, the woman and her property automatically came under the control of the husband. For the woman to remain in the power of her father or guardian, she had to be absent from her husband's home for at least three consecutive nights every year.

If a wife remained in her father's power, whatever property she brought with her to her husband reverted to her father upon her husband's death or the dissolution of the marriage. She could also inherit a share of the family property upon her father's death. After that, however, she would need the approval of a guardian to dispose of her property by gift, sale, or will. If a woman passed into her husband's control through marriage with *manus,* her dowry became her husband's property even after a divorce, but if he died during the marriage, she could inherit a share of his property. Again, however, she would subsequently need the approval of a male guardian to dispose of her property.

If a groom were not independent, he needed the consent of his father or guardian for marriage just as the bride always did. In early Rome, the couple's consent may not have been needed, but later it was required. Since girls were usually only twelve to fourteen years old at first marriage, however, such consent would have been mostly nominal anyway.

Although a wife was never legally free of some man's power over her, there were some compensations if she belonged to the propertied classes. Her position as *materfamilias* within a thriving household brought her honor in society and a significant role in the household economy. While her husband conducted business and public affairs outside the home, she was mistress within. She held the keys to the family storerooms and kept track of all that was brought in or disbursed. She supervised the slaves and dependents who processed food and fiber within the house for use by the rest of the household. She looked after the raising of the children and served as a trusted advisor on matters affecting the family.

Divorce in early Rome seems to have been rare and difficult because of the prevalence of marriage with *manus*. In marriage with *manus,* only the husband or his *paterfamilias* could initiate a divorce and then on very limited

grounds. Such grounds seem to have been attempts to poison him or his children, adultery, and drunkenness. Provisions were made to free the divorced wife from her husband's control and send her back with her dowry to her father, but the husband kept any children. If a husband divorced a wife on other than permissible grounds, he was liable to loss of his property. In marriage without *manus,* a wife or her father could also initiate divorce, but any children still stayed with the husband.

Children and the Family   In early Rome, there seems to have been little of the tenderness and sentimentality toward children that began to manifest itself in the late Republic and early Principate. The hard necessity of a primarily agrarian economy constantly in need of labor and the frequency of infant mortality restricted the growth of affective ties between parents and children. In the hierarchical world of Rome, the needs and emotions of children had to be sacrificed to the greater needs of the parents and the larger welfare of the family, for which the *paterfamilias* was entirely responsible. Strong, healthy children, particularly males, were essential to provide labor and to perpetuate the male line on which the Roman family's continued existence depended. One could not raise too many children, however, because the family property would have been dangerously diminished if there were too many children to provide with dowries and inheritance.

Therefore, the *patria potestas* gave the *paterfamilias* the power of life and death over all children born to him in legitimate marriage. Right after birth, newborns were placed before the feet of the father, who acknowledged a child's legitimacy and his desire to rear it by picking it up. He had the right to kill or expose any child that he did not want. The Twelve Tables even specified that a father should get rid of weak or deformed infants. Girls were likely to be rejected before boys in order to reduce the need for dowries, but the need for all families to have suitable wives for sons must have moderated the pressure against girls somewhat.

So long as children remained under a *paterfamilias,* he had absolute control over their persons as if they were slaves. Unless he were insane or mentally incompetent, he could punish them as he wished. He could sell them into slavery or even kill them. Like slaves, children could have a *peculium,* an amount of money for personal use, but their *paterfamilias* still had legal control over it. His sons were not absolved from his authority even after they had married and set up households of their own, unless he formally freed them (by nominal sale to another person three times). Similarly, a daughter remained under her father's *potestas* unless he permitted her to enter a form of marriage that transferred her to her husband's possession (*conventio in manum*). In the male line of descent, a *paterfamilias* retained this authority not only over his children but also over succeeding generations so long as he lived. The authority of a *paterfamilias,* however, did not take precedence over their rights and duties as citizens or as soldiers.

Indeed, the hierarchical, authoritarian nature of the patriarchal Roman family shaped the early Roman state. Family life fostered obedience to authority and the willingness to do one's duty. On the civic level, the king and later the Republic's magistrates stood in a position of authority similar to that of the *paterfamilias.* They exercised the same duties between members of different families as did the *paterfamilias* within the family. They could expect the same kind of obedience from subordinates. As commanders in war, they had the right to execute anyone who refused to obey, just as the *paterfamilias* had the right to do with anyone under his authority. Under normal circumstances, the obedience to authority fostered by the Roman family helped to hold in check the centrifugal forces that also existed within the state from the pursuit of family interests.

Patrons and Clients   In early Rome, a man who did not have the support and protection of a powerful *paterfamilias* was at the mercy of those above him in the social hierarchy. He could make up this deficiency by attaching himself as a client (*cliens*) to a more powerful man, a patron (*patronus),* who would protect him as a father would protect other members of his family. The connection between the word *patronus* and the word *pater* (father) is obvious. The relationship between patron and client was strengthened by the religiously sanctioned concept of *fides,* faithfulness in performing one's obligations. It was an offense against the gods for either a patron or a client, once having accepted their mutual relationship, to shirk the duties imposed. This view was accepted even in Rome's earliest law code, the Twelve Tables: "Cursed be the patron who has done his client wrong."

The attitudes behind the patron-client relationship also affected dealings between Rome and other states. It was always Roman policy to grant a treaty to others only from a position of strength and not accept one forced upon Rome. Therefore, Rome assumed the superior position of a patron, not the inferior one of a client nor even one of an equal partner. *Fides* obligated the Romans to abide by any treaty and look out for the interests of the other party. Conversely, the other party was expected to be a faithful client to its Roman patron in ways that usually were not spelled out in a written treaty. An ally failing to understand this Roman attitude and thinking itself not obligated beyond the letter of a treaty could quickly find itself the object of unexpected Roman anger.

Slaves and Freedmen   The existence of slavery was never questioned in the ancient world, least of all by the Romans. It seemed to be a logical part of a hierarchical order. In early Rome, however, slaves probably were not numerous, and they constituted an integral part of the family as they worked beside other members of the family at home and in the field. Failure to pay off debts was often the cause of enslavement. Women and children captured in war were usually enslaved and put to work in the home. Because they were valuable and worked closely with their owners and masters, slaves in early Rome generally received fair treatment and could look forward to receiving freedom after some years of faithful service. At that time, they became freedmen or freed-women and remained closely bound to their former masters as clients.

Roman Names and the *Gens*   All Roman citizens belonged to a larger, ostensibly ge-nealogical group called a *gens* (pl. *gentes*), often translated as "clan," The name of one's *gens,* the *nomen gentilicium,* was a person's most im-portant name, which was the second of the three names often borne by a male citizen. The first name, *praenomen,* was the personal name, and the last or surname, *cognomen,* if there was one, indicated the branch of the *gens* to which one's male lineage belonged. For example, Cicero, the famous orator and statesman of the late Republic, was named Marcus Tullius Ci-cero. Therefore, he belonged to the Ciceronian line of the Tullian *gens.* His contemporary Gaius Julius Caesar belonged to the Caesarian line of the Julian *gens.* Originally, Caesar's later rival, Pompey, was named only Gnaeus Pompeius. He acquired the *cognomen* Magnus because of his early military exploits. Since the *nomen gen-tilicium* provided the crucial identification for a Roman, any scholarly book or reference work in ancient history will list an individual under his or her *gentilicium.* In this book, for example, the three men mentioned above will be found in the index under "Tullius," "Julius," and "Pompeius," respectively. When a non-Roman received Roman citizenship, he adopted the *gentilicium* of the man who sponsored him.

Since the male family line was more im-portant than the individual, fathers and sons of-ten bore the same *praenomen* for generations, or two names might alternate between fathers and sons. If there were more than one son each generation, other sons would be named for other male agnates such as a father's brothers. As a result, there were only about sixteen com-monly used male first names during the Re-public, which were usually indicated by easily recognized abbreviations such as "L." for Lu-cius, "M." for Marcus, "P." for Publius, "Q." for

Quintus, and "T." for Titus. Gaeus and Gnaeus are abbreviated "C." and "Cn." because "g" and "c" were not distinguished in the earliest Roman alphabet.

Since women in early Rome counted even less as individuals than men, they usually had only one official name throughout the Re-publican period, the female form of the father's *gentilicium.* Therefore, Cicero's daughter was named Tullia and Caesar's Julia. If a father chose to raise more than one daughter, he merely indicated their numerical order. Hence the three infamous sisters of P. Clodius, the even more infamous enemy of Cicero (p. 192), were named Clodia Prima, Clodia Secunda, and Clodia Tertia. After she was married, a woman was identified by the possessive form of her husband's *praenomen.* Thus Cicero's wife was Terentia Marci (Marcus' Terentia).

***The Origin of the* Gens**   The origin of the *gens* as a genealogical group is hard to discover. Naming patterns in the rest of central Italy in-dicate the existence of similar groups among surrounding peoples. They may have their roots in warrior bands where loyal followers adopted the name of their leader to promote solidarity. The existence of such bands is indi-cated in seventh-century burials where lesser graves are grouped around the princely graves of some wealthy warriors. The story of Attus Clausus (Appius Claudius) and his dependents receiving citizenship *en bloc* in the early Re-public lends support.

During the Monarchy, such war bands may have been incorporated into the Roman army as Rome expanded its territory under the kings. Those men who did not belong to such a band would have been assigned to one or had one created for them. Before the creation of separate rural tribes, Rome was divided into four urban tribes and twenty-six rural districts (*pagi*) or regions (*regiones*). The total of tribes and rural territories combined corresponds to the thirty curia of the early Roman army. Prob-ably each rural district was identified by the name of its biggest *gens.* Significantly, when the rural districts were initially grouped into fewer, larger tribes, each tribe seems to have taken its name from a *gens*.

Patrician and Nonpatrician *Gentes* In keeping with the Roman passion for hierarchical distinction, at some point before the end of the Monarchy and the beginning of the Republic (ca. 500 B.C.) certain *gentes* seem to have become distinguished as patrician. The members of those *gentes*, the patricians, had more prestige and privileges than the members of the other *gentes* and seem to have formed an aristocracy. At some point, the patricians were further divided into greater and lesser *gentes* (*patres maiorum gentium* and *patres minorum gentium*).

How certain *gentes* came to be distinguished as patrician clearly seems to be linked with the *patres* who monopolized the important priesthoods of early Rome, held the office of *interrex,* elected kings, and eventually, as a special group within the senate, claimed the sole right to approve or reject legislation during the early Republic (p. 66). Perhaps the original *patres* were the fathers of the families whose clans headed the early tribes and rural districts that constituted the territory of the early Roman state. The family cults that they maintained might then have become incorporated into the public cults of the early state and secured for their *gentes* the privilege of supplying public priests. Perhaps some patrician *gentes* were designated as "greater" after giving their names to tribes later consolidated out of the original twenty-six rural districts. Unfortunately, much must remain in the realm of learned conjecture and speculation.

As a result of later developments, the nonpatrician *gentes* came to be identified as "plebeian," but for the late Monarchy and the beginning of the Republic, it is best to refer to patricians and nonpatricians. What did not distinguish patricians and nonpatricians was wealth. Many nonpatricians were as wealthy as patricians, although the great majority was not. Neither did the distinction have any particular ethnic basis. Both patricians and nonpatricians were a mixture of Latin, Sabine, and Etruscan

elements. Nor were all nonpatricians clients of patricians, although many probably were.

As Roman citizens, nonpatricians had the right to make commercial contracts, own real property, contract valid marriages, sue or be sued in court, and vote in the popular assemblies of the early state. Although they could not hold public priesthoods, a few outstanding nonpatricians probably had been able to obtain high office and membership in the senate with the cooperation of patricians trying to build up networks of useful supporters, perhaps even to the point of establishing ties of marriage. Over time, however, the patricians tried to assert exclusive rights to political leadership in the face of aspiring nonpatricians, but their claims were ultimately rejected by the citizens as a whole (pp. 58–66).

The Openness of Early Roman Society to Outsiders Despite their penchant for creating hierarchical distinctions, the early Romans, unlike their Greek contemporaries, were remarkably willing to incorporate outsiders as citizens of their community. Even if they are not literally true, many Roman traditions illustrate that openness: the story that Romulus populated his new city by declaring it an asylum for criminals and exiles from all over Italy; the tale of capturing wives from the Sabines and the eventual unification of the two groups; the legend that Traquinius Priscus, the son of a Corinthian Greek immigrant to Etruscan Tarquinia, came to Rome and founded a dynasty of kings; and the tradition that the Sabine war chief Attus Clausus and his followers became Roman citizens and founded the patrician Claudian *gens*. Rome's origin as a community created from several neighboring villages and as a cosmopolitan center of trade among Etruscans, Greeks, Phoenicians, Latins, and other Italic peoples probably explains it.

As Rome expanded by treaty and conquest during the Monarchy and early Republic, it incorporated the inhabitants of new territory as new tribes of Roman citizens. At the same time, their gods were incorporated into the divine community whose public cults constituted the state religion. By the end of the Monarchy, Rome had grown from a few square miles of territory within the radius of the Forum to about three-hundred square miles embracing the northwestern third of Latium. The constant incorporation of new citizens enabled the Roman army to keep pace with expansion and fueled more expansion. Taking over the cults and deities of those newly incorporated gave Romans the self-assured feeling of divine favor toward their actions and lessened the alienation of those who had been forced to join them.

Early Roman Religion   Religion played an important role in the private and political life of early Rome. Both the state and individuals were subordinate to spirits and gods who occupied a hierarchical position of superiority above them. Much of Roman religion involved attempts to please these greater beings and assure their divine favor. A religion of home, farm, and pasture, it was concerned with present rather than with past or future needs. It inculcated the virtues of hard work, discipline, duty, courage, and loyalty. When the religion of the home became the religion of the state, it cemented the people together in a single community and gave the state an internal strength and cohesion that endured for centuries.

Magic and Taboo   Magic, the mechanical use of certain materials, rites, formulae, or spells designed to force nature, spirits, or other people to do one's will, was always a part of popular superstition and played a part in public ritual as well. An example of sympathetic magic was the ceremony of the "Dripping Stone" (*lapis manalis*): A wet stone kept near the Temple of Mars outside the Porta Capena was brought into the city to produce rain during droughts. Another was the *Lupercalia,* which Shakespeare popularized in *Julius Caesar.* Two bands of youths, having brows smeared with the blood of a slaughtered goat and naked except for pieces of goat skin around their thighs, raced around the Palatine and struck the bystanders, particularly women, with strips of goat skin. The purpose of this rite was to dispel

the curse of sterility. Charms and spells were commonly employed to drive away diseases, plagues, and foul weather; to fix broken bones; and to bring good crops and even success in war.

Allied to magic is something usually known by its Polynesian name of *taboo.* In general, it is a prohibition against persons, things, or acts regarded as dangerous to individuals or to the community. In Latin, such things are called *nefas.* At Rome, it was a nefas for a woman to take part in the worship of Hercules, for a man to witness the female-administered rites of the Bona Dea (Good Goddess), or for a horse to enter the sacred grove of Diana. A whole set of restrictive ancient taboos fenced in the life and office of Jupiter's high priest, the *flamen Dialis.* He might not see an army in battle gear nor see or touch a dead body; he could never do any kind of common work; never ride or touch a horse, a she-goat, or a dog; never cut his hair or nails with an iron knife; never wear an unbroken ring or have knots tied in his clothing; and never eat, among other things, fermented wheat, raw meat, or beans. He could not be unmarried, and he had to be united with his wife, the *flaminica Dialis,* by the most ancient form of marriage, *confarreatio.* The *flaminica* performed an equal role in administering Jupiter's cult and was bound by similar taboos.

Numen *or* Mana   From earliest times, the Romans thought of certain sacred objects and places, natural processes, human activities, and gods as being numinous, possessing a mysterious invisible force or influence, which Latin writers of the late first century B.C. and early first century A.D. called *numen* (plural *numina*). Modern anthropologists identify it by the Melanesian name of *mana. Numen* was both a particular and a general concept. A spirit was a *numen* and its life force was *numen* in general. To the early Romans, nothing exists except by virtue of its particular *numen,* and without it no act can be performed. It is not the cobra that strikes, but the *numen* within the cobra; it is not the spear that kills, but the *numen* within the spear. Jupiter is the sky as well as the *numen* of the sky; Janus both the door and the spirit within the door.

Many spirits were considered hostile or malignant powers haunting persons, objects, and places like thick woods, dark caves, volcanoes, or old forest trees struck by lightning. These spirits aroused fear and had to be propitiated with offerings and prayers. As farm and family life became more settled and secure, certain spirits came to be regarded as friendly and helpful beings, if properly placated. They had their abode in such familiar objects in the house and on the farm as the house door (Janus), the fireplace (Vesta), and the boundary stones that marked off one farm from another (Termini). Over all was Jupiter or the sky, the region of light, cloud, and storm.

In addition to the spirits of particular things and places, other spirits presided over definite human activities, especially the ones having to do with the making and storage of farm crops. Of the latter, the most individualized and universal in their worship were Ceres, the spirit of grain crops; Consus, of the stored harvest; Saturn, of planting; Robigus, of rust or mildew; Flora, of flowers; and Pomona, of fruits. As religion became more highly organized, each separate operation of farmwork had a special spirit (plowing, harrowing, sowing, weeding, harvesting, and storing). Each of these many functional spirits received offerings at the proper season of the year. When certain spirits were observed to be operating at the same time in many places and for many families, they tended to become more real, more personal, and more human in form and personality. They gradually acquired names, had special priesthoods and rituals attached to their worship, and eventually attained the status of gods.

Sacrifice and Prayer Like *mana, numen* connotes the triple idea of Power, Life, Will. As Power, it brings about effects beyond human capability; as Life, it possesses a living consciousness; as Will, it can act for good or evil if it wishes. This mysterious Power-Life-Will association evoked the feeling of religion (*religio*) in its primary sense of fear or anxiety and in its secondary sense of a desire to establish right relations with the various *numina* by propitiation, prayer, sacrifice, and other rituals. A Roman sacrifice was made in the conviction that it was good for the spirits as well as for the worshipper, and the accompanying prayer *"Macte esto"* ("Be thou increased") reflects the belief that the offering increased the spirits' power to perform their special functions for the giver's benefit. Sacrifice replenished the store of vital force consumed by the spirit. To restore the vital force taken from Mother Earth by growing crops, the Romans held the annual spring festival of the *Fordicidia,* at which they killed a pregnant cow and made a burnt sacrifice of her aborted calf, in order to "transfer" to the earth the fertility of a cow in calf. Sacrifice was also a means of infusing *numen* into objects not possessing it before. To consecrate a new boundary stone between farms, the Romans used to make offerings of incense, grain, honey, and wine together with the blood of a lamb or sow. To restore the *numen* of all boundary stones each spring, they performed similar rites at the festival of *Terminalia.*

If by sacrifice the *numen* or *mana* of a spirit could be increased, renewed, strengthened, or conferred, it was by prayer that worshippers expressed their desire as to the use and direction of that increased power. To make sure that their desires and petitions were clearly and fully understood, they worded their prayers in exact and unambiguous language called *formulae* (singular *formula*). Any slip of the tongue made it necessary to start all over again. Having correctly and reverently performed the two chief acts of worship—sacrifice and prayer—the worshippers had done their part. The rest lay with the will of the unseen powers.

Gods of the House and Fields The cults and festivals of house and field were the oldest and the most vital; they preceded the founding of Rome and outlived her fall. In the time of her greatness some found expression in the wall paintings of Pompeii, many in the poetry of Vergil, Horace, Ovid, and Tibullus. Greek and Near Eastern cults did not completely supplant them; Christianity did not utterly destroy them. Under various names and disguises, they have survived to modern times among the peasants of Italy and Spain.

The spirits of the house were few. They were partly local, partly functional in character. There was Janus, the spirit of the door, who represented the home in its insecure relation to the outside world. He faced both in and out, letting in friends and shutting out enemies. Family life began with him. At weddings it was the custom for the bride to smear his doorposts with wolf's fat and to be lifted over his threshold. At the birth of a child, the threshold was struck with an ax, a pestle, and a broom to repulse wild spirits from the outside. When someone died in the house, the corpse was carried out feet first for fear that the ghost might find its way back in.

Inside the house was Vesta, the spirit of the fireplace, whose fire gave warmth and cooked the daily meals. She was pure spirit, the *numen* of the living flame. Of her no image or statue was made in early times. Yet she was the center of family life and worship. To her the head of the house presented his bride or newborn child. Before her hearth stood the dining table, also a sacred object. The salt dish was on it and the sacred salt cake baked by the daughters of the house. At dinner the head of the family ceremoniously threw part of the cake into the fire. As Janus began, so Vesta ended the roll of deities invoked in family prayer.

Not far from the fireplace was the pantry. Here dwelt a vague group of nameless spirits collectively known as the Penates. With Vesta they shared the offerings made at the fireplace because they guarded the food that Vesta cooked. In Latin literature, they were a synonym for home. So were the Lares.

Originally, the Lares were probably not gods of the house but of the fields. As spirits of the fields, the Lares were worshipped at the Feast of the Crossroads (*Compitalia*), a thanksgiving festival in which even slaves took part. The plows were hung up as a sign that the season's work was done, and everybody joined in the feasting and fun. Still more picturesque was the festival of the *Ambarvalia,* held toward the end of May to secure divine favor for the growing and ripening crops. The farmer and his family, dressed in white with olive wreaths around their heads, solemnly drove a pig, a sheep, and a bull (*suovetaurilia*) three times around the farm. The three animals were then killed, opened, examined for omens, and burned upon the altar fire. There followed a long prayer for good weather and good crops to Mars, originally the god of agriculture.

Besides the *Fordicidia* and *Terminalia* already described, there took place in spring the *Liberalia,* for Liber (the god of wine); the *Cerialia* for Ceres (the goddess of grain); and the *Robigalia,* at which a red dog was sacrificed to avert mildew or rust, which attacked wheat. Shepherds had their spring festivals too. The *Parilia,* or Feast of Pales, spirit of flocks and herds, took place on April 21, just before the annual trek to summer pastures. At dawn the herdsmen sprinkled the animals with water, swept out the stalls, and decorated the barns with green branches. Then they lit a bonfire of straw, brush, and other stuff, through which both the flocks were driven and the shepherds leaped. After an offering of milk and cakes to Pales and a prayer for the health, safety, and increase of the flocks, they spent the rest of the day in sports, eating, and drinking. Later, the day of this festival was accepted as the anniversary of Rome's founding.

Two festivals held in late summer or early fall are noteworthy because they are coupled with the names of Jupiter and Mars, whose association with agriculture was, in later times, largely forgotten. The first was the Feast of Wine (*Vinalia Rustica*) held on August 19 in honor of Jupiter, whose high priest, after the sacrifice of a ewe lamb, solemnly inaugurated the grape-picking season by cutting the first bunch of grapes. The other was the festival of the October Horse in honor of Mars, in his dual capacity as god of war and god of farming. A chariot race was held. The near horse of the winning team and a spear were sacrificed to Mars. The horse's tail, a phallic symbol, was rushed over to the King's House, where its blood, still warm, dribbled upon the hearth—the seat of vitality in the house, to which the strength and virility of the horse were thus transferred. The horse's head, cut off and decked with cakes, was fought over by the men of two adjacent wards in Rome, the winners being allowed to hang it up as a trophy in their ward.

Greek Influence Contact with the Greeks through trade and the colonies in southern Italy contributed to the rise of anthropomorphic deities among the Romans and the other peoples of central Italy. The Etruscan Uni and Menrva and the Italic Juno and Menerva (the Roman Minerva) came to be identified with anthropomorphic Greek goddesses Hera and Athena. The Etruscan Tinia and Italic Jupiter took on the features of Zeus. This Greek influence was embodied in temples and statues. Unlike the old native spirits, the new anthropomorphic gods had to have houses to dwell in and statues to embody them.

The great temple that was built to the triad of Jupiter, Juno, and Minerva on the Capitoline Hill at the end of the Monarchy and the beginning of the Republic was designed and decorated in a style that incorporated many elements from contemporary Greek temples. Similar temples were appearing in contemporary Etruscan and Latin cities. Cult statues of gods and goddesses that resembled the archaic cult statues of the Greeks were placed in these temples at the same time.

Jupiter and Mars Conceived originally as the sky and the spirit immanent in the sky, as the source and giver of light, and as the unseen force in lightning, storm, and rain, Jupiter had long ago become a spirit of the vine as well, and was associated with Venus, the primitive Italic spirit of vines and gardens. With the growth of political and urban life among the Latins and the Romans, Jupiter lost status as a farmer's god but came into his own as a god of cities and towns. He was the tribal deity of the Latins and the guardian of many Latin towns. In Rome he was the greatest of all gods, the symbol of the Roman state, the giver of victory, and the spirit of law and justice.

Rome similarly exalted Mars, who gave his name to the first month, *Martius* (March), of the early Roman calendar. Once an Italic spirit of the forest, he became the protector of the farmer's crops and herds, but later, as god of war, the defender of the Roman state against its enemies. Thus, with the rise of Rome as a city and a state, Jupiter and Mars lost all connection with agriculture, save the memory preserved in some of the rustic festivals.

Juno and Minerva The most prominent and widespread of the increasingly anthropomorphic cults was that of Juno, Jupiter's wife and queen of the gods, who was worshipped all over Italy and was a special favorite in Latium and southern Etruria. Minerva is closely linked with the cult of Menerva in Falerii, a semi-Etruscan Faliscan town higher up on the north side of the Tiber. She was an old Italic goddess of arts and crafts who was worshipped under the name of Menrva in many Etruscan towns. Perhaps, her worship under the name Minerva in Rome was introduced by immigrant Faliscan workmen skilled in the pottery and metal trades. Her early presence in Rome is clearly in line with the archaeological evidence of close commercial and industrial ties between Rome and south Etruria.

Other Hellenized Cults The expansion of early Roman commercial contacts is likewise pointed up by the erection in the Cattle Market (*Forum Boarium*) of an altar to Hercules, the patron god of the Greek and Italian traveling salesmen. Politically, the transfer of the worship of Diana (identified with the Greek Artemis) from Aricia to the Aventine highlights Roman aspirations to leadership over the Latin League. So, too, does the coming to Rome of two other Latin goddesses destined to have a great future: Fortuna imported from Antium (Anzio) and later identified with Tyche, the Greek goddess of luck or chance; and Venus, formerly worshipped at Ardea as a goddess of gardens and orchards, but later identified with Aphrodite, the Greek goddess of love and beauty.

Of the deities just named, all, except Hercules, had belonged originally to the spirit world of old Italy but had, before their adoption in Rome, been transformed through Greek influence into gods of human personality and form. Even Ceres, the most earthy and the most native of Italic spirits, did not escape the effects of this transforming influence. Identified with Demeter, the Greek goddess of cereals, she had on the Aventine a cult more foreign than that of

Hercules in the Cattle Market. Her Aventine temple was not only the Grain Exchange but, during the early Republic, the refuge of the dispossessed and the political rendezvous of the plebs, who at that time were excluded from the religious and political life of the state.

From Cumae, the nearest and oldest Greek settlement on the mainland, came the worship of Apollo, the god of healing and prophecy, not long after 500 B.C. Despite his unlatinized name, Apollo became in later times one of the greatest gods of the Roman pantheon. Cumae was also the home of the Sibyl, Apollo's inspired priestess, whose oracle must have been known in early Rome, though the story of Tarquin's purchase of the *Sibylline Books* is probably pure legend. The earliest collection of Sibylline oracles seems to have been made around 500 B.C. at the beginning of the Republic. Kept in the temple of Jupiter and guarded in strictest secrecy by a special college of two priests, the oracles were consulted only by command of the senate in time of war, disaster, plague, or famine. Consulted in such times of stress, the *Sibylline Books* played a decisive role throughout the Republic in combining native *numina* with Greek cults to create new Greco-Roman anthropomorphic deities.

Consultation usually resulted in the introduction of some new Greek deity or form of worship. For example, during the famine of ca. 496 B.C., a temple on the Aventine was promised and three years later dedicated to Ceres, Liber, and Libera, a triad of farm gods identical in almost everything but name with Demeter, Dionysus, and Persephone. The following year also saw the dedication on the Aventine of a temple to another Greek god, Hermes, under the name of Mercury. Like Hercules, he was a god of traders and especially of the grain merchants in both Etruria and Greek Italy. His temple was a grain market as well as a rendezvous of merchants and traders.

Seaborne imports from southern Italy seem to account for the early reception of Poseidon, the Greek god of the great open sea. He was identified with Neptune, though the latter was originally not a sea god but the spirit of springs and ponds and other small waters. Nep-

tune quickly received the trident and sea horses of Poseidon and all of the mythology associated with him.

The *Sibylline Books* not only introduced new gods but also prescribed new forms of worship, some exceedingly spectacular and exotic. These innovations, both numerous and of great variety, consisted of funeral and secular games, stage plays and other dramatic performances, ritual dances, religious parades, and banquets of the gods (*lectisternia*) at which images of the gods grouped in pairs of the opposite sex were publicly displayed reclining on couches before tables spread with food and drinks.

Divination   As did other ancient people, the Romans believed that the will and intentions of the gods were revealed by omens and other sacred signs such as thunder, lightning, the flights of birds, and the entrails of sacrificial animals. In particular, hepatoscopy, inspecting the size, shape, texture, and color of a sacrificed animal's liver, was highly regarded. Interpreting such signs is broadly lumped under the term *divination*. The neighboring Etruscans were especially devoted to the practice of divination, which the Romans called the *Disciplina Etrusca,* the Etruscan Learning (p. 16). Roman nobles, whose families provided the public priests, often sent their sons to Etruscan cities to learn this valuable lore. The Etruscan priests who interpreted these signs were called *haruspices,* and on critical occasions the Romans would summon *haruspices* from Etruria when they wanted extra assurance that they understood the divine will.

The State and Religion   The foreign cults just described were not the only factors involved in the changing religious life of the Roman people. Equally important changes occurred when the primitive religion of house and field became organized as the religion of the state. The state itself was essentially a religious institution; it embraced and incorporated all the older and smaller social and religious communities such as the family, the *gens,* and the tribe. According to legend, it had been inaugurated, with religious ceremonies, by Romulus, who established the *pomerium,* a sacred boundary that enclosed the city. As the city grew and expanded, it was the responsibility of the state to extend the *pomerium* and provide for the common religious life of all the people on behalf of the whole community.

Household cults had great appeal because family life was very much the same in town and country. The most popular and successful were those of Janus and Vesta. Janus, the spirit of the house door, became the god of the Sacred Gateway at the northeast corner of the Forum. Probably because the early armies marched through this gate on their way to war, it was kept closed only in peacetime. Another household deity to find a place in the state religion was Vesta, the Sacred Hearth, whose holy fire, relit only on March 1, the New Year's Day of the early state, was kept burning by the Vestal Virgins. The worship of Janus and Vesta fostered a sense of belonging to one great national family. The cults that roused the strongest feelings of pride and love of Rome were those of Jupiter and Mars. Mars was the god of Rome's triumphant armies, his altar the symbol of the city's military power. Jupiter Optimus Maximus (Best and Greatest) sent down upon Rome "the continual dew of his divine favor."

The King and Early Priesthoods The priestly role of the king first as head of state and then as *rex sacrorum* has been described in the previous chapter (p. 30). The Vestal Virgins may have originated as the king's wife and daughters tending his sacred household hearth. Significantly, the later temple of Vesta and its sacred public hearth were built over part of the old royal palace. Besides the king and his family were other important early priests and priestesses. The flamen or chief priest of Jupiter (*flamen Dialis*), his wife the *flaminica Dialis,* and the numerous taboos associated with them have been mentioned above (p. 42). There were two other major flamens (*flamines*), one for Mars and one for Quirinus, a very obscure deity associated with the origins of Rome. Not much is known about these two flamens except that they and the *flamen Dialis* always had to be

patricians even after others did not. The flamen of Mars obviously was associated with the rituals of war, and he officiated at the festival of the October Horse (p. 44). Twelve minor flamens each served a deity characteristic of a largely agrarian people: Ceres, Flora, and Pomona, for example, who respectively represented grain, flowering plants, and fruit trees. Among the early priesthoods were the three augurs, official diviners who interpreted signs from the gods, and three pontiffs, whose name is associated with building bridges but who seem to have acquired a general function as keepers of civil and religious records. This function may explain why the pontiffs eventually acquired oversight of the Vestals and the fifteen flamens (p. 56). Three minor priesthoods of the Republic also seem to have originated in the early Monarchy (p. 57).

The Values of Early Roman Society   People act within a framework of commonly held values and moral assumptions. If one wants to understand how and why people behave as they do, it is, therefore, necessary to understand the ethical framework within which they operate. The early Romans developed a deeply held set of values that affected not only their own history but later ages as well. It is significant that most modern European names of moral concepts stem from Latin, and some of them still retain their original meaning. The English words *virtue, prudence, temperance, fortitude, justice, piety, fidelity, constancy,* and *perseverance* stem from Latin roots. Of these words, *virtue* alone has a distinctly different meaning from that which it had in ancient Rome. All of the corresponding Latin concepts were a vital part of early Roman life. They were enshrined in the *mos maiorum* (ancestral custom) and were consciously fostered by men and women through education and example in private and public life.

***Virtue* (Virtus)**   The word *virtus,* which is derived from *vir* (man, a male) included everything that constituted the Roman ideal of the true man and a useful member of society. It is virtue, says the poet Lucilius (ca. 180 B.C. to 103 B.C.), for a man to know what is good, what evil, what useless, shameful, and dishonorable; to be an enemy of bad men and customs; to be a friend and protector of those that are good; to place first one's country's good, next that of one's parents, and last that of one's self.

Virtue also meant a strong and healthy body, the ability to provide for one's family, interest in and devotion to the state, and heroism in war. If heroism was the greatest of these, it was not the individual heroism of Achilles or Hector; it was virtue only when used for the good and safety of the state. The ideal Roman hero was one whose courage and wisdom saved his country in time of peril. The virtues cited as examples in the moral education of the youths were drawn not from heroic poetry, as in Greece, but from history. Young men were taught that it was glorious to die for their country, as did the heroes of the past. So important was *virtus* as an element of early Roman values and character that it has become the generic term for all kinds of human excellence in many modern languages.

Piety (Pietas) Four virtues were distinctively Roman and of great historic significance: piety, faith, gravity, and constancy. The first, piety (*pietas*), was a family virtue. It implied devotion and loyalty by men and women to the family group and a willing acceptance of parental authority, which gave unity and strength to the family. It further meant reverence for and devotion to the gods as members of the family, as shown in action by the exact performance of all required religious rites and ceremonies. Piety toward the state connoted obedience to the laws, faithful service, and patriotism consistent with justice, law, and the "constitution." In this virtue, patriotic writers saw the prime reason for Rome's greatness.

Faith (Fides) Another virtue in which the Romans took pride was faith, the "foundation of justice," and the "supreme guarantee of human happiness." It had special importance within the community. It meant being true to one's word, the paying of one's debts, the keep-

ing of sworn oaths, and the performance of obligations assumed by agreement with both gods and men. Based on religion and law, it was the foundation of religious, public, and private life. Violation of it was an offense against both the gods and the community. A patron who broke faith with his client by abuse of his power was placed under a curse. A magistrate who broke faith by acts of injustice and oppression against the people gave the latter the right to rebel. Faith rooted in the social conscience was stronger than written law or statute as a force for holding all parts of the society together in a common bond of relationship. Failure to uphold religious obligations would incur divine wrath.

Gravity (Gravitas) and Constancy (Constantia) Faith had to be supplemented by two other Roman virtues: gravity and constancy. The first meant absolute self-control—a dignified, serious, and unperturbed attitude toward both good and bad fortune. To cite some extreme examples, no Roman was supposed to dance in public, nor were husbands and wives supposed to kiss each other outside of their own homes. The second virtue was constancy or perseverance, even under the most trying circumstances, in doing what seemed necessary and right until success was won. Of this virtue Rome herself was the greatest exponent, for in her long history she suffered many disastrous defeats. That she never broke under those defeats and often turned them into victories is no small tribute to Roman moral education.

Dignitas *and* Auctoritas Those who exhibited the four qualities discussed above, especially in public life, acquired *dignitas* (reputation for worth, honor, esteem) and *auctoritas* (prestige, respect). They were highly prized by Roman aristocrats because they confirmed their leading role in society. Those who demonstrated virtue by successfully defending the community in warfare and who promoted the public welfare by faithfully performing their duties as patrons, priests, magistrates, and senators acquired the honor and prestige that set them apart from others and gave them the power to continue to lead. That power gave them the opportunity to earn more *dignitas* and *auctoritas* and thereby to enhance their status in the community in competition with their aristocratic peers.

By 500 B.C., Rome's characteristic hierarchical social structure, centered on the authoritarian patriarchal family and dominated by an aristocratic elite, had become fixed for many centuries to come. The complex religious amalgam of reverence for ancestors, spirit worship, divination, and anthropomorphism and the various rituals associated with them had assumed its form for the future. Along with these social and religious developments had evolved the system of values that defined the Romans' view of themselves as individuals and as a people.

The ultimate effect of these developments was conservative. Roman family life, religion, and morality fostered a conservative type of human being. The authoritarian, patriarchal family and the attitude of dependency inherent in clientage produced an obedience to authority that greatly benefitted the aristocrats who controlled the state. The reverence for ancestors and their customs enshrined in the words *mos maiorum* worked against attempts at radical innovation among all classes, as did the sobriety and piety of the Roman ethical tradition. Furthermore, since established customs had already been sanctioned by the gods, it was an offense against them to change those customs. The resultant abhorrence of innovation is signified by the Roman term for revolution, *res novae* (new things). Therefore, many archaic and obsolete practices, institutions, and offices continued to exist at Rome long after they had lost their original function.

New things had to be justified by finding precedents in the past, a practice at which the Romans became particularly adept as they were forced to adapt to new circumstances. In religion, therefore, the ancient *Sibylline Books,* with their convenient ambiguities and even opportune forgeries, justified the introduction of new cults and rituals from time to time, while priests skilled in the interpretation of divine will could adduce new meanings from old words. Even in politics, in a society where the vagaries of oral tradition often predominated over written records, "ancestral precedents" might be of as recent origin as an orator's latest speech. Therefore, Roman conservatism was saved from being stultifying, and change could occur, while a deep sense of continuity—one of Rome's greatest strengths—was maintained.

V

The Rise
of the Roman Republic,
509 to 287 B.C.

The period of Roman history known as the Republic extended from about 500 (traditionally 509 B.C.) until 27 B.C., the beginning of the principate of Augustus, which marks the beginning of the Roman Empire. The term *republic* (*res publica*) has come to mean a form of government, not necessarily democratic, but essentially different from that which exists under a king or emperor. To the Romans the words *res publica* (common wealth, public thing) originally signified to common property and public affairs, as opposed to private property and affairs. To historians looking back from the time when Rome was ruled by an emperor who had assumed almost unlimited private control over what once had been common and public, *res publica* came to be associated with the form of government that essentially had evolved in the fifth and fourth centuries B.C. In form, it was far from democratic, but the conduct of public affairs was shared equally among the members of an aristocratic class showing at least minimal concern for the lower ranks and working through laws and institutions that limited the arbitrary exercise of power. The creation of that system is not always well documented, but a reasonable outline of the process can be drawn.

Sources of Information for Early Republican History   The sources for this and the following chapter are essentially the same as those

discussed at length in chapter III (p. 24). The two most extensive accounts are in Livy (Books 2 to 10) and Dionysius of Halicarnassus (*Roman Antiquities,* Books 4 to 20). Cassius Dio's *Roman History* is preserved in significant fragments from Books 4 to 10 for this period and in a summary by the Byzantine monk Zonaras. Polybius, a major mid-second-century B.C. Greek historian who lived in Rome, treats the theory and development of the Roman constitution in Book 6 of his universal history of the Mediterranean world, and Cicero devotes thirteen short chapters (25 to 37) to the period in Book 2 of his *De Republica*. A few additional facts and important traditions are included in Plutarch's biographies of Camillus, Coriolanus, Publicola, and Pyrrhus and in Books 10 to 20 (11 to 20 fully preserved) of Diodorus Siculus' world history. The latter's most important contribution is his list of Roman consuls (the chief yearly magistrates) beginning with approximately 486 B.C.

Like the various annalists and historians on whose lost works they based their own, these writers were often guilty of rhetorically exaggerated embellishments and anachronistic interpretation. Again, the surviving works of antiquarian writers mentioned in chapter III preserve many alternative accounts and additional pieces of information culled from previous writers, other traditions, and the more extensive documentation that once was available for this period. Moreover, helpful archaeological evidence and inscriptions become more abundant in this period.

***The* Fasti** The most valuable inscriptions are those that preserve lists of the annual consuls, the consular *Fasti*. In nonmonarchic ancient states, calendar years were not numbered in chronological sequence but named after one or more of the chief annual magistrates: in Athens after the head archon, in Sparta after the chief ephor, in Rome after the consuls. All such officials are known as eponymous (naming) magistrates. Such a system made phenomenal demands upon the memory unless lists were handy for business, legal, and official purposes. Eventually, many such lists must have been available to public officials, priests, and private individuals.

The oldest, perhaps, and certainly the most famous list of Roman magistrates was that kept by the pontiffs, probably from the earliest years of the Republic. At the beginning of each year, the chief pontiff (*pontifex maximus*) had a whitewashed wooden tablet set up in his office. Across the top of the tablet were written the names of the consuls, the other important magistrates, and the priests. Then followed a list of the feast or holy days (*nefasti*) and the regular days (*fasti*) on which it was permitted to do business or hold court. Opposite each day, space was left for noting unusual events such as eclipses, earthquakes, plagues, prodigies, temple dedications, wars, triumphs, and the like. At the end of the year, the information apparently was transferred to linen rolls as a permanent record for future consultation. After the pontiffs stopped setting up the yearly boards in 130 B.C., the accumulated information was edited and made available in published form as the *Annales Maximi*. Thus the *Annales Maximi* recorded the names of the yearly magistrates and other official information from the beginning of the Republic.

Even if all of the early material from the pontiffs' records had not survived until 130 B.C., parallel records and other copies of information from the pontifical records that had been made for public and private use probably filled

many gaps. It was possible, therefore, for the Emperor Augustus in 18 B.C. to set up on the Capitol a marble inscription that listed all of the chief yearly magistrates from 509 B.C. to that time and all of those who had held military triumphs supposedly since Romulus. This inscription is referred to as the *Capitoline Fasti*. The consular list, half complete, has fragments of no year earlier than 483 B.C. The surviving names are remarkably consistent with the *Fasti* preserved in the literary sources and on the fragments of other inscribed lists that have been found. All versions of the *Fasti,* therefore, seem to be based upon a common stock of source material, whose consistency can be attributed to the existence of a stable and fixed tradition from the earliest days of the Republic. Various attempts to challenge the reliability of the *Fasti* have failed, and it is now generally agreed that we have a basically reliable chronological record that allows the beginning of the Roman Republic to be dated to the last decade of the sixth century B.C.

From Kingship to Republic The transition from a kingship to a republic is one of the most disputed questions of Roman history. According to the story popularized by Livy, Tarquin the Proud was an oppressive tyrant who had alienated both the common people and the aristocrats. In 510/09, a series of events led to the overthrow of Tarquin and the establishment of a conservative aristocratic republic headed by two magistrates elected yearly. Tarquin, other members of his family, and the army were besieging the Latin city of Ardea. Tarquin's son Sextus Tarquinius returned from Ardea at one point and raped Lucretia, the virtuous wife of his cousin L. Tarquinius Collatinus. Though held blameless, Lucretia killed herself after revealing the rape to Collatinus, his close friend L. Junius Brutus (also a cousin of Sextus), and others. Outraged, they seized control of the city, won over the loyalty of the army, and drove Tarquin and his sons into exile. Collatinus and Brutus were the Roman Republic's first elected pair of magistrates, but Collatinus was forced to resign because he was part of the male Tarquin line and was replaced by his friend P. Valerius Poplicola (Publicola).

Tyrants and Power Struggles   It looks as if Livy or his sources had taken a complex story of dynastic struggles within the family of Tarquin and turned it into a simplified but dramatic explanation for the end of tyranny and the beginning of republican government. How that change actually took place will probably never be known, but it seems likely that a series of tyrants still called kings in the sources had replaced the traditional kings at Rome in the sixth century B.C. By 550, Rome had grown into a large and complex city comparable to the larger cities of contemporary archaic Greece. The city itself covered about 660 acres and controlled a territory of about 300 square miles with a total population reasonably estimated to have been between 25,000 and 40,000. Similar cities in the contemporary Greek world had fallen under the domination of ambitious "popular" tyrants at this time. Because Rome was in close contact with the Greek world and shared similar social, economic, and political characteristics, it is likely that it followed the same trend.

Servius Tullius, for example, is depicted as having seized control of Rome after the assassination of Tarquin the Elder, and he himself supposedly was assassinated by Tarquin the Proud. Servius is also said to have received important military commands from the elder Tarquin. That could account for the tradition that he was named *Macstrna* in Etruscan (*Mastarna* in Latin). Macstrna seems to be the Etruscan equivalent of *magister* (master), and an archaic Roman term for the commander of the army was *magister populi,* master of the *populus* (the armsbearing men). It looks as if ambitious military leaders had taken the opportunity to overthrow the archaic kings, who had been chosen by the aristocratic *patres,* and had seized personal control with the backing of loyal military forces. After that, the old-style kings were restricted to the religious role of the *rex sacrorum* (king of the sacrifices), whose title conservatively perpetuated the traditional office of king throughout the rest of the Monarchy and the Republic.

The Role of the Army   The creation of the centuriate military organization ascribed to Servius Tullius certainly looks like an attempt to break down the local power of the aristocratic *patres* and create an army that owed allegiance to its leader alone (p. 33). What the "Servian" reform seems to have done was to create new geographic "tribes" as the basis for citizenship in place of the old tribes of *curiae,* made up of hereditary *gentes.* Because the centuries that supplied the field army were then created by combining men from each geographic tribe, every 100-man unit (century) of the hoplite *classis,* for example, would have represented a cross section of each tribe and not been loyal to any one powerful local aristocrat. Therefore, the tyrannical last "kings" of the Regal period probably had risen to power with the backing of loyal soldiers just as some tyrants had risen to power in several contemporary Greek cities.

As did their Greek counterparts, they probably used the army to pursue a popular program of expansion that opened up more land for small farmers, promoted trade, and brought in booty to support public works. Archaeological evidence shows a great deal of building activity at Rome in the late sixth century and confirms that the great temple of Capitoline Jupiter ascribed to Tarquin the Proud was begun right about the end of the Monarchy, as the literary sources claim. Furthermore, the last Tarquin had supposedly taken over the neighboring territory of Gabii and been besieging Ardea when he was overthrown.

The Final Struggles   Brutus, Tarquinius Collatinus, and their friend P. Valerius Poplicola (Publicola) are all portrayed as founders of the Republic in the romantic but compressed saga of the literary sources. More likely they were all struggling to supplant Tarquin themselves. That would explain the story of Collatinus suddenly being forced into exile with other male Tarquins and account for the stories that Poplicola had monarchic ambitions. Indeed, a recently discovered inscription lends some support to that view of Poplicola.

Perhaps the Etruscan Lars Porsenna of Clusium, who is depicted besieging Rome as an ally of Tarquin and even temporarily conquering Rome in some stories, was merely taking advantage of the confusion to seize Rome for himself. Porsenna, however, seems to have overreached himself in further attacks in Latium and then to have withdrawn or been driven from Rome itself around 504 B.C. (p. 69). (Perhaps the arrival of Attus Clausus [Appius Claudius] and his alleged 4,000 followers at Rome in 504 also is connected with Porsenna's loss of power [p. 41].) Tarquin attempted to recapture Rome with help from Latin allies. Nevertheless, the patrician families and their supporters, who had lost power under popular royal tyrants, gained firm control in leading a successful fight against the reimposition of tyrannical rule, and established the republican regime that institutionalized their power.

Archaeology lends support to this scenario with evidence of the violent destruction of sites associated with the monarchy and tyrannical rulers. Around 500 B.C., the Regia was burnt down, as were the Comitium, and the sanctuary of Hercules in the Forum Boarium. The Regia, of course, was the old royal palace, and the Comitium was the place of assembly where popular tyrants could have addressed the people. The sanctuary of Hercules had been built around 530 B.C. in the midst of the bustling market. The iconography of its surviving sculptures indicates that the leader who commissioned it wanted to be identified with the popular patron deity of traders. Significantly, the main statue group shows Minerva escorting Hercules to Olympus and may symbolize divine support for a popular royal tyrant.

Whatever the precise details may be, the Roman tradition seems based on a sound historical core: Around 500 B.C., rule by popular royal tyrants at Rome was abolished in a violent upheaval that led to the establishment of a conservative republican constitution.

The Early Republican Constitution

Although the Roman Republic never had a written constitution, its earliest form looks like a deliberate creation by conservative aristocrats, primarily those identified with the *patres*

(p. 41). It probably was an attempt both to end chaotic power struggles in the last decade of the sixth century and to restore power and privileges that they had lost under popular royal tyrants. They created a system that would make it difficult to acquire too much power at the expense of the rest.

The Consulship The *Fasti* indicate that dual yearly chief executives were a crucial feature of the Republic right from the start. These annual magistrates eventually came to be called consuls but probably were the old *magister populi*, perhaps now known as the *praetor maximus* (chief commander), who commanded the army, and a *iudex*, a civil judge. For the sake of simplicity, however, this book will use the terms *consul* and *consulship* exclusively because they are traditional and the term *praetor* became attached to another office in 367 B.C. (p. 64).

The original formal field army was a legion (legio) of 3,000 heavy infantry (hoplites), 1,200 light infantry (*velites*), and 300 cavalry (*celeres/equites*). Probably by 445 B.C., those figures had doubled, and the army could be split into two legions, each equivalent to the smaller original legion. Regardless of their possible origin, nomenclature, and any ceremonial distinctions between them, the two senior magistrates who eventually came to be known as consuls each commanded one of these later legions. By 311 B.C., there were four legions, and each consul commanded two. As legionary commanders, therefore, they held the earlier kings' power of military command (*imperium*). Furthermore, each had the full power to veto the other. In that way, the risk of one gaining too much power was reduced because each could check the other militarily and legally.

The consuls also shared other old royal powers and privileges. Besides commanding the legions, the consuls acted as judges, summoned meetings of the *comitia centuriata*, and placed legislative proposals before it. They were even surrounded with much of the old royal paraphernalia. Although they wore the purple toga of the old kings at festivals and could be buried in it, only a purple hem distinguished their daily clothes. They were among the curule magistrates, who sat on a portable ivory throne called a curule chair (*sella curulis*). Each was attended in the city by twelve lictors carrying *fasces,* bundles of rods symbolizing the power of punishment. Outside the city on military campaign, a double-headed ax was added to the *fasces* to symbolize the right of execution.

The nonpatrician names in the early years of the *Fasti* are best taken to indicate that the consulship was not the exclusive domain of patrician families. Eventual attempts to make it so, however, proved divisive and produced a strong reaction from wealthy nonpatricians later (p. 57). In the meantime, the criteria for election to the consulship were fairly informal. The prevailing conditions simply favored the election of the leading patricians and, occasionally, one of the wealthy nonpatricians to the two consulships each year.

The Office of Dictator

At times, dire military or domestic crises made it imperative for one man to have sole power, as in the days of the royal tyrants. In that case a magistrate with *imperium* (a consul, an *interrex,* or, after 367 B.C., a praetor) appointed a dictator, who received the sole power of the old *magister populi*. He appointed as his subordinate a man with the old title of *magister equitum*.

The dictator had supreme authority for no more than six months. The consuls remained in office but were subordinate to him. His superior *imperium* was signified by his having twenty-four lictors carrying *fasces* before him.

Junior Military Officers

The tribunes of the cavalry, *tribuni celerum* (*equitum*), and the military tribunes, *tribuni militum* (p. 33), all from wealthy families, continued to be the highest junior officers in the early Republican army. As Romans came to rely on allies for cavalry forces, however, the tribunes of the cavalry seem to have faded away. Because the size of the legion reached 6,000 men before it was split into two smaller legions, the number of military tribunes in each legion became fixed at six. They were all elected until the number of legions exceeded four. After that, twenty-four military tribunes continued to be elected, whereas the consuls appointed those needed for additional legions.

After the legion was reorganized on the basis of centuries, the number of centuries had increased until the legion contained 6,000 infantrymen in 60 centuries. When the legion was split into two smaller ones, 60 became the standard number of centuries in a legion during the Republic even if each century contained fewer than 100 men. The leader of each century was the centurion, a noncommissioned officer from the ranks.

The Senate

At the dawn of the Republic, the senate was, as it had been for the kings, merely an advisory council of prominent and experienced men. It could meet only at the summons of a consul or some other holder of *imperium* (a dictator or *interrex*). Meetings had to take place within a mile of the city's gates in a public, consecrated place like a temple. Its advice was not legally binding. Only the presiding magistrate could make it legal by enforcing it, but he was also free to modify or reject it altogether.

The ancient phrase used in addressing the assembled senators, *patres et conscripti,* indicates that originally there were two classes of members in the early Republican senate. At first, the *patres* of the senate were probably the public priests, whose sanction, the *patrum auctoritas,* as well as the senate's sacred meeting place assured that public actions were in accord with divine will. In a world where the gods were seen as controlling everything, that was of paramount importance, and it helped secure the power of the patrician families, who filled the public priesthoods. To the extent that priesthoods were held for life, the *patres* may have constituted a core of permanent senators and given the senate a certain corporate identity. Gradually, however, the term *patres* probably became extended to cover not just the public priests but all patrician senators; that is, those who came from the families eligible to supply the public priests. The original *conscripti,* "the enrolled," as their name implies, probably were other influential men and friends chosen by the yearly consuls to supplement the *patres.* Many of them must have been ex-consuls, whose experience made them valued as advisors to the current consuls. Their membership probably lasted only for the year in which the appointing consul held office. Because the consuls were usually elected from the patrician families or a few wealthy nonpatricians, the *conscripti* whom they enrolled undoubtedly were from patrician families, too, or from important nonpatrician families who shared the same aristocratic outlook as the *patres,* and therefore, often became identified with them as patricians in the historical tradition. As time went on, these "patrician" aristocrats turned the senate into a major organ of government by which they could dominate the state.

The Comitia Centuriata At the beginning of the Republic, the loyalty of the armsbearing men who made up the *populus* was essential for the success of the new regime. Therefore, the *comitia centuriata,* the assembly of armsbearing men now organized in centuries, probably acquired at the start of the Republic the right to elect the chief magistrates and other officers above the rank of centurion. The *comitia centuriata* also heard the cases of citizens who exercised the right of appeal (*provocatio*) when they had been condemned on capital charges by the magistrates. The tradition that P. Valerius Poplicola (Publicola) had obtained the right of appeal for the people at the beginning of the Republic probably represents another attempt to secure the loyalty of the army. Under the royal tyrants, the centuriate organization may have already been used to approve royal decrees, declarations of war, and the acceptance of peace, and it continued to do so as it became the early Republic's sovereign assembly.

The Comitia Curiata *and Other Assemblies*
The *comitia curiata* probably had already declined after the so-called Servian reforms. In the Republic, it was reduced to a pro forma meeting of thirty lictors representing each of the thirty curiae. It ratified the election of magistrates with *imperium* through passage of a *lex curiata de imperio,* and it also was convened to witness

wills, adoptions, and the appointment of public priests. As time went on, male Roman citizens were organized into other parallel popular assemblies that also had electoral, legislative, and judicial powers (pp. 59–61). Women never had the right to vote or hold political office. Except for the exclusion of patricians in one case, all male Roman citizens were members of all assemblies. No one was elected to an assembly, nor were assemblies like modern parliamentary bodies. No one pursued a political career in an assembly. The members did not formally debate issues. They merely voted on the candidates or bills presented by the appropriate officials who summoned them, or they acted as mass juries in judicial cases brought before them. Speeches and discussions concerning issues to be voted on in assemblies could take place previously in public meetings called *contiones* (sing. *contio*) summoned by elected officials.

The Priesthoods and Priestly Colleges

During the Republic, priestly colleges, boards of public priests organized for the correct performance of public rituals, played a major role in public life. Under the Monarchy, the king, who was himself originally the chief priest, probably appointed all priests, who acted as his assistants and advisors in religious matters. Once the old kings had been reduced to the king of sacrifices (*rex sacrorum*), probably under tyrannical rule (p. 52), the other priests became self-perpetuating colleges. During the early Republic, their membership was limited to men (and women in the case of flamens' wives and the Vestal Virgins) from patrician *gentes,* and in a decidedly nonsecular world, they exercised great power and influence.

There were four priestly colleges: pontiffs (*pontifices*), augurs (*augures*), fetials (*fetiales*), and duovirs for conducting sacrifices (*duoviri sacris faciundis*). In addition, there were a number of societies or associations (*sodalitates*) of lesser priests. Priests were not necessarily men of exceptional piety or endowed with special psychic or clairvoyant powers. They were, rather, men of learning, political experience, and high social rank who did not form any professional priestly class. Their wealth enabled them to perform their priestly duties without financial reward. Some had been magistrates before becoming priests; some were priests and magistrates simultaneously; and many were members of the senate. The chief qualification for a priesthood was an exact knowledge of religious tradition, of divine law, and of correct ritual and ceremonial procedure.

The Pontiffs Originally, a pontiff (*pontifex*) performed rituals and incantations believed to give permanence to the flimsy wooden bridges in early Latium. Under the kings there were three pontiffs (*pontifices*), who also acted as religious advisors. From the birth of the Republic, the membership of the college grew, as the *rex sacrorum,* the fifteen flamens (p. 47), and the six Vestal Virgins came to be included. Under the leadership of the chief pontiff (*pontifex maximus*), the college of pontiffs assumed a larger and larger role in public and private life. The pontiffs were the custodians and interpreters of the sacred law governing both the religious and legal relations of the community to the gods. They alone knew the exact formulae applicable in all legal transactions and the proper forms employed in the making of vows. They were the sole keepers of the temple archives and prescribed the various rituals, prayers, chants, and litanies for use in public worship and sacrifice. They also supervised the dedication and the consecration of temples and altars, the burial of the dead, and the inheritance of religious duties. It was they who organized the calendar that fixed the dates of festivals and the days on which the magistrate might not sit in court.

The Role of Pontiffs in Roman Law The *pontifex maximus,* judge and arbiter of things human and divine, had the power to convene and the right to preside over the Curiate Assembly. Because this assembly passed laws on adoptions and wills, the pontiffs exercised a dominant influence on the law of wills. Equally important was the influence of the pontiffs on legal procedure. Because suits before the courts

had to follow the precise wording of the claim (*legis actio*) being made, they would best stand if drafted with the advice and assistance of the pontiffs, who held a monopoly of jurisprudence throughout the first two centuries of the Republic (500 to 300 B.C.). The first Roman jurists of sacred, private, or public law came from the college of pontiffs, each assisted by a staff of secretaries, copyists, and recorders. They were neither judges nor regularly practicing lawyers. Their contribution arose from their functions as consultants and interpreters of the law. Magistrates consulted the entire college on matters of religious and public law; private disputes were referred to the pontiff appointed by the college to deal with such cases. This authority was not challenged until the later fourth or third centuries B.C., when knowledge of the law passed gradually into the hands of a wide circle of laymen (pp. 143–144).

The Augurs Originally made up of three patricians, the college of augurs (*augures*) gradually increased to sixteen members from both patrician and plebeian *gentes* by the end of the Republic. The augurs were responsible for conducting the auguries, ceremonies of divination to determine if the gods were favorable to an action or a place where an action was to take place or to the person about to undertake it. They looked for special signs in the flight and behavior of birds, the unusual behavior of animals, and heavenly phenomena like thunder and lightning.

They were also experts in the taking of auspices, which involved looking for the same types of signs for the limited purpose of determining if the time was right for an action. Private individuals could take auspices, and public officials did so regularly. They might be assisted by an augur, and they regularly consulted the augurs on questions concerning the correct practice of such rituals. The augurs had the right to block public business, particularly at the popular assemblies, by announcing unfavorable omens.

The Fetials The fetial priests (*fetiales*) were a board of twenty priests who dealt with issues of peace and war. In the early Republic they dealt directly with enemy counterparts in Italy and accepted treaties with a ritual exchange of curses calling down punishment on the first to break them. If the Romans had a grievance with another people, a fetial went to them, stated the Roman case, and demanded satisfaction. If satisfaction was not given in thirty-three days, the priest went to the enemy's border, declared war, and hurled a fire-hardened spear across the boundary. Even after that was no longer practical, fetial law built up over the years governed declarations of war.

Duovirs *for Making Sacrifices* (Duoviri Sacris Faciundis) A board originally of two men (*duoviri*), later ten and then fifteen men (*decemviri* and *quindecemviri*), these priests had the special responsibility of protecting the *Sibylline Books* that Tarquin the Proud supposedly had brought from Cumae. They consulted those sacred texts for guidance at the request of the senate when unusual portents or disasters occurred. They were also responsible for overseeing Greek cults and rituals adopted in response to such occasions.

Sodalitates There were three ancient associations (*Sodalitates*) of lesser priests: the Salii, the Luperci, and the Arval Brothers (*fratres arvales*). The Salii, "Leaping Priests," performed archaic war dances in annual rituals associated with Mars, the god of war. The Luperci, whose name comes from *lupus* (wolf), were young men who took part in the Lupercalia festival, named for the cave where the she-wolf supposedly nursed Romulus and Remus (p.42). The twelve Arval Brothers were the ancient priests of Dea Dia, a goddess of agriculture. They maintained her sacred grove and in conjunction with the Ambarvalia (p. 44) celebrated her festival in May with a special hymn.

Social and Political Conflicts, 509 to 287

B.C. By ca. 300 B.C., many of the priesthoods were no longer restricted to members of patrician *gentes*. The process whereby they were opened to men from plebeian *gentes* appears in the annalistic sources as part of the so-called "Struggle (Conflict) of the Orders." Writers like Livy mistakenly assumed that from the beginning Roman society was rigidly divided into two distinct orders or classes, the aristocratic patricians and the plebeians, nonpatrician commoners. Then, they wove together separate kinds and episodes of conflict during the early Republic into an oversimplified "Struggle of the Orders." As in any attempt to create a clear narrative, convenient labels usually mask a much more complex reality.

For example, it was said that the patricians had a monopoly of the chief magistracies and membership in the senate from the start of the Republic. No amount of convoluted argument, however, can explain away the fact that the *Fasti* show no such monopoly. Between 509 and 486, a number of solidly attested and unassailably nonpatrician names appear in the consular lists. From 485 to 470, however, there are none. Then, only a few appear between 469 and 445, the year when "plebeians" supposedly were specifically allowed to hold the new office of military tribune with consular power (p. 61). The most logical explanation is that at the beginning of the Republic nonpatricians and plebeians were not completely identical and that the sharp patrician/plebeian dichotomy reflected in the late sources is oversimplified. Even in early sources, informal usage may have lumped together as patricians all of those who governed the early Republic as priests, magistrates, and senators. Similarly, those who were not part of the governing elite, even if they were wealthy and influential within certain segments of society, came to be identified with that part of the population labelled as the *plebs*, in other words, the plebeians.

Still, no matter how oversimplified the "Struggle of the Orders" may be, tensions and discontented groups certainly existed within the young Republic. While some wealthy and ambitious nonpatricians managed to get elected to high office and become identified with the patricians, many others would not have been able to make such a breakthrough and would have been resentful. Small farmers, day laborers, shopkeepers, and artisans who did not have the means to serve in the hoplite infantry, the *classis,* which dominated the original *comitia centuriata,* were effectively disenfranchised, even though they may have served outside the *classis* as light-armed and support troops. Not only they but also probably some of those who marginally qualified as hoplites faced serious economic problems that aggravated social and political tensions.

Many farmers suffered losses in the constant attacks by surrounding peoples (pp. 69–78). The need to divide family land among heirs also must have meant that small proprietors, even those who were modestly well off, rapidly found their holdings too small to support them. Moreover, as time went on, large landowners began to monopolize access to public lands for themselves at the expense of poorer citizens.

The expansion of the Persian Empire into the eastern Mediterranean in the late sixth and early fifth centuries B.C. probably disrupted the flow of goods to Italy from Greece and the Near East that had helped Rome prosper and grow. Indeed, archaeological evidence seems to confirm a drop in Greek imports during the early fifth century. Therefore, the urban lower classes probably were feeling hardship, too.

Those who borrowed money from wealthier neighbors ran afoul of Rome's harsh laws of debt. Creditors could summarily seize a defaulting debtor's property, force him to work off his debts (a practice called "debt bondage"), sell him into slavery, or even kill him. The unsettled conditions also created periodic food shortages that posed severe hardship for the poor. Therefore, there were many people who had reason to protest and demand changes from those who governed, usually identified as patricians.

Growing Plebeian Self-Consciousness and Political Organization During the first half of the fifth century, growing discontent and protests fueled the growth of a self-conscious group identified as the *plebs* and constituting an independent political force that expressed the will of the discontented. Moreover,

the constant need for manpower and unity against outside enemies often forced those in power, traditionally labelled patricians, to make concessions to the discontented. Also, some patricians probably sided with some of the discontented to gain support for personal political purposes.

According to tradition, the first step in this process took place in 494 during a war with Rome's Latin neighbors (p. 71). The patricians had refused to curb the abusive practices of creditors during a debt crisis, and large numbers of the lower classes departed the city in protest. They took refuge on what was called the Sacred Mount, north of Rome about three miles from where the Anio River joins the Tiber. During this first "Secession of the Plebs," the protesters constituted themselves as the Council of the Plebs, *concilium plebis,* and elected their own independent yearly plebeian officials to protect their interests outside the regular apparatus of the Roman state.

The first plebeian officials were the tribunes of the plebs (*tribuni plebis*). Originally there were probably only two, modeled on the yearly "consuls," although the sources do not all agree. Only nonpatricians could be tribunes, and the careers of those who are known indicate that they were men of enough wealth to pursue unpaid political leadership. The well-to-do nonpatricians who held the tribunate or supported the plebs probably became identified as plebeians, too. Thus the distinction between patrician and plebeian *gentes* probably emerged.

The duty and function of a plebeian tribune was to protect the life, person, and interests of all plebeians who called upon him for help against the arbitrary power of a magistrate. Always on call, he had to keep his house open day and night and never go outside the city limits. In order that he might perform his duties without fear, his person was declared inviolate or sacrosanct. Anyone violently laying hands upon him or willfully interfering in the performance of his duties was threatened with death in accordance with the *lex sacrata.* The *lex sacrata* was a well-known military oath in ancient Italy. By it, soldiers swore to stand by their commanders to the death. In this case, it rendered the tribunes of the plebs inviolable. Anyone violently laying hands on a tribune in the performance of his duty was subject to lynch law at the hands of an angry mob invoking divine sanction.

Plebeian Aediles The *concilium plebis* also elected two plebeian aediles to assist the tribunes. They were originally caretakers of the temple of Ceres, the goddess of grain, on the Aventine, which was outside the walls of Rome at that time. Appropriately, a grain market and Greek trading center were associated with this site. The presence of resident Greeks may have been a source of democratic inspiration, and the connections with grain and trade indicate the concerns of many protesters with an adequate supply of food. Many of the aediles' functions are linked with providing for the material well-being of the average person. They were custodians of the plebeians' treasury and archives and later of the decrees of the senate. They also acted as police and supervised markets, weights and measures, public works, food and water supplies, and public games.

The Plebeian Tribal Council **(Concilium Plebis Tributum)** In 471, the Aventine itself was the site of a major secession of the plebs in the face of attacks from the Aequi and the Volsci. The interest of small farmers seems to have been a major concern this time. The original *concilium plebis* was reorganized on the basis of the geographical tribes of citizens in order to give more weight to the rural voters. They lived in the more numerous rural tribes (eventually thirty-one) but could not come to meetings near the city so easily as members of the four urban tribes. In this new tribal organization, the plebeian (nonpatrician) members present from each particular tribe voted as a unit. Each tribe thus had one vote based on a simple majority of the members who voted. Therefore, it came to be known as the Plebeian Tribal Council (*concilium plebis tributum*). It may not be coincidental that this new tribal organization was also advantageous to wealthy nonpatrician landowners, who could dominate the votes in rural tribes.

Plebiscita The Plebeian Tribal Council now elected the plebeian tribunes and aediles and could vote on motions placed before it by the tribunes. Such votes expressed the "sense of the plebs" (*plebiscitum*), but these plebiscites (*plebiscita*) were not initially recognized as laws by the patricians. Still, organized popular pressure could not easily be ignored

The success of the efforts by nonpatricians organized as the plebs to obtain relief from their grievances can be seen in two measures passed under popular pressure in the face of more threats from the Aequi and Volsci. The first is the so-called *lex Icilia* of 456 B.C. It was a plebiscite that backed the seizure of public land in the Aventine district for distribution to the needy. The patricians agreed to abide by it only under pressure later. The other measure was a true law, the *lex Aternia-Tarpeia,* promulgated by the two consuls of 454 B.C. It limited to thirty cattle and two sheep the size of a fine that a consul could impose. No doubt, the ones who benefitted most in this case were the better-off nonpatricians.

The Decemvirs and the Laws of the Twelve Tables
One of major sources of popular discontent was the complete domination of the law, which was largely customary and unwritten, by patrician priests. Around 452 B.C., the story goes, after some unsucessful attempts to obtain a code of written laws, the tribunes suggested to the senate that a committee representing both parties be chosen to frame just and equitable laws. The senate turned down the suggestion of plebeian participation but did agree to set up a commission of ten men, *decemviri*, to codify the existing laws. The story that a group of senators went to Athens to study the laws of Solon first may be apocryphal, but many senators must have been aware of contemporary law codes in the Greek colonies of *Magna Graecia*.

The Decemviral Commission The tradition surrounding the work of the Decemvirs is confused and contradictory. Supposedly, at the end of 452 B.C. the regular consulship and tribunate were suspended, and during 451 B.C. the Decemviral Commission—ten patricians chaired by Appius Claudius—ran the government and codified the laws. Apparently, at the end of the year they had not finished their task to everyone's satisfaction, and a second decemvirate—half patrician and half plebeian (nonpatrician) but still chaired by Appius Claudius—was appointed to complete the project.

Appius Claudius supposedly now forced the addition of unfair laws, such as the prohibition against marriages between patricians and plebeians, and acted like a tyrant. For example, he was said to have claimed falsely the beautiful Verginia as his slave to satisfy his lust, so that in desperation her father killed her to save her from dishonor. In protest against Appius and the Decemvirs, the plebeians are said to have seceded again, so that the commission resigned and ten tribunes and two consuls friendly to the plebs were elected for 449 B.C.

While the makeup of the revised decemviral commission may be historical, much of this account seems fanciful. Appius probably was arrogant and high-handed, but it is difficult to see how he could have forced the plebeian members to adopt a ban on patricio-plebeian marriages. That story may be a misinterpretation of an attempt to guarantee a supply of men meeting the traditional requirements for priests (*patres*). The story of Verginia, which looks like a traditional moralizing tale, was attached to Appius Claudius probably because of his prominence and arrogance. The one generally accepted fact is that the Decemvirs did produce a codification of existing early Roman public and private laws, which were set up eventually, if not originally, on twelve bronze tablets in the Forum. This code was henceforth known as the Law of the Twelve Tables.

Style and Content of the Twelve Tables
About one third of the text of the Twelve Tables is preserved in quotations by later authors. The style is archaic, simple, brief, harsh, but legally clear and exact, as in Table I, "If he calls him to court, go he shall; if he doesn't, plaintiff will call witness, then will take him"; or Table VII, "They will keep road repaired, if they don't

cobble it, man may drive team where he wants to"; or Table VIII, "If burglary be done at night, if (owner) kills him, he shall be killed by law, if by day, not, unless burglar defends himself with weapon."

Significance of the Twelve Tables   The law of the Twelve Tables codified the preexisting law of custom but also was capable through interpretation of meeting future needs. It reduced powers of the *paterfamilias* not required for the maintenance of family unity, guaranteed the right to property and testament, provided for the intervention of the state in civil disputes, abolished family revenge, and permitted the referral of capital cases to the *comitia centuriata*. It also abolished torture as a means of obtaining evidence from free men. In short, the basic importance of the Twelve Tables was that they established in principle the equality of all free citizens before the law. Nevertheless, since they primarily codified existing practice, they did not really get at the roots of plebeian discontent.

Post-Decemviral Developments   The creation of written laws at Rome shares clear parallels with the writing down of laws at Athens in the time of Draco. Both represent similar attempts by conservative aristocratic elites to solidify their dominance in the face of social and economic crises typical of archaic city-states. Since they both primarily codified existing practices, however, they did not really get at the roots of nonaristocratic discontent. They merely sharpened the perception of grievances that would lead to even stronger challenges to the existing order as some leaders sought support from outside the ranks of those who had traditionally monopolized political power.

The Valerio-Horatian Laws, 449 B.C.   The laws promulgated by L. Valerius Potitus and M. Horatius Barbatus, the patrician consuls of 449, are a case in point. In cooperation with the tribunes, they opposed the Decemvirs' continuation in office and supported regulations concerning the existing right of appeal from a magistrate and legal recognition of the sacrosanctity of plebeian tribunes. Finally, they provided that what the plebs passed in voting by tribes was binding on the *populus*. In other words, opponents could not negate a plebiscite by citing a previous measure passed in the *comitia centuriata* (i.e., the *populus*).

The Creation of the Comitia Tributa

This last measure may be connected with the creation of another popular assembly, the *comitia tributa*, that came into existence around this time. Modeled on the *concilium plebis tributum*, the *comitia tributa* was an assembly of all citizens voting by tribes. The inclusion of the patrician *gentes*, who were a small minority of the population, probably would have made little difference in the overall voting, which still would have been dominated by the rural tribes. Nevertheless, patrician landowners may have had a little more control over the votes of their rural clients. Because it included all male citizens, however, there was no question that measures passed by it were laws (*leges*) binding on all.

The Quaestors

No more than two years later, the *comitia tributa* was electing two patrician quaestors, who were originally merely appointed assistants to the consuls. Their number was increased to four in 421 B.C., when the office was first thrown open to men from plebeian *gentes*, but it was not until the year 409 B.C. that plebeian quaestors were actually elected. Although their original function was to investigate murders, minor crimes against property also came under their jurisdiction.

Two of the four quaestors accompanied the consuls to the battlefield, where they served as quartermasters in charge of supplies and the payment of troops. The other two remained in the city to serve as keepers of the public treasury and prosecutors of tax delinquents. Since the public treasury was in the temple of Saturn, they were also in charge of the official records and documents kept in that building.

Apparitores

The original quaestors probably were classed as *apparitores*—the scribes, secretaries, accountants, and other skilled appointees who aided the priests and magistrates in the performance of their duties. Those posts were open to ordinary citizens and conferred considerable prestige on their holders. Eventually, they received a salary.

The Lex Canuleia

According to the simplistic traditional account of the "Struggle of the Orders," the tribune C. Canuleius, taking advantage of the Valerio-Horatian law of 449 B.C., struck a blow for the plebeians by obtaining passage of a plebiscite, the *lex Canuleia*, which rescinded the recently adopted law against the intermarriage of *patres* and plebeians. Although the original purpose of the law may have been to preserve the bloodlines required to hold certain priesthoods, some ambitious individuals among both the patrician and the wealthier plebeian *gentes* may have seen the law as preventing politically advantageous marital alliances. Therefore, they may have worked together to overturn it.

Military Tribunes with Consular Power

Another milestone in the traditional accounts of the "Struggle of the Orders" is the supposed compromise of 445 B.C. by which the patricians agreed to create in place of the consulship a new office that would be open to plebeians. These new officials were called military tribunes with consular power (*imperium consulare*); they differed from consuls, however, in that they did not have the right to celebrate a triumph and were not eligible to become senators after their year of office; they each were equal in power and could veto one another; one remained in the city during times of war to carry out civil functions, and the others took the field as commanders of legions. The senate decided whether to have consuls or military tribunes with consular power for a given year. According to the *Fasti*, the latter held office in fifty of the years from 444 to 367 B.C.

One of the difficulties with viewing the institution of the military tribunate with consular power as part of a compromise in the "Struggle of the Orders" is that the first securely attested plebeian holder of the office does not appear until 422 B.C. No plebeian appears again until

400 B.C., and others are found in only five more years after that. Therefore, these statistics may indicate no more than a continuation of what had happened previously in elections to the consulship: the occasional success of a wealthy nonpatrician either through favor directly with the voters or as an ally of some ambitious patrician.

The appearance of military tribunes with consular power in the surviving lists at various times and in numbers varying from three to six may merely reflect incomplete records. More likely, it reveals the need for two or more legions and their commanding officers in years during which Rome faced military threats from Ardea, Veii, the Aequi, the Volsci, and the Gauls until about 376 B.C. (pp. 71–72). At that point, new pressures culminated in the reforms of 367 B.C., which regularized the titles of and qualifications for various magistracies and organized them into the classic hierarchical *cursus honorum,* "course of offices" (pp. 64–65). Until then, however, there probably was no formal provision allowing members of plebeian *gentes* to hold high office.

The Censors In 444 B.C., a new office appeared, the censorship, which seems to have been monopolized by patrician *gentes* until 351 B.C. (p. 65). Two censors were elected at irregular intervals by the *comitia centuriata* to compile the census (the official list of Roman citizens eligible for military service, voting, and taxation). In time, they were elected every five years for a period of eighteen months. They did not have the *imperium* or the right to the *fasces,* they could not call the people or the senate to assembly, nor could they nominate their own successors, but they did sit on the curule chair (*sella curulis*). Eventually, the job of registering citizens and their property, of assessing their liability to taxes and military service, and of assigning them to tribes and centuries for voting made their office, even without *imperium* and the *fasces,* more feared and respected than the consulship. After 339, censors acquired the power of appointing senators and of removing them from the senate if they did not meet the standards of the Roman moral code (p. 65). By

putting a black mark opposite a man's name, the censor could remove a citizen from his tribe, demote him from a rural tribe to a city tribe, or take away his civil rights altogether for at least five years.

The censors also became concerned with the spending of funds appropriated by the senate or released by the consul. They drew up contracts for major public works such as roads, bridges, aqueducts, and public buildings. Control of the tax registers and of the state revenues gave them considerable power. They granted contracts for collecting such revenue; leased public lands, mines, salt works, and fishing rights; and arranged for the collection by private contractors (publicans) of port dues and of taxes owed by squatters on public land. The only kind of revenue with which they had nothing to do was that obtained from war booty.

A New Period of Reform A strenuous war against the Etruscan city of Veii and the disastrous invasion of the Gauls at the beginning of the fourth century B.C., which culminated in the sack of Rome around 390 B.C. (pp. 71–72), probably created the conditions that led to further reforms. Apparently about 376 B.C., in a period of lessened immediate danger, two plebeian tribunes, C. Licinius Stolo and L. Sextius Lateranus, introduced major reforms, the so-called "Licinio-Sextian laws." Both men were very able and dynamic popular leaders whose wealth, social position, and marriages to women of the ancient patrician aristocracy gave them the power to end formally the traditional patrician domination of the highest political office and alleviate economic distress for debtors and small farmers. The sources list three proposals: (1) that interest already paid on debts be deducted from the principal, and the remainder of the debt, if any, be paid within three years in equal installments; (2) that newly acquired public land be allotted to individual private owners, although no one would be allowed to occupy more than 500 *iugera* (ca. 320 acres) of existing public land or graze more than a limited number of animals on public pasture; and (3) that the consular tribuneship be abolished and only consuls be elected, of whom one must be a plebeian. In 367 B.C., these proposals supposedly were enacted into law.

Although there are many problems with details in the existing account of the Licinio-Sextian laws, there is no reason to reject the core of the tradition. That these laws abolished the military tribunes with consular power seems certain, because no more appear after 367. They probably specified, however, only that one of the restored consulships each year *could* be held by someone from a plebeian *gens*. That one *must* be held by a plebeian was probably not specified until a law of L. Genucius in 342 B.C. Some kind of restriction on the growing monopolization of public land, *ager publicus,* by large landowners also seems reasonable. Soon, large tracts of public land were acquired through Roman conquests in central Italy, and many thousands of small holdings were created for impoverished peasants. Accordingly, one of the major economic grievances of the poor plebeians was alleviated for over a century.

The Licinio-Sextian legislation on debt poses no problems and seems to be another attempt to alleviate a major source of discontent, especially among those who had few assets and were threatened with debt slavery. The process continued as regulations restricted interest rates to probably 8 2/3 percent a year in 357 and 4 1/6 percent in 347. In 342, Genucius tried to abolish giving loans at interest completely, but this impractical law soon became a dead letter. A much more practical move was the creation in 352 B.C. of a special governmental board of five, *quinqueviri mensarii,* who helped debtors in trouble by assuming mortgages that could be adequately secured—in many cases probably by the new allotments of land that were now being distributed. Finally, the *lex Poetilia* of either 326 or 313 B.C. so severely limited the circumstances whereby a person could be enslaved for debt that the practice soon disappeared.

Reform of the Comitia Centuriata

Perhaps it was as a result of the Licinio-Sextian reforms that the *comitia centuriata*, which elected the consuls, was reformed to include centuries primarily associated with the plebs, those who could not afford hoplite arms. Centuries no longer supplied specific units of the field army but were grouped in census classes based on the type of military service that their members could afford. In fact, the poorer plebeians now were at a greater disadvantage in the *comitia centuriata,* and the change seems to represent an attempt (perhaps as a concession to certain patricians or the wealthy in general) to minimize the impact of all but the highest census class on the election of the consuls.

The first census class comprised 18 centuries of *equites* (men of the highest census class who were designated as cavalry) and 80 infantry centuries (40 senior and 40 junior). There were 20 centuries each (half senior and half junior) for classes two through four, 30 (half senior and half junior) for the fifth class, and 5 centuries for people below the minimum property assessment (2 for craftsmen, 2 for trumpeters, and 1 for the proletarians). The total, therefore, was 193 centuries. Each century voted as a unit, a simple majority of each century determining its one vote. The voting proceeded in hierarchical order from highest to lowest. It started with the 18 equestrian centuries and continued with the 80 infantry centuries and so on until a majority of 97 votes was reached. At that point the voting stopped. It was very unlikely that centuries below the fourth class, though containing the largest number of citizens, would ever be called upon to vote, and it was possible for the first class alone to dominate the voting because its 98 centuries constituted a majority.

Accordingly, the hierarchical, unit-vote system was far from democratic even for men. The rich, with their 98 centuries, could always outvote the lower census classes. The old could always outvote the young, because the seniors, though numerically fewer, had as many centuries as the juniors. Moreover, close votes within some centuries might mean that the outcome of the unit vote did not reflect the will of the majority who voted, just as in the electoral college system for electing presidents of the United States, in which it is possible for a candidate to lose the popular vote but win a majority of the electoral college. Thus, the organization of this assembly, to which all adult male citizens belonged, favored domination by the conservative, wealthy landowners in the highest centuries. Rich members of plebeian *gentes* benefitted but not those of little or no means.

The Creation of a New Nobility and Further Changes in the Magistracies

The Licinio-Sextian legislation of 367 probably represents a victory of a coalition of certain patrician and plebeian leaders against intransigent proponents of hereditary patrician privilege. It formally opened up the consulship to wealthy members of plebeian *gentes,* whose circumstances permitted a career of unpaid public service. Such a moment was bound to come anyway, because the old patrician families that had dominated the early Republic were inexorably dying out. The universal tendency of upper classes to have small families, many patricians' refusal to intermarry with plebeians even after the *lex Canuleia* of 445 B.C., and deaths in battle during the numerous wars with Rome's neighbors had severely reduced their ranks. For example, only twenty-nine of fifty-three patrician *gentes* recorded for the fifth century appear in the fourth century. With men from plebeian *gentes* frequently (regularly after 342 B.C.) holding the consulship, a patricio-plebeian consular nobility replaced the old, exclusively patrician nobility. It was made up of those families who had a member that had held the office of consul. A man who was the first of his family to reach the consulship was a *novus homo,* new man. He thereby ennobled his family and enjoyed the undying gratitude of succeeding generations.

The New Praetorship

Despite the formal opening of the consulship to wealthy men from plebeian *gentes,* the hardline patricians did not immediately surrender all of their control. The growing complexity of war and public business made it desirable to create a junior colleague of the consuls. In 367 B.C., the patrician-dominated senate, therefore, revived the ancient office of praetor and restricted it to members of patrician *gentes.*

Originally, there was only one praetor. His full title was *praetor urbanus*. Like the consuls, he was elected annually by the Centuriate Assembly. As a junior colleague of the consuls, he possessed the *imperium* and could, if necessary, assume command of a legion. He also could, in the absence of the consuls or if deputized by them, summon meetings of the Centuriate Assembly or the senate and perform all the executive functions of a consul. He had the *fasces* and six lictors, the purple-bordered toga, the curule chair (*sella curulis*), and all the other insignia of a higher magistrate.

The praetor's ordinary duties may have been primarily the administration of justice within the city. That would have allowed the consuls to give their undivided attention to military and foreign affairs, and the patricians could still maintain internal control through the legal system. Eventually, however, men from plebeian *gentes* gained access to the praetorship, too (p. 65).

Around 244 B.C., a second praetor was created, the *praetor inter peregrinos* (later, *praetor peregrinus*). His duties probably involved maintaining Roman authority among the foreign people (*inter peregrinos*) whom Rome had conquered in Italy and Sicily. Thenceforth, the praetorship took on the character of a separate magistracy independent of the consulship, and more praetors were added as the adminstrative needs of the state increased.

The Curule Aedileship

Another office, the curule aedileship, was also created in 367 to help with the expanding burdens of municipal administration. There were two curule aediles, so called because, unlike the two existing plebeian aediles, they had the right to the curule chair. The first curule aediles were patricians, but men from plebeian *gentes* were later eligible in alternate years. Their functions were basically the same as those of the plebeian aediles (p. 59).

The Cursus Honorum

The hierarchical course of offices, *cursus honorum,* that marked an aristocratic political career for centuries was now all in place: quaestor, aedile, praetor, consul, and censor, in ascending order. Because they were officers of the plebs only, not magistrates of the whole state, the tribunes of the plebs stood outside of this *cursus*. So, too, did the office of dictator, which was an emergency creation and not an expected part of a regular career.

After 367 B.C., offices not open to leaders from plebeian *gentes* soon yielded to their pressure. In 356, the distinguished plebeian C. Marcius Rutilius became a dictator, and in 351 he was the first to reach the censorship. Then, in 339, the *lex Publilia* of the plebeian dictator Q. Publilius Philo provided that one censor had to be a plebeian. Finally, plebeians gained access to the praetorship in 337. To prevent any one person from monopolizing high offices, it was also made illegal for a magistrate to hold more than one curule office (one that allowed the holder a curule chair: curule aedile, praetor, consul, censor) in any one year or the same curule office twice within ten years.

Promagistracies As Roman affairs became more complicated, the yearly magistrates were not numerous enough to handle all of the administrative and military tasks required. In order to create officers with the requisite authority, therefore, the senate resorted to the creation of acting magistrates called promagistrates. The first use of this new device was at the siege of Naples in 327 B.C. at the start of the Second Samnite War (p. 75), when it seemed advisable to maintain the consul who started the siege in command after his normal year of office. Therefore, the senate voted to retain him in place of a consul, *pro consule*. A magistrate who had his power extended in this way was said to have been prorogued. Although prorogation was used sparingly at first, its use was gradually extended to other magistrates, and promagistrates became quite common, especially proconsuls and propraetors.

Admission of Plebeians to Religious Offices Another legislative reform of 367 was the admission of plebeian *gentes* to a share in the responsibility of looking after and interpreting the *Sibylline Books*. This task had hitherto been an exclusive prerogative of the patrician *duoviri sacris faciundis* (p. 57), who made use of it to block proposals for social, political, and economic reform. This priestly college was expanded to a board of ten men (*decemviri*), five of whom had to be from plebeian *gentes*, to take charge of these books.

One of the last patrician bulwarks was control of the major priesthoods. In the year 300 B.C., the *lex Ogulnia* increased the number of the pontiffs to eight and of the augurs to nine. Now, four pontiffs and five augurs had to be plebeian. The only priests who still had to be patricians were the king of sacrifices, the flamens of Jupiter, Mars, and Quirinus, and the Salii, or Leaping Priests (pp. 55–57).

Lifetime Senators By the end of the fourth century, appointment to the senate conferred lifetime membership. The almost constant warfare of the previous 200 years, as will be seen in the next chapter, required the existence of some permanent organ of government that could provide informed and consistent guidance in the face of annually changing generals and chief executives. Moreover, strong common interests existed between the senators and the yearly consuls, who had filled the senate mostly from the ranks of ex-consuls. That, plus innate Roman conservatism and respect for tradition, probably had led to the reappointment of many senators from year to year even in the fifth century B.C. The *lex Ovinia* (dated between 339 and 318 B.C.), however, formalized the automatic admission of ex-magistrates to the senate for life. Senators had to be worth at least 400,000 sesterces, and the censors could remove from the senate anyone who fell below that limit or acted immorally. The censors could also add men whom they deemed worthy in order to keep the senate up to strength, probably around 300 by this time.

The number of patrician senators was still overwhelming in the late fourth century B.C. Many of them continued attempts to limit the political power of the lower classes. Nevertheless, there were always nonpatrician and patrician upper-class leaders who were willing for one reason or another to give them help.

Removal of Patrician Control over Law and Voting

In 339 B.C., when the dictator Publilius Philo promulgated the law that one of the censors had to be from a plebeian *gens,* Rome was at war against former Latin allies (p. 74) and the lower classes were angry over the unfair distribution of land. Against that background, he was able to obtain passage of two other laws that reduced patrician power. One reaffirmed that plebiscites were legally binding on all citizens, and the other required that the *patres* give their sanction (*patrum auctoritas*) to bills presented to the *comitia centuriata* before the centuries started voting. In this way, the patricians had to state any objections beforehand and could not find another excuse to block a bill after a vote had occurred. During the Second Samnite War (p. 75), Appius Claudius (not the Decemvir, but the famous blind censor of 312 B.C., who built the Appian Way) was a patrician who sought popular support among the lower classes. To help the urban plebs, he distributed people who owned no land throughout the twenty-seven then-existing rural tribes instead of just the four urban ones. Usually, fewer people voted in the rural tribes, so that an individual's vote carried more weight in them. That is why when the censors of 304 B.C. wanted to reduce the value of freedmen's votes they restricted all freedmen to registration in the four urban tribes.

Despite this discrimination against freedmen, liberal changes continued. Even in 304 B.C., Cn. Flavius, the son of a freedman and a protégé of Appius Claudius, published a useful handbook of procedures and legal formulae to give the average citizen better access to the courts. He even advertised his support of the lower classes by dedicating a temple to Concord (Harmony) in the Forum. In 300 B.C., the consul M. Valerius Maximus obtained a law that guaranteed the right of appeal, *provocatio,* from a magistrate's sentence of death or whipping within the city. About 290, another law abolished the patricians' veto over the election of magistrates and required that they ratify the results of elections in advance.

Finally, in 287 B.C. the aftermath of the long, tedious Samnite wars (pp. 73–76) brought another crisis over debts, and the plebs seceded to the Janiculum Hill across the Tiber. According to the traditional view, the consuls appointed the plebeian Q. Hortensius as a dictator to deal with the situation. He supposedly obtained a law, the *lex Hortensia,* which specified that whatever the plebs had enacted bound the whole people. That principle, however, was already evident in both 449 (p. 61) and 339. The "law" ascribed to Hortensius may be no more than a standard legal formula attached to some unknown plebiscites, or Hortensius may have been only a pontiff issuing some legal ruling. The latter view is consistent with evidence that he also modified the Roman calendar, which the pontiffs controlled, to permit people to conduct legal business in Rome on market days. That would have been popular with small farmers from the countryside because those would have been the days most convenient for them to be in Rome.

The Realities of the Roman Republican Constitution after 287 B.C.

By the time of the so-called *lex Hortensia* in 287 B.C., whatever its true nature might be, many have seen the emergence of a truly democratic constitution at Rome. Others, like the second-century-B.C. Greek historian Polybius, have called it a mixed constitution, a blend of the three "good" types of constitution defined by Aristotle: monarchy, represented by the magistrates; aristocracy, represented by the senate; and democracy, represented by the tribunes of the plebs and the popular assemblies. According to this theory, each branch balanced the other, so that one could not become more powerful at the expense of the other two. Both views are wrong. The Republic was controlled by a powerful oligarchy. It was made up of those wealthy landowners from patrician and plebeian *gentes* who had held the office of consul and constituted a consular nobility within the senate, whose lower-ranking members were also wealthy patrician and plebeian landowners from the highest census class.

In a society that was extremely hierarchical and conscious of rank and prestige, modern egalitarian ideals did not exist; it was naturally assumed that some men were better than others. Business in the senate, for example, was conducted along strict lines of seniority in rank. At each census, the censors designated one of the prestigious ex-consuls as the *princeps senatus,* first man of the senate. This man gave his opinions first in debate. Then followed, usually on strict lines of seniority, the censors-elect and censors (when there were such), ex-censors, the consuls-elect (if elections that year were over), the consuls and ex-consuls, praetors-elect, praetors, ex-praetors, and so on down the ranks. Debate seldom went beyond the ranks of the ex-praetors before the topic was exhausted, whereupon the membership voted by dividing, moving to one side of the room or the other. The men of the lower ranks were called *pedarii* because the only way that they usually had to express themselves was with their feet, *pedes,* as they walked across the room.

Under this system, then, it is clear that senatorial debate would have been framed by the consular nobility and would have proceeded along lines laid down by the early speakers. That is especially true because most of the men of lower rank had been elected to their magistracies through the help of consular nobles and looked to their continued goodwill for election to higher office. Therefore, they were most likely to side with their consular patrons on a particular issue to avoid giving offense.

For the same reason, magistrates during their brief year of office were not really independent of the noble-dominated senate. Not only were they dependent for advice on the collective wisdom of the ex-magistrates who comprised the senate, but they themselves were looking to become senators if they were not already, and those who already were senators hoped to advance in rank. Even the consuls were dependent on the senate for funds and for appointment to prestigious or lucrative military commands and, after the acquisition of an overseas empire, provincial governorships. Accordingly, there was great pressure to conform to the wishes of the powerful consulars in the senate, who formed a virtual oligarchy.

The tribunes of the plebs, wealthy men from plebeian *gentes* who started out as protectors of the common citizens, became co-opted by this oligarchy. As the number of plebeian families who had held high office and joined the senate grew, many of the new tribunes tended to be young men from their ranks who were starting out on political careers. Naturally, most of them desired to cooperate with the consular nobles, who controlled the senate, and they were willing to exercise their vetoes over fellow tribunes in the interest of powerful nobles. Eventually, the tribunes seemed to be so tamed that they, too, were admitted to the ranks of senators, even though they were not strictly part of the *cursus honorum.*

Finally, the various popular assemblies were dominated by the interests of wealthy landowners. During most of the Republic, of course, the *comitia curiata* was merely a *pro forma* carryover from the past, so that there was little need to influence it one way or another. The *comitia centuriata, comitia tributa,* and *concilium plebis* were different, however. They had exclusive rights to elect magistrates and pass legislation, and they had important judicial functions. As already explained, because of the unit-voting procedure, the 193 centuries of the *comitia centuriata* were dominated by the 98 centuries belonging to men of the wealthiest census class, the large landowners (pp. 63–64). The situation was hardly changed by a slight reform, sometime between 241 and 215 B.C., that necessitated voting by the second-highest census class before a majority could be reached.

The unit-vote rule also stifled the vote of the ordinary citizen in the *comitia tributa* and *concilium plebis.* In both of these meetings voting was done by tribes. After 241 B.C., the number of tribes in which all Roman citizens were enrolled became fixed at four urban and thirty-one rural. Obviously, the large number of landless urban dwellers, who had only four votes, were outweighed by the thirty-one votes of the rural tribes. Furthermore, since all voting had to be done at Rome, the small landowners in the rural tribes were at a great disadvantage, compared with the wealthy landowners, who maintained houses in Rome or could afford to go to Rome to vote. Even if a small landowner did get to Rome to vote, he was probably a client of the man who was the largest landowner in his neighborhood and often would have voted as his patron wished. Thus, the votes of many rural tribes were heavily influenced by the same wealthy men who dominated the *comitia centuriata,* the senate, and the magistracies.

After the wealthy landowners from plebeian *gentes* had gained political equality with the patricians, the interests of all large landowners were essentially the same. Therefore, wealthy landowners outside the senate had little incentive to challenge the patricio-plebeian consular nobles who dominated it. The ordinary citizen also was largely satisfied. After 200 years, he had made some important gains: removal of the threat of enslavement for debt, protection from the arbitrary use of magisterial power, a more open legal system, and some successful attempts to obtain land for those without it. Consequently, for a long time there was no serious challenge to the small group of consular senators who exercised great influence over the affairs of state. That would come only after conditions had greatly changed.

VI

The Roman Conquest of Italy and Its Impact, 509 to 264 B.C.

Although the previous chapter has treated them separately, the internal struggles that shaped early Republican social and political history took place during a seemingly endless series of wars between the Romans and the other peoples of Italy. The constant need for manpower to fight the surrounding peoples shaped the army and gave those who served some leverage within the political system. Moreover, it was the values of loyalty and service fostered by the Roman family and the need for unity in the face of enemies that prevented the internal struggles from being too destructive.

Conflicts with Immediate Neighbors

The wars of the fifth century B.C. make up a large part of Livy's narrative from the beginning of the second to well past the middle of his fifth book. A large number are probably glorified plundering raids or border skirmishes over the possession of small amounts of land. Such fights often occurred between Rome and her close neighbors: the Latins, Sabines, Hernici, Aequi, Volsci, and Etruscans. Patriotic Roman historians, of course, claimed that Rome fought others only in self-defense. Hardly any nation ever believes that it is the aggressor, and even fewer admit it. The Romans were as often to blame as their neighbors, and for the same reasons.

The early Romans and other peoples of Italy were mostly subsistence farmers and pastoralists. In primitive agrarian societies such as theirs, shortage of land was chronic as populations expanded. At Rome, for example, one of the poor citizens' constant grievances was lack of land. Moreover, since wealth and status in such societies were based on land, wealthy leaders always wanted more, too. The only way to obtain more for everyone in any community was to take it from another.

Plunder and prestige were additional objects of warfare. The peasant soldier of modest resources found it attractive to increase his wealth by taking someone else's. His aristocratic leaders also looked forward to a large share of war's spoils. Even more, however, leaders sought the prestige that would accrue from conducting a successful armed exploit, which counted heavily in the heroic, aristocratic code of Antiquity.

Rome's first attackers after the overthrow of Tarquin supposedly were the Etruscan cities of Veii and Tarquinia, which backed Tarquin's bid to regain his throne. After they were defeated, the Etruscan Lars Porsenna of Clusium apparently succeeded in capturing the city for himself (p. 53). There seems to be more patriotism than history in the heroic legend of Horatius preventing Rome's fall by single-handedly holding off the attackers at the Sublician Bridge (*Pons Sublicius*) until it could be destroyed.

Italy about 265 B.C.

Porsenna's attempt to expand his control in Latium ushered in a prolonged conflict between Rome and the league of Latin cities that resulted in the Battle of Lake Regillus (496 B.C.). Despite the death of the Latin general and patriotic Roman claims of help from the divine twins Castor and Pollux, the battle seems to have been a draw. As a result, it merely invited the neighboring hill tribes, such as the Aequi and the Volsci, to encroach on both of them during the continued conflict. It also encouraged the poorer citizens and leading nonpatricians at Rome to press for more rights (p.58).

Uniting in the face of common enemies, the Romans and the Latin League decided to settle their differences in 493 with a treaty, the *foedus Cassianum,* negotiated by the Roman Spurius Cassius. This treaty aided Roman expansion in Latium because Rome's position was equal to that of the Latin League as a whole. The Romans contributed half the forces used for common defense; and the League, the other half. Whichever side summoned such an army was to command it, and any spoils were to be split evenly—half to Rome and half to the members of the League. Roman power was bound to increase at the Latins' expense. Rome alone could decide to summon the common army, whereas the League would need a reason satisfactory to individual members before it could do so; thus, the single city of Rome enriched itself with half of any spoils, while the other half was split among several.

Skillful Roman diplomacy also gained another advantage. The territories of the Aequi and the Volsci were separated by that of the Hernici, who feared those tribes more than they feared Rome. The Romans made a defensive alliance with the Hernici around 485 B.C. that isolated the Aequi and the Volsci from each other and thereby made it easier to defeat them in the long run. The principle evident here, divide and rule (*divide et impera*), aided Roman expansion for centuries.

Defeat of the Aequi and the Volsci Having earlier seized Mount Algidus near Tusculum southeast of Rome, the Aequi almost annihilated a Roman army in 458 B.C. According to tradition, the situation was so alarming that a delegation from the senate went out to see Cincinnatus, who was plowing at the time on his four-acre farm. At the delegation's insistence, he accepted the offer of a dictatorship and administered a shattering defeat to the Aequi. Afterward, he resigned his dictatorship, went back home, and yoked up his ox. Still, the Romans did not drive the Aequi off Mount Algidus until 431 B.C.

The Volsci were even more difficult. According to Roman legend, at one point a Roman patrician named Coriolanus, exiled through plebeian hostility, led a Volscian attack against Rome in 491 until his brave mother and wife persuaded him to turn back. Whatever the truth of the story, the Volsci did penetrate as far north as the Alban Mount, and it was not until the end of the century that Rome and the Latin allies pushed the Volsci out of Latium and secured the border with a series of colonies.

The War with Veii Roman aggression during the fifth century B.C. was directed particularly against the Etruscan city of Veii. Veii was located about ten miles north of Rome on the Cremera River, a western tributary of the Tiber. Large, rich, and well fortified, Veii was Rome's chief rival for control of the lower Tiber valley and had a garrison across the Tiber at Fidenae. The Romans fought over fifty years (481 to ca. 426) for Fidenae. Twenty years later, they attacked Veii itself, and finally captured it in 396 after a ten-year siege according to Livy, whose epic account too neatly echoes the *Iliad*.

The Romans subsequently destroyed Veii, sold some inhabitants as slaves, and annexed its territory. That almost doubled the area of the *ager Romanus* (Roman territory) and increased Roman manpower. The dictator Camillus, the victor over Veii, his face and hands painted red like the statue of Jupiter, rode in triumph in a four-horse chariot through the streets of Rome, which was quite unaware of the war clouds even then gathering in the North.

The Gallic Sack of Rome While Camillus was celebrating his triumph over Veii, new invaders, whom the Romans called *Galli* (Gauls), swept into Italy. They were part of the large Indo-European-speaking group of peoples known as Celts (p. 9). Perhaps as early as 500 B.C., successive waves of Gallic tribes had begun to cross the Alps into northern Italy. They gradually displaced the Etruscans until they controlled much of the Po valley from Comum to Ancona and from Mediolanum (Milan) to Verona.

The tribe known as the Senones arrived with the last wave of invaders, found the best land already taken in the North, and marched southward. About 390 B.C., they descended upon the Etruscan town of Clusium (Chiusi). Roman attempts to negotiate peaceful relations failed when an envoy became involved in a fight with a Gallic chief.

The Allia Because Rome was not well fortified, the Romans marched out to intercept the Gauls. They made contact with the Gauls near the Allia, a small stream flowing northward into the Tiber about eleven miles from Rome. The swift Gallic cavalry and light infantry armed with long, well-tempered swords struck the stiff, slow-moving Rome phalanx of spearmen. Their lines broken, the panic-stricken Romans swam across the Tiber and fled to Veii. The Gauls hastened to Rome and captured everything except the Capitol. It was reportedly saved when the alarmed cackling of Juno's sacred geese warned the defenders of a sneak attack. After besieging the Capitol for seven months, the Gauls learned that the Veneti had invaded their lands in the Po valley. Eager to go back home, they readily accepted a ransom of a thousand pounds of gold and marched away.

Up from the Ashes The physical damage to Rome was less than that to her pride and prestige. Having seen the strength of Veii's walls earlier they decided to build similar walls of the same grayish-yellow tufa quarried near Veii at Grotto Oscura. The finished wall was about twelve feet thick and, in places, at least thirty high. It extended about six and a half miles around the city and even included the Aventine

Hill. Mislabeled the "Wall of Servius Tullius," parts of it still stand.

The Romans hastened to shore up their position diplomatically by exchanging the private rights of citizenship with the Etruscan city of Caere, which had been an ally against Veii and gave refuge to the Vestal Virgins during the Gallic attack. They made a similar arrangement with the Greek colony of Massilia in southern Gaul. Massilia apparently helped the Romans pay the ransom that freed their city and may have sent experts to help build Rome's walls. In this way, Massilia could hope for Roman help against restless Gallic tribes that threatened it.

From 389 to 377, the Romans successfully fended off the attacks of a number of neighbors who had hoped to take advantage of Rome's temporary weakness. In 381, they seized control of Latin Tusculum and forcibly absorbed its people into the ranks of Roman citizens, who were subject to taxation and military service. Tusculum thus became the first Roman community known as a *municipium,* an internally self-governing local community whose citizens had all of the obligations of Roman citizens, too. This arrangement became one of the principal means by which Rome eventually united Italy.

By 376, the Romans were clearly dominant in Latium again and lived in relative peace until 370, when they undertook a three-year siege of the Latin town of Velitrae, which may have given tribunes the leverage needed to obtain passage of the famous reforms associated with Licinius and Sextius (p. 62). In 362, Rome's need for more land, perhaps in conjunction with the so-called Licinio-Sextian land reforms, led to conflict with the Hernici and the Latins again. Both the Hernici and the Latin League were forced to revive their old treaties with Rome on terms even more favorable to her in 358. Tibur and Praeneste, however, were not part of the agreement and were not subdued until 354. During that same period, the neighboring Etruscan cities of Tarquinia, Falerii, and even Caere, alarmed at the growth of Roman power, embarked on unsuccessful wars that marked the beginning of Rome's conquest of Italy outside of Latium.

Initial Conquests in Central Italy The reforms attributed to Licinius and Sextius in 367 had preserved internal harmony in the face of external threats after the Gallic sack of Rome. They also created a government and army capable of handling Rome's growing power. Starting around 350, the Romans began to conquer central Italy.

The Gauls had never been able to repeat their performance at the Allia (p. 72). Walled cities were proof against their attacks. When they came back about 349 B.C., the reorganized Roman state easily turned aside their threat despite the Latins' refusal to send help and despite the coastal raids of hostile Greek naval forces. In 348, to counter the Greek naval threat, and assert greater control over the Latins, the Romans renegotiated a treaty with Carthage that dated perhaps from 509 B.C. The Carthaginians received a free hand to attack the Latin coast so long as they did not capture any of Rome's Latin allies and kept only the booty seized from any Latin city not subject to Rome. In turn, the Romans agreed not to found colonies in Sardinia or North Africa or to trade in Carthaginian-controlled territory except through Carthage herself or her ports in Sicily. To counter the Gauls on land, the Romans had already signed an alliance with the warlike Samnite hill people in 354. Both alliances, however, eventually crumbled in the face of Rome's growing power.

The Samnites and Rome The first to crumble was the alliance with the nearby Samnites. For a long time, population pressure and the lack of resources in the Samnites' homeland had been forcing them to expand their territory at their neighbors' expense. Their constant pressure behind the Volsci had long been forcing the latter to invade Latium and wage endless wars with the Romans. To the Greek cities like Tarentum (Taranto) in southern Italy they had been a constant and unnerving menace.

Around 350 B.C., the Samnites seemed much stronger than the Romans. They had more than 4 times as much territory (8,300 as opposed to 2,000 square miles) and had more

than double the population (perhaps 650,000 as opposed to probably 317,400). Even those figures do not convey the initial weakness of the Romans, because they include territories and populations already unreliable and hostile, which 10 years later were at war with Rome. Nevertheless, Rome gradually acquired superiority in manpower and resources.

On the other hand, Samnite expansion into Campania and Lucania did not increase Samnite war-making power. Many of the original Samnite settlers had become rich and had risen to a position of leadership among the local aristocracy. As they did not want the status quo upset by a mass invasion of their have-not kinsmen, they were inclined to line up behind the Romans. Similarly, the Lucanian Samnites, or at least the dominant faction, had turned their backs on their northern kinsmen and wanted to play a big role in the world of the Greek city-states. From time to time, they made alliances with the Romans against their own people.

Samnite relations with related tribes on their northern borders were weak. When the Romans made alliances with the latter they were able to march right into the heart of Samnium. The Samnite homeland itself was divided into four main tribes forming, in time of war, a loose confederacy liable to come apart when unity and cohesion were most required. The confederacy lacked a national assembly that might have enabled the Samnites to formulate a clear, long-range war policy. Their most brilliant victories failed to produce any permanent results.

The Samnites could and did give the Romans many painful lessons in mountain fighting. They had learned that the hoplite phalanx, though irresistible on level ground, was a distinct liability in mountainous terrain. After a while, the Romans mastered the secret of mountain fighting, but the Samnite slowness to copy Roman political and diplomatic methods spelled the difference between final victory and defeat in a long series of wars with Rome.

The First Samnite War, 343 to 341 B.C. About 343, the Samnites attacked the Sidicini, a small group on the northern border of Capua's territory. The Capuans became alarmed and appealed to Rome for help. The Romans readily helped because it made them allies of Italy's second biggest city and gave them a foothold in Campania. The war itself was not a serious one, and the battles recorded are undoubtedly fictitious. The peace terms of 341 B.C. granted the Samnites the right to occupy the Sidicini's territory and acknowledged the Roman alliance with Capua.

The Latin War of 340 to 338 B.C.   The Latin and Campanian allies of Rome regarded the treaty of 341 as a shameful betrayal of the Sidicini and, contrary to Rome's warnings, took up arms in their defense when the Samnite occupation of their territory began about 340. For years, the Latins had been chafing against their Roman alliance, which seemed to them another form of domination. Since the Gauls were no longer a menace after 349, they saw in defending the Sidicini a chance to make their bid for freedom and independence. The Latins were already at war with Samnium, and their insubordination brought them also into a war with Rome. That war gave the Romans a chance to settle the Latin problem (with the help of the now-friendly Samnites) before they got involved in any major conflict.

By 338 B.C., the bitter conflict was over. The Campanians had already accepted the generous terms offered them and deserted their allies. The Latins and the Volsci were soon afterward crushed, never to rise up again, and the Old Latin League was dissolved. From now on, the future of the Latins would be determined at Rome's pleasure.

The Roman System of Alliances and Citizen Communities

The dissolution of the Latin League in 338 marked the creation of a flexible, hierarchical system of alliances and citizen communities that enabled Rome to unite all of Italy under its control and eventually to extend her sway over the entire Mediterranean world.

Latin Allies   Under the terms of the *foedus Cassianum* of 493, the Romans had agreed to share certain rights with their Latin allies. To the Romans, these rights became known collectively as the *ius Latii,* the "Right Belonging to Latium." The citizens of Rome and individual Latin communities shared the rights of intermarriage (*conubium*), the right to do business and make legally binding contracts (*commercium*), and the right to change residence (*migratio*). The children of mixed marriages could inherit either parent's citizenship and both their parents' property. Citizens of one city doing business in the other could sue or be sued in the other city's courts and could enjoy the benefits of its law of sale and of succession. All contracts could be enforced only in the courts of the place where originally drawn up. In early times, Latin and Roman citizens had the mutual right of changing residence and afterward of acquiring citizenship. After 338, the Latin League was destroyed, but certain Latin towns were given individual treaties that allowed them to continue sharing Latin rights with Rome, but not with each other or anyone else. Gradually, the Romans separated Latin rights from their ethnic restriction and granted them to favored allies regardless of ethnicity.

Under this same category may be grouped Latin colonies. They were communities created by Rome or jointly by Rome and her allies for defending strategic locations or to serve some political purpose. The settlers received the standard Latin rights and allotments of land on which to settle. Latin communities and Latin colonies were, strictly speaking, sovereign states allied to Rome. In that way, they were distinguished from *municipia,* which were communities of Roman citizens.

Municipia   The first *municipium* was the Latin town of Tusculum whose independence the Romans had destroyed in 381 and whose free inhabitants received full Roman citizenship (*civitas optimo iure*). In 338, Rome imposed similar status on many of the former Latin allies and later extended it to others as they saw fit. A second class of *municipia* was made up of those whose inhabitants received all the duties and private rights of Roman citizenship (essentially the Latin rights) but not the right to vote (*civitas sine suffragio*). In both cases, municipal status allowed people control over strictly local affairs but always under the watchful supervision of a prefect sent out from Rome.

Roman colonies were different from Latin colonies in that they were generally smaller, about 300 families as opposed to between 2,500 and 6,000 families. They were founded primarily as garrisons to keep enemies in check, and the colonists had full Roman citizenship. From about 338 to 288, the Romans founded several colonies to protect the Latin coast (Rome then had no permanent fleet). Other colonists were sent to Campania and Apulia to occupy key points and forge a ring of fortresses around Samnium, and to Umbria and other points north to keep the Gauls in check. Around 177 B.C., the distinction between Latin and Roman colonies was abandoned, and the size of Latin colonies was combined with the citizenship of Roman colonies. Thereafter, colonies became hard to distinguish from *municipia* with full citizenship.

Socii The Romans also made a number of defensive pacts with Greek and Italian city-states that felt threatened by the Samnites or other neighboring tribes. Those alliances were with states that considered themselves as partners (*socii*) with Rome. Each treaty differed according to circumstances. All *socii,* however, were commonly required to place their military forces at Rome's disposal and agree to leave the conduct of foreign affairs in her hands. In return Rome agreed not to impose taxes upon them and to allow each allied city to raise, equip, and command its own troops, who would fight under the supreme allied command of a Roman general. Rome would also provide the allied troops with food and subsistence pay at her own expense and would share the spoils of war with them. Furthermore, all allied cities could enjoy some, if not all, of the private rights of Roman citizenship.

The Romans created these various types of alliance and citizen states primarily in response to particular circumstances. At first, turning allies into citizens was more of a punishment than a reward because it deprived people of their highly valued independence. Gradually, however, a system emerged that rewarded the progressive Romanization of allies with more and more rights. *Socii* might at some point hope to acquire Latin status and eventually be awarded an equal share in the public life of Rome with a grant of full Roman citizenship. Thus the Romans were able to keep increasing their armies with dependable supplies of loyal manpower despite occasional setbacks. Indeed, after 338 the field army of Roman citizens alone doubled from two to four legions.

The Final Conquest of Central Italy
Though not really intended to provoke hostilities with the Samnites, Rome's system of colonies and alliances effectively cut off the Samnites' chance for expanding westward and was bound to cause friction. Samnite sensibilities were further offended in 334, when the Romans made a move to the east of them by signing a treaty with Tarentum (Taranto), which was fighting neighboring Oscan tribes. Hostilities between the Romans and Samnites finally broke out in 327, when they both backed different sides in an internal dispute at Naples.

The Second (Great) Samnite War, 327 to 304/03 B.C. The military history of this war is obscure. Most of the battles that the annalists record are unimportant even if they did take place, except the battle of the Caudine Forks, which took place in 321. The Romans, attempting to march from Campania across the Apennines to Apulia, were misled by false information into a trap at a pass called the Caudine Forks. They were compelled to surrender, give hostages, and agree not to renew the war. Stripped down to single garments, they were ignominiously driven under a yoke that consisted of two spears stuck in the ground and united at the top by a third, a token of complete defeat and unconditional surrender.

New Military Tactics The battle of the Caudine Forks made clear to the Romans that they needed to learn about mountain fighting. They used the peace to good advantage by reorganizing the legion so as to form three lines separately trained, differently armed, and able to maneuver independently in thirty maniples of two centuries each. The new formations could operate better in mountainous terrain, and some troops were armed with Samnite javelins instead of phalanx spears. Now able to put four legions into battle instead of two, and to fight as well on the plains as the Greeks, and as well in the mountains as the Samnites, the Romans found an excuse in 316 for repudiating the peace treaty and renewing the war.

Despite their military reorganization, the Romans still had a difficult task against the rugged Samnites. Another serious defeat in 315 almost cost the loyalty of Rome's Campanian allies, but the Romans doggedly recovered lost ground and set up strategic Latin and Roman colonies to contain the enemy. Alliances with the Lucanians in the South and with other neighboring peoples enclosed them in a circle of steel.

The Samnites began to copy Roman diplomatic tactics and persuaded some southern Etruscan cities, whose treaties with Rome were about to expire, to create a second front against Rome. There was also a danger that they might induce the Gauls to join them. The Gauls made no move, however, and the Romans continued to create a broad buffer zone across central Italy from which they were able to make devastating raids into the heart of Samnium. By this show of force they also compelled the Etruscans to renew and observe their treaties.

The man who is thought to have masterminded this astute military and diplomatic strategy was the old censor of 312 B.C., Appius Claudius the Blind. A shrewd politician, he built Rome's first great aqueduct and promoted numerous reforms to gain popular support (p. 66). It was also his idea to run a highway from Rome to Capua over which troops could be swiftly moved in any kind of weather. That was the famous Appian Way (*Via Appia*). Finally, to protect the coast of Latium, the Romans built a small fleet of twenty *triremes* (fast, slender ships with three banks of one-man oars).

In spite of their brilliant strategy and their constancy and doggedness in danger and defeat, the Romans did not easily win the long and bloody Second Samnite War. Their victory was by no means absolute, as the peace of 304/03 B.C. clearly shows. The Samnites lost none of their original territory, none of their independence, and none of their capacity to fight again.

The Third Samnite War, 298 to 290 B.C. Nevertheless, the balance of power had gradually been shifting steadily in favor of Rome. After 304/03 B.C., the Romans controlled an area of approximately 9,200 square miles and a population of some 927,000, as compared with about 5,675 square miles and a population of 498,000 for the Samnites. The danger of the growing disparity had become clear to the Sabines, the Etruscans, the Umbrians, and even the Gauls, who all joined forces with the Samnites in 295 B.C. in the hope of stopping Rome. They fought the Romans at Sentinum in Umbria. The consul Publius Decius Mus inspired the Romans to victory by devoting himself to the gods and purposely exposing himself to death at enemy hands. Still, it was not until the victories of Manius Curius Dentatus, consul of 290, that the Romans won the fight for central Italy. The Samnites finally surrendered and sued for peace. Their lands were annexed, and they accepted the status of Roman allies (*socii*). In the same year, Dentatus decisively subdued the Sabines as well.

Etruscans and Gauls The Etruscans and the Gauls fought on, however. After two more defeats the Gauls asked for peace in 282. The Etruscans continued to resist for a number of years but finally surrendered under moderate terms. The only Etruscan city to lose territory was Rome's former friend Caere. It was punished by annexation, probably in 273, and received citizenship without the right to vote, *civitas sine suffragio*.

The Pyrrhic Wars and the Conquest of Southern Italy The Romans had granted the Etruscans moderate peace terms because Rome was now faced with another serious crisis. Victory against the Samnites in central Italy had removed a powerful buffer between Rome and the most powerful Greek city-state in southern Italy, Tarentum. From their side of the Apennines, the Tarentines had been fighting not only the Samnites but also the Bruttians and Lucanians. In so doing, they had called in a number of Greek military adventurers like Alexander of Epirus, uncle of Alexander the Great, from across the Adriatic to help them. Not one had succeeded either in making Tarentum a stronger power or in carving out an empire for himself.

The Tarentines had even become so distrustful of Alexander of Epirus that they withdrew their support, and he was killed in a battle with the Lucanians. Nevertheless, he left them an important legacy. While he was attacking the Samnites in 334, he had negotiated a treaty with the Romans. They had agreed not to come to the aid of the Samnites, who had temporarily become Rome's allies after the First Samnite War. Part of that treaty was a Roman promise not to send ships into the Gulf of Tarentum. With Alexander's death, the Romans considered the treaty dead, too, but the Tarentines thought differently.

They were already upset because Rome had rejected their attempt to mediate between the two sides in the Second Samnite War and had established the colony of Venusia on their Apulian border after the Third Samnite War. Then, in 285, Thurii, a Greek city not far from the western shore of the Gulf of Tarentum and under attack by the Lucanians, appealed to Rome for help rather than to Tarentum, her ally. Perhaps the Thurians believed that Rome was stronger than Tarentum and more reliable, as well as less dangerous. With some misgivings, the Romans answered the appeal, defeated the Lucanians, and stationed a small garrison in Thurii. Other Greeks also asked for and received Roman protection.

These actions upset Tarentum. Therefore, in 282, when Roman ships entered the Gulf of Tarentum in violation of the treaty of 334, the Tarentines attacked without warning, sank four ships, and killed the commander. Then the Tarentines marched to Thurii, drove out the Roman garrison, and sacked the town. Roman ambassadors seeking redress were publicly insulted, ridiculed for their bad Greek, and refused a hearing. The Tarentines called in another Greek adventurer, King Pyrrhus.

Pyrrhus was king of Epirus, a small mountainous country in northwestern Greece. Hugely ambitious, he had delusions of being another Alexander the Great. The invitation from Tarentum presented a real opportunity to establish the empire that he craved.

In the spring of 280, Pyrrhus landed in Italy with 25,000 hoplite mercenaries, 3,000 cavalry, and 20 war elephants, which the Romans had never seen. The more flexible tactics developed against the Samnites enabled the Romans to counter Pyrrhus' hoplite phalanx, but the elephants wreaked havoc. The Romans lost 7,000 men. On the other hand, Pyrrhus won only a tactical victory and lost 4,000 irreplaceable men. (Such an outcome has since been known as a "Pyrrhic victory.")

Nevertheless, encouraged by Rome's rebellious Oscan and Samnite allies, Pyrrhus tried to force a decision by a direct attack on Rome itself. The loyalty of Rome's Latin allies, however, stopped him at Praeneste, forty miles from Rome. The Romans refused an offer of peace and brought him to battle again at Asculum (Ausculum [Ascoli Satriano]) in Apulia. After another costly Pyrrhic victory, Pyrrhus is said to have declared, "Another such victory and I am lost!"

Pyrrhus' Sicilian Venture, 278 to 275 B.C. Stymied, Pyrrhus answered a call from the Greeks of Sicily in 278 B.C. to come to their aid against the Carthaginians, who were on the verge of conquering the whole island. He was obliged to leave half of his forces in Italy, however, because the Carthaginians had promised the Romans enough aid to refuse Pyrrhus' offers of peace in 279. His initial, brilliant successes in Sicily were undone when his Greek allies deserted him and he was forced to return to

Italy. He lost part of his fleet in a battle with the Carthaginian navy on the way back to Italy in 276. In Italy, continued Roman resistance in 275 finally forced him to withdraw to Greece.

The victory over Pyrrhus made it clear that Rome was now a major power in the Mediterranean world. Rome soon received recognition from Ptolemy II of Egypt, who asked for a treaty of friendship in 273. Shortly, in 264, Rome's destruction of the rebellious Etruscan city of Volsinii (Orvieto) made clear that all of peninsular Italy was under her undisputed control, from Pisa and Ariminum (Rimini) in the North to Brundisium (Brindisi), Tarentum, and the Straits of Messana in the South. Within the same year, even the Straits would not be able to restrain Rome's growing power.

Reasons for Roman Success in Italy

Many scholars have sought some particular reason for Rome's success in defeating her numerous hostile neighbors and conquering peninsular Italy in the fifth, fourth, and early third centuries B.C. There is, of course, no single cause sufficient to explain it. Rome had a unique combination of advantages that accounts for her victories. Various of these advantages were, to be sure, shared by one or another of her enemies. The crucial point is that no one shared Rome's combination.

Part of the reason for Rome's success was the reorganization of the government around 367 B.C., which secured greater unity in the face of external danger. Her success was also due in part to her usual willingness and ability to fulfill her treaty obligations and to the statesmanlike quality of her leaders in building strategic alliances. Rome's treatment of her Latin allies had secured their loyalty in the long run. Also, most other Italian communities found their alliances with Rome fair and regarded the Samnites in the South and the Gauls in the North as greater menaces to their security than the Romans.

The strategic advantages of Rome's central geographic location in Italy had allowed Roman armies to move quickly against attacks on more than one front and prevent enemies from combining forces easily. The fertility and population of both their immediate territory and that of their staunchest allies gave the Romans the resources and manpower to recover from initial defeats and eventually wear down their opponents. Compared with the less developed tribes who often encroached on Roman territory, the Romans enjoyed superior military organization and tactics, which they continuously improved. Moreover, the hierarchical social structure produced well-disciplined soldiers who obeyed aristocratic leaders determined to preserve and increase their honor.

Finally, the irrational factor of sheer luck cannot be ignored. The Romans were lucky that their potentially strongest enemies, the highly developed Etruscan and Greek city-states, were both rent by jealousies and rivalries that prevented either group from mounting any unified opposition. It was fortunate that the brilliant military adventurers from Greece who sought Italian empires were poor diplomats. How fortunate for the Romans that the Gauls who sacked Rome around 390 were not in a position to occupy their conquest permanently and left before the Roman people had lost heart.

The Economic and Cultural Position of Rome in Italy by 264 B.C.
The conquest of Italy had made Rome its leading state not only politically and militarily but also economically and culturally. Despite temporary setbacks in the fifth and early fourth centuries, the city of Rome quickly resumed its growth after the Gallic sack as a center of trade and manufacturing and as the largest city in Italy. Between ca. 350 and 300 B.C., the urban population had doubled from about 30,000 to around 60,000 and by 275 it had probably surpassed 90,000.

Trade and Manufacturing To sustain such a large population, food already had to be imported from sources easily reached by water transport along the western Mediterranean coast. Evidence to that effect appears in the treaty that Rome made with Carthage in 348 and, according to Livy, renewed in 306 (p. 73). To obtain what they wanted, the Romans had to agree not to found colonies in Sardinia or North Africa and not to trade in Carthaginian territory except through Carthage herself or her ports in Sicily. That provision presupposes Roman interest in such activities. Indeed, Diodorus Siculus (15.27.4) reports that Rome had sent a colony to Sardinia in 386, and archaeological evidence indicates that she founded Ostia to protect the mouth of the Tiber between 380 and 350 B.C. Further archaeological evidence indicates that these moves were not just to provide physical security but reflect Rome's interest in securing maritime trade.

In the last decade or so of the fourth century, the *Portus* (the harbor facilities along the bend of the Tiber) and the market area (*Forum Boarium*) just behind it underwent major redevelopment and expansion. The first levels of the temple of Portunus, god of the Port, date to this time. In the same period, a temple was dedicated to Hercules Invictus (the Unconquered) beside his existing altar, the Ara Maxima, in the *Forum Boarium*. As the protector of merchants and guarantor of contractual oaths, Hercules had long been prominent there. Just across from the harbor, on the tip of Tiber Island, the healing god Aesculapius (Asclepius), himself a Greek import, became the object of a cult about the same time and received a major temple in 291.

By the beginning of the third century, Rome had become a major manufacturer and exporter of pottery. It has been found all over central Italy, the Mediterranean sea coast from Liguria to Catalonia, the island of Corsica, and Carthaginian sites in Sardinia, western Sicily, and North Africa. Not coincidentally, these are the very regions from which Rome must have been drawing grain to support her burgeoning population.

Another major product of Roman workshops was high-quality bronzes. For example, the magnificently engraved Ficoroni cista, a bronze cinerary container with cast bronze figures for the feet and lid handle from Praeneste (Palestrina), was produced in Rome around 315. At the same time, major pieces of bronze statuary began to be cast and set up in temples and in public places around the city. Other workshops were producing furniture, terra-

The Ficoroni Cista. (From Praeneste. Etruscan, late 4th c. BCE. Engraved bronze. H: 21". Museo di Villa Giulia, Rome, Italy. Scala/Art Resource, NY.)

cotta sculptures, and large and small carved stone monuments such as funeral altars and sarcophagi.

Monumental Construction The wealth that poured into Rome from the Samnite wars and the conquest of southern Italy produced a major building boom at Rome. From 302 to 264 B.C., numerous temples arose in the city. In 312, the blind censor Appius Claudius Caecus inaugurated not only the construction of Rome's first major paved road, the Appian Way, but also Rome's first aqueduct to ensure a supply of clean water for Rome's growing population. In 272 an even bigger aqueduct, the Anio Vetus, was needed to keep up with demand.

Development of Coinage The public works and wars in the late fourth and early third centuries made it increasingly necessary for Rome to finance them with coined money. In the fifth and fourth centuries B.C., irregular lumps of bronze, *aes rude,* which had to be weighed at each transaction, often took the place of the actual cattle or sheep from which *pecunia,* the Roman word for money, was derived. Later, rectangular pieces of cast bronze replaced the irregular lumps, and the state guaranteed the purity of the bronze by a distinctive sign stamped into the metal. The stamped bronze was called *aes signatum.*

By 289 B.C., the fiscal needs of Rome, particularly to pay soldiers, had increased to the point where the Romans created a board of three moneyers, *triumviri monetales,* to supervise an official mint located in the temple of *Juno Moneta* on the Capitoline Hill and from whose name the words *mint* and *money* are ultimately derived. Although it produced *aes signatum,* which was not true coinage because only its purity, not weight or value, was indicated by the stamp, this mint also introduced Rome's first real coins, called *asses* (sing. *as*) or *aes grave* ("heavy bronze"). These coins were cast and circular in shape and were issued in units of one Roman pound (*libra*) or fractions thereof, as indicated by a standard mark. The *libra* equaled twelve Roman ounces (*unicae*), and the Roman ounce (*unica*) was slightly less than the ounce avoirdupois (27.2875 grams versus 28.3850 grams). Therefore, the *libra* weighed 11.536 ounces avoirdupois (327.45 grams).

Gradually reduced in size, the bronze *as* remained the common coin used throughout the Republican period. Nevertheless, as the Romans became more deeply involved with the Greeks of southern Italy, especially during the war with Pyrrhus, they found it necessary to mint silver coins comparable to the silver coins commonly used by the Greeks. Therefore, the earliest Roman silver coins were two-drachma pieces, didrachms, and were clearly modeled on the silver coinage of Campania.

The Agricultural Sector The Roman conquest of Italy was already reshaping Italian agriculture by 264 B.C. From 338 to 264, the *ager* *Romanus* (Roman territory) increased from about 2,000 square miles to over 95,000, about 20% of peninsular Italy's surface area, with a total population estimated at 900,000. In the process, much land had been confiscated to make room for poor Roman farmers. The original owners were often left without anything, deported, enslaved, or killed. Between 20,000 and 30,000 Roman men received allotments from this land. Moreover, another 70,000 Romans and Latins received allotments in 19 Latin colonies established on conquered land between 334 and 263.

Confiscating other peoples' land and enslaving them not only satisfied the land hunger of poor Romans but also allowed rich Romans to amass larger holdings and farm them with slaves. That trend toward large slave-run estates in parts of Italy would increase even more as a result of the first two Punic wars (pp. 124–126). No doubt, however, a growing urban market approaching 100,000 people in 264 was already stimulating the kinds of specialized and commercialized agriculture in which the upper classes increasingly invested the profits of imperialism during the next 130 years.

Impressive Art and Architecture By 300, the growing wealth and power of the Roman elite were creating a market for high-quality arts and crafts like the Ficoroni cista, fine terra-cotta and bronze statuary, and elaborate fresco paintings. Proud aristocrats proclaimed their success in war by building temples vowed in return for victory and decorated them with the finest workmanship.

Upper-class Romans also decorated their private homes with Hellenized art and architectural motifs. Ever since the late sixth century, the wealthy had enjoyed substantial town houses built on stone foundations in the neighborhood of the Palatine. The basic plan was centered on the traditional Italic atrium open to the sky, where the open hearth would have been in earlier times (p. 17). Here would be the family's household gods (*lares* and *penates*) and the funerary masks and busts (*imagines*) of famous ancestors. Across from the front door was the *tablinum,* an office for the family's records, where the *paterfamilias* conducted business.

Off the other sides would be several rooms that might function as bedrooms (*cubicula*) or dining rooms (*triclinia*) as the seasons or need required. In the back would be kitchens, storerooms, and slave quarters.

Temples were constructed in the central Italian style epitomized by a high podium approached only from the front. Deep colonnaded porches projected out from the solid walls, and the whole was topped by a deeply overhanging roof and pediment. Brightly painted molded terra-cottas covered the exposed wooden beams and cornices, and terra-cotta statues inhabited the pediment and rooftops (p. 18).

These temples were conservative in that they still reflected the influence of an already archaic Greek style. In less tradition-bound circumstances, however, the impact of classical Greek art was becoming more and more evident by 300. The scene from the tale of the Argonauts engraved on the Ficoroni cista rivals anything in late classical Greek art, as did the bronze statuary of the time. Indeed, in 293, the Romans supposedly erected statues depicting two famous Greeks, Pythagoras and Alcibiades.

Self-Conscious Upper-Class Hellenism

Prior to ca. 300 B.C., the influence of Greek culture in Italy had been the natural and inevitable result of general contact by non-Greeks with Greek trade goods and colonists. By the time the Romans captured Tarentum in 272, however, the importation of classical Greek culture was part of a self-conscious attempt by Roman aristocrats to appropriate the aristocratic Greek cultural heritage for themselves. Indeed, Romans expropriated Greek or Hellenized art wherever they found it as they conquered Italy and carted off its treasures to decorate Rome. Thus, in 264, the Roman conqueror of Volsinii brought back two thousand fine statues to erect in the Forum Boarium.

Roman aristocrats even began to adopt Greek cognomina such as Philo (Lover), Sophus (Wise), Philippus (Lover of Horses). The cults of the new temples that they built often resembled Hellenistic "victory cults." Not content with only those signs of Hellenization, they appropriated Greek literature, too.

Literature

In early Rome, literature in any significant sense of the word did not exist. Writing, like most everything else, was primarily for practical, mundane purposes such as keeping financial accounts, recording laws, noting important yearly secular and religious events, and preserving oracles and religious rituals. Beginning in the third century B.C., however, the Romans were increasingly influenced by the advanced literary culture of the Greeks.

Greek literature had a certain practical and social value for the Roman upper classes. Greek allowed for the formulation and expression of far more complex concepts and ideas than early Latin and could provide a model for expanding the expressiveness of Latin itself in an increasingly complex world. Greek orators had perfected the principles of persuasive rhetoric, which were very useful to Roman aristocrats in senatorial debates, speeches at trials, and addresses to Roman voters in the Forum. Furthermore, a knowledge of Greek and appreciation of Greek literature was a mark of social distinction, which helped the upper classes set themselves apart from the lower and gave them the sense of their own superiority that all elites crave. Soon there would be a demand for teachers of Greek, who were supplied in the form of educated Greek captives serving as tutors in the homes of their wealthy captors. Those who were later freed often set up grammar schools, where they dispensed their wisdom to the sons of aspiring nonaristocrats for a fee.

Livius Andronicus, ca. 284 to ca. 204 B.C.

One of these teachers was Lucius Livius Andronicus, who had been born in Tarentum about 284 B.C. and had been brought to Rome in 272 as a slave in the house of a Roman senator named Lucius Livius (Salinator?). Upon being freed he had added his patron's name to his own, as was the custom, and became Lucius Livius Andronicus during the Punic wars. Andronicus became not only a teacher of Greek and Latin but also a translator and adaptor of Greek literature for Roman audiences. With his work after 264, the real history of Roman literature begins (p. 137).

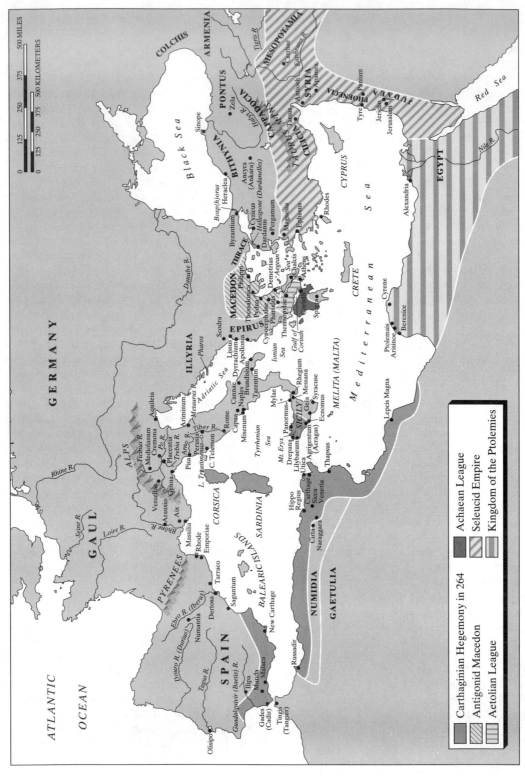

The Mediterranean Sea ca. 264–200 B.C.

VII

The First Punic War and the Beginning of Overseas Imperialism, 264 to 241 B.C.

This and the next six chapters cover the period between 264 and 133 B.C., when the Roman Republic was at its height in many ways. By 264, the internal social and political struggles of the early Republic had largely abated. To preserve unity in the face of hostile neighbors, patrician leaders had gradually granted important men from plebeian *gentes* equal access to the social and political levers of power. The acquisition of booty and territory from conquered neighbors had helped to alleviate the economic distress of the poor plebs. Therefore, between 264 and 133 B.C. the Roman political system remained basically stable under the control of the new patricio-plebeian consular nobility in the senate. Yearly warfare had practically become a way of life during the early Republic. Citizens of all classes had become accustomed to the profits of war, and aristocratic leaders craved military glory and benefitted politically from the popularity won in victorious campaigns. In the process, the Republic had matured militarily and diplomatically into one of the major powers of the Mediterranean world.

With these advantages, therefore, the Romans embarked on a series of wars with Carthage, the Punic wars, which led ultimately to Rome's acquisition of a Mediterranean-wide empire. Imperialism was an appetite that grew with feeding as Rome swallowed Sicily, Sardinia, Corsica, Spain, Macedon, Greece, and large parts of North Africa and Asia Minor. Despite sometimes staggering defeats, the Republic's military strength seemed inexhaustible as all opposition was inevitably and often brutally crushed.

Along with Rome's acquisition of an overseas empire, there was an acceleration of the integration of Roman culture and Hellenistic Greek civilization, which in 264 B.C. still dominated the political, economic, and cultural life of the world from the Himalayan Mountains in the East to the Atlantic coast of Spain in the West. (The term *Hellenistic* is used to designate the distinctive phase of Greek civilization that flourished after Alexander the Great [d. 323 B.C.], when many non-Greek peoples adopted numerous elements of classical Greek civilization.) After 264, Roman culture rapidly matured under the influence of the Hellenistic Greeks, whose poetry, drama, history, rhetoric, philosophy, and art provided the models for Romans to produce a distinctive Greco-Roman civilization that characterized the Mediterranean world for the rest of Antiquity.

Finally, the Republic's imperial success precipitated social, economic, and political changes that set the stage for its own destruction during the century after 133 B.C. Although Rome's conquests provide an interesting narrative, their impacts on the nature of the Republic itself are also fascinating. All of those topics, therefore, will be covered in these next seven chapters.

Sources for Roman History from 264 to 133 B.C.

At this point in Roman history, there are, for the first time, fairly reliable literary sources of information. The early annalistic writers used by Polybius, Livy, and others were contemporaries of this period and had either personally witnessed the events of which they wrote or learned of them directly from those who had. Polybius himself had come to Rome just a century after the outbreak of the First Punic War in 264 B.C. (p. 141). His brief account of that war and his detailed description of the Second Punic War and of Rome's subsequent conquest of the Mediterranean world are quite reliable. Unfortunately, his work is intact only to the year 216 B.C. (Books 1 to 6) and preserved only in fragments to its end with the events of 145/44 B.C. (Books 7 to 40). Livy, however, who used Polybius extensively along with Roman annalists, is complete for the years 219 to 167 (Books 21 to 45). After that he is represented by the summaries of the *Periochae* (Books 46 to 56) and epitomes of the late Empire (p. 471).

From 167 to 133 B.C., Velleius Paterculus, who wrote in the early first century A.D., provides a brief narrative in his compendium of Roman history (Books 1 to 2.1), about whose sources there is considerable question. Cassius Dio used Polybius and the Roman annalists heavily, and extensive fragments of the relevant books of his *Roman History* are preserved (Books 11 to 23). The work of early annalists and Polybius are also preserved in the fragments of Books 23 to 32 of Diodorus Siculus, as well as in Books 6 to 9 and Book 11 of the *Roman History* by Appian, a Greek from Alexandria who wrote in the second century A.D. Although the difficult question of their sources poses problems of reliability, the biographies of the Carthaginian generals Hamilcar and Hannibal by Cornelius Nepos (late first century B.C.) and Plutarch's lives of Cato the Elder, Flamininus, and Aemilius Paullus help to flesh out some of the main characters of the period. The late-first-century-B.C. geographer Strabo also preserves some useful facts, and Book 7 of the *Description of Greece* by the mid-second-century-A.D. traveler Pausanias has important information on Roman activities in 146 B.C.

Moreover, for the first time there are contemporary works of literature, such as the plays of Plautus and Terence and fragments of numerous other works, that help to illuminate the life and culture of the period (pp. 139–140). Contemporary coins now begin to supply abundant numismatic evidence that not only shows economic history but also reveals much about the officials who issued them and the places, events, and concepts depicted on them. Inscriptions are also more numerous. They preserve the texts of treaties and laws and the epitaphs that help to reconstruct the political relationships and careers of famous people and the daily lives of ordinary people. Finally, extensive archaeological excavations at Rome, Carthage, and hundreds of other sites around the Mediterranean reveal much about social, economic, political, and cultural trends.

A New Chapter in Rome's Expansion

The fateful year 264 B.C. emphatically punctuates the completion of Rome's control of peninsular Italy with the destruction of the rebellious Etruscan city of Volsinii (Orvieto). At the same time, it opens up a new chapter in the expansion of Rome's power with the start of the First Punic War. Like ever-widening ripples from a stone dropped in a quiet pool, Roman power had moved outward from its central location. It had already reached the southern tip of Italy when the Greek city of Rhegium (Reggio di Calabria) had accepted Rome's protection as an ally in 285. In 264, the ripple would spread across the three miles of water known as the Straits of Messana (Messina) which separate Rhegium from Sicily.

Carthage The powerful North African city of Carthage had long been vying with the Greek colonies on Sicily for control of that strategic island. By this time, Carthage had become a major Hellenistic power. Although never conquered by Alexander nor an inheritor of any part of his conquests, Carthage had been extensively influenced by the Greeks through constant commercial contact and rivalry in Sicily and the western Mediterranean. The upper classes had adapted Greek models in government, agriculture, skilled crafts, architecture, dress, jewelry, art, metalwares, and even language. Soon Carthage and Rome, which was rapidly rising in the same Hellenistic world, would become locked in a titanic struggle that would make Sicily Rome's first overseas conquest.

Carthage was situated on Cape Bon, a small tongue of land jutting out from North Africa into the Gulf of Tunis, and had been founded around 750 B.C. as a commercial colony by the Phoenician city of Tyre. (The adjective *Punic* is derived from the Latin word for *Phoenician,* which is why Rome's wars with the Phoenician colony Carthage are called the Punic wars.) In a strategically advantageous position at the narrowest part of the Mediterranean and with access to either end, Carthage was in an ideal location for a maritime power. After she had occupied the island of Melita (Malta) between Sicily and North Africa, she was practically able to exclude the Greeks, her toughest commercial and colonial rivals, from the western half of the sea.

After Assyrian, Babylonian, and Persian conquests in the seventh century, Tyre and other Phoenician cities were unable either to control or to protect the Phoenician colonies to the west. Therefore, to protect and expand their mercantile interests, the favorably situated Carthaginians created a navy second to none in the Mediterranean. Eventually, they incorporated former Phoenician colonies and other peoples in North Africa and the Iberian Peninsula into an empire that also included Sardinia, Corsica, parts of Sicily, and the Balearic Islands.

The Carthaginians followed the practice of most imperial city-states in Antiquity by forcing others into becoming tribute-paying subjects and did not integrate them into their own military and civic institutions as the Romans did with allies or conquered foes. Therefore, Carthage lacked large loyal sources of manpower. During her struggle with Rome, she was forced to stamp out numerous revolts among her Spanish and North African subjects, a distraction that seriously hampered her during the war.

Carthaginian Wealth and Trade Carthage controlled by far the richest mining resources of the western Mediterranean basin. Sardinia and Spain produced lead, zinc, copper, iron, and silver. From Gades (Cadiz) on the Atlantic coast of Spain, the Carthaginians had access to Britain for tin from Cornwall and could sail south along the Atlantic coast of Morocco and perhaps as far along the West African shore as the mouth of the Senegal River to obtain gold, ivory, slaves, and war elephants.

By the third century, Carthage's workshops were turning out jewelry, ivory work, pottery, metal goods, and highly prized purple-dyed cloth in great quantities. An even greater source of wealth was the export of Carthaginian agricultural products: wine, olive oil, and various fruits like pomegranates and figs. Carthage no longer had a virtual monopoly on western sea lanes, but she was still a formidable commercial force and eager to secure her advantage whenever she could.

Agriculture The contribution that the Carthaginians made to scientific agriculture and especially to the unfortunate development of slave-worked plantations is usually ignored. They taught the Romans the technique of organizing large masses of slave labor on agricultural estates or plantations for the production of single marketable crops or staples. Although the slave trade and the use of slaves as farm-hands and shop workers were well known in Greece and other ancient countries, slave labor was never able to compete on a large scale with free labor in Greece, in the Seleucid Empire, or in Ptolemaic Egypt. It remained for the Carthaginians, while relying on Greek and Hellenistic treatises for the scientific cultivation of specific farm crops, to work out a system involving the large-scale use of slave labor.

Carthaginian Government As described by Aristotle in the fourth century B.C., Carthage was an aristocratic republic that had both democratic and oligarchic features. The details are not always clear, but four elements stand out: a popular assembly, a senate, a supreme court of 104 picked men, and elected officials including generals and two annual chief magistrates called "judges" (*shophetim* in Punic and *suffetes* in Latin). The popular assembly elected the generals and judges from a small group of wealthy commercial and landowning families who comprised a powerful oligarchy that also dominated the senate and supreme court. The senate, guided by an executive committee of thirty, and the judges presented questions to the assembly only if they could not agree, and the supreme court kept the judges and generals in check.

The Navy and Army Carthage manned her large navy with loyal citizens commanded by naval experts. The army, on the other hand, contained few citizen troops and was composed largely of conscripted natives of Libya, Sardinia, and Spain; troops hired from the allied but independent chiefs of what are now Algeria and Morocco; and mercenaries picked up in every part of the Mediterranean. It was difficult to maintain their loyalty when Carthaginian prestige or funds were low. Moreover, a successful general might be accused of dictatorial ambitions before the supreme court; one who lost might be nailed up on the cross to appease popular anger. The loss of experienced leadership could be critical at times.

Outbreak of the First Punic War in 264
B.C. In Sicily, the two great republics of the western Mediterranean, Rome and Carthage—one strong on land, the other at sea—began a long struggle that neither had wanted. Until 264 B.C., both powers had avoided doing anything to antagonize each other, as indicated by the various treaties that had regulated their commercial and state relations in 509(?), 348, 306, and 279 (pp. 73 and 77). Indeed, many Roman senators sought to avoid giving offense to Carthage over the incident that eventually sparked the conflict.

Roman Intervention in Sicily, 264 B.C. The critical incident involved the Mamertines, a group of Campanian mercenaries. They had been hired by Syracuse, but in 289 B.C. they deserted and seized the strategic town of Messana in the northeastern corner of Sicily on the straits that bear its name. The Mamertines killed the men, took their women, and plundered Syracusan territory. To exterminate them, Hiero (Hieron) II, King of Syracuse, attacked Messana in 265 B.C. The Mamertines appealed for help to the commander of a nearby Carthaginian fleet, who came ashore with a strong force and frustrated Hiero's attempt to capture that strategic location.

Some Mamertines feared that the Carthaginians intended to remain in Messana permanently. They appealed to the Roman senate for military aid and an alliance. The conservative majority in the senate feared that an alliance with the Mamertines might mean war, which they particularly wanted to avoid because victorious generals in the past were often able to acquire political advantage over their fellow senators, and because Rome, without a navy, was unprepared to wage war against the strongest naval power of the Mediterranean. They also argued that it was beneath the dignity of Rome to ally herself with the Mamertines. Their crimes at Messana had been equal to those of the allied Campanian soldiers whom Rome had punished at Rhegium (Reggio) just across the straits in 275. Therefore, the senate decided to do nothing.

Appius Claudius Caudex (a Roman consul and grandson of the famous blind censor) and his friends, who were favorable toward the Mamertine request, brought up the matter before the people. He persuaded them to accept the alliance, with all of its dangers to peace. The practice of willingly taking on an entangling alliance that was bound to create serious problems with third parties was one that the Romans had used in Italy and would often adopt during overseas expansion.

When Appius Claudius sent an advance guard across the straits, it met only token Carthaginian resistance. Meanwhile at the Mamertines' request, the Carthaginian commander withdrew his garrison without a fight. Carthaginian officials, enraged at the loss of Messana, sent an army to reoccupy the city. They also allied with Hiero II of Syracuse. Appius Claudius easily defeated the forces of both. The war had begun.

Causes of the War Although some people had tried to avoid hostilities, a number of underlying factors helped to cause the First Punic War. First, by 264 B.C., Rome had extended her system of alliances to include all of the Greek city-states in southern Italy. Many were heavily involved in commerce and competed with Carthage. If Carthage could have gained control of Sicily and the vital Straits of Messana, she would have had a stranglehold on the shipping of the southern Italian Greek merchants. Many Romans believed that as ally and patron of the southern Italian Greek cities, Rome was bound by *fides* to protect their commercial interests and prevent Messana from falling into Carthaginian hands. They argued that if the Romans did not act, their position and credibility as patrons of their allies would be undermined and their hard-won position as leaders of all peninsular Italy jeopardized.

Another important factor leading to war was the traditional Roman fear of powerful neighbors—fear that had become almost paranoid after centuries of struggle with neighboring peoples like the Etruscans and Samnites. Having gained control of peninsular Italy, the Romans faced the powerful Carthaginians on Sicily across the straits. Pyrrhus had taught them that anyone who controlled Sicily could use it to invade Italy. Therefore, many Romans probably saw an advantage in preventing Carthage from further consolidating her position in Sicily.

A third factor prompting some Romans to provoke a war with Carthage was the desire for military glory among ambitious aristocrats. Many well-established senators had opposed the Mamertine alliance precisely because they feared that a major war would give opportunities for lesser men to move ahead or for rivals to gain an advantage. Appius Claudius Caudex was one of those eager for an important command and the chance of securing a coveted triumph. That is why he brought the issue directly to the voters. It is hardly coincidental that he was the consul put in charge of the force sent to aid the Mamertines.

That many Roman citizens supported Appius points up a fourth factor in the outbreak of the First Punic War: After long years of warfare in peninsular Italy, many citizens were accustomed to supplementing their incomes with booty. Sicily, rich and prosperous, offered easy pickings—which Appius, according to Livy, did not fail to stress in his speech to the assembled people, with momentous consequences for the history of Rome, Carthage, and the whole Mediterranean world.

The Carthaginians, although not prepared for a major war, had to risk fighting. The Romans clearly appeared as the aggressors since they had had no previous interests in Sicily, whereas the Carthaginians had long been one of the dominant powers there. To have tolerated Roman interference would have made the Carthaginians appear weak and unwilling to protect their interests in a situation where justice seemed to be on their side. Moreover, to have negotiated and agreed to the Roman claims of a protectorate over the Mamertines would have left the Mamertines free to cause trouble on Sicily under the umbrella of Roman power. From the Carthaginian perspective, therefore, the Romans had to be opposed.

Initial Carthaginian Setbacks, 263 and 262 B.C. Unfortunately for Carthage, most of her warships had been lying in storage ever since the Pyrrhic War. Ships had to be refitted; crews had to be recruited and trained. Meanwhile, Hiero was alarmed that Carthaginian forces had not even been able to prevent Appius from shipping his main army across the straits in 264. When he did not receive the expected support against a Roman attack in 263, he negotiated peace with Rome for fifteen years and agreed to help her against Carthage. With his help in 262, the Romans captured the Carthaginian stronghold of Agrigentum (Acragas, Gigenti).

Expansion of the War After the fall of Agrigentum, the Romans saw the possibility of driving the Carthaginians out of Sicily altogether. The obstacle was the Carthaginian fleet, which was not fully ready for action. Such a fleet could have cut communications with Italy and starved the Roman army into submission and surrender. It could also have raided the Italian coastal cities without hindrance. Rome realized that she had to build a navy at all costs or else get out of the war.

Rome Builds a Fleet, 261 B.C. The small fleet that Rome had built during the Second Samnite War (p. 76) had lapsed into decay after the war with Pyrrhus. The navies of allied Greek city-states in Italy had transported the Roman armies to Sicily, and their light *triremes* had provided sufficient protection before Carthage had mobilized her full naval power, which was based on the heavy *quinquereme*. A *quinquereme* could have one bank of oars with five (*quinque*) men to an oar, two banks of oars with three rowers over two, or three banks of oars with two rowers each on the upper two oars and one on the bottom oar. In any case, it was heavy and strong with a great bronze beak used for ramming and sinking other ships. Using one captured from the Carthaginians as a model and with the help of allied Greek shipwrights, the Romans built one hundred *quinqueremes* in sixty days. Twenty new *triremes* completed the fleet.

Fortunately the *quinquereme* required only one or two skilled rowers per oar. Those Rome recruited from her Greek allies and used them to train new Roman rowers in simulators set up on land. To the bows of their new ships the Romans added a device that the Athenians had tried during their disastrous expedition to Sicily (415 to 413 B.C.). It was a hinged gangplank raised upright by ropes and pulleys attached to the mast. After an enemy ship was rammed, this gangplank was dropped onto the disabled ship's deck, and Roman marines would rush across to fight as they would on land. The end of the plank had a grappling spike or beak to hold on to the enemy ship so that it could not slip off the Roman ship's ram and escape. This spike gave the device its name, *corvus* (crow or raven). Although it served its purpose very well, it rendered Roman ships unstable in high seas when it was raised upright for transport.

A Titanic Struggle, 260 to 241 B.C. A war of titans commenced in 260 B.C. when the new Roman fleet defeated the Carthaginians in a great naval battle off Mylae not far from Messana. The triumphant Romans erected a column decorated with the rams (*rostra*) of captured Carthaginian ships near the speaker's platform in the Forum. After failing to adapt to Roman tactics and losing another sea fight off Sardinia in 258, the commander of the Carthaginian fleet was crucified.

The Roman Invasion of Africa, 256 to 255 B.C. Having established unexpected naval superiority, the Romans planned a massive invasion of Africa itself to end the war quickly. In 256, the Romans set sail with 250 warships, 80 transports, and about 100,000 men. They defeated another Carthaginian flotilla off Cape Ecnomus on the south coast of Sicily, but new Carthaginian tactics began to counteract the *corvus*.

The Roman consul M. Atilius Regulus landed in Africa in the fall of 256 B.C. He inflicted a minor defeat on the Carthaginians and, thinking that they were just about ready to give up, offered them terms of peace so harsh that they were rejected. Though winter would have been the best season for African fighting, he decided to wait until spring. Meanwhile, Carthage had not been idle. She had engaged the services of Xanthippus, a Spartan strategist skilled in the use of the Macedonian phalanx and war elephants. New mercenaries were hired, and many Carthaginian citizens volunteered for service. All that winter the work of preparation and training continued unabated.

In the spring of 255 B.C., Regulus advanced into the valley of the Bagradas but found the enemy already waiting for him. Here Xanthippus had drawn up his phalanx—elephants in front and cavalry on the wings. The entire Roman army was destroyed, except for 2,000 men who escaped to the coast. Regulus himself was taken prisoner.

A Roman armada sent to blockade Carthage defeated another Carthaginian fleet and rescued the remnants of Regulus' army. As they were approaching the shores of Sicily, a sudden squall caught the ships made top heavy by the *corvus*. All but 80 of 250 ships sank or crashed on the rocks. In 253, a similar disaster occurred.

The War in Sicily, 254 to 249 B.C. After 255, Sicily and its surrounding waters remained the sole theater of military operations. Capturing Panormus (Palermo) in 254, the Romans drove the Carthaginians almost out of the island except for two strongholds at the western tip—Lilybaeum and the naval base of Drepana (Trapani)—both of which they blockaded by land and sea. The Carthaginians concentrated their main effort on expanding their empire in Africa and stamping out native revolts in order to secure their resources at home. In 249, however, they regained the initiative.

Carthaginian Success at Sea, 249 to 247 B.C. Although the Romans had rebuilt their navy after the disasters of 255 and 253 B.C., they had abandoned the *corvus,* partly because the Carthaginians had devised successful defensive tactics against it and partly because its weight made their ships very vulnerable to storms at sea. In 249, the poor tactics of the consul Publius Claudius Pulcher resulted in the loss of 93 out of 120 Roman ships off Drepana (Trapani). Supposedly, when the sacred chickens gave a bad omen by refusing to eat before the battle, he exploded, "Throw the damn chickens into the sea; if they won't eat, let them drink!" A second Roman defeat soon followed Claudius' debacle. The other consul's enormous fleet was completely destroyed, partly by Carthaginian attack and partly by storm. For the next few years, the Carthaginians had undisputed mastery of the sea. They were now able to break the Roman blockade of Lilybaeum, cut communications between Rome and Sicily, and make raids upon the Italian coast itself.

Hamilcar Barca and Carthaginian Failure, 247 to 241 B.C. Never had the picture looked brighter for Carthage, especially after she had sent to Sicily in 247 B.C. the young Hamilcar Barca, the most brilliant general of the war. His lightning moves behind Roman lines and daring raids upon the Italian coast made him the terror of Rome. Well did he merit the name of *Barca,* which in Punic meant "blitz" or "lightning."

Despite the brilliance of Hamilcar Barca and the amazing successes of the Carthaginian navy, Carthage lost the war, chiefly because of her inability to deliver the final blow when Rome was staggering in defeat. Rome's ultimate victory was not wholly due to doggedness, perseverance, or moral qualities, as has often been suggested, but to the weakness of the Carthaginian state itself—a result of the internal division between the commercial magnates and the powerful landowning nobility.

At the very moment when the Carthaginian navy and the generalship of Hamilcar Barca seemed about to win the war, a landowning group headed by Hanno the so-called Great, which had prospered with the conquest of territory in North Africa, came into control of the Carthaginian government. To them, the conquest of vast territories of great agricultural productivity in Africa was more important than Sicily, the navy, and the war against Rome. That the dominant faction in the Carthaginian government was not interested in winning the war was clearly evident in 244 B.C., when the entire Carthaginian navy was laid up and demobilized. Its crews, oarsmen, and marines were transferred from the navy to the army of African conquest.

Meanwhile, Rome saw that her only chance for survival lay in the recovery of her naval power. She persuaded her wealthiest citizens to advance money for the construction of a navy by promising to repay them after victory. In 242, a fleet of 200 Roman ships appeared in Sicilian waters. In the following year, on a stormy morning near the Aegates Islands, it encountered a Carthaginian fleet of untrained crews and ships undermanned and weighted down with cargoes of grain and other supplies for the garrison at Lilybaeum. The result was a disaster that cost Carthage the war. The garrison at Lilybaeum could no longer be supplied. There was no alternative but to sue for peace.

Roman Peace Terms, 241 B.C. The Carthaginian government empowered Hamilcar Barca to negotiate peace terms with the consul C. Lutatius Catulus, the victor of the recent naval battle. Both sides were exhausted. The Roman negotiators, well aware of the slim margin of victory, were disposed to make the terms relatively light. Carthage was to evacuate Lilybaeum, abandon all Sicily, return all prisoners, and pay an indemnity of 2,200 talents in 20 years (for the value of Roman monetary units, see p. 127). These terms seemed too lenient to the Roman voters, who had to ratify the treaty in the *comitia centuriata*. They increased the indemnity to 3,200 talents to be paid in 10 years. The Carthaginians were also required to surrender all islands between Sicily and Italy, keep their ships out of Italian waters, and discontinue recruiting mercenaries in Italy.

As in all major wars, the victors and vanquished both were profoundly affected and underwent significant changes. First of all, the war had exacted enormous tolls in men and matériel on both sides. Although casualty figures are often grossly inflated by ancient sources, Rome and Carthage each had lost hundreds of ships and tens of thousands of men. The sea power of Carthage was broken and her naval dominance of the western Mediterranean was ended for all time. Rome, on the other hand, had become a major naval and overseas power irrevocably involved in the affairs of the wider Mediterranean world. This change not only altered the way in which Rome dealt with foreign powers but also caused major internal changes, as will be seen in the following chapters.

VIII

Between the Wars,
241 to 218 B.C.

The First Punic War made many Romans profoundly suspicious of Carthage and ready to prevent any attempt on her part to even the score. Others had tasted the seductive fruits of overseas conquest and wanted more. Some Carthaginians resented their humiliating defeat and hoped someday to restore Carthaginian prestige abroad, whereas others decided to concentrate on the intensive agricultural development of the territory around Carthage. More immediately, however, Carthage suffered a major crisis because of her inability to pay the mercenary troops that made up the bulk of her army. The temptation to take advantage of this situation at Carthage's expense eventually proved too great for a number of Romans to resist.

The Truceless War and Roman Trickery, 241 B.C.

No sooner had Carthage made peace with Rome at the end of the First Punic War than she had to fight her own mercenaries. Returning from Sicily, 20,000 mercenaries demanded their accumulated pay and the rewards promised to them by Hamilcar Barca. The Carthaginian government, then dominated by unsympathetic landlords such as Hanno the Great, refused. The mercenaries mutinied and were joined by the oppressed natives of Libya, the Libyphoenicians from the East and the Numidians of the West. The mercenaries became masters of the open country, from which Carthage was isolated. It was a war without truce and, therefore, known as the Truceless War. A similar revolt subsequently broke out in Sardinia.

Hanno assumed command of the army, but his "greatness" failed to achieve any military success. The situation deteriorated until Hamilcar Barca took command. After three years of the bloodiest fighting, during which crucifixions and all manner of atrocities were committed on both sides, Hamilcar finally stamped out the revolt.

Carthage received the unexpected sympathy and help of Rome, who furnished her with supplies and denied them to her enemies. Rome permitted her to trade with Italy and even recruit troops there but rejected appeals for alliance from the rebels of Utica and Sardinia. After the revolt against Carthage had been stamped out in Africa, however, a faction unsympathetic to Carthage gained the upper hand in the Roman senate. As Hamilcar was moving to reoccupy Sardinia in 238 B.C., this group persuaded the senate to listen to the appeal of the Sardinian rebels, declare war on Carthage, rob Carthage of both Sardinia and Corsica, and demand an additional indemnity of 1,200 talents. Carthage had no fleet and could not fight back, although the natives of Sardinia fought ferociously against Roman occupation, which was not fully completed until

225 B.C. The two islands were grouped together as the second Roman province.

Carthaginian Recovery   Shortly after the loss of Sardinia and Corsica, Carthage made a strong recovery. Under the leadership of Hamilcar Barca, the loss of the two islands was more than offset by the reconquest of Spain. During the First Punic War and later the Truceless War, Carthage had lost most of her Spanish possessions to native rebellions and most of her trade to the Greek colony of Massilia, her chief commercial rival in the western Mediterranean. Hamilcar recovered those possessions and much more besides. Landing at Gades in 237 B.C., he conquered all of southern Spain, and by a judicious mixture of war and diplomacy founded a bigger and richer empire than Carthage had ever possessed.

After Hamilcar Barca drowned in 229 B.C., his son-in-law Hasdrubal continued the work of empire building. He founded New Carthage (Cartagena) which became the capital, the navy and army base, and the arsenal of the Carthaginian empire in Spain. All the important mining districts were now brought back under Carthaginian control.

Many Romans had been watching these developments with growing suspicion and alarm. They knew that the Barca family, which had been so successful against Rome in the First Punic War, controlled a vast empire in Spain, a small but modern navy, and a fine army that was well equipped and undergoing intensive training in constant warfare against the Spanish tribes. In addition, the mines of Spain furnished them an annual revenue of between two and three thousand talents. This enormous revenue enabled the Barca family to wield almost kingly power in both Spain and Carthage.

Carthaginian expansion in Spain adversely affected neighboring Massilia. Long bound to Rome by ties of friendship and probably a formal alliance by this time, Massilia complained of the Carthaginian threat to her Spanish colonies and especially to her trade, which she had expanded at the expense of Carthage during the First Punic War. About 231

B.C., the Romans sent emissaries to Spain to investigate, but they came back apparently satisfied with Hamilcar's explanation that he was only trying to explore new sources of revenue to enable Carthage to pay her indemnity to Rome.

The Ebro Treaty   Nevertheless, the continued Carthaginian expansion in Spain evoked ever louder complaints from Massilia. At last, in 226 B.C. the Romans negotiated with Hasdrubal the famous Ebro Treaty, which prohibited him from crossing the Ebro River with warlike intent but allowed him a free hand south of the river. This treaty gave him control over almost seven eighths of the entire peninsula. Massilia was guaranteed the security of her two coastal colonies lying between the Ebro and the Pyrenees and was not excluded from peaceful trade with Carthaginian Spain.

Roman Problems after 241 B.C.   Between the First and Second Punic Wars, Rome's most pressing problems were (1) the administration of her two newly acquired provinces, first Sicily and then Sardinia and Corsica; (2) the reform of her government to satisfy the claims of the middle-sized farmer, who had shouldered the heaviest burdens of the war; (3) the conquest of northern Italy to secure her frontiers against future Gallic attack and at the same time to open up more lands for farm settlement; (4) the suppression of piracy on the Adriatic Sea; and (5) the limitation of Carthaginian expansion in Spain.

The Administration of Sicily   The conquest of Sicily presented Rome with the entirely new problem of governing territory outside of Italy. Her old Italian policy of making the newly conquered cities her allies by giving them local self-government in return for military and naval assistance in time of war was impossible to apply in many cases. Rather than be called upon to fight for Rome, most Sicilians preferred to pay tribute in the form of money or farm products, as they had paid to others, and be left alone.

Both Carthage and Syracuse had applied that policy to their Sicilian subjects. They had borrowed it from the Hellenistic successors of Alexander, who had found it long established in Egypt and the Near East, where farmers tradionally paid a tithe, one tenth of their harvested crops, to the pharaoh or king. The Romans found this system spelled out in the laws of Hiero II of Syracuse. They took it over as the *lex Hieronica* and applied it to their newly won holdings in Sicily.

Each year, the magistrates of Sicilian cities subject to the tithe took a census of all the farmers in their territories, both owners and renters, and recorded the size of the farms, the acreage under cultivation, and the amount of seed sown. The records, signed under oath, were filed in the record office of local administrative centers and were open to inspection by contractors, *publicani* (either private individuals or agents of tax-collecting firms), preparing to bid for the collection of the annual tithe. They would compute their estimates of the crop prospects and make their bids, which were based on 10.4 percent of the estimated crop, of which 10 percent went to the treasury, the remaining fraction to the contractor. The highest bidder, receiving the contract and paying the provincial treasury in advance, went to the farmers and drew up signed agreements specifying both the amount of the tithe and the date of its delivery at the public warehouses. The agreements were filed with the local magistrates, who were responsible both for their enforcement and for the delivery of the tithe to the provincial treasury.

The other sources of provincial revenue were custom dues (*portoria*), levied at the rate of 5 percent on all imported and exported goods; the *scriptura,* paid in cash on each head of grazing stock on pasture land; rentals on public lands of one third of the annual crop; and royalties on mines and quarries.

Provincial Governors

The Romans first attempted to govern Sicily by quaestors reporting to the magistrates of Rome. Rome was too far away, however, and a quaestor did not have the powers required to deal with such problems as defense and the maintenance of law and order. Only a magistrate possessing the *imperium,* such as a consul or a praetor, would do. Accordingly, after 227 B.C. the Centuriate Assembly annually elected two additional praetors, one as governor of Sicily, the other for the combined province of Sardinia and Corsica.

The Provincial Edict Although the Roman senate laid down the general principles governing provincial administration, it left the details to be filled in by the praetor as governor of the province. Each newly elected praetor on taking office would publish an edict similar to that of the city praetor and set forth the rules and regulations that he intended to follow during his year in office. The edict would specifically state the rules of procedure that he would apply in his administration of justice. These edicts varied little from year to year and were changed only under special conditions.

Duties and Powers The provincial praetor was assisted by one or more quaestors, who served as treasurers and receivers of revenues derived from taxes. Three *legati*—lieutenants—of senatorial rank, nominated by the praetor and appointed by the senate, acted not only as liaison officers between him and the senate, but as his advisors and often as his deputies. He also had with him a number of comrades or young family friends, who, as members of his staff, might gain an insight into the workings of provincial administration. His staff included clerks, secretaries, and household slaves. He commanded the armed forces within the province, supervised the quaestors, and was responsible for the administration of justice in all civil and criminal cases involving Roman citizens and for the arbitration of disputes arising between the subject communities.

Inside the province, the powers of the praetor were practically absolute. There was no colleague of equal rank to oppose his decisions or acts, no plebeian tribune to interpose his veto in defense of private individuals, no senate to restrain his abuse of arbitrary power, and no popular assembly to pass laws that he had to obey. The provincials had neither the right of appeal nor legal guarantees to the rights of life, liberty, and property. Some cities had local liberties guaranteed in charters granted them by the Roman senate, but an unscrupulous governor could easily circumvent them. Although his term of office was theoretically limited to one year, it was sometimes longer because of the failure through neglect or corrupt influence to elect a successor.

Theoretically, too, the provincials had the right to bring charges against the praetor for misgovernment and extortion, but they rarely did and then only under the most unusual circumstances and for the most flagrant abuse. In time, the practically unlimited power of Roman provincial governors was dangerous to Rome's republican form of government, which depended upon the willingness of individual members of the ruling aristocracy to respect the equal authority of their colleagues in time of conflict and disagreement. Men accustomed to almost royal independence abroad became impatient with republican restrictions at home.

The *Praetor Peregrinus* That praetors rather than consuls were elected to govern provinces seems to have been a logical consequence of the step taken in 242 B.C. of adding another praetor, the *praetor peregrinus*. He dealt with the legal disputes, too numerous for the city praetor to handle, which arose among the foreign merchants and immigrants entering Rome in large numbers. Because Roman law did not necessarily apply to all the points at issue, it was necessary to supplement the Roman civil law (*ius civile*) with models and precedents from the laws of other people and develop rules of procedure based on common concepts of equity.

An International System of Law Provincial governors in framing their edicts and, apparently, the city praetor in dealing with disputes between Roman citizens and foreigners, followed the same practice as the *praetor peregrinus*. Thus a system of international law or law of nations (*ius gentium*) gradually overlaid the narrow civil law of Rome as the Romans became more and more involved in the wider world. In time, this system was vastly expanded and not only was incorporated into the Justinian Code and the Code Napoléon but also became the basis of modern international law.

Gaius Flaminius and the Problems of Reform The period after the First Punic War was an age not only of imperial expansion but also of reform—social, economic, constitutional, and legal. This reform movement arose as a result of the growing tension between the small and less affluent landowners on the one hand and the aristocracy of large landowners on the other. The latter had profited most from the First Punic War through loans to the government, which were frequently paid off by grants of public land. Those who tilled small farms around Rome and in Latium were particularly dissatisfied with their lot. Subject to the draft and forced to fight long campaigns far from home, they had to neglect their crops. During the war many of them had fallen into debt and later could not pay back their loans because the price of wheat was falling as a result of competition with wheat imported from Sicily. Another cause of grievance was the lack of newly conquered land suitable for distribution and settlement, because the new provinces of Sicily and Sardinia offered no opportunity for colonization. These and perhaps other grievances led to political agitation and the demand for reform.

The leader of the reform movement was Gaius Flaminius. As plebeian tribune in 232 B.C., he obtained, without consulting the senate and in spite of its violent opposition, a plebiscite requiring that public lands confiscated south of Ariminum (Rimini) a half century before from the Gauls be cut up into small farms and distributed among poor families. His unorthodox disregard of senatorial authority and privilege set a precedent followed by other champions of popular causes a century later (see p. 147).

The Gallic Wars and Conquest of Northern Italy, 225 to 222 B.C.

An aristocratically biased tradition (preserved by Polybius) alleges that the land distributions after 232 B.C. alarmed the Gauls of northern Italy, who had been peaceful farmers ever since 283 B.C., and provoked them to invade central Italy. Although that may well have been a contributing factor, it certainly was not the only one. Gallic unrest had begun as early as 236 B.C., when the Boii made an abortive attack upon Ariminum. Periodically, expanding Gallic populations had sought new territories to the south, and in 236 the return of now-unemployed Gallic mercenaries, who had served Carthage during the Truceless War, may have caused further unrest.

After 236 the Romans were preoccupied with problems in the Adriatic (p. 96), and the Gallic tribes prepared more thoroughly to challenge Rome. In 225 B.C., an army of Gallic tribesmen crossed the Apennines, pushed down into Etruria, and plundered as they went. The Romans raised two powerful consular armies, which converged upon the Gauls near Cape Telamon on the central coast of Etruria and almost annihilated them.

After this victory, the Romans resolved to end the Gallic menace for good by the conquest of northern Italy. During his consulship of 223 B.C., Gaius Flaminius subdued the Insubrian Gauls by a decisive victory, which led by 220 B.C. to the submission of all the Gauls (except the Taurini of the Piedmont and a few other sub-Alpine tribes). During his censorship in 220 B.C., he arranged for the construction of the great military highway, the Flaminian Way, which ran northeast from Rome to Ariminum on the Adriatic. He also founded Latin colonies at Cremona and Placentia (Piacenza) both to control crossings of the middle Po and to provide outlets for land-starved Roman farmers.

The Reform of the Centuriate Assembly

During the career of Gaius Flaminius, probably in his censorship of 220 B.C., there took place a reform of great constitutional importance — the reorganization of the Centuriate Assembly, which had long since become the stronghold of entrenched wealth. In 241 B.C., two new voting tribes had been added to the Roman citizen body, which brought the number of tribes to a final total of thirty-five. As a result of the reorganization, the tribes became purely administrative divisions to which newly enfranchised citizens were assigned, regardless of place of residence. The Centuriate Assembly subsequently was reorganized with reference to the new tribal organization to make voting in that assembly somewhat more equitable.

Previously, the richest people controlled a majority of 98 out of 193 unit votes in the Centuriate Assembly (p. 63). After the reform, the 18 equestrian centuries remained at the top, and the proletariat kept its 5 at the bottom. In between, however, the 5 property classes were each assigned 70 centuries divided equally between juniors and seniors (men over 45 years old), to make a total of 373 centuries.

To keep the traditional total of 193 votes in the Centuriate Assembly, however, the 280 centuries of the 4 lower property classes cast their ballots together in groups of 2 and 3 centuries each to produce 100 unit votes. In this way, the wealthiest citizens could not alone determine the outcome of the voting, since they controlled only 88 votes (the 18 equestrian centuries plus the 70 centuries of the first class), compared with the 105 controlled by the other citizens (the 5 of the *proletarii* plus the 100 votes controlled by the 280 centuries of the other 4 property classes). Voting would now have to go down to at least the second census class before a majority of the unit votes could be achieved in the *comitia centuriata*.

This reform shows the growing influence of those citizens who met the financial qualifications of the second census class. The difference in wealth between the first and second census classes was not so great, however, as to cause frequent, significant differences in interests, and it was not a great threat to the large landowners to increase the value of the votes controlled by the second property class.

Other Reforms of the Period In the attempt to build up their political support, various politicians promoted other reforms. In 218 B.C., the tribune Quintus Claudius, probably at the instigation of Gaius Flaminius, obtained passage of the *lex Claudia,* which made it illegal for a senator or his son to own or operate ships large enough for overseas trade. Since Flaminius supposedly was the only senator to support this bill, it may be assumed that a significant number of senators had become involved in overseas trade. On the other hand, if the bill's expressed intent had really been to prevent senators from becoming involved in commercial affairs, probably some senators would have supported it. More likely, by limiting senatorial competitors, Flaminius and Claudius were seeking the favor of numerous wealthy nonsenators who had also helped to fill the vacuum in overseas commerce after the defeat of Carthage in the First Punic War.

Earlier, following the trend set by Appius Claudius the Blind, the censor of 312 B.C., and by his freedman Gnaeus Flavius, the aedile of 304/03 B.C., Tiberius Coruncanius, who was the first plebeian ever to hold the office of *pontifex maximus* (254 B.C.), had announced that he was prepared to give free legal advice to any person. In 204 B.C., the learned jurist Sextus Aelius Paetus Catus published his famous commentaries on the Twelve Tables together with the legal interpretations handed down by the pontiffs. Now, anyone, poor or rich, could inform himself about Roman laws.

The Illyrian Wars, 229 to 228 and 220 to 219 B.C.

After the maritime Greek cities of southern Italy had lost their independence and Rome had become preoccupied with Carthage in western waters, the notorious pirates of Illyria along the eastern coast of the Adriatic had grown ever bolder. Queen Teuta, who had been expanding her Illyrian kingdom south to Epirus and the Gulf of Corinth, had been unable or unwilling to stop them. The rugged, broken, and deeply indented coast of Illyria with its myriads of small islands was ideal for hiding light and speedy pirate ships waiting to waylay passing merchant ships. With the Greeks grown weak, pirates roved the seas at will, attacked not only

Greek but Italian ships, and captured or killed their crews. Growing ever bolder, they ransacked towns along the Adriatic shores of southern Italy. Because many of the pirates' victims were Roman allies, Rome was compelled to act.

In 230 B.C., two Roman envoys arrived in the Illyrian capital of Scodra (Scutari, Skadar) to lodge complaints, but Teuta was busy waging war at the moment and had no time to listen to silly complaints about what her subjects claimed a natural right to do. The protests were insolently rejected and the envoys haughtily dismissed. On the way back, one of the envoys was killed.

Rome was not slow to respond. In the summer of 229 B.C., a fleet of 200 Roman ships appeared off the island of Corcyra (Corfu). Demetrius of Pharos, whom Teuta had charged with the defense of the island, betrayed her and surrendered to the Romans without a fight. The fleet then sailed north to support a large Roman army attacking the towns of Apollonia and Dyrrhachium (Durazzo). Teuta sued for peace. She retained her crown on condition that she renounce her conquests in Greece, abandon all claims to islands and coastal towns captured by the Romans, and agree not to let more than two Illyrian ships at a time sail past Lissus, the modern Albanian town of Alessio. For his treachery, Demetrius received control of Pharos and some mainland towns.

Demetrius could not be true to anyone, even the Romans. Conspiring with Antigonus Doson, acting king of Macedon, who disliked Roman interference in Balkan affairs, he stealthily extended his kingdom. After Teuta's death, he invaded Roman protectorates, attacked Greek cities farther south, and made piratical raids far into the Aegean.

The Romans could not overlook these activities. In a speedy campaign they conquered the kingdom of Demetrius, who fled to the court of the youthful Philip V, now king of Macedon. Whispering plots of revenge into the young king's ear, he remained there for several years. The Romans could not further pursue their Illyrian campaign, for at that moment ominous news began to come in from the western end of the Mediterranean.

Further Developments in Spain After Hamilcar Barca died, Hasdrubal, his son-in-law, had brought under Carthaginian control almost all of the Spanish peninsula south of the Ebro River. In 221 B.C., Hasdrubal was assassinated. Hannibal, the eldest son of Hamilcar Barca, succeeded him.

Hannibal Polybius (Book 3.11) tells the romantic story, perhaps true, that Hamilcar, sacrificing before his departure for Spain, consented to take along the nine-year-old Hannibal only after the latter took hold of the sacrificed victims and swore never to be friendly to Rome.[1] From then on, Hannibal spent his entire life in the army. It is said that even after he had become a general, he ate with his men, dressed like them, and, covered only with a cloak, slept among them on the same hard ground. He must have been an exceptional leader. For fifteen unbroken years he commanded an army composed of Africans, Spaniards, Gauls, Phoeni-

cians, and many other ethnic groups, who never once were known to mutiny or rebel. They followed him on long, fatiguing marches, across wide rivers, through swamps, and over the snow-capped Alps.

After two years of preparation, Hannibal advanced northwest from the Carthaginian capital of Spain, New Carthage (Cartagena), toward what is now Salamanca and conquered several tribes of the Upper Tagus and Douro rivers. Carthage now formally claimed all of Spain south of the Ebro, except Saguntum (Sagunto). Saguntum, a town perched on a rocky plateau overlooking the central eastern coast, was a trading partner of Massilia and had become an ally of Rome sometime between 230 and 219 B.C. Since no mention was made of Saguntum in the Ebro Treaty of 226, Saguntum possibly became allied with Rome after 226, no doubt at the insistence of Massilia.

In 219 B.C., Hannibal besieged Saguntum because of what he termed its unprovoked attacks on neighboring tribes subject to Carthage. After a desperate siege of eight months, the town fell. With its fall began the Second Punic War, which made Rome the strongest power in the Mediterranean world and set in motion the events that led to her conquest of the Hellenistic kingdoms of the Greek East.

---

[1] Later, Roman authors said that Hannibal swore eternal hatred of Rome, which implies a more active hostility to Rome than the Polybian version and is, perhaps, a Roman attempt to put all blame for the war on Hannibal and his family.

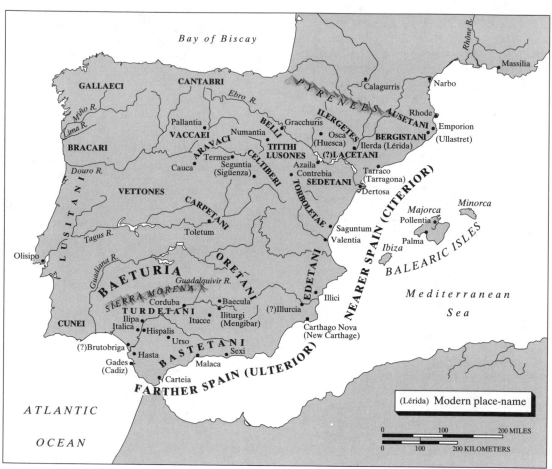

Spain in the Second Century B.C.

IX

The Second Punic War, 218 to 201 B.C.

Neither side had actively sought the Second Punic War. Between 238 and 219 B.C., both the Carthaginians and the Romans had adhered to the treaty of 241 and the Ebro Treaty of 226. The Romans' acceptance of friendship with the city of Saguntum, south of the Ebro, had broached neither treaty. A step taken primarily to keep the good will of Massilia, it indicated no official Roman hostility toward Carthaginian activity in Spain, although some senators may well have thought that Saguntum could provide a strategic base of operations in any unanticipated conflict. At the time, Hannibal apparently had taken no offense when Rome had ruled against a pro-Carthaginian faction in arbitrating a civil dispute at Saguntum, and by not provoking Saguntum he avoided angering the Romans.

Causes of the Second Punic War The simplistic view that Hannibal and the Barcid family had been planning to attack Rome for a long time out of a bitter desire for revenge was a convenient fiction for both sides. The Romans favored it because it absolved them of any blame. Many Carthaginians promoted it because it allowed them to make the Barcids alone their scapegoats in dealing with the Roman victors.

Much more useful for understanding the outbreak of the Second Punic War in 218 B.C. are the mutual fear and misunderstanding that

forced the two parties into a corner and made them willing to support a new war when they reached an impasse in their relationship. Fear arose on both sides because Saguntum—encouraged by Massilia, Carthage's commercial rival in Spain—constantly complained to the Roman senate about Hannibal as he tried to advance his control up to the Ebro. In 220, probably to appease Saguntum and Massilia as well as to check up on Carthaginian intentions, the senate sent ambassadors to investigate the situation. They pointed out to Hannibal that Saguntum enjoyed *fides* with Rome and reminded him of the Ebro treaty. To Hannibal, this action must have seemed like gratuitous Roman interference. Also, he may have feared that the Romans were now trying to use the Saguntines against Carthage, just as they had previously used the Mamertines on Sicily and the rebellious mercenaries on Sardinia. He immediately sent his assessment of the situation to the Carthaginian senate and asked for instructions. The Carthaginian senate apparently agreed with his interpretation, because his next act was to besiege Saguntum in early 219.

That the Romans had no immediate plans to use the Saguntine situation as a pretext for war against Carthage in Spain is clear. They were in the process of sending two consular armies in the opposite direction, to Illyria. When news of Hannibal's attack on Saguntum reached Rome, the senate did not take any action. The fall of Saguntum in early 218, however, must have stirred up public opinion against Carthage: Roman prestige was badly damaged by the destruction of a city that had fruitlessly claimed the protection of Roman *fides*. The senate now had to take serious action against Hannibal. An embassy of leading senators and the two consuls went to Carthage to demand the surrender of Hannibal unless the Carthaginians wanted war. Many may have expected Carthage to capitulate in view of her past actions.

The majority of Carthaginian senators, however, probably could not tolerate the humiliation of abandoning a commander whom they had supported. Resentment must already have existed over the way in which the Romans at the end of the First Punic War had imposed a treaty harsher than the one originally negotiated and had later robbed Carthage of Sardinia and Corsica. To have given in meekly a third time now that Carthage was stronger would have been too much to bear. The Carthaginian senate chose war.

For numerous reasons many Romans also favored war. There was probably a genuine fear, eagerly encouraged by Massilia, that the Carthaginians in Spain and the Celtic tribes in southern Gaul would eventually join against Rome. Also, as the *lex Claudia* of 218 reveals, a significant group of Romans now engaged in overseas trade (p. 96). With the revival of Carthage through expansion in Spain, Roman merchants and traders would have feared stronger competition and would have wanted to weaken Carthage once more. Finally, there were always ambitious aristocrats who sought to increase their prestige and power through successful military commands. Such men were the two consuls of 218, Publius Cornelius Scipio and Tiberius Sempronius Longus. Therefore, both sides accepted the challenge and the Second Punic, or Hannibalic, War was on.

Hannibal's War Strategy Hannibal had a splendid army but no navy to complement and assist it. Roman naval superiority was so great that Carthage could neither safely transport and supply large armies by sea nor prevent the

Romans from establishing beachheads anywhere. The Romans' seapower permitted them to wage war on several fronts simultaneously, to invade Africa and Spain, and to land several armies in both at the same time.

Hannibal's only strong base and source of manpower and supplies was Spain, and he had only one really well-trained and reliable army. His sole chance of success lay in establishing a single front, preferably in Italy. So long as Rome was in danger, the Romans would concentrate the bulk of their forces in Italy. Only an invasion of Italy would enable him to seize the initiative. Only an invasion of Italy would render useless the great Roman navy.

By invading Italy Hannibal also hoped to cut at the roots of Roman military power, which was potentially six or seven times that of Carthage. Only by wrecking Rome's system of alliances and her Italian confederation could he hope to paralyze and destroy that enormous war potential. He knew that the Gauls of northern Italy were already at war with Rome and would rally around him, and he also hoped that her confederate allies in central and southern Italy would break away from the Roman confederation and join him as their liberator.

Roman War Plans The Romans planned to wage an offensive war. Their naval superiority would enable them to seize and hold the initiative at once and to choose the theater of military operations. The army under the consul Publius Cornelius Scipio actually landed at Massilia for the invasion of Spain; another assembled in Sicily for the invasion of Africa. The decision to land at Massilia was theoretically good. The Romans could invade Spain or intercept Hannibal in Gaul, should he decide to invade northern Italy, and they also could use Massilia's fleet for operations in Spanish waters. The Romans, however, landed at Massilia too late to intercept Hannibal. He was already on his way to the Alps.

Hannibal's March to the Alps Around the first of May in 218 B.C., Hannibal set out from New Carthage on the long march north to

Italy. To protect his vital base in Spain, he left part of the Carthaginian army there under the command of his brother Hasdrubal (not to be confused with his dead brother-in-law). By late August or early September, he had crossed the Rhône. Scipio, who had been delayed by revolts in Cisalpine Gaul, arrived too late to intercept him. Wisely ordering his brother to lead the army into Spain, he himself sailed back to Italy in order to lead the two legions in Cisalpine Gaul against Hannibal as he descended the Alps.

Where Hannibal crossed the Rhône and what route he took through the Alps have caused endless speculation but are not known. Neither is terribly important. What stirs the imagination is that it would have been enormously difficult no matter which way he went. To get an army conservatively estimated to have included at the start about 30,000 infantry, 9,000 cavalry, and at least 37 war elephants over the Alps under primitive conditions would have been a great feat even in summer. Hannibal did it at the start of the Alpine winter. His forces suffered great losses because of slippery trails, biting cold, and deep snows. Even worse were the sudden attacks of hostile mountain tribesmen. As he himself recorded on an inscription, only 20,000 infantry and 6,000 cavalry reached the level plains of northern Italy.[1] The Insubres and the Boii, already at war with Rome, eagerly joined his army and made up for the lost men. After a short rest, his army met that of Scipio at the Ticinus River.

Hannibal's Early Victories, 218 and 217 B.C.

The Battle of the Ticinus (218) was a minor cavalry skirmish. It would have been more serious had the seventeen-year-old Publius Cornelius Scipio—the future Africanus, conqueror of Carthage and victor over Hannibal—not saved his wounded father from capture. The father withdrew his army south of the Po, and the Romans recalled the other consul, Tiberius Sempronius Longus, from the planned

[1]How many elephants survived he did not mention, but some did fight in his initial battles in Italy.

invasion of Africa to reinforce Scipio. Hannibal's attempt to maintain a single front was succeeding.

The Battle at the Trebia, 218 B.C. By December of 218, the two consuls had taken up a strong position with 40,000 men on the eastern bank of the Trebia (Trebbia), a small northern tributary of the Po. Against the advice of the wounded Scipio, Sempronius was eager for battle. Hannibal easily tempted him into an ambush and annihilated three quarters of the Roman army. The rich Po valley fell into Hannibal's hand like a ripe plum.

The loss of northern Italy infuriated those who had promoted the conquest and settlement of that region. They helped to elect as consul for 217 B.C. Gaius Flaminius, who had subdued the Insubres and placed the Cisalpina under Roman control in his consulship of 223 B.C. Gnaeus Servilius was the other consul. New legions were called into service. The new consuls were instructed to hold the line and, if possible, recover northern Italy.

The Battle of Lake Trasimene, 217 B.C. Always doing the unexpected, Hannibal invaded Etruria by a difficult but unguarded pass. Feigning a march against Rome itself, he lured Flaminius into a narrow spot between the hills and Lake Trasimene, near Perusia (Perugia). On a foggy morning he ambushed the Roman army from the hills. Most of the 36,000 Romans were either killed or captured, and Flaminius himself was slain. The same fate afterward befell 4,000 cavalrymen whom Servilius had sent down the Flaminian Way, perhaps to support the legions at Trasimene.

The news of Trasimene filled Rome with fear of imminent siege. The fear was groundless because Hannibal knew that the siege of a large fortified city without siege engines and a strong supply base would have been foolhardy. Also, the Romans still had field armies capable of intervening. Hannibal had another plan. He had invaded Italy in the hope of wrecking the Roman alliance system. Victorious battles were only a means to this end, but because they had so far

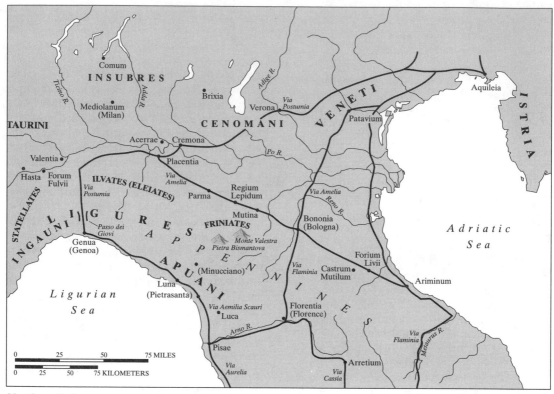

Northern Italy

produced satisfactory results only in the North and not in Etruria or central Italy, he decided to see what could be accomplished farther south.

Fabius Maximus, Cunctator, 217 B.C.

The defeat at Trasimene, the fear of a siege, the daily meetings of the senate, the death of Flaminius (the people's idol), the eclipse of his faction in the senate, and the return to power of more conservative senators all served to revive the dictatorship—an office defunct for thirty years—in the hands of Quintus Fabius Maximus Verrucosus, a man of illustrious lineage and decidedly conservative views on politics and war. For some unclear reason, Fabius was not appointed by a magistrate with *imperium* (perhaps they were all in the field) but was elected directly by the Centuriate Assembly. Nor was he able to appoint his own master of

the cavalry (*magister equitum*). Instead, the Centuriate Assembly saddled him with M. Minucius Rufus, a rash, impulsive, and headstrong person who always disagreed with Fabius' strategy.

Fabius' strategy avoided battles because the Roman cavalry was much inferior to Hannibal's. He waited until Hannibal should inadvertently work himself into an impasse and be forced to fight under highly unfavorable conditions. Meanwhile, Fabius kept his army always on hilly terrain, where Hannibal could not use his superior cavalry to advantage, and attempted to wear him down by constantly dogging his heels, hampering his movements, and preventing him from acquiring allies, feeding his army, or establishing bases. By this frustrating strategy Fabius hoped to prevent Hannibal from destroying the Roman system of alliances.

This cautious strategy of Fabius is to this day known as "Fabian," and in his own time he gained the title Cunctator, the Delayer. Minucius hated his caution, as did many others. The strategy of attrition is a naturally double-edged weapon and puts as hard a strain on the user as on the enemy. During the electoral campaigns of 217 B.C., popular speakers declared that Rome had not yet brought to bear her full force against Hannibal and urged the election of men who would seek a speedy end to the war. After Fabius and Minucius duly stepped down from their posts, the newly elected consuls, Gaius Terentius Varro and Lucius Aemilius Paullus, expected to make short work of the wily Hannibal.

The Battle of Cannae, 216 B.C.

Overconfident in the overwhelming force of an 80,000-man army, the new consuls marched south to engage Hannibal at Cannae, a small fortress town in Apulia. With only about half as many troops, Hannibal concentrated his Gallic and Spanish infantry in the center and posted his heavily armed African veterans in echelon behind them while his superior cavalry protected the wings. While Hannibal's center sagged inward, the Romans became trapped in a cramped pocket as they were outflanked by the Africans and cut off at the rear by Hannibal's victorious cavalry. Rome's loss was frightful. Only about 15,000 escaped death or capture. Many prominent men lay dead on the field with the consul Aemilius Paullus. Among those who escaped were the consul Varro and two future Roman leaders, Marcus Claudius Marcellus and the young Publius Cornelius Scipio.

Further Cartheginian Successes Never was the outlook brighter for Carthage than in the years between 216 and 212 B.C. The Roman allies were exhausted; some began to waver in their loyalty. Several towns in Apulia and most of Lucania and Bruttium went over to Hannibal. The big cities of Capua in Campania and Syracuse in Sicily revolted against their alliance with Rome and opened their gates to him. His capture of Tarentum in 213 was a major blow. Even some of the Latin towns and colonies began to complain about taxes and the terrific drain on their manpower and economies. More serious still, Philip V of Macedon, who was eager to drive the Romans from their bridgeheads in Illyria, had concluded a mutual assistance pact with Hannibal in 215 B.C.

The Roman Recovery

After Cannae, the Romans returned to the Fabian strategy of attrition and the avoidance of battles such as Cannae. They now began to concentrate on keeping their Italian allies loyal and winning back the cities that had gone over to Hannibal. The strategy was to prevent Hannibal from provisioning his army in Italy or obtaining reinforcements from Carthage. Meanwhile, the Romans vigorously prosecuted the war in Sicily, Illyria, and Spain. These tasks required the expenditure of enormous sums of money and manpower, for a fleet of at least 200 ships had to be maintained and 25 legions at home and abroad fed and supplied.

With their enormous manpower and resources, the Romans not only checked Hannibal but also reconquered disloyal cities. Without reinforcement from Carthage or Spain, Hannibal could not protect his Italian allies and keep his army intact at the same time. He had to stand by helplessly and watch the Romans reconquer his new allies one by one. The Romans won back the Apulian cities, then laid siege to Capua. The fall of Capua in 211 B.C. restored all Campania to Roman control. Two years later the Cunctator reoccupied Tarentum.

The Siege of Syracuse The year before Capua's defeat, Syracuse fell to the famous M. Claudius Marcellus after a long siege. Syracuse had been able to defend herself with artillery and other devices invented by the renowned mathematician and physicist Archimedes. During the siege, Carthage gave Syracuse little effective support except some feeble naval assistance, and the city was finally betrayed from within. It was looted after its capture, its art treasures shipped to Rome, and its independence destroyed. After the fall of Agrigentum in 210 B.C., all Sicily fell under the Roman yoke once more.

The First Macedonian War, 215 to 205
B.C. After his alliance with Hannibal, Philip V of Macedon attempted to seize the Roman protectorates and naval bases in Illyria and invade Italy with Carthaginian help. The Romans thwarted him with their superior naval power and created an anti-Macedonian coalition in Greece by an offensive alliance with the Aetolian League and with other Greek states. Although Philip conducted four brilliant campaigns against the Greek coalition, the Greek war kept Philip so occupied that he was unable to give Hannibal any effective assistance in Italy. A temporary stalemate in both Italy and the Balkans ensued. In 206, the Aetolians finally made a separate peace with Philip, much to Rome's displeasure. Nevertheless, Rome was forced to follow suit in 205 with the Peace of Phoenice.

The War in Spain, 218 to 211 B.C.
Having failed to intercept Hannibal at the Rhône, Publius Scipio had sent his brother Gnaeus to blockade Hannibal's brother Hasdrubal in Spain. After his defeat at the Trebia, Publius had joined Gnaeus. Together, the Scipios deprived Hannibal of any aid from Spain. While they blocked the land routes, the Roman navy, with aid from Massilia, controlled the sea. In 216 or 215, they actually defeated Hasdrubal near Dertosa on the Ebro.

After that, many Spanish tribes went over to the Romans, and the Carthaginian position further weakened when Hasdrubal was recalled to North Africa to suppress the revolt of Syphax, the opportunist king of the Numidians. The capture of Saguntum in 212 was another blow. Then, disaster struck the Romans. Hasdrubal returned in 211, recovered many of his Spanish allies, and mounted a three-pronged attack against the Romans. The Roman army was destroyed, and the Scipios perished.

Scipio Africanus
The future Scipio Africanus, son and nephew of the slain Scipios, had survived Cannae and persuaded the other survivors to keep fighting. In 210 B.C., he petitioned the Centuriate Assembly to assign him to his father's old command in Spain. Although only a private person and having held no rank higher than that of a curule aedile, he was granted the *imperium* and the rank of proconsul, an unprecedented occurrence.

Scipio had received a fine Greek education, was more individualistic than most Roman aristocrats, and had a good sense of humor. Although he showed an unusual degree of kindness and clemency to defeated enemies, he could also be unscrupulous and deceitful. As a general, he possessed courage, resourcefulness, self-confidence, and the power to inspire confidence in his men.

In Spain, Scipio improved Roman weapons and tactics by adopting the longer, well-tempered Spanish sword used for either stabbing or slashing, probably the Spanish javelin, and a more open arrangement of the legion's maniples, groups of two centuries. The old formation could advance with terrific force, but could not easily wheel or turn, and so might be readily outflanked, as at Cannae. Also, it tended to act as a whole and did not permit the individual soldier to fight separately or in smaller units. The new formation, similar to that used by Hannibal at Cannae, was capable of expanding or contracting quickly. These innovations necessitated much more drill and training than ever given to Roman legions in the past, but they soon became more efficient instruments of conquest.

Conquest of Spain After training his troops, Scipio boldly marched through enemy territory in 209 and captured the stronghold of New Carthage by taking advantage of an unusual opportunity. The defenders had neglected the walls of the seaward side of the city, where the water usually was deep. A strong north wind, however, had pushed the water back enough for Roman soldiers to wade through and scale the walls. This piece of luck convinced Scipio's soldiers that he was divinely inspired, a belief that he eagerly encouraged, and from then on they carried out his orders with blind faith.

The capture of New Carthage gave Scipio a fine base, access to local silver mines, a number of ships, and immense quantities of booty, money, and weapons along with 10,000 Spaniards whom the Carthaginians had held hostage to ensure the loyalty of their compatriots. Scipio generously allowed the hostages to return home with a share of the booty. That act earned him much valuable goodwill among the Spanish tribes.

Hasdrubal was able to escape with most of his army after being defeated by Scipio in 208, and he marched away to join Hannibal in Italy. With Hasdrubal gone, however, it was easier for Scipio to defeat the other Carthaginian generals in Spain, especially since they did not get on well with each other. Carthaginian power finally collapsed after the battle of Ilipa in 206 B.C., in which Scipio proved himself a master of encircling tactics. Soon the whole of Spain was in Roman hands, and even the ancient Phoenician colonies of Gades (Cadiz) and Malaga voluntarily became Roman allies.

The Battle at the Metaurus and Death of Hasdrubal, 207 B.C.

The years just before Hasdrubal's crossing of the Alps had not been good for Rome. With so many farmers in the army, agricultural production had declined, many fertile districts had been repeatedly devastated, and famine was widespread. Had Rome not succeeded in obtaining some wheat from Egypt, the food problem would have been acute. Some of the Italian and Latin allies were so exhausted by the war that they refused to supply Rome with any more men or money.

If Hasdrubal had succeeded in effecting a junction with Hannibal's army, Rome might have lost the war. Hannibal did move as far north as Apulia but one of the consuls, Gaius Claudius Nero, barred further advance. After the Romans intercepted Hasdrubal's message asking Hannibal to join him near Rome, Claudius Nero left just enough troops to watch Hannibal and headed north against Hasdrubal with the rest. Two Roman armies converged on Hasdrubal at the Metaurus River in 207. His army was destroyed, and he himself was slain. Several days later his severed head was thrown into Hannibal's camp. Hannibal sadly withdrew to Bruttium.

Two other misfortunes for Hannibal followed swiftly. In 205 B.C., a Punic fleet bringing reinforcements and supplies was lost in a storm. That same year, Hannibal's brother Mago, who had landed at Genua (Genoa) with an army, was defeated, wounded, and compelled to withdraw again to Genua, where he received orders from Carthage to set sail for home. During the voyage, he died.

The End Approaches

In 206 B.C., Scipio returned to Rome and was elected to the consulship. The senate debated how to end the war. Scipio, who had already made a pact with two petty kings of Numidia, Masinissa and Syphax, wanted to invade Africa. Fabius Maximus, the Cunctator, leader of the senate, who did not like the young upstart and his bold strategy, vigorously opposed the African venture. Finally, Scipio obtained the senate's reluctant permission to go to Africa, but not to raise troops. He appealed directly to the people for volunteers for the African expedition, and about 7,000 enlisted. They, together with the two legions already in Sicily, made up the African Expeditionary Force. Fabius' certainty that the expedition would fail did not take into account Scipio's extraordinary boldness, cunning, and charismatic leadership. Nor were those traits appreciated by the conservative-minded M. Porcius Cato (Cato the Elder), who was a quaestor in 204 and was assigned to Scipio in Sicily.[2]

In 204 B.C. Scipio landed near Utica in North Africa and immediately became involved in the quarrels of Syphax and Masinissa, both of whom were in love with Sophonisba, the beautiful daughter of Hasdrubal Gisco, the Carthaginian governor of Numidia. Syphax, the stronger of the two petty kings, won the hand of Sophonisba, deposed his rival, and allied himself with Carthage. Masinissa, now a king without love, land, or throne, found refuge in Scipio's camp.

---

[2]Some scholars date Cato's quaestorship to 205, but that is probably too early, and the story that Cato and Scipio quarreled openly in 204 is probably an anachronistic reflection of their later public hostility.

Scipio had perfidiously entered into peace negotiations with Carthage and Syphax for the sole purpose of lulling their suspicions and learning the nature and disposition of their camps. Having learned what he wanted to know, he surrounded Syphax's camp, which was constructed of osiers and reeds, and set it on fire one night. The Carthaginians, thinking that the fire was accidental, rushed out to help, and both armies were attacked and destroyed.

Masinissa then captured Syphax, returned to Numidia in triumph after winning back all that he had lost, and married Sophonisba. Scipio feared that Sophonisba might charm her husband into an alliance with Carthage and insisted that she be turned over to him to parade in his triumph. Not daring to oppose Scipio, but wishing to spare Sophonisba humiliation as a captive, he provided her with a cup of poison that she proudly drank.

The Carthaginians, imitating Scipio's guile, opened peace negotiations with him but recalled Hannibal from Italy. After Hannibal's arrival in Africa, the peace talks suddenly ceased. The war continued until Scipio and Hannibal fought near Naraggara, a three-day march west of Zama, although Zama is the name conventionally given to the battle.

The Battle of Zama (Naraggara), 202 B.C.
Weak in cavalry, Hannibal hoped that his elephants would overcome the Roman legions. As he had learned to do in Spain, Scipio subdivided the legions into small units with spaces for the elephants to run through without breaking up the formations. Panicked by Roman spears and arrows, the elephants crashed into Hannibal's already weak cavalry, which Masinissa then put completely out of commission. The weakness in cavalry, which Scipio's treacherous actions against Syphax had created, had been Hannibal's undoing. Most of the Carthaginians were killed, but Hannibal escaped.

Peace Terms
It was Hannibal himself who advised Carthage to ask for peace, even though he knew that the terms would be hard. In 201 B.C., Carthage was compelled to surrender all territories outside of Africa, to recognize the independence of Numidia and Masinissa's alliance with Rome, to agree not to wage war either outside of or within Africa without Roman permission, to reduce her fleet to 10 light triremes or coast guard vessels, and to pay an indemnity of 10,000 talents, payable in 50 yearly installments. The power of Carthage to challenge Rome was broken forever. Peace declared, Scipio returned to Rome and celebrated a magnificent triumph, which his rivals in the senate had petulantly tried to deny him. He also received the proud title of Africanus.

Reasons for Roman Success
Hannibal's efforts were not negated by political problems at home. Carthage supported Hannibal and the war consistently to the best of her ability. Scipio's guile and generalship had defeated Hannibal in Africa, but the outcome in Italy had been determined by Roman successes in Spain and by Fabius Maximus, the Cunctator, whose favorite tactics of attrition and exhaustion had frustrated Hannibal's main design of wrecking Rome's confederate alliance and afforded time for the mobilization of Rome's enormous war potential. By delaying he saved the state (*cunctando restituit rem*).

The Fate of Hannibal
Hannibal revealed unusual talents as an administrator during his postwar career. After the war, the Carthaginian aristocracy tried to protect its wealth by corruption and by forcing the burden of paying the war indemnity onto the lower classes. The people turned to Hannibal, the popular war hero remembered for his fairness and good treatment of ordinary soldiers, and elected him *shophet,* or judge, in 196 B.C.

Hannibal established a system of taxation based on income and ability to pay and made the government accountable to the people for its expenditures. Hannibal's financial administration was so efficient that in 191 B.C., only ten years after Zama, Carthage offered immediate payment of the forty remaining installments of her war indemnity. Rome refused the offer. Commerce and industry revived as never before, and Carthage again became one of the busiest ports of the Mediterranean. Nevertheless, Carthage soon lost the benefits of efficient administration. Powerful Romans became alarmed at Carthage's remarkable recovery. Acting upon his political enemies' accusation of planning another war, they demanded the surrender of Hannibal as a war criminal. To save his life, Hannibal escaped from Carthage and took refuge in the East. Unfortunately, the Romans' attention now turned in that direction, too. Eventually they hounded him to death in 183 B.C. as they added that part of the world to their growing empire (p. 112–114).

X

War and Imperialism in the Hellenistic East, 200 to 133 B.C.

No sooner had Rome conquered Carthage and won dominion over the western Mediterranean than she began to assert herself in the eastern half, too. The Romans had no consistent policy or program for overseas expansion, but their motives and actions follow a complex pattern similar to that which has been traced through their rise in Italy and their first two wars with Carthage. There is no single explanation. Several factors operated at once, with sometimes one and sometimes another being more prominent, and all interacting to reinforce each other.

The Background of Roman Expansion in the East The empire created by the military genius of Alexander had originally embraced Macedonia, Greece, most of Asia Minor, Egypt, and the entire Ancient Near East, extending from the Mediterranean to central Asia and northern India. After Alexander's death in 323 B.C., that empire had fallen apart in the struggle for power among his generals, not one of whom was able to establish himself as sole ruler and preserve its unity. Before 275 B.C., three dynasties, descended from three of his generals (Antigonus the one-eyed, Ptolemy son of Lagus, and Seleucus Nicator), had established powerful kingdoms: Antigonid Macedon embraced Macedon and from time to time large parts of Greece; Ptolemaic or Lagid Egypt included Egypt, Cyrene, bridgeheads along the Red Sea and East Africa, Phoenicia, several islands in the Aegean, and some cities along the coast of Asia Minor and the Thracian Chersonese (Gallipoli Peninsula); Seleucid Syria laid claim to most of Persia's old empire embracing the western and southern parts of Asia Minor, northern Syria, Mesopotamia, Persia, and at one time even northwestern India (Pakistan), Afghanistan, and Turkestan in central Asia.

Among the minor Hellenistic states was Pergamum, in the northwest corner of Asia Minor. Under Attalus I and his successors in the second half of the third century B.C., Pergamum, enriched by agriculture and a flourishing foreign trade, blossomed as a center of art and literature and became a champion of Hellenism. Another important small state was the island republic of Rhodes, which lay off the southwestern tip of Asia Minor. Like Pergamum, it, too, was a brilliant cultural center, but it owed its material prosperity solely to seaborne trade, which it guarded with a small but efficient navy. In Greece, the once-powerful city-states of Thebes, Athens, and Sparta still maintained a precarious independence. There were also two political and military federations. One was the Aetolian League of small townships and rural communities, which embraced most of central Greece north of the Gulf of Corinth by 250 B.C. The other was the rival Achaean League, which included many minor cities of the Peloponnesus, but not Sparta, Elis, and Messenia.

The existence of the small Hellenistic states depended upon the balance of power established among the three big kingdoms of Egypt, Syria, and Macedon between 277 and 225 B.C. If one of the major powers succeeded in expanding its influence and territory, the other two combined against it. Although none of the three liked this balance of power, it was the salvation of Pergamum, Rhodes, the Achaean and Aetolian leagues, and toward the end of the century, even Egypt. When it was finally disturbed, Pergamum, Rhodes, the two Greek leagues, and Egypt repeatedly appealed to Rome to help restore the balance. They never dreamt that eventually all, both great and small, would become subject to Roman domination.

Antiochus III of Syria and Philip V of Macedon While the Second Punic War was raging in the West, the balance of power was being disturbed in the East by the ambitions and warlike activities of two young monarchs, Antiochus III (the Great) of Syria and Philip V of Macedon. In 223 B.C., when Antiochus became king as a youth of eighteen, the Seleucid Empire had already crumbled into almost total disruption. By 205, however, he had completed the conquest of large areas of Asia Minor, reconquered Armenia and northern Iran, and crossed the Hindu Kush mountains into the valley of the Indus, where he received 150 valuable war elephants as tribute. On his way back to Antioch, he assumed the title of Antiochus the Great, and his exploits were hailed throughout the Greek world as second only to those of Alexander.

In Macedon, Philip V was understandably apprehensive about the Roman attitude toward him at the end of the First Macedonian War (205 B.C.). To strengthen his position on the Adriatic coast vis à vis the Roman protectorates, he apparently acquired some additional Illyrian territory shortly after the war. In the winter of 203/02 B.C., Philip turned his attention eastward to an opportunity to restore Macedonian control over the Aegean. That had always been a major object of Antigonid ambitions in competition with the Ptolemies of

Egypt. Egypt had enjoyed *amicitia* (friendship) with Rome since 273 B.C. and was now badly governed under the rule of the child-king Ptolemy V (Epiphanes), who was at the mercy of corrupt and worthless advisors.

In 203/02 B.C., Philip sought to acquire naval power by supporting the raids of Aetolian pirates in return for a share of the profits. Philip then used those profits to build a fleet of his own. On the Greek mainland, he boldly strengthened his position wherever he could and reneged on his agreement to restore certain territories to the Aetolian League. The Aetolians asked the Romans to intervene in Greece again, but the latter refused because they were still occupied with Carthage. Also, many Roman senators were resentful that the Aetolians had made a separate peace with Philip in 206 B.C.

Having acquired a fleet, however, Philip overplayed his hand in 201. Instead of being content with attacking Egyptian possessions in the Aegean, he attacked many free Greek cities, enslaved their populations, threatened the naval power of Rhodes, and seized control of the Black Sea trade lanes, which were of vital importance to the grain trade of both Rhodes and Athens. Rhodes declared war and persuaded Attalus I of Pergamum, an old friend of Rome, to do likewise. After a number of naval engagements, Attalus and the Rhodians concluded that they were unable to defeat Philip without outside help. In 201 B.C., they appealed to Rome and sent embassies to wait upon the senate. The senate was in a more receptive mood than it had been the year before, when it had rudely rebuffed an Aetolian embassy bringing complaints against Philip.

The ambassadors charged Philip with aggression against Pergamum, and took advantage of the hysterical atmosphere caused by the Hannibalic War and the bitter resentment engendered by Philip's opportunistic alliance with Hannibal after Cannae. They accused Philip of having made a secret pact with Antiochus III to carve up the foreign possessions of Egypt, which had aided Rome with food in the darkest days of the Hannibalic War. They even insinuated that the pact was ultimately aimed at Rome. Though this "fact" may have been a propagandistic lie to scare the Romans, it fell on receptive senatorial ears.

The Romans had used Greek allies during the First Macedonian War and used them badly. Roman prestige among those allies had suffered, and Philip had gotten off rather easily. Now was a chance to refurbish Rome's tarnished laurels by clipping Philip's wings in ways that would help Rome's friends, punish an enemy who had not suffered much before, and preserve the beneficial balance of power that Philip was now upsetting in the East. To show that they were serious, the senators voted to send an embassy of three men to make the rounds of the Greek East and gain support for the conditions that they decreed he would have to accept to avoid war: He must not make war against any Greeks and must submit any disagreements with them to arbitration. In the elections for 200 B.C., P. Sulpicius Galba, who had commanded Roman forces in Greece during the First Macedonian War, succeeded in becoming consul for the second time, with Macedon as his province.

The Second Macedonian War, 200 to 196 B.C.   When Galba took office and proposed that the Centuriate Assembly declare war on Macedon, the proposal was rejected by those who controlled the top two classes of centuries: war-weary veterans and wealthy creditors to whom the state had not repaid money loaned to fight Hannibal. Convinced that he had nothing to fear, Philip ignored repeated warnings and attacked the Greeks more boldly. Now the senatorial leaders had to obtain a declaration of war at all costs. They placated the rich by paying off creditors with public land and mollified many veterans by exempting from service those who had served under Scipio. These measures and, perhaps, reports of Philip's stepped-up attacks were enough to obtain a declaration of war at a second vote of the *comitia*.

Motives and Miscalculations   The last thing that Philip wanted was another war with Rome while he was expanding eastward. He probably thought that Roman interests in Greece were too slight and the Romans' exhaustion after the Second Punic War too great to make them choose war over peace if he called their bluff. Philip did not understand the Romans. There were many reasons why Roman leaders and even Roman voters, once their immediate concerns were satisfied, would be willing to go to war.

Both a need for land and philhellenism, love for Greek culture, can be ruled out. The Romans had more than enough land in northern Italy and Spain and did not keep any territory in Greece after the First Macedonian War. Moreover, Roman senators did not sacrifice Rome's interest to any love of Greek culture.

Several reasons, however, aptly illustrate the general motives for Roman imperialism after the Second Punic War. As was so often the case, fear, pride, and revenge were at work. Although the Romans were not so greatly influenced by concern for markets and raw materials as modern imperial powers have been, economic motives also existed. Rome's maritime allies among the Greek cities of southern Italy and Sicily were very interested in eastern Mediterranean trade, which Philip was disrupting. At the beginning of the Second Punic War, the Romans had taken Malta, Carthage's gateway to the eastern trade routes, and during the war Egyptian grain had become important. As the *lex Claudia* of 218 shows (p. 96), many Romans were now involved in overseas trade. Such individuals would not have been reluctant to speak and vote in favor of a war that could improve their economic opportunities. Moreover, supplying Roman armies could be a lucrative business.

In addition, the Greek East was the source of the most skilled and intelligent slaves. Galba had already profited handsomely from capturing slaves during the First Macedonian War, and the Roman market for such slaves was growing rapidly. Another war with Macedon would also be the source of other valuable booty, which always attracted many Romans, noble and common. In addition, as the experience with Carthage had shown, rich states could be made to pay lucrative indemnities when defeated in war.

Overseas wars had also whetted aristocratic ambitions at Rome. The great military glory won by Scipio against Hannibal had given him preeminent *dignitas* and *auctoritas*. Publius Sulpicius Galba and those who would be eligible for consulships after him could hope to equal Scipio's exploits in another great overseas war. Finally, the huge armies involved in such wars also increased the numbers of ex-soldiers who could become useful clients in the political struggles of the Forum, while the acquisition of rich and powerful friends abroad would increase the resources and prestige necessary for success in competition with other aristocrats. Those who advocated another war with Philip were probably not unmindful of those facts.

The First Two Years, 200 to 198 B.C.

The delay in gaining approval of the war meant that the campaigning season was almost over before Galba could assemble an army. Nevertheless, he went to Greece and established winter quarters to demonstrate Rome's commitment. In the course of the next year, Galba's good behavior and the Romans' determination persuaded the wary Aetolians to join in the new war. Athens, which Philip had earlier attacked, joined also, but other Greeks remained neutral and waited to see which horse they should back in an uncertain race.

Titus Quinctius Flamininus

In 198 B.C., the war took a dramatic new turn with the arrival of the new consul Titus Quinctius Flamininus. Charismatic, cultured, and fluent in Greek, Flamininus electrified the Greek world with the slogan "Freedom and self-determination of all Greeks." With wider support, Flamininus maneuvered Philip out of nearly all Greece except the key fortresses of Demetrias in Thessaly, Chalcis in Euboea, and Corinth in the Peloponnesus. Philip, now confined to Thessaly, sought a peace conference with Flamininus. Although the two men understood and admired each other, the conference itself achieved nothing and broke up over Philip's refusal to surrender the three fortresses, which he had inherited from his ancestors. Flamininus,

however, was rewarded for his military success by being made a proconsul to continue the war.

The Battle of Cynoscephalae, 197 B.C.

The war was decided the next year at Cynoscephalae (Dog's Heads), a ridge of hills in Thessaly. The two armies were about equally matched. The right wing of the Macedonian army made a brilliant breakthrough on the Roman left, but the Roman right routed the Macedonian left before it could close ranks. The Romans gained the victory, however, when a quick-thinking tribune detached some maniples from the rear of the successful Roman right and attacked the ponderous phalanx of the Macedonian right wing from behind. Accordingly, the greater tactical flexibility of the Roman legion's more open manipular organization proved decisive.

Peace Terms

Philip lost the battle of Cynoscephalae and the war. He had no other army, Macedon was exposed to invasion, and peace had to be obtained at any price. The terms were better than expected, for Flamininus and the majority of Roman senators did not want to destroy the Macedonian state (as the Aetolians demanded) now that Philip had been humbled. Macedon served as a buffer against the restless Balkan tribes to the north. Also, Philip might be a useful ally to Rome someday, perhaps more useful than the Aetolians.

Late in 197 B.C., Philip was compelled to recognize the freedom and independence of the Greeks; to withdraw all his garrisons from Greece, the Aegean, and Illyria; to surrender his fleet; to reduce his army to 5,000 men; and to pay an indemnity of 1,000 talents, half at once and the rest in 10 annual installments. The infuriated Aetolians demanded the whole of Thessaly as their share of victory, but Flamininus would concede them only Phocis and the western part of Thessaly. Even worse, he allowed Philip to make jokes at their expense during the peace negotiations.

The Proclamation of Flamininus

In July of 196 B.C., Flamininus made a grand appearance at the Isthmian Games at Corinth and, as proconsul, proclaimed in the name of the Roman senate the promised freedom and independence of the Greek states. They were to be subject to their own laws, without garrisons, and without tribute. A pandemonium of joy and thanksgiving broke loose, unparalleled since the day Alexander proclaimed the right of all Greeks to return to their homes. Gold coins, imitating the famous gold staters of Alexander, were struck bearing the portrait of Titus Flamininus. In some cities he was even worshipped as a god—the first Roman ever to receive divine honors—a point not lost on other ambitious Roman aristocrats.

For a while, some of the Greeks, especially the pro-Roman aristocrats, enjoyed their newly proclaimed freedom enormously. As a Roman aristocrat, Flamininus understood and admired the aristocrats of Greece and desired to perpetuate their domination of the masses. He knew little about the poor and cared less. He regarded their struggle for the cancellation of debts, the redistribution of land, and other social and economic reforms as subversive activity.

Flamininus was even prevailed upon by his aristocratic Greek friends to declare war on Sparta. Nabis, the king of Sparta, had tried to increase the number of landholding citizens who could serve in an enlarged Spartan army and restore ancient Spartan glory. He abolished the malignant plague of debt, broke up the large estates, distributed the land fairly, enfranchised the helots (Spartan serfs), and proclaimed liberty to captives and slaves. His kingdom had become a refuge to homeless exiles. Although Sparta had in a short time become a fairly strong power, she was unable to resist the might of Rome. Flamininus reaped even greater glory, Roman soldiers carried off much plunder, and the Roman treasury received a hefty indemnity of 500 talents.

Flamininus and the Romans had no romantic notions about Greek freedom. Their concern was to keep Greece, with its strategic location and valuable manpower, politically fragmented and out of the hands of any strong power without the trouble and expense of annexing it themselves. Indeed, they expected that as grateful clients the various Greek states would follow Roman policy and preserve the status quo. Unfortunately, there was always someone trying either to upset it within Greece or to take advantage of the situation from without.

The Aggressions of Antiochus the Great, 196 to 192 B.C.

No sooner had Flamininus pulled his legions out of Greece and celebrated a glorious triumph in Rome than the senate became alarmed at the activities of Antiochus III as he continued to reconstitute the empire of Seleucus I. While Philip had been occupied with fighting Rome, Antiochus had attacked and defeated the Egyptians at Panium in northern Palestine in 200 B.C. Seven years later, he concluded a marital alliance between his daughter, Cleopatra I, and the young Egyptian king, Ptolemy V. Then he began to annex the few free coastal cities like Ephesus left in Asia Minor and Thrace.

The growth of Antiochus' power alarmed Pergamum, which had also once formed part of the old Seleucid domains. Pergamum's new king, Eumenes II, decided to follow his father's example of appealing to Rome. In response to the appeals of Eumenes and of some Greek cities in Asia Minor, the senate authorized Flamininus to negotiate with Antiochus in 196 B.C. Flamininus warned the king to keep his hands off the independent Greek cities in Asia Minor, not to cross the Hellespont (Dardanelles), and to evacuate all towns recently taken from Egypt. The king replied correctly that Flamininus had no right to speak on behalf of the Greek cities in Asia Minor, and that if the Romans would leave him alone, he would gladly leave them alone. The Romans were not yet ready to go to war, but influential men were laying the basis of future action, which was eagerly anticipated and promoted by Scipio Africanus and his supporters.

A year later (195 B.C.), Hannibal, forced into exile from Carthage (p. 107), arrived at Ephesus. In response to a question from Antiochus, Hannibal replied that the only chance for victory against Rome lay in the creation of a united front of all her enemies. Antiochus would have to come to terms with Philip V, with Egypt, with Pergamum—perhaps even make concessions. Antiochus thanked Hannibal for his sage advice and ignored it. He decided to ally himself instead with the little powers of Greece, a decision that was to prove extremely unwise.

The War with Antiochus III, 192 to 189

B.C. In Greece, the disgruntled Aetolians had become violently anti-Roman, particularly because the peace settlement of 197 B.C. restricted their favorite occupation, plundering their neighbors. They tried to enlist Philip's help in throwing off the hated Roman yoke, but remembering how they had urged Flamininus to dismantle his kingdom, he rejected their overtures. Antiochus was so ill advised as to accept their invitation; he landed in Greece in 192 B.C. with a puny force of 10,000 men and was promptly elected Aetolian commander-in-chief.

By such actions, Antiochus had triggered the responses that characterized Roman imperialism: fear, vengefulness, greed, and desire for glory. The Romans immediately made common cause with Philip against Antiochus. The Romans were now allied with Philip, Pergamum, Rhodes, the Achaean League, Numidia, and even Carthage. They easily defeated Antiochus at Thermopylae, a position historically impossible to hold. Afterwards, Antiochus made his escape to Chalcis and set sail for Ephesus.

In view of the probable magnitude of further struggles with Antiochus, it would have been advantageous to elect Scipio Africanus, the greatest living Roman general, to the consulship. Because Africanus had been consul in 194 and was not eligible for reelection until ten years later, the people elected his younger brother, Lucius Cornelius Scipio, in the expectation that the latter would appoint him as legate and permit him to assume actual command. Lucius did just that. Early in 190 B.C., the Scipios sailed from Brundisium with a small army, took command of the larger army already in Greece, and began their march through Macedonia to the Hellespont with Philip's active assistance.

The conquest of the East would have been impossible for the Romans without command of the sea, which they secured partly through their own tactical skill and the effective assistance of the Rhodian and Pergamene navies and partly through Antiochus' failure to utilize effectively the talents of Hannibal as a general and strategist. Although Hannibal requested a fleet and an army to open up a second front against Rome in the West, Antiochus merely entrusted him with bringing naval reinforcements from Syria to the northern Aegean. A Rhodian fleet quickly defeated Hannibal, and the Scipios' naval forces defeated Antiochus' main fleet a few weeks later. Having no naval opposition, the Roman army easily crossed the Hellespont.

Antiochus Offers Peace Terms Antiochus offered to abandon Thrace, break off relations with the Aetolian Greeks, and recognize the independence of the Greek cities in Asia Minor, as Flamininus had demanded seven years before. In addition, he agreed to pay half the costs of the war. There was a time when the Romans would have made peace with him, had he merely agreed not to cross the Hellespont and to refrain from attacking the cities of Thrace. Now, his far more sweeping offers came too late. Nothing would satisfy the ambitious Scipios short of the surrender of all Asia Minor north and west of the Taurus Mountains and payment of the entire costs of the war, terms which Antiochus rejected.

The Battle of Magnesia The battle for Asia took place near Magnesia ad Sipylum in 190 B.C. The Romans easily won despite the absence of the Scipios because of illness. Antiochus was hampered by poor generalship, poor equipment, and lack of coordination among the various units of his huge but ill-assorted army. At Magnesia, Antiochus lost the war and the Seleucid Empire lost its power.

The Peace Treaty of Apamea, 188 B.C. A peace treaty was finally worked out at Apamea in 188 B.C. The king was obliged to give up all his possessions in Asia Minor north of the Taurus Mountains and west of the Halys River, to surrender his navy, and to pay 15,000 talents, one of the largest indemnities exacted in ancient times. Some of the vast territory that Antiochus surrendered in Asia Minor to the Romans, who were not yet prepared to administer so large an area, went to the Greek cities and the Republic of Rhodes in return for their help; but the lion's share went to Pergamum, whose original size was increased tenfold to an area almost equal to modern Great Britain's. The enlarged kingdom of Pergamum, writes Polybius, was now inferior to none.

The Aftermath Antiochus the Great was assassinated after robbing a temple at Susa in 187 B.C. After Magnesia, Hannibal had escaped first to Crete and then to Bithynia, which was at war with Pergamum. He won a naval battle for his friend Prusias I of Bithynia, but Flamininus finally arrived in 183 B.C. and compelled Prusias to help him capture Hannibal, who frustrated the plan by taking poison and dying as proudly as he had lived.

Earlier in the same year, Hannibal's greatest opponent, Scipio Africanus, also died under unhappy circumstances. Cato the Elder, jealous of Scipio's military achievements, had never agreed with Scipio's aggressive overseas policy and unorthodox political career. He kept up relentless political and judicial attacks on Scipio, his family, and his friends. In 183 B.C., Africanus finally retired to his country estate and died a short time later.

Philip V had done comparatively well since his defeat at Cynoscephalae, although he did not reap many permanent advantages from his alliance with Rome against Antiochus. He received only a few paltry talents and the promise of a few towns in Thessaly—a promise that the Romans ultimately failed to keep. He did try, when it was almost too late, to cultivate good relations with the other Hellenistic states—Egypt, Syria, and even Pergamum. He also changed the Macedonian constitution to permit the towns under his rule the right of local self-government so that he might pose as the champion of the oppressed masses in Greece. At the same time, Philip set about building up the economic life of Macedon.

Philip's last days, however, were far from happy. He had put his own son Demetrius to death on charges of treason that were later found false. After learning the horrid truth, Philip, tortured with remorse, could no longer sleep and fell an easy victim to illness. He died in 179 B.C., and his eldest son, Perseus, succeeded to the throne.

The Third Macedonian War, 171 to 167
B.C. The Third Macedonian War was caused partly by the reawakening power of Macedon, partly by the intrigues of Pergamum's King Eumenes II, and partly by the chaotic conditions in Greece after the dismal defeat of Antiochus and the Aetolians. They gave convenient pretexts for war to the ambitious aristocrats in the senate who saw Macedon as their next opportune target after intervening wars in Spain and northern Italy had come to a close. The Greeks, moreover, had perverted the freedom proclaimed at the Isthmian Games of 196 into the chaos and anarchy of class conflict. They had become a danger to themselves and a constant source of worry and annoyance to the senate.

The first three years of the Third Macedonian War provided a pitiable exhibition of incompetence on both sides. The Roman commanders marched to and fro to no purpose and made mistakes that a more resolute and daring enemy than Perseus could have turned into defeats as disastrous as those of the Caudine Forks, Trasimene, or Cannae. His excessive caution and misguided hope that he could placate Rome without a humiliating capitulation prevented him from taking these opportunities.

Lucius Aemilius Paullus and the Battle of Pydna, 168 B.C. Lucius Aemilius Paullus had a sincere appreciation of Greek art and culture. He had been consul in 182 B.C. and accepted a second consulship in 168 only on condition that his conduct of the war not be hampered by unsolicited and unwanted advice. He brought Perseus to a decisive battle at Pydna. This battle demonstrated once more, as did those at Cynoscephalae and Magnesia, that the phalanx was now a thoroughly obsolete battle formation.

Rome profited so greatly from the confiscation of Perseus' treasury and the yearly tribute imposed on the Macedonians that all Roman citizens ceased to be subject to direct taxes.

Macedon after Pydna

In Macedon, the Romans decided to try an experiment apparently modeled after the Greek leagues. They abolished the monarchy and replaced it by four independent republics—separate; partially disarmed; and deprived of the rights of alliance, intermarriage, or trade with each other. The Romans also made the royal mines and domains the property of the Roman state, closed the royal gold and silver mines for 10 years, forbade the export of timber, and exacted an annual tribute of 100 talents, which was half the amount of the land tax formerly paid to the kings.

The Macedonians were far less concerned about having their form of government changed than about their unity. They had never regarded their monarchy as an oppressive evil but as the symbol of their national unity. The kingdom of Macedon had more nearly resembled a nation than any other state in the ancient world. It was not a land of city-states like Greece or Italy; it was not a loose confederation of cities like the Achaean League; nor was it a universal state held together solely by the monarchy like the empire of the Seleucids. It was one people in ethnic background, language, religion, customs, and government. The Roman experiment violated the very nature and traditions of the Macedonian state.

The Fourth Macedonian War, 149 to 148 B.C.

It is little wonder, then, that within two decades the Roman experiment failed. Andriscus, an upstart pretender, probably the son of a clothmaker, was able to convince the people that he was the son of Perseus, and they rallied around him. He restored the monarchy in 149 B.C., reunited the kingdom, and even overcame a small Roman army sent against him. After defeating him with a larger army, the Romans converted Macedon into the province of Macedonia in 148 B.C. and thereby ended the political existence of Macedon for the rest of Antiquity.

Greece after Pydna, 168 B.C.

The Roman treatment of Macedon was mild compared with the punishment inflicted upon Greece. In Aetolia, the Romans lent troops to their contemptible henchmen to carry out a purge of Macedonian sympathizers, probably the most intelligent and democratic elements of the population. In Achaea, they deported to Italy 1,000 of the leading citizens (including the historian Polybius), whose names they found among the papers that Perseus had neglected to destroy. For 16 years, the Achaean hostages were kept interned without a trial or hearing and were not released until after 700 of them had died. In 167 B.C., the most horrible and revolting brutality was inflicted upon Epirus, against which Rome had no legitimate complaint, where 70 towns were destroyed and 150,000 people were dragged off to the slave market, to the profit of Aemilius Paullus and his soldiers.

The worst was yet to come. In 146 B.C., Lucius Mummius arrived in Corinth to punish it and the Achaean League for rebellion against Rome. He turned his troops loose upon it, sacked it, and razed it to the ground. He massacred many of its inhabitants, sold many more as slaves, and shipped its priceless art treasures to Rome.

After the destruction of Corinth, the Romans dissolved the Achaean and most of the other Greek leagues to break the last desperate but hopeless attempts of the Greek people to win back their independence. They destroyed the militant democracies and set up petty tyrants or aristocratic oligarchies in their place. Each city-state now had separate relations with Rome, but the governor of Macedonia was empowered to intervene, to settle disputes, and to preserve public order. A century later, Augustus made Greece a separate province.

Rhodes and Pergamum　After Pydna (168 B.C.) the hand of Rome also fell heavily upon Rhodes. This faithful friend had made one mistake. Just before Pydna, she had tried to mediate between Rome and Perseus, not so much out of sympathy toward Perseus as out of fear that Rome might become the unbalanced power in the eastern Mediterranean. Rome took offense at this attempted mediation. A praetor even proposed a declaration of war, and well might it have passed had not old Cato stood up and made a strong plea in defense of the Rhodians.

Although Rhodes humbly repented of her mistakes, she did not escape Roman vengeance. She was stripped of the territories in Asia Minor given to her after Magnesia (an annual loss of 110 talents) and was prohibited from importing shipbuilding timber from Macedonia. Delos was given to Athens in 167/66 B.C. and made a customs-free port. The resulting competition from Delos reduced the income of Rhodes as a banking, shipping, and commercial center from about 166 talents annually to about 25. The loss of revenue from her Asiatic possessions and from harbor dues and banking so crippled the finances of Rhodes that she was compelled to reduce her navy and was no longer able to keep piracy in check in the eastern seas.

Eumenes II, king of Pergamum, who had done so much to betray the Hellenistic world into the increasingly ruthless hand of the Romans, incurred the senate's displeasure because of suspected collusion with Perseus. He was punished by confiscation of territory and hounded by hostile Roman commissions sent to Asia Minor to gather evidence against him. Thus did Rome reward her most devoted and servile ally in the Near East.

When Eumenes died in 159 B.C., he was succeeded by his brother, Attalus II, who followed his policy of friendship and subservience to Rome and of philanthropy toward the Greek city-states. He continued also to promote Pergamum as a cultural and intellectual capital and maintained a Greek cultural offensive against the resurgence of native Near Eastern cultures. He was followed in 138 B.C. by Attalus III, whose parentage is uncertain. Like Louis XVI of France, he preferred his studies and hobbies to being a king. He did serious research in botany, zoology, medicine, scientific agriculture, and gardening. Having no direct heirs, he bequeathed his kingdom to the Roman People and thereby closed, with his early death in 133 B.C., the history of Pergamum as a separate state.

The Seleucid Monarchy　The Seleucid Empire was not a national state like Macedon, nor a city-state like Athens or Rome. It was rather a universal state consisting of many ethnic groups, languages, and even forms of government. All were more or less loosely held together by the military prestige, personality, royalty, and divinity of the Seleucids, heirs of Alexander the Great and of the Persian kings. The power of the king and his claim to royalty and even to divinity rested ultimately upon military victory—a sign of both royal virtue and divine favor. Defeat in war signified the loss of these vital prerequisites and tended to destroy the claim of the Seleucid monarchy to the loyalty and allegiance of the various regional rulers, provincial governors, satraps, and native kings. Therefore, the defeat of Antiochus III at Magnesia dealt a shattering blow to the unity and stability of the Seleucid Empire.

Most of Asia Minor had gone to Pergamum and Rhodes. Armenia freed itself. The Parthians seized large areas of Iran. Farther to the east, the huge kingdom of Bactria, having snatched the eastern portions of Iran, broke off. New Arab kingdoms arose in southern Palestine, Transjordan, and southern Syria. Two decades or so later a new Jewish state sprang up in Judea.

The Jewish Revolt of the Maccabees
Antiochus IV (175 to 164 B.C.), a younger son of Antiochus III, had tried to turn Judea into a strongly Hellenized city-state as a buffer between Egypt and Syria. This program aroused some discontent among the Jews, but no open revolt occurred until Antiochus decided to devote the temple of Jahweh to the worship of

Baal Shamin ("Lord of the Heavens"), a universal deity whom the Greeks identified with Olympian Zeus and Hellenized Jews with Jahweh. Simultaneously, he revoked the decree of his father, Antiochus III, which had permitted the Jews to live and worship according to the law of Moses.

A priestly landowner named Judas Maccabaeus and his brothers, Jonathan and Simon, aroused non-Hellenized Jews to rebellion, gathered together an army, and inflicted a series of defeats upon the king's troops. Aided by the death of Antiochus IV in Armenia late in 164 B.C. and by the subsequent disruption of the Seleucid Empire, the Maccabees rooted out every last vestige of Hellenism in Jerusalem and restored the ancient temple state. In 161 B.C. the Romans saw a chance to erect a barrier to further Seleucid ambitions in Palestine and Egypt by recognizing the Jewish temple state as an ally.

A Review of Roman Imperialism in the East, 200 to 133 B.C.

After the Second Punic War, Rome's attention was drawn permanently to the East out of the desire of many Romans to repair their reputation among the Greeks, gain revenge against Philip V of Macedon for supporting Hannibal, and prevent any of the Hellenistic successors of Alexander the Great from becoming so powerful that they would seek to expand in the West. Other Romans, who may or may not have shared these motives, favored Roman intervention in Eastern affairs in the hope of securing personal glory, political advantage, financial gain, or a combination thereof.

The Romans were not imperialistic in the sense that they wanted to seize the territories of Greece and the Hellenistic monarchies. They did everything that they could think of to avoid a direct takeover. Certainly, however, they were imperialistic in wanting to subordinate the Hellenistic East to their own interests by the use of proxies like Aetolia, Rhodes, and Pergamum, or by the force of their own armies when other tactics failed. On the other hand, the attempts of smaller Hellenistic states to use Rome as much as she used them and the expansionistic moves of the kings of Macedon and Seleucid Syria excited Roman suspicions and invited Roman military intervention even when the Romans were reluctant to get involved.

The Romans were always successful in their eastern wars because the individual Greek states and kingdoms were never able to set aside their own ambitions and petty jealousies to present a united front against Rome. Many Roman leaders in their ambition to win military glory and other benefits of victory became arrogant in the exercise of power and took every advantage of Greek weakness to divide and rule, not directly, but indirectly through subservient allies. Moreover, the Greeks, smug in the confidence of their superiority over the "western barbarians," failed to adopt Roman military improvements and thereby reduced their individual chances of success in battle against Rome's legions.

In the process Rome destroyed the Hellenistic states politically by policies designed to weaken them. She also ruined them economically by wholesale plundering and the imposition of profitable indemnities. Therefore, the vitality of Hellenistic culture was steadily sapped, and the Greek East went into a long period of decline.

XI

Roman Imperialism in the West, 200 to 133 B.C.

While the Romans fruitlessly pursued policies that sought control without territorial takeovers in the East, they were actively engaged in territorial imperialism in northern Italy and Spain. Although the same motives applied to the western wars as to the eastern, the Romans also consciously sought territorial acquisition in northern Italy and Spain because they had no other possible means to exercise control over areas that experience had shown were vital to Roman security and had to be kept out of potentially hostile hands. In both northern Italy and Spain, people were still loosely organized in agrarian tribes. There were no large city-states or territorial monarchies that the Romans could manipulate to maintain control indirectly. There was no sophisticated political elite whom they could co-opt and no shared body of concepts or values that could provide a basis for peaceful coexistence. Therefore, outright conquest was the only possible solution from the Roman point of view right from the start.

Northern Italy   The Gallic tribes of northern Italy had periodically attacked Roman territory or sided with Rome's enemies ever since 390 B.C. Under the leadership of Gaius Flaminius just before the Second Punic War, the Romans had begun to satisfy the need for both land and security by systematically subduing the Cisalpine

tribes and colonizing the area that they called the near side of the Po (*Cispadana* as opposed to the *Transpadana*). This effort had been interrupted and undone by the war with Hannibal, whom the Gauls supported. As soon as the Romans were free of the Second Macedonian War, therefore, they began to settle the score with the Gauls of northern Italy and founded colonies on both sides of the Po between 197 and 175 B.C. For example, they occupied and colonized Mediolanum (Milan) in 196 B.C. Small market towns and administrative centers rapidly sprang up as the country became settled by the many individual farmers who were encouraged to move north and take up land.

After the conquest and settlement of the central region of northern Italy, the Romans turned to the coastal areas. In 181 B.C., they founded a Latin colony at Aquileia, at the head of the Adriatic, which served as a springboard for the later conquest of Istria and the Dalmatian coast. During the late Republic and early Empire, Aquileia was one of the busiest shipping and commercial harbors of Italy (see map on p. 102).

On the west coast, the conquest of the hardy but culturally backward Ligurian tribes was a long and difficult operation attended by several Roman defeats, some victories, and some notorious atrocities. By 172, the Romans had subdued both the Italian and the French Rivieras as far as the borders of Massilia. While these Roman and Latin colonies were being planted along the Ligurian coast in the North, 40,000 Ligurians were moved south and settled on vacant public land near Beneventum in central Samnium (see map on p. 70)

The building of many roads was equally important for the occupation and settlement of the North. In a short time northern Italy had become an integral part of peninsular Italy. The wars ceased, and the use of the Latin language spread. Rome was rapidly becoming the capital of a united Italy.

The Subjugation of Spain

When the Romans had driven the Carthaginians from Spain in the Second Punic War, they stayed to prevent any other state from using it as a base for another attack on Italy. They were also influenced by tales of its fabulous mineral wealth and the remarkable fertility of its soil. They hoped to extract enough wealth from Spain to pay for the costs of its occupation, to recoup the staggering losses suffered from the Second Punic War, and perhaps to finance future wars as well.

The Romans encountered unexpected difficulties. Not only did Spain have no large self-governing states or kingdoms that could be held responsible for the collection of tribute or the maintenance of law and order, but also large areas that the Carthaginians had claimed in the interior and in the western part of the peninsula had never been subdued or even explored by them. The tribes living in these backward areas had long been in the habit of raiding the richer and more civilized parts of Spain formerly controlled by the Carthaginians and now by the Romans. To protect their recent gains, the Romans were obliged to make further conquests.

Spain, however, was cut up by its mountains into thousands of small communities and as many separate clans. Communications among them were difficult, and access to them was practically impossible. The Romans could not conquer them in a few pitched battles, as they had conquered Macedon or Asia Minor, because the Spaniards formed small armed bands skilled in making sudden raids and vanishing as rapidly as they came. The Romans

were completely baffled by this guerrilla warfare. War raged almost continuously until 133 B.C., and even then Spain was not fully subdued until the time of Augustus.

Nearer and Farther Spain For purposes of administration and defense, the senate decided in 197 B.C. to divide Roman Spain into two separate provinces known as Nearer and Farther Spain, each normally to be governed by a praetor but, in time of war and crisis, by a magistrate of consular power. The Mediterranean seaboard from the Pyrenees to a point slightly south of New Carthage (Cartagena) comprised Nearer Spain, rich in silver mines but agriculturally somewhat poor. Farther Spain, roughly coextensive with Andalusia, embraced the fertile Guadalquivir valley as far north as the silver-mining region of the Sierra Morena range. Neither province extended very far into the interior, and both were quite well known, having been visited from the late Bronze Age onward by Phoenician, Greek, and Etruscan traders and sailors.

The costs of provincial administration and defense were defrayed by revenue derived from tribute and regular taxes. The tribute (*stipendium*) was imposed on all tribes, semiurban communities, and a few municipalities such as Malaca (Malaga) and Gades (Cadiz). It was not collected by tax farmers, as in other provinces, but by government agents (prefects). It consisted sometimes of farm products, such as wheat or barley, but more often of payments in silver or gold in bullion or coin. Until 195 B.C., the amount of tribute varied from year to year according to the needs of the provincial government and the rapacity of the governor. As a rule, it was too high for primitive rural communities and often provoked unrest and rebellion. The regular tax, on the other hand, was fairly low, being only a twentieth of farm crops and payable in kind. In addition to tribute and taxes, all communities were required to furnish troops to the Roman army.

In the year in which the two provinces were created, war broke out in both because of the extortions and tryannies of the Roman praetors. The Romans, who had been welcomed as deliverers under Scipio, proved less tolerable than the Carthaginians had been. Even Gades and Malaca, finding themselves denied the promised status of allies, supported the inland tribes in the fight for independence.

Cato the Elder's Governorship of Nearer Spain

In 195 B.C., Cato the Elder, now consul, arrived in northeastern Spain with an army of 50,000 men. Though he was successful in stamping out the rebellion in his own province and even subdued the region as far west as the headwaters of the Tagus, his military achievements were not so outstanding or so permanent as his economic and administrative reforms (which applied to both provinces because he was the senior magistrate).

He did not reduce the tribute but set a fixed amount for each administrative district, so that the people would know long in advance what they would have to pay. More important, he reopened the mines, which had been shut since the Carthaginian defeat. He placed most of them under public ownership, operation, and control to provide new income for the provincial administrations and employment for the poorer people living in New Carthage and other mining districts.

Tiberius Sempronius Gracchus, 180 to 178 B.C.

Tiberius Gracchus, son-in-law of Scipio Africanus and father of the famous reforming tribunes Tiberius and Gaius Gracchus (pp. 146–155), was another governor whose fame rests not on military achievements but on his reforms, fairness, and sympathy. To remove the causes of unrest, he founded many new towns and villages and gave the peasants and workers in Nearer Spain good land for settlement. The faith and confidence that he inspired among the people kept them contented and peaceful for twenty-five years until they were outraged by the brutalities of the later governors. The senate refused to punish their crimes, in spite of bitter denunciations by Cato the Elder and the repeated appeals of the Spanish people, whose resentment festered until the end of the first century B.C.

The Third Punic War, 149 to 146 B.C.

While the Romans were trying to crush native resistance to their rule in the Iberian peninsula, events in North Africa were leading to the final and sorriest chapter in the history of Rome's conflict with Carthage. Even after Zama, Carthage remained a busy industrial and shipping center and controlled the trade between Africa and the Hellenistic world. With peace and order in North Africa, she enjoyed a better market for her industrial products than ever before. The crops grown on her farms and plantations were the envy of the world.

In an effort to please and cooperate with the Romans, the Carthaginians had scrupulously observed all their treaty obligations. They had disavowed Hannibal and had supplied grain for the Roman armies on numerous occasions. They had helped Rome wage war against Philip V, Antiochus III, and Perseus by furnishing both military and naval assistance. Perhaps they would have remained on good terms had it not been for the ambitions and aggression of Masinissa, who unscrupulously expanded his kingdom of Numidia at the expense of the Carthaginians, whose hands were tied by Rome.

Masinissa

The Romans had used Masinissa's small kingdom as a check on Carthage in the same way that they had used the smaller Hellenistic states to exercise indirect control over Macedon and the Seleucid Empire. The end result was also the same. The smaller power tried to manipulate Rome and helped to precipitate a major war.

The treaty that ended the Second Punic War left Carthage in possession of many ports and trading posts along the African coast but confined her home territory to what is now the northern half of Tunisia within frontiers known as the Phoenician Bounds, which enclosed an area of about 30,000 square miles. Masinissa, on the other hand, was permitted to occupy any land that either he or his ancestors had previously held. Another clause forbade Carthage to wage even defensive war without the consent of Rome. Masinissa, with Roman connivance, took full advantage of both clauses of the treaty.

One by one, Masinissa had seized most of the Carthaginian coastal colonies. Not permitted to resist these aggressions by armed force, Carthage appealed to Rome, who sent commissions to arbitrate. These commissions sometimes decided in favor of Masinissa and sometimes left the dispute unsettled. By 154 B.C., Masinissa had whittled Carthage down to about 5,000 square miles, one sixth of her former area. In answer to an urgent Carthaginian appeal, the Romans sent a boundary commission reportedly headed by Cato the Elder. The commission left the matter undecided but, before returning to Rome, made an inspection tour in and around Carthage.

The proud city—overflowing with wealth and luxury, teeming with fighting men, filled with arms and military supplies, and humming with busy shipyards—is said to have stirred in Cato an unreasonable hatred. He demanded an immediate declaration of war, and thereafter ended all his speeches, regardless of the subject, with the hysterical refrain: *censeo Carthaginem esse delendam* ("In my opinion Carthage must be destroyed!").

Motives for War For some Romans, like Cato, an irrational fear and hatred may well have prompted support for a declaration of war against Carthage, their great enemy in two previous wars. Cato, at least, had often opposed unjustified imperialistic adventures in the East. Again, however, economic considerations, though often denied, and the traditional aristocratic desire for glorious triumphs must not be underestimated. Cato, for example, had lucrative investments in shipping firms and companies engaged in foreign trade. (He used a dummy to get around the *lex Claudia* of 218 B.C., which forbade senators from engaging in foreign trade.) Carthaginians were the Romans' major foreign competitors in the West. Therefore, senators like Cato, probably with the support of many wealthy equestrians who had major interests in foreign trade, would have favored a new war against Carthage. Furthermore, only a short sail from Italy, Carthage was a major exporter of agricultural products to the huge Roman market.

While many large senatorial and equestrian landowners could have been concerned about competition with the products of their own rural estates, an even greater concern may well have been assuring that Rome had unhindered access to sufficient food supplies. By 150 B.C., the population of the city had swollen to about 400,000. Food, particularly grain, from the easily accessible parts of Italy, southern Gaul, Sicily, and Sardinia probably was no longer enough to feed it. Having direct control over Carthage's highly productive hinterland would have been very desirable for ensuring Rome's huge population could be fed. Finally, in 152 Carthage had finished paying the huge indemnity imposed after the Second Punic War. Since the rich, fat goose was no longer going to lay golden eggs, many Romans may have found it attractive to carve up the goose itself. Certainly the general victorious in a war with Carthage would celebrate a magnificent triumph and contribute a vast hoard of plunder to the commonwealth.

There is no reason to doubt Polybius' statement that a majority in the Roman senate had been bent on war well before the event. All that was lacking was a pretext that could decorously mark naked aggression. Such a pretext was conveniently provided as a result of Rome's tacit encouragement of Masinissa's unscrupulous seizures of Carthaginian territory. In Carthage, popular, anti-Roman leaders, exasperated by the aggressions of Masinissa and the indifference of Rome, had seized power from pro-Roman oligarchs in 151 B.C. In 150 B.C., war broke out between Carthage and Masinissa with disastrous results for the poorly trained and badly led Carthaginian army. Worse still, in waging war against Masinissa the Carthaginians had violated the treaty of Zama and given Rome a convenient excuse for war.

Hearing that the Romans were preparing to send an army to Africa, the Carthaginians made haste to undo the mischief that they had done. They returned their pro-Roman oligarchs to power and executed popular leaders. Envoys from Rome arrived to investigate the situation and obscured Roman intentions by vague replies when the Carthaginians asked how they could make amends. Meanwhile, the Roman senate, goaded by Cato, prepared for war, which the *comitia centuriata* finally declared in 149. The Carthaginians sent ambassadors to Rome to request peace terms. The ambassadors were told that Carthage would be permitted to retain her territory and independence, provided that she hand over 300 noble hostages and carry out all future orders of the consuls. The consuls demanded the surrender of all arms and weapons. After the Carthaginians complied, the consuls grimly announced the senate's secret final terms: The Carthaginians must abandon and destroy their city and rebuild at least ten miles from the sea—a death sentence for people who made their living by commerce. The Romans probably calculated that they would not submit willingly, but it did not matter. Either way, Rome would have enjoyed a position of great superiority.

The Siege of Carthage and Rise of the Younger Scipio Africanus

Beside themselves with fear and rage, the Carthaginians prepared to defend their beloved city. Supplies of food were hurriedly gathered from the surrounding countryside and brought into the city, where the people were toiling day and night to make new weapons. Prisons were opened, slaves freed, and even temples turned into workshops as the Carthaginians frantically prepared for siege.

The siege lasted three years. Carthage was situated in an excellent defensive location, and its walls were enormously thick and strong. The badly disciplined Roman armies were led by incompetent commanders. One young lieutenant, however, distinguished himself. He was Publius Cornelius Scipio Aemilianus, the son of Aemilius Paullus and the adopted grandson of Scipio Africanus.[1] So impressive were his exploits that when he returned to Rome in 147 B.C. to stand for election as curule aedile—he was

only about thirty and ineligible for any higher office—a special law was passed clearing the way for his election as consul and placing him in command of the besieging army.

The young consul finally took Carthage by storm in the spring of 146 B.C. For six days and nights the struggle raged inside the city from street to street, from house to house, until the beautiful old city was a sea of flames. All survivors were sold as slaves, and Carthage became the province of Africa.[2]

According to the historian Polybius, who was there, Scipio wept at the final destruction of the once magnificent city. He wept not for the suffering of the Carthaginians, which he was only too happy to inflict, but at the thought that Rome might someday suffer a similar fate. At that time, however, Rome was invincible, and Scipio could staunch his tears with pleasant thoughts of returning home in glory as Rome's most admired citizen.

The Viriathic and Numantine Wars in Spain, 151 to 133 B.C.

At the same time that Scipio was destroying Carthage, wars of resistance in the Spanish provinces were raging again. This time the Lusitanians, native inhabitants of Farther Spain, had found a skillful and inspiring leader by the name of Viriathus, who was able to frustrate the Romans for a decade. His name, even after 2,000 years, remains synonymous with freedom among the people of Portugal (ancient Lusitania). Viriathus was a shepherd and a hunter who knew the mountains, glens, and winding paths through which he led 10,000 guerrilla soldiers. For eight years he and his followers held the Romans at bay

---

[1]Aemilianus had also served Rome well when the dying Masinissa asked him to arrange the future of Numidia in 148. Scipio divided Numidia among the old king's three sons and thereby averted the menace of a strong, united kingdom that could have taken the place of Carthage in North Africa.

[2]The common belief that the city was leveled to the ground and a plow run over it is based on the exaggerated account of Orosius (fifth century A.D.). Actually, the ruins remained for generations afterward. In fact, Plutarch says that Marius once sat among them. They remained on such an immense scale that for centuries the old walls, temples, and other buildings were a quarry of ready-dressed stone. Far more thorough agents of demolition, therefore, than Scipio's soldiers were the builders of Roman Carthage, which was founded on the Punic site in 28 B.C., and the insatiable stone hunters of later centuries.

and cut down one army after another. Again and again he would attack and then fade away into the darkness by paths that the Romans could never follow.

In 141 B.C., Viriathus had entrapped a Roman army of 50,000 men, whom he spared in return for a treaty respecting the freedom and independence of his people. The senators ratified the treaty and cynically broke it the next year. The Romans bribed two traitors to slit the throat of the sleeping Viriathus, and the Lusitanians, left without a leader, submitted to the iron yoke of Rome. Some of the captives were forced to go with Roman veterans to found a Latin colony at Valentia (Valencia), where they could not easily resist Roman authority again.

The Siege of Numantia The war in Nearer Spain raged around the Celtiberian fortress town of Numantia. Even for its small garrison of about 4,000 men, Numantia was easy to defend because of its location on a hill at the junction of two rivers that flowed between deeply cut banks through thickly wooded valleys. While besieging Numantia in 137 B.C., the Roman commander C. Hostilius Mancinus saw his army of 20,000 caught in an ambush by 4,000 Celtiberians and was forced to sign a treaty, which the youthful Tiberius Gracchus, son of the former governor with the same name, had persuaded the Numantines to accept. This treaty of 137 B.C., which saved a large Roman army from utter destruction, was later shamelessly broken.

After several such defeats, the Romans in 134 B.C. sent to Spain the best general of the time, Scipio Aemilianus, the destroyer of Carthage, who was looking for another opportunity to earn military glory and prestige among his fellow citizens. He reformed and retrained the demoralized Roman army, drove away the plunder buyers, bootleggers, and prostitutes, and surrounded Numantia with a double-ring wall five miles long, set with towers and guarded by seven camps. He then proceeded to starve Numantia into unconditional surrender and set the town on fire.

The destruction of Numantia in Spain and the inheritance of Attalus' kingdom of Pergamum in Asia Minor in 133 B.C. terminated the remarkable period of a little less than seventy years during which Rome had acquired imperial control over much of the Mediterranean world. It was often a brutal process. Subjugating others, particularly those of different cultural backgrounds, often produces brutality, and brutality in subjugating others certainly was not unprecedented in Roman history. The destructions of Alba Longa and Veii, for example, were prominently featured in patriotic historical tradition. Nevertheless, even with allowance for personal bias or rhetorical exaggeration in the sources, the level of brutality that Roman commanders used against both highly civilized and less civilized peoples does seem to have increased as Rome expanded abroad. Many reasons combined to increase the Romans' use of mass enslavements, wholesale massacres, and total destruction to subdue their adversaries: frustration that people of different cultural backgrounds like the Greeks, Carthaginians, and Spanish tribes would not conform to Roman preconceptions of peace and order; ambition to outdo others in military honor; greed; and the need to keep abreast of political rivals in wealth.

An increase in brutality against non-Romans, however, was not the only change produced by Rome's imperial expansion. The changes produced in Rome's internal life were even greater and often equally lamentable. The following chapters will treat them in detail.

XII

The Transformation of Roman Life, 264 to 133 B.C.

By intimidation and conquest Rome had established her dominion over the Mediterranean world and thus completed the political and economic unification begun by Alexander the Great and continued by the Hellenistic monarchies. In less than a century and a half since the outbreak of the First Punic War, she had passed from city-state to empire. Zama, Cynoscephalae, Magnesia, and Pydna mark the triumph of Rome's armies on three continents. She had reduced the most powerful kingdoms to vassalage and subservience. Vast streams of gold, silver, slaves, and other tribute flowed into her hands. Before her, nations trembled. Although Roman cultural life became much more varied and sophisticated in the process, this phenomenon of world conquest and expansion had begun to work revolutionary effects upon the economic, social, political, and ethical life of the Roman People, which set the stage for the destruction of the Republic itself.

Agriculture One of the most spectacular transformations occurred in agriculture. In the early centuries of the Republic, the small family farm shaped a way of life shared by almost the whole population (p. 42). It formed the idealized view of Rome's past enshrined in the writings of Cato the Elder and the patriotic stories of early heroes like Cincinnatus (p. 71), who purportedly worked their modest farms with their own hands.

Beginning with the middle of the third century B.C., however, farm life in Italy had undergone a radical change. The first two Punic Wars had undermined the relative agricultural stability produced by the reforms associated with the year 367 B.C. The huge casualties suffered in those wars came largely at the expense of small farmers, who made up the bulk of the population and the army. The approximately 285,000 Roman citizens listed before the First Punic War had declined to 214,000 by the year 203 and to only 144,000 in 193. This decline reflected not only battle casualties but the large number of men serving in armies abroad.

Those who survived their tours of duty often did not return to the land in Italy or did not stay long if they did. Some could not resume the dull routine of farm life and enlisted in new wars in the hope of more booty or drifted to cities, particularly Rome, in search of a better life. After long years of overseas duty, many farmers returned to find their farms run down and burdened by debts incurred to support their families. Not a few had been seized for debt or simply taken over by some larger neighbor. For fourteen years during the Hannibalic War, Punic and Roman armies marching up and down the Italian peninsula lived off the land, seized or destroyed crops, killed livestock, and burned down thousands of homesteads. Returning soldiers lucky enough to find houses and fields intact often did not have enough money to buy the necessary tools, animals, and seed needed to restart operations. It made more sense to sell out to a wealthy buyer and take up new land in Cisalpine Gaul or Spain if one wanted to continue farming.

Rome's conquest of the Mediterranean basin also unleashed economic forces that made the old style of agriculture untenable in several areas of Italy. Typically, the small peasant proprietor whose principal crop was grain had dominated Italian agriculture. After the takeover of Sicily, Sardinia, and then North Africa, it became even cheaper for coastal cities, particularly Rome, to import grain by sea from those grain-producing provinces than to cart it from the city's hinterland. For example, grain could be shipped 500 miles by sea for what it would cost to cart it overland 20 miles. Before the Second Punic War, Rome was collecting an annual tribute of a million bushels of wheat a year in Sicily alone. Additional amounts were collected as rent from tenants on land confiscated by Rome and as a result of outright seizure by Roman officials. It could then be sold in Rome at prices with which many small and medium-sized growers in southern Etruria, Latium, and Campania could not compete.

Changing Demand for Agricultural Products

The plunder and tribute from overseas conquests, subsequent commercial expansion, the official exploitation of provincial resources, and the exactions of corrupt officials produced an enormous influx of money that fueled the economic growth of Rome and a few coastal cities like Ostia and Puteoli (Pozzuoli). Urban population expanded rapidly with growing economic opportunities because abundant supplies of grain could be imported by sea. Land once used to grow grain within short distances from the city now could be used more profitably to produce wine, olives, fresh fruits and vegetables, flowers, young meat animals, poultry, eggs, and cheese for lucrative urban markets. Some small proprietors successfully made the transition to the production of these more profitable crops, but other forces made it difficult for all of those who survived the wars to take advantage of the new opportunities.

Latifundia: *Capital, Land, and Slaves* Those who got the biggest share of the profits from overseas wars were the wealthy leaders of Rome and her Italian allies. They invested some of their surplus wealth in shipping, commerce, mining, and craft industries, but most of their investment was in land. Roman senators were officially prohibited from extensive overseas trade, and everywhere in Italy land was the most honorable and prestigious form of wealth. For the *equites,* the wealthy class of nonsenatorial families, the main road to political advancement and social recognition was through landed wealth. In practical terms, the hazards of trade and commerce in the ancient world made land the safest investment anyway.

Many small farms close to Rome were acquired by members of these wealthy elites who wanted to have estates and villas near the city where they competed for social and political prominence with each other. Some of the suburban estates began to resemble large-scale, capital-intensive operations often called *latifundia* (sing. *latifundium*), although the term is not found in Roman writers before the first century A.D. Such estates engaged in specialized production on a large scale for commercial markets.

Many of the large suburban estates were not meant to be profitable. Their elegant villas were for the rest, relaxation, and entertainment of the wealthy owners and their friends. Much of their acreage was given over to pleasure gardens, hunting preserves with stocks of deer and wild boar, ponds of exotic fish, and vast aviaries.

The typical *latifundia* were farther out in the Italian countryside and specialized in high-value products that required large amounts of land and could still be transported to market over longer distances at a profit. After the first two Punic wars large tracts of land were available for such operations. The so-called Licinio-Sextian legislation of 367, which restricted the growth of large estates, was almost completely ignored after the Second Punic War. The senate encouraged wealthy individuals who had made war loans to the government to accept public land as payment. It also encouraged rich investors to rent large tracts of land that would otherwise go unused because of the decline in available citizens. After a few generations, they came to view the leased land as private property and even ceased paying rent to the state.

Latifundia specializing in the raising of cattle, sheep, and pigs spread rapidly in southern Italy, Etruria, and in some parts of Latium. In other parts of Latium and particularly in Campania, large estates producing olives or wine grapes became very common. These *latifundia* ranged at first from 60 to 200 acres, later to as many as 500 acres. Localized risks, such as crop failure or surplus, natural disaster, or insufficient labor at harvest time, encouraged owners to acquire several *latifundia* located in different regions, rather than to operate a single huge one.

Slave Labor Aside from the availability of cheap land and an abundance of investment capital, vast amounts of cheap slave labor fueled the spread of *latifundia*. Some tasks and crops required hired laborers or tenants, whose ranks were often filled by failed small proprietors. Grain needed to supply the rest of the estate and local markets could best be supplied by tenants. It has a relatively short growing season that would leave slaves idle too long and it requires extra labor only at harvest time. Slave labor, was very efficient, however, for systematic application to the year-round activities associated with stock raising, olive and fruit orchards, and vineyards, all of which were very lucrative. Skilled slaves were also in demand as carpenters, masons, weavers, potters, bailiffs, blacksmiths, cooks, and household staff always needed to keep operations going.

The competitive advantages of systematic slave labor were many. It was a stable, flexible supply of manpower, always available when and where needed, and easily replaced. Slaves, unlike tenants, could not be drafted for military service. Because the owner could appropriate any surplus earned by slaves, he was able to produce at prices only slightly above the cost of maintaining them. Moreover, there was probably not enough free labor to meet the agricultural needs after the Second Punic War anyway.

By substituting hundreds of thousands of war prisoners for depleted free manpower, Rome's wars of conquest solved the labor problem that they created. In times of peace, the lack of captives was filled by the victims of pirates and professional kidnappers. Their tasks were made easier by the connivance of Roman officials and the destruction of Rhodian naval power, which had formerly kept pirates in check.

The Growth of Overseas Markets Rome's conquests and political unification of the Mediterranean increasingly gave efficient slave-run estates in Italy access to overseas markets. As early as 167 B.C., Italian wine and oil were exported to Delos and other places in the Greek East. The chief market for Italian farm products, however, was western and northern Europe. Wine exporting to France, where a 6-gallon jug cost as much as a slave, must have been a very lucrative business, and it began surprisingly early. The remains of a Greek ship, which probably foundered around 230 B.C., have been discovered among a group of islands south of Marseilles. It was laden with Campanian tableware and about 10,000 large jars of wine, some of Greek vintage but most of it red Latian produced on the Sabine hills.

The Growth of Industry, Trade, and Commerce

Although agriculture always dominated the ancient economy, Rome's wars and overseas expansion in the third and second centuries stimulated the growth of industry, trade, and commerce in Rome and Italy. Money and other forms of wealth poured into Rome and other Italian urban centers. Successful generals often immortalized their deeds by using part of their booty to build temples vowed to the gods in return for victory, basilicas for public use, roads, and other public amenities. The senate also publicly appropriated profits from the sale of booty, war indemnities, tribute, and state-owned mines for similar construction projects.

The rapid growth of Rome and other urban centers in Italy greatly expanded opportunities in small craft and service businesses such as wine bars, fast-food shops, butcher shops, barbershops, fulling and dying shops, bakeries, potteries, metalworking, shoemaking, furniture making, carting, and the building trades. The construction of large private homes, apartment blocks (*insulae*), warehouses, and baths provided bigger opportunities for investors, builders, and suppliers. The manufacturing of bricks, roof tiles, and fine pottery became big business in rural estates near urban markets. Supplying timber, firewood, charcoal, and quarried stone was very profitable, as were shipbuilding; shipping; and the supplying of crates, baskets, and large clay amphorae as shipping containers. Even more lucrative were public contracts for supplying the legions, the working of state-owned mines, collecting taxes, and building public works such as temples, other public buildings, roads, bridges, aqueducts, and sewers.

The most highly developed areas of Roman business were the financial operations. The huge influx of wealth turned Rome into the banking and money-lending center of the Mediterranean. Well-organized partnerships of investors often made loans to shipowners to finance their cargoes. More frequent and more profitable were loans to provincial taxpayers and whole cities that were hard pressed to pay their taxes or tribute. Although the official rate on such loans was usually limited to 12 percent, the actual rate could reach 24 or even 48 percent. Indeed, whole kingdoms sometimes became indebted to Roman moneylenders at these rates as client kings endeavored to pay for the support that secured their thrones.

Roman bankers became very sophisticated. Individuals could keep open accounts with bankers and use bankers' orders or letters of credit. In that way, payments could easily be made by bookkeeping entries. Coins, the only form of cash, would have been cumbersome and risky in large transactions.

Companies of *publicani*, publicans, who contracted with the state to construct public works, operate state-owned mines or forests, and collect taxes, were uniquely granted incorporation as continuous legal entities. In order to raise working capital, the principal partners, *socii*, offered shares, *partes*, to the public. The company would then submit a bid to the censors for the right to collect a particular tax or to obtain some public contract. In the case of taxes, the highest bidder won, and the investors' profit would be the difference between what they paid and the actual yield of the taxes collected. In the case of other contracts, the profit would be the difference between what the state paid the company and its actual costs. Naturally, there was a temptation for the *publicani* to squeeze the taxpayers as much as they could and to cut corners on public works in order to increase profits. Such work was beneath the dignity of the investors themselves and was left to slaves, freedmen, and laborers supervised by a hired manager, *magister*.

The Integration of Greek and Roman Coinage

During the Second Punic War, as the strain on Roman resources became intense, the Romans introduced a lighter silver coin called the *denarius* (pl. *denarii*). It literally was a "tenner" because the bronze *as* had fallen in weight to only two Roman ounces and the *denarius* was valued at ten *asses*. A few years later, as the Roman economy became integrated with that of the entire Mediterranean world, the *denarius* was slightly reduced in weight to equal the Athenian drachma, the most widely circulated coin in the Mediterranean up to that time. From about 170 B.C., the *denarius,* with its fractions the *quinarius* (one half) and the *sestertius* (one quarter), became the standard silver coinage of the Roman Republic. Six thousand *denarii* equaled a talent. Some idea of what these monetary units were worth in economic terms can be gained from the fact that a *denarius* was about the average daily pay of a hired laborer.

Rising Social Discontent

The rapid growth of the Roman economy as a result of overseas expansion also produced much social change and discontent. The decline of small farmers has already been noted. Those who were left came to resent the hardships imposed by economic change, and they bitterly protested the incessant demands for military service that threatened them further.

The Urban Poor The rapid influx of people to the cities created serious problems. Despite the attractions of the growing urban economy, there were not always enough jobs for the newcomers, especially the unskilled. Unemployment and underemployment caused hardship for many. Housing was in high demand and short supply so that rents were steep for even the worst accommodations. People lived in tightly packed rows of flimsy *tabernae,* one- or two-story buildings with timber frames and wicker walls open to the street except for shutters. In some neighborhoods, the *tabernae* were giving way to multistoried apartment blocks called *insulae,* which often were hardly less flimsy than the *tabernae.* This situation encouraged overcrowding, which in turn produced serious problems in health, sanitation, and safety. Not only did the flimsy buildings often collapse, but many were also firetraps that burned in large numbers without adequate fire protection. The lack of any organized police force encouraged the growth of crime, which the hardships of life fostered. As a result, the urban poor of Italy became increasingly discontent and a threat to public order and political stability.

The situation became especially acute at Rome itself in the latter part of the second century B.C. The economy of Rome no longer rested on an adequate productive base. Its great growth during the first sixty years of the century had depended upon the profits of overseas expansion, which had fueled a great construction boom in the city and created a mass market for labor, goods, and services. After the destruction of Carthage and Corinth in 146 B.C., however, there were no more profitable wars for some time. As the wars against relatively poor Spanish tribes dragged on, they probably did not even recover their own expenses, and they disrupted the regular tribute. In 135 B.C., a slave rebellion in Sicily also required an expensive military effort. The result was a drastic decline in

both private benefaction and public expenditure in the 130s and a serious depression of the city's economy, which greatly aggravated the plight of the urban poor.

The Provincials and Other Overseas People Many inhabitants of the western provinces bitterly resented their loss of independence, the payment of taxes and tribute to Rome, and the depredation of corrupt Roman officials and financiers. The Greeks of the eastern provinces and other people of the Hellenistic East were in particularly difficult circumstances as a result of Roman wars and conquests. Between 201 and 136 B.C., Greece, Egypt, Syria, and other parts of the Near East may have lost as much as 20 to 25 percent of their population. Houses fell into decay, large tracts of land lay fallow or were turned into pasture for want of labor. From 210 to 160 B.C., while wages remained low, the prices of food, rent, and other necessities rose and in times of crop failure, even skyrocketed. Prices finally went down again because of the lack of buying power but not before the people had undergone intense suffering.

Slaves and Freedmen One of the most discontented and potentially dangerous groups was made up of the large numbers of anonymous rural slaves who worked in the fields, forests, and mines of great landlords and commercial operators and were treated like animals. Food and clothing were of the poorest quality, and family life was denied them. When concentrated in groups, they were often chained up in underground prisons at night. Beatings were common. Moreover, because their only value was as the cheapest labor possible, they did not even have the hope of being allowed to acquire any money from the fruits of their labor to purchase eventual freedom. Not surprisingly, many slaves sought escape to become robbers and brigands and even raised serious revolts. Indeed, their ability to do so was considerable because the supervision of rural slaves was often poor and many of them were former soldiers captured in war.

Slave revolts began breaking out all over the Roman world after 138 B.C. In Italy a revolt was suppressed with the crucifixion of over 4,500 slaves at Rome and surrounding towns. An uprising at the great slave market of Delos was put down by force of arms, as was another at the silver mines of Laurium near Athens. In Pergamum, the war of Aristonicus (the bastard son of Eumenes II) and his Stoic "Sunstate" against Rome (132 to 129 B.C.) was simply a major revolt of slaves, proletarians, and soldiers. Worst of all was the slave revolt in Sicily, where normal slave thuggery and mugging had swelled into full-scale war about 136 B.C. under the leadership of a Syrian slave named Eunus. By vomiting fire and uttering oracles, he was able to persuade his 70,000 (some say 250,000) followers that he was Antiochus, the king of the Syrians. Only after several years of hard fighting, the murder of many landlords, and much damage to property were the Romans able to crush this revolt and extinguish its last sparks in 131 B.C.

Not all slaves were forced to work under harsh conditions on *latifundia,* or in mines, quarries, and other places requiring exhausting physical labor. Many trained, educated captives from the lands of the eastern Mediterranean had better lives in domestic service as book-keepers, secretaries, doctors, tutors, cooks, butlers, waiters, maids, hairdressers, and footmen; or as skilled craftsmen like potters, carpenters, masons, decorators, tailors, and jewelers. A vast retinue of such slaves was a mark of status, and the wealthy often competed to impress their peers with the numbers that they owned.

Some masters were even kind and generous to slaves with whom they lived closely, but total control over another person easily led to cruelty and abuse by others. Small infractions might provoke harsh punishment, and if a slave murdered a master, no matter how cruel, all of his fellow slaves had to be put to death with him. Male and female slaves were always vulnerable to sexual exploitation and abuse by their owners. Because adultery was defined for a man only as sexual relations with another citizen's wife, it was commonly accepted that female slaves served their master's pleasure.

The practice of freeing loyal slaves who were part of the household continued. Indeed,

many masters hired out skilled slaves and allowed them to keep part of their earnings as their *peculium.* When a slave had accumulated a large enough *peculium,* he or she could often purchase freedom. A female slave might be granted freedom after producing a certain number of children. Often a slave was manumitted, given freedom, after a number of years of faithful service, and large numbers were manumitted in wills after their owners died. In fact, manumission was so common that the state collected a handsome revenue from a 5 percent tax on the value of manumitted slaves.

The masters who freed their slaves also had something to gain from their generosity. The prospect of freedom in return for faithful service encouraged slaves to be docile and work hard. Many wealthy Romans helped their ex-slaves set up their own businesses in return for a share of the profits. At the very least, any ex-slave was expected to be a loyal client to his former master. For the dead slaveowner, it meant that his tomb would be well cared for by his freedmen, that his memory would be kept green, and that his shade (spirit) would receive the proper ritual offerings. For the living, the increase of clients through manumission had important political implications: Freedmen became voting citizens. Although freedmen (but not their sons) were barred from public office, freedmen clients could be very helpful to an office seeker as voters and political agents.

The political impact of freedmen caused them problems. Lower-class, freeborn citizens resented the dilution of their voting power by the influx of freedmen into the tribes of voters. Many senators feared that their rivals might gain an advantage from having a large number of freedmen clients in the Tribal Assembly. (Freedmen in the *comitia centuriata* were less of a worry because ex-slaves would not usually be wealthy enough to qualify for the highest centuries, which had the most power in voting.) Therefore, the issue of tribal enrollment for freedmen became a source of political controversy.

Customarily, freedmen had been enrolled in only the four urban tribes, where their impact was outweighed by the less populous but more numerous rural tribes dominated by landowners. Some censors, like the famous Appius Claudius Caecus (the Blind) in 312 B.C., had tried to strengthen their *clientela* by enrolling freedmen in all of the tribes. Others had removed the freedmen from the rural tribes and confined them to the urban ones again. In 168, the censors restricted freedmen to only one urban tribe. Many freedmen resented this increased restriction.

The Equites Another increasingly discontented class of citizens was the equestrian class (*ordo equester*), the *equites*. By the third century, the term *eques*, "knight," included any full citizen whose property was equal in value to that of those who were enrolled in the equestrian centuries of the *comitia centuriata*. These men included wealthy nonsenatorial landowners, such as members of the local Italian aristocracy whose families had obtained Roman citizenship, and those people who had prospered with the great growth of business and commerce.

The *equites* have often been identified simply as wealthy businessmen. In practice, however, there was no rigid distinction between well-to-do landowners and prosperous businessmen in the equestrian class. Landowners invested some of their surplus income in business, and people who made money in business usually sought financial security and social status by investing a large share of their profits in land. One reason why the techniques of Roman business and manufacturing never advanced further than they did is that the goal of many businessmen was not to reinvest their profits in ways to improve their productivity, but in estates and villas so that they could live the lives of gentlemen on their rents and agricultural income and even aspire to senatorial office for themselves or their sons.

One source of discontent among the *equites* was that it was very difficult to achieve senatorial office and almost impossible to break into the ranks of the consular nobility. The senators, and especially the consular nobles, jealously guarded their exclusivity. Although members of the great noble families might support an equestrian client for one of the lower offices of the *cursus honorum*, they greatly resented a *novus homo*, new man, who managed to be the first of his family to reach the consulship. While most equestrians probably were content with their status, many must have resented the slight to their class in general implied in the nobility's attitude toward those of their number who wanted to achieve high honors at Rome.

In particular among the *equites*, the *publicani* resented any check that members of the senate might impose on attempts to maximize the amount of taxes collected or of profit made on state contracts. Moreover, the *publicani* were vulnerable to extortion at the hands of magistrates and provincial governors (all senators), who could threaten to interfere with their activities unless they handed over a share of their profits. *Publicani* subjected to such treatment often found the legal system unresponsive to complaints because the juries who heard them were staffed exclusively by senators.

Accordingly, as the equestrian order grew with the prosperity generated by Roman expansion, its members developed interests that sometimes led to dissatisfaction with the senatorial leaders.

The Italian Allies During the second century B.C., the Italian allies found their status more and more burdensome as Rome expanded overseas. They too had suffered enormous losses of manpower during the Second Punic War, and now the Romans were calling upon them to spend long years in wars overseas. Moreover, since the indemnities and tribute imposed upon the conquered went to Rome, the allies were receiving only a minor share of the profits of those wars whereas Rome was getting rich.

Roman leaders became more high-handed in their treatment of the Italian allies as Rome became more and more secure in Italy itself and Romans grew accustomed to dominance abroad. They imposed harsher discipline on allied soldiers, gave allies smaller rewards, and demanded free accommodations and entertainment when they traveled through allied territory. In 186 B.C., the Roman senate interfered in the allies' domestic affairs through a decree that suppressed throughout Italy secret Bacchic cults, whose popularity among slaves and the poor caused the Romans to consider them subversive (p. 144). In short, the Romans more and more began to treat their allies in Italy as subjects. That eventually led allies to demand citizenship and ultimately to rebel when the Romans obstinately refused to grant this just demand.

The Advancement of Upper-Class Women One group whose position did improve in the third and second centuries B.C. was upper-class women. One of the reasons for this improvement was the greatly increased wealth of the aristocracy as Rome acquired and exploited a vast empire. Husbands gained status by their wives' ostentatious displays of wealth. The wife of the elder Scipio Africanus was notorious for such display, and she died richer than her own brother. In 215, during the Second Punic War, the *lex Oppia* limited how much expensive clothing and ornamentation a woman could wear in public. In 195, however, women made mass protests, and the law was repealed, supposedly despite old Cato's vehement objection. As a result of wartime casualties, many women came to possess vast wealth as widows, and in 169 a law was passed to limit female inheritances, but its impact seems to have been limited.

As families became richer and daughters' dowries and inheritances greater, aristocratic families did not want to lose control of such wealth. Therefore, the old-fashioned marriage with *manus,* which transferred a wife to the complete control of her husband, became increasingly rare, and marriage contracts usually contained the stipulation that the dowry be returned to the wife's family if she predeceased her husband. In this way, a woman now lived with a man who did not have legal supervision over her, whereas men who did have it, her male blood relatives or legal guardian, were physically separated from her, particularly because they were often away on overseas service

or business for long periods. Such a situation allowed shrewd and capable women a great amount of room to maneuver. Many of them, surrounded by loyal and able personal slaves, took full advantage of this situation.

The increased level of education among upper-class women also contributed to their independence and influence. The growing wealth and sophistication of aristocratic families prompted them to acquire the most highly trained tutors for their children. The large staffs of domestic slaves meant that girls were not needed for household chores, and were, therefore, allowed to attend the lessons that might have been denied them in earlier times. Also, Roman aristocrats were now being exposed to the Hellenistic Greek model of the educated woman. Soon, a number of educated women were patronizing literary circles and running salons, as did aristocratic women of France in the eighteenth century.

One of the most famous Roman women of the late second century B.C. combines many of the characteristics and accomplishments of such women. She was Cornelia, daughter of the elder Scipio Africanus and mother of the Gracchi (pp. 146–155). Her husband, Tiberius Sempronius Gracchus, had a highly distinguished public career. Cornelia was rich in her own right, but when Tiberius died her wealth increased. Well educated under the influence of her philhellene father, she provided the best education possible for those of her twelve children who survived to maturity, and was well known as a patroness of writers and philosophers. Her own cultured letters were read for generations after her death. Her wealth, family name, and personal accomplishments even brought her an offer of marriage from Ptolemy VIII (Physcon) of Egypt, but she preferred her independence as a Roman widow and turned him down.

Political Developments The general political effect of Rome's wars and the expansion of her power from 264 to 133 B.C. was to increase the conservative upper-class bias inherent in the Republic's constitution. The changes

Woman with a stylus and wax writing tablet; wall painting from Pompeii, A.D. 40–50. (Courtesy National Archaeological Museum, Naples)

in the organization of the *comitia centuriata* around 220 B.C. (p. 95), which seem to have given a greater voice to those enrolled in the second highest census class, who had contributed money and manpower to the First Punic War, were only a minor liberalization of no real consequence. The minimum census qualification of the second class was three fourths of the minimum for the first class. They shared the same economic interests and outlook as the wealthy equestrian and senatorial members of the first census class.

The Senatorial Oligarchy In the century before the First Punic War, the regular election of men from leading plebeian *gentes* to the consulship had brought a number of new families into prominence within the senatorial hierarchy. By the end of the war, however, these newcomers had coalesced with the old patrician families to form a powerful oligarchy dominated by a de facto nobility of consular senators. For example, there were 211 consuls elected from 232 to 133 B.C. Ninety-one came from families representing only 11 *gentes*. Nineteen *gentes* supplied only 1 consul each. Seventeen of those were plebeian. Of those 17 *gentes,* 14 had no previous consuls, and 11 produced no more consuls in the remaining two centuries of the Republic. Clearly, therefore, it was difficult for members of nonconsular plebeian families not only to reach the consulship but also to maintain their consular dignity in competition with candidates from families of more entrenched patrician and plebeian *gentes*.

This restriction of access to the consulship was partly a natural result of the election of only two consuls each year. After the so-called Licinio-Sextian reform of 367 had allowed the election of at least one plebeian consul each year, there was a period of great opportunity for people from nonconsular plebeian families to reach the consulship. After three or four generations, however, successful new families built up the kinds of reputations, alliances, *clientelae,* and connections that gave qualified candidates from their ranks a distinct edge over those who had not yet acquired such advantages.

During the period of the Punic wars and the overseas expansion of Roman power, the consular families who had come to dominate the senate made sure that the opportunities for more families to share in the consular dignity were not created. The senate did not sanction any increase in the number of annual consuls, despite the greatly increased need for high executives. Instead, the senate greatly increased the practice of proroguing (prolonging) a consul's or a praetor's military command or provincial governorship after his normal year of office. Magistrates whose terms of service were prorogued became promagistrates. Such men were able to use their extended terms to capitalize on the opportunities that their positions gave them to acquire clients and financial resources to further their domination of high offices.

The result was a very unhealthy political situation for Rome. Unchecked by any challenges from without, oligarchic nobles often neglected the public welfare. Instead, they competed with increasing intensity among themselves for dominance within the senate and for the corresponding prizes of *gloria* (glory), *dignitas* (esteem), and *auctoritas* (prestige) that came with high office and military triumph. Simultaneously, the holding of high office helped a man to amass the resources of money and patronage needed to maintain or increase his family's advantage in competition with other nobles and lesser aristocrats for political and military advancement.

Political Groupings Political struggles within the senatorial oligarchy were not organized on the basis of political parties, structures, and programs. In a situation where a body of about 300 men with lifetime tenure, who were not held directly accountable to the electorate or any other group, exercised great control over public affairs, there was no incentive to organize in such ways. Candidates for offices might well have different ideas concerning domestic issues or foreign affairs. Nevertheless, their electoral supporters were often organized on a highly personal basis of family connections, friendships, mutually advantageous coalitions, and patronage.

Some outstanding individuals might build up relatively stable factions of personal supporters that would last for some time. Others might last for only one electoral campaign. Although members of a man's family or even *gens* might support his election to high office out of feelings of kinship or family pride, there simply are not enough data to support the thesis that there were lasting factions of related families or otherwise allied groups who consistently supported fellow members for office and promoted concerted political programs in the senate.

Attempts to Check Outstanding Individuals What is apparent, however, is that many members of the senatorial oligarchy feared the rise of any outstanding individual who might amass so much wealth, power, popularity, glory, *auctoritas,* and *dignitas* that he would reduce the chances for them to compete for the same things on an equal basis. Indeed, because the social and financial rewards of political power increased with the power and wealth of Rome, the temptations increased to violate the customary rules governing political behavior as men sought to secure competitive advantage. Values and behavior necessary to preserve a republican form of government gradually began to disintegrate under the pressure. The way was imperceptibly opened for one man to overcome his competitors and dominate all in the manner of Hellenistic monarchs, whom Roman nobles had replaced as the masters of the Mediterranean world.

A good example of the process can be seen in the career of the elder Scipio Africanus during the Second Punic War. After Scipio's father and uncle had been killed in Spain, the well-connected young Scipio obtained from the senate a proconsular command to continue the war there, even though he was only twenty-five and had held no office beyond the aedileship. His successful prosecution of the war in Spain emboldened him to return to Rome and run for the consulship in 206 B.C., although he was far younger than normal and had never held the praetorship, as was normal for a consular candidate. His popularity as a military hero and his promise to invade Africa if elected guaranteed his victory, despite the opposition of rival families and conservative-minded senators who objected to his unorthodox career. Scipio's opponents sought to block him by placing him in charge of the disgraced survivors of Cannae and denying him public funds. He used his popularity to raise enough funds and volunteers to man, equip, and train a first-rate army to invade North Africa in 204 B.C. Such power and independence in one man did not bode well for the Republic, which depended upon the well-established political ground rules.

Other ambitious individuals were quick to follow the path taken by Scipio as they sought to equal or surpass his achievement. For example, T. Quinctius Flamininus had never been elected to any office beyond the junior one of military tribune, but he was made a propraetor in charge of Tarentum in 205 B.C. and while not yet thirty was elected consul for 198 B.C. to prosecute the Second Macedonian War.

The extraordinarily rapid rise of such young men as Scipio and Flamininus disturbed many leaders. Their rivals and many other senators, who saw in their careers a danger to the traditional Republic, procured laws to enforce what custom and tradition could no longer safeguard. Shortly after Flamininus was elected consul, for example, the praetorship was made a prerequisite for the consulship. That change probably was made to reduce the number of candidates for the two consulships each year. The number of praetors had increased from two to four at the end of the First Punic War to cope with administering new provinces, and it was increased to six in 197 after the organization of the two Spanish provinces. Without this new prerequisite, fourteen former quaestors, aediles, and praetors would have been eligible to run for the two consulships. The chances that the voters would pass over an older man for a

more popular younger one and the dangers of overheated electoral competition were too great for many senators to ignore.

In 180 the curule magistracies were systematically regulated by the *lex Villia Annalis:* Minimum ages were set for holding the curule aedileship, the praetorship, and the consulship—probably thirty-six, thirty-nine, and forty-two, respectively—and a minimum interval of two years between the end of one office and the holding of another was required. The status of the quaestorship at this time is not clear, but a minimum age of twenty-five may have been fixed for it, and it became the normal, if not mandatory, first office of the senatorial *cursus honorum.* Finally, in 151 B.C. a law was passed to forbid reelection to the consulship.

Still, the temptation to violate traditional political norms intensified with political competition. Between 181 and 131, several laws were passed to stop bribery and limit the control of patrons over voters in the assemblies. They required secret ballots and even instituted the death penalty for bribery. Two other laws attempted to limit the efforts of wealthy men to extend their private *clientelae* and impress voters with lavish entertainments and dinners. Nothing really worked.

When the prizes are large and the temptations correspondingly great, mere laws are not enough to restrain undesirable behavior. At Rome, the legal restraints on political behavior were especially weak in any case. The political system at Rome was not based on a written constitution that could be altered only after a lengthy process allowing due consideration and requiring the overwhelming approval of those responsible for making any changes. "Constitutional" matters were either merely customary or regulated by normal, ad hoc legislative acts like the *lex Villia Annalis.* All that an ambitious and popular leader had to do to circumvent such restraints was to procure a new law in his favor. For example, in 148 B.C. Scipio Aemilianus, the younger Africanus, obtained a special enactment to run for the consulship although he met none of the conditions set by the *lex Villia Annalis.* Another special law also gave him the command against Carthage, an action that breached the customary right of the senate to assign consuls to military commands. Finally, in 135 B.C. he was granted an exemption from the law that forbade repetition of the consulship so that he could take charge of the war against Numantia.

Other ambitious men dispensed with legality altogether, particularly as provincial governors who exceeded their authority or disobeyed express senatorial orders in order to win military laurels that would enhance their popularity at the polls. Individual governors were practically laws unto themselves in their provinces. They were far from the watchful eyes of their senatorial colleagues, and since they enjoyed supreme judicial and military power in their provinces, the provincials were at their mercy. Because they usually were to govern a particular province for only a year or two, they often had no interest in securing the long-term welfare of their charges; too often they were interested in using their power to extort as much money as they could from hapless provincials so that they would have the resources to advance their careers, pay off their debts, and maintain their status among competing peers back home. That is not to say that there were not many responsible and fair Roman governors who refused to put selfish interest above duty, but the bad ones were numerous enough to cause discontent in the provinces and concern in the senate.

The problem had become acute enough by 149 to inspire the tribune L. Calpurnius Piso to establish Rome's first permanent jury court, the *quaestio perpetua de rebus repetundis,* a tribunal in which provincials could bring charges of extortion against a former governor before a jury of senators and sue for the restitution of their losses (p. 144). Unfortunately, this court often inspired greater rapacity on the part of ambitious governors to make sure that they had money to bribe the jurors in the event of prosecution and still have enough left for other purposes. Also, the court became a weapon in the political competition within the nobility as men tried to destroy their rivals by supporting their prosecution for extortion, the penalty for which was loss of citizenship and exile.

The Republic's entire administrative system tended to intensify political competition at the expense of the kinds of sound, long-range policies needed to cope with the great and rapid changes produced by Rome's expansion. With the exception of the eighteen-month censorship, all of the higher magistracies were held for only one year. No one held office long enough to be able to put into effect consistent, long-range policies, and there was great pressure to think only in terms of what was expedient for gaining election to the next office. Similarly, in a senate rent by oligarchic rivalries present politics rather than the general welfare often dominated senators' actions. In simpler times, with less complex and fewer problems to face, this situation was not dangerous. When, however, Rome had to cope with rapid socioeconomic changes and the government of a far-flung empire, it became a fatal weakness and contributed to the worsening of the crises that these changes had helped to produce. Between 133 and 27 B.C., political infighting among the senatorial oligarchs often prevented solutions to the problems of discontented groups; therefore, discontent increased so that political divisiveness and instability increased still further.

XIII

The Great Cultural Synthesis, 264 to 133 B.C.

The aristocratic craze for things Greek expanded greatly during the period of overseas expansion. Wars on the Greek mainland and in Hellenistic kingdoms exposed the Romans to both the classicizing idealism of Attica and the emotional realism of the wider Hellenistic world. Thousands of plundered paintings, statues, reliefs, and architectural pieces poured into Rome. Thousands of skilled Greek craftsmen and artists came to Italy as slaves or hired craftsmen. In the same way, many educated Greek slaves ended up as secretaries and tutors in elite Roman households, and enterprising Greek philosophers, poets, and publicists sought the patronage of the rich and powerful. In the process, they combined Greek and native Italian influences to create a Greco-Roman classical culture that spread throughout the Mediterranean world.

Architecture and Art Beginning around 264 B.C. with the construction of the *comitium*—a tiered, circular, stone place of public assembly in the Forum—the Romans remodeled Rome under classical Greek influence. The design of the *comitium* probably came from Greeks in Sicily, and in 263 it was adorned with a sundial pillaged (but never recalibrated) from a Sicilian city. In 221/20, Gaius Flaminius celebrated his Gallic triumph by opening up the Campus Martius (Mar's Field), which was then outside the

walls of the city to the northwest along the great westward bend of the Tiber. There he built a new circus for Greek-style chariot racing. Soon, other triumphant generals were adding temples modeled on Greek originals and even constructing Hellenistic-style complexes to display the spoils of their victories over Hellenistic kings. In 184, Cato the Elder seems to have introduced a new style of building—the Greek basilica, a large rectangular covered building with interior supporting columns, where many people could meet for private or public business.

These buildings were still of wood on stone foundations, but expensive all-stone construction became more common after 150. One of the earliest stone structures is a Greek-style round temple (*tholos*) built of plundered Greek marble that still stands on the site of the Forum Boarium. In 142, the first stone bridge across the Tiber appeared, the Pons Aemilius, part of which still stands.

Domestic Architecture Between 200 and 150, Greek influence had also modified domestic architecture. The simple atrium house now received additional amenities such as baths, and gardens flanked by colonnaded walkways off the back. Greek-style fountains, pools, and statuary completed this pleasant setting where the members of well-to-do families could relax.

Innovations in Construction In 196, the first triumphal arch marked the blending of a distinctively Roman form with the Greek style of decoration. Even more important was the development of new construction techniques that allowed the Romans to combine massiveness of form with Greek elegance. The first was the development of molded concrete (*opus caementicium*) whereby a mixture of mortar and small stones was packed into wooden forms that were stripped away once the mixture had set. Buildings could be made more quickly and with less skilled labor than by using dressed stone blocks. This type of construction was also more versatile because it made arches and vaults relatively simple to build. Thus it was easy to provide strong but open supporting walls and vaulted ceilings that required no other support. The same advantages were available with baked bricks, which were fast coming into significant use.

Sculpture and Decoration The tradition of Roman bronze sculpture and terra-cotta relief continued in the second century. Greek sculptors, however, began to produce many neo-Attic marble statues and reliefs for Roman patrons by the second half of the century. Greek artisans also produced frescoes and mosaics in the Hellenistic style to decorate both private and public buildings. By 133 B.C., therefore, the efforts of aristocratic Roman leaders had graced Rome with the best works of art that could be plundered or copied from the Greek world. The spoils of war had also enabled them to adorn the city with public and private buildings built and decorated in the Greek style but with innovative techniques that would soon permit the Romans to build to heights and expanses that the Greeks never imagined.

Literature Just as Roman aristocrats used Greek art to proclaim their triumphs over the older culture that they were appropriating as a mark of social prestige, so they sought to harness the language, literature, and thought of the Greeks to their patriotic and self-serving cause.

Even Cato the Elder, who publicly scorned the "weak Greeklings" whom Rome had conquered, took the trouble to learn Greek. First of all, Greek was the international language throughout the wider world of which Rome had become an important part after the conquest of Italy and Carthage. In order to deal with the leaders of Greece and the Hellenistic kingdoms as equals, it was necessary for Roman senators to understand and speak Greek. Second, there was a certain curiosity and a practical need on the part of the Romans to find out more about the Greeks, whom they increasingly conquered and had to control. Third, despite their feelings of moral and military superiority, many Romans must have felt a certain amount of awe and admiration before the accomplishments of an older, more refined culture and wished to imitate it.

The Works of Livius Andronicus By the end of the First Punic War in 241 B.C., Lucius Livius Andronicus, the former Tarentine slave, had acquired a reputation as a teacher and translator of Greek for eager Roman aristocrats (p. 81). One of his earliest works was a Latin adaptation of a Greek epic poem, the *Odyssey.* Its meter was Saturnian, an accentual Italic one using the stress placed on syllables within a word, not a quantitative meter like that of Greek poetry, which is concerned with the kind of vowel, whether open or closed, in a syllable and how long the syllable is held in speech.

The *Odyssey* was a very good choice to adapt for Roman readers. Its description of travel in exotic lands appealed to Romans, whose horizons were just then extending beyond the narrow confines of Italy. Also, unlike the *Iliad,* it did not dwell on the Greek defeat of the Trojans, whom the Romans by now were claiming as their ancestors. Odysseus' wanderings and hardships even provided the models for those of Aeneas, who supposedly had led the Trojan refugees to Italy. Therefore, if not the first piece of Greek literature adapted to Latin, Andronicus' *Odyssey* was the first to attain wide popularity at Rome. It continued to be used as a textbook by schoolmasters for centuries. In the late first century B.C., the poet

Horace once recalled having to memorize passages from it when he was a boy.

In 240 B.C., the aediles, who were planning the annual festival of the Roman Games, *Ludi Romani,* wanted something special with which to celebrate the recent end of the First Punic War. They asked Livius Andronicus to adapt a Greek tragedy and a Greek comedy for the Roman stage. He not only wrote the texts but also performed as the chief actor. His efforts aroused great enthusiasm and set the trend for Roman drama ever after.

The Creativity of Roman Literature   The fact that all subsequent Roman authors freely borrowed from the Greeks has often led people to charge that Roman literature is wholly derivative and not worthy of respect. That is not a legitimate view. The ancient Greek and Roman concept of creativity is different from the modern. For an ancient artist the supreme challenge was to work within a given tradition in order to refine it and improve it, not to create something startlingly new. What the best Roman authors did was to adapt Greek literary forms to the expression of distinctively Roman themes and ideas. Roman literature was intensely patriotic, even nationalistic, portraying the glories of Roman history and the values that distinguished Romans from other people.

Naevius (ca. 270 to 199 B.C.)   The first native Roman to achieve success as an author was Livius Andronicus' slightly younger contemporary Gnaeus Naevius. He was proficient in tragedy, comedy, epic, and satire. He continued to use the native Saturnian meter and was Rome's first nationalistic poet. He wrote the first important plays that dealt with events of Roman history, *fabulae praetextae,* rather than Greek mythology. He also wrote the first patriotic Roman epic. Appropriately enough, Naevius' subject was the First Punic War, in which he had served. He wove in legends that told of Rome's founding by descendants of Aeneas and thus provided Vergil (70 to 19 B.C.) with useful material for the *Aeneid*. In his plays, Naevius often made critical comments about contemporary political figures. One of them re-

taliated by having him imprisoned. He was freed only after writing two apologetic plays. He then lived as an exile at Utica in North Africa, where he died. His fate more severely limited the use of personal invective on the Roman stage in contrast with the license of Greek Old Comedy.

Ennius (239 to 169 B.C.)   The heir of Naevius as a master of tragic, comic, and epic poetry was Quintus Ennius. The fortuitous circumstance of being a native Italian living near the Greek cities of southern Italy and under Roman domination made him trilingual, knowing Oscan, Greek, and Latin. His talent was equally diverse. He had a thorough understanding of Greek thought, a real ear and feeling for language, and a genuine admiration for Rome. His love of Rome overcame the anti-Hellenism of Cato the Elder, who brought him to Rome in 204 B.C., after they had served together in the Roman army on Sardinia. At Rome, Ennius quickly became acquainted with other leading Romans, such as the elder Scipio Africanus, who acted as his patrons.

Ennius' tragedies were more admired than his comedies. They reveal the influence of Euripides in their subjects, rationalism, and critical liberalism. He also wrote some philosophical books and some shorter poems of a satirical nature. His greatest achievement, however, was his patriotic epic poem entitled the *Annales*. In eighteen books, the *Annales* dealt with the tales of Rome's past and the history of the Second Punic War. Thus, Ennius carried on the process of integrating the legends of Rome's founding with real history. The poem's major innovation was the use of quantitative meter on the Greek model instead of the native Saturnian meter. In both respects, therefore, Ennius served as another of Vergil's major models.

Specialization after Ennius   As Roman authors became more skilled and experienced with various literary genres, it became more difficult for any one person to master them all. Some began to evidence special talents in particular fields. Eventually, individual authors intended to work exclusively in one genre or another.

Pacuvius (ca. 220 to 130 B.C.) and Accius 170 to ca. 85 B.C.)

Marcus Pacuvius and Lucius Accius tried to carry on the Naevian and Ennian tradition of mastering all major poetic genres, but they concentrated their greatest efforts on tragedy. Pacuvius was Ennius' nephew. Extensive fragments of his plays survive and reveal that they had good intellectual content, impressive characterization, and powerful language. Accius seems to have shared these characteristics, so that later Horace and Quintilian counted him among Rome's greatest writers.

Lucilius (ca. 180 to 102 B.C.)

In contrast to Pacuvius and Accius, Gaius Lucilius concentrated his attention on satire, which is Rome's most important contribution to the genres of Western literature. It grew out of a strong native tradition whereby famous people had hoped to avoid excessive pride and the jealousy of the gods by having their faults as well as their virtues pointed out in a jesting manner during such events as triumphal celebrations and funeral processions. Lucilius really made the genre of satire in its modern sense: sharp, biting, witty commentary on the social and political life of various people and the times in general. As a close friend of the younger Scipio Africanus, Lucilius had access to many of the important men who looked to Scipio for leadership. He was particularly critical of Scipio's opponents, as one might expect. Although his Latin was not elegant, Lucilius had a natural, vigorous sense of humor that was highly appreciated by the later satirists Horace and Martial and the critic Quintilian.

Plautus (ca. 254 to 184 B.C.) and Terence (ca. 195 to 159 B.C.)

Tragedy and comedy were the first literary genres to reach their highest stage of development at Rome. In contrast to early tragedy, however, which is known only through fragmentary quotations and comments in later works, Roman comedy is represented by a body of twenty-seven complete plays, twenty-one assigned to Titus Maccius Plautus

and six belonging to Publius Terentius Afer. Few facts are known about the life of Plautus. Even his real name was unknown until 1815, when the oldest manuscript of his plays was discovered. He was not a native-born Roman but an Umbrian from the Italian town of Sarsina, a fact that shows how Roman culture, as in the case of Livius Andronicus and Ennius, was enriched by the incorporation of conquered and allied peoples into the Roman state. Just as with modern New York, London, or Paris, few of the great literary figures associated with ancient Rome were natives of the city itself.

A little more is known about Plautus' younger contemporary Terence, but the issue of his origin is a matter of dispute. According to the second-century-B.C. biographer Suetonius, he had been born at Carthage and was a slave at Rome to a senator named Terentius Lucanus. Suetonius or his source may have inferred Terence's Carthaginian birth from his cognomen, Afer, which, however, usually distinguished other North Africans from Egyptians and Carthaginians. Terence is also called *fuscus,* "dark" or "swarthy," a descriptive word that Romans applied to individuals from all over the ancient world from India, the Levant, and Asia Minor to even Gaul and Spain but not to Black Africans, who were called Ethiopians (*Aethiopes*). It is likely, therefore, that Terence was not born a slave at Carthage but had been captured or bought as a child from one of Carthage's North African neighbors and brought to Rome perhaps by a Carthaginian merchant.

Whatever the case, Terentius is said to have recognized the young man's intellectual gifts and set him free after giving him a good education. Terence's talents brought him to the attention of Scipio Aemilianus, the younger Africanus, who helped launch his career. Unfortunately, his talent was soon extinguished when he died during a trip to Greece in 159 B.C.

The comedies of Plautus and Terence underline the growing impact of Greek culture on the Romans in the late third century and throughout the second century B.C. Both authors freely borrowed their plots, situations, and characters from the Greek New Comedy of the Hellenistic era, especially as represented by Menander, Diphilus, and Philemon. Plautus, however, infused his plays more with the native comic traditions of Italy, which Roman intellectuals had not yet learned to despise, as they did when the influence of older Greek culture became even stronger in the latter two thirds of the second century B.C. Despite the external trappings of urbane Greek New Comedy, Plautine comedy is basically farce inspired by native Italian Atellan farces and the ribald humor of Etruscan Fescennine verses. It is rich in slapstick, fast-paced wordplay, and satirical comment on matters of public concern, elements lacking in the surviving examples of New Comedy. The latter was much more genteel and philosophical in nature.

Terence, the younger author, reveals the greater impact of Hellenism on the younger generation of Romans in the second century B.C. He was patronized by aristocrats like Scipio Aemilianus, who had received a more thoroughly Greek education than their predecessors and had begun to look down on their native culture before it had a chance to reach a greater level of sophistication built more on its own foundations. Terence's plays are much more intellectual and less farcical than the plays of Plautus. Terence's Latin reflects the speech of the educated upper class rather than the less polished, more racy talk of the man in the street. His plays try to teach the psychological lessons of New Comedy. They make good literature but not such entertaining stage productions as those of Plautus. That is why Terence sometimes had trouble holding the attention of his audiences, as he complained in the introductions to his *Phormio* and to his *Mother-in-Law.* Moreover, it is significant that after Terence there are no more important writers of Roman comedy. The growing Hellenism of the educated elite prejudiced them against writing in a manner that would appeal to a mass audience. They turned to other forms of writing, while the average Roman enjoyed revivals of Plautus' and occasionally Terence's old plays, which have continued to inspire comic playwrights down to the present.

The plays of Plautus and Terence not only are important as major contributions to Western comic drama but also are historical reflections of the great cultural, social, and economic changes that affected Rome with the acquisition of an empire. Obviously, the influence of Greek New Comedy on Roman authors mirrors the impact of Greek culture in general. Moreover, New Comedy appealed to the Romans precisely because of the parallels that they saw with their own times. The prominence of slave characters corresponds to the tremendous increase of slavery in Roman society. The conflicts between fathers and sons or husbands and wives that often provide the plots are similar to the conflict between the more cosmopolitan younger generation of Romans like Scipio Aemilianus and Romans of the old school like Cato the Elder and emphasize the growing independence of upper-class women. The prominence of merchants, high-living young men, and gold-digging mistresses mirror the great influx of wealth that Rome was experiencing. The plays may have been set in Greece, but the topics were as much Roman as Greek.

Prose Literature Roman prose took much longer to reach its highest development than did its comedy. In fact, the first significant Roman prose authors were historians who wrote in Greek after the Second Punic War. Many of the early Roman historians are called annalists because, like the official records of the pontiffs, their works were organized on a year-by-year basis. The two earliest known historians, Quintus Fabius Pictor and Lucius Cincius Alimentus, were both Roman senators who had served in the Second Punic War. Fabius came from one of the most famous *gentes* in Roman history and took special interest in the deeds of the Fabii and other great families. Alimentus was from one of the newer, plebeian aristocratic families. As is true of all the early annalists, their works are lost except for quotations and borrowings by later authors. The loss of Alimentus is particularly regrettable because he was captured by Hannibal's army and may have known Hannibal personally. His experience with the Carthaginians seems to be reflected in his reputation for being fair to both sides in the Punic wars. Fabius, on the other hand, was notoriously anti-Carthaginian and blamed the Second Punic War on the Barcids' hatred of Rome.

Two other senatorial annalists, Gaius Acilius and Aulus Postumius Albinus, appeared around 150. Acilius' intellectual interests are reflected in his role as interpreter for three Greek philosophers who represented Athens before the senate in 155 (p. 142). Postumius had fought under Aemilius Paullus against Perseus and had extensive experience in the Greek East. They and their two predecessors all devoted much space to the period of the Monarchy and foundation of the Republic in order to construct a glorious past worthy of Rome's glorious present. They then emphasized Rome's recent greatness with lengthy treatments of the first two Punic wars.

Greek was the logical choice of language for them for several reasons. First, the only models for writing prose history were Greek, and it would have been easier to use existing Greek vocabulary and concepts than to create new ones in Latin. Second, the use of Greek made their works available to both Rome's educated elite and the Greeks, who were becoming more interested in Rome as Roman power grew but seldom bothered to learn Latin, which they considered too crude and beneath their dignity. Third, Roman writers wanted to counteract the favorable view of Carthage that Greek historians presented in their accounts of the Punic wars.

Polybius (ca. 200 to ca. 118 B.C.) In many ways, although he came to Rome as an Achaean Greek hostage after Pydna (p. 115), Polybius represents a continuation of the tradition of Roman historians writing in Greek for a Greek audience. Having obtained the friendship and patronage of Scipio Aemilianus, son of L. Aemilius Paullus, the victor at Pydna, he accompanied Scipio on military and diplomatic missions. In this way, he developed intimate, first-hand knowledge of how Rome's aristocrats thought and acted. Similarly, he personally traveled over much of the Mediterranean world. He even retraced Hannibal's march over the Alps and undertook a voyage beyond the Pillars of Hercules down the West African coast.

Unfortunately, his account of that voyage is lost, but part of his forty-volume *Histories* survives to the enormous benefit of today's historians. All of the first five books and a good part of Book Six are extant. Later authors also preserve numerous excerpts from other books, but five are completely lost. Although he is not without bias, Polybius tries to provide the Greeks with a sophisticated and rigorously analytical explanation of how Rome came to dominate the Mediterranean world from ca. 220 to 167 B.C. He included, however, a background discussion of the First Punic War and its aftermath and analyzed the effects of Rome's conquests on itself and others between 167 and the destruction of Carthage in 146. Though a rigorous intellectual, he was no mere armchair historian. He practiced what he called "pragmatic history" by the careful analysis of documents, the interrogation of eyewitnesses, and the acquisition of firsthand geographical knowledge.

Cato the Elder (234 to 149 B.C.) The first Roman to compose an important history in Latin was Polybius' older contemporary at Rome, Marcus Porcius Cato the Elder. It was entitled *Origines* (*The Origins*) and covered the early history of Italy and the founding of Rome as well as their recent past. For the recent period, by leaving out famous names and including parts of his own speeches, Cato deflated other prominent men and glorified himself. In one well-known episode, Cato underscored the omission of famous names by giving only the name of Surus, one of Hannibal's elephants. Cato gave to Latin prose many important contributions other than his history of Rome. He wrote major works on law, medicine, and agriculture, the last of which, the *De Agricultura*, survives as the earliest extant work of Latin prose and a valuable source of information on Roman life and economic history in the second century B.C. Cato also published a book on rhetoric and was the first Roman to publish his own speeches.

Rhetoric   The publication of Cato's speeches and his work on rhetoric emphasize the growing importance of the art of rhetoric and rhetorical training. With the growth of Rome as a world power, the state needed officials and leaders capable of clearly expounding problems and policies in public meetings, in senatorial debates, and in dealings with foreign governments. The increased complexity of Roman life also meant more lawsuits and, therefore, a need for more trained advocates to plead them. Naturally, great Greek masters of oratory and rhetoric like Demosthenes, Isocrates, and Thucydides served as models for the formal practice of those arts at Rome.

Two of the most accomplished orators of the day were two of the most eager Hellenizers, Scipio Aemilianus and his Stoic friend Gaius Laelius. According to Cicero, Scipio had a reputation for solemnity, as befitted a great aristocrat. Laelius was a little softer and smoother but tended to be austere overall. Unfortunately, all of their works and those of their contemporaries are lost except for a few scraps quoted by later authors.

Philosophy   Hand in hand with history and oratory at Rome grew an interest in philosophy, which meant Greek philosophy, of course. Philosophical systems were useful to the practical-minded Romans because they could provide the conceptual and logical structures for developing ideas in speech, sharpen skill in debate, or clothe personal or partisan purposes with high-sounding phrases. The formal study of philosophy at Rome also received a big boost in 155 B.C. when the Athenians sent an embassy made up of the heads of three major philosophical schools: Critolaus the Peripatetic, Diogenes the Stoic, and Carneades the Academic skeptic. While waiting for an opportunity to address the senate, they gave a series of public lectures that aroused much interest.

Carneades the Academic made the greatest impression. As a skeptic, he had no absolute dogmas or guides on ethical and intellectual questions. He substituted a system of probability and in an eclectic spirit set out to combine the best aspects of all philosophical schools in order to improve the human condition. To show the weakness of absolute dogmas, he argued one side of a question one day and convinced the audience that he was right and then, just as convincingly, argued the other side on the following day. Cato the Elder was scandalized and expressed fear that this skeptical approach would undermine traditional Roman morals.

More compatible with traditional Roman values was the philosophy of Stoicism. The Stoic doctrines of a divinely created world brotherhood and hierarchical order and its stress upon duty, the upholding of established authority, and the natural rule of the wise were tailor-made for Romans seeking to justify their growing empire to themselves and others. These ideas had been popularized by Panaetius of Rhodes, who lived for some time as a guest of Scipio Aemilianus and his famous friend Gaius Laelius, often called *Sapiens,* "The Wise," because of his Stoic learning. Another Stoic, Blossius of Cumae, was the tutor of the tribunes Tiberius and Gaius Gracchus and may have had some influence on their reforms to aid the poor in 133 and 123 B.C. (pp. 146–155).

The fourth major school of Hellenistic Greek philosophy, Epicureanism, did not find many important adherents at Rome until after 100 B.C. The tendency to go to extremes in adopting Epicurus' doctrines about the lack of divine punishments and the primacy of pleasure as life's goal horrified traditional-minded, conservative Roman aristocrats. Therefore, as early as 173 B.C. the senate banished Epicureans from Rome.

The Romans themselves made no notable original contributions to philosophy in this period. They had little patience with the intricacies and hairsplittings of philosophical controversies. They mostly received the established systems of the Greek schools, chose what suited their purposes, and applied it to their lives. For example, those who were concerned with law adopted the rigorous dialectic of the Stoics in order to give structure and order to Roman law.

Law The publication of Cn. Flavius' handbook on the wording of lawsuits and legal formulae in 304 had broken the pontiffs' monopoly on interpreting the civil law. Afterward, a number of aristocrats became private students of the law. They obtained public recognition and gratitude as lawyers and legal interpreters known as jurisconsults (*iurisconsulti*). Around 200 B.C., the jurisconsult Sextus Aelius Paetus published a valuable, systematic legal work in three parts: the text of the Twelve Tables; various interpretations that had clarified and expanded the application of those laws over the years; and a detailed presentation of the various forms of lawsuits and their appropriate *formulae*. It became a classic that influenced Roman jurisprudence for centuries. The systematized exposition and interpretation of Roman law by aristocratic jurisconsults clearly reflected the influence of the Greek philosophy and rhetoric that were part of every Roman aristocrat's education. The spirit of Roman law, however, was always rooted in practical experience. Nowhere was that more visible than in the practical changes resulting in more efficient legal procedures as Roman society became more complex.

Civil Procedure The earliest procedure in civil cases was known as the *legis actio* because it was based on very specific statements of actionable deeds or occurrences called *legis actiones*. Under this procedure, both the plaintiff and the defendant had to appear before a pontiff or, after 367, a praetor. First, the plaintiff stated his case orally according to the precise wording of the appropriate *legis actio*. The defendant, whom the plaintiff could compel to appear, had to reply in the same way, as did the pontiff or praetor conducting the hearing. If the latter decided that there was a basis for a suit, he and the contending parties would by mutual agreement appoint a fellow citizen as judge. The judge would then hear the evidence and arguments in a separate proceeding and render a verdict. If the plaintiff won, he had to take action himself to enforce compliance with the judgment. For example, he could handcuff his

opponent for up to sixty days to compel him or his representative to pay a fine.

Because there were only five *legis actiones*, it became harder to find one that would fit a given complaint as life became more complex. Moreover, the prescribed oral statements were so cumbersome as to produce verbal slips that would cause cases to be rejected. The praetors began to create formulary procedures conducted in writing according to *formulae* published in their annual edicts. The formulary procedure still involved an initial hearing and then an actual trial before a judge or panel of judges, but because the written formulary procedure was less subject to disqualifying slips and because praetors could modify the *formulae* or create new ones as new situations arose, the formulary procedure became much more popular during the third and second centuries.

Criminal Procedure What the Romans called public law (*ius publicum*) dealt with criminal matters. The earliest ways of dealing with crimes, which continued to be widely used in the second century B.C. and beyond, were personal revenge, raising a hue and cry among friends and neighbors who might administer rough and ready justice on the spot, or an informal "trial" before the accused's *paterfamilias*. He had the right to judge anyone who was legally subject to his *patria potestas*. He usually relied on ancestral custom (*mos maiorum*) and the advice of an informal council of friends to determine guilt and punishment.

In the more impersonal world of a large city, however, the private methods of dealing with crime were not always satisfactory. Sometime during the years 290 to 288, special minor magistrates called *triumviri capitales* had first been appointed to deal with serious crimes like murder. They generally exercised jurisdiction over slaves and lower-class citizens. For members of the upper classes, who had power, money, and influence, there could be a trial before one of the higher magistrates with appeal to a popular assembly in capital cases. Cases prosecuted on appeal were usually handled by tribunes and sometimes by quaestors and ae-diles. In special cases of great interest to the governing class, the senate could set up special commissions to conduct a trial.

As public life and politics became more complex, however, laws were passed to set up standing praetorian courts, *quaestiones perpet-uae,* to deal with major crimes. The first per-manent *quaestio* was the extortion court (*de re-bus repetundis*) established by L. Calpurnius Piso in 149 to hear cases against extortionate provincial governors. During the first century, the permanent courts (also called *iudicia pub-lica*) greatly increased in number. One of the major features of the courts was their use of ju-ries made up of fifty senators chosen by lot. Later, the use of nonsenators on these juries would be a matter of great political controversy. As was the case in all courts, prosecution had to be initiated by the aggrieved party. There were no public prosecutors, and except for cases of capital punishment or a state fine, the winner of a criminal case also had to enforce the verdict himself.

Religion   While jurisprudence and legal pro-cedure were becoming more systematic and ef-ficient under the influence of Greek philosophy and practical experience, the Romans were re-sisting the influence of ecstatic mystery cults from the Greek East. The worship of the Greek god Dionysus, or Bacchus as the Romans called him, had become very popular among the Greeks of southern Italy by the third century B.C. The drunken, orgiastic revels of this cult provided a welcome emotional release from the harsh, unremitting routine of daily life faced by the poorer classes, especially the women. Many conservative Romans were not only shocked by the uninhibited behavior of Dionysiac wor-shippers, but as the cult spread they feared that its secret, orgiastic meetings masked a conspir-acy against Roman rule in Italy. In 186 B.C., the senate passed a decree (still extant) against the Bacchants and forbade, under penalty of death, more than five people to meet together for pri-vate worship in Rome or Italy without permis-sion from the praetor.

The senators also sought to restrain the overwrought emotionalism of the worship of Cybele, the Great Mother, which had been im-ported to Rome in 205 B.C. during the dark days of the Second Punic War after consultation of the *Sibylline Books*. The cult of the Great Mother centered around the death and resur-rection of the god Attis, who was both her son and husband. The rites symbolized the annual death and rebirth of vegetation. The actual cult object was a black stone brought from Pessinus in Asia Minor and housed in a temple on the Palatine. Wild celebrations associated with it were performed by gorgeously clad eunuch priests and included riotous outdoor parades, ecstatic dances to the beat of drums and cym-bals, and castrations and self-mutilations per-formed at the climax of religious fervor. Roman leaders were properly horrified and, despite the state's official sponsorship of the cult, denied Roman citizens the right to participate.

Roman religion itself was not immune to the desire for more intense religious activities in the exciting world of a great city. Therefore, partly in response to the needs of the people as well as a result of increased wealth, the state greatly expanded the size and scope of religious festivals, *ludi,* at Rome. They included circus races, perhaps at one point a magical attempt to influence the cycle of the seasons and the rota-tions of the heavenly bodies associated with them; gladiatorial combats (introduced in 264 B.C. from Etruria, where they were part of fu-neral rites for departed spirits to supply them with blood and vitality); and dramatic perfor-mances, the first of which were held at the *Ludi Romani,* September games in honor of Jupiter, in 240 B.C. Other major festivals were the *Ludi Plebeii,* Plebeian Games, to honor Jupiter in No-vember; the *Ludi Apollinares* for Apollo in July; and the *Ludi Megalenses* in honor of the Great Mother, the *Ludi Cereales* for Ceres, and the *Ludi Florales* for Flora, the goddess of plants, all in April. Except for the *Ludi Apollinares,* these festivals were put on by the aediles and brought them so much public recognition and popularity that they had an interest in expanding the num-ber of days and events involved, often at their own expense, as time went on.

The educated Roman elite did not abandon traditional religion but often became more sophisticated in their religious views under the influence of Greek philosophy. Many adopted the ideas of the Hellenistic thinker Euhemerus. He argued that the gods were simply human beings who, like Hercules, had by their superhuman deeds become saviors of the world. His work on the origin of the gods was so popular that Ennius translated it into Latin. It had a significant impact on the Roman aristocracy's ambition for fame and glory and is the underlying assumption behind the deification of Roman emperors later on.

Education Expanded cultural and intellectual life created a need for more formal education at Rome. In the early days, when Roman life was primarily rural for aristocrat and peasant alike, education such as it was had centered around home and family. Slaves were not used as tutors. The mother and other female relatives trained the children at least until the age of seven. After that, girls remained under their mothers' tutelage to learn about household management, whereas boys accompanied their fathers into the fields and Forum to learn how to make a living and be good citizens. Fathers considered it one of their gravest duties to furnish precepts and examples from which their sons could learn their roles as citizens.

At about sixteen, a young male became a man and put on the *toga virilis,* toga of manhood. Soon the young man left his father's personal care. A young aristocrat was often placed by his father in the hands of an old and distinguished friend to further his training for public life. Then, after a year or two, about age seventeen, the young aristocrat entered military service. First, as a soldier in the ranks, he learned how to fight and obey orders. Then, he joined a general's staff to learn the techniques of command. After that, the young man apprenticed himself to another older man at Rome to complete his training in political life.

The purpose of this system was not only to provide a basic education in practical matters but also to inculcate the rigid system of Roman moral values and service to the state as passed on in the ancestral customs, *mos maiorum.* This ideal is seen, for example, in the Roman attitude toward athletic training. The Hellenistic Greeks fostered athletics for health, beauty, and personal satisfaction in excelling through competition as much as for military training. Roman physical education still centered primarily on training for war, and conservative Romans were shocked at the nudity and self-indulgence associated with contemporary Greek athletics.

In the third and second centuries, however, with the increasing interest in Greek culture, Romans began to adopt features of Greek education. Wealthy Romans began to use learned Greek slaves to take care of children and supervise the instruction of the young in Greek language and literature. Greek freedmen set up grammar schools to teach the children of those who could not afford slave tutors. At first only Greek was taught, but as Latin literature became established, Latin grammar schools appeared, too. In the second century, professional Greek philosophers were even coming to Rome to offer instruction at a higher level.

In every way, therefore, Rome's expansion into the wider Mediterranean world between 264 and 133 B.C. had intensified the interaction of Greek and Roman culture. Although Greek influence had been important since the arrival of the Greeks in Italy, it had never been so self-consciously cultivated as it was in this period. During the next century, the Greco-Roman cultural synthesis would progress still further as the Romans became even more closely involved with their Greek subjects.

XIV

The Gracchi and the Struggle over Land Reform, 133 to 121 B.C.

By 133 B.C., the socioeconomic changes resulting from the Punic wars and Rome's rapid expansion overseas were producing serious problems and discontent among a number of groups (pp. 127–131). The attempts of Tiberius Sempronius Gracchus and his brother Gaius to deal with some of these problems and satisfy the interests of disaffected elements ushered in a century of increasingly violent political upheavals that helped eventually to destroy the Roman Republic. Therefore, the careers of these two men and the circumstances surrounding them constitute one of the most intensively studied subjects in Roman history.

Sources for the Period of the Gracchi, 133 to 121 B.C. Unfortunately, the sources for this crucial period are not nearly so extensive or reliable as for the preceding one. There is no extant contemporary source. Although he lived through the Gracchan crisis and it colored the later stages of his writing, Polybius ended his history with the year 145/44 B.C. The continuation of Polybius down to about 78 B.C. by Posidonius (p. 235) is lost. Even the most extensive secondhand account, Books 58 to 61 of Livy, which would have preserved much valuable detail from contemporary or nearly contemporary sources, is also lost except for the brief summaries of the *Periochae* and the sparse outlines derived from him in the late Empire

(p. 471). The few relevant fragments from Books 34 and 35 of Diodorus Siculus and from Books 24 and 25 of Cassius Dio have little value. The same is true for Book 2 (sections 2–7) of Velleius Paterculus. The only extensive accounts are Plutarch's biographies of Tiberius and Gaius, which are naturally limited in scope, and sections 9 to 26 in Book 1 of Appian's *Civil Wars* (Books 13 to 17 of his history as a whole).

The Lack of Military Recruits Traditionally, the Roman legions were recruited from landowning citizens (*assidui*) whose property, usually small family farms, was equal to a certain minimum value. This requirement was supposed to ensure that they could provide the weapons and equipment necessary for legionary warfare. Men without the requisite wealth were used as rowers in Roman fleets or as craftsmen and other service personnel necessary in large armies. Despite successive lowering of the minimum qualification, by 133 B.C. the casualties from a century of almost constant warfare and the decline of small farmers as a result of accompanying economic changes had combined to reduce dangerously the number of recruits available for legionary service.

In 145 or 140 B.C., Gaius Laelius, friend of Scipio Aemilianus (p. 142), had tried to relieve the problem by proposing a law to reinforce the so-called Licinio-Sextian laws of 367, which supposedly limited to 500 *iugera* (about 320 acres) the amount of public land that an individual could hold, and to resettle on surplus land people who had lost their farms. When he met with vehement opposition from many fellow senators, he decided to withdraw his proposal and avoid an obviously sensitive issue. In 133, however, Tiberius Sempronius Gracchus refused to avoid a confrontation under similar circumstances.

The Tribuneship of Tiberius Gracchus, 133 B.C.

When the 30-year-old Tiberius Gracchus took office as tribune of the people in 133 B.C., he bemoaned the impoverishment of Roman citizens and worried about the loss of recruits for Roman legions. Without consulting the senate, he immediately introduced before the *concilium plebis* his famous agrarian bill designed to break up the large estates created out of public land and to divide them among landless Roman citizens. It had been drafted with the support of his father-in-law, Appius Claudius Pulcher, the "first man" (*princeps*) of the senate, and of two learned jurists, P. Licinius Crassus and P. Mucius Scaevola, the consul of 133 B.C. It ordered the state to repossess all public land in excess of 320 acres plus an allowance of 160 acres for each of 2 sons. The holders of estates between 320 and 640 acres were guaranteed clear title, unencumbered by taxes or rent, and reimbursement for any improvements, such as buildings or plantings, on the land to be repossessed. The repossessed land was to be assigned to landless citizens in lots varying in size, probably from 9 up to 18 acres, and was to be subject to a nominal rent payable to the state. The allotments were inalienable and entailed against sale or transfer.

Although it was unusual and inflamed opinion against Tiberius in the senate, his initial failure to consult that body was neither unconstitutional nor unprecedented. In 232 B.C., Gaius Flaminius had obtained enactment of his agrarian law without consulting the senate (p. 94). When Tiberius finally did submit his bill for senatorial approval, it was rejected. Then he made the bill less generous toward the large landholders and rashly refused to abide by the repeated vetos of a fellow tribune, Marcus Octavius. To win his cause in the *concilium plebis*, he took more radical steps to parry traditional constitutional weapons used by his opponents.

Arguing that Octavius was working against the interests of the plebs instead of for them as a tribune should, Tiberius issued the fateful call for a vote of removal. The favorable votes of eighteen of the thirty-five tribes would decide. Even at the last minute, Tiberius gave Octavius a chance to relent. When the first seventeen tribes had voted against Octavius, Tiberius held up the voting for a moment to appeal to his colleague to change his mind. The latter remained obdurate. The voting resumed, and Octavius was divested of his tribunate and forcibly removed from the tribune's bench. Later, the land bill passed.

The Agrarian Commission To carry out the provisions of the land act, Tiberius asked the people to appoint a commission of three members consisting of himself, his younger brother, Gaius, and his father-in-law, Appius Claudius. The commission was later granted full judicial powers with *imperium* to determine which lands were public and which private, to repossess all public land not exempt by the law, and to distribute it to new settlers. Ample funds were required to pay the salaries of surveyors and other officials as well as to help the new settlers make a start by providing them with housing, tools, work animals, seed, and even subsistence till the crops were harvested. Now Tiberius' opponents in the senate, which traditionally controlled appropriations, had a chance to stop him. They appropriated operating expenses of only a denarius and a half a day. Tiberius took another radical step to thwart them.

The Pergamene Treasure Attalus III of Pergamum had upon his death willed his personal fortune and kingdom to the Roman People (p. 116). This matter usually would have been handled in the senate, but Tiberius, it is said, at once requested the people to make these funds available for the use of the commission. It is not completely certain whether such a bill was ever passed or whether the mere threat to deprive the senate of control over provincial revenues caused that body to open up the public treasury for the use of the commission. Thus thwarted, his opponents began to threaten his life. To prepare the ground for violence, they circulated the rumor that he was planning to declare himself king and had retained for that purpose the diadem, scepter, and royal vestments of the Pergamene kings.

Tiberius Campaigns for a Second Term   To protect his legislation from annulment and to save himself from certain prosecution and probably death, Tiberius offered to run for a second term, a step contrary to recent custom but not unconstitutional. The sovereign people could reelect him in spite of law or custom just as they had, in violation of custom, elected his grandfather, Scipio Africanus, to the supreme command during the Second Punic War. Frustrated and embittered by Tiberius' refusal to abide by traditional political rules, his enemies were bent on his defeat and destruction.

The early voting ran so strongly in his favor that opposing partisans interrupted the proceedings by vetoes and bogus religious "omens." Just when the assembly seemed about to break out in open riot, Fulvius Flaccus pushed his way through the milling throng to inform Tiberius that the senate was holding an emergency session in the Temple of Faith. Opponents, he said, had accused Tiberius of wanting to be king and invoked an ancient law under which Tiberius was to be killed as a tyrant.

Scaevola, the consul, had refused in horror to take part in the murder, but Scipio Nasica Serapio, who was *pontifex maximus,* and some other senators rounded up a mob of sympathizers and slaves and hurried to the Forum. The tribunes of the people, who might have interposed their sacred persons between Tiberius and the mob, scurried out of the way. Picking up legs of broken chairs and benches, Scipio Nasica and his men rushed toward Tiberius and clubbed him and 300 of his followers to death. They threw the bodies into the Tiber.

P. Popillius Laenas, consul in 132 B.C., set up a special court to try the Gracchan partisans. The more outspoken ones were executed. To forestall popular retribution, Scipio Nasica was whisked out of danger and sent on a diplomatic mission to Pergamum.

Tiberius' Motives   The struggle over Tiberius Gracchus' land reform bill has often been simplistically portrayed as a struggle between Tiberius on the one hand and the Roman senate on the other: Tiberius appears as some kind of ideologically motivated democratic liberal or radical reformer in the modern mold; the senate merely represents the corporate interest of a wealthy landed oligarchy seeking to protect its financial interests without any regard for the social and economic problems of Rome. Such a view is untenable. Tiberius did not start out with some scheme of radical reform in mind. His reform was essentially a conservative one. It was designed to restore Roman military manpower, which had always depended on the free class of peasants, and to halt the spread of estates worked by slaves. Their increasing numbers posed a serious threat to internal peace and security, as witnessed by the slave revolt in Sicily from 136 to 131 and a brief uprising of slaves in Campania (p. 129).

Insofar as his law would stem the migration of dispossessed rural citizens into the city and even attract back to the countryside some of those who had already come to the city, Tiberius may also have hoped to alleviate some of the unemployment and attendant sociopolitical stress existing in Rome itself. The flow of booty that had sustained economic growth at Rome had ceased with the sacks of Carthage and Corinth in 146. Since then, Rome's wars, mainly against poor tribesmen and slaves, had become an economic burden. The urban economy, heavily dependent upon expenditures for publicly and privately funded construction projects, had become seriously depressed.

Tiberius' reforms, therefore, were not based on consideration of some abstract radical ideology, although it is quite possible that his education at the hands of Greek and Stoic teachers like Diophanes of Mytilene and Blossius of Cumae provided him with arguments to support the rightness and justice of his cause. Nor was Tiberius fighting the senate as an institution or seeking to destroy the primary role of the senatorial aristocracy in governmental affairs. Tiberius himself was a member of the consular families that dominated the senate. The senate was not a monolithic bloc opposed to Tiberius. It is often overlooked that powerful members of the senate worked on his initial reform bill. No doubt, many of those senators who opposed Tiberius did so to protect their own extensive landholdings. Others, however, saw his actions as threats to the "constitution" in which they genuinely believed. Still others opposed him on the basis of personal and factional politics.

The "institutional fallacy" in historical analysis must be avoided. No institution, class, or state does anything. The senate of the United States, for example, does not ever *do* anything. A majority, sometimes all, of those senators who vote on a given issue decide if an action is to be taken or not, and each senator has a unique combination of motives for voting the way he or she does, although each may share many of the same motives with others to one degree or another. Tiberius Gracchus' determination to pursue agrarian reform in the face of bitter opposition from many of his fellow nobles cannot be understood without reference to the personalities and careers of individual senatorial aristocrats.

As expected of members of his class, Tiberius Gracchus was a politically ambitious young noble. A number of factors made him particularly so. His father, now dead, had reached the pinnacle of public success. He had been consul twice, celebrated two military triumphs, earned much good will as a governor in Spain, reached the coveted censorship, and been a member of the prestigious priestly board of augurs. It was the duty of Tiberius, the oldest surviving son, to equal or surpass the achievements of his father and preserve the *dignitas* of the family. Moreover, the Sempronii Gracchi had been closely associated in politics with the Cornelii Scipiones since the time of the

Hannibalic War. Tiberius' mother, Cornelia, was the daughter of the elder Scipio Africanus, victor over Hannibal. Well educated and talented herself, she had had the distinction in widowhood of turning down an offer of marriage from the king of Egypt. Ambitious for her sons, she obtained the rhetorician Diophanes of Mytilene and Blossius of Cumae, a Stoic philosopher, as their tutors. She is said to have urged her sons to live up to the glory of both sides of the family and make her known not only as the daughter of Africanus, but as the mother of the Gracchi! Finally, Scipio Aemilianus, the younger Africanus and famous destroyer of Carthage, not only was Tiberius' first cousin by adoption but also was married to Tiberius' sister Sempronia. (By blood, because Cornelia was also the daughter of the sister of Scipio's natural father, she and Scipio were first cousins, and he was a first cousin once removed of Tiberius and Sempronia.)

At first, the connection with Scipio Aemilianus served Tiberius well. As a youth he had accompanied Scipio to Carthage and won his praise for valor, which would have impressed the voters when he ran for the quaestorship in 138. Nevertheless, there was ill will between Tiberius' immediate family and Scipio over an issue of inheritance produced by their complex relationships. Also, the marriage of Sempronia, which probably had been designed to restore friendly relations, was an unhappy one and merely made matters worse. As so often happened in the Roman aristocracy, complex interrelationships that had arisen from close political cooperation between families in earlier generations led to personal animosities that embittered political differences and rivalries in later generations.

Probably two or three years after he returned from Carthage, Tiberius became betrothed to the daughter of Appius Claudius Pulcher, who happened also to be Scipio's chief rival for preeminence within the nobility. In 137, Tiberius served as quaestor in Spain under C. Hostilius Mancinus, who was besieging Numantia and whose close relative, L. Hostilius Mancinus, was an enemy of Scipio. Mancinus and his whole army were disgracefully captured by the Numantines. Because of his father's reputation, Tiberius was the only one with whom the Numantines would negotiate a treaty. He obtained the release of the whole Roman army and saved much precious manpower for Rome. It looked as if Tiberius would gain the kind of fame and honor that would advance his career.

Tiberius was bitterly disappointed. When he brought the treaty to the senate for ratification, Scipio Aemilianus strenuously opposed it and helped persuade a majority of senators to reject it. Furthermore, Mancinus, Tiberius, and the other officers were prosecuted for cowardice. Tiberius and the others secured acquittal, but Mancinus was ordered stripped, bound in chains, and handed over to the Numantines. (The Numantines showed their contempt for Rome by sending him back.) Hostility to the Hostilii Mancini may well have been a factor in Scipio's actions. Even more important was his desire to keep the war going so that he could obtain command of it and gain the glory of avenging Rome's disgrace with another great victory. He succeeded in 134 and 133 after obtaining exemption from the law forbidding second consulships. In fairness to Scipio, he did help Tiberius escape Mancinus' fate, and he took Tiberius' brother Gaius to Spain as an officer on his staff, but the whole episode had dealt a tremendous blow to Tiberius' prestige.

When he ran for the office of tribune in 134 B.C., Tiberius was desperate to find a means of saving his political career. Land reform was the perfect vehicle. It was urgently needed to help solve some of Rome's pressing socioeconomic and military problems and was a very popular issue with a large bloc of voters in the rural tribes. Once he was elected and succeeded in obtaining a law for redistribution of land, he hoped that those who received land would become a grateful source of votes in the rural tribes for the future. The rural tribes, of course, were the key to the election of tribunes and passing of plebiscites in the *concilium plebis.*

Personal animosities and political maneuvering within the senatorial aristocracy, therefore, go a long way to explain the actions of Tiberius Gracchus and some of the leading opponents of his reform. Tiberius was certainly sincere in his desire to alleviate some of Rome's pressing problems through land reform. Moreover, he also may honestly have believed that there was more long-term danger to Rome's well-being if he bowed to the traditional obstructionist tactics of his opponents within the senate than if he mobilized the sovereign power of the *concilium plebis* to overcome them. Nevertheless, for a politician the most attractive reform is one that is not only just but also politically beneficial to the politician himself. Once set on the path of reform, he could not give up in the face of powerful opponents. To have suffered a second political defeat after the rejection of the Numantine treaty would have meant the end of his career within the senatorial elite. That is why, every time his opponents tried to use traditional constitutional means to stop him, Tiberius resorted to more and more untraditional practices to thwart them.

The Land Commission and Its Impact

That the land commission set up to administer the Sempronian land law was allowed to function even after its creator was slain is another indication that much of the opposition to Tiberius in the senate was not based on ideological opposition to reform or narrow economic self-interest but on personal and factional politics. Because the man who would have reaped the most political benefits from the reform was now dead, it was no longer a threat to his rivals. Indeed, they now tried to reap for themselves the benefits of *gratia* (gratitude) among those who received allotments. The consul Popillius Laenas even boasted of what he had done to carry out the law. On a milestone in Lucania he caused the statement to be inscribed that he was "the first to compel the shepherds to make way for the plowmen."

The commissioners appointed after the death of Tiberius were two active supporters of Tiberius: M. Fulvius Flaccus and C. Papirius Carbo. They worked with zeal and energy. Despite lawsuits and delaying tactics by those who possessed the land, within 6 years the commission may have settled over 75,000 men, an increase of 20 percent in the manpower available for military service. The Gracchan land law seems temporarily to have achieved the objective of strengthening the military power of Rome.

The work of the commission was hard and probably involved some injustice. After the passage of time and with the poor methods of keeping records in ancient times, it was seldom easy to determine what land was public. However conscientiously the commissioners consulted old land registers and summoned neighbors to testify, probably in some cases they seized private property and in others confiscated the only good land that the occupiers possessed. The complaints must have been numerous and bitter.

Rome's Allies and the Death of Scipio

The grievances of Roman citizens probably were not given a sympathetic hearing, but those of the Latin and Italian allies could not have been brushed aside so easily. To have ignored the complaints of the allied states might have constituted a violation of their treaty rights with Rome, disturbed peaceful relations, and perhaps even invited revolt. To the allies, in some cases, whether as individuals or as communities, Rome had assigned public lands by lease or by outright grant. In other cases, wealthy allied landowners simply had encroached on otherwise unoccupied Roman public land, as had wealthy Romans.

In either case, when the allies looked for a patron to champion their interests, they found one in Scipio Aemilianus, the destroyer of Carthage and Numantia. Realizing the value of their military help and anxious to extend his network of clients, he gladly consented to press their claims before the senate and succeeded in having the judicial powers of the commissioners transferred to the consuls, at least as far as the Latin and Italian allies were concerned. If the consuls preferred to go off on long campaigns to avoid involvement in irksome land disputes, the work of the commission would be brought to a standstill.

Scipio's meddling with the land problem in 129 B.C. did not help his popularity. In fact his popularity had waned since he had spoken before an assembly against Carbo's bill to legalize reelection to the tribuneship.[1] In the course of the debate, Carbo asked him what he thought of the murder of Tiberius Gracchus. Scipio replied, "If Gracchus intended to seize the government, he has been justly slain." When the crowd greeted this remark with jeers and catcalls, Scipio roared, "I have never been scared by the shouts of the enemy in arms. Shall I be frightened by your outcries, you stepsons of Italy?"

In May of 129 B.C., Scipio announced that he was going to make a speech about the Latin and Italian allies. It is not known whether he intended to talk about the granting of Roman citizenship. He went home early to work on his speech. The next morning he was found dead in bed. Whether he died from natural causes or was, as rumored, the victim of foul play by one of the Gracchans, perhaps aided by Sempronia, Scipio's wife and sister of Tiberius Gracchus, was never known.

Whereas previously the Romans had been fairly generous in granting citizenship to upper-class individuals in the Latin and Italian towns, there had never been any widespread desire for Roman citizenship among the allied communities. The increasingly inequitable relationship between Roman citizens and the allies (pp. 130–131), however, seems to have been brought into sharper focus by the activities of the Gracchan land commission. A number of Latins and Italians began to press more actively for citizenship. Their overt agitation in Rome made them quite unpopular, and in 126, with senatorial approval, a tribune pushed a bill through the assembly to legalize their expulsion.

The land commissioner Fulvius Flaccus took up the cause of citizenship for the Italian allies. As consul (125 B.C.), he proposed the grant of citizenship to any of the allies that wanted it. All classes opposed his idea—espe-

---

[1]Although Carbo failed to get this bill passed, he had succeeded two years earlier (131 B.C.) in extending the secret ballot to legislative assemblies. No bill was more potent in weakening the hold of politically entrenched nobles, because now they could not easily hold those whom they benefitted to account at voting time.

cially the common people, who did not want to share their privileges with the Italians. Fulvius had to abandon his efforts when his enemies in the senate sent him off at the head of a consular army to help Massilia fight hostile neighbors in southern Gaul.

In the same year, the allied town of Fregellae rose up in rebellion. What, if any, connection this event had with the question of Roman citizenship for the Italians is unclear. The events in Rome may simply have aggravated a particular local conflict among the Fregellans. At any rate, the revolt was crushed with the help of Fregellan "loyalists," who were rewarded, and the rest were stripped of their property and the town destroyed.

Although no other town revolted, the events at Fregellae may have heightened interest in the question of citizenship among other Italians. At Rome, feelings were intensified. Attempts were made to punish those who were suspected of having inspired and encouraged the revolt. Even Gaius Gracchus, who had just returned from Sardinia, was accused but was able to prove his innocence.

Gaius Gracchus, Tribune of the Plebs, 123 to 122 B.C.

The powers and capabilities of Gaius Gracchus were known and feared years before he became tribune. Those who had opposed Tiberius considered Gaius a menace because of his influence over crowds and his membership in the land commission set up by his brother. His enemies were naturally relieved when it fell to his lot in 126 B.C. to go as quaestor to Sardinia, whose pestilential climate, it was hoped, might do him no good, but he returned to Rome in 124 B.C. In spite of hostility from powerful fellow nobles, he campaigned for the tribuneship and was elected for 123. Voters from the rural tribes poured into the city, as they had done ten years before to support his brother. In 123, they voted him into office again for 122 B.C., although he was not an official candidate at that time.

The motives of Gaius Gracchus in promoting reform were essentially those of his brother Tiberius, with two major additions.

First, there was the desire to avenge the murder of his brother and repair the damage to his family's honor. Second, he wanted to build a far more broad and complex coalition of socioeconomic groups not normally part of the political process in order to gain an even broader base of political support than Tiberius had. That would help him win the offices necessary to repair his family's tattered *dignitas*.

The two years of the tribuneships of Gaius Gracchus were politically among the most memorable of the Roman Republic and perhaps the most crucial in the history of the Roman People. He converted the tribuneship, hitherto dominated by the same small number of noble families that also dominated the senate, into an instrument of almost absolute power, whereby an ambitious rival, usually from some other noble family, could effectively circumvent their control. A century later (23 B.C.), the Emperor Augustus strengthened his position against opposition from nobles loyal to the old Republic by invoking not the powers of a consul but the power of a plebeian tribune (*tribunicia potestas*).

The Reforms of Gaius Gracchus

Upon taking office, Gaius Gracchus proceeded to stir the fury of the people against his brother's murderers, who had violated the sacrosanctity of a tribune, and against the procedure by which Popillius Laenas had condemned his brother's followers to death without appeal to the people. The *concilium plebis* responded by passing a bill that prohibited the senate from creating extraordinary tribunals to condemn political offenders without appeal to the people. Under a retroactive provision of this law, Popillius Laenas was condemned and exiled.

Revenged, Gaius Gracchus proceeded to carry out his more constructive program of reform, which was designed to build a solid coalition of political supporters to advance his own career in competition with fellow nobles while dealing intelligently and realistically with the social and economic problems generated by the Roman conquests. The most pressing problems concerned the spreading unemployment and slums, the periodic fluctuations in food prices, the decline of military strength and efficiency, the frequent slave revolts, the continuing problem of provincial administration, and the dissatisfied allies. Therefore, he attempted by a series of measures to organize a coalition of the equestrian class, the proletarian city voters, and the small farmers to advance both his and the public's interests.

Land and Roads To win over the farmers' vote and meet their legitimate needs further, Gaius revived and amplified his brother's legislation. He restored to the land commission the judicial powers that Scipio Aemilianus had perhaps justly persuaded the senate to remove. Most of the public land had by now been assigned, but he was able to benefit the farmers by an extensive road-building program, under which a network of secondary roads was created linking farms with markets, villages with towns, and towns with Rome. These roads not only employed farmers as road builders but also permitted them to move their crops more easily and cheaply to markets and thus improved trade. Also, by facilitating travel to Rome and, therefore, attendance at assembly meetings, they promoted a fuller participation in affairs of government. The extraordinary speed with which this project was completed under Gaius' personal direction further increased the fears of the senate.

The Grain Law To gain the political support of the city masses and relieve their real distress, Gaius persuaded the assembly to pass the famous *lex Frumentaria,* or Grain Law, which provided that the state should buy and import grain from overseas for sale to citizens residing in Rome. It was sold on demand in fixed monthly amounts at six and one-third *asses* per *modius* (about one quarter of a bushel), a price roughly equivalent to one half of an unskilled worker's daily wage for about one quarter of a bushel and not far below the average market price in Rome but often much higher. This law, the most severely criticized of all the Gracchan reforms, did not constitute a dole; it was passed solely to promote price stabilization for the

benefit of the consumer, not, as now, for the producer. A considerable amount of the wheat consumed in Rome came in as tribute and cost the state only the expenses of transport, naval convoy, and storage. The Grain Law even provided for the construction of warehouses and wharves in Rome, a measure designed to relieve unemployment along with implementing the subsidy for grain.

The Grain Law also had a more subtle purpose. It was designed to weaken the patronage of entrenched fellow nobles and increase that of Gaius by using public money. In periods of high food prices, candidates for high office had regularly bought votes by the provision or promise of cheap grain. The Grain Law helped to restore the independence of Roman citizens and rendered more effective the secret ballot law of 131 B.C. It also earned *gratia* for Gaius among the voters resident in Rome.

Military and Monetary Reform Some other important laws passed also brought needed relief to poorer citizens and politically valuable gratitude to Gaius. The Military Law (*lex Militaris*) required the government to clothe and equip Roman soldiers without deductions from their pay, shortened the term of military service, and forbade the draft of boys under the age of seventeen. This law was intended to improve army morale, always a concern of the Gracchi, and to win the political support of soldiers, allies, and voters with small incomes. Furthermore, in 122 B.C. the weight of the denarius was reduced. This measure not only meant that in real terms Roman citizens had to pay less in fixed rents and taxes but also significantly reduced the tribute of the Roman allies without special legislation.

New Colonies Gaius Gracchus' laws authorizing commercial and agricultural colonies in Italy and across the sea were intended to relieve the overpopulation in Rome and provide economic opportunities for farmers, traders, craftsmen, and small businessmen unable to make a living. The sites selected were Capua, Tarentum, and Carthage. The most ambitious of these projects, as authorized by the Rubrian

Law, was the founding of Junonia near the cursed site of Carthage, where 6,000 colonists drawn from Rome and the rest of Italy were to be settled on farms of 125 acres. Gaius went to Africa to supervise in person the initial stages of the settlement.[2]

Provincial Taxes and Jury Service In an effort to drive a wedge between the wealthy equestrian class and his senatorial rivals, Gaius appealed to the economic interests of important *equites.* Those *equites* who had significant interests in business and particularly in tax farming (contracting to collect taxes for the state in return for a share of the proceeds) were already irked by the senatorial aristocracy's control over finance, provincial administration, and especially over the rich revenues of the new province of Asia, where taxes were collected at a fixed rate directly by the governor. Gaius had a law passed overturning this arrangement and directing instead that the taxes of Asia take the form of a tithe. Unlike the system employed in Sicily, where the tithe was auctioned and collected locally, the Gracchan law stipulated that the censors should auction the lucrative contracts for the tithes of Asia to tax-collecting companies in Rome for five-year terms. In that way, the money would come directly to the treasury in Rome, and the companies that won the contracts would then collect the taxes in the province.

The new system of taxation provided the Roman treasury with immediate funds and theoretically at least was less burdensome to the provincial taxpayers than fixed taxes since payments in kind would fluctuate with good or poor crops. It was also beneficial to the Roman tax collectors since clauses were added protecting them against losses due to war and other calamities. It naturally benefitted the richest men of the equestrian class, for the right to bid

was open only to those owning property worth in excess of 400,000 *sestertii* (sesterces), four times the minimum equestrian census. Thus Gaius' law increased the economic power of the wealthiest equestrians, who were expected in turn to use some of their wealth to advance their benefactor's political career. At the same time it weakened the power of his own rivals within the senatorial class.

Another move that tended to divide the equestrians from Gaius' senatorial rivals within the nobility was the Acilian Law, sponsored by one of Gaius' supporters, which excluded senators, the relatives of senators, and all curule magistrates from the juries of the standing courts established under the Calpurnian Law of 149 B.C. to try provincial governors for extortion.[3] This law, therefore, transferred jury service from the senatorial class to the equestrian class. It dealt with a serious abuse and achieved its purpose of widening the breach between the *equites* and Gaius' rivals. Unfortunately, it also gave equestrian business interests the means to punish good governors for preventing the wholesale exploitation and plundering of the provinces by businessmen.

The Italian Question One of Gaius Gracchus' fellow tribunes in 122 was his old ally Fulvius Flaccus. Together they renewed Flaccus' ill-fated earlier attempt to procure citizenship or at least some citizenship rights for the allies in Italy. That bill was a good attempt to address the justified discontent of Rome's allies while it won more voters to Gaius' side. Unfortunately, it enabled those who opposed him for personal reasons or genuinely thought that he was a dangerous demagogue destroying senatorial power to employ demagoguery against him.

Livius Drusus While Gaius was in Africa to lay the groundwork for the colony of Junonia, his enemies within the nobility plotted the destruction of both the Italian citizenship bill and its author. Their agent was the tribune M.

---

[2]Gaius' opponents were strongly opposed to Junonia and, by the use of propaganda and the appeal to superstitious fears of the curse of 146, managed to persuade the people after Gracchus' death to repeal the Rubrian Law authorizing the scheme. Had it been completed, he would have created a colony of loyal supporters in the vital grain-growing area of North Africa. Thus, he had anticipated by almost a century the policy of Augustus and the later emperors.

[3]The justification for the Acilian Law was the charge that the senatorial juries acquitted governors commonly believed guilty.

Livius Drusus, member of a prominent noble family and an eloquent speaker. He pandered to the selfish interests of the Roman populace by pointing out that the benefits of citizenship would be diluted by extending it to greater numbers, and he threatened to veto the Gracchan bill extending citizenship to the Italians. That threat prevented it from being brought to a vote because Gaius knew that it was unpopular and would not pass. Livius then presented a bill to protect Italian soldiers from mistreatment by Roman army officers, which was an important advance, but a shabby substitute for the citizenship bill.

He subsequently introduced a bill to found 12 colonies in Italy, each to consist of 3,000 colonists selected from the poorest class. The land was to be rent free. He also proposed to release from payment of rent the settlers who had been allotted land under the law of Tiberius Gracchus. The proposal to found 12 colonies in Italy was never intended to be carried out, because there was not enough public land left in Italy to permit so ambitious a scheme. After it had achieved its purpose of siphoning support from Gaius Gracchus, it was speedily dropped.

The Fall and Death of Gaius Gracchus

When Gaius returned from Africa, he discovered that Livius had succeeded in splitting the once solid ranks of the city electorate, who had supported him. Too long had Gaius stayed in Africa; too late did he realize the extent of the conspiracy against him. His immense popularity had made him overconfident and forced his rivals into close cooperation against him. Fulvius Flaccus' refusal to be cowed over the proposed rights for the allies reinforced the opposition. Therefore, Gaius was defeated in his attempt to run for a third term. Only his membership in the African commission (granted *imperium* by the Rubrian Law) stood in the way of political enemies now resolved to take his life.

To remove the protecting power of the *imperium,* they hastened to bring about the annulment of the Rubrian Law authorizing the founding of Junonia. No longer tribune, Gaius lacked the authority to summon the people or

the power to resist the threatened repeal. He wished to avoid acts of violence, which might give his enemies the excuse for authorizing extreme measures against him. Nevertheless, the newly elected consul, Lucius Opimius, the destroyer of Fregellae and a vehement opponent of Gaius, deliberately provoked an incident. Then, armed with a final decree of the senate (*Senatus Consultum Ultimum*), virtually declaring a state of martial law (p. 158), Opimius organized an armed posse that killed many Gracchans, including Fulvius Flaccus. Gaius attempted to escape but, seeing the hopelessness of his position, ordered his slave to kill him.

Thus died Gaius Gracchus, who, in his two years of office as tribune of the people, had temporarily broken the monopoly of power enjoyed by a small number of nobles who had dominated the senate and the popular assemblies. He had concentrated in his hands many executive powers and functions. He had supervised the distribution of grain to the populace, changed the composition of juries, awarded contracts for and superintended the construction of highways, presided over meetings of the senate, supported and campaigned for candidates to the consulship, and converted the tribuneship into an office more powerful than the consulship itself. Some of his reforms were truly measures of enlightened statesmanship. Others were dictated by political calculation and must be described as frankly opportunistic. Most were combinations of both.

In death, the Gracchi were mightier than in life. By killing them, their enemies had unwittingly exalted the two tribunes into figures of heroic proportions. Allowed to live they might have been the sooner forgotten. Instead, statues were erected to them in public places, and the spots where they had fallen became hallowed ground. Prayers and sacrifices were offered to them as to gods. Even the proudest noble, regardless of his private opinions, dared not speak of them in public except in respect and veneration. The common people revered them for having brought hope into a world of misery and exploitation. Ambitious fellow aristocrats, seeking advantage against rivals, followed their political strategy.

XV

The Breakdown of the System, 121 to 88 B.C.

The careers of the Gracchi reveal a major reason why the reforms necessary for preserving the stability of the Roman Republic were extremely difficult to make. Reform, however altruistic or patriotically motivated, could not be separated from the highly personalized political competition within the Roman aristocracy. Laws always bore the name of the man who proposed them. Therefore, any law that brought about significant reform benefitting a large number of discontented people would bring the man who proposed it a large increase in supporters among the voters. Envy, jealousy, and political self-interest would cause many current or potential rivals for public office and esteem to resist the attempted reform with every weapon at their disposal—even including violence and, as the competition intensified, eventually civil war.

In addition, violence and murder reinforced themselves through vengeance. The victims of the violence employed by the opponents of Gaius Gracchus seethed in silence until they had an opportunity to retaliate. That, in turn, produced more retaliation and furthered the downward spiral to civil war. Overheated competition and the lust for revenge, therefore, created more and more instability. The Republican system began to lurch from crisis to crisis without hope of a peaceful solution to its problems.

Sources for the Period from 121 to 88 B.C.
As for the Gracchi, the literary sources for this period are also in disarray. The brief summaries of Livy Books 62 to 76 in the *Periochae* and the epitomes largely derived from him in the late Empire provide only a bare outline, as does Velleius Paterculus (Book 2.8–17). The fragments of Books 34 and 35 of Diodorus Siculus have some information on events from 111 to 104 B.C., and large fragments from Books 36 and 37 are valuable for the years from 104 to 88. The fragments of Books 26 to 29 in Cassius Dio are useful for events from 114 to 88, and there are some fragments on the Jugurthine War (111 to 104 B.C.) in Book 8 of Appian. The only lengthy extant sources are *The Jugurthine War* of the mid-first-century-B.C. historian Sallust (pp. 243–244), sections 27 to 54 of the first book from the part of Appian's history known as the *Civil Wars,* and Plutarch's lives of Marius and Sulla, part of which are based on Sulla's *Memoirs.* Some inscribed boundary stones, road markers, fragmentary inscriptions of laws, and excavations of colonial settlements help us to understand the process of land distribution after Gaius Gracchus; and Cicero's speech *Pro Rabirio perduellionis* discusses the civil strife of 101 and 100 B.C. Cicero knew many of the major figures during this period and made numerous references to them in his works, especially his philosophical dialogues and rhetorical treatises (pp. 242–243).

Populares and **Optimates** In analyzing the political struggles that marked the century of Roman history after the Gracchi, two labels are often applied to the protagonists. Those ambitious and even well-intentioned individuals who followed the Gracchi's example of building public support by promoting reforms and policies that benefitted significant discontented groups of voters or potential voters are often referred to as *populares* (sing. *popularis*). In Roman political rhetoric this label was applied to such people by more traditionally minded aristocrats or those whose current domination in the senate was guaranteed by the status quo. They did not approve of seeking popularity among large groups of voters on public issues. Instead, they preferred to rely on the traditional political tools of family reputation, personal alliances with other aristocrats, and the marshaling of clients whose loyalty had been won by individual services. They called themselves *optimates,* the best people, in contrast with the *populares,* whom they accused of using dangerously demagogic tactics. The *optimates* naturally disliked anyone who sought a base of power that they did not control, and many may honestly have feared that *popularis* actions would eventually lead to the creation of a popularly supported tyrant and destroy the Republic.

In no way should the terms *populares* and *optimates* be taken as representing anything like modern political parties with their formal institutional structures and acting within some explicit philosophical framework or theory of government. They do not even signify cohesive factions. The terms mainly indicate in a broad way the two different types of political tactics employed by individual political figures at any given moment in the history of the late Republic.

Insofar as the labels *optimates* and *populares* mean anything, they can be applied only in the context of particular political conflicts between individuals or personal factions. Both the social origins and the goals of the people so labeled were mostly identical. They almost always came from the senatorial aristocracy and sometimes from ambitious equestrian families allied with a powerful noble. Their goals were to retain or increase power and prestige in competition with their peers through public service, which was very important in their aristocratic system of values. Individual *optimates* were often just as much rivals with each other as they were with individual *populares,* and vice versa. For example, individual *optimates* might temporarily ally themselves against a *popularis* who threatened to outstrip them all, but as soon as he was eliminated they would usually resume intense competition among themselves. Nor were *populares* opposed to the dominant role of the senate in the Roman government. They themselves usually were members of the senate. They were looking for ways to establish their own dominance in the senate by utilizing the office of tribune of the plebs and other means of appealing to the mass of voters outside the senate. Many may also have been convinced of the rightness or justice of their positions, but in no way were they seeking to overthrow the power of the class to which they mostly belonged. They wished only to secure their preeminence in it.

Therefore, the political conflicts of the late Roman Republic cannot be viewed as struggles between the senate as a monolithic institution and outside democratic leaders or reform groups. The question was what individual or group of personal allies would control the senate, which controlled Rome. Not even Julius Caesar, for example, ever sought to abolish the senate. In the civil war that Caesar precipitated at the end of the Republic, many senators supported him. He fought against those fellow senators who opposed him in the competition for glory and prestige, *dignitas.* Having beaten them, he merely packed the senate with his loyal supporters to ensure his personal domination.

After the death of Gaius Gracchus, his opponents, who can be broadly classed as *optimates,* kept most of his legislation operate once he could not benefit from it at their expense. They ceased regular grain distributions, but they changed neither the selection of jurors for the extortion courts nor the administration of provincial taxes. Even the land laws, including those pertaining to the founding of colonies, though modified, were not overthrown.

The *Senatus Consultum Ultimum* The reign of terror following the slaying of Gaius Gracchus seems to have silenced temporarily anyone who might have challenged his optimate opponents. When Opimius was prosecuted for murder before the people, he was acquitted, and his acquittal appeared to confirm the legality of the Ultimate Decree of the Senate, *Senatus Consultum Ultimum (S.C.U.)*. That decree advised the consuls to take whatever steps they deemed necessary to preserve the safety of the state and could be construed as a decree of martial law suspending normal constitutional procedures. The senate's right to issue such a decree, however, was not based on any legal statute or ancient customary practice.

Therefore, the question of its validity remained open and subject to the political passions of the moment. *Popularis* politicians shunned it because of its origin as a weapon against the Gracchi and its lack of legal sanction by a popular assembly, but *optimates* always considered it a perfectly constitutional weapon against *popularis* rivals during the late Republic. Because they were dominant at this point, their view temporarily prevailed and even Popillius Laenas, who had been exiled by the people for killing the followers of Tiberius Gracchus, was now allowed to return to Rome. Nevertheless, many *popularis* supporters of the Gracchi who had suffered at the hands of *optimates* wielding the *S.C.U.* nursed their resentment and waited for a popular issue to exploit against them.

Post-Gracchan Land Legislation In the meantime, leading *optimates,* who dominated the senate, pursued policies designed to protect their interests while satisfying those groups to whom the Gracchi had appealed. Three successive laws gradually modified the Gracchan land

legislation to benefit all who had been affected. The first, probably in 121 B.C., permitted the settlers to sell the farms allotted to them. Although this law tended to nullify the purpose of guaranteeing that there would be enough men to meet the property requirements for military service and permitted the rich proprietors to buy or force the sale of small neighboring properties, it was not necessarily unpopular. Trying to earn a living on a small holding was not easy. It would be even more difficult if it were divided among heirs into smaller holdings. Many settlers probably would have been pleased to sell for ready cash.

The second law (perhaps in 118 B.C.) abolished the land commission (whose work probably was already done), halted further division of public land in Italy, and guaranteed legal possession of lands already distributed on payment of a small rent to the state. That would have pleased both large and small proprietors. It also would have been especially welcome to the Italian allies, at whose expense any further distribution of *ager publicus* in Italy probably would have come.

In 111 B.C., the third law abolished all rentals ordered by the second, declared as private property all public lands up to 320 acres assigned by the Gracchan commission, and guaranteed to colonies and municipalities secure tenure of lands already granted. It also forbade further encroachment on public pastures and strictly regulated the number of animals grazed on those lands. Relief from rents benefitted both large and small proprietors, and allies in the municipal towns appreciated the secure tenure of lands granted to them. Small farmers would have welcomed the attempt to keep large neighbors from encroaching illegally on additional public land, and both large and small operators would have benefitted from the regulation against destructive overgrazing.

Colonization The Gracchan program of land settlement in Italy was strongly reinforced both before and after the tribunate of Gaius by the conquest, colonization, and settlement of lands beyond the borders of Italy. Thousands of Roman settlers still remained around Carthage after the formal abolition of the Roman colony. New settlements were made at Palma and Pollentia on the Spanish island of Majorca, and much territory was settled in a new province created in southern Gaul. Between 125 and 120, the Romans took over the coastal strip between the Alps and the Pyrenees except for the small territory of Massilia, which welcomed Rome's suppression of their restless neighbors.

This territory became the province of Transalpine Gaul, later called Narbonese Gaul (*Gallia Narbonensis*) or simply the Province (hence modern Provence). In 118 the Romans founded a citizen colony of discharged veterans at Narbo on the Via Domitia, which linked the Rhône valley to Spain. It not only provided commercial operators a trading center in southern Gaul but also provided new lands for settlement by the small farmers of central Italy. In this way, the number of properly qualified military recruits might be maintained, and those who sold their Gracchan allotments in Italy might use the proceeds to capitalize a fresh start in the rich province of Gaul.

The Jugurthine War and the Rise of Gaius Marius, 111 to 106 B.C.

The outbreak of the difficult and disgraceful Jugurthine War in the North African Kingdom of Numidia finally gave the vengeful and ambitious an issue to exploit in a *popularis* manner against the dominant *optimates* in the senate. Eventually, it brought to the fore Gaius Marius, one of the most powerful *populares* of the late Republic. The war was named after Jugurtha, a grandson of Scipio Aemilianus' old Numidian ally Masinissa. Brave and quick witted, he had attracted Scipio's favor during his service in the war against Numantia. Scipio persuaded King Micipsa, son of Masinissa, to adopt Jugurtha. Trouble followed when Micipsa died in 118 and left Numidia jointly to Jugurtha and his own two natural sons. The Roman historian Sallust, with allowances for rhetorical exaggeration, tells a vivid tale of murder and betrayal as

Jugurtha gained control of the whole kingdom with the connivance and corruption of powerful Roman senators.

In 112 the wealthy *equites* were outraged when Jugurtha besieged one of his rivals in the city of Cirta (Constantine, Algeria), an important center of the North African grain trade. Many equestrian grain merchants and their agents were trapped in the besieged city and were massacred when it fell. This massacre incensed both the common people and the *equites* at Rome. Therefore, it became an issue that could be exploited with *popularis* tactics. In 111 the tribune Gaius Memmius openly accused some senators of taking Jugurtha's bribes and attacked the senatorial leaders so vigorously that they were shamed into asking for a declaration of war.

The commanding consul, however, made only a pretense of fighting and quickly offered Jugurtha easy terms. Popular opinion was outraged, but when Memmius ordered an investigation, another tribune blocked him. Jugurtha then procured the murder of a cousin who was living in Rome and trying to get support against him. Such a slap in the face of the Roman People could not be ignored. The senate repudiated the tainted peace and renewed the war in 110. When Jugurtha defeated the Roman army in 109 and demanded another humiliating peace, the people were even more outraged. Another tribune put through a bill setting up a special court to try senators deemed responsible for the debacle. The jury was filled from the list of equestrian jurors established by Gaius Gracchus for the extortion court. Among those condemned for corruption and sent into exile was the infamous Lucius Opimius, who had used the *S.C.U.* to slay the followers of Gaius Gracchus.

Command of the war finally went to a competent general, Quintus Caecilius Metellus, consul in 109 and a member of the most powerful noble family in Rome at the time. He was incorruptible and an excellent disciplinarian. Unfortunately for him, however, the damage to the army's morale and preparedness could not be repaired overnight. Both the *equi-*

tes and the people wanted speedy results and were inclined to accuse Metellus of prolonging the war for his own glorification.

Gaius Marius (157 to 86 B.C.) If people back in Rome did not understand the difficulties of African warfare, Gaius Marius, one of Metellus' senior officers, did, but he was calculating and unscrupulous enough to exploit them in a *popularis* manner. He urged the equestrian merchants in North Africa to write letters to their friends and agents at Rome in praise of him and in protest of Metellus' conduct of the war. This was the second time in which he double-crossed Metellus' powerful family, and he did so to win enough votes to be elected consul himself.

Born outside of Arpinum, a little town south of Rome, Marius was the son of a wealthy equestrian landowner. His ambition was to reach the consulship at Rome and ennoble his family. He was an excellent soldier and knew how to win popularity among the common recruits, who would remember him at election time. Even after he had become their commander, he slept on the same hard ground as the troops. His rough and ready appearance and his use of common idiom also endeared him to the average man.

He had been with Scipio Aemilianus at the siege of Numantia. His courage, his physical endurance, the care that he took of his horse and equipment, and the attention that he gave to details about the camp had earned Scipio's respect. Later he had become a client of the powerful Metelli family, who had helped him to become a tribune for 119 B.C. At that point, however, he had deserted his patrons for the first time.

He had won the admiration of the common people by his defiance of the aristocracy and his threat to arrest the consuls, one of whom was Metellus' brother, for opposing his bill to make it more difficult for patrons to influence the ballots of their clients. His noble patrons had been outraged and had helped to ensure his defeat in his campaign for the aedileship. He had managed with some difficulty and much bribery, however, to get elected

to a praetorship in 115 B.C., after which he had been sent as a propraetor to Farther Spain, his first military command.

Marius' praetorship had entitled him to admission into the upper ranks of the senate. His money and success had earned him a useful connection with the ancient patrician family of the Julii Caesares through marriage to the aunt of the future Julius Caesar. He also had been able to mend fences with his offended former patrons and get Metellus to appoint him to his post in the war against Jugurtha. Even so, without any noble ancestors of his own, Marius would have found the consulship beyond his reach, except perhaps under most unusual circumstances—circumstances he had helped to create at Metellus' expense.

Marius Campaigns for the Consulship At first, Metellus scornfully refused when asked for a leave to campaign for the consulship. Finally, however, to get rid of a disgruntled officer, Metellus granted Marius permission to go to Rome, where he was elected consul for 107 B.C. Marius, the first of his family to reach the consulship, was a *novus homo,* new man, resented deeply by the old nobility. To add insult to their injury, he also was given the North African command by a plebiscite against the will of Metellus' optimate supporters in the senate.

In recruiting troops for service in North Africa, Marius tried to solve the problem of military manpower by accepting as volunteers all who were physically fit regardless of property qualifications. This move was the logical outcome of a long process of lowering the property qualification for service in order to keep up the supply of recruits. It had occasionally been resorted to in past emergencies. After Marius, it became a regular practice.

Inadvertently, however, this change had serious political consequences. Roman legions became manned more and more by propertyless volunteers personally loyal to their commanders, upon whom they depended for their welfare and whose clients they had become. Successful generals could now more easily compete with their political rivals by mustering the votes of loyal veterans or using them to intimidate their opponents. The value of military commands was thereby raised and the temptation to provoke some foreign military crisis to obtain one became even greater. More ominously, a successful military commander backed by an experienced and personally loyal army was in a greater position to resort to civil war.

Marius Defeats Jugurtha After rigorous training had turned his recruits into serious soldiers, Marius' methodical warfare forced Jugurtha on the defensive by 106. Finally, his quaestor, a capable noble named Lucius Cornelius Sulla, procured Jugurtha's capture by persuading Jugurtha's principal ally, King Bocchus of Mauretania, to betray him. The captured Jugurtha, in accordance with Roman custom, eventually met death by strangulation in the dungeon of the Tullianum after his appearance in Marius' triumph (104 B.C.). As a reward for his treachery, Bocchus received the western and drier part of Jugurtha's kingdom, the eastern part going to Gauda, the half-witted brother of Jugurtha. The business interests of Marius' equestrian friends and relatives were satisfied at last. Numidia was safe for Roman investment and exploitation. Marius was now Rome's most popular military hero. The *comitia centuriata* would elect him, sometimes *in absentia* and always contrary to the law requiring a ten-year interval between repeated offices, to five consecutive consulships (104 to 100) during a formidable series of foreign and domestic crises. First and foremost was the threat of attack from a number of migrating Germanic tribes.

The War with the Cimbri and the Teutones, 105 to 101 B.C. Driven south by overpopulation and coastal inundations, the Cimbri, Teutones, and other Germanic tribes had sought to settle in Transalpine Gaul. Often they had offered to serve in Roman armies in return for land. Met with refusal, they had smashed three Roman armies in 109, 106, and finally at the Battle of Arausio (Orange), in 105. Even if the report of 80,000 Roman casualties is high, this last disaster left Italy open to invasion and recalled the terror of the Gallic sack of ca. 390. Tribunes seized upon popular fear and frustration with corruption and incompetence to attack prominent commanders and other leading senators with prosecutions. They also promoted more laws designed to limit aristocratic influence over voters. Marius' "unconstitutional" five consecutive consulships reflect the impact of fear and popular pressure on the Centuriate Assembly in a period of extreme crisis.

Marius Reorganizes the Legion To meet the tactical problems presented by the Germanic tribes, Marius reorganized the Roman legion. He abolished the light-armed units and divided each legion into 10 cohorts of 500 to 600 men to make a legion of 5,000 to 6,000 heavy infantry armed with javelins (*pila*), short swords (*gladii*), and oblong body shields (*scuta*). Each cohort, in turn, had 6 centuries of 80 to 100 men with a centurion in charge of each century. The cohorts replaced the old maniples and became units strong enough to fight separately but numerous enough to be deployed in various tactical combinations. Thus, without losing its flexibility, the legion acquired a new compactness and cohesion now symbolized by an identifying emblem carried on a standard topped by a silver eagle.

Marius also standardized equipment and training that made soldiers much more professional. Each soldier carried his own cooking kit, construction tools, tent, and rations for three days. "Marius' mules," as they came to be called from their weighty backpacks, were trained to fight as duelists in the cut-and-thrust technique used by gladiators. They were toughened up by long marches and by a great deal of fatigue duty such as ditchdigging. Thus, by a combination of hard training and cohesive organization, Marius made the legion a formidable military machine that in time would also become an effective political weapon in the hands of ambitious generals.

Defeat of the Germans With his newly trained and organized legions, Marius defeated one group of Germans in 102 before they could cross the Alps into Italy. In 101 he himself crossed the Alps to join the consul Quintus Lutatius Catulus in defeating the Cimbri at Vercellae (probably near Turin). After that, a third group of Germans wisely retreated home without a fight. Marius was now a true popular hero.

The Slave Revolt in Sicily, 104 to 100 B.C.

Had the Germans invaded Italy and set at liberty a million slaves or more, the consequences might have been similar to a revolt of the slaves in Sicily that took five years to suppress. In 104 B.C., Marius asked the Roman client-kings of Asia Minor to send troops to assist in the defense of Italy against the Germanic invaders. When the kings sent back word that most of their subjects had been kidnapped and sold as slaves by pirates and that many of them were in Sicily, Marius and the senate ordered the governor of Sicily to release the slaves held illegally. After the release of several hundred persons, the governor allowed himself to be browbeaten by the landowners and harshly ordered the rest of the slaves applying for freedom to go back to their masters. They did not go back. Instead, they took to the hills, and the slave revolt swelled into full-scale war. For four years (104 to 101 B.C.), the slaves had control of the country. Before the end of the Cimbrian War released enough troops to put down the rebellion, 100,000 lives had already been lost.

Piracy in the Eastern Mediterranean

Even before the suppression of the Sicilian slaves, the Romans had to deal with piracy in the eastern Mediterranean. Ever since the destruction of Rhodes as a naval power, the pirates and slave traders of Cilicia and Crete had enjoyed unrestricted freedom of the seas and conducted kidnapping raids upon the coastal regions of Syria and Asia Minor to supply the great slave market of Delos (where 10,000 slaves are said to have been sold every day) and Roman purchasers. Finally in 102 B.C., two years after King Nicomedes III of Bithynia had complained to Rome about the abduction of one half of his able-bodied subjects, the praetor Marcus Antonius (grandfather of the famous Mark Antony) was commissioned to attack and de-

stroy the chief bases and strongholds of the eastern Mediterranean pirates. After destroying many pirate hideouts, he annexed the coastal part of Cilicia as a Roman province and base of future operations against the pirates. These measures may have checked but did not destroy the evil of piracy.

The Political Fall of Marius

Just returned from glorious victories in 101 B.C., Marius was the object of adulation and even worship at Rome: He was seen as "another Camillus," a savior. He enjoyed the unfailing support of a devoted army and found before him a populace that cried out for leadership. He had held five consulships; he wanted more.

Marius entered his sixth consulship in 100 B.C. Unfortunately for him, however, Rome was at peace. All of his jealous enemies in the senate now felt free to work against him. To overcome their opposition to legislation benefitting his veterans, equestrian supporters, and Italian clients, Marius had to rely on two opportunistic *populares,* Lucius Appuleius Saturninus and Gaius Servilius Glaucia, who were prepared to go to greater political extremes than Marius would have liked.

Lucius Appuleius Saturninus and Gaius Servilius Glaucia, 103 to 100 B.C.

Saturninus was an eloquent speaker, an able man, and an ambitious noble whose career had suffered a serious setback. Therefore, he became an active supporter of Marius in an attempt to gain popularity and a position of strength against rivals. When Saturninus entered upon his first tribuneship in 103, he sponsored a law assigning 66 acres of land in Africa to each of Marius' African veterans. A colleague of his, acting in concert with his opponents, attempted to veto the bill but, after a shower of stones, promptly withdrew his veto. Saturninus had no patience with obstructive tactics or legal technicalities. Fists and stones were more effective than vetoes or religious "omens."

During his first tribuneship, Saturninus introduced a law that made it a criminal offense to compromise, injure, or diminish the honor or dignity (*maiestas*) of the Roman People. By the very vagueness of the charge, this law would become dangerous to all as time went on. For his part, Saturninus used it to prosecute unpopular nobles and enhance his own power. For example, he prosecuted the unpopular ex-consul who had obtained passage of a law in 106 B.C. to give the extortion court back to senatorial jurors. In 101 Glaucia was tribune and obtained passage of a law that gave the extortion court back to equestrian jurors again.

In 100 B.C., the year of his second tribunate, Saturninus embarked upon a full program of social legislation. Glaucia, who was now a praetor, supported him. This program included a grain law (possibly dating back to his first tribunate of 103), which restored the regular monthly grain distributions, suspended after the death of Gaius Gracchus, at a selling price below the market rate. The bill seems to have been carried over the vetoes of other tribunes and the violent opposition of the quaestor in charge of the treasury. Saturninus' second bill provided for the founding of veteran colonies in Sicily, Greece, Macedonia, and possibly Africa. A third bill, an agrarian law, assigned land once occupied by the Cimbri and Teutones in Gaul (possibly Transalpine Gaul) to veterans who had fought under Marius.

Lastly, Saturninus proposed a general mobilization of Roman forces against the Cilician pirates and against Mithridates VI of Pontus, a command that was intended for Marius. To this batch of laws, Saturninus appended a clause requiring all senators to take an oath within five days to obey these laws—on pain of loss of their seats, exile, and a fine of twenty talents. In spite of vetoes, "omens," and violence, the laws were passed.

The Fall of Saturninus, Glaucia, and Marius

All eyes were fixed on Marius to see if he would take the oath of obedience appended to the bill assigning land in Gaul to his veterans. At the last minute, he did take the oath to observe the law "as far as it was legal." This express reservation turned the law into a farce. All the senators who took the oath would be able to make the same reservation. Marius' blunder lay in his indecision. He wanted to cooperate with the popular leaders, but at the same time he did not like to offend the powerful senators who opposed Saturninus. Marius thus reveals what was typical of most *populares*. He was quite willing to seek popularity by opportunistic means in order to gain high office and status, but he shared the same basic aristocratic outlook as his foes. Having achieved equality with his former noble opponents and rivals, he instinctively cooperated with them in preserving the political status quo.

Before the end of his second tribuneship, Saturninus had lost the support of both the equestrian class and the city masses. The *equites* disliked his radical and revolutionary methods and feared that he might next attack the sanctity of private property. The city voters turned against him because his agrarian law of 100 B.C. had granted too many benefits to the veterans, many of whom were Italians. Hostile optimate senators and personal enemies were quick to take advantage of the situation to bring down *populares* like Saturninus and Glaucia.

Knowing now that their lives were worth nothing the moment they stepped down from office, Saturninus and Glaucia campaigned successfully for the tribuneship and consulship, respectively, although Glaucia was in defiance of the Villian Law requiring a two-year interval between the offices of praetor and consul (p. 134). In order to rid himself of a possibly successful opponent, Glaucia hired gangsters to kill the former tribune Gaius Memmius. The senate declared a state of emergency and ordered Marius to take action under the *S.C.U.*

Marius did not want to injure or destroy Saturninus, Glaucia, and the other popular politicians to whom he and his veterans owed so many benefits. To save their lives and follow the senate's orders at the same time, he locked up Saturninus and some of his followers in the senate building. An angry mob of nobles and *equites* climbed up to the roof, ripped off tiles, and pelted the prisoners to death. On the same day, they dragged Glaucia from a friend's house and murdered him. Marius, distrusted and disliked by his old enemies among the nobles and despised for his weakness by his former friends, was obliged to look on helplessly as the senate declared the laws of Saturninus null and void. This action apparently ruined Marius' career and gave second thoughts to those who would seek political advantage through *popularis* tactics. It is not surprising that he suddenly "remembered" that he had to go to the East to fulfill a vow.

A Decade of Optimate Reaction Those who had tried to gain an edge in aristocratic political competition through *popularis* tactics had fallen to violence and murder once more. For most of the 90s, public affairs were firmly controlled through the senate by optimate traditionalists, who were largely successful in dealing with Rome's enemies and their own. They had already crushed the Sicilian slave rebellion in 100. In 93 they succeeded in putting down a Spanish uprising. They continued to deny land to Marius' veterans and answered the Italian allies' demand for citizenship by expelling any who resided in Rome. They also enacted legislation that made it more difficult for *populares* to utilize tribunician legislation by requiring an interval of seventeen days between the promulgation of a tribunician bill and its enactment. In that way, those whose power was guaranteed by the status quo would have enough time to marshall their opposition. As a result, serious problems and grievances continued to bubble beneath the surface and build up pressure for another eruption.

The Explosive Reforms of M. Livius Drusus the Younger, 91 B.C. Livius Drusus the Younger, son of the Livius Drusus who had helped to bring down Gaius Gracchus (p. 154), used the office of tribune in 91 B.C. to launch a series of reforms to relieve the worst of the pressure. His goal was to secure power in the hands of his moderate optimate allies in the senate without fear of further *popularis* challenges. Drusus' reforms had three major components: (1) doubling the size of the senate by admitting 300 of the richest and most prominent members of the equestrian class (to remove the chief source of friction between the two classes he

proposed to choose jurors for the standing criminal courts from this expanded senate); (2) providing the poor with subsidized grain and with land through allotments and the establishment of colonies; (3) granting citizenship to the Italian allies.

The compromises represented by these proposals could never satisfy all the powerful optimate aristocrats, all of the *equites,* or even all of the Roman poor and Italian allies. The first two proposals seem to have passed initially, but they provoked such vigorous opposition from extreme oligarchs and those *equites* who would not have been admitted to the senate that they were overturned. Even some powerful Italian allies were against the younger Drusus' citizenship law because they would have had to give up public land and local control of their communities. Before he was able to bring that proposal to a vote, he was stabbed to death by an unknown assassin.

The Italian or Social War, 90 to 88 B.C. The justice that Livius Drusus the Younger had failed to procure for the majority of Italian allies by legal means was achieved in a war that could easily have been avoided had his opponents been able to put aside their own rivalries and selfishness. Never since the Samnite and Pyrrhic wars, not even in the blackest days after Cannae, had Roman supremacy in Italy been more violently shaken than in the months that followed the stabbing of Livius Drusus. With his death vanished the last chance to satisfy the hopes of most Italian allies for securing the rights and freedoms of citizenship through peaceful means. A Roman praetor went to Picenum and addressed the people of Asculum (Ascoli Piceno) in a violent harangue against their agitation for citizenship and their revolutionary societies. The Asculans, enraged by the insolence of his threats, dismembered him and his lictors and massacred all the Romans who lived in the town. The war that Livius Drusus had tried to prevent had begun.

Preparation for War Among the insurgents, the Marsi and the Samnites were the fiercest.

Together with their allies they declared their independence and set up a confederacy, whose capital was at Corfinium, renamed Italia, about 75 miles due east of Rome. The Italian confederacy raised an army of 100,000 men, many of them hardened soldiers trained in the tactics and discipline of the Roman army, as their officers had been.

The landlord-ridden sections of Umbria and Etruria, the more Romanized Latins and Campanians, and the Greek coastal cities from Naples to Tarentum remained loyal to Rome, and her overseas provinces could supply extra manpower and resources. Nevertheless, the Romans fared badly in the first months of the war. Some of their defeats arose from many senators' hostility and spite toward Marius, who had returned from his self-imposed exile in Asia and volunteered his services. They merely assigned him as a legate to an incompetent commander.

The Granting of Roman Citizenship to the Italians, 90 B.C.
Finally, late in the year one of the consuls of 90, Lucius Julius Caesar (cousin of the more famous Gaius Julius Caesar), did what should have been done in the first place. He returned to Rome and carried a bill called the *lex Julia* to confer citizenship on all Latins and Italians still loyal to Rome and to those who would at once lay down their arms. In 89 B.C., two tribunes, M. Plautius Silvanus and C. Papirius Carbo, put through a more comprehensive bill, the *lex Plautia Papiria,* granting citizenship to all free persons resident in any allied community who would register before a Roman praetor within sixty days. A third law, the *lex Pompeia,* proposed by Gnaeus Pompeius Strabo (a consul of the same year and father of Pompey the Great), extended citizenship to all free persons residing in Cisalpine Gaul south of the Po and Latin rights to those living north of the river. The revolts began to collapse.

Strabo was a very good general and an opportunistic politician who backed whatever side in Roman politics seemed most personally advantageous at the moment. Militarily and politically his son, who along with later famous figures like Cicero and Catiline served on Strabo's staff, was much like him but more personally charming. At one point it was only the young Pompey's pleas that saved his father from death at the hands of mutinous soldiers. Strabo ended the war in the North by capturing Asculum and, it was charged, misappropriated the booty. In 88 B.C., Strabo was guilty of complicity in the murder of his cousin, the consul Q. Pompeius Rufus, who was supposed to take over Strabo's command. Thereupon, Strabo continued to fight until the Marsi and their allies were defeated in central Italy.

The other consul of 88 was Lucius Cornelius Sulla, Marius' old quaestor in the Jugurthine War and now a favorite of his enemies. Sulla and his staunch ally Quintus Caecilius Metellus eventually ground down the Samnites in the South. Nola in Campania, however, held out under siege for many years.

The Aftermath of the Social War
The war had exacted a heavy price for the shortsightedness and petty politicking that had blocked Livius Drusus' proposal to grant citizenship to Rome's Italian allies. The human and property losses must have been almost as great as those inflicted by Hannibal. The economic hardships were extremely severe. Food was scarce and prices high; rich and poor were oppressed by debts that they had no means of paying; and the city was crowded with Italian refugees. The city praetor of 89 B.C., A. Sempronius Asellio, attempted to give the debtors some relief by issuing an edict that revived the fourth-century-B.C. law prohibiting interest. He was killed by a mob of angry creditors.

The Social War had actually been a civil war. It pitted against each other communities that in some cases had been fighting side by side for 200 years. Its bitter fighting set a dangerous precedent for civil warfare in Italy and trained a generation of leaders who were willing to resort to it in pursuit of personal political goals.

As for the problems that produced war, the majority of senators seemed to have learned little from the experience. With the war almost over it was politics as usual. There was a move to limit the voting power of the new citizens by enrolling them in only eight or ten of the thirty-five tribes of citizens. This short-sighted action merely fueled more divisive struggles that rent the Republic in the following years.

Nevertheless, the war produced some good results. It added almost 500,000 new citizens to the rolls. From the Po River to the Straits of Messana, all free men were now Romans, and all the many different ethnic elements would in time be fused into a single nation. Local self-government was still continued and all communities and municipalities enjoyed the right to elect their own boards of four magistrates (*Quattuorviri*). Gradually they would adopt Roman private and public law as well as a common Latin language. The enfranchisement of peninsular Italy was a giant stride toward national unification and the development of a common Latin culture that characterized all of Italy in later centuries.

XVI

Marius and Sulla: Civil War and Reaction, 88 to 78 B.C.

Although the Republic had weathered the foreign and domestic crises that had beset it since the time of the Gracchi, none of the basic problems had been solved. Political competition within the aristocracy continued to intensify and so politicized any attempts at necessary reform that nothing could be accomplished without violence and the creation of further instability. At the same time, Rome's wars put so much power in the hands of ambitious military leaders that they were able to resort to everhigher levels of violence in the pursuit of their personal goals. Beginning in 88 B.C., therefore, the Republic was rocked by a series of civil wars that ultimately destroyed it.

Sources for the Years 88 to 78 B.C.   As for the previous period, the only two major sources are Appian and Plutarch. Appian covers the First Mithridatic War (89 to 85 B.C.) in Book 12 (*Mithridatic Wars,* sections 1–63) and the turmoil at Rome from 88 to 78 in Book 13 (*Civil Wars,* Book 1, sections 55–107). Plutarch's lives of Marius and Sulla are particularly important, and pertinent information is also found in the early portions of his biographies of Sertorius, Lucullus, Pompey, Crassus, Caesar, and Cicero. Velleius Paterculus presents a summary in Book 2 (18–29) of his *Histories,* and Books 77 to 90 of Livy are summarized in the *Periochae* and later epitomators. There are a few frag-

ments from Books 30 to 35 of Cassius Dio and sizable fragments from Books 37 to 39 of Diodorus Siculus. There also survive some interesting fragments on the First Mithridatic War from the first-century A.D. Greek historian Memnon of Heraclea in Pontus. For the Mithridatic War, some official documents of both Sulla and Mithridates have been preserved on inscriptions. For internal affairs, numerous references scattered throughout the works of Cicero make him a valuable contemporary witness.

Mithridates VI Eupator (134 to 63 B.C.)
In granting citizenship to the Italians to end the Social War, the senatorial leadership had been prompted not only by the adverse military situation in Italy but also by the aggressive actions of Mithridates VI, king of Pontus. He had taken advantage of several factors: the resentment that often-corrupt Roman rule had aroused in the eastern provinces; Rome's confrontations with Germanic invaders; and the disruptions caused by the Social War. His goal was to overthrow Roman rule in the eastern Mediterranean and create an empire of his own on the model of Alexander the Great's. By 90 B.C., he had gained control of all but the western coast of the Black Sea and most of the interior of Asia Minor. At that time, however, the Romans were thoroughly aroused by his simultaneous seizures of Bithynia and Cappadocia. There-

fore, the senate sent a special envoy, Manius Aquillius, to compel Mithridates to withdraw from both kingdoms and recognize Ariobarzanes as the lawful king of Cappadocia and Nicomedes IV, son of Nicomedes III, as king of Bithynia. That done, Aquillius did a very foolish thing. He incited Nicomedes to raid Pontus in order to seize enough loot to reward the Romans for their intervention in Bithynia.

Mithridates Makes War on Rome When Aquillius persuaded Nicomedes to invade Pontus (89 B.C.), Mithridates, after several unheeded protests, decided to strike. Quickly defeating Nicomedes, he swept the weak Roman forces aside and invaded Pergamum. He captured Aquillius and paid him the money that he had demanded by pouring molten gold down his throat. Many in Asia Minor welcomed Mithridates as a deliverer and a savior and seized the chance of making the Romans pay dearly for their forty years of oppression. By prearrangement they slaughtered many Italians, mostly tax agents, moneylenders, and merchants, although the figure of 80,000 given in the sources is probably highly exaggerated.

Mithridates would not feel secure unless he added Greece to his dominions. He knew that the Romans were hated in Greece almost as much as in Asia and had sent his agents to Athens and other cities to make propaganda for his cause. Meanwhile, his powerful navy had broken out into the Aegean and made a descent on Delos, where he ordered the massacre of 20,000 Italian merchants and slave dealers. Athens overthrew her pro-Roman oligarchic government and made common cause with Mithridates. His general occupied Athens' main port, the Piraeus and from that base conquered most of southern Greece. Meanwhile, another Pontic army was entering Greece from the North. Such was the dangerous situation in the East as Rome slowly recovered from the ravages of the Social War.

The Rise of Sulla (138 to 78 B.C.)   Marius and Sulla eagerly sought the command in the war against Mithridates. Marius wanted to recover

the popularity that he had enjoyed after the Jugurthine and Cimbrian wars but had later lost. Sulla, from an old patrician family that had not been prominent within the consular nobility for some time, wanted the command because he believed that the war would be easily won and a source of power, fame, and also fortune. His rivalry with Marius went back at least as far as the Jugurthine War, when he tried to take credit for the victory because he had captured Jugurtha. He was closely allied with Marius' optimate enemies in the senate. They had assured his election to the consulship of 88 B.C. and an important command in the Social War, whereas Marius had been forced to settle for a legateship. Now Sulla's powerful friends procured him the coveted command against Mithridates.

The Tribuneship of P. Sulpicius (Rufus?), 88 B.C.   The question of the Mithridatic command might well have been settled had it not been for the political aims of the tribune P. Sulpicius (the *cognomen* Rufus is disputed), a close friend and admirer of Livius Drusus the Younger. Sulpicius had strongly opposed the restriction of the newly enfranchised Italians to eight of the thirty-five tribes. Although a member of one of the most ancient and illustrious patrician families and an heir to immense wealth, Sulpicius had given up his patrician status (89 B.C.) to qualify for election as tribune. Like Gaius Gracchus, he was an orator of remarkable power, a little inclined to be showy perhaps, but Cicero declared him to be by far the best that he had ever heard.

As tribune of the people, Sulpicius made four proposals that seem to have been presented in one omnibus bill: (1) to enroll the new Italian citizens as well as the freedmen in all the 35 tribes; (2) to recall all exiles; (3) to exclude from the senate all members owing bills in excess of 2,000 *denarii* (in order to prevent bribery and corruption); and (4) to replace Sulla with Marius in the command against Mithridates. The first proposal was the least acceptable and made it difficult to gain the support of enough tribes to pass in the *concilium plebis*. The fourth provision represented a deal with Marius, who, in exchange for the command against Mithridates, probably carried the required number of tribes through the votes of his veterans. The bill became law, although not without considerable opposition and violence.

Sulla's March on Rome At first Sulla tried to prevent the passage of these laws by declaring religious holidays in order to suspend all meetings of the assembly. Exasperated by the repeated use of that religious weapon, Sulpicius and his armed followers rioted. Ironically, Sulla escaped by taking refuge in the house of Marius. After Sulla had publicly revoked the religious holidays, Marius, like an old soldier doing a good turn for another, allowed him to escape from his house with the expectation that he would go into exile. Instead, Sulla hastened to return to Campania and his army, which was still besieging Nola in the final operations of the Social War. He took part of the troops and marched on Rome. The increasingly bitter competition among ambitious politicians had led to outright civil war for the first time in the annals of the Roman Republic. It is a great irony that this act was made possible in part by Marius' military reforms, which had increased the personal dependence of the soldiers upon their commanders and weakened their loyalty to the state.

The common people of Rome resisted fiercely until Sulla started to set fire to their houses. Once in control, he obtained a senatorial decree declaring Marius, Sulpicius, and ten others to be enemies of the state. He then obtained passage of a law condemning them to death and putting a price on their heads. Marius fled and reached the coast of North Africa after some narrow escapes. Betrayed by a slave, Sulpicius seems to have been the only one executed, but Sulla had set a disastrous precedent for the future.

The victorious Sulla rescinded Sulpicius' laws. Although he introduced a law for the relief of debtors by reducing the maximum rate of interest to 10 percent, he then made a number of reactionary changes designed to make it impossible for anyone outside his group of optimate friends to challenge their dominant position within the senatorial aristocracy. He made the Centuriate Assembly the primary legislative assembly by revoking the right of tribunes to introduce legislation in the *concilium plebis.* The Centuriate Assembly was also reorganized so that the ninety-eight wealthiest centuries had a clear majority once more. Another reactionary step was the requirement that magistrates consult the senate before introducing new legislation.

Sulla's attempt to interfere with the consular elections failed, although he did manage to extract a promise from one of the newly elected consuls, Lucius Cornelius Cinna, not to tamper with any of Sulla's constitutional changes already made. After Sulla had carried out these changes, he departed for the East to make war against Mithridates.

Cinna's Consulship, 87 B.C.
Hardly was Sulla gone from Italy's shores when Cinna attempted to annul the laws of Sulla and reenact those of Sulpicius. The prospect of enrolling the Italians in all thirty-five tribes aroused the opposition of *optimates* like his colleague, Gnaeus Octavius. After some rioting and a massacre of Italians in the Forum, Octavius drove Cinna from the city and had him declared a public enemy by a vote of the senate. In so doing, his enemies committed a very serious blunder, because they gave him the opportunity of appealing to the Italian voters and winning the support of the troops that Sulla had left at Nola. He recalled Marius from Africa and, imitating Sulla's deadly example, marched on Rome.

Marius and His Reign of Terror
Recalled from Africa, the elderly Marius, now well over seventy, stormed Ostia, the seaport of Rome, cut off the food supplies of Rome, and starved her into surrender. Marius, brutalized by years of war and slaughter, embittered by ingratitude and neglect, and maddened by his recent experiences in Italy and Africa as a hunted outlaw, gave full vent to his rage and lust for blood. For days he roved the city like a raving lunatic. His followers struck down all the nobles and senators whom he hated. Their mutilated corpses

littered the streets and their heads, dripping blood, decorated the rostra. Their houses and property were confiscated and auctioned. His outrages made even Cinna quail and finally stop them. In 86 B.C., Marius at last achieved his long-cherished ambition of a seventh consulship, but he did not long enjoy his victory. He fell ill and died a few days after taking office.

The Significance of Marius For a *novus homo,* Marius had made an unusually great impact on Roman history. His military service in making the Roman army more tactically effective, in defeating Jugurtha, and in annihilating the threat of Germanic invasion made him an authentic hero. Politically, however, he was more of a villain. The problem was not with his opening military recruitment to the property-less and its negative political consequences. That would have happened anyway. Rather, the problem was that his only goal was to achieve and continue to hold the consulship. He had no real program to deal with Rome's pressing problems. Therefore, he only made them worse and undermined faith in the political system. Although he was not the first to resort to outright civil war, his willingness to follow Sulla's example in that case helped to set precedents for violence that greatly aided in the destruction of the Republic. Moreover, his reputation as a military hero and the popular policies of Saturninus, Sulpicius, and Cinna, who had become associated with him, created among his veterans, the urban masses, and new Italian citizens a large body of people who would be manipulated by recalling his name in the increasingly bitter political struggles of the late Republic.

Cinna's Time (*Cinnanum Tempus*) After Marius' sudden death in 86, Cinna was in effect left as a dictator. Foregoing elections, he appointed Lucius Valerius Flaccus as consul to replace Marius, and for 85 and 84 he simply appointed himself and Gnaeus Papirius Carbo to the consulship. Cinna attempted, however, to use his power much more responsibly than Marius ever had in order to secure his position.

He overturned Sulla's reactionary laws and tried to satisfy the legitimate grievances of many who supported him, although he disappointed the newly enfranchised Italians on the issue of their enrollment in all thirty-five tribes. Their just demand was not met until the senate passed a decree during the maneuvering after Cinna's death in 84. Flaccus, however, introduced a law that forgave three quarters of all debts, and financial stability was protected by restoring the value of the coinage, which had been thrown into disarray during the recent upheavals and debased by corrupt moneyers.

Under Cinna the senate and courts continued to function, and many nobles supported him. Those who did not support him prudently kept a low profile and waited to see what would happen with Sulla, who, despite being stripped of his command against Mithridates, ignored Cinna's government and continued to press the war. Cinna attempted to come to an amicable agreement, but Sulla would have none of it. As Sulla went from victory to victory and assumed control of the East with all of its resources, support began to shift toward him at Rome, and Cinna was forced to take a harder stand. As he prepared for another disruptive civil war, mutinous soldiers suddenly killed him in 84 B.C.

Sulla and Mithridates, 87 to 85 B.C. Sulla invaded Greece in 87 and captured Athens in 86 after a winter-long siege. He showed the typical Roman love of Greek art by looting every painting, sculpture, and monument that he could put on a ship. During the summer, he chased Mithridates' forces out of Greece and then refused to surrender his command to the consul Flaccus, whom Cinna had sent to replace him. After some of his troops defected to Sulla, Flaccus took his army to Asia to fight Mithridates. There he was murdered by a mutinous legate who seized command, defeated Mithridates' son, and marched on the stronghold of Pergamum. Mithridates, already facing revolts stirred up by his heavy taxation to support the war, decided to make a deal with Sulla, who was anxious to get back to Italy and take revenge on his enemies.

The treaty was signed at Dardanus in the Troad in 85 B.C. All that Mithridates had to do was abandon his conquests in Asia Minor, surrender 80 of his warships, and pay an indemnity of 2,000 talents. Sulla imposed far harsher terms on the province of Asia: an indemnity of 20,000 talents; 5 years' back taxes; and pay, food, and lodging for his troops during the winter of 85–84. To raise the vast sums required, the province had to turn to Roman moneylenders and fell victim to a crushing burden of debt. All Sulla did was create the conditions for another "war of liberation" by Mithridates.

Sulla's Return to Italy, 83 to 82 B.C. In the spring of 83, Sulla set sail for Italy after putting Flaccus' old army under the command of Lucius Licinius Murena to serve as a permanent garrison in Asia. When Sulla landed his own troops at Brundisium, he easily overpowered the two consular armies sent against him. In fact, one simply deserted to his side. The only anti-Sullan who might have been a match for him was Quintus Sertorius, who had fought under Marius. The nobles who had opposed Sulla scorned Sertorius for his equestrian origin and disliked him for his blunt criticism of their actions. Therefore, they had shipped him off to Spain instead of using him in Italy.

Sulla, on the other hand, acquired a number of effective supporters once he arrived in Italy. The first was Quintus Caecilius Metellus Pius, who brought with him a number of recruits from his hiding place in North Africa. Next came the young Marcus Licinius Crassus at the head of a small army returning from Spain. Gnaeus Pompeius (Pompey), the young son of Pompeius Strabo, was an even more valuable addition, both in the number of troops that he brought and in military skill. On his own initiative he had raised three legions in Picenum and on reaching Sulla was hailed, young as he was, with the flattering title of *Imperator.* After Pompey had won several victories, Sulla somewhat facetiously called him *Magnus,* "the Great," and the title stuck.

To bolster their tottering regime, the anti-Sullans elected as consuls for 82 Cinna's old consular colleague of 85 and 84, Cn. Papirius Carbo, and Gaius Marius, adopted son of the elder Marius. Their reputations enabled them to raise large numbers of recruits, but they proved to be inadequate generals against Sulla and his lieutenants. The younger Marius was besieged in Praeneste, where he eventually committed suicide or was killed. Carbo lost his nerve and fled to Africa. (Pompey later captured and executed him.) Nevertheless, thousands of Samnites rose up to fight Sulla, who still treated them as enemies from the Social War (p. 164). Sulla met them late one day just outside Rome's Colline Gate. They actually defeated his left wing, which he personally commanded, but Marcus Crassus won a victory on the right in time to save the day.

Sulla's Reign of Terror, 82 B.C. The bloody battle at the Colline Gate ended all effective resistance in Italy. Then a reign of terror began, during which thousands of persons suffered death often accompanied by torture. Next door to the temple of Bellona, where Sulla was addressing a meeting of the senate, 6,000 Samnite prisoners, whose only crime was that they lost a battle for what they believed was freedom and justice, were tortured to death. As the screams of the dying broke into his speech and distressed some of the senators to the point of fainting, Sulla grimly explained that only some criminals were being punished at his orders.

The Proscriptions To ruthlessness he added the method of proscription. He posted lists of proscribed victims, some carefully selected by himself, others suggested by his henchmen. He listed some for political reasons, others to avenge private injuries, and still others for no reason except that they owned large and valuable properties. The proscribed, with a price set on their head, were to be hunted down as outlaws and murdered. Sulla confiscated their property and revoked the citizenship of their children. Among the thousands he doomed to die were 90 senators, 15 men of consular rank, and 2,600 *equites,* whose property was distributed among Sulla's supporters and veterans. As beneficiaries of his murders they would, when required, rally around him or loyally support the oligarchy that he put in power. He secured additional supporters by freeing 10,000 slaves who had belonged to his victims. He also generously rewarded some freedmen. One, for example, was allowed to buy an estate worth about 1.5 million denarii for about 2,500 denarii.

Unfortunately, the murder and spoliation of rich individuals failed to provide enough money or land to enable Sulla to redeem his promises of pay, pensions, and farms to his discharged veterans. He compelled cities, towns, and other communities to contribute their share to the cause, especially those suspected of having resisted his rise to power or having supported his enemies. Their punishment was in proportion to the duration and strength of their resistance and opposition. The cities that had offered only mild opposition were required to pay fines, have their walls torn down, and surrender most, if not all, of their territory. Others, such as Praeneste in Latium or Florentia (Florence) in Etruria, which resisted him long and stubbornly, were destroyed and their inhabitants sold into slavery. He also turned the richest and most thickly populated districts of Samnium into a desert. Although the confiscations and enslavements were heaviest in Etruria and a few other parts of central and northern Italy, Samnium remained a desolate waste for a long time. Such were the atrocities that resulted from the increasingly bitter rivalries within the Roman ruling elite. The Roman Republic had come to a sorry state of affairs.

Sulla's Dictatorship and Changes in the Constitution

In 82 B.C., a few days before his arrival in Rome, Sulla had demanded and secured from the Centuriate Assembly formal passage of a law known as the *lex Valeria* to appoint him dictator for an undefined period for the purpose of drafting laws and "reconstituting" the state. The assembly, confirming that which had already been established by military force, revived an office held only once since the middle of the third century (by Fabius Max-

imus, Cunctator, in 217 B.C.) and legalized his subsequent murders, confiscations, and other atrocities. Unrestrained by law or custom, by the right of appeal, or by tribunician veto, Sulla's dictatorship could be terminated only by his death or resignation. He had the power of life and death, and his *imperium* was absolute.

In 81 B.C., Sulla increased the membership of the senate to 600. Normally, it had been around 300, but it had been somewhat reduced by the civil war and the murderous activities of Marius and Sulla himself. The new members came from the first eighteen centuries of the Centuriate Assembly, which included the rich, landowning *equites* of the Italian municipalities. The main object of expanding the senate's membership was to make a larger number of persons available for jury service, which he transferred from the *equites* to the senate. In expanding the membership of the senate and in making senators alone eligible as jurors, Sulla was actually carrying out a proposal of Livius Drusus the Younger (p. 164). Moreover, this move not only opened up the senate to equestrians from the local Italian aristocracy, but it packed the senate with grateful clients loyal to Sulla and those who had supported him in the civil war. Finally, Sulla abolished the position of *princeps senatus* to prevent any one man from having too much influence over the other senators.

Reform of the Courts In his reform of the courts, Sulla went much further than Livius Drusus. He abolished trials before the popular assemblies and assigned all trials to a system of standing courts, whose juries were manned by senators. He raised the number of special jury courts for the trials of major crimes to seven: the *quaestio de repetundis* dealing with extortion; *de maiestate,* with treason; *de ambitu,* with bribery in elections; *de falsis,* with forgery; *de peculatu,* with embezzlement of public property; *de sicariis et veneficis,* with murder; and *de vi publica,* with assault and battery. To provide enough judges to preside over these standing courts he increased the number of praetors from six to eight. The reform of the courts was the greatest and the most permanent of Sulla's reforms. It clarified and recast the law dealing with serious crimes and laid the foundation of Roman criminal law (p. 233).

Changes in the Magistracies To regulate the system of officeholding and prevent the unorthodox careers that had increased political competition to destructive levels, Sulla reenacted, in a considerably modified form, the *lex Villia Annalis* of 180 B.C., which prescribed a regular order of holding office (*cursus honorum*)—first the quaestorship, then the praetorship, and finally the consulship. He reaffirmed the rule prescribing an interval of ten years between successive consulships. His revised law advanced the minimum age probably to 29 for the quaestorship, 39 for the praetorship, and 42 for the consulship. Finally, he increased the number of quaestors from around 10 to 20 and made them members of the senate automatically after their year of office. In that way, they not only would replace the average yearly vacancies that occurred in a senate of 500 to 600 members but also would lessen the power of the censors to play favorites, because they no longer controlled admission to the senate.

Changes were made in the tribuneship to destroy the effectiveness of that office and the temptation to use it in a *popularis* manner. Sulla crippled it most by disqualifying a tribune from holding any higher office in order to make it unattractive to able and ambitious men. He limited the veto power of a tribune to the protection of personal rights and restricted or abolished his right to propose laws or prosecute cases before the Tribal Assembly.

Reorganization of the Provinces Before the time of Sulla, there were nine provinces, six in the West (Sicily, Sardinia-and-Corsica, Nearer Spain, Farther Spain, Africa Proconsularis, and Gallia Transalpina) and three in the East (Macedonia, Asia, and Cilicia). Cyrenaica, though accepted in 96 B.C. as a legacy from its king, Ptolemy Apion, was not formally organized as a province until 74 B.C. Sulla made Cisalpine Gaul the tenth province by detaching it from the rest of Italy and sent a governor and a garrison to guard it against the raiders who periodically descended from the Alps.

To fortify the power of the senate even more and prevent ambitious governors from creating positions strong enough to seize control of the state, Sulla limited the independence of provincial governors through his law of *maiestas*. A governor could no longer initiate a war, leave his province with or without his army, or enter a foreign kingdom without express authorization from the senate. A governor also had to leave his province within thirty days of his replacement's arrival. Sulla hoped thus to give the senate full control over the armed forces and limit the war-making potential of provincial commanders.

Sulla's Consulship, Abdication, and Death After Sulla had fully reorganized the government to his own satisfaction and had created a system designed to maintain the dominance that he and his partisans had achieved, he stood for election in 81 as consul for 80 B.C. He probably resigned the dictatorship at the end of 81 or possibly earlier that year. After the consulship of 80, he retired to his country estate near Puteoli (Pozzuoli) in Campania, where he hoped to pass the rest of his life in ease, luxury, and pleasure. He did not enjoy himself long. In 78 B.C., the sixty-year-old Sulla died after experiencing a severe hemorrhage and was cremated at Rome in a magnificent funeral. Before his death, he had dictated the epitaph to be inscribed upon his tomb to the effect that no one had ever surpassed him in rewarding his friends with good, or his enemies with evil. It summed up a code at least as old as Homer, one that had always fueled bitter feuds and factionalism and would continue to do so.

The Failure of Sulla Sulla had named himself Felix, which means "Lucky." He was even more fortunate in death for he never saw the utter futility of the major part of his work. He died in the happy belief that he had created a system that would produce a stable government for Rome under the oligarchic control of the optimate friends whom he had rewarded. They were to dominate the senate, and the constitutional avenues that previously had allowed other ambitious members of the senatorial class to challenge the dominant leaders were to remain blocked. The constitution that he tried to make permanent did have some admirable features, such as the reform of the courts, the admission of new senators from the equestrian class, and the rational ordering of the magistracies and provincial government, but it was doomed to failure. It did nothing to solve the basic social, economic, and political problems that those who did not want to play the political game by his rules could exploit in building bases of power to challenge those whom he had left in control. No sooner had the ashes of his funeral pyre cooled than the whole carefully designed superstructure of his constitution began to collapse upon the sand beneath it.

First of all, his reforms of the magistracies actually increased the competitive pressures for high office by increasing the number of quaestors and praetors. Previously at least one half of the quaestors could hope to reach the praetorship, and one third of the praetors could hope for consulships. Now only two fifths of the quaestors had a chance to become praetors, and only one fourth of the praetors were likely to become consuls. Therefore, the holders of lower offices had to intensify their efforts to reach the consulship. Second, the attempt to limit the war-making potential of provincial commanders was futile. Practically, in the face of an ambitious provincial commander determined to defy the senate with a loyal army as Sulla himself had done, there was little that senators could do except raise up another potentially dangerous commander against him.

Other constitutional safeguards that Sulla had created to check the destructive competition for personal preeminence that had led to civil war in the 80s were inadequate. In fact, they were part of the problem because they also restricted the rights and privileges of the *equites* and the common people. Therefore, ambitious politicians could gain their support by advocating repeal of the safeguards that were supposed to keep them in check. Also, removing the *equites* from juries in the extortion court left no check on corrupt and abusive provincial governors. That only fueled discontent in the provinces, which provided more troubled waters in which the ambitious could fish.

Furthermore, Sulla had left a legacy of bitterness and hate that created many enemies for the oligarchs who succeeded him. The most bitter enemies of these oligarchs were the sons, relations, and friends of the senators and wealthy *equites* who had suffered proscription, exile, or confiscation of their property. In the forests of Etruria roamed bands of once-peaceful and well-to-do farmers whose lands had been confiscated by Sulla for distribution among his veterans. In the city of Rome, the poor had been deprived of their subsidized grain. Of those *equites* who had not been killed, many had suffered financial ruin and all had been deprived of jury service in the extortion court.

As the years passed, no group was more frustrated and rebellious than those veterans of Sulla who had been given confiscated land but had no knowledge of farming or desire for the monotony of rural life. They were soon enmeshed in debt and became one of the most discontented and potentially dangerous elements in Roman society. They were only too happy to support anyone who promised them personal gain without regard to constitutional proprieties. It is not surprising, therefore, that the flawed fabric of Sulla's reforms soon began to fray.

XVII

Personal Ambitions and Public Crises, 78 to 60 B.C.

In creating a constitution designed to secure the oligarchic domination of a select group of optimate nobles within the Roman senate, Sulla had alienated, frustrated, and embittered numerous groups within Roman society. Their hatred, frustration, and desire for revenge, however, could not have found expression without leaders, and in the generation after Sulla, leaders came. Throughout the 70s and 60s B.C., a series of domestic and foreign crises gave ambitious individuals opportunities to gain so much popularity, clientage, and military power that those who controlled the senate became powerless to restrain them. These leaders opened up another round of upheavals and civil wars that led to the destruction of the Republic by 30 B.C.

Sources for Roman History from 78 to 30 B.C. The years from 78 to 30 B.C., which will be covered in this and the following four chapters, are among the best documented in Roman history. Until his death in 43, Cicero's numerous speeches, essays, and letters provide volumes of invaluable information by a keen observer and participant in events (pp. 180–181). Cicero's letters also include letters to him from other important participants or observers. The second largest group of contemporary works covers the conquest of Gaul and the civil war from 58 to 46 B.C.: Caesar's commentaries, namely, the

Gallic War (first seven books) and the *Civil War;* and other accounts by some of his officers, Book 8 of the *Gallic War,* the *African War,* the *Alexandrian War,* and the *Spanish War.* Another valuable contemporary witness is Sallust, whose *Histories,* covering the years from 78 to 67, is preserved only in fragments, but whose account of Catiline's conspiracy (63 B.C.) is extant. Cornelius Nepos was another contemporary historian. Unfortunately, his biography of Cicero is lost, but his life of Cicero's devoted friend Atticus is extant. Other contemporary historians, orators, and antiquarians are preserved mainly in fragments (p. 244–245).

The poems of Catullus (pp. 240–241) and the didactic epic *De Rerum Natura* (*On the Nature of Things*) by Lucretius (pp. 241–242) help to reveal the atmosphere at the time of Caesar's rise, and the *Eclogues* and *Georgics* of Vergil (pp. 287–288) do the same for the time of Caesar's heir, Octavian, the future Emperor Augustus. Fragments of a biography of Augustus' early life by the late-first-century-B.C. writer Nicolaus of Damascus also survive. Most of Augustus' own official summary of his career, *Res Gestae Divi Augusti,* has been preserved because it was set up on stone inscriptions in various cities. The most complete version is the *Monumentum Ancyranum* from Ankara in modern Turkey (p. 291).

Later writers also supply abundant material. The mid-first-century-A.D. commentary by

Asconius on some of Cicero's speeches, particularly some lost ones, is extremely valuable. The biographies of Caesar and Augustus by the early-second-century-A.D. author Suetonius, who often quotes from contemporary writers and documents, are veritable gold mines. So, too, are Plutarch's biographies of Sertorius, Lucullus, Pompey, Crassus, Cicero, Caesar, Cato the Younger, Brutus, and Antony, which are often based on contemporary sources like Asinius Pollio (p. 291). Books 91 to 133 of Livy survive only in the summaries of the *Periochae* and in the brief late Imperial histories, and the relevant books of Diodorus Siculus are lost except for some fragments of Book 40 (71 to 63 B.C.). Nevertheless, there are extensive narrative sources. Appian, in the five books of the *Civil Wars* (Books 13 to 17 of his history), narrates the years 78 to 35 from section 107 of the first book to the end of the work. Beginning with events of 69 B.C., Cassius Dio is complete for the remaining years (Books 36 to 50). Also, Velleius Paterculus' narrative, though brief, is much fuller for this period than for earlier ones (Book 2.30–85).

The Rebellion of Lepidus, 78 B.C. Even before Sulla died, Marcus Aemilius Lepidus had attacked his program. A renegade Marian, he had supported Sulla in 83 and had increased his wealth by buying at cut rates the property of the proscribed. Afterward, as governor of Sicily, he so shamelessly plundered the province that he narrowly escaped prosecution and lost Sulla's favor. He then sought support among the disaffected groups in society. He was elected consul for 78 over Sulla's bitter objections but with the support of Pompey, who felt little loyalty to the now-retired Sulla.

As consul, Lepidus opposed a state funeral for Sulla and proposed the recall of all exiles, the resumption of cheap grain distributions to the poor, the return of all confiscated properties to the former owners, and the restoration of the powers of the tribunes. The first two proposals Sulla's heirs in the senate somewhat unwillingly accepted; the last two they vigorously and successfully opposed. Soon the exiles began to return, men like Cinna's son and Marius' nephew Gaius Julius Caesar. Plots and conspiracies sprang up everywhere.

Those who controlled the senate sought to get rid of Lepidus by sending him to suppress a rebellion of dispossessed farmers near Florence. Instead, Lepidus used the assignment as an opportunity to raise an even bigger rebellion of his own. The opportunistic Pompey accepted a command to help the other consul suppress Lepidus and defeated him. Lepidus died while trying to establish closer ties with the Marian holdout Sertorius in Spain.

The War against Sertorius (ca. 122 to 73 B.C.) Quintus Sertorius is clearly one of the most interesting military commanders in Roman history. For eight years, after some initial setbacks, he and a few Roman officers using native Spanish troops had repeatedly frustrated the armies of provincial governors sent out to fight him. He had opposed only Sulla's government and always proclaimed loyalty to Rome. After Sulla's death he was eager for reconciliation, but Sulla's political heirs were determined to continue the war, which had been under the command of Sulla's old ally Quintus Caecilius Metellus Pius since 79 B.C.

Sertorius in Spain, 82 to 74/73 B.C. In order to challenge those who controlled the senate at Rome, Sertorius attempted to Romanize the native nobility and earn the provincials' loyalty. He accepted many Spaniards and Lusitanians as Roman citizens, admitted some of their leaders into his opposition senate, and established a school for the education of the upper-class youth. Through tact, justice, and moderation, Sertorius won such wide popularity among the Spanish people as no native chieftain, even Viriathus (p. 122), had ever enjoyed. He also appealed to their superstitions by pretending that he received secret information from a white fawn, a gift of Diana, which followed him everywhere. When thousands flocked to his standards, he taught them to fight as Romans but did not destroy their aptitude for guerrilla warfare.

The Rise of Pompey the Great (106 to 48 B.C.)

Metellus had not been able to make much progress against Sertorius by 77, when Pompey the Great returned to Rome after defeating Lepidus. Pompey refused a senatorial order to disband his army and practically demanded to be sent to Spain to join Metellus against Sertorius. A majority in the senate agreed, although many senators were reluctant because they were friends of Metellus or feared to entrust so dangerous a weapon as a major provincial command to a young man not old enough to hold even the lowest office of the *cursus honorum.* Pompey received consular *imperium* and the chief command in Nearer Spain.

As the heir of Gnaeus Pompeius Strabo, Pompey was the largest landowner in the district of Picenum. Therefore, he had a large number of clients and vast personal resources. Although he was personally charming and seems to have inspired great loyalty and love in his children and most of his several wives, he was also extremely ambitious and missed no opportunity to use his resources to advance his personal career. Typically, at the age of twenty-three, after Cinna had refused to grant him the recognition that he wanted, he had raised a large private army and joined Sulla. Later, he willingly divorced his first wife when Sulla wanted him to marry a more politically acceptable partner. Nor did he speak up for former friends who had helped him in trouble when Sulla struck them down before his very eyes. His zealous hunting of Sulla's enemies even earned him the nickname *adulescentulus carnifex,* young butcher. Then, when Sulla asked him to disband his army after killing Carbo and his followers in Sicily and North Africa, he refused and successfully demanded that Sulla grant him a triumph, for which he was ineligible under Sulla's own laws. It was then that Sulla gave him the facetious title *Magnus,* which Pompey opportunistically turned to his own advantage.

As a general, Pompey was not brilliant, and his detractors said with some justice that his victories were prepared by others who had fought before him. Still, Pompey often succeeded where others had not because he planned methodically and seldom attacked unless he had secured an overwhelming numerical superiority. As a statesman, Pompey was somewhat inept and shortsighted. He spoke poorly and awkwardly at times and often fell back on silence because he could think of nothing to say. He had no ideology or political program. His main ambition was simply to be admired as the Republic's greatest hero and enjoy the political prestige that such heroes naturally acquired. He certainly did not want to destroy the Republic that produced him, and he would have been appalled if he had realized that he was helping to do so.

Pompey in Spain, 76 to 71 B.C.

Pompey's arrival in Spain (76 B.C.) proved inauspicious. Sertorius defeated him twice with fewer men. On one occasion, only the timely arrival of old Metellus saved Pompey's army from annihilation. Pompey's threat to withdraw and leave the way open for Sertorius to march into Italy brought reinforcements from the senate, but he was able to end the war in 72/71 only after a traitor had assassinated Sertorius in 74 or 73 B.C.

Although a less skillful tactician than Metellus, Pompey seems to have been a better advertiser, for when the war was over, public opinion gave Pompey the victory. The triumphant Pompey promptly executed Sertorius' assassin. Then, he wisely followed the example of Sertorius and treated the Spanish people with great justice. His honorable peace terms restored prosperity to Spain and were long and gratefully remembered by its people.

Lucullus and the Great (Third) Mithridatic War, 74 to 63 B.C.

While Metellus and Pompey were fighting Sertorius in Spain, the eastern end of the Mediterranean was also ablaze with war. In late 75 or early 74 B.C., the childless king of Bithynia, Nicomedes IV, bequeathed his kingdom to the Roman People. The senate accordingly declared Bithynia a Roman province. This action provoked Rome's old enemy Mithridates VI of Pontus, who feared that Roman control of Bithynia would block his access to the Aegean Sea. Mithridates moved swiftly and occupied Bithynia before the Roman armies arrived.

War had long been expected by both sides. The Roman senate had only reluctantly ratified Sulla's easy peace terms after the first war, and Murena, Sulla's legate in Asia, had touched off the brief Second Mithridatic War in 83 and 82 by an unauthorized attack until Sulla had recalled him. Later, Mithridates had engaged exiled Roman officers, who had been supporters of Marius, to modernize his army. He also made alliances with his son-in-law Tigranes II of Armenia, with the pirates of Crete and Cilicia, and with Sertorius in Spain.

When war broke out with Rome in 74 B.C., the pirates flocked to Pontus and helped Mithridates build up a formidable navy. Sertorius had sent some of the former Roman officers to train the Pontic army to fight with Roman tactics. Tigranes did nothing—at least not yet.

Lucullus in Command, 74 to 66 B.C. Lucius Licinius Lucullus (ca. 116 to 57 B.C.), consul of 74 B.C., was of a very old aristocratic family that had fallen into relative obscurity before Sulla. He loyally served Sulla in civil wars, however, and had been well rewarded. He was now closely linked with the innermost circle of *optimates* who controlled the senate. After his consulship, he was slated to be governor of Cisalpine Gaul but contrived to have himself transferred to the provinces of Cilicia and Asia and the command of the main Roman army in the war against Mithridates. Other commanders had bungled their operations in the war, but Lucullus scored a series of stunning victories. In 72, Mithridates finally fled in exile to the court of Tigranes.

While lieutenants completed the reduction of Pontus, Lucullus returned to the Roman province of Asia to relieve its cities of the crushing indemnity levied by Sulla and the extortionate loans that they had been forced to contract with Roman moneylenders to pay it. He assisted the city treasuries by imposing a tax of 25 percent on crops and special taxes on houses and slaves. He fixed the maximum interest rate on loans at 12 percent, disallowed two thirds of

the debts, gave four years to pay the remainder without interest, and issued a ruling that no debtor had to pay more than one quarter of his income. These regulations rapidly restored the economic health of the province but infuriated the financiers at Rome, who worked for his downfall.

The Downfall of Lucullus, 69 to 66 B.C. When Tigranes refused to surrender Mithridates, Lucullus invaded Armenia in 69 and captured Tigranes' capital Tigranocerta. Unfortunately, he did not have authorization to attack Armenia and agents of his political enemies undermined his efforts. One of them was his own brother-in-law, the young, ambitious, and unscrupulous Publius Clodius Pulcher (p. 187). Lucullus' iron discipline and refusal to permit indiscriminate plunder made it easy for Clodius to stir up a mutiny that forced Lucullus to withdraw from Armenia. That permitted Mithridates to seize the initiative once more and undo all that Lucullus had achieved.

Meanwhile, in 67, Pompey intrigued to have Lucullus removed from command and was put in charge of the war himself a year later. Though cheated of the final victory, Lucullus did eventually obtain the triumph that he deserved and found consolation in his wine cellar, his fish ponds, and his cherry trees, but he seized every opportunity to oppose Pompey.

Spartacus and the Slave War in Italy, 73 to 71 B.C.
While wars were raging at both ends of the Mediterranean, a dangerous slave revolt broke within Italy itself. In 73 B.C. Spartacus, a Thracian slave possibly of royal descent, led a band of gladiators out of the barracks of a training school at Capua. They fortified themselves in the crater of Vesuvius and called upon all farm slaves to join them in a fight for freedom. Many thousands did, especially the Gauls and Germans whom Marius had captured in the Cimbrian War. Some slaves came already armed. The others soon obtained arms by buying them from pirates and unscrupulous traders or capturing them from the Roman armies sent to subdue them. Their force

grew to at least 70,000 as they ranged over the country, broke open the slave prisons, and armed the slaves.

The slaves' rebellion was able to gain momentum because Rome's best soldiers were pinned down in Spain and Asia Minor. The Romans were now locked in a desperate struggle to maintain their power against a loosely coordinated uprising that spanned the whole Mediterranean. Earlier, Sertorius, Mithridates, and the Mediterranean pirates had taken some cooperative steps. Now the pirates were supplying arms and material to the rebellious slaves in Italy.

The government, which had thought the slave revolt would be easily quelled, soon learned that Spartacus commanded a large army and was a master strategist as well. Defeat followed defeat. After Spartacus had vanquished the armies of four praetors and two consuls, the senate in desperation appointed Marcus Licinius Crassus to take command and assigned him six new legions in addition to remnants of the four consular legions that Spartacus had shattered.

Marcus Licinius Crassus (ca. 115 to 53 B.C.)

Like Pompey and Lucullus, Crassus had been a Sullan partisan. He had even played the decisive role in Sulla's crucial victory at the Colline Gate. Accused of manipulating the proscriptions for himself, however, Crassus had lost favor with Sulla and Sulla's most important allies. Now Crassus was in a very difficult position. For three generations his family had enjoyed great prominence among the nobility. His father and brother had died while opposing Marius, and he was the only one left to uphold the family's honor. Therefore, he had set about to acquire the financial resources essential for success in the intense competition of aristocratic politics.

Crassus' financial operations earned him an unfair reputation for greed in ancient times because it was not considered proper for a Roman aristocrat to be so directly concerned with making money. Crassus had to make money, however, if he wanted to compete for high office. Pompey, and eventually Caesar, became much richer through the profits of war, an employment considered very honorable. Crassus, on the other hand, invested in profitable agricultural land, mines, and business loans. He maintained a large staff of highly trained slaves, who could be rented out to those who needed temporary help. He also used them to repair and rebuild property that he bought at bargain prices as a result of the many fires in overcrowded and flimsily built Rome.

Many believe that Crassus maintained a private fire brigade (there was no public fire protection) that would not put out a fire until the unfortunate owner agreed to sell his property to Crassus at a reduced rate. There is no ancient evidence for this story. It was not, however, unusual for wealthy men to maintain private fire brigades in their role as patrons of the less fortunate. Crassus may have done so, too, but it would not have been worth the ill will created to refuse to put out a fire before the owner sold.

Crassus was very skilled at earning good will. He was famous for his willingness to defend anyone in court, even though advocates could receive no fees. He often loaned money to people without interest and in that way earned the loyalty of many lesser-known members of the senate. As a result, Crassus had patiently advanced his career and had reached the praetorship in 73 B.C., a few years after he was first eligible. In 72 the command against Spartacus gave him the chance to earn the kind of fame that would advance him further. He even used his own money to recruit more soldiers.

After he had trained his men, Crassus pursued Spartacus to the southern part of Bruttium. Despite many difficulties, Crassus finally defeated the bulk of the slaves. Spartacus was killed, his body unidentifiable amidst the slaughter, but 5,000 slaves escaped capture. Pompey, returning from Spain encountered them in Etruria and destroyed them. This minor feat of arms enabled Pompey to claim credit for ending yet another war, much to Crassus' chagrin. Crassus, however, made a big show of crucifying 6,000 captured slaves along the Appian Way.

The Consulship of Pompey and Crassus, 70 B.C.

Pompey and Crassus, both victors, marched to Rome and encamped their armies outside the gates. Each expected military honors; both wanted the consulship. Crassus, praetor in 73 B.C., was eligible for the office. Pompey was six years too young to be a consul and had not yet held any of the lower offices that the law required for a consular candidate. The senators could grant Pompey's demands only by violating the Sullan constitution, on which their power was based. Yet they could not reject the demands without the risk of having legions enter Rome. The hope of playing Crassus off against Pompey was equally vain. Although the two were political rivals, they realized that their hopes for consulships could be fulfilled only by cooperation at this point. To increase their popularity and put further pressure on their opponents in the senate, they supported popular demands for the restoration of full powers to the tribunes of the plebs and the placing of nonsenators on juries. Pompey received a dispensation from the legal requirements, and both he and Crassus were elected consuls for 70 B.C.

The consulship of Pompey and Crassus completed the ruin of the Sullan constitution, which had been under attack for several years. The optimate leaders of the senate had made some concessions to popular pressure in the hope of defusing discontent. In 75 the consul Gaius Aurelius Cotta had carried a law permitting the tribunes to hold higher offices. The consuls of 73 B.C., a year of scarcity and high prices, had sponsored a bill to distribute 5 pecks of grain a month to 45,000 citizens at the price set by Gaius Gracchus. Pompey and Crassus now proposed and carried a law to restore to the tribunes all the powers taken away by Sulla. (Pompey hoped that tribunes with full powers would later help him to secure desirable commands. They did not disappoint him.) The tribunes of 70 proposed a law to restore citizenship to all who had fought under Lepidus and Sertorius. The consuls revived the censorship, dormant since Sulla's time, and the newly appointed censors promptly ejected from the senate 64 of Sulla's partisans.

Near the end of this historic consulship,

an optimate praetor, who sought to save something from the wreck, drafted and carried a law to break the senatorial monopoly of jury service and to draw jurors in equal numbers from the senate, the *equites,* and the *tribuni aerarii* ("tribunes of the treasury"). About the *tribuni aerarii* almost nothing is known. They were probably inferior to the *equites* in rank, but like the *equites,* belonged to the upper nonsenatorial classes, which henceforth supplied two thirds of the jurors.

The Trial of Gaius Verres, 70 B.C.

The issue of who should sit on juries was underlined by the famous trial of Gaius Verres in 70 B.C. An old supporter of Sulla, he had become a praetor for 74 B.C. and had received the governorship of Sicily for the following three years. As governor he had cheated, blackmailed, plundered, and even murdered people, some of whom were clients of Pompey. When injured Sicilians charged him with extortion in 70, he assumed that Sulla's old supporters in the senate would procure his acquittal. So did many others, who saw this trial as a test of the integrity of senatorial jurors.

Powerful friends rallied to Verres' support. They persuaded Quintus Hortensius Hortalus, the most famous orator of the day, to defend him. They used the most ingenious tricks and dodges in a vain attempt to quash the indictment or postpone the trial until one of them could preside. They even tried to obtain a friendly prosecutor. They, however, were met at every turn by an eager young orator, Marcus Tullius Cicero, who saw a chance to do Pompey a favor by protecting his Sicilian friends, bolster his own clientele among the Sicilians, and gain fame as an orator by beating Hortensius through successfully prosecuting Verres.

Marcus Tullius Cicero (106 to 43 B.C.)

Cicero, the son of a prominent *eques,* was born in 106 B.C. at Arpinum near the home of Marius, whom his family knew. He had received a fine education, had traveled extensively, had studied philosophy and rhetoric in Athens, Asia, and Rhodes, and had trained himself for the Roman bar. He became one of the world's most renowned orators and greatest literary figures. His writings consist of many legal and political speeches, of which his *In Catilinam* and *Philippics* are the most famous; essays such as *On Old Age (De Senectute)* and *On Friendship (De Amicitia)*; many philosophical and political treatises, of which the best known are the *De Legibus (On the Laws)*, *De Re Publica (On the State)*, and *De Officiis, (On Duties)*; and works on oratory such as the *De Oratore (On the Orator)* and the *Brutus.*

More important from the historical standpoint are his *Letters.* They describe the events of this period not only from year to year but often even from day to day. Cicero's letters are more than historical documents: They reveal the soul of the man as well, his deepest feelings, his weaknesses, his strength of character; and strength of character he certainly had. On the basis of these *Letters,* however, he sometimes has been unfairly judged by modern historians, yet not many men have had the courage, the basic assurance, and the honesty to reveal themselves so fully, unless it be St. Augustine in his *Confessions.*

Throughout his lifetime Cicero continued to unveil the offenses and scandals of the optimate oligarchs, although he never wholly deserted them or ceased to look up to them. His ideal was to join them and convince them to be true, impartial servants of the common good. Nor was he a political coward. In 80 B.C. he defended a young man who was threatened by one of Sulla's henchmen. He had a genuine sympathy for the oppressed people of the provinces. For that reason, as well as to advance his career through a spectacular trial, he undertook the case against Verres in 70 B.C. and marshalled such a mass of damning evidence against him that the great Hortensius gave up the defense. Verres fled into exile to Massilia, where the mullets were delicious and the climate delightful—not a really harsh punishment for a man who had robbed the Sicilian people of millions and had even crucified a Roman citizen.

Cicero's second Verrine oration, never delivered but published as a pamphlet, de-

scribes how Verres plundered his province. The disclosure of Verres' iniquities supplied opponents of the Sullan oligarchs and the system that they controlled with all the ammunition needed. That Verres was not acquitted, however, may have helped to make the compromise of sharing the seats on juries among the senators, *equites,* and *tribuni aerarii* acceptable to the voters. After this reform and the restoration of full tribunician powers, the constitution had for the most part been restored to its pre-Sullan state.

After their historic consulship of 70 B.C., both Pompey and Crassus looked for further ways to enhance their fame and prestige when the next public crisis should arise. Pompey never attended meetings of the senate, where he was most unwelcome, but he was always accompanied on his rare appearances in the Forum by a mass of clients and retainers, to the mingled awe and pride of the populace. He was their idol and mighty protector of their rights. Crassus worked diligently behind the scenes to increase his wealth and network of grateful friends on whom he could depend when the need arose. Eventually, one of those friends was an ambitious young man by the name of Gaius Julius Caesar.

Caesar (100 to 44 B.C.) Caesar was born, probably on July 13, 100 B.C., into a family that was very ancient, very patrician, but which for centuries had been politically obscure.[1] He had strong *popularis* antecedents. His aunt Julia had been the wife of Marius; an earlier relative named Julia had been the wife of Fulvius Flaccus, the Gracchan land commissioner. His own wife was Cornelia, Cinna's daughter, whom he had once refused to divorce in the face of Sulla's command.

Caesar's later fame has led many historians to exaggerate the importance of his early

---

[1]Although some scholars have argued for 102 or 101 as the year of his birth, the traditional date of 100 B.C. is now commonly accepted. Some authorities prefer July 12 as the day. According to Suetonius, *The Divine Julius* (6.1), Caesar boasted of his descent from the goddess Venus and from King Ancus Marcius.

career. His exploits and narrow escapes probably have been romanticized. He may have spoken in favor of restoring the tribunician powers in 70 B.C., but he had little to do with the overthrow of the Sullan constitution. Nevertheless, he certainly took advantage of its unpopularity and the common people's high regard for the dead Marius. For example, as a quaestor in 69, Caesar dared to display the images of Marius, which Sulla had banned, and even dared to extol the deeds of Marius and Cinna at the funerals of his aunt Julia, Marius' widow, and of his own wife Cornelia, Cinna's daughter. Later in the same year, he went to serve in Spain, where he set about to make a name for himself and build up a useful group of Spanish clients. Still, Caesar could not hope to make a mark at Rome without the help of men more powerful than he. For Caesar, whose background made him suspect among many of Sulla's heirs, it would be useful to attract favorable attention from men like Pompey and Crassus.

Opportunistic Tribunes   Other young men were seeking to make their marks too. Several took advantage of the opportunities offered by the office of tribune, whose powers Pompey and Crassus had restored. In 67 B.C., the tribunes Gaius Cornelius and Aulus Gabinius were particularly active. The first law of the tribune Cornelius obliged praetors to administer justice according to the principles that they had laid down in their edicts on taking office—an enactment of supreme importance and the foundation of uniform law and equity throughout the provinces (p. 233). His second law imposed a fine and future exclusion from office for persons guilty of bribing the electorate. His third, as finally passed, made it illegal for the senate to exempt individuals from the laws unless a quorum of 200 members was present. Of his other proposals, later carried by his colleague Gabinius, the first forbade the lending of money to foreign and provincial envoys to enable them to secure audience in the senate by bribery, and the second compelled the senate to give priority to the reception of embassies during its February meetings to protect the Roman

allies against dilatory political tactics. These excellent and salutary laws, enacted in spite of the violent opposition of many leading senators, who stood to lose significant financial and political advantages, seemed to justify the freeing of the tribunes from the restrictions imposed by Sulla.

Still, men like Cornelius and Gabinius were not simply public-spirited reformers. They were doing just what Sulla had feared. As competitors in senatorial politics, they were using the restored powers of the tribunate to get around the dominant senatorial leaders, just as the Gracchi and others had done earlier. Part of their strategy was to attract the favor of other powerful senators, like Pompey and Crassus, who also stood outside the group of Sulla's optimate political heirs, who dominated the senate.

Pompey's Commissions against the Pirates and Mithridates, 67 and 66 B.C.
The fame of Gabinius rests largely upon the passage of a law in 67 B.C. to deal with the scourge of piracy in the Mediterranean. Previous attempts to suppress it had proved ineffective (p. 162), and the menace had recently reached dangerous proportions. Pirates had attacked large coastal cities in Italy itself; had destroyed a large Roman fleet near Ostia; and they so infested the waters around Sicily that grain ships supplying the city of Rome no longer ventured to sail. Food prices had risen and the people, threatened with famine, resolved to clear the seas.

The bill that Gabinius laid before the assembly provided for the appointment of a supreme commander of consular rank to take command with extraordinary powers for three years over the waters and coasts of the Mediterranean basin and gave him authority, superior to that of the provincial governors, over all coastal lands extending 50 miles from the sea. As finally enacted, the law placed enormous power in the hands of one man. He could draw from the public treasury 6,000 talents; raise a fleet up to 500 ships; if necessary, recruit an army of 120,000 infantry and 5,000 cavalry; and appoint a staff of 24 subcommanders (*legati*) of praetorian rank and 2 quaestors.

The consul C. Calpurnius Piso and other senators strenuously opposed this bill because it gave so much power to one man, but the populace mobbed the consul. One of the tribunes vetoed the bill but withdrew his veto when threatened with the treatment that Tiberius Gracchus once dealt out to Octavius. The bill passed. After it became law, the majority of senators appointed Pompey to take the command. They had little choice because there was no one else of equal competence, and, although not expressly named in the law, he was the person whom Gabinius and the voters had in mind.[2] Gabinius in turn was amply rewarded for his efforts on Pompey's behalf. Pompey chose him as a legate in 66 and ensured that he would reach the consulship in 58.

Pompey's excellent organization and the vast concentration of ships, men, and supplies enabled him to sweep the western Mediterranean clean in forty days. He owed his swift victory over the pirates not only to the overwhelming superiority of his armaments but also to his treatment of captives. Instead of following the usual Roman practice of crucifying or selling them into slavery, he adopted the more humane methods that he had used successfully in Spain: He settled all those who surrendered on farms or in villages in Asia Minor. Many of the basic social and economic causes of piracy were thus eliminated, and the resettled pirates later became some of Rome's most loyal and useful subjects. Some were among the first in the East to receive Roman citizenship. They also became loyal clients of Pompey, who later, in his civil war with Caesar, based his strategy on the tremendous support that he enjoyed in the East.

Pompey had long been hoping to take over as commander of the Third Mithridatic War (p. 177). Now, already in the East with a huge force and basking in the glory of his victory over the pirates, he was the logical one to be put in charge after the downfall of Lucullus and the failure of his immediate successor.

While Pompey's friends and enemies in the senate were arguing about giving him the appointment, the tribune Gaius Manilius made a bid for popularity and Pompey's powerful favor by proposing his famous law, the *lex Manilia*, conferring upon Pompey the supreme command of all Roman forces in Asia Minor. Other ambitious young men sought to cash in on the situation, too. Caesar was in favor of the law, and Cicero delivered the *Pro Lege Manilia* on its behalf, a famous oration that he later published. The Council of the Plebs adopted the resolution amid wild enthusiasm, because Pompey was now the idol of the populace as well as of the equestrian class. Though many in the senate, especially the leading *optimates,* opposed the sweeping provisions of the law, no one dared to speak in public against the appointment of this very popular general.

Pompey's Conquest of the East, 66 to 62

B.C. Like a buzzard come to enjoy another's kill, Pompey arrived to take over the command of Lucullus, who had already shattered the armies and destroyed the prestige of Mithridates and King Tigranes II of Armenia. With about twice as many men as Lucullus ever had and a navy cruising about in the Black Sea, Pompey overtook and destroyed the inferior forces of Mithridates, who fled first to Armenia and, when refused haven by Tigranes, to the distant Caucasus. Pompey did not attempt immediate pursuit.

Instead, he invaded Armenia and forced Tigranes to become a subordinate ally of Rome. Then he set out after Mithridates but abandoned the chase at the Caucasus Mountains. After Pompey returned to administer the recently conquered territories, Mithridates made his way through the Caucasus to the Crimea. There he planned a daring invasion of Italy via the Balkans and the eastern Alps, a grandiose idea carried out five centuries later by Attila the Hun (p. 495). Worn out by taxation and conscription, however, Mithridates' subjects rebelled. Shut up in his palace, with all hope of escape or mercy gone, he murdered his wives and daughters and then took his own life.

---

[2]So great was the confidence in his leadership that grain prices fell the very day he received the command.

His son Pharnaces II gave the body to Pompey, who buried it properly and gave Pharnaces the Kingdom of Bosporus. Pompey thereby enhanced his growing new reputation as a just and humane conqueror.

Pompey, Syria, and the Jews, 64/63 B.C.
News of the death of Mithridates reached Pompey in Syria. He was fighting to stamp out the anarchy that had reigned there since Lucullus had driven out Tigranes II and restored Antiochus XIII to the decrepit throne of Seleucid Syria. The Seleucids' eastern territories had been taken over by the resurgent Iranian peoples under the aggressive leadership of the Arsacid kings, founders of the Parthian Empire, which became Rome's chief rival in the East. Tyrants had seized control of the cities; robbers and pirates harassed the people. Pompey disposed of these nuisances and annexed Syria and Phoenicia as a Roman province.

Turning south into Palestine, Pompey found two brothers, Hyrcanus and Aristobulus, fighting over the Judean throne of the Maccabees. Both rivals gave him presents and sought his favor. In Rome's interest he took the side of the rather feeble Hyrcanus, who was supported by the Pharisees, against his more able pro-Parthian brother, the leader of the Sadducees. In making this choice, Pompey, who knew nothing about Jewish theology, unwittingly contributed to the ultimate triumph of the Pharisees over the Sadducees.

The Sadducees, composed mainly of the rich landed aristocracy and of the priestly caste, were conservative fundamentalists who accepted literally the text of the Written Law contained in the Torah or first five books of the Bible. The Pharisees accepted the Written Law, too, but included a mass of interpretations and oral traditions handed down by the scribes. The Pharisaic rabbis or teachers later produced the great commentaries of the law known as the Mishna and the Talmud. In deciding in favor of Hyrcanus on purely political grounds, Pompey may have set the future course of Judaism.

Pompey's Achievements in the Near East
Pompey did not attempt the impossible, as Lucullus had done. Parthia's hostility did not provoke him, nor did Egypt's weakness invite him. Yet his command in the Near East was historic and his achievements solid and enduring. He extended Rome's Empire from the Mediterranean to the Euphrates. He poured into the Roman treasury more revenue from a foreign war than any of his predecessors. In return for the taxes and indemnities he imposed upon the people of the East, he gave such peace and security as they had not enjoyed since Alexander. He cleared the seas of pirates and made them safe for commerce, delivered Syria from anarchy, and all Asia Minor from the scourge and fear of war. More important still, he encouraged city life by granting privileges to numerous existing cities and restoring or founding scores of others.

During Pompey's absence, Lucullus and his other optimate opponents in the senate were bitter and resentful toward him. They prosecuted the former tribunes Cornelius and Manilius, who had favored him. On the other hand, they had little power to inflict real harm, and many feared that with his overwhelming military power Pompey would return like another Sulla and crush his enemies.

The Maneuverings of Crassus and Caesar
Crassus did everything that he could to build up a position of countervailing political and military power. Apparently he was unsuccessful in placing a friend in the governorship of Nearer Spain, but he did get himself elected censor for 65 and supported Caesar's election as aedile as well as that of two others as consuls. A crisis arose when the two consuls-elect were convicted of bribery. Their election was invalidated and they were barred from office. According to Cicero, they then conspired with L. Sergius Catalina (Catiline) to murder their replacements on New Year's Day, 65 B.C. This supposed plot, known as the First Catilinarian Conspiracy, never existed. Cicero was merely twisting certain facts in a later piece of campaign rhetoric designed to blacken his electoral rival Catiline, as well as Caesar and Crassus, who were supporting Catiline in the ongoing attempt to win powerful friends.

Meanwhile, Caesar was winning popularity and entertaining the multitude with money supplied by Crassus. For their delectation he had the Forum decorated, exhibited 320 pairs of gladiators, and armed the criminals condemned to fight lions in the arena with silver-decorated weapons. Early one morning, people entering the Forum saw gleaming gold statues of Marius and his trophies set up everywhere. The old veterans gathered around, tears of pride streaming down their cheeks. Caesar's efforts had begun to bear fruit.

Crassus' ultimate purpose in building a base of popular support was to create an army that would give him the same kind of political strength that Pompey enjoyed. One of the best Roman recruiting grounds was northern Italy. Using the power of censor, he proposed to enroll as full citizens, in all the voting tribes, the people of Cisalpine Gaul north of the Po, a move already advocated by Caesar in 68. Crassus was vetoed by his fellow censor, Quintus Lutatius Catulus, a staunch optimate who trusted neither Pompey nor Crassus and his friends. The impasse was so unbreakable that both Crassus and Catulus resigned. Even so, the proposal won for Caesar and Crassus the continued gratitude of the people north of the Po and future armies were easily recruited there.

Another of Crassus' schemes earlier in 65 concerned Egypt, which was said to have been bequeathed by will to the Roman people earlier. He drafted a bill declaring Egypt a province, which cleverly appealed to several groups. It would have given someone (perhaps Crassus or Caesar) the right to raise an army, the Roman populace a rich source of grain, and equestrian financial interests a store of untapped wealth. Nevertheless, it was foiled by the efforts of Catulus and also Cicero, who was then one of Pompey's staunchest supporters and did not trust the aims of men like Caesar and Crassus.

The Elections of 64 B.C.
Crassus and Caesar continued to build their political bases by supporting candidates for election. In 64, they seem to have backed Catiline (Lucius Sergius Catilina) and C. Antonius Hybrida, who were now running against Cicero for the consulship of 63 B.C. Catiline was already a man of some fame or rather notoriety. Although descended from an ancient and illustrious lineage, Catiline was (if Cicero's and Sallust's accounts are to be believed) a scoundrel, a murderer, and a master of every known vice. He had supported Sulla and had played a notorious role in Sulla's bloody proscriptions. After serving as propraetor in the province of Africa in 67, Catiline was accused of extortion and brought to trial in 65.[3] Bribery secured him an acquittal, and he went on to stand for the consulship in the elections of 64. At the last minute, however, Catiline alarmed the electorate by his violent behavior and his radical talk about the canceling of debts, and Cicero, who had widespread equestrian support, won the election by a large majority. Antonius Hybrida, the other candidate, was a successful but poor second, Catiline a close third. Cicero soon won the allegiance of Antonius by assigning him to Macedonia, a far richer consular province than that which Antonius had originally drawn.

Popular Legislation and Actions in 63 B.C.
Crassus and Caesar seem to have been associated with a number of popular measures in 63 that would win favor with the voters and prove useful in dealing with Pompey. One of them was the proposed land law of the tribune P. Servillius Rullus. This law would have established a land commission that was to control the distribution of public land (which Pompey had promised his veterans), have access to Pompey's war booty, enroll troops, and occupy Egypt by force. Cicero curried favor with Pompey by portraying it as a plot aimed directly at him and helped to bring about its defeat.

Caesar mounted a popular attack on the *Senatus Consultum Ultimum* by prosecuting an old senator named Rabirius. Thirty years earlier, acting under the banner of the *S.C.U.*, Ra-

---

[3]The prosecutor at the trial was Publius Clodius Pulcher, who had helped to undermine Lucullus in Asia Minor. Cicero, though convinced of Catiline's guilt, had at first thought of defending him and even worked out a deal with Clodius but then dropped the idea.

birius had taken part in the shameful murder of the tribune Saturninus (p. 163). Trying to preserve stability in a period of increasing tension, Cicero gave a speech that still exists in defense of Rabirius (*Pro Rabirio Perduellionis*), but a clever strategem ended the trial before the jury voted. No matter, Caesar had focused attention on his hostility to a weapon that the optimate oligarchs had often used against popular challengers.

A friend obtained passage of a voting bill that made it easier for Caesar to get elected *pontifex maximus* against the staunch optimate Catulus. Caesar also was elected praetor for 62, but Cicero blocked his popular proposal to recall and reinstate Sullan exiles. Soon, the rash actions of Catiline would cause him serious trouble.

The Catilinarian Conspiracy, 63 B.C.

Catiline again ran for the consulship in the elections for 62 B.C. Initially, he probably still had the support of Crassus and Caesar, although his rhetoric was more radical and alarming than what they were prepared to support in actual practice. Although his demands for a general scaling down of debts repelled creditors and investors, they had a strong attraction for debtors, ruined aristocrats, Sulla's veterans, and the sons of the persons whom Sulla had proscribed. The more support Catiline received from idlers, hoodlums, criminals, and exiles, the more he caused the well-to-do and respectable citizens to fear him as a public nuisance, if not a dangerous enemy. Cicero did his best to whip up the fear that Catiline, if elected, would resort to violence and revolution.

Upon losing the election, Catiline, frustrated and desperate, formed a conspiracy to overthrow the government, rumors of which reached Cicero. More definite information arrived through the cooperation of Fulvia, mistress of one of Catiline's accomplices. Also, Crassus secretly visited Cicero and entrusted to him a number of compromising letters that he had received from the conspirators.

Still, Cicero's first denunciation of Catiline before the senate was based largely on surmises. Even when he reported that Catiline's lieutenant, Manlius, was busily recruiting an army of malcontents in Etruria to seize control of the government, his evidence was dismissed as incomplete by the senate, which refused to issue a *Senatus Consultum Ultimum* until the news arrived in Rome the next day that Manlius had indeed recruited a substantial army in Etruria. Cicero had not lied.

Cicero refrained from using the emergency decree and waited instead for Catiline's next move. He learned more of Catiline's plans through the cooperative Fulvia. Thus he was able to discredit Catiline and lay a trap for his accomplices. Whereas Caesar courted popularity by calling for the return of Pompey, the arrest and execution of five leading conspirators was a major blow to Catiline, who had already taken the field with the rebels in Etruria. Two thirds of his army melted away.

Caesar, Cato the Younger, and the S.C.U.

During the trial of Catiline's five accomplices, Caesar, now praetor-elect for 62, had taken another opportunity to earn popular favor by speaking out against the *S.C.U.* His eloquence almost persuaded a majority of the senators, even Cicero, to vote for life imprisonment instead of death. Then, Cato the Younger (Uticensis), great-grandson of Cato the Elder, took the floor and attacked the weakness and irresolution of his colleagues. So stinging were his words that a majority of the senators finally voted for the death penalty. That same day the conspirators paid for their crimes in the gloomy torchlit prison of the Tullianum. Their political ghosts would come back to haunt Cicero.

Cicero's Hopes for the Future

In the meantime, Cicero of Arpinum had attained sudden glory. For delivering Rome from danger he was voted a thanksgiving festival and given the title *Pater Patriae,* Father of His Country. Without the support of a proud family name, great wealth, military talents, or strong political following, he had entered the senate, reached the consulship, and ennobled his family—a proud achievement, in proclaiming which he sometimes became tiresome even to his friends. The experience must have had its uncomfortable moments: He was admitted but not accepted; admired for his eloquence but ridiculed for his self-adulation. The first *novus homo* since Marius, Cicero cannot but have been hurt by the aloofness of his colleagues, by their tacit assumption of superiority, and by their frequent rudeness.

Difficult as it must have been for so proud a man to accept such treatment, Cicero was nevertheless convinced that the preservation of the Republic depended on maintaining the supremacy of the senate. The ancient nobility was to give it prestige and continuity with the past, and new men—like Cicero himself—were to bring to it energy, intelligence, and an awareness of present problems. Peace, stability, and freedom depended on the continued harmony (*concordia ordinum*) between the senatorial aristocracy and the wealthy equestrian class of both businessmen and local Italian landed aristocracy. In a slightly expanded form, the concord of the orders was an alliance of all good law-abiding citizens against revolutionary attacks upon property and the status quo. He also insisted upon the *consensus Italiae,* by which he meant that Rome should conduct her affairs in conformity with the interests and sentiments of Italy as a whole —that is, of the class of local Italian notables, from which Cicero himself had come.

Cicero's concept of the ideal state, one governed according to law, reflected the Republic's highest ideal of *libertas.* To the magistrates was to be allotted executive power; to the senate, authority; to the people, liberty. It was to be a state in which the people, undisturbed by social strife or civil war, might live and work in peace and security, and members of the privileged classes maintain their *dignitas* (rank, prestige, and honor) in service to the state. Such a state, Cicero believed, could be neither a monarchy nor a participatory democracy on the Athenian model, but only a free aristocratic republic, flexible enough to incorporate talented

and patriotic men from nonaristocratic circles into the governing elite.

Publius Clodius Pulcher (ca. 92 to 52 B.C.) and the Bona Dea Scandal Unfortunately, Publius Clodius, the man who had done so much to ruin Lucullus' career (p. 178), was about to become an enemy who would drive Cicero from public life when his services were needed most. Late in the year 62, Roman women were celebrating the annual festival of the Bona Dea at the house of the *pontifex maximus,* Julius Caesar. Men were rigidly excluded from this all-female ritual. Clodius, however, disguised as a woman and alleged at the time to have been the lover of Caesar's second wife, Pompeia, managed to enter the house. His presence was detected and a scandal ensued. As a result, Caesar declared that "Caesar's wife must be above suspicion" and divorced Pompeia. Instead of treating the escapade as a joke (Cicero privately regarded it as such.), Cato brought Clodius to trial on a charge of sacrilege. When called as a witness, Caesar, who was about to depart for a provincial governorship in Spain and did not want to make an enemy of a popular and powerful political figure, refused to testify, but Cicero, testifying at the trial, ruined Clodius' attempt to establish an alibi. Conviction seemed certain. Crassus, however, bribed the jurors to vote for acquittal. Clodius never forgave Cato for bringing him to trial or Cicero for testifying against him.

The Reaction against Pompey Toward the end of 62 B.C., Pompeius Magnus, the conqueror of the East, landed at Brundisium. He at once disbanded his powerful army, with which he might have seized dictatorial power, as Sulla had done. His action belies the monarchic ambition sometimes attributed to him. This fiction is based on the literal and serious acceptance of *rex* and *regnum,* two terms of political invective freely and loosely hurled in the late Roman Republic. Even Cicero, because he was a *novus homo* from Arpinum, felt their sting. He was maliciously called "the first foreign king at Rome since the Tarquins."

Against no one has the charge of monarchic ambition been more frequently hurled than against Julius Caesar, who has been described as having perversely dedicated his whole life to the goal of kingly power. He probably never had such a long-range program but had more immediate goals: the acquisition of money to pay his debts (he owed 25 million denarii before he went to Spain) and as a source of patronage; the maintenance of his *dignitas;* and the winning of *gloria* in politics and war. When a Roman achieved those goals, he did not need or want the useless and invidious *ornamenta* of a king. To Caesar, to Pompey, and to every other Roman *nobilis,* the very name of king was still anathema.

The opening days of the year 61 B.C. looked bright for the future of the Republic. In 63 and 62, the optimate generals Lucullus and Metellus Creticus had finally been allowed to celebrate triumphs that had long been delayed by popular opposition. At the same time, the senate had shown unexpected strength and resolution in dealing with the Catilinarian conspiracy. The equestrian class had, in Cicero, a vigorous and eloquent spokesman, whose *concordia ordinum* seemed an answer to social and civil strife, although not a substitute for needed reforms. A truly hopeful sign was Pompey's dismissal of his army and his refusal to seize dictatorial power. Cicero might yet have saved the Republic, could Pompey but have been induced to support the policy of *concordia.*

Unfortunately, these were empty hopes: The jealousy of Crassus, the hostility of the optimate leaders of the senate toward Pompey, Pompey's own ineptness, and Cicero's unconquerable vanity all contributed to the breakdown of the tenuous harmony. Upon his return to Rome, Pompey attended a meeting of the senate with the expectation of being hailed as another Alexander. Crassus solemnly rose and, pointedly ignoring Pompey, dramatically declared Cicero the savior of Rome. Cicero, his vanity flattered, promptly forgot all about Pompey and went on to speak at great length of his own illustrious deeds instead. Cicero had already alienated Pompey by earlier boasts and thereby denied himself crucial support for his

concordia ordinum. Thus he had unwittingly shattered his own hopes of reconstructing the Republic.

Pompey's modest demands, when finally presented to the senate, met bitter opposition. He understandably wanted land for his veterans and ratification of his *acta* or arrangements made in the East. The consul Metellus Celer, whose half-sister Pompey had just divorced, opposed him and so did the ex-consul of 69 B.C., Metellus Creticus, who held a grudge because Pompey had interfered with his command in Crete during the pirate war in 67. Lucullus, emerging from his princely gardens, vindictive and rancorous, insisted on debating Pompey's proposals in detail, not *en bloc* as Pompey requested. He had the support of Crassus, who was a jealous rival, and Cato the Younger, who saw Pompey's power as a threat to the Republic.

Not one of the optimate leaders of the senate opposed Pompey's requests with more rancor than Cato the Younger. Narrow-minded and pedantic, yet honest and fearless, he was one of the few Stoics who lived by the philosophy they professed. Cato's moral courage soon gained him recognition as the spokesman of the optimate heirs of Sulla, and his forceful character won him a power greater than that of any other member of the senate. Because of Cato's obstructive tactics, ratification of Pompey's *acta* was delayed.

After destroying the possibility of good will between Pompey and the optimate leaders of the senate, Cato proceeded to alienate Crassus and the equestrian financial interests by blocking passage of a bill for the relief of tax-collecting companies that had optimistically bid too high for the taxes in Asia and were now requesting a reduction of their contract payments to the treasury. Cicero, though he privately considered the petition outrageous and impudent, had nevertheless supported the bill for the sake of his policy for *concordia ordinum.*

Cato further antagonized the *equites* by forcing passage of a bill that declared as criminal offense the acceptance of bribes by *equites* serving on juries (it had long been so for senators). Again Cicero, as politicians so often must, betrayed one principle for the sake of another; although he thought the bill a fair measure, he opposed it as being detrimental to harmony.

Cato's next object of attack was Julius Caesar. On his return from Spain, Caesar had requested the right to declare his candidacy for the consulship *in absentia* because he had been voted a triumph for some victories against native tribes whom he had found an excuse to attack. It was legally impossible for him to have both in the time available: A recent law compelled potential candidates to declare their intentions in person at Rome before the magistrate in charge of the election; but to cross the city limits would have meant forfeiture of his triumph.

When Caesar learned that Cato opposed the petition, he decided to forego the triumph and stand for the consulship instead. Fearing that Caesar might win the election and thereby be eligible for a province and control of a provincial army, Cato persuaded the senate to assign the mountain roads and forests of Italy as the provinces of the consuls of 59 B.C. If Cato had deliberately set out to destroy the Republic, he could not have been more successful.

Cato and his allies ultimately drove Pompey, Crassus, and Caesar into a coalition that made each of them more powerful than he otherwise could have become. Then, with each aiming for supreme honors, the natural rivalries that were bound to reemerge resulted in the dictatorship of Julius Caesar, who paved the way for the principate of Augustus, which ended the Republic forever. The natural ambitions and rivalries of Roman nobles had reduced Republican politics to a vast game of musical chairs in which only one man would ultimately be left to dominate the rest.

XVIII

The Rise of Caesar, 60 to 52 B.C.

Having surprised Cato and his other optimate enemies by foregoing a triumph to run for the consulship in 60 B.C., Caesar marshalled all of his charm, skill, and resources to guarantee victory. His earlier cultivation of Marius' old followers now bore fruit. After his governorship of Spain, he also seems to have had fairly abundant funds of his own for bribery. In addition, he had those provided by another candidate, Pompey's friend L. Lucceius. Caesar's optimate enemies, determined to defeat him, decided to raise their own bribery fund (to which even the incorruptible Cato contributed) to ensure the election of M. Calpurnius Bibulus, a stubborn and somewhat dull-witted man but son-in-law of Cato. Countering them, Caesar also secured the aid of Crassus and Pompey (probably independently of each other at first). Both of them had, like himself, been thwarted and injured by their optimate enemies in the senate, and they were happy to support a candidate who promised to act favorably toward them as consul. Thus supported, Caesar had little trouble winning election. Lucceius, however, lost to Bibulus, and that posed problems.

The So-Called First Triumvirate The election of Bibulus revealed the strength of Caesar's opponents. It was probably only after the election that Caesar, to strengthen his position as much as possible, persuaded Pompey and Crassus to cooperate together in the coalition that modern writers often call the First Triumvirate. Actually, it is inaccurate to refer to their coalition as a triumvirate, which in Roman terms denoted a legally constituted board of three men with some clearly defined authority. The later triumvirate of Octavian, Antony, and Lepidus, which is often called the Second Triumvirate, was such a board (pp. 213–221). The informal coalition of Pompey, Crassus, and Caesar, the proper Roman term for which would be *coitio* or *factio,* was not. The whole difficulty with the word *triumvirate* might have been avoided had Caesar succeeded in his attempt to add Cicero as a fourth member of the coalition, but Cicero, rightly seeing it as an attempt by three individual dynasts to thwart established constitutional mechanisms, honorably refused.

The three others privately swore that each would seek only those ends not objectionable to the other two. The personal aims of the three were fairly clear: Pompey wanted land for his veterans and ratification of his *acta* in the East; Crassus desired a reduction of the Asian tax contracts of his equestrian friends; Caesar sought command of a province and an army.

At the start, Caesar was clearly less powerful than either Pompey or Crassus. He had a certain long-term advantage, however, because Pompey and Crassus could never completely forget their rivalry and he could maneuver between them. He soon strengthened his position by marrying his daughter, Julia, to Pompey and taking to wife Calpurnia, the daughter of Lucius Calpurnius Piso Caesoninus, who became a consul in 58 B.C. In that and following years, with the help of Pompey and Crassus and others, Caesar obtained passage of legislation favorable to himself that enabled him eventually to amass enough political, military, and financial power to surpass the other two partners in the coalition.

Caesar's Legislation   In 59, however, Caesar's first task was to make good on his promise to obtain the legislation that would fill the needs of Pompey and Crassus. At the start of his term, Caesar sensibly tried to obtain his goals without any unnecessary offense to his opponents and began by being studiously polite both to the optimate-controlled senate and to his optimate colleague, Bibulus. He consulted them on all matters, accepted their suggestions and amendments, and proposed only moderate bills. His friendly behavior may have been interpreted as weakness, or Caesar himself may have tired of the cautious approach, for he soon resorted to more direct methods. When even his moderate bills were endlessly debated and obstructed in the senate, Caesar had Cato, the leader of the opposition, arrested. Upon reflection, however, he apparently decided not to turn the righteous Cato into a martyr and had him set free.

Taking direct action, Caesar presented his land bill for the settlement of Pompey's veterans to the Centuriate Assembly. As the other consul, Bibulus promptly vetoed it and declared all remaining days on which the assemblies could meet during the year to be feast days. He thereby cut off the last constitutional path of action for the three dynasts.

Disregarding this legal obstacle, Caesar presented his land bill to the assembly a second time. The Forum was filled with eager spectators, most of them Pompey's veterans. The law was proposed; three tribunes interposed vetoes. The crowd's murmur rose to an angry roar. Dramatically, Caesar halted the voting and

asked Pompey what other action he was prepared to take. Pompey placed his hand on his hip and declared that he would not hesitate to draw his sword. Bibulus, who had pushed his way into the Forum, jumped to his feet. But before he could say a word, the angry mob had broken his fasces and someone dumped a basket of feces over his head. The assembly passed the bill, and Caesar declared it carried.[1]

The humiliated Bibulus retired from public life and spent the rest of his term shut up in his home. Some wag acutely observed that from then on the names of the two consuls were no longer Bibulus and Caesar, but Julius and Caesar.

Now unopposed, Caesar carried out the rest of his legislative program with speed and efficiency. A law was passed that provided for the distribution of Campanian public lands among 20,000 needy citizens—the only requirement being that each have at least 3 children. A bill was passed to ratify *en bloc* all of Pompey's settlements in the East; another bill remitted one third of the contract payments that the tax collectors of Asia, Crassus' friends, had to submit to the treasury.

Caesar also obtained passage of legislation favorable to himself. One of his partisans, the tribune Publius Vatinius, secured passage of a bill that granted Caesar immediate proconsular power for five years over the provinces of Cisalpine Gaul and Illyricum and an army of three legions. Caesar began at once to recruit his army and held it in readiness near Rome. His opponents within the senate were powerless: They could have declared the law null and void if a meeting of the senate had been summoned by a magistrate, but no one summoned it. Nor could it pass a *Senatus Consultum Ultimum,* which would have been useless anyway, because there was no one to enforce it except Bibulus, who had no troops. After that, no senator dared oppose any of Caesar's measures for fear of incurring his wrath. Those who still at-

---

[1]The authors of the bill had foresightedly included a clause, similar to that inserted into the land bill of 100 B.C. of Saturninus, which required all senators to swear obedience to the law. They all did, including Cato.

tended meetings summoned by Caesar were considerate and polite. When the governor of Transalpine Gaul suddenly died, they voluntarily assigned that province to Caesar.

One of the most enlightened of Caesar's early laws ordered the publication of the *Acta Diurna,* a daily bulletin that contained the texts of all currently enacted laws as well as condensations of the debates and proceedings of the senate and popular assemblies (*Acta Senatus et Populi Romani*). Sold in the streets, posted in the Forum, and sent to all the towns of Italy and to provinces, this publication kept the people informed about foreign and domestic problems. Caesar's purpose in ordering publication of the *Acta Diurna* was also personal, however. Now the actions of his enemies would be made visible to the average citizens, among whom he was very popular. Therefore, his enemies would have to be careful.

The most statesmanly law of Caesar in 59 B.C. was the *lex Julia de Repetundis,* which regulated the administration of the provinces, drastically controlled extortion, and forbade governors, under pain of heavy penalty, to accept presents, sell or withhold justice, transgress the limits of their provinces without authorization, or fail to put their official edicts on deposit: two copies in the provinces and one at Rome. This excellent law served to protect the people of the provinces from oppression and promote their well-being and prosperity. Still, it, too, had a partisan purpose, for it would make it more difficult for his enemies to abuse the provinces in an attempt to obtain power and resources against him and would make the danger of prosecution greater if they did.

P. Clodius Pulcher and the Banishment of Cicero, 58 B.C.

Before leaving for Gaul, Caesar wanted to make sure that his opponents in the senate would not venture to annul the Julian laws of 59 B.C. With his compelling oratory, Cicero was a man who might successfully lead such an attack. In an effort to prevent Cicero from freely speaking his mind, Caesar offered him a remunerative position in the Land Com-

mission. That offer rejected, Casesar then invited Cicero to accompany him to Gaul as his legate. When Cicero turned down this and other offers, Caesar finally decided to leave Cicero to the devices of Publius Clodius, now a tribune and Cicero's sworn enemy after the Bona Dea affair (p. 187). Loose and dissolute, clever and audacious, Clodius was one of the most potent rabble-rousers in Roman history. His armed gangs ruled the streets of Rome. He was a patrician Claudius by birth but used the plebeian spelling Clodius to gain popularity. Early in 58 B.C. Caesar, as *pontifex maximus,* and Pompey, as an augur, presided over his adoption by a plebeian family just so that he could become a tribune and be used to frighten Cicero into silence if necessary.

Clodius' Attack   One of the first bills that Clodius carried abolished the use of "omens" for the obstruction of legislation. Another of his laws provided for the distribution of free grain to the needy. Most notorious is the law that was part of his revenge against Cicero: It forbade the use of fire and water to all persons who had put Roman citizens to death without trial or appeal to the people. The law attacked not only Cicero, who had ordered the execution of the Catilinarian conspirators, but also the *Senatus Consultum Ultimum,* whose legality had been debated since the time of the Gracchi. Cicero, who had believed himself immune from attack, was stunned: He and his friends vainly pleaded with the consuls, Piso (Caesar's father-in-law, Lucius Calpurnius Piso Caesoninus) and Gabinius (Pompey's client), who had once promised him protection, but Pompey, according to Plutarch, slipped out of his house upon Cicero's approach. His pleas denied, Cicero had no choice but to leave Italy.

Clodius next disposed of Cato by a law assigning him to govern the distant island of Cyprus. Clodius dryly observed that Cato was the only man in Rome honest enough to administer the royal treasures of that new province. Cato, who could not justify breaking a duly constituted law, stoically complied.

The removal of his two ablest opponents

ensured for Caesar the perpetuation of the recently enacted Julian Laws of 59 B.C., and he finally set forth for his proconsular provinces.

Caesar in Gaul Caesar, waiting outside Rome for Cicero to be exiled, now hurried north and took command of the legion stationed in Transalpine Gaul, often called the Province or Narbonese Gaul, the eastern part of which is now Provence in southeastern France. Caesar hoped to use his governorship of Transalpine Gaul to pursue great wars and conquests that would earn him undying glory, a large following of loyal veterans, and huge financial resources from booty, all of which were extremely useful in the even more important political battles of the Forum, as the careers of Marius, Sulla, and Pompey had amply demonstrated. At this time, Transalpine Gaul was ideally located for fulfilling these hopes. It bordered the rich and populous lands of the free Gallic tribes in *Gallia Comata,* Long-Haired Gaul, and the political situation both within and without their territory was in an unsettled state that could give ample pretexts for the neighboring Roman commander to intervene "to protect the vital interests of Rome."

***The Situation in* Gallia Comata** According to Caesar, *Gallia Comata* was divided into three parts by three ethnic groups: the Aquitanians, probably a mix of Basques and Celts, in the southwest between the Garonne and the Pyrenees; various Celtic tribes like the Aedui and Sequani in the central area as far east as the Rhine; and the Belgians, warlike tribes of mixed Celts and Germans in the northernmost region from the Seine and the Marne to the estuary of the Scheldt and the Lower Rhine—all with different languages, customs, and institutions. Primarily agricultural people, the vast majority lived in villages and small towns. There were some mining and manufacturing centers on major rivers and trade routes, and a few hilltop fortresses like Bibracte, Gergovia, and Alesia in the interior.

The Gauls, as a whole, were politically weak and unstable. Their largest political unit was the tribal state (*civitas*), a loose confederation of more or less independent clans. There were nearly 100 such states, and they often fought with each other. Also, they were unstable internally. Most had abolished monarchic rule about 50 years earlier and were rent by feuding noble factions.

Defeat of the Helvetians, 58 B.C. When Caesar arrived in the Province in the spring of 58 B.C., the Helvetians (Helvetii) of western Switzerland were ready to set out on a long-projected trek west across Gaul to a land richer and more spacious than their own. Fleeing the aggressions of Germanic tribes under kings like Ariovistus, they had burnt their homes and villages behind them and stood poised on the banks of the Rhône.

Claiming that the migration of the Helvetians would threaten the security of the Province by creating turmoil in free Gaul and would leave their old territory open as an avenue for German tribes to invade Italy, Caesar refused to let them cross. The Helvetians, intending to follow the Saône before crossing and swinging west, turned north. Caesar reacted with the speed and determination that became his hallmarks as a general and the key to his rise as the dominant power at Rome. After a series of minor skirmishes, the two armies clashed in a decisive battle during which the Romans all but destroyed the Helvetian army. Caesar compelled the survivors to return to their native homeland, except for the Boii, whom he allowed to settle in Aeduan territory, at the request of the Aeduan leaders.

Ariovistus There began almost immediately a procession of envoys from many states of central Gaul to Caesar, some to offer congratulations for his recent victory, others to implore his aid against Ariovistus, the powerful German king who had already reduced two states to vassalage and whose aggressions were daily growing more menacing. Caesar at once began negotiations with the king, in whose rudeness and arrogance he found a plausible pretext for war.

Britain and Gaul in the Time of Caesar

Bold, swift marches, a few skillful maneuvers, and a single battle ended in the utter rout and destruction of the Germans. After quartering his legions for the winter, he hastened to Cisalpine Gaul to hold the November sessions of his gubernatorial court and recruit two more legions for another campaign.

The Belgic War, 57 B.C. Caesar's selection of eastern Gaul for winter quarters had aroused the fears and hostilities of the Belgians. A letter from his most trusted legate, Titus Labienus, about their warlike preparations sent the proconsul hurrying back over the Alps with two more legions. Again, speed and resolute action were decisive. The Belgian force proved too unwieldy for unified command and soon ran short of supplies. Torn by mutual jealousies and dissension, the Belgians broke up and dispersed after only one minor skirmish. Caesar could now subdue the Belgian states one by one.

Meanwhile, young Publius Crassus, Crassus' son, whom the proconsul had sent with one legion to western Gaul, had compelled all the tribes along the English Channel and the Atlantic seaboard to submit to Rome. Gaul was prostrate at the feet of the conqueror. Even the Germans beyond the Rhine sent hostages and promised to obey his orders. On receiving report of these triumphs, the senate decreed a public thanksgiving of fifteen days, an unprecedented length.

The Political Situation in Rome, 58 to 56 B.C.

While Caesar was winning battles, Rome itself was the scene of disorder and violence. Constitutional government had broken down. The optimate-controlled senate was too weak to govern, Pompey the Great too inept. Clodius had by his free grain law made himself the idol of the slums, and his armed gangs ruled the streets. They besieged and burnt down houses, hissed at or spat upon political opponents, pelted them with stones, or stomped them to death.

No sooner had Caesar left for Gaul than Pompey and Crassus began to quarrel. The former, in order to restore his ebbing popularity

and win the support of the nobility, began to agitate for the recall of Cicero from exile. Clodius, aroused to fury, incited a series of riots, and the ensuing jeers, insults, and threats drove the general from public life temporarily and confined him to his house. Crassus, who had no liking for Cicero and helped to keep Clodius supplied with funds, although he by no means controlled him, enjoyed his rival's discomfiture.

Cicero's Recall, 57 B.C. Clodius, as tribune, could veto every proposal for the return of Cicero and continued to incite his followers to riot whenever such a bill came up before the assembly. Pompey returned to the political arena during the summer of the Belgic War: He entered into correspondence with Caesar and began to attend assembly meetings in the Forum once more. Usually he was escorted by a large group of followers (many of them veterans of his Eastern wars), headed by the tribune T. Annius Milo. Pompey called upon Cicero's brother, Quintus Cicero, to guarantee that the orator, if permitted to return, would do nothing to upset either the rule of the so-called triumvirs or the Julian laws. Pompey's efforts bore fruit, and that same autumn a bill for Cicero's return passed the *comitia centuriata* with uproarious acclaim. The success of the bill had depended somewhat on the victory of Milo and his followers during a bloody scuffle with the followers of Clodius.

Cicero's return was met with thunderous applause from the watching throngs who scattered flowers in his path. The senate undertook to rebuild (at public expense) his house, which had been destroyed by the followers of Clodius. Unfortunately the same hoodlums drove away the workmen, demolished the reconstructions, and set fire to his brother's house, next door.

After Cicero's return, a sudden and dangerous shortage of grain frightened the optimate leaders of the senate, and they agreed to place Pompey in charge of the food supply. He was given command of a fleet to transport grain and was offered an army, but he solemnly demurred in order not to appear too eager for what he really did want. The *optimates* simply took him at his word. His friends, although exasperated by his lack of frankness, saw a good opportunity for him to acquire an army when Ptolemy the Fluteplayer, king of Egypt, driven from his throne by the citizens of Alexandria, formally requested Roman aid. Unfortunately for Pompey's ambitions, someone took the trouble to consult the books of the Sibyl and found that it was forbidden to use an army to restore a king of Egypt. Much relieved, the majority of senators let the matter drop.

The Conference of Luca, 56 B.C. Caesar was undoubtedly kept informed of the political situation in Rome through correspondence with Pompey, Crassus, and others. He knew that Cicero and Clodius (the latter with the connivance of Crassus) were both attacking the Julian laws of 59 B.C., though for different reasons. He knew from a visit of Crassus to his winter quarters at Ravenna in early April of 56 that Pompey, with Cicero's encouragement, was veering over to the *optimates*. With the coalition of Pompey, Crassus, and Caesar threatened, the time had come for Caesar himself to act. He met with Pompey and probably also Crassus at Luca in mid-April of 56.

It was agreed that Pompey and Crassus should stand for the consulship of 55 B.C., probably that Pompey should afterward be governor of the two Spains for five years whereas Crassus for an equal period should be governor of Syria with the right to wage war against the Parthians, and that Caesar's proconsulship be renewed for another five years. They also agreed that Cicero's acid speechmaking be curbed and the mobs of Clodius and Milo restrained. The conference over, Caesar swept off to Gaul.

The Gallic Wars Continued, 56 to 52 B.C.

The initial conquest of Gaul had been relatively easy. Although Caesar had shown some of the speed and daring for which he would become famous as a general, he had not really been tested. For five years after Luca, however, the heat of many hard-fought battles tempered and annealed the soft Roman aristocrat into the tough and flexible piece of steel that has fright-

ened and fascinated generations of admirers and detractors.

When Caesar returned to Gaul in 56, he put down a revolt of the seafaring Veneti by cleverly employing long poles with hooks to pull down the rigging of their ships. Then he turned to face two large German tribes that had migrated across the Rhine. Provoked, he claimed, by a treacherous attack during negotiations, he engaged in a merciless slaughter. In 55 he overawed the Germans east of the Rhine by an impressive feat of bridgebuilding that permitted lightning raids into their territory. Then in late summer he amazed the Roman world with a showy crossing of the English Channel to invade Britain. It so flattered Roman pride that the senate decreed another public thanksgiving, this time for twenty days.

The hard fighting in Britain came with the spring of 54. Caesar mounted a full-scale invasion with a specially constructed fleet. Soon after he landed, however, a storm destroyed the fleet, and Caesar had to fight for his life before finally defeating the British war-king Cassivellaunus and imposing terms that permitted him to repair his losses and return to Gaul. There he faced a coalition of disgruntled Gallic tribes.

Proud of their glorious past, the Gauls resented their subjugation at the hands of Romans. Moreover, Caesar's perpetual demands for grain in a year of poor crops were driving them to desperation. Caesar's harsh reprisals against the Belgic tribes and reports of disarray in Rome further encouraged the spirit of revolt. Revolt finally came with a vengeance under the leadership of the Gallic chief Vercingetorix. A brilliant strategist and tactician, he forced Caesar to match him or be destroyed. When Caesar surprised him by marching reinforcements from Transalpine Gaul through deep mountain snows, Vercingetorix resorted to guerrilla tactics and a scorched earth strategy. Although Caesar successfully besieged a Gallic army in the center of Gaul at Avaricum (Bourges), Vercingetorix defeated him farther south at the siege of Gergovia.

The Siege of Alesia, 52 B.C. Hampered by impatient allies, Vercingetorix was finally maneuvered into Alesia near the headwaters of the Seine. Failing to thwart Caesar's siege works, Vercingetorix ordered his cavalry, with muffled hooves, to steal away one night, each to his own part of the country and there recruit a relief army in the cause of national independence. Informed by spies, Caesar had an elaborate second line of circumvallation constructed to keep out the relieving army—wide and deep river-inundated trenches interspersed with bastions and towers; beyond and farther out, innumerable turf-concealed pits and booby traps.

The Gauls answered the call for help. From almost everywhere men kept streaming toward the appointed marshalling center. A vast host marched to Alesia. Day after day raged the battle of Alesia, Caesar's time of testing. Cavalry engagements, sorties by the besieged army inside of Alesia, assaults upon the outer defense works by the relieving army occurred simultaneously or in rapid succession. The Romans, hard pressed at times everywhere, were almost overwhelmed in one particular sector. A hard-riding messenger breathlessly told Caesar of the breakthrough; the defenders weary, exhausted; the defense works collapsing under the weight of the mass attack. Into that salient Caesar threw six cohorts, then seven more, and hurried himself to the spot with more reinforcements. The cavalry was ordered to follow; additional cavalry units were ordered to hit the enemy rear. The steadfast Labienus threw in every available man at his command. The legionaries, exhausted and on the point of surrender, caught sight of Caesar's scarlet battle cape fluttering in the wind, took heart, and pressed home a furious attack. The enemy broke and ran, vanishing into the night. While pockets of resistance remained, Caesar had regained the supremacy in Gaul. The last rebel stronghold was Uxellodunum. After its fall, Caesar cut off both hands from every captive. Begging for food everyday thereafter, the handless wretches provided a brutal object lesson to anyone contemplating further rebellion.

Master of Gaul at last, Caesar had established the military and financial basis for realizing his ambition of being Rome's most powerful and respected man.

XIX

Caesar Wins and Is Lost,
Mid-50s to 44 B.C.

In the last years of the Republic, four things clearly mattered: the consulship, the armies, the tribunate, and the role of the preeminent statesmen, which many aspired to play—above all Cicero, Cato, Pompey, Crassus, and Caesar. While Caesar was winning glory, gold, and the loyalty of gallant legions in Gaul, his erstwhile partners—Pompey and Crassus—and the optimate leaders of the senate became increasingly jealous and fearful. As they tried to counter Caesar in the struggle for preeminence at Rome, neither he nor they desired to precipitate the violence and civil war that destroyed the Republic and themselves along with it.

From the Conference of Luca in 56 B.C., Crassus and Pompey had gained renewed strength that promised to keep them on a par with Caesar. Both would again stand for the consulship and command armies and provinces. Their enemies were stunned: Cicero, bound to preserve the peace, turned quickly from invective to softer words of praise and thanksgiving. With Caesar himself Cicero kept up a frequent correspondence; borrowed money from him; and sent him his latest writings.

In 55 B.C., with Pompey and Crassus as consuls, the tribune C. Trebonius carried a law (the *lex Trebonia*) assigning the consuls their provinces for five years as apparently agreed upon at the Luca conference. Pompey received the two Spains but decided, perhaps on Cae-

sar's advice, to remain in the vicinity of Rome to watch the course of events. At last he could again recruit legions. Some he would send under his legates to Spain; others, retain in Italy. Never again would he make the mistake of disbanding them too soon, as he had after his return from the East in 62 B.C. Crassus, Pompey's rival and colleague, received the province of Syria with the right to make war as he saw fit. Parthia was not mentioned in the law, but it was an open secret that he was preparing a war against that rival power on Rome's eastern border.

The Downfall of Crassus, 54 to 53 B.C.
Dogged by controversy and opposition over his planned war against Parthia, Crassus lost no time in setting out for the province of Syria. He did not improve his reputation when he fattened his war chest by looting the Temple of Jerusalem and other rich shrines in his province over the winter of 54–53. During the campaigning season of 54, he had taken his fresh recruits across the Euphrates to scout out his route, establish supply depots, and get some training for a real war in the following year. Despite these precautions, however, neither Crassus nor his army was experienced or trained enough to deal with the tactics and strategems of the Parthians. In the spring of 53, near the town of

Carrhae, Crassus and seven legions met destruction at the hands of mounted Parthian archers. Crassus' grisly head was displayed at the Parthian Court during a performance of Euripides' *Bacchae,* with its equally grisly ending. The proud eagles of his legions now graced Parthian temples.

The Fateful Rivalry between Pompey and Caesar

The death of Crassus was the second blow to the delicate political equilibrium that had existed after Luca. The subsequent estrangement of Caesar and Pompey might have been slower and less severe if Pompey's marriage to Julia, Caesar's only child, had not ended with her untimely death during childbirth in 54 B.C. (Unfortunately, the baby girl died a few days later.) Both men had been very devoted to Julia, and the common people showed their appreciation of her importance by forcing her public burial in the Campus Martius.

Caesar's meteoric rise threatened Pompey's prestige and dominance. To maintain his position, Pompey needed the support of the senatorial leaders. Their hope of wedging the two strong men apart seemed about to be realized. To close the ever-widening breach, Caesar asked for the hand of Pompey's only daughter and was coldly rebuffed. Pompey himself married Cornelia, the young widow of Publius Crassus and daughter of Metellus Scipio, a man from the inner circle of the optimate leadership of the senate.

Meanwhile, disorder prevailed in Rome, corruption and electoral bribery without restraint. The year 53 B.C. began without consuls, the year 52 likewise. Violence and rioting made the streets unsafe. Milo was running for the consulship; Clodius, with Pompey's support, for the praetorship. The bribes were lavish. Blood flowed. The year expired without elections and without magistrates. Authority had broken down. Rome was in anarchy.

The Death of Clodius, 52 B.C.

The murder of Clodius on the Appian Way during a brawl between his retinue and Milo's caused further riots. Egged on by Clodius' widow, Fulvia,[1] a mob in the Forum seized his body, carried it to the senate house, and used the building for his funeral pyre. Pompey exploited the widespread fear and outrage that was aroused. Most people agreed that only Pompey was capable of restoring order and should be given emergency powers. His friends proposed a dictatorship, but that was too much for the *optimates* to accept. Cato and Bibulus came up with a compromise that saw Pompey elected sole consul for 52 B.C. In this way he had great latitude for action but was still subject to tribunician veto and would be held legally accountable for his acts.

Pompey Sole Consul, 52 B.C.

Pompey quickly obtained passage of several laws designed both to restore order and to weaken his rivals. The first was aimed at punishing the perpetrators of the recent violence, even his former ally Milo, who was expendable now that Clodius was dead and who was a rival of electoral candidates whom Pompey preferred to him. The second attacked bribery and was retroactive to 70 B.C., an aspect that troubled Caesar's friends.

Cicero was only too happy to defend Milo when he was charged under the new law against violence, *de Vi,* for the actions leading to Clodius' death. To make certain that no one disrupted the trial to help Milo, Pompey surrounded the court with armed troops. Cicero was so flustered at their sight that he forgot what he wanted to say, and Milo, convicted, went into exile to Massilia. Cicero, who was sometimes amazingly insensitive, sent him a polished version of the speech that he had hoped to give!

While ensuring law and order and passing laws to deal with important problems, Pompey also strengthened his hand against both Caesar and the *optimates,* who saw Pompey only as the lesser of two evils. His law requiring a five-year

---

[1]Not the Fulvia who informed on Catiline (p. 186).

interval between holding a magistracy and governing a province not only made bribery in elections less attractive but also subjected Caesar to immediate replacement by an available ex-magistrate. It even meant that Caesar had to rely on Pompey to keep his province whereas influential men like Cicero and Bibulus who had not held governorships would now have to take up provincial commands and leave the *optimates* even more dependent on Pompey. Furthermore, Pompey had his own command in Spain extended for five years, but by making it more difficult to run for office *in absentia,* he made it more difficult for Caesar to run for consul under the protection of a governor's *imperium.* When Pompey then publicly (and illegally) exempted Caesar from this law, he made Caesar look even more dependent and demonstrated his power to the *optimates.*

Prelude to Civil War   A series of complicated maneuvers followed in 51 B.C. as some of the *optimates* tried to remove Caesar from his command immediately. Pompey persuaded the senators not to raise the issue until March 1, 50 B.C. In this way, Pompey could claim not to have violated his own law of 55 that extended Caesar's command for another five years, yet his stance was a threat to Caesar's hope of retaining his provinces and army while keeping his *imperium* and running *in absentia* for the consulship.

Caesar, however, had not been inactive. His money ensured the election of one friendly consul and ten friendly tribunes for the year 50. One of the tribunes was C. Scribonius Curio, an eloquent speaker and a master of intrigue who had married Fulvia, the fiery widow of P. Clodius. Among Caesar's other useful supporters was the young Marcus Antonius (Mark Antony), pleasure loving and licentious, but a brilliant and loyal soldier who had served with Caesar in Gaul. Curio and the friendly consul blocked meaningful debate on the issue of provincial commands. Curio even called Pompey's bluff by formally proposing that both Caesar and Pompey surrender their provinces at the same time.

In the summer, Pompey used false pretenses to take two legions away from Caesar and station them at Capua. In December, Curio blocked another move in the senate to strip Caesar of his command while letting Pompey keep his. On the next day, the optimate consul, Marcellus, summoned a special meeting of the senate and proposed passage of the *Senatus Consultum Ultimum* against Caesar. When Curio vetoed the motion, Marcellus handed a sword to Pompey and commissioned him to lead the two legions at Capua against Caesar.

Pompey was reluctant to do so because he knew that only a few optimate extremists wanted war. On the day before, when Curio had proposed that both Caesar and Pompey lay down their commands together, the senators had voted 370 to 22 in favor. One crisis followed another: debates in the senate, public mediation, private negotiations. Caesar offered to resign his command if Pompey would resign, too. The *optimates,* however, ignored his proposal, engineered his declaration as a public enemy, and obtained passage of the *Senatus Consultum Ultimum.* The new tribunes Marcus Antonius (Mark Antony) and Quintus Cassius, their veto censured and their very lives in danger, fled the city with Curio and went to join Caesar.

Caesar Crosses the Rubicon   Meanwhile, Caesar had arrived in Cisalpine Gaul, where he had one Roman legion and some detachments of German and Gallic cavalry. He set up his headquarters at Ravenna and summoned two other legions from Gaul. Once more, swift and decisive action tipped the balance in Caesar's favor as it had against the Gauls. When Caesar heard of the senate's action, he decided to act without further delay. Around January 10, 49 B.C., by the calendar then in use (really ca. November 20, 50 B.C.), he secretly sent a few picked men to infiltrate and seize Ariminum (Rimini). It was the first important city south of the Rubicon, which separated Cisalpine Gaul from Italy proper. That night he distracted the rest of his officers with a banquet. Once the guests were engrossed in the festivities, he himself hastened toward Ariminum with a few confidants and a detachment of cavalry. When he reached the Rubicon, he paused to ponder the significance of what he was about to do. Then he resolutely quoted a saying from the popular Greek playwright Menander, "Let the die be cast." At dawn, he arrived at Ariminum to find that he had won the throw. Ariminum was safely in his grasp to the complete surprise of his foes.

Although Caesar claimed to be acting in defense of the lawful rights of the tribunes, a more powerful appeal to his loyal veterans was the request that they help him to avenge his enemies' affronts to his own *dignitas*. Constitutional matters were not unimportant, but the struggle for personal preeminence at Rome was paramount.

Caesar's decision to invade Italy with only one legion and in the dead of winter was a brilliantly calculated risk. Most of Pompey's troops were still untrained and their loyalty uncertain. The two trained legions at his command would not forget their long service with Caesar in Gaul. Resistance to Caesar in Italy crumpled like a house of cards in an earthquake. Panic had gripped Pompey's followers, who fled Rome without even taking the money in the treasury. Pompey himself hastened to Brundisium with all the troops that he could still find and embarked for Greece just before Caesar's arrival.

Caesar's swift conquest of Italy had been made possible by his absolute and uncontested command of his forces, the loyalty of his retired veterans, and his generous treatment of both civilians and captured soldiers. Still, the tasks ahead were stupendous, for Pompey, with undisputed command of the sea, could cut Rome off from the grain supplies of Sicily and North Africa and starve her into submission. Pompey had many battle-hardened legions in Spain and could also draw upon the vast resources and manpower of the East, where he had made and unmade kings. With these forces he could launch a two-pronged attack on Italy. And what if Gaul, recently conquered and weakly held, should raise up another Vercingetorix? Such were the problems confronting Caesar as he hurried to Rome.

Before reaching Rome, Caesar stopped off to call on Cicero to persuade him to come back to Rome and support the new regime by lending it both dignity and prestige. Not quite sure yet which side would win and not able to reconcile his principles with Caesar and Caesar's supporters, Cicero refused. Much disappointed, Caesar went on his way.

Caesar Reorganizes the Government

Caesar entered Rome for the first time in nine years and at once set about reorganizing the government. Summoning all senators still in Rome, he invited their cooperation to avoid bloodshed. Some responded willingly, others less so. They did accept the law granting citizenship to the people living north of the Po, to whom Caesar owed much.

Caesar speedily arranged for the temporary administration of Rome and Italy. He appointed the praetor M. Aemilius Lepidus, son of the rebel leader whom Pompey had defeated in 77 B.C., to take charge of affairs in the city. He made Marcus Antonius governor of Italy and commander-in-chief of all the armed forces. He sent Curio to secure the grain supplies of Sicily and North Africa and others to Illyria to block a possible attempt by Pompey to invade Italy from the northeast. Caesar ordered the doors of the state treasury opened and unceremoniously removed the tribune who attempted to intervene. So much for the rights of tribunes! The administration of Rome and the soundness of his finances thus assured, Caesar set out for Spain, which was controlled by forces loyal to Pompey.

Caesar in Spain, 49 B.C.

Caesar first had to break the opposition of Massilia, which not only endangered the line of communication between Spain and Italy but also might encourage the resurgence of rebellion in Gaul. Leaving part of his army to reduce the city by siege, he hurried on to Spain. Despite some initial difficulty there, the Gallic and Germanic cavalry, whose loyal service proved the value of his years in Gaul, assured victory. Within forty days he had subdued the Pompeian forces in Spain.

On the way back, he accepted the surrender of Massilia, which became virtually an imperial possession of Rome. If Curio had not been killed in North Africa by Pompey's loyal ally Juba, king of Numidia, Caesar's control of the West would have been absolute.

News of Caesar's victory in Spain aroused wild enthusiasm at Rome and greatly increased Caesar's power. A special law proposed by Lepidus made him dictator for eleven days in December to conduct elections for 48. Caesar obtained both a second consulship and a neutral colleague for himself.

Caesar's Second Consulship, 48 B.C.

Caesar's most pressing problem was the relief of debtors and the revival of credit and business undermined by the civil war. He enacted a law that creditors be obliged to accept real estate at prewar valuations; that all paid interest be deducted from the principal (a loss to creditors of roughly 25 percent); and that all interest payments be suspended for one year. In order to make money circulate more freely and encourage lending at 12 percent interest as decreed by the senate in 50 B.C., he reenacted an old law forbidding the hoarding of more than 15,000 *denarii*.

The most humane and enlightened of Caesar's acts was the recall of persons exiled by Pompey and the restoration of civil rights to victims of Sulla's cruel proscriptions. Proposed by praetors or tribunes, the laws rectifying long-standing injustice were duly passed by the Tribal Assembly. The procedure was regular, correct, quite constitutional in fact. Those who benefitted became his friends; those who objected could not accuse him of unconstitutional acts.

The Battles of Dyrrhachium and Pharsalus, 48 B.C.

In a characteristically surprise move, Caesar crossed the Adriatic from Brundisium (Brindisi) during the winter in January 48 B.C. He landed south of the port of Dyrrhachium (Durrazo), where he nearly met disaster. He had only half of his forces, and his old enemy Bibulus, patrolling in Pompey's fleet, captured

his ships as they returned for supplies and the rest of his men. Faced with a lack of supplies and fewer men, Caesar resorted to negotiations and proposed that he and Pompey both disarm and let the senate and people work out the details of peace. In this way, neither would be surrendering to the other. Pompey could never accept, as Caesar probably realized. Pompey's *dignitas* had already suffered from what many saw as an ignominious retreat from Italy. He had to prove that he was not a coward, as he would have been branded if he had accepted an offer of peace from an opponent in Caesar's precarious military position.

Forced to fight at Dyrrhachium, Caesar was outflanked by Pompey's superior numbers and retreated all the way to Pharsalus in central Thessaly. Italy lay open to Pompey, but he pursued Caesar instead. Refreshed by Thessaly's grain harvest, Caesar's experienced veterans defeated the overconfident Pompey, who fled to Egypt.

The Death of Pompey, 48 B.C.

Pompey arrived at Alexandria in the midst of a civil war between Ptolemy XIII (sometimes numbered XII) and his famous sister, Cleopatra VII. Hoping to link their cause to Caesar's rising star, Ptolemy's advisors treacherously procured Pompey's murder. They cut off his head, pickled it in brine for a gift to Caesar, and left the body to rot on the shore.

Caesar in Egypt, 48 to 47 B.C.

When Caesar arrived three days later, he appeared with the dread *fasces* of a consul to show that Egypt was now subject to the authority of the Roman People. Presented with Pompey's head, he turned away in disgust. He wept, ordered the head reverently buried and the perpetrators of the murder executed for daring to do violence to a leader of the Roman People. Caesar had never hated Pompey. They were both men of great charm, and their purely personal relations had often been warm. Ultimately, however, it had simply been impossible for both of them to occupy the same political position at Rome that each craved.

Caesar's high-handed actions at Alexandria aroused the populace against him and made life uncomfortable for Roman soldiers. Caesar, captivated by the brilliant and charming Cleopatra, had peremptorily restored her to her throne and had demanded from the Egyptians payment of a debt owed by her late father. The advisors of Ptolemy XIII ordered out the royal army and kept Caesar under siege for several months. Unable, with his one small legion, to cope with an army of 20,000 men as well as with the mobs of Alexandria, Caesar was in dire peril until the arrival of the 2 legions that he had earlier summoned. The last one to arrive was a mixed force of Jews, Syrians, Arabs, and Cilicians hastily collected by Mithridates of Pergamum, reportedly one of the many bastard sons of old Mithridates VI of Pontus.

When Mithridates, advancing from Syria, had reached the Nile, Caesar took over command and crushed the Egyptian army. Ptolemy fled and was drowned in the Nile. The Alexandrians submitted. The crown passed to Cleopatra and another brother, Ptolemy XIV, who became her dynastic husband. In the spring of 47 B.C. Caesar left Egypt.

From Egypt, Caesar passed through Syria, Cilicia, and Cappadocia on his way to Pontus, where he now planned to settle accounts with Pharnaces II, son of Mithridates VI (p. 184). Taking advantage of the civil war, Pharnaces had betrayed his Roman patrons; had overrun Cholcis, Pontus, Lesser Armenia, and part of Cappadocia; and had committed mayhem and other outrages upon Roman citizens. In a five-day campaign Caesar tracked him down and annihilated his army at Zela. In a letter written to a friend, Caesar proclaimed this swift and decisive victory with the laconic *Veni, Vidi, Vici* (I came, I saw, I conquered). After rewarding Mithridates of Pergamum for his services in Egypt, southern Russia, and Asia Minor at the expense of Pharnaces, and settling other affairs in Asia Minor, the conqueror hastened back to Italy.

Caesar in Italy, 47 B.C. Many tasks awaited Caesar's hand on his arrival in Italy in the summer of 47 B.C. after an absence of eighteen months. Already appointed dictator for a second time, he had to restore order, solve several social and economic problems, find ways and means of raising money, restore discipline among his own legions, who were tired of fighting, and finally take an army over to Africa to subdue the large Pompeian forces assembled for an eventual invasion of Italy.

At Rome, Marcus Antonius, (Mark Antony) master of the cavalry under Caesar, had let the dangerous problem of debt become a catalyst for murder and riot. Even armed force had not restored calm, and mutinous soldiers had already begun to march on Rome when Caesar arrived. The presence of the dictator immediately restored peace and order. He dealt firmly but so fairly with the soldiers that they begged to be accepted back in his good graces. Without publicly disgracing Antonius, he chose the older, more politic Lepidus as his master of the cavalry and instituted moderate debt relief.

The African Campaign, 46 B.C. After Pharsalus, Cato had regrouped Pompey's shattered forces and taken them to Africa. Forced by a storm to land in the Cyrenaica, he led his army for hundreds of miles through the desert from Berenice (Benghazi) to Lepcis Magna (Tripoli) and thence to Utica, where he joined King Juba of Numidia and the Pompeian governor of Africa. After this astonishing military feat, Cato, ever mindful of higher rank, misguidedly resigned the command in favor of Metellus Scipio, Pompey's father-in-law, a senior officer but one of demonstrated incapacity. Scipio was joined by Juba and Labienus, who had been Caesar's right-hand man in Gaul but had ultimately sided with his old family patron Pompey.

Thapsus and the Death of Cato, 47 to 46 B.C. In the fall of 47, the outnumbered Caesar landed in Africa to challenge Scipio. Near Thapsus, he lured the inept Scipio onto unfavorable ground and annihilated his army. When Cato heard the news, he saw the approaching end of Republican liberty. Although he might have obtained Caesar's calculated pardon, he could not bring himself to ask, and preferred to take his own life instead.

Cato's suicide was a cruel blow to Caesar and took some of the glory from his triumph. "O Cato," he exclaimed, "I envy you your death; You denied me the chance to spare your life." Cato became a legend, and his martyrdom became an inspiration to Stoic-minded traditionalists who unwisely resisted the overwhelming power of the emperors later.

Caesar's Homecoming and Triumph, 46 B.C.

The news of Thapsus had preceded Caesar's return to Rome. His followers were in ecstasies. The Forum rang with jubilation. Caesar had reached the pinnacle of preeminence for which he had been aiming. The senators decreed a thanksgiving of forty days and voted seventy-two lictors to attend him at his triumph (three times the usual number). They awarded him a dictatorship renewable annually for ten years and appointed him prefect of morals for three years with powers of a censor. He received the right to express his opinion in the senate first, so that every timid and self-seeking politician could take his cue. His statue, cast in bronze, was to stand on the Capitol opposite that of Jupiter himself. He allegedly rejected many other religious and monarchical honors showered upon him. Some of them are of late report and fictitious, undoubtedly suggested by the history of later Caesarism.

Soon after his arrival at Rome in 46, Caesar celebrated his long-awaited triumphs. There were four, each celebrated on a different day, over the Gauls, Egyptians, Pharnaces, and Juba, but none over Pompey or Scipio. Caesar had no wish to call attention to the deaths of fellow Romans in the civil war that he had started, but he was proud to advertise the 1,192,000 others killed. Gigantic parades; the distribution of millions of *denarii* among soldiers and civilians; 20,000 tables loaded with food and wine for the plebs; elaborate shows, games, and gladiatorial combats; a naval battle in an artificial lake; and a mock battle between two armies on Mars Field were among the highlights of the grandest display ever seen in Rome.

The Spanish Campaign, 45 B.C.

One more campaign had to be fought. Late in 46 B.C., Caesar embarked with eight legions for Spain, where Pompey's two sons, Gnaeus and Sextus, plus Labienus, who had escaped from Africa, had raised a major revolt. Failing to draw the Pompeians into a battle by attacking their fortified towns, Caesar finally caught up with them at Munda (between Seville and Malaga), where his men had to deliver their attack uphill. The battle was one of ferocious savagery as fear and hate on both sides supplied energy to their desperate valor. Superior discipline and generalship at last gave Caesar the decision. Labienus died in battle, and Gnaeus Pompey was caught three weeks later and killed.[2]

Caesar returned to Rome and celebrated another triumph in October of 45. This time, he did not scruple to celebrate a victory over fellow citizens. Many thought it unseemly and feared for the future.

Caesar's Work of Reconstruction

If by war Caesar had saved his life, honor, and dignity, he would now have to save the Roman state from chaos and ruin, heal its wounds, and give to it such peace, justice, and stability as it had not known for almost a century. Otherwise, the very source of his fame and glory would have been destroyed.

Armed with his annually renewed dictatorship, the powers of a censor, and the powers of a tribune of the *plebs,* which Gaius Gracchus had shown so well how to use, he undertook the task of transforming the Roman Republic and its empire into a centralized world state. Unlike Sulla, he did not attempt to resurrect the pre-Gracchan constitution, which events of the past 100 years had shown to be impossible to maintain under circumstances quite different from those that had given it birth. What Caesar, with his customary daring and decisiveness, did not

---

[2]Sextus lived to fight years later against Caesar's successors (pp. 211–219).

realize, however, was that many Romans did not yet recognize that fact or wish to be functionaries in a state controlled by him.

Some of Caesar's reforms were administrative or governmental; some social and economic; others in neither category. Some affected Rome alone, some Rome and Italy, others the empire as a whole. The overall effect of his reforms was to reduce the absolute dominance of the city of Rome and to integrate Rome with Italy and Italy with the rest of the empire while they reinforced his own supremacy over all.

Before he even began his work of reform, Caesar had removed one fatal weakness of the late Republic: separate control of the civilian government and provincial armies. Caesar was both chief executive of the state and commander-in-chief of the army. He sought to prevent anyone from doing what he himself had done with the command of Gaul.

Administrative Reforms The most important of Caesar's administrative reforms had to do with the senate and the magistracies. Traditionally and constitutionally the senate had been a purely advisory council serving first the kings, later the early consuls. During and after the Punic wars, it had necessarily assumed greater control of Rome's increasingly more complex affairs, which increased the competition for leadership among the senators as a whole and thus contributed to the last century of turmoil. To eliminate the senate, however, would have been beyond even Caesar's daring, and it would have destroyed the very body whose expertise and cooperation were needed to run Rome's vast empire. Instead, Caesar raised its membership from 600 to 900 and filled the extra seats with old friends, wealthy equestrians, and even Romanized provincials. To keep up the numbers of this enlarged senate, he raised the number of quaestors from 20 to 40 and of praetors from 8 to 16. This change also provided more administrators for Rome and the provinces and allowed more of Caesar's friends to reach senatorial rank and high office quickly.

In admitting the newcomers into the senate, Caesar had broken down the barriers between Rome and Italy. Rome and Italy for the first time became one, the dominant partners within Rome's empire, and even provincials could aspire to ultimate membership in the senate. Moreover, all of the newcomers were bound to have felt gratitude and loyalty toward Caesar, and they were expected to look out for his interests.

Caesar took a giant stride toward the unification of Rome and Italy when he drafted the Julian Municipal Law (*lex Julia Municipalis*), which was divided into three parts and first enforced after his death. Two of its sections refer to Rome, the first dealing with the reduction of free grain recipients from 320,000 to 150,000, the second with the upkeep and repair of streets and roads in Rome and suburbs. The third relates to the Italian towns, specifically to the age and other qualifications of municipal councilors or senators and to the taking of the local census. The law provided for local self-government and relieved the Roman city praetors of the burden of law enforcement throughout Italy. It laid the basis for the later extension of the municipal system of government to the provinces.

Social and Economic Reforms The immediate purpose of many of Caesar's social and economic reforms was to provide useful employment for those whom he had cut off from the grain dole and to relieve the congestion of population in Rome (then approaching 700,000). He also had to provide for his war veterans. In a society whose industrial capacity was low, Caesar had only two alternatives—public works and colonization.

The object of Caesar's building program in Rome was not only to provide unemployment relief but to make Rome the beautiful and magnificent capital of a great empire. The chief architectural achievements of the period were the Basilica Julia, a covered hall to house the law courts, and the Forum Julium with galleries all around it and a temple of Venus Genetrix in the center. He had plans drafted for a new senate house, a large meeting place for the popular assemblies, a fine public library, a splendid theater, and an enormous temple of Mars.

Even more gigantic were the projects planned for Italy: an artificial harbor at Ostia for seagoing ships (a project later undertaken by Claudius), a road across the Apennines to the head of the Adriatic, and the draining of the Fucine Lake and the Pontine Marshes (a feat often attempted later but never accomplished until modern times). To promote the further economic recovery of Italy, he compelled by law all wealthy citizens to invest half their capital in land and also enacted that at least a third of the cowhands and shepherds employed on *latifundia* be men of free birth. Of course, all of these reforms made Caesar even more powerful by creating goodwill among the population in general.

Colonization and Romanization To relieve unemployment, remove excess population from Rome, and find homes for a large number of war veterans, Caesar resumed, on a much larger scale, the colonizing work of Gaius Gracchus outside Italy. In all he founded no fewer than 20 colonies and provided homes in the provinces for at least 100,000 Roman citizens. In Spain the chief colonies were Hispalis (Seville) and Tarraco (Tarragona); in France, Arelate (Arles), Nemausus (Nîmes), Arausio (Orange), and Lugdunum (Lyons); in Africa, Cirta (Constantine, Algeria) and Carthage; in Greece, Corinth; in Switzerland, Geneva. To promote the commercial importance of the new Corinth, he planned to have a canal cut across its isthmus. Farther east, he founded colonies at Sinope and Heraclea on the Black Sea.

Following the example of Marius, Caesar granted citizenship to the soldiers whom he had recruited in southern Gaul. He enfranchised doctors, teachers, librarians, and scholars who came to Rome from the provinces, and granted Roman or Latin status to many provincial towns: full Roman citizenship to the Spanish cities Gades (Cadiz) and Olisipo (Lisbon) and Latin rights to thirty other Spanish towns; Latin rights also to Tolosa (Toulouse), Vienna (Vienne), and Avenio (Avignon) in Gaul and to all the towns of Sicily. He also founded schools and public libraries in many towns of the western provinces, whence came some of Rome's greatest writers a century or so later.

Even these works do not encompass all that Caesar did for the provinces. In the East he reduced the burden of taxation and transferred, as far as possible, the right of collection from the harsh and corrupt Roman tax farmers, hitherto the curse of provincial administration, to the municipal governments. In Asia and Sicily, he replaced the traditional tithe by a land tax of fixed amounts. His colonies and favorable treatment of the provinces not only were fair solutions to long-standing problems but also increased the reservoir of clients and good will available to support his rule throughout Rome's empire.

Coinage Caesar established Rome's first significant gold coinage by issuing a new gold coin called the *aureus,* worth twenty-five silver *denarii.* His primary motive probably was to provide pay for the armies that he planned to take to Parthia. There, gold was the preferred medium of exchange. Also, as the *aureus* began to circulate, it was destined to play an important economic role in the future Roman Empire.

Reform of the Calendar The most lasting of all Caesar's reforms was a new calendar. He no longer based it on the phases of the moon with a year of 355 days beginning on March 1 but on the Egyptian solar calendar with a year of 365 1/4 days beginning on January 1. The new calendar, worked out by the Greek astronomer Sosigenes of Alexandria, is still in use with a few minor corrections added in 1582 by Pope Gregory XIII. In honor of Julius Caesar, the senate decreed that the month of his birth formerly called Quintilis (the "Fifth") be Julius (July). Later Sextilis (the "Sixth") became August in honor of Augustus, Caesar's heir and successor. Even this reform directly benefitted Caesar, however. The vagaries of the old calendar had given priests and magistrates many opportunities to delay and obstruct the actions of political rivals. The regularization of the calendar made it impossible for anyone to use such tactics against Caesar.

On February 14 of 44 B.C., Caesar obtained unprecedented power. By a decree of the subservient senate, he assumed the title *dictator perpetuus,* dictator for life. This "reform" was totally incompatible with the old Republic and alarmed many who still valued the old traditions.

The Assassination of Julius Caesar, March 15, 44 B.C.

Caesar hoped that with stability and security assured by his sweeping reforms he would be free to pursue a scheme of conquest that would make him even greater than Alexander the Great. The last act of his military career was to be a campaign against the Dacians, who lived north of the lower reaches of the Danube, and against the Parthians in the East, who had defeated and destroyed the army of Crassus at Carrhae in 53 B.C.

His very success, however, had driven many senators to desperation, lest he eclipse them forever. Some had probably voted him excessive honors in the hope of arousing a violent reaction against him. If so, they succeeded. Over sixty senators, led by Gaius Cassius Longinus and Marcus Junius Brutus, incensed at his growing power and unfailing popularity with the people, plotted to kill him at a meeting of the senate on the Ides (15th) of March, 44 B.C., three days before his scheduled departure for the East. Some of the conspirators were pardoned Pompeians like Brutus and Cassius, but the majority were Caesar's old friends and officers. It is said that a soothsayer stopped him on the way to the site of the meeting, ironically a hall in the portico attached to Pompey's theater, and warned, "Caesar, beware the Ides of March!" Undaunted, Caesar continued on his way.

When Caesar took his seat, a number of the conspirators crowded around him as if to make petitions. When the first blow struck, he rose from his chair in surprise and anger, but his cries were of no avail. Bleeding from countless wounds, Caesar died at the foot of Pompey's statue. He had beaten Pompey in the competition for preeminent *dignitas* at Rome, but his undisguised attempt to make his preeminence permanent had unleashed the forces of his own destruction.

The Question of Monarchy

There is abundant evidence that during the last two years of his life Caesar was planning to establish some kind of monarchy. He took or allowed to be taken a number of steps to exalt him above ordinary mortals. It was not enough that the month of his birth was renamed for him; many expensive statues of him also appeared. One showed him standing on a globe, symbol of the world, and another was placed in the temple of Rome's first king, the deified Romulus (Quirinus). In 45 and 44, he issued coins showing a royal diadem and other symbols of kingship. Other coins in 44 bore his portrait, an unusual, if not unheard of, practice at Rome, but a common practice of Hellenistic kings.

Caesar's assumption of the previously unprecedented lifetime dictatorship made him a king in all but name. Along with this dictatorship he received such royal honors as the right to wear a triumphal robe (which was derived from the robes of Etruscan kings) and a laurel crown on public occasions, and to use a gilded chair instead of the ordinary magistrate's curule chair. Finally, Caesar was voted his own special priest (*flamen*), and Marcus Antonius was appointed to the position.

It may well be that some of these measures were prompted by his enemies in order to provoke a reaction against him. Nevertheless, he could have refused them if he had wanted to. It would seem, therefore, that he was assuming the position and trying only to disguise the obvious by denying the hated title king, *rex*, when he rebuked a crowd for hailing him as *rex* earlier in 44. Later, at the Lupercalia festival on February 15, he ostentatiously refused a royal diadem offered him by Antonius and ordered it publicly recorded that he had refused royalty.

One cannot say, however, that Caesar had been planning from an early point in his career to overthrow the Republic and establish a monarchy. There is not any hint of such a plan in his own latest writing, the *De Bello Civile* (*On the Civil War*), probably written in 48 or 47 B.C. Before the civil war, Caesar was merely acting like any other Roman noble in his quest for preeminence *within* the Republic. It was only after the civil war that Caesar found himself faced with the problem of protecting the position that he had achieved while creating a stable government for Rome and the vast polyglot empire that she had become. Previously, Sulla's reforms had failed. Some form of monarchy was the logical alternative, and Caesar's quick mind always cut to the heart of the matter when confronted with a problem.

The Significance of Caesar Despite his quick mind and unconventional daring, too much should not be made of Caesar as an individual. He was not a unique phenomenon, only the culmination of a long series of ambitious nobles who had striven for supreme *dignitas* and *auctoritas* at Rome. For a long time, the military opportunities presented by Roman imperialism had been placing power in the hands of a narrowing circle of rival dynasts backed by large armies of loyal veterans. Caesar had narrowed the competition further during fourteen years of almost continuous warfare by creating the largest and most cohesive body of veterans that Rome had yet seen. Nevertheless, if he had not risen to challenge Pompey's preeminence, someone else would have, just as Pompey had challenged Sulla and his heirs. The timing and the particulars would have been different, but in the end, one man would have established sole domination of some kind, as Caesar's heir did again in the next generation.

XX

The Last Days of the Republic, 44 to 30 B.C.

The assassination of Caesar had solved nothing. It merely set the stage for another destructive civil war to determine who would be the most important man in Rome. At Brutus' insistence, the conspirators had planned nothing other than to murder the "tyrant," Caesar. They naively thought that the old Republic would return miraculously to life. The other senators adjourned in distracted alarm and stole away to their homes. The two archconspirators, Brutus and Cassius, still exulting, arrived to address the populace and found the Forum almost deserted. The few who lingered there were apathetic, sullen, even hostile, and listened to their words in a dazed and stony silence. The uneasy conspirators retired to the Capitol, erected barricades, and planned their future moves.

The Rise of Marcus Antonius (ca. 83 to 30 B.C.)

Sensing a chance to act, Marcus Antonius (Mark Antony), Caesar's colleague in the consulship of 44, improvised a bodyguard, came out of hiding that night, and persuaded Caesar's widow, Calpurnia, to hand over all of his papers to him. Antonius has often been portrayed as a boozing, boorish, bully of the worst kind. As did many young men of his class, he had led a self-indulgent life that had done nothing to enhance his reputation. It must be remembered, however, that his faults, weaknesses, and early follies have been exaggerated

by the propaganda of his enemies, especially Cicero and Augustus, which shaped the "official" version of events reflected in the majority of surviving sources. Antonius had many good qualities as a soldier, general, and politician. His shrewdness and diplomacy helped to avoid serious trouble in the next few days.

While Antonius was securing Caesar's papers, M. Aemilius Lepidus, who had been outside the gates of Rome with a newly recruited legion, was preparing to besiege the conspirators on the Capitol. The next morning Antonius, having sensibly persuaded Lepidus to refrain, took charge of his troops. They then conferred with others of Caesar's old officers and friends and established contact with the conspirators. Both factions also kept in communication with Cicero, the elder statesman, who had declared support for Caesar's murderers immediately after the killing.

The outcome of the various conferences was a meeting of the senate on March 17, over which Antonius presided. Many of the senators wanted Caesar condemned as a tyrant, his assassination approved as necessary and just, his body flung into the Tiber, and all his acts declared null and void. Cool and conciliatory, Antonius urged them to reject such measures as extreme; argued that they owed to Caesar offices, provinces, and political futures; hinted at the danger of uprisings in Rome, Italy, and the provinces; and appealed to them to open their ears and listen to the people outdoors howling for vengeance and the blood of the conspirators. The appeal to fear and self-interest prevailed. Even the adherents of Brutus and Cassius in the senate voted to give all Caesar's acts the force of law, to proclaim an amnesty for the conspirators, and to grant Caesar the honor of a public funeral. After the meeting, Antonius invited the conspirators to a banquet. The toasts that they drank seemed to proclaim more loudly than senatorial resolutions that at last an era of peace, concord, and good feeling had dawned.

March 20 was the day of Caesar's funeral. Marcus Antonius delivered the traditional oration. His speech was brief, factual, and undramatic; quite unlike that popularized by Appian, by Plutarch, and later by Shakespeare. A reader recounted Caesar's mighty deeds, and his will was made public. His benefactions to the Roman People included gardens across the Tiber bequeathed as a public park and 300 sesterces in cash to each Roman citizen. The chief beneficiary of Caesar's recorded will was not Antonius but Gaius Octavius Thurinus, Caesar's grandnephew, the future Emperor Augustus, who became his son by testamentary adoption. He was the grandson of a rich banker from the small Latin town of Velitrae, whom Caesar's sister, Julia, had married. Decimus Brutus, one of the assassins, was mentioned jointly with Antonius as a minor heir.

At the end, with consummate showmanship, Antonius displayed Caesar's bloodied toga and a wax image of the corpse with its oozing wounds. The people went completely berserk and surged forth into the streets to find the conspirators. Returning to the Forum, they cremated Caesar's corpse by burning the senate house and far into the night kept vigil over the ashes of their hero and benefactor.

The Forum was not a safe place for the conspirators. Nor was Rome. Antonius quietly allowed them to proceed to the provinces that Caesar had allotted them: Decimus Brutus to Cisalpine Gaul, Trebonius to Asia. Cassius and Marcus Brutus had not yet gone to their provinces but lingered forlornly among the towns of Latium in a vain effort to recruit support for their cause.

At this time, it seemed that Antonius would succeed Caesar. Although disappointed that Caesar had not made him his principal heir, he profited much from his possession of the dictator's private funds, papers, and rough drafts; much more still from his own skillful diplomacy and conciliatory spirit. He procured for Lepidus the high pontificate. He was not violent toward the conspirators. He reluctantly permitted the demolition of an altar and pillar set up in the Forum for Caesar's worship. He himself had the office of dictator forever abolished in order to assure the senate that there would never be another Caesar. With the senate concurring, he took control over the province of Macedonia and all the legions that Caesar had mobilized for his intended invasion of the Balkans and of Parthia. Antonius' tact and reasonableness certainly had helped save Rome from chaos after Caesar's death, and for that all could be thankful.

Still, Antonius was an ambitious man. He could not resist using his position as consul and executor of Caesar's estate to show special favor to his friends and spend money for his own benefit. These actions caused men like Cicero, who wanted to guide the ship of state himself, to doubt his motives and work against him.

The Opposition of Octavian (63 B.C. to A.D. 14) Even more, it was the unexpected challenge of Caesar's heir that prevented Antonius from smoothly consolidating a position of supremacy. Caesar had sent Octavius to Epirus for military training in preparation for the projected Parthian war. Only eighteen and of a rather delicate constitution, he boldly determined to return to Italy and take advantage of any opportunity that the sudden turn of events might offer. When he learned that he had been made Caesar's principal heir and adopted as his son, he gladly followed the usual Roman practice and took the name Gaius Julius Caesar Octavianus. To capitalize on the magic of the name, he always called himself Caesar, as do most of the sources. (Modern writers all call him Octavian when writing of the period after 44 and before he received the title Augustus in 27 B.C.) Octavian immediately demanded his inheritance, much of which Antonius had already spent. Seriously underestimating the unimposing youth, Antonius contemptuously rebuffed him. More determined than ever, Octavian undermined loyalty to Antonius among Caesar's veterans by playing upon the magic of his new name and by exploiting their resentment of Antonius' leniency with Caesar's assassins.

To strengthen his position, Antonius obtained passage of a law giving him command of Cisalpine and Transalpine Gaul for five years and transferring Caesar's legions there from Macedonia, his original assignment. Obviously, Antonius was hoping to dominate Italy and Rome from this advantageous position, as Caesar had done before him. Pressure from many of Caesar's old officers and soldiers, who did not want to fight each other or lose the political advantages of a united front, kept Antonius and Octavian from intensifying their feud.

Still, Antonius' troubles increased. His new provincial command aroused the fear and jealousy of Marcus Brutus and Gaius Cassius. In July, they demanded more significant provinces than Crete and Cyrene. His patience worn thin, Antonius refused their demands and issued such strong threats that they abandoned Italy in order to recruit armies among Pompey's old centers of support in the East. Moreover, Pompey's son Sextus, who had escaped the Pompeian disasters in Africa and Spain, was now seizing control of western waters and raising a revolt in Spain once more. Antonius was becoming worried, and he began to resent Cicero's absence from the senate, which many would interpret as that influential orator's criticism of Antonius' actions. Indeed, Cicero did feel that the Republic was being subverted, a feeling sharpened by his own lack of power.

Cicero, Antonius, and Octavian On September 1, 44 B.C., Antonius publicly criticized Cicero's neglect to attend meetings of the senate. In reply, Cicero delivered a mildly critical speech but irritating enough to provoke the increasingly sensitive Antonius to an angry attack upon Cicero's past career. Cicero in turn wrote and published an undelivered second speech, in which he branded Antonius as a tyrant, ruffian, drunkard, and coward, a man who flouted morality by kissing his wife in public! Likening his speeches to Demosthenes' famous orations against Philip of Macedon in fourth-century Athens, Cicero dubbed them *Philippics*. Twelve other *Philippics* followed, an eternal monument to Cicero's eloquence but filled with misinformation and misrepresentation. Antonius did not hear them at all. He had other things to do.

Rome had become unbearable for Antonius. Down to Brundisium he went to meet the four legions that he had summoned from Macedonia. He intended to send them north to drive Decimus Brutus out of Cisalpine Gaul, which the latter refused to hand over to Antonius despite the recent law. Antonius' consular year (44 B.C.) was near its end. Should he delay, he might be left without a province or legions to command. Brutus and Cassius had proceeded to the East to take over rich provinces and the large armies stationed there. Cassius had defeated the governor of Syria and had driven him to suicide. Lepidus, in Nearer Spain, was a shifty and precarious ally; Lucius Munatius Plancus in *Gallia Comata* and Gaius Asinius Pollio in Farther Spain were even less dependable. To make matters worse, Octavian had marched on Rome, and two of Antonius' Macedonian legions, seduced by bribes and promises, had declared for the young rebel, whom Cicero eagerly embraced as a means, later to be discarded, of destroying Antonius.

The Siege of Mutina, 44 to 43 B.C. Antonius hastened north and entrapped the recalcitrant and unyielding Decimus Brutus in Mutina (Modena), to whose relief in January the senate finally sent an army under the two new consuls, Aulus Hirtius and Gaius Vibius Pansa, former comrades of Antonius under Caesar. At Cicero's clamorous demand, the senate also sent the young Octavian armed with proprae-torian power and granted senatorial rank. He was promised rich rewards: money and land for his legitimized troops and for himself the right to stand for the consulship ten years before the legal age.

The three enemy armies finally forced Antonius to abandon the siege of Mutina but were unable to prevent his retreat across the Alps into southern Gaul, where he hoped to gain the dubious support of Lepidus and Plancus. Both consuls lost their lives at Mutina: Hirtius killed in battle; Pansa later dying of his wounds. Their deaths left Octavian master of the field.

Mutina was a day of glory for the Republic. Triumph, exultation, delirium! The enemy was on the run. The armies of the Republic would shortly track him down. The entire East fell into the hands of Brutus and Cassius. Decimus still held Cisalpine Gaul, and Sextus Pompey was supreme at sea. Soon the Republicans would close the ring and dispose of Octavian, too. Then would come the day for glorious restoration of the Republic and of constitutional government—so Cicero believed, but he was cruelly deceived.

After Mutina, a decree of the senate declared Antonius a public enemy. Upon Brutus and Cassius it conferred superior command (*imperium maius*) over all Roman magistrates in the East. To Decimus Brutus the dominant senators voted a triumph and supreme command over all the armies in Italy. Even to Sextus Pompey, though really nothing but a successful pirate, they extended a vote of thanks and an extraordinary command over the Roman navy; but for Octavian, who had rescued Decimus Brutus from siege and defeat, they proposed only a minor triumph, *ovatio,* and an inferior command. Even this they finally voted down, refused to reward his troops, and repudiated the promised consulship. Through their own folly they drove Octavian back into the arms of the other Caesarians.

To punish the slights and studied disdain of those who controlled the senate, Octavian marched on Rome. He had eight legions, and when the two legions brought over from Africa

to defend his enemies in the senate declared for him, all resistance collapsed. Octavian entered Rome and had himself elected suffect consul with Quintus Pedius, an obscure relative, as his colleague to fill out the deceased consuls' terms. (Consuls elected to fill out others' terms were called suffect consuls.) Octavian was not yet twenty.

The first act of the new consul was to rifle the treasury to pay each soldier 2,500 *denarii;* the next was the passage of a law instituting a special court to try Caesar's murderers and Sextus Pompey. At the same time, Octavian, who needed allies, had the decree against Antonius revoked. That done, he hastened north to meet Antonius.

Meanwhile, Antonius himself had been neither idle nor unsuccessful. The debacle at Mutina had brought out the leadership, courage, endurance, and self-discipline that had earned Caesar's respect and the loyalty of his troops. After a hard and painful march into southern Gaul, he confronted the far larger army of the aging Lepidus, the governor of Nearer Spain and of Transalpine Gaul, who maintained control over his men solely because of his professed loyalty to Julius Caesar. The two armies lay encamped on either side of a small river.

Antonius cleverly played upon the sympathies of Lepidus' men, many of whom had served with him under Caesar in Gaul. Begrimed, haggard, and thickly bearded, he stole into the camp of Lepidus and addressed the men. Thereafter, the two armies began gradually to fraternize and soon Antonius was in real command. He used the same tactics in approaching the army belonging to the governor of *Gallia Comata,* and returned to Italy with twenty-two legions. He occupied Cisalpine Gaul without opposition, for the defending army of Decimus Brutus deserted. Brutus himself attempted to escape to Macedonia, but he was trapped and slain by a Gallic chief.

When Antonius and Lepidus returned to Cisalpine Gaul, they found Octavian already there with eleven legions. They greatly outnumbered the young pretender, but they did not even try to fight him. Their men might refuse to fight against one who bore Caesar's magic name. Lepidus arranged a conference instead.

The Triumvirate of Octavian, Antonius, and Lepidus

After some preliminary negotiations, the three leaders met near Bologna and agreed upon a joint policy. Carefully avoiding the emotionally charged name of dictatorship, they decided to form themselves into a three-man executive committee with absolute powers for five years for the reconstruction of the Roman state (*tresviri rei publicae constituendae*). The *lex Titia* to that effect was carried by a friendly tribune on November 27, 43 B.C. The consulship survived in name with traditional prestige, title, and conferment of nobility but with greatly reduced powers. Octavian and Pedius agreed to resign the office, and two nonentities took their place. To strengthen the alliance, Octavian also married Claudia, the daughter of Publius Clodius and Fulvia, who was now married to Antonius after being widowed a second time by the death of Curio in North Africa (p. 202).

Octavian was not the dominant member in the triumvirate, as the division of provinces reveals. Antonius secured Cisalpine Gaul and *Gallia Comata;* Lepidus, Transalpine Gaul, and the two Spains. Octavian received a more modest and doubtful portion: North Africa and the islands of Sicily, Sardinia, and Corsica, all disputed and some already seized by the outlawed adventurer Sextus Pompey.

The Proscriptions, 43 B.C.

A few days later the triumvirs sent a chill of horror through Roman society by a proscription as cold-blooded and loathsome as that of Sulla and with little better excuse. Among their victims were 130 senators and, if Appian is correct, 2,000 *equites.* The excuse alleged was the avenging of Caesar's murder, but the real reason was the confiscation of wealth and property in order to raise money for their 43 legions and for the inevitable campaign against Marcus Brutus and Gaius Cassius. When the triumvirs found that the wealth of their victims was insufficient for their needs, they imposed a capital levy upon rich women, laid crushing taxes upon the propertied classes in Italy, and set aside the territories of 18 of the richest cities in Italy for veteran settlements.

In addition to the triumvirs' need for money was a desire to wipe out political enemies. Their most distinguished victim, at Antonius' virulent insistence, was Cicero. Unlike some of the proscribed, he lingered until too late. Abandoning his final flight, Cicero calmly awaited his pursuers along a deserted road and was murdered on December 7, 43 B.C., a martyr to the cause of the dying Republic. His tongue and right hand, the orator's most potent instruments, were nailed to the rostra in the Forum, a brutal reminder of the price that one could expect to pay for opposing the triumvirs.

Cicero may have been vain and shortsighted in his attack on Antonius, but he was one of the few men in the late Republic who had a vision of politics beyond the narrow aristocratic struggle for personal honor and prestige. His ideal of a republic governed by an enlightened elite drawn from meritorious aristocrats and equestrians throughout Italy seems hopelessly naive and paternalistic today. Still, it was an ideal, a consciously constructed vision of a better world based on concerns beyond his own narrow self-interest. That could be said of few, if any, of his fellow senators, even the posturing Stoics Cato and Brutus.

To buttress their regime of terror and violence, of confiscation and proscription, the triumvirs packed the senate with men of nonsenatorial origin who would become their loyal clients. They made the consulship the reward of graft or crime and nominated within a single year several pairs of consuls. To the praetorships, which Caesar had increased to sixteen, they added fifty more.

Formally taking office January 1, 42 B.C., the triumvirs compelled the senate and the magistrates to swear an oath to observe Caesar's acts, dedicated a temple to him in the Forum, and by a special law elevated him among the gods of the Roman state under the name of the Divine Julius. As a result, Octavian called himself *Divi Filius* ("Son of a God"). Now it was time to take care of mortal enemies.

The Battle of Philippi, 42 B.C. After crushing the resistance in Italy, the triumvirs were determined to make war on Brutus and Cassius. Those two had accumulated nineteen legions and had taken up a strong position at Philippi on the via Egnatia in eastern Macedonia. Their navy dominated the Aegean Sea, but in the fall of 42 Antonius and Octavian eluded their naval patrols and landed forces half again as big as theirs. Brutus defeated the less able Octavian, but Antonius defeated Cassius, who committed suicide unaware of Brutus' victory. Instead of letting winter and famine destroy the enemy, Brutus yielded to his impetuous officers and offered battle three weeks later. After a hard and bloody battle, Antonius' superior generalship prevailed and Brutus took his own life.

Antonius, the real victor, received the greatest share of the empire. He took all of the East and the Gallic provinces in the West; although he later gave up Cisalpine Gaul, which was then merged with Italy proper. Lepidus, who was reported to have negotiated secretly with Sextus Pompey while Antonius and Octavian were at Philippi, now began a swift slide into impotence and obscurity. He lost Narbonese Gaul, to Antonius and the two Spains to Octavian, but they allowed him to save himself by conquering North Africa. Octavian returned to deal with problems in Italy and reconquer Sicily and Sardinia, which Sextus Pompey had seized.

Antonius and the East Antonius went to the easternmost provinces to regulate their affairs and raise money promised to the legions. He extracted considerable money from the rich cities of Asia by arranging for nine years' tribute to be paid in two, and he set up or deposed kings as seemed advantageous to himself and Rome. Finally, in 41, he came to Tarsus in Cilicia, where Cleopatra, whom he had earlier summoned to explain why she had aided and financed the conspirators, was soon to arrive. She appeared in a splendid barge with silvery oars and purple sails, herself decked out in gorgeous clothes and redolent with exquisite perfumes. It is easy to follow propaganda and legend and see Antonius hopelessly seduced and subservient to a sensuous foreign queen. Passion notwithstanding, however, both pursued rational political interests. Each had something to gain by cooperating with the other—Cleopatra, the support of Roman arms against her rivals; Antonius, Egyptian wealth to defray the costs of a projected war against Parthia and rivalry with Octavian. In the meantime, Cleopatra bore him a set of twins (p. 218).

Octavian and Italy Octavian, not so good a soldier as Antonius, but a shrewder politician, probably realized that Italy was still the key to ultimate control of Rome's empire, despite the problems that awaited him. Indeed, they may have been greater than even he expected when he chose to return after Philippi. The 18 cities previously earmarked for soldiers' settlement proved inadequate to meet the needs of the 100,000 demobilized veterans who returned with him. The evicted owners angrily protested, and expanded confiscations further increased the groundswell of discontent. The populace of Rome was also in a disturbed and angry mood. Sextus Pompey, who still controlled the seas, had begun to shut off grain supplies. Discontent, confusion, insecurity, and want threatened the stability of the state. Soldiers and civilians were at each other's throats. Octavian himself once almost fell into the clutches of a battling mob.

In 41, intrigue aggravated the difficulties, unpopularity, and danger of Octavian. The firebrand Fulvia (ex-wife of Clodius and Curio and now the wife of Marcus Antonius) and Antonius' brother Lucius, one of the consuls, attempted to stir up against Octavian the suspicion and hatred of both veterans and landowners. In so doing, Fulvia and Lucius hoped to destroy Octavian and catapult the absent and unsuspecting Antonius to supreme power. They well knew that Antonius would disavow their acts and would refuse to repudiate his agreements with Octavian, but they hoped to force his hand.

The Perusine War, 40 B.C. Fulvia and Lucius eventually went too far and drove Octavian to make war on them. His loyal generals Quintus Salvidienus and Marcus Vipsanius Agrippa, who soon became his right-hand man, maneuvered them into the Etruscan hill town of Perusia (Perugia) and put them under siege. Antonius, ignorant of their aims and doings, made no move. Two of his legates marched from Gaul but gave them no concerted or effective help, and starvation quickly forced them to surrender. Although Octavian ruthlessly executed all but one member of Perusia's town council, he spared the lives of Lucius and Fulvia. He sent Lucius as governor to Spain, where he soon died. He allowed Fulvia to leave Italy and join her husband.

Because Antonius' remaining legate in the two transalpine Gallic provinces had now died, Octavian sent some of his victorious forces to seize them.[1] The dead legate's son surrendered without a fight, and Agrippa was placed in charge. Now, militarily, Octavian was virtually in charge of all of western Europe.

Still, it was not the end of troubles for Octavian. Pillage, fire, mass executions, and military control of provinces had not solved his problems nor made him safe from danger. His atrocities served only to increase hatred and discontent in a land still seething with revolt and held in the grip of famine, turmoil, and despair. The hostile fleets of Sextus Pompey menaced Italy's coasts, assailed the provinces, and interrupted grain shipments.

The Pact of Brundisium, 40 B.C.
In his extremity, Octavian sought accommodation with Sextus Pompey, master of the seas. He divorced Claudia, Fulvia's daughter, and in her stead married Scribonia, many years older than he but an aunt of Sextus Pompey's wife. Apparently, he was unaware that Sextus was making overtures to Antonius. The latter had been in Egypt while Octavian was fighting his brother and Fulvia. Antonius had also learned that the Parthians, led by Quintus Labienus, son of Titus, Caesar's famous lieutenant in Gaul and later enemy, had overrun Syria, Palestine, and

parts of Asia Minor. Not yet prepared to fight the Parthians, Antonius sailed for Greece to confer with Fulvia after she left Italy. Fulvia, who died shortly after their reunion, persuaded him to receive envoys from Sextus Pompey and accept the proffered alliance. Only then did Antonius proceed to Italy to recruit legions for a war against the Parthians.

By previous agreement, Antonius and Octavian were to use Italy as a common recruiting ground. How worthless that agreement was Antonius discovered when he found Brundisium closed against him by Octavian's troops. Frustrated and angry, he landed troops and besieged that port. Simultaneously, his Republican ally, Sextus Pompey, struck against southern Italy. When Octavian appeared at Brundisium to oppose his colleague, Caesar's old legions refused to fight and fraternized instead. There followed negotiations, conferences, and finally a new agreement known as the Pact of Brundisium, which renewed the triumvirate. A redistribution of provinces left Octavian in control of Illyricum as well as of all the western provinces; Antonius, of the East; and Lepidus, of Africa. Italy was to remain, theoretically at least, a common recruiting ground for all triumvirs. To seal the pact, Antonius married Octavia, the fair and virtuous sister of Octavian. The covenant between the two powerful rivals filled Italy with joy and thanksgiving. All Rome rejoiced. A golden age of peace and concord seemed near— so men hoped.

The rejoicings were premature. Sextus Pompey, who felt that Antonius had played him false, was threatening Rome with famine. Taxes, high prices, and food shortages provoked riots. The people clamored for bread and peace. When Antonius and Octavian prepared to attack Sextus, popular reaction was such that they were forced to negotiate with him.

Treaty of Misenum, 39 B.C.
At Misenum (near Naples) in the autumn of 39 B.C. the triumvirs met with Pompey, argued, bargained, and banqueted. They agreed to let him retain Sicily and Sardinia, which he had already seized, and gave him Corsica and the Peloponnesus as well. They also allowed him compensation for his father's

---

[1]The larger Gallic province, which Caesar had conquered, eventually was called Transalpine Gaul, and the older transalpine province became Narbonese Gaul, from Narbo, its chief city.

confiscated lands and promised him a future augurate and consulship. In return, he agreed to end his blockade of Italy, supply Rome with grain, and halt piracy on the high seas.

The Predominance of Antonius, 39 to 37 B.C.

The power and popularity of Antonius was now at its height. His influence was especially strong among the senatorial and equestrian orders, old-line Republicans, and most men of property throughout Italy, although that of Octavian was stronger with the Roman populace and the veterans. Moreover, time was on the side of Octavian. Years of Antonius' absence in the East would cause his influence to wane in the West.

For the present, however, the West looked bright to Antonius. Pompey would surely counterbalance the growing power of Octavian —so thought Antonius as he set out for Athens in company with Octavia, his young and loving bride. There he spent two winters enjoying to the full domestic happiness and the culture of that old university town. From there he directed the reorganization of the East. To the Balkans he sent Asinius Pollio to subdue the Parthini; to the East, Ventidius Bassus and Herod (client king of Judea since 40 B.C.) to drive out the Parthian invaders of Syria, Palestine, and Asia Minor. Moving with the speed of Caesar, Ventidius shattered the Parthians in three great battles and rolled them back to the Euphrates. There Ventidius stopped.

Having restored Roman prestige in the East, Antonius moved to subjugate the Parthians and avenge Carrhae. In 37 B.C. he sent Canidius, another of his great marshals, to pacify Armenia. Canidius even carried Roman arms beyond Armenia to the Caucasus. Returning to Armenia, he awaited the arrival of Antonius. He waited long, because new troubles in the West compelled Antonius to postpone his invasion of Parthia. Octavian was the cause.

Octavian Consolidates His Power

To Italy the treaty of Misenum had brought peace and a brief respite from piracy, shore raids, and famine, but to Octavian it meant even greater benefits. Exiled Republicans, aristocrats of ancient lineage, allies worth his while to court and win, returned home. The peace was of short duration, however. Sextus Pompey, upset at Antonius' delay in handing over the Peloponnesus and feeling generally slighted by the triumvirs, resumed the blockade of Italy later in 39. War threatened again and Pompey's ill will was increased when Octavian suddenly divorced Scribonia.

Livia For love and politics Octavian promptly married Livia Drusilla, young, beautiful, rich, politically astute, and anxious to secure the future prominence of her family and her children. Livia is another of the numerous strong-willed and influential aristocratic women—such as Clodia (sister of P. Clodius and wife of Metellus Celer), Servilia (half-sister of Cato, mother of M. Brutus, and reputed mistress of Caesar), and Fulvia (wife first of Clodius, then of Curio, and last of Antonius)—who had a major impact on late Republican politics. Her father was Livius Drusus Claudianus, who linked the great Claudian *gens* with the family of the Livii Drusi through adoption into the latter. Livia herself had married Tiberius Claudius Nero, from another branch of the Claudii, who had fought against Octavian in the Perusine War. Now, both she and her husband decided to pin their families' futures on Octavian. Livia had already borne her husband one son, Tiberius Claudius Nero, the future emperor Tiberius; and she was pregnant with his second son, Nero Claudius Drusus (Drusus I). By mutual consent he divorced her and betrothed her to Octavian, who had obtained special dispensation from the pontiffs to marry her. Octavian was so anxious to consummate this advantageous union with Livia that he divorced Scribonia on the very day that she bore him his only child, Julia, whom he would later use in numerous dynastic marriages. Although she bore him no children, Livia became one of Octavian's most trusted advisors. He consulted her at every major turn for the rest of his life.

The Breadth of Octavian's Support Octavian's marriage to Livia and the noble connections that she secured helped to broaden his support among leading senators and undermine that of Antonius. At the same time, Octavian's origin from an equestrian family of Italian background was also an asset against the noble-born Antonius. It gained him friends among the equestrian class, who had long resented the exclusivity of the old Republican nobility. From this class came two of his most loyal and important supporters: the wealthy patron of the arts who helped to mold public opinion in his favor, Gaius Cilnius Maecenas; and the architect of many of his military victories, Marcus Vipsanius Agrippa. Moreover, he received great sympathy in the countryside of Italy, from which Roman armies were recruited.

War with Sextus Pompey, 38 to 36 B.C.

In 38, Octavian determined to destroy Sextus once and for all. He scored an initial coup when Pompey's traitorous governor of Sardinia defected with his province. Nevertheless, a little later that year, his attempted invasion of Sicily in 38 B.C. was a fiasco, and Pompey destroyed two of his fleets. These reverses compelled him to recall the indispensable Agrippa from Gaul and to invoke the aid of Antonius. Though angry at Octavian for going to war contrary to his advice and for causing a delay in his own campaign against the Parthians, Antonius loyally left Athens with a large fleet and came to his aid. The two triumvirs, both resentful and suspicious of each other, met at Tarentum in 37. Through the patient diplomacy of Maecenas and the alleged good offices of Octavia, they concluded the Treaty of Tarentum. It renewed their triumvirate, which had lapsed on December 31, 38 B.C., for another five years. In exchange for the 120 ships that Antonius contributed for the war against Pompey, Octavian promised 20,000 Roman soldiers for service in the East. Antonius never got them.

The Defeat of Sextus Pompey, 36 B.C.

The ships lent by Antonius and added to those constructed and equipped by Agrippa enabled Octavian to mount a three-pronged amphibious attack upon Sicily. Despite a crippling defeat suffered by Octavian at sea, Agrippa forced Pompey to fight a sea battle at Naulochus near the Straits of Messana. His fleet destroyed, Sextus escaped to Asia Minor.

Octavian had already overcome one rival, and soon he would another. Lepidus, who had come with twenty-two legions under his command and was hungry for glory, insisted on accepting the surrender of Sicily in person. When Octavian objected, Lepidus ordered him off the island. Bearing the magic name of Caesar, Octavian boldly entered the camp of Lepidus and persuaded his legions to desert. Then he stripped Lepidus of any real power, and committed him to comfortable confinement at the lovely seaside town of Circeii in Latium. There Lepidus died twenty-four years later.

The Triumphant Return of Octavian

A sincere and joyous welcome at Rome awaited the homecoming of the victorious Octavian, who had ended wars in the West, restored the freedom of the seas, and liberated Rome from the danger of famine. Although he had crushed the liberty of the old nobility, he brought the blessing of strong and ordered government to a populace exhausted by their civil wars. For his part, he gave vague promises of a future restoration of the civil state (*res publica*).

A grateful and idolizing people heaped honors upon Octavian, even epithets and adorations of divinity: His statues were placed in Italian temples, a golden one in the Roman Forum; and he received the sacrosanctity of a plebeian tribune in addition to the military title of "Imperator Caesar," which he had already usurped.

Octavian had already attained a success beyond reasonable expectation. Frail in health and utterly lacking in military skill, he had triumphed over seemingly insuperable odds. He owed his success to his own coolness, tenacity, good looks and distinguished bearing, his knowledge of men, an ability to take advantage of his opponents' mistakes, an unusual skill as a propagandist, and monumental deceitfulness. He had exploited Caesar's name, Cicero's eloquence, and the prestige of the Roman senate. He had also used and often deceitfully abused Lepidus, Marcus Antonius, Sextus Pompey, the

Roman populace, Caesar's veterans, such loyal friends as Agrippa and Maecenas, and even his own wives.

Antonius and Cleopatra in the East

Having been tricked into spending the better part of two years helping Octavian win mastery of the West while he gained nothing, Antonius returned to the East, to which he henceforth committed himself fully in order to secure his independent power. This commitment was strikingly symbolized by a public ceremony with Cleopatra at Antioch in 37 B.C. That act was not a marriage in any Roman sense, and he did not divorce Octavia. She was too politically valuable, and her status as his legitimate wife was not threatened by his liaison with a noncitizen. By becoming co-ruler of the only remaining independent successor state of Alexander the Great's empire, he was able to lay legitimate claim to that empire, much of which the Parthians controlled. This relationship also allowed Antonius to manipulate popular religious ideas to his advantage. He had already sought favor with the Greeks by proclaiming himself to be Dionysus, the divine conqueror of Asia in Greek Mythology. Now, for the Greeks, he and Cleopatra became the divine pair Dionysus and Aphrodite. To the native Egyptians they appeared as Osiris and Isis.

The religio-political significance of their relationship is also revealed by Antonius' public acknowledgment and renaming of the twins whom Cleopatra had previously borne to him. They became Alexander Helios (Sun) and Cleopatra Selene (Moon). The choice of Alexander as part of the boy's name clearly shows the attempt to lay legitimate claim to Alexander the Great's old empire, whereas the names Helios and Selene had powerful religious implications for his and Cleopatra's political positions. According to Greek belief, the Age of Gold was connected with the sun deity. In Egyptian mythology, Isis (the role claimed by Cleopatra) was mother of the sun. Finally, the Parthian king bore the title "Brother of the Sun and Moon," who were powerful deities in the native religion. Accordingly, Antonius was probably identifying these potent Parthian symbols with himself in order to strengthen his anticipated position as king of conquered Parthia.

Reorganization of Eastern Territories In the past, the dependent kingdoms of the East had owed allegiance not to Rome but to their patron, Pompey the Great. The Parthian invasion had clearly revealed the weakness of their relationship to Rome. Antonius did not disturb the provinces of Asia, Bithynia, and Roman Syria, but he assigned the rest of the eastern territories to four client kings, dependent on Rome but strong enough by means of their heavily armed and mail-clad cavalry to guard their frontiers against invasion.

To Cleopatra he gave part of Syria along the coast, Cyprus, and some cities in Cilicia, territories not more extensive than those given to others but immensely rich. Yet, even they did not satisfy the ambitious queen, who wanted in addition the kingdom of Herod I, who ruled Judea. Antonius firmly rejected this demand, although he did give her Herod's valuable balsam gardens at Jericho. Cleopatra had now regained control over much of what Ptolemaic Egypt had ruled at its height under Ptolemy II Philadelphus. She emphasized this point by naming the son whom she bore to Antonius in 36 B.C. Ptolemy Philadelphus.

The Parthian Campaign, 36 B.C. Antonius' strengthened ties to Cleopatra in 37 had greatly bolstered his position in the reorganized East in preparation for his major invasion of Parthia. He was, however, neither subservient to her nor dependent upon the financial resources of Egypt at that point. He prepared his expedition with the resources of the Roman East and embarked upon it against the advice of Cleopatra in 36. He should have listened to Cleopatra. The expedition was a disaster because King Artavasdes of Armenia, pursuing his own interests, withdrew his support from Antonius at a critical point. Antonius lost his supplies and 20,000 men.

The Approach of Renewed Civil War

Despite his losses, Antonius was still strong in the East and the dominant partner in a divided empire. He also had considerable popular support remaining in Italy and an impressive following of Roman senators, Caesarians, Pompeians, and such staunch republicans as Cn. Domitius Ahenobarbus, L. Calpurnius Bibulus, and several kinsmen of Cato and Brutus. Nevertheless, the defeat in Parthia and, as a result, his increased dependence on Cleopatra's resources, had provided plenty of fuel for Octavian's propaganda machine. Now, Octavian was refusing to send the four legions that he had promised in the Treaty of Brundisium (p. 215) and returned only the 70 ships that survived of the 120 that Antonius had lent him against Sextus Pompey. Even Sextus Pompey tried to take advantage of Antonius' Parthian defeat by attacking Asia Minor, where he was finally captured and killed in 35.

The Divorce of Octavia Octavia, however, remained intensely loyal and set out with a large store of supplies and 2,000 fresh troops to aid her husband in the spring of 35. At Athens a message from Antonius ordered her to return to Rome while sending on the troops and supplies. It was a bitter blow. Still, she dutifully obeyed and continued to look after his interests. It is not that Antonius did not care for her. He was not inhuman, but he was even more concerned with challenging her brother for supremacy in the Roman world, and Cleopatra offered more for achieving that goal than Octavia could. It was not, however, until late in 32 B.C., when Cleopatra's influence was at its height, just before the climactic battle against Octavian, that Antonius finally divorced Octavia, a move that lost him much of the support that he still had in Italy.

Preparations for War After punishing Artavasdes by conquering Armenia in 34 and carrying off the King to Egypt, Antonius celebrated an extraordinary triumph at Alexandria. In a ceremony known as the Donations of Alexandria, he gave Cleopatra and her children

additional territories and recognized Cleopatra as supreme overlord of all eastern client kingdoms. He and Cleopatra then spent the winter of 33–32 B.C. at Ephesus in preparation for the great battle with Octavian. It was not, however, easy for even so crafty a politician as Octavian to go to war against Antonius. The latter had both consuls of 32 and half the senate on his side and was elected consul for 31 B.C. To prove Antonius a menace to Rome was still difficult. Cleopatra was more vulnerable. She was portrayed as a detestable foreign queen plotting to make herself empress of the world and was reported to have said that she would someday hand down justice from the Capitol. In all her alleged machinations, Antonius was made to seem only her doting dupe!

The breach between the two triumvirs constantly widened. In a bitter exchange of letters each hurled recriminations against the other, charges of broken promises, family scandal, and private vices. Poets, orators, lampoonists, and pamphleteers entered the fray at the expense of truth and justice. Both protagonists, just like Pompey and Caesar, were too proud to tolerate the appearance of backing down before each other. Beyond that, however, the truth of the situation lies buried beneath a thick, hard crust of defamation, lies, and political mythology. Had Antonius instead of Octavian won the eventual civil war, the official characterizations of the protagonists would have been equally fraudulent but utterly different. Antonius would have been depicted as a sober statesman and a loving husband and father, not a sex-crazed slave of Cleopatra, and as the savior of the Republic from ruin and destruction, not a tyrant striving to subject the liberties of the Roman People to eastern despotism.

Earlier, Antonius had sent the two friendly consuls of 32 B.C. dispatches requesting the senate's confirmation of all his acts in the East and his donations to Cleopatra and her children. He even promised, for propaganda purposes, to resign from the triumvirate and restore the Republic. Fearing serious repercussions from the first two items, the consuls withheld the contents of the dispatch, but one roundly condemned Octavian in a bitter speech in the senate. A few days later, Octavian appeared before the senate with an armed bodyguard. He denounced Antonius and dismissed the senate with the promise to present incriminating evidence against Antonius at the next meeting. The consuls and more than 300 senators at once fled from Rome to Antonius. Octavian suffered them to depart.

The Will of Antonius   Meanwhile, several adherents of Antonius had deserted him and fled to Rome. One of them brought Octavian a precious gift, none more urgently needed; namely, the knowledge that Antonius had deposited with the Vestal Virgins his last will and testament. Octavian promptly and illegally extorted that will from the Vestal Virgins and read it at the next meeting of the senate. The will allegedly confirmed the legacies to the children of Cleopatra, declared that her son Caesarion was a true son and successor of Julius Caesar, and directed that Antonius after death be buried beside Cleopatra in the Ptolemaic mausoleum in Alexandria.[2] Genuine or forged, the will gave to Octavian his greatest propaganda victory.

Octavian Declares War, 32 B.C.   Capitalizing on the popular revulsion against Antonius, Octavian now resolved to mobilize the power of the West against the East. By various means— local agitations, propaganda, patriotic appeals, and some intimidation, perhaps—he contrived to secure an oath of personal allegiance from the municipalities first of Italy and later of the western provinces. Fortified by this somewhat spurious popular mandate, he declared Antonius stripped of his current *imperium* and upcoming consulship for 31 B.C. Late in the fall of 32 B.C., in order to avoid the appearance of initiating another civil war of Roman against Roman, Octavian declared war on Cleopatra. He then spent the winter in preparation for a spring offensive.

[2]Although regarded as genuine by some scholars, more than one has judged the will of Antonius to be an obvious forgery.

Meanwhile, Antonius himself had not been idle. Having assembled a vast army and fleet at Ephesus, he and Cleopatra, who ordered the execution of the captured Artavasdes, sailed for Greece toward the end of 32 B.C.. They set up camp at Actium, at the entrance to the Ambracian Gulf, in which lay the main part of his fleet.

On paper, Antonius was much stronger than his foe. He was an excellent general and commanded an army numerically equal in both infantry and cavalry to that of Octavian. He also had one of the biggest and strongest fleets the ancient world had yet seen. His weakness, however, overbalanced his strength. Although most legionaries admired Antonius as a man and soldier, they hated war against fellow citizens. His officers detested Cleopatra and in private cursed Antonius for not being man enough to send her back to Egypt. They did not know how much he depended upon her for money, grain, and supplies. She in turn feared to let him out of her sight lest he abandon her and go back to Octavia. Antonius was doomed.

The Battle of Actium, September 2, 31 B.C.   Marcus Agrippa, Octavian's second in command, had set up a blockade that caused a severe famine and an outbreak of plague in Antonius' camp during the summer of 31. Antonius' commanders were divided and quarreling among themselves; his troops were paralyzed by treason and desertions. Apparently, he and Cleopatra decided to make a strategic retreat. While they took only the faster, oared ships and broke out of the bay, the rest of the army, apparently, was to retreat overland to Asia Minor. Cleopatra's squadron of sixty ships got clean away, and Antonius managed to follow with a few of his ships before the rest became too involved with those of Agrippa, who sailed out to block them. Left leaderless, Antonius' men soon succumbed to bewilderment and surrendered some days later to the victorious Octavian. The victory of Octavian was so complete that he felt no immediate need to pursue the fugitives to Egypt. He turned his attention to mutinous legions in Italy instead and crossed

the sea to appease their demands for land and money.

The Deaths of Antonius and Cleopatra

It was not until the summer of 30 B.C. that Octavian, desperate for money, went to Egypt. The legions of Antonius put up only a brief resistance. Alexandria surrendered. While Octavian was celebrating his recent victory, news arrived that Antonius had committed suicide. A few days later Cleopatra followed suit. Thus passed the last of the Ptolemies, a dynasty that had ruled Egypt for almost 300 years. Egypt became part of the Roman Empire, and its rich treasures fell into the hands of Octavian, who was now undisputed master of the world.

The End of the Republic

In form, the Roman Republic, with its diffusion of powers among the citizen assemblies, collegiate magistracies, and senate of aristocratic equals, still remained. In reality, power had become concentrated in the hands of one man, the total antithesis of republicanism. Many reasons have been offered to explain why the Republic collapsed. Ancient authors like Sallust, Cicero, and Plutarch offered moral explanations that often have been favored in modern times: Having conquered most of the Mediterranean world, the Romans no longer had the fear of external enemies to restrain them; they lost their old virtues and self-discipline through the corrupting influences of the alien cultures to which they had become exposed and the great wealth and power that they had attained. Many modern historians have seen the Republic's fall primarily as the work of Julius Caesar in single-mindedly pursuing some long-planned monarchic design or mystical sense of destiny.

Still others have seen the problem primarily in institutional terms: The institutions of a small agrarian-based city-state were inadequate for coping with the great social, economic, administrative, and military problems that came with vast overseas expansion. Some, however, would argue that there can be no general explanation for the Republic's fall because it was essentially an accident: The Republic had weathered the upheavals from the Gracchi to Sulla, had made the necessary adjustments to changed conditions while maintaining its basic character, was functioning quite normally, and would have continued to do so if two egotistical, stubborn, and miscalculating men had not chanced to precipitate the civil war that destroyed it.

None of these explanations is adequate. To a certain extent, all history is accident, but that does not mean that general causes cannot be found or are not important. Accidents occur and have an impact within a general context that make them possible. For example, in one sense the oil crisis that afflicted many nations in the 1970s was an accidental result of politics and warfare in the Middle East, but there would not have been any oil crisis without a whole host of general technological, economic, social, and cultural developments that had taken place in those nations during the previous century to make oil such an important commodity. Similarly, one must look at the outbreak of the particular civil war that destroyed the Republic in the context of general, long-term social, economic, political, and cultural developments.

Those who emphasize the inadequacy of the old Republic's institutions for coping with the new problems of a vast empire have an important point. Institutions that arise from or are designed for a particular set of circumstances will eventually cease to function satisfactorily under radically altered circumstances. For example, the old eighteenth-century New England town meeting form of government is totally impractical in twentieth-century Boston. Old institutions may be modified and adapted up to a point and remain basically what they were, but that process can be carried only so far before they are transformed into something quite different. After 400 years of change, the British monarchy of Queen Elizabeth II is not the same as that of Elizabeth I.

Similarly, after 200 years the old system had ceased to work and minor modifications had not helped to preserve it. In fact, the occasional increases in quaestorships and praetorships that were introduced to keep pace with growing administrative needs helped to increase the intensity of the competition for the annual consulships, which remained fixed at two. Furthermore, annual magistrates limited by collegiate veto and guided by a senate of narrow outlook and experience were not capable of waging long-term overseas wars and governing distant provinces in alien lands. The use of practically independent promagistrates and extraordinary commanders, often with extended terms of duty, to deal with these problems placed in the hands of individuals unprecedented amounts of economic, political, and military power. They could then be used to overcome normal constitutional checks and destroy the equilibrium within the ruling elite that had kept the old system in balance. The tremendous social and economic changes that had accompanied 200 years of imperialism had also greatly altered the composition of the popular assemblies and made them more susceptible to ambitious and/or idealistic manipulators pursuing personal advantage over their peers, the alleviation of legitimate grievances, or both. Sulla's attempt to restore the old system in the face of changed conditions had merely doomed it to failure.

Institutional inadequacies alone, however, do not explain the fall of the Roman Republic. Institutions do not exist or function apart from the people who control them. The character, abilities, and behavioral patterns of the people who control vital institutions do have a bearing on how well those institutions function under given circumstances. For example, during the Great Depression, the American presidency was not an effective instrument of popular leadership under Herbert Hoover, but it was under Franklin Roosevelt, however one judges the ultimate worth of his policies. Therefore, individual leaders like Julius Caesar are important. Although he was not pursuing any mystical sense of destiny or long-meditated monarchic ambitions, he did have particular personality traits, such as self-assurance, decisiveness, and speed, that made him particularly successful in the political and military competition that was destroying the Republic.

Nevertheless, individual differences should not be overemphasized. Caesar was operating within a general cultural context that shaped his thoughts and actions in ways that were typical of men like Pompey, Crassus, Catiline, Clodius, Cato, Curio, Brutus Antonius, and Octavian. They were all deeply concerned with the personal *gloria, dignitas,* and *auctoritas* that were the most highly valued prizes of their era.

Therefore, although mere moralizing is too simplistic, moral considerations, in terms of how the values of a culture affect human behavior, are important in explaining the fall of the Republic. The dominant values of a culture shape the general ways in which individuals who share that culture perceive the world around them and act in it. Such values often arise in response to a particular set of historical circumstances during a formative period and then are perpetuated, reinforced, and amplified in the customs, religion, folklore, art, literature, and institutions that develop along with them. As conditions change over a long period of time, values that produced what may be viewed as positive behavior in earlier times often produce what may be viewed as negative behavior (even as defined by other values in the culture) under new conditions and lead to a period of crisis and change.

For example, during the Dark and Archaic Ages of Greece (ca. 1000 to ca. 500 B.C.), the emerging Greek city-states developed the deeply held values of independence, self-sufficiency, and military success that ensured their survival and promoted their growth, which reinforced their values. Their very success, however, brought them into increasing conflict with each other in the Classical Age (ca. 500 to ca. 300 B.C.) because they could not remain self-sufficient under the changed economic conditions that their growth had generated and could no longer expand except at each other's expense. The only way to achieve the peace that each would have agreed to be desirable would have been to surrender their highly valued independence and give up the ideal of military success as the proof of their independence and self-sufficiency. Such values were too deeply ingrained in their culture, however, and they continued their self-destructive warfare, which allowed Philip of Macedon to destroy the independence that each vigorously fought to preserve.

In the early Roman Republic, the great emphasis on and competition for *gloria, dignitas,* and *auctoritas* produced generations of leaders who eagerly defended the state against hostile neighbors; expanded Roman territory to satisfy a land-hungry population; and ably served the state as priests, magistrates, and senators. So long as Rome expanded within the relatively narrow and homogeneous confines of Italy, there was little opportunity for aristocratic competition at Rome to get out of hand; the values that fueled it were reinforced, and the highly desired stability of the state was maintained. These same values then contributed to overseas expansion along with accompanying disruptive socioeconomic changes at home, both of which made it possible for individual aristocrats to acquire disproportionate resources for competing with their peers. In eagerly seeking these resources in accordance with long-held values, Roman aristocrats raised their competition to levels destructive to the very Republic that they cherished.

XXI

Social, Economic, and Cultural Life in the Late Republic, ca. 133 to ca. 30 B.C.

The political turmoil that began with the Gracchi was matched by continued social, economic, and cultural ferment. In the countryside of Italy, the problems that had contributed to the Gracchan crisis were often made worse by the series of domestic wars inaugurated by the Social War in 90 B.C. The provinces suffered from the ravages of war, both civil and foreign, and from frequently inept or corrupt administration. In Rome and Italy, people's values and behavior changed as the old social fabric frayed. The *mos maiorum* lost its old strength, the state's cults suffered neglect during civil upheavals, and new religious influences from the Hellenistic East gained in popularity. Nowhere, however, was change more evident than in art and literature. Creative, thoughtful individuals responded to the social, economic, and political turmoil with new attitudes, forms, and concepts that mark the late Republic as a period of great creativity as well as crisis.

Land and Veterans Whatever success Gracchan land-redistribution legislation may have had in the late second century B.C., the problems that it sought to alleviate were just as bad throughout much of the first. The economic and military pressures that had impoverished many small farmers earlier still existed, and facts do not support the thesis that beginning

with Marius powerful generals largely solved the problem by enrolling landless men in their armies and providing them with land upon discharge. Those who did receive allotments usually lost them again from a combination of economic pressures, confiscation in civil war, and military conscription. Large-scale, long-term settlements had to wait until after 31 B.C., when the civil wars of the Republic finally ceased.

Until then, instead of receiving their own land to farm, a number of landless or indebted peasants became free tenants, *coloni,* on great estates. This trend is evident primarily in central and southern Italy, where the great estates were concentrated and where the danger of rebellion among large concentrations of slaves had been emphasized by the revolt of Spartacus. Some owners, therefore, found it safer and more productive to settle *coloni* as cultivators on part of their land in return for a yearly rent.

Agriculture In the rural districts of interior Italy, the small independent farmers still concentrated primarily on the cultivation of grain, whose surplus production could be sold in nearby towns. Near large towns and cities, a peasant could engage in market gardening or the specialized production of poultry, honey, and flowers. The great estates continued to specialize in raising sheep, cattle, and pigs to supply wool, hides, and meat for urban markets and Roman armies, or in the growing of grapes for wine and olives for oil.

Wealthy landowners also began to experiment with more exotic crops either for profit or ostentatious display on their own tables. Lucullus deserves to be remembered for transplanting the sweet cherry and the apricot from Asia Minor to Italy, orchards of which expanded rapidly along with those of other fruit-bearing trees. Many large estates were turned into hunting preserves to supply their owners with choice wild game, and seaside properties became famous for their ponds of eels, mullet, and other marine delicacies.

In the western provinces, immigrants from Italy had a great impact on agriculture. In Sicily and North Africa, Roman landowners intensified the production of grain for export to the insatiable Roman market. Settlers in Spain and Gaul were establishing olive groves, vineyards, and orchards that would eventually capture the provincial markets of the exporters in Italy. The provinces of the East, however, were severely depressed as a result of the devastation, confiscations, and indemnities resulting from the Mithridatic wars and the civil wars of the 40s and 30s.

Industry and Commerce Manufacturing and trade in the East had also been severely disrupted by the wars of the late Republic. Many Italian merchants and moneylenders in Asia Minor lost their wealth and their lives in the uprising spurred by Mithridates in 88 B.C. Delos, which the Romans had made a free port to undercut Rhodes in 167/66, never recovered from being sacked in 88 and 69. When commerce did revive between the Levant and Italy, it was carried largely by Syrian and Alexandrian traders, who maintained sizable establishments at Puteoli to service Rome and Italy. Italians, however, dominated the western trade, particularly the export of grain from Africa and Sicily and the exchange of Italian wine, pottery, and metalwork across the Alps in return for silver and slaves.

Two of Italy's most important industries, the production of bronze goods and ceramic tableware, were concentrated respectively at Capua in Campania and Arretium in Etruria. Capua produced fine bronze cooking utensils, jugs, lamps, candelabra, and implements for the markets of Italy and northern Europe. Using molds, the Arretine potters specialized in the mass manufacture of red, highly glazed, embossed plates and bowls known as *terra sigillata,* or Samian ware. It enjoyed great popularity all over the western provinces, which eventually set up rival manufacturing centers of their own.

The copper mines of Etruria were becoming exhausted in terms of the prevailing techniques of exploitation, but the slack was more than taken up by production in Spain, where private contractors operated the mines on lease from the state. Tin, which was alloyed with copper to form bronze, was imported from Cornwall in the British Isles along a trade route that had been opened up by the father of Marcus Crassus during his governorship of Spain in 96 B.C.

The low level of ancient technology in the production and transportation of goods, the extensive use of slave labor, and the concentration of wealth in a few hands limited economic growth. This hampered the development of large-scale industries and mass markets that would have provided high levels of steady, full-time employment for wage laborers. Rather, Rome and other large cities like Capua, Puteoli, and Brundisium were the domain of the *taberna* (retail shop) or the *officina* (workshop) and small individual proprietors, both men and women (p. 232). Helped by family members and a slave or two, the shopkeeper would carry on the retail sale of particular types of food, goods, or services or engage in the specialized production of goods on a handicraft basis. These goods might also be sold at retail on the premises or at wholesale in batches to a merchant who would consolidate them for bulk shipment elsewhere or peddle them individually in smaller towns that could not support a local retailer or producer.

Specific trades were often concentrated

Pompeii, the Street of Abundance, with workshops and stores. (Italian Government Travel Office)

in certain streets or neighborhoods. At Rome, for example, there was the street of the Sickle Makers and the Forum Vinarium, where the wine merchants gathered. In that way it was easy for merchants and craftsmen to exchange information of mutual interest, receive materials, and be accessible to customers looking for what they sold or produced.

In Rome and Italy, the building trades flourished. Sulla, Pompey, and Caesar used the spoils of war to finance many public works in Rome. Wealthy nobles covered the Palatine with sumptuous townhouses. Elsewhere in the city, speculators put up huge blocks of flimsy, multistoried apartment buildings, *insulae,* to house the rapidly expanding population, which probably neared a million by 30 B.C.

Some of the lower-class freedmen or free-born tradespeople and craftworkers could acquire significant wealth and property. People who produced or sold luxury goods for the wealthy in their *tabernae* and *officinae* were very successful. Some owned several shops in their specialties around the city of Rome. People who dealt in gold and silver jewelry, pearls, precious stones, perfumes, luxury furniture, and artwork were quite prosperous. One large-scale baker named Marcus Vergilius Eurysaces was so successful that when he died around 30 B.C. he left for himself and his wife, Atistia, one of the largest and most impressive funeral monuments still in existence from ancient Rome. On it the couple commemorated all aspects of commercial breadmaking in a handsomely

The funeral monument of M. Vergilius Eurysaces, a wholesale miller and baker of late Republican or early Augustan times. The various operations of milling and baking are depicted in the bas-reliefs at the top. (Fratelli Alinari, Art Resource, NY)

sculpted frieze. A freedman named Q. Caecilius Spendo, who specialized in making cheap clothes, built a tomb large enough to include eighteen of his own ex-slaves along with him and his wife.

The business that still produced the biggest profits other than war was finance, both public and private. The numerous annexations in Asia Minor greatly expanded the business of tax farming, which was carried on by companies of *publicani* (pp. 126–127). Moneylending, often to provincial cities who needed money to pay the *publicani,* or to client kings, who needed to borrow to stay solvent after paying huge sums in buying Roman support for their thrones, was an important source of profits to

wealthy financiers. With rates as high as 24 or 48 percent, even the greatest nobles were tempted to exploit this source of revenue. Pompey loaned some of the huge fortune that he had acquired in the East to Ariobarzanes, whom he had confirmed as king of Cappadocia. In 52 B.C., Cicero was shocked to learn that Marcus Brutus was the Roman who indirectly pressured him to use his power as governor of Cilicia to force the Cypriot city of Salamis to make payment on an illegal loan at 48 percent interest.

On the other hand, there were many lenders, mostly well-to-do *equites,* who engaged in the more normal business of advancing money to merchants and shipowners to finance trade or to Roman aristocrats to finance their careers. One of these men was Cicero's confidant, publisher, and banker, T. Pomponius Atticus. Although they were businessmen, they shared the basic outlook of the aristocracy and used much of their profits to invest in land and live like gentlemen. Atticus, for example, acquired vast estates in Epirus, which allowed him to spend the turbulent years from 88 to 65 at Athens (hence his cognomen, Atticus), where he was safe from the political storms of Rome. When he returned to Rome, he patronized the arts and literature from his house on the Quirinal and made so many important contacts that he was protected on all sides during the subsequent civil wars.

The Concentration of Wealth Atticus, with his great wealth, illustrates one of the striking features of the late Republic: the concentration of wealth in a few upper-class hands and the ever-widening gap between rich and poor. This trend had already been evident since at least the time of the Punic wars, but it was greatly accelerated by Marius' and Sulla's introduction of proscription. In times of civil war, those on the winning side, or at least not on the losing side, could acquire the property of proscribed individuals at a mere fraction of their normal value, either through favoritism or because the sudden increase in property for sale temporarily depressed prices. When property values rose with the return of normalcy, their net worth increased enormously. For example, Marcus Crassus had inherited a relatively modest fortune of 300 talents upon the deaths of his father and remaining brother in the civil war of 87. After siding with Sulla in 83, however, he took advantage of Sulla's proscriptions in order to acquire valuable properties. Then, through shrewd management, he increased his wealth still further, so that his vast real estate holdings alone were worth more than 7,000 talents in 55 B.C.

The profits of war and imperial administration that accrued to the nobility were even greater. Despite his failure to defeat Mithridates totally, Lucullus had amassed enough wealth from Asia Minor to live like a king in numerous villas after his recall to Italy. He became so famous for his conspicuous consumption that the term *Lucullan* has come to characterize rich living. The wealth acquired by Pompey and Caesar during their respective conquests in the East and Gaul made them far wealthier than even Crassus, whose only hope of staying even was to conquer the wealthy empire of Parthia.

Provincial governors often abused their power to amass personal fortunes in order to compete with their aristocratic rivals for high office and social status. Verres, the notorious governor of Sicily from 73 to 71, was reported to have said that the illegal gains of his first year were to pay off the debts that he had incurred in running for his praetorship of 74, those of the second year were to bribe the jury to acquit him of his crimes, and those of the third were for himself. Significantly, the artworks that he had plundered from Sicily were said to have earned him a place on Antonius' proscription list in 43. Even an honest governor, such as Cicero had been in Cilicia in 52, was able to profit handsomely from office. In addition, though a man of relatively modest means among the Roman nobility, Cicero acquired enough through inheritances, gifts, and favorable loans from other nobles whom he defended in court to buy a townhouse on the Palatine for 3.5 million sesterces and at least 8 well-appointed country villas. He, too, of course, lost them along with his life in the proscriptions of 43.

Life for the Rural and Urban Poor When not harassed by rapacious neighbors, bad weather, conscription, or dispossession in civil war, the free peasant or tenant farmer could get by. Sometimes he could even earn a little extra by working for hire on the estate of a wealthy neighbor at harvest. His wife worked as hard as he did as she helped at peak seasons in the field, tended the kitchen garden, ran the house, and bore children. Even if she survived the dangers of childbirth under unsanitary conditions, she grew old before her time.

Things had not gotten much better for the urban masses since the Gracchi. The luckier ones might be able to afford some of the better *insulae* that were being built with concrete, which had been introduced in the second century (p. 137), but they, too, were often ill-lit, poorly ventilated, and unsanitary. In fact, overall health conditions in a large preindustrial city like Rome were such that it could not have expanded or even maintained the number of its inhabitants without a constant high level of immigration. Fire and collapse were all too frequent in crowded, rickety slums. There was also danger from frequent floods, because the Tiber often overflowed its banks.

Although there were large numbers of small-scale shopkeepers, such as bakers, fullers, metalworkers, potters, shoemakers, armorers, and wine and food sellers, there were even more unskilled and semiskilled people who had to rely on occasional employment as day workers on construction projects, on the docks, and in odd jobs like porterage and message-carrying for the more fortunate.

As clients of the rich, many of the poor were helped by gifts of food (*sportulae*) and occasional distributions of money (*congiaria*). At election time, one could look forward to selling one's vote as the use of the secret ballot and intense electoral competition increased the use of bribery. Public festivals and triumphs could also produce helpful bonuses. Crassus, for example, feasted the whole city of Rome to celebrate his victory over Spartacus and gave each Roman citizen a three months' supply of grain. The public distribution of free grain to several hundred thousand Roman citizens also helped to keep prices reasonable for those who had to buy all of their grain. Since it was limited to adult men, however, it was not enough to sustain their families. Moreover, the right to receive free grain was not restricted to the needy. It was available only to those who met basic citizenship and residency requirements, rich or poor. Therefore, hunger must have been a constant condition faced by many inhabitants, and abortion and infanticide, especially of girls, were frequent to limit the number of mouths to feed.

Fire and Violence   Life in the cities was precarious in other ways, too. There was no public fire department to control the numerous fires that swept through crowded slums. Nor was there a police force to prevent the growing crime and violence that poverty and crowded conditions bred. Private associations might try to provide local protection, and some wealthy individuals earned popularity by maintaining private fire brigades, as Crassus is believed to have done and as did a certain Egnatius Rufus later. The rich surrounded themselves with private bodyguards when they traversed the city, especially at night. The poor always had to rely mainly on their own efforts or those of family and friends to protect themselves or secure justice from those who committed crimes against them. The principle of self-help was still widely applied. There was no public prosecutor, and the courts, with their cumbersome procedures, were mainly for the rich (p. 143).

Politically inspired violence also increased greatly in late Republican Rome. The most notable examples, of course, are the civil wars and proscriptions, during which many thousands were killed. Increasingly, however, important trials, political meetings (*contiones*), elections, and legislative meetings of the assemblies were marred by violence. Rival politicians hired gangs to intimidate and harass each other. P. Clodius perfected the art of political violence in 58 B.C. by organizing poor citizens into clubs (*collegia*) modeled on legitimate private associations and using them to harass his enemies.

Public entertainment also reflected the increase in violence. Sulla and Caesar both added festivals to the Roman calendar. The accompanying games included chariot races, that excited spectators with high-speed wrecks and the frequent deaths of charioteers. Gladiatorial combats sponsored by candidates for office had become such a common feature of life that special schools for training and supplying gladiators became big business. Bloodthirsty crowds also delighted in staged beast hunts (*venationes*), animals for which were imported from all over the empire. As dictator, Caesar invented a new source of violent entertainment, the *naumachia,* a staged naval battle often on a man-made lake created for the occasion.

Voluntary Associations   To obtain some measure of protection and comfort in the violent, disease-ridden, and unpredictable world of the *tabernae* and *insulae,* the lower classes of Rome and other cities organized themselves into voluntary associations, *collegia,* based on common occupations or religious cults or on their local neighborhoods (*vici*), districts (*pagi*), or hills (*montes*). They elected their own officers and pooled their modest resources to provide banquets and entertainments for themselves, insure proper burial when they died, and protect their interests against the higher authorities if need be. Indeed, aristocrats campaigning for office courted their votes and hoped that the *collegia* would promote their campaigns.

Slaves and Freedmen   Slavery in Rome and Italy continued to grow in the first century B.C. The kidnapping activities of pirates before 67, Pompey's conquests in the East, and Caesar's conquests in Gaul, all produced a flood of slaves. Having finally learned their lesson after the dreadful uprisings of mistreated rural slaves in Sicily (104 to 99 B.C.) and under Spartacus in Italy (73 to 71 B.C.), the Romans improved the treatment of such slaves to prevent future outbreaks. Household slaves and those with skilled trades or professions continued to enjoy many advantages. Those in the service of wealthy and powerful masters fared better than the majority of free citizens. They ran their owners' estates, acted as their business and political agents, and were well rewarded for their loyalty. Many of them acquired considerable personal wealth and even owned slaves of their own.

Roman masters continued to be generous in freeing personal and domestic slaves, whom they came to know and love as members of their own families, personal friends, and bedmates. A good example was Cicero's personal secretary Tiro, whom he treated as a son and eventually freed. Tiro served Cicero faithfully as a freedman, invented a system of shorthand (still extant) to handle his voluminous dictation, wrote a biography of him after his death, and helped to collect his correspondence for publication.

Many of the freedmen who became successful and even wealthy in business got their start with financial help from their former masters, with whom they shared their profits. Ironically, freedmen were able to succeed so well for their former masters because a law of 118 B.C. had removed many of the formal obligations that freedmen once owed their former masters. As a result, many freeborn, upper-class Romans became very ambivalent toward freedmen. On the one hand, they enjoyed the profitable business associations with successful freedmen, but on the other hand they saw the success of freedmen as threats to their own social status. One result was the extremely negative upper-class stereotype of the boorish nouveau-riche freedman later epitomized by the character Trimalchio in Petronius' *Satyricon* (p. 349). Even lower-class freeborn citizens jealously guarded their privileges. Efforts to give freedmen membership in all the voting tribes were bitterly resisted and always failed.

Italians and Provincials Unlike freedmen, the Italians, who had won the franchise as a result of the Social War, were able to obtain equitable enrollment in the voting tribes. Cinna performed that service between 86 and 84, and

Sulla wisely did not anger the Italians by trying to undo the justice that had finally been done. Still, for the average Italian, being allowed to vote on a par with other Roman citizens was a right of little use. The difficulty of going to Rome to exercise the franchise regularly was too great. For the local Italian landed aristocracy, who now became Roman *equites,* it was another matter, however. They joined the older *equites* in demanding a greater voice in public affairs. Sulla's addition of 300 *equites* to the senate did not appreciably alter the status of the rest, who continued to feel that the noble-dominated senate was not doing enough to protect their legal and financial interests. Men like Cicero (who came from the equestrian class), Pompey, Crassus, and Caesar, however, eagerly supported many equestrians. Their money, votes, and influence could be highly useful in the struggles of the Forum. Similarly, powerful Roman aristocrats courted wealthy provincials, provincial cities, and even entire provinces as clients. Their money, manpower, and material resources were great advantages in domestic struggles and foreign wars.

Women in the Late Republic Upper-class women played a significant role in the intellectual and political life of the late Republic. Although fathers did not send their daughters away to places like Athens or Rhodes for higher training as they did their sons (p. 233), some accomplished and loving fathers, like Hortensius, Cicero, and the younger Cato, took great personal interest in educating their daughters beyond the ordinary level. Cicero lavished much attention on his daughter Tullia. He was extremely distressed that while he was in exile his wife had arranged a marriage for her with a man whom he correctly thought was unworthy of her virtue and intelligence. He was inconsolable over her death and even contemplated the establishment of a cult and shrine for her. Cato's daughter, Porcia, was like her father in outspoken Republicanism. She supported her first husband, M. Calpurnius Bibulus, in his opposition to Caesar. She insisted that she participate with her second husband, Brutus, in the planning of Caesar's assassination, and after her death Cicero delivered a powerful eulogy for her. Hortensia, the daughter of Cicero's oratorical rival Hortensius, broke all precedent in 42 when she personally appeared in the Forum to argue against the imposition of a special tax on wealthy women to pay for the war against Brutus and Cassius. She gained public support and won her point. Pompey's last and most beloved wife, Cornelia, daughter of Metellus Scipio, earned praise because she was well read, could play the lyre, and, most significantly, was adept at geometry and philosophy. Nor can anyone ever forget Sallust's picture of the highborn, highly educated, and daring Sempronia who was one of the major conspirators with Catiline in 63 (*Bellum Catilinae,* 25).

Just as dynastic marriages gave shrewd and ambitious royal women more power and status in the Hellenistic Greek world, so the need for powerful marriage alliances in the growing competition for power among the aristocracy of the rapidly expanding Roman Republic gave upper-class Roman women opportunities for power and prestige. Cornelia, Pompeia, and Calpurnia, Caesar's wives; Fulvia, wife of Clodius, Curio, and Marcus Antonius; Octavia, sister of Octavian; and Livia, Octavian's last wife, are prime examples.

One of the most visible signs of the increased power and independence of upperclass women in the late Republic is their sexual liberation. Earlier, a woman like Cornelia, mother of the Gracchi, though quite independent, had held to the ideal of a virtuous Roman matron and widow. During the first century B.C., as traditional values began to break down rapidly under intense political and economic competition, many women became infamous for their uninhibited sexual behavior. Pompey divorced his third wife, Mucia, because she had been notoriously unfaithful while he was fighting Mithridates. Caesar's second wife, Pompeia, was caught in the famous affair with P. Clodius. One of Clodius' sisters, Clodia, the wife of Metellus Celer, was notoriously promiscuous. Among her many lovers were the poet Catullus and Cicero's young friend Caelius Rufus. On his deathbed her husband claimed that

she had poisoned him, and on another occasion Lucullus produced testimony that she and her sister, Lucullus' wife, had incestuous relations with their brother. Sallust claims that a number of talented and dissolute women besides Sempronia became involved in Catiline's conspiracy. These independent, strong-willed, and unconventional women of the late Republic have their counterparts in many of the empresses of the Imperial era.

Lower-Class Women   There were three major categories of lower-class Roman women: slaves, freedwomen, and poorer freeborn women. Female slaves were usually used as household servants, such as nurses, weavers, hairdressers, handmaidens, cooks, and housekeepers. Usually they were available to masters for sexual purposes, to which neither the slaves nor their masters' wives necessarily objected. In such an arrangement wives had less fear of pregnancy and, often, freedom from husbands who had been forced upon them and whom they did not love; also, a responsive female slave might expect eventual freedom from a grateful master. Women slaves could own property, even other slaves. Marriages between slaves were not legally recognized but were often very stable, even when a couple had been separated by sale. A woman slave who saved enough money to buy her freedom or had freedom granted would often then purchase her separated husband and free him.

The most unfortunate group of female slaves was that of the prostitutes. Prostitution was extensive, and prostitutes were often the unwanted female children of slaves and poor free citizens who were sold by masters and parents to procurers who raised them for that purpose alone. In general, they had little to look forward to. Even if they obtained their freedom, they were not trained to do anything else and might be worse off without an owner who had an interest in providing a minimum level of shelter, food, and physical security.

Large numbers of female household slaves eventually gained freedom. Some stayed on as free retainers with their former owners, others practiced the trades that they had learned as slaves, and some rose to a comfortable status by good marriages, generous patrons, or hard work. Often a master would free a woman in order to marry her. Marriage to freedwomen carried no stigma in all but the highest classes.

Ironically, the slaves and freedwomen of the aristocracy often had far greater opportunities in life than freeborn women of the poorer citizen classes. Women of the working poor often had to be content with the lowliest jobs. Laundry work, spinning and weaving, turning grindstones at flour mills, working as butchers, and selling fish are frequently recorded. Inscriptions from Pompeii list some other occupations, such as dealer in beans, seller of nails, brickmaker, and even stonecutter. Many women worked as waitresses in taverns or servers at food counters, where they may also have engaged in prostitution on the side. The names of waitresses and prostitutes are found scribbled on numerous tavern walls with references to their various virtues or vices, attractions or detractions as the case may be. For many unskilled poor women, prostitution was the only source of livelihood, and unlike slave prostitutes, who had at least the protection of a brothel, they had to practice their trade unprotected out-of-doors in the public archways, *fornices,* whence comes the word *fornicate.*

Especially among the poor, daughters were often considered a useless burden and exposed at birth or sold into slavery. Even when such extreme steps were not taken, girls received less attention. That combined with the high incidence of death in childbirth as a result of adolescent marriage, poor health care, and unsanitary living conditions made life for a poor woman very precarious indeed.

New Waves of Hellenization The First and Third Mithridatic wars sent two new surges of Hellenization over Roman arts and letters. In 88, Philo of Larissa, head of Plato's Academy in Athens, fled to Rome, where he became the teacher of important political and intellectual leaders like Quintus Catulus and Cicero. When Sulla looted Athens in 86, he sent home fleets of ships loaded with the finest products of Greek art, literature, and thought. Among them were the works of Aristotle and his successor at the head of the Lyceum. These works had been damaged earlier and had not been widely known for some time. Their intellectual impact was extensive, particularly after Lucullus brought back the captive Greek scholar Tyrannio of Amisus during the Third Mithridatic War, who helped to emend and publish them.

At the end of the third war, Pompey brought back the Greek historian Theophanes of Mytilene and the medical library of Mithridates. Lucullus had already looted a large library of books from Pontus, which he housed in a complex of study rooms and colonnades where Greek intellectuals and interested Roman aristocrats met to study and debate. Indeed, Lucullus set the fashion for large private libraries such as Cicero created. Caesar had planned to outdo them all by building Rome's first public library and filling it with books from the famous library of the Ptolemies at Alexandria. This Roman mania for Greek libraries stimulated a tremendous demand for the copying and selling of books, which made Greek culture even more accessible to the Romans.

Education By the first century B.C., Rome had developed a fairly extensive system of education. Its availability was limited by the ability to pay since the state contributed no support. Primary schools (*ludi literarii*) were open to both boys and girls. There they learned the fundamentals of reading, writing, and arithmetic, often painfully, since corporal punishment was frequently applied. Between the ages of twelve and fifteen, girls and boys took different paths. A girl would often be married to an older man at about fourteen, and unless she were of the wealthy elite, formal education stopped. Roman boys moved on to the secondary level under the tutelage of a *grammaticus,* who taught them Greek and Latin language and literature. No Roman of the first century B.C. could be considered truly educated if he did not speak and write Greek as fluently as Latin and did not know the classical Greek authors by heart.

Since the Romans had come to dominate Italy and the western Mediterranean by the first century B.C., it was essential for other people to know Latin. Therefore, schools of Latin and even Greek, for those who had real ambitions, were becoming common everywhere. They spread the Latin language and Greco-Roman culture widely and produced a remarkably uniform culture among the upper classes of Italy and the western provinces. As earlier, the masters of the primary and secondary schools were frequently freed Greek slaves who had been tutors in the houses of the wealthy. Their pupils were often offspring of middle- and upper-middle-class fathers like those of Cicero, Vergil, and Horace, who had ambitions for their sons to enter Roman politics and rise in social standing.

The prevalence of private tutors among the aristocracy meant that aristocratic girls often received instruction at the secondary level along with their brothers. Sometimes they were even able to participate in the higher training of rhetoric and philosophy, if, as with Sempronia, sister of the Gracchi, their families brought men accomplished in these fields into their homes and supported them in return for instructing their children. Many aristocratic sons as well as those of nonaristocrats were sent to professional rhetoricians for instruction at the highest level. Frequently an upper-class young man capped his formal education with a tour to the great centers of Greek rhetoric and philosophy at Athens and Rhodes.

For a long time Greek rhetoric dominated the higher curriculum. Right at the beginning of the first century, there was a movement to create a parallel course of professional instruction in Latin rhetoric. In 92, however, the censors banned teachers of Latin rhetoric, perhaps out of fear that rhetorical skills, the foundation of political success, might be made too accessible to the lower orders. Julius Caesar finally lifted the ban when he became dictator.

Law and the Legal System Roman law continued to be shaped by private unpaid, learned, aristocratic jurists (*juris consulti, juris prudentes*), but their role became less visible than it had been in earlier centuries. One reason was the establishment of the various permanent jury courts (*quaestiones*) under Sulla (p. 172). By exercising their *imperium* as magistrates in charge of the courts, the praetors created law through their edicts granting relief to plaintiffs, issuing injunctions, and establishing procedural rules. Often, however, they, as could anyone else involved in legal proceedings, consulted with the jurists before issuing their edicts. Praetors from one year tended to adopt the edicts of their predecessors, so that over time there grew up a body of praetorian law that supplemented the traditional civil law and specific statutes.

One of the major trends in the late Republic was a striving for fairness and equity, not just the strict application of the letter of the law. The jurists often resorted to the principle of good faith (*bona fides*) as a way of advancing equity. For the most part, this effort was a practical response to the increasing complexity of the Roman world rather than simply borrowing a concept from Greek law or philosophy as has sometimes been argued. Nevertheless, as in the case of the Gracchan reforms, the Greek law and philosophy may have helped to provide Roman jurists with a vocabulary and rationale for what they were doing or had done.

The same is true in the development of the famous *ius gentium* (law of nations) in the late Republic. Roman civil law and statutes did not always apply in cases where non-Romans were involved, as was increasingly the case with the expansion of Roman power. Therefore, the *praetor peregrinus* at Rome and provincial governors often incorporated into their edicts useful elements from the laws of other people. Greek philosophical concepts like the Stoic idea of a natural law (*ius naturale*) uniting all people supplied useful jargon and justification for what the Romans were doing, but it does not seem to have supplied an ideological motivation.

On the other hand, the principles of logic, debate, and rhetoric worked out earlier by Greeks were important for the rise of forensic orators, who began to take over from the jurisconsults in trying cases before standing courts of nonspecialist judges and jurors. Orators, however, still relied on the expertise of learned jurists like two cousins from the Scaevola family. The older was Quintus Mucius Scaevola the Augur, consul in 117 B.C. He was the son-in-law of Scipio Aemilianus' famous friend Laelius, and he was the father-in-law of his own protégé L. Licinius Crassus. Pupil of the Augur and L. Crassus, Cicero absorbed their idealism and moderation. The younger cousin was Quintus Mucius Scaevola the Pontiff, consul in 95 B.C. The greatest of all legal works published during the Republic was his *Civil Law* (*Ius Civile*), the first systematic exposition of private law and a model for legal commentators down into the second century A.D.

The Religious World of the Late Republic

The commonplace picture of a steep decline in commitment to traditional Roman religion during the late Republic is greatly exaggerated. The cults and festivals of the ordinary rural villagers and urban members of countless *collegia* and neighborhood associations continued to flourish. There is no reason to believe that people had any less confidence in the efficacy of sacrifice and ritual to obtain the divine favor that they eagerly sought for every human activity. The frequency with which augury, divination, and the reporting of omens were used by political rivals against each other shows just how seriously those things were taken. Indeed, the more one thought that he was on the side of the gods, the more convinced he would have been of finding favorable auguries, signs, and omens. One does not have to falsify cynically and consciously what one wants to find, but of course an enemy, who is equally convinced of his rightness, will naturally claim that is what had happened.

If the state for which the great deities were chiefly responsible was not faring well and was being disrupted by partisan conflicts and destructive civil wars, it was not seen as a failure of religion but as a failure of the leaders who were always equally responsible for running the state and carrying out the religious duties that maintained the *pax deorum* vital to its welfare. That Julius Caesar had won the civil war with Pompey and was restoring peace and stability was proof to many of his divine favor and justified bestowing on him such honors as made him seem more than human.

In a way, Julius Caesar was just another in a long line of new deities, going all the way back to Hercules in the Forum Boarium (p. 28), whom the Roman state had officially welcomed into the Roman family of gods over the centuries. It was always wise to have as many gods as possible participate in the *pax deorum* that protected the state and fostered the growth of Roman power. As that power had incorporated new people into Rome's Italian confederacy and overseas empire, the state incorporated their gods. In times of crisis, the senate might even sanction the adoption of a completely foreign deity, as was the case with the Great Mother (*Magna Mater*), Cybele, from Asia Minor during the Hannibalic War in 205 (p. 144).

Nevertheless, Roman authorities were leery of cultic practices and deities that seemed too un-Roman or seemed to promote political loyalties other than to Rome. They still strictly controlled the ecstatic rites of Cybele and would not allow Roman citizens to be one of her eunuch priests, the self-castrating *Galli*. The senate may have viewed Jewish worshippers just like the devotees of Bacchus whom they suppressed in 186 (p. 144). A senatorial decree of 139 ordered the expulsion of Jewish immigrants from Rome, perhaps in part because of their loyalty to the Temple and its high priest in Jerusalem. Only after Pompey captured Jerusalem and established Roman hegemony in Judea during the Third Mithridatic War were the captives whom he brought back to Rome successful in establishing permanent synagogues there. Chaldean astrologers were particularly suspect because of the secret knowledge that they claimed to have and that might be used against established authority. Therefore, a law probably of 67 B.C. expelled them, too. Similarly in the 50s and 40s, when Roman relations with Cleopatra's Egypt were tense, there were several attempts to destroy the increasingly popular worship of the paired Egyptian deities Isis and Serapis (Sarapis), her consort. The priests of Isis and Serapis were independent of the official Roman priesthoods, and they fostered a personal attachment to the loving goddess Isis and her consort, who were closely associated with the Ptolemaic dynasty.

The growing popularity of Isis and other Hellenized mystery cults do show the spread of new religious forces in the Roman world, particularly in the large multiethnic, polyglot populations of cities like Rome. Although traditional Roman religion still had great meaning for the Roman elite, who controlled it, and the native-born citizens whom it served, the large numbers of willing and unwilling immigrants (slaves) from the eastern Mediterranean, who made up an increasingly large percentage of the urban population, often found greater comfort in the more personal, universal mystery cults of their homelands. The conditions that had made them popular there were now being replicated in Rome and other large western cities. People who had been uprooted from the close-knit world of family, village, and local cults, lived in a vast, dangerous, and unpredictable urban world made even more dangerous and unpredictable by partisan conflict and civil war. Sharing the mysteries of an initiation rite helped individuals stripped of previous associations create a new sense of community and belonging to one another. Moreover, deities like Isis, Mithras, and Cybele promised not salvation in the next life, but nurture and protection in this one through a personal connection with a powerful universal deity who was not limited to one city or territory. Such religions would find greater and greater appeal in the increasingly urbanized and cosmopolitan Roman world of the next two centuries.

Greek Philosophy and the Roman Elite

The removal of Greek philosophers and whole libraries of Greek philosophical writings to Rome and Italy during the first century B.C. stimulated the study of philosophy on a scale never seen before among the educated elite. There are those who say that this increased exposure to the rationalism of Greek philosophy undermined the ruling class' belief in traditional Roman religion. That probably was true in some individual instances, but many probably had no difficulty in separating their religion and its important public role from their private intellectual pursuits as gentlemen. After all, many highly trained physicists and biologists today practice religions whose literal scriptures are at variance with many of their scientific suppositions. Cicero, for example, who subjected major aspects of Roman religion to intellectual scrutiny in such works as *On the Nature of the Gods* and *On Divination,* was in no way willing to discard them even if he did not accept them in every single particular. So, for example, in the dialogue *On the Nature of the Gods,* Cicero has one of his speakers say that he still believes in the traditional religion even though he cannot find proofs that meet his standards as an adherent of the Academic school of philosophy.

Stoicism Stoic philosophy, especially as modified in the late second and early first centuries B.C. by the philo-Roman Panaetius of Rhodes (p. 142) and Posidonius of Apamea, appealed to Romans like Cato the Younger and Brutus, who saw support for traditional Roman morality in Stoic ethics. Panaetius emphasized the virtues characteristically ascribed to a Roman noble: magnanimity, benevolence, generosity, and public service. In 87 B.C., as a Rhodian ambassador to Rome, Posidonius had developed a dislike of Marius. Therefore, in his historical writings he favored Marius' optimate enemies and their outlook, which further endeared his Stoic teachings to men like the younger Cato. Cicero and Pompey had both sat at his feet in Rhodes, and Posidonius was so impressed with Pompey that he appended a favorable account of Pompey's wars to the fifty-two books of his continuation of Polybius.

Posidonius saw Rome's empire as the earthly reflection of the divine commonwealth of the supreme deity. Its mission was to bring civilization to less advanced people. Statesmen who served this earthly commonwealth nobly would join philosophers in the heavenly commonwealth after death, an idea that Cicero adopted in his *Republic* to inspire Roman nobles to lives of unselfish political service. Posidonius also believed that the human soul was of the same substance as the heavenly bodies, to which it returned after death. His scientific demonstration of the effect of the moon on earthly tides reinforced this idea and gave great impetus to astrology at Rome. The growing popularity of these ideas, therefore, made it less difficult to accept the notion that the comet seen soon after Caesar's death was his soul ascending to heaven.

Epicureanism   Ironically, Caesar himself and a number of other Romans at this time had adopted the skeptical, materialistic, and very un-Roman philosophy of Epicurus, who had argued that such gods as there were lived beyond this world and took no part in it. He believed that the soul is made up solely of atoms that disperse among the other atoms of the universe upon death. Therefore, he stressed that death is not to be feared and that men should shun the cares of marriage, parenthood, and politics to live quietly in enjoyment of life's true pleasures. Among the Romans, Epicureanism was popularized by Philodemus of Gadara, who came to Italy after the First Mithridatic War and settled on the Bay of Naples at Herculaneum in association with his patron L. Calpurnius Piso Caesoninus, Caesar's father-in-law. Charred papyrus rolls containing some of Philodemus' writings have been found in the remains of Piso's villa, which was destroyed 150 years later by the famous eruption of Vesuvius and has now been spectacularly replicated to house the J. Paul Getty Museum in Malibu, California.

Roman Epicureans were less restrained in taking their pleasures than Epicurus himself would have approved, yet the Epicurean ideal of a life of pleasant retirement in one's garden may help to explain why Sulla at the height of his power retired and why Lucullus, Caesar, and Sallust lavished so much attention on their pleasure gardens. Perhaps Caesar's Epicureanism also explains his lack of concern when he

was warned of plots and bad omens shortly before his assassination.

The Peripatetics and the New Academy   The Aristotelian Peripatetic School and the New Academy of the skeptic Carneades were much less popular than other philosophical schools at Rome. Crassus, however, maintained the Peripatetic Alexander in his household, and Cicero was greatly drawn to the Academic school with its emphasis on the testing of ideas through rational inquiry and debate. Still, in general, Cicero was eclectic. He greatly favored Stoic ethics and attitudes, but Peripatetic influences, especially in political thought, can be found too (p. 242). Cicero and other Roman philosophical writers were not trying to advance original ideas; they were mainly interested in making available to fellow Romans the ideas that they admired and found useful in the works of Greek thinkers.

Art and Architecture   As with philosophy, so with art, the Romans followed Greek models. Italian stonecutters became adept at the standardized reproduction of famous Greek statues. Artists recreated famous paintings in frescoes and mosaics, with which the affluent increasingly decorated the walls and floors of their homes, as can be seen from the ruins at Pompeii. Still, native Roman and Italian traditions in realistic portraiture and landscape scenes flourished and became more sophisticated in technique.

Hellenistic architects stressed the articulated combination of different architectural units into a symmetrical whole along a central axis. The best Greek examples are the acropolis of Pergamum and the Temple of Zeus at Priene. The best example of this influence in Italy is the highly articulated and symmetrical complex known as the Sanctuary of Fortuna Primigenia at Praeneste, the foundations of which date from the second half of the second century B.C. and which Sulla reconstructed. Much of it came to view when allied bombs in World War II destroyed later buildings on the site. The whole sanctuary rose up the side of a

*Model of the Temple of Fortuna Primigenia at Praeneste, which shows the careful symmetrical arrange-
ment of different shapes and architectural elements along a central axis extending from the "notch" at the
center of the covered inclined ramps up the central staircases to the semicircular colonnade at the top.
(Courtesy Fototeca Unione, Rome)*

hill in terraces. Each terrace was architecturally defined in its own symmetrical style on either side of a central axis. The fourth terrace was approached from either side by a pair of unique curved ramps leading to a central staircase on the axis. The whole culminated in a little round shrine centered at the top, behind a semicircular set of steps and a curved colonnade.

Sulla attempted to give a more symmetrical aspect to the Roman Forum when he commissioned the Tabularium (Record Office), which Catulus finished in 78. It was carefully sited on the brow of the Capitoline just behind the Forum. It not only gave a central backdrop to the Forum, but its colonnaded upper story

provided a clear architectural link between the buildings of the forum and the others on the Capitoline to create an articulated whole.

When Pompey built Rome's first stone theater in 55, the Sanctuary of Fortuna Primigenia and his own travels in the East may have inspired him or his architect to design the theater along similar lines. The theater itself, unlike Greek theaters, which were built into solid hillsides, was a freestanding semicircle with the stage and backdrop on the chord and the seats rising in tiers on the arc. To overcome opposition to permanent theaters, Pompey apparently included on the center of the topmost tier a shrine to Venus Victrix. Articulated with this theater was a portico that attached to the back wall of the stage. Two parallel colonnades provided shelter for audiences in case of unexpected rain or places where meetings could be held. The senate was meeting there when Caesar was assassinated at the feet of its builder's statue.

Caesar himself had planned the Basilica Julia to the east of Sulla's Tabularium and across from the rebuilt Basilica Aemilia and approximately parallel to it. In accordance with the new fashion, these roughly parallel buildings introduced greater axial symmetry to the Forum. Caesar also built an entirely new and symmetrical forum known as the Forum Julium in 46 B.C. It was a rectangle completely surrounded by a colonnade with a peristyle temple of Venus Genetrix set toward the back along the longitudinal axis. Centered in front of the temple on the same axis were an equestrian statue of Caesar and a fountain with statues of nymphs grouped about it. This symmetrical forum set the pattern for all fora subsequently built by the Roman emperors.

The combination of both the Roman arch and vault with the Greek column in the structure of Sulla's Tabularium and the Sanctuary of Fortuna Primigenia also set a trend for later Roman architecture. The walls of Pompey's theater rose up on three tiers of arches, each framed in half-columns: the first with Doric, the second with Ionic, and the third with Corinthian capitals. The facade of the Colosseum received the same treatment over 100 years later. Also, just as in Pompey's theater, the tiers of seats in the Colosseum are supported on vaults.

The Romans achieved greater flexibility of design and larger size in their buildings than the Greeks because they used brick and concrete, which are particularly suitable for constructing the arches and vaults that permit more massive structures. The Romans even built columns out of brick and then faced them with stucco or sheathed them with stone. Concrete allowed decorators to achieve numerous textures on exposed surfaces by inserting shaped or colored stones in various patterns. On the most important buildings, however, at Rome and elsewhere in Italy, architects began to use a greater variety of handsome stone, too. Cream-colored travertine limestone from Tibur and the brilliant white marble of Luna (Carrara) came from Italy. Other white and colored marbles of all hues were imported from Greece, the Aegean Islands, Asia Minor, and Africa. Rome and Italy in the late Republic had begun to appear like the imperial centers that they had become.

Late Republican Oratory, Literature, and Thought

For writers, the century from the Gracchi (133 B.C.) to the Battle of Actium (31 B.C.) was one of the most productive in Roman history. Many of the classic works of Roman oratory, poetry, history, and philosophy appeared in that period. Unfortunately, for the first half, from the Gracchi to the death of Sulla (78 B.C.), almost nothing has survived. Beginning with Cicero, Latin authors in the second half of the century so overshadowed their immediate predecessors that later ages lost interest in preserving the earlier writers who inspired them.

Orators and Historical Writers from the Gracchi to Sulla

Between the Gracchi and Sulla, the two most notable orators were Marcus Antonius, father of the triumvir with the same name, and Lucius Licinius Crassus, a relative of Marcus Crassus. Antonius cultivated an emotional style of delivery. Lucius Crassus, one of Cicero's models, was a very sophisticated and witty orator, who could vary the tone and mood at appropriate points as he developed a topic. Antonius had been a consistent optimate and was a victim of Marius' proscriptions in 87. Crassus had once supported Marius but then joined the optimate opposition. In 92, as a censor, he banned the teaching of rhetoric in Latin in order to restrict training in such a politically important skill to the wealthy elite, who could afford the time and money to undergo training in Greek and might be less inclined to the *popularis* programs of the Gracchi and Marius. Ironically, the only surviving book from this period is an anonymous Latin textbook on oratory, the *Rhetorica ad Herennium* (*The Art of*

Rhetoric Addressed to Herennius), which shows marked Gracchan and Marian sympathies.

Gaius Gracchus and P. Sulpicius, the famous popular tribune of 88, were early practitioners of the Asianic style of oratory that is said to have originated in Pergamum. It is a highly emotional style of oratory that uses histrionic gestures, florid verbosity, and musical cadences to overpower the audience's senses. The consummate practioner was Cicero's older rival Q. Hortensius. In reaction to Asianism there arose the Atticist school, which valued a plain, direct, simple style like that of the famous Attic Greek orator Lysias. Cicero was heavily influenced by the Asianists, and Caesar by the Atticists.

Another field of great interest to the politically powerful was history. From the Gracchi onward, the writers of history followed the lead of Cato the Elder and wrote in Latin. They were more interested in presenting their views on important topics to fellow Romans than to Greeks. Many still took the annalistic approach, some from a pro-Gracchan, *popularis* perspective and others from an anti-Gracchan, optimate stance.

In the Sullan period, Licinius Macer supported the *popularis* approach to politics. Valerius Antias, who wrote sometime in the first century, is famous for his sheer bulk. He covered all of Roman history down to at least 91 in at least seventy-five books. About fifty books covered recent history from the Gracchi onward and may have been a major source for Livy, as was Claudius Quadrigarius, who began his account with the Gallic sack of Rome.

Historians like Coelius Antipater, Sempronius Asellio, and Lucius Cornelius Sisenna were more innovative, not always for the better. Dealing with the Second Punic War, Antipater wrote the first Latin historical monograph, which he embroidered with entertaining miracles and fictions. Asellio followed Polybius in an analytical account of events in which he had personally participated, probably from 146 to 91 B.C. Sisenna combined the two approaches in a novelistic work, full of tragedy and melodrama, on the Social War.

Closely related to oratory and history was the emergence of aristocratic autobiography. In the partisan atmosphere after the Gracchi, important men wanted to condemn their enemies and enhance their places in history by writing commentaries (*commentarii*). The two rivals M. Aemilius Scaurus and P. Rutilius Rufus mutually recriminated each other, and Marius' rivals Q. Lutatius Catulus and Sulla (using Greek) wrote accounts of their lives that reflected well on them and poorly on Marius.

The Growth of Scholarship Antiquarian scholarship (research into the origins of institutions, customs, and traditions) was stimulated by patriotic pride in competition with the Greeks and by partisan politics as the proponents of different policies and practices sought precedents in the past. The first great commentator on literary texts was Lucius Aelius Stilo Praeconinus (born ca. 150 B.C.). He published critical editions of Ennius and Lucilius and identified twenty-five plays of Plautus as genuine. Two of his famous students in the next generation were Cicero and Marcus Terentius Varro.

Drama and Poetry, 133 to 78 B.C. By the end of the second century B.C., earlier dramatists had already become classics (pp. 139–140), but they no longer commanded popular audiences. As the magistrates and other sponsors of popular entertainment tried to reach larger and larger audiences in a populace swollen by the uneducated rural poor, ex-slaves, and immigrants of diverse cultural backgrounds, native Italian comic traditions received greater emphasis. In Sulla's day, however, two famous writers, Lucius Pomponius and a certain Novius, imparted a more literary quality to the farce, slapstick, and mime that had been the principal ingredients of native Atellan farce (p. 140).

By the time of Caesar, even the Atellan farces, which kept many of the conventions of serious drama such as masks, stock characters, and all-male actors, were too sophisticated for a mass audience. The mime became the preferred form of popular comedy. The Greek root of the word *mime* connotes the imitation of everyday life. On the Roman stage it came to indicate popular performances like the burlesques and variety shows of modern music halls. The actors, male and female, appeared without masks, in plain shoes, did comic skits from daily life, sang and danced, and even put on stripteases. The skits might parody something from the high culture in the language of the street and include domestic quarrels or risqué love scenes without any sophisticated plot or point. Two contemporaries of Cicero achieved fame as writers of literary mimes, Decimus Laberius and Publilius Syrus. Syrus was famous for moralizing maxims that have been preserved in an anthology from his works.

The *Novi Poetae* In the post-Sullan period, many young aristocrats, thoroughly educated in all Greek literature, were caught up in the fast pace and unconventional mores of cosmopolitan life. Conscious of the difference between themselves and older, more staid generations, they became interested in other, more appealing types of literature. Among such youths in the first half of the first century B.C. were a number of poets who have come to be known as the *Novi Poetae* (New Poets) or Neoteric Poets from some references in Cicero, a traditionalist who disapproved of them. It is not known if they referred to themselves as the New Poets or felt any special identity as a group, but it is likely that they did. Many of them were pupils of Valerius Cato, a *grammaticus* and also a poet. They often mentioned each other in their poems and even commented on each other's work.

The *Novi Poetae* modeled their works on the personal and emotional writings of the early Greek lyric and elegiac poets like Sappho and Alcaeus or later Alexandrian love poets like Asclepiades. They also delighted in the learned, obscure, and exotic allusions to mythology, literature, and geography that characterized Alexandrian poets like Callimachus. They did not write for a large public but for themselves. That is why the works of all but one of them (including the epigrams of Cornificia, the only woman associated with them) have perished except for a choice line or two quoted

by some grammarian or commentator on another work.

Catullus (ca. 85 to ca. 54 B.C.) The one New Poet whose work has survived, albeit in a single manuscript from his hometown, is Gaius Valerius Catullus of Verona. Little is known of his life. He was born about 85 and died around 54 B.C. His participation in public life was limited to a year of service on the staff of Gaius Memmius, governor of Bithynia in 57, and to some scurrilous poems about Caesar, with whom he was reconciled shortly before he died. Nevertheless, these two people and others addressed in his poems show that he moved in the highest circles of the aristocracy.

It was in such circles that Catullus met a woman with whom he had a torrid love affair. He called her Lesbia, but she was really Clodia, sister of the notorious P. Clodius and wife of Metellus Celer. Apparently Clodia's beauty and charm were equaled only by her promiscuity, as Catullus discovered to his bitter sorrow.

The passionate love and hate, joy and sorrow produced by this relationship inspired many of Catullus' most famous poems. Their emotional intensity still burns with a gemlike flame across the ages to kindle a response that reaches a universal human level. Many are written in elegiac couplets. The most famous is number 85:

> *I hate and I love. You ask, perhaps, why.*
> *I know not, but feel it happen and am*
>   *crucified.*

This poem and others like it were probably the main inspiration for Cornelius Gallus, who perfected the use of elegy for love poetry, subjective erotic elegy, in the Augustan Age (p. 289).

Catullus' poetry encompasses many other themes as well. Number 101 is a touching lament for his dead brother, whose grave he visited in Asia Minor. In poem 96 he consoles a friend whose wife has just died, and he can move from a lighthearted drinking song in 27 to a celebration of the beauties of his home at Sirmio, to which he has just returned, in number 31. He could even write a reverential hymn to Diana (34) and a long poem charged with ecstatic frenzy on the god Attis (63). Number 64, on the mythical marriage of Peleus and Thetis, is a masterful little epic, *epyllion,* in the Alexandrian manner. Moreover, in all of his poems Catullus shows himself to be a serious craftsman by being the first to adapt many Greek lyric meters to Latin poetry.

Lucretius (ca. 94 to ca. 55 B.C.)

One of the contemporary poets who did not share the interests of Catullus and other *Novi Poetae,* although he may have known them, was the Epicurean Titus Lucretius Carus. Even less is known about Lucretius than about Catullus. He was born about 94 and died probably in 55 B.C. His patron was Gaius Memmius, the same man whom Catullus served in Bithynia. A house excavated at Pompeii indicates that Lucretius' family may have lived in the area around the Bay of Naples, where Philodemus and other Epicurean philosophers were concentrated. In a letter, Cicero mentions Lucretius' poetry favorably, but not his subject. Romantic legend has it that Cicero published Lucretius' work after the latter had died. Equally unfounded is the story popularized by Tennyson that Lucretius had been driven mad by a love potion and composed his work in lucid intervals before committing suicide.

As both a dedicated Epicurean and a patriotic Roman, Lucretius had little in common with the *Novi Poetae* and their private passions. He wanted to renew the public-spirited epic. His model, however, was not the historical epics of Ennius and Naevius but didactic Greek epics like those of Hesiod and Empedocles. In fact, the latter's poem *On Nature* may have been the direct inspiration for Lucretius' work, the *De Rerum Natura* (*On the Nature of Things*) in six books of dactylic hexameter verse. By teaching his fellow Romans the quietistic philosophy of Epicurus, Lucretius hoped to save them from destroying themselves in violence and civil war. Accordingly, Lucretius used the traditional divine invocation required by epic convention at the beginning of his work to ex-

press the desire for peace. He asked Venus, symbol of the creative power of nature, to seduce Mars, the personification of destructive war, and beg that he grant peace to Rome. In the rest of the poem, however, the gods do not play any role, because he believed that although they do exist, they dwell apart in celestial space and do not concern themselves with human affairs.

Therefore, it is irrational to fear the gods just as it is to fear death. As an atomist, Lucretius held that the universe is made up of empty space and atoms—solid yet invisible particles, infinite in number and differing only in size and shape—that swerve and collide as they fall through space and cluster together to form all animate and inanimate things: the earth, the stars, plants, animals, the bodies, and even the souls of men. All things, even the human soul, must come from something or become something else, because, as the individual object dies or disintegrates, its constituent atoms—themselves eternal and indestructible—separate and drift away into space once more. Death, even that of the soul, being nothing but atomic separation, is a process of nature—inevitable, but not to be feared. All sensation and consciousness simply cease.

For Lucretius, reason, not religion, was the only safe guide to life. Epicurus had saved humankind because his great powers of reason had destroyed the basis of superstitious fears. The only thing to be feared is passionate emotion, which clouds the reason and leads to extremes of behavior, the inevitable result of which is pain. By imparting knowledge of the true nature of reality, Lucretius hoped to convince people that the competition for wealth, fame, and power in order to achieve immortality, or the frenetic search for pleasure to blot out the fear of death are completely vain. Therefore, he argued, people should lead quiet lives, avoid all excess, and preserve the philosophic calm that alone guarantees true happiness free from either pain or anxiety.

Lucretius' originality lay in adapting Epicurus' message to a Roman context, expressing it in poetic language of great power and beauty, and raising the Latin dactylic hexameter verse to a new level of smoothness and flexibility. In the next generation, Vergil, Rome's greatest epic poet, who studied Epicureanism extensively as a young man, owed a great debt to Lucretius. Not only does Vergil's published hexameter verse show clear parallels with that of Lucretius, but the theme of the destructiveness of passion and the powerful scenes that reveal its force in the *Aeneid* vividly recall Lucretius' *De Rerum Natura.*

Cicero (106 to 43 B.C.)

Even Cicero, who viewed Epicureanism as a threat to all the values that had made Rome strong, recognized the talent in Lucretius' verse. Philosophically, however, Cicero's taste ran to the Stoic and Academic schools. One of Cicero's great contributions to western literature and thought is his philosophical works. In them his enlightened philosophy, worthy of the name *humanism,* deals with human beings, their essential nature, the validity of their perceptions, and their place in the universe. From Cicero's Stoic insistence on proper regard for all people stems the modern idea that all are created equal.

Cicero wrote two treatises on political science, *De Re Publica* (*On the State*) and its unfinished sequel, *De Legibus* (*On the Laws*). Both treatises set forth political theories based partly on Stoic teachings, partly on the skepticism of the New Academy as outlined in the *De Officiis* and other philosophical works, and to a large degree on Cicero's own idealized concept of the Roman Republic's constitution. He held that a state guided by an enlightened leader of outstanding prestige, a *princeps civitatis,* with a senate and citizenry observing their separate functions would guarantee a form of government not only stable but also capable of reconciling individual freedom with social responsibility. Such a state would combine the best features of monarchy, aristocracy, and democracy. In it, all social classes would work together for the common good.

Like Lucretius, Cicero was trying to prevent the Roman aristocrats from ruining the Republic with their destructive rivalries for power and *dignitas.* The *princeps,* through the moral authority of his prestige, would be able to stand above and control the ambitious aristocrats. Unlike Lucretius, however, Cicero argued in the *De Re Publica* (*On the State*) that virtuous behavior on behalf of the state would be rewarded with a blessed afterlife among the gods.

Cicero's Oratory Cicero himself was a *novus homo* recently risen from the local Italian aristocracy, which made up the bulk of the Roman equestrian class. His talent as an orator had helped him to break into the exclusive circle of the consular nobility at Rome. For him, moreover, oratory, as the statesman's practical tool for persuading his fellow citizens, was even more important than philosophy. He raised the art of oratory to its highest level as an active force in Roman public life.

Cicero combined substance and style. After delivering a speech, he would polish and refine it for publication by professional copyists, who supplied an even wider audience. Often, note takers using shorthand would copy a speech as he delivered it in order to supply those who could not wait for the official versions. Cicero's sonorous, rolling, rhythmic periods, his pungent and even scurrilous wit, and his marvelous figures of speech constantly delighted a population steeped in an oral culture in which books were rare and mass mechanical or electronic media nonexistent. The art of public speaking, therefore, was a treasured heritage built up by generations of skilled orators. Cicero himself, however, so surpassed his predecessors and contemporaries that only scattered fragments quoted from their speeches by later writers survive.

Probably no orator always used the same unvarying style, least of all Cicero. He combined the Greek Attic and Asianic styles (p. 239) and could be crisp and pointed, grand and verbose, or anywhere in between. Cicero's greatest skill as an orator was in fitting his style to his subject and knowing just what was required for maximum effect as the occasion demanded.

A master of his audience's emotions, Cicero often used this skill to obfuscate and mislead when his case was weak or his purpose polemical, as, for political reasons, they often were. For example, the first of Cicero's four speeches against Catiline (63 B.C.) is a masterpiece of biting invective based on much suspicion about Catiline but too little evidence to warrant strong action. Cicero's political purpose was to stir hostility among Catiline's fellow senators and panic him into showing his hand. By emotional appeals to patriotism, fearful images of murder and conflagration, devastatingly malicious innuendo, and pure bravado Cicero succeeded.

Works on Oratory In the period between the Conference of Luca (April 56 B.C.) and the feverish outburst of the *Philippics* (44 to 43 B.C.), Cicero's opportunities to exercise his oratorical talents were severely limited. He turned them to writing about his craft in a series of instructive works on the theory and practice of oratory. They form an invaluable record of oratory in the late Roman Republic and the principles followed by its greatest practitioner.

Letters Cicero was also a prolific letter writer. He was a keen observer of the political scene as well as one of its participants. Comments to others in his letters provide an invaluable firsthand source for the crucial last years of the Republic from 68 to 44 B.C. The private thoughts of a great man do not always live up to his public image, and Cicero provides no exception to the rule. His excessive vanity, his lack of judgment at critical moments, and his willingness to sacrifice truth to political expediency are there for all to see. Nevertheless, these letters are also full of wit, charm, learning, and grace that have made them a model of epistolary style over the centuries for those who write letters with an eye to posterity.

Poetry Few people remember that Cicero was also a poet. As a young man he seems to have experimented with a number of different meters and genres in the Alexandrian manner, much like the later *Novi Poetae*. All of these works are lost, but most of an early didactic hexameter poem, the *Aratea,* survives. It is a free translation in epic dactylic hexameter of the *Phaenomena,* a verse rendition of astronomical lore by the Hellenistic Greek poet Aratus. Cicero also wrote an epic poem on the life of Marius and two on events of his own life: the *De Consulatu Suo* on his consulship and *De Temporibus Suis* on his exile and restoration.

Sallust (86 to ca. 34 B.C.) Cicero was an *eques* who had broken into the nobility and believed in its basic worth even while he criticized its selfishness and exclusivity. The historian C. Sallustius Crispus, Sallust, was an *eques* who failed to reach the dignity of the consulship and was far less charitable. He, too, had come from a small Italian town, Amiternum in central Italy, and had started on a senatorial career through the *cursus honorum.* He probably was a quaestor in 55, and then in 52 he hoped to advance his career by earning popularity as a tribune. He associated himself with Publius Clodius, the unscrupulous *popularis* politician and personal enemy of Cicero. When Clodius was murdered in 52, Sallust played a leading role in burning down the senate house at his funeral and opposing Cicero, who defended Milo, Clodius' murderer, in court.

Needless to say, there was little love lost between Sallust and Cicero or Clodius' optimate enemies. The optimate censor of 50 B.C., Appius Claudius Pulcher, ironically Clodius' brother, expelled Sallust from the senate. Sallust sought to restore his position by serving Julius Caesar in the civil war against Pompey and Caesar's optimate enemies. His reward was election to the praetorship in 46 and governorship of the revamped province of Africa. He enriched himself scandalously at the provincials' expense and was tried for extortion. Caesar's influence seems to have saved him, but his political career came to an end. Even Caesar apparently did not think of favoring him for the consulship, and his career was certainly lost with the assassination of Caesar a few months later.

Instead, Sallust retired to luxurious gardens and villas financed by his ill-gotten gains and spent the rest of his life in writing moralistic historical monographs condemning the Roman nobility's ambition, corruption, and greed. Hypocrisy? Perhaps. But the disappointing end to Sallust's own ambitions seems to have driven him to reflect on the conditions that had produced the political turmoil in which it had occurred and to present the lessons that he drew to his countrymen, as Thucydides had once done for the Athenians. The glory that he failed to achieve in politics Sallust hoped to replace with the glory of writing profound works of history in a Thucydidean style that would make his countrymen see the errors of their ways and would also put Roman historiography stylistically on a level equal to that of the best Greek historian, Thucydides. To do that in an age without formal academic institutions, research fellowships, or royalty contracts required the wealth of a leisured aristocrat.

Sallust wrote three historical works: first, the *Bellum Catilinae* (*The War of Catiline*); second, the *Bellum Jugurthinum* (*The Jugurthine War*); and finally, the *Historiae* (*Histories*), whose five books covered events from 78 to 67 B.C. and may have been unfinished at his death. The first two works are extant, although only fragments of the *Histories* remain. Two letters addressed to Caesar are also attributed to Sallust, but their authenticity is often doubted for numerous reasons. They may well be later compositions produced in imitation of Sallust under the influence of the rhetorical training that dominated Roman education in the Imperial Age, as is the spurious *Invective Against Sallust* attributed to Cicero.

Caesar (100 to 44 B.C.)   Julius Caesar is usually remembered as a glorious conqueror and an assassinated ruler, but he was also an accomplished orator and consummate literary stylist. His success as a general and politician were based in no small part on both. They enabled him to win the loyalty and devotion of his troops, acquire votes, and overcome the arguments of his political foes. Caesar favored the straightforward, lightly adorned Attic style. He used neither the abrupt, sententious style of Sallust nor the highly colored, ornate writing that Cicero thought appropriate for history. Neither did Caesar concentrate on the personalities and moral characters of those who participated in events. He believed that chance was as big a factor in events as the characters of the participants, and he let actions speak for themselves without overt moralizing on his part.

By 50 B.C., Caesar had published the first seven books of *De Bello Gallico* (*On the Gallic War*). The eighth book was later written by his loyal legate Aulus Hirtius. *De Bello Civili* (*On the Civil War*), in three books, was probably written in late 48 or early 47 B.C. but was not published until after Caesar's death.

The purpose of *De Bello Gallico* has never been clear. It was once held that it was the military report of the democratic general to the people who had given him his command. Most scholars no longer share this opinion. If the commentaries have a motive other than military, it is not apology but more likely self-glorification.

On the Civil War was different in both tone and purpose. The consciousness of war guilt is evident, for civil war was the worst of crimes in Roman society. Therefore, he had to show that it had been waged only under extreme provocation. According to Caesar's account, a small group of ultrareactionaries had perversely driven him to defend his honor and dignity and the good name and best interests of the Roman People. The men are shown as cruel and vain, cowardly in battle and ignominious in defeat. They begged for mercy; he spared their lives. There are no outrageously false statements in the account, but the truth may be said to have been tested for elasticity.

Scholarship and Patriotic Antiquarianism   During the period of military despotism after Caesar, there were no great poets and orators, and Sallust was the only historian of note. On the whole, the writers who continued to produce large numbers of major works were not known so much for their literary qualities as for their scholarship and arcane antiquarian research. These scholars and antiquarians often exhibit a nostalgic longing for a glorious past and a desire to gain control over the present through science and philosophy.

Nigidius Figulus (ca. 100 to 45 B.C.) and Varro (116 to 27 B.C.) The many long works of Publius Nigidius Figulus, Cicero's friend and a staunch Republican, on grammar, natural history, and religion are lost. Marcus Terentius Varro has been somewhat more fortunate. He fought against Caesar at Pharsalus but was pardoned. Caesar admired his great learning in works on history, law, religion, philosophy, education, linguistics, biography, literary criticism, and agriculture, and entrusted him with creating Rome's first great library, which was never finished. Varro's greatest work was probably the *Antiquities Human and Divine,* which contained a vast array of knowledge as well as many errors. It was in this work that Varro fixed the canonical date for the founding of Rome by Romulus as April 21, 753 B.C. Of his numerous works the only ones to survive are his three valuable books on agriculture, six of his twenty-five books on the Latin language, and many fragments of his *Menippean Satires,* a medley of prose and verse on almost every subject under the sun.

Atticus (110 to 32 B.C.) and Nepos (ca. 100 to ca. 24 B.C.) Varro based part of his research in early Roman history on a chronology of Rome produced by his and Cicero's old friend T. Pomponius Atticus. This interest in history had prompted Cicero to request that Atticus write a history of his consulship and the suppression of Catiline, but Atticus politely declined. Cornelius Nepos, born about 100 B.C., was a friend of both Cicero and Atticus. He, too, wrote a Roman chronology, but his main contribution was the popularization at Rome of the Greek genre of biography. He had come to Rome from Cisalpine Gaul but never became involved in politics, so that he survived unmolested until his death around 24 B.C. Before 32 B.C. he published the first edition of his sixteen-volume *De Viris Illustribus (On Illustrious Men),* which contained short biographies of generals, statesmen, writers, and scholars, both Roman and non-Roman.

Twenty-five biographies survive. Their style is very easy to read and once made Nepos a favorite author to assign second-year Latin students. His multicultural emphasis on Persians, Carthaginians, and Greeks as well as Romans is designed to show the Romans that they had no monopoly on talent and virtue. Unfortunately, like most ancient biographers, he is interested more in drawing moral lessons than in historical accuracy. Therefore, he often omits valuable historical details and uncritically reproduces errors in his sources.

Politically, the last generation of the Roman Republic was a failure. Its members had not met the challenges produced by the acquisition of a vast empire and the great social and economic changes that had ensued. Culturally, however, they must be credited with great accomplishments. In art, architecture, rhetoric, literature, and scholarship, they were worthy successors to the Greeks of earlier generations. They had advanced the distinctive blending of Greek and native Italian traditions that was the hallmark of Roman culture to the point where the next generation could produce a new Golden Age, which would rival that of classical Greece and become the dominant cultural force in western Europe for centuries.

XXII

The Principate of Augustus, 29 B.C. to A.D. 14

Octavian's acquisition of undisputed mastery of the Roman world by 29 B.C. is a convenient point for beginning a new period in Roman history. The system of government characteristic of the Republic had now given way in reality to the rule of one man, who came to be known as *imperator* (emperor). Therefore, although the Republic had long ago acquired a vast empire, the establishment of a system of government controlled by an emperor marks the beginning of the Roman Empire.

The first 300 years of the Empire are usually dealt with under the subheading Principate, from the word *princeps,* one of the emperors' chief titles up to A.D. 282. The implication of this title was that the emperor, although the acknowledged head of state, was only *primus inter pares,* first among equals within the Roman nobility, and that he governed in cooperation with them. The period after 282, however, is often called the Dominate, because the emperors were undisguisedly autocratic, the title *princeps* was completely abandoned, and the title *dominus,* lord and master, prevailed.

Sources for the Augustan Principate

Most of the information for the political history of Augustus' rule comes from Suetonius' biography of Augustus, Books 52 to 56 of Dio's history, Book 2.86–123 of Velleius Paterculus' brief compendium, and Augustus' own *Res Gestae.* Unfortunately, Livy's eyewitness account down to A.D. 9, Books 134 to 142 of his history, receive the briefest summaries of all in the *Periochae,* and, therefore, their loss is even more acutely felt.

The literary works of the great authors of the Augustan Age (pp. 286–293) are rich sources for the social, economic, cultural, and intellectual life of the period, as are abundant archaeological remains and the numerous Latin and Greek inscriptions, documents on Egyptian papyri, and coins that have survived. Of great importance for provincial matters is a long Greek inscription from Cyrene, which contains four edicts of Augustus and a senatorial decree and is known as the *Edicts of Cyrene.*

The Triumphal Return to Rome, 29 B.C.

In the late summer of 29 B.C., Octavian returned to Rome in triumph. The senate ratified all his acts, proclaimed his birthday a future holiday, and decreed the erection of triumphal arches at Brundisium and at Rome. The poets hailed the mighty conqueror. On three successive days he held triumphs for Dalmatia, for Actium, and for Egypt, all surpassing in pomp and splendor the triumphs of Julius Caesar. For the first time since the end of the First Punic War in 241 B.C., the doors of the temple of Janus stood closed as the mute but visible sign of peace on land and sea. After a century of civil war and violence, men and women could at last breathe freely, work, and enjoy peace and prosperity without fear of confiscation, proscription, or violent death.

Problems to Be Faced Although peace reigned within the Empire, the frontiers would have to be protected to prevent the outsiders massed beyond the Rhine and the Danube from swarming into rich and peaceful provinces. Imperial defense eventually called for a firm policy of aggressive war, which will be discussed later (pp. 263–271). In the meantime, the Roman armies themselves were an even greater potential menace to internal peace and stability than any outsiders. Under the command of ambitious and ruthless generals, they could again turn and rend the state, as they had in the recent past. After Actium, Octavian had to figure out how to retain supreme command over Rome's legions and reduce their number from seventy to thirty, a number sufficient for defense without bankrupting the treasury. At the same time, he had to find land on which to settle the demobilized veterans without unpopular confiscations of private property or higher taxes. Furthermore, he needed to reconstruct the government to provide stable, centralized control over Rome and her empire without alienating the old governing class traditionally represented by the senate. Finally, he had to reassure the common people that he and his family were looking after their interests, too.

To carry out those difficult tasks might well have taxed the strength of a human dynamo. The sickly Octavian may have seemed doomed at the start. He compensated for his poor health, however, by the same willpower, ruthlessness, and political astuteness that he had demonstrated from the beginning of his arduous climb to power over the previous fifteen years.

He had returned from the East a popular idol, with a prestige and power such as even Caesar had never possessed. East and West were bound to him by oaths of allegiance. He had supreme command of the biggest and best army in Roman history, as well as access to the revenues and resources of a rich and mighty empire. The confiscated treasures of the Ptolemies might alone have sufficed to provide land and bonuses for his veterans, feed and amuse for a time the populace of Rome, and even revive the economic prosperity of Italy by permitting the removal of taxes and the initiation of a vast program of public works.

Octavian had, in addition to his financial resources, an *auctoritas,* a prestige and a dignity unique in Roman history. At first the "soul" of Julius Caesar, "cleansed" of earthly sin and "translated" into a comet, had been called upon to aid Octavian in his struggle for power. Such "divine" aid was now no longer needed, because Octavian, a war hero and popular idol, was also the unchallenged leader of a powerful personal faction and the acknowledged source of all patronage and power.

Even before he had returned from Egypt and the East, the senate and people had been outdoing themselves in voting Octavian special honors, privileges, and titles. He received such visible honors as triumphal arches, games, supplications, and statues. He also received important powers: the tribunician right to aid citizens, apparently not only within the first milestone of the city but also throughout the whole Empire; the right to hear judicial appeals; the power to grant pardons in criminal cases tried in popular courts; and the right to raise men to patrician status.

Special Titles Octavian's foremost title was *Caesar,* his adopted name. It continued to appear on his coins and became a title borne by all succeeding Roman emperors. In more recent centuries it was assumed by the kaiser of Germany and the czar (tsar) of Russia. He also adopted as a permanent *praenomen* the old temporary Republican title *imperator.* Troops had given it to their victorious commanders, who could use it until they had celebrated their triumphs. Octavian hoped that it would inspire the troops' loyalty. Although his immediate successors abandoned it, *imperator* became the standard title of all Roman rulers beginning with Vespasian (A.D. 69 to 79) and survives as the English word *emperor.* Finally, although he did not make it part of his official nomenclature, he emphasized the honorific title *princeps civitatis* ("first man of the state"), a term usually shortened to *princeps,* from which are derived *principate* and *prince.* It, too, had a respectable Republican past and had signified an ex-consul who had been recognized as a person of great prestige and venerability, *auctoritas.*

Creating the Principate Octavian was in a very difficult political and constitutional position in 29 B.C. He had allowed the legally constituted triumvirate to lapse on December 31, 33 B.C., in order to deny its powers to Antonius. During the next year, Octavian's position was purely personal. He justified his public acts by the oath of personal loyalty sworn by most of the inhabitants of Italy and many in the municipalities throughout the West. Such a purely personal position was dangerously unorthodox, however, and he sought a more legitimate stance by obtaining election to one of the consulships for 31. He continued to be reelected consul each year until 23. As consul, however, he initially claimed precedence over his colleagues on the basis of the earlier personal oath and was accompanied by all twenty-four lictors, as dictators had been before the abolition of that office by Antonius.

To counteract criticism, Octavian had promised to give up his extraordinary position and restore the normal operation of the Republican constitution when the war was over. In 29, it was time for Octavian to start making good on that promise, or at least appear to be doing so. If he did not, he could expect the same fate as Julius Caesar or at least some dangerous and difficult opposition. On the other hand, Octavian personally wished to retain the dominant position that he had just won and patriotically realized that if he did not, further destructive power struggles would probably result. Octavian's task, then, was to restore the old Republican constitution enough to satisfy many, high and low, who were deeply attached to it. At the same time, he had to avoid surrendering so much power that he would undermine his own

hard-won supremacy and risk the return of the instability that had characterized the previous century of the Republic.

It was a difficult and delicate balancing act that he had to perform on a very thin rope and without a safety net. He had good examples of what not to do: Sulla had been too reactionary and anachronistic in designing his constitution; Caesar had pursued one-man rule too obviously; Pompey and Antonius had never gained adequate trust from the nobility. His cautiousness, patience, determination, and shrewdness would be taxed to their fullest as he tried to work out an acceptable form of government over the next ten years.

Initial Reforms Octavian took the first visible step on the road to political reconstruction when he and Agrippa took office as consuls on January 1, 28 B.C. He surrendered twelve of his extraordinary twenty-four lictors and handed them over to Agrippa to indicate that equality had been restored to his consular colleague in accordance with normal Republican practice. The next step was to acquire a grant of censorial power for himself and Agrippa in order to register citizens and revise the roll of the senate. Revision of the senate was imperative if his claim to restoring constitutional normalcy was to have any credibility. The senate had been the centerpiece of the old constitution and the pride of the old nobility, whose good will and cooperation Octavian urgently needed.

To bolster respect for the senate, Octavian and Agrippa reduced its number from about 1,000 to 800 by purging many of the outsiders whom Caesar and the triumvirs had appointed in reward for political services during the civil wars. They did not purge anyone on the basis of Republicanism or lack of support in those wars. That would merely have aroused the hostility of those whom he wished to conciliate. With further reductions in 18 and 13 B.C., the senate ultimately returned to about 600, the number established by Sulla.

Octavian had assured that the number of senators would ultimately stabilize at 600 by reducing the number of quaestors to Sulla's 20. He also tried to ensure the prestige of new senators by restricting the quaestorship to men at least 25 years old, of senatorial family and good moral character, who had served in the military and possessed property worth at least 800,000 sesterces (later 1 million). Men of equestrian rank could also hold the quaestorship if they had held one or more of certain inferior magistracies. Octavian pleased traditionalists by cutting back the number of praetors from 16 to 10. Finally, he lowered the minimum ages for the praetorship and consulship to 32 and 35 respectively.

Octavian made admission into the equestrian order dependent, as before, upon a minimum property valuation of 400,000 sesterces. To invigorate both the equestrian and senatorial orders with new blood, Octavian adopted Caesar's policy of admitting a few rich and aristocratic residents from the Italian *municipia* and even from the Roman colonies of Gaul and Spain. Future emperors would continue that policy on a much more extensive scale.

The Settlement of 27 B.C. On January 13, 27 B.C., Octavian dramatically appeared before the purged and rejuvenated senate and offered to surrender all his powers to the senate and the Roman People. That solemn and dramatic act, seemingly portending the full restoration of the Republic, aroused, as he probably expected, more trepidation than joy. Overwhelmed by the noble gesture, the majority of the senators, probably inspired by his close friends, bestowed upon him new honors. To show his honored position in the reformed senate, he became *princeps senatus* (first man of the senate), an honor that censors had bestowed upon the most prestigious member of the senate in the days before Sulla. He also received a grant of proconsular *imperium* for ten years over the large and geographically separated single province of the two Spains, Gaul, Syria, and Egypt, where most of the legions were stationed. As did Pompey during the pirate war, Augustus had the right to appoint legates of consular and praetorian rank and to make war and peace as he saw fit.

In the new division of power, the senate resumed control over Rome and Italy and over the provinces of Sicily, Sardinia and Corsica, Il-lyricum, Macedonia, Greece, Asia, Bithynia, Crete-Cyrene, and Africa. Octavian was to govern the Imperial provinces through his own legates or deputies, whereas the senate controlled the senatorial provinces through proconsuls recruited from the ranks of ex-consuls and ex-praetors.[1] The *princeps,* who continued to be elected consul each year, probably maintained effective control over the governors of the senatorial provinces either through his *auctoritas* or the weight of his *imperium* as both consul and proconsul. He thus retained as much real power after his so-called restoration of the Republic as he had possessed before.

Three days after Octavian's "surrender" of power, the senate met to honor the restorer of the Republic. A laurel wreath was to be placed above the doorposts of his house, and a golden shield inscribed with his virtues of valor, clemency, justice, and piety was to be hung up in the senate. An even greater honor was the conferral upon him of the name *Augustus* (Revered), which had exalted connotations and religious associations.

Further Reforms The new Augustus, in turn, exalted the senate and augmented its powers. He restored its control over public finance and for a time at least, even the right, of coining money in gold and silver. Some time after 23 B.C., the senate became a supreme court to judge cases of extortion in the senatorial provinces and to hear appeals from Italy and the provinces. Although Augustus continued to recognize the popular assemblies as lawmaking bodies, he permitted the senate to issue decrees having the force of law without ratification by the people. Officially, the senate became a full partner in the government. Theoretically, it was even more: the ultimate source of power of the *princeps*. What it had granted it could also take away.

---

[1]The so-called senatorial provinces were, according to Dio (53.12.2 and 53.13.1), generally peaceful and, unlike the Imperial provinces, did not require a garrison of legionary troops. This distinction did not always hold, for the proconsuls of the senatorial provinces of Africa, Illyricum, and Macedonia had legionary troops under their command at various times during the early Principate.

Unanticipated Problems   Hoping that he had effectively solved the constitutional problems that he confronted, Augustus left Rome in late 27 to take control of urgent military operations in his provinces of Gaul and Spain. He was not to return for almost three years (see p. 268). During that time, however, it became increasingly clear that his constitutional sleight of hand had not been so effective as he had hoped. Many of the old nobles were not happy with it. In 26, for example, while he conducted wars in Spain, he had tried to retain control of events in Rome by reviving the ancient office of prefect of the city. His appointee was Marcus Valerius Messala Corvinus, a former partisan of Brutus and Cassius before he had switched to Antonius and finally Augustus. The office had its roots in the pre-Republican monarchy, however, and had fallen into disuse with the growth of the praetorship after 367 B.C. Messala held the office for only six days before he resigned it as being improper. (Eventually Augustus did succeed in reviving the office, but he abandoned it for now.) Obviously, the old Republicans were beginning to grumble.

The lavish honors that Augustus' friends continued to propose in the senate further aroused resentment among the old nobility. After Augustus returned from Spain because of poor health in late 24, they were even more offended when in early 23 he interfered in the treason trial of a senatorial governor and obtained his condemnation. Shortly thereafter, an assassination plot hatched by disgruntled nobles was discovered. It was quietly suppressed, but before Augustus could do anything to remedy the source of discontent, he fell gravely ill.

The Settlement of 23 B.C.   Upon his recovery, Augustus made further constitutional adjustments in order to preserve both himself and political stability. The major irritant to the old nobles was Augustus' continued tenure of the consulship. That was too reminiscent of Marius and Caesar, whose careers were not pleasing to traditionalists. Moreover, the consulship was the goal of every ambitious senator. By holding one of the consulships himself year after year, Augustus was reducing by half those available

to others. After consulting with members of the senate, Augustus resigned his consulship on July 1, 23 B.C. In return, he received (or possibly reemphasized) the full tribunician power, *tribunicia potestas.* He had enjoyed at least tribunician sacrosanctity since 36 and the right of aiding citizens, *auxilium,* since 30. In 30 he had been voted full tribunician power but either refused it or did not make use of it. Now he made it the official legal foundation of his position, and from this date he numbered the years of his principate by the number of years during which he had held the *tribunicia potestas* (abbreviated *T.P.* on his coins). "Constitutionally" Augustus could never actually hold the office of tribune, because he was a patrician by adoption into the patrician family of Julius Caesar.

The power of tribune gave Augustus many important rights and privileges: He could convene meetings of the senate; present legislation for approval by the tribal assembly; and submit motions in writing to the senate, which took precedence over all other business. Nevertheless, he needed more powers to make up for the loss of the consulship. Although no longer consul, Augustus was allowed to retain the consular right to nominate candidates for office. Of course, he had the same prerogative as any high-ranking individual to endorse candidates after their candidacies had been accepted. Once elected, however, all incoming magistrates were required to swear that they would uphold all past and future public acts of Augustus. Also, he received the right to nominate jurors to the various standing courts, which gave him additional control over the administration of justice. Finally, to make up for his loss of the consulship, his proconsular *imperium* was strengthened. He was allowed to retain it in the city, and it was made *maius* (greater) so that he could still override other provincial governors and exercise command over all legions if need be. This *imperium* was renewed at intervals of five or ten years in 18, 13, and 8 B.C. and A.D. 3 and 13.

Other adjustments were also made in 23 B.C. Augustus increased the number of praetors from ten to twelve, the two new ones being placed in charge of the city's treasury. To provide two additional governorships for the increased number of ex-praetors that would result, he transferred to the senate control of *Gallia Narbonensis* (Provence) and Cyprus. (Provinces annexed after 23 needed garrisons and were kept by him.) If not in 23, then sometime later, the senate acquired the right to try fellow senators accused of political or criminal offenses. Suits brought against senatorial governors by provincials simply for the restitution of allegedly misappropriated property were allowed to be tried by a small *ad hoc* committee of fellow senators. The ghost of Sulla would have been pleased!

Acquisition of Further Powers Although traditionalist nobles might have approved of the changes made in 23, the populace of Rome did not. In 22 a combination of flood and famine made life very difficult for ordinary citizens. They were not impressed by how the senate handled matters and riotously demanded that Augustus be given a perpetual consulship or dictatorship and that he take up the censorship and curatorship of the grain supply, *cura annonae.* He refused the consulship, dictatorship, and censorship, but with his vast resources, he was able to alleviate the grain shortage within a few days. Also in 22, because it was less dignified for the senate to be summoned by a person with only tribunician power, Augustus accepted the consular right to summon the senate.

In the spring of 22, Augustus departed to take care of affairs in the provinces, and the senate was left to handle affairs without him. Later that year, the people refused to elect more than one consul, and he had to intervene. He refused to accept the other consulship but persuaded the people to accept his own personal nominee, a noble with good Republican credentials. Much the same also happened in 21, 20, and 19. Also in 19, candidates whom Augustus rejected for the quaestorship refused to withdraw. Worse still, Egnatius Rufus, who had become very popular by organizing a fire department for Rome at his own expense and sponsoring splendid games as aedile, illegally ran for the consulship right after his praetorship. A majority of senators passed the *Senatus*

Consultum Ultimum and begged Augustus to return and restore order.

The Settlement of 19 B.C. Augustus' return on October 12, 19 B.C., was declared a national holiday. He was voted further consular powers: perhaps the right to appoint a prefect of the city in his absence; the use of twelve *fasces;* and the right to sit on a curule chair between the two annual consuls. It must have become clear to Augustus and many traditionalist nobles as well that he had given up too much in 23. Now he had regained everything of importance that he had lost in giving up the consulship. Although he still did not have the title of consul, he was in effect a permanent third consul. The nobles could now happily vie for the two annual consulships, and the common people could be reassured that their hero was in control when they saw him acting with the powers of a consul and being treated like one.

Minor Alterations after 19 B.C. The settlement of 19 B.C. was the last major series of constitutional adjustments and changes in Augustus' power. Occasional alterations were made over the years, however. In 15 B.C., he acquired the sole right to coin gold and silver. In 12 B.C., after his old triumviral partner Lepidus died, Augustus was elected *Pontifex Maximus* in his place. That office gave him great prestige as head of the state religion, and it was kept by all subsequent Roman emperors, even Christian ones, until Gratian (ca. A.D. 375). Further prestige accrued to Augustus in 2 B.C., when the senate voted him the title *pater patriae,* father of his country, an honor formerly voted Cicero after the suppression of Catilinarian conspiracy.

After 18 B.C., therefore, the form of the Augustan principate was fairly well fixed and the stability of the state seemed secure. Augustus himself was confident enough to celebrate the beginning of a new era with the holding of the Secular Games of 17 B.C. Like many ancient peoples, the Romans believed that the history of the world moved in a cycle of epochs (*saecula*: hence the word *secular*). Each *saeculum* was often calculated at 100 or 110 years, and the tenth *saeculum* of the cycle was thought to in-augurate a new Golden Age. With a little prompting from Augustus, who was a member, the board of priests in charge of the *Sibylline Books* indicated that the tenth era of the current cycle was about to begin in 17 B.C. The celebration of magnificent festival games in honor of the event would give Augustus the perfect opportunity to advertise the end of the evil period of political chaos and civil war and the dawn of an era of peace and prosperity under his newly "restored" Republic. The message was clear: The wounds of civil war had now been healed, and health had returned to the body politic. No more fitting symbol of that idea can be found than the fact that the most important religious element of the whole celebration, a joyous hymn to Apollo, was composed by Horace, a man who had once fought against Augustus at Philippi.

The Nature of the Principate With the principate, Augustus had created a stable form of government that enabled the Roman Empire to enjoy a remarkable degree of peace and prosperity for two centuries. Generations of historians, therefore, have sought to determine what kind of government it was. Augustus himself tried to convince people that the old system of the Republic had been restored. Superficially it had. The senate, the magistrates, and the Roman People continued to perform many of their old functions in the familiar way. Augustus' many offices and powers almost invariably had precedents in the Republic. Nevertheless, it was the simultaneous and continuous possession of them that gave him more power than anyone in the Republic (except perhaps dictators) had ever held.

Given Augustus' great personal and constitutional power, the respect that he always showed the senate as an institution, and his eager solicitation of its cooperation in running the Empire, many have characterized Augustus' constitutional settlement as a dyarchy, an equal rule between *princeps* and senate. That, too, is wide of the mark. No matter how much Augustus tried to disguise it or others were willing to overlook it, Augustus was the dominant force

at Rome. Cassius Dio, a Greek from the eastern provinces who wrote a comprehensive history of Rome from the beginning to his own time under Septimius Severus and who was much less squeamish about monarchy than a native Roman, said simply that the Augustan principate was a monarchy.

That judgment is closer to the truth but not wholly satisfactory. It needs refinement and qualification. Augustus' position certainly was monarchic, but it was not like that of the Persian, Hellenistic, or Parthian kings, who provided the standard models of monarchy in both Augustus' and Dio's day. Augustus and his successors did not hold their positions by right of dynastic succession, although in practice dynastic considerations were important, and their powers were not based on any absolute sovereignty of the ruler. Their powers were based on laws and decrees passed by the traditional sources of legitimate authority at Rome—the senate and the people. Gradually, as the traditions of the Republic faded further and further into the past, the force of these restraints weakened. Given the emperor's overwhelming constitutional powers, financial resources, and raw military force, the later emperors became absolute monarchs in every way.

In the first two centuries A.D., however, the principate of Augustus and his successors was more like an elective, constitutional monarchy. Their powers were bestowed and limited by laws not of their own making. The choice of a successor to the previous emperor had to be ratified by the senate, and his powers were voted anew. The senators could be compelled to give their votes by the threat of military force, but that shows that their votes still meant something. Moreover, if an emperor acted like an arbitrary despot, the traditions of the Republic were still strong enough to foster dangerous conspiracies against him and might even result in his condemnation as a public enemy by a vote of the senate, as happened in the case of Nero (p. 317). Sovereignty still lay in the hands of another constitutional body.

In the last analysis, of course, the constitutional settlement created by Augustus was uniquely itself. The man who had clawed his way to the top as a ruthless opportunist in civil war had created an enduring monument of statesmanship. He had performed a delicate constitutional balancing act with consummate patience and skill as he bent and shifted to counteract the conflicting forces that would have toppled others from the tightrope of power. He created a veiled monarchy that was strong enough to ensure his own power and the stability of the state, while it preserved enough characteristics of the free Republic to satisfy many Romans' deep respect for the traditional constitutional forms and institutions that had been the focal point of their public lives for centuries. If politics is the art of the possible, then Augustus became one of its greatest masters.

The Problem of Succession One problem gave Augustus more difficulty than all the rest. The political crisis of 23 B.C. and his almost fatal illness drove him to concentrate attention upon the urgent problem of the succession. Legally and constitutionally, the choice of a successor was not his right, but that of the senate and the Roman People, to whom he owed his power. Nevertheless, he feared that his failure to deal with the problem might bring about a civil war between rival candidates for the throne after his death. Also, he naturally hoped to find a successor in his own family and of his own blood. Unfortunately, he had no sons and only one daughter, Julia, who had been married in 25 B.C. to his eighteen-year-old nephew M. Claudius Marcellus, Octavia's son by her first husband. Augustus assiduously promoted the political advancement of his son-in-law so that he would have accumulated the experience and prestige that would make him the natural one to succeed to the principate.

Unfortunately, Marcellus was not old enough to assume the principate when Augustus fell gravely ill in 23 B.C. Therefore, the *princeps* gave his signet ring to Agrippa, his loyal aide and most successful general, to indicate that he should carry on in his place. When Augustus recovered, he restored Marcellus to first place in the line of succession and compensated Agrippa with a command over the Imperial

provinces and the task of strengthening the East against Parthia.

Marcellus' sudden death in 23 just after Agrippa's departure fueled speculation both ancient and modern that Agrippa and/or Livia had a hand in it to benefit Agrippa or her sons. That seems merely to reflect malicious gossip aimed at discrediting later emperors descended from them. Augustus certainly did not suspect them.

In 21 B.C., he sent for Agrippa and prevailed upon him to divorce his wife and marry Julia. In 18 B.C., he obtained the extension of Agrippa's *imperium* over the senatorial provinces as well and even had the tribunician power conferred upon him for five years. Agrippa, always the faithful deputy, was now son-in-law, coregent, and heir presumptive to the Augustan throne. Nor was that all. In 17 the *princeps* adopted, under the names of Gaius and Lucius Caesar, the two young sons of Julia and Agrippa to settle the problem of succession not just for one but for two generations to come.

When Agrippa's heart failed in 12 B.C., however, Lucius and Gaius were still too young, and Augustus turned to Livia's older son, Tiberius. Tiberius had served Augustus well on numerous military assignments and had held the consulship in 13 B.C. He seems to have been comfortable as a loyal subordinate. He might have happily accepted a secondary role as regent for Gaius and Lucius if Augustus had not made him divorce his beloved Vipsania, Agrippa's daughter by his first wife, and marry Julia, the young widow of Marcellus and Agrippa. It was not long before Tiberius and his new wife became estranged. Julia, pushed about as a political pawn from one husband to another, soon turned for comfort to more congenial lovers.

Augustus came to rely more and more on Tiberius when the latter's popular and talented younger brother, Drusus I, died in 8 B.C. after falling from his horse on campaign in Germany. Tiberius, however, was enraged at Julia's behavior, and once Lucius and Gaius seemed old enough he badgered Augustus to let him retire, bitter and morose, to Rhodes. That Tiberius seems to have broken under the strains placed upon him may confirm Augustus' judgment that he was not really the best man to bear the great burdens of the principate.

Augustus, himself grown disturbed by Julia's flagrant adulteries, had her exiled to a desert island in 2 B.C. He executed some of her paramours (who were guilty more of conspiracy against the regime than of vice) and banished others. Even Tiberius interceded on Julia's behalf, but unsuccessfully. The *princeps* would not relent except to permit her to move to Rhegium, where she eventually died (p. 298). One of her daughters by Agrippa, Julia the Younger, suffered banishment in A.D. 8 for similar reasons.

Fate always seemed to intervene on behalf of Tiberius' succession. In A.D. 2, Augustus reluctantly let Tiberius return after the attractions of Rhodes had worn off. Unfortunately, Lucius Caesar died on the way to Spain a little later that year, and Gaius Caesar died from a wound in Armenia two years later. In grief and frustration, Augustus adopted Tiberius as his son in A.D. 4 and obtained a ten-year grant of the tribunician power for him as well as a grant of *imperium* in the provinces. Over the years, Tiberius clearly acquired the position of a coregent as Augustus became older and more frail. In A.D. 13, when Tiberius' tribunician power was renewed along with another grant of *imperium*

for both him and Augustus, there was no question that he was Augustus' equal partner. When Augustus died a year later, Tiberius was already in place, and the smooth succession for which Augustus had laboriously planned automatically took place.

In his attempt to secure the eventual succession of a member of his own family, the Julii, Augustus had complicated things for the future. At the same time that he had adopted Tiberius, he had adopted Agrippa's surviving son by Julia, Agrippa Postumus. He had also required Tiberius to adopt Germanicus, son of Tiberius' own dead brother, Drusus I. Germanicus' mother, Antonia, had the blood of Augustus' family because she was a daughter of Augustus' sister, Octavia, by Marcus Antonius. The tie was further strengthened by having Germanicus marry Agrippina, another daughter of Julia and Agrippa. Tiberius' own son, Drusus II, who was not a blood relative to Augustus, was relegated to an inferior position because he was only a Claudian. Those attempts to manipulate the succession in favor of Augustus' own Julian side of the imperial family created unfortunate tensions and rivalries in later generations of his Julio-Claudian dynasty. Before he died, however, there were many other important ways in which Augustus had helped to shape the history of the Roman Empire.

XXIII

Systematic Reform under Augustus

Aside from the difficult task of creating an acceptable constitutional solution to Rome's political crisis and providing a successor to himself, Augustus also had to work out an effective and efficient system of administration for the city of Rome and its vast empire, whose population has been estimated at between 50 million and 70 million. Under the Republic, both the city and the provinces had been administered rather haphazardly by the yearly magistrates and provincial promagistrates on short-term assignments. Theoretically, the whole senate, with its collective wisdom, was supposed to offer sound guidance and provide coherence. With the growing complexity of affairs, however, the senate did not have the time to give adequate attention to many problems. Senators often had not gained any more direct familiarity with problems during their short tenure of various offices and posts than those whom they were supposed to advise. Finally, communications to the provinces were slow, so that governors were often left to face crises on their own. In the past, this situation had helped to create emergencies that ambitious men could exploit for their own aggrandizement. Also, the Republican practice of not paying high officials any salary greatly increased the temptation to engage in graft and corruption, which contributed to provincial unrest. Therefore, Augustus was anxious to institute administrative reforms.

The Creation of a Central Administration Augustus did not so much replace the nonprofessionalized administrative system of the Republic's empire as systematize and centralize it under his personal control. Although he systematized career paths and salaries for those who held important administrative posts, the extent to which the system was bureaucratized was minimal. The people who held the most important posts were not trained, professional experts who devoted the majority of their working lives to their duties. They were still basically gentlemen who enhanced their social standing through conspicuous public service. They obtained their posts by patronage from the emperor, who evaluated them not on the basis of professional qualifications but of loyalty, character, and judgment. They were responsible directly to him and not some bureaucratic chain of command.

Senators in Imperial Administration Augustus placed senators in many posts that bestowed great honor on their holders. Between 27 and 18 B.C., he had secured the appointment of a senatorial committee to assist him in preparing the agenda for meetings of the senate. This committee, often called the *Concilium Principis* (Council of the *Princeps*), consisting of the consuls, one representative from each of the other magistracies, and fifteen senators selected by lot, was to change every six months.

255

As reorganized in A.D. 13 and reinforced by members of the Imperial family and from the equestrian order, the committee began to assume functions formerly belonging to the senate. Even as reorganized, it was not a true cabinet or privy council. Meeting more or less publicly, it was an administrative, not a policy-making, body.

The real predecessor of the later Imperial privy council was not this clumsy, rotating committee of the senate, which was abandoned by Augustus' successor, but small coteries of top-flight administrators, close friends of Augustus, high-ranking senators, legal experts, and other specialists, who met informally and behind closed doors. They decided many questions: the policy of the government; the legislation to be presented before meetings of the senate and the popular assemblies; the candidates whom it might please Augustus to recommend at the coming elections; the next governor of such and such a province; and all matters pertaining to public finance, foreign affairs, law, religion, and the administration of the Empire.

Augustus reserved many of the most prestigious provinces like Asia and Africa for senatorial governors. The prefect of the city (*praefectus urbi*), who had under his command the first police force in Rome's history, the three urban cohorts of 1,000 to 1,500 men each, was at first always a senator of consular rank (p. 260), as were the men in charge of the grain supply (until A.D. 6: p. 261), water supply, and flood control at Rome.

Equestrians in Imperial Administration

Although Augustus, especially in the early years of his principate, conferred upon senators positions of dignity and prominence, he drew many of his top-ranking administrators from the equestrian class. The *equites* had acquired valuable experience, especially in the fields of finance, taxation, and commerce, of which senators had little knowledge.

Now somewhat restricted as tax gatherers by the reforms of Caesar and Augustus, they were glad of the opportunity for other, more prestigious service. Augustus, in turn, welcomed their services. He regarded them as more reliable and less politically dangerous than senators because they were more dependent upon him for patronage and future advancement. Eventually, faithful service could advance an *eques* to membership in the senate where, as a *novus homo* obligated to Augustus, he helped keep that vital body loyal to him.

The careers open to equestrians were military, judicial, financial, and administrative. A young *eques* usually began his career as a prefect of an auxiliary cavalry squadron, advanced to tribune of a cohort or legion, then to prefect of a cohort. A prefect of the engineers (*praefectus fabrum*) could also look forward to a future of some importance.

Military service often varied in length. *Equites,* such as the historian Velleius Paterculus, usually served eight years. Others served longer. Some even chose the military life as a career: *Equites* frequently commanded legions on garrison duty, particularly in Egypt, a land forbidden to senators. After a year or two in the regular army, some *equites* served as attorneys in the civil administration; others as officers with the Praetorian Guard (the emperors' personal guard—preserver of law and order in Rome and Italy), the *cohortes urbanae* (the urban police), or the *vigiles* (fire department); or, more frequently still, as procurators, or Imperial agents in the provinces.

In the Imperial provinces, a procurator was the emperor's financial agent, tax collector, and paymaster; in the senatorial provinces, his financial agent, manager of his private estates, and collector of the revenues therefrom. Procurators also served as the eyes of the emperor. A procurator was often more powerful even than a governor of consular senatorial rank. A corrupt and rapacious governor had to be exceedingly wary of a procurator's reports, lest he be liable to stern retribution at the end of his term.

As prefects, *equites* might also govern provinces, especially the more backward and turbulent ones, such as Raetia and Noricum north and east of the Alps, not to speak of Egypt, the richest and most important of all, the eminence and power of whose prefect even the proudest senatorial governor might envy.

Second in power to the prefect of Egypt were the two prefects (also of equestrian rank) to whom Augustus had given joint command over the nine cohorts of the Praetorian Guard in 2 B.C. Under Tiberius, the joint praetorian prefecture was eliminated in favor of a single praetorian prefect. Under later emperors, the praetorian prefect became chief of staff of all armies, head of the bureaucracy, the highest judge of appeals in the Empire, eventually the maker and unmaker of emperors, and on occasion ascended the throne himself.

Two other prefectures, created around A.D. 6, were less important but often served as stepping-stones to higher office. One belonged to the commissioner of the grain administration (*praefectus annonae*); the other to the prefect of the *vigiles* (*praefectus vigilum*), a corps of 7 cohorts, each consisting of 1,000 former slaves, who patrolled the streets at night and guarded the city against riot or fire (p. 260).

Slaves and Freedmen in Imperial Administration The people who most resembled trained professionals were the countless slaves and freedmen whom an emperor employed in carrying out the routine daily tasks that constituted the real work of keeping Rome and the Empire running. They were essential to such vital operations as the grain supply (*cura annonae*), the grain dole (*frumentatio*), the water supply (*cura aquae*), control of the Tiber's floods (*cura riparum et alvei Tiberis*), the mint (*moneta*), and the Military Treasury (*aerarium militare*). They became the nucleus of the great body of Imperial slave administrators and functionaries known as the *familia Caesaris* (the emperor's household). Basically, Augustus was using his slave household and freedmen to run the Roman Empire the way in which a great Roman senator or large landowner ran his far-flung estates and business interests.

Although slaves performed the more menial and obscure jobs, the higher, salaried positions that required managerial talent and judgment went to the emperor's trusted freedmen. Many of them were shrewd and skillful ministers who held positions equivalent to those secretaryships in a modern government such as

state, treasury, defense, war, and transportation. Acting as the emperor's agents, they soon came to exercise great influence over financial affairs: how much the emperor should spend on armaments, public works, games, and spectacles; the weight, fineness, and numbers of gold or silver coins; the taxes or tribute that provinces must pay; the salaries that governors, prefects, procurators, and other appointed officials should receive. Finally, certain freedmen in high positions began to receive petitions and requests from every part of the Empire. The option of ignoring such petitions or bringing them to the emperor's notice gave these freedmen officers positions of real patronage and power.

The Manipulation of the Popular Assemblies

In directing the administration of Rome and the Empire, it was important for Augustus to influence the popular assemblies in their electoral and legislative functions. As did any prominent man, he had the right to canvass voters on behalf of candidates whom he favored. Through his consular *imperium* he shared with the consuls the right to accept or reject men who wished to be candidates. These two rights, *commendatio* and *nominatio*, in combination with his great personal popularity and *auctoritas* gave a major advantage to people whom he preferred.

Still, Augustus did not always get his way by these means, and he was reluctant to interfere too much in consular elections lest he offend the nobles, who continued to dominate the consulship for a number of years and often employed bribery and violence to do so. In A.D. 5, therefore, he induced the consuls to propose the *lex Valeria Cornelia,* which altered the procedure for voting in the Centuriate Assembly. It established in honor of the dead Gaius and Lucius Caesar 10 centuries comprised of the 600 senators and the 3,000 *equites* enrolled as jurors. They were to vote first and indicate their preference for two consular candidates and twelve praetorian. The remaining centuries would then usually follow their lead in the rest of the voting. From that time on, the majority of *equites* in these 10 centuries usually secured the election of "new men," who were much to Augustus' liking.

The common people were pleased with Augustus' attempts to influence the outcome of elections. They wanted him to have loyal magistrates and demanded to know whom he preferred. In A.D. 8, when he was no longer strong enough to canvass for candidates in person, he began to post lists of those candidates whom he commended to the voters.

Augustus' power to influence legislation was also great. By virtue of his *tribunicia potestas* or consular *imperium,* he could submit bills directly. Usually, however, he preferred to have friendly magistrates submit desired bills, as in the case of the *lex Valeria Cornelia* above.

The Administration of Justice Augustus introduced a number of changes to improve the administration of justice and make it more efficient through a series of laws in 18 and 17 B.C. First he established two new standing criminal courts (*quaestiones perpetuae*) for the crimes of adultery, *de adulteriis,* and the hoarding of or speculating in grain, *de annona.* He also increased the representation of *equites* on the jury panels and lowered the age requirement from 30 to 25 in order to increase the pool of jurors for the expanded court system. Several other laws, probably in 8 B.C., further classified the jurisdictions of the various courts so that a comprehensive system embracing all common varieties of crimes was now in place.

In the realm of civil procedure, Augustus seems to have abolished the old *legis actiones* (p. 143) for all practical purposes in 17 B.C. That avoided duplication with the more popular formulary procedure and avoided the possibility that a party who was dissatisfied with a verdict under the formulary procedure would bring suit again under a *legis actio.* More important, however, was Augustus' adoption of a streamlined procedure known as *cognitio extraordinaria* that Republican provincial governors had sometimes used for both civil and criminal proceedings in the provinces. This *cognitio* procedure was constitutionally rooted in the judicial

power inherent in his magisterial *imperium,* which he could delegate to his legates.

Under the *cognitio extraordinaria* there was no two-stage process. The emperor or his appointee each determined the suitability of the case and judged it in a single process. Another advance over the formulary procedure was that under *cognitio* the judge could compel a defendant to answer a summons and could find him guilty by default if he failed to appear. Moreover, the judge did not have to wait for a complaint to be lodged by someone else but could launch an investigation of his own. Because lower judges were merely subordinates of a higher authority, defendants who were citizens had the right of appeal all the way to the emperor. In cases involving important people like senators, the emperor could appoint a tribunal such as the senate to avoid the onus of making a difficult judgment alone. The *cognitio* procedure gradually replaced both the *quaestiones perpetuae* in criminal cases and the formulary procedure in civil cases over the course of the next 200 years.

Military Reforms The armed forces presented Augustus with an even more serious problem than administrative reform. In 27 B.C., to prevent the rise of powerful military commanders who could have undermined his own power and the peace that he earnestly wished to give Rome, Augustus obtained for himself the provinces containing the most legions. He placed them under the immediate command of his own loyal equestrian legates. Moreover, all soldiers were required to take an oath of personal allegiance to Augustus.

Reduced Size of Army Augustus' first step in dealing with military problems, however, had been to reduce the sheer number of men under arms and provide them with their expected grants of land. Both of these steps were necessary to reduce the risk of civil disorder from unoccupied and disgruntled soldiers and to reduce the crushing economic burden that the huge armies of the civil war placed upon the exhausted treasury. After Actium, Augustus had demobilized about 300,000 men and cut the number of legions from over 60 to perhaps 28 (about 160,000 men).

He avoided the harsh confiscations that had accompanied his settlement of discharged veterans in 41 B.C. and established new colonies in Italy and throughout the Empire to provide land for his veterans, who also helped to increase the security and Romanization of the surrounding areas. The vast wealth of Egypt gave Augustus the funds necessary to carry out this colonization scheme without increasing taxes or denying compensation to those whose land was used for colonial settlements.

A Retirement System Eventually, however, it became impractical to give all veterans land upon discharge. To have done so on a regular basis would have required a costly administrative system, and good land would have become prohibitively expensive as peace and stability encouraged the growth of population. Outright confiscation would have revived rural unrest, and distributing cheap waste or marginal land would have left a dangerous number of disgruntled veterans.

Therefore, beginning in A.D. 13, Augustus began to reward many veterans with a system of monetary payments to provide them with financial security upon discharge. Praetorian guardsmen received grants of 5,000 *denarii* and ordinary soldiers 3,000, the equivalent of almost 14 years' pay. That is far more money than the average person could have saved in a lifetime. Moreover, soldiers were encouraged and later required to save some of their pay in a fund kept at legionary headquarters. If spent wisely, their savings and discharge bonuses alone, on the average, would have supplied the daily needs of veterans for as long as they might expect to live after retiring at 35 or 40 years of age. On the other hand, a retired veteran could invest his money in a small farm or open up a small shop to support himself in retirement. A higher-paid centurion might even have enough from his bonus and savings to acquire equestrian status and pursue a career in higher offices

after retirement. The auxiliary troops, however, did not fare as well. Because their bonus, if any, was small, their greatest reward was the diploma of citizenship.

During the years from 7 to 2 B.C., Augustus paid discharged veterans no less than 400 million sesterces from his own funds. Even his resources could not stand that kind of expense forever. Therefore, in A.D. 6 he shifted the burden to the state by setting up a special fund (*aerarium militare*) to which he contributed 170 million sesterces of his own money for a start and funded it for the future with the revenues from certain taxes (p. 261), as well as the gifts and legacies received from his subjects and clients.

Professionalization Augustus created a permanent professional army commanded by men loyal to him and to Rome. Terms of service and rates of pay were regulated. Regular soldiers received 225 *denarii* a year and, at first, were required to serve 16 years. To relieve the strain on manpower and reduce the drain on retirement funds, however, the term was raised to 20 years, though, in practice, men might have to wait even longer before receiving their discharges.

The backbone of the army was the corps of professional officers comprised of the centurions. Under the Principate, they were the lowest commissioned officers and commanded the individual cohorts of the legions. They were often promoted from the ranks of the noncommissioned officers and received triple pay and bonuses. The ranks from military tribune on up, however, were held by equestrians and younger members of the senatorial class in preparation for higher civilian careers. The highest officers were usually members of Augustus' family or were nobles of proven loyalty.

The individual legions were made permanent bodies with special numbers and titles. Through the use of identifying symbols for each legion, a soldier was encouraged to develop a strong loyalty to his unit and strive to enhance its reputation. Each legion tended to be stationed permanently in some sector of the frontier, and around legionary camps many of the important cities of later Europe grew up.

Legionary soldiers were recruited primarily from Roman citizens in Italy and heavily Romanized areas such as Spain and southern Gaul, although freshly enfranchised natives were also used in the East. Each Roman legion was accompanied by an equal number of auxiliary forces, particularly cavalry, from warlike peoples in the less developed parts of the Empire and from allied peoples, who often supplied whole units along with their native officers. Regular pay for auxiliaries was only seventy-five *denarii* a year, and their term of service was twenty-five years.

The combined total of legionary and auxiliary forces under Augustus was between 250,000 and 300,000 men, not too large an army for defending a frontier at least 4,000 miles long. Of the 28 legions, at least 8 guarded the Rhineland and 7 the Danubian region. Three legions were in Spain, 4 in Syria, 2 in Egypt, 1 in Macedonia, and 1 in Africa. The equivalent of 2 others were scattered in cohorts in Asia Minor, Judea, and Gaul.

The Praetorian Guard   In Italy itself, however, Augustus stationed the nine cohorts of the Praetorian Guard. They were specially recruited Roman citizens and were called the Praetorian Guard after the bodyguard of Republican generals. Each cohort probably contained 500 (later 1,000) men. Three were stationed near Rome and six others in outlying Italian towns. As privileged troops, the praetorians served for only 16 years and received 375 *denarii* a year, with 5,000 upon discharge. Many praetorians were promoted to legionary centurions.

The Imperial Roman Navy   The war with Sextus Pompey and the battle of Actium clearly demonstrated the need for a permanent Roman navy. To suppress piracy, defend the shores of Italy, and escort grain transports and trading ships, Augustus created two main fleets, one based at Misenum on the Bay of Naples, the other at Ravenna on the Adriatic. He had other fleets also, especially at Alexandria and, for a time, at Forum Julii (Fréjus) in southern Gaul. The sailors were largely provincials from the Dalmatian coast but included some slaves and freedmen. They served under the command of prefects who were sometimes equestrians but more often freedmen. Auxiliary river flotillas patrolled the Rhine, the Danube, the French rivers, and the Nile.

Vigiles *and* Cohortes Urbanae   The *vigiles* and *cohortes urbanae,* whose duties were to fight fires and maintain public order in Rome, were organized along military lines but were not considered as part of the military. The *vigiles* consisted of 7 cohorts of 1,000 men apiece, and each was in charge of 2 of the 14 regions into which Augustus divided Rome. There were 3 urban cohorts of 1,000 to 1,500 men each. The *vigiles* were recruited from freedmen and were commanded by an equestrian prefect of the watch (*praefectus vigilum*). The *cohortes urbanae* were freeborn citizens commanded by the city prefect (*praefectus urbi*), a senator of consular rank.

Protection of the Emperor   The Praetorian Guard, the *vigiles,* and the urban cohorts not only preserved law and order in Rome and Italy but also were effective means of preventing or suppressing secret plots and rebellions against Augustus. Accompanying the establishment of these protections was Augustus' use of the Law of Treason (*maiestas,* p. 163). It was vague, flexible, and sweeping, comprehending all offenses from conspiracy against the state to insult or even disrespect to the emperor in speech, writing, or deed. Informers, *delatores,* who brought such acts to light received one fourth of their victims' property. In light of Caesar's assassination, conspiracies, such as that uncovered in 23 B.C., and the numerous civil wars of the previous century, Augustus was understandably anxious about plots against himself and the state. He was sensible and restrained in applying the law of *maiestas,* but in the hands of less secure, intelligent, and mentally stable emperors, the law and *delatores* were to become instruments of tyranny and repression.

Fiscal Reforms   Before the principate of Augustus, the civil wars of the late Republic had depleted the funds of the old senate-controlled state treasury, the *aerarium Saturni,* and exhausted its revenues. The old system of tax collection, corrupt and inefficient at best, had completely broken down, and the absence of any formal budget, regular estimate of tax receipts and expenditures, or census of taxable property made an already bad situation worse.

Upon that depleted and exhausted treasury fell burdens both numerous and heavy under Augustus: funds for the grain administration that furnished free grain to 200,000 citizen families in Rome; money for public games and religious festivals; funds for the construction and repair of roads and streets; money for maintenance of the water supply, the sewers, and the police and fire departments of the capital. Providing these services required enormous sums of money. In addition, the ever-mounting costs of Imperial defense, administration, and the provision of pensions for veterans rendered a reform of the fiscal system absolutely imperative.

Despite the urgent need for action, Augustus at first moved slowly and circumspectly, wishing to avoid in every way the suspicion of ruthlessly trampling upon the ancient prerogatives of the senate. In 28 B.C., he requested a transfer of control over the state treasury from inexperienced quaestors to ex-praetors selected by the senate. Their duties were given to two additional annual praetors after 23 B.C. Because Augustus' greater income enabled him to subsidize the state treasury, he soon acquired virtual control over all the finances of the state.

He was content with informal control, however. After 27 B.C., he set up for each Imperial province a separate account or chest called a *fiscus* (literally "fig basket"), into which he deposited the tax receipts and revenues of the province for payment to the legions. The *fisci* not only helped him, as sole paymaster, to assume complete mastery of the armies but also enabled him to take control over the administration of the Empire. Years later, Claudius united the several *fisci* into a single, central *fiscus,* which then became in fact and in law the main treasury of the Roman Empire and was

administered separately from both the *aerarium Saturni* and the *aerarium militare.* Augustus had also continued the Republic's practice of maintaining a special sacred treasury, the *aerarium sanctius,* to provide financial reserves for military emergencies.

Augustus had still another fund, the *patrimonium Caesaris,* of fabulous size, though not strictly a treasury. It consisted of Julius Caesar's private fortune, the confiscated properties of Antonius, the vast treasures of Cleopatra, the revenues from Augustus' private domains in the provinces, and the numerous legacies left him by wealthy Romans. (The legacies alone amounted to the huge sum of 1.4 billion sesterces.) The public treasuries and his enormous personal funds gave Augustus financial control over the entire administration of the Empire.

Taxation   To fund the *aerarium militare,* Augustus instituted two new taxes on Roman citizens: a 5 percent tax on inheritances and a 1 percent tax on sales at auction. He also levied a 20 percent tax on imports from outside the Empire and customs dues of 2 to 2-1/2 percent on the shipment of goods from one province to another. They were collected by tax contractors who paid the *aerarium Saturni* before collecting the taxes themselves. Augustus replaced the old provincial taxes of *stipendium* and tithe with a poll tax called the *tributum capitis* (collected from all adults in some provinces and just adult males in others) and the *tributum soli,* a percentage of one's assessed property. Both of them were determined by a periodic census and were deposited in the provincial fiscs (*fisci*) to cover the expense of Imperial defense and administration. A new 5 percent tax on the manumission of slaves (p. 262) probably went into the special reserve treasury (*aerarium sanctius*).

Social Reforms   Although his constitutional, administrative, military, and fiscal reforms were a great success, the results of Augustus' social reforms were rather mixed. He tried to reinforce the restoration of political order by a renewal of a clear and fixed hierarchical social order that embraced the class structure, women, and the family. Also, by restoring stable family life, he hoped to regenerate the devastated Roman and Italian freeborn population.

Slaves and Freedmen Augustus neither opposed slavery nor did anything to reduce its incidence and importance in Roman life. His wars of Imperial consolidation brought huge numbers of new slaves to Rome and Italy and may have caused him to worry about the impact that the unregulated granting of freedom to many of those slaves would have had on the citizen body. He set limits on the percentages of one's total slaves that could be freed in one's will, with 100 individuals as the absolute maximum, and he instituted a 5 percent tax on formal manumissions. He also strictly regulated the practice of informal manumission and made it less financially attractive for masters who wanted to avoid the 5 percent tax on formal manumissions to free slaves informally. Previously, all property belonging to an informally freed slave upon his death had to go to his former master. Augustus allowed such an informally freed ex-slave to dispose of his property by will as he wished. Finally, he would not permit freedom for any slave who had been imprisoned for a crime or disgraceful deed.

At the same time, Augustus tried to promote the humane treatment of slaves. According to a story told by Cassius Dio, Augustus was dining one day at the home of Vedius Pollio, a rich freedman who had acquired the habit of feeding the lampreys in his fishpond with erring slaves. As Vedius and Augustus were eating, a waiter accidentally broke a precious crystal goblet. Enraged, Vedius ordered that the slave be thrown into the fishpond. The trembling slave knelt before Augustus and begged for his intercession. Augustus, moved, asked Vedius to bring him all the crystal goblets in the house. When they had been placed before him in glistening array, he sent them all smashing to the floor. Vedius flushed, but said not a word. The point was clear.

Furthermore, one of the duties of Augustus' newly established urban prefect was to look into complaints by slaves that they were being denied enough to eat. Of course Augustus was concerned here with only the inhumane treatment of slaves. Perhaps he was influenced by the Stoic view of slaves' basic humanity, but he also probably realized that with the growing number of slaves and fewer chances of manumission, Roman slaveowners would have to treat slaves decently if they were to avoid the kinds of massive slave revolts that had occurred in the late Republic.

Augustus reinforced and rewarded cooperative freed slaves. By the *lex Junia Norbana* (17 B.C.), those who were freed informally had their noncitizen status regularized as Junian Latins with specific provisos for future full citizenship. A slave informally freed under the age of thirty could obtain citizenship by marrying any free Roman or Junian Latin woman and producing a child that was still alive after one year. A freedwoman who produced four children also received extra privileges similar to those given to citizen women who had borne three (p. 263).

To compensate freedmen for being barred from the regular magistracies in Rome and the municipalities, Augustus created new posts just for them. In Rome, they served as *vicomagistri,* who worked with the *vigiles* in fighting fires and maintaining the night watch. They also had charge of the neighborhood festivals. In the municipal towns of Italy, freedmen made up the bulk of local boards of six called the *Seviri Augustales.* The *Augustales* had charge of the emperor's local cult and put on games for their fellow townspeople.

Popular Benefactions The great mass of exploitable common citizens that had built up at Rome since the second century B.C. had been a significant factor in the instability of the late Republic. Augustus had blunted their direct political power by effectively gaining control of the popular assemblies himself. On the other hand, he still had to cope with the potential that they represented for violence and disorder. To limit their numbers, he had contemplated eliminating the distribution of free grain in 2 B.C., but he decided against such a potentially provocative move. Instead, he reduced the number eligible for free grain to 200,000 free-born citizens by eliminating about 120,000 freedmen. He also set up a more efficient system of procuring and distributing the grain needed to supply the recipients of free grain and keep the retail price reasonable for all.[1] At his own expense, he also expanded the number of games and public entertainments, such as the increasingly popular gladiatorial contests. In this way, Augustus set the Imperial policy of "bread and circuses" (*panem et circenses*) that created good will for the emperor among various groups within the population of Rome.

Women and the Family Less effective were the attempts to control promiscuity and regulate marriage and family life. Two Julian laws of 18 B.C. and the *lex Papia Poppaea* of A.D. 9[2] were specifically designed to curb immorality, speed up the birth rate, and revive ancient Roman virtue. These laws prohibited long engagements, regulated divorce, required all bachelors and spinsters to marry as soon as possible, and forced all widows under fifty and all widowers under sixty to marry within three years. Failure to comply carried many penalties and disabilities: partial or complete ineligibility to receive legacies or hold public office and exclusion from public games and spectacles. Married persons who were childless, impotent, or sterile incurred similar disabilities, whereas those with three or more children could advance rapidly in their public careers and social life. For example, women who had borne three or more children were freed from guardianship.

The total effectiveness of the law, however, was somewhat diminished by the conferral of the special and fictitious "right of three children" (*ius trium liberorum*). Persons of influence might claim this right. Thus, the unmarried poets Vergil and Horace, Augustus

himself with only one child, the Empress Livia with two, and even the two bachelor consuls who lent their names to the *lex Papia Poppaea* did not have to comply with the provisions of the law.

The new laws made adultery a criminal as well as a private offense. A *paterfamilias* might kill adulterous females under his power along with their paramours; a husband could kill his wife's lover. A man who refused to divorce a wife caught in adultery or who knowingly married an adulteress was equally guilty before the law. Flagrant adulterers suffered penalties varying from fines and loss of property to banishment and even death.

Although Augustus himself finally admitted that his marriage laws neither curbed immorality nor raised the birth rate, his legislation was not wholly without result: It enriched the treasury and favored the rise of informers, *delatores,* who were to remain the bane of social life in future years.

Religious Reforms In his reformation of the ancient state religion, Augustus resurrected long-neglected ceremonies and priesthoods. It was a difficult undertaking. Many of the ancient priesthoods and rites had fallen into disuse during the disturbed conditions of the civil wars. The archaic language of ancient hymns and incantations was no longer understood. Much antiquarian research went into solving the questions that arose. Nevertheless, it was no meaningless antiquarian task relevant to only a few. It helped to reassure the people that Augustus was doing everything possible to restore the *pax deorum,* that peace of the gods on which their peace and prosperity rested.

In 28 B.C., Augustus undertook the repair of all temples in Rome (eighty-two, according to his own statement). The previous year had witnessed the dedication of the new temples of the Divine Julius (in the old Forum) and of Apollo (on the Palatine), a fitting tribute because both gods were protectors of the Julian dynasty, givers of victory, and saviors of the state from civil war. In 2 B.C., Augustus erected a new temple of Mars the Avenger in the newly built Forum of Augustus.

---

[1] The recipients of free grain were not limited to poor freeborn citizens. Rather, receiving free grain was a mark of status for all freeborn citizens, who were expected to show gratitude to their benefactor for it.

[2] This last was a complete and systematic codification of all previous laws and edicts pertaining to marriage and adultery.

The repair of crumbling temples was a prelude to the revival of many half-forgotten religious rites of Old Rome. In 27 B.C., Augustus reconstituted the ancient college of the Arval Brothers, who once led the people each year at the end of May in the *Ambarvalia* (p. 57). Furthermore, Augustus revived the priesthood of the Flamen Dialis with all its old taboos (p. 47).

The revival of archaic rites may have helped revive the spirit of piety and valor but could not immediately evoke loyalty or devotion to the new government or create propaganda for monarchic Augustan rule. Accordingly, in 13 B.C. the senate voted to erect an altar of Augustan Peace (*Ara Pacis Augustae*). One of the sculptured panels of this superb monument shows Augustus and his family proceeding in solemn pomp to offer sacrifice; another panel shows Mother Earth or Peace seated on a rock and holding on her lap two children and the fruits of the earth (p. 284); a companion panel depicts the armed goddess Roma; and a fourth portrays Aeneas piously sacrificing a sow to his household gods. Thus the altar suggests peace and plenty, which flowed from the martial valor of Augustus and his pious devotion to the gods, on whose favor everything depended.

Augustus was able to push the new religious program with more zeal and vigor after 12 B.C., when he succeeded Lepidus as Pontifex Maximus. By 7 B.C. he had the city divided into fourteen regions and the regions into wards or precincts (*vici*). The *vicomagistri* or ward masters, usually of freedmen status, not only assisted the aediles in fighting fires but also officiated at the shrines dedicated to the worship of the *Lares Compitales,* now called the *Lares Augusti,* guardian spirits of the crossroads and household. At each shrine the *vicomagistri* also offered sacrifices to the Genius of Augustus, his guiding spirit, just as the *genius* of the *paterfamilias* was traditionally honored in the household worship of the *lares* and *penates.* Some Italian cities, especially in the Greek South, actually erected temples to Augustus, but he did not encourage such overt expressions of divinity in Italy. He preferred to promote municipal cults of his *genius* and encourage their maintenance by the colleges of *Seviri Augustales* (p. 262). These religious demonstrations were spontaneous enough but subtly helped organize public opinion behind the government.

During a reign of forty years, therefore, Augustus instituted reforms that touched every part of Roman life. Trying not to attempt too much too soon, but proceeding by gradual steps and building on precedents, Augustus succeeded in a radical reformation of Rome. He created a complex administrative hierarchy that reserved many positions of highest status for the old nobility but brought the equestrians of Italy into positions of real power and made them a loyal part of the system, with chances of obtaining senatorial status as *novi homines.* In some ways, slaves and freedmen were more restricted, but they too had important roles to play in an increasingly complex administrative system and could hope for enhanced status for themselves or their children through loyal service. The urban poor played a much more limited role in political life, but they were kept content with generous benefits. The army became a permanent professional force, and the finances of the state were made more rational and secure. Attempts at reforming the personal morality of individuals did not enjoy great success, but Augustus gave renewed influence to the state religion and promoted the cult of his *genius* as a way of fostering widespread loyalty to his regime.

XXIV

Imperial Stabilization under Augustus

While Augustus had been working out his unique constitutional settlement and making extensive internal administrative, military, fiscal, and social reforms at Rome, he also had to pay serious attention to securing the loyalty of the provinces and the establishment of defensible frontiers for the Empire as a whole. Augustus' primary motive always was to secure for Rome and Italy the benefits of empire in a world safely centered around the unifying core of the Mediterranean sea, *Mare Nostrum* ("Our Sea") as the Romans justly called it. Although he preferred subtler and gentler means, Augustus had no qualms about ruthlessly crushing anyone or anything that stood in the way of that primary goal. He wanted to be remembered as the bringer of peace, prosperity, and increased power to the Roman People. Therefore, the process that created the *Pax Romana* (Roman Peace) was not always experienced as peaceful or benign by those who were to serve Rome's and Augustus' glory.

Improved Provincial Administration
The loyalty of the provinces required stable, efficient, and honest administration with due regard for the provincials themselves. To ensure such administration, Augustus kept firm control over both Imperial and senatorial governors, strengthened the laws against extortion, and reformed the system of taxation by insti-

tuting a census of property at regular intervals. Breaking up the large provinces of Transalpine Gaul, Spain, and Macedonia was another way to achieve greater administrative efficiency and control. He curbed the power of the tax-farming companies and gradually transferred the collection of direct taxes to procurators assisted by local tax officials. Those reforms made possible, particularly in the East, a rapid economic recovery and commercial expansion and helped Augustus win the loyalty of the provincial peoples.

The *princeps* respected local customs as much as possible. He also gave the provincials considerable rights of self-government, which encouraged the growth of urban communities out of villages, hamlets, and temple lands. Accordingly, he allowed the town councils and the councils of the provincial cities and tribes (*concilia* or *koina*) freedom of assembly and the right to express gratitude or homage and bring their grievances to the attention of emperor or senate.

Egypt was a special case. For millennia it had been the personal estate of its kings. To have imposed a new system might have been disruptive, and it was to Augustus' advantage simply to take the place of the ancient pharaohs and Hellenistic Ptolemies in order to keep Egypt's vast wealth and vital grain out of the hands of potential challengers. Therefore, he treated it as part of his personal domain and declared it off limits to Roman senators without

The Roman Empire under the Principate

special permission. He and his successors administered it through special prefects of equestrian rank.

New Territories and Provinces In rounding out the conquest of the Mediterranean basin and extending Imperial borders to the most defensible geographic frontiers, Augustus added a number of new provinces and extended Roman control over other territories. By the time he finished, there were twenty-eight provinces, ten of which were senatorial and eighteen Imperial. From the Roman point of view, his policy was a great success and earned him much prestige in a society that valued military prowess highly. It was not, however, always a pretty story in human terms. A century later, the historian Tacitus grasped the reality faced by the native peoples whose independence and homelands were destroyed in the process of creating the Roman Peace (*Pax Romana*) when he said of the Romans, "They created a desert and called it peace."

The West Augustus applied the policy of conquest most consistently in the West. It was the less civilized part of the Empire, and, therefore, means of control other than brute force were often lacking. There were still large areas near Italy that the Romans had not yet attempted to take over. It was necessary to do so, however, in order to protect Italy, the heart of the Empire, and secure her efficient communications with the outlying territories. From 22 to 14 B.C., therefore, Augustus methodically rounded out Imperial conquests in the West.

Spain and Gaul, 27 to 22 B.C. Augustus personally led the fight against the Cantabrians and Asturians of northwestern Spain in 27, but his always-delicate health failed in 26. Agrippa finally suppressed the rugged tribesmen through the brutal expedients of massacre and enslavement. In Gaul, Caeser's thorough victories left Augustus nothing more than minor campaigns in Aquitania and administrative reorganization. In 22 B.C., he transferred the Province (*Gallia Narbonensis*) to the senate.

He divided old *Gallia Comata* into three administrative parts: Aquitania, Lugdunensis, and Belgica, each under a separate legate subject to the governor, who had his headquarters in Lugdunum (Lyons).

The Alpine Districts, 25 to 14 B.C. Although the Roman Empire now extended from the Straits of Gibraltar to the Euphrates, the Alpine region had remained unsubdued and menaced Italy. Wild and warlike tribes continued to raid their peaceful neighbors to the south and held passes essential to direct communication between Italy and Gaul. In 25 B.C., a decisive victory and ruthless enslavement removed the menace. The foundation of a colony of veterans at Augusta Praetoria (Aosta) gave protection to the Great and Little St. Bernard passes and made possible the construction of a road through the Little St. Bernard from Italy to Lugdunum (Lyons).

In the northern and eastern Alps, Roman armies subdued Raetia (eastern Switzerland, southern Bavaria, and western Tyrol) and Noricum (eastern Tyrol and western Austria) from 17 to 14 B.C. under the leadership of Augustus' stepsons, Tiberius Claudius Nero (Tiberius) and Nero Claudius Drusus (Drusus I). All the tribes near the headwaters of the Rhine and the Danube became Rome's subjects. The upper Danube then became Rome's northern boundary in the West.

The Danubian Lands, 14 B.C. to A.D. 6 Long overdue was the conquest of the Balkans. Illyricum (modern Bosnia, Croatia, Macedonia, western Hungary, northern Serbia, and eastern Austria) was constantly disturbed by the Pannonians living in its northern part or by the Dacians and Bastarnae of what is now Rumania and northern Hungary. In addition, the Dalmatian coastal regions of Illyricum, never completely pacified, were usually in full revolt against Roman authority. In 13 B.C., Marcus Agrippa took over operations begun in the previous year against the Dalmatians and Pannonians. He died during a harsh winter campaign, and Tiberius finished the task in four years of hard fighting from 12 to 9 B.C.

In the eastern Balkans, Thracian uprisings and invasions by the Dacians from across the Danube in 13 B.C. forced Augustus to act. Three years of fighting from 12 to 10 B.C. eliminated the threat but depopulated Moesia (Serbia and northern Bulgaria) along the south bank of the Danube from Illyricum to the Black Sea. Eventually, Roman armies rounded up 50,000 Dacians from across the Danube and settled them in the vacant territory.

By these conquests, Augustus moved the border of the Empire away from northeastern Italy and greatly shortened communications between the vital Rhineland and the East. Moreover, although less economically valuable than many provinces, the Danubian lands soon proved to be the best recruiting grounds in the Empire. In later centuries, many of the emperors who heroically fought to preserve the Empire from outside attacks came from this region.

Failure on the German Frontier, 12 B.C. to A.D. 9

Augustus' only failure on the frontiers was in Germany. The restlessness of German tribes persuaded Augustus to cross the Rhine and push the frontier to the Elbe (Albis), and later, if possible, to the Vistula, so as to shorten the line of defense to the Danube by 300 miles or more. The operations of Drusus I from 12 to 9 B.C. spectacularly accomplished the initial goal. Unfortunately, Drusus broke a leg by falling from a horse and died of complications in the latter year. Tiberius then handled matters effectively in Germany until he was called away to suppress a serious rebellion in Pannonia and Illyricum from A.D. 6 to 9. In 9, however, the harsh policies of Tiberius' successor in Germany, Quinctilius Varus, stirred up a revolt there. The German leader Arminius ambushed Varus and three legions in the Teutoburg Forest. Few escaped, and Varus committed suicide.

News of the Teutoburg disaster was devastating. The *princeps,* dazed, sorrowing, broken, and old, kept moaning to himself, "Quinctilius Varus, give me back my legions." The Teutoburg debacle and the lack of manpower and money to replace the three lost legions persuaded the *princeps* to abandon the hope of further territorial conquests in Germany. Despite all later successes of Tiberius and Drusus' son Germanicus, he relinquished the ambition of making the Elbe a frontier of the Empire in Europe. That decision was fiscally and administratively sound but posed serious strategic problems. The Rhine-Danube frontier was longer and took more men to defend than one based on the Elbe or the Vistula and the Danube would have. In addition, the headwaters of the Rhine and the Danube created a triangular territory, the *Agri Decumates,* which would give attackers easy access to Italy and the western provinces if there were a breakthrough in that sector of the frontier.

North Africa

Caesar had enlarged the old province of *Africa Proconsularis* by the annexation of Numidia. Augustus, however, convinced that the enlarged province was too difficult to defend, consigned the western part of it to the kingdom of Mauretania (modern Algeria and Morocco) and placed upon the vacant throne of Mauretania Juba II of Numidia, who had married Cleopatra Selene (Moon), daughter of Antonius and Cleopatra. Juba, a Latin author in his own right and a connoisseur of art, proved to be an enlightened and effective ruler. He raised the cultural level of his people, fended off the wild tribes of the desert, and assisted Augustus in the work of founding twelve Roman colonies, of which Tingis (Tangier) was the most notable, along the Mauretanian coast.

The East

The problems presented by the East differed widely from those of the West. The eastern provinces were heirs to very old and advanced civilizations and were proud of their traditions. Many had been taken over only recently and were not yet fully reconciled to Roman rule. Beyond the eastern frontier lay the Parthian Empire. It was a territorially vast, polyglot state embracing an area of 1.2 million square miles from the Euphrates to the Aral Sea and beyond the Indus. Within recent memory, Parthia had inflicted three stinging defeats upon the Romans and was still considered a potential menace. As an organized state, however, it was capable of being dealt with through sophisticated diplomacy as well as force.

After Actium, an insistent clamor arose for a war of revenge against Parthia. Without openly defying the demands of public opinion and the patriotic sentiments of authors like Vergil and Horace, Augustus accepted the impossibility of waging war in Spain and Germany, along the Danube, and against Parthia at the same time. The Empire lacked the manpower, resources, and communications for such an undertaking. Augustus would try to strengthen Rome's position and neutralize Parthia by other methods.

Client Kingdoms At first, he continued the policy of Marcus Antonius, which was to maintain client kingdoms as buffer states between Parthia and the Roman provinces. After Actium, Augustus consigned large territories in Asia Minor to Amyntas the Galatian (Galatia, Pisidia, Lycaonia, and most of Cilicia). He also gave eastern Pontus, Lesser Armenia, and the huge realm of Cappadocia to client kings. At the same time, he enlarged Judea, the kingdom of Herod I, the so-called Great (37 to 4 B.C.), a calculating and ruthless ruler who not only was the builder of the splendid Third Temple at Jerusalem but also was an accomplished murderer of wives and sons.

Eventually, all the client kingdoms became provinces. When Amyntas was killed in 25 B.C. while rounding up some savage tribes in the Taurus Mountains, Rome acquired the vast province of Galatia and Pamphylia. A decade after Herod's death, Augustus made Judea and Samaria an Imperial province or rather a subprovince attached to Syria and governed by prefects, the most famous of whom was Pontius Pilate, who held office from A.D. 26 to 36 and authorized the crucifixion of Christ.

Armenia and Parthia In only one kingdom, Armenia, had Roman influence deteriorated after the death of Antonius. Subdued and annexed as a province in 34 B.C., Armenia had slipped away from Roman control just before Actium and had come under the brutal rule of Artaxias, who forthwith slew all Roman residents in Armenia. Augustus did not avenge their deaths and made no effort to recover the region for over a decade, although it provided the best land routes between Parthia and Roman provinces in Asia Minor and Syria. He watched and waited.

In 20 B.C., Artaxias was killed. Augustus immediately sent Tiberius into Armenia with an army. He placed Tigranes III, a pro-Roman brother of the late king, on the throne. At the same time, he frightened the Parthian king into surrendering the battle standards and all surviving prisoners captured from the Romans at Carrhae (p. 199) or in subsequent Parthian victories. A rattle of the saber temporarily restored Roman prestige in the East and wiped away the stains upon Roman honor. Augustus, therefore, shrewdly declared a great victory and silenced further demands for war by advertising his success on coins with such slogans as *signis receptis* (the standards regained), *civibus et signis militaribus a Parthis recuperatis* (citizens and military standards recovered from the Parthians), and *Armenia recepta* (Armenia recaptured).

All was quiet in the East until the death of Tigranes in 1 B.C. Armenian nationalists, aided and abetted by the Parthians, enthroned a king of their own choice without consulting Augustus. He at once sent his grandson Gaius Caesar, armed with full proconsular *imperium* over the entire East, into Armenia at the head of a powerful army. This show of force compelled the Parthians to recognize Rome's preponderant interest in Armenia and accept a Roman appointee on the Armenian throne. The Armenians subsequently revolted but were suppressed after hard fighting. It was a costly victory, however. Gaius, Augustus' heir apparent, had suffered wounds that would not heal, and he died eighteen months later (A.D. 4).

Parthia, as well as Augustus, had reasons for avoiding war. Torn by the dissensions of rival claimants to the throne and continually menaced by Asian migrations, Parthia was in no position to attack and willingly endured diplomatic defeat rather than risk military conflict. Her own diplomacy and intrigue, it was thought, might eventually succeed; overt aggression might fail and would surely be costly.

Both Parthia and Rome also had economic interests that would have been ruined by war. Each wanted to exploit the Euphrates valley as a caravan route for trade with India, Central Asia, and China. Under joint Parthian and Roman protection, Palmyra was rapidly becoming a large and prosperous caravan city with fine streets, parks, and public buildings. Other cities—Petra, Gerasa (Jerash), Philadelphia (Amman), and Damascus—were also beginning to enjoy the rich benefits of caravan trade.

Africa and the Red Sea Zone   Egypt, richest of all Augustan annexations and producer of one third of the Roman annual grain supply (5 million bushels), remained relatively quiet except for some skirmishes on the Nubian border in Upper Egypt. C. Cornelius Gallus, Egypt's first prefect, a distinguished general, elegiac poet, friend of Augustus, Pollio, and Vergil, led an expedition against the Nubians (often called Ethiopians, who actually dwelt farther south) in 29 B.C.[1] A later prefect, C. Petronius, repulsed counterattacking invaders from Nubia and in two campaigns (27 and 22 B.C.) drove them back into the Sudan and destroyed their holy city of Napata. In agreement with Candace, their queen, the *princeps* finally fixed the southern boundary of Egypt about 60 miles south of Syene (Aswan) and the First Cataract, where it remained for the next 300 years.

About this time (25 to 24 B.C.), the *princeps* sent Aelius Gallus, probably prefect of Egypt, on an expedition down the Red Sea against the Sabaeans, who dwelt in the southeast corner of Arabia near what is now Aden. The purpose of this expedition was to gain naval control of the Straits of Bab-el-Mandeb so that Alexandrian merchants might break the Sabaean monopoly on trade with India in precious stones, spices, cosmetics, and other commodities. That expedition, although badly handled by Gallus, paved the way for more suc-cessful ones later. About the same time, a Greek sea captain named Hippalus discovered the principle of the Monsoons, which allowed regular seasonal sailings between southern Arabia and western India. Strabo the geographer says that from Myos Hormos, a port on the Red Sea, 120 ships annually sailed to India.

Road Building   The building of roads went hand in hand with conquest, frontier defense, and provincial communication. Therefore, Augustus devoted much attention to it and greatly expanded the network of roads from Italy to the provinces. By 27 B.C., he had completed the repair and reconstruction of the Italian roads (much neglected since the time of Gaius Gracchus), especially the Flaminian Way, the main thoroughfare between Rome and the North and a vital artery of the Empire. After the conquest of the Alpine and Danubian regions, he began the construction of a road north from Tridentum (Trent) on the Adige in the Venetian Alps to Augusta Vindelicorum (Augsburg) on the Lech in Raetia. Other roads ran through the Alps between Italy and Gaul. The completion of this program brought Raetia and Noricum (modern Switzerland, and parts of Austria and Bavaria) as well as Gaul into close and rapid communication with Italy.

The Imperial Post (*Cursus Publicus*)   Road building made possible another Augustan achievement, the Imperial postal service (*cursus publicus*). Much like that of ancient Persia, the Roman postal service carried official letters and dispatches and transported officials, senators, and other privileged persons. The expense of this service—relays of horses and carriages and the provision of hotel service for official guests—fell upon the towns located along the great highways. That was a burden upon many towns, but it was essential to promote swift communication and the centralization of administration. Moreover, like railroads in the second half of the nineteenth century and national highways in the first half of the twentieth, the routes used by the *cursus publicus* brought business and travelers to towns located along them.

---

[1] Statues of Gallus and boastful proclamations of his exploits incised on pyramids incurred the wrath of Augustus and condemnation for treason by the senate. He took his own life in 27 B.C.

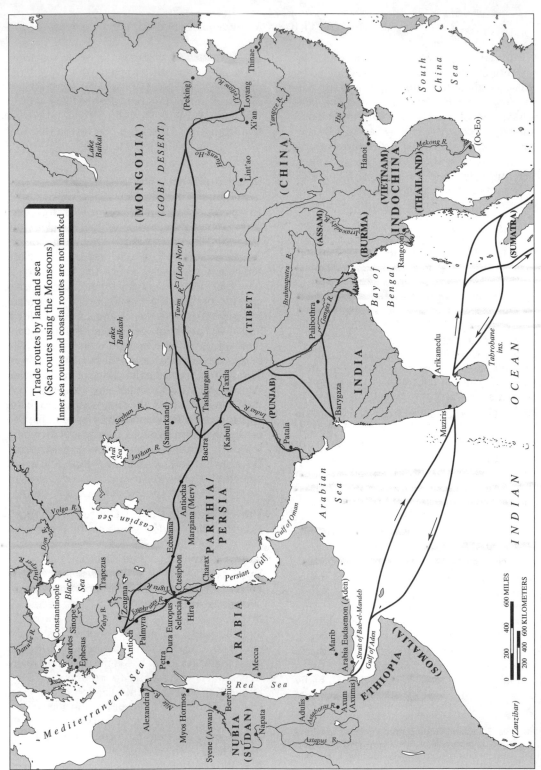

Trade routes by land and sea
(Sea routes using the Monsoons)
Inner sea routes and coastal routes are not marked

East Africa, Arabia, and the Far East

Colonization Throughout his political career from 43 B.C. to A.D. 14, Augustus had founded twenty-eight colonies in Italy and perhaps eighty in the provinces. The Italian colonies, composed mainly of veterans, were centers of tremendous loyalty to the new regime. Unlike Caesar, Augustus seems to have had little interest in the commercial potential of colonies, and he founded few, if any, civilian colonies outside of Italy. Most of his colonies, therefore, were for the settlement of veterans or served as fortresses or military outposts at strategic points to hold down and secure recently conquered territory in the Alps, Gaul, and Spain. As always, while colonies acted as garrisons, they also helped to spread the use of the Latin language and Roman law among the conquered peoples and thus became important agents of Romanization. Whether they were forseen or not, however, large and prosperous communities grew out of many veteran colonies. A number provided the original foundations of well-known modern cities: Barcelona (Barcino), Zaragoza (Caesaraugusta), and Merida (Emerita) in Spain; Vienne (Vienna), Nimes (Nemausus), and Lyons (Lugdunum) in France; and Tangier (Tingis) in Morocco.

Urbanization of the Provinces Colonization probably should be seen as part of a long-term policy to promote urbanization and the growth of urban elites in general. Alexander the Great and his Hellenistic successors had followed that policy in the East. By promoting the growth of cities and their urban elites, the Hellenistic emperors had obtained their cooperation in controlling the surrounding countryside and spreading Greek culture as a unifying factor. Augustus had similar social and political motives for promoting the growth of cities and urban elites in Rome's provinces. They would help to unify the Empire by the diffusion of Roman culture and would serve the central government as convenient administrative units for the collection of taxes and other useful functions. No doubt, too, Augustus realized that since the urban elites would owe their privileged position to the central government, they would in turn support the new Imperial regime with vigor and enthusiasm.

Growth of the Imperial Cult The growth of emperor worship throughout the Empire was also useful in strengthening ties of loyalty to both Rome and *princeps*. The people of the eastern provinces had long been used to worshipping their rulers as gods. After the Hellenistic empires and native kingdoms had been taken over by the Republic, the eastern peoples had showered provincial governors with divine honors. When Augustus became ruler of the Roman world, many easterners began to establish cults for his worship.

Augustus, however, was reluctant to have himself worshipped too directly. It may have been distasteful to him as a religiously conservative Roman, and it certainly would have entailed the political risk of alienating jealous or conservative nobles. He insisted, therefore, that official provincial cults for his worship be linked with the goddess Roma. By 29 B.C., before he had received the title Augustus, temples of such cults already existed in the East at Nicaea, Ephesus, Pergamum, and Nicomedia. Later, with Augustus' encouragement, such cults appeared in the western provinces too, notably at Colonia Agrippina (Cologne) in Germany, Lugdunum (Lyons) in *Gallia Comata,* and, Tarragona (Tarraco) in Spain. Each cult included a yearly festival and periodic games that were managed by a high priest elected from among the leading aristocrats of the city or provincial assembly (*concilium, koinon*) who maintained it. In this way, the provincial elite became identified with and loyal to both Rome and the emperor.

By the end of his life, therefore, Augustus had brought about the pacification of the Roman provinces internally and organized their efficient administration. He had fixed the boundaries of the Empire, with a few notable exceptions, for the future and organized a system of defense that kept them secure for almost 200 years. By cautiously promoting the growth of emperor worship, he had also found a means of building a basis for Imperial unity that

Cities of the Roman Empire

bridged the different local and ethnic traditions of a huge polyglot empire.

The Death of Augustus

At last, after a political career of almost sixty years, on August 19 of A.D. 14 in the Campanian town of Nola, Augustus met a peaceful death. He was ready, serene, cheerful; not plagued by doubt, guilt, or remorse. Dying, he jokingly quoted to his friends these words from a Greek comedy: "Have I played my part well? Then clap your hands and take me off the stage." Played his part well? Indeed he had, and the grateful Roman senators willingly conferred upon him the divinity that he had tactfully refused to claim outright while he was alive.

XXV

The Impact of Augustus on Roman Imperial Life and Culture

The Augustan Age witnessed a general quickening of economic life throughout the Mediterranean. The ending of the civil wars, the suppression of piracy at sea and of banditry and lawlessness in Italy, and the Augustan program of road building in Italy and the provinces brought about a remarkable expansion of agriculture, industry, and commerce. Italy was for a time the chief beneficiary of the new expansion, for the East had not yet recovered from the effects of past wars and exploitation, and the western provinces were still too young to take full advantage of the new order. Italy, therefore, continued to dominate the Mediterranean world not only politically but also economically and culturally.

The Population and Economic Impact of Rome Disturbed conditions during the civil wars from 49 to 31 B.C. probably produced a temporary reduction in the population of Rome, a large part of which was always very fluid and transient. Under the Augustan peace, however, the population rapidly rebounded and probably reached a million as the *princeps* improved the attractiveness of Rome by restoring order, improving public amenities, providing for a steady supply of food, and inaugurating a building program that created much employment. In fact, Rome became the great-

est metropolis of premodern Europe, if not the whole premodern world.

Within Italy and therefore the Empire, the great Imperial metropolis was the driving force of economic and cultural developments. Until recently, it has been fashionable to view Rome in terms of the "consumer" or "parasite" model of the ancient city. According to this model, most large ancient cities produced little of economic value and served mainly their ruling elites. The ruling elite of a region's metropolitan center, it is said, inhibited the development of its hinterlands and subject territories. Surplus wealth was siphoned off in the form of rents, taxes, tribute, and spoils in order to support the metropolis as the physical embodiment of its elite's own greatness. Newer studies, however, based on more extensive archaeological research and comparisons with large cities in other premodern societies, have shown this model to be inadequate.

First of all, it underestimates the real value of a metropolis' central administration in suppressing intraregional conflicts and providing defense from external attack. Second, it ignores the impact of the market created by the metropolis' concentration of surplus wealth, which financed the purchase and transportation of vast quantities of food, goods, and services from the hinterland and subject territories. Under Augustus and a relatively benign central administration, Rome gave the Mediterranean world a prolonged period of internal peace, which freed the whole Mediterranean economy from the destructive conflicts and confiscations of earlier times. As a result, Rome's subjects had more wealth at their disposal to spur local economic growth even after the deduction of Rome's taxes and tribute.

Furthermore, the taxes and tribute used to pay Roman armies on the frontier and build the transportation infrastructure that supported those armies were great stimuli to the economic growth of the frontier provinces. Finally, by subsidizing Rome as the largest metropolis of premodern, preindustrial Europe, the wealth that flowed into the city also flowed out into the Italian hinterland, other parts of the Empire, and even beyond to purchase the foodstuffs, material, services, and luxuries that it demanded. Those expenditures put more money in the hands of people who created even more demand, which supported local and regional economic growth.

From the modern point of view, this economic growth can be considered less than ideal. Much of it was ultimately based on the politically derived purchasing power of the emperor and elite landowners. It was also limited by the lack of many significant technological developments. Profits often rested on the exploitation of slaves and were unevenly distributed in favor of those already privileged. Nevertheless, there was real economic growth, and many ordinary people benefitted.

Agriculture After Actium, because Augustus avoided the disruptive confiscations that had marked his attempts to settle veterans after Philippi, the ranks of the small farmers stabilized throughout Italy. Those near Rome could produce labor-intensive garden crops for the profitable Roman market. Moreover, as Rome's economic impact stimulated urban growth elsewhere in Italy, other small farmers gained access to similar profitable urban markets.

The existence of large urban populations in Rome and other Italian cities greatly reduced the small farmer's perennial problem of subdividing land into smaller, increasingly uneconomical units among heirs. On one fairly conservative estimate, 7,000 fresh immigrants a year were needed just to keep up the numbers of Rome's free population. It and other urban populations were constantly being diminished by the high death rate characteristic of premodern cities with their unsanitary conditions and densely packed housing. Therefore, just to maintain their existing size, urban centers had to siphon away the excess population of the Italian countryside.

Rome's insatiable demand for food had an impact on provincial agriculture similar to that on Italian agriculture. More and more farmers were producing for profitable markets rather than just for subsistence. Although part of Rome's need for grain was met through taxes in kind on provincial producers, the rest was acquired through purchase from both those and Italian producers. Therefore, landowners in the grain-producing areas of Sicily, Sardinia, North Africa, and Egypt profited from the enormous efforts to supply Rome. Similarly, along the Mediterranean coasts of Spain and Gaul and up the valley of the Rhône, vineyards and olive groves were beginning to produce large quantities of wine and oil for the lucrative Roman market.

Agricultural Wealth and Urbanization
In both Italy and the provinces, the larger landowners profited most from the commercialization fostered by Rome, and they largely supported increased urbanization from the time of Augustus. The wealthy local landowners became the backbone and lifeblood of the curial class (*curiales*), the local aristocrats who filled the governing councils (*curiae*) of cities and municipalities all over the Empire. Like their counterparts in the Roman senatorial class, whom they aped, they dedicated a significant part of their agricultural profits to increase their status by building fine residences in the nearest significant city or town and by providing expensive benefactions such as games, gifts of food, temples, theaters, schools, aque-

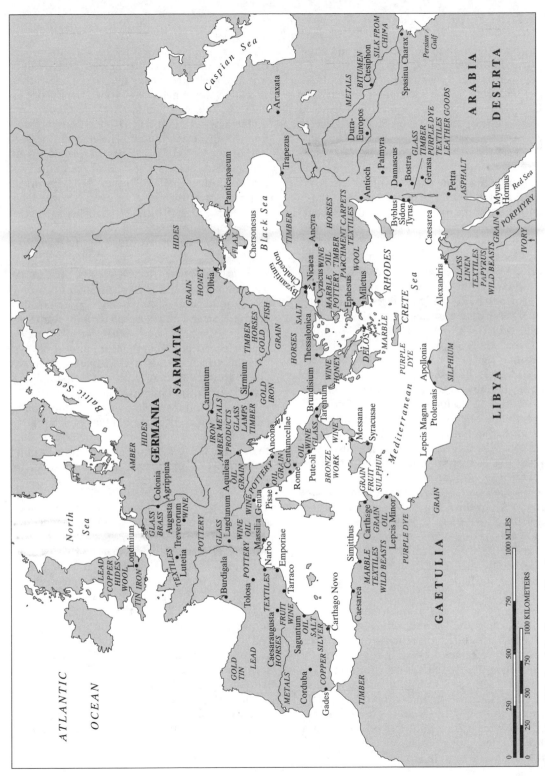

Products and Trade of the Roman Empire

ducts, baths, fora, and porticoes. These activities attracted more population by making the growing cities and towns more attractive places to live and creating employment in the building trades and the provision of goods and services to a growing population. Thus, in many places, there occurred an upward spiral of urban development fueled by the profits of local landowners who were part of an elaborate network funneling food and raw materials from their estates to Rome. Of course, some of these cities were significant markets themselves and further enriched the local landowners, who also produced for them.

Places in Italy that were particularly well situated within the elaborate network of roads and waterways that funneled supplies to Rome had grown to be rather large and significant urban centers by the mid-first century A.D. For example, the crucial ports of Puteoli (Pozzuoli) and Ostia, where ships unloaded cargoes bound for Rome, reached populations of 30,000. Regional centers like Mediolanum (Milan), Patavium (Padua), and Capua had populations from 25,000 to as many as 40,000. About 25 other centers can be classed as major cities like Verona, Cremona, Genua (Genoa), Beneventum, Pompeii, Brundisium, and Rhegium with populations of between 5,000 and 25,000.

On the other hand, being too close to Rome or another growing major center could spell a city's decline. Many old cities of Etruria and Latium are good examples. The wealthy landowners in their territories generally concentrated their efforts on acquiring status in Rome itself, and formerly flourishing centers withered and died. Nevertheless, many more places in Italy prospered.

Supplying Rome also stimulated urban growth around the Mediterranean as old centers were refounded or reinvigorated. Julius Caesar had refounded Corinth in 44 B.C. In 29 B.C., Augustus fulfilled Caesar's intention of refounding Carthage. Both were prime agricultural sites located on major maritime trade routes. As a result, they quickly grew to be major cities once more. The port of Alexandria flourished as never before and probably reached 500,000 in population. Not only was it

the collection point for the vital Egyptian grain that was shipped to Rome in great fleets, but it was also the entrepôt for the luxury goods that flowed to Rome and other cities from the upper Nile and the Red Sea (p. 271). In Gaul, Lugdunum (Lyons), founded in 43 B.C. near the confluence of the Rhône and the Saône, was the hub of the Gallic road system. From its island commercial center at the confluence of the two rivers, Gallic wine and other products were shipped downriver to Arelate (Arles), which grew tremendously under Augustus as a port where seagoing vessels picked up the cargoes from riverboats for transshipment to Rome.

Nonagricultural Trade and Industry

The production and transportation of raw materials and manufactured goods for the vast, lucrative Roman market were also important factors in economic and urban growth under Augustus. Although agriculture almost always was the principal source of their wealth, many cities grew even bigger as centers supplying Rome with certain manufactured goods or raw materials. Moreover, Rome's network of roads and waterways encouraged centers of production to increase output even further and ship their products to distant markets from Jutland (Denmark) to the Caucasus, from Britain to India.

Textiles Until the advent of power-driven, mechanized spinning and weaving, cloth was a very valuable commodity that could be shipped long distances in the ancient world at a profit. Located north of the Po River on what is now the Bacchiglione River in a major sheep-raising district not far from the Adriatic coast, Patavium (Padua) became a great Italian center for the production of woolen goods. Its output was so large that in Augustus' day it is reported to have supplied the huge demand for inexpensive clothing at Rome. Finer grades of woolen goods and purple dye, which was much in demand, came from Tarentum. The silk clothes of the Greek island of Cos were proverbial symbols of luxury for the Augustan poets, and Alexandria supplied the Roman market with linen made from Egyptian flax.

The Glass Industry The thriving glass industry had been revolutionized around 40 B.C. by the Syrian (or Egyptian) invention of the blowpipe, which made possible the production not only of beautiful goblets and bowls but even of window panes. From the glass factories of Campania or of the Adriatic seaport of Aquileia came wares that found their way as far north as the Trondheim fiord in Norway to the southern-most borders of Russia.

Arretine Pottery Manufacturers of red Samian ware, *terra sigillata*, at Arretium in Etruria and later at Puteoli had become highly successful. By the time of Augustus and Tiberius, they had achieved mass production and exported as far west as the British Midlands and as far east as modern Arikamedu near Pondicherry (Poduke?) in southeastern India (p. 371). One Arretine operation had a mixing vat for 10,000 gallons of clay and might well have employed as many as 40 expert designers and a much larger number of mixers, potters, and furnacemen. Some manufacturers were now establishing branch operations in southern and eastern Gaul, in Spain, in Britain, and on the Danube.

The Metal Industries Augustan Italy led the world in the manufacture of metalware. The chief centers of the iron industry were the two great seaports of Puteoli and Aquileia. The iron foundries of Puteoli smelted ores brought by sea from the island of Elba and by a process of repeated forging manufactured arms, farm implements, and carpenters' tools that were as hard as steel. At Aquileia, easy access to the rich iron mines of recently annexed Noricum stimulated the manufacture of equally excellent farm implements for sale throughout the fertile Cisalpina and for export to Dalmatia, the Danubian region, and even Germany.

For the manufacture of silverware (plates, trays, bowls, cups, and candelabra), the two leading centers were Capua and Tarentum; for bronze wares (statues, busts, lamp stands, tables, tripods, buckets, and kitchen pots and pans) Capua, where operators employing perhaps thousands of workmen had evolved a spe-cialization and division of labor usually associated with modern industry. The immense export trade of Capua to Britain, Germany, Scandinavia, and south Russia continued unabated until Gaul had established workshops first at Lugdunum, and around A.D. 80, farther north in the Belgica and the Rhineland.

Building Supplies and Trades The extensive building program of Augustus and the large sums spent on beautifying the Empire's capital stimulated the manufacture or extraction of building and plumbing materials—lead and terra-cotta pipes, bricks, roof tiles, cement, marble, and the so-called travertine, a cream-colored limestone quarried near Tibur. Some of these crafts seem never to have developed large, systematized methods of production. Lead pipes, for instance, were made in small shops by the same people who also laid and connected them. On the other hand, the making of bricks and tiles reached a high degree of specialization, especially on senatorial and Imperial estates, which produced materials in large volumes for public works. Almost nothing is known about the organization of the enterprises that made cement, a mixture of volcanic ash and lime, which was also in great demand.

The queen of building materials was marble. The Romans imported many varieties: the famous marbles of the Greek Aegean; the fine white, purple-veined varieties of Asia Minor; the serpentine and dark red porphyries of Egypt; and the beautiful, gold-colored marble of Simitthus in Numidia. At this time, they also began to quarry marble in Italy: the renowned white Luna (Carrara) marble in Etruria and all those remarkable colored varieties found north of Liguria in the Italian Piedmont, in Liguria itself, and near Verona—brilliant greens and yellows or mixed reds, browns, and whites.

The Roman Imperial Coinage

The Augustan Age also witnessed new developments in the creation of a stable and abundant coinage that served ever-expanding fiscal and economic needs both within the Empire and far beyond its frontiers. Before Actium, the coinages of

Italy and the Roman world had been in a confused and unreliable state as a result of inflation and disruption caused by war and civil strife. The huge amounts of gold and silver available to Augustus after his victory at Actium allowed him to reestablish the credibility of Roman coinage and issue an adequate supply from various mints. His golden *denarius,* the *aureus*, was virtually pure gold and was struck at 40 to the Roman pound, whereas his silver *denarius* was 97.5 to 98 percent silver and was struck at 84 to the pound (p. 251). Twenty-five silver *denarii* equalled one *aureus* for a 12-to-1 ratio of silver to gold by weight. Each coin had its respective half called a *quinarius.* The constant acquisition of more gold and silver through booty, mining, and trade allowed Augustus and most of his successors to maintain similar standards for 200 years. Civic and provincial coins were still produced, particularly in the East, but they were all linked to the Roman *denarius,* which provided the standard of value.

Sometime after 23 B.C. (19 B.C.?), Augustus reopened the mint at Rome and instituted a college of three moneyers (*tresviri monetales*), mint officials who struck coins at the joint direction of the *princeps* and the senate. At that time, Augustus introduced a new series of token coins designed to meet the need for small denominations used in daily transactions. He issued a *sestertius* (one quarter of a silver *denarius*) and its half, the *dupondius,* in orichalcum, brass made of 75 percent copper, 20 percent zinc, and 5 percent tin. Pure copper went into the *as* (one quarter of a *sestertius*) and the quarter *as, quadrans.* Although these coins were not intrinsically worth their official values, they were so well made and useful that they gained universal acceptance.

The Augustan coinage had an important propaganda or publicity value in addition to its purely economic function, for it provided the newborn regime a flexible, subtle, and compelling method of influencing those who used it, particularly the soldiers who received enormous quantities of coins as pay.[1] People all over

the Empire would use and inevitably look at the coins, which could vaguely yet effectively suggest what the government from time to time wanted to be felt and believed. New coin types, appearing as frequently as modern commemorative stamps, kept before the public eye the exalted figure of Augustus sometimes as an associate of Roma (ROM.ET.AUG), as the victor at Actium (IMP.X.ACT), as the preserver of citizens' lives (CAESAR. COS. VII. CIVIBUS. SERVATEIS), as the defender of the *libertas* of the Roman People (LIBERTATIS. P.R. VINDEX), or as the recoverer of the standards lost to the Parthians in 53 B.C. (SIGNIS RECEPTIS).

As media of publicity and mass propaganda, the coinages were more effective and malleable than the monumental arts. Even the most wonderful works of architecture and sculpture could not keep pace with the new messages. Moreover, comparatively few of the Empire's 50 million to 70 million inhabitants ever saw the major monuments, whereas people everywhere daily used and handled the coins. The coinages were also better vehicles than literature for advertising rapidly changing purposes, policies, and resolves of the government, because texts could be reproduced only by hand and slowly. Also, many writers could be unfettered, independent spirits not easily captive to a ruler's shifting moods or yoked in service to the state.

Architecture and Art   As master of Italy and the West after Philippi and before he became Augustus, Octavian continued Julius Caesar's work of beautifying Rome. To this period belong the first public library, a temple to Apollo on the Palatine, a new theater, the rebuilding of the Regia, the completion of the Basilica Aemilia, and the repair of the temple of Hercules. Agrippa, an engineer as well as soldier and admiral, began the repair of the aqueduct *Aqua Marcia* and, as aedile in 33 B.C., the construction of the aqueduct *Aqua Iulia* and other public works.

In the Augustan principate, Roman art and architecture acquired their distinctive Ro-

---

[1]Caesar had increased the base pay for soldiers from 112-1/2 *denarii* per annum to 225.

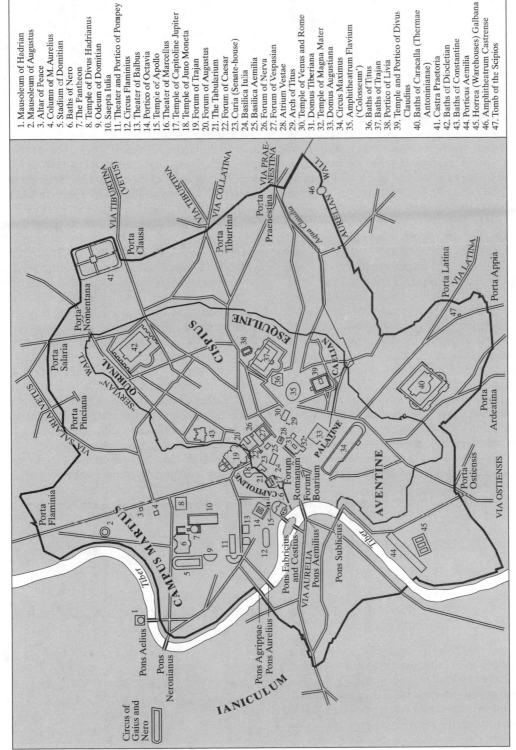

1. Mausoleum of Hadrian
2. Mausoleum of Augustus
3. Altar of Peace
4. Column of M. Aurelius
5. Stadium of Domitian
6. Baths of Nero
7. The Pantheon
8. Temple of Divus Hadrianus
9. Odeum of Domitian
10. Saepta Iulia
11. Theater and Portico of Pompey
12. Circus Flaminius
13. Theater of Balbus
14. Portico of Octavia
15. Temple of Apollo
16. Theater of Marcellus
17. Temple of Capitoline Jupiter
18. Temple of Juno Moneta
19. Forum of Trajan
20. Forum of Augustus
21. The Tabularium
22. Forum of Caesar
23. Curia (Senate-house)
24. Basilica Iulia
25. Basilica Aemilia
26. Forum of Nerva
27. Forum of Vespasian
28. Atrium Vestae
29. Arch of Titus
30. Temple of Venus and Rome
31. Domus Tiberiana
32. Temple of Magna Mater
33. Domus Augustiana
34. Circus Maximus
35. Amphitheatrum Flavium ('Colosseum')
36. Baths of Titus
37. Baths of Trajan
38. Portico of Livia
39. Temple and Portico of Divus Claudius
40. Baths of Caracalla (Thermae Antoninianae)
41. Castra Praetoria
42. Baths of Diocletian
43. Baths of Constantine
44. Porticus Aemilia
45. Horrea (Warehouses) Galbana
46. Amphitheatrum Castrense
47. Tomb of the Scipios

Imperial Rome

man and Imperial character. The conditions that favored this development were the peace and economic prosperity of the period; the publication of Vitruvius Pollio's classic *De Architectura* (ca. 27 B.C.), which has exerted a profound influence on the architecture of Europe until modern times; and the great building activity of Augustus himself. In his *Res Gestae* he briefly refers to the temples that he had constructed and the 82 he had repaired. Before his death he remarked that he "had found Rome a city of brick and left it one of marble," a claim undoubtedly accurate with respect to temples and public buildings but not to the huge blocks of flimsy tenements constructed of light timber and sun-dried brick.

The most important structures erected during the Augustan principate were the Temple of Divus Julius at the eastern edge of the old Roman Forum; the Temple of Mars the Avenger in the newly constructed Forum of Augustus, the first of the four great Imperial fora; the magnificent Temple of Apollo on the Palatine, the first great building in Rome to be constructed entirely of the gleaming white Luna (Carrara) marble. Completed in 28 B.C., it contained two libraries, one for Greek books and the other for Latin. Also imposing are the Theater of Marcellus, with its three rows of arcades supported by Corinthian columns and with a seating capacity of 20,000; the Baths of

Agrippa, the first of a long series culminating in the enormous Baths of Caracalla and Diocletian (all adorned with mosaics, paintings, and statues, and equipped with hot and cold baths, steam rooms, swimming pools, gymnasia, libraries, and recreation rooms); and the huge Mausoleum of Augustus shaped like a mounded Etruscan tomb (*tumulus*). Erected beside the Tiber in 28 B.C., it served as the Imperial family tomb from the death of Marcellus in 23 B.C. to that of Nerva in A.D. 98. The Pantheon ("Shrine of all the Gods") was erected by Agrippa in 27 B.C. and, though reconstructed by Hadrian in the second century A.D. (p. 365), still bears on its facade the famous inscription: M. AGRIPPA. L. F. COS TERTIUM FECIT (Marcus Agrippa, son of Lucius, consul for the third time, built [this] in his third consulship).

Erected after 13 B.C., the altar of Augustan Peace (*Ara Pacis Augustae*), portrays the leading ideas and achievements of the government (p. 264). Its marble panels contain some of the finest sculptured reliefs in the history of art. The figures of Mother Earth or Peace seated among all the symbols of peace and plenty, the armed goddess Roma, Aeneas piously sacrificing, and the solemn procession of the Imperial family and officials epitomize the restrained and idealized classicism associated with the finest works of fifth-century Athens. They are equaled by the celebrated portrait

Sculptured relief from the Ara Pacis, *with fruitful Earth and babes flanked by the East and West Winds and surrounded by symbols of peace and prosperity. (Courtesy Museo delle Terme, Rome)*

Statue of Augustus Imperator with sculptured breastplate (ca. 20 B.C.), from the Villa of Livia at Prima Porta. (Courtesy The Photographical Archives of the Vatican Museums and Galleries, Rome)

statue of Augustus from Prima Porta, which shows the same blend of classical idealism and Augustan ideology. That statue portrays him wearing a decorated breastplate that depicts the Parthian surrender of the captured standards to Tiberius, the final conquest of Spain and Gaul, the fecundity of the earth (*Terra Mater*), and Jupiter's protecting mantle over all. Similar, if not identical, ideas are conveyed in the same style by a marble altar from Roman Carthage with Roma seated on a heap of arms and contemplating an altar with a horn of plenty (*cornucopiae*), staff of peace (*caduceus*), and globe (*orbis terrarum*) resting upon it; by the exquisite Vienna cameo (*Gemma Augustea*) and the Grand Camée de France showing respectively a triumph of Tiberius and the ascension of Augustus into Heaven; by two silver cups from Boscoreale showing the submission of the Germanic Sugambri to Augustus and Tiberius; and by a silver dish of Aquileia, which shows the emperor surrounded by the four seasons and by all the symbols of the fertility, plenty, and prosperity of the Golden Age.

The building and artistic activity of the Augustan period was not confined to Rome. A study of the ruins of the cities of northern and central Italy reinforces the view that the Augustan Age was a period of economic prosperity and of great building activity by the local aristocracy. The western provinces, especially Gaul, copied or borrowed from the newly erected monuments of Rome. The time of Augustus produced the famous Roman temple at Nîmes (Nemausus), the so-called Maison Carrée, notable for its classical harmony, symmetry, and delicate finish; possibly also the lofty Pont du Gard, which rises on three tiers of arches 160 feet above the deep gorge of the river Gard and carries on its top an aqueduct that brought fresh water to Nimes; an unfortified city gate (Porte de Mars) at Reims (Durocortorum, Remi, Rheims); and at Orange (Arausio) a triumphal arch and an immense theater, whose colonnade and central niche housed a colossal statue of Augustus.

Literature The Augustan Age was one of the great periods of world literature, comparable to that of Pericles in Athens, of Elizabeth I in England, and of Louis XIV in France. It has usually been called the Golden Age because, in the judgment of later generations, Roman literature acquired its highest perfection in form and expression during the Augustan principate. The term *Augustan Age,* as applied to English literature of the early eighteenth century, has come to connote the "correct" and "classical" expression of the gracious elegance and polished *urbanitas* of everyday human life in an aristocratic society. It denotes a period in which literature was in perfect harmony with the aims and ideals of the governing class. As in the past, therefore, Roman literature of the Augustan Age often reflects a patriotic concern with Rome's history and contemporary subjects of political importance.

Augustan Rome provided conditions highly favorable to literature. After a century of chaos and civil bloodshed, an era of general peace and ordered government evoked the gratitude, pride, and enthusiasm of the Roman people. It offered themes for literary glorification: a heroic past and a great and glorious present. Already the political capital of the

La Maison Carrée at Nîmes.
(Courtesy French Government
Tourist Office)

Pont du Gard, Nîmes. (Joelle Burrows)

Mediterranean world, Rome was rapidly becoming the cultural center, attracting students, scholars, and writers from abroad.

Unlike the age of Caesar, in which prose writers predominated (Cicero, Caesar, Sallust, Nepos, and Varro), the Augustan Age was notable for its poets (Vergil, Horace, Tibullus, Propertius, and Ovid). It was essentially an age of poetry. Even Livy's great history of Rome, *Ab Urbe Condita,* was no exception, for it was regarded by some critics as an epic in prose form. The *Ab Urbe Condita* began where the *Aeneid* of Vergil left off.

Vergil (70 to 19 B.C.) Publius Vergilius Maro, son of a northern Italian farmer near Mantua, gave up a career in the courts, to study philosophy with Siro the Epicurean at Naples but turned to poetry after Siro's death. In 38 or 37 B.C., he published his *Eclogues* (*Bucolics*), ten short pastorals in the style of the Hellenistic Greek poet Theocritus, poems idealizing country life and the loves and sorrows of shepherds. They were more than pretty pastorals, however. For example, the first and the ninth refer to the dispossession of small farmers to settle Octavian's veterans after Philippi. The fifth and ninth also refer to the deification of Julius Caesar, while the fourth predicts the re-

turn of the Golden Age with the birth of a child. The sixth is reminiscent of Lucretius with its exposition of Epicurean philosophy, and the tenth is a tribute to fellow poet Cornelius Gallus (p. 289).

The *Eclogues* had brought Vergil to the attention of Gaius Cilnius Maecenas, a wealthy equestrian of Etruscan descent, patron of literature, and close friend of Augustus. With Maecenas' support, Vergil began, and by 29 B.C. had completed, his *Georgics,* a didactic poem in four books, like Hesiod's *Works and Days.* Not intended as a technical handbook like Varro's *De Re Rustica,* the *Georgics* nevertheless describe with realism and firsthand experience the various activities of the farmer—plowing, the harvest, the care of vines and orchards, the breeding of cattle, and the keeping of bees. The poem was a hymn of praise to Italy's soil and sturdy farmers and to Augustus for restoring the peace so essential for prosperous agriculture and human happiness.

After completing the *Georgics,* Vergil spent the next decade in the composition of his greatest work, the *Aeneid,* a national epic in twelve books, the first six of which correspond to Homer's *Odyssey,* the last six to the *Iliad.* Written in the smoothest and most beautiful narrative and in stately dactylic hexameter verse, the *Aeneid* unfolds the destiny of Rome from the burning of Troy and the landing of the hero Aeneas in Latium to its rise as a great world empire, of which the Augustan Age was the culmination. It glorifies as the fulfillment of Fate's decrees the achievements of the Roman People from Aeneas to Augustus. Although Aeneas, the legendary ancestor of the Julian family, is nominally the hero, the real hero is Rome: Her mission is to rule the world, to teach the nations the way of peace, to spare the vanquished, and to subdue the proud. The fulfillment of this mission requires of all her heroes the virtues that made Rome great: courage, piety, devotion to duty, constancy, and faith. Vergil's emphasis upon these virtues was in line with the Augustan reformation of morals and the revival of ancient faith (*prisca fides*).

In contrast, Vergil, like Lucretius before him, condemns the lust (*cupido*) and blind emotion (*furor*) that he saw as the causes of prior civil strife. It is these destructive forces that hinder Aeneas and the Trojans from fulfilling the glorious destiny that Jupiter has decreed for Rome and that the virtuous hero Aeneas must overcome. Unfortunately, Vergil usually portrays these evil forces in feminine terms, which help perpetuate the negative stereotype of women in Western literature.

Furious Juno causes constant disasters for Aeneas and his fellow Trojans because long ago Paris had not chosen her as the most beautiful goddess in the famous contest with Minerva (Athena) and Venus (Aphrodite). At Carthage, on whose shores Juno's storm has wrecked Aeneas' fleet, Queen Dido's Juno-inspired passion for Aeneas threatens to divert him from his manly task. Jupiter has to remind him that he has more important things to do than dally in the seductive embraces of a foreign woman. When Aeneas dutifully abandons Dido, her passionate love turns to furious, self-destructive hatred, and her dying curse makes Carthage Rome's implacable enemy forever.

At one point, even the Trojan women tire of the rigors imposed by Aeneas' heroic mission. Weakly succumbing to Juno's temptations and the prospect of settling on the hospitable shores of Sicily, they try to burn the Trojan fleet.

When the Trojans finally do get to Italy, they become embroiled in a desperate war with the native peoples. The Rutilian king Turnus, jealous over Aeneas' betrothal to Lavinia, daughter of King Latinus, is enflamed with lust for war and revenge at Juno's bidding by the Fury Allecto, one of the most powerfully portrayed female demons in literature.

On his deathbed Vergil requested the burning of the *Aeneid*, for he considered it not yet perfected, but Augustus countermanded that request and ordered it published.

Horace (65 to 8 B.C.)   Another great poet of the age was Quintus Horatius Flaccus, son of a fairly well-to-do freedman of Venusia in Apulia. A sincere believer in a good education, his father sent him to school in Rome and later to higher studies at Athens. There Horace met the conservative noble Brutus and, like many young idealistic Romans studying abroad, he fought for the Republic at Philippi. Afterward, he returned to Rome penniless and got a job in a quaestor's office, which, though boring, gave him the time and means to write poetry.

By 35 B.C., he had composed some of his *Epodes,* bitter, pessimistic little poems in iambic meter (in imitation of the Greek poet Archilochus), and the first book of his *Satires* (which he called *Sermones,* informal "conversations" in colloquial style and in dactylic hexameter verse), where he pokes fun at the vices and follies of the capital. His earliest poems, though caustic, sometimes vulgar, and even obscene, were written in such a clear and incisive style and with such wit and cleverness as to win the admiration of Vergil, who introduced him to Maecenas in 38 B.C.

At first, Maecenas provided Horace an independent income and eventually (33 B.C.), a sizable estate in the Sabine country near modern Tivoli.

In 30 B.C., Horace published his second book of *Satires,* in which he is more mellow and less caustic than in the first. Meanwhile, he had begun and for seven years thereafter continued to work on his *Odes* (*Carmina*). The first three books, which appeared in 23 B.C., comprised eighty-eight poems of varying lengths and in a score of meters, most of which he derived from Greek poets like Sappho, Alcaeus, Archilochus, and Anacreon and adapted to Roman lyric form.

The *Odes,* a monument "more durable than brass and loftier than the pyramids of Egyptian kings" (*Odes* 3.30.1–2), on which the fame of Horace chiefly rests, touch lightly on many subjects, their variety adding yet another charm to artistry, compactness, pure diction, fastidious taste, and lightness. Some are so-called "wisdom poems" containing moral exhortations which he himself took seriously: Since Youth and Beauty touch us and soon are gone, let us enjoy them now; since envious time keeps running out, seize the occasion (*carpe diem*), "snatch the day." (*Odes* 1.11.8). Others discourse on friendship, the brevity of life, religion and philosophy, drinking wine, and making love, which for Horace was a pastime lightly comic, not an all-consuming passion as for Catullus. The long, solemn, so-called Roman odes, Pindaric in their splendor, praise the old virtues resurrected by Augustus: moderation and frugality, valor and patriotism, justice, piety, and faith. In proclaiming these virtues as the sole hope of Rome's salvation, Horace anticipated the implementation of the Augustan policy of social regeneration by at least five years.

In his later years, Horace wrote two books of *Epistles,* which were sermons on morals, religion, and philosophy rather than real letters like Cicero's. Although some of these so-called letters are charming and even entertaining, others seem stodgy, uninspiring, even repellent, but they commended themselves to critics of the English "Augustan Age" because of their wit, geniality, *urbanitas,* pretty phrasings, and paradoxes. The longest and most famous of these letters, the so-called *Art of Poetry* (*Ars Poetica*), sets forth the principles for writing poetry, especially tragedy. From it, Alexander Pope in the eighteenth century drew many of the principles versified in his *Essay on Criticism.*

The Latin Elegy

The elegiac couplet consisting of a dactylic hexameter alternating with a pentameter had served in Greek and Latin literature a variety of purposes—for drinking songs, patriotic and political poems, dirges, laments, epitaphs, votive dedications, epigrams, and love poetry. Following the innovations of Catullus (pp. 240–241), the first Roman to use the elegy extensively for love poetry was probably Gaius Cornelius Gallus (ca. 69 to 26 B.C.). His four books of *Amores* firmly established the subjective erotic elegy. Until 1978, none of Gallus' poems were known to exist. In Egypt that year, a piece of papyrus was discovered that contained one complete four-line poem and most of a second. Although not major poems, they do help to see Gallus more clearly in the literary context of the age and his influence on others.

After Gallus, came Albius Tibullus (54? to 19 B.C.); Sextus Propertius (50? to ca. 15 B.C.); Sulpicia (50? B.C.); and Ovid, Publius Ovidius Naso, (43 B.C. to A.D. 17/18). For smoothness and elegance, Quintilian (ca. A.D. 35? to 97?), the famous Roman professor of rhetoric (p. 353), liked Tibullus best. Some modern critics would agree.

Tibullus Of Tibullus there is known only the little he tells about himself in his first two books of sixteen elegies. Several are addressed to Delia and to Nemesis—two fatal attractions who alternately made him swoon with ecstasy or drove him to madness by their vile tempers and infidelities. Tibullus did not belong to the circle of Maecenas but to the smaller circle of the illustrious noble Marcus Valerius Messalla Corvinus (p. 250). He seems to have been handsome, elegant, and rich, but rather neurotic and sometimes even morbid. His two passions in life were girls and the peace and beauty of the country. The attraction of the first was often stronger than that of the second. In spite of his problems, he was a remarkable poet, clear, brilliant, never trite. His verse was smooth, elegant, musical, and he was a master of the elegy of love and of lament.

Propertius Some would prefer the Umbrian-born Propertius. His love was Cynthia, well-born, beautiful, gifted. To her he addressed four books of elegies, the chief burden of which was how she had bewitched him and how she was the sole cause of his joy and pain. In the end, her suspicions, rages, and infidelities drove him away to some other girl despite her charm.

Superior in some ways to Tibullus as a stylist, Propertius is a peculiar poet, bewildering and hard to understand. Frequently he abruptly veers off into some obscure Greek myth, which dulls the most passionate climacteric. Boldest and most original of poets, he yet manages somehow by his obscure allusions to destroy the fine effects achieved by the hard brilliance and sparkle of this verse.

Sulpicia The only poetess to survive from the Augustan Age is Sulpicia, the ward and probable niece of Messalla. Her date of birth can only be approximated to that of her contemporaries, and it is not known how long she lived. Six exquisite short elegies generally accepted as hers are preserved in the manuscripts of Tibullus. They are addressed to Cerinthus, the otherwise unknown object of her unpretentious affections. Notable for their directness and candor, they distill more true feeling than the longer poems of her more celebrated contemporaries.

Ovid The most sensual and sophisticated of the elegists was Ovid, who came to Rome from the little town of Sulmo in the remote mountain region of Samnium. His family were well-to-do equestrians, and for a while he pursued the career in the courts for which he had been trained. He eventually devoted himself to poetry, however. His style was very light, and he became the most prolific of the Augustan poets. He had no particular patron, was friends with both Tibullus and Propertius, and became part of a rather high-living set with low morals.

The two most informative and important of Ovid's works were the *Metamorphoses* (*Transformations*) and the *Fasti,* the first written in hexameters, the second in elegiacs. The *Metamorphoses,* a collection of 250 stories in 15 books, is a storehouse of information about Greek mythology and has been the source of inspiration to poets and painters ever since. More than that, however, the *Metamorphoses* was Ovid's answer to Vergils' *Aeneid,* an epic his-

tory of the world that culminated patriotically in the change of Julius Caesar from a man to a god. The *Fasti* or *Calendar* described and explained the astronomical, historical, and religious events associated with each month of the year, one book per month. It nicely complemented Augustus' attempt to revive the many priesthoods and religious observances that had fallen into disuse. Unfortunately, the work is unfinished and covers only the first six months.

Among his earliest works were the *Amores* or *Love Elegies,* written in the style of Tibullus, with less sincerity but with more polish and virtuosity and greater mastery of erotic verse. One of his most original undertakings was the *Heroides,* a group of fictitious poetic letters from famous legendary women to absent husbands or lovers and presenting the women's view of things. Then came his masterpiece, the *Art of Love,* a salacious handbook, perversely didactic, which explains all the arts of seduction and surveys all the known aspects of heterosexual experience from rape to incest. This thorough piece of research, which the two Julias (daughter and granddaughter of Augustus) both appreciated, gave offense to the *princeps* as an insult to the laws dealing with moral reform and the sanctity of marriage. The *princeps* remembered. Later, in A.D. 8, when Ovid became implicated in a scandal involving the younger Julia, Augustus ordered them banished: Julia to some rocky island in the Adriatic, the poet to the cold and uncivilized town of Tomi (Constantsa) on the Black Sea (his works having been removed from the public libraries and consigned to the flames). From Tomi, Ovid wrote with unusual depth of feeling two books of poems in graceful and melodious verse: the *Tristia* ("Sorrows") and the *Ex Ponto* ("Epistles from Pontus") in which he complains bitterly of the ice and snow on that dismal, treeless rock and the barbarity of the knife-wearing Getae. At Tomi, after many years of useless and pathetic begging for permission to return from exile, Ovid finally died (A.D. 17–18).

Latin Prose Writers The most notable prose writers of the Augustan Age were the soldier and statesman Gaius Asinius Pollio (76 B.C. to A.D. 4), the literary patron Marcus Valerius Messalla Corvinus (64 B.C. to A.D. 8), the Emperor Augustus himself (63 B.C. to A.D. 14), and the patriotic historian Titus Livy (59 B.C. to A.D. 17). Although not so great an orator as Cicero, Pollio had enjoyed an important military and political career as a partisan of Caesar and then of Marcus Antonius before siding with Octavian. He retired from public life after the treaty of Brundisium (40 B.C.) proved ineffective and founded Rome's first public library in a hall adjacent to the Temple of Liberty. He was a minor poet as well as an orator, but his importance is as a historian. Having firsthand knowledge of many important events and access to many valuable sources, he wrote a critical and authoritative history of the civil wars from 60 B.C. to the battle of Philippi. Although most of this valuable work is lost, it directly or indirectly is a major source for Plutarch's biographies of Caesar and Antony and Appian's *Civil Wars.*

Messalla, a respectable orator in his day and devotee of poetry, had served under Cassius at Philippi and then sided with Octavian, for whom he wrote attacks (now lost) on Antony. He wrote an independently minded firsthand account of the civil war following Caesar's assassination that would be very valuable to have. Unfortunately, it, too, is lost, and few traces of its influence can be found.

Marcus Agrippa and Augustus carried on the tradition of self-promotional autobiography started by Sulla. Both of their autobiographies are lost, but some information about Augustus' *Commentaries on His Own Life* remains. It shows that he surrounded himself with an aura of charismatic leadership by describing prodigies and prophesies that had signaled his greatness.

Augustus' *Res Gestae,* a very different type of work, has survived mostly intact thanks to its being published on multiple inscriptions in several provincial cites. A virtually complete bilingual Greek and Latin text is the *Monumentum Ankyranum* found at Ankara in modern Turkey. It officially records the achievements and honors of Augustus and formulates the constitutional position of the *princeps* in the reorganized state as he wished it to be viewed. It also shows Augustus as an excellent prose stylist. He wrote with clarity, brevity, and precision without shrinking from a slang or colloquial phrase that might express his meaning more accurately and vividly than another.

Livy Titus Livius (Livy), the supreme prose writer of the Augustan Age, came from Patavium (Padua) in Cisalpine Gaul. Of his *Ab Urbe Condita,* 142 books on the history of Rome from its founding to the death of Drusus I in 9 B.C., there are extant Books 1 to 10 (from the landing of Aeneas in Latium to 293 B.C.) and 21 to 45 (218 to 167 B.C.). The *Periochae,* short summaries or epitomes (written probably in the fourth century A.D.), indicate the contents of all the books except 136 and 137. Livy blended the styles of Cicero and Sallust with poetical phraseology and great dramatic skill to record the mighty deeds of the Romans as a divinely ordered march to world conquest. His stern preface denounced the luxury and vices of his own age. He proposed to show that Rome's success and greatness resulted from patriotism and traditional virtue: pious devotion to the gods, valor in war, self-control, constancy, *gravitas,* and the sanctity of family life. Although his work was of great literary merit and in full accord with the social reforms of Augustus, Livy had numerous defects as a historian: uncritical use of sources, failure to consult documents and other primary sources, ignorance of economics and military tactics, and failure to interpret primitive institutions in their proper social setting. Nevertheless, Livy succeeded in giving the world a compelling picture of Roman history and character as many Romans wanted to see it. That fact itself is of great significance for the modern historian.

Pompeius Trogus (ca. 50 B.C. to ca. A.D. 25)

A quite different type of historian was Pompeius Trogus. Livy wrote from the patriotic perspective of Rome and Italy and was not interested in other people except insofar as Rome conquered and Romanized them. Trogus wrote from the perspective of a provincial native, albeit a heavily Romanized one. He came from

Transalpine Gaul, and his grandfather had received Roman citizenship from Pompey the Great in return for loyal service against Sertorius. His father had served under Caesar. Like Cornelius Nepos, however, he was much more interested in what Romans could learn from non-Romans than in glorifying an idealized Roman past. Out of the forty-four books of his *Philippic Histories* (*Historiae Philippicae*), only two focussed on Rome. The bulk concentrated on Macedon and the great Hellenistic empires of Macedonian conquerors after Philip and Alexander. Others covered the Near East and Greece to the rise of Macedon. The rest treated Parthia, Spain, and Gaul to the time of Augustus. Unfortunately, the full text with much valuable information is lost, but a condensed version exists in an epitome made by Justin in the second or third century A.D.

The Impact of Augustus on Latin Literature

In a society where writers depend on wealthy or powerful personal patrons, those patrons have a great impact on literary production. Directly, or indirectly through Maecenas, the impact of Augustus was great indeed. That is not to say that he dictated what people wrote. Livy, for example, was no hack writing official history for Augustus. He wrote with a genuine patriotism that happened to coincide with Augustus' own needs and policies. The same can be said for Vergil, Horace, and Propertius, but that is what helped to attract the interest and patronage of Maecenas and Augustus, which in turn enabled them to pursue their writing and ensured a public audience for and the survival of their works. Indeed, Augustus personally intervened to secure the publication of the *Aeneid* against Vergil's own wishes. This situation was not necessarily harmful, but it raises the question of how many talented writers, either through lack of connections or because of incompatible views, failed because they could not find a powerful patron.

Augustus, of course, tolerated disagreement and was too intelligent to exercise any real censorship. Propertius, for example, often resisted Maecenas' request that he write on something favorable to Augustus. Augustus himself even joked with Livy about the latter being a Pompeian in his political sympathies, but Augustus was safely dead before Livy wrote about the sensitive events after Actium. It may not be coincidental that under Augustus' successors the summaries of the relevant books (134 to 142) in the *Periochae* give them the shortest shrift of all. More directly, however, the career of Cornelius Gallus was cut short because he committed suicide after Augustus expressed official displeasure over the way in which he tactlessly publicized his military accomplishments as the first prefect of Egypt. Gallus' disgrace, therefore, may help to account for the disappearance of his work until the recently discovered Egyptian papyrus (which may be contemporary with his own life). Although official disgrace had no such effect on Ovid's work, it did prevent him from finishing the *Fasti* and may well have denied the world better works than the pathetic *Tristia* bemoaning his exile and begging for release.

Greek Writers

Educated men from the Greek-speaking parts of the Empire continued to produce much literature for Greek audiences. Of special note are two who worked in Rome under Augustus. The first is Diodorus Siculus (the Sicilian). He wrote a history of the world in forty books from the earliest days to Caesar's conquest of Gaul. It is not a particularly distinguished work of history as such, but it is similar to the works of Nepos and Pompeius Trogus. It covers not only Greece and Rome but also Egypt, Mesopotamia, India, Scythia, Arabia, and North Africa, about which most ancient authors say little. Moreover, because Diodorus compiled his work from important earlier historians whose works are lost, his history gives an indication of what they wrote.

More important for the history of Rome and Italy is Dionysius of Halicarnassus, who taught Greek rhetoric at Rome from 30 to 8 B.C. and established an influential literary circle. His most famous work is the *Roman Antiquities*. It covered the history of Rome from its founding to the First Punic War in twenty books. Although the work suffers from rhetorical exaggeration, it preserves valuable material from lost Roman annalists and antiquarians on that period of Roman history, which is the most poorly documented.

Dionysius is even more valuable as a literary critic who influenced the tastes of the day. His essay *On the Arrangement of Words* discusses the artistic ordering of words, and his *On Imitation,* which is preserved only in fragments, sets forth the principles to be followed when imitating earlier authors, a practice considered essential for developing a good style. In an essay on the style of Thucydides, he also reveals the impact that Thucydides had on writers of the late first century B.C., and a letter to C. Pompeius, in which he criticizes the style of Plato, reveals some of the stylistic controversies of the period. Especially valuable is his partially preserved *On the Ancient Orators,* which presents biographical and stylistic information about the classical Attic orators.

Also important was a Greek from Pontus named Strabo (64–63 B.C. to ca. A.D. 25). His forty-seven books of history, exclusive of that covered by Polybius, are unfortunately lost, but his *Geography* in seventeen books survives. It covers the known world of the time. Although it is not always based on the best available mathematical, astronomical, and geographic research of the day, it presents in readable form much interesting geographical and historical information that would otherwise be lost.

Scholarly and Technical Writings

Antiquarian scholarship, handbooks, and technical manuals of all types became increasingly popular from Augustus' time onward. The *De Architectura* of Vitruvius became the standard handbook for Roman architects and exercised great influence on the neoclassical architecture of the Renaissance and later classical revivals. Verrius Flaccus, the tutor of Gaius and Lucius Caesar, compiled the earliest Latin dictionary, *De Verborum Significatu,* and Marcus Agrippa set up a large map of the Roman Empire in the Forum, for which he wrote a detailed explanation in his *Commentaries* that summarized the

results of Greek geographic research and Roman surveying. A few years later, under Tiberius, Aulus Cornelius Celsus compiled an important encyclopedia, whose section on medicine still survives as a valuable summary of earlier Greek medical knowledge.

Philology and Literary Scholarship The works of Cicero, Vergil, and Horace were hailed as classics in their own lifetimes. They inspired a steady stream of philologists who analyzed their language and style and scholarly commentators who dealt with literary and historical questions raised by their work. Among the earliest known are Caecilius Epirota, who began to give popular lectures on Vergil even before the *Aeneid* was finished, and Gaius Julius Hyginus, who supervised Augustus' great public library on the Palatine and published a famous series of commentaries on Vergil. Neither's work has survived, but Hyginus is the source of much material preserved in the works of later commentators.

Jurisprudence

The Augustan Age marks the beginning of the classical period of Roman jurisprudence, which lasted until the reign of Diocletian. It saw the creative ideas of the Republic elaborated in great detail. Genius was now slowly giving way to professionalism. As the old Roman families of high pedigree and proud public achievement gradually became extinct, new jurists and legal experts from Italian and even provincial towns came to the fore. Though some jurists held high office in the early Principate, after Vespasian's time (A.D. 69 to 79) another type more commonly appeared, the salaried officials of the Imperial regime. Many of the jurists were practicing consultants, writers, and professors of law.

Responsa Augustus did not abolish the custom established by the early pontiffs and later jurisconsults of giving expert opinions or rulings (*responsa*) on legal questions. Either he or Tiberius may have first given select jurists the right to give responses reinforced by his own personal authority (*ius respondendi ex auctori-*

tate principis). Most praetors and judges respected and accepted these responses but were under no legal obligation to do so. Unauthorized jurists were still free to give responses and magistrates and judges to accept them. Official authorization of jurisconsults did not endure beyond the reign of Trajan (A.D. 98 to 117).

Law Schools As Roman society became more complex and jurists more active in civil and criminal cases than during the Republic, the demand for legal education increased correspondingly. In the first century A.D., two law schools sprang into being. One, said to have been founded by Ateius Capito (*consul suffectus* of A.D. 5), was actually a foundation of C. Cassius Longinus, who died shortly after A.D. 69, but the school is often called Sabinian after Masurius Sabinus, a famous teacher of Cassius. The other school was probably a foundation of M. Antistius Labeo in the time of Augustus even though it later received the name of Pro-

culian from a certain Proculus, who allegedly taught law during Nero's reign.

The Augustan Achievement Law flourishes only in times of peace. Although Augustus had started his career as another self-seeking leader in civil war, he made up for the destructiveness of his early years by earnestly trying to construct for Rome a better future. The restoration of peace and orderly government after Actium and the economic upsurge that followed laid the groundwork for a brilliant efflorescence of art and literature, which Augustus himself did much to inspire and encourage. Augustan art not only achieved complete Romanization but also acquired an empire-wide character, as shown by the sculptures on the Altar of Carthage and numerous monuments in *Gallia Narbonensis*. In Vergil, Horace, Propertius, and Ovid, the Latin language was perfected as a poetic medium, and Latin literature became one of the great literatures of the world.

XXVI

The First Two Julio-Claudian Emperors: Tiberius and Gaius (Caligula), A.D. 14 to 41

Augustus established the longest and most complex family of Roman emperors until the dynasty of Constantine and that of Valentinian and Theodosius 300 years later. Augustus' dynastic successors are called the Julio-Claudians because of their connections with the Claudian family of Augustus' wife Livia and his own Julian family. Of the four following Julio-Claudian emperors, Augustus' immediate successor, Tiberius, son of Livia by her first husband, was the only one without Julian ancestry. The other three, Gaius (popularly known as Caligula), Claudius, and Nero, were members of both families. The four reigns fall conveniently into two pairs, each of twenty-six and one-half years: Tiberius and Gaius (A.D. 14 to 41) and Claudius and Nero (A.D. 41 to 68).

In order to understand fully the characters of these important emperors and the intrigues and complexities of their reigns, it is necessary to keep in mind the intricate relationships of the Julio-Claudian family as seen in the accompanying genealogical chart. In his tenacious attempt to provide a successor closely related to himself by manipulating the marriages of his daughter Julia, his sister Octavia's children, and Livia's children, Augustus created not only a confusing web of relationships but also jealousies, rivalries, and intrigues that bedeviled and even warped those who managed to attain the office of *princeps* that he created.

Sources for the Julio-Claudians Only two surviving ancient writers give significant continuous accounts of the whole Julio-Claudian period. The first wrote in Latin, the second in Greek. They are Suetonius in his *Lives of the Twelve Caesars* and Cassius Dio in Books 57 to 63 of his *Roman History*. Both authors lived after the events that they describe. Suetonius was born about A.D. 69, right around the end of Nero's reign, and died around 140. He practiced law for a time and was the Emperor Hadrian's Secretary in Charge of Correspondence from ca. A.D. 119 to ca. 122. He was dismissed by Hadrian as a result of some scandal and spent the rest of his life writing in retirement. Cassius Dio, a member of the Greek aristocracy of Nicaea in Bithynia, was born about A.D. 150 and died around 235 after a distinguished senatorial career including two consulships and two provincial governorships.

As a child, Suetonius would have heard some firsthand information about the Julio-Claudians from his elders, and while serving Hadrian he had access to archival documents, which he often quotes. As a high-ranking senator, Dio also had access to much official information, but he seems not to have made much use of it. Both he and Suetonius were primarily dependent upon the narratives written by earlier authors. Because the earlier writers were mainly from the senatorial aristocracy, who often resented their loss of real power and privi-

THE JULIO-CLAUDIAN DYNASTY (Emperors are shown boldface)

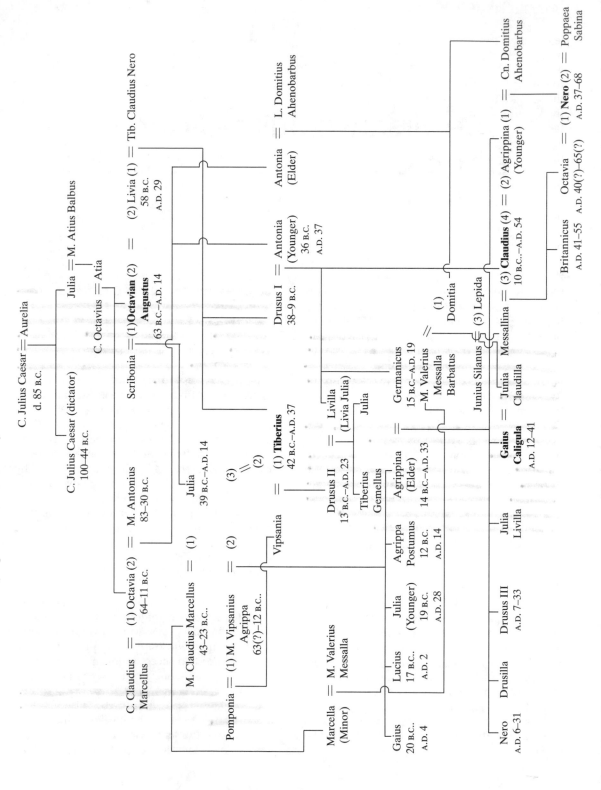

leges under the principate, the words of Suetonius and Dio often reflect a negative bias toward the Julio-Claudians. Moreover, both Suetonius and Dio had an unfailing attraction to the sensational and scandalous. Therefore, in their works, the plain unvarnished truth often takes a back seat to the baseless rumors, damaging innuendoes, and malicious fabrications that they frequently found in other writers.

Other important literary sources exist for individual Julio-Claudian emperors. Velleius Paterculus, who was a loyal cavalry officer under Tiberius, presents a very favorable account of Tiberius' reign in the last part of the second book of his *History of Rome.* For Caligula, the Jewish historian Flavius Josephus in his *Jewish Antiquities,* Books 18 and 19, and the Jewish scholar Philo of Alexandria in his *Against Flaccus* and *Embassy to Gaius* present good contemporary accounts of certain events. Book 19 of Josephus' *Jewish Antiquities* and Books 2 to 7 of his *History of the Jewish War* also cover events under Claudius and the Jewish revolt under Nero. Also, the philosopher Seneca the Younger, who had been exiled under Claudius, is believed to have written a scathing satire of that Emperor, the *Apocolocyntosis* (*Pumpkinification*). The various philosophical and literary works of Seneca and the numerous nonhistorical writings of other authors reveal much about the social, economic, cultural, and even political history of the period (pp. 346–350).

A far more detailed and greater literary source than any of these others is the *Annals* of Tacitus in its surviving books. It originally covered events from A.D. 14 to 69. Now, only Books 1 to 6 (with most of Book 5 missing), covering the reign of Tiberius, and Books 12 to 16, covering the reign of Nero to 66, survive. Just as Edward Gibbon, who greatly admired Tacitus, has exercised a profound influence on modern historians of the Roman Empire because of a superb literary style combined with an intense personal viewpoint, so has Tacitus.

A conscientious historian cannot accept Tacitus' views of people and events uncritically. He came from the ranks of conservative senators who resented the loss of independence and prestige that the senate suffered in the shadow of the emperors. He himself had experienced increasing despotism during the last years of the Emperor Domitian (A.D. 81 to 96) and tended to interpret the actions of previous emperors in that light. In fact, he became rather cynical and disillusioned about life in general. Expecting the worst, Tacitus easily saw it when the opposite could not be clearly proven.

Trained in rhetoric and law, Tacitus approached history as a prosecuting attorney determined, as he himself said, to "preserve the record of virtuous men and to make evil men and evil deeds fear judgment at the bar of posterity." It is often necessary, therefore, that the modern reader of Tacitus act the roles of both the defense and the jury: the one to highlight the favorable evidence that Tacitus usually concedes as he rhetorically builds a case against it; the other to arrive at a balanced judgment.

The modern historian is also aided in this task by the abundant archaeological research that has brought to light numerous coins, artifacts, monuments, inscriptions, and the remains of whole cities and towns from this period. This physical evidence illustrates the social, economic, and administrative developments that the ancient literary sources slight in favor of investigating the emperors' personalities, high politics, court intrigue, and wars. From the nonliterary evidence it is possible to estimate what was happening to the more ordinary inhabitants of the Empire under their rulers, whose lives and deeds are the main focus of the literary sources.

Tiberius (A.D. 14 to 37) The full name of Tiberius was Tiberius Claudius Nero. He was fifty-five years old when he succeeded Augustus in A.D. 14, already past the prime of life for those times. His long years of experience were both a blessing and a curse. On the one hand, his lengthy service first as a successful general on the frontiers and then as Augustus' virtual understudy for ten years made him uniquely fitted to step into the role of *princeps* without having to learn new lines. On the other hand, his personal history had made him an actor quite unsuited to the character whom he had to play.

Born during civil war in 42 B.C., Tiberius had spent his first two years with his parents in fearful exile. In 38, his mother, Livia, persuaded his father to divorce her, though pregnant with Drusus I, so that she could marry the rising star Octavian (Augustus), who seems to have disliked Tiberius, a shy lad with slow, halting speech. Augustus preferred Drusus I, who was born after his marriage to Livia and had a jovial, appealing personality more compatible with his own.

Serious and self-effacing, however, Tiberius had worked hard and dutifully performed all of the Imperial service demanded. Nevertheless, Augustus had chosen to advance Tiberius as his successor only when there was no other choice. Even then, he had tried to arrange that his sister's grandson Germanicus (son of Drusus I) would be preferred to Tiberius' own son as Tiberius' successor. It is no wonder that Tiberius was a sour and tight-lipped man whom many of the nobles in the senate neither liked nor trusted after he became emperor.

Many, for example, believed that he was simply being a hypocrite when he declared that he was reluctant to take up the post of *princeps,* the right to which he had often been denied. Perhaps he was merely imitating Augustus' politic reluctance of 27 B.C., but he may also have been genuinely ambivalent and lacking in self-confidence after his earlier experiences. He eventually accepted with the proviso that he had the right to step down when a suitable successor could be found. Unfortunately, the suitable ones all died before they were ready to relieve him of his heavy burden.

The principate of Tiberius began ominously with the execution of Agrippa Postumus, the grandson of Augustus but a brutal and intractable person, whom Augustus had exiled to a barren island in A.D. 7. It is not known who made the decision or ordered the killing—Augustus, perhaps Livia, or Tiberius. Suspicion fell upon Tiberius. So Tacitus reports in his *Annals* and calls the execution the "first crime of the new principate" (*primum facinus novi principatus*).

Already Tacitus has subtly cast Tiberius as a murderous tyrant by stating the suspicion against him in this case as strongly as possible. Nevertheless, it is quite likely that Augustus had advised that Postumus be executed, and there was good reason to do so. He would have made a very bad emperor, and if he were to remain alive after Augustus, there were those who, for their own ambitions or dislike of Tiberius, would have promoted his claim. Such a situation would have created dangerous political instability for Rome.

Postumus' mother was Julia, Augustus' exiled daughter and Tiberius' ex-wife. Although Tiberius had once tried to save her from exile, he, Livia, and their advisors now probably considered her another potential pawn for those who were opposed to his succession. Therefore, Tiberius cut off the funds that supported her in exile at Rhegium, and she died of starvation not long after her father's death (A.D. 14).

The Mutiny of the Legions   Shortly after the accession of Tiberius, the legions stationed in Pannonia (Hungary) and those in the Lower Rhineland mutinied in protest against the long terms of service, wretched pay, and discipline enforced by beatings and brutalities. Tiberius sent his natural son, Drusus II, to Pannonia to quell the mutiny there, and Germanicus, his adopted son and heir (son of his brother, Drusus I), to the Rhineland. They successfully restored discipline, and through Germanicus, Tiberius proceeded to restore the martial spirit of the legions in Germany and keep the German tribes in check with some vigorous campaigning across the Rhine.

Germanicus   Three successful campaigns from A.D. 14 to 16 gave Germanicus the chance to solidify his reputation as a worthy heir apparent, and a defeat of the German Arminius made it possible to boast that Rome had avenged the defeat of Varus in the Teutoburg Forest (p. 269). Tacitus may well be unfair to Tiberius in claiming that he jealously prevented Germanicus from making permanent conquests across the Rhine. Tiberius probably agreed with Augustus' assessment that Rome did not have the manpower and resources to conquer and hold down a large piece of new territory east of the Rhine. Germanicus' campaigns were designed to destabilize and weaken the Germans, not conquer them permanently. It was a wise policy that soon bore fruit. Arminius and Maroboduus, the powerful king of the Marcomanni in what is now Bohemia, began to quarrel and then to fight. Maroboduus lost his kingdom and fled to Italy as a refugee. Arminius fell victim to an assassin's dagger. Bohemia became virtually a client kingdom of Rome.

After receiving Germanicus at Rome with highest honors (including a splendid triumph), Tiberius sent him to the Near East with powers transcending those of all governors and legates in that area. The purpose of the mission was to negotiate with Artabanus III, the ambitious and aggressive king of Parthia, to place upon the once-more-vacant throne of Armenia a king friendly to Rome, and to superintend the annexation of the kingdoms of Cappadocia, Cilicia, and Commagene as Imperial provinces. Germanicus carried out these difficult tasks with consummate efficiency and success.

All might have ended well had not Tiberius feared that after his successes in Germany Germanicus might impulsively embroil the Empire in an all-out war with Parthia. To act as a brake upon the young prince, he sent the experienced Cn. Calpurnius Piso to the East as governor of Syria. The choice was unfortunate. Piso hated Germanicus and refused to acknowledge him as a superior officer or obey his orders.

Germanicus was guilty of mistakes, too. Without authorization from Tiberius, he went to Egypt, where he accepted divine honors and opened reserve granaries for the relief of starvation in Alexandria. Although that generous act did not endanger the food supply of Rome, his journey to Egypt seemed contrary to the policy of Augustus and naturally irritated the suspicious and legalistic mind of Tiberius, who complained bitterly before the senate.

On his return to Syria, Germanicus found that Piso had contemptuously disobeyed all his

orders, and he had no alternative but to order him out of the province. Shortly after Piso's expulsion, Germanicus took sick at Antioch. In his illness and delirium, he accused Piso of attempting to destroy him by sorcery and poison. Then, calling upon his wife and children to avenge his murder, he died.

The body of Germanicus was hastily cremated. His wife, Augustus' granddaughter Agrippina the Elder, set out for Rome with the ashes. Piso seized the opportunity to regain control of Syria by force, but he was defeated and taken to Rome. There he was brought to trial before the senate on three charges: the murder of Germanicus, insubordination in disobeying a superior officer, and attempting to recover a province from which he had been ordered to depart. Although acquitted of the charge of murder, he was convicted and condemned on the others. Upon hearing of the senate's judgment, Piso committed suicide.

Agrippina suspected Tiberius of complicity in Germanicus' death on the grounds that he was jealous of Germanicus' popularity and wanted to clear the way for his own son, Drusus II, to succeed. The unwillingness of Tiberius and Livia to participate in the extensive public mourning for Germanicus furthered these suspicions. There is no need to impugn their motives, however: Tiberius would have found it difficult to eulogize an impetuous man who had acted unwisely on significant occasions; he might have felt that his own austere personality would suffer in the eyes of the public by comparison with the affable, outgoing man being mourned; and he and Livia may genuinely have wished to remain in the background so as not to appear to be competing with Agrippina, her children, and her dead husband for public attention. Furthermore, Piso's suicide convinced others that he really was guilty of poisoning Germanicus (Piso probably was only trying to avoid execution so that his property would go to his heirs instead of being forfeited to the state), and it made his friends in the senate suspect that he had been made a scapegoat for Tiberius. For much of his reign, therefore, Tiberius had to contend with the slanders of Agrippina, who, along with her children, was a figure around whom those senators who disliked Tiberius could rally.

Sejanus A man who took advantage of the situation for his own self-aggrandizement and made it even worse for Tiberius was L. Aelius Seianus Sejanus. Tacitus portrays him as one of the most infamous and sinister personalities in Roman history. He was a natural target of senatorial resentment because he is a prime example of how the Principate opened up the high levels of government to the equestrian class, whom the Republican nobility had tried to exclude. His father had risen to be a prefect of the Praetorian Guard, and Sejanus eventually became his colleague. After his father's death, he made the guard an even greater base of power for himself by persuading Tiberius to make him sole prefect and allow him to concentrate its nine cohorts, hitherto scattered throughout Italy, into new barracks on the eastern outskirts of Rome. In 20, he raised many eyebrows at Rome by obtaining the betrothal of his infant daughter, Junilla, to the young son that Germanicus' brother, Claudius (the future emperor), had by his first wife. The accidental death of the boy, however, soon ended the possibility of that union with the Imperial family.

Allegations that Sejanus seduced Livilla (Livia Julia), sister of Germanicus and wife of Tiberius' son, Drusus II, and that the two murdered her husband cannot be substantiated but are easy to understand: Drusus II died suddenly in 23, and Sejanus attempted to obtain permission to marry Livilla. Probably he simply took advantage of a fortuitous opportunity provided by Drusus' death in an attempt to maneuver himself into some kind of Imperial partnership with Livilla's son, Tiberius' grandson, Tiberius Gemellus. Tiberius, however, refused to permit the marriage. In the meantime, Agrippina the Elder was doing everything that she could to advance the claims of her three sons by Germanicus: Nero (not the future emperor), Drusus III, and Gaius (Caligula). Because Agrippina made no secret of her dislike of Tiberius, Sejanus needed little effort to convince the suspicious emperor that she and her sons were plotting against him and the accession of Gemellus.

Sejanus' intrigues against Agrippina became increasingly bold in 26, when Tiberius, at his urging, decided to leave the hectic capital for semiretirement on the lovely island of Capreae (Capri) in the Bay of Naples. Using his power and influence as praetorian prefect, Sejanus attacked Agrippina's highly placed friends with charges of treason (*maiestas*) and drove them into exile or procured their deaths by execution or suicide. After the death of the old Empress Livia at the age of eighty-six in 29, he apparently attacked Agrippina and her family directly by convincing Tiberius that they were plotting against the throne. Agrippina and Nero were exiled on desert islands, and Drusus III was cast into prison.

Sejanus' attempt to maneuver himself and his family into the Imperial line seemed to be working. In Rome, the statues of Sejanus and Tiberius stood side by side, and altars to clemency and friendship conjointly commemorated their virtues. Only one obstacle to Sejanus' plans now remained: Agrippina's third son Gaius (Caligula), whom Tiberius had recommended in a letter to the senate as heir to the throne. Sejanus sought to remove that obstacle by a plot against the life of Gaius. Then suddenly something went wrong.

Antonia, the younger daughter of the triumvir Marcus Antonius and grandmother of the young prince Gaius, who was living with her, secretly sent her freedman Pallas to Tiberius, who promptly summoned Gaius to the safety of Capri at the end of August in 30. Apparently, Antonia had succeeded in arousing Tiberius' suspicions against his powerful minister. To keep Sejanus off guard, Tiberius let him become a colleague in the consulship at the start of 31, approved a grant of proconsular *imperium*, bestowed priesthoods on Sejanus and his older son, Strabo, and consented to his marrying either Livilla or her daughter by Drusus II, the princess Julia. In October of 31, Tiberius finally sprang the trap. He sent Naevius Sutorius Macro, prefect of the *vigiles*, to Rome to take over command of the Praetorian Guard and convey to the senate a long and wordy letter. The letter, read out by the presiding consul, began with mild praise of Sejanus. Praise became criticism, criticism reproof, and reproof sharp denunciation and a peremptory order for arrest. The senate at once voted condemnation and death. The populace hailed the fall of Sejanus with frenzied joy, pulled down his statues, dragged his body through the streets, and flung it into the Tiber. The execution of his son Strabo soon followed and a few weeks later that of his second son, Aelianus Capito, and his young daughter, Junilla. Many of his friends and supporters fell victim to the infuriated mob. Still, nothing changed for Agrippina, Nero, and Drusus III. Nero, a victim of murder or suicide, had already died in exile; Tiberius ignored Agrippina, who died in exile, too, and Drusus III was left to starve to death in prison.

Apicata, the divorced wife of Sejanus, committed suicide, but before doing so she wrote Tiberius a letter with the tale that Sejanus and Livilla had murdered Drusus II, the heir to the throne. The former slave attendants of Drusus, when put to torture, understandably confirmed the charge, and Tiberius believed that he had been the unwitting accomplice in a conspiracy against himself. He resolved to eradicate and destroy it.

The Law of Treason (*Maiestas*)

The law of treason (*maiestas*) gave Tiberius a powerful weapon. Under him and Augustus, it had come to include not only high treason (*perduellio*) but also such things as arrogance, sacrilege, slander, extortion, adultery, incest, rape, and murder. Tiberius has been accused of using it to institute a tyrannical reign of terror. Out of 106 known cases, however, only 35 succeeded, because Tiberius often favored acquittal or disallowed convictions handed down in lower courts.

The Informers (Delatores)

Private informers (*delatores*) were encouraged to accuse people under the law of treason because they would usually receive one fourth of a convicted person's property. Unfortunately, they were necessary because there was no system of public prosecutors. Nevertheless, their number and

successes often have been exaggerated at Tiberius' expense. In fact, there were serious penalties for false and malicious accusations, and Tiberius even exiled some unscrupulous *delatores*.

Tiberius and the Senate: The Increasing Power of the *Princeps*

Nevertheless, the increase of *delatores* and treason trials in the latter part of Tiberius' reign embittered his already precarious relations with many senators, which had always been full of irony. They reveal a serious paradox in the nature of the Augustan principate that could not be resolved except in the direction of increased power for the *princeps*. Conscientiously following Augustus' model, as he always tried to do, Tiberius earnestly attempted to make the senate a meaningful partner in the government of the Empire. He styled himself as an equal citizen with the senators and refused such honors as the *praenomen Imperator* and the title *Pater Patriae*. If a worthy senator fell into such financial difficulties that his status as a senator was threatened, Tiberius generously provided the money to remedy the problem. Before abandoning Rome for Capri, Tiberius had tried to attend all meetings of the senate. He encouraged freedom of speech and debate. At least once, he ended as a minority of one when a vote was taken.

Tiberius also increased the powers and responsibilities of the senate. For example, he transferred to it the age-old prerogative of the Centuriate Assembly: the function of electing the consuls and praetors, the most prestigious magistrates. He made the senate a supreme court of justice, especially for the trial of influential persons accused of treason and of both Imperial and senatorial provincial governors accused of extortion and corruption. Though some treason trials even as late as A.D. 20 took place in the regular praetors' courts, Tiberius preferred to have such cases tried in the senate because it was less vulnerable to bribery and intimidation by powerful defendants.

He made it a practice to consult the senate on all affairs of state. Yet all of these attempts to make the senators responsible partners in government did not really work. They knew that in the last analysis Tiberius' powers as *princeps* were far greater than theirs, and his very attempts to encourage senators to speak their minds freely only added to the suspicion that he was trying to set traps for those who did not like him. A remark addressed to Tiberius by Gnaeus Piso aptly illustrates the problem: "I would ask you sire: when are you going to vote? If first, you set me an example to follow; if last, I am afraid that I may unintentionally disagree with you." No matter how much Tiberius might try to disguise the fact, the senators knew that they were the clients of the powerful *princeps,* and it was impossible for them to forget it. Their distress was highlighted after Tiberius retired to Capri and they had to wait for his letters to find out what he wanted them to do.

An Insolvable Problem It is easy, therefore, to accuse many senators of servility, as even Tiberius once did. In a moment of frustration at their refusal of responsibility, he called them "men ready to be slaves." There was, however, no real incentive to counteract the pressures in that direction. A well-intentioned emperor like Tiberius could try to uphold the prestige of the senate or encourage the senators to take responsibility and act independently. Nevertheless, he could not give them the real power and rewards that were the true basis of prestige and incentives for assuming responsibility.

The office of *princeps* depended upon a monopoly of the highest powers, greatest military forces, and most strategic provinces. Those, however, were the very things that brought prestige and for which senators freely strove under the free Republic. If an emperor were to share them with other senators now, however, he would inevitably create rivals to himself. That was something a conscientious emperor could not risk and a despotic one would not tolerate. As a result, even under an emperor who respected the senate, the tendency was for senators to abdicate the responsibilities that he was willing for them to have. Therefore, even a well-meaning emperor had to assume more direct responsibility himself. In

this way, the senate was weakened even further, so that it was even less able to resist the usurpations of a despotic *princeps*. Eventually, the power to flatter an emperor was all that the senate had left.

Stoic Opponents Of course, a significant number of senators resented this situation bitterly. They were descendants of the old Republican nobility or members of newer senatorial families from the conservative districts of northern Italy. Like their famous compatriot the historian Livy, they idealized the virtues of the old Republic. Their heroes were those who had opposed Caesar: men like Cato the Younger and the assassins Cassius and Brutus. Like their heroes, they often professed the philosophy of Stoicism, which became associated at Rome with Republican opposition to the Principate. When persecuted for their opposition, they frequently sought a martyr's death in suicide, which became the ultimate, though futile, act of protest.

The historian Cremutius Cordus was such an individual under Tiberius. He wrote a history of Rome in which he praised Brutus and called Cassius "the last of the Romans." As a result, in 25 he was prosecuted for *maiestas*. Tiberius attended the trial in the senate, and his grim face showed that he disapproved of Cremutius' defense. Cremutius, therefore, gave up and starved himself to death. A majority of senators then sought favor with the emperor by ordering the aediles to confiscate all copies of his history and burn them. Secretly, however, some saved copies that were published after Tiberius' death and helped to inspire more martyrs under later emperors.

Tiberius the Administrator The fame of Tiberius rests chiefly on his knowledge of and skill in Imperial administration. He followed the foreign policy of Augustus by relying on a combination of diplomacy and the cautious application of military force, as when he pursued limited military goals in Germany and took pains to avoid involving Rome in a war with Parthia. The Augustan conquests in central Europe and the East required a pause for consolidation. By strengthening the defenses along the Rhine and other frontiers and by suppressing revolts in Gaul, in Thrace, and in North Africa, he kept the Empire at peace and at an unprecedented peak of prosperity.

To promote the material welfare of the provinces, he kept tribute and taxes at a minimum. By strict economy (the curtailment of expensive spectacles and ambitious building projects), he was able to reduce taxes and still build up a large surplus in the treasury. Unfortunately, his reduced spending on games, spectacles, and grandiose building projects made him unpopular among the common people of Rome. In an effort to procure a more honest and efficient collection of provincial taxes, he restricted the tax-farming companies to the collection of customs dues and severely punished all provincial governors guilty of extortion, floggings, and confiscation of private property, or of corrupt administration. Some of the governors found guilty of such injustices committed suicide rather than face the wrath of the emperor.

Tiberius appointed able and conscientious men to govern the Imperial provinces. As an incentive to honest administration, he increased governors' salaries. He also lengthened their terms of office, perhaps as much out of necessity as by choice, so that they became increasingly familiar with their duties and with local conditions. Many of the governors held office from five to ten years, some even longer. As a result of this policy, cases of extortion and corruption arose less frequently in the Imperial provinces than in the senatorial, where governors normally held office for only one year. In both the Imperial and senatorial provinces, Tiberius encouraged the provincial assemblies (*concilia, koina*) to send delegates to Rome to lodge complaints before the emperor and the senate about the conduct of governors, legates, and procurators.

Policies that were meant to benefit soldiers and frontier defense also promoted commerce and provincial prosperity. For example, eliminating local silver coinage in Gaul probably benefitted the soldiers, who were paid in Roman coins, which no longer needed to be exchanged. A uniform coinage, however, also promoted trade. An extensive road- and bridge-building program in Gaul, Pannonia (Hungary), Moesia (Bulgaria), North Africa, Egypt, and Spain, not only expedited the movement of troops but also stimulated commerce and urbanization.

The new economic prosperity of the provinces, the efficient collection of taxes, and careful financial administration all contributed to increased revenues and a large surplus in the treasury. That enabled the emperor to give prompt and liberal relief to disaster-stricken areas in both Italy and the provinces. Even after making these and other large grants from the treasury, Tiberius was able to reduce the tax on auction sales from one to one-half percent and to leave behind in the treasury the sum of 2.7 billion sesterces (3.3 billion according to some authorities).

Last Years and Succession Tiberius spent the last ten years of his reign in almost continuous seclusion on the Isle of Capri. Three times he journeyed to the outskirts of Rome, but he could never bring himself actually to enter it again. His preference for Capri led to malicious rumors that he spent his time in every vice and debauchery that a perverted mind could invent. Suetonius delighted in publicizing them, but they are highly exaggerated at best. Tiberius actually spent much of his time working for the Empire or enjoying more cultured pursuits. For example, he surrounded himself with scholars and artists, such as the famous Alexandrian scholar Thrasyllus, who tutored the emperor in astrological lore.

One of the most serious questions of state with which Tiberius had to wrestle in his last years was that of a successor. The deaths of Germanicus and Drusus II, plus the deadly plottings of Sejanus against the family of Germanicus, had left as possible choices only Germanicus' son Gaius Caligula and Tiberius' own grandson, Tiberius Gemellus, son of Drusus II. In A.D. 35, at age seventy-five, Tiberius tried to resolve the problem.

He probably would have preferred that Gemellus be his sole immediate successor, but in 35 Gemellus was only sixteen. Caligula not only was older by six or seven years and had already been made an augur, a pontiff, and a quaestor, but he also could trace his ancestry back to Augustus and the family of Caesar through both of his parents, whereas Gemellus could do so only through his mother. Tiberius had also arranged his marriage to Junia Claudilla, like Caligula, a direct descendant of Octavia and Marcus Antonius. Finally, Caligula was the son of the popular Germanicus, so that he enjoyed great support from the common people and the soldiers. It would have been too dangerous to pass over Caligula completely. Therefore, Tiberius made Gemellus and Caligula his joint heirs.

In 37, when Tiberius felt that he was nearing the end, he attempted to return to Rome. He reached only Misenum across the bay from Capri. There he fell into a coma and died. Unsubstantiated rumors reported that when Tiberius momentarily revived, the Praetorian Prefect Sutorius Macro had him smothered in his bedclothes. The story was probably fabricated after Caligula had turned out to be a murderous tyrant, but it received circumstantial support from the fact that Macro had been the one who nominated Caligula as the new *princeps* at a meeting of the senate right after Tiberius' death.

Caligula[1] (A.D. 37 to 41)

The senators accepted Caligula's nomination without objection, and they showed their disapproval of Tiberius by refusing him the deification that they had granted Augustus and Caesar. Caligula's official name, Gaius Julius Caesar Augustus Germanicus, revealed his lineage and probably overshadowed his recent past, which may have given a thoughtful observer pause. In

his later teens, he had lived with his grandmother, Antonia, who threw him into constant companionship with three young Thracian princes, with the young Herod Agrippa I of Judea, and with Ptolemy of Mauretania, a grandson of Antonius and Cleopatra. From them he may have acquired his conception of absolute monarchy. During his stay at his uncle's court at Capri, he practiced the arts of dissimulation and obsequiousness, which probably had been necessary for him to survive during Sejanus' plottings.

Popular Start After the long, stern, and parsimonius reign of Tiberius, however, the people welcomed their new ruler with gladness and thanksgiving. He, in turn, delighted the populace by distributing the legacies of Livia and Tiberius, by abolishing the tax on auction sales (already slightly reduced by Tiberius), and by his splendid spectacles, games, chariot races, and wild beast hunts. He even restored to the popular assemblies their ancient right of electing magistrates. He pleased the senate by his deference and courtesy and by his conciliatory attitude toward the nobility. He abolished all impending trials for treason, curbed the infamous activities of the *delatores,* recalled the exiles of Tiberius, and piously had the bones and ashes of his brother Nero and his mother, Agrippina the Elder, brought back from their islands of exile for interment in the mausoleum of Augustus. He adopted his cousin and cobeneficiary, Tiberius Gemellus, as his son and heir, shared the consulship with his uncle Claudius, and had his three sisters honored throughout the Empire. To cap it all, he stirred the patriotic fervor of all classes by announcing preparations for the conquest of Britain and Germany. In October of 37, however, a serious illness forced him to postpone this enterprise and prompted enormous public outpourings of anxiety and affection.

Increasing Despotism Ancient sources (especially Suetonius) imply that after his recovery Caligula was mentally deranged and succumbed completely to the temptations of supreme power. His earlier efforts at winning

---

[1] Literally, "Little Boot," a name bestowed on him as a child in the Rhineland by his father's soldiers because his mother, Agrippina, liked to dress him in the uniform of a legionary soldier, complete with little military boots, *caligulae,* the diminutive of *caligae,* leather military boots.

popularity as sole emperor despite Tiberius' arrangements for joint rule with Gemellus seem already to have indicated the direction in which he was headed. Nevertheless, a close brush with death certainly could have triggered his subsequent vehement insistence that he was a god incarnate. His acts were those of a man who wanted to show that he was more powerful than a mere mortal, and Tiberius' failure to receive deification may have been a lesson to Caligula to make certain that such an important matter not be left to chance.

Once firmly in power, he began to play the role of an unrestrained despot and indulged in acts of cruelty, megalomania, and caprice. He stripped the senate of military control over *Africa Proconsularis*. He even forced individual senators to swear that they would lay down their lives for him and his sisters, to dress like slaves and wait upon his table, to trot beside his chariot in their togas, and even to kiss his feet in homage.

Like the pharaohs of ancient Egypt, whom he greatly admired and imitated, Caligula asserted the right of eminent domain over the property of his subjects and introduced taxes in the Egyptian manner on shopkeepers and craftsmen. Reports that he lived in habitual incest are not farfetched if he was modeling himself after Egyptian pharaohs, who often married their sisters, and after Zeus of Greek mythology, who was both the husband and brother of Hera. He even longed to be worshipped as a god on earth, the New Sun, *Neos Helios*. Indeed, Egyptian coins represent him as a sun god.

He loved to sit in the Temple of Castor and Pollux and receive divine worship or converse with Jupiter and the other gods. Eventually, he had a temple erected to himself out of public funds, and not only appointed his favorite horse, Incitatus (which he believed to be a reincarnation of Alexander the Great's Bucephalus), as high priest of his cult but even had him made a member of the senate. In 39, he had a bridge of ships built across the Bay of Baiae and celebrated its completion by riding over it and wearing the breastplate of Alexander, whose vast military enterprises he wished to imitate.

Financially, Caligula was equally unrestrained. He squandered money on perfumed baths, banquets, and fabulous drinks, and on horse races, shows, and gifts to the populace. His pleasure barges on Lake Nemi (Lacus Nemorensis) in the Alban Hills south of Rome contained baths, gardens, gem-studded sterns, and the costliest of furnishings. These and many other extravagances soon exhausted the huge surplus that Tiberius had accumulated in the treasury. To obtain new funds, he resorted to extraordinary taxes (on foodstuffs, lawsuits, and the earnings of porters, panders, and prostitutes), forced legacies, and confiscations. He even revived the treason laws as a means of confiscating money and property.

Among his victims were his former father-in-law Junius Silanus; Tiberius Gemellus, his adopted son and heir; Naevius Sutorius Macro, the prefect of the Praetorian Guard who had helped him to the throne; and several members and partisans of the Claudian family. His uncle Claudius escaped only because he seemed to be a harmless dolt.

Caligula's megalomaniacal behavior inspired plots against him. In 39, for example, one of his army commanders in the Rhineland, Cn. Cornelius Lentulus Gaetulicus, conspired to place upon the throne M. Aemilius Lepidus, the widower of Caligula's sister Drusilla. Caligula had both men executed and exiled his other two sisters, Agrippina the Younger and Julia Livilla, both of whom were involved in the plot.

After suppressing the conspiracy in the Rhineland, Caligula crossed the Rhine in late 39 to discourage future German border raids, but in 40 his long-planned invasion of Britain came to nothing more than a march to the Strait of Dover and the erection of a lighthouse 200 feet high at Gesoriacum (Boulogne), which remained standing until 1544.

Caligula's Foreign and Provincial Policies

Although Caligula was autocratic and capricious in foreign and provincial affairs, he generally favored the policies of Pompey and Marcus Antonius rather than those of Augustus and Tiberius. In the East, for example, he preferred client kings with close ties to him instead of provincial governors, who might enter into conspiracies and create armies for rebellion against the throne. He abandoned the kingdom of Greater Armenia as a Roman sphere of influence and allowed Parthia to control it in exchange for Parthian recognition of Rome's interests in the East. He restored Commagene, which Tiberius had annexed as a province, to Antiochus; he made his three young Thracian friends, who probably were his cousins, client rulers respectively of Thrace, Pontus and the Bosporus, and Lesser Armenia; and he placed the Jewish king Herod Agrippa I over the whole of the kingdom formerly ruled by his grandfather Herod the Great. In Africa, on the other hand, Caligula foolishly deposed and executed Ptolemy, the client king of Mauretania (western Algeria and Morocco), and made his kingdom a Roman province. Perhaps Caligula simply resented Ptolemy, who, through Cleopatra Selene, was also a descendant of Marcus Antonius. The murder of Ptolemy provoked a revolt that Caligula did not live long enough to suppress.

In his policy toward the Jews, Caligula was equally erratic and provocative. In Alexandria, where there was a large Jewish community, he permitted a Greek mob to sack the Jewish quarters and forcibly erect his statues in their synagogues. In 40, the Alexandrian Jews sent a delegation headed by the scholar Philo to Caligula but obtained no redress. Meanwhile, Caligula had instructed Petronius, his legate in Syria, to install his statue in the Temple at Jerusalem, but Caligula's death relieved Petronius of the necessity of carrying out the order.

Assassination   Caligula's brief career of extravagance, oppression, murder, and megalomania came to an abrupt end on January 24, A.D. 41, when Cassius Chaerea, a tribune of the Praetorian Guard, whom he had offended with insulting obscenities, struck him down in a secret passageway of the palace. The hand that struck was Chaerea's, but the men behind the deed were prominent members of the senate, administration, and army. Caligula had left himself no adequate basis of support anywhere. The best thing that can be said about Caligula's reign is that it was brief. Fortunately, it had not been long enough to undo much of the good that Augustus and Tiberius had done to improve the administration and defense of Rome's vast empire.

Nevertheless, Caligula had revealed the enormous potential for unfettered despotism in the office of *princeps*. Tiberius, whom his own personality and the paradoxical nature of the principate itself had often frustrated, really had tried to make the senate a meaningful partner in government. Caligula, on the other hand, willfully tried to subordinate it and everything else to his own exalted self. As a result, a significant group of senators, who still preserved the traditions of the free Republic, hoped to restore it, or some better semblance of it, upon the assassination of Caligula. The futility of such fantasies in the post-Augustan world was quickly brought home, however, by the circumstances surrounding the accession of the next Julio-Claudian.

XXVII

Claudius, Nero, and the End of the Julio-Claudians, A.D. 41–68

Claudius (A.D. 41 to 54) After the assassination of Caligula, members of the senate debated what to do. While they were discussing the relative merits of restoring the Republic or creating a truly elective principate, their inability to control events was made painfully clear. Caligula's uncle Claudius, whose full name was Tiberius Claudius Nero Germanicus, had obtained the loyalty of the praetorian guardsmen by promising each one a gift of 15,000 sesterces. Although Tiberius and Caligula had given gifts of money to the guardsmen after they became emperors, Claudius made clear their political power and set a dangerous precedent for the future by promising a reward for their support before he ascended to the principate. When they demanded that the senate confirm their choice, many senators protested. Claudius rightly pointed out that with the guard behind him they had no alternative, and they yielded to the inevitable.

Suetonius depicts Claudius' accession as pure farce: When ransacking the Imperial palace after Caligula's assassination, some soldiers of the Praetorian Guard happened to see two feet sticking out from under a curtain. They discovered that it was Claudius, the brother of Germanicus. Instead of killing him as he expected, they carried him over to their barracks, where the troops tumultuously acclaimed him emperor of Rome. That is just the way in which one would expect a man whom hostile tradition

depicted as a fool to become emperor. This story, however, probably does not give enough credit to Claudius for shrewdly seizing the opportunity that Caligula's assassination presented to make himself emperor. Claudius was no fool, although he did have handicaps that made him an unlikely candidate for *princeps*.

Early Life All of his life, Claudius had had to contend with serious physical and psychological handicaps: persistently poor health, physical deformity, slow mental development, social maladjustment, and timidity. A birth defect or an early illness had apparently left him with a grotesque appearance—wobbly head, spindly legs, a gawky look, and a speech impediment that made him appear simpleminded. Often his Imperial relations either felt ashamed of him and tried to keep him out of sight or else made fun of him. Caligula sometimes made him act the part of a court buffoon.

His ugliness and social awkwardness drove Claudius to drinking and gambling, which also caused embarrassment. Early on, however, Augustus had realized that Claudius did possess a good intellect, and he encouraged its development by providing him with excellent teachers. Under their tutelage, he became a philologist, an antiquarian, and an expert on Roman law and government. The great historian Livy even encouraged him to write history, and he did. He became knowledgeable about

307

Etruscan and Carthaginian history, which he studied by learning Etruscan and Punic and of which he wrote multivolume accounts based on original research.

The study of law and history is not exactly poor training for a head of state. Moreover, Claudius was not without some useful experience. He had been given a prominent role as a representative of the Imperial family among the *equites* and had presided over some of the major games. Under Augustus he had been made an augur and a priest of the Imperial cult; Tiberius had honored him with the consular insignia; and Caligula had made him his colleague in a joint consulship for two months. The senate had even decreed honors for him from time to time. Also, as a Julio-Claudian and brother of the popularly revered Germanicus, Claudius enjoyed the support of the army, the urban populace, the Italian upper class, and the people of the provinces.

The Political Philosophy and Policies of Claudius After his accession, Claudius revealed astonishing strength of character and political acumen. From his study of Roman history and political institutions, Claudius had learned that Rome owed her greatness to her willingness to devise new institutions to meet new needs. Like Augustus, however, whose biography he wrote, Claudius realized that change at Rome could not move too quickly and had to be respectful to the past.

Claudius and the Senate As in the case of Tiberius' reign, the paradox inherent in the nature of the Principate itself strained the relations between many senators and the *princeps* and led to the continued weakening of the senate as an institution of government. Proclaiming Augustus as his model at the beginning of his reign, Claudius had earnestly sought the collaboration of the senate by outward shows of deference. He even restored its control of Macedonia and Achaea, which Tiberius had turned into Imperial provinces, and returned to it the right to elect curule magistrates, which Caligula had given back to the people. Never-

theless, Claudius could not forget that it was dangerous to let senators have too much independent power. Assuming the censorship, which no one, not even Augustus, had held for the past sixty-eight years, he purged the senate of some old members and added new ones in 47 and 48. The old aristocracy was naturally affronted. A few of the new senators were his own clients, tribal chieftains of *Gallia Comata* whose families had received citizenship from Julius Caesar. They were richer than most Italian senators and controlled large and devoted clans. The admission of Gallic senators gave the Gauls political equality with the Italians and made them loyal partners in the new world state. Later emperors recognized the wisdom of such a measure and adopted similar ones on a larger scale.

Claudius struck other blows against the Roman senatorial aristocracy. In order to reduce the possibility of being challenged by a disgruntled or ambitious senator, he weakened the senate's power over the armies and its own provinces. In the name of efficiency, he transferred control of the Roman municipal treasury (*aerarium Saturni*) to two quaestors responsible to him and diverted revenues from several sources to a central Imperial *fiscus*. Furthermore, he placed such vital services as the grain supply, aqueducts, flood control, and Italian roads, canals, and harbors under his control.

Claudius also eagerly put to use his study of the law. The number of trials that took place in the emperor's private court, *intra cubiculum principis,* greatly increased at the expense of the magistrates, provincial governors, and the senate. Claudius' judicial activities were popular with average citizens, but those who saw their powers diminished were naturally offended, and they probably account for some of the exaggerated stories in the ancient sources about Claudius' absentminded, arbitrary, and even capricious behavior as a judge. Ironically, it was his earnest attempt to spare senators the indignity that they had suffered under Tiberius and Caligula in trying their own colleagues for treason that earned Claudius the most ill will. When he himself, however, tried and condemned senators, he was suspected, sometimes with good reason, to have been influenced unjustly by his own ambitious wives and freedmen.

Systematized Control As he sought greater control for himself, Claudius needed more carefully organized loyal help. Therefore, he enlarged the privy council of trusted friends known as the "friends of Caesar" (*Amici Caesaris*) and gave even greater prominence to talented and loyal freedmen, whom he included in his privy council. Their duties were clearly designated by specific titles that created the framework for the bureaus or departments (*scrinia*) that marked more formally bureaucratic administration under later emperors.

Narcissus, Claudius' secretary for correspondence (*ab epistulis*), drafted all laws and decrees sent out around the Empire under the Imperial seal. Callistus headed the department that examined petitions sent to the *princeps* from the provinces (*a libellis*) and had charge of judicial investigations and trials (*a cognitionibus*). Another important official was Pallas (whom Antonia had secretly sent to report to Tiberius the conspiracy of Sejanus). As head of the treasury department (*a rationibus*), he coordinated all the provincial *fisci* and the activities of the procurators. A fourth was Claudius Polybius, keeper of the records' office and reference library (*a studiis*).

The equestrian and senatorial classes bitterly resented that those and other freedmen of mostly Greek or Eastern origin wielded great power in the government and frequently lined their own pockets at Imperial expense. Ancient and modern writers, however, have often been too closely bound to a biased and hostile tradition when they depict Claudius as being under the thumb of his freedmen. For the most part, he was the master and they his faithful and obedient servants.

Popularity through Public Works and Welfare
Following the examples of Julius Caesar and Augustus (and even Caligula), Claudius earned the loyalty and good will of the people through public works and generous benefactions that no one else could match. He curbed some evils of moneylending by forbidding usurers to lend to teenage spendthrifts; he abolished sales taxes on food and relieved stricken communities of their tax burdens; and through his control of the Imperial mint, he both prevented excessive inflation and met the expanding needs of trade and industry, to which public works, such as aqueducts, highways, and canals, gave an added stimulus all over the Empire.

The most spectacular of these projects was the construction of an artificial harbor at Ostia, Rome's port on the mouth of the Tiber, which had become choked with silt. The new harbor allowed grain ships to dock at Ostia, whence their cargoes could easily be barged up to Rome instead of being laboriously hauled overland 138 miles from Puteoli in Campania as before. Ostia soon became a large city with a population of 100,000 from all over the Mediterranean world.

The development of the port of Ostia raised economic problems both difficult and unforeseen. Ships using the port had to leave empty. Rome was now a consumer of the world's products. Her exports were insignificant in comparison with her immense imports. No sooner had Claudius diverted shipping from Puteoli (the outlet of a rich region exporting both agricultural and industrial products) than the shipowners complained of losing money because of the lack of return cargoes. To satisfy them and keep vital supplies moving into Rome, Claudius and his successors had to compensate them with special concessions, such as insurance against shipwreck, tax exemptions, the waiving of inheritance laws, and grants of citizenship to those engaged for six years in the grain-carrying service.

Foreign Policy and Imperial Defense
Just as he dealt aggressively with internal matters, Claudius pursued an aggressive foreign policy, which was more like that of Julius Caesar than that of Augustus after A.D. 9 or of Tiberius and even Caligula. His motives were complex. The security of the *princeps* greatly depended on the loyalty of the provincial armies. The best way to gain their loyalty was

Model of an apartment block at Ostia. (Alinari/Scala, Art Resource, NY)

to command them personally and lead them in conquest. Claudius had not gained any military experience or reputation, and he needed to do so when he became emperor. The danger of his situation became clear within his first year, when the legions in Dalmatia revolted.

As in other matters, Claudius desired to rationalize, systematize, and improve Imperial defense. He restored the peaceful provinces of Macedonia and Achaea to the senate. In 46, he annexed the turbulent kingdom of Thrace as an Imperial province. Annexation of Thrace led to Roman intervention in Dacia (modern Rumania), in the Crimean peninsula, and everywhere north of the Black Sea as far east as the Don. Claudius made the Black Sea almost a Roman lake.

In the Near East, his policy was at once vigorous and cautious: He fomented internal discord and rivalry in Parthia; he reestablished the Roman protectorate over Armenia by reinstating a friendly client king, and, on the death of Herod Agrippa I, annexed Judea as a Roman province. His chief objectives were peace and Roman control over the eastern trade routes.

Early in his reign, Claudius had to suppress the revolt that Caligula had provoked in Mauretania by the murder of King Ptolemy. After crushing the rebels in two years of hard fighting, Claudius organized Mauretania into two Imperial provinces—*Mauretania Caesariensis* in the east and *Mauretania Tingitana* (Tangier) in the northwest. Although the subjugation of Mauretania was a very important and difficult military achievement, it received less fanfare than the conquest of Britain.

The Conquest of Britain, 43 The conquest of Britain probably reflects Claudius' need for military glory, the conviction that the enterprise would arouse strong national sentiment, and a desire to protect Roman traders and their access to the island's reputed wealth in minerals, timber, cattle, and slaves. Nor were pretexts lacking. Claudius had received invitations to intervene from lesser British chiefs who feared the expansive power of the kingdom that Cunobelinus (the Cymbeline of Shakespeare) had established in the southeast, with its capital at Camulodunum (Colchester), northeast of London. After Cunobelinus' death (ca A.D. 40), his son Caratacus had extended the kingdom and had stepped forward as the champion of Druidism. The existence of a strong British kingdom that promoted Druidism was a perpetual threat to Roman authority in Gaul, where Druids fostered Celtic unity and resistance to Roman rule. Augustus and Tiberius had tried to stamp out the Gallic Druids on the grounds that they practiced savage and inhuman rites.

In 43, a Roman army landed in Kent and, after defeating the Britons in a two-day battle on the Medway, advanced to the Thames to await the arrival of Claudius. Taking command, he quickly defeated Caratacus and took Camulodunum, where he accepted the submission of eleven British kings. In tribute to the swift victory, the senate voted Claudius a triumph and the proud name of Britannicus. Within eight years after the celebration of his triumph in 44, his legates had created a province extending from the borders of Wales in the Southwest to the estuary of the Humber in the Northeast near York (Eburacum).

Colonization and Urbanization in the Provinces Hand in hand with conquest and Imperial expansion went colonization, urbanization, and extension of Roman citizenship in the provinces. This process, begun by Julius Caesar, continued with restraint by Augustus, and slowed down by Tiberius, was resumed on a large scale by Claudius. Most of these colonies served at once as military bastions in conquered territory and islands of Roman citizenship. The conversion of rural and tribal communities into organized municipalities (*municipia*) served similar purposes. In all this work of urbanization and Romanization, Claudius paid attention, as his numerous edicts and the extant inscriptions and papyri reveal, to the smallest administrative details and exhibited an amazing knowledge of local conditions. He was hardly the old fool depicted by biased ancient writers.

Claudius' Wives The most troublesome aspect of Claudius' reign was his marital life. After a loveless and lonely childhood, Claudius

had eagerly sought marriage. Unfortunately, his wives never loved him. His first two wives, Plautia Urgulanilla and Aelia Paetina, were merely unfaithful, and he divorced them. His third and fourth wives, however, were not only unfaithful but also ambitious so that their political impact was significant. Claudius' marriage to his third wife, Valeria Messallina, had been arranged by Caligula for political reasons. Through both of her parents, Messallina was a great-granddaughter of Augustus' sister Octavia.

Claudius was 47 and Messallina only 15 when they were married. Claudius was enamored of her youthful beauty, but she was unhappy at being forced to marry a man so much older than she and physically handicapped as well. Although she produced two children, a daughter, Octavia, and a son, Britannicus (named in honor of Claudius' conquest of Britain), Messallina sought her pleasure elsewhere in much the same way that Augustus' daughter, Julia, had when forced to marry men whom she did not love, and her affairs likewise became linked with political conspiracies. She used her influence with Claudius to obtain the condemnation of certain senators on charges of treason, and one of her lovers, Gaius Silius, plotted with her to depose Claudius, marry her, and seize the throne himself.

When Silius was a consul-elect in 48 and Claudius was away at Ostia, the two conspirators put their plot in motion by taking public marriage vows. Claudius' freedmen Narcissus, Pallas, and Callistus, however, informed him of the situation and finally forced him to take action against his treacherous wife. She, Silius, and other conspirators were swiftly executed.

Claudius did not remain a widower long. He systematically cast about for a suitable wife once more. His freedman Pallas, who had been the lover of Agrippina the Younger, Caligula's sister, successfully urged Claudius to marry her, even though she was the daughter of Claudius' own brother Germanicus. By Roman law such a marriage was incestuous. Therefore, Claudius had the law changed.

The needs of both Agrippina and Claudius were met by this marriage. From her mother, Agrippina the Elder, the younger Agrippina had received the ambition of securing the throne for the family of Germanicus, of which she and her son by her first marriage, Cn. Domitius Ahenobarbus, were the only survivors; Claudius, on the other hand, was already fifty-eight years old and needed to provide the Empire with a suitable successor. His own son, Britannicus, was only five and was not yet capable of being trained for the principate. Agrippina's son was of the right lineage and, though only ten, could already begin training for succession. Claudius immediately betrothed his daughter, Octavia, to him. In 50, he adopted him and gave him the name Nero Claudius Caesar, shortened simply to Nero.

The loyalty of the Praetorian Guard to the heir apparent was secured by the appointment of Agrippina's friend Sextus Afranius Burrus as praetorian prefect in 51. Nero's education was entrusted to the learned philosopher Seneca the Younger. Agrippina could now face the future with considerable confidence.

She did not have to wait long. Claudius died in 54 from an undetermined cause. The story that he died as a result of eating a bowl of poisoned mushrooms served him by Agrippina comes from a hostile source (her archenemy Pliny the Elder) and should therefore be accepted with reserve. That Agrippina benefitted the most immediately after his death naturally raises suspicions, but it is quite possible that Claudius, who had a reputation for overindulging in food and drink, accidentally choked to death.

Nero (A.D. 54 to 68) Agrippina, Seneca, and Burrus handled the succession smoothly. The inauguration of Nero was a joyous occasion. A visit to the barracks of the Praetorian Guard (each man was promised 15,000 sesterces); a speech carefully prepared by Seneca and delivered effectively by Nero before the senate (Nero promised to follow the policies of Augustus, respect the prerogatives and powers of the senate, and keep for himself only the command of the armies); cheers; pledges of loyalty; and other obsequious effusions highlighted the first day of Nero's reign.

The First Five Years Nero's first five years formed a memorable unit. Tacitus devoted Book XII of his *Annals* to them, and they are often called the *quinquennium Neronis* ("Nero's five years"), a phrase later attributed to the Emperor Trajan. They were appreciated for peace, prosperity, and good government at home and military success on the frontiers but ended with the spectacular murder of Agrippina, whose own ambitions had fueled intrigue, violence, and murder within the palace.

The good aspects of Nero's early years are usually attributed to the guidance of Seneca and Burrus. They and their collaborators in the senate seem to have found the way to make that institution a real force again. Heeding Seneca's sound advice, Nero applied the ideal of clemency extolled in the philosopher's essay *De Clementia* by putting an end to trials *intra cubiculum principis,* which had engendered the hostility of many against Claudius. Besides respecting the privileges of the senate, Nero provided annuities to assist impoverished senatorial families.

Nero's government maintained peace and prosperity within the Empire, guarded its frontiers, kept piracy in check, and restrained the rapacity of officials by the vigorous prosecution of extortion before the senate. To stimulate trade, in which the wealthy Seneca was not disinterested, oppressive taxation was mitigated, and Nero himself even proposed the total abolition of all indirect taxes and customs duties throughout the Empire. Responsible critics in the senate, however, pointed out such an act's dire consequences for the public finances, and the idea was dropped.

At the beginning of Nero's reign, Agrippina hoped to strengthen her already powerful hand. Even before the end of Claudius' life, she had secured the removal of his powerful freedman Callistus and brought down her rival for influence with Nero, his aunt Domitia Lepida (also mother of Claudius' former wife Messalina). Upon Claudius' death, she and her allies had forced Narcissus, another of his important freedmen to commit suicide. Right after that, she contrived the murder of M. Junius Silanus, great-grandson of Augustus and provincial governor of Asia, who would have been a rallying point for opposition to Nero. In 55, Nero became exasperated with his domineering mother and tried to undercut her by dismissing her strongest ally within the palace, the powerful freedman Pallas.

Agrippina erupted in a cascade of rage and threatened to back Nero's stepbrother, Britannicus, as the rightful heir to Claudius' throne. Shortly thereafter, to forestall any chance of Agrippina's making good on her threat, Nero contrived to have Britannicus poisoned to death right before her eyes at dinner one night. Still, she continued her efforts to build up a base of support against him. Finally, in 59, egged on by his mistress Poppaea Sabina, Nero arranged to entice Agrippina into a boat designed to collapse at sea and drown her. When she managed to swim to safety, he sent assassins to finish the job.

To counter the imperious influence of Agrippina with Nero, Seneca and Burrus had catered to his baser instincts. They had pointed out that, as emperor, he could do what he wanted without his mother's interference. They not only had encouraged him to indulge his taste for art, music, poetry, and chariot racing but also had flattered his vanity and self-importance by pretending that all official acts were the result of his divine guidance. Everywhere, thanks were offered to him with extravagantly worshipful praise. In this way they had inspired Nero to model himself on the absolute, divine Hellenistic monarchs familiar from Greek culture. Ultimately, however, they had turned him into a creature that they could not control.

Nero Asserts Himself Between 59 and 62, Nero began to favor other men like Gaius Ofonius Tigellinus, Prefect of the *Vigiles,* who encouraged his vices even more. When Burrus died in 62, Nero appointed Tigellinus as praetorian prefect in his place. Seneca saw that he could no longer restrain Nero and obtained permission to retire into private life. He was loaded with wealth and honors that he was not destined long to enjoy. Now, freed from any restraining influence, Nero finally dared to divorce and exile his popular wife, Octavia, Claudius' daughter, and marry his long-time mistress, Poppaea Sabina. She had been the wife of M. Salvius Otho, whose compliance was rewarded with the governorship of Lusitania (Portugal), but he eventually rebelled against Nero (p. 317). Shortly after he celebrated his new marriage, Octavia's continuing popularity caused him to have her executed on trumped-up charges.

Freely indulging himself, Nero became more and more extravagant and megalomaniacal. He spared no expense on lavish entertainments and luxuries. He increasingly appeared in chariot races and musical competitions. In 64 he finally went so far as to incur the traditional Roman contempt for actors by appearing publicly in plays.

Much worse, as had been the case under Caligula, wealthy men were condemned again on false charges in order to pay for the emperor's reckless expenditures. Also, Nero's jealousy toward anyone closely related to the Julio-Claudian dynasty became murderous. Rubellius Plautus, a grandson of Tiberius; Cornelius Sulla, a son-in-law of Claudius; D. Junius Silanus, a brother of M. Junius Silanus above; and the latter's son, L. Junius Silanus Torquatus, were quickly eliminated. Naturally, the upper classes came to fear and detest this new oppressor. Tigellinus took a vicious delight in tracking down plots against the throne, with his organization of informers, spies, and secret agents.

Nero and the Great Fire of Rome, 64 In 64 there occurred a long period of hot dry weather. One sizzling night in July, a fire broke out in the slums at the east end of the Circus Maximus between the Palatine and Caelian hills. Fanned by a strong southeast wind, the flames leapt from house to house, from block to block, as they fed on stores of dry wood and olive oil. The fire raged for nine days and left more than half of Rome a charred and blackened waste. Not only had acres of flimsy apartment houses and some of Rome's most venerated temples and shrines gone up in smoke, but

Nero's own palace as well, with its priceless collection of books, manuscripts, and works of art.

Nero had been staying at the time at Antium (Anzio), about thirty-five miles south of Rome. Aroused from sleep, he swiftly sped to the scene of the conflagration. In this crisis, Nero's good qualities shone. After a vain attempt to check the progress of the flames, he converted Mar's Field and his private gardens into shelters for the homeless and hastened the transport of grain supplies from Ostia to feed the destitute. His indefatigable energy in the alleviation of suffering, however, did not spare him from the malicious rumor that he had started the fire in order to acquire the glory of building a new and more beautiful Rome.

Rebuilding Program Although the accusation against Nero is false, it is true that he eagerly seized the opportunity to indulge his passion for esthetic enjoyment and creative activity in rebuilding Rome. Much of what he did or approved to be done was worthy of praise: Nero widened and straightened the streets and had pillared colonnades built on both sides of them to provide shade and lessen the danger of fire. The rebuilt sections of the city had many fountains and open squares. The new houses were required to have their facades and first stories built of fireproof stone and to be separated by alleys, with gardens in the rear provided with fire buckets and supplies of water.

The Golden House The extravagance that Nero showed in rebuilding his own palace, however, helped to fuel the rumors that he was responsible for the fire. No expense was spared. Nero's new palace, the Golden House (*Domus Aurea*), probably rivaled in cost and splendor the great palace of Louis XIV at Versailles. The vestibule was lofty enough to accommodate Nero's colossal statue (120 feet high), and the hall, consisting of three pillared arcades, was almost a mile long. Together with colonnades, gardens, lakes, fields, and game parks, it occupied an area of 120 acres between the Palatine and Esquiline hills.

Nero's Persecution of the Christians

Nero's worst side, a weak and cowardly streak that sometimes resulted in infantile cruelty, is revealed in how he sought to quell the rumors against him. According to Tacitus' *Annals* 15, 44 (written probably as late as 120, perhaps even 123), Nero cast about for scapegoats for the fire in order to avert suspicion from himself. He found them in the Christians, the widespread prejudice against whom Tacitus expressed in the following words:

They were a detestable sect, which owed its name to Chrestus, who, in the reign of Tiberius, suffered under Pontius Pilate. Suppressed for a while, this dangerous superstition, soon revived and spread not only in Judea but even in the city of Rome, the common cesspool into which everything hateful and abominable flows like a torrent from all parts of the world. When some of these depraved and profligate wretches were induced to confess their guilt, Nero had some of them torn apart by dogs, some nailed to crosses, and others burned alive.

Reform of the Currency

The huge sums spent on the rebuilding of Rome and on Nero's Golden House soon completed the bankruptcy of the public treasury and rendered a depreciation of the currency imperative. Nero, therefore, made a virtue of necessity and carried out a currency reform; he introduced a monetary system that remained essentially unchanged until the reign of Septimius Severus (193 to 211). He reduced the weight of the *aureus,* the standard gold coin, by about 10 percent and the silver content of the *denarius,* the standard silver coin, by a similar amount. That brought both coins into a more stable relation with each other and with a new bronze coin. The reform also brought the Roman coinage more closely in line with the local coinages still minted in the Greek East and thus promoted trade within the Empire through the adoption of a more uniform Imperial standard. The currency depreciation perhaps served another purpose: It tended to check the serious drain of gold and silver to India and Southeast Asia by raising the prices for luxury imports such as spices and precious stones and thereby discouraging their purchase.

Plots against the Throne

Nero's outrageous behavior, extravagance, and growing cruelty led to the formation of serious plots against him. A confused tangle of motives inspired them: Some of the conspirators genuinely hoped for a restoration of the Republic; others hated Nero's increasingly vicious despotism and resented his employment of freedmen from Greece and the Near East in positions of power and influence. The most formidable attempt against the throne was the conspiracy of Gaius Calpurnius Piso in 65, which involved many *equites* as well as senators. Nero's reprisals were savage: Among his numerous victims were leading members of the senate and three of the greatest literary figures of the century—the philosopher Seneca, the poet Lucan, and the novelist and satirist Petronius, who obediently committed suicide by cutting open their own veins. One of the most eminent of Nero's victims, although perhaps not actually involved in the conspiracy, was the famous Stoic P. Clodius Paetus Thrasea, renowned for his austere conduct and high moral principles and the champion of *dignitas* and *libertas,* the traditional virtues of the old Roman aristocracy.

Nero's Concert Tour of Greece, 66 to 67

Neither fire nor conspiracy nor the arduous tasks of government interrupted Nero's musical career. After elaborate preparations, Nero set out in the fall of 66 on a grand concert tour of Greece. The tour was a personal triumph, thanks to the shrewd cooperativeness of the Greeks. He made numerous appearances as singer, tragic actor, or charioteer at Olympia, Corinth, Delphi, and many other places and came away as the winner of 1,808 prizes and trophies, many of which were awarded in advance. In 67, pleased with the Greeks' flattering reception and their appreciation of his art, he proclaimed the liberation of Greece from the governor of Macedonia. His words, no doubt intentionally, echoed the speech of Titus Quinctius Flamininus in 196 B.C. (pp. 111–112).

Nero's Foreign Policy

Under the able guidance of Seneca, Burrus, and their friends, Nero had maintained the peace and prosperity of the provinces; chosen, for the most part, honest and able governors, who were held strictly to account; and guarded and extended the frontiers by sending good generals to command the legions. There were two major danger spots: Armenia and Britain. Armenia, a problem since the days of Marcus Antonius, had engaged the attention of all Nero's predecessors. Rugged, mountainous, and subject to summer's heat or winter's cold, Armenia was hard to conquer, difficult to hold, and impossible to annex while Parthia remained strong and unsubdued. Neither Rome nor Parthia could allow the other to occupy it without loss of security and prestige. The only permanent solution to the Armenian problem, as Julius Caesar had foreseen, was the subjugation of Parthia.

The Armenian problem had arisen again at the end of Claudius' reign, when Vologeses I, the young and aggressive king of Parthia, placed his brother, Tiridates I, upon the Armenian throne. Nero sent out to the East Cn. Domitius Corbulo, a strict disciplinarian and one of the ablest generals of the century. In 50, he was able to place Tigranes V, a Roman client, upon the Armenian throne. The brief period of peace and quiet in the East that ensued offered time to resume the conquest of Britain.

Military Operations in Britain, 55 to 61

To Britain, Nero sent C. Suetonius Paulinus, another able general. In 60, after he had conquered the island of Mona (Anglesey), the main center of Druidism, a dangerous rebellion broke out behind his lines among the Iceni and Trinovantes, who then dwelt between the Thames and the Wash. After the death of their king, who had willed his territory to the Roman People, Roman procurators (acting on behalf of moneylenders, such as Seneca, to whom the previous king had fallen into debt) confiscated farmlands and reduced the former owners to the level of serfs. They robbed the king's widow, Queen Boudicca (Boadicea), of her land, flogged her, and permitted the raping of her daughters. The outraged queen collected an army and captured the Roman colony of Camulodunum (Colchester). She destroyed the Roman legion sent against her and marched on Londinium (London), where she caused the massacre of 70,000 Romans. Suetonius Paulinus defeated her army in battle by superior discipline and skill and stamped out the rebellion with ruthless efficiency. The vanquished Boudicca took her own life, and Britain thereafter remained subdued, except for a few border raids.

Armenia Again, 61 to 66 Not so Armenia. After Corbulo had pulled out his army, Tigranes V attacked Media, a powerful Parthian ally, and started a war that he could not finish. Vologeses, king of Parthia, invaded Armenia in force. In 62, he badly mauled and compelled the surrender of a Roman army that Nero had sent, at Corbulo's request, under a commander who proved incompetent. In 63, Corbulo again took command. During 64, he invaded Armenia with overwhelming force and compelled Parthia to accept Roman supremacy. In return, Corbulo allowed Tiridates I to ascend the throne of Armenia on the condition that he go to Rome and receive his crown at Nero's hands.

The long-range Roman plan seems to have been to strangle Parthia rather than make a direct assault. In 64, Nero liberated the Crimea from Sarmatian domination and annexed the kingdom of Pontus on the southeast coast of the Black Sea in preparation for the conquest of the Caucasus region between the Black and Caspian seas. That would secure access to Armenia from the north and block Parthian expansion in that direction. In southern Arabia and East Africa, the Romans took steps to ensure the diversion of trade between the Roman Empire and India from overland routes controlled by Parthia to water routes across the Arabian Sea, through the Gulf of Aden, and up the Red Sea to Roman Egypt. They fortified Aden on the southwest coast of the Arabian peninsula and sent a force up the Nile in preparation for an attack against the Ethiopian kingdom of Axum (Axumis, Auxume, Aksum), whose expansion threatened to block Rome's access from the Gulf of Aden to the Red Sea. In 66, however, all Roman military attention in the East shifted to dealing with a great revolt in Judea.

The Jewish Revolt Because of their unique traditions and often uncompromising monotheism, the Jewish population of the Roman province of Judea had always hated and resisted assimilation with foreign conquerors and had often rebelled against any foreign master since the days of the Assyrian Empire. Their occasional successes, such as the revolt of the Maccabees against the Seleucid Empire (p. 116), also helped to inspire further rebellions under subsequent conquerors. In 66, Greeks attacked their Jewish neighbors in the city of Caesarea. Mob protests in Jerusalem against Roman inaction quickly got out of hand when the Roman procurator, hoping to avoid further trouble, failed to crush the protesters quickly. The Imperial legate of Syria, Cestus Gallus, then besieged Jerusalem. It was late in the year, however, and, not prepared for a long winter siege, Gallus suddenly retreated. The whole province then seized the chance to revolt.

Vespasian Nero, however, gave Titus Flavius Vespasian, who had served well in Britain, a special command to quell the uprising. In 67, Vespasian methodically set about retaking the countryside and drawing a tighter and tighter noose around Jerusalem. Many saw the inevitable success of this strategy and surrendered. Among them was the future historian Flavius Josephus, who had been placed in charge of the rebels in Galilee. Still, resistance was fierce, especially at Jerusalem and later Masada. Vespasian had several years of hard work ahead.

It was fortunate for him that he did. Complete success at an early date might have proven fatal to Vespasian. On the one hand, Nero had no interest in personally conducting military campaigns and visiting troops on the frontiers: He was perfectly happy to let others do that dirty work. On the other hand, he was afraid to let others have too much military success and popularity, lest they become more powerful than himself. Therefore, in 61, for example, he had recalled the successful Suetonius Paulinus from Britain and denied him due honors. In 66 and 67, even more fearful as a result of Piso's conspiracy, Nero compelled the suicides of Scribonius Rufus and Scribonius Proculus, commanders of Upper and Lower Germany, and the great general Domitius Corbulo. These actions, however, merely inspired more plots.

The Revolt of Vindex, 68 Nero had planned to tour Asia Minor and Egypt, but bad news compelled him to cancel the trip and return to Rome: C. Julius Vindex, the governor of one of the provinces of Gaul, had revolted and raised a large army. Vindex also had the support of Servius Sulpicius Galba, the governor of Nearer Spain, and of M. Salvius Otho, the governor of Lusitania (Portugal). North Africa and Rome itself were also seething with revolt.

The rebellion received a sudden check when L. Verginius Rufus, the loyal and able governor of Upper Germany, led three legions into Gaul and overwhelmed the raw and undisciplined troops of Vindex at Vesontio (Besançon). The vanquished Vindex committed suicide. Even then, Nero was unsafe. The victorious legions of Rufus revolted in their turn and proclaimed their commander emperor of Rome. Rufus rejected the acclamation and placed himself unreservedly at the disposition of the senate.

The Fall of Nero, 68 The reasons for the opposition to and rebellion against Nero are not far to seek. He had antagonized the conservative upper classes (equestrian as well as senatorial), from which all provincial governors, high army officers, procurators, and other administrative officials were still recruited. They resented his un-Roman attitudes and activities (as Agrippina pointed out), his seizure and confiscation of large private estates in Italy and the provinces (especially in North Africa), his many tyrannies and executions, and his slow but steady decline toward an absolute despotism. Not only that, but he had failed to win or hold the crucial loyalty and affection of the legions. Toward the end of his reign, he had allowed the pay of the troops to fall into arrears and thereby seriously undermined their loyalty and enthusiasm. Furthermore, he had neglected them. Their *Imperator* they had never seen. They did not know him. It would have been far better for him to have gone to the Rhineland to see his soldiers rather than to have taken his triumphal tour of Greece.

Meanwhile, Galba had not been idle. He sent his agents to Rome to undermine the loyalty of the Praetorian Guard with the promise of 80,000 sesterces to each man. The guards succumbed to the bribe, deserted Nero, and declared for Galba. Soon the armies began to renounce their allegiance. The senate proclaimed Nero a public enemy. Deserted and condemned by all and not having the courage to do himself what he had often coldly ordered others to do, he persuaded a faithful freedman to plunge a sword into his throat. Thus died Nero, the last of the Julio-Claudians. The narcissism that accounts for his obsession with the performing arts and the growing absolutism of his later years is epitomized by his purported last words, "What an artist dies in me" (*Qualis artifex pereo*).

Sources like Tacitus, Suetonius, and Dio Cassius may have correctly conveyed the justified feelings of the upper classes toward Nero, but not that of many common people in Rome, Italy, and the provinces. To the nobles he appeared a madman and a fiend. To the masses he was often a benefactor and friend and a champion in their struggle for survival. Not until his reign had they been so well fed or so royally entertained: He had given them bread and circuses, *panem et circenses!*

The public's adoration of Nero and the flowers placed by unknown hands upon his tomb disturbed Galba and later emperors. Otho, Galba's successor, restored Nero's fallen statues and proudly took the name of "Nero"; Vitellius, who overthrew Otho, publicly praised Nero's name and even offered sacrifices to him. Years later, the Emperor Domitian, who also preferred the absolutism inherent in the principate, revered his memory and executed some of his surviving foes.

XXVIII

The Crisis of the Principate and Recovery under the Flavians, A.D. 69 to 96

Nero, last of the Julio-Claudians, had failed to learn the lessons that had enabled Augustus to establish the position of *princeps* on a solid foundation: In order to gain at least the acquiescence, if not the willing cooperation, of powerful aristocrats, absolute power could not be openly flaunted at the center of the Empire, and the personal loyalty of the legions around the periphery had to be assiduously cultivated so that any attempt to challenge the *princeps* could be quickly crushed before it could spread. Nero's failure now threatened the stability of the Empire with the same kind of destructive competition for preeminence that had characterized the late Republic. With the death of Nero in 68, the principate become a revolving door through which four emperors passed in rapid succession as a result of assassination and civil war in 69. If the process had been allowed to continue, the Roman Empire would have been irreparably damaged. Titus Flavius Vespasianus, Vespasian, was able to halt it, however, and earned the reputation of being the second founder of the principate.

Sources The most important ancient source for the events of 69 and the Flavian emperors (Vespasian, Titus, and Domitian) was Tacitus' *Histories*. Unfortunately, only the books that cover the years 69 and 70 survive. Tacitus also wrote the *Agricola*, a valuable biography of his father-in-law, Cn. Julius Agricola, who governed Britain from 77 to 84; a discussion of the state of oratory during the Principate (*Dialogue on Oratory*); and a rather fanciful ethnographic account of the Germans (*Germania*). Suetonius wrote extant biographies of the three emperors between Nero and Vespasian (Galba, Otho, and Vitellius) as well as of the three Flavians, whereas Plutarch wrote two longer biographies of Galba and Otho. As historical sources, they suffer from both the weaknesses of their authors as scholars and the limitations of biography as a genre. Josephus' *History of the Jewish War* is naturally limited in scope. The only connected historical narrative is provided by Byzantine epitomes of Books 65 to 77 of Cassius Dio's history of Rome. Valuable material can also be extracted from the *Natural History* of Pliny the Elder, the *Letters* of Pliny the Younger, Quintillian's *Institutes of Oratory*, Frontinus' collection of military strategems (*Strategemata*) and his treatise on Rome's aqueducts (*De Aquis Urbis Romae*), and the poems of Statius, Martial, and Juvenal (pp. 352–353). Numerous official and private inscriptions, works of art, buildings, public works, fortifications, coins, and artifacts also supply useful information about political, social, economic, and cultural life.

Galba (68 to 69) Servius Sulpicius Galba, the first to succeed Nero, fell in 69 after reigning only a few months. Although of an old senatorial family, he had little talent for practical politics, and because he was already in his early seventies when he came to the throne, he was too old to learn the half-conscious secrets of empire (*arcana imperii*). Before fully consolidating his power, he attempted two contradictory and impossible things: balancing the budget and winning the support of the armies. He alienated the Roman populace by cutting down the grain dole, the Praetorian Guard by his failure to pay promised donatives, and the armies on the Rhine, already hostile and sullen, by his unwise act of recalling their beloved commander, Verginius Rufus. The two armies mutinied and proclaimed one of their commanders, Aulus Vitellius, emperor of Rome.

Even then, Galba might have saved his life and throne by adopting Verginius Rufus as heir and coregent. He chose instead the aristocratic L. Calpurnius Piso Licinianus, who was very acceptable to the senate but totally devoid of popularity or of political and military experience. Galba's choice turned a former friend and supporter, Marcus Salvius Otho, the ex-husband of Poppaea Sabina, into a jealous and dangerous enemy. Otho hurried off to the camp of the Praetorian Guard and by liberal promises of money persuaded its men to proclaim him emperor. They promptly murdered Galba and Piso.

Otho (69) Although Otho had the support of the Praetorian Guard and the Roman populace and soon won recognition by the senate, the armies on the Rhine, who had already declared for Vitellius, marched against him. An early spring prevented Otho from blocking them at the Alpine passes into Italy. He defeated part of their forces at Bedriacum after a daring encircling movement, but before the Danubian legions on whom he chiefly depended had all arrived, he decided to attack superior Vitellian forces based at Cremona. Defeated after a long, hard-fought battle and hoping to prevent further bloodshed, he terminated his short reign by suicide.

Significantly, Otho was the first emperor who did not have his roots in the old Republican aristocracy. The Julio-Claudians had promoted men in Imperial service from outside traditional senatorial families in order to have a group of loyal officials to counterbalance champions of the old order in the senate. With the end of the Julio-Claudians, there were no loyalties to prevent officials of the new class from attempting the throne themselves.

Vitellius (69) Vitellius came from that class, and hostile sources portray him as one of the most inept and helpless emperors ever to disgrace the Roman throne. His failure to prevent looting and violence after victory is a black mark, but stories that he bankrupted the treasury by extravagant living during a reign of only seven months are not credible. His greatest significance is that he owed his elevation solely to legions from the frontier without any help from the Praetorian Guard.

The armies of the Rhine had already created one emperor. Now, those stationed in the East were about to create another, Titus Flavius Vespasian, the general whom Nero had sent to Judea in 66 to suppress the Jewish revolt (p. 316). Leaving his son Titus in charge of the siege of Jerusalem, Vespasian himself hastened to Egypt in order to prevent the shipment of grain supplies to Rome. In the meantime, the governor of Syria set off with his army to invade Italy on Vespasian's behalf. The Danubian armies did likewise and brutally sacked Cremona after defeating Vitellius' forces there.

In Rome, Vitellius tried to give up to Vespasian's brother Flavius Sabinus, who had become prefect of the city under Otho. Vitellius' soldiers refused to give up and forced him to besiege Sabinus on the Capitoline. The great temple of Jupiter Optimus Maximus was destroyed by fire, and the captured Sabinus was executed. Vitellius' forces, in turn, were defeated. On December 20, 69, he was killed by the Danubian troops, who were in the process of sacking Rome before the arrival of the Syrian army restored order. The senate then chose Vespasian, a man of equestrian origin, as the new emperor. He was able to gain permanent control and replace the defunct Julio-Claudian dynasty with his own Flavian family.

Significant Trends

The birth of a new dynasty was not the sole or the most important change in A.D. 69. Nor did its significance lie wholly in the discovery that emperors could be created elsewhere than in Rome when provincial armies proclaimed their commanders as emperors. The significance lay rather in the reinforcement and culmination of several trends and tendencies that had been slowly evolving since the time of Caesar and Augustus: Besides the growing importance of the frontier armies, there was the progressive decay of the old senatorial aristocracy in the face of men like Otho, Vitellius, and Vespasian; the consolidation of executive power in the hands of the emperors and their administrators; the wider participation of Italy and the provinces in the government and administration of the Empire; and the evolution of a truly integrated world state through liberal grants of citizenship and privileges. For example, Galba enfranchised tribes in central Gaul, and Otho made citizens of the Lignones from eastern Gaul. Vitellius seems to have been generous with Latin rights in Spain and North Africa. Vespasian, moreover, not only let these grants stand but also used his censorial power to add men of ability from the urbanized provinces of the West to the Roman senate itself.

Vespasian (69 to 79)

The accession of Vespasian in the last days of 69 gave Rome a man who was able to end the civil wars, bloodlettings, and pillage. A new day of peace and tranquillity was dawning almost as glorious and as welcome to the Roman People as the day of the august victory at Actium, which had brought to an end the strife, anarchy, and civil wars of the dying Republic. Vespasian lacked the glamour and prestige of Julius Caesar's adopted heir, nor was his reign quite as memorable. It did, nevertheless, usher in a new phase in the history of the Roman Empire and many of the policies typical of the second century.

Born in A.D. 9, Vespasian came from an equestrian family who lived in a small hamlet near the hilltop town of Reate in the Sabine country. His grandfather had been an auctioneer, his father an Imperial tax collector in Asia Minor and, after his retirement, a moneylender in the province of Raetia (southern Bavaria and eastern Switzerland). The father later returned to Italy, married into a family slightly above his own social station, and settled down on a medium-sized estate near Reate.

Young Vespasian had received a fair education and was able to make jokes not only in Latin but even in Greek, some rather corny and at times slightly obscene. His financial and military abilities had won him a number of posts under Claudius and Nero. Coming to the throne in 69 at the age of sixty, bald, wrinkled, and tough, he had behind him much administrative and military experience. He knew the needs of the Empire thoroughly, for in one capacity or another he had known Thrace, Spain, Gaul, Germany, Britain, Africa, Syria, and Egypt. A rugged, hard-bitten old soldier, he had the respect of the armies and could command their loyalty and obedience. They accepted his reforms without murmur or dissent. He was a tireless worker and, although he often took his time making up his mind on a specific course of action, he carried out his decisions with determination and steadfastness. Knowing from past personal experience the value of money, he gave Rome a sound fiscal policy and took endless pains in balancing the budget. Such was the man who rescued Rome from the brink of financial and political disaster and made possible more than another century of peace and prosperity.

The Restoration of Peace

Most urgent was the task of breaking the continued resistance of Vitellius' supporters in Gaul and Germany as well as crushing the revolt in Judea. In Gaul and Germany, Julius Civilis, a chief of the Germanic Batavi and a Roman citizen, had raised a revolt in favor of Vespasian against Vitellius. Apparently, Vespasian's attempts to compromise with Vitellius' forces in 70 led to

Civilis' disaffection and an attempt to combine with those still hostile to Vespasian. They constituted themselves as the Gallic Empire, *Imperium Galliarum*, probably to secure a base from which they could raise up their own candidate for Roman emperor and not, as is frequently claimed, to create an independent Gallic nation. The able Quintus Petilius Cerialis, however, son-in-law of Vespasian, destroyed their hopes in the spring of 70. He then went on to assume command of the legions in Britain and conquer the territory of the Brigantes around Eburacum (York).

Capture of Jerusalem (70) and Masada (73)

Meanwhile, in the Jewish War, Titus, Vespasian's elder son, had stormed and captured Jerusalem. Neither side showed any mercy to the other. The slaughter was frightful, and large numbers of those Jews who survived were sold into slavery. A relief on the Arch of Titus, erected by Domitian in the Roman Forum to commemorate the capture and destruction of Jerusalem, shows a triumphal procession bearing the spoils taken from the Temple —the seven-branched candlestick, the table of the shewbread, and other spoils. Finally, to demonstrate the inevitable punishment that awaited any resistance to Rome, three legions spent three years in crushing pockets of rebels. During the final six months, they built a huge earthen ramp to reach the fanatical defenders of Masada, a sheer rock fortress 1,700 feet above the Dead Sea. When the Romans finally breached their walls, the defenders set fire to their buildings. Josephus says that all but two women and five children committed suicide.

To reduce the chance of organized rebellion in the future, the Jewish council of the Sanhedrin was abolished along with the office of high priest, the Temple was destroyed, and worship there was forbidden. Furthermore, the Jews were forbidden to seek converts, and the Jewish population of the whole Empire was forced to donate the tax formerly paid to the Temple at Jerusalem to Jupiter Capitolinus at Rome instead. All those born into the Jewish faith, however, were still exempted from Caesar worship. Of the various Jewish factions only the Pharisees survived. They devoted themselves chiefly to the study of Jewish law. With Jerusalem destroyed, the small Christian sect was further cut off from its Jewish roots and began to take on an identity more of its own,

Relief from the Triumphal Arch of Titus (A.D. 81), which depicts the spoils from Jerusalem. (Fratelli Alinari, Art Resource NY)

which both helped its spread among non-Jews and soon caused problems over Caesar worship.

Reform of the Army

The part played by the provincial soldiers in the havoc of 69 had clearly indicated to Vespasian the urgent need for a reform of the army. First, he struck from the Roman army lists the legions that had supported the opposition to Vespasian in Gaul and Germany. Next, he stopped the practice of stationing some of the legionary and most of the auxiliary troops in the frontier regions from which they had been recruited, because they were apt to sympathize with local leaders' political ambitions.

To counteract such sympathies, he either formed new auxiliary units of mixed tribal and national origin or transferred units to frontiers far removed from their homeland and under the command of Italian officers. Finally, in order to reduce the chances of military coups by provincial commanders and provide for tighter defense at the same time, Vespasian tended to break up large concentrations of legions, formerly stationed in a few central camps, and space them out singly along the borders.

Another problem was that the popularity of military service had been steadily declining among the population of Rome and Italy as peace and prosperity increased under the emperors. To take up the slack, Vespasian extended legionary recruitment from Italy to the more cultured and educated youth of Gaul and Spain, where military academies for the training of future Roman officers (*collegia iuvenum*) became ever more common. Thus Vespasian's military reforms were part of a process that Romanized and integrated the provinces.

Provincial Policy

Surpassing even Caesar, Augustus, Tiberius, and Claudius, Vespasian inaugurated a new age of municipalization in the Roman world, which lasted until about 260. Completing the work of former centuries, he made Spain an integral part of the new world state by extending Latin rights to about 350 Spanish cities and towns. Even Dalmatia began

in his reign to acquire a degree of urbanization and municipalization that it had never before known. The Danubian provinces were the last regions in the Roman world to receive Roman citizen colonies (*coloniae deductae*) and, during Vespasian's reign, became part of a process inaugurated long before in the historic year of 338 B.C. (p. 74).

Vespasian did more to make the western provinces full partners in the government and administration of the Empire than simply to use them as recruiting grounds or to grant Roman citizenship to officeholders in the newly chartered *municipia*. He went beyond Claudius or any of his predecessors in employing the local aristocracy of Gaul and Spain in Imperial administration. He used his powers as censor to add numerous members of the municipal aristocracy of southern Gaul and of Baetica in southwestern Spain to the rolls of the Roman senate, whose ranks had become depleted through persecutions by former emperors and in the recent civil war of 69. By utilizing the talents and services of the Gallic and Spanish provincials, Vespasian gave them a stake in both defending the Imperial frontiers and maintaining internal peace, order, and tranquility in the West.

Vespasian greatly strengthened the defenses of the northern frontiers by restoring the number of legions serving along the Rhine to eight and by his creation of two new military provinces in Upper and Lower Germany, both entirely separate from the administration of the Gallic provinces. Along the Danubian frontier, he built numerous military roads and new stone fortresses. More important still, he shortened communications along the Rhine-Danube frontier by annexing the triangle of land called the *Agri Decumates* (now largely occupied by the Black Forest) between the upper reaches of the two rivers in what is now southwestern Germany and Switzerland. Vespasian also sent three men of great renown to resume the conquest of Britain, which Claudius and Nero had left unfinished—Petilius Cerialis (71 to 74), who had vanquished Civilis in Germany; Julius Frontinus (74 to 77–78), who wrote the *Strategemata* and *On the Aqueducts;* and Cn.

Julius Agricola (77–78 to 84), about whom his own son-in-law, Tacitus, wrote the *Agricola*.

The Near East   In the Near East, which he knew well from firsthand experience, Vespasian attempted with the limited means at his disposal to remedy some of the fundamental weaknesses in the defensive arrangements of his predecessors. He attempted to maintain peaceful relations with Parthia, even to the extent of resigning control, direct or nominal, over the kingdom of Greater Armenia, but he did not seek Parthia's friendship at the expense of Rome's own interests. His least friendly act toward the Parthians was his refusal to cooperate with them in repelling the Alans, a Sarmatian tribe living beyond the Caucasus, who had overrun Media Atropatene and Greater Armenia and were then a threat to the very existence of the Parthian state. Instead, he only helped the king of Iberia (modern Georgia) to occupy the Porta Caucasica (Dariel Pass), and he built a fortress near what is now Tiflis (Tblisi) in 75.

Some of Vespasian's other measures were also less than pleasing to the Parthian king. First, he strengthened Roman control over the great caravan city of Palmyra and made Judea a separate procuratorial province with one full legion stationed at Jerusalem. He extended the province of Syria from the northern edge of the Lebanon mountain range east of Damascus to the upper reaches of the middle Euphrates by the annexation of the kingdom of Commagene, whose king he deposed. To the north, he created a huge province in Anatolia by adding Cappadocia and Lesser Armenia to the former province of Galatia. There he stationed two legions, one to guard the vital Euphrates crossing at Melitene, the other the important road junction of Satala, whence roads led to Trapezus (Trebizond) and to other naval bases on the Black Sea. Thus Vespasian, except at Zeugma and Samosata, now legionary strongholds, diminished the responsibility of Syria for the Roman defense of the Near East against Parthian attempts to cross the Euphrates and created stronger bulwarks for protecting Rome's eastern provinces.

Vespasian's Relations with the Senate
Although the senate remained a sounding board of upper-class Roman and Italian opinion and, therefore, exerted a powerful influence upon the character of even the most autocratic Imperial regime, it still had been declining steadily as an independent organ of the government since the reign of Tiberius. The extent of its decline was marked in 73, when Vespasian, following the example of Claudius, risked offending conservative senators by assuming the censorship. That gave him the power to remove objectionable and recalcitrant senators and replace them with new men from Italy and the western provinces, who would cooperate and obey. The new men were usually of demonstrated ability and staunch supporters of the regime. The senate had been reduced to about 200 by the actions of Nero and the civil war of 68–69. Vespasian added 800, which must have annoyed the remaining old families but increased the pool of senatorial talent that Vespasian needed to administer the Empire.

The Expansion of Executive Power   The weakening of the senate was accompanied by a steady concentration of powers and functions in the Imperial executive and an increase in appointed officeholders, whose value as the sole means of preserving administrative continuity under rapidly changing emperors had come to light more clearly than ever before in 69.

In his selection of officials, Vespasian made two important innovations: He replaced with equestrians many, but not all, of the freedmen who had held some of the highest positions under Claudius and Nero and appointed more and more Italians and provincials. The reasons for these innovations are clear: The equestrians were less offensive to the senate than were freedmen, who had been offensive to the equestrians as well; also, equestrians usually had considerable business and administrative experience and, often having greater private sources of income, were somewhat less tempted than freedmen to embezzle public funds. The provincials brought with them a knowledge of local conditions that must have been quite useful in the administration of a highly diversified empire.

Fiscal Administration Vespasian's greatest claim to fame was his success in handling fiscal problems—balancing the budget and restoring the public finances, which had been thrown into chaos by Nero's extravagance and the civil wars of 69. Being personally frugal and financially experienced, Vespasian also had firm control over the armies and did not need to buy their loyalty by large donatives. Nor would he tolerate misuse of public funds by government officials. Also, he vigorously increased taxes on the provinces and drastically cut down public expenditures.

Using his powers as censor, Vespasian had a careful census taken of the financial resources of the Empire. He discovered that the provinces after a century of peace and prosperity were able to pay much more tribute than before. He assigned certain "free" cities and islands previously immune from taxation, such as Rhodes, Samos, and Byzantium, to provinces and forced them to pay taxes. He restored to the senate the province of Greece, to which Nero had granted freedom and immunity from taxes, and took back under Imperial control the richer provinces of Sardinia and Corsica. He asserted the government's claim to land seized surreptitiously by private owners or occupied illegally by squatters, took back on behalf of the *fiscus* many estates given by former emperors to their friends, and reorganized the revenues of the other Imperial estates, especially those containing mines, quarries, fisheries, and forests. In short, no source of income, however unorthodox or unsavory (such as a tax on public latrines), was beneath Vespasian's notice.

Despite a reputation for being tight with money, Vespasian spent freely on Imperial defense; on roads, bridges, and fortifications in the provinces; on public buildings in Rome; and on education. After repairing the damage wrought in Italy by the civil war of 69, he commemorated the end of the Jewish War by beginning construction in Rome of the Forum that bears his name (with the Temple of Peace

in the center), the Arch of Titus, and the gigantic stone Flavian Amphiteater or Colosseum (pp. 361–362), a symbol of the might and majesty of Imperial Rome.[1] Another great architectural achievement of the reign was the completion in 71 of a new temple to Capitoline Jupiter.

As an encouragement to literature and education, Vespasian liberally subsidized poets and prose writers. From public funds he endowed schools and established a chair of literature and rhetoric at Rome. Marcus Fabius Quintilianus, the celebrated Spanish rhetorician, was its first holder (p. 353).

The Opposition to Vespasian Despite his conspicuous achievements and services to the Empire, Vespasian never fully escaped the opposition of republican-minded senators and of the Stoic and Cynic philosophers. Many senators objected to his numerous consulships (by which he sought to enhance the nobility of his family), his assumption of the censorship, his practice of admitting Italians and provincials into the senate, and his ill-concealed intention of founding a new dynasty by handing down the office of *princeps* to members of his own family. Yet the senatorial opposition was more vocal than dangerous, and Vespasian paid little attention to it. Far more irritating were the attacks of the Stoic and especially of the Cynic philosophers, who finally nettled him into ordering their expulsion from Rome.

Vespasian's Death, 79 In the spring of 79, after a decade of hard and continuous work, Vespasian caught a fever and died. The hour of death did not deprive him of his sense of humor. As he lay dying he muttered, "Dear me, I think I'm becoming a god!"

Before his death, Vespasian had settled the question of his successor. He had carefully prepared his elder son, also named Titus Flav-

---

[1] The Colosseum owes its name not to its own size but to the size (120 feet high) of the statue of Nero that stood at the entrance. It was placed there by the Emperor Hadrian, who removed it from the court of Nero's Golden House.

ius Vespasianus, to be his successor. Titus, as he is called, had held army commands, the proconsular *imperium,* and tribunician power. He had shared the censorship with his father for one year and the consulship for seven. Vespasian had also appointed him sole prefect of the Praetorian Guard, a wise precaution that enabled Titus to thwart immediately Aulus Caecina's grab for the throne in 79.

Titus (79 to 81)   After Vespasian's death, the senate at once conferred upon Titus the usual honors and titles belonging to the *princeps,* although not without some qualms and misgivings. Titus was handsome, charming, genial, and generous enough, but his moral conduct had reportedly not been of the best. He had associated rather freely with the wilder elements of Roman aristocratic society, and a love affair with Julia Berenice, a sister of the Jewish king, Herod Agrippa II, revived memories of Antony and Cleopatra.

Once seated on the throne, however, Titus became the ideal *princeps,* eager to promote the welfare of his subjects and much beloved by the people. He recalled the philosophers exiled by his father and halted all treason trials. He rewarded unscrupulous informers (*delatores*) with public flogging and enslavement or exile to unhealthy islands. He sent away Berenice to avoid giving offense to conservative senators, and he entertained the people with splendid games and shows to their amazement and delight.

Three catastrophes marred his brief but brilliant reign. In August of 79, Mt. Vesuvius, after centuries of quiescence (except for a severe earthquake in 63) suddenly burst forth into violent eruption near the Bay of Naples. The ground quaked and heaved, the light was blotted from the sky, and tons of smoking pumice, volcanic ash, and mud buried the cities of Pompeii, Herculaneum, and Stabiae. The famous excavations at Pompeii and Herculaneum plus two letters of Pliny the Younger (6.16 and 20), who tells how his uncle Pliny the Elder died trying to rescue some of the victims at Stabiae, bear eloquent witness to this great

cataclysm. Next, a plague, like none ever seen before, descended upon Campania. In Rome, another great fire broke out and raged for three days. These disasters, occurring as they did in rapid succession, put to the severest test the energy and philanthropy of Titus.

In September of 81, after a reign of twenty-six months, Titus contracted a fever just as his father had and died at the family's home. He was only 42. The Roman people mourned the death of their beloved ruler, and the senate showered him with posthumous praises and honors. Deification followed.

Domitian (81 to 96)   The way was now open for Vespasian's younger son, Titus Flavius Domitianus, known as Domitian. Leaving his brother's deathbed, Domitian rode in haste to Rome. He went to the barracks of the Praetorian Guard to be acclaimed emperor. The armies acquiesced; the senate approved. Neither had much choice. The son of Vespasian and brother of Titus had no rival claimants to the throne. It became his, not through any special education or previous military or administrative experience, but by accident of birth.

Vespasian had always made it clear that Domitian was to play a prominent role in the family. His cognomen, *Domitianus,* honored Nero's martyred general Domitius Corbulo, who had been popular with the senate and the people. In 70, the link had become even stronger when Domitian married Corbulo's daughter Domitia Longina. Nevertheless, Vespasian had not entrusted him with early responsibilities comparable to Titus', nor had Titus. Domitian had held seven consulships from 70 to 80, but they were largely honorific, and he had busied himself by writing Greek verse and studying the *Acta* (*Deeds*) of Tiberius, whose reserve, grimness, and austerity he much admired and later imitated. Later gossip predictably accused Domitian of poisoning Titus, but that is unfounded.

Autocratic Behavior   Soon after taking office, Domitian incurred the senate's displeasure and hostility by his autocratic behavior. Appearing before senators in the regalia of a triumphant general, he affronted their dignity. (His triumphal robes marked him as an *Imperator* with power to command. In nonmilitary attire he would have been a *princeps* seeking advice.) Also, his seventeen consulships and his becoming censor for life (*censor perpetuus*) not only defied all tradition but also revealed his intention of establishing an absolute monarchy. Worse still, he outdid even Caligula and Nero by permitting and encouraging poets, courtiers, and appointees to address him as Lord and God (*Dominus et Deus*).

He trampled underfoot the ancient prerogatives of the senate by elevating equestrians to positions of power formerly reserved to senators. He appointed equestrians to his judicial *consilium* to sit in judgment on senators and even named an *eques* proconsul of the senatorial province of Asia. Acts such as these were more intolerable than his premature pretensions to divinity. After his death, the senate damned his memory and ordered the removal of his statues from public places.

Public Benefactions, Religion, and Finance

Although his relations with the senate were bad, Domitian kept the populace happy. Three times he distributed donations (*congiaria*) to citizens resident at Rome for a total of 225 *denarii* a head. For their amusement he organized splendid spectacles: wild beast hunts; mock sea and land battles; gladiatorial contests in the Colosseum, the building of which he completed; and chariot races in the Circus Maximus. He built the Stadium and Odeum (Music Hall) in Mars' Field to encourage competitions in the Greek manner not only in sports but in literature. He also completed the Arch and Baths of Titus and restored the Pantheon and Baths of Agrippa as well as the temple complex of Serapis and Isis. The latter had been gutted in a fire under Titus. In front of it, he placed imported Egyptian Obelisks. He erected a beautiful new temple to the deified Vespasian, a high temple to Jupiter the Guardian (*Jupiter Custos*), and, most magnificent of all, a new temple to Jupiter Optimus Maximus on the Capitol, with columns of Pentelic marble, gold-plated doors, and roof tiles overlaid with gold leaf in place of the rebuilt temple that had also burned in the recent fire.

Domitian had taken a very active interest in Roman religion at an early age. As emperor, he sought to revive and strengthen old practices with a view to their political usefulness. He thereby appeared to be a defender of the *mos maiorum* and the gods who had made Rome great: Jupiter, Minerva, Mars, Venus, Neptune, Vesta, Ceres, and Rome herself. As their champion, he advanced his claim to be one of them. Therefore, he was usually hostile to exotic foreign cults, except that of Isis, as whose acolyte he had disguised himself and escaped danger during the civil war of 69. He seems to have shown particular hostility toward Jews and Christians, which is understandable since their rigid monotheism clashed with his own desire to be recognized as a god. Under him, therefore, treason became linked with impiety and emperor worship became a test of loyalty, which posed great problems for Christians during the next two centuries.

Domitian certainly spent sums of money worthy of a god. Not neglecting himself, he built a grand Imperial palace on the Palatine and a huge mansion on Mount Alba overlooking the placid waters of the Alban Lake. In Italy he constructed a road from Sinuessa to Cumae. In Britain, as well as along the Rhine and Danube he established numerous fortresses and garrison camps. He raised the base pay of legionary soldiers from 225 to 300 *denarii* per annum and also fought several costly wars between 81 and 93.

Where he got the money for everything is a mystery. He apparently never tapped new sources of revenue nor accepted legacies from testators having five or more children. He canceled debts owed to the state for more than five years and, unlike Vespasian, gave clear title to occupiers of public land in Italy. Unlike Nero, he never debased the coinage. To explain how he was able to pass on to his successors a fairly full treasury, it must be assumed that he had his father's financial ability and was an efficient administrator and a strict collector of provincial taxes. In addition he probably raked into the *fiscus,* now reorganized and centralized, the proceeds of considerable property confiscated from persons condemned for treason against the state, of whom there were probably not a few in the latter part of his reign.

The Rebellion of Saturninus, 89   Treason trials occurred more frequently after the rebellion of L. Antonius Saturninus, the governor of Upper Germany and commander of two legions wintering in the double camp at Moguntiacum (Mainz). On January 1, 89, he seized his army's savings and payroll and bribed the troops to proclaim him emperor. He also induced the Chatti, a strong German tribe dwelling east of the middle Rhine, to invade Roman territory. To crush that revolt, Domitian at once sped north with his Praetorian Guard after he ordered Trajan (the future emperor) to bring up a legion from Spain. Both got there too late for the battle. The loyal governor of Lower Germany, aided by a sudden thaw that broke up the ice over the Rhine and prevented the Chatti from crossing to help the rebels, suppressed the rebellion and killed Saturninus.

Upon arriving, Domitian ruthlessly punished the officers and accomplices of Saturninus and expanded the Roman territory to the east of the Rhine and to the north of the river Main (Moenus). He sent the severed head of Saturninus to Rome and later celebrated a double triumph, not over the Roman Saturninus, of course, but over the Chatti and the Dacians, against whom he advanced after having secured the Rhine frontier by shortened defense lines, watchtowers, and fortifications.

The Dacian Frontier, 85 to 93   The revolt of Saturninus in 89 had disrupted Domitian's conquest of Dacia (roughly equivalent to modern Rumania), which he had begun in 85 after the young and aggressive Dacian king Decebalus (85 to 106) had invaded the Roman province of Moesia across the Danube. A Ro-

man army inflicted a great defeat on the Dacians in 88, but in 89, after the suppression of Saturninus, an army led by Domitian himself suffered so sharp a reverse that he gladly came to terms with Decebalus. Decebalus agreed to surrender all Roman captives and accept the role of Roman client. In return, Domitian recognized him as the legitimate king of the Dacians, granted him an annual subsidy, and furnished him Roman engineers skilled in the art of building roads and fortresses.

The Dacian peace treaty, though dictated by expediency and considered by many senators to be an affront to Roman dignity, was of immense value to Rome. It turned Decebalus into a benevolent neutral, if not an active ally, when the Iazyges irrupted into Pannonia in 92 and badly mauled a Roman legion. It also helped Domitian isolate the hostile Marcomanni and Quadi by alliances with the Germanic tribes living to the north of them, with the Semnones east of the Elbe, and with the powerful Lugii of Silesia. Domitian was able to stabilize the Danubian frontier by concentrating nine or ten legions along the river in strongly fortified camps at Vindobona (Vienna), at Carnuntum (Altenburg), at Aquincum (Budapest), and at Troesmis near the mouth of the Danube. By 93, peace prevailed again along the entire Danubian frontier.

Conspiracies and Treason Trials   The rebellion of Saturninus in 89 so upset Domitian that he developed a serious persecution complex and saw conspiracies forming against him everywhere. Spies and informers began to play upon his fears. In 89, he banished philosophers and astrologers from Rome but later struck out most savagely against prominent senators, some able provincial governors, and even members of the Imperial family. In 95 or 96, he executed his cousin Flavius Clemens and exiled his cousin Flavia Domitilla, who was also Clemens' wife.

The Murder of Domitian, 96   Fearing for their own lives, members of the court, possibly including the Empress Domitia, entered into a conspiracy with a number of influential senators. Domitilla's devoted former butler, a certain Stephanus, pretended to have secret information about a conspiracy. Admitted to the emperor's bedroom, he handed him a list of names. As Domitian read the list, Stephanus stabbed him in the groin. The wounded Domitian shouted for his attendant to get the dagger that he always kept under his pillow, but its blade was gone. Stephanus, and others who rushed in to help him, finished the deed.

Despite Domitian's evil reputation in senatorial circles, all three Flavians had done great service to the Roman Empire. They had restored internal peace and prosperity, introduced greater administrative efficiency and fiscal responsibility, continued the process of integrating the status of provincials with that of the Romans and Italians (who had previously exploited them), and set a standard of personal service that inspired their successors during a century of good government.

XXIX

The "Good" Emperors of the Second Century, A.D. 96 to 180

The death of Domitian marked the end of the Flavian dynasty, but the stability established by the Flavians endured. No destructive period of crisis and civil war followed, as had happened upon the death of Nero. Unlike Nero, Domitian had not neglected the legions, and he had been able to crush rebellious commanders quickly. The successful conspiracy against Domitian had originated not among provincial armies but within the Imperial family and senatorial leadership at Rome. The conspirators placed a new emperor on the throne before provincial commanders had time to react. As a result, there was a fairly smooth transfer of Imperial authority at what is considered the beginning of the second century A.D. in Roman history.

Within their own ranks, the senators found the successor to Domitian, Marcus Cocceius Nerva. Sixty years old and long past his prime, he posed no threat of establishing another dynasty. Generous donatives paid or promised kept both the Praetorian Guard and the provincial armies temporarily satisfied and acquiescent. Thus a peaceful transition was effected, and a new period in the history of the Principate was introduced. The emperors Nerva, Trajan, Hadrian, Antoninus Pius, and Marcus Aurelius, from A.D. 96 to 180, are often called the "five good emperors." Under them, the Roman Empire enjoyed its longest single period of stability and good government. They were benevolent rulers, whose chief concern was to promote the welfare of the Empire and the people whom they ruled.

Sources There are only two narrative sources for this period, neither of the first rank as history. The first is Cassius Dio, whose history of Rome covered the reigns involved in Books 67 to 72, which are preserved in only abbreviated form by two later Byzantine epitomes: a lengthy one now missing the reign of Antoninus Pius and the early years of Marcus Aurelius, and a shorter one based on the first. Biographies of the emperors from Hadrian to Marcus Aurelius and also of Lucius Verus and Avidius Cassius are found in a controversial collection known as the *Historia Augusta* and written probably about A.D. 395. It is generally agreed that the first four major lives in the collection are based on a fairly good source and are trustworthy for the main historical outline. The two minor lives are far less reliable and probably contain much sensationalistic fiction. Minor historical summaries and biographies can be found in several fourth-century epitomes (p. 471).

For the reigns of Nerva and Trajan, the contemporary letters of Pliny the Younger and his *Panegyric* (on Trajan) are very useful. The panegyric *To Rome* and the *Sacred Teachings* of the Greek rhetorician Aelius Aristides are useful for the period under Antoninus Pius, and the *Letters* (*Epistulae*) of Marcus Aurelius' tutor Marcus Cornelius Fronto were composed from the time of Hadrian to that of Aurelius. Of course, Aurelius' own *Meditations* provide a firsthand look into his interesting personality. Other literary and technical works and numerous Christian writings are also valuable for reconstructing the social, economic, and cultural milieu of the period (p. 353 ff.), as are Jewish works like the Mishna, Midrash, and Talmud.

Monuments, such as the triumphal arch of Trajan at Beneventum and the columns of Trajan and Marcus Aurelius, present valuable historical information, as do numerous extant coins, inscriptions, and Egyptian papyri from this era. These latter three sources, along with archaeological excavations throughout the Empire, yield interesting data on the provinces. Finally, laws preserved in the *Corpus Iuris Civilis* (*Body of Civil Law*) shed light on the social and administrative developments under the "good" emperors.

Nerva (96 to 98) Though Nerva's family contained several distinguished jurists, it was not an old one and had gained social acceptance only because his maternal uncle had married a woman of Julio-Claudian birth, an ennobling but tenuous link. Nerva himself had not won much distinction as a jurist or as a public speaker and had never governed a province or commanded an army, though he had done fairly well politically. Being a safe and innocuous man and willing to cooperate with any regime, he had had one statue erected to him in the Forum, another on the Palatine during Nero's reign. He had reached the consulship in 71 under Vespasian and again in 90 under Domitian. He also held several priesthoods. In all his past career, he seems to have preferred security to fame.

The senate regarded Nerva as the ideal ruler for many reasons: his deference, his vow never to put a senator to death unless condemned by a senatorial court, his restoration to the senate of the administration of the grain dole, his suspension of the hated law of treason (*maiestas*), and his recall of senatorial exiles and suppression of informers.

On the other hand, Nerva was unable to resist the demand for punishment of Domitian's assassins. When members of the Praetorian Guard besieged his palace and clamored for vengeance against Domitian's killers, he meekly allowed them to kill their former prefect and several other conspirators. Furthermore, despite the initially smooth transition to his new reign, it became apparent early on that Nerva could not hold power long without strong military backing to hold in check ambitious provincial commanders once they had a chance to reflect on the sudden turn of events with Domitian's assassination.

Therefore, the most important act of Nerva's brief rule was his adoption of Marcus Ulpius Traianus, Trajan, as son, heir, and coregent. The very able and respected military governor of Lower Germany, Trajan was an excellent choice. A year after the adoption, Nerva died before his new son had even come to Rome. Thanks to Nerva's action, however, Trajan succeeded without incident.

Trajan (98 to 117) Trajan, the first emperor of provincial origin, was born in Spain at Italica near Hispalis (Seville) in the rich province of Baetica. He was proud of his father, whom Vespasian had admitted not only into the senate but also into the Roman patriciate. His father had achieved the consulship, the Syrian command, the proconsulship of Asia, and numerous triumphal honors in swift succession.

Before his adoption by Nerva, Trajan himself had enjoyed a long and distinguished military career under Vespasian and Domitian on the Rhine, the Danube, and the Euphrates; in Syria; and in Spain. As governor of Lower Germany during Nerva's reign, he had won the proud title of *Germanicus*. Under his own auspices he would win still others: *Dacicus* and *Parthicus* (conqueror of the Dacians and the Parthians). After Nerva's death, two years spent in inspecting and strengthening defenses along the Rhine and the Danube preceded Trajan's long-awaited and much-acclaimed arrival in Rome.

A Model Emperor Toward the senate Trajan was tactful, respectful, often gracious, even indulgent. His was the attitude of the "Best Prince" (*Optimus Princeps*), a title bestowed as early as 100, stamped on the coinage in 105, but not officially assumed till 115. Centuries later, the senate bestowed on every new emperor the supreme compliment: "Luckier than Augustus, better than Trajan" *(Felicior Augusto, melior Traiano).*

The senate with which Trajan had to deal was different in attitude and composition from that of the early Principate. Severely chastened by Nero and Domitian, it had gladly accepted him as being at least a "better *princeps* than the worst" (*melior pessimo princeps*). Change of attitude arose out of change of composition. As inscriptions and papyri show, the senate of Claudius and even Vespasian contained only a few members of provincial origin. Under Trajan, provincial senators made up slightly over 40 percent of the total, more and more of whom now came from the eastern provinces. Enjoying, as he did, the support and eventual affection of the senate, the people, and the provincial armies, Trajan was able to carry out his administrative program without distraction or fear. He was an energetic emperor and tried to give the Empire the best possible government. He pursued many enlightened social and economic programs and inaugurated many public works that added to both the beauty and the prosperity of Rome and the provinces.

The Alimenta: *Public Assistance for the Poor*
Although it may have been instituted under Nerva, a relief program called the *alimenta* to bolster the population of Italy by supporting poor children was strongly promoted by Trajan. In the late first century A.D., viticulture and pottery manufacturing in central Italy were declining because of increased competition from provincial exports, especially from the now highly Romanized provinces of Gaul and Spain (pp. 369–370). The large landowners of Italy were able to adjust to these new circumstances without much difficulty. Land that once might have been used to grow cash crops could be given over to tenant farmers (*coloni*) in return

for a fixed share of their produce, which would keep the owners supplied with foodstuffs.

The impoverishment of smaller farmers and craftsmen, however, had a serious effect on their ability to raise children. A decline of population in the affected parts of Italy resulted. This decline adversely affected Italian recruitment for the army, to which emperors looked not only for the loyal defense of the Empire but also as a means of Romanizing the provinces and promoting Imperial unity. To alleviate this problem, Nerva or Trajan, imitating local private relief efforts by wealthy men like Pliny the Younger, set up the publicly funded *alimenta* to subsidize the care and education of poor freeborn boys and girls.

Under this plan, landowners in a given locality would pledge so much land as collateral for a loan equal to about one eighth of its value. In return, the owners agreed to pay, apparently in perpetuity, about 5 percent interest a year on the amount of money received. The interest paid was put into a fund administered by Imperial officials, who then distributed it to the needy children of the local district. It is not likely that landowners were forced to participate in the *alimenta* or that the members of local town councils, who were large landowners, were excluded. These loans did not make sense for anyone other than the well-to-do. They would certainly not have been attractive or helpful to smaller landowners in difficulties. Such men would not have had collateral to obtain a loan of any consequence, and they would not have wished to burden their precarious finances with a permanent debt. A large landowner, however, could pledge only a part of his holdings and obtain a usable sum of money at relatively little risk and with only a small charge against future income, which he could hope to increase beyond his annual interest cost by using the principal to improve his operations or buy more land in order to increase his profits.

Generosity to Provinces and Municipalities
The measures that Trajan took to improve conditions in the provinces were equally impressive: roads, bridges, harbors, and aqueducts in

almost every province. Unfortunately, many cities in Italy and the eastern provinces had overextended themselves financially as they competed in the splendor of their buildings and public amenities or had to make up for deficiencies in the taxes that they collected for the Imperial government. Trajan unintentionally set a dangerous precedent for interference in municipal affairs by sending out Imperial agents or inspectors (*curatores* or *correctores*) to help municipalities solve their financial problems. The advice of these agents, however polite and friendly, was not to be ignored and eventually contributed to a decay of local initiative.

Trajan's Wars The army, which had been Trajan's life, continued to be his chief delight. In 101, he set out on an invasion of Dacia against King Decebalus. The treaty that Domitian had concluded with Decebalus in 89 had been expedient but galling to Roman Imperial pride. The conquest of Dacia proved neither swift nor easy. Trajan suffered a severe reverse at Tapae near the Iron Gates of the Danube. In the spring of 102, he again invaded Dacia. After several successful battles, he finally occupied the capital city of Sarmizegethusa, where he stationed a permanent garrison. Decebalus surrendered unconditionally and agreed to become a Roman client once more. Trajan then returned to Rome to celebrate his triumph and added *Dacicus* to his titulature.

In 105, Decebalus broke the peace agreement. Trajan hastened to the lower Danube with thirteen legions and broke Dacian resistance (in 106). After the suicide of Decebalus, Trajan annexed Dacia as a province and made Sarmizegethusa a colony (Ulpia Traiana). He settled numerous veterans and colonists from all over the Empire, ancestors of the present-day Rumanians. Fifty thousand Dacian war prisoners ended their days as slaves and gladiators in the Roman arena. Vast revenues from Dacian gold mines made possible magnificent public works in Rome, Italy, and the provinces and temporarily so disturbed the ratio between gold and silver that a slight increase in the cop-

per content of silver coins probably was intended to redress the balance in value between gold and silver coins.

The Parthian Wars, 113 to 117 After seven years of peace, Chosroes, the new Parthian king, provoked Trajan by deposing the king of Armenia without Rome's consent. Trajan's reaction was swift: He set sail for the East in the fall of 113. Within two years he had captured one Parthian capital, Ctesiphon, and extended Rome's dominion from the headwaters of the Tigris and Euphrates to the Persian Gulf. Trade routes to the Far East were now within his grasp, and passage to India might have been his next move.

The Empire, which Trajan had extended to the farthest limits yet attained, was suddenly convulsed by simultaneous revolts. Seleucia, Mesopotamia, Assyria, and even Armenia all were in revolt, and powerful Parthian armies were returning to reoccupy lost territory. The Sarmatians and Roxolani along the Danube were again on the move. In Britain, Roman garrisons were in retreat from the borders of Scotland.

The most serious revolts were those of the Jews in Cyrenaica, Mesopotamia, Adiabene (northern Assyria around Arbela), Cyprus, and Egypt, which were marked by savage massacres. Trajan acted with resolution and promptness; but without help from his able marshal and comrade in arms Lusius Quietus the Moor, he would have failed to restore the rapidly deteriorating situation. Trajan himself pacified southern Mesopotamia by his capture and ruthless destruction of Seleucia on the Tigris, across from Ctesiphon, whereas Quietus reconquered northern Mesopotamia and later, as governor of Judea, stamped out all Jewish riots in Palestine. Trajan's other marshals were less successful in suppressing the revolts in Cyrenaica, Cyprus, and Egypt. Nor was Trajan himself able to hold all of his Parthian conquests: In 116, he surrendered the province of southern Mesopotamia to a Parthian prince, nominally a Roman client, and lost the entire province of Assyria along with part of Greater Armenia.

The Death of Trajan, 117 Three years of hard campaigning in the desert and the strain of recent months had overtaxed Trajan's strength. He was then past sixty. On the road back from Ctesiphon in 116, he became ill. During the winter at Antioch, where he was busily preparing for another campaign in Mesopotamia in the following spring, he grew steadily worse. Reluctantly, he abandoned his preparations. He set out for Rome and left Publius Aelius Hadrianus, Hadrian, the command of the Near East. He never put out to sea. At Selinus in Cilicia, he suffered a stroke and died a few days later (ca. August 8, 117).

The Effects of Trajan's Wars Trajan, one of the greatest of Roman *Imperatores,* was the first to realize at least in part Caesar's plans to conquer Dacia and Parthia. Marcus Antonius had tried but never succeeded; Nero had aspired but never tried. Under Trajan, the Roman Empire reached the high tide of territorial expansion; after him, however, there was to be a slow and inexorable ebb.

The costs of Trajan's expansion were high. He paid the price in health; the Empire, in manpower and resources. Moreover, Trajan had expanded the Empire beyond defensible limits and in the process had weakened, if not totally paralyzed, the capability of three strong buffer states—Dacia, Parthia, and Nabataean Arabia. Rome would later have to absorb and repel the mass invasions of the Goths and other Germans, the Alans, and Iranians. Impelled by the relentless pressure of the Huns from central Asia, they would break and burst through the brittle, overextended defenses of the Roman Empire on the Rhine, Danube, and Euphrates. Undermining the defensive powers of the Dacians, Nabataeans, and Parthians spelled disaster for the Roman Empire of the future.

Hadrian (117 to 138) No sooner had news of Trajan's death reached Antioch than the armies of Syria proclaimed Hadrian to be the new emperor of Rome. Several days later, the senate officially confirmed the acclamation. The rumor that Hadrian owed his throne to a forged instrument of adoption carried little weight against acclamation by the army and the senate's ratification.

Hadrian's birthplace is disputed. According to the *Historia Augusta,* he was born at Rome in 76, but his family on both sides belonged to Italica, the same Spanish town where Trajan was born. An orphan at the age of ten, he became a ward of Trajan, his father's cousin and closest male relative. He received an excellent education and acquired a strong and lasting love of Greek art and philosophy. To that love he owed his half-contemptuous nickname of Graeculus (Greekling). He became a man of refined artistic tastes, an intellectual with a keen, penetrating intelligence.

Like Plato's philosopher king, he had a long military and official career. He had seen military service in Spain, Pannonia, Moesia, Germany, and Parthia. In the First Dacian War, he was Trajan's quaestor, in the Second, the commander of a legion. He was governor of Lower Pannonia in 107 and governor of Syria in 117. To facilitate his climb to power, however, he married Trajan's grandniece, Vibia Sabina, a strikingly beautiful but understandably frustrated woman, whom he probably would have divorced had it not been for his ambition.

Hadrian was more at home hunting or on campaign with the army or touring the provinces than at Rome. Conventional home life did not satisfy him. He seems to have had his share of mistresses in his early years, but the great passion of his life was a handsome young Bithynian Greek named Antinous, whom he met on an Eastern tour in 123. That such a relationship was most satisfying to Hadrian is understandable in light of both his love of Greek art and philosophy, which were heavily imbued with the homoeroticism of aristocratic Greek culture, and, much like an ancient Spartan's, his almost continuous service on active duty in the all-male society of the army.

The Early Years of Hadrian's Principate
Hadrian had fallen heir to a difficult task, not rendered lighter by inevitable comparison with his illustrious predecessor, from whom he had,

ironically, inherited a legacy of disturbance and revolt in Cyrenaica, Egypt, and Cyprus, in Mauretania, on the lower Danube, and in Britain. The man who helped him quell those revolts was his trusted friend, Marcius Turbo, who replaced Lusius Quietus, Trajan's great Moorish marshal.

With the new regime also came a change in foreign policy. Convinced at the outset of his reign that Trajan's wars of expansion were a drain upon the Empire's manpower and resources, Hadrian, playing the role of Augustus after Trajan's Caesar, prudently abandoned all recent conquests east of the Tigris and Euphrates, allowed Greater Armenia to revert to the status of a client kingdom, and made peace with Parthia.[1] False rumors that he also planned to abandon Dacia showed that the new "Pax Augusta" did not please everyone—especially not Lusius Quietus and three former marshals who had admired Trajan's expansionism and disapproved of Hadrian's new frontier policy. The four were executed without Hadrian's sanction or knowledge; or so he averred. To many high-ranking Romans, his disavowals sounded evasive and hollow. Early in July of 118, he appeared before the senate. A tall, bearded, imposing figure, he solemnly promised the assembled dignitaries that henceforth no senator would be put to death without prior condemnation by a senatorial court.

Hadrian tried to court favor on all sides with a magnificent triumph for Parthia's defeat, a large distribution of gifts, and a vast remission of debts and tax arrears. His success was limited, however. To the senate and people of Rome, he always remained something of an outsider. He spent much of his reign looking after the provinces.

Hadrian's Travels The year 121 found Hadrian in Gaul and the Rhineland. The next year, he went to Britain, where he inspected

plans for the construction of his famous wall from Solway Firth to the Tyne to keep marauding tribesmen of the North from raiding farmlands south of the Scottish border. On the way back from Britain, he passed through Gaul and spent the winter in Spain. In the spring, he led a punitive expedition in North Africa against the Moors, who had been raiding Roman towns in Mauretania. There he received news that the Parthians had again broken the peace, and he set sail for Ephesus.

His dramatic arrival in the Near East, backed by impressive troop concentrations, inspired Chosroes, the Parthian king, to negotiate rather than fight. The war over, Hadrian went on to hear petitions and complaints. He punished misgovernment of the provinces, arranged for the construction of municipal temples, baths, aqueducts, and theaters, and built an enormous temple at Cyzicus.

In 128, he again visited North Africa, where he inspected the Imperial estates and studied ways and means for more efficient economic exploitation. He spent the following winter in Athens, where he presided at games and festivals, codified laws, completed and dedicated a huge temple to Olympian Zeus, the *Olympieion,* which the tyrant Peisistratus had begun seven centuries before. In the suburbs of Athens, he built a new city, named Hadrianopolis, and in it erected a pantheon, a stoa, a gymnasium, a library, and another great temple, the *Panhellenion,* which he romantically dedicated to an ancient ideal—Greek unity. In the spring of 129, he toured Asia Minor once more. Towns, temples, libraries, baths, and aqueducts sprang up wherever he went.

Unfortunately, he displayed a singular lack of understanding in Jerusalem. There, he insensitively resolved to found a Roman colony called Aelia Capitolina, and, on the site of the Jewish Temple, he erected a shrine to Jupiter Capitolinus. This act provoked one of the bloodiest rebellions in Jewish history.

Meanwhile, heedless of what he had done, Hadrian went to Egypt to reorganize its economic life and visit the monuments of its glorious past. While he was in Egypt, he was bereft of his beloved Antinous, who drowned in

---

[1]He did not, however, adopt the magic legend of HADRIANVS AVGVSTVS on his coins until the year 123, which happened to be the one hundred fiftieth anniversary of the senate's conferral of the name "Augustus" upon Octavianus.

the Nile. In his honor, Hadrian founded a beautiful new city, Antinoopolis, on the east bank of the Nile near where the youth had drowned. After his death, Hadrian worshipped him as divine, built shrines and temples to him, struck coins bearing his likeness, and set up busts of him all over the Empire.

The Jewish Revolt Hadrian returned to Rome to learn that the Jews had rebelled in the fall of 132 and were waging guerrilla war against the Roman army. Led by a famous guerrilla strategist, Simon Bar Kokhba (Shim'on Ben [Bar] Cosiba in the *Dead Sea Scrolls*), the Jews captured Jerusalem, slaughtered an entire Roman legion, and for a time seemed about to drive the Romans out of Palestine. Hadrian hastened back to Syria, assembled reinforcements from the other provinces, and summoned the able Julius Severus from Britain to take command. Severus began systematically isolating strongholds and inhabited places and starving out the defenders. The Romans may have slaughtered as many as half a million people and enslaved as many more. When the revolt was finally quelled in 135, stillness and desolation descended upon a ruined land.

The surviving Jewish population of Jerusalem was forcibly removed, and Jews were forbidden to enter the city except on one officially designated day each year. The name of the city was formally changed to Aelia Capitolina and remained so until the days of Constantine (324 to 337). The name of Judea was changed to Syria Palestina. Jews who remained there and throughout the Empire were still allowed to practice their ancestral religion and maintain their traditional schools and synagogues, but the vestiges of the national state that had been the focus of their aspirations for centuries were obliterated for 1,800 years.

New Directions under Hadrian A man of ceaseless curiosity and innovative spirit, Hadrian instituted major changes in all aspects of Roman government and policy. His passion for perfection and efficiency is manifest in everything that he did. In many ways, the Ro-

man Empire as an organized state came of age under his leadership.

Frontier Defense Hadrian's renunciation of Trajan's aggressive foreign wars and his surrender of some recent conquests did not constitute a neglect of frontier defense. He was the first emperor to erect large-scale fixed frontier defenses such as Hadrian's Wall in Britain. He extended fortifications for 345 miles in south Germany behind continuous lines of ditches and oakwood palisades nine feet high. These fortifications, with their garrisoned forts and watchtowers, not only protected the frontier from enemy raids and even mass attacks but also marked the frontier and served as checkpoints for the control of trade between the Roman and non-Roman worlds.

Reform of the Army Nor did Hadrian neglect the army. His reforms in discipline, recruitment, and tactics were of lasting importance. Discipline was for him almost a cult. To secure it, he personally inspected army posts all over the Empire; watched soldiers drill, march, and maneuver; inspected equipment, dress, baggage, and mess kitchens; and ordered fatigue marches during which he dressed as a common soldier, marched along with the men, and carried his own knapsack. To no emperor were the armies more devoted, and under none were they more disciplined and efficient.

One of Hadrian's most important military reforms was the progressive removal of distinction between the legions and the auxiliary corps (*auxilia*) with respect to training, equipment, and composition. For the first time, both consisted of Roman citizens and noncitizens recruited more and more in the frontier regions in which they were to serve. Many of the new recruits were soldiers' sons born near the permanent camps, and to them Hadrian granted the right, hitherto withheld, of inheriting their fathers' property.

The traditional *auxilia,* which garrisoned the permanent forts strung out along the frontiers, were armed and organized like Roman legions. Hadrian began to levy, especially in the German and Danubian provinces, in Britain, and in Mauretania, many auxiliary units of a new type called *numeri*. These were small mobile corps, some of them light infantry, some cavalry, others mixed, while some consisted of mounted scouts known as *exploratores*. Although often commanded by Roman excenturions, the *numeri* retained their native languages, arms, and methods of fighting. They were used for patrolling, reconnaissance, and skirmishing.

Hadrian's greatest reform in battle tactics was the introduction of an improved form of the old Macedonian *phalanx*. In offensive operations, the *auxilia* would launch the initial attack whereas the *phalanx* of the legions advanced later to deliver the final blow. If the enemy attacked first, the *auxilia* would take the brunt of the initial assault. The legions held in reserve in camps behind the frontier forts would then advance to destroy the exhausted forces of the enemy. Hadrian's tactics were to remain standard military strategy, except for minor modifications, for over two centuries.

The Provinces Extensive travels and detailed reports from procurators and other agents afforded Hadrian an intimate knowledge of conditions in the provinces. No detail of provincial administration, seemed too small for his personal attention, especially when it involved the defense of the weak against the strong, the poor against the rich (*humiliores contra honestiores; tenuiores contra potentiores*). Also, the urbanization of the Empire reached its peak under Hadrian, and the extension of Roman citizenship kept step with the diffusion of culture and civilization.

Hadrian frequently bestowed the right of Greater Latinity (*Latium Maius*), which conferred citizenship upon all members of town councils or local senates (*decuriones*), as well as upon magistrates. This device was probably not, as is commonly asserted, a sign of municipal decay, nor was it employed simply to make office-holding more attractive but to speed the growth of Roman citizenship everywhere and transform the Roman Empire into a genuine world commonwealth. It also had the very practical effect of extending the tax base and increasing the pool of citizen recruits for the army.

The Reorganization of the Imperial Administration The growing administrative needs of the Roman world commonwealth as well as Hadrian's passion for efficiency led to further expansion and reorganization of the Imperial administration. Gradually, operations were becoming more professional and bureaucratized. The qualities that he demanded from public servants were not unlike those required in most modern states. He insisted that holders of public office be able, well trained, and competent as well as loyal to the emperor and devoted to the state. He paid them well and gave rewards for hard work, initiative, and efficiency.

Vespasian had reversed the policy of Claudius by employing *equites* more than freedmen in high administrative positions. Hadrian followed Vespasian's lead and appointed equestrians as directors of the four executive departments created by Claudius: Imperial correspondence (*ab epistulis*), justice (*a libellis*), treasury (*a rationibus*), and the research and library service (*a studiis*). To enhance their prestige, he bestowed upon the holders of these offices such resounding titles as *vir egregius* ("outstanding man"), *vir perfectissimus* ("most perfect man"), and that of *vir eminentissimus* ("most eminent man"), held by the prefect of the Praetorian Guard. Gradations of salary also differentiated the various executive offices. Procurators, for example, received 60,000, 100,000, 200,000, or 300,000 sesterces per year, according to their rank. Four equestrian prefects commanded even higher salaries.

To the four governmental departments, Hadrian added two new ones of cabinet rank, both pointing not only to increased centralization but also to wider equestrian participation in public service. One of the new departments resulted from his reform of the vitally important system of the so-called Imperial post and communications (*cursus publicus*), formerly a financial and administrative burden laid upon municipalities in Italy and the provinces. Hadrian lightened this burden by his reorganization of the system as a state institution controlled by a central bureau in Rome and headed by an equestrian prefect of vehicles (*praefectus vehiculorum*).

The other new department owed its origin to an overhauling of the tax-collecting system, especially that pertaining to the collection of the 5 percent inheritance tax (*vicesima hereditatum*), which Hadrian, in line with policies set by Caesar, Augustus, and Tiberius, transferred from tax-farming companies to a state agency presided over by an equestrian procurator. The procurator, assisted by numerous agents throughout the Empire, collected these and many other taxes, direct and indirect.

In creating a more professional, bureaucratic system, Hadrian departed from the policy of Augustus by separating the civil and military careers of equestrian officials and by appointing *equites* without prior military experience to civilian posts. Now, *equites* seeking high administrative positions had to begin their civilian careers by accepting such minor jobs as agents or attorneys of the treasury (*advocati fisci*), a newly created class of officials sent all over the Empire to prosecute cases of tax evasion and delinquency. Hadrian probably wanted to attract into government service people of legal and philosophical interests to whom army life seemed irksome and distasteful, but creating a gulf between civil officials and military leaders caused internal divisions that were dangerous during the military crises of later centuries.

Hadrian's separation of civil and military careers was not completely beneficial. It deprived high government officials of requisite military experience and control over the army and left them helpless when confronted, as they were to be in the third century, by a formidable group of army commanders who often alienated the civilian elite, whose cooperation was necessary for maintaining control. In this instance, Hadrian's yearning for administrative efficiency proved injurious to the future stability of the state.

The Reorganization of the Consilium

Having a mania for organization, Hadrian converted the informal conclave of palace friends and advisors, such as Augustus and his successors had consulted, into a genuine cabinet and permanent council of state (*consilium prin-*

cipis). It consisted of the heads of the various departments of the government, the chief prefects, and several distinguished jurists. Besides serving as the chief policy-making body of the Empire, it also acted as a supreme court whose function was to hear cases involving senators and high-ranking officials and to advise and assist the emperor in the creation and interpretation of civil and criminal law.

Legal Reforms

Of all the administrative reforms of Hadrian, the greatest and most enduring were in the field of law. One such reform gave the unanimous opinions (*responsa*) of distinguished jurists the force of law binding upon judges trying similar cases. Only when the opinions conflicted could judges reach their own decisions. These responses later entered into the literature of Roman law and became enshrined at last into the *Digest* and *Code* of Justinian I (p. 509).

More important still was the editing and codification of the *Praetorian Perpetual Edict.* Ever since early Republican times, each incoming Urban Praetor had drawn up and posted edicts setting forth the laws and court procedure that he intended to follow during his year of office. The praetor for aliens (*praetor peregrinus*) as well as the provincial governors had followed suit. Because the praetors normally retained the laws and procedures of their predecessors while adding new ones as need arose, the edicts tended to perpetuate many obsolete rules, contradictions, and obscurities. Hadrian commissioned Salvius Julianus to draw up a permanent edict (*edictum perpetuum*), binding upon all present and future praetors without alteration or addition unless authorized by the emperor or by decree of the senate.

The statutes of the emperors (*constitutiones principum*) thereafter became increasingly important as sources of law. They consisted of the emperor's edicts (*edicta*) issued by virtue of his *imperium;* his judicial decrees (*decreta*) or decisions; his rescripts (*rescripta*) or responses to written inquiries on specific points of law; and his mandates (*mandata*) or administrative directives issued to officials subject to his orders.

To ease the crowded calendar of the praetors' courts in Rome and expedite the administration of justice in Italy, Hadrian divided the peninsula into four judicial districts, each presided over by a circuit judge of consular rank (*iuridicus consularis*) to try cases of inheritance, trust, and guardianship, and probably to hear appeals from the municipal courts. Though the innovation was both salutary and necessary and not intended simply to reduce Italy to the status of a province, it evidently displeased the senate, at whose insistence Hadrian's successor, Antoninus Pius, unwisely abolished it. Marcus Aurelius had to revive it later.

Social Policies In accordance with prevailing Stoic philosophical principles, Hadrian made it illegal for a master to kill, torture, or castrate slaves, or sell them as gladiators, or use them for any lewd or immoral purposes. He also deprived the *paterfamilias* of the power of life and death over his children and safeguarded the right of minors to inherit and own property. Continuing Nerva's and Trajan's policy of using state funds for supporting children of poor families in Italy, he appointed a superintendent of child welfare (*praefectus alimentorum*) to administer the distribution of alimentary funds. In education, he provided funds for secondary-school education in many municipalities of the Empire, endowed advanced rhetorical, philosophical, technical, and medical schools in both Rome and the provinces, and gave pensions to retired teachers.

The Last Years of Hadrian During the Jewish War, Hadrian returned to Rome never to leave Italy again. He spent his last years at his beautiful villa at Tibur (Tivoli) eighteen miles up the Anio from Rome but could not enjoy himself. The man who had traveled so much and seen and done so much had lost all zest for life. Loneliness and despair plagued his mind; a wasting disease racked his body. As his illness grew worse and death seemed at hand, he turned his attention to the problem of choosing a successor. His first choice was his friend, Lu-

cius Ceionius Commodus, and he spent large sums of money to win the support of the soldiers and the people for adopting him as Lucius Aelius Caesar. The money was wasted, for Lucius died early in 138. Hadrian next adopted a rich and virtuous senator, Titus Aurelius Antoninus. Then he required Antoninus to adopt two sons: Lucius Ceionius Commodus, the seven-year-old son of the late Lucius, and Marcus Annius Verus, a youth of seventeen who had originally been adopted by the late Lucius and later became the Emperor Marcus Aurelius. After doing that, Hadrian felt that he had followed the example of Augustus in securing the succession not just for one, but for two generations to come. His last and only wish was to die in peace.

Death came, but not soon enough for him. Maddened by pain, he longed to take his life. He begged his doctor to give him a dose of poison; the doctor took one himself. He ordered a slave to stab him in the heart; the slave ran away. Finally, at Baiae near Naples on July 10, 138, nature granted his wish. His adopted son and heir, Antoninus, had his body placed in a special mausoleum (now the Castel Sant' Angelo) at Rome and, against the opposition of the senate, secured his deification. Another god had now joined the Roman pantheon, and Antoninus won for himself the new name of Pius.

Antoninus Pius (138 to 161) Despite its length (twenty-three years), the reign of Antoninus Pius was singularly uneventful. The Empire was at peace; no major foreign wars or internal revolts disturbed the outward calm. The emperor himself was a man of peace and the possessor of almost every known Roman virtue. According to the *Historia Augusta,* he was tall and handsome, dignified and courteous, eminently talented, eloquent, scholarly, industrious, just, honest, deeply religious, tolerant of others, a cool appraiser of himself, and withal most benevolent and serene. He had few enemies and many friends.

The life of Antoninus had always been simple, but never unpleasant; disciplined, but never strenuous; never dangerous or insecure.

He was born and raised at Lanuvium, a famous old Latin town, but his family came from Nemausus (Nîmes) in southern Gaul, a rich aristocratic old family that owned numerous estates in Italy and valuable brickyards near Rome. Of all his estates, the one at Lorium, about ten miles west of Rome on the border of Etruria, pleased him most. He spent a great deal of time there in personally managing the property. He fed his chickens, entertained his friends, hunted, and fished. Rome and its palaces and Hadrian's villa held little attraction for him.

His Early Career   Having held all the offices of a normal senatorial career, Antoninus intended after his second consulship in 120 to retire to his country estates and enjoy himself. Instead, Hadrian made him a district judge of Italy and, in 135 and 136, proconsul of Asia, where he distinguished himself as an administrator. His expert knowledge of law and his skill in administration led to further appointments, none of which were solicited by him. Hadrian made him a member of the Imperial Council and finally his successor and colleague.

Maintaining the Status Quo   Although Hadrian was a restless innovator, Antoninus Pius was a man who had always played it safe. He saw no need to tinker with Hadrian's smoothly running Imperial machine. Maintenance was his specialty, and he was content to let the system run on its considerable inertia.

Antoninus and the Senate   Antoninus' first act as emperor had been to frustrate the attempt of a number of senators to prevent the deification and annul the edicts and acts (*acta*) of Hadrian, whose nonexpansionistic, philhellenic, and cosmopolitan policies they had always disliked. In return, he agreed to abolish the four hated judgeships of Italy and to spare the lives of senators proscribed by the dying Hadrian. Antoninus further improved his relations with the senate by his deferential attitude, by his attendance at meetings, by seeking its advice on policy, and by rendering financial assistance to insolvent senatorial families.

Public Benefactions   Antoninus allotted to Italy a generous share of the money earmarked for public works and social welfare: harbor improvements ordered at Puteoli, Ostia, and Terracina; baths constructed at Ostia and an amphitheater at Capua; further endowments provided for education and child welfare; and liberal amounts of food and money distributed to the Roman populace. Last, but not least, he sponsored elaborate games and spectacles. Nor did he entirely neglect the provinces. Under his reign of peace, the upper and middle classes prospered, although slaves and the poor continued to be exploited everywhere. Antoninus gave ready ear to the desires and petitions of the ruling classes of the cities of Greece and Asia Minor and some Aegean islands. He frequently reduced their taxes or canceled their debts and came to their aid when they were stricken by earthquake, fire, or flood. Furthermore, he spared them the heavy burden of the Imperial retinue by staying at home. He was content to let his power and beneficence radiate from Rome or Lorium like the peaceful glow of a late summer's afternoon.

Sound Fiscal Management   Before his death, despite his huge expenditures on charity and public works in Rome, Italy, and the provinces, Antoninus had succeeded, through sound fiscal management and personal frugality, in leaving behind in the treasury a surplus of 2 billion sesterces, the largest surplus since the death of Tiberius.

Legal Development   An even prouder achievement was his contribution to Roman law. Never had a Roman emperor surrounded himself with such an array of legal talent, five jurists being members of the Imperial Council. Antoninus himself had an intimate knowledge of both the minutiae and the spirit of the law. He clarified the laws dealing with inheritance, the protection of the legal interests of minors, and the manumission of slaves. He increased penalties against masters who killed or mistreated their slaves, and imposed a severe punishment on kidnapping, hitherto a frightful scourge in Italy and the provinces. Conversely, he reduced penalties for army deserters and released captives after ten years of hard labor in the mines; he permitted Jews the right of circumcision and restricted the persecution of Christians. Of more general interest was his ruling that a man must be considered innocent until proven guilty and in cases where the opinions of the judges were evenly divided, the prisoner must receive the benefit of the doubt.

Foreign Policy Antoninus' prestige and influence transcended the Imperial frontiers. Embassies came to him from Bactria and India. He was known in central Asia and China. Eastern kings sought his advice, and a letter to the king of Parthia dissuaded an invasion of Armenia. He awarded thrones to some, enlarged the territories of others. Even the Quadi of Bohemia accepted his nominee as king.

Despite that, Rome's power was waning. The perception of Roman might rested solely on Trajan's military exploits and on Hadrian's indefatigable efforts to make the Roman army an efficient, hard-hitting force. Antoninus, in his efforts to save money, allowed this force to grow soft and deteriorate, although the nations beyond the frontiers—Germans, Huns, Iranians, and Arabs—were gradually acquiring better military capability by copying Roman arms and tactics. The superior equipment and training that had once made one Roman legionary a match for several Germans or Parthians was now no longer a Roman monopoly. Even such a minor uprising as that of the Moorish tribesmen was not suppressed without considerable difficulty. Similar revolts were occurring from time to time in Britain, Germany, Dacia, southern Russia, Asia Minor, Egypt, and Palestine.

In the only two frontier zones—Britain and Germany—where Antoninus did exhibit energy or initiative, he was simply following Hadrian's policy. In Scotland, he pushed the frontier about seventy-five miles to the north and had a wall of turf and clay constructed between the firths of Forth and Clyde, a distance of some thirty-seven miles, which was about half the length of Hadrian's Wall between the Solway and the Tyne. The purpose of the Antonine Wall, with its nineteen forts spaced two miles apart, was to overawe the natives living north and south of it and check cattle rustling or smuggling. In southwest Germany, he shortened the defensive frontier (*limes*) by pushing it forward from twenty to thirty miles, and strengthened it with new forts and watchtowers made of stone.

The Legacy of Antoninus The defenses that Antoninus erected in Britain and Germany stood firm to the end of his reign, but not long after. The policy of relatively static defense and the failure to keep the army in top form had left the Empire poorly equipped to roll back the tide of massive assault which broke after his death. Perhaps he dimly realized his mistake as he lay dying at Lorium in March 161. In his delirium he talked fretfully about the Empire and all the lying kings who had betrayed him.

Marcus Aurelius (161 to 180) After Antoninus came Marcus Aurelius, one of the most remarkable and certainly noblest of Roman emperors. He was a Stoic philosopher and a man dedicated to peace. It is one of the ironies of history that so peace-loving a man had to spend the greater part of his reign in fighting the Empire's battles against German and Parthian onslaughts upon its frontiers.

Marcus Aurelius was born in Rome in 121 of rich and illustrious Spanish parentage. He enjoyed all the educational advantages money, rank, and high favor could bestow. He was only six when Hadrian had insisted that he be adopted by the elder Lucius Ceionius Commodus.

Educational and Cultural Background Marcus had never gone to public school. He was taught by private tutors from the three R's to grammar, literature (Greek as well as Latin), science and mathematics, music, dancing, and painting. The sports that he learned included ballplaying, of which he was very fond, boxing, wrestling, hunting, and fishing.

The next stage in the education of Marcus was the study of rhetoric and Roman law, the former taught by Cornelius Fronto (ca. 100 to ca. 166), a famous rhetorician and advocate from Africa, the latter by the illustrious legal authority, L. Volusius Maecianus. Herodes Atticus (ca. 101 to 177), a Greek sophist and rhetorician of incredible wealth, came from Athens to teach him Greek oratory. Those were the most distinguished of his teachers, of whom he had altogether almost a score. But the greatest and the most beloved of all was the rhetorician Fronto, with whom he corresponded for many years.

Philosophical Training Quite in keeping with his study of rhetoric, which, according to Fronto's ideals, should produce a person not only learned in literature and effective in speech but also of high moral character, Marcus Aurelius was greatly attracted to the philosophy of Stoicism. He studied under Junius Rusticus, who lent him a copy of the *Discourses* of the Stoic philosopher Epictetus (p. 357), a Phrygian slave, lame, of feeble health, and horribly treated by a freedman in Nero's court. Later freed, Epictetus taught philosophy at Rome until exiled in 90 by Domitian because of his uncompromising Stoic resistance to tyranny.

The most sublime expression of Stoicism, except possibly for the *Hymn to Zeus* by Cleanthes (ca. 310 to 232 B.C.), is contained in the *Meditations* (*ta eis heauton*—"To Himself") of Marcus Aurelius. While encamped along the Danube during the Marcomannic wars (168 to 175, 178 to 180), Marcus spent his nights writing down in Greek his reflections—scattered, disjointed, and unaffected soliloquies or dialogues between himself and the Universal Power. In the *Meditations,* he strongly reaffirmed the traditional Stoic virtues as the basis of morality, from which the spirit is propelled into both direct communion with the divine and unapprehensive resignation to its will.

Persecution of the Christians Like most pious pagan Romans of his time, however, Marcus Aurelius regarded the Christians as not only a depraved and superstitious sect but also an illicit and subversive organization dedicated to the overthrow of the Roman way of life. The willful and obstinate refusal of the Christians to obey a magistrate's order to sacrifice to the gods of the state was regarded as opposition to the efforts of the emperors to restore the ancient Roman culture and religion as a means of strengthening the Empire against the non-Romans from without and disintegration from within. The common people accused the Christians of atheism, incest, and even cannibalism and made them the scapegoats for the calamities that were befalling the state. When angry mobs demanded vengeance, the officials were often sympathetic. For example, Justin Martyr (who adapted Platonic and Stoic philosophy to Jewish and Christian theology) died in Rome along with six companions in 165; twelve Christians died at Scyllium in Numidia in 180; and at Lugdunum and Vienna (Vienne) in Transalpine Gaul numerous Christians were tortured to death in 177.

Marcus Aurelius as Emperor and Soldier

Marcus Aurelius was an able administrator and commander of armies. The first two years of his reign were filled with crises: a serious Tiber flood, an earthquake in Cyzicus, a famine in Galatia, a revolt in Britain, a German crossing of the Rhine, and an invasion of Armenia and Syria by the young Parthian king, Vologeses III. Marcus' first act as emperor was to insist on appointing the younger Lucius Ceionius Commodus, his adoptive brother, as his colleague with the new name Lucius Aurelius Verus, equal in honor, titulature, and power, even against the opposition of the senate, who regarded Verus as a frivolous young man addicted to pleasure and self-indulgence. Verus then went to the East to deal with the Parthian threat while Aurelius handled pressing problems in the West. This division of responsibility between two equal colleagues at the start of a reign, not merely to indicate a successor near the end of a reign, would become an increasingly attractive solution to bearing the increasing burdens of Imperial defense and administration. Eventually, this practice would become formalized, and the Empire would split in two.

The Parthian War, 161 to 165 In the East, Verus cleverly combined pleasure with a thorough reorganization of the undisciplined and demoralized army of Syria and Cappadocia. He had as his subordinates two able generals. One was Statius Priscus, who invaded Armenia, captured and burnt down its capital of Artaxata; the other was the Syrian-born Avidius Cassius, a hard-bitten martinet, who whipped the Syrian army into shape, crossed the Euphrates, and invaded Mesopotamia to capture in rapid succession Edessa, Nisibis, Ctesiphon, and Seleucia, which he burnt to the ground.

Then suddenly two disasters struck. Soldiers returning from the fire-gutted ruins of Seleucia brought back with them a frightful plague. It forced the retreat of the victorious armies of the East, then infected Asia Minor, Egypt, Greece, and Italy, destroyed as much as a third of the population in some places, and finally decimated the armies guarding the frontiers along the Rhine and Danube. The defenses along the Danube had already been weakened by extensive troop withdrawals for service in the East. Now, a host of Germans—the Marcomanni, the Quadi, and many others—reacting at last to the slow but relentless pressure that had for centuries been building up from the vast heartland of Eurasia, attacked the sparsely guarded frontiers in 167 and threatened the Danubian provinces of Raetia, Noricum, and Pannonia.

War along the Danube, 168 to 175 Marcus Aurelius began energetic preparations to reinforce the Danubian frontier, but an outbreak of plague in Rome prevented him and Verus from launching their expedition before the spring of 168. After strengthening the frontier, they suffered an outbreak of plague in their winter quarters and had to return to Rome in early 169. On the way, Verus suffered a sudden stroke and died. Marcus Aurelius, now sole *princeps,* had to contend with a host of troubles: The main enemy—the Quadi, the Marcomanni, and the Sarmatian Iazyges—remained unsubdued and menacing; the Parthian king again invaded Armenia; in 169, the Chatti invaded the frontier regions of the upper Rhine, while the Chauci attacked the Belgic province.

In the fall of 169, Marcus Aurelius returned to the Danubian front after he had sold the gold vessels and artistic treasures of the Imperial palace to finance his efforts. He was determined to destroy the Marcomanni, the Quadi, and the Iazyges one by one, finally annex their lands, and bring to pass the grand strategy of Julius Caesar, which Augustus and Tiberius had abandoned. In 170, however, the Marcomanni and the Quadi defeated Aurelius, swept into Italy, and besieged Aquileia, the big seaport at the head of the Adriatic. Never since the Cimbric and Teutonic invasions in the days of Marius was Italy in greater danger from outside attack. Desperately, Marcus drafted slaves, gladiators, and brigands into the army; hired German and Scythian tribes to harass the enemy's rear; and blocked the Alpine passes and fortified towns in the danger zone. His generals drove the invaders back to the Danube, where the booty-laden Marcomanni were defeated as they tried to cross.

In the meantime, the Moors attacked the shores of Mauretania and invaded the Spanish province of Baetica across the Straits of Gibraltar, and the Costoboci of eastern Galicia joined forces with the Sarmatians, crossed the lower Danube, broke into Moesia, overran the Balkans, and invaded Greece as far south as Attica, where they plundered the Temple of the Mysteries at Eleusis. While the other generals met those emergencies, Aurelius obtained temporary relief on the Danube by granting peace to the Marcomanni and the Quadi, who agreed to settle depopulated land within the Empire and serve in Roman armies.

Once the other emergencies had been met, Marcus Aurelius found pretexts to resume his campaigns against the Marcomanni, the Quadi, and the Iazyges. In 172, he crossed the Danube, attacked the Marcomanni first, then the Quadi, and finally the Iazyges. In 175, however, a revolt in the East forced him to grant terms before he could completely conquer their homelands. He concluded a peace with the proviso that they return all the Roman prisoners whom they had taken, make reparations for the damages that they had inflicted on the provinces, and evacuate a strip of territory ten miles wide running along the north bank of the Danube.

A sculptural record of this part of the Marcomannic wars survives on the spiral frieze of Marcus Aurelius' column in the Campus Martius. Some of the 116 reliefs show Roman soldiers transporting baggage and war material, convoying booty and captives, crossing turbulent rivers, or storming German and Sarmatian strongholds. Others depict the emperor himself, calm and self-assured, riding with his troops, consulting with his aides, receiving foreign envoys, or accepting the obsequious attentions of conquered foes.

The Usurpation of Avidius Cassius, 175

Avidius Cassius, the able governor of his native Syria, but a violent and ruthless man, misled by the false rumor of the death of Marcus Aurelius, had himself proclaimed emperor. Hastily concluding peace along the Danube, Marcus summoned Faustina (his wife) and young son Commodus to Sirmium (Mitrovica, Serbia) and prepared to set out with them to the East. Before his departure, a legionary showed up bearing the head of Cassius, which the emperor refused to look at but ordered reverently buried. The death of Cassius would seem to have removed the need for Marcus to go to the East, but he went anyway, desiring perhaps to make a display of Roman power, receive expressions of loyalty, and remove disloyal officials from their posts. On his way through Asia Minor he suffered the loss of his wife, Faustina, Antoninus' daughter, a woman whom he had loved for thirty years and the mother of his thirteen children.

After traversing Asia Minor, Syria, and Egypt, greeted everywhere by acclamations of loyalty, Marcus arrived in Rome in 176. He was a sad and lonely man, bereft of his wife and one of his best generals. He resolved never again to make a man governor of the province of his birth. To forestall any other potential usurpers, he at once recognized as heir and successor his son Commodus, a remarkably handsome and athletic youth but totally unlike his father in character and ideals. Then, Marcus celebrated his German and Sarmatian (over the Iazyges)

triumphs. In the course of the celebration, he unveiled the famous equestrian statue of himself that still stands on the Roman Capitol, the prototype of most later equestrian statues, and laid the foundation stone of his well-known column in the Campus Martius.

Return to the Danube, 178 to 180

Rumors of fresh troubles along the Danube caused the emperor to hasten north in 178. Leading his men himself, he crossed the Danube and, after a long and strenuous campaign known as the Third Marcomannic War, crushed the resistance of the Quadi and the Marcomanni. He established a new legionary camp on the Danube at Castra Regina (Regensburg in Bavaria) and proceeded to create two new provinces—Marcomannia and Sarmatia—by annexing a vast territory extending as far north as the Erzgebirge Mountains (on the border between the Czech Republic and Germany) and as far east as the Carpathian Mountains (eastern Rumania). Thus he hoped to shorten and strengthen the northern frontiers against future assaults. While engaged in this mighty task, Marcus Aurelius suddenly caught a dangerous infection (possibly the plague) and died in his camp at Vindobona (Vienna) on March 17, 180. His last words were "Go to the rising sun; my sun is setting."

The most important result of the Danubian campaigns lay not in the victories of Marcus Aurelius over Germanic and Sarmatian tribes, nor in his new provinces, which did not survive his death. It was the transplantation and settlement of thousands of Germans in the wartorn and plague-devastated provinces of Dacia, Moesia, Raetia, Pannonia, Dalmatia, Gaul, and even Italy. This measure not only temporarily relieved the pressure on the frontiers of the Rhine and of the Danube but significantly altered the ethnic composition of the Roman Empire.

The Question of Succession

Those who have admired Marcus Aurelius' many fine qualities have often criticized him for designating his own unworthy son, Commodus, as his successor and abandoning the practice of adoption that had produced a series of remarkably able, dedicated, and benevolent rulers from Trajan to Aurelius himself. Such critics forget that the practice of adoption was not any kind of theoretical alternative to dynastic succession. It was not a system based upon the Stoic principle of choosing the most worthy individual regardless of birth. The practice of adoption was a reaffirmation of the dynastic principle. Roman aristocrats had always resorted to adoption to maintain their families' existence in the absence of a natural heir. Nerva and his successors until Marcus Aurelius had happened for various reasons to lack sons to succeed them. The dynastic principle was so strongly favored by the soldiers and common people, moreover, that Aurelius' four predecessors had felt it necessary to create sons where none existed. When it turned out that Aurelius had natural heirs, he had no other choice than to proclaim his eldest son as his successor. Had he not, thousands would have supported Commodus as having a superior claim to the throne, and a disastrous civil war probably would have resulted.

Problems for the Future   Under the five good emperors, the second century A.D. appears to many as the golden age of the Roman Empire. So it was. Beneath the surface, however, were problems and trends that had negative implications for the third century and beyond.

Defense   Trajan's inability to hold on to his conquests in Mesopotamia and Hadrian's decision to adopt a more static defense indicate that the Empire had reached the limits of its power and that its resources were becoming stretched too thin for the defensive burdens that it had to bear. That point is driven home by the great difficulty that Marcus Aurelius had in trying to defend the borders simultaneously in the East and the West. The accident of plague certainly com-

plicated his task, but the extreme measures that he had to take in mounting his last expeditions against the Germanic tribes indicate that the Empire had very little margin of safety when confronted with a major challenge on its frontiers.

Centralization of Political Power   The centralization of power in the hands of the emperor and his increasingly bureaucratized servants accelerated as the problems of governance and defense became more complex. The very benevolence of the emperors naturally increased their power at the expense of the senate and magistrates at Rome and of the local councils (*curiae*) and officials of the provincial municipalities. Everyone came to rely on the emperor to solve all problems. In the third century, this situation rigidified the Imperial system and made it less responsive in times of crisis. Local regions came to feel remote from the central government and were willing to put regional interests above Imperial interests, which undermined the unity of the Empire.

Increasing Militarization   Despite their success as civilian administrators, it was chiefly as military men on the frontiers that Trajan, Hadrian, and Marcus Aurelius made their marks. The civilian side of life was becoming subordinate to the military. The civilian senate became more and more just another municipal council, more prestigious than the others to be sure, but in reality not more powerful. After the reign of Aurelius' son, the Roman senate had little impact on affairs outside of Rome and Italy in the third and subsequent centuries. It still formally ratified the accession of a new emperor, but the real choice increasingly lay in the hands of the provincial armies vital for the defense of a frequently besieged Empire. He who could control the soldiers could control the state; he who could not control them soon perished as the Empire of the third and early fourth centuries was transformed into an absolute, regimented military monarchy.

XXX

Imperial Culture and Society in the First Two Centuries A.D.

The first two centuries A.D. saw the full realization of the potential created by Augustus' establishment of widespread peace within the Mediterranean core of the Roman Empire. Rome had become a giant magnet attracting trade and talent from every quarter and radiating its influence in all directions. Under Imperial patronage, the writers and artists of the Augustan Golden Age had created an Imperial style in literature and art that set the standards for the Empire's urbanized upper classes, who subsequently created a remarkably uniform high culture based upon shared values and educational experience. They became an elite of Imperial service not bound by the parochial ties of language, tribe, or city but the universal ideal of Rome as *the* city, the guarantor of civilized urban life against forces of destruction both within and without. Indeed, the universal rule of a benevolent emperor encouraged many to reject the old particularistic world of individual cities controlled by local elites and see themselves as citizens of Rome's universal commonwealth under the care of a benevolent universal deity either in the form of the emperor himself or one of the savior gods popularized by various Eastern mystery cults.

Socially and economically, the Empire reached great heights. With Italy and the interior provinces enjoying unprecedented peace and prosperity and with threats on the frontiers usually contained, foreign and domestic trade flourished. There was enough surplus wealth to support a vigorous tradition of euergetism (the doing of good works) by the emperors and the upper classes to ameliorate the plight of the poor, and those of moderate means found opportunities for economic and social advancement. At the same time, an enlightened spirit popularized by Stoic and Cynic philosophers was consonant with improved conditions for slaves and women and the integration of provincials as Roman citizens.

Post-Augustan Imperial Literature The late Republic and the reign of Augustus had produced the Golden Age of Latin authors, who had used the great works of Greek literature as their models. The latter continued to be the foundation of traditional *paideia* (the training of youths) in the Greek East. In the West, they were now mediated through the Latin writers of the Golden Age: Cicero, Caesar, Livy, Vergil, Horace, Propertius, Tibullus, and Ovid, who had enshrined the values and ideals summed up in the later word *Romanitas* and now formed the basis of literary education in the West. Educated western provincials thus absorbed patriotic pride in the glories of Rome's past and espoused the ideals believed to have accounted for her greatness. As a result, the high culture of the Imperial capital became indelibly etched on that of the western provinces.

The Latin language and its literature were also the western provincials' passport to the wider world of Rome itself and Imperial service. Consequently, many of the leading figures in the world of Latin letters in the first two centuries A.D. no longer came from the old Roman aristocracy or from the municipalities of Italy, but from the colonies and municipalities of Gaul, Spain, and North Africa. Such men were a constant source of fresh talent and gave Latin letters greater breadth and popularity than ever before.

The Impact of Rhetoric and Politics Despite the pervasive influence of the Greek and Latin classics, the literature of the Empire in the first two centuries A.D. has a very different character, which many modern readers who have been trained on classical models often find inferior. It is different, however, not because writers had inferior talent but because conditions were different. Rhetoric, the art of persuasive speech, had always been an extremely large component of Greco-Roman education. The classics of Greco-Roman literature provided a common stock of values, allusions, vocabulary, and style that a leader could manipulate rhetorically to achieve success in the public arena. Rhetorical skills were needed more than ever under the emperors. The increased crush of legal business in the courts required advocates trained not only in the law but also in the art of persuasive argument. Countless petitions addressed to the emperor and his administrators required skill and polish. Emperors, provincial governors, military leaders, and local officials needed to communicate effectively with large audiences.

At the same time, it was dangerous politically to be too independent or original under an all-powerful emperor, who might view independent and original ideas as a threat to his own leadership. Flattery of the emperor and his agents was much safer. Therefore, the persuasive or argumentative declamations, *suasoriae* and *controversiae,* of the rhetorical schools became increasingly artificial exercises on themes such as "Should Hannibal Have Attacked Rome?"—themes that were completely divorced from real life. As a result, rhetorical style concentrated increasingly on elaborate and exotic technique for its own sake. Style, not substance, became the goal. This constant striving for effect produced a turgid, twisted, and distorted kind of writing meant only to display one's verbal virtuosity in competition with others similarly trained.

This trend was reinforced by the political need of the emperor and local elites to win popular favor by entertaining mass audiences with spectacles, games, and shows. They created a climate in which many writers felt it necessary to be more theatrical and emotional to gain attention. The exotic, the grotesque, and the sensational became appealing subjects. Furthermore, with matters of high politics that would have been the subject of vigorous debate under the Republic now off limits, many Imperial writers chose topics that served private needs.

Of course, the idealized past of heroes and statesmen enshrined in many classical authors was fundamentally incompatible with the autocracy that even the most restrained emperors found hard to mask. In the first flush of peace and "normalcy" under Augustus, this fact had been easily ignored, but as the Imperial monarchy became a permanent fixture under the Julio-Claudians, the contradiction between ideals and reality was difficult for some to overlook, particularly for traditionalists in the Roman senatorial class. Therefore, many of the Latin authors from that class during the first two centuries looked back in nostalgia or protest to the lost liberty of the Republic and took refuge in the teachings of Stoicism symbolized by the great martyr to Republican *libertas,* Cato the Younger. For those, however, who did not come from that class or were only recent arrivals, it was easier to overlook the contradiction between ideal and reality and defer to the emperors in whose service they rose to a prominence that they never could have attained under the old Republic.

Poverty of Literature under Tiberius and Caligula The literary brilliance of the Augustan Age had already begun to fade before the end of Augustus' reign, as the confining na-

ture of the principate began to be felt. No comparable writers took the places of Vergil, Horace, Propertius, Tibullus, Ovid, and Livy under the stern and intrigue-ridden reign of Tiberius or the capricious, megalomaniacal rule of Caligula. For many, there was little to praise, and criticism was dangerous.

History There were only three historians of note under those emperors: Aulus Cremutius Cordus (d. A.D. 25), Seneca the Elder (ca. 55 B.C. to ca. A.D. 40), and Velleius Paterculus (ca. 19 B.C. to ca. A.D. 32). Velleius, an equestrian military officer, wrote a brief history of Rome in a rhetorical style. Its importance is that it reflects the attitudes of his class and is favorable toward Tiberius, with whom he had served, and displays an unusual interest in Roman cultural history. Cremutius Cordus, on the other hand, wrote a traditional history of Rome's civil wars to at least 18 B.C. and reflected the attitudes of Stoic-inspired aristocrats who resented the emperor's monopoly of power and *dignitas*. Sejanus had him tried for treason, his books were burned, and he committed suicide.

Seneca the Elder, Lucius (or Marcus) Annaeus Seneca (ca. 55 B.C. to ca. A.D. 40), fared better, although his history of the same period is also lost. That is unfortunate because he came from Corduba in Spain and was one of the western provincials who were becoming prominent in early Imperial Rome. What has survived of his writings is a handbook of rhetorical exercises (*controversiae* and *suasoriae*) culled from public declamations.

Reference Works Practical handbooks were safe and popular. One of the most famous produced during Tiberius' reign was another compilation for use in rhetorical training, the *Nine Books of Memorable Deeds and Sayings* by Valerius Maximus. He, just as Velleius Paterculus, is highly complementary to Tiberius, but his book is merely a colorless compilation of famous people's words and deeds that provide *exempla* of various virtues under headings such as *De patientia*, *De humanitate et clementia*, and *De religione*. It illustrates all of the virtues expected of a Roman gentleman and was a convenient source for any speaker looking for a quick *bon mot* or handy anecdote to salt a speech. It is useful to the modern historian because it preserves numerous scraps of information about important historical figures from works now lost.

Equally as famous as the work of Valerius Maximus and now more popular is the cookbook whose author is known by the name Apicius. The real author probably was Marcus Gavius, to whom the name Apicius has been falsely attached. Part of it is as late as the fourth century A.D., but Gavius composed the core in the reign of Tiberius, whose reputed taste for the exotic and unconventional certainly could have been indulged by the recipes in the *De Re Coquinaria* of "Apicius."

Poetry Poetry fared almost as badly as prose under Tiberius. He himself seems to have had great difficulty reconciling the illusions of the Augustan principate with its reality. Therefore, he did not encourage celebratory, patriotic historical epic in the tradition of Vergil. Little more than the titles of three or four such works are known from the end of Augustus' reign and the beginning of Tiberius'. They were heavily influenced by Vergil and Ovid but never achieved the kind of popularity that those authors had enjoyed and have disappeared except for chance quotations.

Germanicus (16–15 B.C. to A.D. 19) Tiberius was, however, very interested in astronomy and astrology, which were practically the same by then. Significantly, the only surviving pieces by his nephew and adoptive son, Germanicus, a skillful writer of Greek and Latin verse, are large fragments from his translations of two didactic epics on astronomy and predicting the weather by the Greek poet Aratus. All else is lost.

Manilius (late first century B.C. to early first century A.D.) A better work survives, the *Astronomica* of Germanicus' contemporary Marcus Manilius. Its five books cover the planets, the signs of the zodiac, doing a horoscope, and the influence of the zodiacal signs at various points during their periods of dominance. It is very Stoic in philosophy, and its attempt to find a universal cosmic order reflects the hierarchical structure of Roman society, which Augustus and his successors strove to uphold.

Tiberius and Minor Poetic Genres Tiberius himself was an accomplished amateur poet who preferred the minor genres of poetry that had flourished in Hellenistic Alexandria: the learned little epic, *epyllion,* that was full of obscure allusions and recondite information or parodied a well-known larger work; the pointed epigram; the elegant and refined lyric or iambic; works that displayed a fascination with the exotic and rustic; and even obscene priapic pieces. Examples of all of these appear in a collection known as the *Appendix Vergiliana,* which purports to be a collection of Vergil's youthful writings. They were all written after Vergil's death and show his influence. The latest may date to Nero's reign, but most are earlier and their real authors unknown.

Phaedrus (ca. 15 B.C. to ca. A.D. 50) The most interesting author of the period is Gaius Julius Phaedrus or Phaeder. First of all, as a freed Thracian slave of Augustus, he represents a class whose voice is seldom heard in Imperial Rome. Second, he introduced a whole new minor genre to Greco-Roman literature, the moralizing poetic fable. Taking the popular prose genre of beast fables in the tradition of Aesop, he gave the fable a formal poetic structure, purpose, and voice. It is not the voice of the learned, elegant Alexandrian, but the commonsensical voice of humble people speaking the simple truths of hard experience in a world where they are ignored at best and victimized by the stronger at worst. Thus Phaedrus' fables are often thinly disguised criticisms of the powerful in his own day. In recognition of that, Sejanus unsuccessfully tried to silence him.

Babrius A man named Babrius rendered many of the same fables into Greek verse. He may have been a Hellenized Roman named Valerius Babrius and wrote no later than the second century A.D. The surviving work is incomplete, but it contains some new fables and, with its use of stress in meter and the language of daily life, is useful for tracing developments in popular culture.

The Inauguration of the Silver Age in Literature under Claudius and Nero
The death of the tyrannical Caligula and the accession of Claudius inaugurated a new age of literary vigor at Rome. It surpassed the early years of Augustus in quantity of writing and, with one major break, in length of sustained activity. Because its quality is generally agreed not to equal that of the Augustans, however, it is called the Silver Age. Claudius himself, of course, was a writer and historian of some accomplishment (p. 307). Ironically, under the influence of Messallina early in his reign, he banished Seneca the Elder's son, Lucius Annaeus Seneca (the Younger), an accomplished orator and devotee of Stoicism. This act must have cast a pall over free expression at Rome, but at the prompting of Agrippina, Claudius recalled Seneca the Younger in 49 to tutor her young son, Nero, who had artistic ambitions. From that point until Seneca's fall from power under Nero and Nero's increasing jealousy and fear, there was a great outburst of literary activity, especially among writers from Spain, many of whom were connected with Seneca's family.

Seneca the Younger (ca. 4 B.C. to A.D. 65) L. Annaeus Seneca, the most noted literary figure of the mid-first century A.D., was born to Seneca the Elder at Corduba, Spain, and came as a boy to Rome. There he studied rhetoric and philosophy and became a lawyer. Not only was he an astute politician, but he also made a fortune from banking and viticulture. Furthermore, he was one of Rome's most notable Stoic philosophers and a copious author of varied works: a spiteful burlesque on Claudius (*Apocolocyntosis*); a long treatise on natural science (*Quaestiones Naturales*); nine tragedies, typically

Euripidean in plot and theme, in a highly rhetorical style striving for emotional effect more than real understanding; ten essays (misnamed *Dialogi*), containing a full exposition of Stoic philosophy, such as *De Ira (On Anger), De Vita Beata (On the Happy Life),* and *De Otio (On Leisure); prose treatises (De Clementia and De Beneficiis);* and 124 *Moral Epistles (Epistulae Morales),* brilliant exponents of a Stoic philosophy at once spiritual and humane.

In 65, Nero suspected Seneca of involvement with Gaius Calpurnius Piso in a Stoic plot against him (p. 315). He ordered Seneca to commit suicide. Seneca's wife bravely insisted on dying with him. He opened his veins, which bled slowly and painfully, and died with Stoic fortitude while discoursing on philosophy.

Lucan (A.D. 39 to 65) M. Annaeus Lucan was Seneca's nephew. Born in Corduba, he was brought to Rome in infancy and educated in a rhetorical school. Among his lost works are an epic on the Trojan War and a collection of occasional poems. His sole extant work is the *De Bello Civili* (often called *Pharsalia*), a violent and pessimistic epic poem in ten books, which narrates the war between Caesar and Pompey. It displays a strong Republican bias, a deep hostility toward Caesar, and a rejection of Vergil's patriotic idealism. Also suspected of complicity in Piso's conspiracy, Lucan, too, committed suicide in 65.

Petronius (? to A.D. 66) Nero continued his persecution of Stoic critics in 66 by condemning to death P. Clodius Paetus Thrasea. Others suspected of involvement with him were ordered to commit suicide. One of them was the novelist and satirist Titus (or Gaius) Petronius, probably the Petronius whom Tacitus mentions as the "arbiter of social graces" (*elegantiae arbiter*) at Nero's dissolute court. His *Satyricon* is frequently described as a picaresque novel. It contained at least 16 books, of which are extant most of Book 15 and only fragments of Books 14 and 16.

While the *Satyricon* displays elegant wit and provides piquant entertainment, it also is a serious criticism of the times. Petronius portrays a world in which the old Roman values are stood on their heads. Gross materialism and sensuality are the order of the day, bad rhetoric runs riot, and everyone pretends to be what he is not. Beneath the laughter is the feeling that society has run amok.

Persius (A.D. 34 to 62) and Martial (ca. A.D. 40 to 104) Aulus Persius Flaccus and Marcus Valerius Martialis were both satirists who escaped Nero's purges. Persius may simply have died too soon, because he was connected with Paetus Thrasea, Seneca the Younger, and Lucan. His six surviving hexameter poems, the *Satires,* try to compress his thoughts into the fewest possible words and rely heavily on poetic allusions to express complex ideas succinctly. They are also rather academic attacks on stereotypic human failings more than attacks on the vices of anyone in particular. On the other hand, Martial, a Spaniard from Bilbilis, in the twelve books of his *Epigrams* attacks with shrewd insight the shams and vices of real people in all walks of life. He was probably too young to attract much notice under Nero and wrote mostly under the Flavians (p. 352).

Curtius Significantly, the only important historical work from Caligula to the Flavians was the *History of Alexander* by Quintus Curtius Rufus (ca. A.D. 20 to 80). It was more of a historical romance than serious history. Highly rhetorical, its real significance is that it furthered the romanticized tales that had quickly obscured the real facts of Alexander's career after his death and were the foundation of the popular legends surrounding Alexander in the Middle Ages.

Technical Writing and Scholarship Research and writing on technical subjects were still much safer pursuits than poetry or history. Moreover, practical handbooks were a necessity for men involved in running a complex empire. Therefore, the practical interest in technical subjects that manifested itself in the late

Republic and under Augustus and Tiberius continued under their successors.

Columella (ca. A.D. 10 to 70) Also from Spain, Columella carried on the rich tradition of agricultural treatises. His full name was Lucius Junius Moderatus Columella, he came from Gades (Cadiz), and his *De Re Rustica* is a classic of its genre. Although it is full of sound advice based on firsthand experience and knowledge, it is also a moral exhortation urging large landowners not to neglect their valuable estates but to make them as productive as possible. Thoroughly steeped in Vergil, Columella published his work in twelve books like the *Aeneid* and wrote the tenth in dactyllic hexameter poetry in imitation of Vergil's *Georgics*. In both prose and poetry his style is smooth and clear.

Pomponius Mela (mid-first century A.D.) Rome's acquisition of an empire naturally stimulated a desire to learn more about its lands and people. The earliest Roman geographical treatise that has survived belongs to Columella's contemporary and fellow Spaniard Pomponius Mela. Written in the archaizing style of Sallust, his *Description of Places (Chorographia)* starts at the Straits of Gibraltar, goes counterclockwise around the Mediterranean in three books, and ends up back at Gibraltar. His interest is as much ethnographic as purely geographic, and fantasy sometimes prevails over fact.

Pliny the Elder, Gaius Plinius Secundus (ca. A.D. 23 to 79) Nowhere is the thirst for practical technical knowledge better epitomized than in the encyclopedic *Natural History (Historia Naturalis)* of Pliny the Elder. Pliny's Stoic-inspired goal was no less than to sum up the existing state of practical and scientific knowledge as a service to mankind. Indeed, it was characteristic of the man himself, who died in the eruption of Vesuvius while he combined curious observation with an attempt to rescue victims. Arranged topically in thirty-seven books, his immense work unscientifically but systematically compiles a vast array of information

and misinformation on such subjects as geography, agriculture, anthropology, medicine, zoology, botany, and minerology. Despite his characteristically Roman lack of critical or theoretical method, Pliny is still useful because his indefatigable industry preserved an enormous store of information that, correct or not, provides the modern historian with valuable raw material for fresh analysis.

Frontinus (ca. A.D. 30 to 104) A more technical and practically informed writer is Pliny's long-lived contemporary Sextus Julius Frontinus. A distinguished governor and general in Britain under Vespasian (74 to 78), he turned to the safer occupation of technical writing under Domitian. His compilation of useful military stratagems culled from Greek and Roman history, the *Stratagemata,* has survived, but a more theoretical treatment of Greco-Roman warfare has not. Because military officers building camps, roads, and fortifications need practical information on surveying, he wrote a treatise on that subject, too. Excerpts from it survive in a later compilation of writers known as the *Gromatici* because Roman surveyors used an instrument called a *groma.*

In 77, the Emperor Nerva appointed Frontinus supervisor of Rome's water supply. To guide his successors and people dealing with the problems of water supply in other cities, Frontinus published all that he had found useful in his most famous and original work, the *De Aquis (De Aquae Ductu) Urbis Romae.* In two volumes, it gives an invaluable history of Rome's aqueducts and priceless technical information derived from personal experience, engineering reports, and public documents.

Artemidorus (late second century A.D.) A far different kind of writer is Artemidorus, a Greek from Ephesus. He was very much interested in subjects that today would be associated with popular superstition or the occult—how the divine world makes known its intentions to human beings. Two of his books, one on interpreting the flights of birds and one on palm reading are lost, but his *Interpretation of Dreams* is extant. In it he recorded dreams collected from people during his extensive travels and explained what their significance was for the life of the dreamer. They provide a fascinating look at the popular anxieties and psychology of the time.

Science and Medicine

Abstract science was not a forte of the Romans. What scientific work that did take place was carried on by the heirs of the Greek tradition in the East. Even they were primarily encyclopedists like Pliny the Elder and did little original work but tended to codify and compile the work of predecessors. Their summaries then became standard reference works that remained authoritative until the scientific revolution of the seventeenth and eighteenth centuries.

Ptolemy of Alexandria (mid-second century A.D.)

The most influential scientist of the period was the mathematician, astronomer, and geographer Ptolemy, Claudius Ptolemaeus. With great mathematical skill, he expounded the geocentric theory of the universe in a thirteen-volume work known by the title of its Arabic translation, the *Almagest*. His complex theory of eccentric circles and epicycles to explain the observed motions of heavenly bodies in relation to the earth was so mathematically sophisticated that it dominated Arabic and western astronomy until the Copernican revolution.

In his geographical writings, Ptolemy accepted the view of the Hellenistic scholar Eratosthenes on the spherical shape of the earth and constructed a spherical projection with mathematically regular latitudes and longitudes. Ironically, however, he argued for Posidonius' much shorter circumference of the earth than the more accurate longer one of Eratosthenes. It was Columbus' belief in the spherical shape and short circumference of the earth that led him to think that he could get to the Indies relatively quickly by sailing west.

Medical Writers

A number of Greek and Roman physicians kept up the long-established tradition of medical writing. Under Claudius, the Roman Scribonius Largus produced a prac-

tical handbook of prescriptions that still exists under the title *Compositiones* and provides an interesting glimpse of the kinds of drugs and remedies available at that time. He is greatly surpassed, however, by his Greek contemporary Dioscorides Pedianus, who had traveled extensively as an army doctor. He has left two works on drugs and remedies that became the standard reference in pharmacology for the rest of Antiquity. Under Trajan and Hadrian, Soranus of Ephesus, who was trained in Alexandria but worked in Rome, wrote twenty medical treatises in Greek, and many were translated into Latin. Of his surviving works, the most important are his gynecological writings. They provide a rare resource for studying women in relation to ancient medical theory and practice, which are usually predicated upon experience more with men than women.

Galen (A.D. 129 to ca. 200)

The greatest physician and medical writer of Antiquity was the Greek doctor Galen of Pergamum. He started out as a doctor for gladiators in Pergamum and became Marcus Aurelius' court physician at Rome. Philosophically trained, he was both a theorist and a practitioner. His equal skill in diagnosis and prognosis was highly regarded, and he always sought to confirm his theories with practical experiments. Perhaps his experience with gladiators taught him the value of dissection in that regard. Indeed, through careful dissection he greatly advanced the physiological and anatomical knowledge of the day. His writings, which encompass thirty published volumes, sought to encompass all the medical knowledge of his time. They were so highly regarded as authoritative that medical research in the West largely stagnated for the next thousand years.

Philology and Literary Scholarship

The stream of philological and literary criticism that had begun by the end of the first century B.C. swelled in the next two centuries as the recognized classics of Cicero, Vergil, Horace, and Ovid became the standard texts for Roman rhetorical education. Remmius Palaemon, a self-taught former slave, continued the work of Hyginus (p. 293) in his lost *Art of Grammar (Ars Grammatica),* which definitely enshrined Vergil at the center of the school curriculum. Among his students were the poet Persius and the later rhetorician Quintilian (p. 353). Cicero's importance as a school text is seen in the extant commentaries that Asconius Pedianus wrote for his young sons on five speeches of Cicero. He was born at the end of the first century B.C. and was writing in the 50s so that he had access to good information. Asconius is particularly valuable because two of the speeches on which he wrote, *Pro Cornelio* and *In Toga Candida,* are lost, and his comments help to reconstruct them.

Unfortunately, the authors of many lost commentaries are just names until Helenius Acron and Pomponius Porphyrio, who wrote school commentaries on Horace at the end of the second and beginning of the third centuries. Acron has been reworked by a later pseudo-Acron, but Porphyrio is intact. Both are indispensable for the study of Horace.

On the Sublime

On the Sublime   Sometime in the first century A.D., an author variously identified as "Dionysius" or "Longinus" (once wrongly identified with Cassius Longinus [p. 392]), wrote one of the most important pieces of literary criticism in the ancient world. Written in Greek and entitled *On the Sublime,* it is a highly original analysis of what makes a piece of literature great. It gets beyond the usual discussion of rhetoric and style and stresses the need for greatness of mind and feeling.

Lack of Great Literature under the Flavians, A.D. 69 to 96

Lack of Great Literature under the Flavians, A.D. 69 to 96   Nero's purge wiped out a whole generation of Roman writers just as it was reaching its prime, and the political situation under the Flavians was not conducive to the emergence of a new one. Although Martial did write most of his satires under the Flavians, he eventually left Rome and returned to Spain. Vespasian, Titus, and Domitian were not hostile to learning and literature. Far from it. Vespasian and Domitian generously endowed

chairs of Greek and Latin rhetoric, and Domitian restored Rome's libraries after the disastrous fire of 79. They did not, however, encourage freedom of expression, without which great literature cannot survive. Vespasian set the tone when he banished the Stoic and Cynic philosophers from Rome and executed Helvidius Priscus (p. 324).

In fairness to Vespasian, they had tried his patience sorely with carping criticism and even futile conspiracies against an emperor who understood political reality far better than they. Nevertheless, Vespasian's suppression of philosophers was bound to make any writer cautious. The situation was even worse after the rebellion of Saturninus against Domitian in 88. He banished philosophers from Rome twice, in 89 and 95, and ruthlessly employed informers to muzzle his critics. The only surviving writers who published under the Flavians were "safe" men writing on safe subjects, especially antiquarian epics of no great inspiration or political import.

Poetry   Only three poets other than Martial have survived. Silius Italicus (ca. A.D. 26 to 101) had been one of Nero's prominent informers and governor of Asia under Vespasian. He retired under Domitian to lead the life of a cultured dilettante. He wrote a technically competent but uninspired epic, the *Punica,* in seventeen books on the Punic wars. Valerius Flaccus (A.D. ? to ca. 90) had a similar career and wrote a refined but unoriginal epic, the *Argonautica,* a rehash of Jason's expedition to find the Golden Fleece. Publius Papinius Statius (ca. A.D. 45 to 96), the most talented of the three, was a professional writer patronized by Domitian. He wrote a libretto for Domitian's favorite actor and an epic on Domitian's German wars. Significantly, both are lost. Two other epics, the *Thebaid,* on the quarrel between Oedipus' sons, and the unfinished *Achilleid,* on Achilles, are extant. Modeled on Vergil, they have many individual passages of power and beauty but lack overall structure. Statius' best work is the *Silvae,* thirty-two individual poems, many written to friends. They reveal the warmth and genuine feelings of an affectionate and sympathetic man capable of real poetic charm.

Josephus (b. A.D. 37 or 38) The only important historian who published under the Flavians was their Jewish client Flavius Josephus, a captured Pharisee who allegedly prophesied that Vespasian would become emperor. He wrote the *History of the Jewish War* to point out the futility of resisting Rome. Despite his pro-Roman outlook, however, he defended his people's faith and way of life to the Gentiles in his twenty-volume *Jewish Antiquities*. He also wrote *Contra Apionem* against the anti-Semitic writings of the Alexandrian Greek Apion and defended his own career in an autobiography. His works all survive in Greek but he wrote the original version of the *Jewish War* in Aramaic to reach Mesopotamian Jews.

Quintilian (ca. A.D. 33 to ca. 100) The central role of rhetoric in higher education resulted in a comprehensive handbook of rhetorical training by the Spaniard Marcus Fabius Quintilianus. He held Vespasian's first chair of rhetoric at Rome and tutored Domitian's heirs. His *Institutio Oratoria (Oratorical Education)* deals with all of the techniques of rhetoric and has influenced serious study of the subject ever since. It is also a source of important information on many other Greek and Latin authors.

Resurgence of Literature under the Five Good Emperors The most important authors who came of age under the Flavians did not begin to publish their works until after the death of Domitian. His autocratic nature and constant fear of conspiracies after 88 made it dangerous to express thoughts openly on many subjects. The more relaxed atmosphere between the five good emperors and the educated senatorial elite, however, was more congenial to many writers.

Tacitus (ca. A.D. 55 to 120) and Pliny the Younger (ca. A.D. 61 to ca. 114) The foremost author was Cornelius Tacitus, whose valuable historical works have been discussed above (pp. 297 and 318). He also wrote the *Dialogue on Orators,* observations on earlier orators and how the lack of free institutions in his own day produced mere striving for rhetorical effect instead of real substance in contemporary orators. Nothing underscores Tacitus' point more clearly than the *Panegyric,* a speech of the younger Pliny, Gaius Plinius Caecilius Secundus, nephew of Pliny the Elder. It is full of flattery of Trajan and dares to offer advice only indirectly by safely criticizing the dead Domitian. On the other hand, the ten books of his *Letters* are much better. In smooth artistic prose, they are addressed to Trajan and numerous other important friends. They reveal an urbane, decent individual who tried to live up to his responsibilities, avoid injustice, and do good where he could, as in endowing a school for boys and girls or refusing to accept anonymous denunciations of Christians.

Juvenal (ca. A.D. 55 to ca. 130) A far less pleasant personality is the poet Decimus Junius Juvenalis, an *eques* who may have served under Tacitus' father-in-law, Agricola, in Britain. He suffered banishment under Domitian, which seems to have embittered him permanently. Under Trajan and Hadrian he published 16 hexameter poems, the *Satires,* often vitriolic and sometimes offensive attacks on stereotypic vices. In his early satires he seems to express all of his pent-up rage and hatred for the conditions that had prevailed under Domitian. His vicious characterizations of women in satire 6 may reflect some romantic disappointment, and his vehement attacks on homosexuality in 2 and 9 probably show disapproval of Hadrian's proclivities. Perhaps his most original piece is satire 4, a parody of Domitian, who summons his council to discuss the momentous problem of cooking a huge fish. Juvenal was immensely popular in the Middle Ages because he titillated Christian moralists while confirming their view of pagan Roman decadence.

Suetonius (ca. A.D. 69 to ca. 135) Another writer who fascinated Medieval Christians in the same way was Gaius Suetonius Tranquillus. Friend of Pliny the Younger, he served Trajan and became Hadrian's private secretary and

Imperial librarian. He wrote on textual criticism, famous courtesans, illustrious men, literary figures, Greek and Roman games, and various other curious topics. Nevertheless, most of those works are lost, and his fame rests upon his major biographical work, the *Lives of the Twelve Caesars* (Julius Caesar to Domitian). These biographies, however, aim not so much at serious history as at entertainment. Therefore, although Suetonius preserves much valuable information from lost earlier sources, his portraits must be treated cautiously. Rumor, gossip, and rhetorically embellished scandal are often included, so that judicious skepticism is frequently required on the part of the reader.

Fronto (ca. A.D. 100 to ca. 170) Suetonius' fascination with the bizarre actions of past emperors and his research on obscure topics was symptomatic of a general absorption in arcane and antiquarian subjects that became a definite literary movement, almost a cult of antiquity, under the Antonines (Antoninus Pius through Commodus). The man who seems to have given the most impetus to this movement was Marcus Aurelius' tutor, M. Cornelius Fronto. Significantly, Fronto had been born at Cirta in North Africa, which soon replaced Spain as a provincial source of Roman writers.

Quaestor in Hadrian's reign and consul in 143, as well as Imperial tutor, Fronto moved in Rome's highest circles. He gathered around him a whole circle of literary lights. Their major interest lay in ransacking early Latin literature for archaic and uncommon words. They wanted to expand the rather limited vocabulary of the classical writers like Cicero and Vergil and create what Fronto called an *elocutio novella* (new elocution) to give greater point and variety to their expression.

Unfortunately, as Fronto's letters to Marcus Aurelius reveal, that is about as far as they went. Fronto appears as a thoroughly decent, kind, and generous man, but he discusses only how to express oneself most accurately and never seriously considers what is worth saying. His point of view was that of a professional rhetorician, not a thinker. For him history was merely an exercise in panegyric, and philoso-phy was positively to be avoided, a point on which Marcus Aurelius obviously disappointed his beloved tutor.

Aulus Gellius (ca. A.D. 125 to ca. 175) The danger in Fronto's approach was that arcane archaisms and recondite research would become ends in themselves without any relevance to the real world. A case in point is Fronto's cultured friend Aulus Gellius. Beginning as a student in Athens, he compiled interesting oddities culled from earlier writers and interspersed with accounts of conversations on a wide range of philological and antiquarian subjects. Called *Attic Nights (Noctes Atticae)* in honor of its origin, it is a very valuable work to modern scholars because it preserves much important information from now-lost earlier works. In and of itself, however, it is mainly important as an example of the pretentious rhetoric and antiquarian interests of the age.

Apuleius (ca. A.D. 123 to ca. 180) The works of Apuleius, a rhetorician and popular Middle Platonist philosopher, often exhibit the same pretentious virtuosity. Born at Madaurus in North Africa (Mdaourouch in Algeria), he eventually settled in Carthage, where he was a professional rhetorician. Excerpts from his declamations appear in his *Florida.* In the encyclopedic spirit of the age, he also wrote widely on subjects in such books as *Natural Questions, On Fish, On Trees, Astronomical Phenomena, Arithmetica,* and *On Proverbs.* Although he was inclined to show off, his interests were serious, as seen from his declamation *Concerning the God of Socrates.* His investigations into magic and theurgy eventually led to his prosecution for practicing forbidden magic after he married a wealthy older widow. That led to his two greatest works, the *Apology* based on the successful self-defense in court and his *Metamorphosis* or *Golden Ass,* the only complete Latin novel to have survived intact.

The *Golden Ass* is an original work of real genius. Ostensibly, it is a novel in the form of an old Milesian tale, full of sexual escapades and dramatic reversals of fortune. In it, a certain Lucius is the victim of his own experiments in sex and magic, which turn him into an ass with human senses. Numerous adventures and mishaps cause him to pass through the hands of a cruel youth, thieves, farmers, eunuch priests, a baker, a truck gardener, a cook, and finally a Corinthian circus trainer who wants to teach him to mount a woman as part of a gladiatorial show. That much seems to be part of an existing popular tale. Apuleius, however, has interspersed many additional elements from other stories, such as the beautiful story of Cupid and Psyche, to give it greater depth and in many other cases to ridicule magic and the superstition that riddled the age. In contrast, Apuleius describes the true power of pure faith in the saving grace of the goddess Isis through a moving scene of conversion at the end.

Pausanias (fl. 150)   The peace and prosperity of the first two centuries A.D. and the antiquarianism of the age encouraged travel and the viewing of historical places, monuments, and museums. Therefore, travelogues and guidebooks were in great demand. Fortunately, one of the most valuable survives, the *Description of Greece* by Pausanias, a Greek geographer from Lydia in the mid-second century. Usually, he outlines the history and topography of cities and their surroundings and frequently includes information on their mythological lore, religious customs, social life, and native products. He is particularly interested in historic battle sites, patriotic monuments, and famous works of art and architecture. The accuracy of his descriptions have been very helpful in locating ancient sites and reconstructing what has been recovered.

Resurgence of Greek Literature   It is significant that Pausanias was a Greek writer describing great monuments and locales in ancient Greece. The first two centuries A.D. saw a renewal of cultural activity and local pride in the Greek-speaking half of the Roman Empire. Although the Latin authors of the Augustan Age had established a body of works that were great in their own right and were highly admired by later Roman writers, Greeks could re-

flect with pride that upper-class Romans continued to flock to the great Greek centers of culture to complete their education just as they had done during the late Republic. The vigorous philhellenism of emperors like Nero, Hadrian, and Marcus Aurelius recalled a sense of greatness to many Greeks, which the return of prosperity to Greek cities under the Imperial peace and the growing prominence of influential Greeks in Imperial administration must have reinforced. In fact, many significant Greek writers during this period were men who had successful careers in Roman government.

Plutarch (ca. A.D. 45 to 120)   An outstanding example of such a person is Plutarch (L.[?] Mestrius Plutarchus) of Chaeronea in Boeotia. Under Hadrian, Plutarch was procurator of Achaea. He had spent much of his time at Chaeronea, however, where he taught and wrote. A large collection of miscellaneous ethical, rhetorical, and antiquarian essays (not all genuinely Plutarch's) is entitled *Moralia*. Plutarch's most famous work is, of course, the *Parallel Lives of Noble Greeks and Romans*. The overall theme of the *Lives* is that for every important figure of Roman history, a similar and equally important character appears in Greek history. In that way, Plutarch hoped to show that the Greeks were worthy partners of Rome in the great task of maintaining the Empire. Plutarch chose his material to highlight moral character, not present an objective or critical historical analysis. He also had the instincts of a good storyteller and did not encumber his narrative with exaggerated rhetorical adornment. The subjects themselves provide all the necessary interest, which is why Plutarch remains one of the most widely read ancient authors.

Arrian (ca. A.D. 95 to 180)   Another Greek writer who had served Rome was Flavius Arrianus (Arrian) from Nicomedia in Bithynia. Also a Roman citizen, he became a suffect consul in the early years of Hadrian and was governor of Cappadocia from 131 to 137. Retiring to the cultured life of Athens, he studied philosophy under Epictetus (p. 357). He presented a full account of Epictetus' Stoic teachings in his *Diatribes (Discourses)* and a synopsis in the *Enchiridion (Handbook).* He even went so far as to write a treatise on hunting, *Cynegetica,* and minor biographies in imitation of Xenophon. His *Tactics* and *Voyage around the Black Sea* survive, but unfortunately his *History of Parthia* and *History* of *Bithynia* do not.

Of Arrian's extant historical works, the most important is his account of Alexander's war against Persia, the *Anabasis of Alexander,* in clear, readable prose. It is the fullest and most soundly based account of Alexander that has survived. He further imitated Xenophon by writing a sequel, *After Alexander,* whose loss makes it much more difficult to reconstruct the history of Alexander's successors. All of these historical works on eastern lands probably reflected the contemporary Roman wars against Parthia. They would have reminded the Romans that the Greeks, whose ancestors had conquered those lands before, would be useful partners now.

Appian (ca. A.D. 90 to 165) Appian, a Greek from Alexandria and Arrian's contemporary, also obtained Roman citizenship. After a successful career at Rome, he wrote a universal history in Greek like Polybius' earlier work. His universal *Roman History (Romaika)* in twenty-four books began with the rise of Rome in Italy and then treated various different ethnic groups and nations conquered by Rome. Books 13 to 17, however, form an interlude on the *Civil Wars* from the Gracchi to Actium. Appian often followed valuable, now-lost Greek and Latin sources. He, too, wrote in a simple, unpretentious style that is easy to read.

Lucian (ca. A.D. 115 to ca. 185) The best and most original writer of this period was Lucian, a Hellenized Syrian from Samosata, who held a Roman administrative post in Egypt. He was a master of the classical Attic dialect and was deeply versed in its literature. Lucian's earlier works consist of rhetorical declamations and literary criticism, often laced with wit. His most famous works are humorous, semipopular philosophical dialogues, such as his *Dialogues*

of the Dead, which deflate human pride, pedantic philosophers, religious charlatans, and popular superstitions. He is probably not the author of a novel entitled *Lucius,* or *The Ass,* based on the same original as Apuleius' *Golden Ass.* He vigorously disliked all that was fatuous, foolish, or false and can still be read with pleasure today.

The Second Sophistic Although his interests and the range of his writings are too broad to be categorized easily, Lucian must be seen in the context of a Greek literary movement known as the Second Sophistic. The Greek sophists of the fifth and fourth centuries B.C. had invented formal rhetoric. Hence, the professional rhetoricians of the second and third centuries A.D. were also called sophists. Many sought to revive the vocabulary and style of earlier Greek orators, and from them the Second Sophistic takes its name. Most of them were wealthy, cultured men proud of the Greek past and eager to promote the influence of their native cities within the Roman Empire. In their society they were as popular and influential as modern celebrities. They cultivated relations with Roman aristocrats and were often favored by emperors. Their archaizing tendencies influenced Fronto, whose *elocutio novella* represents a parallel movement in Latin.

The leading figures of the Second Sophistic included Polemon (ca. A.D. 88 to ca. 145), who flourished at Smyrna; Herodes Atticus (A.D. 101 to 177), a wealthy benefactor of Athens; and Aelius Aristides (ca. A.D. 120 to 189), who delivered lectures and ceremonial speeches all over the Empire. Little of Polemon and Herodes Atticus remains, but there are fifty extant works ascribed to Aristides. Aristides is by far the best stylist, but his thought is often shallow and uninspiring. In his panegyric address *To Rome,* however, he movingly gave heartfelt thanks and praise for the peace and unity that Rome had brought to the Mediterranean world so that it had become, in effect, one city. His *Sacred Discourses* records dreams that he attributed to the healing god Asclepius and provides a valuable look at practices associated with the cult of Asclepius and the religious experience of an educated pagan.

Dio Chrysostom (ca. A.D. ***40 to ca. 115)***   The best representatives of the Second Sophistic were popular philosophical lecturers who were earnestly concerned with communicating moral lessons to a wide audience. The most noteworthy such person is Dio Chrysostom ("Golden-mouthed") from Prusa in Bithynia. His message was a mild blend of Stoicism and Cynicism that stressed honesty and the simple virtues that make civilization possible. His speeches show no great original thought, but they communicate deeply held values in a fine syle that avoids the excesses of many contemporaries.

Christian Writers   While Chrysostom was traveling the Empire and propagating what he believed were the best values of his civilization, others, although they shared with him many values of a common Greco-Roman heritage, were spreading new ideas that would eventually transform that heritage into something quite different. Because they, too, had something to say in which they deeply believed, some of the ablest writers of the age were Christian authors writing in Greek. The best-known works are the four Gospels, found in the *New Testament* and ascribed to Matthew, Mark, Luke, and John, which sought to preserve the memory and message of Christ's life and teachings, and the missionary letters of the apostle Paul and those ascribed to him, which make up most of the remainder of the *New Testament* and form the intellectual foundation of much basic Christian theology.

Yet, many other Christian writers often wrote with remarkable intellectual power and fiery zeal. The most notable were Ignatius of Antioch (A.D. 50 to 107), the first great ecclesiastic and the father of Christian orthodoxy; Irenaeus of Lyons (ca. A.D. 130 to 202), the powerful advocate of Christian unity, denunciator of heresy, and father of systematic theology; Tatian (ca. A.D. 120 to 172) "the Assyrian," whose *Life of Christ,* a harmony of the four canonical

gospels in Syriac, was read in Syrian churches for almost three centuries. As Christians began to experience persecutions, Christian writers glorified and exalted the martyrs in works called martyrologies to inspire the living. The earliest such martyrology was the account of Polycarp's martyrdom at Smyrna (Izmir), probably in 155/56.

Philosophy   Hellenistic Greek philosophers like Panaetius and Posidonius had adapted Stoicism to the attitudes and needs of the Romans (p. 2–35). Stoics, along with their Cynic cousins, were the only philosophers to retain any vigor during the first two centuries A.D. Neither Greek nor Roman practitioners in this period broke any new ground, however. Their efforts were directed mainly at popularizing and preaching the accepted doctrines of duty, self-control, and virtue as its own reward.

Seneca had expounded on numerous Stoic themes under Claudius and Nero (p. 348), but his essays did not have so wide an impact in their day as the public lectures of his contemporary Gaius Musonius Rufus (ca. A.D. 30 to ca. 100). Rufus suffered banishment twice, first under Nero, after the abortive conspiracy of Piso; and again under Vespasian's crackdown on Stoic opponents. Many later Stoics were pupils of Rufus, but the most notable was the lame Greek ex slave Epictetus (A.D. 55 to 135), who was banished by Domitian (p. 327). He spent his exile teaching at Nicopolis, across the Adriatic from Italy, and attracted a large following. He did not write anything, but his teachings survive in the *Enchiridion* and the *Diatribes* written by the historian Arrian (p. 355). He emphasized the benevolence of the Creator and the brotherhood of man. He believed that happiness depends on controlling one's own will and accepting whatever Divine Providence in its wisdom might require one to endure.

These teachings of Epictetus came into the hands of Marcus Aurelius and inspired him to exchange the study of rhetoric for that of Stoicism. The same spirit animates the *Meditations* of Aurelius (p. 341). The works of Epictetus and Aurelius together have attracted sensitive readers ever since and have had a significant impact on later Western ethical thought.

Religion Nevertheless, Stoicism did not have such an effect on the first and second centuries as developments in religion. Augustus' renewal of traditional Roman cults, rituals, and festivals had greatly influenced the religious calendars of many other cities. Throughout the Empire, local cults were assimilated into parallel cults of the Roman pantheon, so that Roman paganism took on the appearance of an international religion. Each emperor took his duties as *pontifex maximus* seriously, and emperor worship grew steadily. Many people kept shrines of the emperor in their houses.

More significantly, at all levels of society in a centralized Imperial state that increasingly controlled temporal affairs, people sought access to divine powers in order to achieve some sense of control over their lives and destinies. Oracles, omens, and portents were eagerly sought and studied. Astrology was extremely popular. Miracle workers who claimed to have access to divine powers found eager followings. Under Nero and the Flavians, for example, the Cappadocian Apollonius of Tyana achieved great popularity as a sage and healer, so much so that Domitian banished him from Rome. After his death, he was worshipped with his own cult for a long time.

Under Antoninus Pius, another popular healer and purveyor of oracles was Alexander of Abonuteichos from Paphlagonia (Bithynia). He established a mystery cult that influenced a number of prominent Romans, including Fronto, the tutor of Marcus Aurelius. It, too, continued to exist after his death.

In a universal empire ruled by a powerful central monarch, the traditional local gods and cults were bound to seem diminished in power or not completely adequate. Moreover, the greater mobility of the population also weakened traditional religious ties among cosmopolitan urban populations. Therefore, gods that could claim some more universal power or appeal became prominent features of popular religion.

Mystery Cults The desires of people to connect their lives with greater divine powers and influence their ultimate destinies can be seen in the great popularity of universalized mystery cults whose initiates received assurances of a better future. Dionysiac cults flourished. The initiation procedures of one such cult are vividly portrayed in a series of wall paintings at Pompeii in the Villa of the Mysteries. The cult of Demeter at the Athenian suburb of Eleusis attracted initiates from all over the Empire, one of whom was the Emperor Hadrian.

Isis Alongside traditional Greco-Roman mystery cults such as those, Eastern mystery religions were growing with missionary zeal. Because of the secret nature of their mysteries and because of the complete victory of their Christian rivals later on, information about them is sketchy at best, but a few basic facts are known. One of the most popular was the cult of Isis and her male counterpart, Serapis. Originally, she had been an ancient Egyptian nature goddess, but in Hellenistic times she was transformed into a universal mother figure and savior of mankind. Apuleius celebrated her benevolence in the *Golden Ass*. Those who followed a few simple rules of conduct received promises of happiness in this world and the next. Worshippers also gained psychological satisfaction from direct participation in elaborate, emotionally charged rituals that had caused the senate to ban worship of Isis from Republican Rome. Caligula, however, finally provided a state temple for her in the Campus Martius. A major cult that had spread to every corner of the Empire could not be kept out any longer.

Mithraism Eventually, the Persian god Mithras became even more popular than Isis. The cult originated as part of Persian Zoroastrianism, in which Mithras was a god of light and truth who aided Ahura-Mazda, the power of good, in an eternal struggle with the evil power, Ahriman. He was closely associated with the sun god, an important ally of Ahura-Mazda, and he is sometimes identified as the sun. Among Mithras' divine accomplishments, the most celebrated was the capture and slaying of a sacred bull, from whose body sprang other useful forms of life.

This death and birth are a central element in the Mithraic mysteries. The most common type of Mithraic cult statue shows Mithras sacrificing the bull. The typical Mithraic temple, *Mithraeum,* was an artificial subterranean cave, perhaps symbolizing death and the grave. Initiates had to sacrifice a bull and were baptized with its blood after completing certain ordeals. Among them seems to have been a simulated murder. There was also a sacramental meal. All of that was conducted by a professional priesthood in impressive ceremonies and with promises of immortality. A strong moral code with injunctions to do good works also was imposed.

The worship of Mithras became popular in the western provinces first under the Flavians, especially in military camps and seaports, where there were always many people from the eastern provinces. The cult was restricted to men only and was particularly attractive to soldiers because of Mithras' heroic career as a fighter on the side of good. This restriction eventually, however, put Mithraism at a serious disadvantage and helps to explain why it eventually lost out to Christianity, with which it had much in common.

Christianity Christianity combined the appealing characteristics of many mystery religions: a loving, divine savior in Jesus, who overcame the forces of evil and death; a benevolent mother figure in the Virgin Mary; the promise of a blessed future; a sense of belonging to a special community in an era when local values and civic institutions were losing force in the face of a distant central government. In this third aspect, however, Christianity greatly surpassed the rest. The requirements of a strict moral code and the rejection of all other gods increased the Christians' sense of specialness. Furthermore, Christ's injunction to "love one another" resulted in charitable activities within Christian congregations that increased the feelings of fellowship and communal identity.

Strengths One of Christianity's distinctive strengths was its high degree of organization. During the first century A.D., individual Christian communities established a local system of clergy and leaders—deacons and deaconesses (servants), presbyters (elders), and bishops (overseers)—who ministered to the needs of the congregation, established policies, and regulated activities. Later, the bishops of the early churches became the heads of groups of churches.

Like other new cults, Christianity had spread first to the major urban centers along the trade routes of the Empire. Later, missionaries were sent out under the direction of these larger centers and established churches in the smaller surrounding communities. The urban bishops were the ones who coordinated this expansion and naturally came to exercise great influence and authority, so that by the end of the second century the bishops of the major cities were recognized as the heads of whole networks of churches in their regions. Furthermore, because of the strong sense of Christian brotherhood, the bishops and various churches regularly corresponded with each other to provide mutual support in the face of difficulties. In this way, they also ensured that local practices and beliefs conformed to the authoritative accepted teachings of Christ and his disciples.

It is significant for the development of a strong interchurch organization in the first and second centuries that Christ was a recent historical person and that his immediate disciples or the apostle Paul had founded the earliest Christian churches. These early foundations were seen as direct historical links with the words and deeds of Christ himself through the apostolic succession of their bishops. Churches founded in the generation after Paul and the disciples naturally looked to the apostolic churches for guidance and authoritative teachings when they wished to confirm that they were proceeding in accordance with the words and spirit of Christ's teachings, which they considered imperative for obtaining salvation. Therefore, the bishops of the apostolic churches, especially in the four major cities of Rome, Jerusalem, Alexandria, and Antioch, achieved great respect and authority. Accordingly, they were able to impose their will on the lesser churches, so that Christianity reached a degree of organizational and doctrinal unity matched by no other religion.

Another factor that helped the spread of early Christianity was its openness and appeal to all classes and sexes. Women were not excluded from or segregated within it. In the early Church, deacons and deaconesses shared in ministering to the congregations. The simple ceremonies and the grace-giving rites of baptism and communion posed no expensive obstacles to the poor. Indeed, Christ's teachings praised the poor and the humble and made their lot more bearable by encouraging the practice of charity toward them in the present and promising them a better life in the future.

On the other hand, the foundation of Christianity on written works, such as the Jewish Scriptures, the four Gospels, and the sophisticated writings of Paul, gave it an appeal to the educated upper class as well. Converts from this class provided the trained thinkers and writers who established a tradition of Christian apologetics aimed at counteracting popular misconceptions about Christians and official hostility toward them. Justin Martyr, who went from Flavia Neapolis (Nablus) in Palestine to establish a Christian school in Rome, addressed a defense of Christianity to Antoninus Pius and Marcus Aurelius.

Persecution of the Christians The Christians needed to defend themselves from attack for two reasons. Their rigid monotheistic rejection of other gods and their refusal to participate in traditional activities with their pagan neighbors were an offense to those around them and bred personal hostility toward them. This hostility was fed by the normal human fear of the unfamiliar. Accordingly, people were quick to blame Christians for all manner of misfortunes that befell them individually or collectively and frequently denounced Christians to Roman officials for their "crimes." Moreover, Roman authorities had always been suspicious of secret societies and feared that they were plotting against the state. This fear seemed borne out in

the Christians' case because they refused to propitiate the gods who were believed to protect the state and would not perform the required ceremonies before the image of the emperor.

During the first two centuries, most of the persecutions and resultant martyrdoms were the consequences of purely local personal and political tensions, as when Jewish authorities laid accusations against Paul before Festus, the governor of Judea, or took advantage of Festus' death to execute James, leader of the church at Jerusalem. Nero's execution of Christians at Rome was a purely local act to divert the public in the aftermath of the great fire of 64. Domitian seems to have included Christians among the intellectuals whom he executed or banished as subversives, but he found no justification in the charges leveled at Jesus' relatives in Jerusalem and ordered that persecution of the Christians at Jerusalem stop.

By the beginning of the second century, however, Christianity had become widespread in the eastern provinces, and local agitation against it was frequent. In a famous letter to Pliny the Younger, whom he had placed in charge of Bithynia-Pontus, Trajan agreed that there should be no organized hunt for Christians or acceptance of anonymous accusations. He insisted, however, that those fairly accused and convicted of being Christians be executed unless they renounced their faith and sacrificed to the gods. One of them was Ignatius of Antioch, who was tried and condemned to the beasts in Rome during Trajan's later years. Hadrian demanded that accusations against Christians had to stand up under strict legal procedures or be dismissed. Although he disliked them, Marcus Aurelius himself did not actively promote the persecution of Christians, but he was too occupied with other crises to take action against governors who yielded to popular pressure and condemned Christians to torture and death (p. 341).

The result of the individual martyrdoms in the first and second centuries was to strengthen the resolve of the faithful and impress thoughtful non-Christians, who were often moved to convert by the examples of heroic martyrs. As the spread of the Church proceeded apace, therefore, two mid-third-century emperors did mount active persecutions of Christians in an attempt to appease the traditional gods and enforce unity on an increasingly chaotic Empire (pp. 387–388).

Architecture in the First Two Centuries

A.D. Probably the most creative aspect of Roman Imperial culture in the first two centuries A.D. was architecture. Augustus had used the resources of the state for building projects far more than ever before. His example was followed and enlarged upon by most succeeding emperors during this period. With the resources thus made available, architects found no end of opportunities to use their creative talents.

The possibilities of combining different structural and stylistic elements into a coherent monumental whole had been discovered by Hellenistic Greek architects and imitated in the famous Temple of Fortuna at Praeneste (pp. 236-237). The architects of the first two centuries A.D., many of whom were Greek, developed these possibilities to their fullest. Great complexes made up of diverse elements arranged according to an artistic design became the norm.

Imperial Palaces Each emperor had to have his own splended residence on the Palatine, or at least he had to add to that of his predecessor. Nero took advantage of the fire of 64 to construct a sprawling complex, the Golden House, that mirrored his own megalomania. Its size and complexity, however, made it an architectural achievement of the first order. It covered an area twice as large as that of the Vatican today and was really a complex of palaces, merely one of which had over 80 rooms. It also had its own parks, pastures, groves, and even a zoo. It had an arcaded approach a mile long and 350 feet wide. Two ponds, one fresh and one salt, were fed by aqueducts each 15 miles long. Vespasian destroyed Nero's palace and built a smaller one on the Palatine to symbolize the beginning of a new order. Vespasian's sons, espe-

cially Domitian, continued to enlarge this new palace until it, too, became a huge complex that destroyed or buried many older buildings beneath its foundations. Its remains are visible on the Palatine today.

The Emperor Hadrian was an innovative architect and designed a splendid villa near Tibur (Tivoli), about 18 miles east of Rome. It far surpassed Nero's Golden House in size and complexity of design, and much remains. Covering an area 3,000 feet long and 1,500 wide, this villa contained 8 palaces, each with a different theme or mood: a stadium, a palaestra (for wrestling), a library, a temple of Serapis (Serapeum), two pools, three dining rooms, three baths, numerous porticoes above and below ground level, and many other buildings, such as guest houses, slave quarters, and shrines. What is most striking about the whole complex is the imaginative combination of different geometric shapes—curves, octagons, rectangles, and squares—to create new visual effects.

Public Buildings Augustus' Julio-Claudian successors other than Nero did not contribute greatly to the public architecture of Rome. The Flavians, on the other hand, introduced a dynamic era of public construction. They destroyed the Golden House of Nero and built the Colosseum and baths of Titus on its site. The baths, unfortunately, like many other ancient buildings were almost completely obliterated by builders who used its stones for new buildings in the Renaissance. Titus also began the arch that still bears his name at the eastern entrance to the Forum. It commemorates his triumph over the Jews, and its sculptures depict the sacred objects taken as spoils from the Temple at Jerusalem. Vespasian completed a temple of the Deified Claudius, and began the third Imperial forum—the Forum of Peace (in commemoration of the end of the Jewish revolt), also called the Forum of Vespasian, east of the Forum of Augustus and just north of the original Forum.

Vespasian also probably built what is called the Temple of the Sacred City (*Templum Sacrae Urbis*) between the old Forum and his new one. It was used to house records, and on its outside north wall, which was also the inside south wall of a library in the Forum of Vespasian, a detailed map of the whole city was carved in marble. Many fragments of his Marble Plan still exist and are very useful in reconstructing the layout and monuments of ancient Rome. Domitian built a new stadium, with seats for 30,000 in the Campus Martius. It remained one of the city's most famous structures for centuries. The length of the arena was about 750 feet, and its shape and size are preserved by the modern Piazza Navona. Domitian also completed a Temple of Vespasian at the western end of the old Forum, just to the northwest of the Temple of Saturn and just to the southwest of the Temple of Concord. Only three large Corinthian columns still stand.

The Colosseum Vespasian began and Domitian finished the monumental task of building the Colosseum (Coliseum), the Flavian Amphitheater as it was originally called. It received the name Colosseum from a nearby colossal, 120-foot-high bronze statue of Nero, which Vespasian had reworked into a statue of the sun. The Colosseum's remains stand today as a symbol of Roman Imperial architecture, a massive structure showing a sophisticated blend of decorative styles and impressive engineering. It has an elliptical shape with a main axis of about 620 feet and a minor one of about 515, stands about 160 feet high on the outside, and could hold 45,000 to 55,000 spectators. The facade is a creative blend of architectural forms and styles. Three superimposed arcades of 80 arches each run around the outside of the building. Each arch is decoratively framed with engaged columns supporting an entablature. Thus the curved Roman arch and the horizontal Greek temple facade are joined together. The style of the first level is Doric, the second Ionic, and the third Corinthian. A fourth story has no arches but is decorated with a number of Corinthian pilasters in line with the rows of engaged columns of the lower stories.

Forum of Trajan Many emperors built fora to accommodate the ever-increasing official and commercial business of Rome. Whereas Nerva's is the smallest Imperial forum, that of his successor, Trajan, is the largest. Its remains are still impressive. It was to the west of Augustus'

The Colosseum (Coliseum), or Flavian Amphitheater.
(Courtesy Italian Government Travel Office)

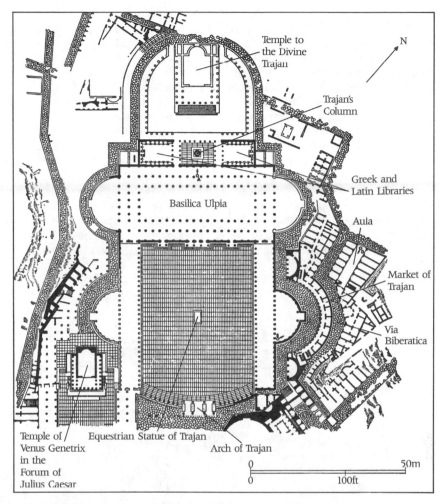

Plan of Trajan's Forum, with Basilica Ulpia, Rome. (from Roman Art, *second edition, Nancy and Andrew Ramage, Prentice Hall, 1996)*

forum, and its southern corner bordered the northern corner of Caesar's in order to complete Caesar's original plan of joining the valley of the Republican Forum with the Campus Martius. The ends of the Capitoline and Quirinal hills had to be cut back to make room for the enormous design roughly 620 feet wide and 1,000 feet long. The main part of this forum consisted of an open space approximately 300 feet by 380 feet. The southeast, southwest, and northwest sides were surrounded by colonnades of different-colored marble. The entrance was in the middle of the southeast side, through a great triumphal arch fronted by six columns and topped by a statue of Trajan driving a 6-horse chariot. Behind the middle of each side colonnade was a large semicircular structure, a hemicycle. The one to the northeast is called the Market of Trajan and had two stories of shops and rooms. More levels rose on terraces behind.

The far end of the forum was closed off by

the front of a great basilica, the Basilica Ulpia, raised about three feet above ground level and approached by three steps. The entrances of the basilica were flanked with columns of yellow marble and had chariots and trophies mounted above. The walls were marble-faced concrete, and there was a large apse at each end. A double row of ninety-six marble columns surrounded the inner hall and supported an upper gallery around the nave, which was about eighty feet wide.

Behind the basilica two libraries (one Latin and one Greek, as was customary) faced each other. In the midst of the courtyard between them stood one of Rome's most remarkable monuments, the column of Trajan (p. 366). After Trajan's death, Hadrian built a magnifi-

cent temple to the Deified Trajan and Trajan's wife, Plotina, on the open side of this courtyard so that the whole area had an architectural balance.

Hadrian's Public Buildings At Rome, Hadrian was primarily concerned with rebuilding and restoring what already existed, but he was responsible for the construction of three unique projects, which epitomize the way that Roman Imperial architecture combined disparate forms and styles into structures that are both massive and interesting. The first was the largest temple in Rome—the Temple of Venus and Roma—between the Colosseum and the northeast corner of the old Forum. It was really two temples with vaulted apses back to back. In

Front view of Hadrian's Pantheon, with inscription from Agrippa's earlier building. (Archivi Alinari/Art Resource, NY)

one apse stood a statue of Venus and in the other, one of Roma. This arrangement took advantage of a convenient Latin pun: Venus is the goddess of love, *amor* in Latin, which is the name of Rome, *Roma,* spelled backward. Only its foundations remain, however.

Hadrian's most famous building is the Pantheon, Temple of All the Gods. A Christian church since 609, it is the best-preserved ancient building in Rome today. It is the perfect example of the imaginative combination of shapes and forms that distinguishes Roman Imperial architecture. The front presents the columned and pedimented facade of a classical Greek temple. This facade may preserve the lines and dedicatory inscription of the original Pantheon built by Augustus' colleague Marcus Agrippa, but it and the rest are almost all Hadrian's work.

The conventional facade joins a huge domed cylinder that is the temple proper. Thus, the rectilinear is uniquely combined with the curvilinear. This theme is carried out further in the rectangular receding coffers sunk in the curved ceiling of the dome, in the marble squares and circles of the floor, and in the alternating rectangular and curved niches around the wall of the drum. Moreover, the globe and the cylinder are combined because the diameter of the drum is the same as the distance from the floor to the top of the dome, so that if the curve of the dome were extended, it would be tangent with the floor. Finally, the whole building is lighted by a round opening, the *oculus* (eye), about thirty feet in diameter in the top of the dome. This hole is open to the weather, but because of its great height, most moisture evaporates before it reaches the floor during a rain.

The dome exemplifies how Roman engineers took advantage of the properties of concrete, whose use the Romans greatly advanced. To reduce the dome's weight, pumice was used instead of ordinary sand or gravel, and the wall was made thinner as it neared the top. The recessed coffers reduced the weight still further and created a grid of structural ribs. Once the concrete set, the dome was a solid, jointless mass of exceptional stability, as its survival for over 1,850 years testifies.

Across the Tiber there arose another architectural marvel of the age—Hadrian's tomb—a colossal mausoleum, massive, solid, round, over 1,000 feet in circumference. On its summit a bronze 4-horse chariot stood poised for flight; inside were walls faced with Parian marble, huge columns of eastern marble or Egyptian porphyry, mosaic floors, and numerous statues. In the Middle Ages that massive structure long served as a fortress and was known as the Castel Sant' Angelo, a name it still bears.

Architecture in the Provinces After Hadrian, the pace of building in second-century Rome slackened considerably, but elsewhere the bustle continued. A fine example of Imperial architecture and planning in a smaller town is Thamugadi (Timgad), a colony established by Trajan for veterans in North Africa. It was laid out on a grid of broad, intersecting main streets and side streets. The main streets were colonnaded, and other amenities, including a large Greek-style theater, baths, and a well-appointed forum, were provided. By A.D. 200, 12,000 to 15,000 people dwelt there in comfort and security.

Sculpture The Roman tradition of realistic portraits and statues continued through the second century A.D., as can be seen in the busts of the various emperors. The best example is a bronze statue of Marcus Aurelius mounted on a horse. It is extraordinary only because it is the single bronze equestrian statue to have survived from Antiquity. It is a skillfully executed representative of a traditional type that could have been seen all over the Roman Empire. It is in the use of sculptured relief that innovations occurred. Beginning with Augustus and the Ara Pacis (p. 284), the sculptured relief became one of the most common forms of official art. Tiberius and Claudius restated Augustan themes in famous reliefs on several altars. The inside of Titus' triumphal arch has vivid sculptured scenes full of the movement and excitement of his own victory procession. Domitian imitated the more restrained classicism of Au-

City of Thamugadi (Timgad) (Art Resource, NY)

gustus' Ara Pacis on a long relief that glorified the Flavian dynasty and, probably, his own campaign against the Chatti. At Beneventum, Trajan erected a triumphal arch that was an exact copy of Titus' arch at Rome, except that he covered every available flat surface with dense relief scenes of himself performing his duties. Moreover, these scenes were very balanced and static in the classical manner.

At Rome, however, in the courtyard behind the Basilica Ulpia, Trajan set up a completely new and extraordinary relief to commemorate his Dacian wars. It is a column about 12 feet in diameter and exactly 100 Roman feet (about 97 English feet) high. Around this column winds a spiral relief depicting the wars themselves. The vast and complex logistical, engineering, and military aspects of the wars

are portrayed in a realistically detailed narrative that leads dramatically to the death of King Decebalus. There are some 2,500 separate figures, but through it all Trajan is a unifying presence appearing over 50 times. The width of the spiral and size of the figures increase as they move upward to compensate for the greater viewing distance from the ground. The top was surmounted by a bronze statue of Trajan, until it was replaced by one of St. Peter in 1588. The large pedestal on which the column rests was Trajan's mausoleum.

Marcus Aurelius imitated Trajan's column with one of his own in the Campus Martius. Its dimensions are the same, and it has a spiral relief depicting the Second Marcomannic War (172 to 175). Artistically, however, this relief is very different from Trajan's. The realistic details of scenery are omitted, there is no attempt at three-dimensional spatial relationships, and there is no unified, dramatic narrative sequence. There is constant motion and striving, almost chaos. Through it all, however, Marcus Aurelius stands out. He is not merely part of the action. He repeatedly faces outward and dominates the viewer's attention to become a solid, powerful presence in the midst of all the confused action. The details of mundane reality are sacrificed to present the viewer directly with the essence of the emperor's role in events. This style approaches the "otherworldly" art of the late Empire and the Middle Ages.

Painting What little is known of Roman painting in the first two centuries A.D. comes from the wall paintings found at Pompeii, Herculaneum, and other sites buried by the eruption of Vesuvius in 79 during Titus' reign. These frescoes are not the work of creative artists but of craftsmen copying on plaster the works of great masters or standardized decorative scenes and following the tastes of their customers. Pleasant or romantic landscapes, still lifes, and scenes from famous myths or epics abound.

Most of these works are set off by painting the surrounding wall in an architectural style. From roughly 14 to 62, the Third (Egyptianizing) Style was most popular. Instead of creating the illusion of depth, the painters used painted architectural forms to provide a flat frame within which the picture could be featured. After 62, the Fourth (Ornamental) Style prevailed. Perspective was heavily used to give the illusion of infinite depth behind the wall. There was also great flamboyance in the design of the architectural forms. They often resembled stage sets, were weighed down with intricate detail to the point of looking like baroque fantasies, and probably show the influence of Nero's tastes on the trends of the time.

Mosaics, Coins, and Medallions The numerous mosaics of the period, which are found all over the Empire, especially in the villas of North Africa, not only are very valuable documents for the social and economic life of the region but also exhibit remarkable taste and

Richly painted walls (ca. 60–79 A.D.) of the dining room (triclinium) *of the house of the Vettii, rich wine merchants of Pompeii. (Art Resource, NY)*

workmanship in an art destined to have a future even more brilliant. The coins and medallions of this period are among the finest in history. The art of medal engraving, which was stimulated by Hadrian's issue of a series of bronze medallions, reveals a love of symbolism and allegory and reached a level of skill and technique comparable to that of the most beautiful coinages in the ancient world.

Social Developments As already seen, the composition of the Roman upper class changed over the first two centuries because emperors recruited administrators from the local Italian and provincial elites as loyal counterweights to the old Republican senatorial families of Rome. Members of those families were understandably resentful. After the purges of Nero and Domitian, however, most of the old Republican noble families had disappeared.

Upper-Class Women In the late Republic, upper-class women had achieved considerable independence and power. In some extreme cases, their sexual conduct was as free as that traditionally permitted to men. As one might imagine, many men felt their traditional male dominance threatened, and in the early Empire there was a concerted attempt to "put women back in their place." This attempt was bolstered not only by the traditional Roman ideal of the virtuous wife and mother but also by widespread Roman exposure to classical Greek literature and philosophy, which tended to view women with a pathological fear, hostility, and insistence on their inherent inferiority. In Roman literature, this view can be seen already in the almost universally negative attitude toward female characters in the *Aeneid* and is paramount in the sixth satire of Juvenal over a century later (pp. 288 and 353). Officially, it is manifest in Augustus' legislation to promote marriage and punish adultery (p. 263).

This attempt to return upper-class women to their former subordination did not work, however. The popularity of Ovid's handbook for philanderers, *The Art of Love,* shows the prevailing upper-class attitude toward Augustus' moralism. Promiscuity increased, and two of the most notoriously promiscuous women of the day were the two Julias, Augustus' daughter and granddaughter.

Women of the Imperial and noble families carried on the tradition of vigorously independent aristocratic women and strove to satisfy their own ambitions. Augustus' wife Livia was a real power in his reign and was given the title Augusta in his will. More than once she annoyed Tiberius with her domineering attitude. Messallina took an active part in a plot to overthrow her husband Claudius. Agrippina the Elder was an implacable foe of Tiberius, and Agrippina the Younger maneuvered her son, Nero, to the throne by murder and intrigue, whereas Trajan's wife, Plotina, helped engineer the smooth succession of Hadrian. Mothers and wives of emperors were often deified or honored in order to exalt their sons and husbands. Their family connections were also advertised in dynastic propaganda as well. Inscriptions and statues honored wives of provincial governors for their benefactions and numerous lesser women for accomplishments as athletes, musicians, and physicians.

After Augustus, the legal status of women also improved in step with social reality. In 126, Hadrian liberalized women's right to make wills. Marcus Aurelius made it legal for mothers, not just fathers, to inherit from children. Eventually, even the guardianship of women was abolished under Diocletian (A.D. 284 to 305).

The Lower Classes The lot of lower-class citizens, freedpersons, provincials, and slaves improved somewhat over the first two centuries A.D. in comparison with the first century B.C., but the poor and the powerless, male and female, in any society seldom see dramatic improvements in their overall conditions. The general internal peace and prosperity of the period fostered traditional upper-class patronage and euergetism. Life became a little more secure and less desperate for the great mass of people, and almost all of the emperors tried to alleviate real hardship. They made great efforts to secure a stable grain supply for Rome in order to sustain those who received free grain and keep the price affordable for the rest. The urban poor also benefitted from the emperors' efforts to improve flood control, housing conditions, and the water supply and to upgrade public sanitation through the construction of public latrines and baths. In many of the great provincial cities, wealthy local benefactors undertook similar projects.

At least in Italy, the rural poor benefitted from private charitable endowments and the *alimenta* of Trajan and his successors, but girls always received less per capita than boys. In the provinces, the emperors' attempts to provide efficient and honest administration must have kept the peasantry from being exploited so mercilessly as they often had been. It would be naive, however, to think that all Imperial officials acted so scrupulously as they were supposed to.

Although some well-educated Greek freedmen and slaves in the Imperial household had impressive careers, the status of most slaves and freedmen had not changed. Some freedmen became very wealthy, others practiced middle-class trades and professions, still others existed at the poverty level, and all remained second-class citizens despite being eligible for honorific posts such as *Augustalis*. It is difficult to know the impact of Hadrian's humane legislation on the treatment of slaves (p. 338). Manumissions were still frequent, as the innumerable funerary inscriptions of freedpersons proves, despite Augustus' attempt to slow down the process by taxing manumissions and limiting the number of slaves that a master could free in his will. Despite more enlightened attitudes on the part of some, slaves were still subject to torture as witnesses, and if a slave killed a master, all of his slaves were punished by death.

Middle-Class Prosperity and Urban Growth

Under the general peace and stability within the Empire during the first two centuries, the wealth of the Empire rose dramatically, and people of moderate means or possessed of talent and enterprise prospered to an extent never known before (and only again in recent times). Increased incomes gave rise to an unprecedented urge to travel, which was further encouraged by the construction of a huge network of excellent roads. Greater prosperity was reflected in the rebuilding of old cities, the colonization of new sites, and the growth of important settlements around major military camps on the frontiers. A traveler in Asia Minor, North Africa, Spain, or Gaul would see familiar-looking temples, theaters, libraries, baths, and fine homes everywhere.

Economic Trends

Economic Trends The growth of Rome and other cities continued to stimulate agriculture, industry, and commerce, but Italy declined as a center of production in relation to the provinces as the products of farm and shop moved freely over land and sea. Foreign trade steadily expanded. The agricultural potential of the less developed provinces was rapidly exploited. In Britain, the Yorkshire valley and the broad fields of the Southeast soon produced enough grain for export. The raising of sheep for wool, much in demand for clothing the northern armies, seems to have been introduced to the Cotswolds in Gloucestershire. Another center of grain production was in the Belgic province along the Rhine. In southern Gaul, regions that are still famous for their wines became major producers and supplanted Italy in the second century as the suppliers of wine to northern Europe. They even competed in the huge market of Rome itself. Olive groves in Spain and Africa Proconsularis (Tunisia) produced huge volumes of oil that were widely exported, also at the expense of Italian producers.

The older agricultural lands of the eastern Mediterranean also prospered. The valley of the Orontes in Syria reached its height as an olive-producing region, grain production flourished on the eastern side of the Jordan River, and irrigated land was increased in Egypt. Moreover, as the number and size of cities grew everywhere, small farmers nearby found ready markets for fruits, vegetables, cheese, eggs, and poultry.

Mining and Manufacturing The creation of stable frontiers and the construction of great roads, harbors, and canals throughout the Empire also opened up new sources of raw materials and encouraged the spread of manufacturing. The production of lead ingots and pig iron was of major importance in Britain. Tin, copper, and silver continued to be important in Spain, and the gold mines of the new province of Dacia were vigorously exploited.

In the East, the old manufacturing centers flourished. The workshops of Egypt and Syria produced papyrus, blown glass, textiles, purple dye, and leather goods. Asia Minor supplied marble, pottery, parchment, carpets, and cloth.

In the West, the Italian producers of glass, pottery, and bronze wares sent their products far and wide during the first century but went into decline as provincial centers, especially in Gaul and the Rhineland, took over their export markets during the second. In the first century, Lugdunum (Lyons) in Gaul became the center of the western glass industry, although Colonia Agrippina (Cologne) in Germany replaced it in the second. *Terra sigillata,* the famous red dinnerware with raised decorations exported from Arretium in Italy, was successfully imitated on a vast scale for western European markets: first at what are now La Graufesenque and Lezoux in Gaul and finally at Tres Tabernae in the Rhineland. Tongres in Belgium produced a popular black pottery, and potteries in Britain made a similar type with a gray slip. Even the famous bronze workers of Capua lost their western markets to skilled Gallic craftsmen who set up shop at Gressnich.

Imperial Commerce The negative social and economic impact on Italy of increased commercial agriculture and specialized manufacturing in the western provinces has been described in the previous chapter (pp. 331–332). The main reason that the Italians could not compete with provincial producers was the inefficiency of ancient transportation, especially by land. Despite the wonderful system of Imperial roads, transportation by wagon or cart was slow and cumbersome, although recent research indicates that the Romans did not so inefficiently harness their draft horses as once thought.

Once provincial farmers and craftsmen produced products comparable to those of Italy, their proximity to local markets gave them an unbeatable advantage over Italian exporters. In fact, provincial farmers near the seacoast or on waterways and enjoying easy access to more efficient water transport had a great advantage over farmers from the interior of Italy in shipping to the lucrative markets of Rome and other coastal Italian cities. For example, it was cheaper to ship an amphora of wine from Arelate (Arles) or Narbo in southern Gaul to Rome by sea than to transport one overland to Rome from only fifty miles away in Italy.

The same factors, however, sharply limited the potential for manufacturing and commerce in the provinces beyond the points achieved by the second century A.D. Only farmers with easy access to water transport could profitably export crops. Moreover, the slowness of transportation and the lack of refrigeration or preservation techniques meant that only spoilage-resistant agricultural products like grain, olive oil, and wine could be shipped long distances. Only expensive manufactured goods whose production was limited by the geographic location of raw materials or highly specialized craftsmen could be profitably exported over significant distances. Therefore, the market for such goods was limited to the well-to-do. The mass of people either had to do without or settle for inferior imitations of local manufacture. As a result, most manufacturing tended to remain small and localized, and large-scale commerce was limited.

Foreign Commerce Because of the greater distances involved, commerce beyond the Imperial frontiers was limited to luxury goods, but the increase that did occur in Imperial prosperity stimulated the demand for foreign luxuries and the exploration of foreign trade routes. Traders traveled north along the coast of Germany and to the Baltic islands in search of amber and furs for Roman markets. Over 4,000 Roman coins have been found just on the island of Gothland. During the first century, the

Parthians had forced diversion of the Chinese silk trade south to India, whence it proceeded by ship to Red Sea ports (p. 316). By the end of the century, however, Greek and Syrian merchants were making regular contact with silk caravans from China at Bactra (Balkh in north-central Afghanistan) and later, under Hadrian or Antoninus, a little farther east at Tashkurgan (Stone Tower).

By the beginning of the first century, Greek merchants had penetrated overland through Bactra to the Punjab. Since the time of Augustus, merchant fleets had also sailed between southern Arabia and western India for perfumes, gems, spices, and cotton cloth (p. 271). Finds of Roman coins across the southern tip of India and the presence of Arretine pottery in excavations at Arikamedu near Pondicherry (Poduke?) on the east coast indicate that in the early first century Roman goods were transhipped overland from places like Muziris (Cranganore) on the southwest side. By the second half of the century, some sailors had braved the dangerous passage around the southern tip to Tabrobane (Ceylon, Sri Lanka) and eventually made their way up to the Bay of Bengal and perhaps to Indochina as far east as Hanoi. In 166, a group even paid court to the Chinese Emperor Huan-ti at Loyang, far up the Hwang-ho (Yellow River), to talk about setting up regular trade by sea with the West. In the long run, however, little was accomplished.

There was also trade with non-Roman Africa. During the first century, merchants traded along the Somali coast for frankincense and may have gone so far south as Zanzibar and Mozambique in search of ivory during the second. Explorers even penetrated inland to the sources of the Nile in lakes Victoria and Albert. Through Fezzan in North Africa, there was a brisk trade from the sub-Saharan regions in exotic animals for the innumerable games at Rome and many other cities.

Inherent Economic and Fiscal Weakness of the Roman Empire

Despite the real economic growth of the first two centuries A.D., serious underlying weaknesses appear as early as the time of Nero. They limited the Empire's economic potential and contributed to a long-term decline beginning in the third century (pp. 397–398). For example, the foreign trade in luxuries had a negative impact. Much of the valuable merchandise was paid for in silver and gold, as the numerous hoards of Roman coins that help document Roman trade routes demonstrate. The elder Pliny complained that under Nero the Indian trade alone drew off 60 million sesterces a year, whereas the rest of the Eastern trade took another 40 million. In the second century, the deficit may have been reduced by the export of some manufactured goods, such as bronze and tin goods, dinnerware, blown glass, woolen cloth, and even rewoven silk. Nevertheless, the most prized Roman products were the Empire's fine coins, and the constant drain of precious metal eventually helped to undermine the stability of the monetary and fiscal systems.

Part of the problem lay with the nature of the monetary system itself. Except for copper, brass, and bronze coins used for small change, the system was based upon the circulation of coins whose value was fixed largely by their actual content of precious metal. Credit, necessary to expand business, was severely limited by the amount of coinage in circulation. If coins were debased to sustain or increase the amount in circulation, prices rose so that no advantage was gained.

By the time of Nero, the productivity of the Spanish gold and silver mines, the main sources of supply, was falling, and that, plus the drain caused by foreign trade and his own overspending, led him to reduce the metallic content of both gold and silver coinage. A serious crisis was temporarily averted when Trajan opened up the gold mines of Dacia to Roman exploitation, but under Marcus Aurelius plague and war put severe new strains on the economy.

In spite of the large surplus that Antoninus Pius had reportedly left behind in the treasury, Marcus Aurelius found himself obliged to sell the palace jewels and treasures in order to finance the Danubian campaigns and to debase the silver currency by raising its copper content to approximately 34 percent. To meet the crises of the third century, later emperors further debased the coinage almost to the point of total collapse, with great damage to trade and commerce and with economic hardship for all.

Further problems were created by the general fiscal policies of the emperors. In times of peace, the revenues of the Empire barely covered expenditures. The mounting costs of government and Imperial bureaucracy; the donatives given to the troops; the vast sums spent on education and public welfare, monuments and public buildings, and relief to stricken communities normally left little surplus to meet unexpected emergencies. The periodic cancellation of arrears and reduction of taxes together with an inefficient system of tax collection kept the state perpetually on the brink of bankruptcy.

Instead of increasing the regular taxes and extending their collection to every part of the Empire, the emperors often resorted to extraordinary taxation; confiscations of capital; requisitions of money, food, and transport for the army; or compulsory labor, almost all of which fell on the agricultural sector of the economy. These disruptive levies increased dramatically during the third century and not only imposed hardship upon the municipalities and rich men made responsible for their collection, but sometimes drove peasants and tenants to strike, revolt, flee their occupations, or become brigands.

The Failure of Ancient Technology Yet it would be erroneous to suppose that the crippling burden of taxation, the aristocratic consumption of imported luxuries, bad financial policies, the prodigious demands of Imperial defense and government, and frequent civil wars after the second century alone provide an adequate explanation of the economic decline that can be traced from the third century onward. The root of the trouble lay rather in the persistent failure of Graeco-Roman society to transform pure science into productive technology. The Greeks had an impressive record of achievement in the history of theoretical science and mathematics. In the Hellenistic period Archimedes (ca. 287 to 212 B.C.), Hero of Alexandria (? to ca. 150 B.C.), and others even invented many mechanical contrivances, such as the endless chain, the compound pulley, the lifting crane, and the reaction turbine. Still, they never succeeded in putting these inventions to practical use to save labor, increase productive capacity, and build an industrial economy capable of bearing the financial load of a highly centralized bureaucratic state.

The clue to the ancient failure to transform science into an industrial technology may be found not only in the heavy use of slave or dependent labor and the aristocratic leisure-class contempt for ordinary work but also in the failure of ancient education, which reflected and perpetuated the attitudes of a class that had little to do directly with economic production. The undue emphasis upon rhetoric to the exclusion of science and practical technological training was designed to produce lawyers, administrators, and professors of rhetoric rather than scientists, industrial engineers, and technicians.

The lack of industrial technology and labor-saving machines that would have met the mounting crises faced by the Empire after the second century was crucial. Without them, the Empire could not meet its greatly increased military needs and maintain a healthy civilian economy at the same time. Therefore, the third century began a period of serious disruption.

XXXI

Crisis and Temporary Recovery, A.D. 180 to 235

The third century A.D. in Roman history really began with the death of Marcus Aurelius in 180 and lasted a little more than 100 years until the accession of Diocletian in 284/85. It is one of the most difficult, confusing, and misunderstood periods of Roman history. Recently, however, scholars have given greater attention to it, and a more detailed and reliable picture than was previously possible has emerged. This century can be divided into two almost equal parts. The first extends from the death of Marcus Aurelius in 180 to the assassination of Severus Alexander in 235. During that time the borders of the Empire remained intact, although under pressure, and there were only two serious internal political crises: from 193 to early 197 and from 217 to 221. The second part stretches from 235 to the ultimate victory of Diocletian in 285, when frequent civil wars and assassinations saw the rapid rise and fall of twenty-six emperors or pretenders, constant breakthroughs on the borders, and the near breakup of the Empire under those two stresses and a devastating plague.

Despite the differences between the first and second parts of the third century, several political trends can be traced throughout that give it unity. The city of Rome itself remained of great symbolic significance, but actual power shifted to more strategic locations near the borders, whose defense demanded ever more attention. The growing importance of defense and the provinces is clearly illustrated by the fact that almost all of the third-century emperors were generals of provincial birth, many from the Danubian provinces, where the problems of defense were often acute and where many of the Empire's best soldiers were recruited.

The growing importance of the provinces and the parallel decline of Roman and Italian primacy also led to increasing regionalism, sectionalism, and disunity. Often the armies and inhabitants of one province or region would support a rival claimant to the throne or oppose a challenger from another part of the Empire because they feared that they and their problems would be ignored while the other province or region received special attention. At times, some areas even broke away under their own emperors.

As defense and personal safety became the overriding concerns of emperors, their office increasingly lost the characteristics of a civilian magistracy that it had retained since the days of Augustus; it was becoming an absolute monarchy resting upon raw military power and the trappings of divine kingship along Near Eastern and Hellenistic lines. Also, as the emperors tried to mobilize all the state's resources to meet its defensive needs, the bulk of its people sank into the status of suffering subjects instead of satisfied citizens. Although the few wealthy and influential senators and equestrians were neutralized and co-opted by grants of greater social and legal privileges and lucrative posts in the Imperial bureaucracy, the lower classes were made legally inferior and subject to even greater oppression in the name of the state, which in better times under more benevolent emperors had afforded them some measure of protection and dignity.

Sources for Roman History, A.D. 180 to 285

The difficulty of understanding the complex period from 180 to 285, especially the second part, arises from the lack of reliable written accounts. Cassius Dio's later and most valuable books (except 79 and 80), which covered his own times, are preserved only in epitomes and fragments. Valuable information about the period from 180 to 238 is contained in the eight extant books of Herodian's contemporary history and the late-fourth-century *Historia Augusta,* but the biographies of emperors after 235 in the latter work are more romantic fiction than history. Minor relevant historical works from the fourth century include biographies like Aurelius Victor's *Caesares* and the anonymous *Epitome de Caesaribus* and brief histories of Rome like those of Eutropius and Festus (p. 471). In the late fifth or early sixth century, Zosimus, a pagan Greek, covered events from 270 to 410 in an account called the *New History.* Unfortunately, the first of its six books is missing the section on Diocletian.

Syriac sources are increasingly important for the period. They include such secular writings as the *Letter of Mara bar Serapion* and several chronicles. Syriac Christian writings such as the *Oration of Meliton the Philosopher before Antoninus Caesar,* the *Acts of Thomas,* and several martyrologies are particularly valuable.

Greek and Latin Christian writers also became more numerous and important during the third century and have supplied much information not only on the history and doctrinal controversies of the expanding Christian Church but on secular affairs as well. Among the Latin Christian authors, the most notable in this period are Tertullian and St. Cyprian (pp. 411–412). Tertullian's works reveal much about the social life of the period. St. Cyprian's works are particularly valuable for the history

of the persecution of Christians that occurred in the 250s and the Donatist controversy over Christians who denied their religion during the persecution and then wanted to be taken back by the faithful afterward. Also valuable for this period are St. Jerome's *De Viris Illustribus* (On Famous Men) and his translation and extension of Eusebius' *Chronicle* (p. 416).

Of the contemporary Greek Church Fathers, Clement of Alexandria and Origen stand out (pp. 411–412). They document the growth of Christian theology and provide unusual glimpses into the pagan Greek mysteries that they combated. Eusebius of Caesarea in Palestine (ca. 260 to ca. 340) produced two historical works that are valuable in reconstructing the third century. The original Greek version of his chronicle of events from Abraham to A.D. 327/28 is lost, but its substance is preserved in an Armenian translation and in Jerome's similar work based largely on it. Fortunately, his *Ecclesiastical History* is intact and is an invaluable general account of the growth of the early Church in the Empire.

Preserved in Justinian's *Corpus Iuris Civilis* are numerous fragments of third-century legal works, which, together with coins, papyri, inscriptions, and archaeological material, are all excellent primary sources. Although these sources have not yet been fully explored or interpreted, they constitute the bulk of information about the third century and are constantly throwing new light upon it. Increasing interest in local archaeology throughout countries once embraced by the Roman Empire has also produced a better understanding of defensive policies and the social and economic conditions of the provinces.

Commodus (180 to 192)

Marcus Aurelius, faced with no viable alternative to allowing his nineteen-year-old son Commodus to succeed him (p. 343), had tried to ensure the continuation of sound leadership by creating a coterie of good advisors close to the throne. For example, he married Commodus' sister Lucilla to Claudius Pompeianus, one of his own most trusted advisors. Unfortunately, they disagreed. Some, like Pompeianus, wanted him to finish his father's great war with the Quadi and the Marcomanni. Others, whether out of conviction or desire to advance in the new emperor's favor or both, advised him to follow the easier path of negotiating a settlement and returning to Rome.

This move seems completely irresponsible at first sight, but a negotiated settlement had much to recommend itself. The war had already placed a great strain on Imperial resources, the Roman army had been weakened by plague, and although a border based on the Elbe River and the Carpathian Mountains did have some strategic advantages over the longer Rhine-Danube line, it would greatly extend the Empire's lines of supply through territory that would take a long time and many troops to pacify adequately.

Moreover, Commodus and those to whom he listened did follow certain well-established precedents in setting terms, which the Quadi and the Marcomanni readily accepted. The latter agreed to surrender Roman deserters and captives, create a demilitarized zone along the Danube, furnish troops to the Roman army, and help feed that army with annual contributions of grain. This settlement was reasonable and produced stability along the Danube for many years. In abandoning Aurelius' scheme of conquest, Commodus also could point to the example of Hadrian, who had wisely abandoned Trajan's expansionistic plans despite objections from Trajan's old advisors.

Unfortunately, the young and inexperienced Commodus was no Hadrian. Once at Rome, he increasingly abandoned himself to physical pleasures, which are predictably exaggerated in the sources but which became more numerous, probably at the urging of those who curried favor and sought to avoid his interference by steering him along a path of self-indulgence. Although he outraged the upper-class sense of propriety by publicly appearing in staged lion and tiger hunts in the Colosseum and calling himself Hercules, he delighted the crowd by his feats. Supposedly he could hit the neck of an ostrich with a javelin at fifty paces, but he exhausted the treasury by his extravagances. Furthermore, he delegated important responsibilities to various favorites, whom he murdered as soon as he tired of them.

As early as 182, a number of senators conspired with Commodus' sister Lucilla to assassinate the irresponsible leader whom they detested and feared to be undermining the Empire. The plot failed, however, and the emperor naturally became fearful, suspicious, and vindictive. Under the guidance of such schemers as the Praetorian Prefect Perennis, who himself was executed for treason in 185, Commodus produced another reign of terror among the aristocracy and courtiers. The accelerating cycle of corruption, extravagance, and terror finally led to a successful plot to strangle him in his bath on the last day of 192.

Pertinax and Didius Julianus, 193 Just as Domitian's assassins had carefully arranged to provide the elderly Nerva as his successor, so Commodus' assassins had arranged for the elderly senator Pertinax, a successful *novus homo* from Africa, who had been influential under Aurelius. He was quickly approved by the Praetorian Guard and by a grateful senate and populace, both of whom condemned Commodus' memory. Pertinax attempted to restore order and refill the treasury. He reduced taxes, granted full possession and ten years' remission of taxes to occupiers of war-torn and plague-depopulated land, and put up for sale the luxuries that Commodus had accumulated in his palace.

Unfortunately, he made two serious mistakes. By selling off high offices to raise needed money, he alienated many senators who had been offended by the practice under Commodus. Also, like Galba after Nero, Pertinax alienated the Praetorian Guard by failing to make promised payments and by his attempt to make the guardsmen submit to strict discipline. Several hundred guardsmen marched on the palace and murdered him. The guardsmen thereupon auctioned off the throne to a fabulously rich senator, M. Didius Julianus, who promised each man the sum of 25,000 sesterces. Helpless, the senate confirmed the nomination.

Goaded to action by this outrageous affront to the august Imperial office, the populace of Rome assailed Julianus with vile names and pelted him with stones as he made his way in and out of his palace under armed escort. Then they thronged into the Circus, where they passed a resolution calling upon Pescennius Niger, the governor of Syria, to rise in arms and seize the throne. The legions of Syria saluted the governor as emperor. Simultaneously, the armies of Britain and the Danube declared for their respective commanders, Clodius Albinus and Septimius Severus, and made a dash for Rome. Septimius got there first and with boldness and decision seized the throne. At first Julianus attempted to resist Severus and then to negotiate, but deserted by the praetorians who had sold him the throne and deposed by the senate, he sought refuge in the palace, where a guardsman murdered him.

The Accession of Septimius Severus

Septimius Severus, born in 146 at Lepcis (Leptis) Magna, a town not far from modern Tripoli (ancient Oea), was the second native of Africa to hold the throne, proof of the growing importance of the provinces. He had enjoyed an active career: a student of literature and philosophy in Athens, a lawyer in Rome, a tribune of the people, a praetor in Spain, and governor of Gallia Lugdunensis and finally of Pannonia. Although he spoke Latin with a Punic accent, he was well educated and loved the company of poets and philosophers. His first wife had died without producing any children. His second was a rich and shrewd Syrian woman named Julia Domna, who bore him two sons—Caracalla and Geta.

Severus moved swiftly to consolidate his power. He seized the various treasuries, restocked the depleted granaries of the city, and avenged the murder of Pertinax, whose name he assumed. He increased the pay of his own troops to make sure of their continued loyalty and disbanded the Italian Praetorian Guard. He then replaced it with 15,000 of his best legionary soldiers, largely from Illyria and Thrace. The change in the composition of the Guard helped to remove the special privileges of Italy in the choosing of emperors and in the government of the Empire.

The War against Pescennius Niger, 193 to 194

Severus thereupon set about dealing with one rival at a time. He temporarily acknowledged Clodius Albinus in Britain as his adopted successor with the title of Caesar in order to secure his rear as he advanced east against Niger. Niger had meanwhile won the support of Roman Asia and Egypt and had seized Byzantium as a base from which he could threaten the Danubian provinces of Severus. In a swift and savage campaign, Severus defeated Niger and captured Antioch. Niger was overtaken and killed as he attempted to escape to the Parthians across the Euphrates.

First War against Parthia, 194 to 195

After Niger's defeat and death, Severus attacked Parthia, whose king, Vologeses IV, had not only offered assistance to Niger but had tampered with the loyalty and allegiance of the king of Osrhoene, a Roman client in northwestern Mesopotamia. In 194 and 195, Severus overran Osrhoene, northern Mesopotamia, and Adiabene (northwestern Iraq). Here the campaign came to an abrupt end. At the other end of the Empire, Albinus had amassed an army in Britain for the conflict with Septimius.

Albinus had been growing suspicious of the emperor's sincerity in acknowledging him as Caesar and successor. Supported by a large following in the senate, he decided to make a bid for supreme power. To enforce his claim, he crossed over into Gaul and set up headquarters at Lugdunum (Lyons). It is no coincidence that he received considerable support in Gaul, Spain, and Germany as well as Britain against Severus, who was closely tied to Africa, the Danubian provinces, and Asia Minor. Severus hastened west, and the two fought a furious battle that ended in the defeat and suicide of Albinus. Severus allowed his victorious troops to sack and burn the city of Lugdunum and carried out a ruthless extermination of the adherents of Albinus in the provinces and in the Roman senate.

New Sources of Imperial Authority and Legitimacy

Although Septimius had arrived in Rome at the head of an army in 193, he had tried to conciliate and cooperate with the senate in order to legitimize his claim to the throne against his rivals. He had already taken the name of Pertinax so that he could pose as the avenger of the previously slain senatorial appointee. In Rome, he had donned civilian dress and had sworn to the senators that he would never execute a senator without a trial by his peers. He also had promised not to encourage the use of informers.

Septimius had little chance to prove himself. Many in the senate either distrusted him or, because he had been born a provincial of only equestrian rank, disliked him. Clodius Albinus had been much more acceptable to them because he was of the hereditary nobility and had served faithfully under Marcus Aurelius, a scrupulous protector of senatorial prestige. By obviously promoting the fortunes of Albinus they had inevitably provoked Septimius' wrath. Therefore, after he had secured the East against Pescennius Niger and Parthia, Septimius dropped the policy of conciliation with the senate and formally relied on the army as his principal source of authority in establishing himself and his family as a new dynasty at Rome.

In the past, the army had been used to force the senate, which was still the recognized source of legitimate authority, to authorize the appointment of a new emperor. Septimius, however, went a long way to making the army the recognized source of authority instead. For example, in 195 he had the army in Mesopotamia declare Albinus a public enemy in order to legitimize the war against him. In the same year, he also had the army ratify his adoption into the family of Marcus Aurelius, the Antonines, and proclaim the deification of his "brother" Commodus. (Because the senate itself had condemned the memory of Commodus, he also forced it to revoke its previous action.) In 195 or 196, he also had the army proclaim his elder son, Septimius Bassianus (Caracalla), as Caesar in place of Clodius Albinus and bestow the name Marcus Aurelius Antoninus upon him in order to emphasize the family's new Antonine pedigree.

This pedigree not only legitimized the claim of Septimius and his sons to the throne through dynastic succession but also allowed Septimius to claim the support of divinity for himself and his family, because he was now the "son" and "brother" of deified emperors. Along with publicizing numerous omens and portents foretelling his accession to the throne, Septimius officially reinforced his claims to divine sanction through coins, inscriptions, and the Imperial cult. In the military camps, the statues of Septimius and other members of his family were worshipped as the *domus divina* (Divine House). Septimius unofficially came to be called *dominus* (lord), a title with increasingly divine overtones. On one coin, his younger son, P. Septimius Geta, is depicted as the sun god crowned with rays, giving a benediction, and identified as "Son of Severus the Unconquered, Pius Augustus," a designation that recalls the Unconquered Sun, an increasingly popular deity. Severus' wife, Julia Domna, is portrayed as the Great Mother Cybele on some coins and on others as seated on the throne of Juno, Mother of the Augusti, Mother of the Senate, or Mother of the Fatherland (*Mater Patriae*). Severus is also referred to in inscriptions as a *numen praesens* (present spirit), and dedications were made to him as a *numen,* clear indications of his divinity.

Systematic Reform

Having defeated Albinus and clearly established new bases of Imperial authority and legitimacy, Septimius Severus initiated the most comprehensive series of changes in the Roman government since the reign of Augustus. Up to his time, many changes had occurred, but they had been subtle and evolutionary. What Severus did was often in line with changes that had been gradually occurring, but he was the first to give them formal expression, and he was revolutionary in ruthlessly following their implications to create a clearly new system that gave an entirely different spirit to the Principate.

Major Downgrading of the Senate

With his rivals out of the way, Severus took his revenge on the senate. He revoked its right to try its own members and condemned 29 of them for treason in supporting Albinus. He also appointed many new members, particularly from Africa and the East, who would be loyal to him, so that Italian senators became a minority. Moreover, he favored *equites* of military background over senators in administrative appointments as deputy governors in senatorial provinces and used as temporary replacements when regular senatorial governors became ill or died. When he added 3 new legions to the army, he put equestrian prefects instead of senatorial legates in command. He also abolished the senatorially staffed standing jury courts (*quaestiones perpetuae*) and placed cases formerly heard by them under the jurisdiction of the city prefect (*praefectus urbi*) within a 100-mile radius of Rome and the praetorian prefect (*praefectus praetorio*) everywhere else.

As the result of a process of evolution dating back to Augustus, the senate had become simply a sounding board of policies formulated by the *princeps* and his Imperial Council, which had now become the true successor of the old Republican senate. Since its inception the Council had grown in membership and now included not only many of the leading senators and equestrians but also the best legal minds of the age—Papinian and, later, Ulpian and Paul.

The powers of the praetorian prefect were greatly increased: He was in charge of the grain supply, was commander-in-chief of all armed forces stationed in Italy, and was vice-president of the Imperial Council, now the supreme court of the Empire and its highest policy-making body. From 197 to 205, the senior prefect was C. Fulvius Plautianus, a man of extreme ambition, arrogance, and cruelty, who wielded almost autocratic power because of his overpowering personality and his influence over the emperor. He finally fell from favor and was assassinated. The next senior prefect was the distinguished jurist, Papinian.

Fiscal Reforms

The confiscations of property belonging to political enemies in both East and West were so enormous that Severus created the *res privata principis* (the private property of the *princeps*), a new treasury department separate and distinct from the *fiscus* (the regular Imperial treasury) and from the *patrimonium Caesaris*. The new treasury, administered by a procurator, gave the emperor stronger control not only over the fiscal administration of the Empire but also over the army, whose annual base pay he raised from 300 to 400 *denarii* per man. Popular with the soldiers, this increase was also necessary in order to compensate for the inflation that had raged since the reign of Commodus. The resulting need for more coins forced Severus to reduce the silver content of the *denarius* to about 56 percent by the end of his reign. Although that ultimately increased inflationary pressure, it temporarily produced a revival of economic prosperity and a fairly respectable surplus in the treasury.

Legal Reforms

Several legal reforms under Septimius were already implicit in those under Hadrian, especially in the jurist Julianus' revision of the *Perpetual Edict*. The major Severan reform was the already mentioned abolition of the regular standing jury courts of Republican times and the transfer of their cases to the jurisdiction of the urban prefect and the praetorian prefect. Another significant Severan innovation, however, was the introduction of different scales of punishment for the two social classes into which the citizen body was now divided—the *honestiores*, consisting of senators, *equites*, all municipal magistrates, and soldiers of all ranks; and the *humiliores*, the lower orders. A privileged person might be exiled or cleanly executed, an underprivileged one sentenced to hard labor in the mines or thrown to the beasts for the same crime. Furthermore, *honestiores* had the right of appeal to the emperor; *humiliores* did not.

Provincial Administration In general, the provincial policy of Septimius Severus was a corollary to that of Hadrian and the Antonines, who had begun to make the status of the provinces equal to that of Italy. Severus continued this policy mainly because of political and dynastic motives. His disbanding of the Italian Praetorian Guard, his stationing of a newly created legion in Italy, and his appointment of Near Eastern and African senators had been measures undertaken principally to consolidate his regime. Although he spent money liberally in Rome and Italy on public works, on the feeding and amusement of the Roman populace, and on the resumption of the public alimentary and educational program (which Commodus had suspended), he spent equally vast amounts in Africa and Syria. Thus the Severan regime saw the consummation of earlier policies leading to a balance, equalization, and fusion of the various geographical and cultural elements of the Greco-Roman world under the leadership of the emperors.

At the same time, Septimius had to prevent the dangerous concentration of power in the hands of provincial governors who might prove as dangerous as Pescennius Niger and Clodius Albinus. He followed the policy of Augustus, Trajan, and Hadrian and partitioned large legion-filled provinces. He divided Syria and Britain each into two separate provinces and detached Numidia from Africa to create smaller provinces and correspondingly weaker provincial governors.

Military Reforms Owing his power entirely to the soldiers and genuinely concerned to provide adequate defense, Septimius made significant improvements to the army, not only by increasing its size from thirty to thirty-three legions but also by making army life as attractive as possible. He allowed junior officers to organize social clubs, to which all contributed for drinks, entertainment, and financial insurance during service and after discharge. He legalized marriages between soldiers defending the Empire's frontiers and native women living near forts and encampments. Thus he abolished anomalous marriages long in existence, but not officially countenanced. The Praetorian Guard, though no longer composed solely of Italians, western provincials, and Macedonians, continued to be an elite corps trained in the best Roman tradition and renowned as a training school for future army officers.

In his reorganization of the army, Severus began to replace senatorial commanders with *equites,* who were often ex-centurions promoted from the ranks. The commanders of his three new legions were no longer senatorial *legati* but equestrian prefects with the rank of *legatus,* some of them eligible for provincial governorships. Severus democratized the army by making it possible for a common soldier of ability and initiative to pass from centurion on to the rank of tribune, prefect, and *legatus,* and eventually to the high office of praetorian prefect, if not emperor. Even ordinary veterans became a privileged class rewarded with good jobs in civilian posts after discharge. While raising the pay of the legionaries, he also permanently leased lands from the Imperial estate to certain auxiliary units, who thus became a permanent peasant militia in their sector of the frontier.

The Second Parthian War, 197 to 199 In foreign policy, Septimius adhered closely to his predecessors. He continued the historic war (interrupted under Hadrian and Antoninus Pius) against the Parthian Empire without realizing that such a policy had become untenable and even dangerous in view of changed world conditions. He was unaware that the steppes of central Asia had for centuries been the spawning ground for migrating Huns and other tribal groups who would one day descend like an avalanche upon both the Roman Empire and its neighbors. The resources and manpower of the Empire, though huge, were inadequate for waging war simultaneously against migrating tribes and the Parthians. Another dangerous consequence of the Severan resumption of war against Parthia was the continued weakening of the feeble and ineffectual Arsacid dynasty, which had held sway over Parthia ever since 238 B.C., and its final overthrow by A.D. 227.

The War in Britain, 208 to 211 In the last years of his reign, Septimius, accompanied by Julia Domna and their sons, Caracalla and Geta, led an expedition into the heart of Scotland but failed in his attempt to bring the natives to battle. They resorted instead to guerrilla tactics and inflicted heavy losses upon the Roman army. Despite the losses and the apparent failure of the whole campaign, Septimius achieved important results: The display of Roman power and the thorough reconstruction of Hadrian's Wall effectively discouraged future invasions of England from the north and gave Britain almost a century of peace. Septimius, however, was not to see Rome again: He died at Eburacum (York) in 211. According to Dio, Severus on his deathbed advised Caracalla and Geta to "agree with each other, enrich the soldiers, and despise everyone else." Probably these words are rhetorical inventions, but they are significant in their emphasis upon favoring the military and their contrast with the failure of his heirs to work together.

Caracalla (211 to 217) With Septimius dead, Caracalla and Geta together ascended the throne, but their attempt at joint rule proved hopeless because of their long-standing mutual jealousy. Each lived in mortal dread of the other until Caracalla treacherously lured Geta to their mother's apartment and there murdered him, supposedly in his mother's very arms. Afterward, he carried out a pitiless extermination of Geta's supposed friends and supporters, among them the illustrious jurist and Praetorian Prefect Papinian. To silence the murmurs of the soldiers over Geta's killing, he increased their basic pay from 400 to 600 *denarii,* an expenditure that exhausted the treasury and compelled him to raise more revenue by doubling the tax on inheritances and the manumission of slaves and by continuing to reduce the weight and fineness (ratio of precious to base metal) of coins. He issued a new coin called the *Antoninianus,* supposedly a double *denarius* but actually not double in weight. He also earned the undying hatred of many nobles by continuing his father's policy of downgrad-

ing the importance of the senate while favoring the soldiers and the provincials.

Caracalla, who got his commonly used nickname from a long Gallic cape that he used to wear, was a fairly good soldier and strategist and had some of the instincts of the statesman. The most historic act of his reign was the extension of citizenship in 212 to all free inhabitants of the Empire, the culmination of a process initiated by Julius Caesar. By his promulgation of the famous *Constitutio Antoniniana,* Caracalla obliterated all distinction between Italians and provincials, between conquerors and conquered, between urban and rural dwellers, and between those who possessed Greco-Roman culture and those who did not. Henceforth, every free inhabitant of the Roman Empire was a Roman citizen and, of course, a Roman taxpayer.

Another manifestation of Caracalla's statesmanship was his proposal of marriage to the daughter of Artabanus V of Parthia in order to bring to pass his dream of uniting the Roman and Parthian empires. He hoped that the two great civilizing powers might present a common front to the less civilized tribes beyond the frontiers, but it is difficult to see how either the Roman or Persian aristocracy would have tolerated such an arrangement.

German and Parthian Wars Attempts at diplomacy notwithstanding, Caracalla spent the major part of his reign fighting wars and proved himself a real soldier emperor: He ate and marched with his men and helped them dig trenches, build bridges, and fight battles. In 213, he proceeded to the Raetian *limes* to attack the Alemanni, a formidable but newly organized confederacy of mixed resident and displaced Germanic tribes that had migrated westward and settled along the right bank of the upper Rhine. After decisively defeating them at the river Main, he built and restored forts, repaired roads and bridges, and extended a 105-mile stone wall from 6 to 9 feet high and 4 feet thick along the Raetian frontier, which successfully withstood numerous assaults for the next 20 years.

After similarly strengthening the defenses in Pannonia and along the lower Danube, Caracalla proceeded to the East. He brutally suppressed an uprising in Alexandria and resumed the war against Parthia. In 216, he marched across Adiabene and invaded Media, but after sacking several fortified places, he withdrew to winter quarters at Edessa. There he made preparations to mount a more vigorous offensive the following spring, but he did not live to witness the consummation of his plans. On April 8, 217, while traveling from Edessa to Carrhae to worship at the temple of the Moon, he was stabbed to death at the instigation of the Praetorian Prefect M. Opellius Macrinus.

Macrinus (217 to 218)

As ringleader of the plot against Caracalla, Macrinus secured the acclamation of the army and ascended the throne. He was a Mauretanian by birth, an *eques* in rank, and the first *princeps* without prior membership in the senate to reach the throne. To affiliate himself with the Severan dynasty, he adopted the name of Severus, bestowed that of Antoninus upon his young son Diadumenianus, and even ordered the senate to proclaim Caracalla a god. Realizing that he needed some military prestige to hold the loyalty of the army, he continued the war with Parthia but proved to be a poor general. After a few minor successes and two major defeats, he lost the respect of the army by his agreement to surrender to the Parthians the prisoners whom he had captured and to pay a large indemnity. This inglorious settlement, together with his unwise decision to reduce the pay for new recruits and the opposition of Severus' family, ultimately cost him his life and throne.

Impressive Syrian Queens

Through his second marriage, Septimius Severus was connected with a family of remarkable Syrian women who actively sought a leading role in Imperial politics. His wife, Julia Domna, and her sister, Julia Maesa, were well educated, shrewd, and tough. Their father was the high priest of the sun god Elagabalus (Heliogabalus)

at the Arabian city of Emesa (Homs) in Syria and probably was descended from its old royal house. They were accustomed to power and influence. Domna had enjoyed great influence at the beginning of Severus' reign but had been outmaneuvered for a time by the ambitious Praetorian Prefect Plautianus and had devoted herself to creating a circle of influential intellectuals. She was able to recover her former strength after the fall of Plautianus, to which she had probably contributed through Caracalla, and she had accompanied Severus to Britain in 208. After his death she had tried to promote the interests of her more even-tempered son, Geta, but failing to prevent his murder, she had made the best of it with Caracalla. She accompanied Caracalla to Antioch on his Parthian expedition in 215 and died there soon after his assassination. Macrinus then forced her sister, Maesa, to retire to Syria.

In Syria, Maesa plotted to restore her family's Imperial fortunes. She had gone back to Emesa with her two daughters, Julia Soaemias and Julia Mamaea. There, Varius Avitus, the fourteen-year-old son of Soaemias, had inherited the high priesthood of the sun god Elagabalus and he himself came to be known by that name as emperor.

Elagabalus (218 to 222)

Knowing how the army cherished the memory of Caracalla, Maesa concocted the rumor that Varius Avitus was the natural son of Caracalla and, therefore, was a real Severus. She presented him to the legions of Syria, who, further convinced by the offer of a large donative, saluted him as emperor under the name of Marcus Aurelius Antoninus. Macrinus, deserted by most of his troops and defeated in battle, fled but was later hunted down and killed.

A year later, wearing a purple silk robe, rouge on his cheeks, a necklace of pearls, and a bejeweled crown, Elagabalus arrived in Rome. He had brought from Emesa a conical black stone—the cult image of the god Elagabalus—which he enshrined in an ornate temple on the Palatine and worshiped with un-Roman sexual practices (which probably have been exaggerated in the retelling by hostile and sensationalistic sources) and outlandish rites to the accompaniment of drums, cymbals, and anthems sung by Syrian women. What shocked the Roman public even more than any of these strange rites was his endeavor to make that Syrian sun god the supreme deity of the Roman state.

In order to devote more time to his priestly duties and (in Roman eyes) scandalous ceremonies, Elagabalus entrusted most of the business of government to his grandmother and appointed his favorites to the highest public offices—a professional dancer, for example, as praetorian prefect, a charioteer as head of the night watch (*vigiles*), and a barber as prefect of the grain supply (*annona*). Maesa, realizing that the un-Roman conduct of Elagabalus would lead to his downfall and the ruin of the Severan family, tactfully suggested that he ought to adopt Gessius Bassianus Alexianus, her grandson by Julia Mamaea, as Caesar and heir to the throne. When Elagabalus saw that Alexianus, whom he adopted under the name of Marcus Aurelius Severus Alexander, was preferred by the senate and the people, he regretted his decision and twice attempted to get rid of the boy.

Maesa and Mamaea appealed to the Praetorian Guards, who were happy to hunt down Elagabalus and his mother, Soaemias. They seized the two in their hiding place—a latrine—, cut off their heads, and dragged the corpses through the streets to the Aemilian bridge. There they tied weights to them and hurled them into the Tiber.

Severus Alexander (222 to 235)

The accession of Severus Alexander was greeted with rejoicing. Although he was studious, talented, and industrious, he was only fourteen, and his domineering mother, Mamaea, held the reins of power. She was virtually, even to the end of his reign, the empress of Rome.

The reign of Alexander marked the revival of the prestige, if not the power, of the senate, whose support Mamaea enlisted in order to strengthen the arm of the civil government in controlling the unruly and mutinous armies. She accordingly set up a council of sixteen prominent senators to exercise at least a nominal regency, though actually, perhaps, to serve only in an advisory capacity. Senators also probably held a majority in the enlarged Imperial Council. The president of both councils was the praetorian prefect, normally of equestrian rank, but now elevated while in office to senatorial status in order that he might sit as judge in trials involving senators without impairing the dignity of the defendants. At this time, the praetorian prefect was the distinguished jurist Domitius Ulpianus. Thus the new regime not only enhanced the dignity of the senate but also enlarged the powers of the praetorian prefect at the expense of the old executive offices. Under Severus Alexander, the tribunes of the plebs and aediles ceased to be appointed.

Social and Economic Policy The government seems to have tried to win the good will and support of the civilian population by providing honest and efficient administration. It reduced taxes and authorized the construction of new baths, aqueducts, libraries, and roads. It subsidized teachers and scholars and lent money without interest to enable poor people to purchase farms. One major reform was the provision of primary school education all over the Empire, even in the villages of Egypt. Another was the legalization, under government supervision and control, of all guilds or colleges (*collegia*) having to do with the supply of foodstuffs and essential services to the city of Rome. Under this category fell wine and oil merchants, bakers, and shoemakers. In return the guilds enjoyed special tax favors and exemptions and the benefit of legal counsel at public expense.

The Military Problem The fatal weakness of Alexander's regime was its failure to control the armies. In 228, the Praetorian Guard mutinied and murdered, in the emperor's palace itself, their prefect, Domitius Ulpianus, because he seemed too strict. The soldiers in Mesopotamia mutinied and murdered their commander. Another excellent disciplinarian, the historian Cassius Dio, would have suffered the same fate had not Alexander whisked him off to his homeland of Bithynia.

Never had the need for disciplined armies been greater. Rome's recent wars with Parthia had so weakened the decrepit Arsacid regime that it was overthrown between 224 and 227 by the aggressive Sassanid dynasty of Ardashir (Artaxerxes) I (A.D. 224 to 241) and his son Shapur (Sapor) I (A.D. 241 to 272), who sought to reestablish the old Persian Empire of the Achaemenid dynasty (ca. 560 to 330 B.C.). By 331, Ardashir had already overrun Mesopotamia and was threatening the provinces of Syria and Cappadocia. After a futile diplomatic effort, Alexander himself had to go to the East. He planned and executed a massive three-pronged attack that should have ensured a decisive victory, but, because of poor generalship and excessive caution, it resulted only in heavy losses on both sides and produced nothing more than a stalemate at best. Alexander returned to Rome to celebrate a splendid but dubious triumph in 233.

Meanwhile, the Alemanni and other German tribes had broken through the Roman defenses and were pouring into Gaul and Raetia. Accompanied by his mother, Alexander hurried north in 134. After some early successes, he followed his mother's suggestion and bought peace from the Germans with a subsidy. His men, who would have preferred to use some of that money themselves, were disgusted. Under the leadership of a Thracian named Gaius Iulius Verus Maximinus (Maximinus Thrax), commander of the Pannonian legions, they mutinied in 235 and killed both Alexander and his mother. Thus they terminated the Severan dynasty and ushered in almost a half century of civil wars that were made more intractable by such problems as Severus Alexander had faced on the borders of the Empire.

The Importance of the Severi The Severi had been responding to a number of circumstances that made necessary many of the things that they tried to do, however one may wish to criticize the manner in which they often acted. The greatest task facing any emperor by this time was defense of the frontiers. Therefore, it was necessary for an effective emperor to spend much of his time with the frontier armies. To protect both himself and the Empire, he had to secure the favor and loyalty of the troops more than the senate.

Nor was it any longer practical or fair for the senatorial class and Italy to enjoy privileged positions within the Empire. The provinces now provided the bulk of Roman manpower and bore most of the expense for defending the frontier. Broadening the outlook of the senate to an empire-wide perspective by admitting many new provincials was useful, but even that was not enough to meet Imperial needs. Despite reaching 900 members under the Severi, the senate was still too small to provide the large number of capable officers and administrators that an empire the size of Rome's needed. To provide more personnel it was necessary either to increase the size of the senate further by the wholesale admission of *equites* or to use more *equites* directly as officers and administrators. In either case, the hereditary senators would have resented their corresponding loss of exclusivity and would have opposed any change.

Finally, with the rising importance of the provincials in the army and civilian bureaucracy, it was no longer possible to maintain Imperial unity through the figure of the emperor as a Roman magistrate. In an Empire dominated by the Roman citizens of Italy, who had shared the political culture of the old Republic, that was a useful role for the emperor. For the most part, however, the provincials did not share that political culture, nor was there any other secular role that would have sanctioned the emperor's dominant position on an empire-wide scale. The only universally acceptable sanction was the religious one of the emperor's divinity, which could be accommodated easily in the religious outlook of all but a few extraordinary rationalists in a basically religious age and the relatively small sects of the Christians and Jews.

XXXII

The Third-Century Anarchy, A.D. 235 to 285

The murder of Severus Alexander in 235 ushered in fifty years of unprecedented crisis for the Roman Empire. The frontiers were under repeated attack. The office of emperor became a football tossed back and forth among a bewildering number of usurpers. Whole regions broke away under their own emperors, and the Empire seemed about to disintegrate completely. Many painful, long-term adjustments had to be made before order could be restored and the Empire preserved for the future.

Reasons for the Crisis   Many interrelated factors combined to create this crisis. A number of them had existed for some time and had been the reasons for Septimius Severus' efforts to make fundamental changes in the Imperial system. Others were more recent. The combination was almost lethal.

The Failure of the Severan Dynasty   One of the major factors was the failure of the Severi to produce another emperor of Septimius' stature. Under increasing stresses and strains, there was no one person powerful enough to maintain firm control over the whole in the face of regional needs and interests. Therefore, the crisis was intensified by numerous civil wars between regionally backed rivals for the throne.

Internal Tensions   Septimius Severus had grasped the essential need to eliminate the dominant position of the senate and Italy in order to create a stronger, truly united Empire in accordance with geopolitical reality. Unfortunately, the integration that he had promoted had not yet been completed. Jealous in protecting their prestige and privileges, many traditionally minded senators and Italians worked to undermine emperors of equestrian and provincial origin, whom they had had no hand in making. Because, however, they did not have the military power to protect their nominees, all that they succeeded in doing was creating more chaos.

Interregional jealousies were just as bad. The legions and inhabitants of one province or group of provinces often believed that an emperor who came from another part of the Empire was not paying enough attention to their problems. Therefore, they often rebelled and set up an emperor who would look after their needs. For example, the Pannonian legions, to whom the northern frontiers were a special concern, had mutinied against the Syrian Severus Alexander because in their eyes he had shown weakness in dealing with the invading Germans.

Defensive System and Increased Pressure on the Frontiers   Rome's system of frontier defense essentially went back to Hadrian, who had formalized a policy of static defense, with units stationed in fixed camps all along the frontiers. Septimius had increased its fixed and static nature by allowing the legionary troops to marry legally and by encouraging auxiliary units to take up farming in the countryside surrounding their camps, so that they became a peasant militia. So long as the level of attacks on the frontiers remained relatively low or infrequent, this system could work. Local units could handle small-scale incursions, and if a major threat occurred in one sector, units could be called up temporarily from others to mount a major campaign.

In the second half of the third century, this system clearly was no longer effective. Not only did the level and frequency of hostile incursions along the Rhine and the Danube increase, but Rome was faced with the active belligerence of the new Sassanid Persian dynasty on the eastern frontier. Throughout much of the period, in effect, Roman emperors confronted every military strategist's nightmare, major simultaneous wars on two fronts. Meeting an emergency on one front by summoning troops from another merely invited a dangerous attack on the second. Knowing that, the men who had become closely attached to their areas because of permanent marriages and settlement were reluctant to leave the fronts entrusted to their care to fight on another. Thus, they often backed their local commanders as emperors in the hope of securing greater Imperial concern for their region.

Shortage of Manpower and Money

The only way in which the system of static defense could have been made to work in the face of mounting pressure on all fronts would have been to increase dramatically the size of the army, particularly in the number of well-trained and well-equipped legionary troops. As Augustus had long ago realized, however, the Imperial economy could not easily support more than twenty-eight or thirty legions, and even he had left the number at about twenty-five after the loss of Varus' three legions in A.D. 9. The number of permanent legions had not reached thirty until Marcus Aurelius, and Septimius had raised it to thirty-three. To have exceeded that number would have had a negative impact on the economy both by requiring an excessive burden of taxes and by drawing away vital manpower as well.

This problem was made even worse by a declining supply of precious metals for coinage and an imbalance in foreign trade. It was compounded by the outbreak of a devastating plague in the middle of the third century. Therefore, in order to have met the Empire's defensive needs, it would have been necessary to develop either new defensive strategies or new sources of revenue and manpower or both. Such tasks would have been difficult under the best of circumstances. In light of all the other complications that the Empire faced, they were almost impossible. It took fifty brutal years just to stabilize the situation.

Maximinus Thrax (235 to 238)

Having led the mutiny against Alexander Severus in 235, Gaius Julius Verus Maximinus, otherwise known as Maximinus Thrax (the Thracian), became emperor. Although he was hardly the ignorant peasant depicted in the *Historia Augusta,* he had come from the ranks, and the soldiers under his command feared, respected, and admired him. He knew their moods and aspirations, and he doubled their pay after they had saluted him as emperor. They followed him deep into Germany, defeated the Germans near Württemberg, and took thousands of prisoners and vast quantities of booty. After defeating the Sarmatians, Dacians, and perhaps even the Goths on the lower Danube, Maximinus laid plans for the total conquest of Germany.

The chief problem facing Maximinus was that of obtaining money to pay his troops. He sent his collectors all over the Empire. They plundered all classes, especially the rich. One particularly ruthless procurator created a violent reaction in North Africa. Big landowners, faced with the loss of their estates, fomented rebellion. They killed the procurator, repudiated Maximinus, and proclaimed the extremely rich but elderly M. Antonius Gordianus as emperor and his son of the same name as joint-emperor. The senators, many of them Africans appointed by the Severi, who had always considered Maximinus a Thracian upstart, hailed the nomination with delight and declared Maximinus a public enemy. When the two Gordians had lost their lives, the younger by falling in battle against Maximinus' governor of Numidia, the elder by suicide, the senate then appointed two of its members, M. Pupienus Maximus and D. Calvinus Balbinus as joint emperors, and the thirteen-year-old Gordian III, a grandson of Gordian I, as Caesar. The rejuvenated senate of Alexander Severus acted with amazing resolution and speed. For a time its prestige was high.

Events in Africa and Italy forced Maximinus to set out on an immediate march against Rome. Finding his way barred at Aquileia by hostile Italian forces, he laid siege to the city but failed to take it. Finally, his own men, starving and desperate, mutinied and killed both Maximinus and his son. They acclaimed the two senatorially appointed emperors, Balbinus and Pupienus, whose arrival in Rome was hailed with delirious joy. The joy did not last. Less than two months after the death of Maximinus, the Praetorian Guard killed the two emperors and acknowledged Gordian III as the new emperor.

Gordian III (238 to 244)

At the accession of the boy emperor, two powerful and dangerous enemies had begun or were about to assail the weakened frontier defenses of the Empire. The Goths were now streaming over the lower Danube and, in alliance with the Sarmatians and the Carpi, were overrunning Moesia and Thrace. In the Near East, the Sassanid Persians were invading the provinces of Mesopotamia and Syria. In 241, the mighty Shapur (Sapor) I was marching toward Antioch on the Orontes.

Rome might well have suffered a disaster of unparalled magnitude had not Gordian III been able to count on the loyalty, experience, and brilliance of his own father-in-law, C. Fu-

rius Timesitheus, the Praetorian Prefect, who was not only a fine army commander but a superb organizer. In 242, they set out from Rome together and, after stabilizing the situation on the Danube, proceeded to Syria, where they relieved Antioch and recovered the Roman provinces. They were on the point of taking the Persian capital of Ctesiphon when Timesitheus died. Then Gordian himself died, apparently after falling from his horse in battle, although another tradition says that the new praetorian prefect, Philip, an Arab sheik from Jordan, took advantage of a threatened food shortage and engineered a mutiny, which resulted in the death of Gordian.

Philip the Arab (244 to 249)

The army accepted Philip as emperor, and he made peace with Shapur (Sapor). New evidence indicates that the peace was neither hasty nor ill-considered. He obtained recognition of Rome's control over the provinces of Lesser Armenia and Mesopotamia and perhaps the ransom of recently taken captives. That freed him to deal with restless tribes along the Danube. After a minor victory over the Dacian Carpi, he returned to Rome in 247 to make preparations for the celebration of Rome's thousandth anniversary.

Although he courted the goodwill of the senate and gave painstaking attention to the government, events were beyond his control. Even during the magnificent festival, the Goths and Carpi were thundering across the Danube. Understandably, the Danubian legions revolted and proclaimed one of their commanders emperor. Two other pretenders appeared in the East. These calamities compelled Philip to send an experienced senator, C. Messius Quintus Decius, to the Danube. After restoring discipline in the army, Decius drove the Goths back over the Danube. Out of respect for him as a disciplinarian and general, the soldiers of the Danubian front saluted Decius as emperor, who promptly marched into Italy against Philip. In 249 a great battle was fought near Verona, during which Philip was defeated and slain. Thus ended the principate of Philip the Arab, the last eastern provincial to occupy the Imperial throne for many years.

Decius (249 to 251)

Meanwhile, the Goths, led by their able king, Kniva, took advantage of the gaps that the absence of Decius and his troops left in the Danubian defenses and poured into Dacia, Lower Moesia, and Thrace. The invasion brought Decius hurrying from Rome. Although he inflicted a severe defeat on one of the Gothic armies, his forces were too weak, his marches too slow, and the support that he received from his sluggish subcommander, C. Vibius Trebonianus Gallus, too dubious and ineffectual to enable him to overtake and destroy the enemy. Finally, in 251, Kniva succeeded in luring Decius into a trap on boggy ground at Abrittus near Adamclisi in the Dobrudja (south of the Danube, along the Black Sea), where the Romans suffered one of the most disastrous defeats in their history. Decius and his son Herennius were slain. Gallus, proclaimed emperor by the soldiers, made a disgraceful treaty with the Goths, which permitted them to return home with all the plunder and high-ranking Roman prisoners that they had captured and guaranteed an annual payment of tribute by Rome.

Few emperors have aroused more controversy in ancient and modern times than Decius. Pagan Latin writers, who usually were prejudiced in favor of the senate, praised Decius highly because he was connected to an old senatorial family on his mother's side and was himself a consular senator who maintained cordial relations with the senate during his reign. In their eyes he was an admirable ruler and a man of boundless energy and iron will. Christian writers have condemned him because he instituted the first systematic persecution of the Christians all over the Empire. Lactantius, for example, called him "an execrable animal." Pagan writers generally justified the persecution on the grounds that the Christians belonged to a subversive organization that refused to recognize the state religion and obstructed the defense of the Empire by preaching peace.

Gallus (251 to 253) and Aemilianus (253)

Trebonianus Gallus legitimized his seizure of the throne by adopting Decius' younger son. He had to deal with a severe outbreak of plague and did not respond adequately to renewed Persian aggression in Syria. Troops on the Danubian frontier proclaimed their commander Aemilius Aemilianus emperor in 253, and Gallus was killed by his own men before he could respond. An old and respected senator named Publius Licinius Valerianus (Valerian), whom Gallus had sent to raise troops in Raetia, was acclaimed by his soldiers and marched on Italy. The murder of Aemilianus quickly cleared the way for Valerian's recognition by the senate and the acceptance of his son, P. Licinius Egnatius Gallienus, as co-emperor.

Valerian (253 to 260) and Gallienus (253 to 268)

The period encompassed by the reigns of Gallienus and his father, Valerian, is often called the Age of Gallienus. It witnessed the culmination of the destructive trends originating in the past and laid the groundwork for future recovery. It began in catastrophe: New invaders were breaking through the shattered and weakly defended frontiers along the Rhine and the Danube. In the Near East the Persians had invaded the provinces of Mesopotamia, Syria, and Cappadocia. Scarcely a province escaped the havoc wrought by invasion: the widespread destruction of property, the sacking and burning of cities, and the massacre and enslavement of citizens.

Pirates infested the seas as in the days before Pompey; bands of robbers and thieves raided the countryside; earthquakes rocked both Italy and Asia Minor. At the height of the devastating invasions, a plague broke out in Egypt and infected the entire Empire, where it raged for more than 15 years. The death toll was staggering: Two thirds of the population of Alexandria died and as many as 5,000 a day in Rome alone. It created a shortage of rural and urban labor and production fell sharply. Worse still, it severely depleted the ranks of the army. The impact of all these blows occurring simultaneously or in rapid succession aggravated the problems that broke the resistance and shattered the unity of the Empire.

The breakdown of Imperial defense increased the localist spirit of the troops on the frontiers. This localist spirit, together with the constant desire for more pay as the shortage of goods drove up prices, increased the number of locally supported usurpers. During the reign of Gallienus alone, eighteen usurpers made vain attempts to seize the throne.

Foreign Affairs Alarming reports from the Near East began to reach Rome. In 252, Shapur (Sapor) I had engineered the assassination of the Roman client king of Armenia and replaced him with his own puppet to open the way for the conquest of Roman Asia Minor. He invaded Mesopotamia and Syria in 253. Shortly after that, the Goths plundered cities along the eastern and southern shores of the Black Sea and began a naval attack upon the coasts of Asia Minor.

The gravity of the situation impelled Valerian to leave Rome, probably in 256, and appear in the East, where he proved utterly incompetent. Despite a few minor skirmishes described on his coinage as major victories, he failed to restore Roman prestige. Frustrated and depressed, he took out his resentment on the Christians and subjected them to a major persecution. Finally, in desperation, he sent his plague-stricken army to meet the main Persian army at Edessa. The results were disastrous to both his army and himself. He fell into the hands of Shapur (Sapor) in 260 and ended his days in captivity, one of the most pathetic figures in Roman history.

Meanwhile Gallienus, constantly at war since 254, had been busy clearing the Alemanni and the Franks out of Gaul and the Rhineland. He beat back further attempts to cross the river, and strengthened Roman fortifications. Farther south, the Marcomanni and the Alemanni, who had been hammering away at the Danubian defenses, broke through and pushed down into Italy. The former had penetrated as far as Ravenna in 254, the latter reached Mediolanum (Milan) four years later. Gallienus first halted the Marcomanni by concluding an alliance with them and granting them land south of the Danube in Upper Pannonia. Then, in 258 and 259, he crushed the Alemanni near Milan. During the next year, he had to suppress two dangerous rebellions in Pannonia, where legions irked by his continued absence on the Rhine had thrown their support first to one pretender then to another.

The situation in the Rhineland had rapidly deteriorated during his brief absence. The Alemanni had crossed the upper Rhine and invaded the Rhone valley and the Auvergne. The Franks had surged over the lower Rhine and overrun Gaul, Spain, and even Mauretania (Morocco). The Saxons and the Jutes, who dwelt along the coasts of Germany and Denmark, had begun roving the seas and raiding the shorelands of Britain and Gaul. Nor was that all. In 259, the legions on the Rhine in fear and desperation mutinied and renounced their allegiance to their absent emperor in favor of Postumus, the general whom Gallienus had left in command of the Rhineland. The armies of Spain and Britain later followed suit.

Gallienus did not recognize the usurpation of Postumus but, hampered by the German and Gothic invasions of the Danubian provinces as well as by the rebellions of other pretenders to the throne, could do no more than compel Postumus to confine himself to the western provinces. Left alone, Postumus drove the Franks and the Alemanni out of Gaul, energetically defended the frontiers, issued his own coinage, and established an efficient administration. Gallienus himself could not have done better.

The Eclipse of Roman Power in the East

After their defeat and capture of Valerian in 260, Shapur and the triumphant Persians plundered Antioch, occupied all of Mesopotamia, overran Cilicia and Cappadocia, and cut across Asia Minor to the Black Sea. They might have occupied all of Asia Minor permanently, had they maintained their military organization. Instead, they broke up into small, isolated looting bands.

All the while Rome was preparing her counterstroke. Macrianus, one of Valerian's old generals, aided by his lieutenant Callistus, had rallied the shattered remnants of Valerian's army. Putting some of the troops aboard transports, Callistus made landings along the Cilician coast, where he surprised and defeated thousands of Persians and captured the king's baggage train together with his harem. That embarrassing loss impelled Shapur to evacuate Asia Minor and retreat to Ctesiphon with all his plunder and hordes of captives. On the way back, he came into conflict on the banks of the Euphrates with an unexpected enemy, Odenathus, the Roman client sheik of Palmyra. That disastrous encounter left Shapur crippled for a long time. To the end of his reign, the war-weary Shapur devoted himself to internal affairs and to his ambitious building projects, whereas he left the future of Asia Minor to Odenathus of Palmyra and Gallienus.

Palmyra Palmyra was an oasis in the Syrian desert. It lay astride the main caravan routes from the Mediterranean to central Asia and to the Persian Gulf. Piled high in its marketplace were such goods from China, India, Persia, and Arabia as textiles, spices, perfumes, jewelry, and precious stones. By the second century, it had become one of the major cities of the Near East with fine wide streets and highways, shady porticoes, stately arches, and magnificent public buildings.

Since the time of Trajan, Palmyra had been an important recruiting ground for the Roman army. The famous Palmyrene cohorts of mounted archers and armored cavalry had rendered invaluable service all over the Empire. Later on, the Severi, who gave Palmyra the rank of titular colony and admitted some of its leading citizens into the senate, allowed these units, though officially part of the Roman army, to serve as a semi-independent Palmyrene army in Syria and along the Parthian (Persian) frontier. That was the army with which Odenathus humbled the pride of the mighty Shapur on the western banks of the Euphrates.

The services that Odenathus had performed for Rome on his own initiative were not lost upon the shrewd and opportunistic Gallienus, who showed his gratitude by rewarding him with flattering high-sounding titles and by making him commander of all the Roman forces in the Near East.

Macrianus, meanwhile, had broken with Gallienus and had persuaded the army to proclaim his two sons, Macrianus and Quietus, joint emperors. The long-suffering East hailed them with delight, and all might have gone well had the elder Macrianus been content to limit his ambitions to the East. He resolved instead to reach out for the rest of the Empire. Leaving Quietus behind in the East, he and his elder son set out for the Danube. There they were defeated and killed by Aureolus, whom Gallienus had sent to intercept them. Then Odenathus hunted down and put to death the other pretender, along with his praetorian prefect, Callistus.

In his second campaign against Persia (267), Odenathus turned from the siege of Ctesiphon to drive out the Goths. They had invaded Asia Minor by land and sea, had laid waste the rich cities of Chalcedon and Nicomedia, and had destroyed the great temple of Artemis (Diana) at Ephesus. He failed to overtake them, however, for they had already boarded ships at Heraclea Pontica with all their loot and captives. Shortly after that, an unknown assassin stabbed Odenathus to death. His capable widow, Zenobia, assumed power in Palmyra and held it until the reign of Aurelian.

The Last Battles of Gallienus, 268 Much encouraged by their success in the previous year and joined by the Heruli, the Goths began the largest invasion experienced in the third century. An armada of 500 ships (some say 2,000) put to sea, and a land army unbelievably reported at 320,000 men invaded the Balkans and the Aegean area, ravaged Greece, and sacked the cities of Sparta, Argos, and Athens. After the Athenian rhetorician and statesman Dexippus counterattacked with a hastily recruited local army, the invaders passed north through Epirus and Macedonia and finally arrived at Naissus (modern Niš, Nish) in Moesia. There, in 268, Gallienus intercepted them and, in the bloodiest battle of the third century, destroyed thousands of them. This victory might have been the end of the Gothic peril, had not Gallienus been compelled to break off pursuit and hasten back to Italy to suppress the rebellion of Aureolus, the cavalry general to whom he had entrusted the defense of Italy against Postumus. Gallienus defeated Aureolus in battle near Mediolanum (Milan), only to be assassinated by his own staff officers, all of them Illyrians who may have felt that Gallienus had not devoted enough energy to the defense of the Danubian lands.

The Reforms of Gallienus

Before his death, however, Gallienus had laid the foundation of future recovery and prepared the way for the reforms of Diocletian and Constantine. His purpose was to strengthen the hands of the central government in restoring discipline in the armies. That helped to prevent the rise of usurpers and made it easier to defend the Empire against increased attacks on the frontiers.

Administrative The most radical of the reforms of Gallienus was the normal exclusion of senators from the command of legions and their replacement by equestrian prefects, many of whom were now coming up from the ranks. One purpose of this reform may have been to prevent rebellions and attempts by ambitious senatorial commanders to usurp power. It also aimed at the restoration of military discipline and efficiency by providing an adequate supply of professional officers willing to endure the hardships of army life on the frontiers and capable of enforcing strict military discipline. The reform not only completed the process of professionalizing the army but dealt a heavy blow to the prestige of the senate.

Equestrians also gradually replaced senatorial governors in most of the Imperial and occasionally even in the senatorial provinces. Gallienus did not, however, strip senatorial governors of their military powers. Civil and military powers at the provincial level generally remained linked. In the most devastated provinces, he even combined fiscal responsibilities with civil and military powers in the hands of experienced equestrian officers who had worked their way up from the ranks. In that way, they could deal effectively with crises.

Military While promoting from the ranks to provide experienced senior officers, Gallienus also made some major tactical and strategic changes. They were not part of any grand preconceived system but practical responses to sometimes temporary situations and were not always permanent. A major and permanent tactical change, however, was to place greater emphasis on cavalry units to increase the mobility of the Roman army and meet the challenges posed by the notoriously effective Persian and Alemannic horsemen.

The new cavalry corps consisted of Moorish bareback-riding javelin men, Dalmatian horsemen, Osrhoenian and Palmyrene mounted archers, and the heavily man-and-horse armored cavalry of the Persian type (*cataphractarii*). Gallienus regarded this cavalry corps so highly that in 263 he placed it on a par with the Praetorian Guard. Its commander soon rivaled and later eclipsed the praetorian prefect and, though only of equestrian rank, became the most powerful in the Empire next to the emperor. Claudius Gothicus, Aurelian, Probus, and Diocletian were later to use this command as the springboard to the emperorship.

Temporarily, Gallienus strategically abandoned the eastern and western extremities of the Empire to regional dynasts so that he could concentrate on saving the central core of Egypt, western Asia Minor, Greece, the Balkans, Italy, and Africa. Although he distrusted Postumus and never recognized his authority as legitimate, Gallienus left him in de facto control of the westernmost provinces and responsible for defending the Rhine. He maintained nominal suzerainty over Odenathus and Zenobia in Syria and Mesopotamia but left them on their own to deal with Persia. Gallienus' immediate need was to defend the

Alpine and Danubian frontiers. He maintained and strengthened fortifications and infantry units as a first line of defense in the frontier zones themselves. Behind the frontiers, he also fortified numerous cities capable of resisting and absorbing attackers who broke through the first line of defense.

Finally, in response to various large incursions, Gallienus stationed large cavalry detachments (*vexillationes*) at strategically located major cities in the rear. From these secure, well-supplied positions, they could move swiftly in any direction to meet emergencies in their sectors. Such bases were located at Mediolanum (Milan), Verona, and Aquileia to protect Italy and defend the Alpine frontier; at Poetovio in Noricum and Aquincum (Budapest), and Sirmium in Lower Pannonia to protect the Middle Danube; at Lychnidus in Macedonia and Byzantium in Thrace to protect the Balkans, Greece, and the Aegean. Once the core of the Empire had been secured and the frontiers stabilized, the *vexillationes* would be shifted elsewhere

The constant need for the emperor to be in personal charge of defense from bases like Mediolanum (Milan) reduced the political importance of the city of Rome and the senate. Emperors had to transfer to major military centers not only the mint and arms factories but their own residences as well. Where the emperor was, there Rome was also. In the fourth century, Mediolanum in the West and Byzantium in the East would displace Rome as principal Imperial residences.

An Assessment of Gallienus Of all his Imperial predecessors, Gallienus seems to have resembled Hadrian most closely. He had the same keen intelligence, indefatigable energy, and capacity for swift decision. Gallienus shared Hadrian's love of poetry and the arts, and his admiration for Greek culture, literature, and philosophy. He also, however, abandoned his father's persecution of Christians and established a policy of toleration that lasted for forty years, a period known as the "Little Peace of the Church."

Claudius Gothicus (268 to 270) Upon the assassination of Gallienus, one of his murderers, Claudius II, a member of that group of brilliant young Illyrian officers whom he had promoted from the ranks, was proclaimed emperor. Claudius' first task as emperor was to drive back the Alemanni, who had invaded Italy as far as Lake Garda. Then he rounded up the Goths who had escaped Gallienus, as well as those who had later invaded the Balkans. He enrolled some of the captured Goths in the Roman army; he settled others on abandoned farms in Thrace, Moesia, and Macedonia. So thoroughly had he liquidated the Gothic menace that it did not again recur on a mass scale for more than a century. For this great contribution to the Empire's reconstruction, he received the richly deserved title of Claudius Gothicus.

Aurelian (270 to 275) When Claudius Gothicus died of the plague, the army, which now had become the major power in the state, chose as his successor another brilliant Illyrian officer, Lucius Domitius Aurelianus, whom Claudius had put in command of the cavalry corps during the Gothic War. He was a tough, skillful general whose harsh discipline earned him the nickname *Manus ad Ferrum* ("Hand on Steel"). So severe were his punishments that he seldom had to inflict them.

The tasks awaiting Aurelian were numerous and difficult. He had to secure the long Danubian frontiers from attack and Italy from invasion, restore both the western and eastern provinces to the Roman Empire, and solve several political and military problems. The immediate task was to rescue Italy from the invasion and depredations of the Juthungi (kinsmen of the Alemanni) living north of the upper Danube. At Aurelian's approach they attempted to retreat quickly with their plunder, but he caught them from ambush at the Danube and destroyed half their army. He next defeated the Asdingian Vandals, who had invaded Pannonia, and forced them to supply 2,000 cavalrymen for the Roman army. Meanwhile, the Juthungi, aided by the Alemanni and the Marcomanni, invaded Italy again, besieged Mediolanum, and occupied Piacenza. There they set an ambush for Aurelian and defeated his army, which had been wearied by the long march from the Danube. The invaders could easily have marched on and taken Rome had they kept together instead of spreading out into scattered marauding bands, which Aurelian easily destroyed. His victories on the Metaurus and near Ticinum sent the invaders scurrying back to Germany.

Reforms Aurelian, free for other tasks, returned to Rome to suppress a serious revolt of the mint officials who were aggrieved at the emperor's efforts to check their profiteering from debased coins. Aurelian immediately closed the mint for a time as a preliminary step toward his projected reform of the coinage. In order to protect Rome from future assault and capture by invaders, he began the construction of a brick wall around the city in 271. The wall was twelve miles long, twenty feet high, and twelve feet thick. It had eighteen gates as well as many sally ports and towers for artillery. Convinced of the impossibility of permanently holding Dacia with its irreparably broken defenses, Aurelian withdrew all the garrisons and most of the civilians from the province. The withdrawal not only shortened the frontier defense line of the Empire but also released troops for service elsewhere. The evacuated civilians were resettled in the ravaged and depopulated provinces of Pannonia, Moesia, and Thrace, and Dacia was abandoned to the Goths.

The Reconquest of the East, 272 to 273 With Italy and the Danubian provinces temporarily safe from attack, Aurelian was free to attempt the reconquest of the East. The enemy whom he had to conquer was not the Persian king, but Zenobia, the ambitious and capable queen of Palmyra, who matched the Egyptian Cleopatra in intellect, personality, and ambition. She not only maintained a court of pomp and splendor but also gathered about her scholars, poets, and artists. Her chief advisor was Cassius Longinus (213? to 273), a celebrated Athenian rhetorician, polymath, and philosophical writer. Tak-

ing advantage of Aurelian's preoccupation in Italy and on the Danube, Zenobia had seceded from the Empire and extended Palmyra's dominion over Egypt and Asia Minor as far north as Bithynia. She had even concluded an alliance with the Persians but received little help from them.

Aurelian entrusted the reconquest of Egypt to Probus and advanced through Asia Minor himself. He encountered little opposition until he reached Antioch on the Orontes, where he had to battle a Palmyrene army of mounted archers and heavy cavalry. He overcame them and proceeded to Emesa, where he engaged another Palmyrene army. The Romans won a second resounding victory and set out under the broiling desert sun for the city of Palmyra, eighty miles away. Well prepared for a siege, Palmyra resisted long and stubbornly. It finally capitulated when the panic-stricken queen attempted to flee to Persia for help. Brought before Aurelian, the captured queen saved her life by accusing Longinus and her other advisers and friends of inspiring her aggressions. Longinus had to die, but Aurelian was very lenient with the people and city of Palmyra. He stationed a small garrison there and at once set out for Europe.

He got as far as the Danube when word came that Palmyra had risen in rebellion and massacred the garrison. Aurelian's return was swift, his vengeance terrible. Not even women or children escaped his wrath. He had Palmyra's treasures carted away, tore down the walls, and reduced the once proud and powerful city to a small desert town, which it has remained to this day. Soon after, he suppressed a rebellion in Alexandria with similar ruthlessness.

The Reconquest of Gaul, 273 to 274 The reconquest of Gaul was less difficult. After the murder of Postumus in 268, the Gallic succession passed first to Victorinus and then to Tetricus. Tetricus was a harmless old senator who could neither keep out the German invaders nor maintain authority over his own army officers. His opposition to Aurelian was halfhearted and ineffectual. When his subordinates finally compelled him to fight, he deserted his troops and surrendered to Aurelian. He was forced to walk through the streets of Rome in Aurelian's triumphal parade together with a more spirited captive, the fabled Zenobia. After the triumph, Aurelian treated both captives with unparalled leniency and dignity. He appointed Tetricus chief inspector of Lucania. (*Corrector Lucaniae*) in southern Italy and presented Zenobia with a villa at Tibur (Tivoli), where she ended her days as the wife of a Roman senator.

Upon his recovery of the lost provinces, Aurelian received the proud title of *Restitutor Orbis* ("Restorer of the World").

Economic Reforms In 274, Aurelian grappled with another gigantic task: the restoration of internal stability. The most pressing problem was the regulation of the coinage, which had depreciated so much since 267 that people had to use *denarii* and *antoniniani* by the sackful (3,125 *antoniniani* to the sack). Aurelian reduced the official valuation of the *antoninianus* (double *denarius*) from eight sesterces to one in order to bring it in line with the eightfold rise in the price level after 267, but whether the change actually halted inflation is debatable. He increased the number of provincial mints and permanently abolished the senatorial mint at Rome, a blow against municipal autonomy and the prerogative of the senate.

To relieve the distress that had resulted in Rome from the rise of food prices, Aurelian placed the bread-making industry under the direct control of the state, which sold wheat for milling to the bakers' guild and fixed the price of bread. He suspended the monthly grain dole and arranged instead for the daily distribution of two pounds of bread to all eligible citizens. For the same citizens he instituted regular distributions of pork, oil, salt, and possibly wine. Following the example of Alexander Severus, Aurelian placed all guilds or colleges engaged in the transport and processing of food and other necessities under state control and thereby made them agencies of the government.

Autocracy and Monotheism Two long-term developments approached their culmination during the reign of Aurelian. The tendency toward absolute monarchy in government and the monotheistic trend in religion began at this time to achieve a sure dominance, and even a certain interrelation, as emperors sought religious sanctions for their authority. The rapid changing of emperors during the third century had not destroyed the monarchy; it served rather to transform the Principate into autocratic absolutism. The trend toward monotheism in religion was equally pronounced. The rise of the universal cosmopolitan state, together with the far-reaching influence of Near Eastern culture and of the westward-spreading Eastern cults, had precipitated the decline of the old national and local polytheism and the rise of a more universal and monotheistic religion. Even the Imperial cult lost its potency as a moral basis for Imperial unity and power and gave way before the twin emergence of autocracy and monotheism.

In Rome, Aurelian erected a resplendent temple to the Unconquered Sun (*Sol Invictus*). He even established a college of pontiffs of senatorial rank to superintend the worship of this supreme god of the universe and divine protector of the Roman state. A single divine power was now to watch over the single earthly ruler.

Unfortunately for Aurelian, the new divinity did not save him from the fate of many other third-century emperors. A corrupt secretary, caught in a lie and fearing for his life, forged a list of the chief officers of the guard and spread the false rumor that Aurelian planned their execution. The "condemned" officers acted swiftly; they murdered Aurelian in the fall of 275. When the truth finally came to light, the horror-stricken officers repented, but it was too late.

Tacitus (275 to 276) Contrite and dismayed, the military leaders deferred to the senate in the choice of the next emperor. After some hesitation and delay, the senate nominated its own leader, M. Claudius Tacitus, a man in his middle seventies. In spite of a fairly successful campaign against the Goths and Alans in Asia Minor, he too fell victim to a conspiracy of his own soldiers. His six-month reign marked a fleeting resurgence of senatorial power that, meteor-like, rose, briefly flashed, and was gone forever.

Probus (276 to 282)

After Tacitus' death, the power of making and breaking emperors reverted to the army. It soon disposed of Florianus, the late Emperor Tacitus' half-brother, who had seized the throne without consulting army or senate. The army of the East had already proclaimed emperor the mighty M. Aurelius Probus, another great Illyrian, who was the equal of Aurelian as a general and perhaps his superior in intellect and culture. Probus continued the work of Imperial consolidation by restoring peace and order in the provinces.

The first task was the liberation of Gaul from the Franks and the Alemanni, who had overrun the entire province after Aurelian's death, seized some 70 cities, and laid waste countless fertile fields. Within a year the invaders were in full retreat. In relentless pursuit, the victorious Probus killed them by the tens of thousands and drove the rest back into Germany. Probus built strong redoubts along the eastern bank of the Rhine opposite the Roman cities on the western bank. He also recruited 16,000 German soldiers for the Roman army and assigned them in small units to the various provinces. Except for the rebellions of two disloyal and ambitious generals (which he firmly suppressed), Gaul remained quiet through the reign of Probus.

In 278, Probus cleared the Alemanni and Burgundians out of Raetia and the Vandals out of Pannonia. He settled on abandoned land in Thrace some 100,000 Scythians and Germanic Bastarnae who had been dislodged from their southern Russian homelands by the Goths. In 279, he subdued the Isaurian brigands of southern Asia Minor and established colonies of veterans there to keep the peace and breed young recruits for the Roman army. His generals also liberated Egypt from the Blemmyes, who had invaded from the Sudan. Apparently Probus himself had been planning to invade Persia, where Shapur's own son's successor Bahram

(Vahram, Veharan, Varanes) II (272 to 293) was hampered by a rebellious brother. Bahram was able to obtain a truce probably because Probus had to return to Gaul to put down a rebellion in 280.

After celebrating a magnificent triumph at Rome in 282 for his various victories, Probus set off to resume the war against Persia. At Sirmium he fell victim to yet another mutiny. The sources say that the soldiers turned on him because he worked them too hard on land reclamation and public works projects. A more compelling reason may well have been the troops' reluctance to be drawn away from their posts for another war in a far-off land that had been the graveyard of many a Roman general and army. In Raetia, the troops were already putting up the Praetorian Prefect Marcus Aurelius Carus as Emperor, and Probus' troops declared for him.

Carus and His Sons, Carinus and Numerianus (282 to 285)

Carus, the new emperor, was another Illyrian. He, too, was a professional soldier and a fairly competent general. He did not even bother to seek senatorial confirmation of his position as emperor, and upon his accession, he conferred the rank of Caesar on his two sons, Carinus and Numerianus. Later in 82, leaving Carinus to defend Italy and Gaul, he set out for the East with his other son. Early in 283, after defeating the Quadi and the Sarmatians, who had come over the Danube, he marched against the Persians. He crossed the Euphrates, took Seleucia, and then crossed the Tigris to capture Ctesiphon. This series of successes came to an abrupt halt in 284 with his mysterious death, which was attributed by the ancient sources to a bolt of lightning. It is far more likely that Carus fell victim to foul play at the hands of his father-in-law, the Praetorian Prefect Arrius Aper, who later secretly arranged the assassination of Numerianus. He had probably correctly gauged the troops' reluctance to continue farther into Persia.

The army of the East acclaimed one of their own officers, Diocles, as Numerianus' successor. The first act of the new emperor (who is better known as Diocletian [284–305]) was to run Aper through with his sword. Carinus, who had acquired the rank of Augustus in the West, refused to acknowledge Diocletian as his colleague and marched East in 285. The two foes clashed in Moesia in the valley of the Margus (Morava). In the fierce battle that ensued, the superior army of Carinus had almost achieved victory when Carinus himself received a dagger's thrust through the heart by a military tribune whose wife Carinus had seduced. His victorious but leaderless army accepted Diocletian as their emperor. Diocletian, however, dated his reign from his initial acclamation in 284.

XXXIII

Changes in Roman Life and Culture during the Third Century

Traditionally, historians have portrayed the third century as one of catastrophic decline from the economic, social, and cultural heights of the first and second centuries A.D. Since the 1960s, however, more intensive and sophisticated research and analysis have shown that the heights of the earlier centuries have been overemphasized and that changes in so vast an entity as the Roman Empire varied enormously in pace and scale with local conditions. What might be true of one area might not hold in another. For example, there was often a contrast between the Greek East and the Latin West. The political and military crises of the third century may have accelerated some trends or retarded others. In either case, there were striking continuities as well as significant breaks with the past.

Economic Life The basically underdeveloped economy of the Roman Empire had reached its limited potential for expansion during the relative peace and stability that had prevailed between Augustus' victory in the civil wars of the late Republic and the death of Antoninus Pius in 161. Beginning with Marcus Aurelius, invasions, civil wars, and plague disrupted production and trade in significant parts of the Empire. The increased size of the army and the civil bureaucracy in the third century as emperors tried to cope with these crises created

demands for money and manpower that were very difficult to meet with an economy capable of producing only small surpluses per capita under the best of conditions. Scarcity and high inflation were the results.

The Inflationary Spiral Up until the end of the Severan dynasty, the available evidence indicates that the rate of inflation had remained stable at a modest 1 percent or less a year. By about A.D. 250, however, the rate of inflation had soared to ruinous heights. One of the contributing factors was that the production of precious metals was not enough to maintain the weight and fineness (ratio of precious to base metal) of the coins issued. Both had started to decline precipitously with the reign of Marcus Aurelius. For example, the number of silver *denarii* struck from a Roman pound of silver went from 107 to 120, and the fineness of the coins went from 88 percent silver to 78.5 percent. By the time of Severus Alexander, the number of *denarii* to a pound of silver had more than doubled to 226.8, and the fineness had dropped to 45 percent. Even worse, this debasement was accompanied by a great increase in the number of coins produced. For example, from Nero through Commodus, the average output of silver *denarii* has been estimated at 16.4 million per year, but under the Severi the figure is 30.8 million per year. Even under the Severi, the debasement by itself might not have had much impact on inflation, but as the great increase in the money supply worked its way through an essentially stagnant economy, inflation began to accelerate. By 250, the debasement of the coinage had become so bad that both it and the continued increase in the number of coins in circulation helped to push inflation to dizzying heights. Between 267 and 274, for example, prices had increased as much as 700 percent.

The emperors needed to mint ever larger numbers of coins to keep up with the costs of the Imperial budget, particularly the increased costs of pay and donatives to the army and cash distributions (*congiaria*) to the *plebs urbana* at Rome. For example, the costs of military salaries are estimated to have ranged from 643 million to 704 million sesterces around 150 A.D. but from 1 billion 127 million to 1 billion 188 million by about 215. The combined estimates for donatives and *congiaria* rose from 50 million to 100 million sesterces around A.D. 150 to 100 million to 150 million around A.D. 215.

The direct impact of inflation was not the same everywhere. In the countryside, where 90 percent of the Empire's population lived, the outright exchange of goods and services that kept their relative values regardless of their prices in monetary units could lessen the ravages of inflation. Taxes, however, were hard on the small farmer. Taxes on produce had often been paid in kind, but some, like the poll tax, required cash, which was usually acquired through the sale of a pig, a goat, or a little surplus produce in the local market town. Rapid inflation made it difficult to save up enough to satisfy the tax collector, particularly when inflation was increasing the amount of extortion in which tax collectors had habitually engaged.

Although the urban poor did not pay taxes, their wages did not keep pace with rapid inflation, and they had nothing with which to barter. They and their country cousins had several options, however. They could become *coloni,* tenants of the great landowners, try to find government handouts (*congiaria*) at Rome and some other favored cities, join the army, become outlaws and brigands, or flee beyond the frontiers.

The great landowners were strong enough to resist the tax collectors and supply their wants from their own vast estates. The curial class, those of middling wealth who made up the bulk of municipal councils (*curiae*) and were responsible for collecting local taxes, could shift some of its tax burdens onto the peasantry or seek refuge by joining either the bureaucracy or the army. Soldiers were in a good position to demand raises and bonuses, which were often the objects of their mutinies and rebellions. On the average, however, their wages no more than kept pace with inflation, and they often resorted to extortion or force against civilians to obtain what they could not buy.

Inflation, combined with the disruptive effects of military and political turmoil and destructive plagues that assailed the Empire from 235 to 285, had many negative economic consequences. The public and private alimentary and educational trust funds that had been one of the finest achievements of the Principate were wiped out. Credit, which had never been a very highly developed aspect of the economy, became almost unobtainable. Poverty, always extensive, became even worse.

Decline of Trade and Commerce The volume of trade and commerce, both internal and international, declined severely in many parts of the Empire during the third century, particularly after 235. The lack of a reliable coinage forced a decline in banking, which principally involved money changing. Banking probably was hurt further by a decline in the volume of trade. The smaller number of commercial shipwrecks found in the Mediterranean from the third century may indicate such a decline, because there were no significant advances in shipbuilding or in seamanship. The coastal raids of the Saxons and Jutes and the virtual collapse of the Rhine-Danube frontier severely disrupted trade in the northwestern provinces. Evidence is provided by the declining production and distribution of *terra sigillata* (fine red Arretine-style dinnerware) from central and eastern Gaul, which could compete with lower-quality locally made products only by "piggybacking" on the shipment of commodities such as wine, grain, and building materials. In the East, the disintegration of the Parthian Empire after Septimius Severus and the collapse of the Han Empire in China at the same time disrupted the overland trade with the Far East and India. The sea routes to India across the Arabian Sea seem to have been abandoned early in the third century, too. The need for importing large amounts of grain to Rome kept trade flowing between North Africa and Italy, but even it suffered temporarily in the third century.

Disruption of Agriculture The decline of trade and commerce went hand in hand with the disruption of agriculture. A major component of trade was the transportation of major agricultural products such as grain, wine, and olive oil. If the markets for these products declined or if the producing areas ceased to produce, trade between the two declined or ceased, too. Available archaeological surveys indicate that the rural population shrank in Italy during the third century. In southern Spain, the rich olive-producing region of the Guadalquivir Valley, in the region of Baetica, which specialized in producing olive oil for the Roman market, went into decline even in the late second century. In northeastern Spain, a similar decline is visible in the third century, but in the more geographically protected northwestern area of Galicia, agricultural villa estates underwent vigorous development at the same time.

Northeastern Gaul seems to have been hard hit by the third-century invasions. The Northwest prospered during much of the third century but suffered a collapse at the end. Only the southwestern coastal region seems to have enjoyed continual agricultural prosperity during this period. The British countryside, which was relatively well protected, also remained fairly prosperous. The grain- and olive-producing regions of North Africa did not maintain so high a level of prosperity as they had in the first and second centuries, but decline was not severe.

Egypt, which was plagued by high taxes and raids by the Blemmyes from the south, suf-fered some serious decline in productivity, but it was not irreparably harmed. In Syria, however, the rich olive-producing inland plateau continued to enjoy prosperity throughout the century. The agricultural prosperity of the Levant, Asia Minor, and the Aegean Islands also held up well. Much of mainland Greece and the Balkans, however, was badly affected because of the area's exposure to raids from across the Danube.

Farmers suffered not only from "barbarian" raiders and impoverished Romans turned brigands but often even more from Roman armies sent to drive off the attackers or, as so often, fighting each other in civil war. Whether his crops, animals, and supplies were stolen, requisitioned, or destroyed in the fighting, it made little difference to the farmer who was left destitute even if he had not also lost his buildings, equipment, and family. Even an army just passing through a district en route to some other destination could spell disaster. Ancient armies on the march needed enormous amounts of local provisions, and the emperor and the exalted personages of his retinue had to receive lavish hospitality commensurate with their high station even if the locals were reduced to beggary. Should a farmer have escaped the previous calamities, he still faced extraordinary taxes and requisitions to support unexpected wars and the expenses associated with the accession of the latest new emperor or local usurper. As a result of all of those pressures, much land, particularly of marginal quality or on unstable frontiers, went out of production.

Increase of Great Estates In many cases where agriculture still prospered, particularly in the West, it tended to become the domain of great landlords residing in fortified villas. In the prosperous days of the first and second centuries A.D., the spread of *latifundia* in Italy had halted, and everywhere freehold family farms or medium-sized estates were dominant. The troubles of the third century, however, caused the rapid growth of *latifundia* once more. The hereditary senatorial magnates and provincial elites or new men from the army and bureaucracy were the only ones with the resources to buy extra land or take over what others had abandoned. Often small farmers willingly surrendered their holdings to larger neighbors and agreed to pay rent as *coloni* (tenants) in return for the protection that powerful landlords with their social connections, fortified villas, and private retainers could provide against tax collectors, military recruiters, brigands, and outside attackers.

Like medieval manors, these villa estates were largely self-sufficient. They produced most of what was needed for local consumption. Tenants paid their rents in kind, which supplied the landlords with raw materials, food, and fiber, and resident artisans provided most of the items needed for everyday use. Only specialized products, such as iron and luxuries for the landlord, had to be bought from outside.

Mining and Manufacturing The widespread decline in other areas of economic activity is paralleled by declines in mining and manufacturing. The inability to produce enough gold and silver to keep up with the demand for coins contributed heavily to the monetary chaos and inflation of the third century. The decline of trade and agricultural prosperity in many regions reduced the demand for manufactured goods like tools and equipment, high-quality pottery and cloth, building materials, furniture, and decorative artwork, and carts, wagons, boats, and ships. The decline was so bad by the end of the third century that when Diocletian and Constantine increased demand for the products of many trades with their building programs and military expansion in the early fourth century, they found a shortage of people with the skills to provide them.

Social Trends In the third century, the Roman Empire was, as it always had been, a vast multi-ethnic, multicultural conglomeration of peoples on three continents. By Caracalla's *Constitutio Antoniniana* of 212, all of those who were of free status shared a common citizenship. In many ways that was the culmination of a process that had begun with the first extension of Roman citizenship in Italy during the

Republic. It is significant, however, that Caracalla was the son of a Syrian mother and a father born of Punic stock in North Africa. Whatever pragmatic consideration may have been involved in his grant of universal citizenship, it is not likely that an emperor from the old elite of Italian origin would have taken such a step so soon. His father, Septimius Severus, had reduced the privileged status of Italy and the Italians by enlarging the senate with appointees from the provinces, particularly Africa and Syria, replacing the old Praetorian Guard recruited mainly from Italians and heavily Romanized western provinces with one manned by regular legionaries, and giving important military commands to provincial equestrians.

Social Role of the Army During the third century, the army had made it possible for provincials of non-Italian origin to rise to the top of the Imperial hierarchy. Septimius Severus himself is a perfect example. Maximinus, the Thracian whom the Pannonian legions had made emperor after Severus Alexander, had been appointed to several equestrian military offices by Septimius. The Emperor Philip the Arab came from an Arabian family that had been favored by Septimius Severus, and he had been promoted to the office of praetorian prefect in 243. Claudius Gothicus and Aurelian were talented military officers from Balkan provinces who rose to become emperors, the first in a series that culminated with Diocletian and Constantine.

The constant movements of troops from one region of the Empire to another during the crisis of the third century also did much to integrate soldiers from one part of the Empire with another. It was a long-standing Roman policy to post soldiers far from their home provinces. Under Septimius, for example, there were Arabs serving in Gaul and Goths serving in Arabia. After completing their terms of services, soldiers frequently retired where they had been stationed, a trend that was encouraged by Septimius' abolition of the prohibition against soldiers' marrying. Although native soldiers from the provinces had learned Latin and become Romanized, they also brought some of their own traditions and customs to the areas where they settled.

Greater Public Recognition of Important Women

During the Republic and the first two centuries A.D., the women of elite families and emperors' households had always been important as vehicles for building useful marital alliances and often played important informal roles in politics. In the late Republic and under the Julio-Claudian emperors, individual women like Clodia, Fulvia, Livia, Messallina, and Agrippina the Younger played more active, openly political roles. Still, they received little public recognition except as the subjects of scandal and censure by horrified males. The wives and mothers of emperors in the first and second centuries A.D. were sometimes portrayed on coins for dynastic and propagandistic purposes and were occasionally honored with statues and dedicatory inscriptions, but the scope of the roles in which they were portrayed was limited to the domestic and religious functions to which Roman women were traditionally restricted.

Septimius Severus and his family, however, came from Syria and Africa where there was a tradition of giving greater public prominence to important women. Syria and Egypt had been major parts of the monarchial Hellenistic Empires, which produced a series of powerful and active Hellenistic queens that culminated in Cleopatra, who had ruled Egypt in her own right. Near Eastern and Egyptian religions gave greater prominence to priestesses and female deities like the Anatolian Great Mother Cybele, the Egyptian Isis, and the Syro-Phoenician Astarte, whom the Phoenician colonists in North Africa had worshipped as Tanit at Carthage.

According to a deep-seated tradition, Carthage had been founded by the great Queen Dido from Phoenician Tyre. More recently, Zenobia, queen of Palmyra in the Syrian desert, had wrested control of the eastern provinces, including Egypt, away from Rome, and soon the region would see the rise of Mavia, queen of the Saracens (see p. 451). More immediately, women of prominent families received more public recognition as patronesses of their communities in Roman Africa than anywhere else in the Empire. It probably seemed natural, therefore, to an emperor of Punic descent from North Africa to give public prominence to the role played by his Syrian wife, Julia Domna.

No Roman woman had ever before received the kind of honors bestowed upon Julia Domna. Not only was she depicted on coins as Cybele or seated on the throne of Juno with titles such as "Mother of the Camps and Senate" or "Mother of the Fatherland," but statues and honorific inscriptions were set up everywhere. At Aphrodisias, on the coast of Asia Minor, she even was hailed as the goddess Demeter and given a temple. Under Caracalla, she functioned almost as a prime minister or secretary of state with her own Praetorian Guards. She carried on much of the Imperial correspondence in Latin and Greek all over the Empire. Julia Maesa and Julia Mamaea achieved even greater public prominence under Elagabalus and Severus Alexander.

Salonina, wife of the Emperor Gallienus (253 to 268), did not gain the prominence of Domna, Maesa, and Mamaea, but she figured heavily in dynastic propaganda on the coins of Gallienus' reign. Her portrait appears on literally hundreds of issues from the period, particularly in those minted at Milan. That was Gallienus' main residence, and she often maintained the Imperial presence among the troops there while Gallienus was off fighting elsewhere. She also supported Gallienus' cultural agenda and was noted for accompanying him to hear the philosopher Plotinus lecture. Under the soldier-emperors who followed Gallienus, the women of the Imperial Court became less visible again, but the stage was set for the emergence of women who would play dominant roles in the Imperial Court, particularly in the eastern half of the Empire during the fourth, fifth, and sixth centuries.

At Carthage in 203, a young aristocratic woman named Vibia Perpetua and a pregnant slave named Felicitas achieved an entirely different kind of public prominence. These two women were among the early martyrs of the Christian Church. Their deaths are told in *The*

Passion of Perpetua and Felicitas, most of which purports to be Perpetua's own account of her experiences between being arrested and marched off to face death in the gladiatorial arena. In her confrontations with her father and the Roman governor and in her various dreams, she completely overturns the existing male-dominated social and political order. She, ordinarily a powerless woman, feels empowered by her sufferings and impending death. The traditional hierarchy is turned upside down. She is called a *domina* (mistress), victorious over her normal masters as she, her slave, and their fellow martyrs turn suffering and death into joy and eternal life. Unbowed and in control to the very end, she guides the sword of the trembling gladiator to her own throat. *The Passion of Perpetua and Felicitas* became a popular and powerful tool for converting others to a faith that promised the power to overcome suffering and powerlessness and would, in less than 125 years, itself overpower its persecutors to become the religion of the Roman Emperor himself.

Decline of Cities The problems and changes of the third century caused suffering, anxiety, and a sense of powerlessness for many people. Urban dwellers were hard hit in numerous areas. Natural disasters, such as plague and the large earthquakes that hit much of the Empire between 242 and 262, economic decline, and attacks during invasions or civil wars caused many cities to shrink and decay. In the 260s, for example, Augustodunum (Autun) in Gaul was heavily damaged in a siege by troops loyal to the usurper Postumus; Athens was devastated by the Goths and Heruli; and even Antioch was sacked by the Persians. To survive at all, cities had to erect fortresses and walls that characterized cities in Europe and the Mediterranean world for centuries thereafter. Between 271 and 275, Aurelian surrounded Rome with battlements over 20 feet tall and 12 miles long. Square towers projected out every 100 feet, and gates with round towers protected the entrances

A sign of shrinkage is that walls sometimes enclosed only a fourth of a city's former area, although there are cases where extensive habitations remained outside the walls. Inside

the walls public buildings and monuments often decayed as can be seen in third-century Trier (Augusta Treverorum). Even Rome, which was becoming the capital of the Empire in name only, began to recede from the high tide that it had reached in the first and second centuries. Only a few cities like Milan, Verona, Aquileia, Sirmium, and Antioch, which became major defensive centers, revived or experienced any growth, although the cities of the East did not fare so badly as those in the West.

The Plight of the Curial Class The decline of trade, manufacturing, and agriculture and the shrinking of cities were accompanied by the progressive weakening of the decurions or curial class (*curiales*): the merchants, businessmen, and medium-sized landowners who made up the *curiae* (municipal senates or councils) of their local cities or towns. In the past, as municipal magistrates and councillors, the *curiales* not only appropriated municipal funds for public works, baths, temples, entertainments, and welfare but through traditional euergetism often supplemented those appropriations with their own private wealth to gain reputations as benefactors of their communities. They also served as collectors of Imperial taxes and provided for the feeding and bedding of troops in transit and for changes of horses for the Imperial post (*cursus publicus*).

As the government and the army made more and more demands on the communities in the form of requisitions and taxes, the *curiales* had less and less to spend on private benefactions. Unable to put pressure on the great senatorial landlords, they put more and more pressure on those below them to relieve their own financial burdens. What had once been a highly sought after honor, the position of decurion became more and more a cruel burden to be avoided. Many *curiales* sought escape by gaining positions in the Imperial bureaucracy, becoming soldiers, or subordinating themselves to some great landowner as his tenants (*coloni*).

The Urban Poor Only in Rome and a few other favored cities did the urban poor find any significant relief. In those cities, usually major

Imperial residences, the poor received food and entertainment on an incongruously generous scale as the emperor tried to maintain his traditional role as patron and benefactor. In most cities, which had to depend upon local revenues and benefactors to support such generosity, the poor could no longer be fed and entertained. Life became desperate for many, and crime, prostitution, the selling of children, military service, and flight to the countryside or even beyond the Imperial frontiers were among the few options for survival. Those who professed Christianity, however, found relief through the growing charitable activities of the local churches, which encouraged more fortunate members to share what they had with the poor. Not coincidentally, the number of urban Christians increased significantly.

***Slaves and* Coloni**   Slavery remained a major feature of Roman social and economic life in the third and subsequent centuries, as is clear from the amount of attention devoted to issues involving slaves in the Imperial law codes, but by the second half of the third century, the supply of cheap unskilled slaves for agricultural labor probably was shrinking. When they were successful in defeating attackers, emperors preferred to enroll captives in the Roman army or settle them in deserted lands. Therefore, the owners of *latifundia* increasingly welcomed *coloni,* free tenants, who farmed a portion of the landlord's holdings as renters and share-croppers.

The Expansion of the Upper Class and Villa Society   As is so often the case in times of great economic stress, the ranks of the very rich increased at the expense of those even greater numbers who were sinking lower and lower on the socioeconomic scale. The great landowners of hereditary wealth and status were able to profit by taking over the property of smaller landowners who could not withstand the simultaneous blows of shrinking markets, high inflation, confiscatory taxation, and rapacious officials. Some of the old senatorial families in the West would reach a princely level of wealth, status, and power. Below them was a growing class of large, if not truly grand, landowners. Their ranks were swollen by an influx of numerous newcomers, often former government officials and military men who had risen from a lower station through the army and bureaucracy to positions where they had the power to enrich themselves. Among the military men were former non-Roman auxiliaries and soldiers from key frontier provinces like Illyricum, Pannonia, and Thrace.

The newcomers had conservatively invested their gains in land. When they retired, they imitated those of hereditary wealth by deserting the faltering cities for fortified villas and self-sufficient estates in the country. Their wealth enabled them to enjoy the luxuries that still came by way of foreign and domestic commerce, and they acquired more land whenever they could.

Increasing Stratification and Regimentation   The militarization of the government in the third century was reflected in the increasing stratification and regimentation of society in general. A primary example is Septimius Severus' legal distinctions between *honestiores* and *humiliores* and the harsher penalties for *humiliores* than those for *honestiores* (p. 378). As the great landowners deserted the cities, there was pressure to reduce the *curiales* to lower status and to tie the *coloni* to their landlords.

Third-Century Cultural Life   The disruptions of the third century severely reduced the resources and leisure available for maintaining the cultural life of the old Greco-Roman elites. That was especially true in the hard-hit West, although some areas did better than others. In the East, where the urban and economic declines were generally less severe, the Greek-speaking urban elites more vigorously carried on the traditions of their class. Everywhere, however, the old elites' control of the cultural agenda was weakened, so that long-scorned native and popular influences began to make themselves felt at all levels. Nowhere was that more true than in the matter of religion.

Religion The Roman Empire continued to exhibit much religious diversity during the third century. In the countryside, where the bulk of the population lived, the familiar spirits of nature and the hearth received pious devotion as they always had among the peasantry and continued to do so for centuries, as witnessed by the term *pagan,* which comes from the word *paganus* (of the countryside) and which the Christians applied to nonbelievers after Christianity became dominant in the cities. On the other hand, the religious changes that were already visible in the cities, army camps, and administrative centers of the Empire during the first and second centuries were accelerating in the third. Local civic deities, who had enjoyed real meaning as the gods of sovereign cities and peoples, were increasingly irrelevant to individuals' lives. The army, trade, and the movement of people from one part of the Empire to another had already exposed the urban classes and administrative elites to a much wider range of deities and religious experience.

Caracalla's grant of universal citizenship in 212 had given legitimacy to people and traditions that the old Roman and Greek elites had not sanctioned. As the third century progressed, the state came more and more under the control of emperors and officials who even themselves were not from the old elites. Moreover, the disasters of the second half of the century made many people question the power and value of both the old pantheon of Greco-Roman gods and the rationalistic philosophies of happier times. In an increasingly grim and chaotic world where individuals had little direct influence over events, people were attracted to deities, religions, beliefs, and occult practices that had more universal appeal and promised to empower those who felt powerless. People wanted to feel divine power working directly through them to make a difference in their lives. In the cities and army camps of the third century, various popular mystery religions, particularly those that dealt with the very relevant subjects of the forces of evil and how to overcome them, continued to gain adherents. Magicians and charlatans who claimed to have supernatural powers also attracted wide followings.

Traditionalists at Rome and among the old Greco-Roman urban elites continued to cling to the old, but their power and influence shrank.

Religion and the State The all-too-obvious mortality and fallibility of emperors between the Severi and Diocletian destroyed emperor worship as a serious practice, and none of them was deified after death. Therefore, various emperors tried to enlist religious support for the state by claiming the personal favor of some divinity who would protect the state. Decius, who mounted the first general persecution of the Christians (250), tried to regain the favor of the traditional anthropomorphic deities, to whom Rome's success in better days had been attributed.

Many traditionalists in the Roman senate welcomed and participated in this movement, and pagan senators at Rome remained a bastion of the traditional state religion for at least another 150 years. Decius wanted to restore what the Romans had called the *pax deorum* (Peace of the Gods), which the old public priesthoods and festivals had been supposed to preserve. Other emperors were more innovative, however. Gallienus was deeply interested in the Neoplatonic philosophical mysticism of Plotinus (see p. 407), through which a person could attain knowledge of the divine One, who ruled the universe. Aurelian tried to promote the syncretistic, almost monotheistic cult of Sol Invictus, the Unconquered Sun, as a way of uniting the Empire under one leader.

Isism and Mithraism The mystery cult of Isis did not continue to gain strength as it had in the first and second centuries A.D. Partly it became submerged in a general syncretism of mystical eastern cults, magic, and symbolism (pp. 473–474), and partly it failed to satisfy those seekers of religious truth for whom the question of evil in the world was a major concern. Mithraism, however, although it was open only to men, continued to attract devotees, particularly in the mostly male worlds of soldiers, seafarers, and merchants. The struggle of its savior-hero Mithras on the side of light and life (Ahura

Mazda) pitted against the Zoroastrian forces of darkness and death (Ahriman), could easily be interpreted in terms of good and evil. Mithraism was favored by the Severi, and numerous shrines from the third and fourth centuries are found in cities and military camps all over the Empire.

Manichaeism One of the most potent forces in the second half of the third century and for the next 200 years was Manichaeism, the religion of a Persian prophet named Mani. Mani was a friend of the Sassanid Persian king Shapur (Sapor) I and started preaching with his support in 242. A little over 30 years later, however, he was executed by Shapur's grandson Bahram (Vahram, Varahan, Varanes) I under the influence of a conservative religious reaction.

Because Jesus plays a central role as the agent of ultimate salvation, Manichaeism can be classed as a heretical offshoot of Christianity. It also shared many similarities with the Gnostic heresies of Christianity (p. 405) and grew up in the same intellectual atmosphere. This atmosphere was a product of the Hellenistic Age, during which Greek philosophy, Persian Zoroastrianism, Babylonian astrology, and various Eastern mystery cults all interacted with each other over the vast territories of the Hellenistic empires as far east as India. Mani had even traveled to India and included Buddha along with Zoroaster and Christ as prophets.

The Zoroastrian element is clear from the fundamental starting point of Manichaean belief—the existence of the Two Principles or Roots, the Light and the Dark. They are two completely opposite, eternal, palpable physical realms. The realm of Light contained everything orderly, peaceful, intelligent, and clear; the Dark contained everything disordered, turbulent, crass, and muddy. At some time in the past, according to Mani, the Dark invaded the Light, and that was the beginning of evil. In the ensuing struggle, this world was created from the bodies of the forces of Darkness, who had swallowed part of the realm of Light. Therefore, this world and all that is in it are an admixture of particles of Light and the material of Darkness.

It was Jesus who revealed to Adam this miserable state of affairs and pointed out how he could gradually free the Divine Substance, the particles of Light, within him from its physical prison and join in the process of distilling the Light from the Darkness to restore the original perfect state. Unfortunately, the agents of Darkness created Eve to entice Adam from his task, and through their children the particles of Light were scattered still further. Jesus, however, using the moon and the sun, set up a mechanism to distill the souls of the dead and reconstruct the Perfect Man. Eventually, Mani claimed, the world will end with Jesus' second coming, and a great fire will refine its remains for 1,468 years until all heavenly material is freed and the Realm of Light is completely restored.

This blend of Zoroastrian dualism and Christian salvation was a strong rival of orthodox Christianity. It even claimed the allegiance of St. Augustine in the late fourth century before he became a true Christian. Manichaeism's major weakness in competition with orthodox Christianity, however, was its lack of personal salvation. In Manichaeism, the focus of salvation was reconstructing the Realm of Light into which the particles of Light that had been trapped inside the physical person were submerged. There was no survival of the individual personality and no personal victory over the forces of evil in this world and over death in the next, which Christianity promised and many found more appealing. Also, the Manichees never enjoyed the advantage of converting a Roman emperor and lost the support of the Persian emperors, whereas Christianity eventually became the religion of Rome's rulers.

Judaism and Christianity Judaism maintained itself among the Jewish population dispersed throughout the Empire, but its missionary impetus had been destroyed by Hadrian's ban on Jewish proselytizing, so that conversion was rare. Within that restriction, Judaism remained a protected religion. Therefore, there was no official persecution, although local outbreaks of violence against Jews did occur, particularly in Greek cities like Alexandria with large Jewish communities that claimed both special status and full citizenship contrary to the whole tradition of Greek civic life.

Because Christianity had assumed an identity quite distinct from its Jewish origins, it had lost any claim to special protection when Christians refused to worship the gods of the state, and it became subject to official persecution. Persecution was still mainly local under the Severi, as in the case of Perpetua and her companions at Carthage in 203 (p. 400). Then, it became systematic in the mid-third century as Decius and Valerian sought unity through religious means (p. 387). Persecution, however, helped Christianity by strengthening its organization and attracting publicity. Early Christian writers support the oft-repeated popular view that great numbers of Christians suffered martyrdom through horrible forms of execution at the hands of Roman persecutors. The actual number, however, was quite modest, probably under a thousand. Still the impact of the martyrs was enormous because Christian authors endlessly retold or replicated stories of martyrdom to demonstrate the power of Christianity to triumph over pain and suffering.

The blood that martyrs spilled in fact and fiction nourished the spirits of the urban middle and working classes. Facing an increasingly uncertain future and largely cut off from the upper-class civic life and institutions of the cities in which they lived, the excluded found refuge in the tightly knit, yet accepting, communities of Christians. Therefore, during the period of toleration known as the "Little Peace of the Church" after Valerian's death (260 to 302), the numbers of Christians continued to grow geometrically, and the Church became more firmly rooted than ever in the cities of the Empire's core while it spread deeply into the smaller cities and towns of the peripheral provinces. The soldier-emperors from remote rural villages in the Danubian provinces were too busy defending the frontiers or putting down usurpers to notice or care until Diocletian began to rebuild the Roman state.

It was during this period, moreover, that the New Testament canon of scriptures and the major theological doctrines of the Church were established, a period of tremendous ferment that resulted in the establishment of official orthodoxy at the Council of Nicaea a little later (325). One of the major forces in this ferment was the influence of Greek philosophy and pagan mystery cults that permeated the world in which Christianity was developing and from which it was drawing its converts. The commonest manifestation of this influence was the spread of various Gnostic heresies. They paralleled the elaborate cosmologies and dualistic views of many Greek philosophers and pagan cults and saw the divine immortal soul trapped in an evil mortal body. Gnostic Christians believed that Christ was the one who brought knowledge (*gnosis*) of these things. It was the acceptance of the truth of this knowledge that would free the soul from its mortal prison and allow it to return to the pure heavenly realm where it naturally belonged.

Two factors, however, prevented Christianity from becoming just another Hellenized Eastern mystery cult. First, was its acceptance of the Holy Book of the Jews (the Old Testament, as Christians came to call it), with its completely different spirit, as the foundation for and proof of its faith in Jesus as the Messiah. Second, was its unique organizational structure based on the idea of apostolic succession. That could check the spread of beliefs and practices too radically divergent from the spirit of the Old Testament and the early Christian writings canonized in the third century as the New Testament, which were written largely by men whose background was still more Jewish than Gentile. This system appears already worked out in all its major details between 180 and 190 in the works of Irenaeus, bishop of Lyons, particularly his *Five Books against Heresies* and the *Demonstration of Apostolic Preaching.*

By 200, the Church in the West had already matured to its familiar form. Irenaeus, a Greek from Asia Minor, was the last major Christian writer in the West to use Greek. Latin became the standard language of the Western Church for both theology and daily use. The form and order of Sunday worship and the celebration of the Eucharist had assumed their standard outlines. By now the bishop of Rome was recognized as having primacy over other bishops and churches and was looked up to by even the bishop of Carthage, the second largest Western see and home of an important school of thinkers.

In the mid-third century, disputes between Rome and Carthage arose over the question of treating apostates who wanted to return to the Church and over the validity of baptism by heretics. The Roman bishops tended to be liberal on both counts. The Carthaginians led by Cyprian (p. 411) favored the more strict view of the Roman priest Novatian; but the threat of persecution from without prevented a serious breach. Eventually, of course, the issue erupted into the Donatist schism of the fourth century (p. 431), but in the third, Carthaginian bishops generally remained loyal to the bishop of Rome. The church at Rome also rejected the Eastern practice of commemorating Christ's death on the Jewish Passover and established the observance of Easter Sunday. Complicated theories about the relationship of the divine Logos (Word) to God the Father along the lines of Greek philosophical speculation were also rejected. Eventually, this question would cause great dissension between Rome and Alexandria, but during the third century even Alexandria followed Rome and accepted the Roman New Testament as canonical.

On the whole, however, the state of the Church in the East was much more fluid than in the West during the third century. Egypt was full of gnostic heresies, and the close relationship between Rome and Alexandria was part of the effort to control them. Nevertheless, Greek-speaking Alexandria was much more open to the influence of Greek philosophical thought than the Latin-speaking West. By the end of the second century, the famous catechetical school of Alexandria was becoming a veritable Christian university, and the intellectual influence of Greek philosophy stirred up many theological disputes in the East (p. 476–479).

East of the Roman province of Syria, in the Mesopotamian client kingdoms and border lands, a Syriac-speaking church was founded around A.D. 170 by Tatian, a disciple of Justin Martyr. He provided a Syriac harmony (unified version) of the four Gospels known as the *Diatessaron (Four-in-One),* which became its basic testament. The conversion of King Agbar of Edessa gave great impetus to the Syriac church, and it remained strong and orthodox for many centuries. It did produce one major heretic, however, Bardaisan (Bardesanes), who became a Christian about 180. He was a highly educated Aramaean trained in astronomy and astrology. He combined many of the ideas that he had picked up earlier with his new faith. This heretical synthesis of Christian and non-Christian ideas was the basis of many of the views later espoused by the prophet Mani and Christianized Mesopotamian Gnostics known as Mandaeans.

In Asia Minor, whose churches were the earliest outside Palestine, the Christians were numerous and tended to remain on good terms with their pagan neighbors. In the mid-third century, there arose an internal dispute over the question of readmitting to the Church those who had lapsed during the Decian persecution. A number of Christians in Asia Minor adopted the strict position of Novatian, whose followers had become a schismatic sect and extended to all major sins his view on the inability of the Church to grant absolution. The Novatians, therefore, were very puritanical. They tried to lead completely sinless lives, called themselves *Cathari* (Pure Ones), and insisted on the rebaptism of converts.

In the late second century, a popular heresy had been introduced by Montanus, a convert in Phrygia. He began prophesying in the belief that the Second Coming was near. If the validity of this prophetic movement had been granted, the doctrines of the Church would have been thrown into chaos by the constant occurrence of new revelations among those claiming divine inspiration, and the vital unity of the Church would have been destroyed before it had had a chance to consolidate its position in the Empire.

The only other controversy of note involving the churches of Asia Minor was the refusal to bow to Rome over the question of Easter.

Magic and Superstition Although Christianity was winning many converts and working out its formal theology, many people of all classes turned to various forms of magic and superstition. A collection of works under the supposed authorship of Hermes Trismegistus (Thrice-Greatest) that dealt with astrology, alchemy, magic, and theurgy (the art of summoning and controlling divine powers) was very popular. Theurgy became a subject of great interest in the late third century as people sought more and more for a means of controlling an increasingly chaotic world.

Science and Philosophy

The temper of the times was not conducive to objective scientific thought. The last creative, rigorously systematic philosopher of Antiquity was Plotinus (205 to 270), a Greek from Egypt. He had studied under a mysterious philosopher named Ammonius Saccas at Alexandria and had joined the expedition of Gordian III to Persia (243) in the hope of studying the wisdom of Persia and India. When Gordian was killed the next year, Plotinus went to Rome, where he joined a group of ascetic philosophers and set up a school.

Starting with Plato's philosophy, he propounded a systematic explanation of the universe that gave birth to a new school of thought called Neoplatonism. This system is expounded in a magnum opus known as the *Enneads (Groups of Nine)* in six sections of nine books each. It is heavily influenced by the mystical Pythagorean elements in Plato. For Plotinus, everything is derived from the One, a single, immaterial, impersonal, eternal force from which reality spreads out in a series of concentric circles, the utmost one of which is matter, the lowest level of reality. Each level of reality depends upon the next highest: Matter depends upon Nature, which depends upon the World-Soul, which depends upon the World-Mind, which depends upon the One. A person contains all of these levels of being in microcosm and by focusing the power of the intellect can attain a level of being equal to that of the World-Mind. At that point, one may be able to achieve such a complete unity of self that an ecstatic union with the One itself is achieved.

Obviously, Plotinus' goal was shared by contemporary religions, but it was philosophical in that it was reached through pure, contemplative intellect, not through magic, ritual, or an intermediary savior. Such rigorously intellectual mysticism was far beyond most of his contemporaries, however, and Neoplatonism soon became overlaid with the magical musings of people like Iamblichus (p. 473).

The *Enneads* was actually published by Plotinus' pupil and assistant Porphyry (232/233 to ca. 305). Porphyry was not a creative thinker, but he was quick to grasp the ideas of others and was an accurate interpreter and publicist. He did the most to popularize Plotinus' ideas and saw them as the bulwark of pagan philosophy and religion against the Christians, who threatened the old ways. He wrote a massive fifteen-book defense of tradition against the Christians, which set the stage for his own pupil Iamblichus' even more vehement effort to rally the forces of paganism and block the spread of Christianity in the fourth century.

Education and the World of Letters

During the second century A.D., the city of Rome ceased to be the center of literary activity in the Roman world. A writer no longer had to go there and write for its elite to gain a significant audience and reputation. By the third century, authors from many different parts of the Empire were writing to satisfy the needs of diverse audiences in many different fields and genres. The need for literate personnel in the army and civil bureaucracy and the upper classes' need for marks of social distinction had produced increased support of higher education in the first and second centuries. Therefore, education in literature and rhetoric was still strong in the first half of the third century, but it suffered heavily in the crisis of the second half.

Paideia Despite public support, however, education remained an expensive luxury reserved for the wealthy and well-to-do. Most teachers and professors demanded fees on top of their salaries, and advanced education usually meant the expense of sending students away from home in late adolescence to teachers of rhetoric and philosophy in major cities like Rome, Carthage, Athens, Antioch, and Alexandria. Women, therefore, were generally excluded. To a large extent, the system defined the upper-class men whom it taught and set them apart from ordinary men. Educated aristocrats from diverse provinces all over the Empire often had more in common with each other than with the lower-class inhabitants of their hometowns, whose native language they might not share. In the eastern provinces, the local notables all spoke Greek and studied the same canon of classical authors beginning with Homer and ending with the Attic orators. They had learned many by heart and had all absorbed a uniform dialect of Attic Greek that allowed them to recognize one another instantly.

In the West, elite boys first acquired a basic knowledge of Greek and a thorough grounding in the Latin classics of the late Republic and early Principate: Catullus, Cicero, Caesar, Vergil, Horace, Livy, and Tacitus. Then, they capped their studies with a stint at one of the major educational centers in Greece so that they could deal as equals with the local leaders of the eastern provinces. In Greek terms, they had acquired the distinctive *paideia* that marked them out as sharers in a common elite culture and code of gentlemanly conduct. It allowed them to blunt the invidious distinctions between the rulers and the ruled and to maintain a civil discourse based on mutual understanding and respect that facilitated the smooth functioning of Imperial rule.

The system's heavy emphasis on literature and rhetoric produced innumerable people who could turn a quick hexameter verse or make a fine-sounding speech. Hundreds of competent but second-rate examples exist, particularly in the Greek East. Many of the emperors were products of this system and shared the literary interests of the educated upper class, on whom they depended to run the Empire. Septimius Severus was well educated in literature and law and wrote his autobiography

(now lost) in Greek. His wife, Julia Domna, was very interested in philosophy and religion and patronized pagan sophists. Severus Alexander had an intellectual circle that included historians, orators, and jurists. Gordian I was a poet, as was Gallienus, who also took an interest in Plotinus and had plans to set up a Neoplatonic state headed by Plotinus in Campania. Carus' son Numerianus was highly regarded as a poet.

Introduction of the Codex Book   Along with the spread of education, there arose a greater need for a less expensive and cumbersome form of the book than the old *volumen* (roll). The need was met in the third century by the introduction of the parchment codex, individual leaves of parchment bound together in a stack along the left-hand edge in the manner of wooden-backed wax writing tablets. It was much more useful for taking notes and writing out individual exercises. Because it was cheaper and more convenient, it made books written in codex form accessible to a wider public, which made it particularly attractive to Christian writers.

Biography and History under the Severi   Julia Domna's role as patroness has been exaggerated in the past to include almost every literary and intellectual figure of note in Rome at the time. The only known important member of her circle whose work has survived is Philostratus (b. ca. 170), a Greek sophist. He wrote a collection of biographies of previous sophists and, at Domna's request, a biography of the first-century-A.D. Cappadocian mystic and miracle worker Apollonius of Tyana, who is presented as a pagan equivalent of Christ. Probably not long after Philostratus, Diogenes Laertius, another Greek biographer, produced a collection of biographies of ancient philosophers that is extremely useful in reconstructing the history of Greek philosophy.

Under Alexander Severus in 229, the Greek historian Cassius Dio produced his history of Rome from its founding. Although not a historian of the first rank, Dio used good sources and supplied much valuable information in the absence of other sources. A few years later, Herodian produced his valuable Greek narrative of events from 180 to 238. Marius Maximus, a contemporary of Dio and Herodian, wrote a continuation of Suetonius with Latin biographies of the emperors from Nerva to Elagabalus. These accounts often included spicy fiction with the facts but also contained much of value. Although they are now lost, they provided the basic framework for the parallel biographies in the first and best part of the notorious *Historia Augusta* (p. 472).

Roman Scholarship and Legal Science The Severan and early post-Severan period saw the production of many commentaries on classical Latin authors and learned treatises on technical subjects. They were aimed at teachers, students, and officials whose native culture was not Roman or who found that the material to be mastered was increasingly difficult to understand with the passage of time and too voluminous to be managed in its original form. Some authors catered to the desire for many to learn more about the diverse places and peoples that made up the Empire. Under the Severi, Claudius Aelianus (Aelian), a Roman writing in Greek, preserved much curious information on animal and human life in his *De Natura Animalium* and *Varia Historia*. Gaius Julius Solinus covered the whole Empire in a wide-ranging Latin compedium called *Collectanea Rerum Memorabilium*. First, he traced Rome's rise from its foundation to the creation of Augustus' principate. Then, after treating the Italian and Greek core of the Empire, he worked counterclockwise to Germany, Gaul, Britain, Spain, Africa, Arabia, Asia Minor, India, and Parthia. In the process, he gathered together from previous authors much information on plants, animals, people, and customs.

Roman civil law, *ius civile,* was the glue that bound together the diverse peoples and places that made up the Empire. Previous officials and emperors had modified Roman law to fit new conditions and peoples as the Empire expanded. Over the years, a huge number of individual laws, edicts, and decisions had been issued. There was a great need to organize and explain them for ease of use. Three major jurists from different parts of the Empire took up the task under the Severi. Papinian (Aemilius Papinianus), probably a North African, became Septimius' praetorian prefect in 203 and was executed in 212 after criticizing Caracalla. His legal commentaries in 56 books were so useful that later German kings used them as guides for establishing their own courts. Ulpian (Domitius Ulpianus) was a Phoenician from Tyre and praetorian prefect to Severus Alexander from 222 to 228, when he was murdered by disgruntled Praetorian Guardsmen. Among his numerous works are 81 books commenting on the praetor's edict. Paul (Julius Paulus) succeeded Ulpian as praetorian prefect (228 to 235). His 319 books of commentaries surpassed both of his predecessors' combined. Later in the third century, Herennius Modestinus analyzed the differences between similar-appearing cases, and near the end of the century the *Codex Gregorianus* collected the rescripts of emperors from the previous two centuries.

Poetry and Greek Romances The third century was primarily an age of prose, not poetry. A late compilation called *The Latin Anthology* preserves only one or two good pieces of poetry from this period. The first is Pentadius' celebration of spring in clever yet elegant "echoing couplets," in which the first part of the hexameter is repeated in the second half of the pentameter. The other poem (probably from the third century) is the anonymous *Vigil of Venus (Pervigilium Veneris)*. It is a fresh and spontaneous expression of joy at the coming of spring as celebrated in Hybla on Sicily. Venus, linked with legends of Rome's founding, is the procreative force of nature, who brings love to humankind and fertility to the field.

The best Latin poet of the age was Marcus Aurelius Olympicus Nemesianus in the late third century. Nemesianus was from Carthage and was close to the Emperor Carus and his son Numerian, upon whom he had hoped to write an epic. His four surviving eclogues are worthy successors to Vergil's, and his didactic poem on hunting, the *Cynegetica,* is in the tradition of the *Georgics*. In Greek, there are only two poets of note. At the beginning of the third century, Oppian composed two didactic poems on rural themes. The first is the *Halieutica,* which deals with fishing, and the second is another *Cynegetica* on hunting. The other poet is Babrius, who is not a great poet but wrote over 130 extant fables in the tradition of Aesop.

Much more typical writings of the age are the Greek romances. They usually involve a virtuous heroine and steadfast hero who are separated by some mischance after falling in love. They experience all manner of hair-raising adventures, disasters, and narrow escapes until they are happily reunited in marriage at last. This genre originated at least as early as the first century A.D., and five representatives have survived: Achilles Tatius' *Leucippe and Cleitiphon,* which is now dated to the mid-second century; *Chaereas and Callirihoe* by Chariton of Aphrodisias is probably around 180; Heliodorus of Phoenician Emesa probably wrote his *Aethiopica* or *Theagenes and Charicleia* around 220; Longus (of Lesbos) and Xenophon of Ephesus, respectively, seem to have written *Daphnis* and *Chloe* and the *Ephesiaca* or *Anthia and Habrocames* at some time in the third century.

The style of these works and the quality of production evident from surviving papyrus fragments indicate that they were aimed at the urban elites of the Greek East. They reflect the values of a privileged class that had the resources to withstand life's misfortunes without really suffering. They also seem to promote the standards of male and female behavior designed to confirm the elite position of the upper class within the social hierarchy by reinforcing the stable family structure and harmonious social relations that helped it to perpetuate that position.

Secular Literature after the Severi The mid-third century saw a steep decline in literary production, and little of note except in philosophy survives. Two relatives of the sophist Philostratus, a father and grandson each confusingly named Philostratus, wrote three volumes entitled *Eikones (Images),* which, in the sophistic style of rhetoric, describe over eighty works of art. More important than Longinus (p. 392) in

the post-Severan period was the Athenian sophist Dexippus, who had helped to drive off the Goths and Heruli from Athens in 268 (p. 389). He wrote a history of Alexander's successors, a chronological summary of history down to 270, and a history of the Gothic wars from 238 to 275. Unfortunately, all three are largely lost, but quotations from later authors like Zosimus (p. 536) show that he was a worthy historian who modeled himself on Thucydides.

Christian Literature The audience and purpose of Christian literature, which came into its own during the third century, was often very different from that of secular works. Writings such as the Church's official accounts of various martyrdoms and the less formal passion narratives were aimed at people from the bottom of the social hierarchy. The first in Latin appears around 180 and recounts the deeds of the martyrs of Scillum in North Africa, *Acta Martyrum Scillitanorum.* The *Passion of Perpetua and Felicitas* follows in 203, and there are many others, such as the *Acts of Marcellus,* throughout the century.

These accounts of suffering and death were subversive of the prevailing political and social order. In them, Roman authorities were delegitimized as they, often unwillingly, imposed violent and unjust punishments on innocent sufferers ("passion," from the Latin *passio,* means "suffering"). Christians defined themselves through these narratives as a community of sufferers that rejected the bonds of the dominant social order reaffirmed by the happy endings of Greek romances. Wives, husbands, children, parents, and friends were abandoned in the joyous pursuit of a death that others saw as an ignoble defeat and punishment, but that Christians viewed as a glorious triumph. Through suffering, they rejected this world and entered the glorious life with Christ in heaven:

> Whoever comes to me and does not hate father and mother, wife and children, brothers and sisters, yes, even life itself, cannot be my disciple (Luke 14:25–26).

For Christians, death *was* the happy ending.

The Christian rejection of prevailing norms also appears in the works of Tertullian (ca. 160 to ca. 240), a North African from Carthage. Son of a centurion in the Roman army and trained as a lawyer, he was the first of the Latin Church fathers and a master of the art of defending the faith (apologetics). He became one of the founders of Western Christian thought. With biting irony and fiery rhetoric, he defended a strict version of Christianity while he attacked both pagans and heretics. For example, in a tirade on the immorality of public games, *De Spectaculis,* he claimed that theaters and temples were all that was left to pagans because Christians controlled the centers of power, namely, the cities, senate, and army. Thirty more of his works survive on such subjects as martyrdom, the soul, baptism, the resurrection of the flesh, marriage, and the proper behavior of women, whom he regarded with puritanical distrust. He was a brilliant pleader full of aggressive zeal in proclaiming a new Christian vision of the world, although he eventually became an adherent of the Montanist heresy (p. 406).

Not all Christian apologists were so hostile to the pagan world as Tertullian and the writers of passions and martyrologies. For example, although he, too, was a lawyer from North Africa, Tertullian's contemporary Minucius Felix was more upper class in origin. He shows how Christianity was beginning to penetrate the social elite, to whom he tried to appeal on their own terms. His surviving work is an elegant dialogue, the *Octavius,* in which Minucius' friend Octavius convinces their mutual pagan friend of the superiority of the Christian religion. Stamped with the *paideia* of upper-class culture, it exhibits none of the crude language, fiery zeal, and emotionalism of Tertullian but rather the dignified calm of friendly gentlemen having a rational debate in Ciceronian Latin. Nothing intrudes to threaten the social world that they share as friends.

Occupying the middle ground is St. Cyprian (ca. 200 to 258), another Carthaginian and a younger contemporary of Tertullian. A well-educated member of the upper class, he was a famous teacher of rhetoric. After converting to Christianity and giving all of his goods to the poor in 246, he was appointed bishop of Carthage in 248. He admired Tertullian's rigorous morality and wrote on many of the same subjects, but he was more refined and less strident. He conducted his duties as bishop like an upper-class Roman magistrate striving for equity and justice. In his writings he introduced legal language and concepts that helped to shape the Catholic Church in the West.

He fought against heresies and schisms in *De Catholicae Ecclesiae Unitate (On the Unity of the Catholic Church)* and dealt in *De Lapsis* with the divisive issue of readmitting to the Church those who had lapsed under the pressure of Decius' persecution. He took the moderate position that those who had renounced their faith could be readmitted to communion after rigorous penance. Although he had courageously protected his flock during Decius' persecution, he was ultimately martyred under Valerian. The *Life of Cyprian,* by his deacon Pontius, is the earliest known Christian biography.

The only Christian Latin poet in the third century probably was Commodian (ca. 250). He wrote at Carthage and mirrored Tertullian in his zeal and harshness. He uses accent rather than long and short syllables to produce his hexameter verses, which give voice to the hopes and prejudices of the lower classes. Poems like his *Instructiones* and *Carmen Apologeticum* have, unfortunately, crude attacks on pagans and Jews but present an emotionally compelling picture of the coming of God's Kingdom and justice for the downtrodden.

Christians who wrote in Greek had produced the earliest apologetic works and accounts of martyrs. Many such Greek writers were active in the third century. They were usually well-educated members of the urban Greek upper class, and their writings furthered Christianity's appeal to that class in ways that reflected its traditions. Titus Flavius Clemens, Clement of Alexandria (ca. 150 to ca. 215), for example, was born a pagan, most likely at Athens. He was steeped in Platonic philosophy and classical literature before he was converted and went to study at the informal Christian school at Alexandria. He eventually became head of the school and an influential apologist. In such surviving works as his *Exhortation to the Greeks,* he argues with grace and serenity that Christianity is superior to paganism.

Origen, Origenes Adamantius (ca. 185 to ca. 255), was Clement's student and successor as head of the Christian school at Alexandria. He also may have studied with the Platonist Ammonius Saccas, Plotinus' famous teacher. He had a famous personal library, wrote voluminously on textual and interpretive problems in the Bible, systematically explained Christian beliefs in *On First Principles,* and countered the anti-Christian arguments of the philosopher Celsus in *Against Celsus.*

In many ways, Origen was the founder of systematic theology. He made logic, dialectic, natural science, geometry, and astronomy standard parts of the curriculum. With such training, the Alexandrian Church fathers skillfully used Greek philosophy against their pagan critics and gave a more intellectual cast to Christian thought, which gained greater respect among the pagan intellectual elite of the Empire.

It was precisely the influence of Platonic thought, however, that caused Origen to develop the heretical views that this world resulted from evil and was not a perfect creation before the Fall and that the Trinity is three separate entities, not one. On the one hand, therefore, he encouraged certain gnostic ideas, and, on the other, he set the stage for the divisive Arian heresy in the fourth century under Constantine (pp. 432–433).

After a dispute with the bishop of Alexandria, Origen settled in at Caesarea in Palestine and opened a school there. Tortured horribly during Decius' persecution, he died a little later at Tyre, but his influence remained very strong in Palestine through students like Pamphilus, who inherited his library, and it contributed to more arguments about the Trinity. The most notable involved Paul of Samosata in Syria, who had become bishop of Antioch in the 260s. He viewed the Logos as one with the Father and the Son as wholly human. The Origenist bishops condemned his views as heretical mostly on the ground of his joining the Logos with the Father in the same essence. Thus they supplied even more ammunition for the controversy that rent the Eastern Church over the Arian heresy.

Origen's friend Sextus Julius Africanus was a learned Christian from Jerusalem. He eventually went to Rome on an embassy to Elagabalus and later set up a library in the Pantheon for Severus Alexander. His *Chronographies* was the first attempt to rationalize biblical and Church history with secular history. It formed the basis of Eusebius' later *Chronicle* (p. 477).

Less is known about the influential writer Methodius. One of Origen's detractors, he wrote *On the Resurrection* to counter Origen's denial of a bodily resurrection of the flesh. He also countered the gnostics in his *On the Freedom of the Will*. Although these are now fragmentary, his popular *Symposium of the Ten Virgins,* in which the Christian heroine Thecla gives a prize oration on virginity, is complete (p. 459).

The tales of Christian martyrs and the apologetic and theological writings of the Latin and Greek Church fathers had helped to spread Christianity among all classes during the third century and made it strong enough to withstand the greatest persecution of all that was soon to come.

Art and Architecture

Sculpture Despite all the troubles of the age, considerable art was produced for emperors and wealthy magnates. Portraiture on coins maintained a high standard of realism as vehicles of official propaganda. Portrait sculpture also continued the vigorous Roman tradition. From the Severi to Gallienus, sculptors strove for psychological realism in order to emphasize the true character of the subject. Under Gallienus there was a preference for the more idealized portrait in the classical Greek style, but after that, the influence of Neoplatonism caused a shift to a more schematized, geometric style that gave a transcendent quality to the subjects, a style that prefigured the Middle Ages.

Although there were not many opportunities to produce monumental public relief sculptures through the difficult times of the third century, relief sculpture became a striking feature of the elaborately decorated stone sarcophagi that wealthy Christians and pagans began to use as the new religious influences of the age caused the practice of bodily burial to replace cremation. Some feature groupings of classical figures around a philosopher or poet, who symbolize the triumph of wisdom over death. Others feature a heroic figure in the midst of a chaotic battle to symbolize the triumph of good over evil. Christians depicted the Good Shepherd or Old Testament stories of God's deliverance. Despite the unclassical lack of balance in many of these scenes, the individual figures are very skillfully carved and are thoroughly in the tradition of Greco-Roman realism.

Painting and Mosaics Painting and mosaic art continued to flourish throughout the third century. Painting is represented mainly by murals preserved on the excavated walls of homes, public buildings, tombs, synagogues, temples, and churches from around the Empire. Excellent mosaics also adorned many of these build-ings, particularly their floors. The level of technical skill remained very high, and the scenes represented are valuable in reconstructing the life of the times.

Architecture Despite the Empire's serious economic problems, the building activity under the Severi was more than had been seen for many years. At Rome the Arch of Septimius Severus still stands in the Forum. Massive new additions were made to the Imperial residence, whose foundations are visible on the Palatine. Caracalla built a huge new complex of baths and a new camp for the Imperial bodyguards, both of which are now in ruins. In North Africa, Septimius' hometown, Lepcis (Leptis) Magna, received a whole complex of monumental buildings, whose remains today provide a striking example of Imperial architecture and urban planning. All of these remains, moreover, show solid Roman craftsmanship.

During the anarchy between the Severi and Diocletian, there was not much opportunity for public architecture other than defensive works such as Aurelian's partially preserved twelve-mile-long wall around Rome and fortifications in the provinces. Christian churches in various cities, however, had begun to accumulate enough wealth to erect some significant buildings. Little is known about these churches, however, because many were destroyed in the persecutions early in the follow-

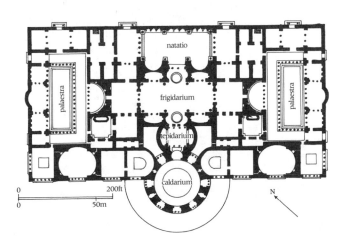

Baths of Caracalla, Rome, plan. (from Roman Art, *second edition, Nancy and Andrew Ramage, Prentice Hall, 1996)*

ing century or were replaced by more impressive structures after the persecutions ended.

Summary and Prospect As do all ages, the third century of the Roman Empire had one foot in the past and the other in the future. The massive inflation of the latter half of the century was rooted in the basic nature of the ancient Mediterranean economy. In the West, many cities and the once-prosperous curial class declined. Small landowners, unable to withstand the pressure of Roman tax collectors, military requisitions, raids on the frontiers, and pressures from rich neighbors, were often reduced to dependent *coloni,* foreshadowing Medieval serfs. On the other hand, the wealthy became ever richer as they assessed huge amounts of land and withdrew from the declining cities to their great villas in the country. In the East, the cities and small farmers fared better and were poised for revived prosperity in the next century. In either case the bulk of the population lived in the countryside as it always had and followed the traditional rhythms of life in a peasant economy that functioned largely apart from the inflation-ravaged commercial economy.

Although the free inhabitants of the Empire acquired citizenship, and military service brought "barbarians" and people from different parts of the Empire into greater contact with each other, it was mainly the upper classes from the provinces who found greater opportunities for advancement in the army and government. Similarly, a few women of the privileged classes achieved greater public prominence, but most women saw little improvement in their conditions. Women and the lower classes, however, increasingly found refuge among the growing ranks of the Christian Church, which was much more inclusive than aristocratically dominated secular society.

Christianity and other popular mystery religions gave greater expression to the cultural traditions of those who could not afford to acquire the educated polish of upper-class *paideia*. In fact, Christianity often represented a challenge to all that the privileged classes held dear. Nevertheless, as Christianity began to penetrate the upper classes, they began to shape Christian institutions, thought, literature, and art along familiar lines. By the beginning of the fourth century and the conversion of the Emperor Constantine, Christianity was as much a force for spreading classical culture to the previously excluded as it was a challenge to it.

XXXIV

Diocletian: Creating the Fourth-Century Empire, A.D. 285 to 305

In Roman History, the fourth century is often reckoned from the acclamation of Diocletian as emperor in 284 to the death of Theodosius in 395. The real turning point between the third and the fourth centuries, however, is Diocletian's victory over Carinus in 285. Only at that point did the unprecedented barrage of political, military, and natural disasters characterizing the third century begin to lose intensity in the face of Diocletian's reforms.

The gigantic mobilization required to meet Rome's difficulties had accelerated the trend toward an absolute military monarchy. Under Diocletian, the Principate gave way completely to the Dominate. The term comes from *dominus*, "lord and master," which was synonymous with absolute monarchy and was now used to refer to the emperor in public documents. Diocletian instituted sweeping military, administrative, and fiscal reforms to ensure the survival of the Roman Empire united under his command as the senior of four ruling partners, tetrarchs, who formed the Tetrarchy.

Sources for Roman History during the Fourth Century A.D. Although the latter part of the fourth century A.D. is one of the best documented in Roman history, Diocletian's crucial reign lacks many major secular sources. The pagan Greek Zosimus (p. 536) portrayed Diocletian very favorably in his *New History*

(ca. A.D. 500), but the sections that cover Diocletian's reign in detail are missing. On the other hand, the rest of the narrative, which is very biased against Constantine and the Christians, is complete. Unfortunately, Ammianus Marcellinus' excellent *History* (or *Res Gestae*) has not completely survived, but it is extant for the period from 353 to 378. The staunch pagan upholder of senatorial tradition at Rome, Quintus Aurelius Symmachus, has left a major body of letters that provide valuable insights into the world of well-connected Roman aristocrats.

The letters and poems of Ausonius, a Gallo-Roman aristocrat and rhetorician, illustrate the life of the increasingly Christian elite of the western provinces. Themistius, a philosopher and rhetorician, and other skilled orators produced numerous panegyrics on Constantine and members of his dynasty. The voluminous letters and speeches of the great Greek rhetorician Libanius of Antioch shed light on many personalities and events during the second half of the fourth century.

Secular sources of secondary importance include the biography of Diocletian at the close of the *Historia Augusta* and several *breviaria*, brief historical surveys of Roman history, the last parts of which are of real value since they record events of the authors' own time. Of these the best are the *Caesars* of Aurelius Victor, short biographies of the emperors from Augustus to Julian the Apostate (361 to 363);

the *Breviary* of Eutropius, which ends with the year 369; the *Breviary* of Rufius Festus, which ends with the year 371; and the anonymous *Epitome of the Caesars,* which ends with the death of Theodosius I in 395. A number of interesting fourth-century technical treatises and handbooks on military affairs have also survived (pp. 470–471).

Christian writings for the fourth century are very extensive, and they are full of quotations from otherwise lost documents such as Imperial statutes and edicts, proceedings of Church councils, Imperial correspondence, and letters written by bishops and other ecclesiastical officials. Their biases are obviously counter to those of secular or pagan authors and often involve partisan or theological controversies within the Church as well. One of the best and most biased Christian writers is Lactantius (ca. 240 to ca. 325). Aside from his doctrinal works, important for the history of the evolving Christian Church, his Latin tract *On the Deaths of the Persecutors* presents a very hostile view of the policies and personalities of Diocletian and those with whom he shared power. Of great importance are works of the Greek writer Eusebius of Caesarea. In addition to versions of his *Chronicle* and his *Ecclesiastical History* mentioned earlier (p. 374), his *Life of Constantine* (unfinished) and *Praise of Constantine* (with the *Tricennalian Oration,* which celebrate Constantine's thirtieth anniversary as emperor) are invaluable despite their obvious favoritism. Other Greek histories of the Church are those of Theodoret, Sozomen, and Socrates, which end in 408, 425, and 439, respectively.

Many other great churchmen writing in both Greek and Latin provide a wealth of material for all aspects of history in the latter half of the fourth century through their histories, biographies, letters, sermons, and doctrinal writings. In Greek there are the bishops Basil of Caesarea, his brother Gregory of Nyssa, Gregory of Nazianzus, Synesius of Cyrene, Athanasius of Alexandria, and John Chrysostom (Golden-Mouthed), the renowned preacher and moralist of Constantinople. Among the important Latin Church fathers, St. Jerome, the famous Latin translator of the Bible, translated Euse-

bius' *Chronicle,* too, and continued it from 325 to 378. He also wrote a *De Viris Illustribus* on the lives of 135 illustrious men (St. Peter to himself). Rufinus of Aquileia, who translated Eusebius' *Ecclesiastical History,* extended it from 324 to 395, and bishops such as Ambrose of Milan, Hilary of Poitiers, Sulpicius Severus, Paulinus of Nola, and St. Augustine of Hippo, greatest of all the Latin fathers, are rich sources for their times. Augustine's magnum opus, *The City of God,* powerfully states the Christian view of history, whereas works such as his *Confessions, On Christian Learning,* and *On the Teacher* reflect the uneasy relationship between pagan classical culture and Christianity. The Spanish priest Orosius covers the fourth century in the last part of Book 7 of his *Historiae Adversus Paganos,* and the Gallic theologian Prosper of Aquitaine picks up where Jerome left off and carries his *Chronicle* down to 455.

Christian biographers after Eusebius wrote numerous lives and accounts of martyrdoms that are valuable sources of social history. The most famous Christian biography is probably the *Life of St. Anthony* ascribed to Athanasius of Alexandria. It represents the ideals of Christian asceticism that had an enormous influence on monasticism and asceticism throughout the Empire. Jerome imitated the *Life of Anthony* in his *Lives* of Hilarion, Paul, and Malchus. The great lay Christian poet Prudentius (348 to post 405) glorified many martyrs and the ideals of Christian life. The accounts of female martyrs vividly illustrate the impact of Christianity on the role of women in society, as do Gregory of Nyssa's biography of his sister, *Life of Macrina,* and Gerontius' very popular *Life of Melania the Younger.*

Other sources include inscriptions, papyri, coins, archaeological materials, and especially Imperial statutes (*constitutiones*[1]). The

---

[1]The *constitutiones principum* ("statutes of the emperors"), which had the validity of laws, included (1) *edicta* or edicts (official proclamations of the emperor as a Roman magistrate, which were valid during his term of office for the whole Empire); (2) *decreta* or decrees (court decisions of the emperor having the force of law); (3) *rescripta* (written responses to written inquiries on specific

latter are preserved in numerous documents: inscriptions, papyri, various juristic and literary works, the Theodosian Code (published in 438 during the reign of Theodosius II, 408 to 450), and the Justinian Code (first published in 529 during the reign of Justinian I, 527 to 565). The two most important inscriptional texts are Diocletian's famous *Edict on Maximum Prices,* and the great Paikuli inscription of Narses I of Persia (293 to 302), wherein the king recounted his triumphs and the acts of homages paid him by Roman envoys and the vassal kings of Asia.

Another major document is the *Notitia Dignitatum (List of Offices)*, an apparently official, illustrated register of military units and their postings throughout the provinces. As it stands, it comes from the western half of the Empire after the division that prevailed from 395 onward, but the information in the East is earlier. Because it reflects the ideal of stated policy, it does not necessarily represent actual practice and must be used with caution when trying to determine what was really happening at any particular moment.

The archaeological evidence for the fourth century is enormous. Diocletian, his co-emperors, Constantine, and Constantine's heirs spent prodigiously on building in Rome, Constantinople, and various other important cities where emperors frequently resided, such as Trier, Milan, Sirmium, Nicomedia, and Antioch. Fortifications, camps, guard stations, and signal posts were constructed all over the Empire. The elite spent huge sums on building and expanding rural villas as they focused more and more on a self-sufficient life in the countryside. Christians built shrines, monasteries, and major urban churches with great fervor after persecution ended early in the century and official support began.

---

points of law). Although the *constitutiones* were originally valid only during the principate of their author, they later remained in force as sources of public and private law unless revoked by a later Imperial constitution. The emperor also became a source of law through the responses of eminent jurists to whom he had delegated the *ius respondendi* (p. 294).

The Rise of Diocletian The humbleness of Diocletian's origins has been exaggerated by hostile or overly dramatic sources. One of a series of talented, well-trained officers from the Danubian provinces, he probably came from a relatively well-to-do provincial family. He had been a cavalryman under Gallienus, a *dux* or cavalry commander in Moesia, and a commandant of the Imperial mounted bodyguard. His excellent military record is nevertheless overshadowed by his career as an organizer, administrator, and statesman. He inspired excellent advisors and generals to assist him loyally in restoring stability to the Empire.

The chief military and political problems facing Diocletian were the strengthening of the power and authority of the central government, the defense of the frontiers, the recovery of the rebellious and seceding provinces, and the removal of those conditions that favored constant attempts to seize the throne. Diocletian's first act was to find a loyal representative who could take over the defense of the West and permit him to concentrate his energies upon the protection of the threatened Danubian and eastern frontiers. Such a loyal representative would convince the western legions of his concern for western problems and would lessen the danger of revolt. His choice fell upon Maximian, an old comrade in arms, whom he elevated to the rank of Caesar and sent to Gaul.

In Gaul, Maximian quickly crushed a rebellion of desperate peasants (the Bacaudae) and drove out the Germans into the region east of the Rhine. In recognition of these victories, Diocletian raised Maximian to the rank of Augustus in 286. Maximian was to rule jointly with Diocletian and to be second only in personal prestige and informal authority.

Maximian had not been so successful at sea. To clear the English Channel and the North Sea of the Frankish and Saxon pirates who had been raiding the shores of Gaul and Britain, he established a naval base at Gesoriacum (Bononia, Boulogne) on the coast of Gaul and placed Marcus Aurelius Carausius in command of the Roman fleet. Carausius, a native of the German lowlands and an experienced and daring sailor, overcame the pirates within a few weeks. He ambitiously enlarged his fleet with captured pirate ships and men, seized Gesoriacum and Britain, and conferred upon himself the title of Augustus. Because Diocletian was too occupied to do more than protest and Maximian's fleet was wrecked at sea, Carausius maintained undisturbed sway over Britain for seven years as Emperor of the North.

Meanwhile, Diocletian himself had not been idle in the East. Displaying the might of Rome on the Danube and the Euphrates between 286 and 291, he had repelled invasions and strengthened frontier defenses. In 287, successful negotiations with the Persian King Bahram (Vahram, Varahan, Varanes) II (276 to 293) obtained Persian renunciation of claims to Roman Mesopotamia and recognition of Rome's ally Tiridates IV (261 to 317) as the legitimate king of Armenia.

The Tetrarchy, 293 to 312 In order to strengthen Imperial control of the armies and forestall usurpers such as Carausius, Diocletian resolved in 293 to create the four-man ruling committee known as the Tetrarchy. Two Caesars were to be appointed to serve as junior emperors and successors to two Augusti, one to serve under Diocletian, the Augustus in the East, the other under Maximian, the Augustus in the West. Diocletian selected Gaius Galerius another Danubian officer and a brilliant strategist, as his Caesar. Maximian's choice was yet another Danubian, C. Flavius Julius Constantius, commonly called Chlorus or "Pale Face," who proved himself an excellent general, a prudent statesman, and the worthy father of the future Constantine the Great.

The Tetrarchy was held together by the personality and authority of Diocletian, the senior Augustus. It was doubly strengthened by adoption and marriage, for each Caesar was the adopted heir and son-in-law of his Augustus. The Tetrarchy was indivisible in operation and power: Laws were promulgated in the names of all four rulers, and triumphs gained by any one of them were acclaimed in the name of all. On the other hand, each member of the Tetrarchy had his own separate court and bodyguard and

had the right to strike coins bearing his own image and titulature.

Each Augustus and Caesar oversaw those provinces and frontiers that he could conveniently and adequately defend from his own headquarters: Maximian protected the upper Rhine and upper Danube from Mediolanum (Milan) and Aquileia in Italy; Constantius shielded the middle and lower Rhine, Gaul, and later Britain from Augusta Treverorum (Trèves, Trier) in Gaul; Galerius seems initially to have guarded the Euphrates frontier, Palestine, and Egypt from Antioch in Syria (293 to 296) and then the lower Danube and the Balkans from Thessalonica in Macedonia and Serdica in Thrace (299 to 311); for most of his first ten years, Diocletian oversaw the middle and lower Danube and Asia Minor from his bases at Sirmium on the Save River and Nicomedia on the Sea of Marmara (Marmora, Propontis); from 299 to 302, he looked after affairs in Asia Minor, the Levant, and Egypt at Antioch and then at Nicomedia (302 to 305).

Theoretically, the Tetrarchy also provided for a quiet and orderly succession to the throne. On the death or abdication of an Augustus, his Caesar, also his adopted son and heir, supposedly would take his place and would, in turn, select a new Caesar. Unfortunately, the system was held together only by the dynamism of Diocletian. Once he was removed, his successors began struggling among themselves for personal dominance, and the Empire was plunged into another debilitating series of civil wars.

The Tetrarchy in Action While he held the reins of power, however, the Tetrarchy fully justified Diocletian's expectations as each of the four rulers set about restoring peace and unity in his own part of the Empire. Constantius weakened Carausius by capturing the port of Gesoriacum (Bononia, Boulogne) and defeating his German allies. In 293 a treacherous rival assassinated Carausius, and in 296 Constantius successfully reestablished Roman rule in Britain. Returning to the Continent, he strengthened the fortifications along the Rhine frontier and established a long period of peace after a spectacular victory over the Alemanni in 298.

The activities of Diocletian and Galerius in the East are poorly documented, but recent research supports the following outline. Between 293 and 296, Diocletian waged a series of successful campaigns against the tribes along the lower Danube and restored Roman defenses in the area while events in Persia and Egypt occupied Galerius' attention. In Persia, a new king, Narses (293 to 302), overthrew Bahram II and began to subvert the treaty of 287. He also promoted the religious beliefs of the Manichees, whose missionary activities raised Roman suspicions. At the same time, Egypt was being disturbed by the raids of the Blemmyes from the Sudan, who could no longer be left unchecked. Galerius probably spent all of 294 and the first few months of 295 in Egypt in order to drive out the Blemmyes and strengthen Egypt's defenses.

Meanwhile, Narses was causing increasing alarm on the Euphrates frontier. By the fall of 296, hostilities could no longer be avoided. Narses had driven Tiridates IV out of Armenia and was poised to strike at Roman territory. Diocletian brought reinforcements from the Danube and guarded the Euphrates while Galerius rushed off to intercept Narses. After an initial defeat (early 297?), reinforcements enabled Galerius to turn the tables in the following year. He captured the King's harem, regained control of Mesopotamia, and seized the strategic fortress of Nisibis as well as the Persian capital of Ctesiphon.

While Galerius was fighting Narses, increased taxation precipitated a serious revolt in Egypt under the leadership of Domitius Domitianus and Aurelius Achilleus.[2] Diocletian brought an army from Syria in mid-297 and besieged Alexandria for eight months. After subduing the whole of Egypt during the rest of 298, he returned to join the victorious Galerius at Nisibis for the final peace negotiations with Narses.

[2] Manichaeism may have provided some link between their revolt and Narses' hostile actions. At least Diocletian may have thought so by the time he outlawed Manichaeism in 302.

The loss of his wives and children obliged Narses to accept harsh peace terms. He agreed to surrender Mesopotamia, which now extended to the west bank of the upper Tigris, and five small provinces east of the Tigris. He acknowledged as Roman protectorates Greater Armenia and the kingdom of Iberia south of the Caucasus. He also agreed that merchants traveling between the Roman and Persian empires must pass through the Roman customs center at Nisibis. The victory of Galerius was so complete that the Persians did not risk war with Rome for another fifty years.

The creation of the Tetrarchy had been fully justified by the victories of Constantius in the West and of Galerius in the East; by the construction of strong defenses in Britain, along the Rhine, Danube, and Euphrates rivers, and in Egypt and Mesopotamia, and by the systematic settlement of captured invaders to repopulate and help defend lands adjacent to the frontiers. That four-headed, seemingly decentralized, but actually united power, gave Rome 20 years of stable rule. Defenses were repaired and resources mobilized so that the Roman Empire was able to survive for another 200 years in the West and lay the foundations for the Byzantine Empire in the East.

Diocletian's Reforms In addition to establishing the Tetrarchy and consolidating the military defenses of the Empire, Diocletian carried out sweeping reforms in almost every department of the government. These reforms were not wholly without precedent. They were not the innovations of a radical but rather the continuation and strengthening of the trend toward absolute monarchy.

Court Ceremonial To promote stability by ensuring the personal safety of the emperor, Diocletian surrounded himself with an aura of such power, pomp, and sanctity that an attempt to overthrow him would appear not only treasonous but also sacrilegious. Diocletian assumed the title of Jovius as Jupiter's earthly representative sent to restore the Roman Empire. He bestowed upon his colleague, Maximian, the name of Herculius as the earthly analog of Hercules, helper of Jupiter. Together they demanded the reverence and adoration due to gods for the Jovian and Herculian dynasties that they had founded. Everything about them was sacred and holy: their palaces, courts, and bedchambers. Their portraits radiated a nimbus or halo, an outer illumination flowing from an inner divinity.

In order to dazzle his subjects with the Emperor's power and majesty and infect them with a feeling of mystery and awe, Diocletian adopted an elaborate court ceremonial and etiquette, not unlike that prescribed at the royal court of Persia. The emperor became less accessible and seldom appeared in public. When he did, he wore the diadem and carried the scepter. He arrayed himself in purple and gold sparkling with jewels. Those to whom he condescended to grant audience had to kneel and kiss the hem of his robe. This act of adoration was incumbent also upon members of the Imperial Council (*consilium*), which acquired the name of Sacred Consistory (*sacrum consistorium*) from the necessity of standing while in the Imperial presence.

Provincial Administration To increase the control of the emperor and prevent ambitious governors from amassing too much power, Diocletian completely reorganized the administrative system. Following a trend initiated by Septimius Severus, he completed the abolition of Italy's privileged status and divided it into a dozen provinces. In addition, by subdividing the old provinces, he increased the total number of provinces from about 40 to about 105. He also deprived most governors of their former military functions.

The new provinces were grouped into twelve administrative districts known as dioceses. Each diocese was subject to a vicar (*vicarius*) of equestrian rank who supervised all governors, even those of senatorial rank except the three proconsuls of Africa, Asia, and Achaea. Like all governors (except those of Isauria in Asia Minor and Mauretania in North Africa), the vicars were civilian officials whose main function was the administration of justice

and supervision of tax collection. The dioceses, in turn, were grouped into four prefectures, Gaul and Italy in the West and Illyricum and the Orient in the East. A praetorian prefect supervised the vicars in each prefecture and reported directly to the tetrarch who resided at the headquarters of that prefecture.

Diocletian assigned command over the armies and garrisons stationed in the provinces to professional military men known as dukes (*duces*). To assure close supervision and the mutual restraint of ambitious impulses, he made the dukes dependent for military supplies and provisions upon the governors and other civilian officials. In some dioceses, several dukes might serve under the command of a higher officer known as a count (*comes*).

Military Reforms During the third century Rome's system of frontier defense had essentially collapsed. It was only by withdrawing the armies to the central core of the Empire that Gallienus and the capable Illyrian cavalry commanders who succeeded him were able to check the momentum of outside attackers and then regain effective control over the periphery. Diocletian represents the culmination of this process. Having regained political and military control within the territory of the Empire, Diocletian instituted military reforms to give better protection to the frontiers and enable more effective responses to major attacks before they did irreparable harm.

The details of Diocletian's solution are a matter of great debate, but a general outline is clear. First of all, he increased the size of Roman military forces (infantry, cavalry, and naval, both regular and auxiliary) by as much as 100,000 men to a total of around 500,000. He probably kept the official manpower of individual legions at around 5,500, but they and the other forces were often spread out in numerous smaller detachments. They manned small, heavily constructed forts and guard posts along roads and supply routes in frontier zones or served as easily mobilized forces billeted in strategically located fortified cities and towns within the frontier provinces. In this way the army could guarantee the safe acquisition, transportation, and storage of supplies, protect communications in general, sound the alarm when any sector of the frontier was attacked, and quickly bring up mobile forces as needed.

There is no major shift in Roman defensive strategy here. The fortified roads were built in forward areas to provide protective zones for the provinces proper. That fits a pattern going all the way back to Augustus. Units stationed in the rear performed the same function as those once stationed in large legionary camps. It was easier to supply them, however, by stationing smaller detachments in various cities and towns. Furthermore, the dispersal of provincial troops in small units made it more difficult for provincial commanders to win over large numbers of troops quickly for a rebellion.

To ensure that large armies necessary to meet major emergencies along the most vulnerable frontiers remained in loyal hands, each of the four tetrarchs commanded a different prefecture from their strategically located headquarters. Constantius kept an eye on the Rhine from Trier; from Milan, Maxentius could defend the dangerous triangle formed by the upper reaches of the Rhine and Danube rivers; Galerius guarded the rest of the Danube from Sirmium; and Diocletian protected the eastern frontiers from Nicomedia in Bithynia. With each tetrarch were highly mobile troops, especially cavalry. They constituted his *comitatus* (personal escort) and formed the nucleus of the large field armies that would be assembled from smaller provincial units where and when they were needed.

Recruiting enough soldiers for Diocletian's expanded army was a real problem. Conscription had fallen into disfavor, and the government could not afford to call too many men away from most occupations anyway. Diocletian employed conscription cautiously, enforced hereditary military obligations, utilized voluntary enlistment, and hired foreign mercenaries. To make sure that Imperial armies were adequately armed and equipped, Diocletian instituted a system of state-owned workshops (*fabricae*) that produced directly for the military. Those located near sources of iron ore in Asia Minor specialized in armor or weapons.

Some were located in strategic western cities such as Sirmium, Salona, and Ticinum. A number of shops produced cloth or leather, which other shops turned into clothing, headwear, and footwear.

Diocletian's administrative and military reforms added fuel to the inflationary fires of the time. When he increased the number of provinces from about 40 to about 105 and created separate military commanders and civilian governors for each, he increased the number of highly salaried provincial officials fivefold. On top of that he added the four praetorian prefects and twelve vicarii and all their staffs. The creation of various new Imperial residences for the four tetrarchs, the building of frontier forts and roads, and monumental building programs in Rome entailed even more expense. Between 150 and 300 the basic rate of military pay had increased sixfold. By increasing the number of soldiers by somewhere between one-fourth and one-third and by giving donatives at regular intervals throughout the year, Diocletian raised the government's cost for manpower and supplies even more.

The Reform of the Coinage, 286 to 293 Diocletian attempted to end the frightful monetary chaos of the third century by reforming the coinage. His system of silver and gold coinage, though not a long-term success itself, served as a model for his successors. In 286, he began to replace the old *aureus* with a new gold coin at the rate of 60 to the standard Roman pound of 327.45 grams (12 Roman ounces, 11.536 ounces avoirdupois). In 293, he introduced a silver coin, the *argenteus,* at 96 to the pound and roughly equivalent to the *denarius* of Nero's time. To answer the need for small change, he struck three denominations: a copper *denarius,* a silver-washed copper piece worth two *denarii,* and a more heavily silvered bronze *nummus* worth five *denarii.*

The Edict on Maximum Prices, 301 Diocletian's monetary reforms were not very successful in combating inflation. He was not able to mint enough good gold and silver coins to satisfy the government's needs, and the copper

The Dioceses and Provinces of the Roman Empire in A.D. 314

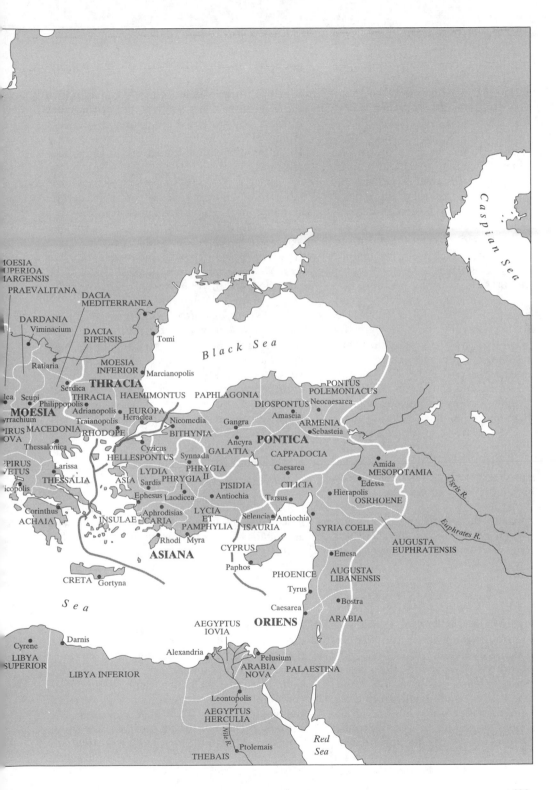

MOESIA
SUPERIOA
MARGENSIS

PRAEVALITANA

DARDANIA
Viminacium

DACIA
MEDITERRANEA

DACIA
RIPENSIS

Tomi

Ratiaria

MOESIA
INFERIOR
Marcianopolis

Black Sea

Serdica

THRACIA

lea Scupi
Philippopolis

MOESIA
rrachium

Adrianopolis
Traianopolis

IRUS MACEDONIA

Thessalonica

THRACIA HAEMIMONTUS PAPHLAGONIA

EUROPA
Heraclea

RHODOPE

Nicomedia

BITHYNIA

Gangra

DIOSPONTUS

Amaseia

PONTUS
POLEMONIACUS
Neocaesarea

ARMENIA
Sebasteia

Ancyra

PONTICA

Caspian Sea

EPIRUS
VETUS

icopolis

Larissa

THESSALIA

Cyzicus

HELLESPONTUS

ASIA

LYDIA
Sardis

Ephesus

Synnada
GALATIA

PHRYGIA
II

PHRYGIA
I

Laodicea

PISIDIA

Antiochia

CAPPADOCIA

Caesarea

CILICIA

Tarsus

Amida
MESOPOTAMIA

Edessa

Hierapolis

OSRHOENE

Tigris R.

Corinthus

ACHAIA

INSULAE

CARIA

Aphrodisias

Rhodi

LYCIA
ET
PAMPHYLIA

Myra

Selencia
ISAURIA

Antiochia

SYRIA COELE

Euphrates R.

AUGUSTA
EUPHRATENSIS

ASIANA

CYPRUS

Paphos

Emesa

AUGUSTA
LIBANENSIS

CRETA
Gortyna

PHOENICE

Tyrus

Caesarea

Bostra

ARABIA

Sea

ORIENS

Cyrene

Darnis

LIBYA
SUPERIOR

LIBYA INFERIOR

AEGYPTUS
IOVIA

Alexandria

ARABIA
NOVA

Pelusium

PALAESTINA

Leontopolis
AEGYPTUS
HERCULIA

Nile R.

Ptolemais

Red
Sea

THEBAIS

denarii and the billon (silver-coated base metal) coins were issued in huge numbers that only added to inflation. Diocletian made the situation even worse in early 301 by issuing his famous *Edict on Maximum Prices*. This edict is one of the most valuable Roman economic documents available. It has been reconstructed from numerous fragmentary Greek and Latin inscriptions largely in the eastern part of the Empire but more recently also in Italy. It set a ceiling on the prices of over a thousand different items from wheat, barley, rice, poultry, vegetables, fruits, fish, and wines of every variety and origin to clothing, bed linen, ink, parchment, and craftsmen's wages.

In a remarkable preamble to the edict, Diocletian sharply condemned speculators and profiteers who robbed the helpless public. He was particularly concerned about the purchasing power of soldiers, who had little other than money to exchange in the marketplace. The penalty for those who overcharged was death. With the prices for goods and services fixed and the value of money falling, it became unprofitable to sell goods at the official prices. Therefore, people either refused to produce goods, sold them illegally on black markets, or simply relied on barter, which had always played a strong role in the everyday economy, particularly for the countryside. In the face of economic realities, the edict had to be relaxed to encourage production and the availability of goods for sale in markets. The edict had become largely a dead letter by the end of Diocletian's reign.

Tax Reform In order to meet the increased needs of the government and reduce the impact of inflation on the Imperial budget, Diocletian instituted a thorough rationalization of the tax system to make it more efficient and dependable. Although he did away with many taxes, Diocletian based his new system on two basic types of taxes that had traditionally been used throughout the ancient Mediterranean world, the land tax and the poll tax. It was also traditional that many taxes were paid in kind; that is, in the form of agricultural products (such as grain, oil, wine, and meat) or manufactured goods (such as cloth, leather, tools, building materials, and arms), the so-called *annona,* by which the emperors fed, clothed and equipped the armies, paid the soldiers and government officials, and sustained the poorer residents of Rome. What Diocletian tried to do was regularize these traditional practices on an empire-wide basis.

Under Diocletian's system, agricultural labor and land were taxed according to certain standard units. The system for assessing labor is usually referred to as *capitatio* and that for land as *iugatio,* which are derived respectively from *caput* (pl. *capita*), "head," and *iugum* (pl. *iuga)* "yoke" ("the amount of land that could be ploughed with a yoke of oxen). Theoretically, all of the land throughout the Empire was divided into *iuga,* which varied in size with the types of crops grown and the quality of the soil, whereas all agricultural labor, human and animal, was reckoned in *capita,* with women and young teenagers being counted at half the value of men, and draft animals proportionally lower. The property owner was then assessed at so many *capita* and so many *iuga.* Every five years until 312 and then every fifteen thereafter a new assessment called an *indictio* (indiction) would be made. Thus the term *indictio* came also to be used for the period of time that the assessment was in force. For each year during an indiction, the government would calculate how much food, material, and labor it would need and divide those amounts by the total number of units to find out how much would have to be collected per unit from each property owner.

On paper, this system looks like the soul of simplicity and fairness. In practice, however, it was neither. Surviving documents show that sometimes taxes in kind were converted to taxes in gold *solidi.* There was also great variation in the terminology actually used and even in the meaning of the same term. In some cases, *caput* may refer to the labor equivalent of one adult male. In other cases, *caput* may be interchangeable with *iugum* and represent the amount of labor needed per *iugum*. Figures from one estate indicate that such a *caput* may be equivalent to the labor of 1⅓ adult males. In southern Italy, land was assessed in units of 50 Roman *iugera* called *millenae* (sing. *millena*), and in North Africa, the *centuria* of 200 *iugera* was the standard unit. If, as has been argued, the standard *iugum* equaled 12½ Roman *iugera,* then the *millena* and *centuria* can easily be divided into 4 and 16 *iuga,* respectively, but certainty is impossible.

Moreover, it is not reasonable to expect complete consistency in so vast an empire as Rome's, with its strong regional differences and traditions. Insofar as Diocletian did not include provisions for taxing merchants and craftsmen, his system was unfair to the owners of agricultural land. Moreover, although rural landowners were supposed to be taxed in proportion to what they owned, there were many inequities and injustices in the way in which assessments were actually made and taxes collected. It was always easier for the wealthy landowners, who were responsible for collecting the taxes at the local level, to shift a disproportionate share of the tax burden onto the poor through dishonesty and extortion.

The great virtue of Diocletian's system was that it gave taxpayers relief from the totally unexpected and unregulated ad hoc requisitions characteristic of the late third century, and it created a dependable source of supply for the government that did not have to rely on the government's own worthless money.

Persecution of the Christians

The end of Diocletian's career has been overshadowed by his persecution of the Christians, which brought his reign to a tragic and bloody close. Why he broke the forty-year religious truce proclaimed by Gallienus has been the subject of much speculation, particularly because his wife was a Christian. Some scholars have seen his persecution based on religious principle: He, the self-proclaimed representative of Jupiter, sought to restore the old Roman faith and moral code. The circumstances under which the persecution began give some support to this view, but they also show that Diocletian was politically concerned about ensuring conformity and uniformity among the population in order to strengthen the state in pursuit of security. Enemies of Christianity, like the Caesar Galerius and the Neoplatonist Hierocles, were quick to brand the Christians as subversives and evil influences on the Empire.

The persecution had begun in 299. At a public sacrifice offered to determine the will of the gods from an inspection of the entrails of the slaughtered animals, the augurs reported that the presence of hostile influences had frustrated and defeated the purpose of the sacrifice. Diocletian, suspicious and furious, gave orders that all persons in the Imperial palace—including his own wife—offer sacrifice to the traditional gods of the state or, upon refusal to do so, be beaten. He next permitted Galerius to post orders that all officers and men in the army be required to offer sacrifice on pain of dismissal from service.

In 303, he drafted an edict that ordered the destruction of the Christian churches and the surrender and burning of sacred books, prohibited Christian worship at any time or place, and restricted the rights of prosecution and defense formerly enjoyed by Christians in courts of law. One evening in the winter of 303, without having waited for the official proclamation of the above-mentioned edict, the Imperial police suddenly entered, ransacked, and demolished the Christian cathedral that stood opposite the emperor's palace in Nicomedia. The edict was posted throughout the city the next day. An enraged Christian tore down one of the posters, was arrested, and burned at the stake.

Within the next fifteen days, two fires of unknown origin broke out in the Imperial palace in Nicomedia. Numerous Christian suspects were imprisoned, tortured, and killed. At the same time, revolts ascribed to Christians in Syria and Cappadocia, though easily suppressed, led to the proclamation of two more edicts: one ordered the imprisonment of the clergy; the other sought to relieve the overcrowding of the prisons by offering liberty to all who would consent to make sacrifice to the gods of the state and condemned to death those who refused.

After his visit to Rome, where he had just celebrated the twentieth anniversary of his accession, Diocletian became very ill and ceased to attend to public affairs. According to Eusebius, Galerius seized the opportunity to draft and publish a fourth edict, which required all Christians to offer the customary sacrifices under pain of death or hard labor in the mines. None of the four edicts, except perhaps the first, was enforced everywhere with equal severity. In Gaul and Britain, Constantius limited himself to merely pulling down a few churches, whereas Galerius and Maximian were far more zealous in their domains. When Diocletian abdicated in 305, the persecution was at its height and would not end until 311.

The Abdication   On May 1, 305, in the presence of the assembled troops at Nicomedia, Diocletian formally abdicated. With tears in his eyes, he took leave of his soldiers. He told them that he was too old and sick, probably from a stroke, to carry on the heavy tasks of government. On the same day at Milan, in fulfillment of a promise previously extracted by Diocletian, Maximian also resigned. Diocletian nominated Constantius Chlorus and Galerius as the new Augusti, with seniority for Constantius, who received as his special provinces Gaul, Britain, Spain, and Mauretania. Galerius took the Balkans and most of Asia Minor. Galerius, in turn, nominated his nephew Maximinus Daia as his Caesar in the East and ruler over the provinces in the rest of Asia Minor, Syria, and Egypt. Constantius accepted Galerius' friend Flavius Valerius Severus, who was to rule over Italy, Roman Africa, and Pannonia, as his Caesar in the Herculian dynasty.

After their abdication, the two ex-Augusti went into retirement. Maximian, fuming over his enforced abdication, went to Lucania to await the first opportunity to snatch back his share of the Empire. Diocletian retired to an enormous fortress palace on the Dalmatian Coast outside of Solin (Salona, Salonae) at Spilt (Spalatum, Spalato), where he spent the last eight years of his life in the manner of a good Roman gentleman. He tended his estate and intervened directly in events only once. Whatever influence he may have kept at Court disappeared in 311 with the death of his son-in-law, Galerius. Weary and disappointed with the course of events, Diocletian himself died in 312. Sadly, his widow, Prisca, and their only child, Valeria, widow of Galerius, were exiled under Maximinus. In 313, they were beheaded by his successor, Licinius (p. 431).

Ultimately, many of Diocletian's reforms and policies did not work. He had created a huge administrative and military machine that was a drag on the economy, impeded communication between the center and the periphery, encouraged corruption, and reduced citizens of all ranks to subjects whose response to an oppressive system was frequent disobedience. Still, his stable twenty-year reign and the subsequent modification of his reforms by Constantine, enabled the Empire to survive more or less intact for at least a hundred years.

XXXV

Constantine the Great and Christianity, A.D. 306 to 337

Diocletian had lived to see the disintegration of the Tetrarchy and the recognition of a religion that he himself had persecuted. He saw his own great fame fade into obscurity before the blazing light of Constantine's rising sun and died in the belief that he had worked in vain. In principle, however, after gaining control of the Empire, Constantine continued many of the social, economic, military, and administrative policies established by Diocletian.

Constantine the Great, as he came to be called by Christian writers, was the son of Constantius Chlorus, Maximian's Caesar and eventual successor as Augustus in the West. His mother was named Helena, but her origin and the details of Constantine's early years are hard to discern. The existing information is scanty and distorted by the biases of his Christian boosters and pagan detractors. For example, the former call Helena a virtuous Christian wife and mother, but the latter call her only a concubine of low birth and questionable morals.

Although certainty is impossible, the best evidence indicates that Constantine was born in 272 or 273, probably in or near Naissus (Niš or Nish) in what was then the Balkan province of Moesia, later Dardania, and now Serbia. By 289, his father had set aside his mother in favor of a politically advantageous marriage to Theodora, the stepdaughter of Maximian, who was then Diocletian's Caesar in the West. Subsequently, Constantine was sent to Diocletian's court in the East, where he received excellent training in the arts of politics and war.

Constantius may have had little choice in these matters, because his own military success marked him as a potential rival for power. Demonstrating his loyalty by accepting Maximian's stepdaughter in marriage and sending his son to live under the watchful eye of Diocletian may have been a way to guarantee the safety of himself and his family. Certainly Constantine never seems to have held his father's actions against him, and he rejoined his father soon after Diocletian and Maximian abdicated.

The Rise of Constantine, 306 to 312 By 306, Constantine had distinguished himself militarily during Galerius' victorious Persian campaigns of 298 and was becoming a popular figure with the troops. Although Constantius was nominally the Senior Augustus after 305, Galerius was the actual master of the Empire. He still basked in the glories of his Persian victories, and the two Caesars, Maximinus Daia in the East and Flavius Valerius Severus in the West, were both devoted to him. The presence of the young Constantine at what was now his court also gave him leverage with Constantius and a popular advocate with the army.

Galerius' leading role in the last persecution of the Christians engendered a strong bias against him in the later sources, which are largely Christian and favor the Christian hero Constantine. For example, Lactantius tells the following story about how Constantine rejoined his father: When Constantius asked Galerius to let Constantine help him battle the Picts, who had invaded Britain from Scotland in 306, Galerius was unwilling to let him go. One day, however, after dinner, when Galerius was in a good mood, he gave Constantine a pass to use the Imperial posting system (*cursus publicus*) to go wherever he wanted. Taking no chances, Constantine left in the middle of the night to rejoin his father. As he had feared, Galerius changed his mind the next morning and sent pursuers. Constantine foiled his enemies by killing or laming the remaining post horses after each change of mounts.

The truth is probably more prosaic. In fact, it can be shown that instead of reaching Constantius on his deathbed in Eburacum (York), as the story goes on to claim, Constantine joined him at the port of Gesoriacum (Bononia, Boulogne) on the English Channel. From there, they set sail for Britain and successfully defeated the Picts before Constantius died at Eburacum on July 25, 306. Contrary to the principles of the Tetrarchy, the army immediately proclaimed Constantine as the Herculian Augustus in his father's place.

That title, however, now rightly belonged to Constantius' Caesar, Severus. Constantine remained loyal to Diocletian's system by accepting the title of Caesar from Galerius and not contesting Severus' elevation to the position of Augustus in the Herculian dynasty. The actual behavior of Constantine, Galerius, and Severus challenge the sources' picture of Constantine reluctantly accepting an insultingly inferior position from a fearful and hostile Galerius until he was better prepared to challenge both him and Severus. The real challenge to the system came from Maximian's son Maxentius.

The Usurpation of Maxentius, 306
Maxentius was incensed by Constantine's appointment as Caesar. He believed that he, as the legitimate son of an ex-Augustus, had a better right to the throne. At Rome, the Praetorian Guard and population in general backed him

because they resented the loss of privileges that Diocletian, Galerius, and Severus had gradually removed as they sought to increase the revenues of the state. Severus' attempt to dislodge Maxentius and his allies failed, and, with Maximian's support, Maxentius declared himself Augustus. Severus sought safety at Ravenna but was treacherously murdered by Maxentius when Galerius invaded Italy in 307.

Complex Maneuvers
In 308, Galerius tried to stabilize the situation after Severus' death by calling a summit meeting with Diocletian and Maximian, who had turned against Maxentius. He obtained approval of his old comrade Licinius as a replacement for Severus and condemnation of Maxentius as a usurper. Constantine and Maximinus Daia, neither of whom attended the meeting, were told to be content with the inferior status of Caesars and were quite angry at the sudden elevation of Licinius to the rank of Augustus ahead of them.

Meanwhile, Constantine had prudently concentrated on building up the defenses and loyalties of his own provinces and avoided direct involvement in the conflicts of the others while courting favor wherever it seemed helpful. For example, although he had not sent any aid to Galerius and Severus in their struggle against Maxentius, he had received support for his own legitimacy and showed loyalty to the senior Augustus by holding the consulship with Galerius for 307. Early that same year, he had divorced his first wife, an obscure figure named Minervina, mother of his son Crispus, and married Maximian's daughter Fausta, to whom his father had originally betrothed him fourteen years earlier. It would have been dangerous to leave Fausta free for Maximian and Maxentius to use for attracting some other ally, and as the daughter of the former senior Augustus of the Herculian dynasty, she strengthened Constantine's dynastic position even further. In 308, Constantine helped Maximian after the latter had turned against Maxentius. Two years later Maximian tried to subvert the loyalty of Constantine's troops and apparently committed suicide after Constantine had captured him.

By 310, it probably was apparent to Constantine that the tetrarchic system of Diocletian would never work and that he had the opportunity to consolidate the whole Empire under his own leadership. Galerius was dying of cancer, Maximinus Daia and Licinius hated each other, and Maxentius' position in Rome and Italy was rapidly deteriorating. At that point, Constantine repudiated the Herculian dynasty as the basis of his claim to rule and sought a new sanction by announcing his descent from the renowned Claudius Gothicus. In place of Hercules, he adopted as his patron deity the Unconquered Sun (*Sol Invictus*), who was identified in Gaul, it seems, with Apollo. This deity had also been the protector of Claudius Gothicus and Aurelian. Constantine's claim of descent from Claudius Gothicus would enable him to assert not only his right to the throne by inheritance but also his right to undivided rule over the whole Empire. Fortified by this new sanction, he declared Maxentius a usurper and a tyrant, but he postponed further action to await more favorable circumstances after the death of Galerius.

The Edict of Religious Toleration, 311

After the abdication of Diocletian, the persecution of the Christians had continued in Galerius' dioceses (Illyricum, Thrace, and Asia Minor) and particularly in those of Maximinus Daia (Syria and Egypt). Finally, near death in 311, Galerius became convinced of the futility of the Christian persecutions. As senior Augustus, he issued his famous Edict of Toleration that granted Christians all over the Empire freedom of worship and the right to reopen their churches, if only they would pray for him and the state and do nothing to disturb public order. He explained his change of policy by stating that it was better for the Empire if people practiced some religion than none at all. A few days after the proclamation of this edict, Galerius died.

Predictably, after the death of Galerius, Maximinus Daia at once overran and seized the Asiatic provinces of Galerius and threatened Licinius' control over the Balkans. In anticipation of war with Maxentius, Constantine had made an alliance with Licinius and betrothed to

him his half sister Constantia. Meanwhile, Daia had come to a secret understanding with Maxentius.

Constantine's Invasion of Italy, 312

Constantine launched his long-awaited invasion of Italy in the spring of 312. He set out from Gaul with an army of nearly 40,000 men and crossed the Alps. Near Turin he met and defeated a large force of armored cavalry dispatched by Maxentius. Quickly seizing northern Italy, he advanced against Rome. Maxentius had originally intended to defend the city behind the almost impregnable walls of Aurelian because Constantine's army probably was too weak either to take the city by storm or to conduct a long siege. Nevertheless, whether through belief in religious "omens" or through fear of a popular uprising, Maxentius changed his plan and went out to meet Constantine in open battle.

The Battle of the Milvian Bridge, 312

Maxentius led out his army and crossed the Tiber over a pontoon bridge hastily constructed to replace the old Milvian Bridge, which he had ordered destroyed as a defensive measure in accordance with his earlier strategy. The pontoon bridge consisted of two sections held together with chains, which could be quickly cut apart to prevent pursuit by the enemy. He advanced along the Flaminian Way as far as the *Saxa Rubra* ("Red Rocks" about ten miles north of Rome). There Constantine had encamped the night before.

Lactantius says that on the night before the battle a vision appeared to Constantine and bade him place upon the shields of his soldiers an ancient symbol of Christ, a monogram consisting of an X with a vertical line drawn down through it and looped at the top to represent the first two letters of Christ's name, *Chi* and *Rho*. With less plausibility, Eusebius asserts that Constantine told him years later that sometime before the battle he saw in the sky across the sun a flaming cross and beneath it the Greek words ἐν τούτῳ νίκα ("By this sign thou shalt conquer," or as handed down in the more familiar Latin form, *in hoc signo vinces*). Whatever vision Constantine may have had, when he went forth into battle, he soon drove the enemy back to the Milvian Bridge and won a total victory.

The next day, Constantine entered Rome in triumph. In the forefront of the procession, a soldier carried the head of Maxentius on a spear. The jubilant throng hailed Constantine as liberator. The senate damned the memory of Maxentius, declared his acts null and void, and proclaimed Constantine senior Augustus of the entire Empire.

A Victory for Christianity Although the senate undoubtedly hailed the elevation of Constantine as the triumph of *libertas,* the true victor would turn out to be the Christian Church. Constantine's arch of triumph inscriptionally attributes the victory to the intervention of an unnamed divine power (*instinctu divinitatis*) and to his own greatness of mind (*mentis magnitudine*), but a victory statue of Constantine held a cross in its right hand. That publicly recognized the valuable support of the Christians, which he had cultivated by his tolerant policies in the provinces under his control.

Although Constantine eventually came to ascribe his victory to the intervention of Christ, he did not become an exclusive believer in Christianity upon his victory at the Milvian Bridge. On the other hand, he clearly was a believer before his baptism at the end of his life. Exactly when his conversion took place cannot be said. The interactions of political considerations and personal developments made it a complex, gradual process. He was obviously too keen a statesman to attempt to impugn or suppress immediately the religious beliefs of 80 to 90 percent of his subjects, not to mention the senate Imperial bureaucracy, and army. Also, one victory, however brilliant and decisive, could not in one day completely change his old beliefs, which only gradually were fully replaced. As emperor, Constantine continued to hold the ancient Roman office of *pontifex maximus*. His triumphal arch represents the Unconquered Sun as his patron deity. A set of gold

medallions struck in 315 represents a blending of typical Roman and Christian symbolism: It shows the emperor with the Christogram on his helmet, the Roman she-wolf on his shield, and a cruciform-headed scepter in his hand. Constantine continued to strike coins in honor of Mars, Jupiter, and even Hercules until 318; and coins in honor of the Sun until 323. Thus Constantine's reign was a link between the pagan Empire that was soon to pass and the Christian Empire that was to come.

As senior Augustus, Constantine ordered Maximinus Daia to discontinue his persecution of the Christians in the East. Daia obeyed. In 313, Constantine instructed his proconsul in Africa to restore to the churches all confiscated property, to furnish Caecilianus, the newly elected bishop of Carthage, funds for distribution among the orthodox bishops and clergy in Africa, Numidia, and Mauretania, and to exempt them from all municipal burdens or liturgies. That done, Constantine left Rome for Milan (Mediolanum) to attend a conference with Licinius.

The Conference of Milan, 313 At the conference of 313 in Milan, not only the long-expected marriage of Licinius and Constantia took place, but also the two emperors reached a general agreement regarding complete freedom of religion and the recognition of the Christian Church or rather of each separate local church as a legal "person."[1]

The publication of an actual Edict of Milan is open to some doubt, but the agreements reached included not only the Edict of Toleration of Galerius but also all the western rescripts of Constantine concerning the restitution of property and exemption from public burdens in favor of the churches. Licinius applied this "Magna Carta" of religion not only to his own domains in Europe but also to the East, which was soon to be liberated from the persecutions of Maximinus Daia.

---

[1]In much the same sense, modern business and nonprofit corporations are legally "persons." They can own property, make contracts, and sue or be sued in court.

The End of Maximinus Daia, 313 Maximinus Daia was undoubtedly a man of some principle, military competence, and statesmanship, but he is understandably vilified by Christian writers. Since the publication of the Edict of Galerius, he had sporadically persecuted the Christians in his dominions or subjected them to humiliating indignities. Constantine's order to desist was obeyed, but with neither alacrity nor enthusiasm.

After the defeat and death of his ally Maxentius, Daia stood alone against the combined forces of Constantine and Licinius. Constantine's departure for Gaul to repel a Frankish invasion of the Rhineland presented Daia with an excellent opportunity to attack Licinius. In the dead of winter, Daia crossed the Bosphorus (Bosporus) and captured Byzantium. Licinius rushed from Milan with a smaller but better-trained army. The two forces met near Adrianople (Adrianopolis). Defeated in battle, Daia disguised himself as a slave and escaped. Licinius pursued him into Asia Minor, where he took sick and died. Licinius, with the East now in his hands, granted the Christians complete religious freedom and, as he had agreed at the conference of Milan, restored to them their confiscated churches and properties.

The Empire Divided, 313 to 324 Once again the Empire was divided, as it had been in the days of Marcus Antonius and Octavian. Mutual fear and suspicion led to war between Constantine and Licinius in 316. Licinius was defeated with heavy losses in Pannonia but fought to a draw in Thrace. Because neither wished the inconclusive struggle to continue, they arranged a truce: Licinius agreed to abandon his claim to any territory in Europe but Thrace; Constantine agreed to waive his claim as senior Augustus to the right of legislating for Licinius' part of the Empire.

The compromise peace was neither destined nor intended to last. After a few years of apparent harmony and cooperation, relations between the two emperors slowly deteriorated. Constantine did not really want peace. Licinius' eventual reversal of the policies agreed upon at

Milan presented Constantine a ready-made, though specious, pretext for the war that gave him the whole Empire. Unlike Licinius, Constantine had drawn closer to Christianity ever since the battle of the Milvian Bridge. The benefits which Constantine at this time bestowed upon the Church were to render thanks to God for the aid that he believed he had been given in battle. In turn, he recognized the Christian Church on earth and made it an effective partner of the state.

Although he had to take into account the predominance of pagans in the population, army, and bureaucracy, he authorized measures that went far beyond the Edict of Milan by granting Christians ever more privileges and immunities. An important feature of his religious policy was to permit the pope (bishop of Rome) and the orthodox clergy to determine correct doctrine and discipline within the Church and enforce their decisions by the authority of the state. In a constitution published in 318, he recognized the legality of decisions handed down by bishops' courts. In a rescript of 321, he not only legalized bequests by Roman citizens to the Christian Church, but assigned to it the property of martyrs dying intestate. In the same year, he proclaimed Sunday a public holiday and day of rest for people working in law courts and state-run manufacturing operations.[2] Symbolic, too, of Constantine's growing personal acceptance of Christianity was his adoption after the battle of the Milvian Bridge of the *labarum,* a standard consisting of a long-handled cross with a *Chi Rho* monogram at the top.

The Donatist Schism Constantine's personal experiences and mentors such as Bishop Hosius of Corduba had convinced him of the power of the Christians' deity, and he also saw the benefits that the state could derive from being united with the strong effective organization that the Christian Church had become. Therefore, Constantine took a serious view of a

---

[2]The proclamation could have been interpreted either way: by a Christian as "the Lord's Day," by a pagan as "the holy day of the Sun."

schism that was rending the Church in Africa and destroying unity in the state. The schism derived its name from Donatus, the fanatical leader of a radical group of dissident clergymen. This group had protested strongly against the election of Caecilianus as metropolitan bishop of Carthage. They claimed that he was too ready to grant pardon and restore to clerical office those who had betrayed the faith during Diocletian's persecution and surrendered the holy scriptures for burning. Contrary to the will of the Roman pope, the Donatists had elected as bishop of Carthage Donatus himself, who had endured six years of prison and torture without breaking.

The African dispute rose to a crescendo of fanaticism when Constantine denied the Donatists a share in the benefactions that he had recently granted the clergy and congregations in Africa. Two church councils summoned by Constantine in 313 and 314 ruled against the Donatists. They appealed to the emperor to judge their case himself. At last he agreed. After much deliberation, he reaffirmed the decisions of the councils and ordered the military suppression of the Donatists and the confiscation of their churches. In 321, realizing that persecution only heightened their fanaticism and increased the turmoil in Africa, Constantine ordered the persecutions to cease. He scornfully left the Donatists "to the judgment of God." His first attempt to restore peace and unity in the Church had failed dismally.

The Arian Heresy Similar religious problems confronted Licinius, but he handled them differently, yet not more successfully. At first he faithfully observed the decisions reached at Milan, but, when the Arian heresy arose in Egypt and threatened to disrupt the peace and unity of his realm, he resorted again to systematic persecutions of the Christians. Arius, a priest associated with a group in Egypt that also opposed leniency toward Christians who had given in under Diocletian, held views about the nature of Christ that his opponents could use to discredit him as a heretic. He argued that Christ was not "of the same substance" (*homoousios*)

as God the Father but "of different substance" (*heteroousios*). Since he was the Son of the Father, he must, therefore, have been subsequent and posterior. Although begotten before all worlds, there must have been a time when he was not.

Although it was not substantially different from the occasional utterances of some great Church fathers of the early third century (e.g., Origen, St. Dionysius of Alexandria, and, in his old age, Tertullian), Bishop Alexander of Alexandria argued that the Son was of the same substance with the Father, and that all the three persons of the Trinity (the Father, the Son, and the Holy Spirit) were one in time, substance, and power, representing the three aspects of the Almighty Power of the universe.

Alexander, whose position eventually became orthodox, excommunicated Arius and touched off a raging controversy that even drew in Licinius' wife, Constantine's half sister Constantia. Never really sympathetic toward the Christians, Licinius now saw in their controversies a disruptive element all the more dangerous in view of his impending power struggle with Constantine (on whose behalf he perhaps suspected they were saying their prayers). Accordingly, in 320 he renewed the persecution of the Christians.

The Defeat and Death of Licinius, 324

Although renewed Christian persecutions provided Constantine with a moral issue in his war against Licinius, he found a more immediate cause in the Gothic invasion of Moesia and Thrace in 323. To repel the invasion, Constantine had no other recourse but to trespass upon the Thracian domains of Licinius. Licinius made an angry protest; Constantine rejected it. Both sides at once mobilized.

In the middle of 324, Constantine attacked and defeated the forces of Licinius. Licinius surrendered, but an appeal by Constantia moved Constantine to spare his life. He was exiled to Thessalonica (Salonica). Six months later, however, Constantine had him put to death for treason. Constantine was now sole emperor over an Empire united for the first time in almost forty years. The new slogan of the Empire came to be "one rule, one world, and one creed."

The Council of Nicaea, 325

The military victory had reunited the Empire politically but did not so quickly and decisively restore the religious unity that Constantine had striven to bring about. In all his efforts to promote religious unity, Constantine labored under one distinct handicap: He failed to see the religious importance of the controversy between Arius and the bishop of Alexandria. Because his chief aim was to achieve unity within the state, it made little difference to Constantine whether the Father, Son, and Holy Spirit represented one indivisible godhead or were three separate deities. Accordingly, writing to Arius and Bishop Alexander, he urged them to get down to fundamentals and abandon their battle of words over abstruse and unimportant points of theology. His letter naturally failed to end the controversy.

Still hoping for an amicable solution to the problem, Constantine summoned an ecumenical council at Nicaea in Bithynia, to which bishops from all over the Empire might travel at state expense and at which he himself would also be present. The council opened on May 20, 325, with some 300 bishops present. In his brief opening address, Constantine avowed his own devotion to God and exhorted the assembled bishops to work together to restore the unity of the Church. All else, he declared, was secondary and relatively unimportant. Reserving for himself only the right to intervene from time to time to expedite debate and deliberation, he then turned the council over to them.

The Council of Nicaea defined the doctrine and completed the organization of the Catholic Church. Its decisions affected not only the problems of 325, but Christianity for all time. It formulated the Nicene Creed, which, except for some minor modifications adopted at the Council of Constantinople in 381, has remained the creed of most Christian churches to this day. It declared Christ *homoousios* and the Trinity indivisible, excommunicated Arius, and

ordered the burning of his books. Easter was fixed to fall on the first Sunday after the first full moon following the spring equinox, and twenty canons (rules) were formulated for the regulation of Church discipline and government throughout Christendom.

The negative consequences of the Council of Nicaea were momentous. First of all, it made compromise on the issue of Christ's nature more difficult and split the Church into two hostile camps for years. It also bedeviled Imperial politics since some emperors were Arian and others upheld the Nicene Creed. While enjoying official favor under Constantius II and Valens, Arians were able to spread their version of Christianity across the Danube to many of the Germanic tribes who eventually took over much of the western half of the Empire, which had remained staunchly Nicene.

Sectarian hostility between the Orthodox population of old Roman territories and the new German overlords hindered unity in the face of worse invasions later. Ironically, the problem would have been less severe if the Germans had remained pagans. They could have been forgiven their ignorance and more easily converted. The Arian Germans considered themselves true Christians already and resented the attitude of the Orthodox.

The Council of Nicaea also deeply influenced future relations between Church and state during the remainder of Roman and subsequent Byzantine history. The formal role that Constantine played by convening the council reinforced the already close association that had developed between the head of state and the Church during the Donatist Schism. Constantine's actions at the council of Nicaea provided the model for the Caesaropapism of later centuries, when the emperors dominated the Church and manipulated it for purposes of state. Constantine himself claimed to be *Isapostolos* ("Equal of the Apostles") and the elected servant of God.

Constantine's Secular Policies

Although Constantine's religious preference was quite different from Diocletian's, the policy of centralizing religion under state control was very similar, and he followed Diocletian's lead even more clearly in other spheres, such as monetary reform. He created a stable gold *solidus* minted at 72 to the Roman pound by slightly reducing Diocletian's *aureus* (60 to the pound) and replaced the *argenteus* with a new silver coin, the *miliarense* (denoting a thousandth part of the gold pound). Silver remained in short supply, however, and the overproduction of base-metal coins continued to fuel inflation in terms of the ratio of base-metal coins to gold (p. 445). He supplemented taxes in kind with taxes in cash like Rome's first tax on business, the *collatio lustralis* or *chrysargyron* (p. 456).

Military Developments The idea that Constantine abandoned a strong perimeter defense and substituted a policy of defense in depth for one of preclusive security has been largely discredited. That idea rests on two mistaken assumptions: first, that the Romans shared the modern idea of borders as fixed lines that clearly demarcated Roman territory from non-Roman; second, that Constantine withdrew the best troops from the frontier rearward to fortified positions and service in a mobile field army while he left only a weak peasant militia to sound the alarm when invaders appeared. The Romans did not think in terms of fixed borders. The walls, roads, and rivers that are often viewed as boundaries were really part of a system of broad frontier zones. Within the frontier zones, they served to display Roman power, observe and control the movement of people, ensure military communication, and provide for the transportation of troops and supplies.

Both Diocletian and Constantine essentially kept this traditional Roman system of frontier defense, but they did disperse small detachments of soldiers in the cities and towns of frontier provinces to break up large concentrations of troops or oversee and protect the collection and storage of supplies as taxes in kind. Therefore, the troops responsible for guarding the frontier became more interspersed among the civilian population of frontier provinces. Over a long period of time, the distinction between soldier and civilian in the frontier zones became blurred, particularly after it became common in the late fourth and in the fifth century to settle invaders on vacant land in return for military service.

Constantine's major military innovations were to increase the size of the mobile forces attached to the Imperial Court (*comitatus*), to accelerate the enrollment of Germans in Imperial armies, and to appoint them to the highest governmental offices. To the regular troops of the *comitatus* (the *comitatenses*) Constantine added a new elite corps composed of some infantry, but mainly of cavalry and known as the Palace Guards, *palatinae*. He also replaced the old Praetorian Guard, which he disbanded in 312, with a personal bodyguard of crack troops, most of whom were German. To this bodyguard he gave the distinctive name of "Palace Schools" (*scholae palatinae*).

Another important military development was the reorganization of the high command and the complete separation of military and civil functions. Constantine gave the military functions of the praetorian prefects to two supreme commanders known as master of the infantry (*magister peditum*) and master of the cavalry (*magister equitum*). Similarly, he abrogated the authority of the provincial governors over the dukes and counts, who commanded the frontier garrisons.

Though stripped of their military functions, the praetorian prefects were still very powerful dignitaries. Each exercised the powers of a deputy emperor in one of the four great prefectures of Gaul, Italy, Illyricum, and the East. After 331, all judicial decisions handed down by them were final and were not subject to appeal even to the emperor. They supervised the administration of the Imperial posting system (*cursus publicus*), the erection of public buildings, the collection and storage of taxes, the control of craft and merchant guilds, the regulation of market prices, and the conduct of higher education. Even more important, their executive control over the recruiting and enrollment of soldiers, the construction of military installations, and the provision of supplies acted as a powerful brake upon ambitious army commanders.

Expansion of the Imperial Court The master of the infantry and the master of the cavalry were members of a vastly expanded Imperial Court (*comitatus*). In keeping with Diocletian's policy of surrounding the emperor with an elaborate court ceremonial to promote an aura of sacredness, Constantine increased the number of personal attendants, many of whom, in Persian style, were eunuchs and became powerful by controlling personal access to the emperor. The most important of them were the chamberlain or keeper of the sacred bedchamber (*praepositus sacri cubiculi*) and the chief of the domestic staff (*castrensis*).

Numerous palace officials (*palatini*) helped to make up the Sacred Consistory, the Imperial Council. They handled governmental business and along with their staffs were exempt from the burdens of ordinary citizens. The most powerful was the master of offices (*magister officiorum*). He controlled the sacred secretariats (*agentes in rebus*), who carried dispatches, gathered intelligence, and controlled the movement of troops. He also oversaw the Imperial bodyguards, arsenals, and arms production. He even controlled appointments with the emperor, received ambassadors, and thus influenced foreign policy.

Final Decay of Old Offices and the Senate
Although Constantine and his successors continued to hold the office of consul on occasion, retained the title *pontifex maximus,* and still advertised their *tribunica potestas* in the tradition of Augustus, the old magistracies continued to decline. By 300, the praetors, who had lost their judicial functions under Septimius Severus, and the quaestors, who no longer had senatorial revenues to handle after the militarization of all provinces during the third century, had been reduced to one each. Their only duty was to conduct the games and entertainments during festivals at Rome. Two consuls continued to be appointed, one at Rome and one at Constantinople, but their office was merely honorary. The last real function of the consuls, as presidents of the senate, had already been transferred at some point to the urban prefect, whose court heard the civil suits of all the senators and the criminal suits of those domiciled in Rome. All of the consuls' other previous functions, however, now belonged to a vicar of the praetorian prefect for Italy.

The Roman senate became, with the urban prefect, only the municipal council of Rome. It no longer ratified the appointment of emperors, and its advisory function had been taken over by the Sacred Consistory. The emperor now merely informed the senate of his decisions, for which courtesy he received fulsome thanks.

In keeping with a long-standing trend, Constantine finally abolished the distinction between senators and equestrians. Because the need for competent officials was great, offices previously restricted to one class or the other were now open to both. *Equites* who were appointed to senatorial offices became senators, and the number of senators swelled to about 2,500. Ironically, however, this change increased the prestige of the senators as a class despite the institutional decline of the senate itself. Now senators became a part of the highest strata of Imperial government, especially in the less urbanized West, where the great senatorial landowners were in a position to monopolize the highest posts. Constantine even revived the term *patrician* as an official honor for senators who had performed particularly important services.

The Founding of Constantinople, 324 to 330 Since the time of Hadrian, the city of Rome and peninsular Italy had gradually lost their earlier dominance within the Empire. Citizenship, privileges, wealth, and political power had steadily spread outward toward the provincials until they came to make up the bulk of the soldiery, the bureaucracy, and the senatorial class and finally occupied the throne itself. Although the city of Rome still had much symbolic value for its possessor, it was no longer strategically well placed in relation to the constantly threatened frontiers and was eventually supplanted by Milan as the strategic Imperial residence in the West. As had Diocletian, Constantine realized that the Empire had to be de-

fended and administered from strategically located Imperial residences in both the East and the West. Also, Rome's loss of privileges and Constantine's increasing favor toward the Christian Church alienated the old pagan families that dominated Rome. Therefore, the idea of a new Rome strategically located in the East and free from the deeply rooted pagan traditions of the old Rome greatly appealed to Constantine. His choice for his Eastern residence was the old, decaying Greek city of Byzantium, which he began to transform in 324 and was eventually renamed Constantinople in his honor.

This choice was a stroke of genius. At Constantinople, now the Turkish city of Istanbul, where the Black Sea flows through the straits known as the Bosphorus (Bosporus) into the Sea of Marmara (Marmora), Europe meets Asia. Through the city passed roads linking the Near East and Asia Minor with the Balkans and Western Europe, roads with easy access to two of the main battle fronts of the Empire, the lower Danube and the Euphrates. Situated on a promontory protected on two sides by the sea and strong land fortifications on the third, Constantinople occupied an almost impregnable position and could not be taken by storm for more than 1,000 years. It also enjoyed an excellent deep-water harbor (later called the Golden Horn), the entrance to which could be quickly and easily closed against attack by sea. Ideally located for trade, it captured the commerce of the world passing East and West, North and South: furs from the North, silk from the Orient, spices from India and Arabia, fine wines and olive oil from Asia Minor and the Mediterranean, grain, precious stones, and exotic animals from Egypt.

In all else save religion, Constantine made the new Imperial city an exact equivalent of Rome. Rome was still the capital, but it was no longer limited to one place, an idea conveyed by replicating Rome's essential features in Constantinople. It had to have a share of the senate, which he filled with the heads of Rome's most illustrious families and the grandees of the eastern provinces, a *Populus Romanus,* privileged and exempt from taxation, and, above all,

a *plebs*—one as in Rome, recipient of free entertainment and food.

To beautify the new city, Constantine ransacked ancient temples and shrines—even Delphi, from which he removed the tripod and the statue of Apollo. His confiscations, (amounting perhaps to 60,000 pounds of gold) made it possible for him to build in Constantinople an enormous Imperial palace, a huge hippodrome, a university, public schools and libraries, and magnificent Christian churches—Holy Peace (*Hagia Eirene*), Holy Wisdom (*Hagia Sophia*), and Holy Apostles (pp. 513–514). After dedicating the new city on May 11, 330, Constantine resided there most of his remaining life.

The Death of Constantine the Great, 337

Domestic tragedy marred an otherwise glorious reign. In 326, Constantine had his eldest son Crispus, a youth with a brilliant military future, put to death on a trumped-up charge of raping his stepmother, the Empress Fausta (who, it appears, had engineered the story to remove him as a possible rival of her own three sons—Constantine II, Constantius II, and Constans). In the same year, the empress herself died, scalded in a hot bath after the emperor's mother, Helena, supposedly, had revealed that Fausta had committed adultery with a slave.

In 337, while preparing to lead an army against Persia in retaliation for unprovoked aggression against the Roman protectorate of Armenia, Constantine fell ill. A visit to the hot springs of Helenopolis failed to help. On the way back to Constantinople, near Nicomedia, he felt the relentless approach of death. He asked Bishop Eusebius of Nicomedia, who had vigorously defended Arius at Nicaea, to administer the sacrament of baptism. (It was not uncommon to put off baptism until late in life in order to die in a blameless state.) While still arrayed in the white robes of a Christian neophyte, Constantine died. His tomb was the mausoleum connected with the Church of the Holy Apostles.

It would be difficult to overstate the significance of Constantine's reign. He had taken Christianity, a small, persecuted sect, and given it the impetus that made it one of the major religions of the world. Indeed he greatly influenced the formulation of its most widely accepted creed and institutional structure.

Finally, by following up and skillfully modifying Diocletian's reforms and by his splendid choice of a new residence, Constantine laid the foundations of the Byzantine Empire, which was to last 1,000 years and have an incalculable impact upon Europe and the Near East.

XXXVI

From Constantine's Dynasty to Theodosius the Great, A.D. 337 to 395

Diocletian and Constantine had helped to save the Roman Empire from the chaos that had threatened to engulf it in the last half of the third century. They had singlemindedly mobilized Rome's diminishing resources for the supreme effort of self-preservation. As a result, the Empire survived intact for the rest of the fourth century, despite bloody feuding among Constantine's heirs, two serious military defeats, distracting struggles between Christians and pagans, and the increasing need to man the armies with Germanic recruits or mercenaries.

Murder and Civil War   Although Constantine had provided for the safe transfer of his soul from the earthly to heavenly realm, he could not provide for the safe transfer of power within the earthly realm. After his death, bloody rivalries and power struggles soon erupted. His two half brothers and most of their sons were butchered by troops acting on false rumors that the half brothers had murdered Constantine. Only two young nephews of Constantine survived, the half brothers Gallus and Julian.

The false rumors allegedly originated with Constantius II (337 to 361), second son of Constantine's wife Fausta. Previously appointed Caesars, he and two other sons of Fausta assumed the rank of Augusti and di-

vided the Empire among themselves. Constantine II (337 to 340), the oldest son, received the western half of the Empire, with the youngest, Constans (337 to 350) governing Africa, Italy, and Illyricum under his supervision. Constantius II held the East. In 340, Constantine II was killed in attacking Constans, who took over the West. Although Constans vigorously defended the British and German frontiers, his harshness as a commander and inability to relieve inflation led to his overthrow and execution in 350 by Magnentius, a high-ranking officer of British and Frankish ancestry. Constantius II had been occupied with defending the East against the Persian King Shapur (Sapor) II (309 to 379). He disengaged himself from the Persians and defeated Magnentius in a series of battles beginning in 351. Magnentius finally committed suicide in 353, and Constantius II was left as sole emperor.

Constantius' Search for a Partner   Soon after moving west, Constantius II had realized that he needed a loyal subordinate to hold the East. Even Constantine had relied on his sons to help him hold together the vast Empire, whose unity external forces and internal pressures constantly threatened to destroy. Yet, close ties of blood did not guarantee harmony between those who shared power, as the execution of Constantine's son Crispus, the murder of his

438

half brothers and nephews, and the civil war between Constantine II and Constans attest. Still, it was too dangerous not to have someone share the burdens of power, and family ties were usually the most reliable.

After much hesitation, Constantius II chose his cousin Gallus as Caesar and put him in charge of the East. Gallus, one of the two who had been spared in the massacre of Constantine's male relatives, received Constantius' sister Constantia (Constantina), as a wife in order to bind the Augustus and Caesar more closely. Unfortunately, Constantia soon died, and Gallus' success against the Persians, his hot temper, and his actions against powerful interests at Antioch aroused the jealousy and suspicion of Constantius. Constantius recalled him to Italy and had him beheaded in 354.

Constantius' next choice was Julian, Gallus' twenty-three-year-old half brother. While Constantius was fighting restless tribes along the Danube, Gaul was thrown into turmoil by a combination of military rebellion and Germanic invasion. Eusebia, wife of Constantius, urged Julian's appointment as Caesar. A totally inexperienced young man who had spent all but his last four years under close house arrest in an atmosphere of suspicion and intrigue, Julian did not have Constantius' complete trust. Nevertheless, he had the advantage of a much more congenial personality and a sharp intellect well trained by his tutors in rhetoric, history, and philosophy. Without repeating Gallus' political mistakes, he became a popular commander and administrator and methodically restored Roman defenses in Britain and all along the Rhine between 357 and 359.

By 359, court intrigue and the death of the Empress Eusebia began to weaken Julian's position and arouse Constantius' jealous suspicions. Using a threat from Persia as an excuse, Constantius demanded many of Julian's troops. The troops refused, and in February of 360, they proclaimed Julian emperor, ostensibly against his will. For the next year, while Constantius was securing the eastern frontier, Julian negotiated for a peaceful settlement of the situation. Constantius adamantly refused all offers of joint rule and set out to attack Julian in 361. Julian had already seized the initiative by marching east first, but before their two armies could clash, Constantius suddenly took ill and died. Because Constantius had no son to succeed him, Julian became sole emperor without a struggle.

The Empire under Constantius II Although not one of history's more pleasing characters, Constantius II had not been a bad emperor. In many ways he was a Tiberius to Constantine's Augustus. Insecure and indecisive, he was often unduly influenced by unscrupulous members of his court and resorted to deviousness to secure his ends. To the best of his limited abilities, however, he had dutifully followed the path marked out by his father. "One Empire" and "one Church" were the foundations of his policies, as they had been for his father. The former helps to explain his role in the cold-blooded actions of 337, his subsequent refusal to recognize either Magnentius or Julian as co-emperors, and his willingness to resort to civil war in each case. Constantius II never neglected the arduous duties of protecting the frontiers. Most of his reign was spent in the military camp, not the sumptuous accommodations of the new capital, and although he was not so bold a general as his father or his rival Julian, he did maintain the Empire's territorial integrity.

As an administrator, Constantius II continued the centralizing tendencies of Diocletian and Constantine. At the same time, his legislation shows an honest attempt to mitigate the abuses of bureaucratic power that the system fostered. Finally, he zealously encouraged the union of the Christian Church and Roman state that Constantine had begun. He reaffirmed Constantine's earlier ban against pagan sacrifices and ordered the closing of all pagan temples in 356. Theologically, Constantius II espoused a moderate Arian position and promoted doctrinal unity from that perspective. In 359, he summoned two regional councils of bishops—in the West at Ariminum (Rimini) on the Adriatic coast of Italy and in the East at Seleucia on the Calycadnus in Cilicia.

Both councils eventually accepted a creed that declared Christ to be "like the Father," and this creed was confirmed by a general council at Constantinople in the following year. Had Constantius lived longer and defeated Julian, he might have been able to make the compromise stick, but his death in 361 quickly threw religious matters into turmoil once more.

Julian the Apostate Emperor (361 to 363)

As had all of his relatives, Julian had been raised a Christian. His secondary education had been supervised by Bishop George of Cappadocia, and he had even taken lower orders as a lector in the Church. George, however, had a fine library of classical literature and Greek philosophy, especially Neoplatonist philosophy. Julian found the spirit of Hellenism in these works more attractive than the Christianity espoused by those who had murdered his family and forced him to endure years of lonely exile. When released from exile, Julian had gone to Pergamum to study rhetoric and then to Athens and the study of philosophy. Sometime in the course of these studies he became convinced that paganism was the path of true religion and secretly converted. Soon after he entered Constantinople in 361, however, Julian openly proclaimed his devotion to the old ways by rescinding laws hostile to paganism.

Officially, Julian merely proclaimed religious toleration for all; in practice, he used all the subtle powers of his office to advance paganism at the expense of the Church. While he hoped that toleration would produce the unedifying spectacle of uncompromising adherents of the Nicene Creed fighting with Arians, he worked to create a Neoplatonic syncretism of pagan cults with the sun god as the Universal One. He even tried to give this unified Neoplatonic paganism an ethical emphasis and organizational structure modeled on those of the Church, which he had renounced. To the Christians, Julian was a demonic agent of Satan, an impression reinforced by his emphasis on magic, divination, omens, theurgy, and elaborate sacrifices, which even many of his friends thought excessive. Nevertheless, the sudden

and dramatic turn that his fortunes had taken since 354 had convinced Julian that the gods were on his side, and he forged ahead.

The Persian War   Convinced of his own destiny, Julian did not want to wait to prove his prowess. He quickly prepared to invade Persia in order to gain permanent security for the neighboring provinces and glory for himself as another Alexander the Great. While he was using Antioch as a base for preparations, Julian promoted his pagan revival among the inhabitants of this great city, one of the most staunchly Christian in the whole Empire. At best the Antiochenes ignored him; at worst they laughed at him. For the first time since his meteoric rise, Julian met failure, and it shook his self-confidence.

Confidence returned with the success of his initial invasion of Persia. He was tempted to push on into the interior, although he had not brought the main Persian army to battle and had no clear strategic objective. He reached the Persian capital of Ctesiphon but failed to take it. Retreating in the deadly heat of summer and low on supplies, the Roman army was now constantly harassed by the main force of King Shapur II. While riding off without his breastplate to rally the troops in a sudden attack on the rear guard, Julian received a mortal spear wound in the side. Some say that it was hurled by a Christian in his own ranks. In the days following, the Persians taunted the retreating Romans with this idea to undermine morale. In the confusion of battle, however, no one had been able to tell who threw the spear, and certainty can never be attained. Julian lingered for a while and died on June 26, 363.

The early death of Julian was a major turning point in Roman history. Had he enjoyed a long reign like Diocletian's or Constantine's, his policies would have had a great impact. Certainly he would not have been able to eliminate Christianity, as he fervently wished, but with official support the kind of theologically and institutionally unified paganism that he advocated could have become a strong counter force to the Christian Church and might have jeopardized the whole Empire by splitting it between two large antagonistic religious camps.

Jovian Proclaimed Emperor (late June 363)

Julian had no heir, and like his hero Alexander, he refused to designate a successor as he talked on his deathbed with friends. Upon his death, Julian's generals, the legionary commanders, and cavalry officers met to choose a successor. Their first choice was Julian's close advisor Salutius Secundus, praetorian prefect of the East, a moderate pagan and a popular individual in general. Old and unambitious, however, he refused. After considerable further debate, the officers finally settled on a Christian officer ironically named Jovian.

The Romans struggled on, and after they forced a crossing to the east bank of the Tigris, Shapur, who still feared a pitched battle, offered to negotiate. Jovian, irresolute, insecure, and perhaps anxious to confirm his claim to the throne at home, accepted very disadvantageous terms. They included the surrender of Nisibis, the almost impregnable stronghold that was the anchor of Roman defenses in Mesopotamia, abandonment of Roman provinces beyond the Tigris, cessation of the Roman protectorate over Armenia, and payment of an annual subsidy to Persia to defray the expenses of defending the Caucasus. In return, Shapur granted peace for thirty years.

Jovian died after reigning only eight months. His one major act after negotiating the treaty with Shapur was to rescind Julian's anti-Christian legislation. Though pro-Christian, he did not pursue repressive policies toward pagans. Julian's pagan friends and supporters did not suffer for their earlier allegiance, and all were free to worship as they wished.

Valentinian I and Valens, 364 to 378

With the death of Jovian, the chief military officers and civilian officials chose as his successor Flavius Valentinianus, an experienced Christian Pannonian officer, though only of secondary rank. They also insisted that he choose a co-emperor so that equal Imperial attention could be given to problems in the East and West. Valentinian chose his brother Valens and left him in charge of the East while he oversaw the West from Milan. Julian's old Gallic legions, pagans, and many who favored the house of Constantine the Great supported Procopius, a relative of Julian's mother. He attempted to usurp the throne in late 365 but was suppressed and executed in early 366.

As military men, Valentinian and Valens energetically defended the Empire. Unfortunately, Valentinian died in 375 after suffering a stroke during angry negotiations with the Quadi. He left his share of the Imperial title to his sixteen-year-old son Gratian. In the East, Valens fought back the Goths in Thrace from 365 to 369. He turned his attention to Persia in 371 but managed only to restore Roman control over Armenia before he had to rush back to face a rising tide of Goths on the Danube.

The Battle of Adrianople (August 9, 378)

Pressured by the onrushing Huns, thousands of Ostrogoths and Visigoths begged Valens for permission to resettle in Roman territory. Welcoming such an increase in manpower for Rome, Valens agreed on the condition that they surrender their arms. The Romans were not prepared to handle such a vast influx of refugees, and corrupt officials mercilessly exploited their plight. The Romans sold them bad food, even dog meat, at high prices or in exchange for other Goths, whom they sold into slavery. Abused and frustrated, the Goths rose up in mass revolt in 377, and an incompetent Roman commander lost control of the situation.

Valens arrived in the summer of 378 to take personal command. Impatient and not wanting to share the laurels of victory with his young nephew Gratian, Valens sought battle without waiting for Gratian's reinforcements. On the afternoon of August 9, 378, after a morning march and no midday meal, between 15,000 and 20,000 Romans suddenly found themselves fighting on a hot, dusty plain near Adrianople (Adrianopolis) in Thrace. They did not have a chance. The slaughter was frightful. Two thirds of the army, scores of officers, and the foolish emperor himself perished. The Balkans were the Goths' for the taking.

The Policies of Valentinian I and Valens Except for the disaster at Adrianople, the joint reign of Valentinian I and Valens had been militarily successful. They had strengthened the Roman army by recruiting mercenaries from the warlike tribes along Rome's frontiers, and they had successfully defended those frontiers until Valens' foolish haste at Adrianople. In civil matters, however, they had been much less successful. Men of the camp, they had little sympathy with the civilian upper class and vice versa. They tended, therefore, to choose as their civil administrators less educated and more opportunistic men of their own social class.

By their legislation, the two tried to protect the poor, ensure justice, and prevent fiscal abuse. For example, Valentinian created an empire-wide office of *defensor civitatis,* an ombudsman, whose duty was to protect citizens from arbitrary officials. Nevertheless, the good intentions of the co-emperors were frequently thwarted by ruthless and rapacious officials like those who so fatefully abused the Goths. Honest officials had little chance against the influence of the corrupt. For example, when Theodosius, who had put down a revolt by Firmus in Africa, uncovered official wrongdoing in that province, powerful men at court turned the emperor against him, and he was executed.

On matters of religion, both emperors were tolerant of pagans and banned only sacrifices and the attendant practices of magic and divination. In the West, Valentinian was an orthodox adherent of the Nicene Creed (p. 433), but he kept out of theological disputes and allowed the religious authorities to work out their own problems. He did, however, forbid unscrupulous clerics from taking advantage of widows and unmarried women to obtain lucrative gifts. In the East, Valens adhered to the official moderate Arianism established by Constantius II in 359. Unfortunately, he tried to impose it forcibly and caused clerical discontent, popular unrest, and persecution of dissenters.

Gratian and Theodosius the Great, 379 to 395

When Valens died, the young Gratian was at a disadvantage. He had received a good education and was guided by competent advisors, but as a young man he was in a precarious position. To ensure the loyalty of Illyricum after the debacle at Adrianople, the troops of Illyricum had proclaimed Gratian's four-year-old half brother Valentinian II as co-emperor. Gratian accepted their move but gave Valentinian II no further territory and left him with his mother (Justina, Gratian's own stepmother [p. 454]) and a Frank named Merobaudes as regents. Gratian himself recalled from exile Theodosius, son of the Theodosius who had been unjustly executed after suppressing Firmus' revolt, and made him his colleague in 379.

Theodosius' first task was to confront the Visigoths, who had been plundering the Balkans since their defeat of Valens. Theodosius pursued them for three years without inflicting a decisive defeat. Unwilling to prolong the costly conflict, he agreed to let the Visigoths settle within the Empire as autonomous federate allies with their own kings. In return, they agreed to fight for Rome under their own national commanders. The settlement of foreign tribesmen after capture in war or after terms of military service in Roman armies had been common, but to grant anyone autonomous status within Imperial territory was a radical departure from previous policy. At the time, there was little else that Theodosius could have done. Unfortunately, his innovative settlement to meet the needs of the moment set a precedent that would tempt other invaders to press for similar treatment later on and thus further undermine the integrity of the Empire.

Maximus Overthrows Gratian, 383 In the West, Gratian, who had been given the finest education possible in order to receive the respect that the upper classes had denied his father, had replaced with his own, more refined friends the rougher Pannonian advisors provided by his father. He became more interested in the pursuit of game on royal estates than of the enemy on the frontiers. He also was intensely interested in promoting orthodox Christianity. He had issued an edict of general religious toleration upon the death of Valentinian I but had soon rescinded it, probably under the influence of the talented and zealous Bishop Ambrose of Milan. In 381, Gratian renounced the title *pontifex maximus*, removed the Altar of Victory from the senate house at Rome, and confiscated the endowments of the Vestal Virgins and ancient priestly colleges. The next year, pagan senators petitioned for a reversal of these measures, but Pope Damasus and Ambrose helped him to keep his resolve.

Absorbed in those interests, Gratian fatally neglected his troops. In 383, soldiers in Britain proclaimed Magnus Maximus, their commander, as emperor. He seized Gaul, captured Gratian, whom the army had promptly abandoned, and had him executed. Not wishing civil war in the face of Persian and Ostrogothic enemies, Theodosius accepted Maximus as his colleague in charge of Britain, Gaul, and Spain. Valentinian II, under the sole regency of his mother, kept Illyricum and received Italy, Dacia, and Macedonia as well.

In 387, however, after Theodosius had defeated the Ostrogoths and reached a settlement with Persia, Maximus tried to seize Italy. Theodosius gave refuge to Valentinian II, married his sister Galla, and marched west. After two defeats, Maximus' own troops surrendered him to Theodosius in 388. Theodosius' Frankish master of the soldiers, Arbogast, recovered Gaul from Maximus' son Victor, and Valentinian II was placed in charge of the West under the guidance of Arbogast.

The Revolt of Arbogast

Arbogast was one of many Germans to reach high rank under Theodosius, who relied heavily on Germanic tribes to make up for the chronic shortage of military manpower. In 392, Arbogast quarreled with the young Valentinian, now twenty, who was eager to assert his own independence as a ruler. Valentinian failed in his confrontation with Arbogast and was found hanged soon after, whether by his own or another's hand is not clear. Arbogast, however, had little to gain under the circumstances and did not dare to proclaim himself, a "barbarian," as emperor. Only after his overtures expressing loyalty to Theodosius were rebuffed did he set up a puppet in

the West, the rhetorician Eugenius, head of the secretarial office and a tolerant Christian, if not a secret pagan. Eugenius unsuccessfully negotiated for recognition and sanctioned a revival of the traditional public cults to gain support from powerful pagan senators at Rome. Theodosius reluctantly prepared to invade the West again. On September 6, 394, the two armies finally met at the Frigidus River near Aquileia. After an initial repulse, Theodosius gained the victory with timely aid from a storm and the defection of some enemy troops. Eugenius was killed, and Arbogast committed suicide, whereupon Theodosius became sole emperor of the reunited Empire.

The Death of Theodosius and the Division of the Empire, 395

Theodosius' health had been failing for some time, although he was only forty-eight. He died at Milan in early 395, five months after his victory. Some say that by leaving the West to his ten-year-old son Honorius and the East to his seventeen- or eighteen-year-old son Arcadius, Theodosius permanently split the Empire, whose unity he had so recently preserved. Still, Theodosius was probably convinced of the strategic necessity of having an equal representative of Imperial authority in both the East and the West. It was the illegitimacy of Eugenius' rule in the West that Theodosius could not countenance, not the division of authority, which had long become an accepted principle. He had shown no predisposition to challenge the legitimate western emperors Gratian and Valentinian II, and it is clear that he intended his dynasty to be the vehicle for continued unity between East and West.

Much more difficult for Theodosius were the expenses of civil wars and the defense of frontiers. The taxes and manpower required were more than the economy and population could safely bear. The situation was also made worse by Theodosius' return to an elaborate court and the inauguration of a costly building program to increase the splendor of Constantinople. The operation of a vast bureaucracy needed to meet the increased military and fiscal burdens produced ever more problems as numerous officials corruptly sought their own interests at the expense of everyone else.

It was primarily because of his religious activities that later, Christian ages called Theodosius "Great." A pious orthodox Christian, he increasingly supported those who accepted the Nicene Creed. In this effort he was encouraged by the zealous Ambrose of Milan. At first, he applied his orthodox piety only to Christians themselves, but late in his reign, edicts of 391 and 392 legally banned the outward expression of pagan worship. Theodosius did not reverse the long-standing official Roman policy of religious freedom for the Jews, but he was often unable to protect them from the ethnic and religious bigotry of their neighbors.

Paganism certainly did not disappear in the face of Theodosius' hostility, but without official sanction and financial support, its public manifestations gradually decayed. Many representatives of old families whose political and social prominence had been reinforced by their control of time-honored priesthoods, cults, and ceremonies kept hoping for a restoration of the old religious order. Their hopes were momentarily raised when Arbogast and Eugenius sought their support by sanctioning a revival of public pagan cults. Those hopes were quickly chilled by Theodosius' victory at the Frigidus River and were doomed in the long run by the general transformation taking place.

XXXVII

The Evolving World of Late Antiquity in the Fourth Century A.D.

The restored Empire of Diocletian and Constantine was still recognizably Roman. Nevertheless, such changes had taken place in the Roman world by the beginning of the fourth century that scholars have seen the beginning of a new period of ancient Greco-Roman history called late Antiquity. In the more stable atmosphere created under Diocletian and Constantine, economic, social, and cultural changes in the fourth century were more evolutionary and less revolutionary than they had threatened to become in the latter part of the third. Furthermore, the pace and scope of change remained uneven. Many economic problems continued to a greater or lesser degree. Some geographic regions and types of economic activity prospered; others did not. Several social developments visible in the third century continued and even accelerated in the fourth, but there were modifications, too. The cultural conflict between paganism and Christianity apparently climaxed with the political victory of Christianity by the end of the century. Still, the majority of the Empire's population, particularly the peasantry, clung to its religious traditions, while pagan intellectual and artistic influence remained strong. Even Christians made more accommodations and experienced more internal divisions than the rhetoric of victory would acknowledge.

Economic Conditions   A lack of silver undermined Constantine's attempt to revive the silver coinage, and hyperinflation caused by the overproduction of copper and billon coins continued throughout the fourth century. In 334, for example, the ratio of the *denarius* (now only a unit of account based on copper or bronze *nummi*) to gold was 300,000 to the Roman pound. By Constantine's death in 337, it was 20 million to the pound, and 330 million by 357! (For the weight of the Roman pound, see p. 80.)

Constantine did, however, manage to stabilize the gold coinage with his new *solidi* by minting them at 72 instead of 60 to the Roman pound and by measures designed to release hoarded gold. He forced large taxpayers to make some payments in gold, confiscated the supplies of gold forcibly amassed by his rival Licinius, and eventually confiscated some of the treasures held by pagan temples, although not to the extent claimed by hostile pagan sources. The long-term stability of gold, however, rested on the increased measures to recover gold coins through taxation and forced purchases from moneychangers and the rich. The production of gold mines was also steadier as a result of increased security and political stability.

In effect, the Roman government created

a two-tiered system, a stable one based on gold and an unstable one based on copper. The gold system benefitted the government and the wealthy. The stable purchasing power of gold enabled the government to retain the loyalty of the armies by regular cash donatives that held their value and supplemented the in-kind rations (*annona*) that constituted much of their ordinary pay. The government also used gold to pay officials, to buy and subsidize food and entertainments for the urban plebs of Rome and Constantinople, and for annual subsidies and diplomatic payoffs to ensure peaceful frontiers. The rich were the only ones with enough income to acquire gold in sufficient quantities to protect themselves against inflation. The lower ranks of the curial class and the poor saw their copper and billon currency continually lose its purchasing power and had to find ways to avoid using money as much as possible. Under such conditions, the rich got richer and the rest got poorer.

Agriculture The economic advantage enjoyed by wealthy senatorial landowners meant that the amassing of vast landholdings in a few hands continued during the fourth century, although the total amount of land under cultivation continued to shrink. Particularly in the West, the disruptions of the third century had caused much hardship and led to the abandonment of large amounts of good land. The large landowners who had been able to protect themselves or find refuge elsewhere were able to buy or take over the lands of the less fortunate when more favorable conditions returned. They shrewdly spread their holdings over many provinces, particularly in relatively productive and protected areas. It was not unusual, therefore, to find one owner with large holdings in Britain, the Moselle Valley, Aquitaine, Spain, southern Italy, Sicily, and North Africa. The wealthiest senatorial landowners reportedly had incomes averaging 4,000 Roman pounds of gold a year, while the average senator could count on 1,000 to 1,500. A peasant was lucky if he could scratch together 5 *solidi,* less than one fourteenth of a Roman pound.

In the East, land continued to remain more in the hands of smaller independent proprietors, particularly in Asia Minor, Syria-Palestine, and Egypt. Those areas had not suffered so badly during the third century, and a senate at Constantinople had only recently been created from the ranks of moderately wealthy local aristocrats, who had not had the opportunity to emulate the wealth of the old western senatorial families. The proximity of more large and relatively prosperous cities also gave eastern farmers access to urban markets where they could find good prices.

Trade and Industry On the whole, markets were more restricted during the fourth and subsequent centuries than earlier. The government tried to supply most of its usual needs through taxes in kind and state-run workshops and utilized its own transportation and distribution systems. The great landowners needed to purchase little on the open market. Each estate had its own complement of dependent workers and slaves with the skills needed to supply much of what was used on the spot. Whatever could not be produced or found on one estate could be supplied from another by the owner's own ships and wagons. Even when owners exchanged among themselves, such exchanges were in the form of gifts befitting the magnanimity of aristocrats.

That is not to say that the great landowners were not interested in selling anything. Their estates produced many valuable commodities for sale. Such products included grain, olives, olive oil, wine, meat, leather, wool, flax, cloth, timber, quarried stone, roof tiles, pottery, metallic ores, raw metal, and metal products. Handsome profits could be made by selling in bulk to municipal governments and wholesale traders and even to the army and the Imperial government. As the fourth century progressed, some taxes in kind were commuted to payment in gold, and troops were paid more in gold than in rations. Therefore, the buying and selling of supplies increased. When owners or their contractors and agents sold commodities to large buyers, they tended to work through *negotiatores,* who were more like brokers and middlemen than merchants who bought and sold. Naturally, such transactions were affected by the forces of supply and demand, but the army and the Imperial government always had the option of forcing sales at their own price or confiscating outright.

The trade in luxuries from beyond the Empire revived in the fourth century. Native middlemen brought gems, spices, and silk from India and East Africa up the Red Sea to Egypt. Egyptian traders took them to the Nile and down to Alexandria, where they were shipped to other Roman ports. Exotic animals for beast hunts at the public games were imported from sub-Saharan Africa and North Africa or from the northern forests. Slaves and amber also made their way south again from the Baltic regions.

The state tried to control foreign trade through a few official gateways such as Clysma (Suez) in Egypt, Hieron on the Bosphorus (Bosporus), Nisibis in Mesopotamia, and Carnuntum on the Danube. Exports of strategic material were forbidden, and a duty of 12½ percent was collected on imports. In comparison, the levy on goods transported internally was only 2 to 2½ percent.

Internal tariffs, then, were no barrier to private traders. Internal trade in western Europe and the Mediterranean was as free as it had been in the glory days of the second century or would be until the creation of the modern European Economic Community. The high cost of transportation, however, and the limited private market still kept private trade and industry restricted to a few basic commodities, luxuries, and specialized craft goods. Cities and towns with access to the sea or navigable rivers were generally well supplied with what goods were available from around the Empire because they could be brought in by ship. The difficulty of land transport, however, restricted inland cities and towns to what itinerant merchants could carry in their packs or what local craftsmen could produce.

In the West, private craft manufacturing tended to shift from declining cities (p. 448) to the great estates of the large landowners. In the East, where large cities and towns had always been more numerous and were more able to re-cover from the third century (p. 449), demand from private purchasers was enough to support a significant number and variety of independent craftsmen and shopkeepers. Itinerant merchants made the rounds of smaller villages that could not support specialized craftsmen. The craftsmen and shopkeepers of the larger cities and towns had their own guilds for regulating the quality and prices of goods, collecting the tax on businessmen, maintaining the nightwatch, and supplying labor for things such as public buildings and the public post (*cursus publicus*) in their district.

The Economic Impact of the State   Clearly, the state had taken a larger role in the production and distribution of goods during the fourth century through greater reliance on taxes in kind, the establishment of large state-run workshops (*fabricae*), and heavy utilization of the *cursus publicus*. Approximately forty *fabricae* turned out all of the arms and armor needed by the army. Others turned wool and linen into some of the uniforms and clothing worn by soldiers and government officials. State-owned dyeworks produced their own dyes and dyed the cloth. The *fabricae* were originally under the praetorian prefects and then the master of the offices later in the fourth century. The count of the sacred largesses oversaw the other operations. Hereditary groups of workers supplied the labor. They received rations, fuel, and raw materials from in-kind taxes and had to meet annual production quotas. The state also had its own mines and quarries. Some were worked regularly and used convicts for labor. Others were worked with labor requisitioned from local landowners as needed.

Because transport by water was much more efficient than by land, the state tried to ship large cargoes like grain, stone, timber, and military supplies by water as much as possible. Seaborne goods were carried by state-mandated guilds of shippers (*navicularii*). They were wealthy individuals who financed ships dedicated to government service. They were paid half the commercial rate but received valuable reductions in taxes, freedom from curial duties, and protection against loss from shipwreck. They could also carry deck passengers and consignments of small high-value items for extra revenue. Similar guilds of barge operators on the Tiber between Rome and Ostia brought grain and firewood to Rome. The state also ran its own boats on major rivers like the Rhine and the Po.

The state-run *cursus publicus* provided enormously expensive transportation over land. It operated two levels of service. The express post (*cursus velox*) supplied light transportation from saddle horses to four-wheeled carriages pulled by eight to ten mules for fast couriers, small loads of valuables, and authorized travelers. The wagon post (*cursus clabularis*) carried heavy freight such as food, clothing, building materials, arms, and military baggage.

There were way stations every ten or twelve miles on the trunk roads: *Mansiones* provided travelers' services as well as fresh animals; *mutationes* provided changes of animals only; and both were staffed by public slaves who repaired equipment and took care of the animals. They were given rations of state food and clothing. The state acquired animals through an annual levy, local landowners provided fodder as a tax in kind, and provincial governors had to maintain the buildings out of provincial taxes.

The praetorian prefects and master of the offices issued warrants to use the *cursus publicus*. Provincial governors received only two, one for sending messages to superiors and one for local matters. Important senators, bishops, and dignitaries often obtained warrants, too, but special inspectors from the Secret Service (*agentes in rebus*) watched out for unauthorized users.

The Growing Economic Impact of the Church

After the end of persecutions and with growing official support after Constantine, the Christian Church became a major economic influence. Constantine first allowed churches to inherit property, and by the end of the century, churches had acquired vast landholdings. Many wealthy Christians piously donated their land and wealth to their local churches or founded monasteries and church-run charities. Bishops, who often came from the class of wealthy aristocratic landowners, operated these holdings just as any secular owner. Taking on the traditional aristocratic role of public benefactors, the bishops distributed food, clothing, and money to the needy from the Church's own resources.

The Church also replaced aristocratic benefactors and municipal councils as the biggest local builders of the fourth century. The building of magnificent public buildings gave way to the building of magnificent churches as more and more wealth flowed into the Church and away from secular benefactions. Other buildings included hospitals, orphanages, homes for the elderly, shrines to martyrs, and even baths.

Pilgrimages to the shrines of saints like that of St. Martin at Tours and Felix at Nola, to the Holy Land, and to the abodes of renowned holy men brought prosperity to those places and stopping points along the way. Pilgrims needed food, accommodations, and transportation. They bought souvenirs, amulets, holy water, and pictures or statuettes, while saints' feast days provided the opportunity to hold lively market fairs.

The Social Context The fourth century saw continuing demographic change, increasing social stratification and regimentation, the declining status of the curial class, and a growing public role for upper-class women. The eastern and western halves of the Empire experienced these changes differently, however. Demographically, for example, the western provinces do not seem to have recovered population lost during the third century, but by the end of the fourth, the East was growing in population, a factor that helped the eastern economy recover, too.

The Urban Scene After the shocks of the third century, cities in the West generally continued to decline. Compared with eastern cities, they suffered from decreasing trade, a greater frequency of civil wars and "barbarian" attacks, and a less deeply rooted tradition of urbanism. Sometimes, special circumstances produced exceptions to the rule. For example, being Imperial residences or other strategic centers on the great military highways allowed western cities like Augusta Treverorum (Trier), Arelate (Arles), Mediolanum (Milan), Ravenna, Aquileia, Vindobona (Vienna), and Sirmium to prosper from the stimulus of public expenditures. The continued export of grain from North Africa also provided a solid economic base for cities like Carthage, Hippo Regius, and Thamugadi (Timgad).

In many other western cities, however, there was not enough economic activity to support the former levels of urban life. The wealthiest members of the communities had either fled to their rural estates or taken up residence in cities of political and military importance. Many well-to-do decurions had escaped into the Church or Imperial service to avoid their increasing civic burdens. The withdrawal of the upper classes from many cities meant even less business to support the local artisans, shopkeepers, and tradesmen, on whom curial burdens weighed even more heavily. They did not have the resources to keep up the temples and public buildings that wealthy benefactors had helped to erect in more prosperous times. By the end of the fourth century, laws in the West show that they, too, had abandoned many cities to ply their trades or become *coloni* in the countryside.

Rome in the fourth century, on the other hand, largely recovered from the disasters of the third. The emperors maintained and even expanded benefactions of food and entertainment, while new construction and the restoration of old buildings provided employment. The last great period of secular public building in Rome occurred during the reigns of Diocletian and Constantine (p. 475), and Christian emperors from Constantine onward lavished enormous resources on the building of Christian churches (p. 487). The great nobles also built extravagant private mansions for themselves that rivaled Imperial palaces. By 367, therefore, Rome's population seems to have approached a million again.

In Rome and many other western cities, local leadership began to shift to the Christian bishops during the fourth century. Bishops could have useful influence over a Christian emperor, as did the powerful St. Ambrose, bishop of Milan, and the growing economic impact of their churches increased their influence and patronage at the expense of secular elites. Indeed, their charitable activities created large groups of loyal dependents. In the late third century, the bishop of Rome was already supporting between 1,500 and 2,000 widows, orphans, and poor men. No comparable figures for western cities are available from the fourth century, but the fourth-century bishops of Antioch in Syria supported 3,000 needy widows and virgins alone. Porphyry, the fourth-century bishop of Gaza, used his own personal fortune to establish a charitable endowment for the needy.

In the East, however, the secular municipal councils still played an important and active role in the lives of their cities. The shift of political and military resources to the defense of the eastern frontier, and the generally more favorable economic and political situation in the East enabled many eastern cities to recover and even begin to prosper again in the fourth century. In contrast with the West, there was no concentration of extreme wealth in the hands of a few senatorial landowners. Although members of eastern elites were individually less wealthy, they were more numerous. If some wealthy decurions were drawn away to Imperial service or the senate in Constantinople, enough remained to keep up the traditional competition for patronage and prestige that gave Greco-Roman urban life its vitality.

Often now the competition centered around the ability to gain the favor of the emperor or his representatives, who had the vast wealth and power to provide the benefits that they could not supply by themselves. Indeed, Imperial patronage underwrote many of the building projects and amenities that gave eastern cities the outward signs of growth and prosperity. In expending great sums on building up the defenses on the eastern frontier, Diocletian helped to stimulate the prosperity of the region in general.

Whereas the elites of Rome and Italy had previously drained off the wealth of the East to the West, the emperors based in the East spent their revenues there. Thus, Nicomedia and Antioch benefitted greatly from the money that Diocletian spent on them. Constantine, his family, and subsequent pious emperors lavished benefactions on Jerusalem. Constantine and Constantius II provided funds to build the Great Church at Antioch. Thirty years later, Valens gave Antioch a new forum. After the disaster at Adrianople, Theodosius spurred the growth of Thessalonica as the anchor of Imperial strategy in the Balkans. Constantinople, splendidly founded by Constantine and nourished by later fourth-century emperors, grew into one of the great cities of the world and became an economic engine that pulled other major eastern cities in its train. Alexandria, for example, always prosperous, prospered even more as it supplied grain to the new Imperial city and turned imported materials from Africa, India, and the Far East into luxuries for the Imperial Court. The prosperity of the major cities then rippled through the smaller surrounding cities and towns into the countryside.

The Political Role of Cities The decline of cities in the West had serious implications for control of the West in the future. If a monarchy is not to be a tyranny, rule depends upon the consent or at least the acquiescent awe of the governed. In many ways, the politics of the Empire were an elaborate form of theater with the cities as the stage and their large lower-class populations the audience whose applause and approval validated the emperor's legitimate power. Imperial subsidies supplemented the local funds expended on the distribution of food and popular entertainments such as theatrical performance, beast hunts (often involving public executions), chariot races, and athletic games. Imperial processions marking the visit of the emperor were elaborately theatrical. Diocletian sprinkled gold dust in his hair on such occasions to create a soft halo of reflected light. Ammianus paints an unforgettable portrait of Constantius II's triumphal state visit to Rome in 357:

. . .he was seated by himself alone on a golden coach that gleamed with the brightness of various gems, and as it glittered, a second sort of daylight seemed to be intermingled. And after multitudes had passed by first, he appeared, surrounded by dragons made of purple cloth attached to the golden and gem-encrusted points of spears, so that with their gaping mouths open to the breeze they hissed as if roused to anger and streamed their inflated tails in the wind . . . . The Augustus, having been hailed as such by cheering shouts, did not stir at the thundering echo of the hills and shores. He showed himself so motionless and just such a one as he was frequently seen in his provinces . . . . As if his neck were held fast, keeping the gaze of his eyes fixed straight ahead, he turned his head neither right nor left, and as if he were a statue, he was seen neither nodding when a wheel lurched nor spitting nor wiping or rubbing his nose or face nor moving his hand in any way. (Book 16.10.6–10)

When bread, circuses, and other spectacles failed to keep the masses happy, however, a grimmer drama was often played out. Religious tensions, conflicts between the infamous circus factions, food shortages, higher taxes, and other sources of discontent often led to violence and mass riots. They might undermine an emperor's authority if not properly handled with theatrical displays of rage, clemency, or some combination of the two. Two incidents in the reign of Theodosius are illustrative.

First, in 387, rioters at Antioch insulted Theodosius' name and dragged the toppled statues of him and his wife through the streets. Theodosius sent in troops, executed many rioters, and ordered harsh penalties for the city and its leaders. Then he kept the populace in a state of suspense and anxiety while he listened to lengthy appeals for clemency from the local pagan notables and Christian leaders. Dramatically yielding to the Christians' entreaties just in time for Easter, Theodosius solidified his support among the single most powerful group in Antioch and reinforced their growing dominance in the city's affairs.

The second incident occurred three years later, in 390, at Thessalonica, the city most closely linked to Theodosius' rise to power. After rioters had lynched a local Gothic military commander, Theodosius and his military advisors ordered the execution of the perpetrators. In carrying out their orders, the Gothic soldiers instituted a vengeful massacre that sent shudders throughout the Empire. After his point had been made, Theodosius again donned the mask of Christian piety by performing a minor act of penance before St. Ambrose at the cathedral in Milan, which then became the setting for another great theatrical show of Imperial pomp in celebrating the concord of his dynasty with Honorius and Valentinian II. By such displays, Theodosius maintained his authority in the cities that constituted the essence of the Empire.

Growing "Barbarian" Presence A common demographic feature was the continued intermingling of the Roman and "barbarian" populations along the frontiers. In fact, the distinction between so-called barbarians and Romans was largely an artificial one. It reflects the attitudes of the educated upper classes toward those who did not have the level of education, refinement, and social pedigree that they considered to be hallmarks of civilized life. Upperclass authors were primarily the ones who left the literary records that have shaped the modern view of uncouth barbarian hordes destroying the Roman Empire. From their narrow perspective, it might have been true, but in terms of Roman society at large, assimilation between the Roman and non-Roman populations in the frontier zones had been going on for a long time. The fourth century saw only an intensification of an ongoing process in both the East and the West.

In the East, Egypt, and North Africa, the situations along the frontiers were very fluid. Trade and the movements of nomadic peoples produced a constant flow of goods, people, and influences. Whereas Christianity spread Roman influence in Persia, Manichaeism spread Persian influence in the Roman Empire. The mutual capture of each other's soldiers and towns as a result of frequent warfare further mingled the populations. Both used nomadic

Arabic tribes (often identified as Saracens) as proxies against each other. Many of the Saracen tribes bordering Rome's eastern provinces were ruled by Roman-appointed tribal chiefs (phylarchs). For example, in the early fourth century, the Lakhmid tribe centered at Hira was allied with Rome. In the second half of the fourth century, it was probably allied with Persia but then sided with Rome again after its leaders converted to Christianity. The Lakhmids' most famous leader is Queen Mavia, who took over after her husband's death and attacked Roman provinces from Syria-Palestine to Egypt in 376. She came to terms with Valens and became Rome's ally again on the condition that a famous Christian Arab hermit named Moses be appointed bishop for her people. He converted many more Arabs, and Mavia faithfully sent Arab troops to protect Constantinople from the Gothic threat of 378.

Archaeological evidence shows that along the northern frontiers there was little difference in the material cultures of the Romans and non-Romans. Romans had adopted the local style of dress, which was more suited to northern climes, utilized wood more extensively for construction, drank beer, bought Germanic slaves, and may have adopted such non-Roman innovations as coulters and asymmetrical plowshares for agriculture. The non-Roman upper class adopted villa-style agriculture, drank imported Roman wine, ate off imported Roman tableware, and eagerly sought other high-status Roman goods such as silver plate, gold coins, spices, and jewelry.

Northern tribesmen by the tens of thousands had served directly in Roman armies and acquired the rudiments of Latin and Roman culture. Evidence from hoards of Roman coins indicate that heavy recruitment of tribesmen from beyond the northern frontier had begun under Marcus Aurelius. He had also enrolled defeated invaders in the Roman army and settled many in the Danubian provinces, Germany, and even Italy. These practices continued in the third century and were increased in the fourth. Diocletian and Constantine recruited many of their best units from Germanic tribes like the Franks and the Alemanni and probably granted them citizenship. Allied tribes were often required to supply troops to Roman armies, and prisoners of war continued to be taken directly into service. Non-Roman prisoners or refugees were also settled on abandoned lands as *laeti* governed by Roman prefects and were required to supply soldiers to Rome. More than thirty settlements of Sarmatians, Franks, and Suevi are listed throughout Gaul and Italy at the end of the fourth century.

By then, even Germanic tribes that were relative newcomers on the Roman frontier had been undergoing heavy Romanization for over a century. The Franks, Vandals, Burgundians, and Alemanni in the West and the Goths (also called Tervingi and Scythians in the sources) in the East had all occupied territories along the frontier since the mid-third century. Constantius II had supported efforts of the Arian bishop Ulfila to convert the Goths to Christianity. When they petitioned for admittance to the Roman Empire as *laeti* in 376 to escape the terrifying Huns, the Romans had already used some of them as auxiliaries in the Persian campaigns of Gordian III (242) and Julian. Valens, therefore, welcomed them as a permanent source of valuable military manpower.

Under Valens, Valentinian, Gratian, and Theodosius, strongly Romanized Germans were providing more and more of the forces that accompanied the emperor (the *comitatenses*) and occupied the most important military offices. In 379, Theodosius appointed the Gothic noble Modares as his first master of the soldiers. One of Valentinian's greatest generals, Merobaudes, was a Frank and was consul twice. He and two other Franks, Arbogast and Bauto, commanded Roman armies under Gratian. Theodosius made first Bauto, then Arbogast his new masters of the soldiers and married his son Arcadius to Bauto's daughter. After the revolt of Arbogast, Theodosius chose the Vandal Stilicho as still another master of the soldiers and married him to his niece Serena. Stilicho's daughter, in turn, married Theodosius' son Honorius.

These Germanic generals were usually the sons of men who had fought in Rome's armies and settled in Roman lands. They fought and thought as members of Rome's military elite and loyally served their emperors or advanced their own personal careers within the Imperial system. The civilian aristocratic literati who labeled such men "barbarians" had no objection to them doing Rome's fighting. They were jealous that a new class of Romans was achieving the political power and social prestige that they considered their birthright. The contemptuous aristocrats conveniently forgot their origins. Almost to a man their families had come from defeated and allied peoples whom earlier elite families had despised as barbarians and foreigners, although they were just as Romanized as those whom their descendants now despised.

The dynamic, long-standing, but not always pretty, Roman process of integrating new ethnic and cultural groups into the state and society was still at work. It was a process that became somewhat more difficult to control after Theodosius had to agree to settle as many as 100,000 Visigoths inside Roman territory as independent federate allies (*foederati*) under their own kings in 382. Basically, however, the federate leaders used their strong positions to compete even more successfully as aspiring Romans in the internal politics of the Empire. Ultimately, of course, the newcomers gained political control in the West during the fifth century with momentous consequences for the future. In the meantime, traditionalists continued to look down upon "barbarians" from their lofty perch atop the social pyramid.

The Ruling Class Diocletian had greatly increased the size of the Empire's ruling class. His administrative and military reforms dramatically increased the number of high-ranking bureaucrats and officers, and local notables were now directly responsible for meeting the local tax levies. Ironically, this broadening of the ruling class had the effect of increasing the height and steepness of the hierarchical pyramid that had always characterized Roman society.

Before the third century, the social pyramid had not been very complex or high, and its angle had been fairly shallow. Following more recent trends, the fourth century saw the top of the pyramid reach dizzying heights, particularly in the West, while the angle became much steeper and the levels of stratification ever more complex. Under Diocletian, the senatorial class at the top of the pyramid consisted of 500 or 600 families. A man of that class held the rank of *clarissimus* (most renowned). The men who held administrative posts under Diocletian often rose from the ranks of the army and were granted equestrian titles of various degrees. The highest was *eminentissimus* (most eminent), the lowest *egregius* (outstanding).

The tendency was to cheapen the value of these ranks by letting people have titles of higher rank without higher achievement. Ever-higher ranks had to be created to distinguish those at the top of the pyramid from those lower down. Constantine, for example, watered down the rank of *clarissimus* by appointing many holders of equestrian rank to it or by increasing the number of offices that bestowed such rank. For the highest-ranking senators he revived the title *patricius* (patrician). Constantius II created a completely separate senate at Constantinople. It had 300 members drawn largely from new families. By the time of Theodosius, it reached 2,000 members, and the senate at Rome increased correspondingly. Already, therefore, Valentinian I, had begun to distinguish a senator who had held the office of consul or been made *partricius* by calling him *illustris* (illustrious). Below the *illustris* now were the *spectabilis* (notable) and *comes* (companion, count). In the next century, the *gloriosus* overtopped the *illustris*.

Rank, of course, does not always equal status. Many of the men who reached high senatorial rank under the fourth-century emperors were of relatively low social status. Emperors promoted loyal and talented men from non-senatorial families to offices that bestowed senatorial rank, or they gave outright grants to those who had earned their favor. Other men, particularly from the curial class, obtained senatorial rank through bribery and influence. Therefore, the senatorial class in the fourth century was characterized by great social, geographic, and ethnic diversity. It included men who originated from every class and province and not a few foreign tribes and nations. A number of Persians, Germans, and Sarmatians, for example, had become generals in Roman armies and thereby achieved senatorial rank. Slaves, peasants, and higher civil servants all found their way into the senatorial class through service in the army and Imperial ministries and via successful careers as doctors, lawyers, architects, and professors.

There were strong reasons for wanting to achieve senatorial rank in the fourth century. For most of it, senators were free of extraordinary taxes and did not have to supply corvée labor or perform curial duties. By the end of the fourth century, however, those privileges had been legally denied to all senators except those of the highest rank (the *illustres*). Nevertheless, senatorial rank gave a man the kind of influence that enabled him to flout the law and get away without performing curial duties or paying his taxes. Above all, it freed him from the humiliation of being flogged by public officials. Legally, the curial class was free from such demeaning treatment, but high-ranking officials increasingly violated the law as they sought to assert their own or the state's authority. They would not dare, however, to establish the precedent of abusing a man of equal rank. Some men even hoped to pursue high political office and join those families who already enjoyed elite social status from generations of power and privilege.

Opportunities were particularly available in the East because Constantinople and its senate were new foundations. Unlike Rome and the senate there, they had no noble families who had controlled them for generations, and it was easier for men of obscure origin to found great families. For example, the low-born Flavius Taurus, who started out as a notary under Constantius II, became praetorian prefect (355) and consul (361), as did his son and grandson. Flavius Philippus, son of a sausage manufacturer, also went from notary to consul (348) and founded the family that included a praetorian prefect, two consuls, and the Emperor Anthemius. The Pannonian peasant Gratian became a high-ranking military officer and father of the emperors Valens and Valentinian.

Members of new senatorial families in the fourth century (or those aspiring to be) improved their social status through the pursuit of land, education, friendship, and marrige. To be accepted by the best families, one had to acquire the cultural accoutrements of upper-class *paideia* through rigorous training in rhetoric and the ancient classics. Landed wealth and education opened the way to influential friendships (often formed at school) and intermarriage. They, in turn, linked large landowning families together in ever-growing networks of wealth and influence that were as strong and supple as spiders' webs. By the end of the fourth century, these elite families had attached their webs firmly to the highest-ranking offices and often managed to ensnare the emperor himself.

For example, Justina, mother of the Emperor Valentinian II and stepmother of the Emperor Gratian, came from a prominent Roman family. As a young girl, she had become the second wife of Gratian's father, Valentinian I, son of the peasant-born Pannonian officer Gratian mentioned above. She brought up her stepson and son in the traditions of the landed nobles, whom they favored with Imperial appointments instead of the rough Pannonian officers preferred by their father. When Gratian needed someone to take over the East after the death of his uncle, the co-emperor Valens, at Adrianople, he chose Theodosius, who came from a prominent landowning family in Spain. The name of Theodosius' first wife, Aelia Flaccilla, even recalls the Hispano-Roman family to which Aelius Hadrianus, the Emperor Hadrian, belonged.

Theodosius' father (p. 442) had been well connected with prominent senatorial families at court. His friends even included Symmachus, the great senatorial champion of paganism at Rome. After the death of Valentinian, he had fallen victim to a powerful faction of Pannonian officers at court, whom Gratian later purged. After coming to power, Theodosius appointed many senatorial aristocrats from Gaul and Spain to positions at court and eventually took Justina's daughter Galla, sister of Valentinian II, as his second wife.

Widening Gap between Rich and Poor By the end of Theodosius' reign, the networks of aristocratic power and patronage had produced higher and higher concentrations of wealth and power in the hands of a few fabulously rich families, particularly in the West. For example, about 20 great families in 6 large clans owned most of the land in Gaul and Italy. Some of them like the Acilii Glabriones, Anicii, Caeionii, Petronii Probi, and Valerii traced their lines back to the Republic and the Principate. Others like the Aurelii Symmachi were more recent arrivals, but Q. Aurelius Symmachus, consul at Rome in 391 and famous champion of traditional paganism, had 19 houses or estates in Italy, Sicily, and North Africa and could spend 2,000 pounds of gold on his son's praetorian games. One of his close relatives, probably his sister, was married to one of the Anicii. His daughter married Nicomachus Flavianus, son of the very influential Virius Nicomachus Flavianus, twice praetorian prefect and consul in 394. Symmachus' son married a granddaughter of that same man, and one of his son's great-grandaughters married another of the Anicii.

The aristocrats who dominated the eastern court were not so wealthy or so closely intermarried as those in the West. The senate at Constantinople was too new to be dominated by a handful of families, and the economic forces that had fostered the amassing of large amounts of land in a few hands were not so strong. Power and wealth were distributed among a number of major cities and their notables, the large local landowners whose families had dominated them for generations. Antioch alone had ten such families, one of them being that of the famous rhetorician Libanius, friend of Julian the Apostate and zealous supporter of paganism. In the past, these families had competed for influence and prestige by outdoing each other in providing public buildings, entertainment, and food for their fellow citizens. To some extent, they still did so, but not on the same lavish scale as before. Rather, they spent much of their efforts in gaining Imperial offices and influence at Court in order to protect their cities and themselves from the oppressive workings of the fiscal and adminstrative system. The man who could use his influence to obtain relief from taxes or avert the wrath directed at his fellow townsmen by an offended governor or emperor was the greatest benefactor of all.

The Middle Classes Beneath the small number of great senatorial landowners and office-holders, the *honorati* (literally, "honored with public office"), there was a broad middle class often distinguished as *honestiores* (more honorable). Soldiers comprised the largest single group in the class. Although military life could be hard and dangerous, the prospect of regular pay, food, clothing, and shelter plus a nice bonus along with a grant of land upon retirement could be very attractive to men in the less developed provinces.

After the soldiers, the second largest bloc among the *honestiores* was the *curiales,* the men of property who comprised the decurions of the local municipal councils (*curiae*). Their position continued to deteriorate in the fourth century. As the demands of the government and exactions of corrupt Imperial officials increased, being a decurion could easily mean financial ruin. The local decurions were personally liable for any shortfall in the Imperial tax receipts from their territory and were subject to heavy requisitions of labor and supplies to support the *cursus publicus* and nearby troops.

The class as a whole became poorer in both status and wealth. Local magnates like Libanius were able to obtain high offices and senatorial rank, which conferred immunity from curial obligations. Some, by the sheer weight of their wealth and influence, could with impunity refuse to perform their curial duties. Others gave their property to the Church in return for clerical appointments, which, since the time of Constantine, procured exemption from curial burdens. Repeated decrees to prevent the desertion of decurions show the extent of the problem. As those who had the resources escaped, their places had to be filled by men of lower wealth and status. Diocletian decreed that anyone who owned at least twenty-five

iugera (about sixteen acres) of land—even the illiterate, illegitimate, or slave born—belonged to his local curia. By 376, the status of *curiales* was so low that they became legally subject to flogging. To that extent, they were now no better than slaves and lowest-ranking citizens, the *humiliores.*

Still, despite their increasing problems and justified complaints, the *curiales* remained a vital group throughout the fourth century. Although their status was supposed to be hereditary, the constant need for educated personnel to run the machinery of government and provide vital services presented opportunities for advancement to those with the proper education. Many decurions, even of restricted means, did everything they could to ensure that their sons (rarely their daughters) received such an education. Doctors, lawyers, and professors were in high demand and received good incomes. Successful lawyers in the Imperial courts could look forward to obtaining high-ranking offices. Professors of rhetoric, literature, law, and philosophy sought Imperial appointments to salaried chairs. Major cities like Rome, Constantinople, Athens, Alexandria, and Berytus (Beirut) had many such chairs, and important smaller cities such as provincial capitals all had at least two. Any city of consequence had at least one publicly salaried doctor. Carthage, for example, had five. There were also private doctors and teachers who could make good incomes on private fees, and even those with public salaries could receive extra fees and gifts.

During the fourth century, the clergy of the Christian Church became paid professionals and attracted the educated sons of decurions. Men like St. Augustine and other bishops like Athanasius of Alexandria, Eusebius of Caesarea, St. Basil, Gregory of Nyssa, Gregory of Nazianzus, and Synesius of Cyrene all came from the curial class. Augustine's father was only a minor decurion from the African town of Thagaste. He struggled to pay for Augustine's education, but he had connections. After he died, Augustine was able to continue higher studies at Carthage with the help of a wealthier family friend. As bishops, these men achieved tremendous power and influence by controlling the resources, wealth, and income of their churches (p. 448). Being born into the curial class, therefore, could still be a ticket to success.

The Lower Classes The lower classes, *humiliores* ("more humble"), had less chance to improve their lot than the *curiales*. In the cities, they were generally the merchants, shopkeepers, craftsmen, and wage laborers. The tax on businesses, the *collatio lustralis* or *chrysargyron* (gold and silver tax), instituted by Constantine weighed heavily on craftsmen and small businessmen. It was payable every five years in gold or silver on the total worth of the business. Assessments were very subjective and left much room for official abuse. It was very difficult for small operators to save up the gold or silver required, and tax collectors used beatings and torture to extract what they demanded. Poor workers were lucky to earn between one twenty-fourth and one forty-eighth of a *solidus* per day and often could not survive without handouts from the emperor and wealthy benefactors or, increasingly, the highly effective charity of the Church.

The vast majority of the *humiliores* and the Empire's population were the peasants of the countryside. The numbers of independent proprietors continued to shrink in the fourth century, and more became *coloni* on the great estates (p. 446). Given the high rate of taxation and extortion that they often faced, the small farmers could not produce enough surplus to keep them going after disease, bad weather, or man-made disasters like a plundering raid or a war caused heavy losses. A wealthy neighbor might be willing to loan the unfortunate peasant money at a high rate of interest, but that was often the prelude to foreclosure and loss of his property. Sometimes, for a fee, a local military commander used his power to protect peasants from the even greater demands of tax collectors. The situation was less severe in the East, where greater security, better economic conditions, and more vigilant emperors made rural life a little easier.

In both East and West, laws were made to bind both peasant proprietors and *coloni* to their lands in order to ensure production and the collection of taxes. They were, however, difficult to enforce. The demand for labor was so high that landlords were willing to protect fugitives, who could, therefore, bargain for favorable terms of tenancy.

The Persistence of Slavery Slaves in the home, workshop, and field remained a major part of Roman life in the fourth and later centuries. Sometimes slaves on great estates became tenants as the practical difference between *coloni* and slaves became blurred. Supplies of new slaves were not so cheap and plentiful as in the days of Imperial conquest, but Roman victories on the frontiers still resulted in large numbers of captives. Those who were not settled as *laeti* or made to serve in Roman armies right away were enslaved. Kidnappings, the sale of children by the poor, and slave breeding also kept up the numbers. An idea of the scale of slave ownership by the rich can be found in 8,000 slaves freed by the Christian noblewoman Melania the Younger when she adopted the life of an ascetic (p. 459). Nor was Christianity a force against slavery. Melania was not making a statement about slavery in granting her slaves freedom. Rather, she was freeing herself from property. In view of the increasingly harsh treatment of free citizens from all but the highest rank, there is no reason to believe that the treatment of slaves improved significantly either. Slavery remained as the brutally logical consequence of a social system that emphasized hierarchical power relationships right through the Middle Ages.

The Status of Women In some ways a woman's position in the male-dominated social hierarchy remained no better than that of a slave. St. Augustine's mother, Monica, actually urged that a wife accept the fact that she was the slave of her husband, and during the fourth century, Christian emperors issued laws that restricted a wife's ability to divorce a husband. Constantine even ruled out a husband's drinking, gambling, and philandering as valid causes for divorce. The only permitted grounds for divorcing a husband were murder, sorcery, or desecrating tombs. If a wife sought divorce and could not prove one of those charges, Constantine called her "presumptuous" and required that she forfeit everything she owned down to her last hairpin and suffer deportation to an island. A man could not divorce a woman except for adultery, sorcery, or pimping, but he suffered much lighter punishment if he sent away a wife for any other reason. He had to give back her dowry and could not remarry. If he did remarry, his first wife could confiscate the second wife's dowry. Notice how the man's second marriage is not voided and the second wife pays for his transgression!

Julian returned to more lenient earlier laws, which gave women greater freedom in obtaining a divorce, but the double standard for sexual behavior still remained. Women who had sex outside of marriage or formal concubinage continued to be condemned, but even under Christian emperors the law allowed married men to have sex with slaves, prostitutes, and unmarried women of low status. Women who worked in certain occupations, actresses and waitresses, for example, were considered to be no better than prostitutes. The assumption always was that any woman who appeared unchaperoned in public and had contact with men was sexually available. Therefore, a man was not guilty of unlawful intercourse (*stuprum*) with such a woman.

On the other hand, Constantine blamed even a respectable woman if a man abducted her: If she connived in the abduction to force her father to consent to a marriage that he opposed, she had robbed him of his rights (having been abducted, she was no longer a suitable bride for any but her abductor); if she had truly been abducted, she had not screamed loud enough for help from her family; and if she had been where her family could not have come to her aid, she should not have been there. Although a woman might not always have been without a share of blame, there was no reason to treat the man as if he had no fault in the matter and blame only the woman, a situation that Justinian reversed (p. 529).

On the prevailing assumption that women were weak and needed protection, they were normally excused any ignorance of the law. Constantine ruled, however, that women could not be allowed to profit from ignorance of the law either. By the end of the fourth century, women were legally excused from the public obligations that their fathers, brothers, and husbands often resented. On the other hand, a woman was required to fulfill certain obligations if she were the heiress of a man who died before he was able to discharge them, but she could not claim any higher status that fulfilling an obligation might entail. Legally, women were also excluded from being guardians and standing surety for another's debts. In 373, however, widowed mothers and grandmothers were allowed to become guardians of their children and grandchildren if they promised not to remarry. Moreover, widows who had demonstrated competence in managing affairs were allowed to do so regardless of the law, as many particular examples indicate.

There had always been great pressure on widows not to remarry. It was feared that the children of a former husband might suffer at the hands of a stepfather if a widow remarried. During the fourth century, the growing power of Christianity, with its great emphasis on virginity and celibacy, increased the pressure on widows not to remarry. At the same time, the Church made widowhood more bearable by supporting impoverished widows and giving them status within the Church. As in Antioch (p. 449), bishops in major cities kept legions of widows on their charity rolls. Many widows performed valuable services as members of Christian religious communities or served as deaconesses in the Church.

The Ascetic Rejection of Sex Many factors combined in the fourth century to cause both men and women to advocate and adopt a life that emphasized sexual continence, celibacy, virginity, and asceticism. The more stringent sexual morality of Christianity meshed with secular medical theories and pagan beliefs to convince many educated men that they should do everything possible to conserve and retain their sperm and expend it only rarely for the sole purpose of obtaining legitimate children. According to Galen and many doctors after him, it was necessary for men to retain their sperm as much as possible because it contained the vital spirit, *pneuma,* which was essential for their strength and health. Therefore, many men had begun to practice rigorous continence and even give up sexual activity after obtaining children. Contrary to Aristotle, Galen and late Roman medical writers like Soranus and Oribasius believed that women also produced *pneuma*-laden sperm that was expended during intercourse. Therefore, many women wished to avoid sexual activity as much as possible, too.

Retaining the *pneuma* allowed it to be concentrated and refined into purely psychic *pneuma,* which strengthened the soul and brought one closer to the divine as one became a more spiritual being. That seems to be the motivation behind the self-castration of the priests of the Great Mother (Cybele) and the requirement that her priestesses be virgins. These ideas also seem to be inherent in the words ascribed to Jesus in Matthew 19:12, "For there are eunuchs who have been so from birth, and there are eunuchs who have been made eunuchs by others, and there are eunuchs who have made themselves eunuchs for the sake of the kingdom of heaven. Let anyone accept this who can." In the same vein, St. Paul reinforced the idea that a life of continent celibacy is spiritually superior for Christians (First Corinthians 7:8 and 25–39). It probably was ideas like these that influenced Constantine to abolish the Augustan penalties for men who did not marry. That in turn may have decreased some of the pressure on women to be married.

Women in the Church   The powerful image of the Virgin Mary in Christianity further encouraged Christian women to accept the superiority of virgin or celibate status. The story of Eve and the serpent causing the Fall in the Garden of Eden only reinforced the negative view of women that had often prevailed in the classical Greco-Roman world. The central role of the Virgin Mary in Christ's nativity, however, provided a countervailing positive image that forced Christianity to treat women and men as spiritual equals. That is one reason why women were attracted to the early Christian missionaries. The imitation of Mary as virgins and celibate widows then earned them status that they could not otherwise obtain in pagan society, and it gave them a control over their own bodies that traditional society and Roman law had denied them. Today, people might think that giving up a sexually active life in exchange was a poor bargain. Yet, in view of the accepted medical and religious ideas that the educated classes held about the physical and spiritual superiority of the unmarried state, many women would have disagreed.

Of course, the theories and ideology concerning virginity were articulated primarily by men. Fourth-century Church fathers like saints Ambrose, Jerome, John Chrysostom, Basil of Caesarea (the Great), and Gregory of Nazianzus preached and wrote to persuade women to choose virginity and the celibate life. Many women, including those of wealthy and illustrious families, happily followed suit. Often to the dismay of their families, they dedicated their fortunes as well as their bodies to the service of God. Attempts were made to ensure that wealthy heiresses and widows did not deny their children and other close kin their rightful shares of family fortunes, but nothing could stop them from using their own money for good works after taking a religious vow of celibacy. Indeed, such women were eagerly cultivated by bishops and influential churchmen, who sometimes became suspected of impure motives.

St. Jerome had such a large following of pious noblewomen at Rome that suspicions finally forced him to leave and resettle in Palestine. Some of the women followed him there, women like Fabiola, a rich widow who sold her property and used the proceeds to finance a hospital, monasteries, and a trip to Palestine. Similarly, the wealthy widow Paula and her daughter Eustochium left Rome in 385 for Palestine. They founded monasteries in Bethlehem and helped take care of the cantankerous Jerome until they died (p.534). Widowed at twenty-two, Melania the Elder went to Egypt to visit Christian hermits in the desert and then settled in Palestine for over twenty-five years after founding a monastery in Jerusalem. She was a friend of Jerome's erstwhile friend and later rival Rufinus.

Melania's more famous granddaughter, Melania the Younger, was heiress to one of the great aristocratic fortunes in the West. She was married at thirteen to Pinian (Valerius Pinianus) from one of the wealthiest families at Rome. Their two children died as infants, and at age twenty she persuaded her husband to join her in a life devoted to continence and Christian charity. They supported the work of Paulinus at Nola, founded monasteries in Africa, visited the hermit monks of Egypt, and finally settled in Palestine, where they built more monasteries and became acquainted with Jerome. The sale of properties in Britain, Spain, Gaul, Italy, Sicily, and North Africa supported all of these activities. At Constantinople, the young widow Olympias used her great wealth to support its bishop, Nectarius, as well as numerous other churchmen like John Chrysostom there and in other cities.

By getting young girls and widows to take vows of chastity, the male advocates of celibacy undoubtedly hoped to minimize the danger that they always feared the "daughters of Eve" represented for men. If a man chose to marry, churchmen could not advocate dissolution of a union "sanctioned by God," but they could hope that the couple would give up sexual relations after the birth of a child or two, as the Gallic Bishop Sidonius Apollinaris urged a young friend and his wife to do and as Pinian and Melania the Younger did. They railed, however, against the common practice of cohabitation by unmarried men and women who had taken vows of continence. That situation created too many temptations to be tolerated!

The Church fathers of the fourth century inherited all of the traditional ancient stereotypes about the physical, intellectual, and emotional weaknesses of women. They still used woman's physical weaknesses, the story of being created after Adam in Genesis, and the belief that her reproductive role was divinely ordained punishment for the Fall to justify subordinating women to men. Nevertheless, they also had to take women seriously as spirit-ual beings, parishioners, and patronesses. In the Bible, woman was still God's creation, and God's son, Savior of the human race, had been born of a woman. It was agreed with Plato and against Aristotle that the soul was not sexed and that women, though physically inferior, were men's equals in soul and potential for virtue. Therefore, by the fourth century, to an extent not seen before in the ancient world, women had achieved prominence as role models worthy of public attention by both sexes.

Increasingly, women became the subjects of serious attention by male authors. The biography of St. Melania (Melania the Younger) appeared in both Greek and Latin and was widely read. Gregory of Nyssa wrote a loving biography of his sister Macrina as a model of the Christian virgin. In it he compares her to Thecla, one of the most famous female figures in works of the fourth-century fathers. Her first appearance in Christian literature may be as early as the second century A.D. in the apocryphal work known as the *Acts of Paul and Thecla.* As a young girl, she supposedly heard St. Paul teaching at Iconium in Asia Minor, was converted, and immediately took a vow of chastity. Her horrified mother and fiancé unsuccessfully tried to force her to relent and then had her and Paul arrested. After a series of miraculous escapes from horrible punishments, she accompanied Paul briefly and then settled in Seleucia as a holy woman teaching and healing for many years. In the third century, Methodius, author of the *Symposium of the Ten Virgins,* actually designated her as a disciple of Paul and portrayed her as giving the prizewinning speech in a rhetorical contest on virginity. Whether she really existed or not is of little consequence. Christians of the fourth century believed that she did, and just about every major Christian author of the period praised her as the paragon of Christian womanhood.

Educated Women Educated men increasingly wanted women who were sufficiently educated to be able to appreciate them and support the education of their children. Although young women still were not allowed to pursue advanced education outside the private sphere of family and friends, they often learned a great deal from fathers, brothers, and private tutors and could even achieve intellectual distinction. The most notable in the fourth century are Sosipatra of Pergamum (ca. 315 to 375) and Hypatia of Alexandria, (ca. 355 to 415). Sosipatra's wealthy father gave her an expensive education in mystical religious and Neoplatonic lore because she was thought to have clairvoyant powers. She married a famous Neoplatonic follower of Iamblichus, Eustathius of Cappadocia, and after his death she established herself as a highly sought after teacher at Pergamum. Coincidentally, her son Antoninus became a famed pagan priest and theurge at Canopus, near Alexandria, where Hypatia was studying mathematics, astronomy, and Neoplatonic philosophy with her father, Theon. She collaborated with Theon on many of his mathematical and astronomical works, and, as a renowned teacher and scholar in her own right, she produced her own work in those fields, too (p. 474). Among her many well-to-do male students was the famous fifth-century bishop and Church father, Synesius of Cyrene (p. 537).

Although the Church fathers were adamant about not letting women be public teachers and preachers, they often formed intellectual friendships with women that would have been unthinkable in earlier centuries. Because Christianity rested on a body of scriptures, upper-class Christian women often received a thorough grounding in the Bible and other important Christian texts. Jerome discussed many theological issues with his friends Marcella and Paula. Paula and her daughters, like Jerome, had learned Hebrew, and Jerome even dedicated some of his biblical commentaries to Paula. St. Augustine addressed a book on widowhood to the great noblewoman Anicia Juliana, and John Chrysostom carried on a vigorous correspondence with his friend Olympias at Constantinople, who is also the subject of a significant biography. These and many other heroines of fourth-century Christian writings were forerunners of an impressive number of remarkable women in the next two centuries.

Marriage, the Family, and Children   The fourth century saw some significant developments in ideas and attitudes concerning marriage, the family, and children, particularly as Christianity became a powerful force in Roman life. Influential Christians like St. Augustine, Basil of Caesarea, and John Chrysostom tried to eliminate the double standard enshrined in Roman custom and law by defining adultery as the infidelity of either husband or wife. In general, they had little success. Men did not want to lose their sexual freedom, and wives often found it convenient to let them have it in order to avoid ill temper or an unwanted pregnancy. Constantine, however, did rule that married men could not have concubines.

Both pagan and Christian moralists condemned contraception and abortion. One of the main purposes of ancient marriage was the production of legitimate children. Contraception in both pagan and Christian eyes was for prostitutes, and using it in marriage was considered to reduce nuptial relations to a sordid transaction for the gratification of lust. To Christian writers like John Chrysostom, contraception was even equivalent to murder because it took away life from the child who would have been born. For the moralist therefore, the only way to avoid pregnancy in marriage was abstinence.

Despite the moralists, however, contraception was neither illegal nor even officially condemned by a council of the Church until 572, and various forms of contraception were available. They ranged from practicing intercourse in ways that would avoid fertilization to charms, spells, and amulets. Some, such as suppositories made from wool dipped in olive oil or vinegar, worked fairly well and safely. A number of herbs and drugs could be useful, but others were often dangerous poisons. The latter frequently resulted in an abortion if a woman were already pregnant.

Both pagan and Christian moralists as well as Roman law condemned abortion and infanticide. Disagreement arose over what constituted abortion. Hippocratic medical writers did not think that conception was complete before the end of the first three months of pregnancy. Therefore, they considered ending a pregnancy in the first trimester contraception, not abortion. Christian writers, however, viewed voluntary termination of a pregnancy at any stage as murder. A law of 374 agreed with the Church in considering infanticide a capital crime, but there was no law against the widespread practice of exposure, the parental abandonment of infants whom passersby might or might not rescue as chance would have it.

The fourth century saw considerable disagreement over who might be permitted to marry and have children. All agreed that incestuous marriages should be forbidden, but the definition of incest in the Greek-speaking East traditionally was less strict than in the Latin West. For the Romans, "degree of kinship," which determined incest, was measured by "acts of generation." A parent and child or brother and sister were the products of two acts of generation and were in the second degree of kinship. An aunt and nephew or uncle and niece were in the third degree as products of three acts of generation, and first cousins were in the fourth degree through four acts of generation. Except for the special law passed as a favor to the Emperor Claudius that allowed a man to marry his brother's daughter, Roman law had forbidden marriage within the third degree. Moreover, Roman custom frowned heavily upon marriages in the fourth degree.

During the fourth century, both Roman law and the Church were imposing tighter restrictions. Citing Leviticus 18 from the Old Testament, the Church banned all marriages within the fourth degree. In 295, Diocletian had reiterated the prohibition on marriage within the third degree (except for the exemption noted above) and also banned marriage between all ascendants and descendants or between a man and his former stepmother, stepdaughter, mother-in-law, or daughter-in-law. In 355, a brother's former wife or the sister of a former wife were excluded. Sometime later, Theodosius I outlawed marriage between first cousins. In the Greek East, however, marriages in the third and fourth degrees or even between half siblings had been a common practice to keep property within the family. As a result there

were constant petitions from eastern subjects for exemption from the law and constant opposition from the Church fathers to practices they thought immoral.

Except for the rare and archaic form of Roman marriage known as *confarreatio* (p. 37), a pagan marriage ceremony was basically a civil act that served the interests of the state and family. It was usually symbolized by the giving of rings and the joining of right hands. Juno was thought to have favored the union, and it would be preceded by appropriate sacrifices on the day of the wedding but not as part of any wedding ceremony presided over by priests and fraught with religious meaning. Its celebration was mainly secular, with much feasting and entertainment among those who could afford it.

For Christians in the fourth century, marriage took on greater and greater spiritual meaning as a divine institution, not just a civic or familial duty. To the traditional customs, which also included veiling and, in the East, crowning the bride, Christians added the consent of a bishop, prayer, and often Holy Communion. Instead of Juno, Christ was depicted as joining the couple. Attempts to eliminate the feasting and entertainment were not successful, however.

Because the Christian model of marriage was the love of Christ for the Church, mutual consent and conjugal love received greater emphasis in Christian thought on marriage. Although heretical extremists might reject marriage in favor of holding women in common or rejecting sex entirely, orthodox thinkers declared that God approved sex with pure motives within marriage and that marriage was no hindrance to salvation. It was a sacrament worthy of praise for those who remained faithful to each other. In emphasizing mutual respect and love, the Christian ideal emphasized the equal spiritual worth of men and women. Nevertheless, because the male leaders of the Church viewed women as being weaker and less able to resist sin than men, they still advocated the subordination of wives to husbands. On the other hand, when a pagan man married a Christian woman, they adamantly rejected the traditional notion that woman should follow her husband's lead in religion.

Clearly, the more spiritual view of marriage among Christians raised problems for non-Christians. The fourth-century Church fathers disapproved of marriage between Christians and Jews or pagans. Under civil law, marriages between Christians and Jews could even be punished by death.

Marriage, of course, was the foundation of the family, which both pagans and Christians from Cicero to St. Augustine viewed as the foundation of the state and society. The affections of husband, wife, and children for one another were supposed to extend outward to embrace relatives, friends, fellow citizens, and humanity in general. The ideal family was the nuclear family, but the actual experience of family often involved much more. The high mortality rate, particularly for women of child-bearing age, meant that many families might include the children of two or more wives. Fathers often died before their children were grown, so that a stepfather and children from the new marriage were not unusual in a household. The orphaned children of relatives might also be present. A further complication might be the presence of a child born to the husband by a slave or concubine.

Among the upper classes, there were not only numerous household slaves but also clients, relatives like a widowed mother or unmarried sister, and long-term house guests. The result was a houseful far more complex than the "normal" nuclear family. The opportunities for significant interactions between diverse individuals in such an environment were extensive. For example, many upper-class Roman mothers used slave wet nurses to care for their young children. Strong affective bonds often developed between nurses and their charges as witnessed by numerous inscriptions.

There is plenty of evidence from grave inscriptions and literary sources that parents often had much love and affection for their children in previous centuries. Nevertheless, affective bonds between parents and children and the value of children as human beings seem to have received more stress during the fourth century. That is also reflected in Christian sources. It has been argued, for example, that the use of wet nurses reduced the affective bonds between mother and child. Significantly, the fourth-century Church fathers condemned the practice for that reason.

Christian writers also condemned the exposure of infants. Bishops established funds for widowed mothers, set up homes for abandoned babies, and urged families to adopt orphans. Constantine, perhaps motivated as much by a concern for manpower as by sentiment, reinstituted the *alimenta* for the whole Empire to help poor parents so that they would not be driven to infanticide or selling their children. Interestingly, he provided for boys and girls equally instead of favoring boys. He also ruled that parents who had abandoned a child could not reclaim it later from a person who took it in. (He also, however, gave the finder the option of raising it as free or slave.)

Children's legal rights were reinforced in relation to their parents. For example, although the age of adulthood was twenty-five, Constantine ruled that boys could take over their savings or inheritances at twenty and girls at eighteen. The need for Christians to be able to read the Scriptures spurred churches to set up grammar schools open to all boys and girls. Thus the status of children as well as women was not revolutionized during the fourth century but seems to have become greater than in earlier centuries.

Summary The fourth century, therefore, had seen many changes that established the economic and social characteristics of the Late Antique Roman world. The gap between rich and poor had continued to widen after the third century as the expanded fiscal and administrative needs of the emperors increased the size and complexity of the senatorial class and further depressed the status of the middle and lower classes. Trade in foreign and domestic luxuries and specialized craft products revived with the support of the Empire's network of military roads and waterways, the *cursus publi-*

cus, and the subsidized shipping of food and supplies to major cities and military bases. Despite Contantine's stabilization of the gold currency, the unchecked inflation of the common copper and billon coinage and harsh or corrupt taxation weighed heavily on small landowners and urban tradesmen. Particularly in the West, population still tended to shift from cities to great estates in the countryside except in the case of Rome and a few strategic provincial cities. In the East, the growth of Constantinople and the accompanying shift in resources to eastern defense reversed the decline of old centers and spurred prosperity.

The interpenetration of so-called barbarians and Romans was blurring the distinctions between the two. At the same time, Christians were advocating new attitudes toward sexual behavior, marriage, and children. Moreover, the greater emphasis on spirituality fostered by both Christianity and Neoplatonism provided greater, though still limited, opportunities for women to become prominent intellectually, religiously, and, as will be seen, politically.

XXXVIII

Christianity and Classical Culture in the Fourth Century

The fourth century is one of the most culturally rich periods in Roman history. Not only was there a revival of classical Greco-Roman traditions after the disruptions of the previous fifty years, but there was a creative interaction with the diverse traditions of native cultures that had been overshadowed in the period when Rome and Italy had dominated the life of the Empire. Christianity, having been freed from persecution and even enjoying Imperial favor, became a major factor in that process.

Christianity and the Expansion of Classical Culture Eusebius in Greek and Rufinus in Latin loudly proclaimed the total victory of Christianity over the old gods of classical pagan culture between Constantine and Theodosius. For obvious reasons, that became the accepted position of the Christian Church, and it is still widely repeated. St. Augustine, however, rightly rejected this smug triumphalism. Even under Christian emperors, coins and inscriptions hailed the restoration of the traditional world order (*Reparatio Saeculi*). Indeed, despite Christianity's adamant rejection of the pagan gods and their sacrificial rites, the world views of pagan and Christian thinkers had begun to converge under the influence of Neoplatonism (p. 407). They both had come to see an hierarchically layered universe in which the highest divinity inhabited the remotest reaches

beyond the stars and touched the secular world only through the agency of a myriad of lower spirits, *daemones,* and invisible powers. Spells, charms, amulets, and people of unusual spiritual power could give one access to these spirits in ways common to both pagans and Christians for centuries to come.

Even in the third century, Origen, the great Christian apologist from Alexandria (p. 412), who was thoroughly educated in traditional upper-class *paideia,* had pointed the way to a reconciliation between Christianity and much of the cultural tradition that leading pagans held dear. Early in the fourth century, at the time of the last persecution of the Church, his successors like Lactantius in Latin (p. 476) and Eusebius in Greek (p. 477) worked mightily to show that Christianity was the ultimate fulfillment of the quest undertaken by the great pagan philosophers of the past. Moreover, it was, they argued, the natural ally of the universal Roman Empire founded under Augustus at the same time as Christ's birth and without which his Church could not have flourished.

Appealing to the educated urban elites, Christian apologists argued that their religion was the guarantor of civilization against the barbarianism that seemed to be pressing in from all sides. As the "sublime philosophy," Christian revelation was called the ultimate source of truth for the best teachings of the classical philosophers and the firm foundation of the high ethical standards imparted by traditional *paideia*. Only the Christian God, they said, had saved the tottering edifice of the Roman Empire from collapsing during the shocks of the third century; through Christ, the solid steel of true philosophy could reinforce it for the future. In visual art aimed at elite audiences (frescoes, mosaics, elaborately carved sarcophagi, and expensively crafted small objects), Christ is no longer the simple carpenter's son of the Gospels who preaches to equally humble disciples and people of the countryside. He is now the Divine Schoolmaster dressed in a philosopher's robe, seated on a professor's *cathedra,* holding a book, and lecturing to similarly dressed well-bred men of philosophic visage. The classical figure of the cultured man seated in his study and holding a scroll of some famous author is transformed into a similarly seated Christian saint or evangelist with a book open before him.

At the same time that the Church was claiming to champion the civilization of cultured pagan elites, it accepted those whom they scorned. Although classical culture had spread far and wide over the Roman Empire, it had done so like a net, not a blanket. It had been restricted largely to those who had acquired traditional *paideia,* the educated Latin- and Greek-speaking elites of the Empire's cities. The Mediterranean sea lanes and Rome's famous roads were the threads that tied together the urban knots into a strong net of Imperial control. The poorly educated peasants of the countryside and lower classes of the cities, whose native language was often neither Latin nor Greek, constituted a large mass of "inner barbarians" who were excluded from the dominant culture of the urban elites.

Christianity had grown precisely because of its appeal to the excluded populations of the Empire. Christians believed that God had sent Christ to save the souls of the poor and the humble just as much as those of the rich and powerful. The Christian Church actively sought to include the excluded through its missionary activities, charitable works, inexpensive rituals, and communal worship. Ironically, however, the original language of the Church was the premier language of the Empire's educated classes, Greek. St. Paul, the writers of the Gospels, and the other authors of the New Testament all spoke and wrote Greek. Even the Old Testament used by Paul and other Hellenized Jews, who constituted many of Christianity's early converts, was the Greek translation of Hebrew Scriptures known as the Septuagint. Therefore, one had to have a certain level of elite education to be able to read and study the texts that were the basis of Christian doctrine if one were to become an authoritative Christian leader. Translations culminating with the great vulgate Bible of St. Jerome (ca. 385) eventually made these texts available in Latin, the dominant language of the elites in the West, and Latin still remains the official language of the Roman Catholic Church even though mass is now celebrated in the various vernacular tongues.

Therefore, Christianity not only was open to those who had been excluded from elite classical culture but also gave them access to the elite culture through the Greek and Latin of its fundamental texts. That may explain in part the attractiveness of Christianity to Constantine, on whose willing ear the words of Christian apologists like Bishop Hosius of Corduba and Eusebius of Caesarea frequently fell. Like Diocletian and his third-century predecessors, Constantine had come from a rough frontier province along the Danube. To the civilian population of the Mediterranean provinces, they and the rest of the Roman army were hardly different from the attackers whom they were supposed to fight. In the process of converting to Christianity and settling in Constantinople, Constantine sought to shed his uncouth military image and appear as a champion of the more civilized, civilian elements in Roman society. In the West, he promoted the recovery of the landed aristocracy, and in the East he gave the notables of the Greek cities extensive access to power in his new regime. Under Constantine and his Christian successors, political success lay open not just to military officers but once more to the men of civilian virtues fostered by traditional *paideia*.

Paideia fostered a common code of cultured civility that allowed the civilian elites to create a system in which those religious issues that did divide them did not lead to constant conflict and intolerance. Pagan and Christian symbols were combined in ways that were acceptable to many in both camps. Constantine, for example, kept the title *pontifex maximus,* which indicated the emperor's care of religious matters. After Gratian ceased to use it, it became a title of the bishop of Rome. Images of the old pagan deities in exquisite neoclassical style were used to represent the power, peace, and prosperity of the restored order, which was also protected by the Christians' God, whose cross now appeared on such things as the foreheads of statues honoring Rome's first emperor, Augustus, and his wife Livia outside the city hall of Ephesus and on the milestones along Roman roads.

Many of the old pagan ceremonies and rituals of power were taken over with minor changes by emperors who loudly proclaimed their Christianity. Circus festivals were held on their customary dates, but they no longer were explicitly religious occurrences. Christian and pagan holders of the consulship received their offices during the annual New Year's festival as the planets and stars that make up the ordered universe were paraded past in the guise of pagan gods who were their traditional personifications.

Christian emperors could not afford to be tyrannically intolerant no matter how much they might favor Christianity publicly in laws and proclamations. A wise Christian emperor did not persecute a pagan community that paid its taxes faithfully. He usually tried to persuade in a serene and civilized style appropriate to his exalted station. Although Gratian and Theodosius I increasingly banned the public manifestations of pagan forms of worship in the late fourth century, they did not interfere in the private devotion of pagans who did not challenge their authority. Under Theodosius, for example, two great pagan orators, Themistius in Greek and Symmachus in Latin, both reached high office. Theodosius even pardoned Symmachus for supporting the usurper Magnus Maximus after Symmachus publicly proclaimed his loyalty

again. Many of the talented and ambitious men who had acquired elite *paideia* in order to become part of the restored Empire's new ruling class in the fourth century had come from Christian homes or had converted to Christianity. Accordingly, they often ended up as leaders of the growing Church, which had intertwined itself tightly with the dominant culture of the restored Empire. By continuing to include the excluded "inner barbarians," they also could mobilize an impressive number of supporters and become powerful forces in their local communities and even Imperial politics.

Through thousands of sermons, hymns, pastoral letters, inspirational writings, and devotional books in Greek and Latin, they inculcated into their flocks the languages and many other attributes of their own classical educations. Celtic dialects at last gave way to Latin in the countryside of Spain and Gaul. Similarly, Punic yielded to Latin in North Africa. Latin became so dominant among the peoples of the Danubian provinces that Romanian is one of the most Latinate of the Romance languages. In the East, Christians made Greek the language of lower Egypt in the Delta through the pervasive influence of Alexandria. In Upper Egypt, the Coptic language of the native Egyptians became a literary language as Christians spread their message and thereby introduced Christianized classical culture to those who had had little access to classical culture in any form. Similarly, whereas the Greek of cities along the coast of the Levant became the language of the Christianized peasants in the surrounding countryside, Syriac became the vehicle for spreading Christianity and classical culture through the churches of Aramaic-speaking people in Syria and western Mesopotamia. In Anatolia, vigorous Greek-speaking bishops and missionaries effectively made Greek the language of the rough natives of the interior, who had largely been untouched by classical civilization. Armenia, whose kings had converted to Christianity even before Constantine, remained firmly in the orbit of the late classical world for centuries (pp. 544).

In the churches of great fourth- and early fifth-century bishops like St. Ambrose at Milan,

St. Augustine at Hippo, St. Paulinus at Nola, St. John Chrysostom at Constantinople, St. Basil at Caesarea in Cappadocia, and St. Athanasius at Alexandria, congregations were exposed to sermons that displayed the highest standards of Greco-Roman rhetoric. The logic and metaphysical speculation of the Greek philosophical schools informed the theological debates surrounding the Trinity, the nature of Christ, and the status of the Virgin Mary. By incorporating the legal and administrative system of Rome into its institutional structure, the Church reinforced the political and social values of the old Greek and Roman elites at the grassroots level.

For Christian as well as pagan, therefore, education in the Greek and Latin classics remained the key to cultural literacy and success in both secular and ecclesiastical careers. When the Emperor Julian forbade Christians to teach the classics, many leaders of the Church protested vehemently, for they understood how Christians would be marginalized without access to the traditional *paideia*. Even those who saw the pagan classics as a threat to Christian beliefs understood the importance of the forms and standards of classical literature. Attempts were made to create substitutes for the pagan classics in Christian schools, but they had little success, particularly after Julian's ban was shortly reversed upon his death.

Monks, Holy Men, and Christian Paideia

There was a great division between those Christians, usually from the relatively well-to-do, who valued traditional *paideia* and those, usually of more humble origin, who did not. The latter believed that Christian baptism and revelation could produce the same moral excellence and wisdom previously reserved for those fortunate enough to have the time and money required to pursue traditional *paideia*. Through such claims, the poor and uneducated, who had been consigned to subordinate positions in society, could assert their worth as moral and intellectual equals, nay, even superiors, to the culturally dominant upper classes. By ostentatiously rejecting all that upper-class culture held dear, ordinary Christians could claim to have beaten their "betters" in what traditionally mattered most, moral excellence and wisdom.

That attitude was manifest to the extreme in the great growth of Christian asceticism (from the Greek *asketikos,* "characterized by rigorous training") during the fourth century. Great numbers of Christian men and women sought to live alone as monks (from the Greek *monachos,* "solitary") and hermits (from the Greek *eremites,* "dweller in the desert [*eremos, eremia*]") or anchorites (from the Greek *anachorites,* "one who has retreated"). As already noted in the earlier discussion of virginity and celibacy (pp. 457–458), there was a growing interest in the ascetic rejection of the body and physical world in favor of spirituality during the fourth century. The ideal of the solitary holy or wise person living a pure life apart from the world became especially attractive to Christians: Christ is said to have told people to give up their worldly goods in order to enter the kingdom of heaven. The ideal, of course, had had its counterpart for centuries in that of the pagan philosopher who dressed in a simple cloak and gave up the pursuit of worldly fame and riches for that of goodness, beauty, and truth. If Christianity was the sublime philosophy, then the untutored Christians, who gave up the comforts of a civilized community to pursue holy wisdom in their desert cells, became the sublime philosophers. One learned, as it were, directly from the open book of the natural world created by God and fought in their savage lairs the demons who were always trying to subvert it.

Those who took up such an arduous task became popular heroes. People saw in them superhuman concentrations of wisdom and spiritual power similar to those of the old pagan oracles and miracle workers. Many sought their advice and their healing power. Others, who hoped to emulate their example, set up camp nearby. Soon the surrounding desert became as crowded and busy as the society that they had left behind. If one wished to remain free of the distractions of human society, it was necessary to strike out farther into the desert.

Early Christian monasticism is illustrated by St. Anthony, the son of prosperous peasants near Thebes in Upper Egypt, who took literally

Jesus' reported challenge to give up everything and follow him. Anthony became a hermit on the outskirts of his village around 270. By 285, he had moved his cell much farther into the desert proper away from the nearest habitation. Even there, however, he attracted others, and by 305 he had organized them into a loose community called a *laura*. The monks remained completely autonomous. They met together for common worship once a week but were not bound by formal rules or institutions. This movement gained further momentum from a highly fictionalized Greek biography of St. Anthony, which was ascribed, probably falsely, to St. Athanasius of Alexandria. It achieved wide popularity and quickly appeared in the West via Latin translations.

Soon some monks began to live together and share a common life under fixed regulations and the directions of a leader. They came to be known as cenobites from the Greek words meaning common life (*koinos bios*). Their leaders were eventually called abbots from the Aramaic word for father (*abba*). The first known such community was founded at Tabennisi, near Thebes in Egypt, by St. Pachomius in 326. He enforced strict discipline and physical labor under the abbot.

Both eremitic and cenobitic monasticism spread rapidly among men and women in the East. By 330, Hilarion had founded a *laura* at Gaza in Palestine. In 360 St. Basil of Caesarea (Cabira, Niksar) in Pontus set up a new form of cenobitic monastery. His rules were more elaborate and humane than Pachomius'. He prescribed more study and communal labor rather than excessive asceticism. Basil's rule was widely imitated and became the model for Greek monasticism.

Monasticism did not spread so rapidly or become so popular in the West as in the East. St. Martin of Tours pioneered the movement in Gaul at Poitiers about 360, but only two or three other Gallic monasteries existed by 400. It was also around 400 when St. Ambrose brought monasticism to Italy and St. Augustine introduced it into North Africa. There is no evidence for Spain at this time. Rather, a wealthy convert named Priscillian (ca. 340 to ca. 387)

preached the ideal of personal asceticism without total withdrawal from the world in Spain in Southern Gaul. His growing popularity caused such bitter disputes with established ecclesiastical authorities that the Emperor Gratian and the usurper Magnus Maximus became involved. Maximus eventually executed Priscillian and several supporters, who became martyrs for the ascetic ideal in Gaul and Spain.

The ascetic rejection of the civilized ideals embodied in the traditional concept of *paideia* took particularly striking forms in Syria. Asceticism had already been popularized there by Gnostic sects, Manichees, and Marcionite Christians, but the Syriac Christian writer Ephrem of Nisibis in the mid-fourth century popularized an extreme brand of asceticism that inspired truly bizarre behavior in many Syrian holy men. Some lived for years on small platforms atop columns as stylites (*stylos:* "column" in Greek), some literally became wild men who dressed in a few skins and ate grass and roots as "grazers," and others immobilized themselves in chains under the most deprived circumstances.

Not all of them were so uneducated as stereotypical, pious biographies indicate. A number were educated people of fairly privileged background who had decided to abandon their previous ways of life for an ascetic one as the path to true wisdom and virtue. They often used their skills as writers, orators, and thinkers to promote the ascetic ideal and advocate their own positions on theological issues.

Ostensibly cut off from the outside world, those who followed the ascetic life were kept in touch with what was going on through many letters and visitors. They also had to go to neighboring villages and towns to get their grain ground and exchange produce or handicrafts for the bare necessities that even they occasionally needed. Many monks hired themselves out as seasonal laborers to acquire the meager rations of grain needed to sustain them. In the East, the ascetics who settled on marginal lands, particularly in the Egyptian, Syrian, and Judaean deserts, helped to pioneer the settlement of those areas for the region's expanding population. In the West, where population was declining, they more often represented the shift in focus from an urban to a rural style of life.

Many monks and holy men in the East became embroiled in the religious and theological disputes of neighboring cities and towns. They often engaged in fanatical actions against Jews, pagans, and Christians whose views differed from theirs. For example, in 386, bands of Syrian monks attacked the temples of local villages, and in 388 one group destroyed the house of worship used by Valentinian Christians (who were labeled heretics because they held certain Gnostic beliefs) and even burned down the Jewish synagogue at Callinicum. In 391, under the urging of Bishop Theophilus at Alexandria, a mob of monks tore down the Serapeum, the great temple of Serapis that had been at the heart of the city's pagan identity for centuries.

In these and many other episodes, powerful Christian bishops and zealous monks made Christianity the dominant religion of the Empire. Often they had the tacit consent of Theodosius, who could not risk openly attacking shrines and practices dear to many of his subjects. Christian leaders were satisfied, however, with banishing the pagan gods and sacrifices from public life. As yet, they made no concerted moves against educated and influential pagans, with whom they shared much else in common and who continued to express themselves in art and literature in traditional ways. In fact, both Christians and pagans contributed to a fourth-century cultural flowering that was pollinated from many sources in the Empire's diverse landscape.

The Educated World of Letters Political instability, the virtual collapse of frontier defenses, and disturbed economic conditions had greatly reduced the scope of cultural life from the middle of the third century until the latter part of Constantine's reign. Moreover, the old educated Greco-Roman elites, who had patronized similarly educated artists and writers, had been pushed aside by the practical soldiers who had stepped in from outlying provinces to salvage the situation. During the disasters of the latter half of the third century, men like Arnobius in North Africa, Porphyry at Rome,

and Dexippus at Athens had kept up the formal teaching of philosophy and rhetoric in the heart of the Empire, but it was not easy. Although Dexippus had remained at Athens after the sack of 268, the rhetorician Longinus had moved to the court of Zenobia at Palmyra. In many smaller, provincial cities, the formal schools had ceased to function, as at Augustodunum (Autun) in Gaul. There could be no significant revival of literature without the widespread revival of formal education.

The Revival of Education The return of stability under Diocletian and Constantine and their expansion of the Imperial bureaucracy created a heavy demand for education. Many leading families throughout the Empire felt the need to reestablish continuity with Rome's glorious past after the disruptions of the previous half century. Members of the newly risen ruling elite needed to become better acquainted with the core culture of the Empire and acquire the refinements appropriate to their new status. For example, even Germans who achieved military and political importance in Imperial service sought the education of Roman aristocrats, as can be seen from the Germanic origin of the Latin rhetorician Marcomannus.

Therefore, generous public salaries were once more provided to teachers of rhetoric and philosophy, and students, like swallows in springtime, flocked back to their schools from all corners of the Empire. In the late 290s, for example, Eumenius, the newly appointed teacher of rhetoric at Augustodunum (Autun), praised the tetrarchs for their generous support of education. At the same time, he sought permission from the governor of Gallia Lugdunensis to donate his salary of 600,000 sesterces to the reconstruction of the school building where his grandfather had once taught in Augustodunum. By the middle of Constantine's reign, there were so many schools at Athens that the students of rival teachers were physically dragooning newly arrived youths into their ranks. At times, the clashes of rival teachers' students resembled gang warfare.

People trained in the schools that had survived the third century helped to produce the new gerneration of teachers that spread throughout the Empire. Arnobius' famous pupil Lactantius (p. 476), had gone to Nicomedia to teach Latin rhetoric during Diocletian's reign. After becoming a Christian, he went back to North Africa during the great persecution, but in 317 Constantine summoned him to become his son's tutor at Augusta Treverorum (Trier, Trèves). Iamblichus (ca. 250 to 325 [p. 473]), the famous Neoplatonic philosopher, miracle worker, and rhetorician, had studied under Porphyry in Rome (or earlier in Sicily) before he established his own school in Syria, probably at Apamea, where he trained many famous teachers of the next generation. Julian of Cappadocia (ca. 275 to 330) had gone for advanced training to Athens, where he himself taught several talented successors. Among their many famous students at Athens was Libanius of Antioch (314 to ca. 393), one of the most influential Greek orators and teachers of the fourth century (p. 475).

Minor Secular Latin Literature in the Fourth Century   Recovering and reconstructing the elite culture of the Latin West was particularly difficult because it had not been so deeply rooted outside of Italy as elite Greek culture had been in the Greek-speaking cities of the East. Therefore, during the first half of the fourth century, demand for basic textbooks, reference works, commentaries, and technical handbooks was particularly great in the Latin West. For example, the early fourth-century North African grammarian Nonius Marcellus produced the encyclopedic *De Compendiosa Doctrina* in twenty books. He illustrates each grammatical point with quotations that are often all that survive from the works of early Republican writers. Other grammars are similarly valuable. The *Ars Grammatica* of Dositheus is of particular interest as a Latin textbook for Greek-speaking easterners. The *Exempla Elocutionis* of Arusianus Messius canonized the four best models of Latin for all aspiring orators: Terence, Cicero, Sallust, and Vergil.

Aelius Donatus wrote two valuable grammars, *Ars Minor* and *Ars Maior,* which remained the most popular beginning Latin texts through the Middle Ages. He also wrote important commentaries to explain the texts of Terence and Vergil. Most of the Vergilian commentary is lost, but another Donatus (Tiberius Claudius Donatus) wrote a major surviving commentary, the *Interpretationes Vergilianae,* on each of the *Aeneid*'s twelve books. Aelius Donatus' student Servius also wrote extant long and short commentaries on Vergil.

The full flavor of fourth-century Latin rhetoric can be found in a unique collection of twelve model Latin panegyrics, mostly by Gallo-Roman aristocrats trying to gain influence at court. Other than the younger Pliny's panegyric on Trajan, they range from the time of Constantine to the reign of Theodosius the Great, but most relate to Constantine. One is Eumenius' speech on the restoration of the rhetorical schools at Augustodunum.

Textbooks and summaries for other technical subjects besides grammar and rhetoric were needed to help those who were trying to meet the complex demands of life in the restored Empire. Medical and veterinary science, military science, agriculture, practical mathematics, and geography all found their fourth-century muses. Several collections of medicines, medicinal herbs, and home remedies survive.

The army's need for healthy mules and horses led a certain Pelagonius to compose a volume on diseases of the horse, whereas the *Mulomedicina Chironis* took ten volumes to summarize a Greek original on the treatment of mules. Even more famous on that topic is the *Mulomedicina* of the practical military officer Flavius Vegetius Renatus. Vegetius also authored the four-book *Epitome Rei Militaris* covering such topics as formations, siege tactics, and naval warfare. Late in the century, the anonymous *De Rebus Bellicis (On Matters of War)* proposed a number of interesting technological and economic innovations to restore Roman military superiority against outsiders.

Technological and social changes in agriculture can be seen in the *Opus Agriculturale* or *De Re Rustica* of Palladius. After a general, introductory book, he devotes one book to the types of work appropriate for each of the twelve months and then shows his liberal education at the end by composing a book on grafting in hexameter poetry like the last book of Columella's *De Re Rustica* from the early first century. Remius Favinus (or Remmius Flavianus) went Palladius one better and composed a whole work in hexameters on Greek and Roman weights and measures and how to convert from one to another.

Geographical subjects were particularly popular among Latin writers. Latin was still the language of administration throughout the Empire, and the elite needed to have an idea of the vast and diverse regions under their control. Furthermore, pious Christians from the Latin West who made pilgrimages to the holy shrines of the Greek East wanted to know what to expect along the way. Various maps, handbooks, and travelers' accounts called itineraries survive from the fourth century. Pilgrimages are the subjects of two interesting itineraries. One is a trip by an anonymous author to Jerusalem in 333, the *Itinerarium Hierosolymitanum,* which starts in Burdigala (Bordeaux) and returns to Milan via Rome. The other is the *Itinerarium Egeriae* (or *Peregrinatio Aetheriae*) by an aristocratic woman named Egeria (or Aetheria). Probably from Spain, she traveled on her own to Sinai, Palestine, and Mesopotamia in the late fourth century.

There was also a great demand for brief summaries of Roman history among the numerous officials and emperors who came from provinces not steeped in the traditions of Rome. The North African Aurelius Victor sketched the lives of the emperors through Constantius II in his *Caesares*. His advice on how an emperor should act reflects the biases of the educated upper class when he says that it is best if an emperor is both virtuous and cultured but that at least he should be cultured. Shortly after the death of Theodosius (395), someone summarized Victor in the *Epitome de Caesaribus* and extended his account to 395. Another unknown writer also included Victor in a collection known as the *Tripartite History* to create a complete summary of Roman history by including the *Origo Gentis Romanae (Origin of the Roman Nation),* which covered

the mythological past from Saturn to Romulus, and the *De Viris Illustribus Urbis Romanae (Concerning the Illustrious Men of the City of Rome),* sketches of famous men from the Alban kings to Mark Antony.

Two minor historians were members of the court of the Emperor Valens. Eutropius, who had served in Julian's Persian campaign, wrote the *Breviarium ab Urbe Condita (Summary from the Founding of the City),* which covered everything from Romulus to the death of Jovian (364) in ten short books. Clearly written and concise, it became very popular, was translated into Greek, and was often used in schools until recent times. Rufius Festus wrote a similar summary that competed for the attention of Valens, to whom he dedicated it. Called the *Breviarium Rerum Gestarum Populi Romani (Summary of the Deeds of the Roman People),* it too extended from Romulus to A.D. 364, but it gave greater stress to wars of conquest.

Popular Latin Historical Novels A large popular audience seems to have enjoyed history in highly novelized form during the fourth century. Curiously, it showed a greater interest in the Greek past rather than the Roman. Many stories concerned the Trojan War or the deeds of Alexander the Great. One is the *Ephemeris Belli Troiani (Diary of the Trojan War),* which claims to have been written by one of the Greek fighters, Dictys of Crete, and translated into Latin by Lucius Septimius. Julius Valerius Polemius may have written two of the popular tales of Alexander, the *Historia Alexandri Magni (History of Alexander the Great)* and *Itinerarium Alexandri (Alexander's Journey).* They are written in highly colloquial Latin and include much that is fanciful and absurd. They are similar to the anonymous and incomplete *Epitome Rerum Gestarum Alexandri Magni (Epitome of the Deeds of Alexander the Great).* Probably contemporary with those tales of Alexander is the anonymous and even more fantastic *Historia Apollonii Regis Tyrii (History of Apollonius King of Tyre).* Amid episodes involving love, rape, incest, prostitutes, and pirates, Apollonius suffers exile from Antioch and ends up as king of Tyre.

The Revival of the Great Tradition in Latin Literature The work of reconstruction and recovery during the first half of the fourth century led to a veritable Indian summer of Latin literature among the great senatorial landowners during the second half of the fourth century. Not all were pagan, but they wanted to link themselves firmly to the great traditions of Rome's glorious past and reinforce their power and influence in the Latin West by fostering a sense of community and renewal, a true *Reparatio Saeculi*. One of the central figures in this group was Quintus Aurelius Symmachus (ca. 340 to ca. 402). His family took a special interest in preserving copies of Livy's history, and he became the most famous Roman orator of his day. Holding many high offices, he fought Ambrose over removing the Altar of Victory from the senate (p. 443). Ten books of letters survive along with fragments of his speeches. They present a vivid picture of the life of the wealthy senatorial class in fourth-century Rome.

It was probably in this same circle that the strange biographical pastiche of fact and fancy known as the *Historia Augusta* was composed. It covers the emperors from Hadrian to the accession of Diocletian and was allegedly written by six different authors in the reigns of Diocletian and Constantine. Computerized stylistic analysis, however, confirms the theory that it was really written by one person. Perhaps it was someone who was having a good joke while playing the role of Suetonius. That such a work could be written at all, however, indicates the existence of a bold and confident spirit at the time.

Although its substance contrasts markedly with the *Historia Augusta,* the serious history of Ammianus Marcellinus (ca. 330 to ca. 400) reveals a similar spirit. The last great Roman historian, Marcellinus boldly took up the mantle of Livy and Tacitus by carrying the history of Rome from where Tacitus left off in A.D. 96 to the Battle of Adrianople in 378. Born probably a pagan at Antioch, he was a native speaker of Greek, but he retired to Rome after a successful military career and wrote in Latin. He used good sources and exercised a well-balanced judgment even though he had a definite agenda of his own. Devoting over one third of the work to the lifetime of the Emperor Julian, he showed approval for the idea of a revived paganism, but he was critical of Julian's overzealous hostility to Christianity, and he censured the moral failings of the great senatorial aristocrats. He seems to have been hoping that a tolerant and enlightened pagan would provide the leadership necessary to block what he saw as a tyrannical partnership between the emperor and the Christian Church.

It was probably in this same late-fourth-century period that Julius Obsequens sought to bolster the pagan cause in the little treatise *De Prodigiis (On Prodigies)*. He summarized the prodigies recorded by Livy from 196 to 12 B.C. and showed how the Romans had avoided the calamities that they portended. He wanted to emphasize, therefore, that the old reliable rites should not be abandoned in favor of the Christianity that condemned them.

On the more literary side, the same point was made by Ambrosius Theodosius Macrobius, who straddles the fourth and fifth centuries. As a young man he was acquainted with the circle of Symmachus, and his major work, the *Saturnalia,* purports to be the learned conversations of Symmachus and his friends at a banquet held during the Saturnalian festival. Their discussions about the festival, Roman antiquities, grammar, and literary criticism preserve a wealth of ancient scholarship otherwise lost. Macrobius also wrote a commentary on the "Dream of Scipio" from Cicero's *Republic.* The idealized view of the Roman statesman and the Platonized Stoicism that underlay Cicero's thought at that point were very attractive to the Neoplatonic antiquarian pagans of Macrobius' day.

Any educated man worth his salt was expected to be able to turn out a competent poem, and some produced work that, if not equal to those of the Golden Age, at least measured up to the Silver. The most prolific and well-known poet of the fourth century is the Christian Decimus Magnus Ausonius. Born about 310 and dying about 394, he embodies much that typifies the society and culture of the western aristorcracy in the restored Empire. A member of the provincial aristocracy from Burdigala (Bordeaux) in Gaul, he received a rigorous education in the classics and became a professor of rhetoric in his hometown, which had become a thriving educational center. There he taught many important young aristocrats and developed an influential circle of friends with whom he carried on an extensive correspondence. Eventually, he attracted the attention of the Emperor Valentinian, who placed him in charge of educating the future Emperor Gratian. His connections and close relationship with Gratian led to a successful political career at Court and the coveted honor of a consulship in 379.

Much of Ausonius' poetry reveals the life and outlook typical of his class. As befits an academic, he exhibits great care in his choice of words and skillful command of meter, and his poems are full of learned references and allusions to classical Roman mythology, literature, and history. Many of the poems deal with the personalities and topics of interest to his colleagues and students. His *Commemoratio Professorum Burdigalensium* honors and sometimes gently satirizes many of his professional colleagues through a series of fictitious epitaphs. Other poems deal with ethical, historical, and cultural subjects that comprised the academic curriculum. One group, the *Ephemeris,* is a diary of the typical daily activities of his life as a high Imperial official.

There are also poems that deal with more personal subjects and reveal an attractive warmth and sensitivity. The *Parentalia* are short fictitious epitaphs honoring the dead of his own family, whereas the *Bissula* is a longer work about a German slave woman of that name, whom he educated and freed. There are also 139 epigrams and epistolary poems to various friends. His longest work, the *Mosella,* is an epyllion (little epic) in 483 hexameters and celebrates the delights of the Moselle River valley with its lovely landscapes and prosperous estates.

Although he was a Christian, Ausonius delighted in the recovery and preservation of Rome's classical heritage, which he skillfully reworked in carrying on a centuries-old literary tradition. What mattered most was whether something furthered the image of Rome's lasting greatness, not whether it was pagan or Christian. Through Ausonius and other teachers like him, the classical tradition lived on in both pagan and Christian writers who made the early fifth century one of the major ages in Latin literature (pp. 532–536).

Hellenism in the Fourth Century During the fourth century, the educated upper classes of the Greek-speaking East were firmly attached to Hellenism, the elite Greek culture fostered by traditional *paedeia.* In the schools that flourished once more, Hellenism became closely linked with Neoplatonic philosophy, which blurred the distinctions between religion, rhetoric, science, and philosophy. Of the vast body of writings by fourth-century Neoplatonic teachers and scholars, however, only a fraction survives.

Iamblichus (ca. 250 to ca. 325) stands out as one of the most influential men of the century. Born at Chalcis in southern Syria, where he received his early education, he ultimately studied Neoplatonic philosophy under Plotinus' successor Porphyry. He then used Neoplatonism, particularly its Pythagorean elements, to support the ritualistic magic and superstitions of traditional paganism. Establishing his own school at Apamea in Syria, he spent his life trying to counteract the growth of Christianity and restore paganism. He created a vast synthesis of mystery religions and pagan cults centered on Mithras and buttressed with elaborate symbolism, sacrifices, and magical spells. He became a renowned theurge, and his followers claimed that he caused spirits to appear, glowed as he prayed, and levitated from the ground.

Through Iamblichus' writings, several of which survive, and the work of his students, Julian the Apostate was inspired to abandon the Christianity of Constantine's dynasty and put the full weight of the Imperial office behind revitalizing paganism in opposition to Christianity. As a young man, Julian had eagerly attended the lectures of Aedesius, one of Iamblichus' students, who had a famous Neoplatonic school at Pergamum. Later he turned to Aedesius' own students Chrysanthius of Sardis, Eusebius of Myndus, Priscus the Thesprotian (or Molossian), and Maximus of Ephesus. When Julian became emperor, Priscus and Maximus, who was an enormously popular theurge and miracle worker, joined his circle of advisors. Julian also brought Iamblichus' former student Eustathius, husband of the famed Sosipatra (p. 460), to court and appointed Chrysanthius high priest of Lydia.

Except for a letter from Eustathius to Julian, the only writings to survive from this group are those of Julian himself. The first three of his orations are typical panagyrics that show his mastery of standard rhetorical techniques. The next four are on philosophical and religious topics that show his devotion to the Neoplatonism of Iamblichus' school, and the eighth is a consolation to himself upon the departure of a friend who shared his philosophical doctrines. Like the rest of his work, it is packed full of quotations and references to classical philosophy, literature, and history that demonstrate the enormous erudition produced in the schools of the fourth century. Three long literary letters and about eighty shorter ones to numerous recipients are valuable historical sources for his life and times. The long letter to the sophist (orator) Themistius (p. 475) sets out his program for a pagan revival, while the long letter to the Athenians amounts to an autobiography. Two rhetorical pieces, *The Caesars* and *Misopogon (Beard-Hater),* poke fun at all the previous Roman emperors and himself, but always with his characteristic seriousness of purpose.

The contemporaries to whom Julian wrote and often referred would not be so well known if it were not for Eunapius of Sardis (ca. 354 to ca. 420). Eunapius was a relative and student of Julian's former teacher Chrysanthius and shared Julian's hatred of Christianity and zeal for pagan Hellenism. His *Lives of Philosophers and Sophists* does for the fourth-century sophists what Philostratus (p. 408) did for the third. After a brief survey of some previous historians of philosophy and sketches of Plotinus and Porphyry, Eunapius covers many of the leading teachers and scholars of the fourth century from Iamblichus to Sosipatra (p. 460) to

Zeno of Cyprus (see below) all the way to 396. These lives are full of fascinating details that reveal the social, political, and intellectual life of the educated class. They also contain many absurd tales of mystical powers, magic, and miracles as Eunapius tries to create the pagan counterparts to the *Lives* of Christian saints. Unfortunately, Eunapius' *Universal History,* which continued the work of Dexippus (p. 410) from 270 to 404, is lost. Although it was heavily biased in favor of Julian, it was based on much good information and was a valuable source to later historians.

Science and Mathematics Like many of the Neoplatonic philosophers and sophists, Eunapius also had scientific interests. One of his interests was in medicine, which he shared with his friend Oribasius of Pergamum (ca. 320 to ca. 400). Of several famous Neoplatonic doctors and rhetoricians, including his teacher Zeno of Cyprus, Oribasius is the only one whose work survives. At the request of the Emperor Julian, whom he served as personal physician and trusted advisor, Oribasius produced a collection of extracts from the great second-century physician Galen and an even more ambitious collection of excerpts in seventy or seventy-two books from medical writers as early as 500 B.C. Although the first is lost, most of the latter survives in whole or in summaries that he made for Eustathius and Eunapius.

Alexandria flourished again in the fourth century as a center of medicine and science. With public support, Magnus of Nisibis, another student of Zeno's, founded a thriving school of medicine there. He was a close contemporary of Theon of Alexandria (ca. 335 to ca. 400), a famous Neoplatonic teacher of mathematics and astronomy, and father of Hypatia (ca. 355 to 415). Several of Theon's works survive: editions of Euclid's *Elements, Optics,* and *Data;* a commentary on the astronomer Ptolemy's *Almagest;* and long and short commentaries on Ptolemy's *Hand Tables.* Four poems and the known titles of other works indicate a strong interest in both astronomy and astrology. Hypatia collaborated with her father on mathematical research and may well have prepared the texts on which he commented. She gained an even greater reputation than her father in mathematics and astrology, which in her teaching she combined with an interest in Hermetic and Orphic religious teachings. As a result, she was very popular and attracted many students, who are mentioned in the works of her most famous student, the fifth-century Christian bishop of Ptolemais, Synesius of Cyrene (p. 537).

The election of the ambitious and aggressively contentious Cyril as bishop of Alexandria led to serious riots and disturbances. He persecuted pagans, heretics, and Jews in order to strengthen his own position at the expense of the Imperial prefect, who tried to curtail his activities. Cyril's partisans were so afraid of Hypatia's support of the prefect, that they ambushed her as she was returning home one day, dragged her into the courtyard of a church, stripped her, and hacked her to death with potsherds. They then burnt her remains at a spot outside the city.

The Sophists   Of the many men who concentrated on the teaching of rhetoric in the fourth century, only three are still represented by extant works: Himerius of Bithynia (ca. 310 to ca. 390); Themistius of Paphlagonia (ca. 317 to ca. 388); and Libanius of Antioch (314 to ca. 393). Of the three, Himerius is the least important. About a third of his known speeches survive. Except for six on topics from Athenian history and a eulogy for his son, they are ceremonial set pieces untouched by history, politics, or philosophy, full of poetic eloquence but little else. More important are his students such as Gregory of Nazianzus (p. 478) and St. Basil (p. 477), who became important fathers of the Christian Church.

Themistius is a very interesting person. He had an unusual interest in Aristotle during a Neoplatonic age and has left extant paraphrases of several of Aristotle's major works. It was as a rhetorician, however, that he made his mark. Establishing a school of rhetoric in Constantinople about 345, he soon attracted Imperial favor. He received appointment to a public chair of rhetoric and to the senate in Constantinople. Though a pagan who strongly supported Julian the Apostate, he also had the ear of every Christian emperor from Constantius II to Theodosius the Great because he was a willing promoter of the Imperial monarchy among the eastern notables. Constantius II sent him on a mission to the senate at Rome in 357, and Theodosius made him not only prefect of the city in 383 but also tutor of Arcadius, heir to the eastern throne. Many of his surviving thirty-four speeches contain important information on fourth-century political history and reveal the outlook of an influential pagan senator living under Christian emperors.

Without the writings of Libanius, our knowledge of the fourth century would be far poorer than it is now. He was the most famous literary figure in the Greek-speaking East. In sheer volume of surviving work, only Aristotle and Plutarch are comparable to him from all of Greco-Roman Antiquity. His 64 speeches, 51 classroom declamations, various model exercises, minor rhetorical works used in teaching, and approximately 1,600 letters take up 12 volumes of standard classical text and span the years from 349 to 393. They are gold mines of social, political, and cultural history because Libanius was one of the central figures of his time and place. His vast correspondence linked him with emperors, prefects, governors, and many of the prominent men of his day like Themistius, Himerius, and even the Jewish Patriarch Gamaliel.

A vigorous defender of pagan Hellenism, he was one of the most highly regarded teachers of his time. Talented and ambitious young men of the eastern provinces flocked to his school in Antioch, where he held the chair of rhetoric from 354 to his death. Although he eagerly supported Julian's attempt to restore Hellenic paganism to cultural and religious dominance, he advocated tolerance toward the Christians. Indeed, a number of leading Eastern Christians, such as St. John Chrysostom, St. Basil, St. Gregory Nazianzus, and Theodore of Mopsuestia (p. 477–479), were his students and friends. Julian's death almost drove him to suicide, and he lived in constant fear of reprisals under the militantly Christian Valens. His courage revived after Valens' death at the battle of Adrianople, however, so that he became influential under Theodosius, who appointed him honorary praetorian prefect in 383.

Christian Literature of the Fourth Century

Christian writers of the fourth century basically came from the same social and intellectual milieu as their pagan counterparts. In fact, they had often studied together at the same schools and exhibited the same Neoplatonic influences and rhetorical styles. For example, one of the most famous sophistic teachers of rhetoric in Athens was an Armenian Christian named Prohaeresius (276 to 367–368). The pagan Eunapius (p. 474) was one of his students and Julian even exempted him from the ban against Christian teachers of pagan literature. Many Christian writers had not even become Christians until they were adults as Christianity began to penetrate the upper classes in greater numbers under Christian emperors.

Christian Latin Authors

A good example of an upper-class convert in the Latin-speaking West is Arnobius (ca. 250 to ca. 327), who had been a pagan rhetorician at Sicca Veneria in the North African province of Numidia. He suddenly converted to Christianity around 295 and became a powerful critic of pagan beliefs. He wrote an attack on paganism called *Adversus Nationes (Against the Nations)*. His attacks on Neoplatonism and pagan practices reveal more familiarity with them than with Christian Scriptures and doctrine. He is a master of rhetoric and satirical invective but not a good guide to the theology of contemporary Christian leaders.

One of the greatest Latin Church fathers, however, was Arnobius' student and fellow North African, Lactantius (Lucius Caecilius Firmianus Lactantius [ca. 250 to ca. 325], p. 470). He surpassed even Tertullian as the Christian Cicero. Writing in a calm and well-balanced style, he argued that Christianity had absorbed and confirmed what was best in the old pagan world and would usher in an even better one through God's salvation. His ideas

can be seen in such works as the *Divinae Institutiones (Divine Institutes)*, which shows God upholding justice through the ultimate punishment of the wicked, and the *De Mortibus Persecutorum (On the Deaths of the Persecutors)*, which contrasts the unhappy deaths suffered by those emperors who persecuted Christians with the happiness of tolerant or helpful emperors, particularly Constantine. Lactantius' stress on the triumph of the Church and the glorification of Constantine became the hallmark of much subsequent Christian historiography.

Gaul produced a series of major Christian writers. Hilary of Poitiers (Hilarius Pictaviensis [ca. 315 to 367]) started out as a well-to-do pagan but converted to Christianity and ended up as bishop of Poitiers around 350. His strong opposition to the Arian heresy is apparent in all his work, such as the twelve books *De Trinitate (On the Trinity)*, and resulted in his being exiled for four years under the Arian Emperor Constantius II. Unfortunately, only three of his hymns, which were highly original and the first in Latin whose author is known, have survived.

An even greater writer of hymns was also born in Gaul, St. Ambrose, who became bishop of Milan (339–340 to 397). He came from a wealthy Christian family related to the great pagan traditionalist Symmachus at Rome. Ambrose himself was sent to Rome, where his family connections allowed him to pursue the finest education and a major political career. As governor of northern Italy, he was so successful that the people insisted on making him bishop of Milan in 374. Despite his initial reluctance, he became a zealous voice for orthodoxy against Arianism and used his powerful see to overshadow popes and browbeat emperors. Too numerous to list, his hymns, sermons, essays, and letters are invaluable for understanding the history of his time.

Of the numerous other extant anti-Arian writers in the fourth-century Latin West, the most important is Marius Victorinus (ca. 300 to ca. 370?). He left his native North Africa for Rome, where he became a successful rhetorician with a strong Neoplatonic bent. He even was recognized with a statue at public expense in 353. Two years later, he made a startling conversion to Christianity. After Julian's edict against allowing Christians to teach pagan authors, he used the rhetorical and logical skills that he demonstrated in his early works on Plato, Aristotle, and Cicero to write commentaries on letters of St. Paul, a major attack on Arianism, and anti-Arian hymns.

One of the greatest writers of early Christian hymns was Prudentius (ca. 348 to after 405), a lawyer from Spain in the Imperial administration at Ravenna. His two collections of hymns, *Hymns for Every Day* and *The Martyrs' Crowns,* have had a great impact on western Christian hymnology. He also composed a series of short poems to accompany paintings on sacred subjects and supported the removal of the Altar of Victory from the senate house in two books *Against Symmachus.*

The writing of hymns in the fourth century paralleled the growth of Christian poetry in general. Around 330, Juvencus, a priest from Spain, blended Christianity and classical epic by rewriting the Gospel of Matthew in Vergilian hexameters. In that way, he hoped to make the Christian message more acceptable to the educated pagan elite. Vergil also provided a model for Pope Damasus I (ca. 305 to 384) in writing a series of epitaphs carved on the tombs of Christian martyrs. The Christian poetess Proba (ca. 310 to 380) was a convert from the high aristocracy. Her knowledge of Vergil was so thorough that she was able to weave together different lines and partial lines from his works into a type of poem called a cento to express Christian ideas. Unfortunately, her epic on the civil war between Magnentius and Constantius II is lost.

Christian Writers in the Greek East

With the victory of Constantine and the building of Constantinople as a primarily Christian city, ecclesiastical writers raised their triumphal trumpets throughout the Greek-speaking East. The man who contributed most to the paean of the Church triumphant in the fourth century was Bishop Eusebius of Caesarea in Palestine (ca. 260 to ca. 340). He was a learned student of Pamphilus, the student to whom Origen had bequeathed his library (p. 412). He had sought a

compromise between Arians and anti-Arians at the Council of Nicaea (p. 433). An ardent admirer of Constantine, he praised Constantine and his sons in his *Praise of Constantine* and unfinished *Life of Constantine.* He also produced several apologetic works refuting attacks on Christianity and arguing for the truth of Christian beliefs, but he is remembered primarily as the first Christian historian. His *Chronicle,* preserved in Armenian and Latin translations, summarized the history of the world from Abraham to A.D. 327/28. The *Ecclesiastical History* is an innovative work that detailed the growth of the Church from Christ's birth to 324. In it he abandoned the exclusively rhetorical approach used by most ancient historians and relied on extensive direct quotations from documents and his other sources to support his narrative.

Rhetoric, however, informed much of Eusebius' work and that of many other Church fathers in the Greek-speaking East. For example, St. Athanasius (ca. 295 to 373), bishop of Alexandria, had received a good classical education in grammar and rhetoric, which he utilized against pagans and heretics in a vociferous defense of orthodoxy. As a deacon at the Council of Nicaea (325), he had played a major role in rejecting Eusebius' compromise position on the Trinity in the Arian controversy (see above). Three years later, he was made bishop of Alexandria, where bitter political and theological conflicts caused his exile five times. Twice he spent his exile in the West, where he introduced monasticism. He has left behind a large body of apologetic, dogmatic, ascetic, and historical writings along with numerous letters, which are all essential for understanding the crucial religious dispute of the century.

St. Basil of Caesarea in Cappadocia (330 to 379) and his friend St. Gregory of Nazianzus (329 to 389) studied with Himerius at Athens and probably Libanius at Antioch. Basil is famous as the author of two sets of regulations, *Long Rules* and *Short Rules,* that formalized the monastic practices of the Eastern Orthodox Church. He also wrote a very influential work entitled *An Address to Young Men,* which discussed ways of adapting the traditional classical curriculum to the needs of Christians. Staunchly orthodox and a great benefactor of the poor, he was made bishop of Caesarea in 370. He has left an impressive body of elegant, thoughtful, and moving sermons, essays, and letters. The latter number over 350, providing a fascinating look into his life and times.

Basil's fellow student Gregory of Nazianzus, another Cappadocian, also was a staunch defender of orthodoxy against Arianism. He served briefly as bishop of Constantinople after the victory of the orthodox Emperor Theodosius. Ultimately, however, he preferred a life of contemplation and writing to Church politics. He has left forty-five excellent orations on topics ranging from the Trinity and love for the poor to eulogies. His lively letters also provide many details of interest to the historian. More astonishing are the 17,000 lines of poetry that employ all of the verse forms of classical poetry on a myriad of theological, moral, and personal topics.

St. Gregory of Nyssa (ca. 330 to 395) was the younger brother of Basil, who made him bishop of Nyssa in 371 or 372. He combined deep philosophical learning with genuine pastoral care and faith in the ability of people to develop their inner spirituality. His thirteen books *Against Eunomius* form one of the best defenses of orthodoxy against Arianism, whereas his dialogue *On the Soul and Its Resurrection* rivals Plato's *Phaedo*. One of his most interesting works is a biography of his sister Macrina, whom he presents as the ideal of Christian womanhood.

Trained in Antioch and probably in Athens, one of the most influential Christian intellectuals was Diodore of Tarsus (d. ca. 390). He vigorously defended Christianity against Julian the Apostate and other pagan opponents and supported Nicene trinitarianism against the Arians. Eventually, he established an influential monastery and school near Antioch. He advocated a historical approach to the interpretation of biblical texts, which became the hallmark of biblical exegesis at Antioch in contrast with the allegorical approach favored at Alexandria. Diodore's insistence that Christ was both man and God led to his later being attacked as a forerunner of the Nestorian heresy

(p. 478). In 372, the Arian emperor Valens forced him into exile in Armenia, but he returned to become bishop of Tarsus after Valens' death (378).

The greatest orator among the fourth-century Greek Church fathers was John Chrysostom (ca. 354 to 407), as indicated by his last name, which means "Golden-Mouthed." Born to a leading family at Antioch, Chrysostom studied first with the great Libanius, who would have chosen him as a successor had he not converted to Christianity under the influence of his second teacher, Meletius, bishop of Antioch. After six years as a monk in the Syrian desert, Chrysostom was ordained a deacon at Antioch and preached his first sermon in 386. In 387, he made his mark in twenty-one sermons *On the Statues* as he counseled and comforted his parishioners while Theodosius threatened harsh punishment for the destruction of his statues during riots over increased taxes that year (p. 450). His skill won him great admiration, and for the next ten years he was the greatest preacher in the greatest church in Antioch.

In 397, Chrysostom was made bishop of Constantinople, where his preaching made him an instant celebrity but aroused the enmity of other bishops, high officials, and the Empress Eudoxia (p. 500). Other bishops did not like the increased prominence of the see of Constantinople, and Eudoxia and other members of the court resented his moral crusade against vice, luxury, and corruption and the great popularity gained from his charitable work with the poor, sick, and oppressed. Eudoxia eventually obtained his exile to Armenia, where he died. Almost a thousand of his impressive and moving sermons survive.

Another famous student of Libanius and Diodore of Tarsus was John Chrysostom's schoolmate Theodore of Mopsuestia (ca. 354 to 428). He opted for the monastic life apparently after preparing for marriage and a career in law. Becoming bishop of Mopsuestia in Asia Minor (392 to 428), he faithfully followed the example of Diodore in the historical approach to biblical exegesis and as a staunch defender of Nicene orthodoxy and believer in the two natures of

Christ: the true union by association of two personal subjects, God the son and God the man. Because of his latter views, his writings were later condemned along with Diodore's in association with the Nestorians (p. 538). As a result, his original works are lost and have to be reconstructed from fragments surviving in Latin or Syriac translations.

Many Greek-speaking Christian authors adopted the pagan forms of biography and the novel to write hundreds of hagiographies (lives of saints) and martyrologies (accounts of martyrdoms). Fiction often overpowers fact, but they still have historical importance by providing insight into the values and ideals being communicated. The most famous such work is the *Life of St. Anthony* (p. 468).

Fourth-Century Art and Architecture

The establishment of the Tetrarchy under Diocletian and his colleagues ushered in a new era in Roman art and architecture. New styles developed alongside the classical Greco-Roman traditions to serve the needs of Imperial propaganda and, from the time of Constantine, the rapidly expanding Christian population and Church. In an increasingly spiritual and religious age, the hieratic traditions of Near Eastern art became more and more prominent in the arts of painting, mosaic, and sculpture. The tradition de-emphasized worldly full-bodied, three-dimensional naturalism and strove for a flatter, transcendent, spiritual quality. Human figures were often posed in a rigidly frontal manner in order to focus on the full face. Facial features were frequently rendered schematically to de-emphasize the mortal person in favor of some greater reality, particularly through the treatment of the eyes as the "windows of the soul." The rest of the body was hidden under simple drapery, and the use of flat, perspectiveless presentations emphasized detachment from the world by making figures "float" on the surface of a relief, fresco, or mosaic. The importance of a figure like the emperor or Christ was emphasized by making it bigger than the surrounding figures and reducing humbler folk to small, schematized, even crude figures.

Imperial Portraiture and Relief In the official art of the emperors, many of those stylistic devices are often used to focus on the emperors' extraordinary power, the permanence of their rule, and the subordination of themselves as individuals to higher things. A perfect illustration is a group portrait of the four tetrarchs that probably once stood in Constantinople but is now built into an outside corner of St. Mark's Cathedral in Venice. It is made out of dark-purple Egyptian porphyry, an extremely hard durable stone reserved for Imperial use. The four are divided into two pairs with arms clasped around each other's shoulders to indicate the loyalty of each Caesar to his Augustus. Aside from a beard to indicate the older Augustus in each pair, the four are indistinguishable from each other to symbolize their unity and the primacy of their office over themselves as individuals. Their solid, squared-off shapes give the impression of the firmness and uniformity of their rule, while their wide-open eyes, deeply drilled pupils, and furrowed brows show their vigilance, commitment, and care. Similar features can be seen in Imperial portraits on fourth-century coins.

Under Constantine, sculptors adopted the convention of carving the pupils of the eyes in the shape of a crescent with the ends turned upward to emphasize the upward, spiritual aspect of the gaze. That is strikingly evident in the 8½-foot-high head from a colossal marble statue of the seated Emperor Constantine. It was originally placed in the apse of the great Basilica of Maxentius and Constantine (p. 485). Enough fragments of the rest remain to show that it reached to a height of 30 feet and had the same heavy, square proportions that give the tetrarchs' statues their powerful effect. The left hand probably held an orb to symbolize the emperor's worldwide rule, whereas the right arm was held straight out from the side and bent 90 degrees upward at the elbow with the index finger pointing to the heavenly source of that rule.

As that statue was meant to dwarf everyone in the presence of the divinely appointed, all-powerful emperor, so were the depictions of Constantine on the famous friezes that adorned

These stylized figures at St. Mark's in Venice are thought to represent Diocletian and the other three tetrarchs (Art Resource, NY)

his triumphal arch in Rome. In one, he stands in a full-frontal pose on the rostra in the Roman Forum and addresses a crowd. Although his head is missing, the space for it shows that he was taller than the officials accompanying him on the rostra and was surpassed in height only by the enthroned statues of two emperors at either end. To either side of the rostra are rows of adoring Romans looking up to the emperor or commenting to their neighbors. The other frieze shows an enthroned Constantine in a pose much like that of his colossal statue. He towers over ranks of poor citizens reaching out to receive donations of money that officials, as depicted in four small panels above the crowd, were giving out in his name. Although there are some attempts at variety, the overall effect is one of flatness and regimentation.

Large head of Constantine. c. A.D. 325. (The Metropolitan Museum of Art, New York, bequest of Mary Clark Thompson.)

The Continuation of the Classical Style

Despite the very unclassical elements found in fourth-century Imperial sculpture and portraiture, much of the classical tradition survived. For example, the portrait of C. Caecilius Saturninus Dogmatius, who rose to praetorian prefect under Constantine, clearly shows the traditions of realism in Roman portraiture, although it also exhibits many of the stylistic conventions found in less individualistic portraits of the tetrarchs. Another larger than life-size head of Constantine maintains the squared-off look of the tetrarchs and the upraised look of the eyes, but the modeling of the chin, mouth, and nose is very classical, reminiscent of the Augustus

from Prima Porta. Indeed, the slight tilt of the neck and the prominence of the ears enhance that resemblance.

It is hard to imagine that the parallels were not intentional. They reinforced the idea that the age of Rome's greatness had been restored (*Reparatio Saeculi*). Constantine further linked himself with the classical age of the High Empire by reusing reliefs and sculptures from the monuments of Trajan, Hadrian, and Marcus Aurelius. Therefore, the classical and newer, hieratic styles were found side by side on his triumphal arch (p. 479).

Constantine's own hieratic friezes probably had been executed by sculptors who were used to carving the reliefs that decorated sarcophagi. Workshops producing sarcophagi were about the only source of steady employment for sculptors in the late third century. Therefore, when the tetrarchs and Constantine

C. Caecilius Saturninus Dogmatius. A.D. 326–333. (Scala, Art Resource, NY)

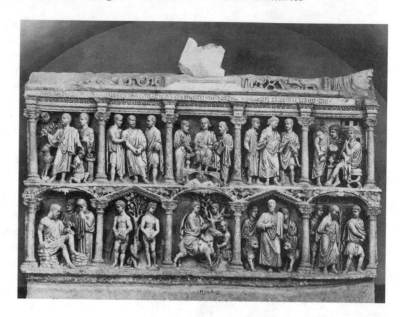

Marble sarcophagus of Junius Bassus. (Direzione Generale Musei Vaticani)

revived public sculpture on a significant scale in the fourth century, they probably utilized skilled artisans from those workshops. Such is clearly the case, for example, with the reliefs on the arch of Galerius begun in 296 at Thessalonica to commemorate his campaign against the Persian Empire. Their style and composition reflect the battle sarophagi from the third century (p. 413).

By 350, there was a revival of the classical style in carved sacophagi. The wealthy new ruling elite of the fourth century linked itself to Rome's glorious past through the classical style of these elaborate funerary monuments just as it did through the revived study of classical history, rhetoric, and literature. Even as Christian members of the new elite took over much from classical pagan literature, rhetoric, and philosophy to express their new faith, so they adopted pagan symbols, motifs, and styles in the visual arts for their sarcophagi. A prime example is the great porphyry sacophagus made for Constantine's daughter Constantia (or Constantina) around 350. Dionysiac symbols of grapes, grapevines, and cupids (erotes, putti, cherubs) preparing the vintage cover the sides and are accompanied by peacocks (pagan symbols as-

sociated with immortality) and a lamb, which may be associated with Christ (the Lamb of God) or the saved soul of the deceased (the lost sheep saved by the Good Shepherd).

The richly carved marble sarcophogus of the Roman aristocrat Junius Bassus, who was urban prefect when he died in 359, spectacularly portrays Christian subjects in high classical style. The front is divided into ten equal bays, five on top and five below. Each bay is framed by Corinthian columns, which support a straight entablature across the top row and alternating arches and pediments across the bottom. The scenes depicted in the bays are from the Old and New Testaments, but the sculpting of the figures and clothes in each scene is clearly in the same tradition as the Parthenon frieze in Athens or the Ara Pacis of Augustus (p. 284). In the center of the top row, Christ sits enthroned like a Roman emperor between Saints Peter and Paul. The two bays to his right depict Abraham preparing to sacrifice Isaac and St. Peter being arrested. The two to Christ's left show him facing charges before Pontius Pilate. Below, the central scene presents Christ riding on a donkey to Jerusalem. To his right, are Job on a dung heap and the naked Adam and Eve flanking the serpent and the Tree of Knowledge. To his left, are Daniel being brought into the lion's den and St. Paul being led to execution.

Many other works of art produced for wealthy Christians and pagans reflect the classical revival of the fourth century. The fact that a work of art depicted a purely pagan scene did not mean that it belonged to a pagan any more than the owner of a copy of the *Iliad* or the *Aeneid* had to be a pagan. A large ornate silver dish from the mid-fourth century site of Mildenhall in Britain is a good example. It depicts a Dionysiac revel in a graceful, flowing classic style without any hint of Christian symbolism. Yet, some other items found with it do have Christian iconography.

Another great silver dish combines elements of the hieratic and classical styles, while it also combines Christian and pagan motifs. Commemorating Theodosius' tenth anniversary as emperor in 388, it depicts him flanked by his son Arcadius and the western Emperor Valentinian II. They are all presented in the standard frontal hieratic, though not excessively rigid pose, and each, like a Christian saint, has a nimbus projecting a divine aura around his head. Theodosius' seniority in status and age is indicated by his greater size, and the armed guards are simply placed on different levels without any use of perspective to convey depth.

On the other hand, the three enthroned figures are depicted within an architectural framework that closely resembles the entrance to Diocletian's palace at Split (Spalatum, Spalato [p. 485]). Four classical Corinthian pilasters support a pedimental entablature with a central arch over the two inner pilasters. In the corners of the pediment, classically modeled winged putti bear victory wreaths, while in the space below the enthroned figures, more putti raise up the fruits of peace, and a fluidly curved partially draped Earth Mother figure reclines amid stalks of ripened grain in a scene reminiscent of the Ara Pacis of Augustus (p. 284).

More purely classical is a scene from the panels of a carved ivory diptych. Such diptychs became popular among the wealthy elite to commemorate important events like marriages

Ceremonial silver dish depicting Theodosius I, Valentinian II, and Arcadius. (Giraudon, Art Resource, NY)

and consulships. This one seems to commemorate a marriage between two families associated with support of traditional paganism at Rome, the Symmachi and Nicomachi. The modeling of the figures and clothing is very classical, and there is an attempt to portray depth, although the decorations on the altar are rather flatly incised instead of being carved in the round. Because a pagan sacrifice is depicted, the person who ordered it probably was making a religious statement, but it clearly became appreciated as a work of art to survive during the centuries when all members of the elite had embraced Christianity.

Mosaics and Wall Paintings The great traditions of decorating the homes of the wealthy and well-to-do with mosaics and wall paintings continued in the fourth century. Two superb mosaics depicting hunt scenes come from early fourth-century villas at Hippo Regius in North Africa and Piazza Amerina in Sicily. They show great technical skill in the use of color and pattern but prefer the new style of flat figures and perspectiveless representation of space. The mosaics that decorate the mausoleum of Constantia (Constanina) combine the grape and peacock imagery from her sarcophagus with other fruits and birds floating randomly in an off-white background to create a surface that vibrates with richly colored light. The owners of villas in Britain, however, preferred black-and-white mosaics often rendered in elaborate geometric patterns such as one from Sparsholt near Winchester.

The painting of walls in an architectural style also continued in the fourth century, as indicated by the surviving interior walls of houses at Ephesus, but figured wall painting is known mainly from tombs, whose owners probably were not rich enough to afford mosaics. Frontality, the lack of perspective, and the upraised eyes seen in other media are apparent in both pagan and Christian tomb paintings. Despite their differences, the painting of the bearded Christ from the Catacomb of Commodilla and the painting of a bearded professor sitting with his students at an anatomy lesson from the Catacomb of the Via Latina are stylistically similar. Christians also increasingly decorated their churches with mosaics

Ivory diptych of the Symmachi. A.D. 388–401. (Victoria and Albert Museum, London)

and wall paintings. Unlike pagan temples, which served primarily to house cult statues and dedicatory offerings, Christian churches were houses of worship, where congregational activities took place inside. Therefore, once they were secure and increasingly wealthy after Constantine's rise to power, Christians began to build elaborate churches (p. 487) and decorated them in the tradition of fine homes and public buildings such as baths.

Minor Arts Minor arts flourished in the fourth century. Ivory carvers produced not only commemorative ivory diptychs but also small, elegant, round lidded boxes, hair combs, and jewelry. Gem carvers and goldsmiths fashioned rings and jewelry of all kinds for the rich and powerful. Glassblowers and molders mass-produced bowls, cups, pitchers, and vases in many colors, shapes, and sizes for larger numbers of people. An interesting art that developed in the fourth century was the striking depiction of minor scenes and portraits by engraving glass with gold leaf, often on the bottoms of bowls or dishes or on round medallions.

Architecture Diocletian and the tetrarchs revived the Severan policy of constructing massive public buildings and palaces to celebrate their power and the restored Empire. Diocletian's baths in Rome were the biggest ever constructed. Today Michelangelo's great church of Santa Maria degli Angeli occupies only the central hall, whereas much of the rest is occupied by the Museo Nazionale Romano delle Terme. The only other Diocletianic building of note in Rome is the small Senate House that he built on the site of earlier senate houses in the Forum.

 Diocletian poured much money into construction at Nicomedia, his Imperial residence in the East, and at his great fortified retirement villa on the Dalmatian Coast at Split (Spalatum, Spalato). The latter was laid out like a great military camp surrounded by thick walls between square towers. In the middle of the three landward walls were gates fortified with projecting octagonal towers and entering onto colonnaded streets corresponding to the *cardo* and *decumanus* of Roman camps and planned towns. It covered almost eight acres and included not only the living quarters along the seaward wall but also barracks, exercise grounds, a temple, and an octagonal mausoleum.

 Maximian expanded Milan (Mediolanum) for his Imperial residence, and Galerius built up Thessalonica for his. Little survives at Milan,

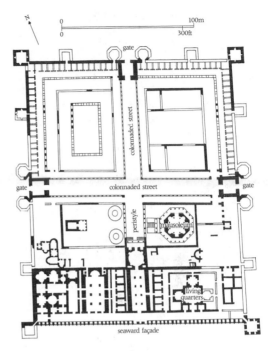

Plan of the Palace of Diocletian, from Roman Art, *second edition, Nancy and Andrew Ramage, Prentice Hall, 1996*

but part of Galerius' complex survives at Thessalonica. His triumphal arch with its marble reliefs was really a four-sided gateway where the colonnaded road leading to his palace from his mausoleum intersected with a colonnaded section of the Via Egnatia, the main military road from Italy to the East. The palace has totally disappeared, but the round, domed mausoleum, which is reminiscent of the Pantheon, survives as the church of St. George. At Rome, Constantine both restored such monuments as the Circus Maximus and Porta Asinaria and was a great builder himself. He not only built the great triumphal arch that bears his name but also finished the huge basilica begun by Maxentius. Three of its six massive side vaults still soar 114 feet into the air, but originally a vaulted clerestory rose another 40 feet above them. It covered an area approximately 350 feet by 220 feet and housed the colossal seated statue of Constantine (p. 479) in an apse projecting off the back. Both he and his mother, Helena, also built large baths for the people of Rome.

Constantine continued the tradition of round or polygonal buildings like the mausolea of Augustus, Hadrian, Diocletian, and Galerius. His mother was buried in the round mausoleum originally built for himself near the Via Casilina. The round mausoleum of his daughter Constantia (Constantina) was built about ten years after his death and is now the church of Santa Costanza. Even more interesting in design is the earlier decagonal building known as the Temple of Minerva Medica.

Constantine was an even greater builder outside of Rome. He spent much on construction and reconstruction in Italy, North Africa, and along the Rhine frontier in Gaul. Of course, his greatest concentrated program of public construction was at Constantinople. Unfortunately, nothing of his remains there. It has all been replaced by centuries of later building. The remains of his work in Gaul, however, are significant for the development of Medieval Western architecture. The crenelated walls and round towers of his great fortified camp at Divitia (Deutz) across the Rhine from Cologne (Colonia Agrippina) even look like the bailey

Basilica of Maxentius and Constantine, Rome, plan, from Roman Art, *second edition, Nancy and Andrew Ramage, Prentice Hall, 1996*

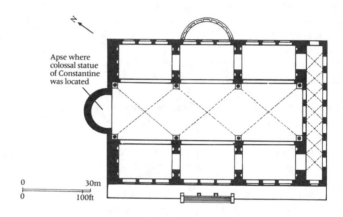

Apse where colossal statue of Constantine was located

0   30m
0   100ft

Basilica of Maxentius and Constantine, Rome, architectural reconstruction, from Roman Art, *second edition, Nancy and Andrew Ramage, Prentice Hall, 1996*

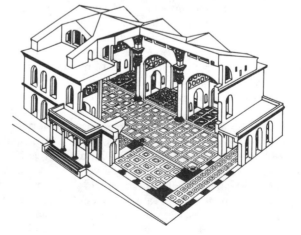

of a Medieval castle. The buildings that he built as the Imperial residence at Augusta Treverorum (Trier, Trèves) in Gaul foreshadowed the Romanesque architecture of early Mediaeval Europe, as one can see there from the ruins of his great baths and the large audience hall of his palace, which still survives as a Lutheran church. The latter is a rectangular basilica measuring 190 feet by 95 feet with an apse on one end. It stands 100 feet high and has a trussed roof with a flat, coffered wooden ceiling. Heating ducts were built into the walls, and a hypocaust supplied heat beneath the floor. Constantine also built a circus, which was said to rival Rome's Circus Maximus, and a 50-room summer palace outside of town.

Constantine's biggest contribution to architecture, however, was his program of building impressive Christian churches all over the Empire. The amount of money, men, and material mobilized for this effort was enormous, and Constantine himself gave personal attention to the choice of architects and designs. At Rome alone, he sponsored the building of two major churches inside the walls and at least a half dozen at the sites of major martyr cults outside the walls. Some of them were large basilicas with apses like that at Trier, some removed the apse and added side aisles to create a central nave, and others were round or polygonal. Many of them have disappeared in their original form or have been extensively reconstructed in later centuries. Nevertheless, much is known from pictures, written descriptions, and archaeological excavations.

The first of Constantine's churches was the great cathedral of St. John Lateran, built inside the walls on the site of the former Lateran palace. The original cathedral was a great basilica with four side aisles separated by rows of massive columns, and it measured 250 feet by 180 feet. Substantial parts of the foundation walls are incorporated into the present Lateran Cathedral. It had an apse on the west end, and attached to it was a round baptistry. Constantine dedicated 29 estates in Italy, Sicily, Greece, and North Africa to support its upkeep, and he spared no expense on its decorations. An elaborate silver screen separated apse and nave. On one side, a silver statue of the resurrected Christ stood between four angels and faced the clergy inside the apse; on the other side, a silver statue of Christ in the role of teacher stood between Apostles and faced the worshippers. Gold and silver glittered everywhere: gilded roofbeams; seven gold altars; gold and silver chandeliers and candlesticks; a solid silver basin with a golden lamb spouting water between life-size statues of John the Baptist and Christ for the font and seven silver stags forming subsidiary fountains. Red, green, and yellow marble columns marched down the side aisles. Those of the baptistry were of porphyry.

St. Peter's Basilica was the last and greatest of Constantine's Roman churches. It was located across the Tiber on the slope of the Vatican Hill where an ancient tradition said St. Peter was buried. Begun around 332, it took over 60 years to complete. Although it was razed to make way for the present St. Peter's in the late fifteenth century, pictures and descriptions survive. It measured a stupendous 368 feet by 190 feet. The central nave and four side aisles ended in a transept with an apse in the middle of the far side. In the middle of the transept, in front of the apse, four spiral columns held up a large canopy over the purported burial site of Peter himself. The canopy was topped by a cross made from 150 pounds of pure gold.

The preparation of the building site alone was an enormous undertaking. A huge terrace had to be created by cutting down the upper side of the slope and building up the lower side to a height of twenty-five feet. Again, no expense was spared on the internal decorations, which were resplendent with gold, silver, and precious stones. From the spoils of his victory over Licinius, Constantine set aside rich rural estates in the eastern provinces and revenues from houses, gardens, baths, and bakeries in Antioch to support its operation.

At Antioch itself, Constantine began a great octagonal church surmounted by a gilded dome. Located on an island in the middle of the Orontes River, it was surrounded by subsidiary buildings and courtyards and connected with the Imperial palace. Many other cities, like Tyre and Nicomedia, received major churches, but

Jerusalem and the Holy Land, of all places besides Rome and its vicinity, benefitted most from Constantine's church-building activities. His mother, Helena, went to Jerusalem on a pilgrimage in 326 to identify the sites associated with Christ's birth, crucifixion, resurrection, and ascension. Constantine then supported the building of major churches at these sites. By 333, in amazingly short order, four basilica churches had been completed. The largest was the Church of the Holy Sepulcher on the supposed site of Calvary and Christ's tomb in Jerusalem. A round martyrium (martyr's shrine) stood over the cave identified as the tomb, and a courtyard attached to the back of the basilica surrounded the Rock of Calvary, where Helena claimed to have found the True Cross. The great four-aisled basilica itself rivaled those of St. John Lateran and St. Peter at Rome in size and lavishness of decoration.

Pagan temples, particularly in the countryside, continued to be built or rebuilt throughout the fourth century despite the lack of Imperial patronage. In the middle of the century an interesting complex connected with the triple cult of Celtic earth mother goddesses (the Matronae) and the Great Mother (Cybele) was built outside of Colonia Agrippina (Cologne) at the modern town of Pesch. There was a square Romano-Celtic temple consisting of a solid-walled cella (central room) surrounded on the outside with a narrow open portico, whose low, sloping roof was attached to the walls of the cella. Opposite it was a freestanding L-shaped portico that provided shelter for spectators during festivals. The most interesting building was a temple similar to a Christian basilica. It had a square apse raised above a vaulted crypt and seating in the nave for those watching the performance of rituals.

Several octagonal versions of Romano-Celtic temples appeared in Britain. An interesting elongated hexagonal temple was built at Montmaurin, a great villa in southwestern Gaul. At Rome, in the time of Julian, a temple to the Syrian gods appeared on the Janiculum, and an underground shrine shaped like a stadium sixty-five feet long and possibly dedicated to some fountain cult was built along the Via Livenza. At Carthage, an eclectic group of buildings possibly connected with some Dionysiac cult has been excavated. The most interesting has a floor plan like a three-leaved clover.

The revived prosperity of cities in the East prompted the restoration of many temples and other public buildings as well as the construction of some new ones. Valens, for example, gave Antioch a new forum, and a proconsul restored a temple dedicated to Hadrian at Ephesus. Large lavishly decorated villa complexes sprouted up all over the Empire. Excavations of a villa at Yakto in Daphne, a suburb of Antioch, revealed a large number of beautiful floor mosaics. The great villa of Montmaurin in Gaul boasted a mansion of 200 rooms floored in expensive marble and geometric mosaics. Numerous rural villas in Britain from the same period are similarly decorated.

After the reign of Julian, however, the pace of building slowed for the rest of the fourth century. Theodosius did stimulate building in strategic Imperial cities like Milan, Thessalonica, and Constantinople but not on such a scale or with such creativity as Constantine. Milan received a number of churches during the bishopric of St. Ambrose, but the only Theodosian church at Rome is the basilical church of St. Paul, which replaced a smaller structure. The basilica would be the standard model for church architecture for some time until new forms emerged in the Byzantine East. Unfortunately, Theodosius' strictures against paganism led to the destruction of a significant portion of the Empire's architectural heritage because of the zealous destruction of pagan temples by increasingly militant Christians. Nevertheless, the conversion of major pagan temples such as the Pantheon at Rome and the Parthenon at Athens to Christian churches also preserved some of the great monuments of classical architecture and symbolizes the way in which Christianity and classical culture creatively interacted during the late Empire despite the tensions that also existed. Although Christianity became more dominant and more intolerant from Theodosius onward, it could not eliminate or escape the cultural context of which it was part.

XXXIX

The Fifth-Century West:
The Localization of Imperial Power
under Germanic Kings

The fifth century, which effectively extends from 395 to 518, saw the radical political transformation of the Roman Empire in the West. Beginning with Diocletian, the fourth century had shown that the simultaneous pressure from aggressive Persian kings in the East and land-hungry Germanic tribesmen in the West required a strong Imperial presence on both fronts at all times. That necessitated the sharing of the Imperial office between two or more colleagues dynastically united either by marriage or, preferably, by blood. Theodosius had fully recognized the need for such a system when he married Galla, sister of Valentinian II. That he had two sons was not the reason for creating eastern and western emperors; it was the need for dynastically joined eastern and western emperors that caused him to choose his two sons. As we shall see later, for more than 200 years after Theodosius, the East was able to survive intact under emperors who maintained an unbroken line of political succession and kept centralized control over Imperial officials. In the West, however, emperors gradually lost power until they themselves finally disappeared, replaced entirely by local Germanic kings holding Imperial titles that legitimized their rule over "Roman" territory and preserved the shadow, if not the substance, of the Roman Empire in the West.

Sources for Roman History from 395 to 518
With the notable exception of Ammianus Marcellinus and far less so of the fourth-century epitomators, the sources for the first twenty-five years of this period are much the same as for the fourth century (p. 415). After Zosimus and Orosius, however, whose works end in 410 and 417 respectively, there are no general narrative sources of even their limited breadth on which to rely. The more narrowly focused, though useful, ecclesiastical histories of Theodoret, Sozomen, and Socrates end in 408, 425, and 439, respectively. Evagrius began his *Ecclesiastical History* with the Council of Ephesus (431) and carried it down to 594. Its attempt to be impartial is sometimes marred by credulity. It and the other ecclesiastical histories have one great virtue, however: They often quote official documents, a practice that secular historians usually avoided.

From 439 onward, the only connected accounts are some thin chronicles such as that of Prosper of Aquitaine, who continued Jerome's *Chronicle* from 378 to 455. The Byzantine scholar John Malalas and the learned Spanish Bishop Isidore of Seville (Hispalis) both cover the fifth century in chronicles that start with Creation. Another Spanish bishop, Hydatius, continued Jerome to 468. Medieval Byzantine compilers like Photius and Constantine Pophy-

ATLANTIC
OCEAN

NORTHMEN

*North
Sea*

Baltic Sea

PICTS

S C O T S

*ANGLES
AND
SAXONS*

WALES

CORNWALL

FRISIANS

SAXONS

THURINGIANS

SLAVS

Vistula R.

"CELTIC
FRINGE"

KINGDOM

Meuse R.

Rhine R.

Aachen

Elbe R.

Dnieper R.

BRITTANY

Soissons

Le Mans

Paris

Châlons

Loire R.

Seine R.

Troyes

Main R.

Vouille

Tours

Poitiers

ALAMANNI

LOMBARDS

Dniester R.

OF THE

GASCONY

BURGUNDY

AQUITAINE

FRANKS

BASQUES

Garonne R.

Toulouse

Rhone R.

KINGDOM

Milan

Ravenna

Prut R.

SUEVI

Ebro R.

OF THE

Danube R.

*Black
Sea*

Tagus R.

KINGDOM

CORSICA

OSTROGOTHS

Adrianople

THRACE

Constantinople
(Istanbul)

OF THE

Rome

VISIGOTHS

Seville

*BALEARIC
ISLANDS*

SARDINIA

ASIA

MINOR

Strait of Gibraltar

SICILY

Carthage

KINGDOM OF THE VANDALS

Athens

EAST

M e d i t e r r a n e a n

CRETE

ROMAN

EMPIRE

S e a

Alexandria

EGYPT

✕ Battle sites

| 0 | 200 | 400 | 600 MILES |
| 0 | 200 | 400 | 600 KILOMETERS |

Germanic Kingdoms about 526

rogenitus preserve many valuable fragments from lost works. For example, Porphyrogenitus' compilation of diplomatic sources preserves Priscus of Panium's fascinating look at Attila and the Huns in his account of an embassy to Attila's camp. Isidore of Seville gives a sympathetic view of Germanic invaders in his *History of the Goths, Vandals, and Suevi.* Also important for the non-Roman side of events is Jordanes, a sixth-century monk, whose history of the Roman world includes the unsettled tribes of northern Europe and whose *On the Origin and Deeds of the Goths* is based on the lost twelve-volume account of Cassiodorus (p. 535). The British monk Gildas covers the Anglo-Saxon invasions of Britain in his *De Excidio et Conquestu Britanniae (On the Destruction and Conquest of Britain).*

Important documentary evidence is supplied by the various compilations of Roman law beginning with the *Code* of Theodosius II, which was published in 438 and contained many of the laws issued during the previous forty years. Subsequent collections of new laws, *novellae,* issued by Valentinian III and Theodosius II also contain valuable explanations for their issuance. Summaries of other laws issued by Theodosius II are contained in Justinian's *Code.* Cassiodorus' *Variae* contains 468 official letters written during his tenure of important public offices. The *Notitia Dignitatum,* a later fourth- or early fifth-century official list of the major civilian and military officials of the Empire, gives important insights into the administrative structure and military dispositions of the time. Other useful contemporary writings are the poems of Rutilius Namatianus and Claudian (p. 532), the poems and letters of Sidonius Apollinaris (p. 533), and the numerous biographies of saints, churchmen, and upper-class individuals that begin to appear in this period. What they lack in breadth they make up in detail about social, economic, and cultural conditions.

The amount of archaeological, epigraphical, and numismatic evidence is rapidly expanding and constantly adding new insights into this crucial period of Roman history.

Problems and Weaknesses Various problems and weaknesses contributed to the undermining of Roman power in the West. Compared with the East, the West faced a greater number of external threats along more permeable frontiers. Whereas the East could pursue war and diplomacy more effectively with the centralized Persian Empire on the long eastern frontier, the West was exposed to the more volatile tribal peoples on a frontier that stretched along the Rhine and the Danube for 1,000 miles. The East, however, had to guard only the last 500 miles of the Danube. In addition, the East had much more material and human resources with which to pursue its military and diplomatic objectives. The East also had a more deeply rooted unity in the Greek culture of the numerous Greek and Near Eastern cities that Rome had inherited from the Hellenistic empires. Latin culture had not achieved comparable penetration of the less urbanized West outside of Italy. The penetration of Germanic culture had been so extensive along the more permeable Rhine-Danube frontier that it was often difficult to distinguish between "barbarian" and "Roman" in those regions by the fifth century anyway.

Child Emperors The accessions of Arcadius and Honorius illustrate the unfortunate pattern of child heirs that weakened the whole dynasty of Theodosius in both East and West. When Arcadius died in 408, he was succeeded by his seven-year-old son, Theodosius II. Honorius was succeeded in 423 by his nephew Valentinian III, who was only five. Because of their young ages, Theodosius' sons and grandsons could not rule without older advisors and regents, upon whom they naturally became dependent and from whom they were unable to break away after reaching maturity. As powerful individuals vied for influence and dominance at court, the general welfare was often sacrificed to private rivalries and ambitions. Moreover, it was the women of the dynasty— Galla Placidia, half sister of Honorius and Arcadius and mother of Valentinian III; Placidia's daughter, Honoria; The Empress Eudoxia, wife of Arcadius; Pulcheria, sister of Theodosius II; and the latter's wife, Eudocia—who were far the more capable and interesting characters. Holding the keys to succession through birth and inheritance, they became active players in the political arena.

Under the youthful successors of Theodosius, the nominal unity of the Empire was maintained by having one of the two annual consuls nominated at Rome and the other at Constantinople. The facade of unity was reinforced by the public display of the emperors' statues together and the publication of Imperial laws with the names of both in the headings. Frequently, however, laws issued by one were not reciprocally issued by the other, and the administration of the East and the West went in separate ways despite instances of cooperation in times of military or dynastic crisis. Theodosius had already proclaimed his elder son, Arcadius, as Augustus in 383 and had left him nominally in control of the East when he marched west against Maximus in 387. In 393, Theodosius declared his younger son, Honorius, Augustus for the West before he undertook the expedition against Arbogast and Eugenius. Upon Theodosius' death in 395, Arcadius, now seventeen or eighteen, obtained sole authority in the East, and the ten-year-old Honorius, who had been summoned to Milan upon his father's last illness, was left alone as the western Emperor.

Germanic Commanders in Imperial Service
One of the outstanding features at the beginning of this period was the prominence of Germanic generals in the high Imperial commands. The trend had become significant under Gratian, and several practical reasons can explain it. The foremost probably was the sheer need for military manpower that made it attractive to recruit warlike bands of Germanic peoples for the armies, which, in turn, gave able chieftains and warlords the opportunity to gain Imperial favor and advance in rank. Second, one way to turn Germanic chieftains from potential enemies into loyal supporters was to offer them good positions in the Roman military, as Theodosius did by making the Visigoths federate allies af-

ter Adrianople. Also, although Theodosius had risen to power as a military leader, as a cultured aristocrat, he preferred to emphasize the civilian role of the emperor and to rely for protection on "barbarian" generals whose loyalties were primarily to him, their patron.

Internal Rivalries Unfortunately, the high positions achieved by Germanic officers often aroused the jealousy and hostility of high-ranking Roman military and civilian officials. Such positions also gave their Germanic holders a chance to pursue both personal and tribal animosities in the arena of Imperial politics. Internal Roman rivalries and power struggles aggravated the situation. Rival Roman emperors and factions often granted Imperial titles and conceded territory to one Germanic leader or another in return for help against fellow Romans. While the Romans were thus distracted by internal conflict, other tribes seized the opportunity to cross into Roman territory unopposed. When the Romans could not dislodge them, peace was bought with further titles and territorial concessions as federate allies. Accordingly, as the career of Stilicho under Honorius illustrates, all of these situations could prove dangerous to the peace and safety of the West.

Stilicho Son of a Vandal who had served in the Roman army, Stilicho served in the *protectores,* officer candidates who formed part of the emperor's bodyguard. He soon caught Theodosius' eye and married the latter's niece, Serena. He had risen to the supreme military command as *magister utriusque militiae,* master of both cavalry and infantry, when Theodosius marched west against Arbogast. Finally, before dying, Theodosius charged Stilicho with protecting the young heirs to the throne.

Rivalry with Rufinus Stilicho, however, hoped to elevate his own son to the purple and soon came into conflict with Rufinus, Arcadius' corrupt and powerful praetorian prefect. The immediate question at issue was control of the strategically important prefecture of Illyricum, which Gratian had transferred from the West to

Theodosius in the East to aid him after the Battle of Adrianople. Stilicho claimed that Theodosius had intended to transfer it back to the West, but Rufinus persuaded Arcadius to reject Stilicho's position.

In the spring of 395, Stilicho arrived in Illyricum with troops whom he claimed to be returning to Constantinople, from which they had come with Theodosius in 393. While he was there, Stilicho captured the Visigothic king Alaric, who had recently ravaged Macedonia and Thrace before heading west. Fearful that Stilicho would gain the credit for destroying the Visigothic menace and thereby strengthen his claim to Illyricum, Rufinus persuaded Arcadius to order Stilicho to send the eastern legions immediately to Constantinople and return west. Stilicho obeyed. Perhaps he did not feel strong enough to ask the troops to disobey an order of their sovereign; perhaps he feared for his wife and children at Constantinople. He also let Alaric go free, a move that put the latter in his debt for the future and would earn Arcadius the displeasure of the defenseless Romans of the Illyrian prefecture.

The eastern troops returned under the command of Gainas, an Ostrogoth with whom Stilicho plotted the assassination of Rufinus. On November 27, 395, Rufinus appeared along with Arcadius to review the troops at Constantinople. Gainas and his accomplices crowded around Rufinus with friendly gestures and flattering talk. Then, with the trap closed tight, they cut him down. His severed head was mocked through the streets, and his severed right hand was shown to passersby with requests for gifts, as a commentary on his notorious rapacity.

Alaric and the Downfall of Stilicho For the next ten years Alaric and Stilicho alternately fought and cooperated with each other as they both sought to increase their power at the expense of Honorius and Arcadius. Arcadius tried to undercut Stilicho by making Alaric a *magister utriusque militiae* of Illyrium and stirring up trouble for Honorius. Alaric invaded Italy in 401 while Stilicho was fighting German tribes across the Alps. Stilicho had to strip the northern defenses to drive off Alaric. Subsequently, a mass of Ostrogoths and other Ger-

mans swept into Italy in 405. On the last day of 406, large numbers of Vandals, Suevi, Alans, and other tribes crossed the frozen Rhine into Gaul and precipitated the usurpation of power by another Constantine, a provincial commander in Britain.

When Stilicho broke off his long-delayed invasion of Illyricum to put down Constantine, Alaric invaded Noricum and demanded 4,000 pounds of gold as a subsidy plus military employment for his men. Stilicho persuaded a reluctant Roman senate to acquiesce. This action gave jealous Roman officials at court ammunition to attack him with charges of treasonable collusion with Alaric. They also rumored that he planned to set up his son as a third emperor in the Illyrian prefecture. Palace plotters turned Honorius against Stilicho and brought about his arrest and execution along with his son in August of 408.

Alaric Attacks Rome Internal power struggles merely made relations between Honorius and Alaric worse. Honorius now refused to honor the agreement with Alaric, who immediately invaded Italy and besieged Rome while Honorius cowered in the safety of Ravenna's swamps. Lacking aid from Honorius, the Roman senate negotiated with Alaric, who agreed to lift the siege in return for a huge payment. This ransom was approved on communication with Honorius, who also agreed to hand over hostages as a token of good faith. Again, however, Honorius did not live up to his promises, and Alaric marched on Rome once more in late 409. Negotiations resulted in the city's being spared. With senatorial approval, the urban prefect, Priscus Attalus, was declared emperor and agreed to cooperate with Alaric. Alaric himself was given Stilicho's old post as supreme *magister utriusque militiae,* while his brother-in-law, Athaulf (Adolph), became count of the domestics. Other important posts were filled by friends of Attalus, all of whom belonged to the circle of powerful pagan senators that had been headed by the late Quintus Aurelius Symmachus, who had clashed with St. Ambrose about the Altar of Victory (p. 472).

A terrified Honorius offered to negotiate for a joint rule, but Attalus refused. Just as Honorius was about to flee Ravenna for Constantinople, 4,000 troops arrived from the East and strengthened his resolve. Differences arose between Attalus and Alaric about using non-Romans to fight Romans. Alaric decided to revoke his support of Attalus and come to terms with Honorius. Unfortunately, Sarus, a Visigothic rival of Alaric, intervened on behalf of Honorius and destroyed any chance of peace. Alaric then besieged Rome again and did not spare it this time (August 24, 410). For the first time in 800 years, Rome was sacked by foreign invaders. For two or three days, Alaric allowed his men to plunder, loot, and burn. Although contemporary sources exaggerated the physical damage to the city, much valuable loot and many captives, including Honorius' half sister, Galla Placidia, were carried off.

Alaric did not long enjoy what he had seized, however. After marching south and having a fleet wrecked before he could get to Sicily, he died at Consentia (Cosenza). His followers diverted the nearby Busentus River, buried him in its exposed bed, and then turned the river back into its natural course so that his final resting place could never be desecrated.

The Visigothic Migration and Settlement after Alaric

The Visigoths elected Alaric's brother-in-law, Athaulf, as their new king. After spending almost a year in raiding Italy, they crossed the Alps into Gaul in 412 and supported a rebellion there. Later they switched support to Honorius' efforts to regain control of the province. Honorius, who had not learned his lesson before, refused to reward them afterward. Athaulf promptly seized Narbo, the capital of Narbonese Gaul, along with other important towns. He then married Honorius' captive half sister, Galla Placidia. She shrewdly cooperated in his attempt (ultimately futile) to gain recognition and cooperation from Honorius. Honorius sent out his supreme commander, Constantius, who had long wanted Placidia for himself, to dislodge the Visigoths. They fled to Spain, where Athaulf was assassinated (415).

After a few days of turmoil, Wallia was elected to succeed Athaulf. He failed in an attempt to lead his people to Africa. Faced with starvation because of a Roman blockade, he negotiated with Constantius. In return for food, Wallia agreed to return the widowed Placidia, become allied with Rome, and attack Vandals and Alans who had invaded other parts of Spain. His success against them frightened Constantius, who recalled the Visigoths to Gaul (where he could more easily oversee them) and settled them in southern Aquitania (Aquitaine).

The Visigoths settled as federate allies governed by their own kings and bound to serve Rome militarily. Lands of Roman owners were partially divided among the Visigoths, whereas the Romans retained the rest of their property and remained subject to Honorius without any Visigothic control. The Visigoths wanted an independent kingdom, however, and eventually Wallia's successor, Theoderic I, forced the Romans to grant him sovereignty over Aquitania.

The Vandals, Alans, and Suevi

After the Vandals, Alans, and Suevi had crossed the frozen Rhine in 406, they had raided and plundered their way south into Aquitania. They had remained there until 409, when the usurper Constantine had driven them across the Pyrenees to Spain. After a Roman blockade of supplies had denied them food, they had agreed to settle as Roman federates in return for land, until the Romans had persuaded Wallia and the Visigoths to attack these unwelcome guests. Eventually only the Asding branch of the Vandals, which absorbed the remnants of the other tribes, remained free under Gunderic. In 428, Gunderic was succeeded by his able and ambitious brother Gaiseric.

Galla Placidia, Valentinian III, and Aetius

Constantius' success in finally marrying Placidia (417) and producing an heir, Theodosius' grandson Valentinian III, increased jealousy at the eastern court. Furthermore, after the death of Constantius (421), Placidia and Honorius became estranged, and followers loyal to each rioted against each other. Placidia and her children took refuge with Theodosius II at Constantinople in 423. Then, when the childless Honorius died a few months later, no immediate successor was available in the West, and a certain John was proclaimed emperor at Ravenna. The West now had to be reconquered for the five-year-old Valentinian III with a large force supplied by Theodosius II, who further tied the western branch of the Theodosian dynasty to the East by betrothing his infant daughter, Eudoxia (named for his famous mother, the Empress Eudoxia), to Valentinian.

Instead of fighting outsiders, the Romans now fought among themselves. Placidia, who served as regent, was also supported by Boniface, count of Africa, while a talented officer named Aetius supported John by raising an army of Huns, with whom he had spent his youth as a hostage. They arrived too late to save John but secured favorable terms for Aetius as count and master of the cavalry to defend the Gallic provinces against the Franks and Visigoths (425). Aetius was able to force Placidia to appoint him master of cavalry and infantry in 429. In the meantime, Boniface had revolted in Africa and called in Gaiseric's Vandals, who began to seize North Africa for themselves in 429. Nevertheless, Boniface became reconciled with Placidia, and she replaced Aetius with him. Aetius called in the Huns and secured restoration to power with the rank of patrician in 434.

The Huns The Germanic tribes had pressed the borders of the Roman Empire partly because of pressure from the Huns, a Mongolian people who had been driven westward from their central Asian homelands by other people pressing on them. Short, dark, wiry, excellent horsemen, fierce fighters, and inured to hardship by a nomadic life, they terrified the more settled Germans in their path. By the time of Theodosius the Great, they had halted in the old Roman province of Dacia and exacted tribute from the Germanic tribes living in southern Russia: the Ostrogoths, Heruli, and Alans. Sometimes, they raided the Roman borderlands; sometimes, they served in Roman armies.

Greater political unity seems to have been reached under their energetic king Rua (Ruas, Rugula, Rugila), who was able to exert greater pressure in dealing with the Romans. In 422 or 424, the Emperor Theodosius II agreed to pay a yearly subsidy of 350 pounds of gold to him to avoid attacks on the Balkans. It was in the following year that Rua sent a large army under Aetius to help the usurper John against the forces of Galla Placidia and Valentinian III. When John fell, Aetius was able to save himself in return for a promise from the Huns to quit the Pannonian provinces, but in 433 and 434 Rua successfully supported Aetius against his rivals and received territory in Pannonia again.

Attila Rua was succeeded in 434 by his nephews Attila and Bleda, who divided the kingdom. The aggressive Attila soon eclipsed Bleda and united all the Huns under his rule after executing Bleda in 443. Attila continued to harass the Balkans and demand increasingly larger subsidies until about 450, when he suddenly turned his attention to the West in an attempt to create a vast European empire of his own. Honoria, sister of Valentinian III, had called on Attila to help her gain part of the West for herself, and the Vandal Gaiseric was encouraging the Huns to attack his Visigothic enemies in Gaul.

Attila was overextended when he attacked Gaul in 451 and was already in retreat when Aetius, King Theoderic of the Visigoths, and other Germans, such as the Burgundians and Franks, fought him to a draw on the Mauriac Plain. Aetius, however, allowed the Huns, who had been very useful to him in the past, to escape. Attila then attacked Italy to demand the hand of Honoria. The diplomacy of Pope Leo, the timely outbreak of a plague in Attila's army, and the arrival of an army from the East induced him to withdraw in 453 without Honoria. In 454, before he could attack again, he died while consummating a marriage with the sister of the Burgundian king. Without Attila's forceful leadership, his empire quickly broke up under the attacks of the eastern Germanic tribes that he had dominated.

The Burgundians   In the wake of the Vandals, Alans, and Suevi, the Burgundians, under King Gundahar (Gunther), crossed into Gaul from the east bank of the Rhine in 407. They settled near Worms and cooperated with a Roman usurper. Subsequently, Honorius recognized them as federates. Later, Aetius enlisted the Huns to attack them for not supplying promised troops to the Roman army. In 443, he settled them in southeastern Gaul in what is now Savoy between Lake Geneva, the Rhône River, and the Graian Alps, and they fought for him against the Huns in 451. After the deaths of Aetius and Valentinian III, the Burgundians extended their domain down the Rhône to the Druentia (Durance). Officially their kings remained federate allies of Rome because they valued the prestige that association with the ancient Imperial throne entailed. In fact, however, they were autonomous rulers who served the emperor at their own discretion, not his.

The Franks   Just as the Burgundians had taken advantage of the disturbed conditions in Gaul during 407 to carve out territory there for themselves, so did the Franks. There were two groups of Franks: Ripuarians and Salians. The Ripuarians had been settled along the middle Rhine on the German side for some time. They now crossed over and established themselves on the left bank as well. They too used their arms to serve Rome and helped defeat Attila in 451.

More numerous and important, however, were the Salian Franks, who had been expanding southward from the shores of the North Sea near the mouth of the Rhine. They had already crossed the lower Rhine and seized control of Toxandria, between the Mosa (Meuse) and the Scaldis (Scheldt), before 350. Julian had halted their expansion and made them federates of Rome, but they were able to take advantage of the problems in Gaul after 406 to expand farther south to the Samara (Somme). As federates again, however, they aided Aetius against the Huns in 451 and remained loyal until 486, when Clovis (Chlodovechus), king of the Franks and founder of the Merovingian dynasty, overthrew the last vestiges of Roman

power in Gaul and extended his rule to the Liger (Loire), which was the border of the Visigothic kingdom.

Angles, Saxons, and Jutes   While these events took place on the Continent, German tribes along the North Sea—the Angles, Saxons, and Jutes—began to raid Britain. In 408, the Saxons made a devastating raid that undermined British loyalty to the usurper Constantine, who was in Gaul by that time. Eventually, Roman political and military authority was reestablished, but the western emperors could never really spare the resources to provide adequate security. By 428, Angles, Saxons, and Jutes were making permanent settlements along the English coast. Around 442, the Roman garrison left Britain and never returned. The Germanic invaders steadily gained ground, therefore, in the whole area north to the Tweed and west to the Severn.

The Vandals in Africa   By 431, only Cirta and Carthage held out against Gaiseric in Africa, despite the reconciliation of Boniface and Galla Placidia. A grant of federate status in Numidia bought only temporary peace in 435. Gaiseric seized Carthage in 439 and then began to raid Sicily and other islands. In 442, Valentinian III recognized the Vandals as an independent kingdom, and relations stabilized until the death of Aetius in 454.

The End of Aetius' Ascendancy   For twenty years, Aetius had been the power behind the throne and responsible for preserving what was left of the western Empire by skillfully playing off the Huns and Germanic tribes against each other. He was also able to betroth a son, probably Gaudentius, to one of Valentinian III's daughters, the younger Placidia. Understandably, however, neither the elder Placidia nor Valentinian III appreciated being dominated by the man who had once supported the usurper John against them and thwarted their earlier attempts to get rid of him. It was easy, therefore, for Petronius Maximus, head of an old and powerful senatorial family at Rome, and the chamberlain Heraclius to enlist Valentinian III in a scheme to assassinate Aetius, which was successfully carried out on September 21, 454. With his own hand, the foolish Valentinian III slew the one man really capable of defending his throne. Chaos ensued.

The Death of Valentinian III and the End of Theodosius' Dynasty in the West

Valentinian now promised the younger Placidia to Olybrius, a powerful senator. Expecting to be made patrician in place of Aetius, Maximus was now blocked by Heraclius. Maximus then arranged with friends of the murdered Aetius to assassinate both Heraclius and Valentinian III (March 16, 455). Because Valentinian III had no male heirs, a struggle for the throne ensued. Maximus' money obtained the support of the soldiers against both Aetius' friend Maximian and Majorian (Julius Valerianus Majorianus), an ambitious senator eager for the purple. To strengthen his position, Maximus forced Valentinian III's widow, Eudoxia, to marry him and Valentinian's elder daughter, Eudocia, to marry his son Palladius. Eudocia, however, previously had been pledged to Huneric, son of the Vandal king Gaiseric, a match that Gaiseric wanted badly. Therefore, perhaps even with the cooperation of Eudoxia, Gaiseric invaded Italy and carried off her and both of Valentinian III's daughters back to Africa after sacking Rome, June 3, 455. Soon thereafter, Huneric married Eudocia.

The Final Collapse of Central Authority

By the time Gaiseric sacked Rome in 455, only Italy, the islands of the western Mediterranean, and the parts of Spain and Gaul where powerful provincial aristocrats still held sway were under the authority of the western emperor. By 476, even those places had generally fallen under German overlords, and the western emperor ceased to exist. The events that transpired between those two years are mind-numbingly complex. A brief outline will show that the same combination of general weakness, East-West rivalries, internal factionalism, and ambitious Germanic generals and kings was still at work.

Because the city of Rome depended heavily upon North African grain, the emperors made many efforts to dislodge Gaiseric and Vandals from North Africa. The failure of these efforts was often a factor in the downfall of western emperors. In the fateful year 476, the eastern Emperor Zeno accepted reality and acknowledged the Vandals' possession of Roman Africa, Lilybaeum in Sicily, Sardinia, Corsica, and the Balearic Isles.

After the angry Roman populace had killed the usurper Maximus as he fled the Vandal advance in 455, there was a year and a half of chaos. The Visigothic King Theoderic II and Gallo-Roman aristocrats supported one of Aetius' former subordinates, the Praetorian Prefect Avitus. The eastern emperor recognized Avitus, but Gaiseric and the Roman senators and soldiers opposed him. They favored Majorian.

The Ascendancy of Ricimer Majorian also obtained the backing of Ricimer, grandson of the former Visigothic King Wallia and recently appointed *magister utriusque militiae* under Avitus. As a Visigoth and an Arian Christian, however, Ricimer could never be accepted as an emperor himself. Therefore, he worked assiduously to be the power behind the throne for the next sixteen years. On April 1, 457, he succeeded in getting the eastern Emperor Leo I to appoint him as a patrician and confirm Majorian as western emperor (457 to 461). Although Majorian succeeded in punishing his Visigothic and Gallo-Roman opponents, he lost public support for his failure to recapture Africa. Therefore, Ricimer stripped him of office and executed him (August 21, 461).

After three months, Ricimer persuaded the Roman senate to elect Libius Severus as emperor (461 to 465), but the eastern Emperor Leo would not concur. After Severus died amid suspicions of poisoning by Ricimer, Leo eventually appointed a Greek named Anthemius as western emperor (467 to 472). He also arranged a marriage between Ricimer and Anthemius' daughter. Then he coordinated a vast three-pronged attack on Gaiseric in 468, after he had obtained the release of Valentinian III's widow, Eudoxia, and her daughter Placidia the

Younger. Unfortunately, intrigues and jealousies caused the expedition to fail. Gaiseric was more firmly entrenched than ever.

Anthemius himself enjoyed little success. He was unable to stop Euric, king of the Visigoths, from seizing more territory in Spain and Gaul, and as a Greek he was merely tolerated by the Romans in preference to the "barbarian" Ricimer. Eventually, Ricimer overthrew Anthemius and raised up Olybrius, who seems to have obtained Gaiseric's permission to marry the younger Galla Placidia while she was still captive. Olybrius reigned briefly in 472 and had the rare distinction of dying a natural death.

Gundobad, Orestes, and Romulus Augustulus
After the deaths of both Ricimer and Olybrius that same year, Leo and Ricimer's Burgundian nephew Gundobad struggled to appoint their candidates to the western throne. *Magister utriusque militiae,* Gundobad succeeded in elevating Glycerius (473 to 474). After Gundobad left to become king of the Burgundians, however, Leo put his own relative Julius Nepos (474 to 475) on the throne in place of Glycerius.

Gundobad was succeeded by a certain Orestes, who had been secretary to Attila the Hun. He replaced Nepos with his own son, Romulus, whose name was that of Rome's legendary founder and whose nickname, Augustulus, mocked that of the first Roman emperor, Augustus. Nominally the last western Roman emperor, he was never recognized in the East, and Nepos remained the official Roman emperor of the West until his murder in exile (480).

Odovacer (Odoacer) and Theoderic the Amal (476 to 493)
Orestes' German soldiers overthrew him and Romulus Augustulus in 476 because Orestes would not grant them land in Italy. They proclaimed Odovacer their king, but he obtained the support of the eastern Emperor Zeno and the Roman nobility by refusing to become king and accepting Zeno's appointment as patrician. Zeno did not trust Odovacer, however, and wanted to get rid of him.

In the meantime Theoderic the Amal, king of the Ostrogoths, had been plundering Illyricum, Dacia, and Thrace right up to the gates of Constantinople. In 488, Zeno hit upon the idea of enlisting Theoderic to overthrow Odovacer and govern Italy as his representative. Persuaded by a subsidy of gold, Theoderic invaded Italy in 489. After four years, Odovacer surrendered in February of 493. A few weeks later, Theoderic slew Odovacer with his own hand on the pretext that Odovacer had been plotting against him. Officially, Theoderic ruled Italy as the patrician appointed by Zeno. His position as a subordinate representative of the eastern emperor was confirmed and refined by the Emperor Anastasius in 497. For all practical purposes, however, Italy had now become the newest Germanic successor state of the western Empire.

By 500, therefore, the localization of Imperial power in the West under Germanic kings was complete. Anglo-Saxon chiefs held sway in most of Britain, with the Romano-Celtic Britons confined to the far-western enclaves of Cornwall, Wales, and Cumberland. The Franks under Clovis held the old German provinces along the Rhine and Gaul south to the Loire. Soon, they would take much of Aquitania from the Visigoths, who would continue to rule a good portion of Spain for 200 years. The Burgundians would rule along the Rhône until they were conquered by successors of Clovis in 534. The Vandals under the family of Gaiseric would rule North Africa and the islands west of Sicily, and the Ostrogoths under Theoderic and his family would rule Italy until the Emperor Justinian's ultimately unsuccessful reconquest of those lands (pp. 515–523).

Still, it was almost impossible to conceive of legitimate rule in old Roman territories as other than Roman. Clovis, for example, gloried in being made honorary consul (and probably *patricius* [patrician]) in 507. Gundobad, king of the Burgundians, and Theoderic, king of the Ostrogoths, also held the title of *patricius,* and the Vandal King Huneric had actually married the daughter of a Roman emperor. The idea of the universal Roman Empire lived on in the Imperial titles of Germanic kings and inspired their successors' dreams of imperial glory for almost 1,500 years.

XL

Fifth-Century Empresses
and the Survival of the Empire
in the East, A.D. 395 to 518

During the fifth century, the Theodosian dynasty and its successors in the West had not been able to prevent Imperial power from becoming increasingly localized under Germanic kings. The East suffered many of the same problems as the West: attacks on the frontiers, weak minor emperors, "barbarian" generals and ambitious aristocrats hungry for power, and divisive religious controversies. These problems, however, were not so disastrous for the East as they were for the less fortunate West. The East was wealthier, more populous, and, therefore, not so dependent as the West on the manpower of Germanic mercenaries and federates, who could be counterbalanced by native troops and commanders. The East's greater wealth also meant that attacking tribes could be bought off and induced to cause trouble elsewhere. On the easternmost frontier, Persia was a centralized monarchy, with which it was easier to deal militarily and diplomatically. Furthermore, weak eastern emperors were often balanced by a remarkable series of able Imperial women who dealt effectively with the dynastic and religious problems that constantly threatened political stability.

In the East, therefore, the substance of the Empire survived, albeit in geographically contracted form. During the fifth century, Latin remained the official language of the army, government, and law; the emperors still thought in social, economic, political, and military terms

little different from those of their predecessors in the previous two centuries. They still viewed the East and West as one, and they and their eastern subjects always called themselves *Romaioi* ("Romans" in Greek). To the Turks who eventually conquered them, their land was Rome, *Rum,* a word preserved in the name of Rumania, a country whose language is derived from Latin.

The Weak Men and Powerful Women of the Theodosian Dynasty (395 to 450)

Theodosius the Great left the East to his seventeen- or eighteen-year-old son Arcadius (395 to 408). Initially, Arcadius was dominated by the Praetorian Prefect Rufinus. Gainas the Ostrogoth, after he had assassinated Rufinus (p. 493), aimed for the same power in the East as Stilicho enjoyed in the West. Many aristocrats and average citizens at Constantinople bitterly resented the power of the Germans in the army. On July 12 of 400, a major riot broke out in the city, and large numbers of German soldiers were massacred. Gainas himself fled for his life. The overthrow of Gainas did not spell the end of powerful Germanic generals in the army and at court, but after that, they never became so numerous or entrenched as they became in the West.

Arcadius' wife, Eudoxia (grandmother of Valentinian III's wife of the same name), and the aristocratic Praetorian Prefect Aurelian led the anti-German faction at the eastern court. Eudoxia was determined that nothing would be able to challenge or weaken the Theodosian dynasty and that the throne would pass to Theodosius II, the son that she eventually gave Arcadius. Her elevation to the rank of Augusta in 400 had been part of the attempt to rally public support for the dynasty against Gainas. Her forceful and highly public political activity brought her into conflict with the eloquent, popular, and austere bishop of Constantinople, St. John Chrysostom (Golden-Mouthed). Influenced by Christian asceticism, he had a very narrow view of the place and behavior proper for the women, whom he viewed as dangerous daughters of Eve.

His harsh public criticisms of Eudoxia threatened to undermine the popularity of the dynasty. She cooperated with his rivals and jealous detractors within the Church to depose and silence him (p. 478). Shortly thereafter, she suffered a fatal miscarriage, but she had already stamped her powerful influence on her eldest daughter, the nine-year-old Pulcheria, who grew to be a worthy successor.

Pulcheria, Eudocia, and Theodosius II (408 to 450)

When Arcadius died, Pulcheria's brother, Theodosius II, was only seven and her two sisters even younger. The youth of all four presented an opportunity for ambitious individuals to build up positions of power and influence in order to supplant the Theodosian dynasty. The very able and well-connected Praetorian Prefect Anthemius might have raised his own family to the purple if it had not been for the strong and precocious Pulcheria. Indeed, his grandson and namesake eventually became the ill-fated Emperor Anthemius (467 to 472) in the West after both branches of the Theodosian dynasty perished.

By publicly swearing a pious vow of perpetual virginity at fourteen, Pulcheria thwarted the efforts of the elder Anthemius and his aristocratic allies to establish claims to the throne through marriage and inheritance. She induced her younger sisters to do likewise. In 414, Pulcheria was made an Augusta and became re-

gent for Theodosius II after age or intrigue removed Anthemius. She took control of Theodosius' education to keep him from morally and politically corrupt influences and under her control. In the highly religious atmosphere of Constantinople, the dynasty's reputation for piety was a powerful factor in its favor. Her formal regency may have ended officially with Theodosius' fifteenth birthday, but she remained of paramount influence at court for several more years.

Powerful aristocrats in the senate of Constantinople, many of whom still championed traditional Hellenism, which radical Christians opposed, eventually undercut Pulcheria's influence by finding Theodosius a wife in 421. Although later romantic legend has Pulcheria initiate the marriage, contemporary sources like Olympiodorus and Synesius allow us to see how influential aristocrats and intellectuals connected with Anthemius and his friends contrived to bring about Theodosius II's marriage to Athenais, daughter of the pagan philosopher Leontius, for whom they had obtained the chair of rhetoric at Athens. Although she had to convert to Christianity and take the pious name Eudocia, her becoming empress was a great comfort to the Hellenists, and her brothers, her uncle, and their friends rapidly advanced to the highest offices.

Eudocia and her supporters helped to inspire two of Theodosius' greatest accomplishments. In 425 he created a real university at Constantinople to compete with those of Alexandria and Athens. Lecture rooms were provided in the Capitol, and ten chairs each were endowed in Greek and Latin grammar along with five in Greek rhetoric, three in Latin rhetoric, two in law, and one in philosophy. Four years later, Theodosius inaugurated his most famous work, the Theodosian Code, in which all the laws issued by emperors from Constantine to himself were collected and compiled into a single work of reference. After nine years and the labor of sixteen jurists, it was jointly issued by Theodosius II and Valentinian III on February 15, 438.

Naturally, Pulcheria resented her loss of influence and sought to eclipse her rival. Pulcheria emphasized her virgin piety to gain the support of the populace and powerful bishops like Cyril of Alexandria, who all feared a resurgence of paganism. Eudocia, who bore two daughters, Eudoxia (wife of Valentinian III) and Flavilla (d. 430), was hampered by her failure to bear a son. The Council of Ephesus in 431, which declared the Virgin Mary to be *Theotokos* (Mother of God), represents a triumph for the virgin Pulcheria, who exploited Mary's reflected glory.

Both women were outmaneuvered by the eunuch Chrysaphius. Pulcheria withdrew to the suburbs of Constaninople in 441, and Eudocia's downfall on suspicion of adultery followed in 443. Eudocia, who had become a friend of the famous Christian ascetic Melania the Younger, spent the rest of her life doing pious good works in Jerusalem. Pulcheria, however, eventually maneuvered herself back into power and was able to control the appointment of a successor when Theodosius II died in 450.

Persians and Huns, 408 to 450 After Theodosius' treaty of 387, relations with the Persian Empire had become stable, even friendly. The Persian King Yazdgard (Yazdigird, Yezdegerd) I (399 to 420) was tolerant of Christians, and about 409 Anthemius succeeded in obtaining the king's help in settling the disputes of Persia's Christian bishops. Subsequently, Yazdgard gave legal recognition to the bishop of Ctesiphon as head of the Church in Persia. There is even a credible story that the dying Arcadius asked Yazdgard to protect the young Theodosius II from Roman usurpers. Unfortunately, relations with Yazdgard soured in the last year of his reign when a fanatical Christian bishop demolished a fire alter belonging to Persia's official Zoroastrian religion. His son and successor Bahram (Vahram, 420 to 439) instituted a persecution that produced a stream of Christian refugees begging for help from Theodosius. Persuaded by the pious Pulcheria, Theodosius immediately mobilized Roman forces to attack Persia in 421.

The war did not go well. In 422, Rua the Hun took advantage of the situation to attack

Thrace. Pulcheria's policies were disgraced. Her aristocratic opponents, who had regained ascendancy through the marriage of Theodosius to Eudocia, negotiated a peace that many sources claim as a great victory for Theodosius. At the same time, Rua was bought off with a subsidy of 350 pounds of gold a year to keep the peace.

Unfortunately, Rua and his successor Attila knew a good thing when they saw it. Whenever the East's forces were distracted on another front, they attacked Thrace. Constantinople itself was impregnable, thanks to the earlier actions of Anthemius. He had initiated the construction of a massive western wall from the Propontis (Sea of Marmara/Marmora) to the Golden Horn, strengthened the navy, and provided for a secure food supply. Nevertheless, the treasury was saddled with increasingly ruinous subsidies to get rid of the Huns. During a Persian attack in 441 and 442, for example, Attila extorted an immediate payment of 6,000 pounds of gold and an annual tribute of 2,100. The wealthy aristocrats' resentment of taxes needed to pay these sums contributed to the downfall of the eunuch Chrysaphius after he bungled an assassination attempt against Attila.

Christian Controversies and Imperial Politics In the late Roman Empire, theological disputes among Christians always had great political significance. Because Nestorius, bishop of Constantinople (428 to 431), claimed that Christ had two separate natures, human and divine, in one person but not mixed, he opposed calling Mary *Theotokos* (Mother of God) and thus threatened to lower the status of the Virgin Mary, with whom the virgin Pulcheria was associated in the minds of common people to Pulcheria's great political advantage. After Pulcheria and her allies, particularly the contentious and unscrupulous Cyril of Alexandria, defeated Nestorius at the First Council of Ephesus (431), he was exiled. Many of his perscuted followers were welcomed by Rome's enemy Persia, where they spread the Nestorian sect of Christianity. Another theological dispute helped to undermine her enemy

Chrysaphius in 450. He supported the influential monk Eutyches, who held the Monophysite view that Christ's nature was wholly one. Eutyches' trial for heresy in 448 and the disgraceful politicking that led to his restoration at the Second Council of Ephesus in 449 ultimately damaged the prestige of his patron Chrysaphius to the advantage of Pulcheria.

German and Isaurian Generals   The final nail in Chrysaphius' coffin was the problem of ambitious Germanic generals. After the downfall of Gainas, Anthemius had kept Germanic officers out of the high military commands, but when Pulcheria eclipsed him, she resorted to the dynasty's traditional practice of utilizing the political and military support of powerful Germanic generals. That led to the rise of Aspar, part Goth part Alan, which displeased senatorial leaders at Constantinople. Chrysaphius tried to check Aspar by promoting the use of warlike mountain tribesmen from the Roman province of Isauria on the south coast of Asia Minor. The Isaurian chief Zeno, however, soon realized that he was more powerful than his patron. When Chrysaphius refused to do his bidding, Zeno helped to procure his downfall in 450, and Pulcheria resumed her dominance in the court of Theodosius II. Soon thereafter, the emperor died after falling from his horse while hunting.

Pulcheria and Marcian (450 to 457)
Backed by Aspar, Pulcheria firmly controlled political and religious affairs, but he, a "barbarian," and she, a woman, could never be accepted as holders of the throne themselves. They chose, therefore, to elevate one of Aspar's close subordinates, the tribune Marcian, a Roman from Illyricum or Thrace who was acceptable to the leading senators. A pro forma marriage was arranged with Pulcheria to give Marcian a dynastic claim and protect her politically crucial virginity. To forestall scandal among the pious, a commemorative gold *solidus* depicts Christ standing between the couple as sponsoring the marriage of his virgin "bride" to the new emperor.

Marcian and Pulcheria continued to reverse the policies of Chrysaphius. They refused to continue payments to Attila, who was too involved in the West to retaliate before he died. His death and the breakup of his empire allowed them to resettle Germanic federates, particularly Ostrogoths, in abandoned territories along the Danube. Without having to pay the Huns anymore, they also tried to accommodate the senatorial class by reducing taxes, alleviating the expenses of holding offices, and trying to halt the sale of offices, too. The marriage of Marcian's daughter by his first wife to Anthemius, grandson of Anthemius, also pleased the senate. When Pulcheria died in 453, she had overcome all obstacles to her control of dynastic power. Paradoxically, however, her reliance on her own virgin status for authority and her success in coming between Theodosius II and her rival Eudocia before they could produce a son meant that the dynasty could no longer continue in the East and would pass away altogether with the death of Valentinian III two years later in the West.

Leo I (457 to 474)   When Marcian died, most senators probably would have preferred to elect Marcian's son-in-law Anthemius as his successor. Instead, Aspar forced them to elect one of his officers as Leo I. Leo, however, did not want to be Aspar's puppet. Leo surrounded himself with Isaurian bodyguards, the Excubitors, and married his daughter Ariadne to an Isaurian officer named Tarasicodissa, who took the Greek name Zeno. They worked to weaken Aspar.

In foreign policy, Leo asserted his independence by installing Anthemius as emperor in the West and by mounting a massive joint expedition to North Africa against Gaiseric the Vandal in 467. The failure of that expedition weakened Zeno so that Aspar and his two sons intrigued against him more boldly. In desperation, Leo and Zeno lured them into the palace, where the emperor's eunuchs ambushed them. Aspar and one son were killed, while the other was captured and allowed to live (471).

The Ostrogothic general Theoderic Strabo

used Aspar's murder as an excuse to demand appointment in his place and lands in Thrace for his Ostrogoths, who now elected him their king. Leo refused, and Strabo ravaged Thrace. In 473, a compromise was reached, by which Strabo received Aspar's old post and the Ostrogoths received a subsidy of two thousand pounds of gold a year.

Leo II (473 to 474) and Zeno (474 to 491)

In 473, Leo I also made Zeno's son by Ariadne, another Leo (II), his colleague and destined successor. Leo I died some months later in early 474. In turn, Leo II took his father, Zeno, as co-emperor. He died before the end of the year and thus left Zeno in sole possession of the throne. Zeno was resented because he was an Isaurian outsider. He soon had to face a serious revolt led by Theoderic Strabo and the widow of Leo I, Verina, another strong eastern empress. In 476, Zeno temporarily succeeded in defeating his domestic enemies but still had to deal with Theoderic Strabo, whom he tried to fight with a rival Ostrogoth, Theoderic the Amal. Zeno adopted Theoderic the Amal, made him master of the soldiers, and sent him to fight Strabo in Thrace. The Amal, however, turned the tables on Zeno and tried to play Strabo off against him. More domestic plots involving Verina followed and were not completely suppressed until 488. Meanwhile, Theoderic Strabo had died, and in 488, Zeno was also able to come to a satisfactory agreement with Theoderic the Amal, whom he authorized to overthrow Odovacer in Italy. Zeno had finally rid himself of serious foes and was free from plots for the remaining three years of his life.

Religious Controversies Continued The theological disputes that bedeviled the East from Theodosius II to the Arab conquest of Syria and Egypt two centuries later had their roots in the questions raised about the nature of Christ in the Arian heresy (pp. 432) and in the jealousies of rival bishops (patriarchs) vying for preeminence with each other at Rome, Constantinople, Alexandria, Jerusalem, and Antioch.

Cyril, bishop of Alexandria (d. 444), had been a powerful and violent ally of Pulcheria against Nestorius, bishop of Constantinople and ally of Cyril's archrival, John, bishop of Antioch (d. 441/42), who also believed that Christ had distinct human and divine natures. Cyril supported the Monophysites, who argued that Christ's two natures had been fully combined into one nature (*monophysis*). After the Council of Ephesus, Pulcheria had used her renewed influence to force John and Cyril to accept a compromise in 433 to preserve the unity of the Church. The resultant Formula of Union stated that there had been a "union of two natures" resulting in "one Christ, one son, one Lord." Many Alexandrians had refused to accept the compromise and elected Dioscorus bishop in 444, who adhered to the extreme Monophysite position. He immediately persecuted Cyril's old followers and also attacked the views taught at Antioch again. Dioscorus' powerful ally at Constantinople was Chrysaphius' friend Eutyches, who was convicted of heresy at Constantinople in 448. His restoration through Dioscorus' blatant manipulation at the Second Council of Ephesus in 449 had given Alexandria primacy over religious affairs in the East and provoked further disorder and disharmony in the Church.

The Emperor Marcian and Pulcheria could not ignore the political dangers of this situation. In cooperation with Pope Leo I, they brought about the Fourth Ecumenical Council, held at Chalcedon in 451, to try to settle the divisive issue of Christ's nature. Chalcedon condemned Eutyches for heresy, deposed Dioscorus, and adopted a theological position based on the Formula of Union from 433 and the views of Pope Leo I as set forth in *The Tome of Leo*—namely, that Christ is completely human and completely divine, one and the same Christ having two natures, without confusion or change, division or separation, each nature concurring into one person and one substance (hypostasis). This Chalcedonian formula still prevails in the Greek Orthodox and various Christian churches of the West, but it was widely unpopular in Syria, Palestine, and Egypt, where the Monophysites had extensive appeal.

Disorder between Monophysites and Chalcedonians over control of major bishoprics had multiplied after the death of Marcian. Finally, in 482, Zeno and Acacius, bishop of Constantinople, had tried to end the disruptive religious controversy by issuing a decree of union, the *Henotikon,* which asserted the orthodoxy of the view set forth at Nicaea in 325 and Constantinople in 381, condemned the views of Nestorius and Eutyches, and anathematized anyone who had deviated at Chalcedon or would at any future council. This document had not pacified the extreme Monophysites and Chalcedonians, and Pope Felix had refused to ratify a document that ignored *The Tome of Leo.* Instead, he had excommunicated Acacius, who, along with Zeno, ignored his action.

The *Henotikon* was flexible enough that Monophysite patriarchs (bishops) could assent to it and thereby hold on to their sees. As a result, Alexandria, Jerusalem, and Antioch all had Monophysite patriarchs under Zeno. The problem did not really disappear, however. It continued to cause difficulties in later reigns and subsequently had serious consequences for the unity of the East in the face of the Moslems. Their views on the oneness of God were more compatible with the Monophysite position than with that of the orthodox Chalcedonians, who dominated Constantinople. Significantly, the Monophysite sects of Coptic and Jacobite Christians still survive in Egypt and Syria today.

Anastasius (491 to 518) Reflecting the important role of women in Imperial politics, Ariadne held the key to the election of the Emperor Anastasius after the death of Zeno in 491. Internal and external conflicts plagued Anastasius' reign. Isaurians disappointed that Zeno's brother had been passed over in favor of Anastasius eventually revolted and took seven years to be suppressed. Between 502 and 506, Anastasius fought King Kawad (Kavadh, Kavades, Cawades, Qawad) I (483 to 531) of Persia to a draw and finally effected a lasting peace that enabled him to check the devastating raids of the Bulgars, a Mongolian tribe that had united the remnants of Attila's Huns. They had been able to attack Illyricum and Thrace after the departure of the Ostrogoths under Theoderic the Amal. Anastasius' first response was to build the Long Wall (probably in 497), a defensive bulwark about forty miles west of Constantinople from the Propontis (Sea of Marmara/Marmora) to the Black Sea.

In religion, Anastasius was a Monophysite. Therefore, Euphemius, bishop of Constantinople, had refused to permit his coronation until he signed a pledge to support Chalcedonian orthodoxy. For twenty years, Anastasius had kept his pledge by upholding Zeno's *Henotikon*, but religious extremists brought his efforts to naught. By 511, the Chalcedonians had taken over the sees of Antioch and Jerusalem, and Anastasius began to intervene on behalf of the Monophysites. That led to a dangerous rebellion of Vitalian, count of the federates in Thrace, between 511 and 515.

Reforms The most successful part of Anastasius' reign entailed his fiscal reforms. In 498, he abolished the *chrysargyron (collatio lustralis),* the gold and silver tax on urban craftsmen and shopkeepers. Whatever revenue was lost from this measure was made up by setting aside an equivalent amount of income from the private Imperial estates. In 513, he even began to phase out the *capitatio,* which was a severe burden on the peasantry.

This latter move was probably made possible by the increased revenues that resulted from the scrupulous and systematic fiscal management that he imposed to eliminate fraud and waste. He clamped down on bureaucratic "fees" and made certain that soldiers received their proper pay. He demanded a careful accounting of military rations to prevent the theft of supplies. He also made the procurement of supplies more efficient by switching much of the land tax from payment in kind to payment in gold, so that only supplies actually needed were acquired.

Anastasius further tightened the system of tax collecting by appointing *vindices* (protectors) to oversee provincial officials and the municipal councilors, *curiales.* The *vindices* saw to it that the taxes were honestly collected and that the wealthy did not receive preferential treatment. Finally, Anastasius introduced a series of copper coins useful for small daily transactions. Previously, there had been nothing between the gold *solidus* and the almost worthless copper *nummus*. The new coins were denominated in units of forty, twenty, ten, and five *nummi*. Their convenience was greatly appreciated by the people, and they were profitable to the treasury because they cost less to produce than gold *solidi*, which the treasury received in exchange.

All of these reforms increased the Imperial revenues while they actually reduced the burden of taxation. By being prudent and scrupulous in normal operations, Anastasius could be generous to cities and provinces that suffered damage from wars or natural disasters and still not strain the Imperial finances. When he died, he left a surplus of 320,000 pounds of gold in the treasury, a precious legacy to his immediate successors.

Despite dynastic upheavals and divisive religious controversy in the century and a quarter since the death of Theodosius the Great, the East had survived intact, whereas the West had disintegrated into a number of separate Germanic kingdoms. Germanic king makers had been purged, the Ostrogoths had been lured off to Italy, a stable peace was in place with Persia, and the finances of state were unusually sound. For the moment, the future of the Empire in the East appeared to offer the hope of stability if the problem of finding a successor to Anastasius could be handled quickly.

XLI

Justin and the Establishment of Justinian's Autocracy, A.D. 518 to 532

The death of Anastasius without a direct heir in 518 produced another crisis of succession, but most people seemed anxious to avoid a destructive struggle. Through intrigues that are not entirely clear, Justin, head of the Excubitors, the emperor's personal bodyguards, obtained nomination from the senate and approval of the populace and chief ministers. He was an Illyrian of fairly humble origin and limited education. Having risen to high rank, he had promoted his family's fortunes by bringing his nephews to Constantinople and obtaining for them every advantage of education and rank. Already in his sixty-sixth year, Justin groomed his favorite nephew, Justinian, for succession by closely associating him with his reign right from the start. The well-educated and energetic Justinian exercised much influence on his uncle's whole reign (518 to 527).

Sources for the Period of Justin and Justinian

The sources for Justin's reign are limited. In *On the Ceremonies of the Byzantine Court,* Constantine Porphyrogenitus preserves the official account of Justin's election and coronation. About twenty-five of his laws appear in Justinian's *Code,* and his letters on religious matters are extant. The principal narrative sources are the contemporary account of the Byzantine chronicler John Malalas, the chronicle of Isidore of Seville (Hispalis) [p.

535], and the ecclesiastical histories of Evagrius (p. 537) and John of Ephesus—the former from the Chalcedonian point of view, the latter from the Monophysite and written in Syriac.

Justinian's reign (527 to 565), on the other hand, is one of the best documented in ancient history. Procopius of Caesarea records, often as an eyewitness, military and diplomatic history in his *Persian War, Gothic War,* and *Vandalic War* up to 552. Writing immediately after Justinian's death, Agathias covers the events from 552 to 558 in his *Histories* (p. 537), and large fragments of a continuation to 582 by Menander the Protector are preserved in the *Historical Excerpts* of Constantine Porphyrogenitus. Corippus' Latin epic, the *Johannid,* also gives a detailed picture of military action in Africa from 546 to 548 (p. 533).

For internal affairs, John the Lydian's *On the Magistracies of the Roman People* and Procopius' *On Buildings* are very useful. Procopius' *Secret History* is full of scurrilous gossip and scandal designed to present Justinian and his wife, Theodora, in the worst possible light. It does, however, give insights into the working of the bureaucracy, whose abuses are blamed on the emperor himself. The most important sources for internal affairs are, of course, the laws preserved in Justinian's law code, the *Codex Iustinianus.* The laws are quite complete up to 534, when the second edition of the Code was published. Of his subsequent laws, 180, mostly from 534 to 544, are preserved in other collections. Saints' lives and ecclesiastical documents in great number from this period are also valuable sources of information.

For Italy in this period, the philosophical writings of Boethius, a Roman noble who had an important political career in Ostrogothic Italy, are very important, as are the writings of Cassiodorus and Jordanes (p. 491). Of paramount importance are the writings of Pope Gregory the Great (540 to 604), guardian of papal power in the political and ecclesiastical struggles of the period (p. 543). Venantius Fortunatus wrote informative saints' lives and panegyrics in prose and poetry relating to the kingdom of the Franks (p. 533). Most important for the Franks is the *History of the Franks* by Gregory of Tours (538 to 594) [p. 535]. Isidore of Seville documents events in Visigothic Spain, and through the excellent *Ecclesiastical History of the English People* (*Historia Ecclesiastica Gentis Anglorum*), the Venerable Bede (672–673 to 735) preserves much valuable material on events at the outer edge of the western provinces that Justinian hoped to recover.

The Reign of Justin (518 to 527)

Justin's first acts as emperor were to execute his two most immediate rivals and reverse the pro-Monophysite policies of Anastasius. As natives of Latin-speaking Illyricum, Justin and Justinian sided with Rome in favoring the Chalcedonians. Justin immediately convened a council of bishops in Constantinople and instituted a brutal purge of Monophysite bishops and their supporters, but he failed to unseat Bishop Timothy IV at Alexandria. Having weakened the Monophysites, he then turned on the powerful orthodox military commander Vitalian and had him assassinated while he was consul in 520. Justinian succeeded to his offices.

Militarily, Justin's reign was a success against "barbarian" tribes but not the Persians. His other nephew, Germanus, regional commander in Thrace, prevailed on the Thracian frontier for ten years. The Tzani, a fierce tribe on the borders of Colchis and Armenia, were pacified and Christianized. That cut off Persian access to the Black Sea. Late in his reign, Justin intervened in the religious affairs of Iberia, a Persian client state, and rejected the proposal of Kawad I that Justin adopt Chosroes (Kosroes, Khusro, Khusrau) I (531 to 579), Kawad's favorite son, to secure his succession to the Persian throne. It was a clever ploy that would have given Chosroes claim to the Roman throne. Justin's insulting reply triggered a Persian attack, but before any decisive battles took place, Justin died after designating Justinian as his successor (August 1, 527).

Justinian's Goals

In the prime of life and as a native speaker of Latin inspired by the history of Rome's great accomplishments, Justinian yearned to recover the West and restore the territorial integrity of the Empire. A passionate believer in Chalcedonian orthodoxy as the true, universal Christian faith, he also hoped to root out paganism and heresy in the united realm and spread the "true faith" to other realms. Those two goals were tightly linked, and his devotion to them bordered on the fanatical. By championing orthodoxy, Justinian hoped to earn divine favor for his secular goals, and by his secular success, he hoped to have the opportunity to enforce his version of the true faith on God's behalf. In the process, he increased the emperor's control over administration, defense, finance, religion, and commerce and created the model of Byzantine autocracy.

Justinian's faith was buttressed by serious theological study, which also seems to have reinforced a penchant for system, order, and fairness in secular affairs. Throughout his reign, Justinian sought answers to thorny theological questions in his desire to promote orthodox uniformity in Christian doctrine. He also streamlined and reformed the legal, administrative, and fiscal systems of the Empire to promote efficiency and strengthen the state. Even his building program reflects the same love of order and system found in his other work.

This passion for order, system, and efficiency also reflects a man who wanted to be in control of everything. The difference between a conscientious, talented administrator pursuing lofty goals with systematic efficiency and an autocrat who demands uniform obedience for the good of the state in whose name he rules is not very great. Justinian's desire for religious orthodoxy led to the systematic persecution of nonbelievers and heretics. Jealous of his authority, Justinian was also reluctant to take advice from others and was too willing to listen to charges of disloyalty against those who were trying to serve him best. Finally, he loved elaborate ceremonials and rules of etiquette designed to exalt him far above his most distinguished subjects. Even senators had to abase themselves by prostration in the presence of either the emperor or empress, now called Lord and Mistress, and high officials and members of the court referred to themselves as their slaves.

Theodora   Justinian's empress was the beautiful, intelligent, witty, self-confident, and bold Theodora. She carried on the tradition of effective female leadership established in the eastern court by Eudoxia and Pulcheria. Her importance to Justinian's reign is difficult to overestimate. She acted with great independence, and Justinian publicly acknowledged her as a partner in counsel. He bestowed upon her the palace of Hermisdas and great estates, whose income allowed her to maintain a large number of loyal followers ready to do her bidding. She was a powerful friend, whose patronage could advance the careers of some, and a formidable foe, whose enmity could destroy those of others. She was even bold enough to act contrarily to Justinian's policies when it seemed best to her.

Theodora's power and her undeniably humble origin naturally aroused the jealousy and resentment of the male senatorial aristocrats. As a result, many scandalous rumors were circulated concerning her past and her activities as empress. Because so much about her comes from obviously hostile and biased sources, however, it is difficult to separate fact from fiction. That her birth was too humble to be acceptable for marriage to the heir to the Imperial throne probably accounts for the adamant refusal of Euphemia, Justin's wife, to

agree to let Justinian marry her. Procopius, in his untrustworthy *Secret History,* tells an elaborate story of her birth as the daughter of a bearkeeper from the circus and of a sordid career, first as a child actress, then as the most profligate of prostitutes.

No doubt Theodora's early life was not perfect, but much of Procopius' pornographic portrait probably was inspired by a few simple facts. Her father probably was the bearkeeper for a circus faction known as the Greens (p. 512). She may well have become an actress, although the coincidence that Justin abrogated the law forbidding senators to marry actresses about the time that Justinian married Theodora may be the only basis for the story. It does seem that she had borne a daughter to a lover prior to her relationship with Justinian, but that and her interest in saving impoverished young girls from the all-to-common fate of enforced prostitution may be the only facts behind the lurid tales of her youth as told by her enemies.

Protection of Women   Theodora deserves much praise for her attempt to protect women from abuse and secure better rights for them. She actively worked for laws to prohibit the sale of and traffic in young girls for prostitution. She even paid her own money to free those already held captive. To provide for their refuge and rehabilitation, she converted a palace across the Bosp(h)orus into a home called *Metanoia,* Repentance. She also protected women from harsh and arbitrary divorce on charges of adultery, charges that husbands often trumped up to get rid of unwanted wives.

Religious Policies of Theodora and Justinian   Another group that benefitted from Theodora's concern was the Monophysites, whose views she favored against the orthodox Chalcedonians whom Justinian staunchly supported. Against such heretics as the Manichees and Montanists, he employed harsh measures at the start. In the case of the more widespread Monophysite heresy, his hope was to find a theological formula that would reconcile Chalcedonians and moderate Monophysites so that extreme Monophysites could be isolated and then eliminated by harsh actions if necessary.

In 532, he convened a committee of six Chalcedonian and six moderate Monophysite bishops. They worked out a formula that condemned the views of Nestorius and Eutyches (p. 501) and mentioned neither a double nor single nature of Christ. It was accepted by Pope John II in 534. In 535, Timothy IV, the extreme Monophysite patriarch of Alexandria died, and Justinian forcibly replaced him with Theodosius, a moderate. His policy seemed to be gaining ground, but Pope John II died and was succeeded by Agapetus, who was doctrinally less flexible. He rejected the compromise that John had accepted and persuaded Justinian to abandon it, too. An extreme Chalcedonian patriarch, Menas, was installed at Constantinople, and he convoked a new council, which condemned the moderate Monophysites. Justinian then supported harsh persecutions of them in Syria and Egypt.

Nevertheless, Justinian still searched for a theological compromise. In 543 to 544, he published an edict called *Three Chapters*. Each chapter condemned certain Chalcedonian ideas offensive to Monophysites. Eastern Chalcedonian patriarchs accepted the edict, but Pope Vigilius alternately rejected and accepted it until he was forced by threats of being deposed to give it his full blessing in 554. This action merely caused a schism among the western bishops because many refused to follow Vigilius' lead.

In the East, the *Three Chapters* also failed to placate the Monophysites, who were rapidly developing a strong independent church under the pressure of persecution. In 564, Justinian tried a new formula for compromise by accepting the extreme Monophysite doctrine of the incorruptibility and impassibility of Christ's body, but he died without success in 565, and the Church, upon whose unity he believed the Empire's welfare to rest, was more fragmented than ever.

Justinian had also acted on many other religious matters during his long reign. With his fanatical passion for systematization and good order, he passed numerous laws regulating such internal affairs of the Church as the election of bishops, the behavior and character of the clergy, monastic discipline, and the management of Church property. He also pursued strong measures against pagans and other non-Christians. In 529, he ordered all pagans to be instructed in the Christian faith and to be baptized or lose their property and be exiled. He even closed the Platonic Academy in Athens and executed some prominent pagan aristocrats at Constantinople. Moreover, Justinian enacted laws against Jews and Samaritans that denied them honorable status, restricted their civil liberties, and forced them to bequeath their property to orthodox Christians only. Later, he even dictated the rules for worship in Jewish synagogues, and in 562, he persecuted pagans with renewed vigor.

Legal Reforms Justinian's legal reforms were more praiseworthy and successful than his religious policies. The disorganized mass that Roman law had become after centuries of growth and change needed rationalization and systematization. On February 13, 528, Justinian appointed a commission to collect all previous codified and uncodified Imperial edicts; update, edit, and simplify them; and codify them in a single, compact work. This task was completed by Justinian's quaestor, Tribonian, and the other commissioners on April 7, 529.

In December of 530, Justinian set Tribonian to codify the legal commentaries of the classical jurists. This *Digest* was completed in three years. It was then time to update the *Code* to include the large legislative output of Justinian up to that time. This second edition, which survives today, appeared on November 16, 534. A year earlier the *Institutes* had been published as a textbook to simplify the study of law.

Administrative Reforms In the administration of the Empire, Justinian earnestly tried to eliminate corruption and increase efficiency. Although corruption and abuse in Imperial administration had never been eliminated under the Principate, the early emperors had rigorously enforced higher standards than had prevailed in the late Republic. The chaos of the third century and the tremendous growth of the bureaucracy since the reforms of Diocletian and Constantine, however, had undermined standards, increased the chances for corruption and the number of officials susceptible to it, and made it much more difficult for a conscientious emperor to oversee the system.

One of Justinian's most beneficial reforms was the elimination of *suffragia,* payments for offices, which were then recouped by graft and corruption. He also issued standard rules for provincial governors and strengthened the powers of the civic defenders, *defensores civitatis,* who were supposed to act as ombudsmen for the provincials. He streamlined provincial administration by abolishing the vicars, who had been in charge of dioceses, by combining the office of civil governor and military commander in provinces where there were no serious external threats, and by giving Christian bishops powers to oversee public officials and provide for the general welfare.

In the capital, Justinian bolstered the office of police chief, *praefectus vigilum,* and gave him a new title, *praetor plebis.* He took measures to provide for the populace's security and supply food for the armies. He also created a new office, that of *quaesitor,* investigator. This official made sure that visitors to Constantinople left upon completion of their business, returned illegal immigrants to their homes, and found work for unemployed legitimate residents.

These administrative reforms were ably carried out through Justinian's praetorian prefect, John the Cappadocian. As with so many reforms, however, they sometimes worked better in theory than in practice. With the abolition of the vicarates, lawless bands could escape capture by moving from one provincial jurisdiction to another. The corruption and abuse of power that thrive in large bureaucratic organizations, especially in societies where some people are viewed as superior and others as inferior, continued. In fact, with the elimination of the middle-level vicars, who, if strengthened, might more easily have checked corruption and abuses at the provincial level, the reforms prob-

ably did little more than enhance the power of John the Cappadocian.

John the Cappadocian John used his power to great advantage in the sphere of Imperial finance. Justinian's ambitious wars, diplomacy, and building projects needed vast sums of money. The surplus left by Anastasius was soon spent, and Justinian had to finance everything out of current revenues. John's success in securing those revenues made him very valuable to Justinian but aroused the hatred of those who had to pay more taxes and the jealousy of those who resented the power and favors that he received from the emperor. No doubt, he was ambitious, often ruthless in his methods, and eager to maximize his own financial rewards, but one must discount considerably the monstrous picture painted of him by sources like Procopius and John the Lydian. The former was a jealous courtier, and the latter reflected the views of wealthy aristocrats and officials who had evaded taxes or enjoyed profits from corruption and felt the sting of John's strong fiscal administration most severely.

The wealthy landowners must have bitterly resented John's supplementary land tax, the "air tax," which, nevertheless, they were quite able to pay and which added 3,000 pounds of gold to yearly revenues. Throughout Asia Minor, the Levant, and Egypt, except on the strategic route from Constantinople to the Persian border, John also eliminated the public posting service, *cursus publicus,* an expensive service often abused by wealthy citizens and government officials. He likewise abolished four expensive *scholae,* ceremonial military units to which the wealthy sought appointment to enhance their prestige, and he ordered others to the front unless their members agreed to forfeit their pay to avoid active duty. These units were a useless expense, and it was worth incurring their members' animosity to free their pay for better uses. A less wise economy, however, was the suspension of pay for frontier troops in the East during a period of peace with Persia, because they were demoralized and useless when war broke out again.

To check the misappropriation and mishandling of public funds, John sent out special auditors to examine records, especially municipal and military accounts. They exposed the corruption of local notables, removed absentee and unqualified soldiers from military payrolls, and stopped officers from reporting undermanned units at full strength and pocketing the difference in pay and supplies. This system was bound to anger vested interests and provoke complaints. Some auditors were themselves corrupt, but Justinian personally sought to ensure the appointment of men with integrity, and their honesty was rewarded by giving them one twelfth of the monies saved for the state.

The Fall of John the Cappadocian Early in 532, during the shocking Nika Rebellion (p. 512), Justinian was forced to replace John with the less aggressive Phocas, a representative of aristocratic interests. In less than a year, however, when he had recovered firm control, Justinian reappointed John as praetorian prefect. Nevertheless, John remained the object of machinations by his enemies, particularly Theodora, who resented his influence with her husband and may honestly have thought that he had ambitions for the throne himself. Finally, in 541, with the help of Antonina, wife of Justinian's great general Belisarius, who wanted her husband to be supreme in Justinian's favor, Theodora secured John's banishment and forced ordination. After Theodora's death, however, Justinian freed John and allowed him to return to Constantinople as a priest.

Administration and Finance after John

After John, Justinian adjusted the administrative system to provide a middle level of authority over groups of provinces. In the diocese of Oriens, the old *comes Orientis,* count of the East, who had been reduced to one of the provincial governors, received authority over some of the lesser governors again (542). In 548 a *vicarius* was reappointed for the diocese of Pontus with military authority to preserve order in its provinces, and a similar official was appointed for Asia and for Thrace. Justinian

also continued to issue laws designed to improve administrative procedures and control abuses.

Peter Barsymes In the financial sphere, John's role was assumed by Peter Barsymes, first count of the sacred largess and praetorian prefect in 543. When he tried to increase revenues by selling off grain stored at Constantinople in 544 and then had to make compulsory purchases of grain in 545 after a bad harvest, he became very unpopular and had to be removed in 546. Nevertheless, he was soon in charge of the sacred largess again and became praetorian prefect once more in 554 or 555.

Peter Barsymes, too, is portrayed negatively by Procopius, but laws inspired by him show that he was concerned to protect both revenue and small taxpayers by fair procedures. That would not have appealed to the wealthy and powerful, who often tried to shift taxes onto the weaker citizens and exploit them. They also must have resented the innovation whereby he took advantage of the shortage of silk caused by wars with Persia to establish a state monopoly over the sale of silk at high prices and great profit to the treasury. In 552, a plan was devised by some monks to smuggle some silkworms' eggs out of China in a hollow bamboo cane, and the manufacture of raw silk was soon part of the state's monopoly. Peter also may have introduced the practice of selling monopolies in other types of business to appropriate guilds, *collegia.*

Justinian also created a state monopoly in the manufacture of arms. His motive in this case seems to have been to keep arms out of the wrong hands rather than a desire for revenue since the state's manufacture of arms for its own needs had existed since Diocletian. Now, however, only the state could manufacture arms.

The Monetary System Despite the financial strains caused by Justinian's programs, the gold coinage of the Empire remained strong and was the standard medium of exchange throughout the civilized world from Gades (Cadiz) to Tabrobane (Ceylon, [Sri Lanka]). The Germanic successor states in the West found it politically and economically wise to duplicate Imperial gold coins. The Merovingian kings of the Franks even put Justinian's bust on their coins with only their own initials. In Spain, the Suevi continued the coin types of Honorius and Avitus, and in Italy, the Ostrogothic kings merely revived the bust and legends of Anastasius rather than replace the Imperial coinage with another after Justinian attacked them. Bronze and silver coinage, however, became less and less viable (p. 525–526).

The First Persian War   When Justinian became sole emperor upon Justin's death in 527, he inherited the war with Persia, which was going badly. He had no desire to conquer Persian territory and hoped simply to put enough military pressure on the Persians to force them to accept a long-term peace that would free him to reconquer the West. The war seesawed back and forth until the death of the Persian king, Kawad, in September of 531, and Chosroes, who wanted to be free to meet any challenges to his succession, entered serious negotiations with Justinian's ambassadors. Finally, in the spring of 532, a treaty of Eternal Peace was signed. The prewar boundaries were accepted by the Persians, and Justinian paid Chosroes 11,000 pounds of gold as the price for Chosroes' agreement not to demand an annual subsidy for defending the Caucasus.

Circus Factions and the Nika Rebellion
In the middle of the negotiations with Chosroes, Justinian almost lost his throne in an uprising involving the factions of the circus at Constantinople. Circus factions had originated during the time of the late Republic, when chariot races became the most popular spectacles at public festivals. Each race normally required four chariots. The official in charge of the games would hire the chariots and their respective drivers and horses from four different groups organized for that purpose. They came to be known as factions, and each one distinguished itself by a special color—red, white, blue, or green. Just as modern athletic teams,

each one had its fiercely loyal fans, and successful charioteers earned sums as extravagant as today's multimillion-dollar professional sports stars.

The popularity of the chariot races and successful charioteers explains why all of the Roman emperors, who often relied on the good will of the masses as a counterweight to the jealousy of the senatorial aristocracy, were generous patrons of the races. Some, like Nero, Domitian, and Commodus, had even driven in the races themselves. As Roman culture spread through the Empire in the first and second centuries A.D., each provincial city of any significance had its own group of reds, whites, blues, and greens. In a society where the people had been denied any meaningful role in politics and where the urban poor often led otherwise useless and frustrating lives, the excitement of the circus and the chance to obtain money by betting on the races aroused intense interest. The restless and bored, much like the members of modern motorcycle and street gangs, attached themselves to individual factions in groups called partisans. They distinguished themselves by special dress, harassed ordinary citizens, and even committed crimes. Clashes among partisans of different factions were also frequent and sometimes erupted into full-scale popular riots.

The Blues and the Greens   In Constantinople by Justinian's day, the Reds and the Whites had been completely overshadowed by the Blues and the Greens. These two factions had acquired such widespread followings and organizational strength that they were a significant element in the political life of the capital. Emperors and powerful senators sought to manipulate the two factions for their own political and religious ends. The Emperor Anastasius, for example, had favored the Greens, who became associated with his Monophysite views. The orthodox Justin and Justinian, therefore, had catered to the Blues by putting some in governmental posts, supplying them with money for their activities, and protecting them from punishment for their disorders and crimes.

Neither faction, however, was strongly

committed to any one theological doctrine, and once Justinian had secured his own power, he tried to curb the lawless behavior of both the Blues and the Greens. On January 13, 532, when Justinian refused to commute the sentences of two men, one Blue and one Green, who had survived a bungled hanging, the two factions decided to cooperate to force their release. They adopted the word *nika* ("conquer") as their watchword, which gave the subsequent popular uprising its name.

That evening, rioters set fire to a number of public buildings, including the entrance hall of the Great Palace and the Church of the Holy Wisdom, *Hagia Sophia.* Renewal of the chariot races the next day failed to divert their attention, and they set fires at the northern end of the Hippodrome, where the races were held. The ranks of the original rioters were now swollen by those who had suffered from Justinian's fiscal policies, such as the numerous small farmers who had abandoned their land in the face of heavy taxes and had migrated to Constantinople. Encouraged by powerful senators who also resented Justinian's autocratic ways and his fiscal maneuvers, they were now demanding removal of three key ministers: Eudaemon, prefect of the city; Tribonian, Justinian's quaestor; and John the Cappadocian.

No matter what Justinian did, he could neither calm nor crush the howling mobs. When they proclaimed Anastasius' reluctant nephew Hypatius emperor in his stead, Justinian decided to flee. At the crucial moment, however, the dauntless Theodora, who had known deprivation once, argued that death in defense of the throne was far better than exile. Justinian ordered his loyal eunuch Narses to sow dissension between the Blues and the Greens with bribes and reminders of Anastasius' former favoritism toward the Greens. Then, two loyal generals made a surprise attack on the tightly packed mob in the Hippodrome. The subsequent slaughter broke the back of the revolt. The unfortunate Hypatius and his brother were executed, suspect senators were exiled, and the circus factions ceased to be a problem. Justinian was then able to consolidate his autocratic rule, which had fueled resistance in the first place.

The Rebuilding of Constantinople   Just as an earlier promoter of Imperial autocracy, Nero, had used the great fire of 64 to rebuild Rome on a magnificent scale suitable for the capital of an exalted emperor, so Justinian rebuilt Constantinople after the conflagrations of the Nika Rebellion. In autocratic fashion, Justinian also took the opportunity to renovate his palaces entirely and decorate them with splendid mosaics glorifying his reign.

In keeping with Justinian's desire for divine favor to support his rule, churches received special attention. The Church of Holy Peace, *Hagia Eirene,* was rebuilt on a scale second only to that of the neighboring *Hagia Sophia,* Holy Wisdom. The earthquake-damaged Church of the Holy Apostles was replaced at this time, too.

Hagia Sophia was the most ambitious project and took five years to build. The best available architects, Anthemius of Tralles and Isidore of Miletus, were in charge. Anthemius, who had specialized in domed churches, conceived the novel plan of combining a domed roof with a floor plan in the shape of a Greek cross. It was about 250 feet by 225 feet with a dome 180 feet high above the 100-foot square where the arms intersect. To support the dome and fit its circular base over the square opening, the architects placed massive arches over each side of the square with great piers on which they rested at the corners. In each corner they constructed a pendentive, an arched and curved triangle of masonry whose apex rested on the pier, whose sides followed up the curves of each adjoining arch to its center, and whose resulting curved base formed a 90-degree arc (one quarter of a circle) between the centers of the adjoining arches. For stability, half domes rested against the east and west sides of the building below the main dome, and great vertical buttresses secured the north and south. The basic structural material was brick, with the ribbed dome being built of special lightweight tiles.

The outside, as is typical of Byzantine churches, for which *Hagia Sophia* became the archtype, was plain, but the interior was richly decorated. Different-colored marbles from around the Empire were used for pillars and floors and to sheathe the walls. The domed ceil-

Hagia Sophia with the four minarets added by the Turks. (Erich Lessing, Art Resource, NY)

ing was covered with pure gold, and huge mosaics, the largest being a great cross on a field of stars at the top of the dome, decorated the church throughout.

The new *Hagia Sophia* was dedicated on December 26, 537. Unfortunately, however, Anthemius and Isidore had miscalculated the stresses in its innovative design, and the dome eventually collapsed in 558. Isidore the Younger built a new dome over twenty feet higher to provide more vertical thrust. It was finished in 562 and has endured to this day.

To make it a worthy monument of both Holy Wisdom and Justinian's reign, thousands of pounds of gold were spent on the construction and furnishing of *Hagia Sophia*. The pulpit was covered with gold and jewels, the altar was solid gold, and the bishop's throne was constructed of thousands of pounds of gilded silver. One source places the total cost at 320,000 pounds of gold. Even if it is exaggerated by a factor of ten, the cost would still be staggering. Perhaps Justinian would have been wiser to put off such huge domestic expenses until he had completed his great scheme of reconquering the West. He launched that campaign right after the Nika Rebellion and the signing of the peace treaty with Chosroes, but his failure to devote enough resources to operations in the West after his initial success almost ruined the whole enterprise and caused serious long-term problems in both the East and the West.

XLII

The Impossible Dream of Universal Empire, A.D. 532 to 602

The unity of Imperial power had been destroyed by its localization under Germanic kings in the West during the fifth century. Still, the dream of universal empire was very much alive during the sixth century in the Imperial offices and titles that legitimized the new local rulers, whose dynastic ambitions were thoroughly Imperial, and in the universal Church, whose bishops preserved the power and influence of the old ruling class. For no one did this dream seem more real than Justinian, who devoted more than thirty years in an attempt to make it come true. The task proved more difficult than he had ever imagined. Opening hostilities in the West left him more vulnerable to attacks elsewhere. He was forced to spread the Empire's resources dangerously thin and thereby make the task even more difficult. Finally, as always in Imperial politics, the jealousies, ambitions, and intrigues of others undermined his efforts.

Reconquest of the North African Provinces, 533 to 534 By 532, conditions in the Vandals' kingdom of North Africa were favorable to Justinian's hopes of reconquest. The previous Vandal king, Hilderic, had been a descendent of Theodosius the Great. His mother was Valentinian III's daughter Eudocia, who had married Gaiseric's son Huneric (p. 497). Clearly hoping to be more than a Van-

dal king, he had stopped persecuting the orthodox Roman Catholics in his realm and had entered into a treaty with Justinian. Unsuccessful against Moorish raiders, however, he had been deposed by his cousin Gelimer. Invoking the treaty with Hilderic, Justinian prepared to attack North Africa. His generals and advisors, recalling the disastrous human and financial losses of earlier expeditions against the Vandals, protested. Justinian rejected their advice nevertheless, and in 533, Belisarius sailed for North Africa with between 15,000 and 20,000 soldiers. Commanding with Belisarius was his able and fearless wife, Antonina, close friend of Theodora and a real power in politics at court.

Victory was deceptively easy. Gelimer was incompetent and distracted by revolts. Belisarius and Antonina swooped down on North Africa without opposition, and they were helped by the Catholic population, who resented the Arian Vandals. Within a year, by two battles that were won more because of Gelimer's astounding incompetence than the skill of Belisarius and Antonina, North Africa was reconquered. In 534, it and Sardinia were formally organized into the separate praetorian prefecture of Africa. Unfortunately, the unexpected ease and speed with which the African operation proceeded were a disaster in disguise. They would commit Justinian wholeheartedly to his great scheme of reconquering western territories, which proved extremely difficult and costly to retain after the initial victories.

Italy Soon after the recovery of the North African provinces, an attractive opportunity arose to restore Roman power in Italy. From his capital at Ravenna, Theoderic the Amal had provided an enlightened Ostrogothic regime for Italy throughout most of his long reign (471 to 526). He greatly admired Roman culture and institutions and, though an Arian, had tried not to provoke his orthodox Catholic Roman subjects. For all classes in Italy, therefore, life had gone on much as before, and they had enjoyed relative peace and prosperity. The only major difference was that taxes were now paid to Theoderic, who held the political and military power. Unfortunately, neither the orthodox Roman aristocracy nor Theoderic's fellow Ostrogoths always appreciated his policies, but he had managed to prevail over both until his death in 526.

Theoderic was succeeded by the ten-year-old Athalaric, whose mother, Theoderic's daughter Amalasuntha, acted as regent. She continued Theoderic's policies and gave Athalaric a classical education. A powerful anti-Roman faction among the Ostrogoths, however, insisted that Athalaric be raised as a German warrior. They ultimately prevailed, and Amalasuntha entered into negotiations with Justinian for asylum. The intemperate behavior fostered by Athalaric's peers, moreover, led to his alcoholic death in 534.

Amalasuntha then offered the throne to her cousin Theodahad, with the proviso that he be guided by her. Once securely enthroned, however, Theodahad ordered her imprisoned and executed (535). The Empress Theodora may even have secretly maneuvered him into doing so in order to give Justinian the chance to act as Amalasuntha's avenger.

At any rate, Theodahad's actions gave Justinian a convenient pretext to intervene. First, he seized Sicily and Illyricum and then opened negotiations with Theodahad. Ultimately, Theodahad promised to hand over Italy to Justinian in exchange for luxurious exile on rich eastern estates. When a Gothic army momentarily recovered Illyricum, however, he reneged, and Justinian ordered the invasion of Italy. Belisarius and Antonina finally arrived in Italy with fewer than 10,000 men in June of 536. He made good progress because the feckless Theodahad scarcely opposed him and the Catholic population of Italy generally supported his cause. Naples, however, had to be taken by a long siege and clever strategem before he could march on Rome.

Vitigis and the Siege of Rome In the meantime, the Ostrogoths had replaced the faint-hearted Theodahad with Vitigis (Vitiges, Witigis), a successful general unrelated to the Amal royal clan. Therefore, he had forcibly married Amalasuntha's daughter Matasuntha to legitimize his rule. Although he negotiated unsuccessfully with Justinian and called on the Franks for aid, the majority of Romans led by Pope Silverius and the senate brought about the surrender of Rome to Belisarius. Vitigis then mounted a siege that Belisarius stoutly resisted for over a year.

Rival Commanders Belisarius was unable to break the siege when John, the ambitious nephew of the Vitalian assassinated under Justin (p. 507), brought reinforcements to Italy. John soon became insubordinate, however, and hampered Belisarius' success. The problem was compounded when the eunuch Narses brought more reinforcements and also refused to take orders from Belisarius. Justinian finally recalled Narses and clearly designated Belisarius as the supreme commander.

The Capture of Ravenna (Spring 540) Firmly in command and aided by an attack of the double-dealing Franks against the Ostrogoths, Belisarius methodically attacked the Ostrogoths' stronghold in the North. He was kept supplied by sea while war-induced famine worked enormous hardship on both the Ostrogothic garrisons and the civilian population. From Ravenna, Vitigis vainly summoned the Lombards from beyond the Danube and secretly encouraged Chosroes to divert the Romans by starting another war on the Persian front. Learning of the latter move, Justinian offered generous terms to Vitigis, who readily agreed. Belisarius, however, resented losing five years of hard work on the eve of total victory and refused to sign the treaty on Justinian's behalf. Fearing bad faith on Justinian's part, the Ostrogoths ceased dealing with him.

On the other hand, seeing signs of Belisarius' disappointment with Justinian's policy, they proposed to accept Belisarius as a new western Emperor. He pretended to accept the offer and was received into Ravenna with an armed escort. He then treacherously seized Vitigis and Matasuntha, many Ostrogothic nobles, and the royal treasury and took them all back to Constantinople (May 540).

Justinian was not wholly pleased by Belisarius' unauthorized actions and did not give him a triumph, as he had after the Vandalic War. Despite the superficially spectacular results, the situation in Italy was left worse than Justinian's terms would have made it. The Ostrogoths north of the Po refused to surrender to anyone after Belisarius' duplicity was revealed. Bound by no treaty, they created the problem that Justinian had hoped to avoid —major wars on two fronts.

Troubles in North Africa

Justinian's haste to invade Italy before securing adequate control of North Africa had already produced an example of that strategic difficulty on a smaller scale. Right after Belisarius' victorious departure in 534, Moorish tribes began devastating incursions, which had taken two years to quell, and they still remained restive. No sooner had the Moors been repulsed than about two thirds of the Roman army in North Africa mutinied for various reasons: Slowness in collecting taxes in the new province caused long delays in paying the soldiers; many soldiers resented the harsh discipline of their new commander, Solomon; non-Roman auxiliaries felt that they had been poorly rewarded with booty; men who had taken Vandal women as wives were aggrieved that the emperor would not allow the Vandal women to inherit their fathers' and for-

mer husbands' estates, which he confiscated instead; and many of the Romans' Germanic allies were Arian Christians, who resented Justinian's suppression of Arianism among the conquered Vandals.

The mutineers besieged Carthage, which was rescued only when Belisarius interrupted his invasion of Italy and returned from Sicily. Belisarius soon had to return to Sicily, and Justinian placed his own capable cousin, Germanus, in charge of restoring order in North Africa. He defeated the rebels decisively in the spring of 537 and consolidated control during the next two years. In 539, Solomon returned and purged the army, exiled the troublesome Vandal women, and made sorties against the Moors. For the time being at least, those actions reduced Justinian's worries in North Africa.

The Second Persian War, 540 to 562

By 539, Justinian's biggest worry was the threat of renewed war with Persia. The situation on the eastern frontier was already unstable. In Armenia, which had always been a bone of contention between the Romans and Persians, a revolt had broken out because of Roman fiscal exactions. Unable to defeat the Romans, the rebels had appealed for help from the Persian king, Chosroes. With additional encouragement from Vitigis in Italy, Chosroes opened the war in 540, and it was not officially ended until 562.

In Chosroes, the successor of Kawad, Sassanid Persia had an energetic and able leader comparable to the Roman Empire's Justinian. He continued administrative and land reforms begun by his father, he made the army more efficient, and he took great interest in literature, philosophy, and religion. In every way, he hoped to increase the glory and greatness of the Sassanid Persian Empire.

Justinian's successes in Africa and Italy had aroused both fear and envy in Chosroes. He scarcely needed the pleas of either Ostrogoths or Armenians to prompt his breaking of the Eternal Peace of 532 and renewing war on Justinian's eastern flank in 540. In the meantime, fortunately for the Romans, Justinian had carefully rebuilt or strengthened frontier fortresses and the walls of cities in Mesopotamia and Syria. Chosroes' main goals, therefore, were not so much to capture Roman territory as to make a show of strength by successfully besieging some major strongholds in Syria, to obtain plunder or money from those whom he besieged or threatened, and to force Justinian to pay tribute in return for peace on the frontier. He demolished Sura, Beroea, and Antioch but had to be content with only money from Hierapolis and Edessa after failing to take them. Justinian would have agreed to pay the 5,000 pounds of gold plus an annual subsidy of 500 pounds that he demanded if Chosroes had not then unsuccessfully besieged the great fortress of Dara during negotiations.

In 541, Chosroes scored a major coup by seizing the Romans' client kingdom of Lazica, ancient Colchis, at the eastern end of the Black Sea. After garrisoning the fortress city of Petra in Lazica to secure his control of the kingdom, Chosroes then returned to Persian territory to face Belisarius, who had arrived to take command and had captured a major Persian stronghold. When Chosroes failed to take a Roman stronghold the next year, he and Belisarius made a temporary truce (542).

Resumption of War in Italy, 541 to 543

Justinian probably was anxious to secure some kind of truce, however imperfect, because he needed the incomparable Belisarius back in Italy. The new Ostrogothic king, Ildebad, had been determined to continue the war in Italy, and Roman policies made it easy for him to do so. First, with the departure of Belisarius in 540, military command in Italy was left fragmented among his former subordinates. Second, the harsh fiscal policies of Imperial administrators were alienating both the soldiers and the very people whom Justinian claimed to be freeing from tyranny. Murder ended Ildebad's success.

A cousin, Totila, became king shortly thereafter (541). He took the offensive against the divided Roman commanders in 542 and quickly recovered most of southern Italy except Naples, which fell in the spring of 543 only af-

ter a lengthy siege. He increased the ranks of his army by recruiting slaves and wisely refrained from plundering the countryside for supplies. Instead, he collected the regular taxes and rents, which provided regular income without ruining the territory. His humane treatment of captured cities and towns also advanced his cause. He did, however, demolish their fortifications because he did not have enough troops to garrison them against Roman counterattacks.

Troubles Everywhere

In 542, the Romans had to battle not only the Ostrogoths and Persians but also a far more destructive enemy as well—plague. The initial outbreak was enormously destructive, and its appearance in Syria contributed to Chosroes' willingness to sign a truce. As many as 300,000 people may have died in Constantinople alone. Justinian himself fell ill but survived. Those who did survive were immune from the subsequent attacks that appeared with diminishing severity during the next 20 years, until a general immunity had built up in the Empire's population.

The truce of 542 was not highly effective. Immediately afterward, Chosroes demolished a Roman fortress. In 543, he was preparing an invasion of Roman Armenia but was thwarted by an outbreak of plague and the revolt of a son. On the other hand, the Romans successfully invaded Persarmenia near the headwaters of the Euphrates. Finally, in 545, after again failing to take Edessa (544), Chosroes consented to a meaningful five-year truce. In return, Justinian paid him 2,000 pounds of gold, but operations in Lazica were exempted from the agreement. The truce was subsequently renewed for another five years on similar terms in 551.

Belisarius Returns to Face Totila in Italy

After the initial truce with Chosroes in 542, Justinian had reassigned Belisarius to take charge of the war against the Ostrogoths in Italy. No doubt Belisarius' preparations were hindered by the outbreak of plague at Constantinople in 543. He and his intrepid wife, Antonina, did not arrive at Ravenna until 544. Also, he desperately lacked manpower. Plague and lack of funds, because of the war with Persia and Justinian's expensive building program, probably hindered recruitment. He brought only 4,000 men with him and found that many of the soldiers originally sent to Italy had deserted because they had not been paid for years. He finally persuaded Justinian to divert some troops from the East now that there was a truce with Chosroes, but they were not adequate.

Totila besieged Rome and captured it with the help of treachery after Belisarius had to break off relief efforts because of disobedient subordinates (545/46). Belisarius was able to reoccupy the depopulated and devastated city, but the 6,000 assorted troops that Justinian sent in 548 were not nearly enough to enable Belisarius to take the offensive.

Clearly, Belisarius was Justinian's best general, but even he could not successfully prosecute a war without adequate forces. Therefore, he sent the resourceful Antonina to Constantinople in the hope that she might obtain more men through her influence with Theodora. Unfortunately, Theodora had died on June 28, 548, just before Antonina arrived, and Justinian was preoccupied with finding enough men to prosecute the war in Lazica, which had been exempted from the truce with Chosroes in 545. Seeing her husband in a hopeless situation, Antonina then asked that he be recalled. It was futile to remain. He returned to Constantinople in early 549 and was reappointed chief military commander for the East, but he never actively assumed the post.

The Lazic War, 549 to 557

Chosroes was determined to preserve his unprecedented access to the Black Sea by consolidating his hold on Lazica (Colchis). Justinian was just as determined to prevent Rome's ancient enemy from retaining this strategic naval advantage. The Lazi had soon begun to dislike Persian oppression even more than the Roman kind. They asked for Roman help, and Justinian sent 7,000 men to retake Lazica in 549. Petra was recaptured in 551, but the war stalemated after that.

Peace in the East

In 557, another 5-year truce was signed, and that one included Lazica. Finally, Justinian and Chosroes worked out a 50-year peace in 562. In return for evacuating his positions in Lazica, Chosroes received an annual subsidy of 30,000 gold pieces. He also agreed to guard the Central Caucasus against outside attackers. Other provisions regulated commercial, military, and diplomatic relations between the Persian and Roman empires, and rules for arbitrating personal disputes between Persians and Romans on the frontier were set up to prevent them from growing into wider conflicts. In a separate agreement, Chosroes promised to tolerate the Christians in his empire as long as they did not seek converts.

Disaster in Italy, 549 to 551

After Belisarius' departure in 549, things went from bad to worse in Italy. The ease with which Belisarius had initially reconquered both North Africa and Italy had deceived Justinian and caused him to discount the seriousness of subsequent problems in the West. Also, he needed large amounts of money to mount campaigns against Chosroes in the East or to buy him off with subsidies and to expend on buildings or art to glorify God and the Empire. Therefore, he was even more willing to believe that Belisarius and others in the West wanted more than they needed. Already undermanned, therefore, Roman armies in both Italy and North Africa suffered mutinies and betrayals by troops angry over the lack of pay.

Just such a situation caused some Isaurian soldiers to betray Rome in 550 to Totila again after Belisarius left. That finally spurred Justinian to take more vigorous action. He rejected Totila's offers to renegotiate. The latter then promptly invaded Sicily, which previously had been spared. At last Justinian placed his cousin Germanus in charge of the war. Using private as well as public money, Germanus prepared a proper expedition to recover Italy.

The Recovery of Italy, 552 to 562

Unfortunately, Germanus, who shrewdly married Amalasuntha's daughter, Matasuntha, granddaughter of Theoderic, in the hope of dividing Ostrogothic loyalties, died before he could depart for Italy. In his place, Justinian appointed the popular and capable eunuch Narses. Narses arrived in Italy with at least 25,000 men, almost half being Lombards, Heruli, Gepids, and Huns. He promptly defeated Totila in a set battle (Busta Gallorum), and Totila was killed in flight (A.D. 552).

In the same year, Narses won another great battle against the Ostrogoths at Mons Lactarius. After that, Ostrogothic resistance was confined to a number of fortified cities, which Narses systematically reduced. On the other hand, he had to face a large army of Franks and their Alemannic subjects, who swept into Italy from the north in 553 to reap what Narses had sown. Narses kept to the fortified towns whereas the Franks dissipated their energies in plundering much of the rest of Italy. Finally, in 554 Narses annihilated them at a great battle outside of Capua. Italy south of the Po was free at last from warfare, but it was not until 562 that Narses finished taking Ostrogothic strongholds between the Po and the Alps.

The Pragmatic Sanction, 554   In 554, Justinian issued what is known as his *Pragmatic Sanction* to restore order and provide proper Imperial administration to Italy. It restored rights and property to prisoners and exiles, slaves to their masters, and *coloni* (tenants) to their landlords. Gothic landowners of long standing were left in enjoyment of their property, however. Justinian also forbade the kind of fiscal and administrative abuses that had caused so much discontent after the initial reconquest, and he provided for the proper provisioning of troops without undue burdens on the people.

Wars on Other Fronts, 544 to 561   While Justinian was confronting simultaneous wars or uneasy truces on the eastern frontier and in Italy, he was not free of trouble elsewhere. Remarkably, he even continued to pursue his grand scheme of reconquering other parts of the West before he had adequate control of

North Africa and Italy. In 544, the Moors revolted once more in North Africa. They were aided by the Roman general in charge of Numidia, who wished to rule Africa independently, and by troops who had not been paid. This revolt was not crushed until 547, but the Moors then remained subdued (except for a brief rebellion in 563) for the remainder of Justinian's reign.

After 550, Justinian seems to have devoted greater energy to the West. At the same time that he finally committed adequate resources to prosecute the war in Italy, he also unfairly took advantage of a dynastic struggle among the Visigoths to recapture part of southern Spain along both the Atlantic and Mediterranean coasts on behalf of a pretender named Athanagild. The Visigoths then accepted him as king, but the Romans refused to hand over to him what they had captured. Instead, they organized the territory, which included such important cities as New Carthage, Malaca, and Corduba, into the province of Baetica.

In the Balkans, various frontier tribes had periodically raided Thrace and Illyricum since 529. Three tribes combined for a massive invasion in 559. One group penetrated Macedonia and Greece as far south as Thermopylae, another attacked the Chersonese (Gallipoli Peninsula), and another drove through Thrace right up to the walls of Constantinople.

Belisarius, who had long learned to do much with little, saved the day once more. With a makeshift army of his 300 loyal bodyguards and some hastily recruited, poorly armed civilians, he set a clever ambush for the 2,000 Huns that confidently rode to attack his small force before Constantinople. Without any losses, his men killed 400 Huns, while the rest retreated in panic. At Thermopylae and at the entrance to the Chersonese, Roman defenses held, and the invaders went back across the Danube after Justinian promised them an annual subsidy. A similar offer dissuaded the Avars in 561, and the Balkans remained calm for the rest of Justinian's reign.

Invading tribes could be persuaded to accept subsidies because it was impossible for them to remain in the Balkans for very long after an initial breakthrough. Between 540 and 549, Justinian had expended much effort on building and repairing defenses and forts at hundreds of places along the Danube and throughout the Balkan peninsula. Perhaps that is why he did not feel able also to commit adequate resources to Italy during this period. At any rate, his expenditures in the Balkans proved their worth. Although raiders could sweep through the open country, the Romans could hold the well-supplied fortified places with a few men and harass the enemy when they scattered to plunder, or could attack them in the rear after they had exhausted available food and were returning encumbered with spoils.

Successes and Failures of Justinian's Reign
Justinian was one of the most important emperors in Roman history. He stood at the crossroads of Antiquity. His often spectacular successes and failures demonstrated that the empire of Old Rome was gone forever but left a legacy that shaped the Byzantine Empire of the New Rome at Constantinople for centuries to come.

Law and Administration   Justinian's policy of codifying and revising the corpus of Roman law was a great success and is what one recalls first about his reign. The elimination of outdated and contradictory laws and the systematic presentation of those retained provided a uniform and efficient body of law such as is necessary for the well-being of any large, complex state. It still provides the model for the legal systems in most European nations.

Justinian's attempt to provide more efficient and honest adminstration by increasing salaries, combining functions to lessen the number of officials, and centralizing authority at Constantinople was not always successful. No system is immune to corruption. Justinian remained flexible, however, corrected mistakes and abuses when he could, and definitely improved upon what had existed before. During his reign the interests of both the ordinary person and the state as a whole were better served by Imperial administrators.

Byzantine Autocracy   Both Justinian's legal and administrative reforms contributed to the creation of a fully autocratic monarchy, which was characteristic of the succeeding Byzantine Empire. The office of emperor had grown more and more autocratic since the time of Augustus—sometimes faster, as under Caligula, Nero, Domitian, Septimius Severus, or Diocletian; sometimes more slowly, as under Vespasian, Antoninus Pius, Tacitus, Probus, or Gratian. The personalities of the individual emperors had affected the pace, but in the long run the need for a powerful, efficient, central authority to deal with increasingly large and complex problems pushed the emperors in the direction of autocracy. Justinian's policies were the culmination of that process. The Byzantine autocracy had all the unpleasant faults of any highly centralized, bureaucratically administered monarchy, which resulted in the pejorative meaning of the word *Byzantine* when applied to the complex politics of large organizations. Nevertheless, Justinian's successors and their ministers were able to maintain armies and organize resources enough to preserve Greco-Roman civilization in the East from being overwhelmed by a constant stream of outside attackers for centuries.

Long Reign   Perhaps Justinian's greatest success was in living so long. A well-disciplined man of Spartan habits, Justinian enjoyed a sound constitution that enabled him to survive the plague that killed countless thousands. He also seems to have been safe from plots. Only two conspiracies after the Nika Rebellion are noteworthy, and they were revealed before he was in any serious danger.

Unfortunately, the involvement of two of Belisarius' men in one of these plots raised suspicions against him. He was forced to dismiss his armed retainers and was disgraced. Contrary to legend, however, he did not end his life as a blind beggar. Justinian restored him to favor after less than a year, and they passed the rest of their days together. Belisarius died in March of 565, and Justinian followed a few months later on November 14, 565.

Religious Persecution   Despite notable accomplishments, on balance Justinian's reign was a failure. One of his biggest failures was in the sphere of religion. His policy of seeking divine favor by uniting the Empire under the orthodox Catholic version of Christianity as defined at Chalcedon only created deep animosities toward the Imperial government among inhabitants who espoused different faiths or other versions of Christianity. Persecution of the Jews and Monophysite Christians in Egypt and the Levant so embittered many of them that they welcomed the Moslem conquerors who seized those lands seventy-five years after Justinian's death. Similarly, the Arian Christians of North Africa resented the continued attempts to impose Catholic orthodoxy, and the resultant divisiveness made it easier for the Moslem conquerors in the mid-seventh century. Likewise, the devastating Ostrogothic rebellion after the initial reconquest of Italy was fueled by the Arian Ostrogoths' resistance to the imposition of orthodoxy.

Bankruptcy of the Empire   By the time Justinian died, the Imperial treasury had been exhausted by the expenses of his grandiose building projects, his impetuous wars, and the ruinous subsidies that he agreed to pay some enemies in order to be free to fight others. The desperate state of the treasury subsequently contributed to his successor's decision to risk war with Persia rather than continue subsidies. Ironically, that war dragged on for twenty years and weakened the Empire even further.

Mishandling of Succession   Justinian compounded problems by his poor handling of the arrangements for providing a successor. The choice of an Imperial heir lay between Justin, an able general and son of his cousin Germanus, and another Justin, a nephew whom Theodora had greatly favored. Although the latter had no conspicuous abilities, Justinian had advanced him to high rank. Nevertheless, Justinian had not clearly indicated who was to succeed. Unfortunately, the inferior Justin was well placed to seize the throne and had his rival executed when Justinian died. Justin II (565 to 578) had pretensions that bordered on megalomania and led to disastrous foreign policies. He eventually continued disruptive religious persecutions, too, and his fiscal frugality so overcompensated for Justinian's overspending that he undermined Imperial security. Finally, he became so mentally unbalanced that he could not rule. In 572, the Empress Sophia persuaded him to appoint as Caesar a man named Tiberius, commander of the bodyguard (*comes excubitorum*), who added the name Constantine after Tiberius when he became the Emperor Tiberius II (578 to 582).

Reconquest of the West   Even Justinian's reconquest of the North African provinces, Italy, and part of Spain must be counted as a failure—his biggest. He had to weaken the defenses on other frontiers to pursue these unprovoked wars and thereby invited attacks from Persia and various aggressive tribes. The net result was to overstrain the resources of the Empire and weaken it for the future.

Furthermore, the reconquered provinces did not repay the costs of their conquest and subsequent defense. The North African provinces suffered periodic revolts and constant raids from the surrounding Moors. By the time Italy finally had been pacified, the long years of warfare had devastated its cities and permanently impaired its prosperity. The Imperial province in Spain was under constant pressure from the surrounding Visigoths, from whom it had been treacherously seized.

After all of the trouble and expense of reconquering these western provinces, they began to be lost right after Justinian's death. In 568, the Lombards and their allies invaded northern Italy. By 572, they held everything between the Po and the Alps. By 590, much of the rest of Italy had been lost also. About sixty years after Justinian's death, the Visigoths wrested back the territories in Spain, and after little more than a century, the Moslems had swept away Imperial power in North Africa.

Tiberius II and his successor Maurice (582 to 602) achieved some success on the Persian frontier, but Maurice's attempt to regain control of the Balkans from Slavic invaders without adequate pay for his troops led to his assassination and disastrous political instability just as the first wave of Arabic Moslem conquests was about to crash upon the provinces of the East. The smaller state that eventually survived was no longer the eastern Roman Empire that had evolved between Constantine and Theodosius I but had clearly become what is now called Byzantine Greece.

If Justinian had devoted his considerable talents mainly to strengthening the defenses of the Roman Empire that he had inherited in the East instead of trying to recapture the West, and if he had not sown bitterness and discord within by his religious policies, the Roman Empire of the East might not have suffered the severe losses of the seventh century. Moreover, the Germanic successors to Imperial power in the West might have been better able to resist subsequent conquerors, who did more damage to Roman civilization in Europe than they had. The historical conditions that had made possible the universal Roman Empire of the first two centuries A.D. no longer existed. The resources needed to maintain it under changed circumstances had not been there to prevent the loss of the West in the first place. They were not available now. Justinian's effort to revive the dead had only weakened the living.

XLIII

The Transformation of the Late Antique Roman World, A.D. 395–600

The restored Roman Empire of the fourth century had disintegrated during the fifth and sixth. Since the time of Montesquieu and Edward Gibbon, many modern thinkers great and small have proposed various particular causes to explain Rome's fall. A process such as the disintegration of the Roman Empire, which took place over such a vast extent of territory for a long time, is extremely complex in detail. The factors involved are so numerous, their interactions so involved, and our evidence so limited in comparison that a definitive analysis is impossible. At the general level, however, it is clear that given its geographic, economic, social, political, and cultural characteristics, the Roman Empire was unable to sustain the frequent and simultaneous blows of "barbarian" migrations and invasions in the West and war with the Sassanid Persians in the East. Without those external factors, the Roman Empire might have continued indefinitely, despite what proved to be weaknesses when it was faced with them.

During the fifth and sixth centuries, many of the internal characteristics that identified the world of the Roman Empire in Late Antiquity as still Roman underwent a major transformation. The changes that took place did not occur at a uniform pace or even in the same way everywhere within the vast territories of the late Roman Empire. By the early seventh century, however the cumulative effects had cre-

ated a world that was quite different from that of the fourth and was recognizably Medieval despite significant continuities with the classical Roman past.

The Economy In general, the economy of the late Antique Roman world declined in the fifth and sixth centuries, sooner and more steeply in the West than in the East and more in some ways than in others. Despite overall economic decline, there were major shifts in wealth that enriched some even while others saw their wealth reduced or became impoverished. In the West, Germanic kings and their loyal warriors were enriched at the expense of Roman landowners, who often lost anywhere from one third to all of their property to their new overlords. In the East, wealth poured into the new capital at Constantinople to the benefit of the eastern emperor and a growing class of Imperial functionaries. Everywhere, Christian churches, monasteries, and shrines received countless donations of land, money, gold, silver, jewels, and other precious goods from those who piously sought divine favor or shrewdly hoped to acquire influence in an increasingly powerful institution.

Economic Fragmentation and Declining Trade Although reduced in volume, long-distance trade in luxury goods continued to follow traditional patterns. Those who had retained their wealth or were newly rich were willing to pay for high-status goods at prices that attracted suppliers no matter what the risks and hardships. Therefore, writers still make occasional references to Syrian, Greek, and Jewish traders and eastern luxury goods in Spain and southern France during the fifth and sixth centuries. Archaeological excavations have revealed that some Syrian glass and amphorae from the eastern Mediterranean still reached the small marble-shipping port of Luna (Luni) in Etruria until about 600, and that better quality tableware known as African Red Slip Ware was still imported to Rome and its environs in decreasing amounts until the same time.

In general, however, the collapse of the Roman state in the West fragmented the economy of the Roman world and caused major changes in the production and distribution of goods. The Roman armies and the system of taxation and supply to maintain them had been powerful forces promoting the production and transportation of a wide range of goods in large quantities over considerable distances. Roman administrative centers and major military posts had stimulated the development of profitable urban markets. The state's system of roads and transport had subsidized commercial shipments. The government's demands for taxes and supplies had spurred the higher levels of organization and production that had sustained a larger and more sophisticated private sector than would have been possible otherwise.

After 410, the withdrawal of Roman armies from positions on the Rhine ended the export of grain from Britain and caused a major contraction in the production of pottery and glass in Augusta Treverorum (Trier) and the surrounding region. The Vandal conquest of Carthage (439) freed that city from the Roman government's demands for grain to feed Rome. Between then and the Roman recapture of Carthage in 534, more and more of the city's trade was with the eastern Mediterranean as the increasing amounts of eastern pottery found from that period show. In the meantime, Rome had to develop more local sources of supply.

In the East, traditional trade and production held up until the Arabic Moslem conquest. Alexandria supplied Constantinople and other eastern cities with grain and luxury goods until the Arabs captured it in 642. A shipwreck found off the coast of Turkey from about A.D. 625 shows that coastal trade was still significant. It was carrying 900 amphorae of wine, and it was well equipped with high-quality tableware, metalware, glassware, and coins. Ephesus remained a wealthy and commercially thriving city until the Persian sack of 616. Further Persian attacks and then the permanent Moslem conquests eventually destroyed long-distance eastern Roman trade, too.

Decline of Monetization and the Monetary System Hand in hand with the decline of trade and breakdown of the Roman administrative and military structures went a decline of the Roman system of coinage and monetary ways. For four centuries the Roman Empire had promoted a higher degree of monetization in western Europe and the Mediterranean than was reached again until the modern era. Moreover, the European Economic Community is only now attempting the uniformity of currency that the Roman Empire had achieved.

During the fifth century, the Empire shifted completely to a gold standard. Gold coins continued to circulate because the government insisted on collecting its revenues in gold *solidi*. Silver, however, quickly disappeared into private hands as hoarded coins or the elaborate silver plate that adorned churches and the homes of the wealthy. The almost worthless debased bronze (or copper) *nummi minimi* ("tiniest coins") were so easy to counterfeit that the flow of fakes made the problem of inflation caused by official overproduction even worse. The numbers of *nummi* needed for a transaction were so numerous that hundreds or even thousands were sealed up in leather bags and exchanged by weight. Therefore it was even easier to pass off counterfeits.

After 430, the Roman Empire fragmented into three monetary zones comprising the Iberian Peninsula and the former northwestern provinces; southern Gaul, Italy, and

North Africa; and the eastern provinces ruled from Constantinople. The major withdrawal of Roman troops from Britain in 410 ended the influx of coins from their pay, and local issues ceased after 430. Earlier the destruction of Roman defenses along the Rhine and upper Danube between 406 and 410 disrupted the coining of money in Gaul. Gaul produced gold and silver coins again only intermittently and in greatly reduced volumes during the fifth century under powerful Roman commanders like Aetius, Aegidius, and Syagrius. The Visigothic, Burgundian, and Frankish successors to the Romans in Gaul and Spain tried to maintain the Roman commercial, fiscal, and monetary system and minted imitations of Imperial gold and silver coins in small numbers. Gradually, however, they surrendered control of taxation and the right to coin money to local magnates and towns, so that by the early seventh century, coins ceased to circulate widely. Many coins remained locked up in the coffers of kings and bishops, were melted down to make fancy plate, or were used to purchase luxuries from the East.

In the sixth century, some trade continued to link southern Spain, southern Gaul, Italy, Dalmatia, and North Africa, where bronze *nummi* continued to circulate after 430. To a certain extent the old Roman administrative system continued and required small denominations of bronze and silver. Trade linking Italy and North Africa with the East even kept gold coins circulating. The Vandal kings in Carthage and the Ostrogothic kings in Italy had some success in reforming their coinages in the late fifth century on the basis of older Roman and Carthaginian types.

In 498, the Vandal and Ostrogothic reforms inspired the Emperor Anastasius to reform the coinage of the eastern Roman provinces. He recoined the bronze denominations into good-looking, well-made coins called *folles* (sing. *follis*). They held their value, and Justinian continued to improve them until the wars of the 540s, when war debts and the need for bronze to make arms forced him to debase the bronze coins once more.

As a result, inflation wracked the econ-omy of the eastern Empire. Tiberius II (578 to 582) and Maurice (582 to 602) stabilized the coinage temporarily, but the chaos that followed the assassination of Maurice, the wars with Persia, and the Arab conquests threw the monetary system of the East into turmoil. Inflation raged, most Imperial mints ceased to function, and uniform, regular denominations of coins for daily use could not be maintained.

Agricultural Trends As trade and the Roman monetary system that supported it declined in the fifth and sixth centuries, the amount of cultivated lands in Roman territory declined, too. Contrary to older views, soil exhaustion was probably not a general problem. Often good or potentially good land was abandoned, and the process was uneven. Therefore, local circumstances were often very important.

Lack of military security in times of invasion or civil war were major factors. The devastation visited on Augusta Treverorum and its vicinity in northern Gaul in 406 and subsequent decades caused the flight of many landlords and tenants and the takeover of their land by the newcomers. For both those who remained and the new settlers, agriculture was reduced to a more subsistence level than before, although the great wine-producing estates in the Moselle valley seem to have flourished at least into the sixth century.

In Italy, the revenues from agricultural land dropped in many regions after the invasion of Alaric and the Visigoths. By 418, the tax on cultivated land in Etruria, Campania, and Picenum had been reduced by almost 90 percent. Justinian's long war against the Goths in Italy did incalculable damage to Italian agriculture. In North Africa, the raids of Moorish tribes before the even more disastrous invasion of the Vandals had already disrupted agriculture. By 422, for example, one third of the Imperial estates in the province of Africa Proconsularis and one half in Byzacena were deserted.

In the East, the periodic devastation of the Balkans on the Danubian frontier produced large tracts of deserted land, but in more protected areas agriculture flourished and expanded until well into the sixth century. The olive-producing area of northern Syria's limestone massif continued to prosper. In southern Palestine, there was an impressive expansion of population, particularly in the arid Negev. An elaborate system of dams, cisterns, and water-delivery systems allowed the spread of vineyards and olive groves in this unpromising landscape.

Even those areas that had remained agriculturally prosperous, however, show evidence of decline by the end of the sixth century. All around the Mediterranean basin, the river valleys have an alluvial deposit called the Younger Fill built up between 400 and the economic revival of around 900 that sparked the high Middle Ages. This Younger Fill began with the abandonment of the terraces that supported hillside fields, vineyards, and olive groves. As they deteriorated from neglect, heavy winter rains eroded the fragile soil and left it in the river valleys.

Many other factors besides invasions and internal conflicts caused agricultural production to decline. Beginning in 541, serious outbreaks of plague periodically occurred for the rest of the century. The decline of trade and the monetary system reduced the market for agricultural products. Farmers who once could have sold enough to obtain the money needed for rents and taxes were less and less able to do so. At the same time, the emperors were levying higher and higher taxes on land to meet the increasingly heavy demands of defense and warfare. Those who leased land or farmed marginal land found it increasingly difficult to make ends meet. They could abandon the unprofitable land, look for more profitable land to buy or lease somewhere else, or become the *coloni* of those with greater resources.

The Villa System   The concentration of remaining agricultural land in fewer and fewer hands accelerated in the fifth and sixth centuries. With the decline in trade and monetization, the great estates worked by slaves and *coloni* produced more and more to fill their own or local needs rather than distant markets or destinations. Although large landowners still exchanged commodities over considerable distances as gifts among friends or bestowed them

upon dependents, agriculture by the end of the sixth century began to resemble more that of Medieval manorialism than that of the High Empire.

Social and Demographic Changes

The economic trends of the fifth and sixth centuries accompanied major social and demographic changes. Although the population of the Empire had always been overwhelmingly rural, it became more so. At the same time, the total population declined. By the end of the sixth century, the late Antique social world had given way to one that would characterize the Medieval world for centuries.

The End of the Classical City   Although the urban population of the Roman Empire as a whole was probably never much more than 10 percent, the classical Greco-Roman city gave Roman civilization its distinctive character. Maintaining and spreading the distinctive form of the classical city (with its civic institutions; its typical architectural style; its standard public buildings and monuments like baths, temples, theaters, amphitheaters, circuses, markets, libraries, fora, statues, commemorative arches, and shrines; its common amenities, such as aqueducts, fountains, sewers, and well-paved streets) had provided the social, cultural, and administrative glue that had held together Rome's far-flung empire. During the fifth and sixth centuries, the cities of the Roman Empire were either abandoned, destroyed, or transformed into something quite different in every way from what they had been before. Those that remained inhabited shrank to shadows of their former selves; their economic function became much more limited primarily as local or regional market towns; the classical style and construction of buildings gave way to local vernaculars; ecclesiastical institutions replaced civic; and the amenities disappeared.

The decline of Roman cities was both a function of and a contributor to the other changes taking place in the late Antique Roman world. Attacks by invaders and usurpers weakened them so that they were more vulnerable to attack. The decline of trade and agriculture undermined them economically so that there was even less of a market for trade goods and agricultural products, and the inability or unwillingness of urban elites to perform increasingly burdensome civic duties weakened civic institutions still further.

Like lights progressively going out on an overloaded power grid, Roman cities declined in a pattern beginning on the fringes of the less heavily urbanized West and culminating in the older, more heavily urbanized East. Those along the northeastern frontier in Britain, northern Gaul, and Germany rapidly declined at an early date. Between 400 and 500 urban life disappeared in these areas. Many sites were abandoned altogether but some places like London, York, and Augusta Treverorum survived mainly as the locations of major churches and ecclesiastical residences.

Even Rome had practically collapsed by 550. By the mid-fourth century, the population of Rome had recovered to around a million after the disasters of the third century. By 419, however, nine years after Alaric's sack, it had fallen to less than half of that. Between then and the Vandal sack of 455, it had risen by between 50,000 and 100,000 but then steadily declined after that. During Justinian's Gothic War, it may have been reduced to 20,000, and Procopius reports that at one point it was abandoned. After 600, Rome seems to have been primarily a site of monasteries and churches inhabited by clerics and a few Byzantine officials.

Carthage, the queen city of Roman North Africa, decayed badly after Justinian's reconquest. Many of the occupied areas were abandoned in the seventh century. Burials, which used to be forbidden within the walls of the city, began to intrude upon ruined structures. After it fell to the Arabs in 698, it was abandoned altogether. By the time of the Arab conquest, Lepcis (Leptis) Magna, on the coast between Carthage and Cyrene, had shrunk from a city covering 320 acres at its height to only 70.

In general, the cities of the East fared much better than those of the West in the fifth and sixth centuries. The cities of the northern Balkans, however, went into decline when the Huns and Ostrogoths invaded in the second half of the fifth century. Greek cities like Athens, Corinth, Argos, and Sparta declined precipitously after the Slavic attacks in the 580s. Athens remained inhabited, but the others were eventually abandoned.

The cities of Asia Minor and the Levant show new building activity accompanying growing wealth and population until the Persian and Arab invasions of the seventh century. Thereafter, rapid decline set in. The Sassanid Persians sacked Antioch in 611, Damascus in 613, and Jerusalem in 614. Between the Persian sack of 616 and the Arab attack of 654/55, the great city of Ephesus shrank to little more than a fortress. The Moslem capture of Alexandria in 642 ended its role as the supplier of grain to Constantinople and caused it to decay.

Constantinople itself had reached its apogee under Justinian. While Rome was shrinking, Constantinople had grown in population to about half a million. As it lost control of the cities from which it drew its wealth, however, it too began to contract. Although it withstood a siege by the Avars and Sassanid Persians in 628 and a series of Arab attacks between 698 and the year-long siege of 717, its power was now limited to Asia Minor and a few coastal enclaves in Greece and Italy. Preoccupied with its own internal political intrigues and religious factionalism, it had lost the spirit and resources of a classical city.

Changing Patterns of Rural Settlement The amount of archaeological information available for the countryside in Late Antiquity is not so great as that for cities, nor is it easy to interpret. Nevertheless, evidence for the transition to later patterns of settlement in the fifth and sixth centuries is beginning to come to light in some places. Around Augusta Treverorum in Gaul, for example, many rural villas were abandoned, and Frankish settlers took up the flatter, more easily worked land, particularly in the basin between the Saar and the Moselle. Pockets of older inhabitants remained, however, often grouped around an old fortified site or church and can be traced in place names with Celtic or Latin roots.

The shift from the classical pattern of dispersed settlement in open land to the Medieval pattern of hilltop villages can be seen in parts of Italy. Archaeological surveys in South Etruria indicate a drastic drop in population and the creation of fortified hilltop settlements to protect the area from invading Lombards. A similar trend is evident in the upper valley of the Volturnus River. Although much more work needs to be done in other parts of Italy and to confirm the details, it is safe to say that the transformation from the classical to the Medieval countryside was well underway by A.D. 600.

Attempts to Improve the Position of Women and Children in Society

In the fifth and sixth centuries, there were attempts at improving conditions for women and children. How much these attempts actually affected the daily lives of most is hard to assess, but that efforts were even made is significant. Emperors could not make up their minds on whether to permit divorce by mutual consent or not. There was always a fear that liberalized divorce would break up families too easily and harm the interests of the children in family property. In 440, Theodosius II allowed a woman to divorce a husband unilaterally on the grounds of outrageous acts of infidelity in their own home or wife beating, but a woman who divorced without grounds had to wait five years to remarry, whereas a husband who did so did not have to wait. Anastasius allowed divorce by consent and required that a woman wait only one year to remarry (to allow for the birth of any recently conceived child of the husband) if a groundless divorce was by consent.

Justinian at first permitted consensual divorce. In 442, however, although he added that a woman could divorce a husband for impotence or if he stayed with another woman in the same city after repeated warnings not to, Justinian disallowed consensual divorce and wife beating as grounds for divorce. (He did, however, institute heavy fines in an attempt to stop husbands from beating their wives.) He also ruled that a woman who divorced without legitimate grounds had to enter a convent, and he

made the penalty for divorce without grounds equal in 548, when he ruled that men also had to enter a monastery. A year after Justinian's death, Justin II returned to the more lenient position that men and women should be allowed to dissolve unhappy marriages by mutual consent without formal grounds. Working within a long legal tradition, even Christian emperors in their most strict legislation never adopted the teachings of churchmen like Basil of Caesarea, Augustine, or Jerome that a woman could never divorce her husband and that neither could remarry until the death of the other.

Justinian's legislation made a concerted effort to improve conditions for lower-class women, particularly prostitutes or those equated with prostitutes. There is good reason to believe that the powerful influence of Theodora had something to do with it (p. 508). Leo I had unsuccessfully tried to ban prostitution in 460. In 535, Justinian made it a crime to force or trick girls into prostitution. During the fourth century, laws had forbidden actresses and their daughters to change professions unless they converted to Christianity, whose moral code required a chaste life thereafter. Justinian added that such converts could legally marry.

Justinian tried to protect all women from *raptus,* which encompassed seduction, abduction, and rape. Contrary to previous law, there was now no class of women with whom it would be impossible to commit *stuprum* (unlawful intercourse), and he put the blame for *raptus* squarely on the man committing the deed. The penalty was execution. A woman's relatives or master could summarily kill her *raptor* if they caught him in the act. If the victim were a slave or freed woman, the executed man's heirs could receive his property. A freeborn victim got to keep the executed man's property plus that of any accomplices, and she was free to marry without stigma. If she were in an adulterous relationship with a seducer, a woman could, if the family wished, be divorced and prosecuted with the man, but she could also simply be given a whipping and sent to a convent for two years. After that she could return to her husband if he would have her.

Justinian tried to protect the property rights of children in their mother's family by asserting that consanguinity should be reckoned through females as well as males. He also decreed that a child could not be enslaved to pay off a parent's debts, a long-standing evil in the ancient world. Finally, he declared that no foundling could be raised as a slave. An unintended consequence, however, might have been a greater reluctance of people to take in exposed infants. On the other hand, the organized efforts of the Church to provide for such infants may have filled any gap.

Romans and Germans The western Roman aristocracy was seriously affected by the imposition of Germanic rule. In Gaul, when the Visigoths and Burgundians were settled in Aquitania and Savoy in 418 and 443, the Roman inhabitants had to surrender one third of their arable land, cattle, *coloni,* and slaves to the newcomers. Later they had to give up another third. Both the Visigoths and the Burgundians governed the old Roman inhabitants under special, Roman-based codes of law. That not only tended to segregate the Romans and Germans, but made disputes between them more complicated. The Visigoths also forbade intermarriage between Romans and themselves.

In Italy, Odovacer took only one third of the Romans' possessions for his men, and Theoderic merely assigned those thirds to his Ostrogothic followers when he took over in 493. He allowed many landowners simply to pay one third of their rents as taxes to the king instead of losing the land itself. Theoderic also tried to preserve the Roman administrative system intact and not segregate the old Roman inhabitants, who could even serve as military officers.

The Vandals under Gaiseric in North Africa confiscated all the property of the old Roman inhabitants and probably reduced to serfs those who did not flee. In northern Gaul, the Franks were completely different. After their initial conquests, they left the Roman inhabitants in possession of all of their property.

Understandably, the relations between the old inhabitants of the West and the newcomers were frequently strained. The Germanic tribesmen were not used to settled ways and orderly government despite the earnest attempts of some of their kings to preserve it. Germanic officials were just as corrupt as the Roman ones had been, and lawlessness and violence were common everywhere.

Moreover, there was the added problem of the religious differences between the Arian Germans and the orthodox Catholic Romans. The old Roman upper class turned to the administration of the Church when other opportunities for leadership were restricted by their new overlords. Ethnic antagonisms and religious differences tended to become intertwined. The situation was especially acute in the Vandal kingdom, where the kings were particularly fanatical Arians. Huneric banished about 5,000 Catholic clergy to the desert and used Catholic bishops for forced labor on Corsica.

The Burgundians, Visigoths, and Ostrogoths were more tolerant and tried to cooperate with the Catholic hierarchy. The Burgundian king Gundobad (474 to 516) even allowed his children to be converted to Catholicism. Theoderic the Ostrogoth, however, was not that flexible and found that orthodox clergy cooperated with his enemies. The Franks were unusual because they converted directly from paganism to orthodox Catholic Christianity after Clovis, founder of the Merovingian dynasty of Frankish kings, was baptized through the influence of his Burgundian wife, Clotilda, Gundobad's daughter.

Pagan Survivals Although the public cults and rituals of paganism declined rapidly after Theodosius' attacks at the end of the fourth century, pagan intellectuals lived relatively undisturbed. Theodosius had not instituted the ancient equivalent of the Inquisition. Only the outward practices of paganism, not belief itself, were attacked. Pagan books freely circulated, and pagan thought still dominated the schools of law, rhetoric, and philosophy, where pagans and Christians freely mingled. During the fifth and early sixth centuries, many high Imperial officials, who were usually trained in the schools, continued to be pagans, both openly and secretly. Even after the brutal murder of the pagan scholar Hypatia by the partisans of Cyril in 415 (p. 475), Alexandria remained a center of Neoplatanic thought with an Aristotelian twist. Athens continued as another center of Neoplatonism and even increased its intellectual prestige.

Justinian was the one who initiated what might be called an inquisition to eradicate pagan thought. He encouraged civil and ecclesiastical officials to investigate reports of continued pagan practice and forbade anyone except baptized Christians to teach. When the leaders of the schools at Athens refused to conform, Justinian confiscated the schools' endowments (529). Some of the scholars fled to the court of Chosroes I in Persia but soon found life uncongenial there. Chosroes did them one great service, however: In his treaty of 532 with Justinian, he stipulated that they be allowed to return to the Empire and live in peaceful retirement.

Justinian also sought to root out the paganism that had persisted among the simple folk of the countryside. He sent out aggressive officials to close out-of-the-way shrines that had escaped previous attempts at closure, and he supported wide-ranging missionary activities to convert the unconverted. The task was made easier, however, because there had already occurred a certain synthesis of Christian and pagan practices. The former simple services of the Primitive Church had now given way to more elaborate ceremonies that included the use of incense, lights, flowers, and sacred utensils. A myriad of saints and martyrs had taken over the competing functions of many pagan deities and heroes. It is no mere coincidence, for example, that the Parthenon at Athens, home of Athena the Virgin (*Parthenos*), became a church of the Virgin Mary; that the celebration of the Nativity came to coincide with the date of Mithras' birth and the season connected with pagan celebrations of the winter solstice; or that sleeping in a church of Saints Cosmas and Damian could now produce the cures that used to be found in the temple of Castor and Pollux. Nor would the distinction between theurgy and the celebration of the Eucharist be clear to the unsubtle mind.

Christians and Jews Many important developments in late Imperial Christianity involved heresies and schisms, such as Arianism, Monophysitism, and the Donatist schism. They have been discussed in the chapters on the political events with which they were intimately bound because they had aroused popular passions on a large scale. Other heresies have been noted in connection with religious developments during the third century (pp. 406–407). Although it did not touch off any great popular conflict, the Pelagian heresy in the early fifth century is worthy of note because it raised fundamental questions about sin and salvation that have exercised Christian thinkers ever since.

The Church taught that saving grace could be obtained through only two sacraments, baptism and penance. Baptism, which could not be repeated, would wash away the taint of Adam's original sin and any personal sins incurred in this life up to the moment of baptism, and penance could eliminate those committed thereafter. As a result, in the fourth century, many who espoused Christianity put off baptism until the last possible moment in order to die sinless in a state of grace. After baptism in childhood or early adulthood became more common in the fifth century, penance was relied on as the means of wiping out sins committed before death. Therefore, many people paid little attention to the strict Christian moral code. They lived just as sinfully as non-Christians. Indeed, there was even less need to show restraint because they knew that all could be wiped away by baptism or penance.

Among those who were troubled by this unedifying state of affairs was a Welsh layman named Morgan, later known as Pelagius, who denied the doctrine that Adam's original sin derived from his nature and was transmitted to posterity. Therefore, he argued, it was possible to gain salvation through one's own efforts in leading a righteous life. Pelagius' views were originally accepted in the East, but St. Augustine (p. 534) led an attack on them in the West at a council in 416. Eventually, after numerous intervening councils, they were condemned at the Third Ecumenical Council at Ephesus in 431.

Justinian was anxious to root out heretics as much as pagans. He barred heretics from the professions of law and teaching, forbade them the right to inherit property, and would not let them bear witness in court against orthodox persons. He was just as harsh against the Samaritan offshoot of Judaism, whose synagogues he destroyed in 529. He even instituted the death penalty for Manichees and relapsed heretics.

Justinian was no friend of orthodox Jews either. For centuries, the Greek and Jewish communities in the cities of the East had been at odds over the rights and duties of citizenship and at times rioted against each other. In general, the Roman emperors had tried to maintain order without favoring either side too much. With the Greek population becoming more and more Christian, however, the explosive element of religious hatred had increased proportionately, and, as Theodosius had found, the growing power of the Christian Church was making it increasingly difficult for civil authorities to protect the basic rights of Jews (p. 444). At Alexandria, for example, riots between Christians and Jews gave the newly elected bishop Cyril an opportunity to solidify his leadership of the Alexandrian church and increase its power in the city by conducting a virtual pogrom against the Jewish population. It was Hypatia's support of the Imperial prefect's efforts to curb Cyril's violence that led to her murder in 415 (p. 475).

Justinian, who clearly wanted to secure his autocratic rule by uniting the Christian population behind him—"one Church and one Empire"—abandoned the secular toleration that the Roman government had traditionally maintained toward the Jews. Although he did not forbid them to practice their religion, he subjected them to the same civil disabilities as heretics and Samaritans. These policies resulted in two serious revolts of Jews and Samaritans in Palestine in 529 and about 550, which produced much bloodshed and no relief for the oppressed.

The New Cultural Spirit   The tree planted during the cultural revival of the fourth century continued to grow in the fifth and sixth, but as cities declined, it increasingly required the special environment of the church, cloister, or Imperial court to flower. On the stock of elite pagan rhetoric, philosophy, literature, and art, Christianity had grafted the traditions of those formerly on the social and geographical fringes of the Roman world. The pagan stock still produced new shoots, but they were completely overshadowed by the luxuriant growth of the new graft, which transformed the cultural landscape of the age. It was a landscape dominated by theological debate, experiencing holy mysteries, discovering allegories, and a sense that in the face of change what was useful from the past needed to be collected before it was lost.

Latin Poetry   Two poets who represent the old pagan stock in Latin literature are Claudian, Claudius Claudianus (ca. 370 to ca. 404) and Rutilius Namatianus (d. after 416). Claudian was a pagan Greek from Alexandria. He wrote some early poems in Greek, but he moved to the West in 395 and became a professional poet at the court of Honorius, where he enjoyed the patronage of the powerful Germanic general Stilicho. Between 395 and 404 he turned out a prodigious volume of highly polished classicizing poems in epic dactylic hexameter verse in praise of Honorius, Stilicho, and members of Stilicho's family. His poems are full of rhetorical color and descriptive detail and show an interest in mythology connected with Orphic and mystical views. Two of his long poems treat mythological subjects, the *Gigantomachy* (*Battle of the Giants*) and *De Raptu Proserpinae* (*On the Rape of Persephone*). Numerous short occasional poems, epigrams, and idylls round out his extensive corpus.

Rutilius Namatianus was a wealthy pagan from Gaul. Not a professional poet like Claudian, he became part of the circle of prominent Neoplatonic senators at Rome and achieved public prominence. In 416, he sadly left Rome to attend to his estates in Gaul, which had been badly damaged in Germanic raids. He described his journey in the long elegiac poem *De*

Reditu Suo (*On His Return*). He gives a moving tribute to the city of Rome and keenly observes the country through which he passes, but crudely condemns the "barbarian" Stilicho, Judaism, monasticism, and all else that he saw as destroying paganism and the Empire.

Far different in outlook from Namatianus is the court poet Flavius Merobaudes. A provincial from Spain who modeled himself on the court poet Claudian, Merobaudes combined a deep knowledge of Latin literature with Christian faith in service to the court of Valentinian III and the general Aetius. In 435, he received a public statue in reward for his panagyrics and poems celebrating his patrons. His major work is the *De Christo* (*On Christ*) in epic verse. Unfortunately, much of his work is badly preserved in a palimpsest, a manuscript that was erased and written over.

A more famous Christian contemporary is Paulinus of Nola, Meropius Pontius Paulinus (353 to 431). He came from an extremely wealthy Gallo-Roman family in Burdigala (Bordeaux) and was a prized pupil of Ausonius (p. 472). After being consul at Rome (378) and then governor of Campania, he married a wealthy woman from Spain. They both became attracted to the growing ascetic movement associated with St. Martin of Tours and abandoned worldly fame and fortune to devote themselves to pious works. They eventually settled in the Campanian town of Nola, where they devoted themselves to the cult of St. Felix of Nola and to converting the local peasants. Each year for the saint's feast day, he composed one of his *Natalicia,* poetic sermons that use familiar rural themes and everyday experiences to communicate Christian ideas to the pagan peasants. Paulinus' large correspondence links him not only with Ausonius, but many of the leading Christian figures of his day like St. Ambrose, St. Augustine, St. Jerome, Melania the Elder, and Melania the Younger. His position, expressed in one of his letters, is that cultivating pagan learning is proper if it is used to propagate the faith.

Sidonius Apollinaris (ca. 430 to ca. 480), famous bishop of Clermont (Augustonemetum) near Gergovia (p. 546), was another wealthy Gallo-Roman aristocrat who gave up a prominent public career for the Church. He represents a perfect blend of classical culture and Christianity, which he saw as allies against uncouth Germanic invaders. Before giving up his public career, he wrote the *Carmina,* a collection of twenty-four poems that include hexameters in praise of the emperors Avitus (his father-in-law), Majorian, and Anthemius and various occasional poems that reflect his social world. Of great historical value are the nine books of letters that he published as bishop.

North Africa produced two notable poets who combined Christianity with a thorough grounding in the classics. In the last part of the fifth century, Dracontius (died ca. 500) wrote a collection of classicizing poems called the *Romulea* that included the *Tragedy of Orestes,* the *Rape of Helen,* and the *Medea* in hexameter verse. His *Satisfactio* in elegaic couplets and his three books of hexameters *On Praises of God* show his Christian piety in an attempt to win the pardon of his Vandal overlord for some indiscretion. After the reconquest of Africa, Corippus wrote celebratory poems in classical epic style. In eight books modeled on the *Aeneid,* the *Iohannis* recounts the exploits of the general John in the Moorish War (546 to 548). Another work in four books praises Justinian's successor, Justin II.

The last Latin poet of note in the sixth century was Venantius Fortunatus (ca. 530 to ca. 600). Born near Ravenna, where he was educated, he left Italy around the time of the Lombard invasions and traveled widely through the old provinces of Gaul and Germany. He supported himself by celebrating local lords and bishops in poems that he wrote in return for hospitality. In 567, he became secretary to the widowed Frankish queen Radegunda, who joined a convent in Poitiers, and he took holy orders as a priest. He composed a biography of Radegunda and several saints' lives, including four books in hexameters on St. Martin of Tours. Much more notable, however, are his powerful hymns and short poems. The Latin is fresh and striking, but it does not follow classical models closely and foreshadows the poetry of the Medieval troubadours.

Latin Prose The two greatest masters of late Latin prose were St. Jerome (ca. 347 to ca. 420) and St. Augustine (354 to 430). Educated at the height of the fourth century, their writing in the early fifth reflected high classical standards. As Paulinus of Nola advocated, however, they applied their skill on behalf of propagating the faith, yet, steeped as they were in the classical tradition, they were devastated by the sack of Rome in 410.

Jerome, Sophronius Eusebius Hieronymus, was born at Stridon in Dalmatia. Going to Rome, he studied with the famous pagan Vergilian scholar Aelius Donatus (p. 470). Later he left Rome to travel and study in the Greek East. After learning Greek, he returned to Rome and rose to prominence as secretary to Pope Damasus I and confessor for a number of wealthy ladies. His learning easily allowed him to adapt old forms to the new faith, and Damasus asked him to undertake his most enduring work, the Latin translation of the Bible, commonly known as the *Vulgate*. After he started, he realized that he had to learn Hebrew because the Septuagint, the Greek translation of the Old Testament, could not be the authoritative text for a translation into yet another language. When hostility toward his strong asceticism forced him to leave Rome, he settled in Bethlehem, where he learned Hebrew and completed his task with help from devoted women like Paula and Eustochium (p. 458).

Jerome was also a prolific commentator on the Bible and harsh polemicist in theological debates. The word *adversus* (against) occurs in many of his titles. His eventual doubts about the orthodoxy of Origen (p. 412) embroiled him in a particularly nasty dispute with his former friend Rufinus and John, bishop of Jerusalem. He carried on many of his disputes through a vast correspondence with people like St. Augustine. These letters and his historical works (p. 416) make him a major witness to his age.

The greatest example of the complex blend of pagan learning and Christian faith, at least in the West, is Saint Augustine, bishop of Hippo Regius in North Africa (354 to 430). Born of a pagan father and a Christian mother, he studied rhetoric at Carthage and then went to Rome to make his mark. There he became acquainted with Symmachus and his circle. Through them, he gained appointment to a professorship of rhetoric at Milan. He was greatly influenced in thought and style by Cicero, and he was a Manichee before he became an orthodox Christian at Milan through association with Saint Ambrose, who was part of an influential circle of Christian Neoplatonists.

Augustine's voluminous letters, sermons, and commentaries show the influence of pagan classical literature and philosophy everywhere. Two works stand out—his *Confessions,* which trace his intellectual and spiritual development from a callow student smitten with Cicero to a Manichee, to a Neoplatonist, and finally to a baptized Christian; and his *magnum opus,* the *Civitas Dei* (*City of God*), which was stimulated by Alaric's sack of Rome in 410 and the flood of upper-class pagan refugees to Africa, where their example threatened to undermine the recently won supremacy of orthodox Catholicism.

In his best Latin rhetorical style, Augustine met them on their own terms. He made a systematic critique of the ancient myths and historical views on which they based their paganism, and he presented a philosophically rigorous refutation of Neoplatonism. Even in arguing for his radically Christian view of reality, however, he argued on the basis of major shared concepts, such as Divine Providence and the quintessentially classical sociopolitical concept of the *civitas,* a community of citizens. For Augustine, the Christian is a citizen of God's perfect heavenly community and longs for it while dwelling as a resident alien in this earthly community. Yet Augustine does not reject the alien city for Christians. As part of God's creation it is good, though not perfect; and the good Christian can work to eliminate its faults while enjoying its virtues. There is no puritanical rejection of the old earthly *civitas* that pagans loved. It is simply augmented by the vision of another that is even better.

Jerome and Augustine tower over many lesser writers who carried on Latin prose in countless sermons, theological treatises, and historical works. Augustine's younger friend

Paulus Orosius (ca. 390 to after 417), a priest from Spain, wrote treatises on the controversies surrounding Origen, Priscillian, and Pelagius. His major work, a history of mankind in seven volumes, was the *Historia adversus Paganos.* He wrote it for Augustine to use in writing the *City of God* and argues that God had created the Roman Empire in order to spread Christianity and that Romano-Christian culture would eventually absorb the Germanic invaders. Salvian of Marseilles (ca. 400 to ca. 480), however, in his *De Gubernatione Dei* (*On the Governance of God*) argued that God had sent the invaders to punish sinful Christians.

Gennadius, Prosper of Aquitaine, and Gildas were three minor chroniclers and biographers (p. 490). Sulpicius Severus (360 to ca. 420) on the other hand, who was a friend of Paulinus of Nola, wrote another minor chronicle and an extremely influential biography of Saint Martin of Tours (Limonum): It was one of the earliest saint's lives in the West. A Latin historian who bridges Antiquity and the Middle Ages is Gregory of Tours (538 to 594). As bishop of Tours after 573, Gregory was well situated to view the events around him. His *History of the Franks* starts with Adam but concentrates on the murderous doings of the Merovingian Franks. He reveals familiarity with ancient historiographical models, but his interest in what happens in daily life and the value that he places on personal observation make him worth reading in his own right.

A number of authors carried on the Roman tradition of technical and encyclopedic writing (p. 349). One of the most difficult but important is Martianus Capella. A resident of Carthage, he wrote between the sack of Rome (410) and that of Carthage (439) and sought to sum up the essence of classical culture in an encyclopedic work entitled *On the Marriage of Mercury and Philology*. Heavy with allegory, it reflects the religious-mystical world of Late Antiquity and establishes the model for the Medieval educational curriculum based on the seven liberal arts: the trivium of grammar, dialectic, and rhetoric plus the quadrivium of geometry, arithmetic, astronomy, and music. Similarly important is the great grammar by

Priscian, the *Institutio de Arte Grammatica,* which passed on the accumulated grammatical thought of Antiquity to Medieval schools.

Three great preservers of the classical tradition in the West mark the sixth century. Boethius (ca. 480 to 524) was a philosopher who had enjoyed the patronage of Theoderic the Ostrogoth but was later executed on suspicion of treason. Attempting to sum up the best of ancient thought, he wrote on mathematics, music, Aristotle, and Cicero and had started the monumental task of translating all of Plato and Aristotle into Latin. He also wrote defenses of the orthodox view of the Trinity. His most popular work is the *Consolation of Philosophy,* written to comfort himself in jail. There, in a dialogue with the allegorical figure Philosophy, he espouses many pagan philosophical views that show how blurred the distinction could be between Neoplatonic paganism and Christianity.

More fortunate than Boethius was Cassiodorus (487 to 583). Of a distinguished Italian family, he was one of the last Roman consuls, master of offices, and praetorian prefect. During his career, he published two large historical works, the *Chronica,* a world history from Adam to 519, and the *History of the Goths,* which comprised twelve books (mostly lost). Upon retirement he founded a monastery in Bruttium, where he promoted the study and preservation of literature and useful knowledge that would enable the Romans and Germanic newcomers in Italy to forge a new nation. His treatise *Educational Principles of Divine and Secular Literature* was widely used as a guide to reading in the Middle Ages.

Isidore of Seville (Hispalis) (ca. 570 to 636) is most famous as an encyclopedist, although he wrote an important historical account of the Goths, Vandals, and Suevi as well as a *Chronica* and *De Viris Illustribus.* Succeeding his brother as bishop of Seville in 600, he worked hard to promote orthodox Catholicism in alliance with the Visigothic throne, but he also embraced ancient learning. He summarized rational explanations of natural phenomena in his *De Natura Rerum* dedicated to King Sisebut in 613. In 620, the king commissioned an even greater encyclopedia, the *Etymology* or

Origins. Unfinished when Isidore died, it was edited into twenty books. Through etymology, he tries to get back to and preserve the original meaning of the words that embody the skills, techniques, and tools essential for maintaining civilization.

Classicizing Greek Poets The rigorous *paideia* maintained in the Greek cities continued to produce writers who could mimic the ancient classics with ease. Much of their work has an artificial air, but sometimes there is real merit. A remarkable example is Nonnus, a Christian from the Egyptian Thebaid who flourished around 400. A master of Greek epic verse, he paraphrased the Gospel of John in dactylic hexameter. His *magnum opus,* however, is an amazing epic in forty-eight books on the life and loves of the god Dionysus, the *Dionysiaca.* Thoroughly pagan in spirit, it weaves together mythological traditions from Egypt, India, and the Near East and revels in lush sensuality. More traditional than Nonnus is his contemporary Quintus of Smyrna, who wrote a sequel to the *Iliad* often called *Posthomerica.* In fourteen books, he fills the gap between the *Iliad* and the *Odyssey* by recounting such things as the death of Achilles and the building of the Trojan horse.

The *Greek Anthology* preserves a large number of epigrams in classical style from a collection called *The Cycle.* It was comprised of short poems by a number of high-ranking officials at Justinian's court. They can be clever, charming, and entertaining but also tedious. They are, however, a good example of the high level of technical skill that was still expected in the sixth century. Surprisingly good, however, are the larger poems of a court official named Paul the Silentiary, who wrote around 540. His love poetry has been much imitated by later writers, and his poems describing the Church of the Hagia Sophia and the Pythian baths are full of interesting detail and evocative language. Finally, a poem that has inspired countless retellings is Musaeus' romantic *Hero and Leander.* In 340 hexameters, Musaeus tells how the young Leander is smitten by the beautiful Hero when he sees her at a religious festival, convinces her of his love, and swims across the Hellespont each night to join her secretly in her family's lofty tower by the shore. One night, overpowered by a storm, he drowns, and when Hero spies his body washed up below, she hurls herself from the tower to join him in death.

The Late Greek Historians History is the premier Greek genre in the fifth and sixth centuries and is represented by several important authors whose work survives. The first is Zosimus, an official of the Imperial treasury in the first half of the fifth century. His *New History* is an account of the Roman Empire from Augustus to Alaric's sack of Rome in 410. It is particularly valuable for the third and fourth centuries in the East because he used sources like Dexippus (p. 410) and Eunapius (p. 474). He was outspokenly anti-Christian and constantly blamed Rome's troubles on neglect of the old gods.

Three important historians of the Church wrote in the mid-fifth century. The most significant is Socrates Scholasticus (ca. 380 to 450), whose *Church History* continued Eusebius from 306 to 439. He was not a cleric but a lawyer at Constantinople. Well-read in philosophy, theology, and logic, he respected Hellenism and brought a balanced sense of judgment to his work. That quality and his careful citation of sources make him particularly valuable. Although he, too, was a layman writing in Constantinople, Sozomen (ca. 400 to 460) had been born near Gaza in Palestine. He drew heavily on Socrates Scholasticus for his *Church History* and covered almost the same period (325 to 425). He is not entirely derivative, however, and uses some different sources of his own. He criticizes bishops who misused their power and is interested in literary affairs in Constantinople, monasticism, and the spread of Christianity to the Armenians, Goths, and Arabs. The Syrian bishop Theodoret of Cyrus (393 to ca. 460) wrote another *Church History* covering virtually the same period as Socrates and Sozomen (323 to 328). As a bishop and theologian deeply involved in the controversy between Nestorius and Cyril over the nature of Christ (p. 503), he brings an interesting perspective to the history of doctrinal issues. His *History of the Monks of Syria,* which also includes three women as subjects, is an important source for the ascetic movement in the East.

A later church historian from Syria was a well-connected lawyer named Evagrius at Antioch (ca. 535 to 600). He admired Eusebius, Socrates, Sozomen, and Theodoret, whose work he continued in a *Church History* from 428 to his own time. Like Socrates, he was careful about his sources, which he quoted frequently, but was too credulous at times. He was hostile to the Monophysites and attacked the anti-Christian views of Zosimus. Pessimistic about people's ability to control events, he ascribed many developments to God's hand.

The outstanding figure of late Greek secular historiography is, of course, Procopius (ca. 500 to 565), who chronicled the age of Justinian as private secretary to the great Belisarius (p. 506).

The last secular Greek historian of the sixth century was Agathias (ca. 530 to ca. 582). He studied law and became an official at Constantinople. He was also one of the love poets at court and married the daughter of Paul the Silentiary. He edited *The Cycle,* which contained many of his own poems. After Procopius died, however, Agathias decided to carry on the topic of military history in a *History* of his own. Unlike Procopius, however, he does not allow fortune to determine events. His interest in the Franks and Persians and his use of Persian sources make him valuable. Unfortunately, he had written only five books on the campaigns of Narses in Italy and the end of the Lazic War when he died.

Philosophy   At Alexandria and Athens, philosophy remained a major enterprise and provided a refuge for pagan intellectuals in the Neoplatonic tradition, although the distinction between Neoplatonism and Christianity became more and more blurred. A good example of the way in which the two tended to merge is Synesius of Cyrene (ca. 370 to ca. 414). He belonged to an old aristocratic family from the province of Libya in North Africa. After his studies with the pagan philsopher Hypatia in

Alexandria, he successfully represented Libya at Constantinople in a plea for a reduction in the province's taxes. Later, he organized local efforts to defend Libya from the attacks of Berber tribes. Synesius had married a Christian woman, and the Christians in Libya were so impressed with his leadership abilities that they insisted on electing him bishop of the important city of Ptolemais in 410. Synesius accepted only on the condition that he not be forced to give up his wife or some of his most cherished philosohical beliefs. In return, he accepted basic Christian doctrines like the Resurrection. He wrote some typical rhetorical/philosophical essays on subjects like kingship and the decline of humanistic learning in the face of Christian asceticism and peasant superstition. He also wrote hymns that show his poetic talent and an important collection of 156 letters that provide a valuable look at life in his part of the late Roman world.

There were no major original thinkers in the fifth and sixth centuries, but Proclus (ca. 410 to 485), who headed the Academy in Athens, was a significant synthesizer. He wrote commentaries on some of Plato's dialogues and compiled encyclopedic works on physics, Platonic theology, and astronomy. Living a very ascetic life like a monk and even writing Neoplatonic hymns, he, too, illustrates the shared religious-mystical views of the day. Another important commentator was Simplicius, who studied at both Alexandria and Athens in the sixth century. He wrote extensively on Aristotle. After Justinian officially ended the teaching of philosophy in Athens, Simplicius somehow kept on working. There is even a hint that he established a new school at Carrhae (Harran) in Persian territory.

Theology   By this time, it was very difficult to separate philosophy and Christian theology. Simplicius' great rival, for example, was John Philoponus, a Christian who was the principal philosopher at Alexandria. He was a Monophysite and wrote numerous works, among which was an attack on Proclus' belief that the world had no beginning. It was, however, the Christological disputes over Monophysitism that dominated the theological debates of the Greek East in the fifth and sixth centuries. They began with the dispute between Nestorius, bishop of Constantinople, and Cyril, bishop of Alexandria (ca. 375 to 444), over granting Mary the title *Theotokos,* "Mother of God" (p. 501). Nestorius (ca. 381 to 451), no original theologian himself, came from Antioch and followed the views of Theodore of Mopsuestia that Christ was the true union by association of two personal subjects, God the son and God the man (p. 478). The aggressive and ambitious Cyril, who wanted to assert the supremacy of his see over Antioch and Constantinople, speciously accused Nestorius of teaching the heresy that Christ had two separate natures. John, bishop of Antioch (died 441/442), naturally allied with Nestorius against Cyril. After Nestorius was condemned at the Council of Ephesus (431), John and Cyril reached a compromise called the Formula of Union (433). Some of Nestorius' supporters, however, did take what is called the Dyophysite (two natures) position and established a separate Nestorian church that Nestorius himself never supported.

Unlike Nestorius, Cyril was a prolific writer. He left a large body of exegetical works on various books of the Bible, a lengthy refutation of the ideas of Julian the Apostate, several works on the Trinity, and numerous letters. Cyril's teachings as embodied in his *Second Letter to Nestorius* were accepted as orthodox at the Council of Chalcedon in 451.

The church historian Bishop Theodoret of Cyrus (p. 536), who was also a prominent theologian, defended Nestorius in writings that actually provided the basis for the Formula of Union, which he himself rejected. As a result, after his attack on Cyril's teachings in his *Eranistes* of 447, he was stripped of his office at the "Robber Council" of Ephesus in 449. He was restored at the Council of Chalcedon, but later his writings against Cyril and the Council of Ephesus were condemned at the Council of Constantinople in 553, and most of those, except the *Eranistes,* have perished. His histories, commentaries on Paul's letters and various books of the Old Testament, treatises against heresies and paganism, and about 200 letters survive.

The bitter Christological debates of the fifth and sixth centuries aroused passionate interest at the time, but the writings surrounding them fell into obscurity once the politics that drove them were settled by the Arab conquest. On the other hand, one of the most influential theological works from this period is a group of spurious writings by an author purporting to be a first-century Athenian Christian named Dionysius the Areopagite, now called Pseudo-Dionysius. It was really written around 500 by a person at Athens who was trying to reconcile Christianity and Neoplatonic philosophy. The ideas expressed are heavily influenced by the teachings of Proclus. They teach the Neopla-

Tombstone with relief showing Mary suckling Jesus. Fifth- to sixth-century, from Fayum, Egypt. (Bildarchiv Preussischer Kulturbesitz)

Third-century Egyptian picture of Isis suckling Horus. (Editions Gallimard.)

ings of the New Rome. Many old pagan temples were used as quarries for the building of Christian churches, despite official attempts to preserve the great monuments of the past. Early Christian churches generally adopted the style of the Roman basilica, a simple rectangular building with arched windows, a semicircular apse at one end, and a pitched wooden roof. Eventually, side aisles were added, and then in Justinian's Church of the Holy Apostles at Constantinople, two short wings or transepts were added near one end to produce a plan in the shape of a cross. Justinian's Church of the Holy Wisdom (Hagia Sophia), of course, set a whole new style of church architecture (pp. 513–514).

Under the patronage of the Church, emperors, kings, and the fabulously wealthy few, the decorative arts reached new heights during the fifth and sixth centuries. Gold and silver plates with finely chased reliefs; goblets, chal-

Bishop Abraham, sixth- or seventh-century icon from Middle Egypt. (Jahr, Bildarchiv Preussischer Kulturbesitz)

tonic idea that God cannot be known directly and interacts with people through a series of nine angelic emanations. Contemplation and prayer, however, can free the soul for ecstatic union with God. Because Dionysius the Areopagite was thought to have been one of St. Paul's converts at Athens, these ideas had wide influence among Medieval thinkers, for whom philosophy was the handmaiden of theology.

Art and Architecture No significant new ground was broken in architecture until the time of Justinian. Except at Constantinople, there was little building activity beyond defensive works and churches. From the time of Constantine onward, great works of art from pagan temples were carried off to decorate the build-

Mosaic depicting Justinian and attendants, San Vitale, Ravenna. (Fratelli Alinari, Art Resource, NY)

Mosaic of Theodora with attendants, San Vitale, Ravenna. (Fratelli Alinari, Art Resource, NY)

ices, crosses, and crowns encrusted with gemstones; exquisitely carved ivory plaques and containers; richly embroidered tapestries and robes; elaborately designed rings and jewelry; fancy reliquaries; beautifully decorated books; and lavishly wrought icons, wall paintings, and mosaics were all marks of piety and status.

Icons received particular attention during the fifth and sixth centuries. An icon is the image (*eikon*) of a particularly holy person, object, or scene. Icons were often painted on wooden panels with egg tempera or molten wax (encaustic). Their use stems from the cultural traditions of Egypt and the Near East, which influenced the Hellenistic and Roman practice of creating similar portraits of gods, emperors, king officials, and renowned men of letters. These classical and preclassical predecessors often influenced the pose, grouping, and symbolism found in Christian icons. For example, the popular icon of the seated Virgin holding the infant Christ child on her lap has its parallel in similar Egyptian depictions of Isis and Horus.

By the fifth century, the popularity of icons increased as people began to believe in their ability to ward off evil. During the next century, it was common to bow and genuflect before icons. A cult of icons emerged supported by theological speculation of a Neoplatonist bent about the relationship of an image to what is being imaged.

Icons employed the same flat, perspectiveless, otherworldly style that had become popular in wall paintings and mosaics during the fourth century (p. 479). Their otherworldly quality was enhanced by the use of powerful symbols, rich color, and a skillful handling of light. The combination of color and light is particularly impressive in the mosaics of the period. Subtle patterns created by richly colored bits of glass and stone make them glow with inner life. Many stunning examples can still be found at Ravenna in churches like San Vitale and Sant'Apollinare in Classe from the time of Justinian.

To enter these glowing sanctuaries is to enter a completely different world from that of the first Roman emperor 600 years earlier. The pieces of the mosaic that constituted Roman culture had been rearranged into a very different pattern. Still, something of its substance remained, and memories of the old pattern endured.

XLIV

The Church and the Legacy of Rome

The social, political, and cultural values promoted by Christian emperors, clergymen, artists, and writers played a powerful role in the transformation of the Late Antique Roman World into the Medieval West and the Byzantine Empire. It should be clear by now, however, that Christianity and its ecclesiastical institutions were not alien imports to that world but organically grew out of it. Although Christianity is deeply rooted in Judaism, the popular Judaism of Christ and his Apostles had been permeated by the culture of the Hellenistic Greek world in which the Jewish people had lived for 300 years before the Roman annexation of Judea. St. Paul, the man who did so much to spread Christianity beyond the Jewish community in the first century A.D. and shape Christian theology, was himself a highly Hellenized Greek-speaking Jew who claimed Roman citizenship. The new religion spread by converting the pagan population of the Roman world, and for 300 years many of the great leaders and thinkers among Christians were converts who had been steeped in classical literature, rhetoric, and philosophy. The Christian desire not to be of the world while in it was, of course, impossible for any human being, even the most rigorous ascetic, to attain fully. Christianity, then, must be seen as part of the systemic evolution of the Roman world, of whose gradual transformation it was as much an effect as it was a cause.

Transmitting the Roman Classical Legacy Even as Christianity was helping to transform classical Roman civilization, it was spreading the legacy of that civilization far beyond its traditional boundaries. Ireland (Hibernia) had been known to Greek and Roman mariners and geographers since at least the late seventh century B.C., and the famous Roman general Agricola had even contemplated invading it from Britain under the Flavians. Nevertheless, active contact with the Greeks and Romans had been minimal, and their cultural impact had been commensurate. By the fifth century A.D., however, contact with the Celts in Britain had brought Christianity to some of those living in the south of Ireland. Prosper of Aquitaine says that in 431 Pope Celestine I sent a deacon named Palladius to believers in Ireland. A few years later, a British bishop named Patricius (Patrick) came to missionize pagans in northern Ireland, where he had once been taken as a slave before escaping back to Britain. In thirty years, he had founded a flourishing church based in rural monasteries because Ireland was devoid of cities.

Although they were independent of the episcopal system led by the bishop of Rome, the Irish monks were deeply immersed in the Latin Christian tradition. They produced an extensive Latin literature of poetry, letters, sermons, saints' lives, biblical commentaries, and inspirational tales. Safe from the Germanic migrations that swamped the Roman West, the Irish developed a strong scholarly tradition, which Irish missionaries like Columba (ca. 521 to ca. 597) and Columbanus (d. 615) transferred to northern Britain and Gaul in the sixth and seventh centuries. Some of the earliest manuscripts of late Latin authors and the Latin Bible are preserved in Irish manuscripts.

By 595, Britain had been lost to the Roman Empire for at least 150 years. The pagan Saxons had driven the Christianized Celtic population to the western parts of the island, and Irish missionaries had reevangelized mainly the North along the Scottish border. At that point, however, Pope Gregory I, the Great, saw an opportunity to convert the Saxons to Christianity through the Roman Catholic Church. The Saxon king Ethelbert of Kent had married Clovis' great-granddaughter Bertha, a Roman Catholic. Gregory appointed a Benedictine monk who came to be known as St. Augustine of Canterbury (not to be confused with the earlier St. Augustine of Hippo) to lead a missionary party to Ethelbert's court at Canterbury in hopes of converting his kingdom. After a two-year delay, the missionaries finally arrived at Canterbury. They quickly succeeded in converting Ethelbert, and Gregory made Augustine the first archbishop of Canterbury. After that, he rapidly evangelized neighboring Anglo-Saxon kingdoms. The Celtic Christians of the West and North differed with the Roman Church over the proper date to celebrate Easter (the Paschal controversy), the appropriate tonsure for monks, and the independence of bishops. Many of these issues were finally resolved at the Council of Whitby (663 to 664), and Celtic Christianity was effectively united with the Church of Rome.

In East Africa, Arabia, and the Far East, Christian sects that have been labeled heretical did the most to transmit the Greco-Roman legacy beyond the traditional bounds of the Roman world. Although the Ethiopian kingdom centered at Axum (Axumis, Auxume) and the kingdoms of Nubia had considerable commercial and diplomatic contact with the Empire for a long time, their conversion to Christianity linked them much more closely to the cultural and intellectual world of Late Antiquity. Nubia, extending up the Nile between Aswan and Ethiopia, comprised three kingdoms that were eventually united by the kingdom of Nobatia. In 542, the Empress Theodora sent Monophysite missionaries to convert Nobatia. As a result, Nubian Christians aligned with the Monophysite Copts in Egypt, along with whom they were cut off from the Orthodox Church at Constantinople by the Arab conquest. The cultural heritage of this wealthy Christian kingdom has only recently received serious attention.

South of Nubia, the Ethiopian royal family at Axum had been converted to Christianity by the mid-fourth century apparently through the efforts of two brothers, of whom Frumentius supposedly was consecrated the first bishop of Axum by Athanasius of Alexandria. After the Council of Chalcedon in 451, Ethiopian Christians sympathized with the Monophysites and received a number of influential Monophysite refugees from Syria and Egypt. They founded so many churches and monasteries that Cosmas Indicopleustes, a sixth-century merchant in the Indian trade, asserted that it was thoroughly Christianized.

A rich body of Christian writings appeared in the ancient Ethiopic language, Ge'ez. The Septuagint and New Testament, the life of St. Anthony, the monastic rules of Pachomius and many other Greek texts were translated into Ge'ez. The only complete text of the apocryphal book of *Enoch* exists in an Ethiopian translation. Many other Ethiopian translations of important Greek, Arabic, and Coptic originals are still awaiting proper scholarly attention.

In 523, the Ethiopian King Kaleb (514 to 542) sent an expedition across the Red Sea to South Arabia in alliance with Justin I to rescue Christians who were being persecuted by an ally of Persia. Syriac Christians had been particularly active in spreading Christianity to the Arabian Peninsula. They were so successful that Islamic traditions mention a Christian cemetery and an icon of Mary and Jesus at Mecca and claim that Mohammed conversed with monks and other Christian Arabs. Indeed,

Syriac Christians communicated Greek logic, rhetoric, and science along with Christian mysticism and even theology to the Arabs.

In the Far East, Syriac Monophysite and Nestorian missionaries spread Christianity to India and China. The so-called "Thomas Christians" in India today are descended from the early Indian converts. A Nestorian missionary named Mar Sergis was working in Lint'ao (Lintan) 300 miles west of the Chinese capital at Xi'an (Sian) by 578. A-lo-pen was preaching Nestorian Christianity in Xi'an itself by 635 and placed Christian Scriptures in the library of the Emperor T'ai-Tsung. He probably helped to translate the still-extant *Treatise on Jesus the Messiah* into Chinese. The story of his career and a list of thirty-five Chinese Christian books are preserved in the *Treatise of Veneration.* Many later writings, artifacts, and ruins of the early Chinese Christians have survived and show the interaction of Christianity and Buddhism along the ancient Silk Road. Buddhism survived later official persecution in China, but Christianity did not.

In the Caucasus region, Armenia had become the first officially Christian nation when Gregory the Illuminator (ca. 240 to 332) converted King Tiridates III. The Armenian Bishop Mashtots (361/62 to 440) and Sahak, the Syriac bishop of Samosata (Samsat), invented the first alphabet for Armenian and turned it into a literary language by initiating the translation of the Bible and countless other early Christian texts, which provided the foundation for later original work by Armenian scholars and theologians. Works by many important Greek authors whose originals are lost survive in Armenian translations. After Chalcedon, the Armenians, too, became Monophysites and spread that version of Christianity to other peoples of the Caucasus.

The Imperial Church As Christian missionaries spread Rome's cultural legacy beyond the traditional boundaries of the Classical World, the Church was also preserving Rome's imperialistic spirit. In the East, where Constantinople preserved the Imperial political and military apparatus, the Byzantine emperors and Orthodox patriarchs (bishops) became so firmly united in the cause of empire that the term *Caesaro-papism* has often been used to describe the relationship between the Church and the secular state. In the West, where the secular apparatus of the senate and the Caesars disappeared, the bishops of Rome (popes) erected an ecclesiastical one in its place.

The Rise of Ecclesiastical Power While the power of the Roman emperors and their officials declined during the fifth and sixth centuries, Christian ecclesiastics gained increasing control over civic and secular affairs. During the first three centuries A.D., Christians had created an ecclesiastical administrative structure outside of but parallel to the secular administrative system. It had spread through the network of cities that were the basis of Roman Imperial control. By the fourth century, many cities had churches headed by an official whose title was the Greek word for overseer, *episcopos,* which Latin transliterated as *episcopus,* from which are derived *episcopal* and related words in English. Germans corrupted the pronunciation of the Latin *episcopus* into *Bischof,* which came into English as *bishop* through the Anglo-Saxon dialect of German.

The bishop's church was called a cathedral (from the Greek word for this throne, *kathedra*), and from it he might control other churches and Christian institutions such as hospitals, orphanages, old-age homes, and homeless shelters in his city and its surrounding territory, which constituted his "see" (from the Latin *sedes,* "seat"). Other churches and institutions within the see might be independent dioceses and parishes with their own endowments and clergy, but a bishop and his cathedral church would certainly have the most prestige in comparison.

Christian bishops in individual Roman provinces had created provincial councils called "synods" ("congresses") modeled on the secular provincial councils made up of leading representatives from municipal *curiae* (p. 265). Bishops usually met once or twice a year to discuss common issues in the provincial capital (*metropolis*), with the bishop of the *metropolis* presiding. Therefore, the metropolitan bishop came to exercise influence over the bishops in other churches of the province. The council of Nicaea formalized the authority of metropolitan bishops in 325 and also recognized the extraprovincial primacy of sees in great cities like Alexandria, Antioch, Rome, and Carthage. As a result, a hierarchy of bishops reflecting the administrative hierarchy of cities in the Roman Imperial system had emerged. Thus the administrative organization of Christian churches mirrored that of the Roman government.

When Constantine sought to enlist this organization in the effort to restore peace and stability to the Roman world under his leadership, it became even more like the administrative apparatus of the Roman Empire. In 314, Constantine summoned bishops from the western provinces to the largest synod yet held. It met at Arelate (Arles) to deal with the Donatist controversy in North Africa (p. 432). In 325, he summoned the Council of Nicaea, which was the first ecumenical council because it included bishops from the whole Empire (p. 433). The next six ecumenical councils, which are the only other ones accepted as such by both the Greek Orthodox and Roman Catholic churches, were also summoned by emperors.

Clearly, bishops were now very important people. The ecclesiastical and Imperial hierarchies had been joined at the top. Bishop Hosius of Corduba (ca. 257 to ca. 357) was one of Constantine's major advisors. After the establishment of the eastern court at Constantinople, resident and visiting bishops, whom subsequent emperors frequently consulted, constituted a perpetual (endemic) council. As Constantine and his Christian successors bestowed money, power, and privileges upon the Church and its clergy, aristocrats saw an opportunity to acquire leadership and prestige through the control of important episcopal sees. In Constantine's restored Empire, the Church became a new vehicle of civilian power for the traditional aristocracy of a world that had become increasingly dominated by upstarts and "barbarians" through the military.

Christian congregations gave a bishop a well-organized group of supporters whom he could mobilize against secular and ecclesiastical rivals through effective preaching. He also had significant wealth at his disposal. Imperial donations and private bequests to churches and Christian charitable foundations had placed large amounts of money and property in episcopal hands. Constantine himself had set a precedent by granting to the churches of Rome estates with incomes totaling over 400 pounds of gold a year. Leaving something to the Church in one's will became customary for Christians of all classes. Moreover, the Church had to pay only the regular taxes on its lands, which were free from extraordinary imposts and the burdens of corvées.

As a result, bishops of large churches enjoyed impressive incomes. John Chrysostom said that the church of Antioch had revenues equal to those just below the wealthiest citizens. In the first half of the sixth century, Ravenna enjoyed annual rents of 12,000 *solidi,* and at the beginning of the seventh century, the bishop of Alexandria had 8,000 pounds of gold in his treasury. Such resources allowed the bishops of major sees to exercise patronage and maintain staffs or retinues greater than those of secular aristocrats and even rivaling those of Imperial officials.

According to one document, the bishop of Ravenna annually received 3,000 *solidi,* 880 fowls, 266 chickens, 8,800 eggs, 3,760 pounds of pork, and 3,450 pounds of honey as well an unspecified number of geese and volume of milk to feed his household and provide gifts and banquets for the people whom he cultivated in maintaining the dignity of his office. At the great church in Constantinople, Justinian tried to limit the ordained staff to 525, and that did not count additional personnel like gravediggers, funeral attendants, and parabalans (stretcher-bearers for the sick and infirm). At Constantinople alone, the funeral attendants numbered 950 under Justinian, and at Alexandria in the early fifth century, Cyril had a force of 600 rugged parabalans at his disposal as he tried to cow the Imperial prefect and other rivals in the violence that led to the murder of Hypatia (p. 475).

It is no wonder that emperors and Imperial officials were willing to grant as much respect to bishops as they did to wealthy secular aristocrats, renowned pagan orators and philosophers, or charismatic holy men. They needed the cooperation of these powerful men to maintain control at the local level. Bishops, therefore, could exercise greater freedom of speech, *parrhésia,* than many in dealing with Imperial authorities and had a greater opportunity than others to catch the ear of a Christian emperor. They could use this influence on behalf of their cities to obtain relief from taxes, assuage the wrath of an angry emperor, or secure Imperial gifts and benefactions.

The Church was the natural heir of the Empire that bore it. Some churchmen like Salvian (p. 535) probably were happy to see the parent die in order to gain full control of their inheritance, but many rallied to its defense and were devastated at the thought of its passing. The resources and respect commanded by a bishop could allow him to assume the leadership of his entire community when the secular powers failed. In 451, for example, Bishop Anianus of Orleans (Cenabum, Aurelianum) [d. 453], successfully organized the defense of his city against the Huns. The great Gallo-Roman aristocrat Sidonius Apollinaris (p. 533) had risen all the way to consul and prefect of Rome when he turned to the Church and became bishop of Clermont (Augustonemetum) near Gergovia ca. 470. He organized resistance to the Visigoths and was imprisoned when they were victorious. They soon reinstated him, however, and acknowleged his leadership of the local Roman population. In 540, Megas, bishop of Beroea (Aleppo) in Syria, vainly tried to save his city from the Persians in the face of apathetic Roman authorities.

In the East, the great metropolitan bishops of Alexandria, Antioch, and Constantinople had perpetuated the intercity rivalries of the old civic elites. These rivalries frequently manifested themselves in bitter doctrinal disputes as each bishop tried to assert the dominance of his city's position. The Arab conquests of the seventh century put an end to that situation by leaving Constantinople as the largest surviving Christian see of the Greek East. After that, the interests of church and state in the Byzantine Empire became indissolubly linked.

The Rise of Rome   In the West, the abandonment of Rome as the principal Imperial residence increased the power and prestige of the pope, bishop of Rome. When Alaric and the Visigoths besieged the city in 408, Pope Innocent I stepped into the political vacuum and tried to save the city. Pope Leo I intervened to save Rome from Attila the Hun in 450 and managed to negotiate with the Vandals in 455 to lessen the fury of their sack. Indeed, Leo was one in a long line of popes who increased the power of the bishop of Rome in the West as the city's political position in the Empire was eclipsed by Ravenna and Constantinople. Under Julius I (337 to 352), the Council of Sardica (343), which tried to settle the dispute between Athanasius and his Arian opponents (p. 477), declared that as the apostolic see of St. Peter, Rome could hear appeals from other bishops. Carthage was the only real rival of Rome in the West, but it did not have an apostolic connection. Therefore, Roman bishops increasingly held primacy in the West and claimed it in the East, where Constantinople had been proclaimed as the "New Rome," second in primacy only to "Old Rome" at the Second Ecumenical Council (381).

The emperors Gratian and Valentinian III issued decrees in support of the popes in ca. 378 and 445. After the western line of emperors ended in the late fifth century, Pope Gelasius I (492 to 496) virtually proclaimed himself joint ruler in a letter to the eastern Emperor Anastasius. There he declared the doctrine of the "two swords" that governed the world: the spiritual authority of the bishop of Rome as "Vicar of Christ" and the temporal power of the emperor. After the adversities following Justianian, Pope Gregory the Great (590 to 604) set out to conquer the West for Rome once more, not with new legions but with loyal missionary bishops, who would enlist the armies of heretic and pagan kings in the cause by converting them to Rome's faith. Thus the Imperial spirit of the senate and the Caesars lived on in the Medieval papacy. Rome in the West was now the Church.

Bibliography

In the interest of economy, this bibliography has been limited to books in English, primarily of recent publication, that will be reliable guides to the subjects covered. Important journal articles and other books in all languages on these subjects will be readily available in the notes and bibliographies of the works listed here. Serious students will also consult various scholarly journals in classics and ancient history to find additional mate-rial, especially that published after the compilation of this bibliography (June–October 1997). Students should also familiarize themselves with the annual publication known as *L'Année Philologique*, which lists, in the language of publication, the books and articles published each year on various topics in classics and ancient history. It and other bibliographical aids are also available electronically.

I General Histories and Reference Works

Atlas of Classical History, ed. R. J. A. Talbert. London and Sydney: Croom Helm, 1985.

Atlas of the Classical World, ed. A. A. M. van den Heyden and H. H. Scullard. London and New York: Thomas Nelson, 1959.

Bickerman, E. J., *Chronology of the Ancient World* (2nd ed.). London: Thames and Hudson, 1980.

Broughton, T. R. S., *The Magistrates of the Roman Republic,* 3 vols. New York and Atlanta: American Philological Association, 1951–1986.

Burstein, S. M., R. MacMullen, K. A. Raaflaub, and A. M. Ward, *Ancient History: Recent Work & New Directions.* Claremont: Regina Books, 1997.

The Cambridge Ancient History, vols. 11–12, ed. S. A. Cook et al. Cambridge: Cambridge University Press, 1936–1939.

The Cambridge Ancient History (2nd ed.), vols. 7.2–10, ed. F. W. Walbank, A. E. Astin, et al. Cambridge and New York: Cambridge University Press, 1989–1996 (vols. 11–14 of the new edition will appear after 1996).

Cornell, T. J., and J. Matthews, *Atlas of the Roman World.* Oxford: Phaidon, 1982.

Encyclopedia of Early Christianity (2nd ed.), ed. E. Ferguson. New York and London: Garland Publishing, 1997.

Grant, M., *The Roman Emperors: A Biographical Guide to the Rulers of Ancient Rome 31 B.C.– A.D. 476.* New York: Scribner's, 1985.

———, *A Guide to the Ancient World: A Dictionary of Classical Place Names.* New York: H. W. Wilson, 1986.

———, *The Visible Past: Greek and Roman History from Archaeology 1960–1990.* New York: Scribner's, 1990.

Grant, M., and R. Kitzinger, *The Civilization of the Ancient Mediterranean: Greece and Rome.* New York: Scribner's, 1988.

Jones, A. H. M., J. R. Martindale, and J. Morris, *The Prosopography of the Later Roman Empire,* vols. 1–3. Cambridge and New York: Cambridge University Press, 1971–1991 (a projected fourth volume of additions and corrections has not yet appeared).

Lewis, N., and M. Reinhold, *Roman Civilization* (sources in translation), 2 vols. New York: Harper and Row, 1966.

Lintott, A., *Imperium Romanum: Politics and Administration.* London and New York: Routledge, 1993.

The Oxford Classical Dictionary (3rd ed.), ed. S. Hornblower and A. Spawforth. Oxford and New York: Oxford University Press, 1996.

The Oxford History of the Classical World, ed. J. Boardman, J. Griffin, and O. Murray. London and New York: Oxford University Press, 1986.

The Penguin Encyclopedia of Ancient Civilizations, ed. A. Cotterell. Harmondsworth: Penguin Books, 1988.

The Princeton Encyclopedia of Classical Sites, ed. R. Stillwell. Princeton: Princeton University Press, 1976.

Richardson, L. Jr., *A New Topographical Dictionary of Ancient Rome.* Baltimore and London: The Johns Hopkins University Press, 1992.

Scarre, C., *The Penguin Historical Atlas of Ancient Rome.* Harmondsworth: Penguin Books, 1995.

Who Was Who in the Roman World, 753 B.C.–A.D. 476, ed. D. Bowder. Oxford: Phaidon, 1980.

II Geography

Cary, M., *The Geographic Background of Greek and Roman History.* Oxford: Clarendon Press, 1949.

Dilke, O. A. W., *Greek and Roman Maps.* London: Thames and Hudson, 1985.

Grant, M., *The Ancient Mediterranean.* New York: Scribner's, 1969.

Smith, C. D., *Western Mediterranean Europe: A Historical Geography of Italy, Spain, and Southern France since the Neolithic.* London and New York: Academic Press, 1979.

III Early and Non-Roman Italy

Balmuth, M. (ed.), *Studies in Sardinian Archaeology, Volume II: Sardinia and the Mediterranean.* Ann Arbor: University of Michigan Press, 1986.

Brown, A. C., *Ancient Italy before the Romans.* Oxford: Ashmolean Museum, 1980.

Pallottino, M., *The Etruscans,* trans. J. Cremona, ed. D. Ridgway. London: Allen Lane, 1975.

———, *A History of Earliest Italy,* trans. Martin Ryle and Kate Soper. Ann Arbor: University of Michigan Press, 1991.

Richardson, E. H., *The Etruscans: Their Art and Civilization* (2nd ed.). Chicago and London: University of Chicago Press, 1976.

Ridgway, D., *The First Western Greeks.* Cambridge and New York: Cambridge University Press, 1992.

———, and F. R. Ridgway, *Italy before the Romans: The Iron Age, Orientalizing, and Etruscan Periods.* London: Academic Press, 1979.

Salmon, E. T., *Samnium and the Samnites.* Cambridge: Cambridge University Press, 1967.

Trump, D. H., *The Prehistory of the Mediterranean.* Harmondsworth: Penguin Books, 1981.

IV Early Rome

Cornell, T. J., *The Beginnings of Rome: Italy and Rome from the Bronze Age to the Punic Wars (c. 1000–264 B.C.).* London and New York: Routledge, 1995.

Holloway, R. R., *The Archaeology of Early Rome and Latium.* London and New York: Routledge, 1994.

Smith, C. J., *Early Rome and Latium.* Oxford: Oxford University Press, 1996.

V The Republic

Astin, A. E., *Cato the Censor.* Oxford: Clarendon Press, 1978.

Badian, E., *Foreign Clientalae (264–70 B.C.).* Oxford: Clarendon Press, 1958.

———, *Publicans and Sinners: Private Enterprise in the Service of the Roman Republic.* Ithaca: Cornell University Press, 1972.

Beard, M., and M. H. Crawford, *Rome in the Late Republic.* London: Duckworth, 1985.

Bernstein, A. H., *Tiberius Gracchus: Tradition and Apostacy.* Ithaca and London: Cornell University Press, 1978.

Brown, F. E., *Cosa: The Making of a Roman Town.* Ann Arbor: University of Michigan Press, 1980.

Brunt, P. A., *The Fall of the Roman Republic and Related Essays.* Oxford: Clarendon Press, 1988.

Clarke, M. L., *The Noblest Roman: Marcus Brutus and His Reputation.* London: Thames and Hudson, 1981.

Crawford, M. H., *The Roman Republic* (2nd ed.). Cambridge, MA: Harvard University Press, 1993.

Dudley, D. R., and T. A. Dorey, *Rome against Carthage.* Garden City, NY: Doubleday, 1972.

Eckstein, A. M., *Senate and General: Individual Decision-Making in the Roman Republic.* Berkeley, Los Angeles, and London: University of California Press, 1987.

Flower, H., *Ancestor Masks and Aristocratic Power in Roman Culture.* Oxford: Clarendon Press, 1997.

Gelzer, M., *Caesar: Politician and Statesman* (6th ed.), trans. P. Needham. Cambridge, MA: Harvard University Press, 1968.

———, *The Roman Nobility,* trans. R. Seager. Oxford: Blackwell, 1969.

Gruen, E. S., *The Last Generation of the Roman Republic.* Berkeley, Los Angeles and London: University of California Press, 1974.

Gruen, E. S., *The Hellenistic World and the Coming of Rome.* Berkeley, Los Angeles, and London: University of California Press, 1984.

Harris, W. V., *Rome in Etruria and Umbria.* Oxford: Clarendon Press, 1971.

———, *The Imperialism of Mid-Republican Rome.* Rome: American Academy in Rome, 1984.

Huzar, E. G., *Mark Antony: A Biography.* Minneapolis: University of Minnesota Press, 1978.

Kallet-Marx, R. M., *Hegemony to Empire, the Development of the Roman Imperium in the East 148 to 62 B.C.* Berkeley, Los Angeles, and Oxford: University of California Press, 1995.

Lancel, S., *Carthage, A History,* trans. A. Nevill. Oxford and Cambridge, MA: Blackwell, 1995.

Lazenby, J. F., *Hannibal's War: A Military History of the Second Punic War.* Warminster: Aris and Phillips, 1978.

Lintott, A. W., *Violence in Republican Rome.* Oxford: Clarendon Press, 1968.

Mitchell, R. E., *Patricians and Plebeians: The Origin of the Roman State.* Ithaca and London: Cornell University Press, 1990.

Mitchell, T. N., *Cicero: The Ascending Years.* New Haven and London: Yale University Press, 1979.

———, *Cicero: The Senior Statesman.* New Haven and London: Yale University Press, 1991.

Nicolet, C., *The World of the Citizen in Republican Rome,* trans. P. S. Falla. Berkeley and Los Angeles: University of California Press, 1980.

Raaflaub, K. A. (ed.), *Social Struggles in Archaic Rome: New Perspectives on the Conflict of the Orders.* Berkeley, Los Angeles, and London: University of California Press, 1986.

Riddle, J. M., *Tiberius Gracchus: Destroyer or Reformer?* Lexington, MA: D. C. Heath, 1970.

Salmon, E. T., *The Making of Roman Italy.* London: Thames and Hudson, 1982.

Scullard, H. H., *Scipio Africanus, Soldier and Statesman.* London: Thames and Hudson, 1970.

———, *A History of the Roman World 753–146 B.C.* (4th ed.). London: Methuen, 1980.

———, *From the Gracchi to Nero: A History of Rome from 133 B.C. to A.D. 68* (reprint of 5th ed.). London and New York: Routledge, 1988.

Seager, R. J., *Pompey: A Political Biography.* Oxford: Blackwell, 1979.

Staveley, E. S., *Greek and Roman Voting and Elections.* London: Thames and Hudson, 1972.

Stockton, D., *The Gracchi.* London: Oxford University Press, 1979.

Syme, R., *The Roman Revolution.* Oxford: Clarendon Press, 1939.

Vanderbroek, P. J. J., *Popular Leadership and Collective Behavior in the Late Rome Republic (ca. 80–50 B.C.).* Amsterdam: J. C. Gieben, 1987.

Wallace, R. W., and E. M. Harris (eds.), *Transition to Empire: Essays in Greco-Roman History 360–146 B.C., in Honor of E. Badian.* Norman and London: University of Oklahoma Press, 1996.

Ward, A. M., *Marcus Crassus and the Late Roman Republic.* Columbia and London: University of Missouri Press, 1977.

Warmington, B. H., *Carthage* (2nd ed.). New York: Praeger, 1969.

Warrior, V. M., *The Initiation of the Second Macedonian War, An Explication of Livy, Book 31.* Stuttgart: Franz Steiner Verlag, 1996.

Wiseman, T. P. (ed.), *Roman Political Life 90 B.C.– A.D. 69.* Exeter: Exeter University Press, 1985.

Yavetz, A., *Julius Caesar and His Public Image.* Ithaca: Cornell University Press, 1983.

VI The Principate

Birley, A. R., *Marcus Aurelius: A Biography.* New Haven and London: Yale University Press, 1987.

———, *Septimius Severus the African Emperor* (2nd ed.). New Haven and London: Yale University Press, 1988.

———, *Hadrian the Restless Emperor.* London and New York: Routledge, 1997.

Blagg, T., and M. Millet (eds.), *The Early Roman Empire in the West.* Oxford: Oxbow, 1990.

Brunt, P. A., *Imperial Themes.* Oxford: Clarendon Press, 1990.

Campbell, J. B., *The Emperor and the Roman Army 31 B.C.–A.D. 235.* Oxford: Clarendon Press, 1984.

Chisholm, K., and J. Ferguson, *The Augustan Age.* Oxford: 1981.

De Blois, K., *The Policy of the Emperor Gallienus* (rev. ed.). Leiden: E. J. Brill, 1976.

Garnsey, P., and R. Saller, *The Early Principate: Augustus to Trajan.* Oxford: Clarendon Press, 1982.

Jones, A. H. M., *Augustus.* London: Chatto and Windus, 1970.

Jones, B. W., *The Emperor Titus.* New York: St. Martin's Press, 1984.

Levick, B. M., *Tiberius the Politician.* London: Thames and Hudson, 1976.

———, *Claudius.* London: B. T. Batsford, 1990.

MacMullen, R., *The Roman Government's Response to Crisis, A.D. 235–337.* New Haven and London: Yale University Press, 1976.

Millar, F., *The Emperor in the Roman World (31 B.C.– A.D. 337).* London: Duckworth, 1977.

———, and Erich Segal (eds.), *Caesar Augustus: Seven Aspects.* Oxford: Clarendon Press, 1984.

Nicolet, C., *Space, Geography, and Politics in the Early Roman Empire.* Ann Arbor: University of Michigan Press, 1991.

Nicols, J., *Vespasian and the Partes Flavianae.* Wiesbaden: Steiner, 1978.

Raaflaub, K. A., and M. Toher (eds.), *Between Republic and Empire: Interpretations of Augustus and His Principate.* Berkeley, Los Angeles, and London: University of California Press, 1988.

Randsborg, K., *The First Millennium A.D. in Europe and the Mediterranean: An Archaeological Essay.* Cambridge and New York: Cambridge University Press, 1991.

Syme, R., *The Augustan Aristocracy.* Oxford: Clarendon Press, 1986.

Talbert, R. J. A., *The Senate of Imperial Rome.* Princeton: Princeton University Press, 1984.

Wells, C. M., *The Roman Empire* (2nd ed.). Cambridge, MA: Harvard University Press, 1992.

Yavetz, Z., *Pleb and Princeps* (2nd ed.). New Brunswick and Oxford: Transaction Books, 1988.

VII The Late Empire

Barnwell, P. S., *Emperor, Prefects, and Kings: The Roman West, 395–565.* Chapel Hill and London: University of North Carolina Press, 1992.

Bowersock, G. W., et al., *Edward Gibbon and the Decline of the Roman Empire.* Cambridge, MA, and London: Harvard University Press, 1977.

———, *Julian the Apostate.* London: Duckworth, 1978.

Brown, P. R. L., *The World of Late Antiquity: 150–750.* New York: Harcourt and Brace, 1971.

———, *The Making of Late Antiquity.* Cambridge, MA, and London: Harvard University Press, 1978.

———, *Power and Persuasion in Late Antiquity: Towards a Christian Empire.* Madison: University of Wisconsin Press, 1992.

Browning, R., *Justinian and Theodora* (2nd. ed.). London: Thames and Hudson, 1987.

Cameron, Alan E., and J. Long, with a contribution by Lee Sherry, *Barbarians and Politics at the Court of Arcadius.* Berkeley, Los Angeles, and Oxford: University of California Press, 1993.

Cameron, Averil, *The Later Roman Empire: A.D. 284–430.* Cambridge, MA: Harvard University Press, 1993.

———, *The Mediterranean World in Late Antiquity A.D. 395–600.* London and New York: Routledge, 1993.

Clover, F. M., *The Late Roman West and the Vandals.* Aldershot, Hampshire, and Brookfield, VT: Variorum, 1993.

Dzielska, M., *Hypatia of Alexandria,* trans. F. Lyra. Cambridge, MA, and London: Harvard University Press, 1995.

Fowden, G., *Empire to Commonwealth: Consequences of Monotheism in Late Antiquity.* Princeton: Princeton University Press, 1993.

Goffart, W., *Barbarians and Romans, A.D. 410–584: The Techniques of Accommodation.* Princeton: Princeton University Press, 1980.

Grant, M., *Constantine the Great.* New York: Scribner's, 1994.

Hodges, R., and D. Whitehouse, *Mohammad, Charlemagne & the Origins of Europe: Archaeology and the Pirenne Thesis.* Ithaca: Cornell University Press, 1983.

Holum, K. G., *Theodosian Empresses: Women and Imperial Dominion in Late Antiquity.* Berkeley, Los Angeles, and London: University of California Press, 1982.

Jones, A. H. M., *The Later Roman Empire, 284–602.* Norman: University of Oklahoma Press, 1964.

Kelley, J. N. D., *Jerome: His Life, Writings, and Controversies.* London: Duckworth, 1975.

MacMullen, R., *Corruption and the Decline of Rome.* New Haven and London: Yale University Press, 1988.

Mathisen, R. W., *Roman Aristocrats in Barbarian Gaul: Strategies for Survival in an Age of Transition.* Austin: University of Texas Press, 1993.

Matthews, J., *Western Aristocracies and the Imperial Court, A.D. 364–475.* Oxford: Clarendon Press, 1975.

O'Donnell, J. J., *Cassiodorus.* Berkeley, Los Angeles, and London: University of California Press, 1979.

Pohl, W. (ed.), *Kingdoms of the Empire: The Integration of the Barbarians in Late Antiquity.* Leiden and New York: E. J. Brill, 1997.

Van Dam, R., *Leadership and Community in Late Antique Gaul.* Berkeley, Los Angeles, and London: University of California Press, 1985.

Williams, S., *Diocletian and the Roman Recovery.* New York: Methuen, 1985.

———, and G. Friell, *Theodosius: The Empire at Bay.* New Haven and London: Yale University Press, 1995.

VIII Cities, Provinces, and Neighbors of the Empire

Alcock, S. E., *Graecia Capta: The Landscapes of Roman Greece.* Cambridge and New York: Cambridge University Press, 1993.

Bowersock, G. W., *Roman Arabia.* Cambridge, MA, and London: Harvard University Press, 1983.

Bowman, A. K., *Egypt after the Pharaohs 332 B.C.–A.D. 642.* (2nd ed.). Berkeley and Los Angeles: University of California Press, 1989.

Churchin, L. A., *Roman Spain: Conquest and Assimilation.* New York and London: Routledge, 1991.

Colledge, M. A. R., *The Parthians.* New York: Praeger, 1967.

Drinkwater, J. F., *Roman Gaul: the Three Provinces, 58 B.C.–A.D. 260.* Ithaca: Cornell University Press, 1983.

Dyson, S. L., *The Creation of the Roman Frontier.* Princeton: Princeton University Press, 1985.

Elton, H., *Frontiers of the Roman Empire.* Bloomington: University of Indiana Press, 1996.

Engels, D., *Roman Corinth: An Alternative Model for the Classical City.* Chicago: University of Chicago Press, 1990.

Grew, F. and B. Hobley (eds.), *Roman Urban Topography in Britain and the Western Empire.* London: Council for British Archaeology, 1985.

Koester, H., *Ephesos, Metropolis of Asia: An Interdisciplinary Approach to its Archaeology, Religion, and Culture.* Valley Forge: Trinity Press International, 1995.

Millar, F., *The Roman Near East 31 B.C.–A.D. 337.* Cambridge, MA, and London: Harvard University Press, 1993.

Mocsy, A., *Pannonia and Upper Moesia; A History of the Middle Danube Provinces of the Roman Empire,* trans. S. Frere. London and Boston: Routledge and Kegan Paul, 1974.

Reynolds, J. (ed.), *Libyan Studies: Select Papers of the Late R. G. Goodchild.* London: P. Elek, 1976.

Rich, J. (ed.), *The City in Late Antiquity.* London and New York: Routledge, 1992.

Smallwood, E. M., *The Jews under Roman Rule from Pompey to Diocletian: A Study in Political Relations.* Leiden: E. J. Brill, 1976.

Stambaugh, J. E., *The Ancient Roman City.* Baltimore and London: The Johns Hopkins University Press, 1988.

Stoneman, R., *Palmyra and Its Empire: Zenobia's Revolt against Rome.* Ann Arbor: University of Michigan Press, 1992.

Thompson, L. A. and J. Ferguson (eds.), *Africa in Classical Antiquity.* Ibadan: Ibadan University Press, 1969.

Todd, M., *The Northern Barbarians.* London: Hutchinson, 1975.

Wacher, J. S., *Towns of Roman Britain.* Berkeley and Los Angeles: University of California Press, 1975.

Whittaker, C. R., *Frontiers of the Roman Empire: A Social and Economic Study.* Baltimore and London: The Johns Hopkins University Press, 1994.

Wightman, E. M., *Roman Trier and the Treveri.* New York and Washington: Praeger, 1971.

———, *Gallia Belgica.* Berkeley, Los Angeles, and London: University of California Press, 1985.

Wilson, R. J. A., *Sicily under the Roman Empire: The Archaeology of a Roman Province 36 B.C.–A.D. 535.* Warminster: Aris and Phillips, 1990.

IX Society and the Economy

Bauman, R. A., *Women and Politics in Ancient Rome.* London and New York: Routledge, 1992.

Boer, W. Den, *Private Morality in Greece and Rome: Some Historical Aspects.* Leiden: E. J. Brill, 1979.

Bonner, S. F., *Education in Ancient Rome from the Elder Cato to the Younger Pliny.* London: Methuen, 1977.

Bradley, K. R., *Slavery and Rebellion in the Roman World, 140 B.C.–70 B.C.* Bloomington and Indianapolis: Univeristy of Indiana Press, 1989.

———, *Discovering the Roman Family.* New York: Oxford University Press, 1991.

———, *Slavery and Society at Rome.* Cambridge and New York: Cambridge University Press, 1994.

Brown, P. R. L., *Society and the Holy in Late Antiquity.* Berkeley, Los Angeles, and London: University of California Press, 1982.

Brunt, P. A., *Italian Manpower, 225 B.C.–A.D. 14.* Oxford: Clarendon Press, 1971.

Cameron, A. E., *Circus Factions: Blues and Greens at Rome and Byzantium.* Oxford: Clarendon Press, 1976.

Cantarella, E., *Bisexuality in the Ancient World.* New Haven and London: Yale University Press, 1992.

Champlin, E., *Final Judgments: Duty and Emotion in Roman Wills, 200 B.C.–A.D. 250.* Berkeley, Los Angeles, and Oxford: University of California Press, 1991.

Clark, G., *Women in Late Antiquity: Pagan and Christian Lifestyles.* Oxford: Clarendon Press, 1993.

Cornell, T. J., and K. Lomas (eds.), *Urban Society in Roman Italy.* New York: St. Martin's Press, 1995.

Cunliffe, B., *Greeks, Romans & Barbarians: Spheres of Interaction.* New York: Methuen, 1988.

D'Arms, J. H., *Romans on the Bay of Naples: A Social and Cultural Study of the Villas and Their Owners from 150 B.C. to A.D. 400.* Cambridge, MA: Harvard University Press, 1970.

———, and E. C. Kopff, *The Seaborne Commerce of Ancient Rome: Studies in Archaeology and History.* Rome: American Academy in Rome, 1980.

Dixon, S., *The Roman Family.* Baltimore and London: The Johns Hopkins Univeristy Press, 1992.

Duncan-Jones, R., *Money and Government in the Roman Empire.* Cambridge and New York: Cambridge University Press, 1994.

Edwards, C., *The Politics of Immorality in Ancient Rome.* Cambridge and New York: Cambridge University Press, 1993.

Evans, J. K., *War, Women, and Children in Ancient Rome.* London and New York: Routledge, 1991.

Fantham, E., et al., *Women in the Classical World.* New York: Oxford University Press, 1994.

Frank, T. *An Economic Survey of Ancient Rome,* 5 vols. and index. Baltimore: The Johns Hopkins University Press, 1933–1940.

Garnsey, P. (ed.), *Non-Slave Labour in the Greco-Roman World.* Cambridge: Cambridge Philological Society, 1980.

———, *Famine and Food Supply in the Greco-Roman World: Responses to Risk and Crisis.* Cambridge: Cambridge University Press, 1988.

———, and R. Saller, *The Roman Empire: Economy, Society and Culture.* Berkeley and Los Angeles: University of California Press, 1987.

Grant, M., *The Jews in the Roman World.* London: Weidenfeld and Nicolson, 1973.

Greene, K., *The Archaeology of the Roman Economy.* Berkeley and Los Angeles: University of California Press, 1986.

Grubbs, J. E., *Law and Family in Late Antiquity: The Emperor Constantine's Marriage Legislation.* Oxford and New York: Clarendon Press, 1995.

Hands, A. R., *Charities and Social Aid in Greece and Rome.* London: Thames and Hudson, 1968.

Harris, H. A., *Sport in Greece and Rome.* London: Thames and Hudson, 1972.

Hawley, R. and B. Levick (eds.), *Women in Antiquity: New Assessments.* London and New York: Routledge, 1995.

Hopkins, K., *Conquerors and Slaves.* Cambridge: Cambridge University Press, 1978.

Joshel, S. R., *Work, Identity, and Legal Status at Rome: A Study of Occupational Inscriptions.* Norman and London: University of Oklahoma Press, 1992.

Konstan, D., *Friendship in the Classical World.* Cambridge and New York: Cambridge University Press, 1997.

Lewit, T., *Agricultural Production in the Roman Economy, A.D. 200–400.* Oxford: British Academy in Rome, 1991.

Lomas, K., *Rome and the Western Greeks.* London and New York: Routledge, 1993.

MacMullen, R., *Roman Social Relations, 50 B.C.–A.D. 284.* New Haven and London: Yale University Press, 1974.

Morley, N., *Metropolis and Hinterland: The City of Rome and the Italian Economy 200 B.C.–A.D. 200.* Cambridge and New York: Cambridge University Press, 1996.

Nippel, W., *Public Order in Ancient Rome.* Cambridge and New York: Cambridge University Press, 1995.

Parkin, T. G., *Demography and Roman Society.* Baltimore and London: The Johns Hopkins University Press, 1992.

Peacock, D. D. S., and D. F. Williams, *Amphorae and the Roman Economy*. London and New York: Longman, 1986.

Perkins, J. B., *The Suffering Self: Pain and Narrative Representation in the Early Christian Era*. London and New York: Routledge, 1995.

Rawson, B. (ed.), *Marriage, Divorce, and Children in Ancient Rome*. Oxford: Clarendon Press, 1991.

Rickman, G., *The Corn Supply of Ancient Rome*. Oxford, Clarendon Press, 1980.

Rostovtzeff, M. I., *Social and Economic History of the Roman Empire* (2nd ed.), revised by P. M. Frazer. Oxford: Clarendon Press, 1957.

Saller, R. P., *Personal Patronage under the Early Empire*. Cambridge: Cambridge University Press, 1981.

———, *Patriarchy, Property, and Death in the Roman Family*. Cambridge and New York: Cambridge University Press, 1994.

Sherwin-White, A. N., *The Roman Citizenship* (2nd ed.). Oxford: Clarendon Press, 1973.

Taylor, D., *Work in Ancient Greece and Rome*. London: Allen and Unwin, 1975.

Thompson, L. A., *Romans and Blacks*. Norman and London: University of Oklahoma Press, 1989.

Treggiari, S., *Roman Freedmen during the Late Republic*. Oxford: Clarendon Press, 1969.

———, *Roman Marriage: Iusti Coniuges from the Time of Cicero to the Time of Ulpian*. Oxford: Clarendon Press, 1991.

Veyne, P., *Bread and Circuses: Historical Sociology and Political Pluralism*, abridged with an introduction by Oswyn Murray and translated by Brian Pearce. Harmondsworth: Penguin Books, 1990.

Wallace-Hadrill, A. (ed.), *Patronage in Ancient Society*. London and New York: Routledge, 1989.

Whittaker, C. R. (ed.), *Pastoral Economies in Classical Antiquity*. Cambridge: Cambridge Philological Society, 1988.

Wiedemann, T., *Emperors and Gladiators*. London and New York: Routledge, 1992.

Witherington, B., *Women in the Earliest Churches*. Cambridge and New York: Cambridge University Press, 1988.

X Literature and Rhetoric

Anderson, G., *The Second Sophistic: A Cultural Phenomenon in the Roman Empire*. London and New York: Routledge, 1993.

Bartsch, S., *Actors in the Audience: Theatricality and Doublespeak from Nero to Hadrian*. Cambridge, MA, and London: Harvard University Press, 1994.

Binns, J. W. (ed.), *Latin Literature of the Fourth Century*. London and Boston: Routledge and Kegan Paul, 1974.

Bloomer, W. M., *Valerius Maximus and the Rhetoric of the New Nobility*. Chapel Hill: University of North Carolina Press, 1992.

———, *Latinity and Literary Society at Rome*. Philadelphia: University of Pennsylvania Press, 1997.

Bowersock, G. W., *Fiction as History: Nero to Julian*. Berkeley, Los Angeles, and Oxford: University of California Press, 1994.

Cambridge History of Classical Literature, ed. P. E. Easterling and E. J. Kenney. Vol. 2: Latin Literature. Cambridge: Cambridge University Press, 1982.

Cameron, Averil, *Christianity and the Rhetoric of Empire: The Development of Christian Discourse*. Berkeley, Los Angeles, and London: University of California Press, 1991.

Clarke, M. L., *Rhetoric at Rome: A Historical Survey* (3rd ed.), revised and with a new introduction by D. H. Berry. London and New York: Routledge, 1996.

Conte, G. B., *Latin Literature, A History*, trans. J. B. Solodow and revised by D. Fowler and G. W. Most. Baltimore and London: The Johns Hopkins University Press, 1994.

———, *Genres and Readers: Lucretius, Love Elegy, Pliny's Encyclopedia*, trans. G. W. Most; with a forward by Charles Segal. Baltimore and London: The Johns Hopkins University Press, 1994.

Cooper, K., *The Virgin and the Bride: Idealized Womanhood in Late Antiquity*. Cambridge, MA, and London: Harvard University Press, 1996.

Edwards, C., *The Politics of Immorality in Ancient Rome*. Cambridge and New York: Cambridge University Press, 1993.

———, *Writing Rome: Textual Approaches to the City*. Cambridge and New York: Cambridge University Press, 1996.

Fantham, E., *Roman Literary Culture from Cicero to Apuleius*. Baltimore and London: The Johns Hopkins University Press, 1996.

Fox, M., *Roman Historical Myths: The Regal Period in Augustan Literature*. Oxford: Clarendon Press, 1996.

Gleason, M. W., *Making Men: Sophists and Self Rep-

resentation in Ancient Rome. Princeton: Princeton University Press, 1995.

Gold, B. (ed.), *Literary and Artistic Patronage in Ancient Rome.* Austin: University of Texas Press, 1982.

Harris, W. V., *Ancient Literacy.* Cambridge, MA and London: Harvard University Press, 1989.

Humphrey, S. (ed.), *Literacy in the Ancient World.* Ann Arbor: University of Michigan Press, 1991.

Hunter, R. L., *The New Comedy of Greece and Rome.* Cambridge and New York: Cambridge University Press, 1985.

Hutchinson, G. O., *Latin Literature from Seneca to Juvenal: A Critical Study.* Oxford: Clarendon Press, 1993.

Kennedy, G. A., *A New History of Classical Rhetoric.* Princeton: Princeton University Press, 1994.

Leach, E. W., *The Rhetoric of Space: Literary and Artistic Representations of Landscape in Republican and Augustan Rome.* Princeton: Princeton University Press, 1988.

Oberhelman, S. M., *Rhetoric and Homiletics in Fourth-Century Christian Literature.* Atlanta: Scholars Press, 1991.

Ogilvie, R. M., *Roman Literature and Society.* New York: Barnes and Noble, 1980.

Quinn, K., *Texts and Contexts: The Roman Writers and Their Audiences.* London and Boston: Routledge and Kegan Paul, 1979.

Ramage, E. S., *Roman Satirists and Their Satire: Fine Art of Criticism in Ancient Rome.* Park Ridge: Noyes Press, 1980.

Rawson, E., *Intellectual Life in the Late Roman Republic.* Baltimore: The Johns Hopkins University Press, 1985.

Reynolds, L. D., and N. G. Wilson, *Scribes and Scholars: A Guide to the Transmission of Greek and Latin Literature.* London: Oxford University Press, 1974.

Richlin, A., *The Garden of Priapus: Sexuality and Aggression in Roman Humor.* New Haven and London: Yale University Press, 1983.

Russell, D. A. (ed.), *Antonine Literature.* Oxford: Clarendon Press, 1990.

Santoro L'Hoir, F., *The Rhetoric of Gender Terms: "Man," "Woman," and the Portrayal of Character in Latin Prose.* Leiden and New York: E. J. Brill, 1992.

Sullivan, J. P., *Literature and Politics in the Age of Nero.* Ithaca: Cornell University Press, 1985.

Tatum, J. (ed.), *The Search for the Ancient Novel.*
Baltimore and London: The Johns Hopkins University Press, 1994.

Wilkinson, L. P., *Golden Latin Artistry.* Cambridge: Cambridge University Press, 1963.

XI Art and Architecture

Andreae, B., *The Art of Rome.* London: New English Library, 1978.

Boatwright, M. T., *Hadrian and the City of Rome.* Princeton: Princeton University Press, 1987.

Boethius, A., and J. B. Ward-Perkins, *Etruscan and Roman Architecture.* Harmondsworth: Penguin, 1970.

Dunbabin, K. M. D., *The Mosaics of Roman North Africa.* Oxford: Clarendon Press, 1978.

Hannestad, N., *Roman Art and Imperial Policy,* trans. P. G. Crabb. Aarhus: Aarhus University Press, 1988.

Harden, D. B. (ed.), *Glass of the Caesars.* Milan: Olivetti, 1987.

MacCormack, S. G., *Art and Ceremony in Late Antiquity.* Berkeley and Los Angeles: University of California Press, 1981.

MacDonald, W. L., *The Architecture of the Roman Empire,* 2 vols. New Haven and London: Yale University Press, 1982 and 1986.

Matt, Leonard von, *The Art of the Etruscans,* trans. P. Martin. New York: H. N. Abrams, 1970.

McKay, A. G., *Houses, Villas and Palaces in the Roman World.* Ithaca: Cornell University Press, 1975.

Ramage, N. H., and A. Ramage, *Roman Art: Romulus to Constantine* (2nd ed.). Englewood Cliffs: Prentice Hall, 1996.

Toynbee, J. M. C., *Roman Historical Portraits.* London: Thames and Hudson, 1978.

Zanker, P., *The Power of Images in the Age of Augustus,* trans. A. Shapiro. Ann Arbor: University of Michigan Press, 1988.

XII Religion

Beard, M., *Religions of Rome.* Cambridge and New York: Cambridge University Press, 1997.

———, and J. A. North, *Pagan Priests: Religion and Power in the Ancient World.* Ithaca: Cornell University Press, 1990.

Bernstein, A. E., *The Formation of Hell: Death and Retribution in the Early Christian Worlds.* Ithaca: Cornell University Press, 1993.

Bregman, J., *Synesius of Cyrene, Philosopher Bishop.* Berkeley, Los Angeles, and London: University of California Press, 1982.

Brown, P. R. L., *Authority and the Sacred: Aspects of the Christianization of the Roman World.* Cambridge and New York: Cambridge University Press, 1995.

De Labriolle, P., *History and Literature of Christianity from Tertullian to Boethius.* New York: Barnes and Noble, 1968.

Doran, R., *Birth of a World View: Early Christianity in Its Jewish and Pagan Context.* Boulder: Westview Press, 1995.

Dorcey, P. F., *The Cult of Sylvanus: A Study in Roman Folk Religion.* Leiden and New York: E. J. Brill, 1992.

Dumézil, G., *Archaic Roman Religion: With an Appendix on the Religion of the Etruscans,* trans. P. Krapp, foreword by Mircea Eliade. Chicago and London: University of Chicago Press, 1970.

————, *Camillus: A Study of Indo-European Religion as Roman History,* ed., with an introduction, by Udo Strutynski; trans. Annette Aronowicz and Josette Bryson. Berkeley, Los Angeles, and London: University of California Press, 1980.

Edwards, D. R. *Religion and Power: Pagans, Jews, and Christians in the Greek East.* Oxford and New York: Oxford University Press, 1996.

Ferguson, J., *Greek and Roman Religion: A Source Book.* Park Ridge: Noyes Press, 1980.

Fishwick, D., *The Imperial Cult in the Latin West: Studies in the Ruler Cult of the Western Provinces of the Roman Empire.* Leiden and New York: E. J. Brill, 1987.

Fowden, G., *The Egyptian Hermes: A Historical Approach to the Late Pagan Mind.* Cambridge and New York: Cambridge University Press, 1986.

Frend, W. H. C., *Archaeology and History in the Study of Early Christianity.* London: Variorum Reprints, 1988.

Garrison, R., *The Graeco-Roman Context of Early Christian Literature.* Sheffield: Sheffield Academic Press, 1997.

Ladner, G. B., *God, Cosmos, and Humankind: The World of Early Christian Symbolism,* trans. T. Dunlap. Berkeley and Los Angeles: University of California Press, 1996.

Liebeschuetz, J. H. W. G., *Continuity and Change in Roman Religion.* London: Oxford University Press, 1979.

Lieu, S. N. C., *Manichaeism in the Later Roman Empire and Medieval China* (2nd ed.). Tubingen: J. C. B. Mohr, 1992.

————, *Manichaeism in Mesopotamia and the Roman East.* Leiden and New York: E. J. Brill, 1994.

————, and D. Montserrat (eds.), *From Constantine to Julian: Pagan and Byzantine Views: A Source History.* London and New York: Routledge, 1996.

MacBain, B., *Prodigy and Expiation: A Study in Religion and Politics in Republican Rome.* Brussels: Collection Latomus (177), 1982.

MacMullen, R., *Christianity and Paganism in the Fourth to Eighth Centuries.* New Haven and London: Yale University Press, 1997.

Markus, R. A., *The End of Ancient Christianity.* Cambridge and New York: Cambridge University Press, 1990.

Potter, D. S., *Prophets and Emperors: Human and Divine Authority from Augustus to Theodosius.* Cambridge, MA, and London: Harvard University Press, 1994.

Sawyer, D. F., *Women and Religion in the First Christian Centuries.* London and New York: Routledge, 1996.

Scullard, H. H., *Festivals and Ceremonies of the Roman Republic.* London: Thames and Hudson, 1981.

Shaw, G., *Theurgy and the Soul: The Neoplatonism of Iamblichus.* University Park: Pennsylvania State University Press, 1995.

Simmons, M. B., *Arnobius of Sicca: Religious Conflict and Competition in the Age of Diocletian.* Oxford: Clarendon Press, 1995.

Solmsen, F., *Isis among the Greeks and Romans.* Cambridge, MA, and London: Harvard University Press, 1980.

Staples, A., *From Good Goddess to Vestal Virgins: Sex and Category in Roman Religion.* London and New York: Routledge, 1997.

Turcan, R., *The Cults of the Roman Empire,* trans. Antonia Nevill. Oxford and Cambridge, MA: Blackwell, 1996.

XIII Philosophy and the World of Ideas

Adcock, F. E., *Roman Political Ideas and Practice.* Ann Arbor: University of Michigan Press, 1959.

Anderson, G., *The Second Sophistic: A Cultural Phenomenon in the Roman Empire.* London and New York: Routledge, 1993.

Champlin, E., *Fronto and Antonine Rome.* Cambridge, MA, and London: Harvard University Press, 1980.

Dillon, J. M., and A. A. Long (eds.), *The Question of "Eclecticism." Studies in Later Greek Philosophy.* Berkeley, Los Angeles, and London: University of California Press, 1988.

Francis, J. A., *Subversive Virtue: Asceticism and Authority in the Second-Century Pagan World.* University Park: Pennsylvania State University Press, 1995.

Galinsky, K., *Augustan Culture: An Interpretive Introduction.* Princeton: Princeton University Press, 1996.

Gibson, M. (ed.), *Boethius: His Life, Thought, and Influence.* Oxford: Blackwell, 1981.

Griffin, M., and J. Barnes, *Philosophia Togata: Essay in Philosophy and Roman Society.* Oxford: Clarendon Press, 1989.

Gruen, E. S., *Studies in Greek Culture and Roman Policy* (reprint of 1990 ed.). Berkeley, Los Angeles, and London: University of California Press, 1996.

———, *Culture and National Identity in Republican Rome.* Ithaca: Cornell University Press, 1992.

Jones, P., and K. Sidwell (eds.), *The World of Rome: An Introduction to Roman Culture.* Cambridge and New York: Cambridge University Press, 1997.

Lewis, N., *The Interpretation of Dreams and Portents.* Toronto and Sarasota: Samuel Stevens, Hakkert and Co., 1976.

Minyard, J. D., *Lucretius and the Late Republic: An Essay in Roman Intellectual History.* Leiden: E. J. Brill, 1985.

Rawson, E., *Intellectual Life in the Late Roman Republic.* Baltimore and London: The Johns Hopkins University Press, 1985.

Wickham, L. R., and C. P. Bummel (eds.), *Christian Faith and Greek Philosophy in Late Antiquity.* Leiden and New York: E. J. Brill, 1993.

Wirszubski, C., *Libertas as a Political Idea at Rome during the late Republic and Early Principate.* Cambridge: Cambridge University Press, 1950.

XIV Science, Technology, and Material Culture

Aicher, P. J., *Guide to the Aqueducts of Ancient Rome.* Wauconda, IL: Bolchezy-Carducci Publishers, 1995.

Bass, G. F. (ed.), *A History of Seafaring Based on Underwater Archaeology.* New York: Walker, 1972.

Brecher, K., and M. Feirtag, *Astronomy of the Ancients.* Cambridge, MA: MIT Press, 1979.

Chevallier, R., *Roman Roads.* London: Batsford, 1976.

Dilke, O. A. W., *Mathematics and Measurement.* Berkeley, Los Angeles, and London: University of California Press/British Museum, 1987.

Greene, K., *Roman Pottery.* Berkeley and Los Angeles: University of California Press/British Museum, 1992.

Hamey, L. A., and J. A. Hamey, *The Roman Engineers.* Cambridge: Cambridge University Press, 1981.

Healy, J. F., *Mining and Metallurgy in the Greek and Roman World.* London: Thames and Hudson, 1978.

Jackson, R., *Doctors and Diseases in the Roman Empire.* Norman: University of Oklahoma Press, 1988.

Johnson, S., *Rome and Its Empire* (The Experience of Archaeology). London and New York: Routledge, 1989.

MacDougall, E. B., and W. F. Jashemski (eds.), *Ancient Roman Gardens.* Washington, DC: Dumbarton Oaks, 1981.

———, *Ancient Roman Villa Gardens.* Washington, DC: Dumbarton Oaks, 1987.

Neugebauer, O., *A History of Ancient Mathematical Astronomy.* Berlin and New York: Springer-Verlag, 1975.

Nielsen, I., *Thermae et Balneae: The Architecture and Cultural History of Roman Public Baths.* Aarhus: Aarhus University Press, 1990.

O'Connor, C., *Roman Bridges.* Cambridge and New York: Cambridge University Press, 1993.

Scarborough, J., *Roman Medicine.* London: Thames and Hudson, 1969.

Stahl, W. H., *Roman Science: Origins, Development, and Influence to the Late Middle Ages.* Madison: University of Wisconsin Press, 1962.

Strong, D., and D. Brown (eds.), *Roman Crafts.* London: Duckworth, 1976.

Thurston, H., *Early Astronomy.* New York: Springer, 1994.

Vallance, J. T., *The Lost Theory of Asclepiades of Bithynia.* Oxford: Clarendon Press, 1990.

White, K. D., *Farm Equipment of the Roman World.* Cambridge and New York: Cambridge University Press, 1975

———, *Greek and Roman Technology.* Ithaca: Cornell University Press, 1984.

Wiseman, S. U., and W. S. Williams, *Ancient Technologies and Archaeological Materials.* Langhorne, PA: Gordon Breach Science Publishers, 1993.

XV Law

Crook, J., *Law and Life of Rome.* Ithaca: Cornell University Press, 1967.

Daube, D., *Forms of Roman Law.* Westport: Greenwood Press, 1979.

Gardner, J. F., *Women in Roman Law and Society.* London and Sydney: Croom Helm, 1986.

Honoré, T., *Emperors and Lawyers.* London: Duckworth, 1980.

Jolowicz, H. F., and B. Nicholas, *Historical Introduction to the Study of Roman Law* (3rd ed.). Cambridge: Cambridge University Press, 1972.

Jones, A. H. M., *The Criminal Courts of the Roman Republic and Principate,* ed. J. Crook. Oxford: Blackwell, 1972.

Kunkel, W., *An Introduction to Roman Legal and Constitutional History* (2nd ed.), trans. J. M. Kelley. Oxford: Clarendon Press, 1973.

Watson, A., *Law Making in the Later Roman Republic.* Oxford: Clarendon Press, 1974.

———, *The Making of the Civil Law.* Cambridge, MA, and London: Harvard University Press, 1981.

———, *The Evolution of Law.* Baltimore and London: The Johns Hopkins University Press, 1985.

———, *State, Law and Religion: Pagan Rome.* Athens, GA: University of Georgia Press, 1992.

———, *International Law in Archaic Rome: War and Religion.* Baltimore and London: The Johns Hopkins University Press, 1993.

XVI Coinage

Brooke, C. N. L. (ed.), *Studies in Numismatic Method Presented to Philip Gierson.* Cambridge and New York: Cambridge University Press, 1983.

Burnett, A. M., and M. H. Crawford (eds.), *The Coinage of the Roman World in the Late Republic.* Oxford: British Academy in Rome, 1987.

Carson, R. A. G., *Coins of the Roman Empire.* London and New York: Routledge, 1990.

Crawford, M. H., *Roman Republican Coinage.* Cambridge: Cambridge University Press, 1974.

Foss, C., *Roman Historical Coins.* London: Seaby (Distributed by B. T. Batsford), 1990.

Harl, K., *Coinage in the Roman Economy, 300 B.C. to A.D. 700.* Baltimore and London: The Johns Hopkins University Press, 1996.

Jones, J. M., *A Dictionary of Ancient Coins.* London: Seaby, 1990.

Mattingly, H. et al., *The Roman Imperial Coinage,* 10 vols. London: Spink, 1923–1994.

Nicklas, S. D., *A General Survey of Coinage in the Roman Empire A.D. 294–408 and Its Relationship to Roman Military Deployment.* Lewiston: E. Mellen Press, 1995.

Sutherland, C. H. V., *The Roman Imperial Coinage,* vol. I (revised). London: Spink, 1984.

XVII Military and Naval Affairs

Bishop, M. C. (ed.), *The Production and Distribution of Roman Military Equipment.* Oxford: Clarendon Press, 1985.

Breeze, D. J., and V. Maxfield (eds.), *Service in the Roman Army.* New York: Columbia University Press, 1987.

Campbell, (J.) B., *The Emperor and the Roman Army 31 B.C.–A.D. 235.* Oxford: Clarendon Press, 1984.

———, *The Roman Army 31 B.C.–A.D. 337: A Source Book.* London and New York, Routledge, 1994.

Casson, L., *Ships and Seamanship in the Ancient World.* Princeton: Princeton University Press, 1971.

Connolly, P., *Greece and Rome at War.* London: Macdonald, 1981.

Elton, H., *Warfare in the Roman World, A.D. 350–425.* Oxford: Clarendon Press, 1996.

Gabba, E., *Republican Rome, the Army and Allies,* trans. P. J. Cuff. Oxford: Blackwell, 1977.

Garlan, Y., *War in the Ancient World: A Social History.* London: Chatto and Windus, 1975.

Isaac, B. H., *The Limits of Empire: The Roman Army in the East* (2nd ed.). Oxford: Clarendon Press, 1992.

Keppie, L. J. F., *The Making of the Roman Army: From Republic to Empire.* Totowa: Barnes and Noble, 1984.

Luttwack, E. N., *The Grand Strategy of the Roman Empire from the First Century A.D. to the Third.* Baltimore and London: The Johns Hopkins University Press, 1976.

Marsden, E. W., *Greek and Roman Artillery, Historical Development.* Oxford: Clarendon Press, 1969.

Maxfield, V. A., *The Military Decorations of the Roman Army.* Berkeley, Los Angeles, and London: University of California Press, 1981.

Rich, J., and G. Shipley (eds.), *War and Society in the Roman World.* London and New York: Routledge, 1993.

Speidel, M. P., *Riding for Caesar: The Roman Emperors' Horse Guards.* Cambridge, MA and London: Harvard University Press, 1994.

Starr, C. G., *The Roman Imperial Navy* (2nd ed.). New York: Barnes and Noble, 1959.

Warry, J., *Warfare in the Classical World.* London: Salamander, 1980/ Norman: University of Oklahoma Press, 1995.

Watson, G. R., *The Roman Soldier* (2nd ed.). London: Thames and Hudson, 1983.

Webster, G., *The Roman Imperial Army* (3rd ed.). London: A. and C. Black, 1985.

Index